THE HANDBOOK OF
COMMUNICATION ETHICS

INTERNATIONAL COMMUNICATION ASSOCIATION (ICA) HANDBOOK SERIES

Robert T. Craig, Series Editor

Cheney/May/Munshi — *The Handbook of Communication Ethics*

Strömbäck/Kaid — *The Handbook of Election News Coverage Around the World*

Wahl-Jorgensen/Hanitzsch — *The Handbook of Journalism Studies*

THE HANDBOOK OF COMMUNICATION ETHICS

Edited by
George Cheney
Steve May
Debashish Munshi

First published 2011
by Routledge
270 Madison Ave, New York, NY 10016

Simultaneously published in the UK
by Routledge
2 Park Square, Milton Park, Abingdon, Oxon OX14 4RN

Routledge is an imprint of the Taylor & Francis Group, an informa business

The right of the editors to be identified as authors of the editorial material, and of the authors for their individual chapters, has been asserted by them in accordance with sections 77 and 78 of the Copyright, Designs and Patents Act 1988.

Typeset in Times and Helvetica by EvS Communication Networx, Inc.
Printed and bound in the United States of America on acid-free paper by Edwards Brothers, Inc.

Library of Congress Cataloging in Publication Data
The handbook of communication ethics / edited by George Cheney, Steve May, and Debashish Munshi.
p. cm.
1. Communication—Moral and ethical aspects. I. Cheney, George. II. May, Steve (Steve Kent), 1961–
III. Munshi, Debashish.
P94.H353 2010
175—dc22
2010017324

ISBN 13: 978-0-415-99464-4 (hbk)
ISBN 13: 978-0-415-99465-1 (pbk)
ISBN 13: 978-0-203-89040-0 (ebk)

*To the further pursuit of values, ethics
and justice in the field of communication,
recognizing that the very discussion of those matters
must be inclusive, complex, conflictual, and ongoing.*

Contents

Foreword   xi
ROBERT T. CRAIG, THE UNIVERSITY OF COLORADO AT BOULDER

Preface   xvii

Author Biographies   xxi

1   Encountering Communication Ethics in the Contemporary World: Principles, People, and Contexts   1
GEORGE CHENEY, DEBASHISH MUNSHI, STEVE MAY, WITH ERIN ORTIZ

UNIT 1: THEORY OLD AND NEW

2   A Contribution to Ethical Theory and Praxis   15
JOHN STEWART

3   Ethics, Rhetoric, and Discourse   31
MICHAEL J. HYDE

4   Situating a Dialogic Ethics: A Dialogic Confession   45
RONALD C. ARNETT

5   Feminist Discursive Ethics   64
PATRICE M. BUZZANELL

6   Power and Ethics   84
DENNIS K. MUMBY

7   What Are We, Then? Postmodernism, Globalization, and the Meta-Ethics of Contemporary Communication   99
BRYAN C. TAYLOR AND LEONARD C. HAWES

8   Decolonizing Communication Ethics: A Framework for Communicating *Other*wise   119
DEBASHISH MUNSHI, KIRSTEN J. BROADFOOT, AND LINDA TUHIWAI SMITH

UNIT 2: CONTEXTS OF APPLICATION AND THEORY DEVELOPMENT

9   Interpersonal Communication Ethics   135
SALLY PLANALP AND JULIE FITNESS

viii   CONTENTS

10 Ethical Challenges in Small Group Communication   148
JOHN GASTIL AND LEAH SPRAIN

11 Communication Ethics and Organizational Contexts: Divergent Values and Moral
Puzzles   166
MATTHEW W. SEEGER AND TIMOTHY KUHN

12 Journalism Ethics in Theory and Practice   190
CLIFFORD G. CHRISTIANS

13 Ethical Dimensions of New Technology/Media   204
CHARLES ESS

14 Public Relations and Marketing: Ethical Issues and Professional Practice in Society   221
JACQUIE L'ETANG

15 Visual Communication in Traditional and Digital Contexts   241
SEAN CUBITT AND VIOLETA POLITOFF

16. The Search for Social Justice and the Presumption of Innocence in the Duke
University (USA) Lacrosse Case of 2006–2007: Implications for Contemporary
Legal and Ethical Communication   258
GLEN FEIGHERY, MAROUF HASIAN, JR., AND RICHARD RIEKE

17 Political Communication Ethics: Postmodern Opportunities and Challenges   273
STEVEN R. GOLDZWIG AND PATRICIA A. SULLIVAN

18 Ethics in Health Communication   293
NURIT GUTTMAN AND TERESA L. THOMPSON

19 Science, Democracy, and the Prospect for Deliberation   309
KEITH R. BENSON AND JOHN ANGUS CAMPBELL

20 Intercultural Communication Ethics: Multiple Layered Issues   335
STELLA TING-TOOMEY

UNIT 3: CONTEMPORARY ISSUES

21   Diversity, Identity, and Multiculturalism in the Media: The Case of Muslims
in the British Press   355
NASAR MEER AND TARIQ MODOOD

22 Hierarchies of Equality: Positive Peace in a Democratic Idiom   374
ROBERT L. IVIE

23 Democracy, Publicness, and Global Governance   387
SLAVKO SPLICHAL

24 Religion, State, and Secularism: How Should States Deal with Deep Religious
    Diversity?   401
    RAJEEV BHARGAVA

25 Truth, Evils, Justice, and the Event of Wild(er)ness: Using Badiou to Think
    the Ethics of Environmentalism   414
    KEVIN MICHAEL DELUCA

26 Economic Justice and Communication Ethics: Considering Multiple Points
    of Intersection   436
    ZACHARY A. SCHAEFER, CHARLES CONRAD, GEORGE CHENEY, STEVE MAY,
    AND SHIV GANESH

27 The Polyphony of Corporate Social Responsibility: Deconstructing
    Accountability and Transparency in the Context of Identity and Hypocrisy   457
    LARS THØGER CHRISTENSEN, METTE MORSING, AND OLE THYSSEN

28   When Unreason Masquerades as Reason: Can Law Regulate Trade and
    Networked Communication Ethically?   475
    RADHA D'SOUZA

29. Response and Conclusion: A Vision of Applied Ethics for Communication Studies   494
    JOSINA M. MAKAU

    Index   517

Series Editor's Foreword

Robert T. Craig

The Handbook of Communication Ethics offers the most comprehensive current guide to ethical studies across the field. No previous work has explored this fundamental aspect of communication theory, research, and practice in broader scope. Moreover, the editors and authors have attempted not only to represent diverse ethical topics and approaches but also to overcome the field's current state of fragmentation by illuminating common themes and opening new conversations across topics and approaches.

While scholars who specialize in particular areas such as dialogue, journalism, or environmental justice will find useful chapters related to their specialties, those who read further in the *Handbook* may profit even more from the discovery of unexpected links to other areas. The *Handbook* forges integrative links both implicitly in the selection and arrangement of topical chapters and explicitly in the introductory and concluding chapters that frame the volume. This effort toward integration expands the horizon of ethical/moral inquiry in communication, affording glimpses of a communication ethics that is more than an application of ethics to communication but rather includes an array of original contributions to ethical thought essentially informed by communication concepts and practices.

The selection and arrangement of 27 chapters in three main units composing the volume implicitly invites authors and readers to weave each topic through others in a three-dimensional array of theories, contexts, and problems. The first unit presents seven chapters addressing ethical theory from various viewpoints. Here as elsewhere in the volume the reader will find commentaries on classic ideas like utilitarianism and virtue ethics, but the chapters do not focus centrally on traditional schools of ethics. Instead, each chapter advances a particular communication approach to ethics, featuring themes like interactively emergent choice (Stewart), otherness and dialogue (several chapters), feminist discursive ethics (Buzzanell), or postcolonial praxis (Munshi et al.).

Most of these theoretical themes, both classic and new, recur in one or more of the 12 chapters in the second unit, each of which treats a specific context of communication (interpersonal relations, journalism, new technologies, law, and politics, among others). Empirical research abundantly informs many of these essays, elucidating ethical problems and dilemmas that arise in particular contexts and often resemble those in other contexts, thus inviting comparison across contexts. Specific kinds of communicative practices, for example, privacy management or deliberation, also become important in multiple contexts.

Empirical research, as was just noted, has a prominent role in many of these chapters on particular contexts of communication. Empirical research has a similarly large role in chapters of the following unit on contemporary ethical issues. These chapters illustrate the merit of Donsbach's (2006) argument that empirical studies in communication science, no less than critical studies, can and should be conducted so as to address significant normative problems.

The third unit includes eight chapters on contemporary issues ranging from multiculturalism to peace, secularism, and corporate social responsibility. Each issue connects contexts and (re) introduces theories in different ways. For example, Badiou's ethic of truths, introduced by Taylor and Hawes in relation to postmodern theory in the first unit (chapter 7), recurs in the context of visual communication in the second unit (Cubitt & Politoff, chapter 15), and again as grounds for a critique of environmental justice in the third unit (DeLuca, chapter 25).

Explicit integration is provided by Makau's concluding chapter, in which she comments extensively on the preceding chapters while reflecting on the central place of communication in a field of applied ethics, and by the editors in their introductory chapter. Editors Cheney, Munshi, and May (with Ortiz) integrate the field with reference to several key "dialectics," including, for example, the dialectic of theory and practice and the dialectic of reason and emotion. The editors relate each chapter to one or more dialectics. They also reflect on the distinct contribution of communication studies to ethical thought in general, a theme I would like to pursue a bit further.

The editors' introduction opens with the interesting claim that "Communication, as both a discipline and an 'interdiscipline' or field, is poised to play a unique role in advancing discussions of ethics because the field offers an array of concepts and principles attuned to the examination of ethics writ large" (p. 1) . On my reading the *Handbook* provides ample evidence in support of this claim. To be sure, no one moral/ethical view dominates, and chapters differ in many ways. Even so, the volume as a whole suggests the influence of a broad but distinguishable tendency of ethical thought informed by a family of communication-theoretic concepts. Without attempting a definitive family portrait it is still possible to offer partial and preliminary sketches of a few of those concepts.

A good place to begin is by noting four senses of communication ethics embraced by the *Handbook*, according to the editors. First, communication ethics is especially concerned with specific forms of action, such as deception and free expression that are both inherently communicative and morally fraught. Second, as currently exemplified by Habermasian discourse ethics, generalized ethical principles can be constructed on a basis of communication theory. Third, a sense the editors particularly emphasize, communication ethics attends to the rhetorical dimension of ethical/moral discourses in which material conditions are framed symbolically, revealing, for example, how the rhetorical framing of economic globalization in neoliberal discourse obscures questions of social justice. Fourth, communication ethics, by attending to comparative and multicultural moral/ethical views, challenges the status of ethics as an autonomous sphere of thought that transcends particular cultures and practices.

The four senses are different and even contradictory in some respects, yet each is a recognizable member of the communication family. Characterizing these and perhaps other senses of communication ethics are conceptual family traits that members display in different combinations. Consider the following examples, each of which appears in some form in a range of *Handbook* chapters.

PROCESS

Communication theory tends to favor a process understanding of human action. Communication is not a linear series of independent acts chosen by purely autonomous agents; it is an ongoing process of social interaction from which actions, meanings, and identities all continually emerge. Individuals participate in the process but with limited ability to control it. Stewart (chapter 2) draws implications of this concept for a theory of ethical choice. Ethical action requires choosing what to do next in a process that one contributes to but does not control, and requires openness to revising one's choices as the process unfolds. With the recognition that moral/ethical choice always occurs in the context of a communication process, the emphasis of ethical theory shifts from rules and principles of individual action to characteristics of the contextual process, variously conceived in terms of an ideal speech situation, genuine dialogue, democratic deliberation, or power and resistance, among other concepts. A communication ethics informed by empirical studies of human interaction has much to contribute to ethical thought in this vein, as Stewart points out and other chapters illustrate. Several of those chapters also share with others a second family trait of communication ethics: the idea that the communication process involves dialectical tensions.

DIALECTICAL TENSION

The process of communication involves a constant negotiation of tensions among conflicting values and principles. People faced with ethical dilemmas, whether involving tensions between disclosure and privacy or between cultural sensitivity and universal rights, must make highly contextual choices of how to proceed. The shifting process allows no final, principled resolution of dilemmas but requires, again, contextual sensitivity in the negotiation of momentary resolutions. As Christensen et al. (chapter 27) show in the case of corporate social responsibility, a communication approach reveals the ambiguous status of an ideal that can only be pursued in a complex communication environment, yet also reveals a progressive potential that inheres in that very ambiguity. The constant negotiation of dialectical tensions does not arise only from the contingency of consequences in uncertain situations. It also arises and has ethical significance as an experience of otherness, the idea of which may be regarded as a third family trait of communication ethics.

OTHERNESS

Unlike the autonomous agent of modernist ethics, the self as understood in major traditions of communication theory exists only in relation to others who are ontologically equal and different from the self in ways that can be experienced in communication but never fully known. The self, therefore, is always incomplete and has much to learn in dialogue with others. The incompleteness of the self implies an ethical imperative to learn from others and openness to ethical choices that are not determined in advance by an autonomous rational act but that emerge in a communication process. But if I as a self am incomplete, then our group, our culture, is also incomplete. To acknowledge otherness is to acknowledge a pluralistic, multicultural world in which every group, no less than every individual, has much to learn from others. The *Handbook* abounds in references to self-incompleteness and partiality, other-orientation, dialogue, and multiculturalism. For example, Buzzanell (chapter 5) writes of the need for self-questioning, and Ess (chapter 13) of pluralism. Christians (chapter 12) reviews several kinds of dialogic ethics for journalism. Bhargava (chapter 24) describes an Indian model of adaptive secularism in which the state is not walled off from religion but is actively involved in negotiating arrangements within and among religious groups, again illustrating how a communication ethic replaces an absolute principle (whether theocracy or church-state separation) with the imperative to engage with others in an open communication process.

DISCOURSE

A fourth family trait of communication ethics is to theorize the communication process that produces ethical choice as both material and symbolic, that is, as discourse: the practical use of language and other expressive resources in complex situations. Whereas traditional and modernist ethics tended to regard rhetoric as inherently unethical, studies in communication ethics more often find that rhetorical discourse has ethically necessary roles in framing problems, articulating differences, and constructing resonant narratives of moral choice within a communication process. Classical rhetoricians theorized discourse as a practice oriented to audience and situation; postmodernists theorize discourse as a practice enmeshed with social habitus and material circumstances. Rhetorical strategy has an inevitable presence in both views. Concepts including discourse, rhetoric, and narrative occur frequently throughout the *Handbook*. The editors discuss rhetorical framing of material conditions as an ethically significant problem exemplified by varying interpretations and classifications of "human rights" in ordinary as well as legal discourses. For Mumby (chapter 6), the experience of otherness is constituted by discursive articulations of difference bound up in relations of power. Other chapters focus on democratic deliberation as an ethically significant discourse practice enmeshed in material conditions. Splichal (chapter 23), for example, reflects on the normative implications of new forms of participation in democratic deliberation afforded by global networks, while Benson and Campbell (chapter 19) examine practices of popular deliberation in relation to technical science.

Process, tension, otherness, and discourse are not the only family traits of communication ethics manifested in the *Handbook* and not necessarily the most important. Other prominent traits could have been discussed under headings such as technology, media, culture, and performance, among others. As well, it should be emphasized again that members of the communication ethics family do not all share the same traits; they show a family resemblance but are not identical. Finally, to tweak the metaphor and acknowledge what is obvious, this is not a biological family. Anyone can join, and the *Handbook of Communication Ethics* extends a welcome invitation. Though it does not provide us with a definitive family portrait of communication ethics, the *Handbook* invites scholars across the field to consider how their work might contribute to possible versions of that picture.

REFERENCE

Donsbach, W. (2006). The identity of communication research. *Journal of Communication, 56*, 437–448.

THE ICA HANDBOOK SERIES

The ICA Handbook series is a joint venture between the International Communication Association and Routledge. It will be a series of scholarly handbooks that represent the interests of ICA members and help to further the Association's goals of promoting theory and research across the discipline. These handbooks will provide benchmark assessments of current scholarship and set the agenda for future work. The series will include handbooks that focus on content areas, methodological approaches, and theoretical lenses for communication research.

We seek proposals from prospective editors of handbooks. We especially seek proposals that cross the boundaries of established disciplines and fields to address timely problems of international scope, not just representing different specialties but bringing them together collaboratively to address intersecting interests and research problems of broad interest. For example, such problems might be formulated as topical concerns (e.g., globalization, virtual environments), theoretical approaches (e.g., social cognition, critical studies), or matters pertaining to communication or communication research in general (e.g., methodological innovations, communication theory across cultures).

For more information about this series, contact:

Robert T. Craig
ICA Handbook Series Editor
Department of Communication
University of Colorado at Boulder
270 UCB
Boulder, CO 80309-0270
303-492-6498 voice
303-492-8411 fax
Robert.Craig@colorado.edu

or

Linda Bathgate
Senior Editor, Communication Studies
Routledge
270 Madison Avenue
New York, NY 10016
212-216-7854 phone
212-643-1430 fax
linda.bathgate@taylorandfrancis.com

Preface

George Cheney, Steve May, and Debashish Munshi

The need to address ethics in today's world hardly requires explanation. Still we should ask why ethical concerns are not considered a more integral part of discussions of an array of issues ranging from economic to social to environmental dimensions of our lives. Unfortunately, the study of ethics often remains a sideline to other areas of investigation and, in certain respects, an afterthought in everyday public discourse. Such marginalization of ethics is ironic, of course; yet it persists in contexts from education to professional training to popular culture. In this way, ethics has not fulfilled its promise as a system of reflection and guidance in part because it has not been presented in such a way as to be broadly compelling.

This volume is the first of its kind to bring together in one place considerations of communication ethics in contexts ranging from interpersonal to global. Moreover, the reader will readily see microlevel implications of macrolevel treatments, and vice versa, in part because the chapter authors have themselves bridged levels of analysis in vivid and thought-provoking ways. In prioritizing ethical insight and practice, the volume also bridges "explicit" treatments of ethical issues in communication and "implicit" considerations of ethics. That is, we have put under one umbrella analyses and applications that draw upon recognized ethical theories and those which, while they do not cite traditional ethical theorists, nevertheless engage important questions of power, equality, and justice. As has been noted by the three editors in recent publications, supported by their classroom and professional experiences, even *applied* ethics suffers from a kind of "ghettoization" because neither students nor scholars make some of the important (and necessary) connections between matters of social justice as conceived in several domains and ethical theory as applied to a variety of social contexts. Thus, for example, the writers on matters of "difference" and those who typically make applications from what is called "ethics" or ethical theory do not cross paths nearly as much as they should. This volume seeks to move beyond this limited cross-pollination by bringing together a wide range of authors who conceive of ethics from a wide range of theoretical perspectives and from a variety of contexts. We hope that readers find it innovative, comprehensive, and provocative.

This collection has three major sections: one on resources for theoretical understanding and insight, a second on application to specialties of communication study, and a third on contemporary issues of social and economic justice. The 27 regular chapters are followed by an expansive commentary. In addition, we have encouraged the cross-fertilization and cross-referencing of chapters when possible. The reader will see, for example, that certain theories, concepts, and principles appear in more than one chapter; importantly, their treatments will vary according to context and perspective. For example, the influences of postmodernism appear in various forms and bring discussions to varying conclusions. Further, some concepts and sets of processes, like globalization, are featured in a number of different ways although there is no chapter on globalization per se.

Finally, we note that some chapters are more traditionally "reviewlike," while others are constructed as single arguments; still others are case-based. In all instances, however, we encouraged authors to look beyond their accustomed bases of knowledge and citation networks. We urged everyone to strike a reasonable balance by offering some state-of-the-art observations and at the same time presenting a perspective or advancing a point of view. All authors took seriously the charge of putting forth ideas to stimulate further research, and a few were deliberately provocative with respect to existing or anticipated debates. Moreover, this volume has provided a platform for diverse viewpoints to comingle. In the process of assembling the essays that comprise this handbook, there has occasionally been healthy debate between the editors and contributors. We hope that the chapters presented here will stimulate further discussion and debate, as well as forays into new areas of research and practice.

We believe that this volume fills an important niche in the literature of communication studies, through consolidating knowledge about the multiple relationships between communication and ethics, by systematically treating areas of application, and by "introducing" explicit and implicit examinations of communication ethics to one another.

This *Handbook* is primarily intended for scholars and graduate students although some advanced undergraduates will find it accessible and stimulating as well. We are pleased to present this volume as the single most comprehensive compendium on the study of communication and ethics. Moreover, we hope that this volume will help to reinvigorate the discussion of ethics in our field, including not only explicit treatments of ethics but also what we call "implicit" treatments of ethics located outside the strictly philosophical to look at specific social, political, and cultural issues. Some of these issues are not traditionally considered within the purview of ethics. In addition, to the extent possible, the volume manifests an international outlook, in terms of analyzing diverse cultural contexts, detailing comparative assessments, and considering the tensions between universalism and particularism.

We see the primary audiences for the *Handbook* as three: (a) scholars in communication and related disciplines who will use the *Handbook* as a resource for their research; (b) instructors who will use the *Handbook* as a main point of reference in graduate and upper-division undergraduate courses in communication and ethics; and (c) university libraries that seek a comprehensive resource for research in the study of communication and ethics. Also, we fully expect scholars in other fields where applied ethics holds interest to benefit from this volume as well. These disciplines, specialties, and interdisciplinary arenas include Philosophy (Ethics), Sociology (Social Issues), Psychology (Positive Psychology), Political Science (Political Theory), Anthropology (Cross-cultural Studies), Economics (Political Economy), Environmental Studies, Peace and Conflict Studies, Gender Studies, Ethnic Studies, International Relations, Global Justice Studies, Law, and of course Ethics across the Curriculum.

ACKNOWLEDGMENTS

We express gratitude to Bob Craig of the University of Colorado at Boulder, who initiated this project with a call to George 4 years ago and whose input and encouragement have been invaluable along the course of its development. We thank Linda Bathgate, Senior Editor for Communication Studies at Routledge, who has been helpful, flexible, and patient at every stage. We are grateful for the work by Kate Ghezzi, Editorial Assistant, who moved the book into production. We are indebted to Erin Ortiz, doctoral candidate at the University of Utah, whose careful work as part of a research assistantship enabled us to complete and expedite the final editing process.

George is grateful for Sally's enduring love, support, and patience. Also, he acknowledges the University of Utah for a Faculty Fellowship in the spring of 2006 and a half-time sabbatical from the College of Humanities during academic year 2008–2009 which generously supported work on this book on communication ethics and the one preceding it. Steve thanks Geriel for her continuing love, support, and encouragement and Arcadia for her constant reminder that ethics matters for our futures. He also thanks the Arthur W. Page Center at the Penn State College of Communications for their support during his work on the book. Debashish thanks Priya, Akanksha, and Alya for helping him refine his thoughts and for being part of a collaborative quest for the meaning of life. He also thanks the Department of Management Communication at the University of Waikato for its ongoing support to his scholarly pursuits.

Finally, we are pleased to have worked closely with so many wonderful colleagues who produced the fine work that comprises this volume.

1

Encountering Communication Ethics in the Contemporary World

Principles, People, and Contexts

George Cheney, Debashish Munshi, Steve May, with Erin Ortiz

Communication, as both a discipline and an "interdiscipline" or field, is poised to play a unique role in advancing discussions of ethics because the field offers an array of concepts and principles attuned to the examination of ethics writ large. That is to say, the conceptual and practical orientation of communication studies enables us to probe questions about how ethics come to the forefront of consciousness and experience (or not). Communication is especially well suited for meta-ethical analyses as well as examinations of specific ethical issues, dilemmas, and decisions because of how it is attuned to the very construction of arguments about what "counts" as relevant information, opinion, and choice. The rhetorical framing of ethics broadly considered, where ethics can be treated as integral to the life-world or ancillary to it, is but one obvious but powerful example.

This edited volume embraces the following senses of communication ethics. First, the book includes treatments of communication phenomena from the standpoint of ethics and morality, with attention to such clearly communicative phenomena as deception, openness, free expression, and so forth. In fact, these are the types of issues that come most readily to mind for most scholars, practitioners, and students when they hear the term *communication ethics*. Following the linguistic turn in mid-20th century philosophy, we take the position that communication *is* action but also recognize that such is most apparent in cases where the very accomplishment of something is almost completely encompassed by a communicative act (such as an apology or a promise; see Austin, 1965). At the same time, and especially from a theoretical standpoint, a number of our authors deal directly with the question of how communication itself has inherently ethical or moral dimensions. This line of thinking can be traced back at least to Plato's (1994, 2002) considerations of different types of messages and their ethical–moral implications (including the capacities for seduction and corruption). This point of view is most fully developed in our day by the work of Jürgen Habermas (1979), for whom ethical communication is implicated by our reflexive uses of language and indeed reinforced in one way or another by our every interaction. From this point of view, it is impossible to step outside the context of ethical considerations in our uses of symbols with one another, although the question of what constitute ideals,

1

constraints, and possibilities for free and open (or profoundly democratic) communication is still subject to debate. Third, there are chapters which consider how material conditions (such as the economy and the environment) are necessarily framed, "translated" (Latour, 1993), and affected by our use of symbols (see, e.g., Cheney, Lair, & Kendall, 2010). Therefore, the debates over issues such as human rights for species other than *Homo sapiens*, the urgency of global warming or climate change, and the need for economic justice fall indirectly though importantly within the domain of communication ethics. Along the way, the chapters of this book also question the very notion of ethics as a separate sphere of thought, discussion, and practice; indeed, this is one of the most important lessons of the still-emergent area of comparative and multicultural ethics (see, e.g., Singer, 2002).

WHAT ARE KEY DIALECTICS IN THE STUDY AND PRACTICE OF COMMUNICATION ETHICS?

While no introductory or overview essay could possibly account for all the visions and nuances of communication's relationship to ethics, we would like to offer five dialectics as means of charting key issues at this intersection and suggesting how each of the following chapters in this volume might be viewed in relationship to at least one dialectic. This exercise risks being a bit reductionistic in the placements of chapters; however, we offer these pairings in a heuristic spirit to stimulate further thought, discussion, and research.

Theoretical-Practical

This is a classic division: it is well-recognized in current discussions of the disjuncture between ethical theory and ideals and "on the ground" experience (e.g., Sabini, 1982). The theory and practice of ethics are only possible by placing the ethical dimensions of communicative acts in conversation with ethical dimensions of everyday life. As Appiah (2008) writes, "because making a life is an *activity* [emphasis added]…we should expect to learn more from experiments in living than from experiments in philosophizing" (p. 203). The theory–practice divide is beginning to be transcended in the arena of applied ethics today as the ancient method of casuistry is reclaimed for our present day, putting cases in ongoing conversation with theory and therefore allowing for the modification and even supplanting of certain theoretical perspectives.

A number of chapters in this volume give special attention to theory–practice relations. These include contributions by Buzzanell; Christians; Ess; Gastil and Sprain; L'Etang; Mumby; and Stewart. Patrice Buzzanell's chapter takes, as a starting point, that the field of communication can offer a fundamentally different lens on ethics—one that cuts across dualisms that pervade ethics literature and contributes to contemporary debates. She explores the means by which feminist scholars have integrated theory and practice. More specifically, Buzzanell proposes the metaphor of discursive acts "to accommodate inconsistencies and tensions on micro and macro levels" (p. 77), including socially constructing context, promoting dialogue through human values, designing vision, reframing, embedding iterativity, and making processes and outcomes transparent. In his discussion of power, ethics, and communication. Dennis Mumby similarly notes that the field of communication is well positioned to address the ethics–power nexus in the context of a nonfoundational world. He explicates the ways in which theorizing about power and ethics has been limited because scholars rarely view them as complex and frequently contradictory phenomena, in practice. He suggests that a viable "communicative ethic always recognizes the social character of self and other as they are situated within a broader political, economic, and historical context that embodies particular configurations of power" (p. 95). John Stewart, in a chapter on ethical theory and praxis, argues that ethical inquiry has much to learn from empirical work and vice versa. He reminds readers that "important ethical dimensions that are warp and weft of the fabric of interpersonal, organizational, cultural, and mediated communicating, but also of the contributions to ethical analysis and theorizing that emerge from studies of events of verbal–nonverbal articulate contact; that is, of communication" (p. 15).

Clifford Christians contends that both the theory of and practice in the journalistic profession are at a crossroads, with the primary challenge being cultural relativism. He suggests that four explicit issues for theory and practice stand out as the most demanding and complicated for journalism ethics: social justice, truth-telling, nonviolence, and human dignity. In his view, the most productive framework for addressing each of them is social responsibility theory. In his chapter on the ethical dimensions of new technologies and media, Charles Ess reminds us that responses to current and emerging issues such as privacy and online participation must recognize how diverse cultural values and communicative preferences shape and influence these responses. He calls for a "pluralistic" global information and communication ethics that conjoins theory and practice via both "shared ethical norms along with the irreducible differences between diverse cultural traditions and communicative preferences" (p. 205), thereby avoiding ethical relativism and ethical monism.

John Gastil and Leah Sprain explore the ethical challenges in small group communication by discussing the range of scholarly research that clarifies how groups, in practice, conceptualize and confront ethical dilemmas and how these microdecisions in small groups intersect with the larger social system. Jacquie L'Etang similarly identifies a range of ethical dilemmas common to public relations that require healthy debate among scholarly and professional groups. Developing core ethical practices in the profession, she argues, requires "taking into account competing, multiple discourses including the official occupational aims (encompassed in codes of ethics and the formal statements of professional bodies), the normative literature, and empirical evidence regarding aims and impacts" (p. 221).

Academic/Philosophical Discourses-Popular/Lay Discourses

Somewhat mirroring the theory–practice divide in ethics is the disjuncture between philosophical discourses about ethics and lay understandings of ethical situations. For many communication practitioners, ethics is more about "doing the right thing" in a given situation (that is, a decision focus) and less about philosophical treatises on virtue, morality, deontology, or *eudaimonia* (currently translated into English more as flourishing than as happiness, per recent writings in applied ethics and classics). Just as theory and practice lean on each other, philosophical and popular discourses have important points of intersection. If indeed, the "end of philosophical ethics is to make sense of the project of *eudaimonia*," Appiah (2008) maintains, it "cannot do that on its own" (p. 203). There is a need to mix the accustomed analytical purity of philosophy with the moral messiness of everyday situations, where the clash between ethical principles is in fact more the norm than the exception. Still, relatively little has been written about the *framing* of ethics writ large in popular or lay discourses, including popular culture, although more has been said about how, for example, the media treat specific ethical issues such as scandals. Recent meta-ethical discussions have featured not only abstract analyses of multiple ethical systems but also broad views of the ways ethics are approached or framed in a variety of spheres, including politics, the media, work, and the home.

While many of the chapters in this volume comment upon lay or popular as well as on scholarly or academic discourses, several are especially attuned to making observations across that boundary. These include the contributions of Cubitt and Politoff; DeLuca; D'Souza; Goldzwig and Sullivan; Hyde; and Schaefer, Conrad, Cheney, May, and Ganesh. Michael Hyde, for example, explores how a focus on rhetorical analysis, as a middle ground between the academic and the popular, is concerned "not only with what a given text means, but also and primarily with how it means: the various ways that its discourse produces understanding, attitudes, and beliefs, calls for critical judgment, and encourages action" (p. 32). Arguing that ethics, rhetoric, and discourse lie at the heart of human beings, he explains how the nexus of these three phenomena should be understood, empirically, from the ground up, "from the fundamental spatial and temporal fabric of existence to the constructed social and political domains that we create and inhabit on a daily basis" (p. 32). Schaefer et al. consider the variety of ways that economy, ethics, and communication intersect, in popular as well as academic discourses. They focus on the master narrative of neoliberalism especially because of the way it has masked its own ideological, persuasive, and power-related dimensions.

Sean Cubitt and Violeta Politoff also explore the boundaries of the academic and the popular in their chapter on visual communication and ethics. There, they consider a diverse range of images. They explore the scholarly and popular understandings of these images as the "increasing ease of production, manipulation and circulation of images forms the condition for contemporary ethical obligation" (p. 254). Kevin DeLuca similarly explores the framing of academic and popular discourses that impact environmental ethics and the practices surrounding it. He claims that displacing a historical emphasis on wilderness with a new focus on social justice ironically limits the environmental movement. As DeLuca argues "justice within the frame of humanism and identity politics renders environmentalism incapable of responding to the crucial issues of global warming, ocean pollution/depletion, and other catastrophic global threats" (p. 415).

In the realm of law, trade, and networked communication, Radha D'Souza addresses a comparable issue with regard to the bifurcation of scholarly and popular arenas of knowledge. D'Souza explains, for example, that "ethical problems in trade and networked communication are usually examined within disciplinary enclosures of law, trade, and communication technologies, each with their own normative codes" (p. 475), creating a disjuncture between theoretical inquiries in communication ethics, on the one hand, and popular, applied communication ethics at the user end, on the other. Steven Goldzwig and Patricia Sullivan acknowledge that scholars of communication ethics in political contexts "have moved away from prescriptive models in suggesting possibilities for negotiating ethics along a continuum balancing the interests of individuals and community, private and public spheres" (p. 276). Regardless of how political discourse circulates in both scholarly and popular realms, though, they suggest that "rhetors have the responsibility to communicate with humility, frame narratives of integrity, and invite critical responses from their audiences…and audiences also have the responsibility to be engaged as critical receivers" (p. 284).

Universal-Particular

The tension between the universal and the particular is a classic division in thought and debate about ethics. This matter is entangled with the dominance of particular perspectives: for example, in the ways Western European (e.g., Enlightenment-based) conceptions of ethical standards and, indeed, the ethical sphere itself, have been taken as universal without question except, notably, in cultural anthropology. The Canada-based indigenous scholar, Taiaiake Alfred (1999), for example, links presumably universal ideas about ethics to the colonialist agenda in that colonial regimes equated peace with their concepts of order and stability and then used the idea of maintaining "order" to oppress native peoples. In fact, he makes a strong argument for what he calls the "ethic of courage" which involves a "struggle for personal transformation and freedom from the dominance of imperial ideas" (p. 11). Clearly, context is a core dimension of communication ethics (the traditional attention to the importance of audience reminds us of this), and it is the context of the particular that is often in tension with what is deemed to be universal. Indeed, as Henderson and Waterstone (2009) put it, "ethical positions are themselves sites of contestations and struggle" (p. 191).

Within this volume, several chapters provide a snapshot of some of these sites of struggle. These contributions include those of Arnett; Bhargava; Christensen, Morsing and Thyssen; Taylor and Hawes; and Ting-Toomey. Ronald Arnett, for example, examines the " interplay of communication ethics and dialogue, assuming a hermeneutic bias that there is no one universal understanding of what constitutes communication ethics and, additionally, that there is no one universal understanding of what constitutes dialogue" (p. 45). As Arnett notes, any attempt to construct a theory of communication ethics and dialogue is necessarily rhetorical, situated within a given bias and identified as a perspective that gives shape to a particular world. Doing so in an era of narrative and virtue contention requires attention to multiplicity, minimalism, historicity, and dialogic confession. Bryan Taylor and Leonard Hawes acknowledge the importance of ethical contestation and struggle in their chapter on postmodernism, globalization, and the meta-ethics of contemporary communication. As they note, the deconstruction that has resulted from postmodern theory "has affected the theory and practice of ethics, rocking foundational premises such as universally applicable moral principles, the moral autonomy of the individual, and the linkage between questions of human rights and the authority of nation states" (p. 99).

In a religious context, Rajeev Bhargava also examines the universal/particular tension: "Of all available alternatives, secularism remains our best bet to help us deal with ever deepening religious diversity and the problems endemic to it" (p. 401). Bhargava proposes a modest, nuanced, and adaptive secularism that "seeks to modify religious ethics, to make them more inclusive by reducing intrareligious domination, or to provide a relatively independent moral standpoint from which to free religions of interreligious domination" (p. 402). Stella Ting Toomey's chapter on intercultural communication ethics notes that "much of the complexity of an intercultural ethical decision-making process derives from the tension between whether ethics is a culture-bound concept or whether ethics should be understood apart from the culture" (p. 335). She proposes a meta-ethical approach that emphasizes in-depth fact-finding, layer-by-layer interpretations, and seriously considers the importance of culture, context, persons, intentions, means, consequences, and global humanism to cultivate creative visions and alternative options for globally inclusive solutions to ethical dilemmas.

In their chapter on the polyphony of corporate social responsibility, Mette Morsing, Lars Thoger Christensen, and Ole Thyssen also acknowledge the importance of context in discussions of ethics. They note, for example, that the incorporation of social virtues into the practices of business corporations is more complex and contextually situated than is often assumed. They explain that corporate social responsibility coexists with other organizational concerns, including economic, legal, and technological considerations. As a result, these different concerns—or premises for decision making—"must often be attended to simultaneously, since their integration is contextually defined; it cannot be handled in any automatic or technical manner, but must constantly be readdressed and renegotiated" (p. 457).

Global-Local

This dialectic at first appears to be identical with the one above and, indeed, there is a significant overlap as is evident in a number of chapters. However, in articulating the global versus the local, we mean to emphasize the contexts of cultural expressions for ethics themselves. These we see readily in competing conceptions of the processes of globalization and what may be considered as inevitable as opposed to particular configurations of power and choice. Treating this dimension or dialectic together with the one above, we necessarily ask questions about the (re)framing of local expressions of and standards for ethics as universal, and vice versa. Ethics, as conceived by Henderson and Waterstone (2009), "is about the development of new concepts that potentially open up new political practices and new or revised alliances and identities for those politics" (p. 191). The interplay between the global and the local in fact opens up possibilities for the reconsideration of established theories as well as the development of new ones.

Many of the chapters in this volume articulate what J. K. Gibson-Graham (2009) calls "an ethics of the local" which looks at how local practices can help construct "different Universals and new communities" (p. 355). A number of authors demonstrate how local formulations of ethical practice can redefine some of the taken-for-granted universals and reshape the theory of communication ethics. The following chapters in this volume are especially sensitive to local–global dimensions of communication ethics in practice. These contributions include: Feighery, Hasian and Rieke; Meer and Modood; Munshi, Broadfoot, and Smith; Seeger and Kuhn; and Splichal. Glen Feighery, Marouf Hasian, and Richard Rieke, for example, explore the specific, local, cultural construction of guilt and innocence in legal cases. They argue that local knowledge should not supersede the importance of multiple perspectives on communication that are necessary to address the ambiguities that result when legal and ethical assessments intersect. They conclude that "no matter how pure the motives, individuals, groups, and even powerful organizations are not free to impose their sense of justice to replace well-defined, properly established systems of public justice" (p. 268). Nasar Meer and Tariq Modood also address the question of the global and the local in their chapter on diversity, identity, and multiculturalism. In it, they suggest that "multiculturalism must necessarily engage with ideas of citizenship when the latter are oriented toward a reciprocal balance of rights and responsibilities, assumptions of virtue and conceptions of membership or civic status" (p. 355), since broad, global practices of multiculturalism may ignore the sensibilities of local minorities marked by social, cultural, and political differences.

Debashish Munshi, Kirsten Broadfoot, and Linda Tuhiwai Smith, in a chapter on decolonizing communication ethics, remind us that "communication ethics are always already historically, materially, politically, socially situated and yet the universalizing framework through which they are often constructed is still overwhelmingly Western" (p. 119). They aim to decolonize communication ethics by arguing that Western Enlightenment notions such as rationality, justice, and humanity are not necessarily transferable to other contexts "without an engagement with issues of social injustice that arise from the ideological, intellectual, and imperial domination of Western thought and theory" (p. 119).

In their chapter on organizational ethics, Matthew Seeger and Timothy Kuhn note that organizations are fraught with dialectical tensions "between individual values and collective morality, between profitability and social justice, between centralized managerial authority and organizational democracy and between rhetoric and practice" (p. 182). As they argue, "communication in organizations is both part of the process of constituting an ethical climate and a specific domain of ethical praxis" (p. 166) and, as such, organizational ethics are woven into the fundamental structural/cultural fabric, taken-for-granted assumptions, patterns of language and interaction, and day-to-day routines of organizational life that reflect broader, cultural assumptions and practices. Slavko Splichal addresses the local–global dialectic by exploring the extent to which the principle of publicity, "the public," and "the public sphere" is related to personal freedom of expression, the expansion and diversification of mass communication, democratic process, and global governance. He explains that technological achievements and globalization have profoundly changed communication in both transnational and local contexts, creating both new opportunities and challenges for citizens' participation in public discourse to "materialize the principle of deliberative publicness and the personal right to communicate" (p. 387).

Rational-Emotional

We hesitate to call this pair dialectical in the usual sense insofar as current conceptions of ethics are moving toward a more integrative view of these dimensions of human experience, following advances in information processing, decision making, and affect. Still, it is important to highlight these terms and their different but overlapping orbits of meaning because of the long-standing bifurcation of rationality and emotionality in European and North American thought which has only recently been bridged to any significant extent (e.g., Solomon, 1990).

Perhaps one of the most important intellectual currents in this regard is the rise of the trans-disciplinary studies of happiness, grounded in positive psychology but extending their wings across fields from philosophy to economics. One of the key lessons of this research has been to reconnect happiness with the pursuit of a meaningful life, and therefore with happiness (Diener & Seligman, 2002). Interestingly, this linkage also harks back to Aristotle's (trans., 2009) for-mulations of the ethical life as an ongoing process that incorporates practical wisdom as well as virtue. From a communication standpoint, several implications become evident, including the framing of "the good life," the narrative of life's meaning, the articulation of transcendent goals, and the importance of interaction.

Several chapters in this volume deal with such issues, and focus especially on the inter-relations of ethics, "being with others," and well-being. These contributions include those of Benson and Campbell; Guttman and Thompson; Ivie; and Planalp and Fitness. Keith Benson and John Campbell, for example, manifest the hope that "deliberation will play an enhanced role in contemporary political culture and the anxiety that deliberative democracy is threatened by a combination of technical reason and government by opinion poll" (p. 309). They suggest that a lay-initiated, lay-directed, deliberatively centered, and environmentally conscious worldview would redeem, in a postmodern context, belief in the scientific potential of ordinary people and hope in the emancipatory power of reason. In a related argument, Robert Ivie's chapter points out the inherent tensions between war and peace, with particular attention to our culture's violent quest for peace as an ethical quandary for all citizens. He seeks to engage the irony of represent-ing war as a mission of peace by "reviewing the meaning of positive peace in relation to the myth of just war and examining the democratic idiom as a resource for articulating peace-building hierarchies of equality" (p. 374) that balance reason and emotion.

The tensions between rational and emotional dimensions are perhaps no more pronounced than in health care contexts. In their chapter on health communication and ethics, Nurit Guttman and Teresa Thompson note that little scholarship has focused on ethical issues and, in addition, benevolence of medical interventions are taken for granted and ethical issues are minimized in the health care industry. Tensions related to rational decision making and emotional affect are common, they note, among issues such as "power relations, privacy, disclosure and truth-telling, and range from issues regarding what to tell or not tell to patients, presumably for their own bene-fit, what to keep confidential, and whether to disclose medical mistakes" (p. 306). In their chapter on interpersonal relationships, Sally Planalp and Julie Fitness argue for the need to recognize the fundamental role of ethics in all aspects of relational communication and to "promote a 'culture of caring' that enables human beings to flourish, both individually and in relationship with one another" (p. 136). They remind us that relationships are always necessarily embedded in, and draw on, physical, biological, social, economic, and cultural environments that either enable or constrain ethical relational practices related to inclusion, respect and dignity, interdependence, fairness, and autonomy and privacy.

AN EXEMPLAR: HUMAN RIGHTS CONSIDERED FROM THE STANDPOINT OF COMMUNICATION STUDIES

The dialectics outlined above can serve as one set of organizing principles for the examination of communication ethics. A domain that features all of these dialectics is human rights. The arena of human rights readily suggests issues such as classification and interpretation (e.g., what "counts" as a human right and how it will be interpreted), agency and authority (e.g., who determines what rights should be considered and in what contexts), and negotiation and enforcement (e.g., how are differences within human rights discussed, managed, resolved, and perhaps adjudicated). Along with Cynthia and Michael Stohl (e.g., 2005, in press), we recommended that communication scholars engage more fully with the area of human rights, particularly as the discipline becomes increasingly international in scope. Here we outline the context for human rights investigation and identify several issues pertinent to the study of human rights from the standpoint of communication studies.

As a category, human rights may be viewed as heartfelt moral justifications (Clapham, 2007); as fictions in the sense of how they are called into being (MacIntyre, 1984); as opportunities for reshaping state conduct (Apodaca, Stohl, & Lopez, 1998) as baselines for acceptable treatment, protection, aid; and as political tools to enhance the power of one state and delimit that of another. The variety of perspectives suggest that human rights do not really resolve the tension between competing interests and various visions of how the world should be; rather, human rights ideas provide the *vocabulary for arguing* [emphasis added] about which interests should prevail and how best to achieve the ends we have chosen. (Clapham, 2007, p. vii)

The framing of human rights writ large brings us into consideration of their ontological, epistemological, and axiological statuses. Rights-oriented discourses lean on social-contract perspectives (e.g., Rousseau, 1762/1968) as well as on the organization of politics around the sovereignty and authority of nation-states since the Treaties of Westphalia in 1648. The assertion of a human right is a type of a priori position that can be challenged both in terms of its foundation and its pragmatic effects: that is, that such assertions can have unintended consequences such as the further division of communities and the relegation of protections solely to institutional actors (e.g., Cheney, 2009). Beyond this, of course, there is also the matter of how rights, once established, are interpreted and negotiated by various actors: a prime example being widely differing interpretations of principles related to economic justice (see Schaefer et al. in this volume).

A communication-related perspective can be seen within a panorama of disciplinary treatments of human rights. For example, moral and political philosophy (e.g., Shute & Hurley, 1993) looks primarily at the influence of natural law and social-contract theories in order to establish a basis for human rights. Legal theorists tend to view human rights in terms of key institutions and standards, extending to issues of application and enforcement (e.g., Gross & Compa, 2009). Sociologists sometimes examine social and power relations within domains of human rights by considering "the coverage, content, inclusions, [and] exclusions of rights texts [which] tell us not only who is protected against what, but also what sort of people…are especially valued (or not)…" (Woodiwiss, 2005, p. xiv). Sociologists, including demographers, also consider human rights standards in terms of dimensions of identity such as gender (Bamforth, 2005) and race (Banton, 2002). Historians trace the development of human rights as both an ideal and a set of institutions (Ishay, 2004), while religious studies scholars emphasize the interrelationships and distinctions between secular and faith-based perspectives on human rights. Communication studies is poised to complement these perspectives by examining not only formal means of communication surrounding human rights but also how human rights are positioned in everyday talk on a variety of levels and in an array of social contexts, including professional standard-setting, social-movement mobilization, and family socialization (Stohl & Stohl, personal communication, 2010).

A major problematic that communication scholars could investigate is the *classification and interpretation* of human rights. In other words, what "counts" as a human right, and how it will be interpreted? For example, even though torture is described in absolute terms by the U.N. Convention against Torture (1994), torture has risen to the level of international disputes as well as subterfuge in recent years, as many nations claim not to be practicing torture by either adopting extremely strict definitions of torture or through transporting prisoners to other nations with even fewer compulsions about practicing torture. In the wake of the September 11, 2001 terrorist attacks on the United States, there were attempts to define torture in particularly narrow ways (e.g., intentional infliction of "excruciating" and "agonizing" pain, according to a 2002 memorandum of the U.S. Justice Department).

Parallel contestations are evident for other "rights" as well, such as privacy (Rozenberg, 2004), food, housing, work, education, and free movement across borders (Ghai & Cottrell, 2004; Ortiz, Agyeman-Budu & Cheney, in press), to name a few domains. Questions of privacy have become especially vexing because of the simultaneous possibilities for democratization, control, intrusion, and exposure that come with the digital age (Clapham, 2007). While some of these domains of rights, like privacy, are more explicitly communicative in nature, even the most material of them can be examined from the standpoint how debates and formulations of rights proceed.

A second major ethical problematic is *agency and authority*, concerning the parties to be protected and the parties to determine policies of protection. Ethical questions center on isolating and characterizing the actual and potential violators (i.e., states, corporations, groups, and individuals) and who has the authority to protect potential victims (i.e., governments, corporations, or nongovernmental agencies). Questions of agency and authority also implicate where human rights should be promoted. For instance, some observers argue that human rights should are relevant to the workplace (Ewing, 1977; Gross & Compa, 2009) and to the internal affairs of religious institutions (Lotz, 2003) while others disagree and apply human rights in distinct ways in different spheres (e.g., Alston, 2005).

A third major ethical problematic, *enforcement and negotiation,* considers questions revolving around decision making, resolution, and agreement. In specific terms, how are differences discussed, managed, resolved, and perhaps adjudicated? What is the future role of the state in these processes? What nongovernmental institutions are best equipped to deal with these problems? What should be expected on transnational corporations? How is legitimacy established? These questions focus on the *processes* of rights creation, maintenance, and application (or non-application).

These ethical questions and problematics serve as starting points for communication scholars and students to enter into discussions of and research on human rights. Although this volume has not explicitly addressed human rights in a specific chapter, we offer this brief sketch of what such an area of investigation might look like.

NOTE TO THE READER

A handbook such as this one will typically be used as a resource to consult for specific topics and, therefore, chapters rather than a volume to read from start to finish. This makes perfect sense given the structure of the work and the diversity of the chapters. Nevertheless, in the spirit of debate and dialogue, we ask the reader to place chapters in conversation with one another just as our respondent has done. By doing so, each of you can help to develop further the ethical thought and practice of communication as a discipline and as an interdisciplinary field.

REFERENCES

Alfred, T. (2005). *Wasase: Indigenous pathways of action and freedom*. Peterborough, Ontario, Canada: Broadview Press.

Alston, P. (2005). *Labor rights as human rights*. New York: Oxford University Press.

Apodaca, C., Stohl, M., & Lopez, G. (1998). Moving norms to political reality: Institutionalizing human rights standards through the United Nations system. In C. F Alger (Ed.), *The future of the United Nations system: Potential for the twenty-first century* (pp. 185–220). Tokyo, Japan: United Nations University Press.

Appiah, K. A. (2008). *Experiments in ethics*. Cambridge, MA: Harvard University Press.

Aristotle. (2009) *Nicomachean ethics*. Oxford, UK: Oxford University Press.

Austin, J. L. (1965). *How to do things with words*. New York: Oxford University Press.

Bamforth, N. (Ed.). (2005). *Sex rights*. Oxford, UK: Oxford University Press.

Banton, M. (2002). *The international politics of race*. Cambridge, UK: Polity Press.

Cheney, G. (2009, December 10). *Ten observations about human rights in today's world*. Paper presented at National Human Rights Day, Salt Lake City, UT.

Cheney, G., Lair, D. J., Ritz, D., & Kendall, B. E. (2010). *Just a job? Communication, ethics and professional life*. New York: Oxford University Press.

Clapham, A. (2007). *Human rights: A very short introduction*. Oxford, UK: Oxford University Press.

Diener, E., & Seligman, M. (2002). Very happy people. *Psychological Science, 131*, 81–84.

Ewing, D. W. (1977). *Freedom inside the organization: Bringing civil liberties to the workplace*. New York: McGraw-Hill.

Ghai, Y., & Cottrell, J. (2004). *The role of judges in implementing economic, social, and cultural rights*. London: Interrights.

Gibson-Graham, J. K. (2009). The ethics of the local. In G. Henderson & M. Waterstone (Eds.), *Geographic thought: A praxis perspective* (pp. 355–370). New York: Routledge.

Gross, J. A., & Compa, L. (Eds.). (2009). *Human rights in labor and employment relations: International and domestic perspectives*. Champaign, IL: Labor and Employment Relations Association.

Habermas, J. (1979). *Communication and the evolution of society*. Boston, MA: Beacon Press.

Henderson, G., & Waterstone, M. (2009). *Geographic thought: A praxis perspective*. New York: Routledge.

Ishay, M. R. (2004). *The history of human rights: From ancient times to the globalization era*. Berkeley, CA: University of California Press.

Latour, B. (1993). *We have never been modern*. Cambridge, MA: Harvard University Press.

Lotz, L. A. (2003). All religions believe in justice: Reflections on faith community support for worker organizing. In J. A. Gross (Ed.), *Workers' rights as human rights* (pp. 183–202). Ithaca, NY: Cornell University Press.

Ortiz, E., Agyeman-Budu, E., & Cheney, G. (in press). How should corporate social responsibility address labor migration, in light of market globalization? In K. Korinek & T. Maloney (Eds.), *Migration in the 21st century: Rights, outcomes, and policy*. Routledge.

MacIntyre, A. (1984). *After virtue: A study in moral theory* (2nd ed.). Notre Dame, IN: University of Notre Dame Press.

Plato. (1994). *Gorgias*. Oxford, UK: Oxford University Press.

Plato. (2002). *Phaedrus*. Oxford, UK: Oxford University Press.

Rousseau, J. (1968). *The social contract* (M. Cranston, Trans.). London: Penguin Group. (Original work published 1762)

Rozenberg, J. (2004). *Privacy and the press.* Oxford, UK: Oxford University Press.

Sabini, J. (1982). *Moralities of everyday life.* New York: Oxford University Press.

Shute, S., & Hurley, S. (Eds.). (1993). *On human rights.* New York: Basic Books.

Singer, P. (2002). *One world: The ethics of globalization.* New Haven, CT: Yale University Press.

Solomon, R. C. (1990). *A passion for justice.* Reading, MA: Addison–Wesley.

Stohl, M., & Stohl, C. (2005). Human rights, nation states, and NGOs: Structural holes and the emergence of global regimes. *Communication Monographs, 72*(4), 442–467.

Stohl, M., & Stohl, C. (in press). Human rights and corporate social responsibility: Parallel processes and global opportunities for states, corporations and NGOs. *Sustainability Accounting, Management and Policy Journal.*

Woodiwiss, A. (2005). *Human rights.* New York: Routledge.

Unit 1
THEORY OLD AND NEW

2

A Contribution to Ethical Theory and Praxis

John Stewart

Ethics, as every school child knows, is a philosophical topic. As a result, since at least the early 20th century, almost no responsible Western scholar associated with any discipline outside philosophy has undertaken a project focused on ethics without acknowledging that he or she could only be a visitor to this intellectual terrain, perhaps an informed one, but more likely a kind of conceptual voyeur, never a native. Anthropologists and educational theorists interested in epistemology have suffered from the same status as strangers, as have cognitive theorists and neuroscientists interested in philosophy of mind and even some theologians interested in making ontological and metaphysical claims.

Early in his important book, *Experiments in Ethics* (2008), Kwame Anthony Appiah reminds his readers how short-lived and wrongheaded this narrow disciplinarity actually is. "Plato and Aristotle had almost physiological theories about the nature of the soul and the nature of life," Appiah notes (p. 7). Descartes devoted much of his attention "to geometry and optics, and for a period he was revered among scholars as, principally, a sort of mathematical physicist.... He also spent time and energy dissecting cows and other animals" (p. 7). Similarly, Immanuel Kant developed theories of the winds of the earth's rotation, dispensed advice about training the young, and wrote, "Concerning the Volcanoes on the Moon."

Whether Plato's interpreters are to be blamed for focusing philosophy on the noumenal world, or Appiah is right that philosophy was narrowed to conceptual analysis after World War II, today it is at least uncomfortable for any scholar with a terminal degree in another discipline and no publications in *Ethics* or *Philosophical Quarterly* to undertake a project on a topic as closely associated with the philosophical silo as is ethics.

But Appiah argues that ethical inquiry has much to learn from empirical work. In fact, he writes, it would not be "novel" for philosophy to turn to "experimentation." "What's novel was the turn away from it" (p. 6). Appiah effectively makes the case that philosophical projects can and should profit from work done in such empirical disciplines as psychology and social psychology (his favorites), and, by apt extension, communication. The present volume clearly responds to some elements of Appiah's call. It reminds readers not only of the important ethical dimensions that are warp and weft of the fabric of interpersonal, organizational, cultural, and mediated communicating, but also of the contributions to ethical analysis and theorizing that emerge from studies of events of verbal-nonverbal articulate contact; that is, of communication. In other words the channel of contribution runs in two directions.

GLOBALIZATION

From the empirical vantage offered by communication and its sister human studies, globalization is the primary 21st century reality that contextualizes any consideration of ethics.[1] What "information" and then "technology" were to the end of the 20th twentieth century, globalization is to the beginning of the 21st. As Joanne Myers (2002) puts it,

> Although there was a time when it was possible for citizens of one country to think of themselves as owing no obligation to the people of other nations, admittedly that was long ago. Today national borders have less meaning as issues of trade, environment, and health, along with incredible technological advances of the last century, have left us with *a legacy of connectedness we cannot ignore* [italics added]. Globalization has changed the way societies work and the way individuals think and interact with one another. In such a world, what do we ethically and morally owe our fellow human beings?

Although Myers' characterization of globalization is abstract, every citizen in developed countries and nearly every citizen in developing countries can tell personal stories about their concrete experiences of the effects of globalization, including international job outsourcing, OPEC's impact on corporate and personal finances, security responses to terrorism, air and water degradation across international borders, global cell network communication, threats and realities of pandemics, and world music and media.

The first and often the most lasting and influential outcome of these concrete, empirical experiences of globalization is contact with Otherness, the sometimes stark and, for some people, intensely uncomfortable realization that people with whom I am in contact really don't see and do things the way I do. In philosophy, Michael Theunissen (1984) identified "the problem of the Other" as an historically prominent one "in ethics and anthropology, in legal and political philosophy" (p. 1). In a complementary project, Maurice Friedman began *The Confirmation of Otherness in Family, Community and Society* (1983) with Martin Buber's urging that people develop the ability to affirm that our conversation partner is essentially other than myself, that this one or that one does not have merely a different mind, or way of thinking or feeling, or a different conviction or attitude, but has also a different perception of the world, a different recognition and order, of meaning, a different touch from the regions of existence, a different faith, a different soil (Buber, 1965, pp. 61–62). As Buber's work and attempts to apply this view demonstrate, the challenge to consistently affirm Otherness in this way is daunting.

Of course, every human experiences a version of the contact with Otherness in the childhood recognition that a sibling or cousin is "different from me" and that adults have priorities that seem unusual. But the European American high school student shocked by the raucous verbal play of African American classmates, the Jew's or Christian's discovery of radical Islam's rationale for suicide bombing, the traveling European college student's direct encounter with tribalism and AIDS in central Africa, and the businessperson's face-to-face work with a Chinese entrepreneur all produce a more profound and often more troubling realization: My ways are not the only ways; sane people act on what seem to me to be alien values; nothing in my experience equips me to predict what some people in the actual situation will do.

Again, the initial response to this experience is as predictable as it is ethically freighted. "They're wrong." "How could she do that?" "I can't accept that people actually believe those ideas." One important goal of secondary and tertiary education is to moderate this ethnocentrism that is such a familiar first response to contact with Otherness. But the educational project is complex and often frustrating. Most learners begin without the awareness that their attitudes and actions embody presuppositions—cultural values and beliefs that are initially as invisible as the air they breathe. When—or if—the educator succeeds in facilitating the discovery that unreflectively adopted presuppositions have this power, learners then have to cope with the fear that accompanies the loss of comfortable cultural certainty. Then, the cure can seem as threatening as the disease. "If I can't apply my values, where do I turn? Am I really supposed to honor standards that are foreign to me?" Not many years ago, substantial populations were born, lived, and died without confronting Otherness and being forced to cope with its implications. But today, as Myers writes, all of us inhabit "a legacy of connectedness we cannot ignore." The empirical facts of globalization confront virtually every world citizen with the inescapable necessity of mediating between conflicting value systems on issues that matter. In this way, globalization broadly and deeply prioritizes applied ethics.

A CONCEPTUAL INVITATION FROM COMMUNICATION SCHOLARSHIP

Many disciplines host programs for responding to the ethical challenges engendered by globalization, including philosophy, anthropology, psychology, sociology, education, business, and communication, and this volume focuses in part on the contributions of the discipline of communication. For hundreds of years, communication scholars have helpfully highlighted ethical dimensions of communication events in politics, organizations, and families. Aristotle left both *The Rhetoric* and *The Nicomachean Ethics*; Quintilian and the pedagogical programs based on his work blended communication ethics and rhetorical effectiveness; Kenneth Burke (1966) integrated elements of Spinoza's and Kant's ethical works into his analysis of the centrality of the human as "inventor of the negative"; and a list of contemporary communication scholars with interests in ethics would include the 47 contributors to this volume, Christopher Lyle Johnstone, Richard L. Johannesen, Julia T. Wood, Pat Arneson, Kenneth E. Andersen, Arneson's edited volume (2007), Walter R. Fisher, and others.

But I believe that communication scholarship can contribute something more to ethics than analyses of ethical dimensions of varied interactions, important as those are. Influential works in communication theory address presuppositions that are central to ethical theory and practice, and I want to outline and trace implications of one of them here. I believe that communication theorizing about the problematic of choice has produced insights into ethical praxis that invite ethicists across the human studies to reconsider central theoretical and practical issues, especially in the context of globalization.

Choice

Ample literature indicates that it is almost impossible to undertake an analysis of ethics without the construct of choice. Sissela Bok (1999), in her influential book *Lying: Moral Choice in Public and Private Life,* begins the chapter entitled, "Truthfulness, Deceit, and Trust" with a section on "Lying and Choice," starting with the claim, "Deceit and violence—these are the two forms of *deliberate assault* [italics added] on human beings" (p. 18). Bok also argues that, not only does lying centrally involve choice, it also affects others' choices. As she puts it,

> Such a manipulation of the dimension of certainty is one of the main ways to gain power over the choices of those deceived. And just as deception can initiate actions a person would otherwise never have chosen, so it can prevent action by obscuring the necessity for choice. (p. 20)

Bok's remedy has a parallel focus. She writes, "What paths, what means of inquiry into the troubling questions of truth-telling and lying remain if systems help so little? I believe that any method, to be of help, should originate with the actual choices people make" (p. 54).

Ethics of communication scholars interviewed by Pat Arneson (2007) expressed similar positions. For example, in 2001, Richard L. Johannesen identified as a central challenge in the development of communication ethics the question, "Can we develop a viable concept of the 'self' as an ethical agent in communication?" (pp. 126–127). In Arneson's book, Johannesen notes that he does not differentiate between rhetorical ethics and communication ethics: "I think both of them have a communicator with the intent or purpose to influence others in some way to some degree. Both involve choices among communicative means" (p. 38).

Similarly, in 1969, James Chesbro identified the "universal humanitarian" as one of four "categories" of communication ethics, and Arnett, Arneson, and Bell's (2007) contemporary appropriation of this category emphasizes that it embodies "the Enlightenment commitment to rational discernment of the truth" (p. 157), where rational beings are understood as choice-makers. Arnett, Arneson, and Bell approvingly cite Christopher Lyle Johnstone's argument that "This humane knowledge…is always a potentiality inherent in the relating of one human being to another. When we attempt to 'reason together' in order that we might live together productively and happily, we lead each other and ourselves to the edge of the human soul" (Johnstone, 1981, p. 188).

Communication professor Elaine Englehardt introduces the first reading in her *Ethical Issues in Interpersonal Communication* (1999) with closely related claims:

> Ethicists generally hold that while reason is not the only guide the [sic] truth, it provides the best direction. Ethics involves our analysis of and reflection on moral choices and judgments. Other guides to truth may involve religion, intuition, or advice from trusted others. However, within the study of ethics and interpersonal ethics, each of us must accept the difficult challenge of rationally defending our choices and actions. (pp. 2–3)

Englehardt's description of "the five moral systems" (duties, rights, utility, virtues, and relationships) highlights the importance of intentional "human actions." For example, deontological or "duty" ethics focuses on how "moral action discharges duty," "rights" ethics highlights how "moral action preserves individual rights," and utilitarian ethics clarifies how "moral action produces favorable consequences" (p. 18).

Englehardt's book also hosts communication scholar James Anderson's (1999) argument that "answers to questions of right and wrong" depend on an understanding of the self as "acting agent—the entity we would point to in answer to the question, 'Who did this?'… First, the agent is a particular and identifiable *agent of* action…second the agent is an *agent for* some recognizable intersection of cultural signs…. The self acts within some domain of agency" (p. 37).

Clearly there is a tradition among scholars in the human studies generally and particularly among communication ethicists to consider centrally the intentional choices of the individual moral agent, the rational subject, the choice-making communicator. Many classic Western ethical theories have been built around this construct, and a great deal of ethical advice focuses on the communicating subject's willingness and ability to make appropriate, humane, reasoned, empathic, or otherwise principled *choices*.

The Invitation to Reconsider Choice

Volumes of late 20th and early 21st century scholarship challenge the efficacy of understanding the human as a Cartesian rational *cogito*, the choice-making "subject" of Enlightenment theory and practice, including structuralism and poststructuralism, philosophical hermeneutics, and much of what has been termed "postmodern." But before many of these works were written, and before many seminal European writers were translated into English, a group of communication theorists and practitioners working in the United States challenged the centrality of choice when they produced, in 1967, one of the late 20th century's most influential books about human interaction, *Pragmatics of Human Communication*. The authors included transplanted Austrian psychotherapist Paul Watzlawick, young social psychologist Janet Helmick Beavin, and psychiatrist Don D. Jackson, all of whom were strongly influenced by their collaborations with British anthropologist, semiotician, and linguist Gregory Bateson. The book they published has been translated into German, Dutch, Spanish, French, Italian, Portuguese, Japanese, and Greek, and 42 years after publication, it still generates 232,000 Google references. Its contents continue to appear in multiple accounts of communication by both interpretive and social scientific interpersonal, organizational, rhetorical, and cultural communication scholars and authors of textbooks for courses in multiple disciplines.

The first chapter of *Pragmatics* outlines a Batesonian, ecological "frame of reference" that substitutes a *relational* perspective focused on "organism-environment interaction" for the dominant "monadic" view of humans (p. 29). The guiding metaphor of this frame of reference is the mathematical concept of "function" in which "variables do not have a meaning of their own; they are meaningful only in relation to one another" (p. 24). This frame of reference significantly includes central constructs from systems theory and cybernetics, and when it is used as a lens to view human interaction, the first insight that emerges is, as Watzlawick, Beavin, and Jackson (1967) put it, "the impossibility of not communicating." The authors express this insight as the first of five "tentative axioms of communication," "One cannot not communicate" (pp. 48–51). They reason to this tentative axiom in three short steps: First, there is no such thing as nonbehavior; one cannot *not* behave. Second, all behavior in an interactional situation has message value; that is, all behavior that is in any way observed may be interpreted; it "means something" to the observer. Thus, "it follows that no matter how one may try, one cannot *not* communicate" (p. 49), because, regardless of one's intent or choice, others can construct meaning from one's behavior.

Subsequent distinctions outlined in *Pragmatics* have functioned powerfully as theoretical, empirical, and clinical heuristics, including the distinctions between content and relationship "levels" of communication, between symmetrical and complementary relationships, and between analogic and digital communication codes. But the first axiom, with its catchy syntax and compelling intuitive coherence, has the potential to reorient the work of virtually every theorist and practitioner in the human studies who fully understands and adopts it. No longer is it satisfactory to understand humans communicating in Aristotelian-Quintilian-Ciceronian terms as speakers inventing, arranging, clothing, memorizing, and delivering ideas in and with language, or as a linear process involving a source, encoder, channel, decoder, destination, and noise, as information theorists argued, or even as a process linking Sender-Message-Channel-Receiver as outlined in David Berlo's influential *The Process of Communication* (1960). All these subject-, intent-, choice-, and for the most part verbal-centered conceptualizations are undercut by the effacement of the crucial notion of *purpose, choice, or intent*. If all behavior in an interactional situation may be interpreted as meaningful by others, then one's choices do not determine the outcomes of the behavior. If "one cannot not communicate," then one's communicative intent (purpose, choice) is only one among many parts of the puzzle. Elements that make up a communication event are meaningful in relation to each other, just as the elements are that make up a mathematical function. What one means is disconnected from what the other(s) may take one to mean. "Communication" thus becomes a label for *outcomes emerging in relationships* from interpretations of verbal and nonverbal cues. The term can no longer be simply a noun for the *effects* of *choices*, as in "He communicated his determination" or "Her communication was not ethical."

One indicator of the heuristic value of Axiom #1 was the publication of several essays that explored, clarified, and critiqued it (Bavelas, 1990; Beach, 1990; Motley, 1990a,1990b; Weiner, Devoe, Rubinow, & Geller, et al., 1979). Some respondents argued that the axiom claimed that "all behavior is communication," which led Weiner et al. (1972) and later Bavelas (1990) to emphasize that Axiom #1 applies only to behavior in an interactive situation. Others took issue with Watzlawick et al.'s disinterest in cognitive or "covert" operations that, they assert, "find their way into ongoing overt interactional behaviors" (Motley, 1990b, p. 616). Motley (1990a, 1990b) argued that the decision whether to attend to or ignore cognitive operations is methodological, and that "communication" may fruitfully be studied from either perspective. Bavelas (1990) and subsequently scholars self-identified as social constructionist (Gergen, 1994; Gergen & Gergen, 2003; Pearce, 2007; Stewart, Zediker, & Witteborn, 2005) countered that the decision to highlight or efface such cognitive operations as purpose, choice, or intention is much more than merely methodological. Gergen (1994), for example, described how the deconstruction of authorial intent in works by Derrida (1978), Wittgenstein (1953), and Rorty (1979) contributed to what is widely known as the "crisis in representation," a critique of the fundamental claims that language externally manifests internal states and that words "represent" aspects of "the world." The epistemological version of this claim is, in Gergen's (1994) words, that "The terms and forms by which we achieve understanding of the world and ourselves are social artifacts, products of historically and culturally situated interchanges among people" (p. 49). Especially because it focused on "situated interchanges among people," Watzlawick et al.'s "pragmatic" perspective shared with social construction these fundamental assumptions. Axiom #1 and the theoretical and empirical projects that have appropriated it demonstrate that communicative outcomes cannot be adequately accounted for as merely or even primarily the external manifestations of covert cognitive operations such as "intent" and "choice."

As my reference to social construction indicates, the metatheoretical move that is made in Axiom #1 is familiar to students of contemporary intellectual history. In the last third of the 20th century, dozens of authors identified as postmodern essayed implications of the effacement of the Cartesian *cogito*. To cite just one example, Hans-Georg Gadamer (1989) announced in the Foreword to the second edition of *Truth and Method,* "My real concern was and is philosophic: not what *we do* [italics added] or what we ought to do, but what happens to us over and above our wanting and doing" (p. xxviii). Choice, in other words, does not determine outcomes, and Gadamer was interested in significant outcomes.

There are also accounts in the recent ethics of communication literature of what can emerge when choice is effaced. For example, Ronald C. Arnett (2008) begins his reflection on terrorism with Levinas's rejection of "the sanctity of the originative communicative agent, displacing our understanding of ethics grounded in an individual agency" (p. 70). Arnett argues that, when guided by Levinas, the ethicist's concern with "the autonomous moral agent" is replaced by a relational understanding that, when applied to his topic, leads to the conclusion that "terrorism does not live merely in the lives of those who contend against us, but within any effort, including our own, that defaces another.… Levinas calls us to take humanism [and choice] off the map in order to remind us to attend to the face of all, even those who seek to deface our own" (p. 85).

In a conceptually related essay, Leslie A. Baxter and Chitra Akkoor (2008) demonstrate how Mikhail Bakhtin's dialogism replaces subject-centered understandings of romantic love with an understanding that decenters the sovereign self, its choices, and its intent. Baxter and Akkoor argue that, for Bakhtin, consciousness is not monadic but "a mutual process of authoring, an ongoing dynamic of joint action" (p. 27). Bakhtin (1990) terms this mutual authoring "answerability," which he views as "the ethical obligation of being human." "In essence," Baxter and Akkoor note, Bakhtin's position is that "our very consciousness as human beings depends on answering an Other—giving the Other the 'gift' of our excess of seeing" (p. 27). Concretely, answerability occurs in three "intertwined" events: empathy, difference, and meeting. First, "I must experience—come to see and to know—what he experiences" (p. 25). The second moment is a return "into myself, a return to my own place outside…" (p. 26), and the third "interanimates" unity and difference in human meeting. Baxter and Akkoor apply this analysis to an understanding of romantic love by contrasting monologic ideologies of romantic love that identify it with internal emotion, self-interested pursuit of similarity, or a finalized outcome of attraction (pp. 30–34). From Bakhtin's vantage, love is "the ongoing accomplishment of respectful attention" that emerges as partners mature together. The relational or social construction understanding of romantic love that Baxter and Akkoor develop positions them to clarify how love understood in this way is often deeply fostered in arranged marriages between subcontinent Indians. The authors conclude that when "romantic love is conceptualized as a psychological construct, communication is positioned as a conduit—a way to transmit to the Other one's feelings of love" (p. 40). A relational alternative is to "position communication as constitutive. It is through communication between persons that love—mutual, lingering attention—is constituted" (p. 40).

The Invitation Refused

Arnett, Baxter, and Akkoor are three communication scholars who have begun to consider the concrete impact of a relational understanding of communication on ethical praxis. But a glance at the current literature that is assigned to hundreds of thousands of English-speaking communication students—and read by at least many of them—demonstrates that this relational understanding is not yet a widely adopted part of communication pedagogy. Discussions of ethics in contemporary communication textbooks still generally treat choice as an unproblematic construct.

For example, the 2007 edition of one of the most widely adopted interpersonal communication texts (Verderber, Verderber, & Berryman-Fink, 2007) begins its discussion of the ethics of interpersonal communication with, "In any encounter we choose whether or not we will communicate ethically" (p. 12). "When we communicate," the authors continue, "we make choices with ethical implications. So we should understand the general ethical principles that form a basis for ethical interpersonal communication" (p. 13). They elaborate five of these choice-guiding principles: truthfulness and honesty, integrity, fairness, respect, and responsibility.

Several recent texts begin their ethics discussions with Richard Johanneson's argument that ethical issues are those that arise when behavior has significant impact on other persons, when the behavior involves conscious choice of means and ends, and when the behavior can be judged by standards of right and wrong. One authorial team writes, "We need to understand that because ethical choices can have lasting physical, emotional, financial, and psychological consequences, a sense of ethics should guide us on a daily basis" (West & Turner, 2009, p. 37). Another widely adopted text dependent on Johanneson begins with eight "principles of interpersonal communication," the third of which is "Interpersonal communication involves ethical choices" (Wood, 2007, p. 30). Importantly, the first principle is, "We cannot not communicate" (p. 29), but this author does not clarify how her first principle significantly changes the meaning of the third. Similarly incomplete accounts of choice can be found in many other widely adopted communication texts (e.g., Beebe, Beebe, & Redmond, 2008; Canary, Cody, & Manusov, 2008; DeVito, 2007; McCornack, 2007).

Incomplete analyses of choice-making also appear in accounts of applied ethics authored by philosophy teacher-scholars and others outside the discipline of communication. Since the 1970s, philosophy bibliographies have reflected increasing interest in practical ethics related to decisions about such topics as sexuality, family, abortion, treatment of animals, environmentalism, gender, race, privacy, immigration, and euthanasia. Some of these works display the ethical elements of debates over these issues without directly addressing the impact of varied analyses on individual choices (e.g., Baggini & Fosl, 2007; Cohen & Wellman, 2005; Singer, 1993). Others foreground choice in ways that echo the advice from communication textbook authors. For example, Scott B. Rae's *Moral Choices* (2000) focuses on "the moral life and moral decision-making" (p. 11). Similarly, James R. Otteson's *Actual Ethics* (2006) is dedicated to helping its readers "develop good *judgment*.... And we do so only when we enjoy the freedom to make decisions for ourselves and enjoy or suffer, as the case may be, the consequences of those decisions.... Judgment cannot develop if we are not required to take responsibility for our decisions" (p. x). Rita C. Manning and Scott R. Stroud (2008) include a chapter about communication in their book, *A Practical Guide to Ethics*, but their analysis focuses primarily on strategies for "finding the purpose of your speech," organizing ideas, gathering support, and developing effective delivery (pp. 130–138). These authors approvingly cite Foss and Foss's (2003) "invitational rhetoric" without appearing to recognize inconsistencies between elements of that view and their simplistically choice-focused analysis.

ETHICS, CHOICE, AND A NEXTING HELIX

What justifies calling these analyses "simplistic?" What is praxically problematic about these accounts of choice? My response, as noted earlier, is that they fail to acknowledge that *individual choices cannot assure ethical communication outcomes*. As Axiom #1 clarifies, one person's choices do not determine the outcomes of the communication events in which he or she participates—not the informational outcomes (whether "the others get it" or "I am understood"), the affective outcomes (the emotions experienced by the persons involved), or the ethical outcomes (whether participants are perceived to be respectful, fair, honest, etc.). This much is clear in a great deal of contemporary communication theorizing: What happens when people communicate is a function of events much more complex than the effects of any person's choices. Outcomes of communication emerge from multiple-events-in-context.

Does this mean that personal choices don't matter? Not at all. Each individual's choices contribute importantly to the complex from which communication outcomes emerge. But when one attends to the empirical realities of persons communicating, the critical piece of practical communication advice, for all aspects of communicative transactions (informational, emotional, ethical, etc.), is that one must endeavor consistently and continuously to attend and respond to what happens *next*. Especially because of the pervasive and local influence of globalization on emergent outcomes, every person wishing to engage ethically in communicating needs not only to make careful choices but also to attend the outcomes of these choices *and* to respond appropriately to the uptake from Other(s). In other words, one must attend not only to his or her own considered and principled choices but also, and continuously, to the outcomes affected by those choices as they inform and promote subsequent choices. This is the advice that follows from the combination of full awareness of Axiom #1, a relational understanding of communication, a commitment to ethical communicating, and acceptance of the reality of globalization.

Karen Zediker, Saskia Witteborn, and I (Stewart et al., 2005) call this practice "nexting," and argue that it is "the most important single communication skill" (p. 46). We also describe how choices reveal ethical standards and commitments (pp. 37–38) while cautioning readers that "no one individual has complete control" over communication outcomes and that "all of our choices are made within the context of our personal experience and are evaluated in accordance with cultural norms and expectations" (p. 38). Our discussion of nexting, however, does not thoroughly explain the connections between that vital skill and the ethics of communicating. I hope the present discussion helps remedy this shortcoming.

The topics and insights that I am attempting to integrate here—applied communication ethics, a relational understanding of communication, Axiom #1, and globalization—lead me to suggest that teacher-scholars of ethical praxis might want to respond to the invitation to reconsider Enlightenment accounts of choice by exploring the effectiveness of the metaphor of a "nexting helix." As is well-known, a helix is a three-dimensional curve that lies on a cylinder or cone, so that its angle to a plane perpendicular to the axis is constant (*American Heritage Dictionary,* 1992, p. 839)—the threads of a wood screw. Visually, the figure of a helix depicts ongoing circular movement that never returns to itself—as does the line of a circle—but that continually changes incrementally. Communicating individuals might usefully visualize themselves as moving together along this helical line, integrating individual and shared expectations and actions with new interpretations that result in outcomes being more than just "the same thing over and over"; in other words, understanding that outcomes are *continuously emergent.* If ellipses or infinity symbols are added at the beginning and end of this helix, then the figure can also represent the fact that communication was ongoing when each of us was born and will certainly continue after our death. This means, as Bakhtin (1986) emphasized, that every communicative contribution that any person makes can be understood to be *responsive* to what preceded and contextualizes it *and* that communicative outcomes, what Gadamer (1989) termed "what happens to us over and above our wanting and doing" (p. xviii), are continuously emergent—always opening out into what happens *next.*

Bakhtin's (1986) insight about responsiveness is particularly apt here, because he explains how the realities of what he terms "speech communicating" illustrate the oversimplified quality of choice-based accounts. Bakhtin writes,

> Thus, all real and integral understanding is actively responsive, and constitutes nothing other than the initial preparatory stage of a response (in whatever form it may be actualized). And the speaker himself is oriented precisely toward such an actively responsive understanding. He does not expect passive understanding that, so to speak, only duplicates his own idea in someone else's mind. Rather he expects response, agreement, sympathy, objection, execution, and so forth.... Moreover, any speaker is himself a respondent to a greater or lesser degree. He is not, after all, the first speaker, the one who disturbs the eternal silence of the universe. And he presupposes not only the existence of the language system he is using, but also the existence of preceding utterances—his own and others. (p. 69)

Neither speaker nor listener, in other words, is originating the interaction they experience together; both are responding to global and local elements that contextualize their communicating and affect what emerges between them.

A. J. Conyers (2009) highlights the contrast between this understanding of responsiveness and the focus on choice in his explanation of the Christian concept of "vocation." Conyers argues that one residue of Enlightenment thinking was a subject-based philosophical anthropology that eventuated in the "distinctly modern prejudice" that "might be called the 'Invictus' principle. We think for ourselves; we are the masters of our souls" (p. 19). Our choices, in other words, determine the outcomes we experience. "Over against this," Conyers (2009) writes,

> is the understanding of life that has always struck human beings as belonging to the province of common sense. We came into a world that existed before us. We leave this world long before things resolve themselves.... So, in order to live here with any semblance of wisdom, purpose, and order, we need "the guidance of another." (p. 19)

From Conyers's theological vantage, this guidance comes as a call from the human's divine author. And this "is the opposite of 'choice,' or of freedom in the sense of self-determination" (p. 17). But the acknowledgment that human life is fundamentally responsive is valid with or without the theological overtones, especially human life with others. Choices clearly make a difference, and one must make choices in order to engage the people and topics one encounters. But individual choices do not determine outcomes.

One important benefit of using this helical figure to understand each communication event—face-to-face, online, at home or work, with intimates or enemies—can be that one becomes continuously aware of what happens *after* one's own communication choices, and that this awareness can direct one's decision about what to do *next*. Importantly, the helix does not imply that what happens *after* happens simply *because* of what I do; the Other(s) is (are) living out consequential choices, too. But insofar as I attend to emergent outcomes, I am positioned to choose next actions consistent with my preferences, values, goals, etc. One's choices are wide-ranging. I may choose to withdraw in order to protect myself from, or to reduce the escalation of, certain outcomes. I may choose to restate, engage in face-saving or face-repair, defer, cite more evidence, apologize, circumscribe, or insist. But in each case, insofar as I am attending to emergent outcomes and integrating them into my next-actions, I am being response-able. And response-ability, understood as the willingness and ability to respond, is a key feature of ethical communicating. As Buber (1965) wrote, "Genuine responsibility exists only where there is real responding" (p. 16).

There are significant differences between this approach and treatments of applied ethics anchored in an Enlightenment understanding of choice. In *Ethics for the Real World* (2008), Stanford professor of management science and engineering Ronald A. Howard and his coauthor Clinton D. Korver offer "practical advice on how to make more effective decisions every day" and "to create a personal ethical code" (cover). These authors argue that ethical decision making involves four phases:

> In the first phase, we develop awareness of ethical temptation and compromise... In the next phase, we learn how to use ethical logic and principles to foster clear thinking... In the third phase, we learn to make ethical choices.... In the final phase we go beyond ethical basics to using ethics as a lever for better living. (pp. 5–6)

The central chapter of Howard and Korver's book, *Choose Action: Systematic Ethical Decision Making*, presents a guide to "quality decisions," by which the authors mean "decisions where we have followed a high-quality process and adhered to proven principles" (p. 93). In this chapter, they detail each of the crucial "phases": Clarifying the salient ethical issues, creating alternatives, evaluating alternatives, and making a best choice. These authors do note that, if one's ethical position is consequentialist, one must "add three steps to our process: Characterize consequences of each alternative. Assess uncertainties. Evaluate trade-offs" (p. 106). But their focus is consistently on consequential actions, not *next*-actions. As the authors themselves note, their focus on "high quality" choices and actions

> is not to be confused with high-quality outcomes, the results of the decision. None of us can know the future, which means we can make a good decision and end up with a bad outcome; or we can make a bad decision and end up with a good outcome. Of course, in most cases, the worse the decision, the worse the outcome. (p. 93)

These authors reiterate in the final paragraph of their book that they focus on "find[ing] convincing reasons to take right action" (p. 154).

Problems arise if one attempts to follow this advice, especially in a global context. For example, Irene's acculturation as traditionally Japanese may have contextualized her awareness of what Howard and Korver call "ethical temptation and compromise" and her development of "ethical logic and principles" to the point that she chooses to respond to a moral challenge with face-saving deference. Although she understands the challenge and privately supports the position she hears, Irene smiles, lowers her eyes, speaks softly, and offers neutral or mitigating comments. David, her traditionally North American conversation partner, interprets Irene's actions as indecisive, compromising, and morally suspect—far from what she intended. He doubts Irene's ethical courage and has no evidence that she supports the position he articulated. David responds with scorn, an outcome which puzzles and threatens Irene, who attempts to respond again with more conflict avoidance, to the point where the two end their conversation in mutual misunderstanding. In this situation, both Irene and David may be effectively following the advice of applied ethicists and communication ethics scholar-teachers to make considered and principled choices. But because they are not focused on outcomes-and-next-choices, their communication is less than effective or satisfying.

If Irene were to understand the exchange helically, she would be paying attention not just to her choices but also to the outcomes of her choices-in-context and their implications for her next actions. When the outcome—in this case David's scorn—reveals the nature of his uptake of her turn at talk, Irene would be positioned to repair the misunderstanding, for example, with metacommunication—"I don't mean that I don't care"—or an alternative expression of her position—"That happened to me when…and I decided that I definitely believe.…" Of course, since these options require Irene to move culturally toward David's position, they presume that she is biculturally competent and motivated to connect effectively with David. In a parallel way, if David were to understand the exchange helically, he might respond to Irene's defensive uptake of his scorn with his own repair attempts. A helical frame for understanding does not guarantee outcomes that are consistently ethically apt, but it does position conversation partners to make optimally effective next-choices.[2]

Of course, the example of Irene and David is oversimplified, because cultural commitments are virtually always multifaceted rather than simply "traditionally Japanese" and "traditionally North American." Hybridity is the norm. Living, spontaneous human events mix multiple embodiments of gender, age, ethnicity, class, and other cultural influences. This complexity makes it even more difficult to predict or control the outcome of one's ethical choices and thus even more important to attend and respond to what happens next.

It may appear that I am only proposing an incremental change in applied communication ethics, from a focus only on first choices to consideration of all choices that communicators make. But I understand this position to be transformational, not just incremental. The combination of a full awareness of Axiom #1, a relational understanding of communication, a commitment to ethical communicating, and an acceptance of the reality of globalization results in a conceptualization of communication that is fundamentally different from the model that is implicit in most current accounts of ethical choice-making. The majority of those accounts are monadic, or at best, interactional. They presume *actions* performed by individual *subjects* engaged in processes understandable as *causally* related and thus producing predictable *effects*—"She confused me." "He lied," "She told the truth but he took advantage of her." These accounts' focus on choice embodies either the assumption that choice will cause the desired outcome or that the individual communicator's "responsibility" ends when he or she makes a carefully considered choice. But when one understands communication as relational and emergent, and one focuses on outcomes, the inadequacy of these assumptions becomes apparent. There is no direct, causal relationship between choices and outcomes. Responsibility, understood as the willingness and ability continuously to respond, does not end with one's choices. When accounts that embody these assumptions are mobilized in the service of applied ethics, they generate the kinds of subject-centered advice reviewed earlier in this essay. From this incomplete perspective, a primary feature of ethical awareness is ethical integrity, understood as the sense that *one* can (and should) "choose what's right."

But one's *choices cannot "rightness" make*. And this is why the understanding outlined here embodies more than an incremental change. In practice, "rightness," to continue the awkward construction, cannot be guaranteed by an individual's choices; rightness is an outcome that may emerge-in-context. No one individual determines the ethical outcomes of a communication transaction, whether face-to-face, on line, in print, or otherwise mediated. Meanings or understandings are a function (cf. Watzlawick et al.) of the multiple contributions that make up each communication event. Especially because of the pervasive and concrete effects of globalization, one should never focus exclusively or even primarily on the processes of ethical choice-making and implementation, as challenging as those processes are. Rather than assuming closure or finality in ethical events, one should focus continuously on the uptake of choices by others, as they move with us through next events. As Howard and Korver (2008) emphasize, "…we can make a good decision and end up with a bad outcome; or we can make a bad decision and end up with a good outcome" (p. 93). What Howard and Korver fail to recognize, however, is that this realization should compel students of communication ethics to move beyond simplistic analyses of choice to something akin to the helical understanding proposed here.

An undergraduate discovered first-hand the inadequacy of "Choose what's right" advice when, over several months, she witnessed an escalating relationship between her roommate and a young, charismatic faculty member. Many evenings, the faculty member made himself available at neighborhood bars for conversations with students about their science projects. He saw himself as mentor and coach, and students appreciated his accessibility and attention. But it became obvious, especially to Anna, that the professor and her roommate were becoming more than friends. Anna's awareness of ethical issues and principles had been enhanced by her involvement in a campus-wide ethics-across-the-curriculum program. As Anna told the story, she felt torn between her friendship with her roommate and her realization that the professor's relationship with Beth was inappropriate. Anna and Beth had been roommates for 3 years, and many shared challenges and celebrations had made them best friends. Anna couldn't bear the thought of betraying Beth, but she also knew that what was happening between Beth and the professor was wrong. After listening to an on-campus speaker discuss the importance of ethical courage, her anguish escalated to the point where it seriously interfered with her sleeping and eating. Finally, Anna confided in a trusted faculty member who accompanied her to the dean's office, where Anna tearfully recounted what she'd seen and heard.

It was obvious to the professor and the dean that Anna understood the ethical dimensions of the situation and knew what was right. She acknowledged this herself. But she was unable to act for many weeks primarily because of what she believed would happen *next*, after she implemented her ethical choice. For her, the advice, "Choose what's right," was not praxically adequate. Anna was convinced that if she said anything about the relationship, she would lose her best friend, seriously damage the life of one of her favorite professors, and be condemned by her student friends who were also enjoying the professor's attention. The faculty member in whom she finally confided did his best to present other possibilities—her roommate might be grateful rather than enraged; future young women would be protected from the professor's predatory behavior; Anna would be respected for her courage. He and the dean promised to help Anna cope with what happened after she made her choice.

The university corroborated Anna's testimony, confronted the faculty member, and, when he admitted the inappropriate relationship, terminated his employment. But Anna experienced first-hand the practical challenges of what she had studied in her ethics classes. She discovered that when one develops what Howard and Korver (2008) call "awareness of ethical temptation and compromise" it can be as painful as it is enlightening. She discovered that, to her credit, she did know "how to use logic and ethical principles to foster clear thinking" (p. 5) and arrive at a right ethical choice. But, as an intensely practical matter, she was for a long time unable to act because of her assumption that, when she made her choice, that would determine what happened next, and the outcomes would unquestionably be negative. She had been taught that individual choice, right action, was the end-goal of applied ethics, yet she knew otherwise. She was effectively paralyzed by her beliefs about what would happen after she made her ethical choice. Anna was able to move forward only when she discovered resources to help her cope with movement along the helix, in this case, a supportive faculty advisor, and an institutional system willing to deal decisively with inappropriate faculty behavior. She also found support for what would inevitably happen after she spoke up. She was protected from public scrutiny, discovered peers who respected her courage and affirmed her action, and, over time, was even able to repair important aspects of her relationship with Beth.[3]

CONCLUSION

In 2009, while this essay was being completed, a Forum sponsored by the editors of *Communication Monographs* and *Journal of Applied Communication Research* was addressing the question, "Has communication research made a difference?" Invited essays by Celeste Condit (2009), Matthew Seeger (2009), Lawrence R. Frey (2009), and Mary Lee Hummert (2009) set the stage for next turns-at-talk invited from interested readers, and the Forum was scheduled to be concluded by statements from Dennis S. Gouran and Charles R. Berger. One theme of the first four contributions to this Forum was that, like other academic projects, some communication research has made some differences, *and* the discipline's scholars could do much more to make their findings accessible and relevant to policy-makers, activists, and other change agents.

This chapter responds to a similar impetus. Communication research can indeed make a difference, because the focal interest on what I have called verbal–nonverbal articulate contact (Stewart, 1995) that distinctively characterizes the work of communication scholars empowers researchers in this discipline to critique and reformulate assumptions about human contact that can significantly affect theorizing and empirical efforts across the human studies. In this essay I offer one example of this potential. I argue that the shift in focus by communication researchers and teachers from linear, subject-, intent-, choice- and for the most part, verbal-focused models of communication to relational, social-construction understandings requires a reformulation of at least one basic construct that is central to applied ethics, the construct of choice. When verbal–nonverbal articulate contact is understood helically, as sketched here, ethical advice becomes focused not simply on individual choices but on the complex of choice-uptake-outcome-next-choice…, with the ellipsis an important part of the formulation. When applied ethics scholar-teachers across the human studies accept the invitation of communication scholarship to reconsider choice, this, it seems to me, is where their acceptance might fruitfully lead.

NOTES

1. Appiah (2006) prefers the term *cosmopolitanism,* because "globalization…once referred to a marketing strategy, and then came to designate a macroeconomic thesis, and now can seem to encompass everything, and nothing" (p. xiii). But his preference has not yet been adopted. Hence, I use the more widely accepted term.

2. Conversation analysis (Arundale & Good, 2002; Hopper, Koch, & Mandelbaum, 1986) is one empirical approach to the study of communication that takes seriously the helical understanding outlined here.
3. Elements of this story have been changed to protect the identities of the parties. "Beth" gave permission to publish this version. The story is less an example of Anna "doing nexting ethically or well" and more an illustration of the practical, concrete inadequacies of choice-based advice and of how the nexting helix can facilitate a nuanced understanding of a complex and poignant human communication situation.

REFERENCES

American heritage dictionary of the English language (3rd ed.). (1992). Boston, MA: Houghton Mifflin.

Anderson, J. (1999). Identify and self. In E. Englehardt (Ed.), *Ethical issues in interpersonal communication* (pp.35–39). Fort Worth, TX: Harcourt College.

Appiah, K. A. (2006). *Cosmopolitanism: Ethics in a world of strangers.* New York: Norton.

Appiah, K. A. (2008). *Experiments in ethics.* Cambridge, MA: Harvard University Press.

Arneson, P. (Ed.). (2007). *Exploring communication ethics: Interviews with influential scholars in the field.* New York: Lang.

Arnett, R. C., Arneson, P., & Bell, L. M. (2007). Communication ethics: The dialogic turn. In P. Arneson (Ed.), *Exploring communication ethics* (pp. 143–184). New York: Lang.

Arnett, R. C. (2008). Provinciality and the face of the other: Levinas on communication ethics, terrorism—otherwise than originative agency. In K. G. Roberts & R. Arnett (Eds.), *Communication ethics: Between cosmopolitanism and provinciality.* New York: Lang.

Arundale, R. B., & Good, D. A. (2002). Boundaries and sequences in studying conversation. In A. Fetzer & C. Meierkord (Eds.), *Rethinking sequentiality* (pp. 121–150). Amsterdam, the Netherlands: John Benjamins.

Baggini, J., & Fosl, P. S. (2007). *The ethics toolkit: A compendium of ethical concepts and methods.* Oxford, UK: Blackwell.

Bakhtin, M. (1986). *Speech genres and other late essays* (V. W. McGee, Trans.). Austin: University of Texas Press.

Bakhtin, M. (1990). *Art and answerability: Early philosophical essays by M. M. Bakhtin* (M. Holquist, Ed.; V. Liapunov, Trans.). Austin: University of Texas Press.

Bavelas, J. B. (1990). Behaving and communicating: A reply to Motley. *Western Journal of Speech Communication, 54,* 593–602.

Baxter, L. A., & Akkoor, C. (2008). Aesthetic love and romantic love in close relationships. In K. G. Roberts & R. C. Arnett (Eds.), *Communication ethics: Between cosmopolitianism and provinciality* (pp. 23–46). New York: Lang.

Beach, W. A. (1990). On (not) observing behavior interactionally. *Western Journal of Speech Communication, 54,* 603–612.

Beebe, S. A., Beebe, S. J., & Redmond, M. V. (2008). *Interpersonal communication* (5th ed.). Boston,MA: Pearson Education.

Berlo, D. (1960). *The process of communication.* New York: Holt, Rinehart & Winston.

Bok, S. (1999). *Lying: Moral choice in public and private life.* New York: Vintage.

Buber, M. (1965). *Between man and man* (R. G. Smith, Trans.). New York: Macmillan.

Burke, K. (1966). *Language as symbolic action: Essays on life, literature, and method.* Berkeley: University of California Press.

Canary, D. J., Cody, M. J., & Manusov, V. L. (2008). *Interpersonal communication: A goals-based approach.* Boston, MA: Bedford/St. Martin's.

Chesbro, J. (1969). A construct for assessing ethics in communication. *Central States Speech Journal, 20,* 104–114.

Cohen, A. I., & Wellman, C. H. (Eds.). (2005). *Contemporary debates in applied ethics.* Oxford, UK: Blackwell.

Condit, C. M. (2009). You can't study and improve communication with a telescope. *Communication Monographs, 76*, 3–11.

Conyers, A. J. (2009). *The listening heart: Vocation and the crisis of modern culture.* Waco, TX: Baylor University Press.

Derrida, J. (1978). *Writing and difference* (A. Bas, Trans.). Chicago, IL: University of Chicago Press.(Original work published 1967)

DeVito, J. A. (2007). *The interpersonal communication book* (11th ed.). Boston, MA: Pearson Education.

Englehardt, E. E. (1999). *Ethical issues in interpersonal communication.* Fort Worth, TX: Harcourt College.

Foss, S. K., & Foss, K. A. (2003). *Inviting transformation: Presentational speaking for a changing world* (2nd ed.). Long Grove, IL: Waveland Press.

Frey, L. R. (2009). What a difference more difference-making communication scholarship might make: Making a difference from and through communication research. *Journal of Applied Communication Research, 37*, 205–214.

Friedman, M. (1983). *The confirmation of Otherness in family, community and society.* New York: Pilgrim Press.

Gadamer, H-G. (1989). *Truth and method* (2nd rev.). In J. Weinsheimer & D. G. Marshall (Ed. & Trans.). New York: Crossroad.

Gergen, K. J. (1994). *Realities and relationships: Soundings in social construction.* Cambridge, MA: Harvard University Press.

Gergen, K. J., & Gergen, M. (Eds.). (2003). *Social construction: A reader.* Newbury Park, CA: Sage.

Hopper, R., Koch, S., & Mandelbaum, J. (1986). Conversation analysis methods. In D. G. Ellis & W. A. Donohue (Eds.), *Contemporary issues in language and discourse processes* (pp 169–186). Hillsdale, NJ: Erlbaum.

Howard, R. A., &. Korver, C. D. (2008). *Ethics for the real world: Creating a personal code to guide decisions in work and life.* Boston, MA: Harvard Business Press.

Hummert, M. L. (2009). Not just preaching to the choir: Communication scholarship does make a difference. *Journal of Applied Communication Research, 37*, 215–224.

Johannesen, R. L. (2001). Communication ethics: Centrality, trends, and controversies. In W. B. Gudykunst (Ed.), *Communication yearbook* (Vol. 25, pp. 201–235). Mahwah, NJ: Erlbaum.

Johannesen, R. L. (2007). A conversation about communication ethics with Richard L. Johannesen. In P. Arneson (Ed.). *Exploring communication ethics: Interviews with influential scholars in the field* (pp. 37–52). New York: Lang.

Johnstone, C. L. (1981). Ethics, wisdom, and the mission of contemporary rhetoric: The realization of human being. *Central States Speech Journal, 32*, 177–188.

Kant, I. (1785, March). Über Vulkane Im Monde [On the volcanoes of the moon]. *Monatsschrift*, 199–223.

Manning, R., & Stroud, S. R. (2008). *A practical guide to ethics.* Boulder, CO: Westview Press.

McCornack, S. (2007). *Reflect & relate.* Boston, MA: Bedford/St. Martin's.

Motley, M. T. (1990a). On whether one can(not) not communicate: An examination via traditional communication postulates. *Western Journal of Speech Communication, 54*, 1–20.

Motley, M. T. (1990b). Communication as interaction: A reply to Beach and Bavelas. *Western Journal of Speech Communication, 54*, 613–623.

Myers, J. (2002). *One world: The ethics of globalization.* Retrieved from http://www.cceia.org/resources/transcripts/164.html

Otteson, J. R. (2006). *Actual ethics.* Cambridge, UK: Cambridge University Press.

Pearce, W. B. (2007). *Making social worlds: A communication perspective.* Oxford, UK: Blackwell.

Rae, S. B. (2000). *Moral choices.* Grand Rapids, MI: Zondervan.

Rorty, R. (1979). *Philosophy and the mirror of nature.* Princeton, NJ: Princeton University Press.

Seeger, M. (2009). Does communication research make a difference? Reconsidering the impact of our work. *Communication Monographs, 76*, 12–19.

Singer, P. (1993). *Practical ethics* (2nd ed.). Cambridge, UK: Cambridge University Press.

Stewart, J. (1995). *Language as articulate contact: Toward a post-semiotic philosophy of communication.* Albany, NY: SUNY Press

Stewart, J., Zediker, K. E., & Witteborn, S. (2005). *Together: Communicating interpersonally* (6th ed.). New York: Oxford University Press.

Theunissen, M. (1984). *The Other: Studies in the social ontology of Husserl, Heidegger, Sartre, and Buber* (C. Macann, Trans.). Cambridge, NJ: MIT Press. (Original work published 1982)

Verderber, K. S., Verderber, R. F., & Berryman-Fink, C. (2007). *Inter-Act* (11th ed.). New York: Oxford University Press.

Watzlawick, P., Beavin, J. H. & Jackson, D. D. (1967). *Pragmatics of human communication.* New York: Norton.

Weiner, M., Devoe, S., Rubinow, S., & Geller, J. (1979). Nonverbal behavior and nonverbal communication, *Psychological Review, 79*, 185–214.

West, R., & Turner, H. (2009). *Understanding interpersonal communication: Making choices in changing times.* Boston: Wadsworth.

Wittgenstein, L. (1953). *Philosophical investigations* (G. Anscombe, Trans.). New York: Macmillan.

Wood, J. T. (2007). *Interpersonal communication: Everyday encounters* (5th ed.). Belmont, CA: Thompson.

3

Ethics, Rhetoric, and Discourse

Michael J. Hyde

Intellectual assessments of the relationship between ethics, rhetoric, and discourse date back to the ancient Greeks and their concern with the ethical function of public moral argument in the workings of the body politic. The most famous philosophical starting point of the assessments arises when Socrates and Plato (trans., *Gorgias; Phaedrus; Sophist*; 1973a, 1973b, 1973c) take exception to how the discursive practice of coming to terms with "the truth" is too easily and too readily impeded by the manipulating and deceptive ways of the orator's art. Hippocratic physicians, for example, had to deal with this problem when these first men of scientific medicine sought to define and defend their *techne* during public debates against traveling sophistic lecturers and those quack doctors whose practice still admitted the use of magical charms (Edelstein, 1967; Hyde, 2001).

With the Hippocratics in mind, Socrates and Plato argued that as medicine is currently developing a rational understanding of the body and its diseases, so must rhetoric develop a rational understanding of the soul and of any topic that is discussed to influence it. Rhetoric, in other words, must become scientific in scope and function; it must know itself to be a true medicament of the soul. Aristotle modifies this claim somewhat so as not to destroy what he takes to be rhetoric's "true nature" *(physis)*. For unlike medicine, rhetoric is not a science; it has no definite subject matter to call its own. Rather, it makes its living by dealing "with what is in the main contingent" (Aristotle, *Rhetoric*, trans., 1357a15). Rhetoric is there to help human beings deliberate about the certainty of their uncertain existence. It stands ready to answer the call of those who find themselves in situations where "definitive evidence" that can guide moral action is lacking, but where such action, nevertheless, is required (Blumenberg, 1987). Rhetoric is a competence that gives expression to our ability to be persuasive, to make known the useful and the inexpedient, the fitting and the improper, the just and the unjust, thereby enabling us to engage others in collaborative deliberation about contestable matters (Farrell, 1993).

A history of the Western rhetorical tradition is documented throughout the many entries composing *The Encylopedia of Rhetoric* (Sloane, 2001). With this 837 page book in hand, one gains a sense that the literature on the art's relationship with ethics and discourse is, to say the least, immense and complex. Indeed, the scope and function of the relationship is such that it warrants the attention of many disciplines besides rhetoric and philosophy that recognize the relationship's necessary presence in the midst of their teaching and research interests. Theology, literature, sociology, political theory, law, economics, science, and, of course, communication studies, are cases in point. Within this last mentioned field, rhetoric's relationship with ethics and discourse is most commonly associated with the related professional divisions "Communication

Ethics" and "Rhetorical Theory and Communication" (National Communication Association) and "Philosophy of Communication" (International Communication Association) (Arneson, 2007a, 2007b; Arnett, Fritz, & Bell, 2009; Cook & Holba, 2008; Hyde, 2004; Johannesen, Valde, & Whedbee, 2008).

Communication scholars interested in "discourse analysis" also speak to the importance of rhetoric's relationship with ethics in their investigations of language-in-use, the interactive production of meaning in conversational encounters (Bavelas, Kenwood, & Phillips, 2002) and the moral implications of the media in contemporary public life (Chouliaraki, 2006; Chouliaraki & Fairclough, 1999). Jacobs's (2002) observation regarding the history of this research procedure is noteworthy: "Knowing what language does has commonly been thought to be superfluous to knowing what language is. While this attitude has begun to fade, the term *language* has been so thoroughly appropriated by the technical structural interests of sentence grammarians that any effort to study the uses of language or the structures of language beyond the sentence requires use of a whole new term: *discourse*" (p. 213). Discourse analysts make much of *how* language is actually employed in structuring specific interpersonal communication transactions (e.g., the physician/patient/family relationship; see Beach, 2008). Focusing on how language functions in such transactions necessarily brings a rhetorical perspective to the circumstances under consideration; for rhetorical analysis, as the ancient Greeks first made clear, is concerned not only with what a given text means, but also and primarily with how it means: the various ways that its discourse produces understanding, attitudes, and beliefs, calls for critical judgment, and encourages action (Farrell, 1993). Discourse analysts distinguish their research agenda from those of rhetorical scholars by attending to how, for example, "turn taking" and creating "openings" in conversations affect their evolving meaning and establish power relationships between the involved parties (Sacks, Schegloff, & Jefferson, 1974; Schegloff & Sachs 1973).

Ethics, rhetoric, and discourse show themselves in our everyday existence. Their display admits an ontological status. Ethics, rhetoric, and discourse lie at the heart of human being. The purpose of this essay is to clarify this fact of life by offering a phenomenological assessment of the phenomena's relationship. Such an assessment allows us to appreciate the empirical presence of the phenomena from "the ground up": from the fundamental spatial and temporal fabric of existence to the constructed social and political domains that we create and inhabit on a daily basis with the help of ethics, rhetoric, and discourse. The assessment thereby also enables us to appreciate certain ontological presuppositions that inform all else that can be said about the relationship's existential presence and dynamics (no matter what discipline has the floor). The presuppositions I emphasize here include: the "dwelling place" (*ethos*) of ethics, the "call of conscience," "emotion and the happening of truth," "the life-giving gift of acknowledgment," and "otherness." The relationship of ethics, rhetoric, and discourse calls to mind a host of matters that, as I hope to make clear in what follows, are crucial for the well-being of humankind.

THE *ETHOS* OF ETHICS

Ethics is a discipline that deals with what is good and bad and with moral duty and obligation. The Greek for ethics is *ethos*. This specific term is also commonly associated with a person's "moral character." This second sense of *ethos* is what Isocrates has in mind when considering the nature of the orator's art: For "who does not know that words carry greater conviction when spoken by men of good repute than when spoken by men who live under a cloud, and that the argument which is made by a man's life is more weight than that which is furnished by words?" (Isocrates, trans., 1982, p. 278). *Ethos* is both a legitimating source for and a praiseworthy effect of the practice of rhetoric. Heeding the call of public service as a person of "good repute," the orator's presence and rhetorical competence are a display of a "principled self" that instructs the moral consciousness and actions of others and thereby serves as a possible catalyst for them to do the same for the good of their community (Hyde, 2004, pp. xiii–xxviii; Hyde, 2010, p. 63).

Isocrates anticipates the doctrine of *ethos* developed in Aristotle's *Rhetoric*, but with this doctrine comes a significant change in the technical use of the term. For Aristotle, *ethos* is not primarily associated with the orator's reputation for being a wise and honest soul, but rather with the actual rhetorical competence displayed in the orator's discourse. The practice of rhetoric constitutes an active construction of character; *ethos* takes form as a result of the orator's abilities to argue and to deliberate and thereby to inspire trust in an audience. Aristotle thus directs our attention away from an understanding of *ethos* as a person's well-lived existence and toward an understanding of *ethos* as an artistic accomplishment (Garver, 1994).

Although Isocrates and Aristotle emphasize different senses of *ethos*, there nevertheless exists a more fundamental existential and ontological connection between the two. Aristotle's understanding of artful ethos presupposes that the character that takes place in the orator's specific text is itself contextualized and thereby made possible by past social, political, and rhetorical transactions that inform the orator's and his audience's ongoing, communal existence: the "places," "habitats," and "haunts" (*ethea;* plural of *ethos*) wherein people dwell and bond together. This use of *ethos* as "dwelling place" dates back to Homer and Hesiod (Chamberlain, 1984; Heidegger, 1977/1947; Miller, 1974). Aristotle develops this particular usage of *ethos* when, in the *Nicomachean Ethics*, he discusses how, beginning in childhood, "ethical" virtues can be trained and made habitual (2.1.1103a17-30).

What I am emphasizing about *ethos* and its relationship to rhetorical discourse directs our attention to the "architectural" function of the orator's art (McKeon, 1971): how, for example, its practice grants such *living room* to our lives that we might feel more *at home* with others and our surroundings. The *ethos* of rhetoric would have one appreciate how the *premises* and other materials of arguments are not only tools of logic but also mark out the *boundaries* and *domains* of thought that, depending on how their specific discourses are *designed* and *arranged*, may be particularly inviting and moving for some audience. The *ethos* of rhetoric makes use of our inventive and symbolic capacity to construct dwelling places—or what discourse analysts term "architecture[s] of intersubjectivity" (Heritage, 1984; Jacobs, 2002; Rommetveit, 1974)—that are stimulating and aesthetically, psychologically, socially, and morally instructive. With architecture in mind, we might also speak of the construction as an "edifying" discourse (to edify, Latin: aedificare: aedes, "dwelling" + ficare, "to make" or "to build") whose communal character (ethos) takes form as the communication and rhetorical architect uses materials (e.g., tropes, figures, topics, arguments, narratives, emotions) to attract our attention, maintain our interest, and encourage us to judge the work as being praiseworthy and persuasive.

As we direct our communicative and rhetorical competence toward achieving this goal, we accept the responsibility of becoming *home-makers*, builders of those special places where "the heart" is suppose to be and where others thus feel welcome and at home while thinking about and discussing the truth of some matter of interest. The genuine enrichment of interpersonal relationships and public opinion require as much. Indeed, it is discomforting to feel "out of place" in the company of others (Casey, 1993; Hyde, 2006, pp. 60–116; Hyde, 2010, pp. 243–279).

In meeting this challenge, people place their own characters on the line and in the text. The ethical practice of rhetoric entails the construction of a speaker's or a writer's *ethos* as well as the construction of a dwelling place for collaborative and moral deliberation. The process was at work when Hippocratic physicians made their case for the importance of scientific medicine. The same can be said whenever people are constructing, deconstructing, and reconstructing their social and political ideologies. An ideology is a dwelling place: a discursive habitat offering a worldview that, for "good reasons," commends certain habits of thinking and acting, promotes with its guiding narratives notions of progress and perfection, and thereby encourages specific ways of being with and evaluating others (Aune, 1994; Fisher, 1987). Discourse analysts and rhetorical critics make their living by analyzing data housed in these habitats. Here, too, is the founding place of research in organizational communication (Cheney, 1991; McMillan & Hyde, 2000); for in addition to whatever else can be said about their nature, organizations present concrete forms of what is being defined here as a dwelling place.

THE CALL OF CONSCIENCE

Ethics and moral character presuppose a dwelling place wherein they can take form and be cultivated. Heidegger (1977) makes much of this point in his ontologically oriented discussion of humankind's ethical nature. He emphasizes that, in its most primordial form, *ethos* "names the open region in which man dwells" (p. 233). This open region shows itself in the ongoing and future-oriented process of human being: the way the objective uncertainty of our spatial and temporal existence—*before* it is reduced to the measurements of clocks, calendars, and maps—is forever opening and exposing us to the unknown and thus challenging us to assume the ethical responsibility of affirming the burden of our freedom of choice. The challenge calls us to think and act such that we can bring a sense of order and meaning to our lives and to our relationships with others. This is how systems of morality (e.g., institutionalized religion) come into being in the first place. The perfectionist driven language of morality is the language of responsiveness and responsibility that is called for by the ontological workings of human being (Hyde, 2010).

History is the recorded consequences of our answering this challenging call—a call that permeates the fabric of our being but that *is not* a human creation. We had nothing to do with creating the original dynamics of our spatial and temporal existence that came about approximately 15 billion years ago with a Big Bang and that appear to be infinite. The *ethos* of human being thus has something about its nature that is *more* and thus *other* than what we decide to make of it—something whose objective uncertainty is the basis of "mystery." What will happen tomorrow? Who can say for sure? Otherness lies at the heart of human existence; it makes its presence known even when we are all alone.

Ontologically speaking, this otherness of human existence is its own evocation and provocation, an event of deconstruction-reconstruction in its most primordial form. Before we have anything to say about it, the open-ended dwelling place of our spatial–temporal being is at work calling us into question and demanding a response. The *ethos* of human being functions first and foremost in accordance with a challenge–response logic. When this logic occurs "within" a person, on an intrapersonal level, we speak of it as an "act of conscience," whereby the person is judging his or her own character, thoughts, and actions. Pointing to its original revelation in and through the spatial and temporal workings of human being, Heidegger (1927/1962) identifies its dynamic character as the most original and empirically verifiable "call of conscience" (pp. 313–325). The ontological structure of human existence places before us the challenging tasks of ethical responsibility, freedom of choice, thoughtful action, living a meaningful life, and being with others. Compared to a particular person's conscience, the call of conscience that comes with human being never rests.

This call defines an epideictic display of existence in its most original form: a "showing forth" (*epi-deixis*) or "saying" (*logos*) of the truth of something that is and that can be represented symbolically for others to understand. The call of conscience is existence disclosing itself to the one who is living it and who can and must respond to its challenge (Hyde, 2001, pp. 108–115). Here, at this ontological level of existence, the logos of the call, its discourse, is not understood first and foremost as a capacity of communication but rather as the original and silent manifestation of what is. "The call dispenses with any kind of utterance," writes Heidegger (1927/1962). "It does not put itself into words at all; … [c]onscience discourses solely and constantly in the mode of keeping silent" (p. 318).

Heidegger speaks to us of a discourse, a silent "voice," that is more original than anything he or anyone else has to say about it and that defines the "being of language" (*Logos*) in its most primordial state: the original presenting and "saying" of all that lies before us.

> *The essential being of language is Saying as Showing.* Its showing character is not based on signs of any kind; rather, all signs arise from a showing within whose realm and for whose purposes they can be signs….
>
> Even when Showing is accomplished by our human saying, even then this showing, this pointer, is preceded by an indication that it will let itself be shown. (Heidegger, 1959/1971, p. 123)

Elsewhere Heidegger (1987/2001) provides a description of what he is doing in describing the saying/showing of the call of conscience when he notes: "To speak means to say, which means to show and to let [something] be seen. It means to communicate and, correspondingly, to listen, to submit oneself to a claim addressed to oneself and to comply and respond to it" (p. 215). The call of conscience (of our being and its otherness) is nonverbal communication in its purest, most original form. We are "voiced" before we learn to speak.

Regarding the genre of rhetoric (epideictic) most steeped in this primordial discourse, Quintilian (trans., 1921/1985) has said: "Indeed I am not sure that this is not the most important department of rhetoric in actual practice" (2.1.10). The above assessment of the call of conscience lends ontological support to this claim. Although epideictic rhetoric is typically associated with discourse that bestows praise or blame on the actions of others, its most original form takes place before any such assessment is made. Recall, the disclosing of our spatial and temporal existence defines the most primordial form of epideictic speech and "public address." There is something fundamentally rhetorical about the call of conscience that happens at the heart of human being and that speaks to us of something other than our own making.

The call of conscience is an empirical phenomenon, although the otherness that it announces registers a "transcendence" of material reality that is known to send us metaphysical creatures toward spiritual realms in the hope that we may someday understand how and why it is that we are here on earth (Eco, 1993/1997). Cognitive scientists have shown that the brain has evolved to accommodate the impulse at work here, thereby explaining, at least for the time being, "why God won't go away" (Gazzaniga, 2005; Hamer, 2004; Newberg, D'Aquili, & Rause, 2001). We are wired to be ethical and moral creatures.

The rhetoric of religion offers itself as a way of understanding the "true" origins of this evolutionary happening. "In the beginning was the Word": Its proclamation informs the ontological structure of our existence, with its deconstructive–reconstructive dynamics, its challenge–response logic, its call of conscience. The *ethos* of human existence exhibits a self-questioning design that motivates us with its mystery to ponder the One who brought this design into being. God uses the spatial and temporal structure of existence to call attention to Itself. God interrupts our everyday routines, our habits of thinking and acting, with *the* call of conscience, with an ever-present happening that encourages us to question what, why, and how we are and "to know together" (*con-scientia*) with God and the rest of humankind as much of the truth as possible. This particular interruption serves a crucial rhetorical function: It calls for acknowledgment.

Hence, the memorable question–answer sequence found throughout the Old Testament: "Where art thou?" "Here I am!" (Hyde, 2006).

One of the most famous Christian enactments of the sequence is found in the influential rhetoric of St. Augustine's *Confessions*, with its many suggestions about how the orator's art can and must open others to the teachings of the Almighty. The word *confess* is from the Latin *confiteri*, meaning "to acknowledge." Augustine (trans. 1992) acknowledges that "the language" of God that inspires the Scriptures is "rich in meaning," allowing for a "diversity of true views." He also confesses: "I would not be using the language of my confessions [appropriately] if I fail to confess to you that I do not know" which of these views correspond "supremely" to both "the light of truth and to the reader's spiritual profit" (XII.xxx.41).

Still, for Augustine, this truth exists. In moments of existential crisis and great emotion, he heard its call of conscience. This call was there all along—as soon as God initiated the "beginning" with a specific speech act, an "avowl": "Let there be…." God is the Great Avower: the One who declares most assuredly, openly, bluntly, and without shame. Such an open declaration or avowal is also known as an instance of acknowledgment. By way of acknowledgment, God created the dwelling place—the cosmos; the earth—where all other acts of acknowledgment could happen. Without acknowledgment, God is a rather vacuous concept.

EMOTION AND THE HAPPENING OF TRUTH

Is the empirical and ontological phenomenon of the call of conscience, with its vivid affirmation of otherness, a product of God's will? What is more "Other" than this most famous heavenly source of ethical and moral behavior? Science rightly cautions against accepting the all too "easy" suggestion raised by this question. As the physicist and cosmologist Paul Davies (1983) notes: "Our ignorance of the origin of life leaves plenty of scope for divine explanations, but that is purely a negative attitude, invoking 'the God-of-the-gaps' only to risk retreat at a later date in the face of scientific advance."… Hence:

> To invoke God as a blanket explanation of the unexplained is to invite eventual falsification, and make God the friend of ignorance. If God is to be found, it must surely be through what we discover about the world, not what we fail to discover. (Davies, 1983, pp. 70, 209)

A phenomenological assessment of the matter sides with this position. Empirically oriented assessments and descriptions of "the things themselves" should go as far as they possibly can in disclosing the truth of these things before we allow our metaphysical impulses for order and completeness to encourage a rush to judgment and a corresponding "leap of faith."

Science and phenomenology share a specific ethic of inquiry: With the greatest diligence and for as long as possible, remain open to the materiality and dynamics of the data in question. This ethic abides by the *ethos* of human being: its openness to otherness, its call of conscience. The Nobel Prize winning physicist Richard Feynman (1998) has this ethic in mind when he emphasizes how in science "openness to possibility is an opportunity. Doubt and discussion are essential to progress" (pp. 49–50). Openness allows us to become what Feynman describes as "atoms with curiosity" that look at themselves, wonder why they wonder, and thereby help to promote the evolution of knowledge and moral consciousness (p. 39).

Although curiosity can have its drawbacks, it nevertheless demonstrates an ontological aspect of our existence. It is a way of taking an interest in, being attuned to, and showing concern for the world. Attunement is a "state of mind," a moodful way of being with things, others, and oneself (e.g., "I am in a curious mood"). Everyday existence defines a realm of emotional orientations and attachments (moods) that are constantly attuning us to and helping to disclose the situations of which we are a part and that are forever unfolding before our eyes. This disclosing capacity of emotion is ontologically significant in that it calls attention to how the phenomenon serves a "truthful" purpose.

The validity of any truth claim (e.g., "It is raining.") presupposes at least two specific acts of disclosure: (1) the presence of some subject matter disclosing itself to a witness, and (2) the ability of the witness to disclose in some symbolic manner this original disclosure. Truth thus shows itself as an event of disclosure, an act of revelation, of something "that is the case"—something that shows some aspect of itself in the openness of the light of day and thereby makes itself available for interpretation and understanding. Something making itself available "means" nothing, however, if it is not perceived, interpreted, and understood by a witness. This hermeneutic process of perceiving, interpreting, and understanding takes place only to the extent that the witness takes some interest in an original act of disclosure. Emotion thus becomes a crucial factor in the situation. Matters may be as simple as "$1 + 1 = 2$." Or a bit more complicated: $E = mc^2$. Sometimes the truth of a given disclosure requires the artistic genius of a Vincent Van Gogh or Abraham Lincoln to show us what, for example, the meaning of a "wheat field" or a "civil war" truly is. But in every case some emotional involvement with the matters at hand is a prerequisite for coming to terms with the truth.

The cognitive determining of "clear reason" poses no exception here. Even when reason is couched in the most positivistic language (such that it can be "objective" in its registration of "facts"), its announcements will always be rooted in what emotion makes possible: an interpretation of some matter of interest, a concern for being. Hence, the so-called dispassionate claims of reason—as made by science, for example—can never escape the emotion that begets their existence. The scientist claims to be a "disinterested" observer. Disinterestedness, however, is a state of mind, a particular way of being attentive to the presence of some object or subject. As commented on for years by health communication researchers, it is this "cold" and "calculating" emotional orientation that too often deadens the heartfelt attention that patients are known to desire in their interpersonal communication with their physicians (Charon, 2006). When we are ill, it is nice to be in a dwelling place where people are willing to go out of their way to make us feel at home by seeing us as being more than some diseased body in some bed. Physicians are trained to understand and treat the pathophysiology of a patient's disease. Acknowledging a patient's personhood requires additional emotional and rhetorical effort.

THE LIFE-GIVING GIFT OF ACKNOWLEDGMENT

The phenomenon of acknowledgment was mentioned previously in conjunction with Augustine's responding to what he considered to be the true and Holy source of the call of conscience. Such metaphysical speculation (God-of-the-gaps thinking), however, is not necessary in order to advance an empirical assessment of the phenomenon that relates it to ethics, rhetoric, and discourse.

Acknowledgment is a capacity of consciousness that enables us to be and remain *open* to the world of people, places, and things so that we can "admit" (Middle English: *acknow*) its wonders into our minds and then "admit" (Middle English: *knowlechen*) to others the understanding that we have gained and that we believe is worth sharing. This entire "admission" process is mandatory for establishing the truth of anything and the knowledge that comes with it. Recall that truth happens first and foremost as an act of disclosure, an epideictic display of something that shows itself to us and that, in turn, can be disclosed by us to others in some symbolic manner for the purpose of knowing together what *is* the case regarding some matter of concern. Acknowledgments initiate and continue to sustain our being open to the status of some truth claim. "Knowledge," insists Ludwig Wittgenstein (1969/1972), "is in the end based on acknowledgments" (p. 378). Emmanuel Levinas (1990) stresses the importance of the interpersonal function of the phenomenon when he argues that acknowledgment of otherness is a moral act that "accomplishes human society" as it promotes "the miracle of moving out of oneself," of egoism becoming altruism (p. 9). It is this moral act that is consistently emphasized by communication scholars and philosophers whose research focuses on the role played by "dialogue" in fostering and sustaining the health of interpersonal relationships and the body politic in general (Anderson, Baxter, & Cissna, 2004).

Those who remain unacknowledged in everyday life are isolated, marginalized, ignored, and forgotten by others. They suffer the disease of "social death." The suffering that can accompany this state of being is known to bring about fear, anxiety, sadness, anger, and sometimes even death in the form of suicide or retaliation against those who are rightly or wrongly accused of making our lives so lonely, miserable, and unbearable. Social death is present, for example, whenever people are victimized by racism, ageism, and gender inequality; mocked for their sexual orientation; denied equal rights, freedom of speech, and educational opportunities because of their physical and mental disabilities; forced to live in abject poverty; refused decent medical care; or otherwise left to live a hellish existence that defaces the human spirit (Hyde, 2006, 2010).

Acknowledgment provides an opening out of such distressful situations, for the act of acknowledging is a way of attuning consciousness toward others in order to make room for them in our lives. With this added living space comes the opportunity for a new beginning, a second chance, whereby we might improve our lot in life and feel more at home with others. There is hope to be found with this transformation of space and time as people work to construct dwelling places that make us feel wanted and needed. Offering positive acknowledgment is a moral thing to do. I know of no theory of communication ethics worth the name that does not acknowledge and encourage the doing of this act.

Notice that my remarks about acknowledgment do not contain the word *recognition*. People oftentimes speak of these two phenomena as if they were synonymous. For the purpose of the present discussion, however, their difference must be kept in mind. As Calvin Schrag (2002) reminds us, "The blurring of the grammar of acknowledgment with the grammar of recognition is one of the more glaring misdirections of modern epistemology" (pp. 117–118). The definition of "recognition" found in the *Oxford English Dictionary* reads: "The action or fact of perceiving that some thing, person, etc., is the same as one previously known; the mental process of identifying what has been known before; the fact of being thus known or identified." The phenomenon of acknowledgment, however, entails more than the mental process of identifying what has been known before.

For example, it is often quite easy to recognize that one of the eight graduate students taking my seminar in "Communication Ethics" is for whatever reason during class showing some signs of distress about the seminar or about something else that is going on in their lives. Acknowledging this student's situation at the appropriate time and place initiates a transformation of the situation. The *ethos* of acknowledgment establishes an environment where the student and I can take the time to know together the reasons for the distress, perhaps gain a more authentic understanding of the matter, and feel more at home with each other as we deal with it. *Recognition is only a preliminary step in this process of attuning one's consciousness toward another and his or her expression of a particular concern in order to facilitate the development of such existential knowledge and personal understanding.* Acknowledgment makes possible the moral development of recognition by enabling us to remain open to what is other than ourselves, even if, at times, matters become boring or troublesome.

The process should not be taken for granted. What would your life be like if no one acknowledged your existence? How would you feel if you found out that some assumed benefactor was actually deceiving you with his or her initial show of acknowledgment (at best, you were only being recognized; the person did not really care about your welfare)? Research in deception tells us that in such situations the "bedrock of civilized society"—that is, "trust"—is weakened, if not totally destroyed. Trust, "is accomplished in no small measure through principles of mutuality, cooperativeness, and truthfulness in discourse" (Burgoon, 2005, p. 5). These principles, however, presuppose the workings of acknowledgment, which, as they open us to others, begin the process of our learning to establish trustful relationships with them. This same process, of course, is also one that makes us vulnerable as it opens us to the deceptive practices of others. Acknowledgment entails risk (Hyde, 2006).

Rhetorical discourse and acknowledgment go hand in hand. Rhetoric is at work whenever language is being employed to *open* people to ideas, positions, and circumstances that, if rightly understood, stand a reasonable chance of getting people to think and act wisely. Orators are forever attempting to create these openings, for this is how they maximize the chance that the members of some audience will take an interest in what is being said. Neither persuasion nor collaborative deliberation can take place without the formation of this joint emotional interest. "We interest a man by dealing with his interests," writes Kenneth Burke (1954, p. 37). Acknowledgment happens as such dealing transpires. The "good" speaker is always seeking acknowledgment from some audience whose "good" members are also waiting for the speaker to acknowledge their interests in some meaningful way. Rhetorical competence has a significant role to play in providing dwelling places (openings) where a life-giving gift can be received.

Training in rhetorical competence, or what Cicero termed the "art of eloquence" (*oratio*) in developing his social, political, and moral theory of civic republicanism, instructs one on how to equip (*ornare*) knowledge of a subject in such a way that it can assume a publicly accessible form and function effectively in the social and political arena. Rhetorical competence displays the human capacity to be inventive, to arrange materials in an appropriate, orderly, and beautiful way, to favor the good and the just, and, of course, to speak "the truth" of what *is*. For Cicero, such symbolic activity admits the potential of being "heroic." Robert Hariman (1995) makes much of this point when he notes that "The republican politician achieves greatest glory as the heroic individual seizing the moment by voicing immortal words at the height of great events (p. 121). Ralph Waldo Emerson's way of stating the point in his discussion of "eloquence" is also noteworthy. "Certainly there is no true orator who is not a hero.... The orator must ever stand with forward foot, in the attitude of advancing.... His speech is not to be distinguished from action. It is action, as the general's word of command or shout of battle is action" (cited in Whicher, 1957, p. 306).

This claim calls into question a well-known maxim of our culture—"Actions speak louder than words"—that is famous for its "put-down" of the practice of rhetoric. And the metaphor that informs the eloquence of Emerson's claim lends it further force for, indeed, heroes and war are readily related. When speaking of the true orator's heroism, however, Emerson's understanding of "war" emphasizes what he terms "a military attitude of the soul" that is not directed toward the actual killing of others. Instead, this attitude is needed by the orator who would "dare the gibbet and the mob," the rage and retribution of a misinformed and closed-minded public, when attempting to move its members beyond the blinders of their "common sense" beliefs and toward a genuine understanding of what, for the orator, is arguably the truth of some immediate matter of concern. For Emerson (2000/1836), the heroism of the true orator is made possible not only by one's "power to connect his thought with its proper symbol, and so to utter it," but also, and primarily, by one's "love of truth and...[the] desire to communicate it without loss" (pp. 15, 228).

Eloquence is born of such power, love, and desire. Kenneth Burke (1968) puts it succinctly:

"The primary purpose of eloquence is not to enable us to live our lives on paper—it is to convert life into its most thorough verbal equivalent" in order to better understand, appreciate, and deal with the reality of which we are a part (p. 167). The true orator, the rhetor as hero, is a person committed to this task of eloquence, of constructing dwelling places where the well-being of humankind is respected and advanced. Hence, Cicero's (trans. 1942) praise for the art: For

> what function is so kingly, so worthy of the free, so generous, as to bring help to the suppliant, to raise up those who are cast down, to bestow security, to set free from peril, to maintain men in their civil rights?... The wise control of the complete orator is that which chiefly upholds not only his own dignity, but the safety of countless individuals and of the entire State." (1.8.32)

Cicero's words certainly speak to the importance of the relationship between acknowledgment and rhetoric. In his phenomenological study of the functions of speech and its corresponding theory of communication ethics, Georges Gusdorf (1953/1965) expands on and further clarifies the matter by associating the rhetorical artistry needed to acknowledge the truth, others, and to cultivate civic virtue with what he terms "the ceaseless heroism necessary in pursuing the struggle for style"—a struggle where "Concern for the right expression is bound up with the concern for true reality: accuracy (*justesse*) and integrity (*justice*) are two related virtues" (pp. 74–75). The phenomenon of rhetorical style discloses itself in discourse dedicated to opening people to the truth of some matter of concern as well as to each others' judgments about the matter. Working together, these openings define a dwelling place, an *ethos*, where people can "know-together" (*con-scientia*) and, at least to some extent, experience the life-giving gift of acknowledgment.

These related goals of open-mindedness, conscience-formation, and civility lie at the heart of Jurgen Habermas's (1981/1984) highly influential theory of "communicative action" and "discourse ethics." Here he speaks to us of "the pragmatic presuppositions," "the substantive normative rules" or "validity conditions" of argumentation that promote "the ideal community of communication"—a community that thrives on the capacity for acknowledgment and thus the open-mindedness of its participants toward each other and toward discovering the truth of some matter of concern. These conditions include: choosing a comprehensible expression, intending to communicate a true proposition, expressing intentions truthfully, and choosing an appropriate expression with respect to the rhetorical situation at hand. Anyone who sincerely participates in argumentation, according to Habermas (1983/1990), "has already accepted these substantive normative conditions—there is no alternative to them. Simply by choosing to engage in argumentation, participants are forced to acknowledge this fact" (p. 130). Indeed, we are not the creators of these conditions and the open-mindedness that they call for. Rather, these conditions come with the very nature of human existence, with our "given" (*es gibt*) way of being *homo loquens*—creatures distinguished by our unique and related abilities to acknowledge others and to communicate with them about all that can be understood in our everyday lives. Habermas would thus have us acknowledge that "morality as grounded by discourse ethics is based on a pattern inherent in mutual understanding in language from the beginning" (p. 163).

Habermas grants us a way to "ground" the life-giving gift of acknowledgment in the "rational" workings of language-use, especially as they show themselves in interpersonal contexts where argumentation is necessary for adjudicating some contested matter. I have suggested throughout this essay that this grounding actually goes deeper than Habermas is willing to dig. He is not interested in developing a phenomenological and ontological understanding of the relationship between the ethos of human being, its call of conscience, and our capacity for acknowledgment. Rather, he is content to disclose the validity conditions of communicative action that are "already built into" this action and that thereby assume a "transcendental" status (pp. 99–100).

With these conditions in mind, Habermas (1983/1990) makes a crucial distinction between his theory and what he terms "the *model of strategic action*":

> If the actors are interested solely in the *success*, i.e., the *consequences* or *outcomes* of their actions, they will try to reach their objectives by influencing their opponent's definition of the situation, and thus his decisions or motives, through external means by using weapons or goods, threats or enticements. Such actors treat each other *strategically*. In such cases, coordination of the subject's actions depends on the extent to which their egocentric utility calculations mesh. The degree of cooperation and the stability is determined by the interest positions of the participants. By contrast, I speak of *communicative* action when actors are prepared to harmonize their plans of action through internal means, committing themselves to pursuing their goals only on the condition of an agreement…about definitions of the situation and prospective outcomes. (pp. 133–134)

Clearly, Habermas's conception of strategic communication harkens back to what Plato condemned in his critique of rhetoric. The importance of this critique and all that it warns against should never be taken for granted and forgotten. But the actual workings of rhetorical discourse are a far more complicated matter than what Plato had to say about them. Habermas avoids the issue. He thus ends up marginalizing a major empirical concern of the rhetorical critic and discourse analyst: *how* discourse is specifically invented and arranged with style, eloquence, and other forms of communicative and rhetorical know-how in order to be expressed in an appropriate, truthful, and effective manner. By way of this heroic process of acknowledgment, we create the dwelling places or openings where collaborative deliberation, conscience-formation, and civility become possible. Acknowledgment is a life-giving gift.

OTHERNESS: A MORAL VOCATION

The giving of this gift defines a moral vocation, one of learning to "let beings be" and, in turn, of trying to know together (by way of discussion, argument, and persuasion) the truth of all that stands before us. It is a vocation that requires ethical and rhetorical fitness. Jacques Derrida (1978) offers the following description of this vocation:

> It conditions the respect for the other as what it is: other. Without this acknowledgment, which is not a knowledge, or let us say without this "letting-be" of an existent (Other) as something existing outside me in the essence of what it is (first in its alterity [or "otherness"]), no ethics would be possible.… To let the other be in its existence and essence as other means that what gains access to thought, or (and) what thought gains access to, is that which is essence and that which is existence; and that which is the Being which they both presuppose. Without this, no letting-be would be possible, and first of all, the letting be of respect and of the ethical commandment addressing itself to freedom. Violence would reign to such a degree that it would no longer even be able to appear and be named. (p. 138)

We are saved from an all-encompassing violence by our ability to attune our consciousness toward things and others so that they can be acknowledged and respected for what, who, and how they are. Derrida's above description of this vocation echoes Heidegger's assessment of the fundamental relationship that holds between Being and human being (*Dasein*): we are those beings who exist in such a way that we make a dwelling place for Being to show and call attention to itself. This showing and calling for thought and resolute action define the primordial "ethical commandment" upon which all moral systems are based. The commandment calls for a respecting of the Being of beings, for a letting-be of what gives and shows itself to and for thought and that thus is "other" than the consciousness that perceives it.

Derrida (1984) aligns his "deconstructive" way of doing criticism with the necessity of answering this call. He writes: "…deconstruction is, in itself, a positive response to an alterity which necessarily calls, summons or motivates it. Deconstruction is therefore vocation—a response to a call" (p. 118). Moreover, Derrida would have us understand that deconstruction offers itself to others as a way of helping them to realize that "every culture needs an element of self-interrogation and of distance from itself, if it is to transform itself" and thereby become something different, something other and perhaps "better" than what it presently is under the "official political codes of governing reality" (pp. 116, 120). Deconstruction, in other words, is especially attuned to that deconstructive dimension of the moral vocation of human being that shows forth in the temporal openness of this being's existence and that continually calls into question the truthfulness of whatever human beings create in order to make their lives meaningful. Deconstruction does something of what existence tells it to do: it is a critical activity; it *"intervenes"* in meaning systems in order to call attention to the potential pitfalls that accompany our strict adherence to these systems and that are too often taken for granted and forgotten when "all is well" with the system's functioning. This act of rhetorical intervention is done out of respect for the "otherness" of the other, which calls for acknowledgment. The cultural theorist Jean Baudrillard (1995/2008) would have us place no limits on the enactment of such respect: "All that seeks to be singular and incomparable, and does not enter into the play of difference, must be exterminated…. We must reconcile nothing. We must keep open the otherness of forms, the disparity between terms" (p. 123). The ethical challenge is immense.

CONCLUSION

We are back to the beginning: The otherness of the other is an ontological feature of human existence. It shows itself in the presence of other things, other people, the validity conditions of argumentation that are already built into communicative action, and the fundamental spatial and temporal dynamics of our very being. This last instance of otherness is known to call to mind "God's presence." Taken all together, the otherness that permeates human being is an awesome presence that is never without absence. The empirical relationship between ethics, rhetoric, and discourse originates in the presence of this absence, disclosing itself as a call of conscience that intervenes in and interrupts our everyday existence, stimulates emotions, and opens us to the objective uncertainty of our existence. Faced with the awesomeness of this uncertainty, we are called to think, act, and construct dwelling places where moral consciousness can be cultivated. It is a heroic thing for us to do: create those habitats or openings where collaborative deliberation, moral consciousness, and civility become possible and where a life-giving gift can be shared with others.

REFERENCES

Anderson, R., Baxter, L. A., & Cissna, K. N. (Eds). (2004). *Dialogue: Theorizing difference in communication studies.* London: Sage.

Aristotle (1984). *Nicomachean ethics.* (W. D. Ross, Trans., revised by J. O. Urmson). In J. Barnes (Ed.), *The complete works of Aristotle* (Vol. 2). Princeton, NJ: Princeton University Press.

Aristotle. (1954). *Rhetoric* (W. R. Roberts, Trans.). New York: Modern Library.

Arneson, P. (Ed.). (2007a). *Perspectives on philosophy of communication.* West Lafayette, IN: Purdue University Press.

Arneson, P. (Ed.). (2007b). *Exploring communication ethics: Interviews with influential scholars in the field.* New York: Lang.

Arnett, R. C., Fritz, J. M. H., & Bell, L. M. (2009). *Communication ethics literacy.* Los Angeles, CA: Sage.

Augustine. (1992). *Confessions* (H. Chadwick, Trans.). New York: Oxford University Press.

Aune, J. A. (1994). *Rhetoric and Marxism.* Boulder, CO: Westview Press.

Baudrillard, J. (2008). *The perfect crime* (C. Turner, Trans.). New York: Verso. (Original work published 1995)

Bavelas, J. B., Kenwood, C., & Phillips, B. (2002). Discourse analysis. In M. L. Knapp & J. A. Daly (Eds.), *Handbook of interpersonal communication* (3rd ed., pp. 102–129). London: Sage.

Beach, W. A. (2008). *A natural history of family cancer: Interactional resources for managing illness.* Cresskill, NJ: Hampton Press.

Blumenberg, H. (1987). An anthropological approach to the contemporary significance of rhetoric (R. M. Wallace, Trans.). In K. Baynes, J. Bohman, & T. McCarthy (Eds.), *After philosophy: End or transformation?* (pp. 429–458). Cambridge, MA: MIT Press.

Burgoon, J. K. (2005). *Truth, lies, and virtual worlds* (Carroll C. Arnold Distinguished Lecture). New York: Pearson/Allyn & Bacon.

Burke, K. (1954). *Permanence and change* (2nd rev. ed.). New York: Bobbs-Merrill.

Burke, K. (1968). *Counter-statement.* Berkeley: University of California Press.

Casey, E. S. (1993). *Getting back into place: Toward a renewed understanding of the place-world.* Bloomington: Indiana University Press.

Chamberlain, C. (1984). From "haunts" to "character": The meaning of ethos and its relation to ethics. *Helios, 11,* 99–103.

Charon, R. (2006). *Narrative medicine: Honoring stories of illness.* Oxford, UK: Oxford University Press.

Cheney, G. (1991). *Rhetoric in an organizational society: Managing multiple identities.* Columbia: University of South Carolina Press.

Chouliaraki, L. (2006). *The spectatorship of suffering.* New York: Sage.

Chouliaraki, L., & Fairclough, N. (1999). *Discourse in late modernity.* Edinburgh, Scotland: Edinburgh University Press.

Cicero. (1942). *De oratore* (H. Rackham, Trans.). Cambridge, MA: Harvard University Press.

Cook, M. A., & Holba, A. N. (2008). *Philosophies of communication: Implications for everyday experience.* New York: Lang.

Davies, P. (1983). *God and the new physics.* New York: Simon & Schuster.

Derrida, J. (1978). *Writing and difference* (A. Bass, Trans.). Chicago, IL: University of Chicago Press.

Derrida, J. (1984). Deconstruction and the other: Interview with Richard Kearney. In R. Kearney (Ed.), *Dialogues with contemporary continental thinkers: The phenomenological heritage* (pp. 107–126). Manchester, UK: Manchester University Press.

Eco, U. (1997). *The search for the perfect language* (J. Fentress, Trans.). Oxford, UK: Blackwell. (Original work published 1993)

Edelstein, L. (1967). *Ancient medicine: Selected papers of Ludwig Edelstein* (O. Temkin & C. L Temkin, Eds., C. L. Temkin, Trans.). Baltimore, MD: John Hopkins University Press.

Emerson, R. W. (2000). *The essential writings of Ralph Waldo Emerson* (B. Atkinson, Ed.). New York: Modern Library. (Original work published 1836)

Farrell, T. B. (1993). *Norms of rhetorical culture.* New Haven, CT: Yale University Press.

Feynman, R. (1998). *The meaning of it all: Thoughts of a citizen-scientist.* Reading, MA: Pereus Books.

Fisher, W. R. (1987). *Human communication as narration: Toward a philosophy of reason, value, and action.* Columbia: University of South Carolina Press.

Garver, E. (1994). *Aristotle's rhetoric: An art of character.* Chicago: University of Chicago Press.

Gazzaniga, M. S. (2005). *The ethical brain.* New York: Dana Press.

Gusdorf, G. (1965). *Speaking (La Parole)* (P. T. Brockelman, Trans.). Evanston, IL: Northwestern University Press. (Original work published 1953)

Habermas, J. (1984). *The theory of communicative action: Vol. 1. Reason and the rationalization of society* (T. McCarthy, Trans.). Boston, MA: Beacon Press. (Original work published 1981)

Habermas, J. (1990). *Moral consciousness and communicative action* (C. Lenhardt & S. W. Nicholsen, Trans.). Cambridge: MIT Press. (Original work published 1983)

Hamer, D. (2004). *The god gene: How faith is hardwired into our genes.* New York: Doubleday.

Hariman, R. (1995). *Political style: The artistry of power.* Chicago, IL: University of Chicago Press.

Heidegger, M. (1962). *Being and time* (E. Robinson & J. Macquarrie, Trans.). New York: Harper & Row. (Original work published 1927)

Heidegger, M. (1971). *On the way to language* (P. D. Hertz, Trans.). New York: Harper & Row. (Original work published 1959)

Heidegger, M. (1977). Letter on humanism. In D. F. Krell (Ed.), *Basic writings* (pp. 189–242). New York: Harper & Row. (Original work published 1947)

Heidegger, M. (2001). *Zollikon seminars: Protocols-conversations-letters* (F. Mayr & R. Askay, Trans., M. Boss, Ed.). Evanston, IL: Northwestern University. (Original work published 1987)

Heritage, J. (1984). *Garfinkel and ethnomethodology.* Cambridge, UK: Polity.

Hyde, M. J. (2001). *The call of conscience: Heidegger and Levinas, rhetoric and the euthanasia debate.* Columbia: University of South Carolina Press.

Hyde, M. J. (Ed.) (2004). *The ethos of rhetoric.* Columbia: University of South Carolina Press.

Hyde, M. J. (2006). *The life-giving gift of acknowledgment.* West Lafayette, IN: Purdue University Press.

Hyde, M. J. (2008). *Perfection, postmodern culture, and the biotechnology debate* (The Carroll C. Arnold Distinguished Lecture, 2007). New York: Pearson/Allyn & Bacon.

Hyde, M. J. (2010). *Perfection: Coming to terms with being human.* Waco, TX: Baylor University Press.

Isocrates (1982). *Antidosis* (G. Norlin, Trans.). Cambridge, MA: Harvard University Press.

Jacobs, S. (2002). Language and interpersonal communication. In M. L. Knapp & J. A. Daly (Eds.), *Handbook of interpersonal communication* (3rd ed., pp. 213–239). London: Sage.

Johannesen, R. L., Valde, K. S., & Whedbee, K. E. (2008). *Ethics in human communication* (6th ed.). Long Grove, IL: Waveland Press.

Levinas, E. (1990). *Difficult freedom: Essays on Judaism.* (S. Hand, Trans.). Baltimore, MD: John Hopkins University Press. (Original work published 1963)

McKeon, R. (1971). The uses of rhetoric in a technological age: Architectonic productive arts. In L. F. Bitzer & E. Black (Eds.), *The prospect of rhetoric.* (pp. 45–52). Englewood Cliffs, NJ: Prentice-Hall.

McMillan, J., & Hyde, M. J. (2000). Technological innovation and change: A case study in the formation of organizational conscience. *Quarterly Journal of Speech, 86,* 20–48.

Miller, A. B. (1974). Aristotle on habit and character. *Speech Monographs, 41,* 309–316.

Newberg, A., D'Aquili, E., & Rause, V. (2001). *Why God won't go away: Brain science and the biology of belief.* New York: Ballantine Books.

Plato. (1973a). *Gorgias.* In E. Hamilton & H. Cairns (Eds.), *Plato: The collected dialogues* (R. Hackford, Trans.) (pp. 229–307). Princeton, NJ: Princeton University Press.

Plato. (1973b). *Phaedrus.* In E. Hamilton & H. Cairns (Eds.), *Plato: The collected dialogues* (R. Hackford, Trans.) (pp. 475–525). Princeton, NJ: Princeton University Press.

Plato. (1973c). *Sophist.* In E. Hamilton & H. Cairns (Eds.), *Plato: The collected dialogues* (R. Hackford, Trans.) (pp. 957–1017). Princeton, NJ: Princeton University Press.

Quintilian. (1985). *Institutio oratoria.* (H. E. Butler, Trans.). 4 vols. Cambridge, MA: Harvard University Press. (Original work published 1921)

Rommetveit, R. (1974). *On message structure.* London: John Wiley.

Sacks, H., Schegloff, E. A., & Jefferson, G. (1974). A simplest systematics for the organization of turn-taking for conversation. *Language, 50,* 696–735.

Schegloff, E. A., & Sacks, H. (1973). Opening up closings. *Semiotica, 7,* 289–327.

Schrag, C. O. (2002). *God as otherwise than being: Toward a semantics of the gift.* Evanston, IL: Northwestern University Press.

Sloane, T. O. (Ed.). (2001). *Encyclopedia of rhetoric.* New York: Oxford University Press.

Whicher, S. W. (Ed.). (1957). *Selections from Ralph Waldo Emerson.* Boston, MA: Houghton Mifflin.

Wittgenstein, L. (1972). *On certainty* (G. E. M. Anscombe & G. H. von Wright, Eds., D. Paul & G. E. M. Anscombe, Trans.). New York: Harper & Row. (Original work published 1972)

4

Situating a Dialogic Ethics
A Dialogic Confession

Ronald C. Arnett

This essay examines the interplay of communication ethics and dialogue, assuming a hermeneutic bias—there is no one universal understanding of what constitutes communication ethics
and, additionally, there is no one universal understanding of what constitutes dialogue. Thus,
any attempt to render a theory of dialogic ethics requires public articulation of biases and assumptions, permitting the reader to understand the particular rendition of dialogic ethics framed
within a given essay or theory. This interpretive essay exemplifies the theoretical and practical
communicative consequences of engaging the terms *communication ethics* and *dialogue* through
a lens of difference and multiplicity, pragmatically accepting the necessity of engaging in a dialogue through the meeting of two historical stories, stories marked by profound differences—
"communication ethics" and "dialogue." This essay works from a particular dialogic perspective
with public admission of the rhetorical nature of such an enterprise—such a perspective does not
seek to *describe* the world, but to *confess rhetorically* the construction of a dialogic ethic that is
both situated within a given bias (Gadamer, 1975) and identified as a perspective that gives shape
to a particular world (Levinas, 1969): in this case, a theory of dialogic communication ethics.

INTRODUCTION

This essay offers a public construction of theory that depends upon histories of communication
ethics and dialogue; the interplay of these theories invites the possibility of a public framing of a
theory of dialogic communication ethics. This interpretive task works within the dialogic tradition of Gadamer's (1976) "philosophical hermeneutics" centered upon three major terms: *bias,
horizon,* or the *text,* and the interpretive dialogic result emerging from the meeting of bias and
text (Arnett, 2007a). Doing philosophical hermeneutics begins with two texts—dialogic theories
and communication ethics theories—with the resultant theoretical contribution emerging from
the dialogue between them. This essay, "Situating a Dialogic Communication Ethic: A Dialogic
Confession," celebrates complexity, difference, and multiplicity in an effort to render a particular dialogic communication ethics theory, making the task more one of theoretical confession
(Arnett, 2005) than definitive proclamation.

  The primal assertion of this essay is that there is an wide array of communication ethic and
dialogue standpoints, and the interplay of these histories meets the bias of this historical moment,

called postmodern (or if one tires of the overuse of that term, one might suggest the notion of *counter modern*) set of assumptions, which is actually more in line with the work of Hannah Arendt.

The final public dialogic interplay of two histories constitutes a theory of dialogic communication ethics dependent upon a basic set of guiding coordinates that theoretically and practically reflect the demanding task of engaging communication ethics in an era of narrative and virtue contention (Arnett, Fritz, & Bell, 2009): (1) multiplicity, (2) minimalist, (3) historicity and the existential life-world, and (4) tainted ground and dialogic confession. These metaphors form an image of "walls with bridges," a central metaphor used by this author in detailing a postmodern engagement with diversity from a standpoint of conviction (Arnett, 2005).

The above four metaphors constitute the final section of this essay, "Dialogic Confession and the Rhetorical Turn," which examines the constitution of a dialogic ethics theory based upon a storied history and ultimately a publicly acknowledged perspective that offers a particular and necessarily limited understanding of dialogic communication ethics (Levinas, 1985). The task of this essay is to reveal the beginning ground of a dialogic ethic situated within prejudice (Gadamer, 1975) about the importance of communicative content. Such a theoretical treatment lives not in agreement on style or concurrence on process, but in the recognition that the narrative ground upon which a communicator stands functions as a moral source, an ethical position of content (Taylor, 1989) that constitutes ground upon which the identity of the communicative ethic finds shape. Such a perspective makes a conversation derivative of the narrative ground that accompanies a communicative agent in a given human meeting. This essay assumes that one cannot stand above history and offer an opinion through objectivity or through self-proclaimed confidence from one's own subjectivity. To paraphrase Bernstein's (1983) call for philosophy beyond objectivism and relativism, we must search for something beyond objectivity and subjectivity, something that takes us once more to the mud of everyday life (Buber, 1966). Such a dialogic ethic lives within existence, not above the demands of life or in the self-assurance of a given communicator.

A dialogic communication ethic illuminates the following exchange contrary to convention. A faculty member sat with a colleague and commented on a student who was having much difficulty in the class. The faculty member first stated how the objective standards of the course were not being met. Then the same faculty member stated, "I certainly would not engage a class like this student." The conversation offered opinionated answers, leaving little room for the complexity of existence that might ask, "Why is a student who has done so well in the past doing so poorly at this time?" Such a question might best be answered in conversation with the student, not gossip with a colleague. The dialogic goal of any professor should not be to fix the student, but rather to meet the existence that is now making learning a challenge for a student who has long prospered in the classroom. Such a dialogic ethic guarantees no answers; the only assurance is that maybe, if we stop telling long enough, we can listen for existential answers that may assist our questions and the student.

ETHICS AND COMMUNICATION

This essay begins with a basic presupposition—there is no one universal communication ethic; there are multiple communication ethics (Arnett, Fritz, & Bell, 2009). A communication ethic understood as such is best understood within the terminology of gestalt, which consists of background and foreground. A communication ethic functions as a gestalt involving the interplay of a narrative background and foreground communicative practices.

A given narrative informs the sense of the good and the practices that shape the ongoing communicative actions that compose the whole or the gestalt of what this essay understands as a communication ethic. In gestalt form, a communication ethic is larger than the sum of its parts. The narrative and the practices together offer an entrance into a communication ethic that points to what Arendt (1992) and Kant (1951) understood as an "enlarged mentality." With the understanding that there is no one form of communication ethics, this essay turns to the history of communication ethics to find footing for this essay.

This history of communication ethics invokes Aristotle's *Nicomachean Ethics* as a beginning foundation with more contemporary engagement framed initially by the work of Jim Chesebro (1969), Richard Johannesen (1983), James Jaksa (1988), Josina Makau (Makau & Arnett, 1997), Cliff Christians (2003), Brent D. Ruben and Lea Stewart (2005), and Michael Hyde (2001), to name a few intimately associated with communication ethics. As stated above, there are numerous ways to define a communication ethic; the following treatment offers one way to understand a given scholarly and conceptual lineage of communication ethics.

A Scholarly Lineage

One line of research or particular way of making sense out of the diversity of theory in communication ethics was begun by Chesebro (1969), adapted and added to by Arnett (2001), and then further tailored by Arnett, Arneson, and Bell (2006). This lineage of research engaged communication ethics through metaphorical analysis, propelled by the following privileged metaphors: *democratic ethics, a universal ethic, contextual ethics, ethical codes and procedures, a narrative ethic,* and *a dialogic ethic.* Each of these metaphors privileges a different conception of what is "good" in communication ethics. This diversity of perspectives leads the way for a dialogic perspective that seeks to learn from the complexity of a given communicative environment and all those situated within that environment. This essay understands communication ethics as a dialogue among differing perspectives. Communication ethics inquiry that begins with diversity of metaphors and stresses the reality of bias or prejudice of narrative ground casts necessary pragmatic suspicion upon undue confidence in any one person's ability to tell another *the* ethical stance or position.

The most recent comprehensive history of communication ethics theory, "Communication Ethics: The Dialogic Turn," penned by Arnett, Arneson, and Bell (2006), assumes this pragmatic admission of difference. This review essay has kinship with a number of early projects indebted to the conceptual groundbreaking work initiated by Chesebro (1969). The story that Chesebro offered about communication ethics was both insightful and innovative. The categories he placed communication ethics theories within were important, but the fundamental contribution was the heuristic value of his essay—his work framed communication ethics within *difference*; there is no single approach to communication ethics. His essay was the first to take us into a dialogue about difference in the theoretical construction of communication ethics.

Chesebro understood the beginnings and the evolutionary nature of the discipline of communication ethics as difference, with "telling" only one perspective functioning as propaganda. First, he outlined the discipline's operational commitment to *democracy* shaped around one basic presupposition; each person's voice counts and has a right to be heard. Second, Chesebro reminded us of the Enlightenment assumption of the *universal,* which assumes in the case of ethics that each person has basic inalienable rights, regardless of status or position in life. Third, he introduced a counter to the universal with the notion of a *contextual* view of communication ethics; this perspective offered a textured response to the universal perspective. In retrospect, the democratic framework outlined by Chesebro was a combination of a contextual and a universal approach; together, these two orientations unite the importance of personal rights and attentiveness to the environment which a democratic ethic, at its best, offers a people. Additionally, Chesebro delineated *codes and procedures* as an approach with both a universal component and a core focused on an organizational context.

The essay "Paulo Freire's Revolutionary Pedagogy: From a Story-Centered to a Narrative-Centered Communication Ethic" in *Qualitative Inquiry* by Arnett (2002) continued this dialogue on communication ethics framings with the addition of *narrative ethic*. A narrative can be understood as a *contextual universal,* functioning as a "unity of contraries" (Buber, 1965, p. 111) with privilege going first to the contextual and then to the universal. A narrative is a story-laden context that people take as true within a given context, unlike a metanarrative, which is a universal truth system that has no qualifying limitations. What differentiates a narrative from being just a story-laden context is that a group of people actually believe in the narrative. People do not fight and die for stories, but they will fight and die for narrative ground that holds the key to their identity. What distinguishes this concept, a narrative, from a metanarrative is that the notion of universal must play second fiddle to a contextual understanding of ethics in a narrative, and a metanarrative takes on universal characteristics without such tempering.

A communication ethics background is a narrative or a worldview upon which a communicator stands in a given moment of discourse. The foreground components of a communication ethic are the communicative social practices that derive action and meaning from a given narrative location. In essence, a communication ethic involves social practices that are derivative of a larger narrative or worldview. Regardless of the term used, whether *narrative*, *worldview,* or *theory*, there is commonality in the philosophical essence of these notions suggesting that communication ethics requires a "background" for interpretation and comprehension of "foreground" social practices or communicative ethics in action. A communicative background offers ongoing guidance and structure to any foreground communicative practice.

This essay's presupposition that there is no one legitimate communication ethics understanding of the good necessitates understanding the importance of a narrative background of a communication ethic, which (1) houses a given view of the "good" and (2) gives birth to foreground social practices that display an understanding of the good in action. For instance, following the classical insight of Aristotle, a genuine friendship centers itself on a "good" called "reciprocity of goodwill" (Aristotle, trans. 1985). The background narrative of friendship houses a given understanding of a reciprocal goodwill that, in the foreground, unites the social practices of human bonds, connecting human beings to one another in discourse practices that display various renderings of the good of a genuine friendship that wants the best for the Other, with the Other rejoicing in like motion and cheering for the friend.

The final addition in this understanding of communication ethics came in "Communication Ethics: The Dialogic Turn" in *The Review of Communication* by Arnett, Arneson, and Bell (2006); they frame the emerging understanding of *dialogic ethics*. This approach, understood through the work of Buber, Gadamer, Levinas, Arendt, and Bahktin, requires knowledge of a particular narrative that grounds dialogue. Dialogue is derivative of a petite narrative. Narrative is the ground upon which a human being finds moral direction; this understanding of narrative and its connection to moral identity is fundamental to the work of Charles Taylor, particularly in *Sources of the Self* (Taylor, 1989) and his most recent book, *A Secular Age* (2007). Dialogue in the works cited here takes on the practices and the moral fiber of a given narrative ground; in short, dialogue does not begin with the conversation but with narrative content that shapes the identity of the communicative agent. We discover what is "good" in and from the narratives that shape us. This approach to communication ethics is anathema to what Alasdair MacIntyre (1981) called *emotivism* or decision making by personal preference. The notion of narrative connected with dialogue moves ethics to a question of *content*—the good in word and deed or speech and action (Gadamer, 1980).

Ethics as Content

This essay assumes that ethics constituted by content is narrative based; a "good" is a form of content that shapes communication ethics, begins in narrative, and is made present in dialogic discourse. Calvin Schrag (1986), in his description of communicative practice, outlines communicative praxis as communication *by, for,* and *about.* In the discussion of communication ethics the "about" is a particular content or rendering of the "good" that both explicitly and implicitly provides a value-laden understanding of communication. The "for" is the audience, and the "by" is the communicative agent. The key is that communication begins with content; it is about something.

In *Communication Ethics Literacy; Dialogue and Difference,* Arnett, Fritz, and Bell (2009) illustrate the diversity of communication ethics metaphors that carry content, a sense of the *good,* in a given communicative setting; additionally, they emphasize the importance of reading what people consider the good—what they protect and promote. In a postmodern age, the basic, fundamental assumption is that one cannot assume that the Other embraces or conforms to an understanding of the good similar to one's own. Communication ethics literacy from a dialogic standpoint begins with attentiveness to the historical moment that both guides and shapes a given dialogic engagement between persons.

The complexity of reading the good of a given communication ethic begins with an understanding of diversity and multiplicity; again, there is no one "universally right" understanding of communication ethics. This era is a demanding historical moment for those wanting a universal in which all must adhere to the same moral principles or suffer the fate of being termed "unethical."

This section frames a story of communication ethics and diversity, which leads to the inevitability of dialogue if we are to avoid the raw use of power in forcing the weaker to adhere to "our" ethics. Such a perspective involves the bully interpersonally and invokes, on an international scale, the problem of imperialism. I offer the following example of street validity of the reality of difference in communication ethics.

A neighborhood group gathered to generate the "guiding rules" for the inhabitants. A time was set for the meeting, and some could not attend—they protested the results of the meeting. Those wanting no more building on any of the sites were happy with their homes, yet newer owners wanted to change their structures. Those with cement driveways made a resolution that no asphalt driveways be permitted, yet some of both existed already. When one person wanted quiet hours at 9:00 p.m., some began to agree, but not all, with some simply beginning to leave, walking slowly home. The only thing that was clear was that few would attend the "block party" in a month, and fewer would read the suggested "guiding rules" for the neighborhood. Maybe if the "good" protected by all was a safe place for a diverse population, then the meeting might have offered a communication ethic that could have united the people; instead, the evening ended with some displaying a wry smile and others displaying a bit of sadness from a recognition that seemingly nothing united the neighborhood. However, there was one sense of the "good" present that night—a reminder in an age of narrative and virtue contention that diversity lives in one's own neighborhood, whether or not the Other looks like "me."

DIALOGIC THEORY

Dialogic theory has a long and diverse history; the scholarship in this area consists of differing schools of thought. This section outlines some of the approaches to dialogue and concludes by framing the particular manner in which dialogue is used in this essay to approach dialogic ethics. Additionally, this section suggests that dialogue has a twofold kinship with communication ethics. First, both dialogue and communication ethics have a history of diversity. Second, both of these terms are too often used in a cavalier fashion, which can easily lead to their employment as personal assertions against another—for instance, this or that person is just not ethical or refuses to do dialogue. In most cases, these terms are used to cloak a personal demand against another and to hide the decision-making criteria of "emotivism" (MacIntyre, 1981) under the guise of terms that seem to offer a warrant for inflicting a thinly veiled, self-righteous set of accusations upon another.

Just as communication ethics has responded to the historical moment and grown increasingly sophisticated in its content, the notion of dialogue enters the conversation with similar complexity. It is simply inaccurate to suggest that there is one understanding of dialogue, for this theory has shifted and changed since the early essays on dialogue by Poulakos (1974) and Johannesen (1983). The connection of dialogic theory to communication ethics is central as Arnett, Fritz, and Bell (2009) define communication ethics as the protection and promotion of a given understanding or rendering of a good. This definition presupposes a world of diversity that requires consideration of a multiplicity of goods before us—with particular attentiveness to what "good' is protected and promoted in a given communicative setting.

This essay centers on dialogic theorists prominently cited in communication literature. The notion of dialogue, however, extends beyond these theorists. One can make the case that there is a connection between dialogue and the social construction work of Kenneth Gergen (2003), Maurice Friedman's (1985) use of dialogue in psychotherapy, the ongoing insights of Robert Bellah and his critiques of individualism in both *Habits of the Heart* (1985) and *The Good Society* (1992), and Fred Dallmayr's (1987) work on Hannah Arendt and questions of policies of peace. Additionally, a dialogic emphasis is central to the work of Nel Noddings (1984) in psychology and education, Jean Gebser's (1949–1950/1985) phenomenological examination of consciousness, and José Ortega y Gasset's (1946) uniting of dialogue within the meeting of existential circumstance. The more contemporary work of Seyla Benhabib (2000) engages the work of Arendt and Habermas (1979) in feminist discourse related to communication and ethics. And the thoughtful work of Amit Pinchevski (2005) brings the connection of dialogue and Levinas to the field of ethics. The above authors are but a small number of the major contributors to the ongoing understanding of dialogue. The following rendering of dialogic theory does not omit their scholarship; but inevitably does as Levinas predicts; human life manifests an ontological sense of violence—as one turns toward one group of authors, one simultaneously turns away from another, displaying a form of ontological neglect, no matter how temporal. As one writes one must not forget the possibilities offered by numerous textured insights left unengaged, particularly as one examines the ongoing influence of dialogue.

Additionally, this essay works with the limitation of citing authors primarily from a Western perspective. The richness of intercultural dialogue will without doubt be a major quest in the years to come. This view of dialogue is akin to understanding dialogue as a form of philosophy of communication. Philosophy of communication requires us to examine presuppositions that ground intercultural philosophies; intercultural exchange was the first meeting of difference (Arnett, 2007a). Postmodernity, within the West, presupposes that philosophies of communication hold a fundamental postmodern value in common with intercultural communication. Intercultural dialogue and dialogue within the West dwell within a postmodern commonality, privileging the notion of difference as the penultimate, if understanding and learning are to occur in this historical moment.

To avoid falling prey to the conventional use or misuse of the term *dialogue*, this essay frames the schools of dialogue and then situates this essay within a particular perspective on dialogue. It is not beyond the scope of scholarly documentation to suggest that there is such a wide array of approaches to dialogue that, at times, the only commonplace between varied uses of the term rests with the term itself.

The previous section on communication ethics was engaged with a dialogic spirit, examining the ongoing additive conversation of colleagues in a given line of communication ethics inquiry. This section on dialogue brings ethics to the table in the manner of Sissela Bok (1999), who insists that positions be able to withstand public scrutiny. Confession in the public domain is one of Bok's major criteria for ethics, which makes practical sense when dealing with terms that come replete with multiple meanings and contrasting histories. For instance, most of us in the field of communication repeatedly hear about the importance of dialogue and the dangers of monologue; yet, from the standpoint of Martin Buber, the outright rejection of monologue makes dialogue impossible. The reason for this reality is as follows: (1) dialogue cannot be demanded; (2) to discount all monologue implies placing dialogue in a supreme position; and (3) when dialogue is unduly privileged, it becomes monologue. Put more simply, it is impossible to "make" a person be spontaneous. We need to be careful about our demands; sometimes the demand actually makes impossible what our insistence seeks to secure. For instance, have you ever had someone demand to be your friend? One wants to run, not meet the Other, when such a demand defines a relationship. The conclusion of this essay highlights the importance of monologue, or what has been often called the "I-It" relationship, which actually makes dialogue possible (Arnett, 2006).

Before detailing a particular scholarly lineage of dialogue, it is important to delineate the manner in which the term *Other* is used within this essay. The notion of Other or Otherness, in this essay, adheres to the insight of Immanuel Levinas, reminding us of alterity, extreme difference, and the recognition that when the difference of the Other is denied colonization is invited. It is this constructive understanding of Otherness that guides this essay. There are multiple scholars, from Simone Beauvoir (1948) to Gayatri Chakravorty Spivak (1999), who have assumed a contrary position on the notion of the Other. Ironically, the spirit of their projects and that of Levinas rests within a common denominator: rejection of totalitarian, colonial, and oppressive efforts that ignore the uniqueness of the human face. The differences among these scholars are beyond the scope of this essay but the unique manner in which this essay frames the Other bears admission.

A Scholarly Lineage

This section outlines differences in the various dialogic schools or positions, relying heavily upon an essay entitled "Dialogue as an 'Enlarged Mentality:' Review, Assessment, and Ongoing Difference" published in *Communication Research Trends* (Arnett, Grayson, & McDowell, 2008), which delineates differences in the schools of dialogue while providing an additive contribution to dialogic study with the addition of vocabulary and insight from Hannah Arendt. The act of theory construction in the area of dialogic studies is not complete; additional perspectives and authors continue to emerge, without presupposing a conclusion to this accumulative process. This essay offers an understanding of dialogue that begins with bias and the particular, assuming the reality of a multiplicity of dialogic positions.

Martin Buber (1965), in the "History of the Dialogic Principle," begins discussion of the inseparability of "Thou and I" in the work of Friedrich Heinrich Jacobi in 1775; Buber suggests that the specific scholarly dimension of "I and Thou" has a history of three centuries. He stresses the long history of the "Thou" calling out the "I." Buber's essay examines a number of important common places in the advancement of dialogue: (1) he offers a starting date for a theory of dialogue; (2) he outlines the importance of "calling," in which the "Thou" calls forth to an "I"; and (3) he stresses the contributions of scholars working around the time of World War II who emphasize the importance of existentialism, citing Karl Jaspers as central in this effort. What we learn about the dialogic principle is that it does not begin with "me," but with "existence" and a "Thou" that then shapes my "identity." Dialogue is one of the first communication theories to offer an understanding of identity construction as it suggests that the "I" is derivative from the call of existence and the Thou of the Other.

The next major summary and interpretive look at the history of dialogue is put forth in *The Interpretation of Dialogue* by Tulio Maranhão (1990). This work understands dialogue as a "dialogic hermeneutic," suggesting that the way in which dialogue is constructed shapes our interpretation of the communication process before us. He outlines a number of schools that offer different hermeneutic entrances into the study and use of dialogue, placed within two large categories of "descriptive" and "idea" dialogue, with the former aiming for clarity and the latter tied to the shaping and reshaping of human identities.

In the field of communication, the most thorough reviews of dialogic schools emerge in essays by Cissna and Anderson (1990, 2002). They describe four approaches: (1) the work of Buber with an emphasis upon human meeting; (2) those working from an ethnographic or conversation analyst perspective on human conversation; (3) the work of Mikhail Bakhtin that connects dialogue to cultural knowing; and (4) the textual analysis and philosophical hermeneutic work of Hans-Georg Gadamer. Their understanding of dialogue is that it presupposes sociality. In a later work, they added Jurgen Habermas and his commitment to ideal speech that exposes "interests" that make it difficult for others to join the conversation (Habermas, 1984). In the Cissna and Anderson special edition of *Communication Theory* (2008), they continued to offer the reality of differences in the approaches to dialogue. Their work is central to dialogic theory as Chesebro's is to communication ethics; they offer categories of difference in the engagement of the notion of dialogue. Additionally, major articles by Richard Johannesen (1971), John Poulakos (1974), John Stewart (1978), and Ronald C. Arnett (1981) are but a few of the essays that began the movement in dialogue in the 1970s in the discipline of communication, with Stewart (1978) being the first to bring the philosophical hermeneutic work of Gadamer to the table. This move took us from a psychological understanding of dialogue within the person to understanding the larger communication environment in which persons gather as a text, both constructed dialogically and understood dialogically. More recent work by Pete Kellett and Dalton (2001), Jeffrey Murray (2003), Michael Hyde (2001), Jeanine Czubaroff (2000), and Joohan Kim and Eun Joo Kim (2008) continue the philosophical and identity shaping understanding of dialogue. This essay considers this line of inquiry very promising, particularly due to the reality of increasing questions about identity formation in a time in which routine understandings of everyday life are placed at risk, as Ronald L. Jackson's (2010) project with the *Encyclopedia of Identity* suggests. The connections of philosophical content and identity as content shape this particular lineage of dialogue—dialogue begins with content, not process or subjective intent.

Dialogue as Content

It is the philosophical and identity part of the dialogic tree that this essay follows. The key is to focus upon content within dialogue. In quick summary, this understanding goes as follows. First, Buber's history of the dialogic principle states the importance of content through an emphasis upon *existence* and *calling* that reshapes the content of human identity through the ongoing construction of the "I." Second, there is the content of *philosophy*; the moment one must use philosophical terms for understanding dialogue, a term leaves what is called the "natural world" and moves into a phenomenological world in which dialogue becomes not a process, but a phenomenon that has a life of its own, uncontrolled by a technique or process. Third, the importance of *identity* is central in dialogue, but this view of dialogic identity stresses the derivative, not the originative. We cannot make ourselves; dialogically, we have a derivative sense of identity. Fourth, the traditional emphasis on the notion of the *between* stresses that no one person is in control; the phenomenon of dialogue has a life of its own that can be invited, but not demanded. Fifth, the author of this essay connects this view of identity and the notion of the between to Arendt's view of the *public* as a place of difference where all are invited and no one feels like a landowner; in such a place the better metaphor is *guest*, a guest who is but one short step from feeling like a stranger.

Dialogue is not a communicative phenomenon that brings out only our warm feelings; from the standpoint of a continental view of dialogue, each "I" feels some discomfort and, at times, much uneasiness, for the phenomenon of dialogue has a life outside our control. Such a view of dialogue works within an ironical spirit, calling us into places of discomfort, rejecting our efforts at ownership, reshaping our identity without our permission, making us attend to a content of communicative life more akin to the "mud of everyday life" than the pristine hope of "rising above it all" and helping the less fortunate or demanding that another help me. To paraphrase a title from another essay, dialogue works to enlarge our mentalities whether we like it or not—such is the reason that Bakhtin could connect dialogue to the ongoing fabric and background of life driven on its own with our being mere participants.

This view of dialogue drove the following discussion in class. Students asked, "What is the most important concept in communication?" I replied, "Content." The students then asked, "What happens when another talks to you in a manner that makes it difficult to hear the content?" I stated that we then have to make a choice: "Do we want to learn the content or confirm our current position?" Of course, we want to have friends who care for us in style and content, but all too often in a world of diversity the style of discourse may not fit our expectations or hopes. At such a moment we must decide whether to focus upon style or content. If we choose the latter, we risk new content's reshaping us, and if we choose the former, we begin to demand "our" form of "dialogue" that we deem acceptable. If we walk in dialogue toward content we would not choose, we open the door to learning as we meet the unwanted—opening the face of dialogue before us. It is as if dialogue lurks and hides in counterintuitive places, unwilling to be owned and unwilling to be called forth upon demand. As the class ended, a student asked, "Does dialogue rest in the shadows?" I simply said, "Sometimes—I guess it does." But, perhaps the real home of dialogue is in an "enlarged mentality," a sense of hope that is bigger than our desire for comfort and more comprehensive than our singular perspective. Such a home of dialogue is ever-demanding of the participants to discover at the end of an exchange that their worlds have been made larger, that the reality of an enlarged mentality has followed them, all the while shaking their heads and saying within the spirit of Arendt's *public,* "I still feel like a guest here."

DIALOGIC ETHICS—DIALOGIC CONFESSION AS AN ETHICAL RHETORICAL TURN

This project engages the terms discussed in the previous section in a tradition that inherits Chesebro's early insights on communication ethics and the necessary linkage to the public arena, offering a public admission of the biases that shape and continue to constitute given understandings or theories of communication ethics, etched in the words of Gadamer's (1975) view of dialogue as a "fusion of horizons" between a given text and the question and bias that guide the interpreter. The text, in this case, consists of both the stories of communication ethics and dialogue, and the bias of this essay rests within their connection to a postmodern age of narrative and virtue contention, defined by difference. Specifically, this dialogic effort consists of the meeting of two horizons centered upon the two lineages discussed above—the *metaphorical lineage in communication ethics* begun by Chesebro and the *philosophical and existential lineage of dialogue* begun in

1775 by Jacobi. In both cases, these lineages explicitly and implicitly announce how one can meet a world of diversity, or, put more directly in communication ethics terms, meet an era of narrative and virtue contention.

This essay constructs the theoretical construct of dialogic ethics in a manner congruent with the discussions of communication ethics and dialogic theory in the previous section, including *dialogic ethics as lineage* and *dialogical ethics as content*. This particular construct of dialogic ethics has a deep and rich heritage that rejects the modern assumption that we can stand above history and render an objective ethical pronouncement or enter a dialogue in such a fashion. This approach to dialogic ethics begins with a confession that we live within the mud of everyday life; there is no way to escape such a reality. The messiness of existence haunts us not only in time of war, death, loss of friendship, and in economic collapse, but in our engagement with the everyday. It is, however, the assertion of this author that this same existential reality gives us meaning and a place to stand; in the words of Levinas (1969), existence, wanted or not, is the place in which we must and we do, reluctantly or eagerly, dwell.

Dialogic Ethics as Lineage

The lineage of dialogic ethics involves a large number of persons, with representative voices being Chesebro (1969), Rob Anderson (2004), James Jaksa (1990), Richard Johannesen (1983), Josina Makau (1990), Arnett (1981), and more recently Michael Hyde (2001) and Jeffrey Murray (2003), with each pointing to the importance of engaging existence, meeting difference, and finding metaphors that touch that existence and help us understand the diversity around us. This lineage of communication ethics scholars has one major *praxis* action in common; they all integrate philosophical and practical lived experience. Their collective work illuminates the difference between an analytic understanding of philosophical ethics and communication ethics, with the latter engaged in existential questions about the influence of communication ethics on and between persons.

Additionally, these authors point to philosophical content as necessary in understanding different practical implications resulting from dissimilar approaches to communication ethics and dialogue. A philosophical meeting of dialogue and communication ethics attempts to account for dissimilarities in the standpoint one takes to meeting contrasting approaches to cultures, organizations, contexts, and race and ethnicity. These stories have three ongoing mantras. First, these authors pay attention to the content of ideas; indeed, they have consequences and shape our conversation, often in metaphorical form. Richard Harvey Brown was one of the initial voices who sought to conceptualize the power and importance of metaphors as ideas that shape theory construction (Brown, 1989, pp. 77–112), and Arnett and Arneson (1999) built the notion of "dialogic civility" within a metaphorical horizon. Second, they attend to existence; we must meet what is before us, not what we want or demand to meet us. Neither dialogue nor communication ethics can stand above existence and still have "street value'" in communicative lives. Third, difference is not just a motto or slogan; it is the life-blood of the human condition in an era in which we must learn increasingly more about the Other. The insightful work of Benhabib from a different perspective tied to Kant, Habermas, and discourse ethics reminds us of the fundamental nature of difference as we meet Otherness in this historical moment (Benhabib, 1996).

It is important at this juncture to recognize a scholarly lineage that is related to, but different from, the approach pursued here. The very mention of one lineage presupposes other ones from which to choose. The discourse ethics to which Benhabib adheres is another such family of scholarship from which one can construct a dialogic ethic. This reality of differentiation reveals that lineage matters, that, to our good fortune, approaches to this topic are plentiful, and that the differences reveal the power of narrative ground in their assertions. This essay does not have the space to frame yet another dialogic ethic, but it is essential to draw attention to the provinciality of theory, which even Benhabib does in her citing of Kant's cosmopolitan aims with the term *cosmopolitan federalism* (Benhabib, 1996). This is a project worthy of engaging (a dialogic discourse ethic perspective), but right now the aim of this essay is to play out an understanding of dialogic ethics framed upon temporal narrative ground.

The stress on difference in this essay moves us to the importance of temporal narrative ground, akin to the work of Alasdair MacIntyre (1981), Robert Bellah (1975), Stanley Hauerwas (1981), Charles Taylor (2007), and in the discipline of communication, Walter Fisher (1984).[1] It is narrative ground that gives one something upon which to pivot, to push off of, something that functions as a source of identity in decision making and action. It is from such ground that one can engage in what Calvin Schrag (1986) termed, "the rhetorical turn." The turn starts with a narrative that, in the words of Charles Taylor (1989), offers the source of moral life and identity that gives us moral content to guide our discourse as we make a rhetorical turn.

The work of Schrag influences a number of communication scholars engaging ethical issues from a philosophical perspective with perhaps the most well known representative being one of Schrag's former students—Michael Hyde (*The Call of Conscience*, 2001; *The Ethos of Rhetoric*, 2004). The notion of the rhetorical turn assumes that all communication, including dialogue, assumes a public admission of perspective or tainted ground from which the discourse begins (Arnett, 2008a). Calvin Schrag's "rhetorical turn" brings communication ethics and dialogue together only when the taint of bias shapes our understanding of dialogue. This perspective resonates with Buber and his view of ground, Stewart's (1978) introduction of Gadamer to the field, in the reclamation of prejudice as a central theme in dialogue, and Leslie Baxter's emphasis of Bakhtin's (1981) connection between dialogue and the one not present, the third. It resonates with the work of Anderson and Cissna providing a detailed look at the dialogic ground of Rogers and Buber, in its similarity and difference, and it resonates with the work of Arnett and Arneson in their framing the necessity of narrative ground if we are to offer an alternative to conventional humanistic assumptions about the autonomy of the communicative agent.

A dialogic ethic, as framed in this essay, assumes narrative ground that is not easily altered and functions, reflectively or not, as a persuasive position in engagement with the Other. Such is the reason why, when Martin Buber was at Union Theological Seminary and he was asked, "What is it like to be a Jew?" and with glaring eyes he asked the student, "Do you really want to know?" that the student gulped and withdrew the question, fearing he might be converted on the spot. This understanding of a dialogic ethic in operation admits the reality of a rhetorical turn—there is narrative ground upon which we stand, and the content and social practices of our discourse are given birth from that narrative ground. The ontological nature of the rhetorical turn shapes this essay's vision of a dialogic ethic, formed through a lineage of scholarship that engages the philosophical complexity of dialogue and ethics while understanding that both ethics and dialogue begin with narrative ground, not the discourse itself, suggesting the impossibility of avoiding a rhetorical turn in the doing of either communication ethics or dialogue.

The previous authors point to a dialogue that begins with ground under our feet. Is it any wonder that Bonhoeffer stated that the most immoral thing one can do to another is to remove narrative ground from under another's feet without having something other than individualism as an alternative (Arnett, 2005, pp. 10–11, 106–107)? Such a view of dialogue that begins somewhere on some kind of ground has the taint of persuasive deliberation and is not to be confused with a pristine world in which interlocutors stand above history and engage in discourse about ethical ground that does not matter. Dialogic ethics begins with the assumption that the content of ethics shapes the ground from which the discourse begins. In the paraphrased words of Martin

Buber, dialogue begins with the ground on which one stands with an openness to learn from the Other, but never a willingness to forego the ethical ground that propels and shapes the identity of a communicator speaking about a topic more substantial than an emotivistic outburst with the Other. The two lineages of communication ethics and dialogue point to narrative ground and difference, with metaphors giving us insight into both.

The scholarly lineage that shapes this essay suggests that a dialogic ethic begins first with a *narrative ground*, then assumes *difference*, and is made public and recognizable by the *metaphors* that emerge in conversation with Others—on the surface, our rhetorical turn takes those metaphors into engagement with others, and the deeper text of narrative ground shapes the identity of those using such terms in the meeting of Others. To this dialogue, this author adds an additional metaphor—dialogic confession. Arnett (2005) uses this term in a book on Dietrich Bonhoeffer, who lost his life in a conspiracy against Adolph Hitler. The term *dialogic confession* is a central metaphor for illustrating how an ethical position of conviction can meet and address a tyrannical age in which a dominant group seeks simply to destroy the narrative and virtue guidance of dominated people (Arnett, 2005). This lineage leads to a metaphorical content in the study and engagement of a dialogic ethic.

Dialogic Ethics as Content

Dialogic ethics as content is more akin to Arendt's understanding of the story-laden nature of action. The difference between behavior and action for Arendt is whether or not there is a story associated with the behavior; if the answer is yes, the behavior moves to action. This final section seeks to answer a basic question, "What is the basic content of a dialogic ethic from the perspective of this essay and how do these metaphors together constitute a story that lends itself to the action and praxis genres of Arendt and Schrag, respectively?"

Paraphrasing Sandra Harding's (1991) understanding of standpoint, this section frames a dialogic ethic from a given standpoint, publicly disclosing the limits and possibilities of this perspective. This section concludes in openness, not in closure, in the admission and confession of particularity—the importance of provinciality that seeks to meet the Other (Roberts & Arnett, 2008). This particular view of dialogic ethics works with the genre of petite narratives (Rorty, 1979) that function with walls of necessary provinciality and bridges attentive to the alterity of the Other. Each historical moment requires answers to its own unique questions, and any understanding of pluralism must begin by privileging provinciality that engages in a communicative bridge to difference.

This perspective on dialogic ethics assumes the pragmatic currency of understanding communication ethics in a postmodern age that embodies a "unity of contraries" (Buber, 1965, p. 111), difference, and the importance of temporal narrative ground attentive to the following coordinates: (1) *multiplicity,* (2) *minimalist,* (3) *historicity and existential life-world,* and (4) *tainted ground and dialogic confession,* which all begin with the presupposition that one cannot assume the Other is like "me" or "my people." These five coordinates shape a general understanding of communication ethics central to this essay, with the last, dialogic confession, assuming a particular way of engaging a world of diversity (Arnett & Makau, 1996). The following is an outline of dialogic communication ethics in that it works within the unity of contraries of difference and narrative ground.

Multiplicity is an open admission of perspective in communication ethics, rejecting the assumption of the universal, with a constant demand to learn from difference. In this historical moment we must learn from those who are different from us. The struggles in the international community and our own local communities provide empirical evidence for this necessity. Multiplicity is a postmodern mantra, intimately tied to the work of Foucault (1973) and Derrida (1976) and, additionally, representative of renderings of communication ethics and dialogue that assume that different schools of dialogue and communication with contrasting metaphors have not been imposed upon reality, but reflect the actual diversity of the world before us. The reality of multiplicity shifts the conversation from a posture of accusation and weaponry in the hands of a single communicative agent who claims that something is unethical or not dialogic when the agent's own personal disposition or self-perceived interests do not govern the discourse.

The focus on multiplicity is an invitation to understand that a given good is protected and promoted by a particular communication ethics theory. In the case of dialogic ethics, the good to be protected and promoted is dialogue. *A dialogic ethic assumes multiplicity, which counters any presupposition that there is only one understanding of dialogue or one communication ethic that can be imposed upon another as the only good, turning a supposed good into a form of "interpersonal colonization"* (Arnett, Fritz, & Bell, 2009). The notion of multiplicity, as understood within this essay, works within the genre of Bakhtin and his emphasis on heteroglossia (1981). Bakhtin has a textured understanding of this term that stresses the multiplicity of language spoken between people of difference and linguistic tradition. Additionally, Bakhtin has a phenomenological view of heteroglossia that is akin to Husserl in his work, *Crisis of European Sciences and Transcendental Phenomenology* (1970), in which Husserl outlines genetic phenomenology. A genetic phenomenology presupposes a layered texturing of multiple traditions and voices that comprise the ground of presupposition for a particular understanding at a particular time. Heteroglossia, as Bakhtin understood it, presupposes this multinature, multilayered rendering of discourse between persons. In a Bakhtinian sense, our discourse is encircled within multiple layers, both textured voices of the past and attentive to the future. In short, conversation is never simply about "what is." It always carries markers of what has been and what might be emergent in a given moment. This genetic phenomenological focus was also central to the genealogical work of Foucault (1971).

This specific essay's emphasis on multiplicity and understanding in communication ethics and dialogue rests within the pragmatic and philosophical assumptions of Sissela Bok, who suggests that as we engage one another together in public space, we should pursue minimal, not maximal, points of agreement.

Minimalist engagement presupposes recognition of difference and multiplicity and the accompanying pragmatic reality of controlling our expectations about agreement with one another. This *minimalist* position is central to the work of Sissela Bok (1995). She thoughtfully frames the dilemma before us, moving us from an unreflective maximalist position that assumes that the Other holds an idea that is isomorphic to our own, offering as an alternative a minimalist position that looks for minimalist concurrence in the search for temporal commonality. Unbridgeable divisions emerge when we demand that another assume our position; such actions work within a colonialist spirit. *A minimalist position on dialogic ethics begins with the assumption that we do not have to hold a great deal in common, but we must be willing to learn from the Other as we minimize our impulse to tell, even as we recognize the inevitability of the "rhetorical" nature of our meeting.* Multiplicity and a minimalist expectation reflect awareness of the existential demands upon us in this historical moment.

Historicity and existential life-world are placed together; they coinform one another. The existential life-world has a long history from Husserl to the work of Karl Jaspers (1971), who was Hannah Arendt's dissertation director. Arendt begins her understanding of existential life in her dissertation on Augustine, whom she considers the first "existentialist" (Arendt, 1996). Gadamer knew this tradition well and worked out a manner in which one can listen to the existential life-world via the notion of historicity, which, for Gadamer (1975), manifests itself in the form of a question.

A theory then becomes a temporal answer to a given question that emerges from a given existential setting. This Gadamerian view of historicity came to the discipline in Stewart's work on Gadamer, making the connection to *historicity* a natural part of this construction. Both communication ethics and dialogue are historically, not universally, constituted. Historicity moves the conversation into temporality, a temporality shaped by questions announced by a given historical moment. Historicity does not live within linearity, but offers the possibility of communicative companions across time whenever similar questions emerge in a given historical moment. Take, for instance, those following Moses across the desert day after day, week after week, month after month. We can imagine the questions asked regularly of this leader of a people so long ago: "How far? How much longer? Remind us again why we are doing this." Such stories continue to live because they ask questions that we, today, at times, feel bearing down upon us: "How far? How much longer? Remind us again why we are doing this." Clearly there are different circumstances in the 21st century than in approximately 1400 BCE. But the questions form a kinship of historicity across time. The notion of historicity is not to be confused with history; historicity is inherently dialogic.

This work follows Gadamer's (1975) framing of historicity as a question that emerges from a given existential setting. Gadamer situates historicity, the question emerging from a given existential setting, as the origin of dialogue. The dialogue does not begin in me or in the Other, but in the historical situation itself. *Dialogic ethics assumes that the existential life-world is the home of historicity or questions to which we must respond and the repository of dialogic companions who have engaged similar questions long before our own first breath.* Dialogic ethics assumes the importance of listening attentively to the historical moment, not just to the visceral impulses of communicative agents. The fundamental importance of this approach, historicity in communication, in an existential engagement is framed in "Bridges Not Walls: The Communicative Enactment of Dialogic Storytelling" (Arnett, Arneson, & Holba, 2008) with a stress on dialogic storytelling as attentive to questions emerging in the historical moment. A dialogic ethic attentive to multiplicity, a minimalist position, and the dialogic character of historicity within the existential life-world acknowledges that we bring a dialogic ethic not "in" a process between persons, but "upon" tainted ground that each brings to the encounter.

Tainted ground and dialogic confession abides by Gadamer's project of renovation, in opposition to the tyranny of modernity in favor of a rootless sense of progress; he reclaimed the ontological reality of "prejudice" and "bias" in our making sense of the world. This stress upon temporal narrative ground that is biased or prejudiced is at the heart of the essay, "The Rhetoric of Communication Ethics" (Arnett, 2008), which states that tainted or biased ground is the beginning of a dialogic ethic engaged in the meeting of the Other. The dialogic ethics emphasis upon tainted ground requires, in addition, a pragmatic admission of bias as a public warning, a form of *dialogic confession* in an era of narrative and virtue contention.

Dialogic confession works within an existential assumption that one cannot stand above history, making this construct an ethical warning about one's own position and the reality of fallibility—dialogic confession warns the Other and reminds oneself of one's own pragmatic admission of fallibility. Dialogic confession acknowledges the tainted ground of communicative partners. Dialogic ethics confesses tainted ground as the beginning of learning. We work from where we are, not from where we pretend to be—above the fray of perspective and interests.

A dialogic ethic that begins with knowing the ontological reality of tainted ground and a willingness to confess a perspective assumes the pragmatic position of communication from a position that is not universal but committed to the particular, respectful of distance between persons of difference, and ever attentive to learning from the acknowledgement of one's own position and learning from that of another (Arnett, Fritz, & Bell, 2009). Dialogic ethics is a meeting of radical alterity that does not seek to impose upon the Other, while simultaneously recognizing the reality of a rhetorical turn that naturally emerges from a dialogic ethic situated within tainted ground.

This essay assumes that any sense of the good will be met by varied and different other renderings of the good. Such a historical realization requires this essay to contend that in a postmodern age, dialogic ethics is a knowing rhetorical task that simultaneously seeks to learn from the Other. The oddity of a rhetoric of dialogic ethics is intentionally offered as a pragmatic metaphor situated in a commitment to provinciality; a rhetorical rendering of communication ethics and dialogue begins with the recognition of the synergy between provinciality and a given understanding of the good. *This communication ethics model of dialogue embraces provinciality while tempering provinciality with learning attentive to alterity and difference. This dialogic ethic functions as a bridge to alterity, difference, and learning, linking provinciality and cosmopolitanism within the spirit of what Buber (1965) called a unity of contraries.*

The rhetorical understanding of a dialogic ethic goes so far as to suggest that the knowing use of monologue sometimes is more akin to a dialogic ethic than any effort that attempts to turn communication ethics and dialogue into a universal ought, a demand that must be met on "my" or "our" terms, missing the confession of tainted ground. Dialogic ethics seeks to counter self-deception that turns dialogue and ethics into monologue under the guise of a self-donned mask of dialogic care. Dialogic ethics affirmed by one's own self-assessment and self-applause is contrary to a "dialogic ethic" attentive to Otherness. In the conceptual spirit of Chesebro, a dialogic ethic must end modestly or morph into the shadows of the dwelling of that which one seeks to counter. A dialogic ethic works in a confessional fashion from tainted ground and naturally works within a prescriptive and rhetorical communicative impulse, working simultaneously to fight the impulse to link "truth" too quickly to "me" and evil too quickly to another who stands upon narrative ground that refuses to conform to "my" demand.

Such a dialogic ethic does not often lend itself to the answer we demand or the reaction we wish to find in the voice of the Other. I end with an example tendered while waiting for a delayed plane to arrive so I could go on home. The two people next to me were discussing President Bush and his policies. The word *immoral* was used repeatedly and discussion of his arrogance dotted many a phrase. The exchange went on for more than 45 minutes; it was so loud I could not read, there was no other place to sit, and the night had brought me too much weariness. I sat somewhat numb, listening, but, in general, nodding with approval of their critique. As the conversation became more and more of a drone of complaint, I noticed a woman walking toward us. The woman paused and said: "Are you educators? If so, this is sad. If you get your students to think like this, we are in serious trouble. You only complain about the man, offering one personal accusation after another. Stop using the word *unethical* and begin to focus upon his policies. I agree that they are wrong, but when you use terms like *immoral,* you give us the impression that such problems will go away when he is not in office. You are wrong if you think the problem is simply a man and not the policies." This woman demanded content in the conversation. When she left, I lowered my head and wrote notes on the encounter, thinking that I had somehow been in the presence of Hannah Arendt lecturing us in monologic style about the "banality of evil" (Arendt, 1963). Discussion of the man and not policies is where she witnessed evil hiding from common view. If Arendt were here as I pen this essay, she might warn me once again in a monologue that looks more like a dialogic ethic of the danger of a "banality of evil" lurking in the most surprising places—perhaps even in communication ethics and dialogue when the demand of "me" trumps genuine conversation about content. In the words of Tevye in *Fiddler on the Roof*, "on the one hand" I begin with narrative ground that propels me long before I meet the Other and "on the other hand," I must give the Other the same opportunity that I demand, to bring new tainted ground to the table of conversation.

I end this essay with a dialogic confession (Arnett, 2005): that I have never been this happy after a political election. The reason for my enthusiasm, in terms of dialogic ethics, is that we have witnessed a moment that Arendt might have penned as an opening for an "enlarged mentality." We have opened the public sphere of influence and politics in a manner that just a few years ago would have seemed impossible. Dialogic ethics presupposes the importance of learning and opening the public sphere for more to enter and for less to feel like settlers, possessors of the public sphere. Perhaps, in a world attentive to difference, our goal in the public sphere is a place that invites us all to join as guests with the nagging feeling that we are one step away from being a stranger; it is the feeling of being decentered that makes genuine public space possible.

Decentering is a dialogic reminder that only by our discomfort are there openings for those different from ourselves. Dialogic ethics does not render a life of comfort for us; but it does work at making space for Otherness as we no longer try or can possess or totalize public space. I end with one story. After the election, a friend with political views much different from my own sat with me and looked carefully into space and said, "I voted for John McCain. But I am still aware that this is a glorious moment to be alive. The world is a little bigger place today, and the world is asking me to be a part of it. I am reminded today how glorious it is to be a part, not the owner, the proprietor, the controller, the totalizer, or the colonizer of public space." This historical moment seems to offer a dialogic confession that dialogic ethics begins with the realization that we are only a part—it is good to be a part, pragmatically contending against the dialogic diseases of totalization and domination.

NOTE

1. I have said publicly that Fisher's introduction of narrative to the field is the most important contribution to the study of ethics in my professional stay with the discipline. The notion of narrative opened the conversation beyond objective and subjective readings of ethics.

REFERENCES

Anderson, R. (2004). *Dialogue: Theorizing difference in communication studies.* Thousand Oaks, CA: Sage.

Anderson, R., & K. N. Cissna. (2008). Fresh perspectives in dialogue theory. *Communication Theory, 18,* 1–4.

Arendt, H. (1963). *Eichmann in Jerusalem: A report on the banality of evil.* New York: Penguin.

Arendt, H. (1992). *Lectures on Kant's political philosophy* (R. Beiner, Ed.). Chicago: Chicago University Press.

Arendt, H. (1996). *Love and Saint Augustine* (J. V. Scott & J. C. Stark, Eds.). Chicago: University of Chicago Press.

Aristotle. (1985). *Nichomachean ethics* (T. Irwin, Trans.). Indianapolis, IN: Hackett. (Original work written 350 BCE)

Arnett, R. C. (1981). Toward a phenomenological dialogue. *Western Journal of Speech Communication, 45,* 201–212.

Arnett, R. C. (2001). "Dialogic civility as pragmatic ethical praxis: An interpersonal metaphor for the public domain." *Communication Theory, 11,* 315–338.

Arnett, R. C. (2002). Paulo Freire's revolutionary pedagogy: From a story-centered to a narrative-centered communication ethic. *Qualitative Inquiry, 8,* 489–510.

Arnett, R. C. (2005). *Dialogic confession: Bonhoeffer's rhetoric of responsibility.* Carbondale: Southern Illinois University Press.

Arnett, R. C. (2006). Through a glass, darkly. *Journal of Communication and Religion, 29,* 1–17.

Arnett, R. C. (2008a). The rhetoric of communication ethics. In *International encyclopedia of communication* (W. Donsbach, Ed.). Malden, MA: Wiley-Blackwell.

Arnett, R. C. (2008b, June 13). *Communication ethics as Janus at the gates: Responding to postmodernity and the normativity of crisis.* Keynote speech for 10th National Communication Ethics conference, Pittsburgh, PA.

Arnett, R. C., & Arneson, P. (1999). *Dialogic civility in a cynical age: Community, hope, and interpersonal relationships.* Albany, NY: SUNY Press.

Arnett, R. C., Arneson, P., & Bell, L. (2006). Communication ethics: The dialogic turn. *The Review of Communication, 6,* 2–92.

Arnett, R. C., Arneson, P., & Holba, A. (2008). Bridges not walls: The communicative enactment of dialogic storytelling. *The Review of Communication, 8,* 217–234.

Arnett, R. C., Fritz, J. M. H., & Bell, L. M. (2009). *Communication ethics literacy: Dialogue and difference.* Thousand Oaks, CA: Sage.

Arnett, R. C., Grayson, C., & McDowell, C. (2008). Dialogue as enlarged communicative mentality: Review, assessment, and ongoing difference. *Communication Research Trends, 27,* 3–35.

Arnett, R. C., & Makau, J. (Eds.). (1996). *Communication ethics in an age of diversity.* Carbondale: University of Illinois Press.

Bakhtin, M. M. (1981). *The dialogic imagination: Four essays.* Austin: University of Texas Press.

Beauvoir, S. (1948). *The ethics of ambiguity* (B. Frechtman, Trans). New York: Citadel. (Original work published 1947)

Bellah, R. (1975). *The broken covenant: American civil religion in time of trial.* New York: Seabury.

Bellah, R. (1985). *Habits of the heart: Individualism and commitment in American life.* Berkeley: University of California Press.

Bellah, R. (1992). *The good society.* New York: Vintage Books.

Benhabib, S. (Ed.). (1996). *Democracy and difference: Contesting the boundaries of the political.* Princeton, NJ: Princeton University Press.

Benhabib, S. (2000). *The reluctant modernism of Hannah Arendt.* Thousand Oaks, CA: Sage.

Bernstein, R. J. (1983). *Beyond objectivism and relativism: Science, hermeneutics and praxis.* Philadelphia: University of Pennsylvania Press.

Bok, S. (1995). *Common values.* Columbia: University of Missouri Press.

Bok, S. (1999). *Lying: Moral choice in public and private life.* New York: Vantage.

Brown, R. H. (1989). *A poetic for sociology.* Chicago: Chicago University Press.

Buber, M. (1965). *The knowledge of man: A philosophy of the interhuman.* New York: Harper & Row.

Buber, M. (1966). *The way of response: Martin Buber; Selections from his writings* (N. N. Glatzer, Ed.). New York: Schocken.

Chesebro, J. W. (1969). A construct for assessing ethics in communication. *Central States Speech Journal, 20,* 104–114.

Christians, C. (2003). *Special issue: Virtual reality and communication ethics.* Mahwah, NJ: Erlbaum.

Cissna, K. N., & Anderson, R. (1990). The contributions of Carl Rogers to a philosophical praxis of dialogue. *Western Journal of Speech Communication, 54,* 125–147.

Cissna, K. N., & Anderson, R. (2002). *Moments of meeting: Buber, Rogers, and the potential for public dialogue.* Albany, NY: SUNY Press.

Czubaroff, J. (2000). Dialogical rhetoric: An application of Martin Buber's philosophy of dialogue. *Quarterly Journal of Speech, 86,* 168–190.

Dallmayr, F. (1987). Public or private freedom? Response to Kateb. *Social Research, 54,* 617–628.

Derrida, J. (1976). *Of grammatology* (Trans. G. C. Spivak). Baltimore, MD: John Hopkins University Press.

Fisher, W. R. (1984). Narrative as a human communication paradigm: The case of public moral argument. *Communication Monographs, 51,* 1–22.

Foucault, M. (1971). *The order of things: An archaeology of the human sciences.* New York: Pantheon.

Friedman, M. (1985). *The healing dialogue in psychotherapy.* New York: Aronson.

Gadamer, H. G. (1975). *Truth and method.* New York: Seabury.

Gadamer, H. G. (1976). *Philosophical hermeneutics*. Berkeley: University of California Press.
Gadamer, H. G. (1980). *Dialogue and dialectic: Eight hermeneutical studies on Plato*. New Haven, CT: Yale University Press.
Gasset, J. O. (1946). *Concord and liberty* (H. Weyl, Trans). New York: Norton.
Gebser, J. (1985). *The ever-present origin* (N. Barstad & A. Mickunas, Trans.). Athens: Ohio University Press. (Original work published 1949–1950)
Gergen, K. (2003). *Social construction: A reader*. Thousand Oaks, CA: Sage.
Habermas, J. (1979). *Communication and the evolution of society* (T. McCarthy, Trans.). Boston, MA: Beacon Press. (Original work published 1976)
Habermas, J. (1984). *The theory of communicative action*. Boston, MA: Beacon.
Harding, S. (1991). *Whose science? Whose knowledge? Thinking from women's lives*. Ithaca, NY: Cornell University Press.
Hauerwas, S. (1981). *A community of character: Toward a constructive Christian social ethic*. Notre Dame, IN: Notre Dame University Press.
Husserl, E. (1970). *Crises of European sciences and transcendental phenomenology: An introduction to phenomenological philosophy* (D. Carr, Trans.). Evanston, IL: Northwestern University Press. (Original work published 1954)
Hyde, M. J. (2001). *The call of conscience: Heidegger and Levinas, rhetoric and the euthanasia debate*. Columbia: University of South Carolina Press.
Hyde, M. J. (Ed.). (2004). *The ethos of rhetoric*. Columbia: South Carolina University Press.
Jackson, R. L. (2010). *Encyclopedia of identity*. Thousand Oaks, CA: Sage.
Jaksa, J. (1990). *Communication ethics: Methods of analysis*. Belmont, CA: Wadsworth.
Jaspers, K. (1971). *Philosophy of existence* (R. F. Grabau, Trans.). State College, PA: Pennsylvania State University Press.
Johannesen, R. (1971). The emerging concept of communication as dialogue. *Quarterly Journal of Speech, 57, 373–382*.
Johannesen, R. L. (1983). *Ethics in human communication*. Prospect Heights, IL: Waveland.
Kant, I. (1951). *Critique of judgment* (J. H. Bernard, Trans.). New York: Hafner Press.
Kellett, P., & Dalton, D. (2001). *Managing conflict in a negotiated world*. Thousand Oaks, CA: Sage.
Kim, J., & Kim, E. J. (2008). Theorizing dialogic deliberation: Everyday political talk as communicative action and dialogue. *Communication Theory, 18*, 51–70.
Levinas, E. (1969). *Totality and infinity: An essay on exteriority* (A. Lingis, Trans.). Pittsburgh, PA: Duquesne University Press. (Original work published 1961)
Levinas, E. (1985). *Ethics and infinity* (R. A. Cohen, Trans.). Pittsburgh, PA: Duquesne University Press. (Original work published 1982)
MacIntyre, A. (1981). *After virtue: A study in moral theory*. Notre Dame, IN: Notre Dame University Press.
Makau, J. (1990). *Reasoning and communication: Thinking critically about arguments*. Belmont, CA: Wadsworth.
Makau, J., & Arnett, R. C. (Eds.). (1997). *Communication ethics in an age of diversity*. Urbana: University of Illinois Press.
Maranhão, T. (1990). *The interpretation of dialogue*. Chicago, IL: University of Chicago Press.
Murray, J. (2003). *Face to face in dialogue: Emmanuel Levinas and (the) communication (of) ethics*. New York: Rowman & Littlefield.
Noddings, N. (1984). *Caring: A feminine approach to ethics and moral education*. Berkeley: University of California Press.
Pinchevski, A. (2005). *By way of interruption: Levinas and the ethics of communication*. Pittsburgh, PA: Duquesne University Press.
Poulakos, J. (1974). The components of dialogue. *Western Journal of Speech Communication, 38*, 199–212.
Roberts, K. G., & Arnett, R. C. (2008). *Communication ethics: Between cosmopolitanism and provinciality*. New York: Lang.
Rorty, R. (1979). *Philosophy and the mirror of nature*. Princeton, NJ: Princeton University Press.
Schrag, C. O. (1986). *Communicative praxis and the space of subjectivity*. Bloomington: Indiana University Press.

Spivak, G. C. (1999). *A critique of postcolonial reason: Toward a history of the vanishing present.* Cambridge, MA: Harvard University Press.

Stewart, J. (1978). Foundations of dialogic communication. *Quarterly Journal of Speech, 64,* 183–201.

Ruben, B. D., & Stewart, L. (2005). Communication and human behavior. Boston, MA: Allyn & Bacon.

Taylor, C. (1989). *Sources of the self: The making of the modern identity.* Cambridge, MA: Harvard University Press.

Taylor, C. (2007). *A secular age.* Cambridge, MA: Belknap Press.

5

Feminist Discursive Ethics

Patrice M. Buzzanell

Andrew, Keller, and Schwartzman (2005) note the increased range of urgent national and international issues with which feminist philosophers and ethicists grapple. To sexual harassment, human rights violations, sexist media portrayals, chilly climates, inadequate social care policies, and everyday diminishment of women's agency and potential in varied communication contexts (Buzzanell, Meisenbach, Remke, Sterk, & Turner, 2009), Andrew et al. add immigration policies, a "just war theory in the context of terrorism" (p. 3), and oppression in the global south. In these ethical considerations, feminist communication scholars orient toward "gender justice, a goal that takes into account the ways that gender always already intersects with race, ethnicity, sexuality, and class" (Dow & Condit, 2005, p. 449).

Feminists' particular orientation toward gender justice is controversial. Indeed, feminist activists have decried "armchair" philosophers who (purportedly) simply report the shape and textures of contemporary feminisms. Feminist academicians explore the nuances of controversial issues and range of feminist advocacies. These advocacies are derived from theory development, the use of theory as resource, and a "deep interaction between sustained theoretical articulations and textual analyses that employ and embroider upon a theoretical framework" (Dow & Condit, 2005, p. 464). It is at these intersections of theory–practice dialectics that I sketch out a feminist discursive ethics.

To do so, Part I foregrounds the distinctive qualities of communication that are brought to bear on this topic as well as the metatheoretical and metaphorical underpinnings of a feminist discursive ethical approach. In a nutshell, communication's distinctive contributions include adherence to the importance of messages within larger societal and global discourses through sense making and narrativizing of experience and courses of action (Carbaugh & Buzzanell, 2010). Through feminist discursive ethics, communication scholars position *feminisms* as the *process of embracing and embodying struggle, resistance, and contradictory enactment on behalf of vulnerable groups, most especially but not exclusively women and children*. Feminist discursive ethics applies to everyday interactions through social networks and global infrastructures to take seriously the ways communication constitutes community values and caring responsibilities (Steiner, 2008).

In Part II, a feminist model with six interrelated processes for interrogating ethical dilemmas combines sensemaking, poststructural inclinations, narrative, feminist empirical work, and praxis—an admittedly eclectic array of epistemological, ontological, and axiological positionings. Using processes rather than stages, phases, or steps "enable[s] creative ways of reflecting on social policy" (DiQuinzio & Young, 1997, p. vii). Ethical processes are dialectical. For feminist dialectics, ethicists expose and work to transform the gendered hierarchies that are their bases. They work to unseat the different ways in which the masculine typically dominates the feminine (for diverse ways in which gender hierarchies come to be and are sustained in communication research, see Buzzanell, 1994). These dialectic processes are at the heart of feminist ethical dilemmas because they order social relations. As such, they can be mapped to illuminate how and why gendered relations of power continue to devalue the feminine in everyday talk (discourse) and cultural formations or macrodiscourses (Discourse). The dialectics discussed in this chapter include: justice-care, moral-ethical, abstract-context, human-individual rights, public-private, sustainable-ephemeral and culture sensitive-centered, and community-individual.

The final section, entitled Part III: Epilogue, offers a continuation of ethical questioning. This section poses challenges as well as some ways that feminist visions of ethical dialogue respond to human moral and ethical dilemmas.

PART I: UNDERPINNINGS OF FEMINIST ETHICAL DISCURSIVE PROCESS

Questions about what constitutes justice and care have become increasingly complex in today's technological, intercultural, and global world. Justice ethics provide rights, rules, and responsibilities; care ethics incorporate other resources, such as different ways of knowing and experiencing the world, into moral considerations (Hamington & Miller, 2006). Neither seems adequate to deal with the complexities at hand. For both justice and care, ethical responsiveness may be perceived as too removed from immediate concerns or abilities to affect change. Indeed, morality seems to be more rhetorically compelling than the linguistic choice of "ethics" among today's students (Cheney, Lair, Ritz, & Kendall, 2010). There seem to be insurmountable barriers to action and a lack of accountability erected by institutional hierarchies and community practices (Johannesen, Valde, & Whedbee, 2008; Redding, 1996). Furthermore, legal remedies and common policies (e.g., systems of professional ethics) fail to guide action because they do not include the relational and contextual considerations that make ethical decision making so difficult (Buzzanell, 2004; Mattson & Buzzanell, 1999). Finally, notable cases attesting to equal treatment, publicity about crackdowns on crimes against women (and children), and reports about equitable divisions of labor and parity between men and women lead people to assume that there no longer are needs for activism regarding gender justice.

Yet, issues pertaining to feminist justice and care ethics are very much a part of mundane activities and communication research. Researchers investigate who does (paid and unpaid) caregiving work and how power and social location are negotiated in these contexts (Buzzanell & D'Enbeau, 2009; Medved, 2007, 2009; Tronto, 1993, 2006; Wood, 1994). Media celebrate feminisms as forces that change cultural meanings and practices but then undermine progressive content and reaffirm the status quo (Dow, 2009; Maddux, 2008). Women still strive to frame assaults on their physical well-being as criminal acts (Okin, 1998). Underrepresented group members still seek discourses to construct diverse kinds of labor, relationships, race/ethnicities, and sexual–social orientations as normal and worthy of treatment with dignity (e.g., Cheney, Zorn, Planalp, & Lair, 2008; Dixon, Schell, Giles, & Grogos, 2008; Kroløkke & Sørensen, 2006). Cyberfeminists struggle in their use of new media interfaces to queer and race their identities, interactions, and cultural products (Gajjala, Rybas, & Altman, 2008). Health communication campaigns designed to enhance quality health care still are undermined by professional and gendered hierarchies including lack of culture centeredness (e.g., Dutta, 2008; Ellingson, 2005). Many stakeholders' concerns still are not integrated into internal corporate and institutional decision making and policy (DeBussy, 2008; Deetz, 2008; Haas & Deetz, 2000; Liu & Buzzanell, 2004). Resolving these challenges falls within feminist communication considerations (see Buzzanell et al., 2009) because processes are influenced not only by participants in particular cases, but also by fundamental polarities in society—namely, justice/care and public/private.

Justice/Care and Public/Private

With regard to *justice/care* tensions, *justice* corresponds with the abstract and dispassionate moral theory of the public realm (Tronto, 1993) and often is associated with rights that may overemphasize individual autonomy in ways that have significant political and economic implications (McLaren, 2007). As a set of discourses, justice is concerned with rationality and reasons for adopting norms, that is, with justifications (Ruiz, 2005). Conversely, *care* connotes caring *for* others in the altruistic or nurturing fashion associated with the private sphere (Jaggar, 1994a; Sullivan & Turner, 1999). Different logics underlie justice and care: "Whereas justification discourses rest on arguments that there are sufficient grounds to adopt a norm *under unaltered circumstances*, application discourses rest on arguments that a given norm is the most appropriate one to regulate a particular situation *all circumstances considered*" (Ruiz, 2005, p. 782).

  Public/private also is implicated, perhaps inherent, in thinking about feminist ethics because this dualism is reconstituted socially in numerous contexts and continues to operate as a means by which societal members construct knowledge, determine which arguments and experiences are worthy of public and private scrutiny, and indicate where advocacy and solutions for equity are located (e.g., in courts, corporations, not-for-profits, home, and community; e.g., Belenky, Clinchy, Goldberger, & Tarule, 1986; Buzzanell, 1994; Griffin, 1996; Mumby, 2000; Tronto, 1992, 1993). Public typically corresponds with reason, agency, male, work, justice, and public speaking; private usually means emotion, communion, female, home, caring, and relational speaking (e.g., Mumby & Putnam, 1992). Public and private realms define privilege and subordination, particularly what discourse is admissible into discussion and who is valued. Public/ private and its associated dualities exist in the core of human identities (Bem, 1993) and the heart of interpersonal relationships (see Campbell, 1973, 1999; Wood, 1998) as well as political processes in government and grassroots organizations (Jaggar, 1998; M. Papa, Singhal, & Papa, 2006; Sullivan & Goldzwig, 1995; Sullivan & Turner, 1999). They should mutually inform each other so that there is greater equity in all aspects of everyday lives. Yet, people have difficulty bridging public/private and justice/care divisions.

  Feminist discursive ethics reconsiders the artificial barriers between justice/care and public/ private. To develop this ethics, I first delve into epistemological and ontological assumptions and implications underlying common images of public/private and justice/care in different contexts of communication theory and research. I argue that the pervasiveness of these common metaphors (i.e., container and voice images) prevent the kind of creative and flexible thinking that is needed to transcend their limitations (see Putnam & Boys, 2006). To act with justice and care not only requires that individuals comprehend situational imperatives, but also that ethicists locate the rhetorical means of subverting identity restrictions and complicated role relations with others that are guided by sophisticated identification and control processes.

Common Images of Public/Private and Justice/Care in Communication Studies

Reasons for the bifurcation of public/private concerns are located in interrelated human tendencies. People often frame experiences hierarchically, create boundaries around phenomena, and devalue approaches associated with the private world and its inhabitants (e.g., Bem, 1993;

Chodorow, 1994; Tronto, 1993). This bifurcation is so deeply rooted that the first (container) metaphor for public/private and justice/care dominates communication studies of ethics and approaches to advocacy. A second image, voice, has emerged as one that can overturn the privileged status of public, male, and justice by encouraging expression of those often silenced by others or themselves. These two metaphors encompass much research on and thinking about public/private and justice/care but ultimately fail to create a space for change.

The most common image, the *conduit/container metaphor*, is fundamental to understandings and language about what constitutes appropriateness in society and organizations (see Putnam & Boys, 2006). Conduit or container images imply that certain information, behaviors, and roles are deemed most suitable for a particular realm. Because these images are established as dualities, the spheres-as-containers metaphor implies two aspects germane to feminist ethics discussions: barriers for entry of data from one sphere to the other; and hierarchical ordering that privileges one over the other.

These two aspects are evident in conventional ethical systems that correspond with the abstract, rational thinking of the public sphere. These traditional ethical systems include: utility issues, cost/benefit analyses of actions focusing on consequences; utilitarianism, the greatest good for the greatest number; deontology, intent to perform actions because such actions fall within one's duty; Rawlsian ethics, justice as fairness through treatment of others as equals; and Kant's categorical imperatives of universalization (application for every person in a similar situation), respect for individual human beings (respect as an end in itself not as a means), and rightness of behavior (as acceptable to all rational human beings) (Bok, 1979, 1982; Johannesen et al., 2008; Liu & Buzzanell, 2004; Seeger, 1997; Seeger, Sellnow, Ulmer, & Novak, 2009; Tong, 1993; Tronto, 1993). These systems usually rely on universal others to whom standard categories can be applied reliably (see Haas & Deetz, 2000; Ruiz, 2005). For instance, downsizing occurs for utilitarian reasons but the greatest good may not be achieved as individuals, families, and communities are devastated (Buzzanell, 2000). The incorporation of relational issues into ethical decision making also proves unsatisfactory because relationships are framed as personal concerns rather than as politicized sites (Noddings, 2006; Tronto, 1993, 2006; Tucker, 2006).

Although the definitional and role clarity available through container thinking may seem advantageous in moral decision making, the benefits of clarity are outweighed by the difficulty with which societal members can transcend spheres. Changes to the status quo are highly controversial because they may violate common sense and equality desires, even though appropriation of values and means of evaluating moral arguments occur routinely (e.g., appropriation of life interests or spiritual issues into work; see Nadesan, 1999). Researchers of close personal relationships describe the tensions that emerge when partners, friends, and roommates confront either/or dilemmas as they work through, for instance, self- and other expectations to be autonomous (valued in the public, male sphere) or interconnected (valued in the private, female sphere) (see Baxter, 2010; Baxter & Montgomery, 1996; Rawlins, 1992). The container metaphor draws boundaries around public and private, making it extremely difficult to break from dualistic thinking.

Even when discussions attempt to deconstruct the dualisms, they inadvertently replicate polar structures. Themes and values of feminisms (e.g., cooperation, community, emotional and personal knowledge, integrated thinking) may be described in idealistic terms and almost always in opposition to traditional terms (see this tendency in Buzzanell, 1994; Mumby & Putnam, 1992). This inclination to replicate separate spheres also is found in moral development and values (Gilligan, 1982; Kohlberg, 1981, 1985).

Communication scholars understand how people may categorize messages and related practices as public or private, admissible into debate or relegated to private conversation, and under demands of justice or care, but still find it difficult to discuss how public/private or justice/care reinforces dominant hegemony and where or how resistance to hegemonic practices can occur. For instance, Redding (1996; for further destructive messages and ideologies, see Lutgen-Sandvik & Sypher, 2009) developed a prototypology of unethical organizational messages such that discourse knowingly designed and exchanged to be destructive, deceptive, coercive, intrusive, secretive, or manipulative-exploitative can be classified as unethical. Yet, Mattson and Buzzanell (1999) critiqued Redding's typology from feminist perspectives to reveal two biases: how managerialist thinking inherent in the form and content of his system (when taken to extremes) could lead one to argue for use of unethical messages that preserve utilitarian goals; and how omission of emotions into unethical message taxonomies reaffirms separate spheres and leads to incomplete analyses of ethical dilemmas (an implicit claim in their study).

In sum, conduit/container thinking sustains the bifurcations between public/private and justice/care that offer definitional clarity and classification ease, but that cannot account for the complexities of lived moral decision making. One remedy might be encouragement of multiple public and private realms. However, this solution by itself does not unseat the duality, does not prepare researchers for the politicized nature of public and private, and does not alter the structures of one's society or find a passage among spheres. The danger of the multiple realms approach is that dominant members may simply appropriate that which is useful to their interests.

Whereas most discussions of morality operate with implicit notions of immutable categories and privileging of the public, the other prominent metaphor of public/private and justice/care presents a different image that focuses on the particularities of lived experience. The voice metaphor offers a contrast to container or compartmentalized thinking but still may not prevent dualistic thinking. Simply put, the container metaphor differentiates public from private and privileges abstract qualities of morality; the voice image introduces a personalized account of justice and care through the presentation of lived experiences. As Dow (1997) concludes, voice is "a political issue; that is, it is about power" that is, the result of political struggle (p. 245). The presentation and arrangement of lived experience into a political statement about structural inequities in society constitutes a standpoint.

In standpoint perspectives, women (and other members of traditionally underrepresented groups) account for their experiences within the complex intersections of race/ethnicity, gender, sexual-social orientation, and class. Emphases on feminist standpoints and intersectionalities give voice to "others" by externalizing marginalized members' struggles to recognize how social orders are constituted and sustained (Hallstein, 1999; Harding, 1991; Wood, 1992). In keeping with the metaphor of voice, issues of public/private and justice/care focus on who can speak, when, and why (Putnam & Boys, 2006; Putnam, Phillips, & Chapman, 1996). Voice constitutes an affirmation of boundary permeability between public and private realms when those who typically cannot speak or be heard (i.e., those who are not members of the "appropriate" realm for their concerns), gain access and resist silencing by others. For instance, Hegde (2009) shows how a woman from the global south is rendered voiceless—perceived as completely irrational and barbaric—when she refuses to comply with others' directives for talk about female infanticide. Instead, she continues to protest lack of assistance for her poverty. In addition to silencing, voice also entails distorted, dominating, and different voices, as well as access.

Distorted voices are suppressed. Individuals and collectivities speak but not in ways that represent their interests. In other words, they do not find the language and arguments that can transcend public/private boundaries. For instance, Pankhurst's strategy for the "Importance of the Vote" speech was that she "worked within the separate spheres orientation which her audience accepted" and, in doing so, "tried to transform not the orientation but the view that female suffrage was 'impious' within that orientation" (Jorgensen-Earp, 1990, p. 86). The fact that suffrage did not alter the fundamental motif of political and private lives leaves doubt about the long-term effectiveness of a tactic that reaffirms separation. In this sense, the voice becomes distorted.

In the voice of domination, discourse forms "patterns of activity and institutional arrangements [that] culminate in common sense, thus concealing the choices and interests of the dominant group" (Putnam et al., 1996, p. 389). Domination occurs through overt and unobtrusive controls. In his culture-centered approach to health campaigns, Dutta (2008; see also McLaren, 2007) draws attention to the erasures in dominant epistemologies and subaltern sectors that have been ignored in research. Waymer and Heath (2007) remind crisis communication practitioners and researchers about forgotten publics who are disenfranchised and voiceless in disasters.

Moreover, while the different voice approach highlights concerns rendered invisible by ordinary societal and organizational patterns, long-term dangers are that realm differences are givens and that male norms constitute the standard against which difference is articulated (Jaggar, 1994b). For instance, Nodding's (1984) ethic of care situates "caring for" others as an admirable quality and as one belonging in the private realms. Yet, ethical systems that take devalued feminine values as a springboard for social change may replicate traditional gender ideologies and sustain dependency in relationships (Hoagland, 1991; Johannesen, 2001; Johannesen et al., 2008; Noddings, 2006; Perrons, McDowell, Fagan, Ray, & Ward, 2006; Tong, 1993; Tronto, 1992). For example, family researchers have questioned the ethics of unpaid labor and disenfranchisement of some to give care for others (Buzzanell & D'Enbeau, 2009; Medved, 2007, 2009; Townsley, 2006).

Access to voice is the challenge of providing balanced, open forums for multiple stakeholders. Following Benhabib, Haas and Deetz (2000) propose that internal corporate decision making can be enhanced by including both the perspectives of concrete or specific others and viewpoints of generalized or universal others. They note that marginalized stakeholder voices need to be heard (without intermediaries) because dominant members may be unable to sponsor minority causes and the nuances of minority interests. Through their approach, public and private should find voice in the simultaneous integration of general and specific concerns. However, they admit that one disadvantage of their position is finding mechanisms for implementation. Another difficulty is that most stakeholder approaches still adhere to masculinist orientations and hierarchical arrangements in member configurations such that some stakeholders (e.g., stockholders) have interests that are more protected than others (Wicks, Gilbert, & Freeman, 1994). Finally, marginalized group members may have difficulty framing responses in language that crosses justice/care boundaries.

These four aspects of the voice image are useful for discussions of public/private and justice/care in diverse communication contexts. In general, gaining voice appears to be a necessary but not sufficient condition for transforming power dynamics. The accounting of others' achievements gives face and form to injustice in a way no other method can. Yet the strength of voice also is its weakness. Specifically, access to a realm may not transform everyday life or policies. Individuals simply may consider the speaker who raises consciousness an anomaly. When this happens, the change advocate may receive critical acclaim for eloquence and argument construction but may not affect any sustained societal change (see Kendall & Fisher, 1974). Similarly, aligning with members of the other realm, but positioning oneself in the background to gain acceptability of ideas, may backfire if the sponsor can no longer support the cause. These change agents became members *of* but not *in* the public realms. As a case in point, the depth of change needed to fulfill the promise of women's liberation is so fundamental to society that admission of women's full and equal public participation would alter *every* aspect of society (Campbell, 1973, 1999; Japp, 1985). Third wave feminist communication scholars note consciousness changing *not* raising is required and must involve transnational, intercultural, and social networking opportunities (e.g., Kroløkke & Sørensen, 2006).

In sum, the metaphor of voice can infuse the public realm with expressions of those often silenced and rendered invisible in our society. Without structural interventions and empirical studies, this heightened awareness may not go beyond the personal level and women and people of diverse cultures become objects of study. Moreover, the voice metaphor defies the value neutrality of the container metaphor by encouraging engagement with difference and resistance through overt challenges, silence, and hidden transcripts (see Fleming & Spicer, 2007, 2008; Mumby, 2005; Murphy, 1998). One problem with voice is that individuals may talk about situations but feel (or physically be) powerless to act (e.g., Hallstein, 1999). While voice suspends the normalcy of separate spheres, the image itself may be insufficient for generating pragmatic solutions that maintain collective action for structural change (see Hekman, 1999). To create communicative processes necessary for sustained and iterative change, we turn to feminist ethical processes driven by metaphors of discourse.

PART II: FEMINIST DISCURSIVE ETHICS

My analysis is feminist in that it promotes feminist values, advocates destabilization of commonly accepted categories, and views the boundaries drawn around public/private and justice/care as contested sites whose meaning is not fixed but is stabilized momentarily in the discourse and related practices of people embedded in socio-historical-economic contexts. Although more elaborate feminist frameworks exist (e.g., Buzzanell, 1994; Calás & Smircich, 1996, 2006; Tong, 1989), I use Jaggar's (1994a) definition of feminisms as movements "dedicated to ending the subordination of women" and enlarge it to include other marginalized members so that I can center on core values and avoid polarization in debates about specific issues and means of goal accomplishment (p. 2).

Specifically, debates splinter justice and care, public and private, and diverse feminisms in ways that certainly bring depth and complexity to this discussion, but also operate against the generation of a feminist discursive ethics that can incorporate differences. My discussion is embedded within different poststructural feminist, postmodern, and critical theories that can be extended to end patriarchy. In addition to those ethicists already noted, Fraser (1995) suggests that a pragmatic view in which "discursive phenomena may be fruitfully approached from several different angles, depending on one's situation and aims" (p. 167) might remedy the lacunae in varied approaches. She elaborates on Benhabib's quasi-Habermassian (i.e., intersubjective aspects of discourse and normative critique), Butler's quasi-Foucauldian (i.e., individual situated performances of creativity and constraint), and Cornell's quasi-Lacanian-Derridean (i.e., denaturalizing with ethical-utopian critique) approaches. She recommends that conceptions of discourse and subjectivity be "treated as tools, not as the property of warring metaphysical sects" (p. 167) so that the goal of feminism to oppose male domination can be achieved. Ashcraft and Mumby (2004) aim to "articulate a distinctly communicative feminist approach" (p. x) in which extensions on postmodern deconstructive turns and critical theory's emphases on emancipatory visions can be mutually informative, challenging, and productive (see pp. xix–xxii).

Building on these approaches, discourse provides the most fluid image of communication and ethics because it emphasizes process, envisions structures that continuously redesign themselves, and imagines change on multiple levels through collaborative action within particular contexts. Discourse "foregrounds language as the nexus for untangling relationships among meaning, context, and praxis" (Putnam et al., 1996, p. 391). Language shapes discursive practices that, in turn, shape the form, content, and ways of knowing, feeling, and valuing what happens. Within discursive acts, language enables "'fluid' negotiation of meanings through interplays among texts (actions performed at any given moment) and context (the circumstances in which those actions take place)" (p. 391; see also Ruiz, 2005; Weedon, 1987, 1997).

Discursive acts perspectives examine emotional expression, certain communication genres or templates for social interaction, paradoxes and irony, and dialogue with the central theme being the ways in which contextual understandings are (re)produced (Putnam & Boys, 2006). In this image, public/private and justice/care become contested sites open to variable meanings over time, location, and participants. What is appropriate for the different spheres is of less importance than how, when, and why (i.e., under what circumstances) public/private and justice/care are (re) constituted.

In the image of discourse acts, individuals and groups are seen as active, albeit constrained, agents in usurping the boundaries of opposing spheres. Extending Steiner's (1997, 2008; see also steps for moral discernment in Makau, 2009) original five phases, agents consider six dialectic processes. These processes act as dialogic points for analysis, for deriving a flexible ethical system, and for formulating moral responses to ethical dilemmas. The heart of a feminist discursive ethics is the constant questioning of human behavior in particular contexts. The six interrelated processes are: (1) social constructing context; (2) promoting dialogue through human values; (3) designing vision; (4) reframing; (5) embedding iterativity; and (6) making processes and outcomes transparent. The first four describe the doing of feminist ethics; the final two act as root processes underlying feminist ethics. Together, they offer a feminist discursive ethics with some rhetorical techniques and material implications.

Social Constructing Context

The social construction of context means both that the interwoven issues of public/private and justice/care are studied historically, and that the personal histories and loyalties of investigators, change agents, and societal/organizational members are part of the process. In exploring *historical context*, ethicists react to and ponder the meanings and (re)construction of knowledge and material conditions. Investigation of historical context underlying a practice or injunction is both a defining characteristic of feminist discursive ethics as well as a rhetorical technique for enlarging boundaries of public/private and justice/care. Historical context means delving into particular circumstances to uncover whether or how a situation could be considered unethical and what could be effective strategies to encourage change. For instance, when Antoinette Brown Blackwell was barred from ministerial work, she developed a reinterpretation of Paul's message against female speech in church by exploring Paul's life, his entire set of epistles, and the socio-political environment of Paul's time (Munson & Dickinson, 1998). Rather than disagreeing unilaterally with contemporary interpretations of Paul's message, Brown Blackwell agreed with Paul's admonition as "embedded in Paul's larger discussion about the proper use of spiritual gifts" (p. 113). Through contextualization, she could argue for education of women in the ministry and, later, for her radical vision of what constituted just divisions of labor.

Historical context also necessitates the interrogation of politically embedded systems of logics. As a case in point, Gheaus (2008) challenges ideologies of social welfare states (i.e., a political system in which care is redistributed via public institutions). Arguments supporting welfare states align with the distributive justice stance insofar as care is regulated and rewarded through economic incentives that protect people from market risks associated with global economies (i.e., neoliberalism). However, dependencies wrought by gendered domestic and public matters such as male heads of households, women as natural caregivers and child-raisers, and divisions of labors within the family often continues inequities that some services, such as extended family leaves and child care systems, intend to rectify (see Mandel & Semyonov, 2005).

Besides grounding in material and ideological conditions of the times and places in which ethical dilemmas occur, a second aspect of contextualization is the infusion of *personal histories and loyalties*. In their discussion of feminist organizational communication ethics, Mattson and Buzzanell (1999) explain why they did not use Steiner's (1997) entire template for phases in feminist ethical analyses in their fifth endnote. They say that the category of loyalties, or the use of biases and responsibilities in ethical analyses, was tangential to their analyses.

While their analyses do exhibit the ongoing questionings to which Steiner refers, their dismissal of further discussion of loyalties seems antithetical to the spirit of feminist ethical analyses and to a discursive treatment of ethics. Based on Steiner's framework, loyalties can be defined as the admission of personal biases, allegiances, and responsibilities into analysis of specific situations. Loyalty means the protection of those most vulnerable in a given situation with ongoing tensions surrounding issues of agency, duty, and responsibility. But it also means rendering oneself vulnerable to the kinds of self-questionings that must occur if ethical analysts are to uncover how self-interest and close personal relationships with individuals involved in cases could stand in the way of living a moral life. For instance, Rowe (2000) interrogates the extent to which the paradox of privilege and subordination blinds White feminists to possibilities of alignment with women of color. Rowe's findings may be painful for White feminists who apply well-meaning but insufficient forms of research on, and resistance to, the power of Whiteness. Similarly, Buzzanell (2004) and Buzzanell and D'Enbeau (2009) challenge understandings of and responsiveness to cases involving academic sexual harassment and treatment of pregnant graduate students using feminist sensemaking and poststructural approaches. Finally, Ellis (2007) presents a relational ethical approach whose implementation for conduct goes beyond research texts. She contrasts formal or procedural approaches with situational tensions, boundaries, and engagements (i.e., "the unpredictable often subtle, yet ethically important moments that come up in the field," p. 4). Despite ethical responses determined by procedural factors, Ellis recalls the persistent tugs into self-questioning and analyses that her forays into research participants' lives and friendships prompted. She advocates self-scrutiny as a radical reciprocity. Her self-scrutiny can be circumvented through enlisting participants as coresearchers; that is, by giving participants a voice in the research design, writing, and interpretations (see also Steiner, 2008, ¶10).

The notion of loyalties rounds out the historical-economic-social background of a situation by infusing guidance of *both* emotional/rational, private/public, care/justice, sustainable/ephemeral, and culture sensitive-centered into ethical decision making. Loyalty mandates the public scrutiny of feelings and of possibilities of misplaced allegiances and bias (e.g., classism, racism, colonialist thinking). Reworking loyalty tensions may enable feminist communication ethicists to better manage complications to context. In particular, Drichel (2008) says that the a-temporality or fixated representations that often accompany postcolonial discussion is

> at least one reason we cannot move "post-*the other*"—this other is not only the other as constructed by (post)colonialism but also postcolonialism's *other* other—the ethical other who cannot be reduced to the (re)presence of representation, and who reminds us of our responsibilities and obligations. (p. 589)

Context is further complicated in postcolonial contexts when feminist ethicists and rights advocates focus on justice with Western lenses:

> theorists who apply rights cross-culturally without attention to context, run the risk of Western cultural imperialism.... Simply applying rights without addressing these [contextual] concerns can actually serve to undermine feminist and other causes that rely on a different paradigm for political action and social change. (McLaren, 2007, p. 162)

Specifically, McLaren (see also Gheaus, 2008) argues that while rights discourses can protect women in public areas, it does little to usurp familial and other private abuses and fails to account for economic issues in its focus on political and legal reform and far-reaching consequences in global issues.

Through adherence to loyalties and contexts, feminist ethicists can grapple with the degrees to which agency is constrained, conditioned, empowered, and contested in situ (see Boudreau, 2009; Butler, 1995a, 1995b; Hallstein, 1999). Through assessment of material conditions, contextualization offers techniques of boundary enlargement (enlarging the "appropriate" scope of public and private); through inquiry into loyalties, contextualization provides avenues to engage in boundary enrichment (adding depth and linkages among constructs, values, and emotions that can transcend specific spheres).

Promoting Dialogue Through Human Values

Guidance by human values means exploration of criteria by which action and inaction can be evaluated. To gain access to decision makers and have ethical appeals heard, the human values process means that ethical decisions are guided by engagement through dialogue and by appeals to values. In dialogue, participants "suspend defensive exchange, share and learn from experiences, foster deeper inquiry, and resist synthesis or compromise" (Putnam et al., 1996, p. 394). When ethical appeals adhere to core values, public/private and justice/care can be transcended by gearing discourse toward (a) human rights and by maintaining (b) openness to alternatives.

In feminist discursive ethics, *human rights* does *not* operate as a monolithic category that is insensitive to local customs. Instead, discussions of human rights aim to continue conversations by proposing controversial stances and resolutions that continue discussion. Okin (1998, 1999) takes to task the standard practices of regarding human rights abuses as within the purview of specific cultural or religious practices. Her highly controversial stance attempts two goals: to center human, rather than women's, rights as positions that combine justice/care and public/private; and to make visible the ways in which interpersonal violence as well as institutionalized forms of slavery and abuse (e.g., rape defined as a war crime) are unethical across cultures. She admits that what she regards as violations of human rights often "would be regarded as quite within the limits of normal, culturally appropriate behavior in parents or husbands" and institutional rights in many parts of the world (p. 35). Okin (1998) promotes human rights for women and children and calls for government accountability, reorientation of the law, and discourse that reaffirms women's rights when cultural or religious justifications for subordination continue (p. 37).

However, what is of critical importance in feminist discursive ethics is that these decisions of what is broadly defined as human rights' violations must be recognized as continuously (re) constructed rather than established as truth. The diverse opinions in essays edited by Cohen, Howard, and Nussbaum (1999) on Okin's ideas display human rights as a contested site. Through the constant critiquing of one's own and others' positions about human rights (see Cohen et al., 1999; Jaggar, 1998; Wood, 1998), increasingly sophisticated responses to ethical dilemmas may be able to overcome boundaries such as morality/politics (see Tronto, 1993). The appeal to infuse ethical consideration with each person's contribution through dialogue might seem an impossible task, particularly in large heterogeneous societies and organizations. However, a feminist discursive ethical process offers the template for inclusion of different voices through the creation and evaluations of alternatives.

Besides the continual assessments of human rights, *the creating and evaluating of alternatives* also is essential to a feminist discursive ethical process. My emphasis here is *not* on the development of multiple possible courses of action that then are scrutinized against feasibility, plan-meets-needs, and other stock criteria, but on the ways thinking about options can prevent premature closure that excludes specific others.

The creation and assessment of options, or potential routes for addressing problems, include the development and evaluation of several alternative courses of action (see Steiner, 1997). When thinking through and judging options, the ethical analyst recognizes that short- and long-term consequences are not pleasing to all stakeholders. Indeed, the goal is not to have a middle ground between extreme responses, but to develop adequate moral theory through the process of understanding and evaluating responses to specific ethical dilemmas. In this way, "a central part of the process...[is how] people commit themselves to some principles rather than others" (Jaggar, 1994a, p. 9). Commitment to principles put choice, ethics, empowerment, and contested and constrained agency into uneasy conversation with each other. How does one make sense of and assist in end of life planning and quality for children who have exhausted bone marrow replacement and other treatments (Monteverde, 2009)? What happens when two older lesbian mothers, one of whom lives with profound disability, refuses to engage procedures potentially aligned with replaceability ethics (i.e., parents' termination of "disabled fetus" with a more able zygote upon results of amniocentesis, see Atkins, 2008)? How might one explore the ramifications of sexuality, bioethics, disability, aging, and "responsible" decision making (in light of health care and financial crises) or reaffirmation of cultural Discourse that diminish value in the lives and contributions of people with disabilities (Atkins, 2008)? Movement between justice and care can provide a kind of fluid ethical approach in which discursive processes are pivotal for addressing human values and alternatives.

Designing Vision

Vision generally means a future-oriented set of desired possibilities that can motivate oneself and others toward actualizing the imagined goal. Feminist ethical systems develop a combined ethic of care and justice based on a vision of what life could look like if feminist values were accorded the same privileges as male values in public and private decision making (Daly, 1994; Haney, 1994). Feminist visions are grounded in core feminist values but differ greatly in specific portrayals (e.g., Wright's utopian communities, Kendall & Fisher, 1974; as distinguished from Atwood's, 1986 and 2003, disturbing accounts of institutional attempts to silence women and bioengineer all life). These versions produce contrastive projections of what could be if feminist values are—and are not—implemented in society.

While the first element of a vision in a feminist discursive ethics, creation of an *ideal vision*, offers an image of a world for which communication scholars can strive and contribute, it is the second aspect of vision, *embodiment of the vision*, on which a feminist discursive ethics concentrates. The embodiment of the vision is the daily struggle of redefining and reframing talk, societal Discourses, and related practices in such a way that the gap between what happens and what is desired can be lessened. Embodiment emphasizes active engagement as well as social (re) construction of what is an ethical vision at a particular point in time and space. Although similar to Haney's (1994, p. 5) vision criterion, "present community" or "doing ethics," a feminist discursive ethics focuses on discourse elements of paradox, irony, contradictions, and tensions (see Ruiz, 2005) and their inscription on human bodies.

Indeed, communication scholars describe ways of handling tensions that emerge when visions confront practice. Among these approaches are organizational processes constituted by contradiction, tensions, and irony (Ashcraft, 2000; Barker, 1999; Cheney et al., 1998; M. Papa et al., 2006; Putnam & Boys, 2006). Although an embodied vision means living or "doing" ethics within episodes of contradiction, emphasizing these tensions could disillusion people confronted with moral dilemmas. Therefore, the embodiment of the vision requires a safe "place" in which individuals and groups can explore opportunities for capitalizing on the benefits of these tensions. This safe "place" emerges through carefully crafted strategies. For instance, Mary Ashton Rice Livermore created a vision of what society as well as personal relationships could look like if her relational ethics were implemented (Gayle & Griffin, 1998). Her society founded on women's rights, care, and public voice was displayed in her rhetorical inventiveness. Her strategy of mainstreaming or embedding arguments for change within commonly accepted positions implied that the desired effects of action would not be as radical as they actually were. Livermore accomplished what Hekman (1999; see also Jamieson, 1995) describes as telling a new story (i.e., creating a new vision by working within existing language, imagery, and myths to reassemble the old and tell a different narrative) and third wave feminists label as a new manifesta that cuts across communication contexts (Baumgardner & Richards, 2000; see also Hernández & Richman, 2002; Labaton & Martin, 2004). Drawing notions of ideal and embodied vision together means that the resulting desire for greater synthesis of public and private (including its numerous values, such as reason/emotion, justice/care, male/female) would have to incorporate contradictions and tentativeness. This vision uses reframing.

Reframing

Framing prompts individuals to accept one version of reality over another (Entman, 2007). Use of framing admits that there are multiple possible realities of which some are promoted as preferred ways of addressing ethical and other dilemmas. The ways of analyzing and (re)constructing power relations is through language.

Because a goal of a feminist discursive ethics is to understand how identities can (re)form around more equitable social relations, poststructuralist feminism can provide the analytic lens for consciousness raising and for solution generation (Flax, 1987, 1990; Scott, 1988; Weedon, 1987). Through a discursive analysis, researchers better understand how women and men can act as active (albeit constrained) agents in challenging meanings and options, and how they can develop transformational change incrementally and radically while accounting for resistance/ complicity and empowerment/disempowerment in specific contexts. Emphasis on discourse and discursive practices provides individual and systemic interventions to revision the double bind that traps people in either/or thinking.

With regard to public/private spheres and gendered moral orientations toward justice/care, it is the *inventional skill* that marginalized members and supporters use when advocating causes that provide models of reframing (Campbell, 1995). Janet Reno spoke with emotion *and* reason as well as tentativeness *and* authority when describing her decision making during the Waco tragedy (Sullivan & Turner, 1996). The beauty of Grimké's letter to Garrison in 1835 was its ability "to change problems into solutions and despair into resolve.... Grimké's identity [as a White Southern woman whose family owned slaves] within the text is itself a source and result of this process (Browne, 1996, p. 60; see also Daughton, 1995). Development of reframing such as Grimké's repositioning of violence as proof of abolitionists' success (because opponents were so threatened that they found no other recourse except violence) is time consuming and difficult (Browne, 1996; see also Carlson, 1994; Fairhurst & Sarr, 1996; Mason, 1997). In short, the inventive skill required by reframing must not only manage what is acceptable to audience members, but also must be self-reflexive (see iterative nature section). Inventive skills require appropriation of linguistic elements, such as irony, as well as rhetorical or performative strategies.

In exploring the tensions and ironies of change with the status quo, there is such a fine line between what is acceptable and what is not, that speakers or writers may display two separate selves, almost in a schizophrenic manner as they work through the usual audience expectations and their own public and private "violations" (e.g., Campbell, 1995). Other speakers and writers may express conflicted feelings, as in the case of Emily Newell Blair who acted as vice-chair of the Democratic National Committee (DNC) between 1922 and 1928 and whose "continuing efforts to secure equality for women in politics—help us appreciate the tangled paths she and others negotiated as new options and constraints unfolded" (Anderson, 1997, p. 50). Newell Blair's essays, unpublished autobiography, and letters provide a glimpse into her "agonizing self-reflection" and role conflicts (Anderson, 1997, p. 52).

Still other speakers, writers, and change advocates may at times incur hostile exchanges when they overstep expected boundaries and need to construct a modified rhetorical strategy for change. Exceeding acceptable boundaries may happen when the speaker or writer is seen as advocating changes that are too different from conventional gendered behaviors, values, and emotions (e.g., feminist texts of Lillian Gilbreath; see Graham, 1999). Moreover, blatant violations of sacred values (among other reasons) can end change possibilities, as was the case of Frances Wright who drew large audiences and praise even from her critics when speaking about women's rights, education, and other issues but who was avoided when she practiced consensual sexual relationships without marriage (Kendall & Fisher, 1974). In the 20th century, Zoe Baird was seen as flaunting values when she tried to position herself both as upholding U.S. legal codes and as rationalizing her own breach of law (displaying elitism and privilege; see Sullivan & Turner, 1999).

Through (re)framing discourse, feminist communication ethicists can fragment identities and locate power within systems that normalize discursive practices (see Putnam et al., 1996). Because meanings are never fully formed, societal and organizational members are able to see that realities are (re)constructed—thus opening up further ethical possibilities.

Embedding Iterativity

The fifth process of feminist discursive ethics, embedding iterativity, is a root process that underlies the other four processes already discussed. In her discussion of the ethics of hybridity, Drichel (2008) describes an iterative inversion of colonial–postcolonial logics and hierarchies. In talking about identity, Drichel says that iteration

> captures the strange double logic whereby identity is both self-identical and forever different from itself; identity emerges from (identical) repetition, but in that repetition identity is no longer self-identical…thus [iteration] offers the possibility to reintroduce, quite literally, the sense of alterity that had been disavowed in the stereotype as a fixed form of otherness. (p. 601)

Similarly, moments for revision embedded in feminist discursive ethics and founded on temporal disjunctures may help maintain the other without falling prey to stereotypes (though an affirmation of otherness with the second step of displacement, brought about through temporality).

As stated earlier, a feminist discursive ethics requires self-reflexivity or constant questioning throughout ethical decision making and moral theorizing. Jaggar (1994a; see also M. Friedman, 1985, p. 40) suggests that feminists develop "flexible policies designed to change as women and men succeed in changing themselves" although she admits that flexibility could be constructed as inconsistency (p. 14). However, "new social circumstances require creativity in institutionalizing justice and equality.… feminists must live with the contradictions resulting from divergent and sometimes incompatible strategies for gaining equality (p. 14).

Liu and Buzzanell (2004) address inconsistencies when different stakeholders' expectations are taken into consideration during U.S. maternity leaves. They note that leaves often are perceived as disruptions to routine organizing, dilemmas in un/equal application of standards, and instances where expectations for treatment not only shift over time and circumstance but also reveal justice/care tensions in stakeholders' discourse. Without understanding that there are profound differences in stakeholders' stances and agency during role negotiations, bosses, coworkers, and the women themselves may envision themselves as operating within contradictory moral and ethical expectations, rights and responsibilities, policies and practices, and constrained and contested agency. Rather than treating justice/care as dualisms, an iterative approach offers possibilities for integrating feminist ethics in organizing processes as multiple series of dialectic and sub-dialectic tensions with possibilities for productive responses (e.g., Gibbs, 2009). A similar iterative approach can be offered in health care settings when personalized approaches to medical procedures, such as gynecological exams, can guide care providers' and patients' participation in treatment decisions (Brann & Mattson, 2004).

Making Processes and Outcomes Transparent

The final process is a hope, a value, and a root process. Transparency occurs when stakeholders are treated as mature, involved parties who deserve to be appraised of ongoing concerns. Transparency demystifies technical details of accounting and making processes public. Transparency can be considered a moral obligation to stakeholders insofar as transparency idealistically seeks to describe current practices and ways of improving organizational, journalistic reporting, political, and media operations (e.g., Akhtar, Malla, & Gregson, 2000; Dascal, 2003; Livesey & Kearins, 2002). Whereas some contexts, such as blogs, assume transparency (Duke, 2008), other contexts, such as scientific communication, may demand degrees of opacity (Dascal, 2003). Transparency is intended to establish trust, promote learning, develop systems to produce knowledge, work through difficulties of making knowledge public, manage tensions of openness and operating in a competitive environment, and work toward good governance and information and computer technology use (see Akhtar et al., 2000; Livesey & Kearins, 2002). Issues of how to accomplish transparency are difficult, especially in ethical considerations where premature disclosure of accusations or proprietary technologies and practices could produce great harm to individuals and collectivities.

PART III: EPILOGUE

When people consider different positions regarding, and solutions for, moral and ethical dilemmas, they often invoke justice/care and public/private dynamics. Metaphorically, these bifurcations defeat possibilities of transformational change because they are so deeply embedded within every life aspect and communication context that it is difficult to conceive of different ways of thinking, being, and acting. Feminist discursive ethics transcends dualisms by proposing fluid processes and structures able to accommodate inconsistencies and tensions on micro- and macrolevels.

Discursive ethical processes validate the fragmentation of a postmodern world with desires for common ground in assessing ethical dilemmas and building moral theory (Buzzanell, 2004; Hallstein, 1999; Jaggar, 1994a, 1998; Ruiz, 2005). A feminist discursive ethical system recognizes constrained and contested human agency (Boudeau, 2009; Hallstein, 1999) while simultaneously enhancing possibilities for empowerment (defined as communicative processes occurring when decisions or actions are negotiated collaboratively; M. Papa et al., 2006) and transparency. Through discourse imagery, feminist researchers can explore: *how* moral boundaries change over time, space, and particular groups of people; and *how* interventions can be designed to transcend boundaries and integrate interests of specific individuals and collectivities. Justice and care are seen as contested sites rather than immutable entities.

Through six interrelated processes in a feminist discursive ethics, public/private and justice/care can be reconsidered: (1) social constructing context; (2) promoting dialogue through human values; (3) designing vision; (4) reframing; (5) embedding iterativity; and (6) making processes and outcomes transparent. The first four describe the doing of feminist ethics; the final two act as root processes underlying feminist ethics. Taken together, these processes enable participants and other stakeholders need to position gender as fundamental to ethical considerations within and across communication contexts to affect everyday interactions and global policy changes (Buzzanell et al., 2009). Even so, feminist discursive ethical processes are difficult to achieve. Controversies and challenges continue. These challenges include: feminist responses and proactive stances toward transcultural and international ethical and human rights issues; recognition of the role of diversity and marginalization in ethical processes and outcomes; gendered violence, privacy, safety, and identity dilemmas posed by cyberspace, gaming, and social networking (see Johannesen, 2001). Communication scholars offer unique ways of surfacing, interrogating, and resolving ethical dilemmas for today's world. In this chapter, I promote communication work as essential to feminist undertakings in ethics.

REFERENCES

Akhtar, S., Malla, M., & Gregson, J. (2000). Transparency, accountability and good governance: Role of new information and communication technologies and the mass media. *International Journal on Media Management, 2* (3/4), 124–132.

Anderson, K. (1997). Practicing feminist politics: Emily Newell Blair and U.S. women's political choices in the early twentieth century. *Journal of Women's History, 9*(3), 50–72.

Andrew, B. S., Keller, J., & Schwartzman, L. (2005). Feminist interventions in ethics and politics: An introduction. In B. S. Andrew, J. Keller, & L. Schwartzman (Eds.), *Feminist interventions in ethics and social theory* (pp. 1–13). Lanham, MD: Rowman & Littlefield.

Ashcraft, K. L. (2000). Empowering "professional" relationships: Organizational communication meets feminist practice. *Management Communication Quarterly, 13,* 347–392.

Ashcraft, K. L., & Mumby, D. K. (2004). *Reworking gender: A feminist communicology of organization.* Thousand Oaks, CA: Sage.

Atkins, C. (2008). The choice of two mothers: Disability, gender, sexuality, and prenatal testing. *Cultural Studies ↔ Critical Methodologies, 8,* 106–129.

Atwood, M. (1986). *The handmaid's tale.* Boston: Houghton Mifflin.

Atwood, M. (2003). *Oryx & Crake.* New York: Random House.

Barker, J. R. (1999). *The discipline of teamwork: Participation and concertive control.* Thousand Oaks, CA: Sage.

Baumgardner, J., & Richards, A. (2000). *Manifesta: Young women, feminism, and the future.* New York: Farrar, Straus & Giroux.

Baxter, L. A. (2010). A dialogic approach to interpersonal/family communication. In D. Carbaugh & P. M. Buzzanell (Eds.), *Distinctive qualities in communication research* (pp. 13–31). New York: Routledge.

Baxter, L. A., & Montgomery, B. M. (1996). *Relating: Dialogues and dialectics.* New York: Guilford.

Belenky, M. F., Clinchy, B. M., Goldberger, N. R., & Tarule, J. M. (1986). *Women's ways of knowing: The development of self, voice, and mind.* New York: Basic Books.

Bem, S. L. (1993). *The lenses of gender: Transforming the debate on sexual inequality.* New Haven, CT: Yale University Press.

Bok, S. (1979). *Lying: Moral choice in public and private life.* New York: Vintage Books.

Bok, S. (1982). *Secrets: On the ethics of concealment and revelation.* New York: Pantheon.

Boudreau, T. E. (2009). Human agonistes: Interdisciplinary inquiry into ontological agency and human conflict. In D. Sandole, S. Byrne, I. Sandole-Staroste, & J. Senehi (Eds.), *Handbook of conflict analysis and resolution* (pp. 131–143). New York: Routledge.

Brann, M., & Mattson, M. (2004). Reframing communication during gynecological exams: A feminist virtue ethics of care perspective. In P. M. Buzzanell, H. Sterk, & L. Turner (Eds.), *Gendered approaches to applied communication* (pp. 147–168). Thousand Oaks, CA: Sage.

Browne, S. H. (1996). Encountering Angelina Grimké: Violence, identity, and the creation of radical community. *Quarterly Journal of Speech, 82,* 55–73.

Butler, J. (1995a). Contingent foundations: Feminism and the question of "postmodern." In S. Benhabib, J. Butler, D. Cornell, & N. Fraser (Eds.), *Feminist contentions: A philosophical exchange* (pp. 35–57). New York: Routledge.

Butler, J. (1995b). For a careful reading. In S. Benhabib, J. Butler, D. Cornell, & N. Fraser (Eds.), *Feminist contentions: A philosophical exchange* (pp. 127–143). New York: Routledge.

Buzzanell, P. M. (1994). Gaining a voice: Feminist perspectives in organizational communication. *Management Communication Quarterly, 7,* 339–383.

Buzzanell, P. M. (2000). The promise and practice of the new career and social contract: Illusions exposed and suggestions for reform. In P. M. Buzzanell (Ed.), *Rethinking organizational and managerial communication from feminist perspectives* (pp. 209–235). Thousand Oaks, CA: Sage.

Buzzanell, P. M. (2004). Revisiting sexual harassment in academe: Using feminist ethical and sensemaking approaches to analyze macrodiscourses and micropractices of sexual harassment. In P. M. Buzzanell, H. Sterk, & L. Turner (Eds.), *Gender in applied communication contexts* (pp. 25–46). Thousand Oaks, CA: Sage.

Buzzanell, P. M., & D'Enbeau, S. (2009). Stories of caregiving: Intersections of academic research and women's everyday experiences. *Qualitative Inquiry, 15,* 1199–1224.

Buzzanell, P. M., Meisenbach, R., Remke, R., Sterk, H., & Turner, L. (2009). Positioning gender as fundamental in applied communication research. In L. Frey & K. Cissna (Eds.), *Routledge handbook of applied communication research* (pp. 181–202). New York: Routledge.

Calás, M. B., & Smircich, L. (1996). From "the woman's" point of view: Feminist approaches to organization studies. In S. R. Clegg, C. Hardy, & W. R. Nord (Eds.), *Handbook of organization studies* (pp. 218–257). London: Sage.

Calás, M. B., & Smircich, L. (2006). From the "woman's point of view" ten years later: Towards a feminist organization studies. In S. R. Clegg (Ed.), *Handbook of organization studies* (pp. 284–346). Thousand Oaks, CA: Sage.

Campbell, K. K. (1973). The rhetoric of women's liberation: An oxymoron. *Quarterly Journal of Speech, 59,* 74–86.

Campbell, K. K. (1995). Gender and genre: Loci of invention and contradiction in the earliest speeches by U.S. women. *Quarterly Journal of Speech, 81,* 479–495.

Campbell, K. K. (1999). "The rhetoric of women's liberation: A oxymoron" revisited. *Communication Studies, 50,* 138–142.

Carbaugh, D., & Buzzanell, P. M. (Eds.). (2010). *Distinctive qualities in communication research.* New York: Routledge.

Carlson, A. C. (1994). Defining womanhood: Lucretia Coffin Mott and the transformation of femininity. *Western Journal of Communication, 58,* 85–97.

Cheney, G. Lair, D., Ritz, D., & Kendall, B. (2010). *Just a job? Communication, ethics and professional life.* New York: Oxford University Press.

Cheney, G., Straub, J., Speirs-Glebe, L., Stohl, C., DeGooyer, Jr., D., Whalen, S., Garvin-Doxas, K., & Carlone, D. (1998). Democracy, participation, and communication at work: A multidisciplinary review. *Communication Yearbook, 21,* 35–91.

Cheney, G., Zorn, T., Planalp, S., & Lair, D. (2008). Meaningful work and personal/social well-being: Organizational communication engages the meanings of work. *Communication Yearbook, 32,* 136–185.

Chodorow, N. J. (1994). *Femininities, masculinities, sexualities: Freud and beyond*. Lexington: University Press of Kentucky.

Cohen, J., Howard, M., & Nussbaum, M. (Eds.). (1999). *Is multiculturalism bad for women? Susan Moller Okin with respondents*. Princeton, NJ: Princeton University Press.

Daly, L. K. (Ed.). (1994). *Feminist theological ethics: A reader*. Louisville, KY: Westminster John Knox Press.

Dascal, M. (2003). Transparency in scientific communication: From Leibniz's dream to today's reality. *Studies in Communication Sciences, 3*, 155–180.

Daughton, S. M. (1995). The fine texture of enactment: Iconicity as empowerment in Angelina Grimké's Pennsylvania Hall Address. *Women's Studies in Communication, 18,* 19–43.

DeBussy, N. (2008). Stakeholder theory. In W. Donsbach (Ed.), *The international encyclopedia of communication*. Retrieved fromss http://www.communicationencyclopedia.com/subscriber/tocnode?id=g9781405131995_chunk_g978140513199524_ss101-1

Deetz, S. A. (2008). Organizational ethics. In W. Donsbach (Ed.), *The international encyclopedia of communication.*.Retrieved from http://www.communicationencyclopedia.com/subscriber/tocnode?id=g9781405131995_chunk_g978140513199520_ss25-1

DiQuinzio, P., & Young, I. M. (1997). Introduction. In P. DiQuinzio & I. M. Young (Eds.), *Feminist ethics and social policy* (pp. vii–xv). Bloomington: Indiana University Press.

Dixon, T., Schell, T., Giles, H., & Grogos, K. (2008). The influence of race in police–civilian interactions: A content analysis of videotaped interactions taken during Cincinnati police traffic stops. *Journal of Communication, 58*, 530–549.

Dow, B. J. (1997). Politicizing voice. *Western Journal of Communication, 61,* 243–251.

Dow, B. J. (2009). Feminist approaches to communication. In W. F. Eadie (Ed.), *21st century communication: A reference handbook* (pp. 82–89). Los Angeles, CA: Sage.

Dow, B. J., & Condit, C. M. (2005). The state of the art in feminist scholarship in communication. *Journal of Communication, 55*, 448–478.

Drichel, S. (2008). The time of hybridity. *Philosophy & Social Criticism, 34,* 587–615.

Duke, S. (2009). Educating public relations students to enter the blogosphere: Results of a Delphi study. *Journalism & Mass Communication Educator, 63*, 317–332.

Dutta, M. (2008). *Communicating health: A culture-centered approach*. London: Polity.

Ellingson, L. (2005). *Communicating in the clinic: Negotiating frontstage and backstage teamwork*. Cresskill, NJ: Hampton.

Ellis, C. (2007). Telling secrets, revealing lives: Relational ethics in research with intimate others. *Qualitative Inquiry, 13*, 3–29.

Entman, R. M. (2007). Framing bias: Media in the distribution of power. *Journal of Communication, 57*, 163–173.

Fairhurst, G. T., & Sarr, R. A. (1996). *The art of framing: Managing the language of leadership*. San Francisco, CA: Jossey-Bass.

Flax, J. (1987). Postmodernism and gender relations in feminist theory. *Signs, 12*, 621–643.

Flax, J. (1990). *Thinking fragments: Psychoanalysis, feminism, and postmodernism in the contemporary West*. Berkeley: University of California Press.

Fleming, P., & Spicer, A. (2007). *Contesting the corporation: Struggle, power and resistance in organizations*. Cambridge, UK: Cambridge University Press.

Fleming, P., & Spicer, A. (2008). Beyond power and resistance: New approaches to organizational politics. *Management Communication Quarterly, 21*, 301–309.

Fraser, N. (1995). Pragmatism, feminism, and the linguistic turn. In S. Benhabib, J. Butler, D. Cornell, & N. Fraser (Eds.), *Feminist contentions: A philosophical exchange* (pp. 157–171). New York: Routledge.

Friedman, M. (1985). Abraham, Socrates, and Heinz: Where are the women? (Care and context in moral reasoning). In C. B. Harding (Ed.), *Moral dilemmas: Philosophical and psychological issues in the development of moral reasoning* (pp. 25–41). Chicago, IL: Precedent.

Gajjala, R., Rybas, N., & Altman, M. (2008). Racing and queering the interface: Producing global/local cyberselves. *Qualitative Inquiry, 14*, 1110–1133.

Gayle, B. M., & Griffin, C. L. (1998). Mary Ashton Rice Livermore's relational feminist discourse: A rhetorically successful feminist model. *Women's Studies in Communication, 21,* 55–76.

Gheaus, A. (2008). Gender justice and the welfare state in post-communism. *Feminist Theory, 9,* 185–206.

Gibbs, J. (2009). Dialectics in a global software team: Negotiating tensions across time, space, and culture. *Human Relations, 62,* 905–935.

Gilligan, C. (1982). *In a different voice.* Cambridge, MA: Harvard University Press.

Graham, L. D. (1999). Domesticating efficiency: Lillian Gilbreth's scientific management of homemakers, 1924–1930. *Signs, 24,* 633–675.

Griffin, C. L. (1996). The essentialist roots of the public sphere: A feminist critique. *Western Journal of Communication, 60,* 21–39.

Haas, T., & Deetz, S. (2000). Between the generalized and the concrete other: Approaching organizational ethics from feminist perspectives. In P. M. Buzzanell (Ed.), *Rethinking organizational and managerial communication from feminist perspectives* (pp. 24–46). Thousand Oaks, CA: Sage.

Hallstein, D. L. (1999). A postmodern caring: Feminist standpoint theories, revisioned caring, and communication ethics. *Western Journal of Communication, 63,* 32–56.

Hamington, M., & Miller, D. (Eds.). (2006). *Socializing care.* Lanham, MD: Rowman & Littlefield.

Haney, E. H. (1994). What is feminist ethics? A proposal for continuing discussion. In L. K. Daly (Ed.), *Feminist theological ethics: A reader* (pp. 3–12). Louisville, KY: Westminister John Knox Press.

Harding, S. (1991). *Whose science? Whose knowledge? Thinking from women's lives.* Ithaca, NY: Cornell University Press.

Hegde, R. (2009). Fragments and interruptions: Sensory regimes of violence and the limits of feminist ethnography. *Qualitative Inquiry. 15,* 276–296

Hekman, S. (1999). Backgrounds and riverbeds: Feminist reflections. *Feminist Studies, 25,* 427–448.

Hernández, D., & Richman, B. (2002). *Colonize this! Young women of color on today's feminism.* New York: Seal Press.

Hoagland, S. L. (1991). Some thoughts about "caring." In C. Card (Ed.), *Feminist ethics* (pp. 246–263). Lawrence: University of Kansas Press.

Jaggar, A. M. (1994a). Introduction: Living with contradictions. In A. M. Jaggar (Ed.), *Living with contradictions: Controversies in feminist social ethics* (pp. 1–17). Boulder, CO: Westview.

Jaggar, A. M. (1994b). Sexual difference and sexual equality. In A. M. Jaggar (Ed.), *Living with contradictions: Controversies in feminist social ethics* (pp. 18–28). Boulder, CO: Westview.

Jaggar, A. M. (1998). Globalizing feminist ethics. *Hypatia, 13*(2), 7–31.

Jamieson, K. H. (1995). *Beyond the double bind: Women and leadership.* New York: Oxford University Press.

Japp, P. M. (1985). Esther or Isaiah? The abolitionist-feminist rhetoric of Angelina Grimké. *Quarterly Journal of Speech, 71,* 335–348.

Johannesen, R. L. (2001). Communication ethics: Centrality, trends, and controversies. *Communication Yearbook, 25,* 200–235.

Johannesen, R. L., Valde, K., & Whedbee, K. (2008). *Ethics in human communication* (6th ed.). Prospect Heights, IL: Waveland.

Jorgensen-Earp, C. R. (1990). The lady, the whore, and the spinster: The rhetorical use of Victorian images of women. *Western Journal of Communication, 54,* 82–98.

Kendall, K. E., & Fisher, J. (1974). Frances Wright on women's rights: Eloquence versus ethos. *Quarterly Journal of Speech, 60,* 58–68.

Kohlberg, L. (1981). *Essays on moral development.* San Francisco, CA: Jossey-Bass.

Kohlberg, L. (1985). Resolving moral conflicts within the just community. In C. B. Harding (Ed.), *Moral dilemmas: Philosophical and psychological issues in the development of moral reasoning* (pp. 71–97). Chicago: Precedent.

Kr, C., & Sørensen, A. S. (2006). *Gender communication theories and analyses: From silence to performance.* Thousand Oaks, CA: Sage.

Labaton, V., & Martin, D.L. (Eds.). (2004). *The fire this time: Young activists and the new feminism.* New York: Anchor.

Liu, M., & Buzzanell, P. M. (2004). Negotiating maternity leave expectations: Perceived tensions between ethics of justice and care. *Journal of Business Communication, 41*, 323–349.

Livesey, S., & Kearins, K. (2002). Transparent and caring corporations? A study of sustainability reports by The Body Shop and Royal Dutch/Shell. *Organization & Environment, 15*, 233–258.

Lutgen-Sandvik, P., & Sypher, B. D. (Eds.). (2009). *The destructive side of organizational communication.* New York: Routledge.

Maddux, K. (2008). The *Da Vinci Code* and the regressive gender politics of celebrating women. *Critical Studies in Media Communication, 25*, 225–248.

Makau, J. M. (2009). Ethical and unethical communication. In W. F. Eadie (Ed.), *21st century communication: A reference handbook* (pp. 435–443). Los Angeles, CA: Sage.

Mandel, H., & Semyonov, M. (2005). Family policies, wage structures, and gender gaps: Sources of earnings inequality in 20 countries. *American Sociological Review, 70*, 949–967.

Mason, K. M. (1997). Mary McDowell and municipal housekeeping: Women's political activism in Chicago, 1890–1920. In L. E. Murphy & W. H. Venet (Eds.), *Midwestern women: Work, community, and leadership at the crossroads* (pp. 60–75). Bloomington: Indiana University Press.

Mattson, M., & Buzzanell, P. M. (1999). Traditional and feminist organizational communication ethical analyses of messages and issues involved in an actual job loss case. *Journal of Applied Communication Research, 27*, 49–72.

McLaren, M. A. (2007). Women's rights in a global context. *Journal of Developing Societies, 23*, 159–173.

Medved, C. (2007). Investigating family labor in communication studies: Threading across historical and contemporary discourses. *Journal of Family Communication, 7*, 1–19.

Medved, C. (2009). Crossing and transforming occupational and household divisions of labor: Reviewing literatures and deconstructing divisions. *Communication Yearbook, 33*, 457–484.

Monteverde, S. (2009). The importance of time in ethical decision making. *Nursing Ethics, 16*, 613–624.

Mumby, D. K. (2000). Communication, organization, and the public sphere: A feminist perspective. In P. M. Buzzanell (Ed.), *Rethinking organizational and managerial communication from feminist perspectives* (pp. 3–23). Thousand Oaks, CA: Sage.

Mumby, D. K. (2005). Theorizing resistance in organization studies: A dialectical approach. *Management Communication Quarterly, 19*, 19–44.

Mumby, D. K., & Putnam, L. L. (1992). The politics of emotion: A feminist reading of bounded rationality. *Academy of Management Review, 17*, 465–486.

Munson, E., & Dickinson, G. (1998). Hearing women speak: Antoinette Brown Blackwell and the dilemma of authority. *Journal of Women's History, 10*, 108–126.

Murphy, A. G. (1998). Hidden transcripts of flight attendant resistance. *Management Communication Quarterly, 11*, 499–535.

Nadesan, M. H. (1999). The discourses of corporate spiritualism and evangelical capitalism. *Management Communication Quarterly, 13*, 3–42.

Noddings, N. (1984). *Caring: A feminine approach to ethics and moral education.* Berkeley: University of California Press.

Noddings, N. (2006). Caring and social policy. In M. Hamington & D. C. Miller (Eds.), *Socializing care* (pp. 27–48). Lanham, MD: Rowman & Littlefield.

Okin, S. M. (1998). Feminism, women's human rights, and cultural differences. *Hypatia, 13*(2), 32–52.

Okin, S. M. (1999). Is multiculturalism bad for women? In J. Cohen, M. Howard, & M. C. Nussbaum (Eds.), *Is multiculturalism bad for women? Susan Moller Okin with respondents* (pp. 7–24). Princeton, NJ: Princeton University Press.

Papa, M. J., Singhal, A., & Papa, W. H. (2006). *Organizing for social change: A dialectic journey of theory and praxis.* Thousand Oaks, CA: Sage.

Perrons, D., McDowell, L., Fagan, C., Ray, K., & Ward, K. (2006). Introduction: Work, life and time in the new economy. In D. Perrons, C. Fagan, L. McDowell, K. Ray, & K. Ward (Eds.), *Gender divisions and working time in the new economy: Changing patterns of work, care and public policy in Europe and North America* (pp. 1–15). Cheltenham, UK: Edward Elgar.

Putnam, L. L., & Boys, S. (2006). Revisiting metaphors of organizational communication. In S. R. Clegg (Ed.), *Handbook of organization studies* (pp. 541–576). Thousand Oaks, CA: Sage.

Putnam, L. L., Phillips, N., & Chapman, P. (1996). Metaphors of communication and organization. In S. R. Clegg, C. Hardy, & W. R. Nord (Eds.), *Handbook of organization studies* (pp. 375–408). London: Sage.

Rawlins, W. K. (1992). *Friendship matters: Communication, dialectics, and the life course.* New York: Aldine de Gruyter.

Redding, W. C. (1996). Ethics and the study of organizational communication: When will we wake up? In J. A. Jaksa & M. S. Pritchard (Eds.), *Responsible communication: Ethical issues in business, industry, and the professions* (pp. 17–40). Cresskill, NJ: Hampton.

Rowe, A. M. C. (2000). Locating feminism's subject: The paradox of white femininity and the struggle to forge feminist alliances. *Communication Theory, 10,* 64–80.

Ruiz, B. R. (2005). Caring discourse: The care/justice debate revisited. *Philosophy & Social Criticism, 31,* 773–800.

Scott, J. (1988). Deconstructing equality-versus-difference: Or, the uses of poststructuralist theory for feminism. *Feminist Studies, 14,* 33–50.

Seeger, M. W. (1997). *Ethics and organizational communication.* Cresskill, NJ: Hampton.

Seeger, M. W., Sellnow, T. L., Ulmer, R. R., & Novak, J. M. (2009). Applied communication ethics: A summary and critique of the research literature. In L. Frey & K. Cissna (Eds.), *Routledge handbook of applied communication research* (pp. 280–306). New York: Routledge.

Steiner, L. (1997). A feminist schema for analysis of ethical dilemmas. In F. L. Casmir (Ed.), *Ethics in intercultural and international communication* (pp. 59–88). Mahwah, NJ: Erlbaum.

Steiner, L. (2008). Feminist ethics. In W. Donsbach (Ed.), *The international encyclopedia of communication.* Retrieved from http://www.communicationencyclopedia.com/subscriber/tocnode?id=g978140513 1995_chunk_g978140513199511_ss19-1

Sullivan, P. A., & Goldzwig, S. R. (1995). A relational approach to moral decision-making: The majority opinion in *Planned Parenthood v. Casey. Quarterly Journal of Speech, 81,* 167–190.

Sullivan, P. A., & Turner, L. (1996). *From the margins to the center: Contemporary women and political communication.* Westport, CT: Praeger.

Sullivan, P. A., & Turner, L. (1999). The Zoe Baird spectacle: Silences, sins, and status. *Western Journal of Communication, 63,* 413–432.

Tong, R. (1989). *Feminist thought: A comprehensive introduction.* Boulder, CO: Westview.

Tong, R. (1993). *Feminine and feminist ethics.* Belmont, CA: Wadsworth.

Townsley, N. (2006). Love, sex, and tech in the global workplace. In. B. Dow & J. T. Wood (Eds.), *The Sage handbook of gender and communication* (pp. 143–160). Thousand Oaks, CA: Sage.

Tronto, J. C. (1992). Women and caring: What can feminists learn about morality from caring? In A. M. Jaggar & S. R. Bordo (Eds.), *Gender/body/knowledge: Feminist reconstructions of being and knowing* (pp. 172–187). New Brunswick, NJ: Rutgers University Press.

Tronto, J. C. (1993). *Moral boundaries: A political argument for an ethic of care.* New York: Routledge.

Tronto, J. C. (2006). Vicious cycles of privatized caring. In M. Hamington & D.C. Miller (Eds.), *Socializing care* (pp. 3–26). Lanham, MD: Rowman & Littlefield.

Tucker, J. (2006). Care as cause: Framing the twenty-first-century mothers' movement. In M. Hamington & D. Miller (Eds.), *Socializing care* (pp. 183–203). Lanham, MD: Rowman & Littlefield.

Waymer, D., & Heath, R. L. (2007). Emergent agents: The forgotten publics in crisis communication and issues management research. *Journal of Applied Communication Research, 35,* 88–108.

Weedon, C. (1987). *Feminist practice and poststructuralist theory.* New York: Basil Blackwell.

Weedon, C. (1997). *Feminist practice and poststructuralist theory* (2nd ed.). Oxford, UK: Basil Blackwell.

Wicks, A., Gilbert, D., Jr., & Freeman, R. (1994). A feminist reinterpretation of the stakeholder concept. *Business Ethics Quarterly, 4,* 475–497.

Wood, J. T. (1992). Gender and moral voice: Moving from woman's nature to standpoint epistemology. *Women's Studies in Communication, 15,* 1–23.

Wood, J. T. (1994). *Who cares? Women, care, and culture.* Carbondale: Southern Illinois University Press.

Wood, J. T. (1998). Ethics, justice, and the "private sphere." *Women's Studies in Communication, 21,* 125–149.

6

Power and Ethics

Dennis K. Mumby

One of the interesting things about living in a postlinguistic turn world is that many of the shibbo-leths of high modernity have been cast into doubt. As we enter the second decade of the 21st cen-tury there are few remaining apodictic truths that provide a moral and epistemological foundation from which to make judgments about the world in which we live. This "crisis of representation" (Jameson, 1984) has not only cast doubt on the possibility for—or indeed the value of—universal truths; it has also subjected to detailed scrutiny the ways in which *any* claims to truth are not only always partial, but also rooted in a particular constellation of discourses, power relations, and positionalities. In a post-Foucauldian world, we have largely come to accept that not only is any claim to know always partial; it is also always an effect of power.

In this context, various perspectives on power—be they Marxist, feminist, poststructuralist, postcolonial, and so forth—have at least in part sought to counter the possibility of some kind of universal ethic that prescribes human thought and action, regardless of situation. Instead, each of these perspectives attempts to "highlight the sectional interests and strategic exclusions that pretensions to ethical universality mask" (Wray-Bliss, 2009, p. 269).

Given this—admittedly deeply glossed—characterization of the power–knowledge relation-ship, whither ethics? Once we have jettisoned the possibility of foundational, universal principles upon which to build a normative, moral framework for practicing the good life, where do we look for guidance? In the wake of antifoundationalism, antiessentialism, and suspicion of any kind of master narrative that smacks of totalizing thought, are we left with anything beyond relativism and radical contingency to provide a secure mooring for any sense of ourselves in the world? If ethics and morality are, by definition, dependent on some coherent notion of a sovereign moral subject, do the various poststructuralist efforts to "decenter" the subject cast doubt on the very notion of ethics itself?

In this essay I want to use this initial framing to address the relationships among ethics, power, and communication. There is a very real sense in which the field of communication is especially well positioned to address the ethics–power nexus in the context of a nonfoundational world. In particular, I want to explore some ways in which one can adopt a communicational mode of explanation in thinking about ethics in the context of power and politics. In other words, in the wake of the linguistic turn, how might one productively conceive of the relationship be-tween ethics and power in a context where communication is a defining—rather than peripher-al—feature of the human condition? First, let me address the relationship between power, ethics, and modernity.

POWER, ETHICS, AND MODERNITY

The relationship between power and ethics takes on a particular resonance with the rise of modernity precisely because power, as a phenomenon, becomes more complex. In traditional, premodern societies, systems of domination largely predetermine one's place in society (slave, serf, aristocrat, etc.). But with the emergence of the modernist imperative to "Dare to know" (Kant), replete with new conceptions of human identity, knowledge (celebrated in the new human and natural sciences), and imbued with an emancipatory ethos, configurations of power become more contested.

In the context of this contested terrain, modernity and modernist knowledge formations take many forms, and I do not wish to rehearse old arguments and debates here (see Mumby, 1997, for one take on these debates). However, in terms of the power–ethics relationship Marxism and neo-Marxist thought takes on a particular importance. For Marx (1867/1967), capitalism functions as a system of exploitation by virtue of its expropriation and alienation of the sellers of labor power, who are reduced to mere "hands" in the capitalist mode of production, violently separated from their own means of production. For Marx, then, power takes on a specific historical and material form upon which a particular dominant ideology is constructed, such that "The ideas of the ruling class are in every epoch the ruling ideas, i.e., the class which is the ruling <u>material</u> force of society, is at the same time its ruling <u>intellectual</u> force" (Marx & Engels, 1845/1970, p. 64, emphasis in original). In this reading, power is located with the owners of capital and is sanctioned by the state, both through coercion (police, army, prisons, etc.) and ideology (religion, education, etc.). But relations of power in capitalism are also constructed on systems of contradiction that harbor its potential demise. As Marx indicates, the very process of capital accumulation is founded on the contradiction between the socialized nature of capitalist production, and the privatized character of the accumulation process. In other words, the sellers of labor power produce wealth through the creation of surplus value (the production of which is hidden); the owners of capital accumulate it. As Marx pithily states, "Capital is dead labor, that, vampire-like, only lives by sucking living labor, and lives the more, the more labor it sucks" (1867/1967, p. 224).

The wage relation in capitalism is therefore an unethical and exploitive relationship by virtue of the vampirism that Marx describes above. Freedom and self-determination are possible only through revolution and the ownership of the means of production by those who labor. From an ethical perspective, Marx is a Utopian in his vision of an ideal communist state that will be realized out of the emancipation of the proletariat. Indeed, Marx imbues the realm of philosophy itself with an ethic of social transformation that is quite different from early idealists such as Kant and Hegel. As Marx states in his 11th thesis on Feuerbach, "The philosophers have only interpreted the world, in various ways; the point is to change it" (Marx & Engels, 1955/1969, p. 15).

The Frankfurt School of Critical Theory takes up Marx's agenda in a somewhat different historical, political, and economic context, and in the full knowledge that capitalism has confronted and survived several legitimation crises since Marx wrote *Capital*. Writing both before and after World War II, Adorno, Horkheimer, and others (Adorno, 1966/1973; Horkheimer, 1968/1986; Horkheimer & Adorno, 1944/1988) focus on the superstructural elements of capitalism and the processes through which culture and ideology maintain and reproduce capitalist relations of production. From a power–ethics perspective, the project of the Frankfurt School is at least twofold. First, they extend Marx's critique of capitalism to address in detail the various ways in which the "culture industry" serves to present "enlightenment as mass deception." This interdisciplinary critique of "totally administered society" focuses on the ways in which ideological processes foreclose possibilities for social transformation and emancipation. Second, the Frankfurt School takes on the Enlightenment project itself, arguing, in Horkheimer and Adorno's memorable phrase, that "In the most general sense of progressive thought, the Enlightenment has always aimed at liberating men from fear and establishing their authority. Yet the fully enlightened earth radiates disaster triumphant" (Horkheimer & Adorno, 1944/1988, p. 3).

The target here is the perversion of Enlightenment thought by instrumental rationality and the subsumption of all forms of knowledge within a narrow technical, administrative frame. In a move that is in some ways redolent of Foucault's conception of power/knowledge, Horkheimer and Adorno explore the ways that ostensibly "progressive" conceptions of knowledge have disastrous consequences for the possibilities of human liberation from structures of oppression. Indeed, in a famous essay, "Traditional Theory Versus Critical Theory," Horkheimer (1968/1986) argues that traditional social science theory and research functions merely as a handmaiden to administrative logic and the reproduction of dominant relations of power. Critical theory, on the other hand, with its dialectical sensibility, works in opposition to dominant knowledge structures creating possibilities for envisioning alternative realities and emancipatory logics. In a similar manner, Adorno (1966/1973) argues that it is only through "negative dialectics" and the refusal to accept "identity thinking" (characteristic of both traditional theory and popular, administered culture) that truly progressive thought and social transformation is possible.

From an ethical perspective, then, the Frankfurt School sheds light on the ways that rationality and the production of knowledge in the name of enlightenment can lead to the impoverishment of the human spirit. Knowledge gets appropriated by narrow interests and used as justification for the oppression of "the other." Indeed, Horkheimer and Adorno saw the Holocaust as the inevitable endpoint and nadir of the Enlightenment project ("disaster triumphant"). The Nazi extermination of the Jews was the ultimate expression of a rationalized system of truth detached from a critical, ethical framework that examined knowledge claims in terms of their political interests and their consequences for humanity.

Of course, in addition to their ultimately pessimistic view of the emancipatory possibilities of capitalist modernity, the first generation Frankfurt Schoolers also adopted an élitist disdain for popular culture and rejected the notion that everyday social interaction contained any possibilities for realizing alternative social realities or resisting received power relations. However, the return of "the popular" occurred in the second half of the 20th century with the emergence in the early 1960s of the British tradition in Cultural Studies, institutionalized in the work of the Birmingham University Centre for Contemporary Cultural Studies (CCCS), as well as the work of second generation Frankfurt School theorists like Jürgen Habermas. CCCS scholars took up popular culture as a site of contestation where issues of meaning, identity, power, and resistance get played out in ways that shape the cultural and political landscape (Hall, 1983, 1985, 1988, 1997; Hebdige, 1979; Willis, 1977). In this work, popular culture is not administered from above, but is the context through which agentic raced, classed, and gendered social actors construct systems of representation that contain both progressive and conservative possibilities in terms of their relationship to hegemonic meaning systems. While the British Cultural Studies tradition is explicitly Marxist in its orientation, it is, in Stuart Hall's (1983) emblematic phrase, a "Marxism without guarantees" that refuses any deterministic relationship between the economic infrastructure on the one hand, and cultural and political superstructure on the other hand. Marxism provides no guarantees in its reading of the complex and contradictory configurations of the cultural and political landscape, nor does it guarantee that progressive systems of thought and inclusive political institutions will prevail. As such, British cultural studies provides a "radically contextual" reading of the political and cultural landscape and its relationship to everyday practices.

Jürgen Habermas's (1976/1979, 1981/1984, 1985/1987a, 1981/1987b, 1962/1989) work reclaims the emancipatory impulse of modernity in a related manner given his focus on ideology critique, but his agenda is more explicitly articulated around ethical questions. The importance of

Habermas's work lies in part with his efforts to articulate the power–ethics relationship in a manner that directly addresses questions of communicative praxis. That is, if we replace the Kantian transcendental, a priori structures of consciousness as the foundation for critical reflection, what takes its place? For Habermas, the answer is language or, more specifically, communicative action. Thus, he shifts the frame of reference from Kant's solitary, reflecting moral consciousness to a community of moral subjects who are in dialogue. Critical reflection, truth, and ethics are placed firmly in a communicative context.

One of the most interesting aspects of Habermas's work is that he makes a connection between the structures of moral judgment and the structures of social interaction. According to McCarthy (1990), Habermas sees the task of moral theory and philosophy as being to "reflexively articulate, refine, and elaborate the intuitive grasp of the normative presuppositions of social interaction that belongs to the repertoire of competent social actors in any society" (McCarthy, 1990, p. x). Truth, in such a context, is fundamentally intersubjective and rooted in the ability of appropriately socialized social actors to engage in the discursive testing of claims to validity. By definition, power is exercised strategically when truth claims are not subject to discursive testing and forms of discursive closure occur (Deetz, 1992). In Habermas's terms, then, communication is unethical to the extent that it functions in a systematically distorted manner to foreclose possibilities for full, open, and noncoercive dialogue aimed at achieving consensus.

As is well known, Habermas argues that any act of speaking implicitly engages in three claims to validity, each associated with a specific referential domain. First, a specific utterance can be deemed true or false based on knowledge of the objective world (claims to truth); that is, "the totality of all entities about which true statements are possible" (Habermas, 1984, p. 100). Second, a speaker can present claims for the legitimacy of an utterance in terms of the normative context in which it is spoken (claims to rightness); such claims take as their referential domain the social world, defined as "the totality of all legitimately regulated interpersonal relations" (Habermas, 1981/1984, p. 100). Third, speakers lay claim to the sincerity of their utterances (claims to truthfulness); here, the referential domain is the subjective world, or "the totality of the experiences of the speaker to which he [or she] has privileged access" (1984, p. 100).

The significance of such a framing of truth claims is that it conceptualizes human autonomy and agency in terms of its embeddedness in shared forms of life, or what Habermas describes as the *Lebenswelt*, or Lifeworld. Here, Habermas frames moral philosophy as a fundamentally practical endeavor in that it investigates the normative structure of social interaction. As Habermas states, "As long as moral philosophy concerns itself with clarifying the everyday intuitions into which we are socialized, it must be able to adopt, at least virtually, the attitude of someone who participates in the communicative practice of everyday life" (1990, p. 48).

Habermas's project, then, explores the possibilities for genuine dialogue and action oriented to understanding in the context of the colonization of Lifeworld practices by the system (principally characterized by the steering media of money and power), the latter of which is a product of modernization processes and capitalism's response to various legitimation crises. The system has colonized the Lifeworld by replacing genuine communicative action with media-steered interactions; capitalism reproduces itself by regulating social integration via administrative and economic systems. A simple example of this would be the colonization of the educational sphere such that education functions strategically as a means to produce workers, managers, and an administrative élite, rather than as a means to enhance possibilities for emancipation and social transformation. Habermas's goal then, is to rescue modernity from these colonization processes and recreate possibilities for self-reflection and emancipation through ethically and morally grounded communicative processes.

Let me turn now to a brief discussion of contemporary theories of power, particularly as they have emerged in social and political theory. Although they do not necessarily address the question of ethics directly, they nevertheless implicitly invoke a conception of the relationship between power and ethics.

THEORIES OF POWER

> Power is the most fundamental process in society, since society is defined around values and institutions, and what is valued and institutionalized is defined by power relationships. (Castells, 2009, p. 10)

The above quotation from Castells, in a recent book appropriately named *Communication Power*, provides a useful starting point in framing our discussion of power. Power has been studied for a long time, but it hasn't always been credited with the central role among social theorists that Castells bestows on it. Moreover, the connection between communication and power has more often than not been articulated in a way that positions communication as playing a handmaiden role to power; it is invariably framed as a vehicle for expressing and reproducing existing power relations rather than playing a constitutive role in their production and instantiation. Elsewhere (Mumby, 2001) I have argued that so-called functional, representational models of power (e.g., strategic contingency theory and its cousin, resource dependency theory) are largely guilty of assigning this sort of peripheral role to communication, so I will not reproduce that argument at any length here, other than to note that the following quotation by Pfeffer (1981) effectively exemplifies this approach:

> The view developed here…is that language and symbolism are useful in the exercise of power…. However, in this formulation, language and the ability to use political symbols contribute only marginally to the development of the power of various organizational participants; rather, power derives from the conditions of resource control and resource interdependence. (p. 184)

Such conceptions of power, while clearly operating in a prelinguistic turn universe, also seem to implicitly treat power as having a sovereign, structural quality that functions independently from the agency of communicating social actors. Moreover, power is largely framed as extralinguistic; in Pfeffer's quotation, for example, the juxtaposition of resource control over and against communicative processes overlooks the fact that not only is communication itself a resource, but that precisely what count as resources and their control is frequently defined through the communicative construction of organizing.

In contrast, I would suggest that all viable conceptions of power must adequately account for the communicative construction and operation of human agency and subjectivity. Ethically speaking, a central issue thus becomes how particular forms of subjectivity and agency are communicatively constructed and privileged over other forms. That is, in what ways does the power–communication nexus work to construct a hierarchy of subjectivities that create greater life chances for some than others? In Gregory Bateson's (1972) terms, a communicative conception of the power–ethics relationship explores how "differences that make a difference" (race, gender, class, sexuality, etc.) are constructed and sedimented in society. In other words, whose voices are privileged and whose are marginalized in the communicative construction of meaningful difference?

Furthermore, and ethically speaking, one could argue that all theories of power at least implicitly provide a normative judgment about the possibilities for what Jürgen Habermas describes as autonomy and responsibility (*Mundigkeit*). In other words, theories of power address the relationships among social actors, communities, and the broader society, including the state. Castells (2009) places these relationships in context when he states, "societies are not communities, sharing values and interests. They are contradictory social structures enacted in conflicts and in negotiation among diverse and often opposing social actors" (p. 14). Power, then, refers to the ability of social actors (where actors here refers to individuals, groups, and organizations) to achieve their goals in the face of conflict and opposition from other social actors. Where community (in Habermas's terms, the *Lifeworld*) is the sphere where connection and what it means to be a social human being is realized, society is where division and difference is instantiated. In this sense, institutions—as part of society rather than community—are "crystallized power relationships" that provide the "generalized means" (Castells, 2009, p. 14) by which social actors are able to exercise power over other social actors.

From an ethics perspective, then, power—and various theories of power—needs to be read in terms of how it intervenes in the process by which social actors are provided with the life chances that enable them to realize particular goals, identities, forms of difference, and so forth. In what follows, then, I want to examine various treatments of power and address how they speak to the critique of systems of oppression and colonization on the one hand, and articulate possibilities for the realization of freedom and democracy on the other.

The Community Power Debate

The arguments of the "community power debate" have been rehearsed in a number of places (e.g., Clegg, 1989; Clegg, Courpasson, & Phillips, 2006) so I will not spend a great deal of time on them here. However, while they do not explicitly address issues of ethics, the various positions in this debate implicitly articulate a vision of the good life and, to varying degrees, suggest possibilities for emancipation from oppression. In many respects, the community power debate revolved around the question of enfranchisement; that is, to what extent is community power spread evenly amongst a broad cross-section of stakeholder groups or, to the contrary, concentrated with political élites?

Dahl's (1957, 1961) study of the local politics in New Haven, CT, argued for the former position, making the case for a pluralist view of power as distributed widely, with no one stakeholder group exercising a monopoly over power and authority. On the other hand, the so-called "élitists" (Bachrach & Baratz, 1962, 1963; Hunter, 1953; Mills, 1956) argued that, to the contrary, such a plural view of power was naïve in its characterization of the landscape of U.S. politics, and that there existed an élite in which much of the political decision-making power was concentrated.

While there is certainly an important empirical question here regarding the structure of power in contemporary U.S. society, what is perhaps more interesting for our purposes here is that much of this debate revolved around definitional and theoretical—not to say methodological—questions regarding what counts as power. Dahl's behavioral conception of power limits it conceptually to those contexts in which there are observable conflicts between stakeholder groups, and in which such conflicts are resolved by the more powerful group causally effecting change in the behavior of the less powerful group. Dahl's famous definition of power perfectly captures this causal, behavioral model: "A has power over B to the extent that he [or she] can get B to do something that B would not otherwise do." Inherent in this model is a conception of sovereign, politically self-aware subjects who struggle against each other in order to maximize their resources through achieving particular political decisions or outcomes. Furthermore, and methodologically speaking, such a model presumes the ability to accurately measure behavioral change, and hence exercise of power. In other words, it is a deeply modernist conception of power rooted in modernist assumptions about subjectivity, causality, and knowledge.

The élitist model, on the other hand, problematizes the pluralist view by at least partially undermining its assumptions about subjectivity and causality. Perhaps most famously embodied in Bachrach and Baratz's (1962) "two faces of power" essay, this position challenges the sovereignty of the political subject in Dahl's model, and articulates a model of power that presumes a much greater sense of uncertainty and ambivalence about the positionality of the subject in the "face" of power. In brief, Bachrach and Baratz argue that power resides not only in the ability to prevail in situations of overt conflict, but also in the ability to shape decision-making agendas in ways that favor particular interests. In speaking of the "mobilization of bias," Bachrach and Baratz suggest that power is most effectively exercised when a particular power élite has the ability to organize and exploit some forms of conflict (those that are in their interests) and suppress others (those that endanger their interests). Power, then, resides in the ability to manage both overt conflict and covert forms of conflict. Thus, groups are disenfranchised not only in situations where they lose a battle over resources or political power, but also in situations where their grievances are organized out of the sphere of public debate, and hence cannot even be addressed. This "Janus-faced" view of power argues that it is precisely this second face of power that political élites in society exercise in order to protect and enhance their interests.

From an ethical viewpoint, the pluralist and élitist views of power represent two distinct perspectives of the possibilities for autonomy and enfranchisement. For pluralists such as Dahl power is exercised among sovereign subjects who compete on a relatively even terrain to realize life possibilities. For élitists, on the other hand, a "discourse of suspicion" (Mumby, 1997; Ricoeur, 1970) frames their reading of power such that the very possibility for autonomy and enfranchisement is short-circuited by the machinations of a power élite bent on preserving their own sphere of influence. In such a model, sovereignty is limited to the privileged few.

The last position in the tripartite community power debate is provided by Steven Lukes's (1974) theoretical treatise. Arguing that both the pluralist or one-dimensional, and élitist or two-dimensional, models of power are seriously flawed, he articulates what he describes as a radical, three-dimensional view of power that both incorporates and extends the earlier models. Both models, Lukes argues, are rooted in behavioral conceptions of power that focus on conflict— overt in the pluralist model, and covert in the élitist model. For Lukes, the most effective exercise of power resides not in the way that groups are able to prevail in conflicts or set agendas wherein their needs and interests are privileged. Rather, power works most effectively in the absence of conflict (whether overt or covert) and where A prevails over B "by influencing, shaping, or determining his [or her] very wants" (1974, p. 23). Lukes goes on to argue that even the existence of a consensus and apparent lack of grievances among different actors does not mean that power is not being exercised. Indeed, he makes the compelling case that "to assume that the absence of grievance equals genuine consensus is to rule out the possibility of false or manipulated consensus by definitional fiat" (1974, p. 24). As Castells (2009) succinctly puts it, "the most fundamental form of power lies in the ability to shape the human mind" (p. 3).

Ethically speaking, Lukes's model presents some conceptual and pragmatic difficulties. In arguing, following Gramsci (1971), that power works through ideology to shape social actors' very wants and needs, he makes the case that their real, objective interests (and hence potential grievances) are distorted and obscured. For example, Lukes might argue that under U.S. capitalism the real interests of the working class are obscured by virtue of an ideology of individualism that constructs everyone as having an equal opportunity to succeed, and frames failure as an individual responsibility. Such an ideology limits possibilities for the working class to think about its relationship to the capitalist mode of production and its position as expropriated, commodified labor that produces wealth for the "vampiric" capitalist class.

Of course, there are significant problems with such a position. First, it presumes that one can identify and articulate those real, objective interests presumably in some kind of empirical fashion. Second, the claim that social actors who are subject to power are not able to assess their "best interests" by virtue of their ideological interpellation by the powerful, positions them as cultural dupes who are unable to adequately reflect on their own subject positions. Third, Lukes's notion of "objective interests" necessarily requires a position outside of power, outside the process of ideological interpellation, that is able to identify and assess how power works and how the process of ideological interpellation is privileging certain interests and marginalizing others. Finally, the notion of "real interests" necessarily entails that the exercise of power constructs a set of "false" interests that people take on as their own. Again, this position requires a view of the ideologically interpellated individual as someone who lives in a perpetual state of false consciousness from which he or she must be liberated.

Using the intersection of power and ethics as an interpretive lens, this position contains a number of problems. Knights and Willmott (1999) argue that Lukes's theory is grounded in a radical humanist, essentialist position that is dualistic in its characterization of the relationship between the sovereign, autonomous subject and the exercise of power. For Lukes, the interests from which power is exercised appear to exist in an a priori relationship to power; that is, the interests of various groups are built on a set of objective conditions that exist in society, and power is exercised as a means to protect certain interests and deny or marginalize others. Power, then, impedes the autonomy of a fully formed, sovereign subject who, under ideal conditions, functions outside the realm of power. For Lukes, then, power is a distortion that mediates between sovereign subjects and their objective interests. Powerful subjects use power to enhance their interests and realize the good life; powerless subjects live in a perpetual realm of ideological distortion and are doomed to support and realize the interests of the more powerful.

From an ethical perspective, then, Lukes makes an explicit connection between power and responsibility. That is, "to identify a given process as an 'exercise of power', rather than a case of structural determination, is to assume that it is *in the exerciser's or exercisers' power* to act differently" (1974, p. 55, emphasis in original). Thus, for Lukes, "The point...of locating power is to fix responsibility for consequences held to flow from the action, or inaction, of certain specifiable agents" (p. 56). Here we can clearly see the image of the sovereign, modernist subject-agent who can be held morally responsible for his or her actions. Lukes, then, articulates an "ethics of power" (Clegg, 1989) that, at its root is founded on at least the possibility of clearly identifying an essential human agency, objective interests, and the consequences for various groups of particular configurations of power.

Thus, we can summarize the three views of power in the community power debate by suggesting that they represent progressive conceptions of power as an increasing intervention in, and threat to, the sovereignty and autonomy of the modernist subject. The pluralists' behavioral model treats power as exercised among sovereign subjects who are fully aware of the issues at stake. The élitists view power as exercised by a sovereign few, with those who are disenfranchised aware of their marginalization but unable to shape the "mobilization of bias" to their own interests. Finally, Lukes's "radical" model sees power as fundamentally undermining the sovereignty of those social actors who are its victims, in that they are unaware that their needs, wants, and beliefs are the outcome of power. Lukes, then, articulates a dualistic model in which the agents of power are responsible for its consequences, and hence for its effects on those whose interests are shaped for them.

While the community power debate has significantly influenced theorizing about power, it is limited in its efforts to address power as a complex and frequently contradictory phenomenon. The relationships among power, truth, ethics, and subjectivity are not easily addressed by causal understandings of "real" interests, identifiable moral responsibilities, measurable consequences of power, and so forth. In the rest of the chapter I want to further complicate these issues by examining more recent interventions in debates about power, the subject, and ethics. Let me first turn to the work of Foucault.

Foucault and Power

One could argue that debates around ethics are primarily concerned with how one engages with the other. That is, how do we treat those who are different from us (whoever "us" may be)? Behavior and forms of communication that are considered unethical are those that in some way position the other as less than human, as objectified or normalized in some fashion. In such contexts, the other becomes an object for measurement and manipulation rather than someone with whom one engages in genuine dialogue. Insofar as ethics is concerned with engagement with the other, it is also centrally about difference; that is, how is difference treated, marked, and encoded in society (Bourdieu, 1984, 1991)?

In this context, the work of Michel Foucault represents a significant intervention in our understanding of the relationship between power and ethics. Indeed, James Bernauer (1988) has argued that Foucault's entire project can be seen as an "embrace of otherness" (p. 71) and an effort to understand the ways in which particular forms of subjectivity are normalized in the contest of certain power knowledge regimes.

In the context of the power–ethics relationship, Foucault can be read as providing a particular response to the crisis of representation that I addressed at the beginning of this chapter. Given the loss of faith in the Enlightenment, and its efforts to establish foundational truths via a sovereign, unitary subject, Foucault's writings respond to the "new agnosticism" (Bernauer, 1988, p. 73) that emerged from the various disasters of the 20th century. While the Frankfurt School philosophers descended into cynicism and despair regarding the way knowledge had been harnessed to a vast administrative apparatus, Foucault's response is to interrogate that knowledge itself. Rather than view knowledge production as a cumulative, unfolding process with a particular historical *telos*, Foucault deconstructs the radical contingency of history by, in effect, constructing a history of truth; that is, how do particular "truth effects" make particular subjects possible? Moreover, within these "games of truth" (Foucault, 1986), who gets to tell the truth, and who are the subjects/objects of this truth telling? Moreover:

> What are the moral, the ethical, and the spiritual conditions which entitle someone to present himself as, and to be considered as, a truth-teller? About what topics is it important to tell the truth?… What are the consequences of telling the truth?… What is the relation between the activity of truth-telling and the exercise of power? (Foucault, quoted in Bernauer, 1988, p. 72)

Here we see emerging a very different conception of power than those discussed earlier, which Foucault would characterize as "sovereign" models (Foucault, 1980a). Such models adopt a largely top-down, negative conception of power in which the role of power in social formations is to forbid, prohibit, oppress, and so forth. Whether Marxist models of the state, neo-Marxist theories of ideology, or political theories of community decision making, power is conceived as limiting and controlling human agency and possibility.

Foucault, on the other hand, articulates a disciplinary, positive analytics of the practices of power (I avoid the word *theory* here, given Foucault's aversion to such totalizing concepts). Rather than view power as creating a veil of illusion that obscures truth, Foucault conceives of it as productive—producing subjects, producing truths, producing systems of inclusion and exclusion (e.g., Foucault, 1975/1979, 1980a, 1976/1980b, 1982, 1988).

Given the kinds of genealogical analyses in which Foucault engages, there is a very real sense in which, for him, philosophical inquiry is itself an ethical enterprise. As he states in an interview given a few months before his death:

> On the critical side…philosophy is precisely the challenging of all phenomena of domination at whatever level or under whatever form they present themselves—political, economic, sexual, institutional, and so on. The critical function of philosophy, up to a certain point, emerges right from the socratic imperative, "Be concerned with yourself, i.e., ground yourself in liberty, through the mastery of self." (Foucault, 1988, p. 20)

Thus, in writing histories of discipline, of madness, of sexuality, and so forth, Foucault is, in part, opening up to interrogation the regimes of power/knowledge that produce "the other" as a particular object of knowledge and, hence, normalization. Foucault's focus is therefore on knowledge as a practice (i.e., as something that organizes subjects in a particular manner); he asks the question, "What does knowledge do?" How does it intersect and articulate with certain regimes of power to construct not only particular subject effects, but also certain relationships of self to the self?

This last issue is central to Foucault's framing of the power–ethics relationship, and provides important insights into how his understanding and analyses of "the subject" differ from modernist conceptions. For Foucault, the self is invented, rather than discovered. For example, while Freud might be said to have "discovered" the unconscious and thus changed both societal understandings of, and practices toward, the self (as well as our own relationship to ourselves), Foucault is interested in how particular power–knowledge configurations produce "games of truth" through which the subject is constituted, and which create a particular relationship of self to self. This rejection of any a priori theory of the subject enables Foucault to start his analyses from a different point. Rather than start with a particular theory of the subject and then explore what forms of knowledge are thus made possible, Foucault instead asks "how the subject constituted himself as a mad subject or as a normal subject, through a certain number of practices which were games of truth, applications of power, etc." (1988, p. 10).

This process, which Foucault refers to as "governmentality," does not have a specific origin (such as the State), but is dispersed in a capillary fashion through the social body, functioning through a number of intersecting discursive and nondiscursive practices. For example, in my own area of research—critical organization studies—much analytic focus has been placed on the discursive and nondiscursive practices through which the subjects/objects of organizing practices (workers, managers, customers, etc.) come to view themselves as part of a culture of enterprise in which the relationship of self to self and self to other is constituted entrepreneurially (Du Gay & Salaman, 1992; Holmer Nadesan & Trethewey, 2000; Knights & Morgan, 1993; Tracy, 2000; Trethewey, 2001). In this work, focus is on the subject's self-constitution as an object of knowledge that can be judged in terms of its commercial viability, productivity, free agency, adaptability to consumer needs, and so forth. For example, Trethewey's (2001) study shows how older professional women's narratives of self are framed around their relationship to this enterprise discourse, even in cases where they deliberately resist a "master narrative" that constructs aging subjects as nonviable in an enterprise culture.

In this context, then, how does Foucault frame the possibility for freedom in a disciplinary regime where power appears to be everywhere? His answer is to argue that, "if there are relations of power throughout every social field it is because there is freedom everywhere" (1988, p. 12). For Foucault power only exists as a relationship; indeed, the exercise of power would not be necessary if freedom did not exist. But in Foucault's antiessentialist perspective, just as there is no such thing as absolute power, so freedom does not exist in an absolute, utopian sense. There is no "state" of liberation, but rather experimental acts of transgression that engage liberty as a practice. In framing liberty this way, Foucault makes it a moral issue. As he states, "What is morality, if not the practice of liberty, the deliberate practice of liberty?" (1988, p. 4).

For Foucault, this practice of liberty is framed as an aesthetics of existence that engages with and transgresses the current "order of things" in order to cast it into doubt. As Bernauer points out, Foucault

> taught us to recognize that the articulation of a domain in terms of the true and the false is no less significant and dangerous in its implications than was the appearance of discourses which defined the holy and the profane, the saved and the damned, the good and the wicked. (1988, pp. 72–73)

Truth, then—or, more accurately, what counts as truth—has profound ethical implications that must be closely examined and challenged. This in itself is a moral project for Foucault, but one that "must be understood as the creation of a work of art rather than the execution of a program" (1988, p. 71).

CONCLUSION: COMMUNICATION, POWER, AND ETHICS

The crisis of representation represents some unique challenges and opportunities for conceptualizing the relationship between power and ethics. While the resort to foundational principles provides a moral and epistemological center from which to adjudicate social relations, it also creates a "will to totality" that homogenizes otherness and difference, and effectively obscures the sectional interests that inhere in all knowledge claims. On the other hand, decentered and antiessentialist conceptions of truth and subjectivity run the risk of lapsing into a moral relativism whereby difference is celebrated in an uncritical manner; one could argue that this is simply another form of the will to totality that renders critique impossible.

But examined from a communication perspective, another reading of the power-ethics relationship is possible. As I stated earlier in this chapter, the study of ethics is centrally concerned with the ways in which one engages with "the other"; to what extent is the other treated as an object to be strategically manipulated or as a human who fully engages and interrogates our own sense of self? For Levinas (1991), ethical questions arise precisely from exposure to the other—from the call of the other that affects me despite myself. As such, the other demands a response and sensorial engagement that threatens to make us vulnerable.

Deetz (1992) adopts a similar position in his claim that "communication is not for self-expression but for self-destruction." Such a move positions communication not as a conduit for the articulation of already formed identities, but as the process through which self and other are constituted in relationship to each other. Communication, then, is political in that it is intimately connected to processes of identity and meaning construction; however, the opportunities to shape such processes are not evenly distributed amongst social actors and interest groups. Access to communicative and discursive resources heavily shapes abilities to participate in the process of reality construction; that is, to shape what is, what is good, and what is possible (Therborn, 1980).

As we think about the future of a communicative approach to power and ethics, then, we might view it as primarily concerned with how "the differences that make a difference" (Bateson, 1972) are produced, maintained, and reproduced through discursive and material resources. It might focus on how the construction of particular institutionalized differences creates privileged, voiced identities on the one hand, and marginal, voiceless identities, on the other hand. A power–ethics perspective would thus be interested in examining the processes by which a hierarchy of values is strategically and discursively constructed, and in exploring the consequences of this hierarchy for various interest groups; whose interests are constructed as central and privileged, and whose are constructed as marginal and unworthy of consideration?

Power must be examined, then, in terms of how it impacts—either positively or negatively—the possibilities for realizing human beings' life chances. Power and human agency (either individual or collective) is ethical to the extent that it creates possibilities for the greater realization of human community and well-being; it is unethical to the degree that it forecloses life possibilities, or else arbitrarily privileges the realization of some life-chances over others. Such a position is not an argument for—in a relativistic sense—"letting difference be," that is, for letting a thousand differences bloom (Ferguson, 1997), but rather for systematically interrogating the character and consequences of particular articulations of difference. What forms of conflict are suppressed in order that certain configurations of difference prevail (Deetz, 1992)? In a Foucauldian sense, how is difference constructed and institutionalized through games of truth and power–knowledge regimes that normalize subjects as objects of knowledge, both to themselves and others?

Certainly the emergence of feminist, poststructuralist, and postcolonial approaches to human behavior have complicated the ethical landscape precisely because any claims to knowledge and certitude become, well, more uncertain. But at the same time we now have greater and more interesting possibilities for exploring the ways that ethics, power, and communication intersect. Complicating the theoretical landscape produces new ways of looking at the world, new ways of understanding how power functions as a dynamic and multivalent process. Theoretical monotheism tends to lead to bifurcated ways of looking at the world—you either accept the dominant view or you don't. Multiple perspectives enable us to both see the world in a more complex and nuanced manner, and to recognize that no perspective has the answer—each simply provides us with a certain vocabulary, a certain set of possibilities for understanding the world and others, but in each instance that understanding is provisional, contingent, and lacking in certitude (and, one hopes, dogma).

In a postfoundational world, then, ethics do not function to provide a universal set of principles that guide people's lives. Rather, from a communicative perspective, "acting ethically" is a dynamic practice that requires an ongoing awareness of the everyday operation of power, and a willingness to engage "the other" in a manner that is both responsive to his/her/their difference and that opens up the possibility for self-transformation. Ethical practice in the face of power is a risky business because it rejects the monological worldview of "identity thinking" (Adorno, 1973)—of reducing "the other" to "the one" (e.g., a melting pot, assimilationist approach to race)—and embraces dialectical thinking that rejects essentialism, discursive closure, and easy or imposed consensus. Dialectical thought views contradiction as a reality of everyday life and a catalyst for dialogue that is productive of a new, intersubjective, truth, not the reproduction of an existing, sedimented truth (Gadamer, 1960/1989).

Thus, while there is some appeal to Foucault's aesthetics of existence and the kind of ethical agency that he imputes to "the care of the self," ultimately his project seems to be a relatively isolated and lonely affair; as McNay (1994) suggests, Foucault appears to articulate a form of "heroic masculinity" that leaves little room for collaborative engagement with others. I suggest that a true (with a small "t" of course) communicative ethic always recognizes the social character of self and other as they are situated within a broader political, economic, and historical context that embodies particular configurations of power. A communicative ethic explores and opens up the human interests that lie behind knowledge and value claims.

Future power–ethics research thus needs to explore the ever more complex character of the ways that identity, community, and power intersect. The increasing fragmentation of everyday life means that the very idea of community and shared understanding is more fragile, or at least more difficult to sustain in meaningful ways. Human identities are more vulnerable as people are confronted with ever more disparate and yet powerful corporate efforts to shape meanings, values, and the moral frameworks that guide behavior. There has probably never been a time when more vigilance was needed to examine the ways that meanings and identities are appropriated for corporate gain. Communication scholars are particularly well-positioned to critically explore the processes and practices through which meaning systems are strategically constructed to serve the interests of particular groups. Communication ethics research must, at its heart, be an examination of the ways that the possibilities for human growth and community are either constrained or enabled by social actors (individual, group, or institution). Do communication practices work to serve narrow interests and construct politically expedient divisions and differences, or do they work to produce understanding, connection, and a sense of the possibilities that inhere in the human communication condition? It is only by understanding and critiquing the complexities of power and politics as communicative processes that such research agendas can be successfully realized.

REFERENCES

Adorno, T. (1973). *Negative dialectics* (E. B. Ashton, Trans.). New York: Continuum. (Original work published 1966).

Bachrach, P., & Baratz, M. (1962). Two faces of power. *American Political Science Review, 56*, 947–952.

Bachrach, P., & Baratz, M. (1963). Decisions and nondecisions: An analytical framework. *American Political Science Review, 57*, 641–651.

Bateson, G. (1972). *Steps to an ecology of mind*. New York: Ballantine.

Bernauer, J. (1988). Michel Foucault's ecstatic thinking. In J. Bernauer & D. Rasmussen (Eds.), *The final Foucault* (pp. 45–82): Cambridge, MA: MIT Press.

Bourdieu, P. (1984). *Distinction: A social critique of the judgment of taste*. Cambridge, MA: Harvard University Press.

Bourdieu, P. (1991). *Language and symbolc power*. Cambridge, MA: Harvard University Press.

Castells, M. (2009). *Communication power*. New York: Oxford University Press.

Clegg, S. (1989). *Frameworks of power*. Newbury Park, CA: Sage.

Clegg, S., Courpasson, D., & Phillips, N. (2006). *Power and organizations*. Thousand Oaks, CA: Sage.

Dahl, R. (1957). The concept of power. *Behavioral Science, 2*, 201–215.

Dahl, R. (1961). *Who governs? Democracy and power in an American city*. New Haven, CT: Yale University Press.

Deetz, S. (1992). *Democracy in an age of corporate colonization: Developments in communication and the politics of everyday life*. Albany, NY: SUNY Press.

Du Gay, P., & Salaman, G. (1992). The cult[ure] of the consumer. *Journal of Management Studies, 29*, 615–633.

Ferguson, K. (1997). Postmodernism, feminism, and organizational ethics: Letting difference be. In A. Larson & R. E. Freeman (Eds.), *Women's studies and business ethics: Toward a new conversation* (pp. 80–91). Oxford, UK: Oxford University Press.

Foucault, M. (1979). *Discipline and punish: The birth of the prison* (A. Sheridan, Trans.). New York: Vintage. (Original work published 1975)

Foucault, M. (1980a). *Power/knowledge: Selected interviews and other writings 1972–1977* (L. M. Colin Gordon, John Mepham, Kate Soper, Trans.). New York: Pantheon.

Foucault, M. (1980b). *The history of sexuality: An introduction* (R. Hurley, Trans. Vol. 1). New York: Vintage. (Original work published 1976).

Foucault, M. (1982). The subject and power. In H. F. Dreyfus & P. Rabinow (Eds.), *Michel Foucault: Beyond structuralism and hermeneutics* (pp. 202–226). Brighton, UK: Harvester.

Foucault, M. (1986). *The use of pleasure.* New York: Vintage. (Original work published 1984).

Foucault, M. (1988). The ethic of care for the self as a practice of freedom. In J. Bernauer & D. Rasmussen (Eds.), *The final Foucault* (pp. 1–20). Cambridge, MA: MIT Press.

Gadamer, H.-G. (1989). *Truth and method* (J. W. D. G. Marshall, Trans. 2nd ed.). New York: Continuum. (Original work published 1960)

Gramsci, A. (1971). *Selections from the prison notebooks* (Q. Hoare & G. N. Smith, Trans.). New York: International Publishers.

Habermas, J. (1979). *Communication and the evolution of society* (T. McCarthy, Trans.). Boston: Beacon Press. (Original work published 1976)

Habermas, J. (1984). *The theory of communicative action: Reason and the rationalization of society* (T. McCarthy, Trans. Vol. 1). Boston: Beacon Press. (Original work published 1981)

Habermas, J. (1987a). *The philosophical discourse of modernity: Twelve lectures* (F. Lawrence, Trans.). Cambridge, MA: MIT Press. (Original work published 1985)

Habermas, J. (1987b). *The theory of communicative action: Lifeworld and system* (T. McCarthy, Trans. Vol. 2). Boston: Beacon Press. (Original work published 1981)

Habermas, J. (1989). *The structural transformation of the public sphere* (T. Burger & F. Lawrence, Trans.). Cambridge, MA: MIT Press. (Original work published 1962)

Habermas, J. (1990). *Moral consciousness and communicative action* (C. Lenhardt & S. W. Nicholsen, Trans.). Cambridge, MA: MIT Press. (Original work published 1983)

Hall, S. (1983). The problem of ideology: Marxism without guarantees. In B. Matthews (Ed.), *Marx: 100 years on* (pp. 57–84). London: Lawrence & Wishart.

Hall, S. (1985). Signification, representation, ideology: Althusser and the poststructuralist debates. *Critical Studies in Mass Communication, 2,* 91–114.

Hall, S. (1988). *The hard road to renewal: Thatcherism and the crisis of the left.* London: Verso.

Hall, S. (Ed.). (1997). *Representation: Cultural representations and signifying practices.* London: Sage/ Open University Press.

Hebdige, D. (1979). *Subculture: The meaning of style.* London: Methuen.

Holmer Nadesan, M., & Trethewey, A. (2000). Performing the enterprising subject: Gendered strategies for success (?). *Text and Peformance Quarterly, 20,* 223–250.

Horkheimer, M. (1986). *Critical theory* (M. O'Connell et al., Trans.). New York: Continuum. (Original work published 1968)

Horkheimer, M., & Adorno, T. (1988). *Dialectic of enlightenment* (J. Cumming, Trans.). New York: Continuum. (Original work published 1944)

Hunter, F. (1953). *Community power structure.* Chapel Hill: University of North Carolina Press.

Jameson, F. (1984). Foreword. In J-F Lyotard, *The postmodern condition* (pp. vii–xi). Minneapolis: University of Minnesota Press.

Knights, D., & Morgan, G. (1993). Organization theory and consumption in a postmodern era. *Organization Studies, 14,* 211–234.

Knights, D., & Willmott, H. (1999). *Management lives: Power and identity in work organizations.* London: Sage.

Levinas, E. (1991). *Otherwise than being or beyond essence.* Dordrecht: Kluwer Academic Press.

Lukes, S. (1974). *Power: A radical view.* London: Macmillan.

Marx, K. (1967). *Capital* (S. Moore & E. Aveling, Trans.). New York: International. (Original work published 1867)

Marx, K., & Engels, F. (1970). *The German ideology.* New York: International. (Original work published 1845)

Marx, K., & Engels, F. (1969). *Karl Marx and Frederick Engels: Selected Works* (Vol. 1, W. Lough, Trans.). Moscow: Progress. (Original work published 1955)

McCarthy, T. (1990). Introduction to Jürgen Habermas, *Moral consciousness and communicative action* (pp. vii–xiii) (C. Lenhardt & S. W. Nicholsen, Trans.). Cambridge, MA: MIT Press.

McNay, L. (1994). *Foucault: A critical introduction*. Cambridge, UK: Polity Press.

Mills, C. W. (1956). *The power elite*. Oxford, UK: Oxford University Press.

Mumby, D. K. (1997). Modernism, postmodernism, and communication studies: A rereading of an ongoing debate. *Communication Theory, 7*, 1–28.

Mumby, D. K. (2001). Power and politics. In F. Jablin & L. L. Putnam (Eds.), *The new handbook of organizational communication: Advances in theory, research, and methods* (pp. 585–623). Thousand Oaks, CA: Sage.

Pfeffer, J. (1981). *Power in organizations*. Cambridge, MA: Ballinger.

Ricoeur, P. (1970). *Freud and philosophy: An essay on interpretation* (D. Savage, Trans.). New Haven, CT: Yale University Press.

Therborn, G. (1980). *The ideology of power and the power of ideology*. London: Verso.

Tracy, S. J. (2000). Becoming a character for commerce: Emotion labor, self-subordination, and discursive construction of identity in a total institution. *Management Communication Quarterly, 14*, 90–128.

Trethewey, A. (2001). Reproducing and resisting the master narrative of decline: Midlife professional women's experiences of aging. *Management Communication Quarterly, 15*, 183–226.

Willis, P. (1977). *Learning to labor: How working class kids get working class jobs*. New York: Columbia University Press.

Wray-Bliss, E. (2009). Ethics: Critique, ambivalence, and infinite responsibilities (unmet). In M. Alvesson, T. Bridgman, & H. Willmott (Eds.), *The Oxford Handbook of Critical Management Studies* (pp. 267–285). Oxford, UK: Oxford University Press.

7

What Are We, Then?

Postmodernism, Globalization, and the Meta-Ethics of Contemporary Communication

Bryan C. Taylor and Leonard C. Hawes

INTRODUCTION

Not so long ago, use of the term *postmodernism* provoked widespread enthusiasm, anxiety, and outrage in audiences as they confronted growing disenchantment with traditional sources of authority and dramatic upheavals of tradition. More recently, however, the concept has aged and settled, scarred by the reactionary vitriol of its critics, and encrusted by its institutionalization in contemporary architecture, business, education, and religion. There (and seemingly everywhere), "postmodernism" has become a condition, a topic, a slogan, and a bid for legitimacy. It has been enshrined, condemned, and generally sustained as the master-sign of a controversial, "rapidly-changing world" (see Best & Kellner, 2001; Hutcheon, 2002).

Nonetheless, there may still be "news" for communication scholars about postmodernism and its discontents, including the growing articulation of postmodernist questioning with the phenomena of *globalization* (see, e.g., the chapters by Munshi, Broadfoot & Smith, and Splichal in this volume). Increasingly, these two fields of discourse converge around the challenges posed by economic, political, technological, and environmental change for adequate knowledge and just conduct of the social world. In this process, postmodernism is resituated as a counterdiscourse that is affiliated with oppositional projects such as feminism, postcolonialism, and queer theory. Its subsequent identity politics display "a focus on difference and ex-centricity, an interest in the hybrid, the heterogeneous, and the local, and an interrogative and deconstructing mode of analysis" (Hutcheon, 2002, p. 166). Unavoidably, this deconstruction has affected the theory and practice of ethics, rocking foundational premises such as universally applicable moral principles, the moral autonomy of the individual, and the linkage between questions of human rights and the authority of nation states (Benhabib, 1992, p. 2).

It is our task in this chapter to interpret and illustrate the consequences of such developments for *communication ethics*. We proceed below by first, reviewing key premises of postmodern ethical philosophy. Next, we consider the implications of this work for the distinctive theory and practice of communication ethics. Then, we illustrate the variety and potency of these implications by profiling the work of two philosophers who have interrogated ethics at the meta-theoretical level: Alasdair MacIntyre and Alain Badiou. In each case, we review major claims in the key works of these authors, and discuss their contributions to scholarship in postmodern communication ethics. Throughout, we are guided by the claim that "[Postmodern] ethics is not a mere vision of things to come…rather, it is a way of mediating and transforming hierarchical relations between ideas and things, self and others, so that they become interactive, resourceful, and creative" (Ilcan, 2004a, p. 27).

CONSEQUENCES OF POSTMODERNISM FOR THE THEORY AND PRACTICE OF ETHICS

Surveying the body of work denoted by "postmodern ethics" is a formidable task. It encompasses over four decades of dense and complex argument conducted by Anglo-American and European Continental scholars who work in a variety of disciplines, and whose positions have evolved over that period. That work is characterized as much by dispute as by agreement, and the possibility of characterizing core ideas in this genre is challenged by postmodernism's premise that certain knowledge-claims are at best illusory. Thus, we offer here a selective discussion of key themes and issues that organize this ongoing conversation as a relatively coherent enterprise. Readers desiring further discussion should consult primary sources by figures such as Jean Baudrillard (1990), Zygmund Bauman (1993, 1995), Seyla Benhabib (1992), Gilles Deleuze (1984), Jacques Derrida (1965/1978), Michel Foucault (1975/1979, 1976/1980), Jean Francois Lyotard (1979/1984; Lyotard & Thébaud, 1985), and Richard Rorty (1997).

In our reading, the following four claims are central to the postmodern conceptualization of ethics:

First, *"ethics" is a central—not auxiliary—discourse in human affairs*. In politicizing the expression and regulation of "otherness," postmodernism undermines the traditional positioning of ethics within academic and cultural hierarchies (e.g., as a derivative of analytic philosophy). Instead, postmodern theorists breach the boundaries opposing politics and ethics in several ways. Most importantly, they deny the independent existence of prior knowledge from which ethical priorities may be reliably derived. As a result, postmodern ethics is classified variously as a postfoundationalist, postessentialist, and postmetaphysical project (Gabriel & Ilcan, 2004; Madison & Fairbairn, 1999; McCance, 1996). Its associated theory is developed according to "a *non-specific normative purpose* as it unsettles our comfortable sense of there being authoritative descriptions of ethics and/or ethical norms upon which we can confidently depend" (Wilmott, 1998, p. 79; emphasis in original). Postmodern theorists such as Michel Foucault also assert that claims of morality, knowledge, and power are *mutually constituted* (Ilcan, 2004a). In this view, such claims arise simultaneously and interdependently in cultural discourse; not discretely in sequence, or according to logics of subordination. One consequence of this condition is that social structure is an inherently ethical human "project," because it is devoted to ensuring the predictability of preferred meanings and practices (Baumann & Tester, 2001, pp. 44–45). Additionally, postmodernists reverse the priority of ontology over ethics in social theory by noting that, rather than an ethic depending upon a particular social reality for its justification, a social reality must first justify itself by recourse to an ethical discourse (Baumann & Tester, 2001, p. 54).

Second, *alterity—the conceptualization and practice of Otherness—is the central concern of ethics*. If nothing else, postmodernity is a condition of heightened sensitivity to Otherness, in which cultural subjects increasingly encounter mysterious, stimulating (and sometimes threatening) difference. The objects of those encounters include both mediated representations, and also immediate companions and interlocutors. While this situation is capable of producing many different outcomes (e.g., cosmopolitan self-regard), it is frequently experienced as conflict and uncertainty, in which the grounds for ethical agreement are not only unknown but impossible to determine (Baumann & Tester, 2001, p. 46): "We have too many competing and incommensurable sacred names" (Caputo, 1993, p. 34). While this concern is not unique to postmodern ethics, that work is distinctive in asserting Otherness as a primordial precondition that organizes the very possibilities for meaningful and moral encounter.

Crucial to this claim is the work of French philosopher Emmanuel Levinas (1982/1985), whose concepts of "face" and "responsiveness" emphasize the haunting imperative created by excluded, repressed, and deprived others (e.g., the child, the homeless, the insane, the outcast, etc.). This effect is created as those actors exercise their signifying capabilities, which include *being chosen by* a spiritual "third party" as a vehicle for ethical animation. In all cases, human witnesses are required, somehow, to answer the summons issued by another's face (Kearney, 1999; Rutland, 2004). Generally, this work depicts our existence as fundamental susceptibility to modes of influence expressed by others with whom we work, play, struggle, love, and die (Wyschogrod, 1996). Caputo (1993, p. 6) summarizes this condition as: "Obligation happens." For Levinas, we continuously orient to voices that instruct, seduce, assert, plead, and command. We are always-already addressed, and there is no escape, no liberation, from this sentence (Caputo, 1993, p. 14; Kearney, 1999, p. 22). What is at issue, instead, is our production of an utterance (a *said*) that resonates with the possibilities for approach and relationship (i.e., for *saying*) evoked by these types of encounters.

Ethics, in this view, arises from mutual and reflexive vulnerability and engagement. It emerges through the symbolic practices by which we invite each other to empathize with our respective situations, and by which we respond to those invitations (Butler, 1996). This is particularly true in "disasters" (such as genocide) where the Other's performance of suffering does not serve our convenience, and ruptures our otherwise-comforting presumption that we are, as a species, willing and able to care for each other (Caputo, 1993, p. 28). Such performances stimulate in us powerful forms of feeling such as surprise, disgust, fear, and compassion. They induce a range of noncognitive responses, including duty, tolerance, indifference, resentment, and rejection (Carroll, 1996). In contrast to the traditional Western presumption of reciprocity, likeness, and symmetry in personal relationships, this perspective emphasizes asymmetry and heterogeneity.

A third theme central to postmodern ethics is that *the ethical agent is constituted in and through discourse.* This claim arises from a convergence of poststructuralist, feminist, and psychoanalytic challenges to the modernist narrative of the knowing, ontologically primary subject (Rutland, 2004). Historically, that "humanist" narrative emphasizes features and capabilities such as the prior existence of an objective Self, whose depth and uniqueness is revealed through its actions; a disembodied consciousness which disdains the unreliability of emotion in favor of cognitive rationality; and a unitary identity which serves as the engine of intention.

Central to these challenges is the claim that human identity arises from *subjectivity* formed in the "hailing" of human consciousness by cultural discourses which have preorganized the possibilities for self-understanding in the service of ideological narrative (Benhabib, 1992; Wilmott, 1998). In postmodern ethical theory, this claim is coupled with an understanding that the human ego (particularly that of the liberal, Western "individual") misunderstands its linguistically contingent Self as distinctive and autonomous, and mistakenly believes that it is according the Other in social interaction a similar ontological status. However, the subject in these encounters is actually engaged in unacknowledged practices of desire, reduction, assimilation, and projection. These unconscious practices are animated by myth and irrationality; they engulf the Other's actuality, and confine its potential to those identities of difference (e.g., infidel, client, etc.) upon whose reproduction the ethical subject depends for its fulfillment and coherence (e.g., as modern, care provider, etc.) (Wyschogrod, 1996). In this process, the integrity of the Other is compromised by its subordination to the binary, Self-serving logic of the Same.

As a result, the Other *persists*. For Levinas, the Other's face bears a *trace* of "infinity that we cannot see, but that nevertheless enters into language" (Jovanovic & Wood, 2004, p. 317). That trace resonates as "an indescribable depth of the difference between the self and the other" (p. 317); it both compels and forever exceeds ethical communication. The Other is thus a ghostly figure resurrected by our nostalgia and regret. It returns through the gaps and failures of our logic to beckon, admonish, parody, and generally stimulate our wisdom. It lingers around and beyond our encounters as a poetic and hyperbolic remainder, a radical singularity that resists all efforts at totalization and annihilation (Caputo, 1993; McCance, 1996).

This theory thus alerts us to the productivity of judgment and service as ethical practices which appear to be performed in the interest of their object, but which are more properly understood as the mastery of difference necessary for refreshing the otherwise precarious and transient subjectivity of their agents (Bernstein, 1992). However, the shift in Foucault's *oeuvre* between the themes of *power-knowledge* (which held that ethics is inseparable from the institutional constitution of the subject as an object of both "truthful" discourse and disciplinary power), and of *technologies of the self*, indicates how this position also allows for more positive and expansive conceptions of agency. In the latter set of studies, Foucauldian "ethics" involves the creative and dynamic process by which the self invents, cultivates, and deploys itself *as a particular kind of subject*, through the intensively embodied practices of technical-aesthetic fashioning and stylized transgression. Potentially, in these practices of self-care, the masterful subject resists limited and oppressive subject positions offered by culture, and approaches transcendence and fulfillment (Bernstein, 1992, p. 146; Bevir, 2007, p. 140; McCance, 1996, p. 127).

In any case, however, postmodern theory establishes the ethical encounter not as the rational execution by transcendental subjects of universal strategies (i.e., those conforming to moral codes), but as the *mutual talking into presence and consequence* of ethical possibilities for immediate and embodied relationships.

In our final theme, *the deconstruction of moral organization is both necessary and insufficient*. As discussed above, postmodern theory "impiously" refuses to specify or endorse a fixed, natural, or original source of ethics (and thus a foundation for critique) that would permanently resolve controversy among the participants in moral conflict (Bernstein, 1992, pp. 148–152). Traditional touchstones rejected by this post-Nietzschean philosophy include Being, Freedom, God, History, Reason, and Spirit. Here, Caputo's (1993, p. 5) whimsical confession is apt: "I have…lost all communications from On High. My satellite has been knocked out." As a result, postmodern ethics studiously defers the development of concrete prescriptions and interventions in conflicts. This position is taken partly out of solemn respect for the failure, tragedy, absurdity, and violence that potentially arise when we presume certain knowledge of the Other, and employ that knowledge in derivative disciplines (e.g., of instruction, conversion, and cure). Here, the assumption is that, in prescribing speech, moral codes also render us (partly) speechless (Caputo, 1993, p. 12). Deconstruction thus seeks to remember what the moral law, in its quest for generality, prefers to minimize: its dependency for accuracy and success on fulfilling the complex and evolving needs of actors in their local situations (Caputo, 1993, p. 88). This position also arises from the recognition that specifying the content of ethical programs renders resistance vulnerable to distortion and appropriation by the institutions of bourgeois society (Bevir, 2007).

Philosophically, this rejection of the "treacherous" promise of universal guarantees enjoins ethical actors to engage in the longest possible "earthbound" conversation about the role of difference in their situations. As a result, they may approach (but never exhaust or possess) the ideal of justice (i.e., by letting each other *be*; Bernstein, 1992, pp. 73, 185). In this view, ethical action is both impossible (i.e., as a perfect fulfillment of abstract ideals) and inevitable (a practical human activity). However, continuous questioning and reflection by actors—their observation of a "flashing yellow [traffic] light" (Caputo, 1993, p. 4)—increases the possibility that they can interrupt and revise the otherwise facile, automatic, and "terrorizing" administration of truth-as-moral-priority (McCance, 1996, p. 40). For Derrida, for example, an ethical "decision" does not achieve *its own* ethical potential unless the actors engaged in that process concede the hopelessness of their completely considering all relevant possibilities, and reject the presumption that conventional wisdom and formal codes are adequate to achieve the justice sought (Bernstein, 1992, p. 214). In this counterintuitive logic, acknowledging the "self-deceptive illusion" that we can "eliminate violence from our language, institutions, and practices" is held to *contribute to* the realization of ethical integrity (Bernstein, 1992, p. 217).

This position is, not surprisingly, itself subject to judgment, with verdicts ranging from a brilliant, facilitation of acute vigilance and humility, to a mystifying—even nihilistic—abandonment of necessary grounds for resolving ethical dispute in favor of "narcissistic hedonism and an irrationalist relativism" (Bevir, 2007, p. 145; see also Caputo, 1993, p. 3; Feldman, 1998). In particular, postcolonial and feminist scholars dispute the apparently limited and frivolous dimensions of postmodern ethics that deprive oppressed groups of practical resources (i.e., necessary fictions of agency) to address the injustice of their situation as raced and gendered subjects (Benhabib, 1992, p. 214; Hutcheon, 2002, p. 174). One aching question, then, remains how this theory may normatively ground its claims (e.g., in the necessity of practicing reversible perspective-taking to achieve sound moral judgment; Benhabib, 1992, p. 54), and assist ethical actors to achieve the desirable ends of increased self-understanding, dignity, solidarity, and representation.

One sympathetic interpretation of this situation is that the rigorous deconstruction of ethical tradition creates the possibility of a new kind of relationship between human freedom and responsibility. We may not yet have adequate language to express this relationship, but in our capacities as "finite, embodied and fragile creatures" (Benhabib, 1992, p. 5), we are nonetheless invited—if not compelled—to develop it. For dedicated postmodern ethical actors, the question subsequently arises: *What might we become for each other, here and now, if we are no longer certain of our requirements in this situation, if we do not repeat what we already know how to do, and if we instead seek to adequately understand and respond to the difference that we embody and express?* Here, actors reject the allure of *monologue* (i.e., distancing the Other through unaccountable judgment) and *analog* (unreflectively assimilating the Other by using familiar models and categories). They seek, alternately, to achieve a dialogic encounter that "challenges rigid cultural boundaries, fosters voices from the margin, and forms a counter-position to hegemonic practices" (Ilcan, 2004b, p. 227). New possibilities emerge as these actors tentatively, unexpectedly, collaboratively, and intuitively develop alternate wisdom. In this vision, one speaking turn may build upon another to create a sufficiently binding intimacy: "The only sacred names we require are proper names" (Caputo, 1993, p. 34). For ethical actors, this wisdom is potentially compelling because of its adequacy for their situation, and because they (mostly) made it themselves. Examples of this kind of useful heresy include: "We might be more 'secure' if we were less 'safe'"; "We might do better work if we did less work"; "We might have more agreement if we were more tolerant of dissent"; and, "We might do more Good if we acknowledged how we also do Evil." Postmodern ethics thus involves radical openness to human plurality and creativity in the service of innovating virtue. "Of the Good, I can only say: come. I cannot say what it is, but what it is not. Let it happen" (Caputo, 1993, p. 40).

CONSEQUENCES FOR THE THEORY AND PRACTICE
OF COMMUNICATION ETHICS

The implications of postmodernism for the theory and practice of communication ethics have been rich and provocative. Postmodern ethical theory engages phenomena that have historically been central to the communication discipline's claim upon ethics, including: language, discourse, meaning, practice, culture, dialogue, argument, narrative, identity, relationship, and community. These implications have been developed by various scholars in attempts to conceptualize a distinctive agenda for the postmodern theory and practice of communication ethics (see Arneson, 2007; Arnett, 2001; Arnett, Arneson & Bell, 2006; Cooper, 1996; Hallstein, 1999; Hawes, 1998; Johannesen, 2001). In our reading, two themes are central to this project.

The first theme involves *the necessity of reconceptualizing communicative agency following the decentering of the ethical subject*. Here, scholars focus partly on assimilating the challenge posed by postmodernism to modernist traditions (e.g., empiricism) in communication theory and research. Smith (1997), for example, notes how the enduring conception of *a priori* subjects who constitute phenomena in the service of certainty and sameness inhibits recognition of their subjection to Otherness, and of their constitution through "adventurous" responsiveness to mystery. Not all voices present in an ethical encounter, Smith notes, are obviously recognizable to researchers. Those voices are no less effective, however, in interrupting, hailing, and refashioning us, operating outside our orthodox conceptions of communication form and content.

This focus also entails developing a compelling and coherent image of the subject in order to represent the integrity of ethical practice. If, as some postmodernists hold, "fragmented" moral agents are not preexisting or autonomous, and are merely effects of determining discourses, how may we explain their choice to affiliate with or diverge from particular discourses of responsibility? Here, the commitment of communication scholars to document the granularity of social action adds fleshy substance to theoretical images of ethical actors. As a result, we may better understand how they are hailed by multiple discourses, and how their response provides them with capabilities (however imperfect) for managing tension (e.g., arising from disappointment and discomfort) generated through their encounters with difference. Significantly, in this view, actual ethical agency is a site of struggle between determining and resistant forces. It "emerges from a dialectical synthesis of free will and [the] recognition of situatedness within cultural and institutional constraints." As a result, ethical agency represents freedom "discovered" by actors within those obligations, and yields "embedded significant choice" (Arnett, 2001, p. 317). In postmodernism, then, "responsible" ethical agents are those whose abilities to respond are developed and supervised in ongoing relationships. If there is virtue still to be found in communication, in this view, it does not emanate from the objective validity of a particular theory, or the character of an individual speaker. Instead, it is accomplished by actors in reflectively nurturing the potential for mutual recognition and transformation that is opened through the process of their encounter (Bracci, 2007, p. 29).

Our second theme involves *affirmation of the ongoing quest "to find meaningful ways to deliberate across differences about ethical issues"* (Makau & Arnett, 1997, pp. x–xi). This affirmation identifies another opportunity opened by postmodern ethics for conceptualizing communication outside of modernist principles such as binarism, consensus, linearity, persuasion, stability, and strategy. For social actors and theorists, the challenge of achieving ethical deliberation and judgment is particularly acute in postmodern contexts of fragmentation (Johnstone, 2007, p. 14). In these contexts (e.g., of identity politics), "difference" is increasingly embraced by actors as a warrant for their creation of exclusive groups nurtured by a shared narrative of grievance, and of self-protection dependent on the maintenance of internal similarity and cohesion.

In this view, however, while difference has emerged as a central trope of postmodern communication ethics (Arnett et al., 2006, p. 64), its immanence in actual situations requires the temporary configuration of interests through practices such as negotiation. Potentially, this condition inspires optimism toward postmodernism as "the era of welcome…to learning and difference" (Arnett, 2007, p. 62).

Generally, then, postmodern theory creates new possibilities for communication ethics by reprivileging traditionally marginalized elements such as fragility, ephemerality, suspension, tactics, "gender, empowerment, decentered selves, multiple narratives, and ethical pluralism" (Bracci, 2007, p. 29). Developing these possibilities requires communication scholars and practitioners to *stay put and be questioned by* [Otherness] if one hopes to make a difference…" (Smith, 1997, p. 343; emphasis in original). As a result, they may promote humane forms of contestation that meet the needs of postmodern culture. If they wish their projects to succeed, however, those actors must sensitively design and administer normative constraints in order to encourage the broadest possible participation from Others, without perpetuating structures of exclusion and alienation (Bracci, 2007). Additionally, the absence of ethical foundations in postmodernism requires an enhanced tolerance by communicators for the immediate, embodied performance of difference as *narrative* (i.e., that successfully evokes its integrity for the purposes of just deliberation and desirable cultural change). This process, as noted above, requires a modification—if not rejection—by ethical actors of the presumption that logical *argument* should be the sole, default mode of communication in ethical dispute.

GOING DEEPER: EXPLORING THE WORKS OF TWO CONTEMPORARY PHILOSOPHERS AND THEIR IMPLICATIONS FOR COMMUNICATION META-ETHICS

Alasdair MacIntyre

Alasdair Macintyre's *After Virtue* (1981/2007; hereafter, *AV*) is considered "the most influential work in the field of virtue ethics" today (Herrick, 1992, p. 142). Scholars in this field believe that the central focus of morality involves habits and knowledge developed in response to the question of how one should live one's life. In this view, good moral judgment arises from the development of a virtuously formed character, in which one's moral action is consistently directed to its correct ends. As a result, the exercise of good judgment by a virtuous person in an ethical dispute is considered more important than the standardized administration of rules. Also, the excellence of a virtuous practice is considered a superior criterion for evaluating an ethical action, compared with its conformity to obligatory customs, or the nature of its produced consequences (see Johannesen, 2001, pp. 214–215).

After Virtue offers a scathing indictment of modern moral philosophy, and a proposal for its correction. Specifically, MacIntyre argues that contemporary culture is profoundly disordered, characterized by "unresolved and apparently unresolvable" (*AV*, p. ix) ethical conflicts in which the normative statements of participants are not only opposed, but lack an adequate metadiscourse in which their incommensurability might be worked out. These statements commonly invoke impersonal standards of morality, but their alleged objectivity and rationality is belied by their "shrill and assertive" tone (*AV*, p. ix).

MacIntyre attributes these interminable performances to a cultural condition of "emotivism," in which moral judgments are believed to be the unique creations of sovereign "individuals," who express their personal attitudes and partisan preferences (*AV*, pp. 11–12). Emotivism is, for

MacIntyre, an ahistorical discourse which prevents willful and competing assertions of moral claims from achieving rational conclusion through the use of inherited tradition (it also prevents actors from recognizing this very condition). Additionally, emotivism is problematic because its indifference to external accountability (e.g., to shared criteria for evaluating proffered good reasons) reduces ethical argument to contests of personal influence and irrational "manipulation" (e.g., involving the use of charisma; *AV*, p. 23). In this process, ethical debate devolves to consider the selection of means, because conflict over ends cannot be concluded. The modern ethical self developed in emotivism, then, is mobile and fragmented, inhabiting roles with associated codes, but with no unifying, overarching narrative to provide coherence. That subject subsequently oscillates between the existential experience of excessive freedom and of oppression by arbitrary authority (*AV*, p. 35).

MacIntyre attributes this sterile and frustrating situation to philosophy's abandonment during the European middle ages and early Modernity of a continuous historical foundation for grounding moral precepts in "a shared conception of the human good" (*AV*, pp. ix–x). In the absence of this grounding, Enlightenment philosophers from the 18th-century on were able to produce only "rival and incompatible" (e.g., Kantian and contractarian) accounts of moral judgment. The philosophical and public discourses of morality subsequently "passed from a state of order to a state of disorder," in which key terms of moral philosophy, and the historical logic that organized them as a coherent project, disintegrated. Such projects were doomed to failure (*AV*, p. 52).

That abandoned foundation is Aristotelian moral theory (principally encoded in the *Nicomachean Ethics*), which depicts ethics as the science enabling humans to move from their current state to fulfill their true, potential nature—the *telos* which represents *both* a desired end-state *and* a continuous spur to faithful ethical practice (*AV*, p. 175). "Virtues," for MacIntyre, are thus those qualities of action which enable us "to achieve that good of rational happiness which it is peculiarly ours as a species to pursue" (*AV*, pp. 52–53)—the *eudaimonia* of "being well and doing well in being well…in relation to [both oneself and] the divine" (*AV*, p. 148). In discarding this scheme, Enlightenment-era philosophers rejected a conception of human nature which provided consistent justification for the content of specific moral injunctions. Modern ethical actors are subsequently unable to answer "what it is in virtue of which a particular moral judgment is true or false" (*AV*, p. 60). In this view, the ethical question "What sort of person am I to become?" is superior to the question, "What rules ought we to follow?" (p. 118).

For MacIntyre, the ancient and classical traditions of Western culture idealize heroic virtues such as courage (particularly in the service of friendship), cunning (as compensation for lack of courage), agreeableness, and *phronesis* (i.e., knowing how, based upon an accurate assessment of one's relevant rights and responsibilities, to exercise judgment in particular situations). The protagonists of ancient myth are continually engaged in conflicts which typify a culture's narratives for how an individual may live well in the face of inevitable fragility, vulnerability, and misfortune, and also for what is exemplified by that form of living. In this process, irony (i.e., self-aware detachment) is precluded from ethical action; instead, the integrity of that action is located "inside" a particular worldview, and its associated performance is accountable to local bonds of social structure such as friendship, family, and community (*AV*, pp. 126–127, 137–138). This constraint constitutes the authority and legitimacy of our situated moral judgments. As a result, they may acquire adequate properties of truth and falsehood in our debate with others. Universal morality is thus, for MacIntyre, an illusion, as is a complete escape from inherited traditions.

MacIntyre argues that in order to understand the historical concept of virtue, it is necessary to understand three contributing stages in its development. The first stage involves a virtue's enactment as a *practice*—as a cooperative, social activity in which "internal goods" are realized as actors conform to relevant rules and standards of excellence that define a performance of that activity as successful. Such conformity sustains both the integrity of a skillful performance, and its collective (and often intangible) benefits for both the performer and his or her society. In this process, the devotee of a practice communes both with current ethical actors, and also with the ghostly community of historical performers from whom current actors inherit a tradition of good form (*AV*, p. 194). In this process, however, the exercise of virtue potentially conflicts with the interests of *institutions*, who are concerned with appropriating the "external goods" of practices—and thus with disciplining those practices to ensure their predictability, productivity, and profitability (*AV*, p. 194).

The second stage in the development of a virtue outlined by MacIntyre involves its embedding within "the narrative order of a single human life" (*AV*, pp. 187–188), such that a virtuous performance "enabl[es] an individual to make of his or her life one kind of unity rather than another" (*AV*, p. 203). Here, the performance of virtue ideally repairs modernity's liquidation through aggregation of the self as a collection of dissociated roles. Ideally, a virtuous performance enables us to integrate our accounts of our short-term intentions with accounts of our long-term goals, and, finally, with accounts of how those goals support a particular *telos*. For MacIntyre, all ethical practice presupposes a *conversation* in which that practice may be depicted as intelligible and legitimate; its performance constitutes a statement which can only be understood within actors' biographical narratives—which ideally reflect cultural *telos* (*AV*, pp. 211–212). Ethical practices are thus events in unfolding stories that actors are continuously authoring and narrating, both to themselves and to other actors. Within these stories, ethical actions are justified as alternately realizing and foreclosing the achievement of particular personal and cultural futures. Statements concerning "What I am doing and why I am doing it" thus do not represent the emission of personal beliefs, but are instead events in the ongoing, collaborative constitution of the self-as-ethical-story. In particular, virtues confirm the story of life as a particular kind of journey: "as those dispositions which—sustain us in the relevant kind of quest for the good, by enabling us to overcome the harms, dangers, temptations, and distractions which we encounter, and which will furnish us with increasing self-knowledge and increasing knowledge of the good" (*AV*, p. 219). The virtuous society, notes MacIntyre, creates social contexts in which quests can successfully be conducted. Significantly, the good is not so much *discovered* by persons in these quests (i.e., as the preexisting, known object of a search) as it is *constituted* through their associated interaction, reflection, and learning. In this way, *telos* partly—but not entirely—determines a quest.

The third stage involves the contribution of a virtue to a particular moral tradition. For MacIntyre, virtuous practice directly affects the "inheritance" of cultural knowledge which actors must draw upon in order to render their actions intelligible to each other. It alternately maintains and transforms associated institutions as ongoing sites of "argument" about the viability of that tradition. More specifically, virtues sustain "those traditions which provide both practices and individual lives with their necessary historical context" (*AV*, p. 223), thus enabling actors to make successful choices from among candidate maxims. One disaster of modernity, in MacIntyre's view, is that its moral philosophy has failed to foster a durable, rational understanding of how—beyond the mere following of rules—a human being's quest to achieve their individual *telos* may articulate with the quest for the common good (*AV*, p. 232).

The argument of *After Virtue*, subsequently, forms one vision of how that disaster may be mitigated. This repair occurs as ethical actors strive to understand and debate what a virtuous life should be in the period of late modernity. In this process, they contemplate what the good life should be for human beings, including seeking after the good life for all persons, and cultivating smaller "goods" such as friendship. They continuously reflect on their practices, not to relativize and dismiss tradition, but to enhance their awareness. This is because those practices indicate their performers' intentions, which depend for their coherence on accountability to the biographical narratives of those performers, and to their respective cultural narratives of excellence and purpose. Finally, ethical actors seek to construct "local forms of community, within which civility and the intellectual and moral life can be sustained" (*AV*, p. 245). In maintaining the mutual constitution of virtuous practices, personal biographies, and cultural narratives, MacIntyre concludes, those actors may also redeem the value of moral philosophy.

MacIntyre's vision of virtue ethics[1] has proven compelling for communication scholars in a variety of subfields and affiliated disciplines (Arnett, 2001; Aucoin, 1992; Farrell, 1984, 1991; Fisher, 1984, 1990; Frentz, 1985; Herrick, 1992; Lambeth, 1990; Leeper & Leeper, 2001; McNamee & Gergen, 1999; Pearce & Freeman, 1984; Shotter, 1997; Sullivan & Martin, 2001). These disciplinary responses display three central themes.

The first theme involves endorsement of MacIntyre's characterization of emotivism, and of the traditions, as *dynamic contexts of communication*. Here, connections are drawn to related concepts of postmodern communication such as dialogue, difference, fragmentation, multiplicity, narrative competition, reflexivity, situated interests, and undecidability (Arnett, 2001; Shotter, 1997). "In a world lacking full dialectical closure for practical questions," notes Farrell (1991, p. 207), rhetoricians must "ask what proofs and possible modes of conviction might best adjudicate conflicts among partisan positions." McNamee and Gergen (1999, p. 9) note that the competitive individualism associated with emotivism inhibits actors' development of "responsibility" towards *relationships* as the proper source and object of ethical communication.

A second theme involves affiliation with those elements of MacIntyre's argument which establish communication (and its august relative, rhetoric) as *the principal means by which virtue is socially developed*. Here, for example, Shotter (1997, p. 106) characterizes MacIntyre's conception of tradition as a source of "second-order arguments" that shape the form, content, and style of cultural members' specific argumentation. Arnett (2001, p. 333) argues that establishing the narrative foundation of virtues revises their monolithic and canonical status, rendering them available for collaborative and consensual development through reflective ethical *praxis*. Pearce and Freeman (1984, p. 68) characterize MacIntyre's argument thus: "Historically, moves to new ways of moral decision making depend on and occur in pockets of people of good will, who can explore with each other novel ways of relating without threatening or being threatened." Finally, rhetorical theorist Walter Fisher has invoked MacIntyre's observation "that human beings are essentially storytellers" (1990, p. 246) to develop his Narrative Paradigm, which focuses on audiences' use of the principles of "coherence" and "fidelity" to assess their communication experience.

Rhetoricians take issue, however, with MacIntyre's denouncement of emotivism. Specifically, they protest his limited—even Platonic—conception of rhetoric for ignoring its historical status as the necessary, ongoing process of morally deliberating contingent matters of public interest under inevitable conditions of disagreement and uncertainty. In this way, they argue, MacIntyre fails to appreciate rhetoric as the medium through which narrative traditions are made available to actors *as* potential resources for ethical argument (e.g., through modes of address inherent to cultural institutions of education and socialization), thus forming a crucial bridge between abstract tradition and local practice. In this view, traditions can only be perpetuated through persuasive acts of appeal and justification, and their viability sustained through practical demonstrations of their situational appropriateness. Should MacIntyre's bias go unanswered in moral philosophy and civic life, these scholars conclude, the "internal goods" of rhetoric itself—including its cultivation of practical wisdom and identification in the reasoned interaction between speakers and audiences—would be stifled (Farrell, 1984; Fisher, 1990; Frentz, 1985; Peters, Lyne & Hariman, 1991).[2]

As suggested by this opposition, the third theme in Communication's reception of MacIntyre's work is reflexive, and concerns the extent to which communication and rhetoric *may them-*

selves be conceptualized as a virtuous practice. Here, for example, journalism is considered as a communal craft that is historically embedded in professional tradition (e.g., public service), that strives for moral standards of excellence (e.g., justice, courage, honesty, and rigor), and that struggles in the process against temptation (e.g., for "revenge on deadline"; Aucoin, 1992, p. 170) and the corrupting force of media-ownership institutions (Lambeth, 1990). The virtuous practice of public relations, similarly, realizes its "internal goods" of developing and maintaining community among an organization and its stakeholders (Leeper & Leeper, 2001). And for technical communicators, narrative accounts are a superior form of deliberation in ethical conflicts because they depict how their subjects' actions are (or should be) sensitively oriented towards particular others and traditions. In this process, those subjects may avoid "unpersuasive" stories that "justify…actions by defining them as mere technical operations designed to achieve a predetermined end outside the agent's control" (Sullivan & Martin, 2001, p. 269). Finally, Herrick (1992, p. 133) argues that rhetorical virtues "are discovered by examining the goods inherent to rhetoric"—such as responsible invention, public advocacy, and testing of claims through the clash of debate— "as well as the sources of cooperation and the standards of excellence implied by the practice of rhetoric." Three virtues which realize these goods include: (1) skillful "acumen" in inventing and evaluating arguments; (2) the "honest" tendency to not "willingly mislead" audiences; and (3) the "cooperative" willingness to resolve conflict through means other than violence and coercion.

Having completed this review, we are now able to reflect on the relationship between MacIntyre's virtue ethics and postmodern ethics. While we may wish to definitively classify or reject the former as a case of the latter, that path leads to problems arising from the internal complexity and ambiguity of each discourse. As a result, it seems better to ask where and how they affiliate and diverge in their respective positions.

Regarding *similarities*, we can say that both MacIntyre and postmodern theory represent critiques of the shortcomings and liabilities of modernity—particularly the rise of scientific rationality and bureaucratic domination (McMylor, 2001; Watson, 2001, pp. 678–679). Both also reject the conduct of inquiry from a standpoint independent of a particular tradition. Both accept that permanent resolution of ethical dispute may not be possible—although situated dialogue and persuasion are. Both emphasize the constitution of personal and group identity through relationships with traditional narratives; as a result, both invite the critical analysis of cultural practices and texts as media for this constitution.

Regarding their *differences*, we can say that MacIntyre seeks to repair the chaos of emotivism by reviving Aristotelianism, while the more celebratory strands of postmodernism privilege continuous and productive play between competing traditions. In this way, although MacIntyre and the postmodernists *agree* about the contemporary condition of virtue fragmentation, he does not *endorse* it. Second, to the extent that postmodernists oppose historical narrative as a determination of human conduct, they oppose both the general principle of scripted *telos* which founds MacIntyre's vision of right human development, and the necessity of submitting to a particular cultural tradition. In this way, MacIntyre's dutiful quest for virtue contrasts with Lyotard's (1984; cited in Tsoukas & Cumming, 1997, p. 673) conception of "the inventor's paralogy," in which ethical actors practice openness and experimentation, and tolerate even incomplete and inconclusive outcomes. Finally, we may note that MacIntyre is no post-structuralist in his conceptualization of the role of discourse in shaping identity and agency. That is, his account of the subject arguably contains ontological residues of "robust individuality" (if not individualism; on this point, see Solomon, 2004, p. 1023) and voluntarism. These residues conflict with strong postmodern traditions concerning the linguistic constitution of intersubjectivity as a radically situated, material, embodied, spatial, and temporal micropractice (see Collier, 1998; Hancock, 2008; Hawes, 1998). As a result, future communication research utilizing MacIntyre could usefully depict ethical actors engaged in virtuous quests for narrative integration while preserving the discursive contingency of that process.

Alain Badiou

We turn now to profile our second contemporary ethical metatheorist. Alain Badiou's *Ethics: An Essay on the Understanding of Evil* (2001; hereafter *Ethics*) is an aggressive critique of contemporary liberal-humanist and neoliberal ethical thought. In this work, Badiou argues that contemporary ways of framing ethics, such as bioethics and human rights, predicated as they are on a tolerance of difference and a reverence for Other, are little more than "a jumbled confusion of legalistic formalism, scandalized opinion, and theological mystification" (Hallward, front cover of Badiou, 2001/1998). For Badiou, ethics thus amounts to a thoroughgoing critique of "the ideology of ethics." In its place, he offers "an ethic of truths."

What does this critique involve? Contemporary liberal-humanism and neoliberalism, Badiou argues, operate between two philosophical poles: a vaguely Kantian pole grounded in the abstract universality of human rights, and a vaguely Levinasian pole predicated on the irreducibility of the alterity of the Other. For Badiou, the ideology of ethics begins from the *a priori* Kantian assumption that the world is Evil; the responsibility of ethics is to identify Evil, to intervene in order to do Good to Evil, and to do this out of reverence for the Other. Countering, Badiou claims that the world is neither inherently Good nor Evil. Rather, it is simply what it is: *immanent*. In fact, the *a priori* of Evil actually *reproduces itself* in the process of intervening to do Good. Without the innate capacity to do Good, there could be no Evil.

Let us further consider Badiou's argument. Specifically, he argues that an "ethic of truths" sustains and inspires a disciplined subjective adherence to a truth. Rather than insisting on and enforcing the objectivity of some universal Truth, Badiou stipulates four domains of truth. It is disciplined adherence to a truth of these domains, he argues, that constitutes an ethic of truths. These four domains of truth define four associated domains of philosophy, including love, art, science, and politics. Each of these domains demarcates the possible subjectivities that a truth affirms and that a subject bears. Love, for example, pertains to individuals, and politics to collectivities. Art and science combine individual bodies, which in turn serve as collective vehicles. We suggest, however, that these four domains of truth extend beyond philosophy and point toward a uniquely postmodern communication ethics that entails a love, art, science, and politics of rhetorics and truths.

Badiou further explicates an ethic of truths, in which a truth is considered a universal singularity rather than the general universality. For Badiou, a universally singular truth is universally true in its singular address, reception, and application. Such a truth is universally true for one speaker or another, but it is not necessarily true for both of them, or for anyone else. Nor should, Badiou believes, a universally singular truth be imposed on others as though it were a general universality. Making this critical distinction between general universality and universal singularity, we argue, makes it possible to install a love, art, science, and politics of rhetoric, and thus a postmodern communication ethic of truths.

Following this thread, we see that Badiou advocates a rigorous and disciplined adherence to affirming an ontological truth (or a cause). He distinguishes between the militaristic imposition of the Truth on Other (i.e., as supposedly for the Good of Other) and a militant adherence to a truth that overtakes a body's mere mortality. Militaristic imposition in ethical conflicts, he argues, insists on its Truth, on an ethical ideology of Other and a reverence for Difference whose hegemony supposedly increases as the population of its adherents increases. Badiou thus appeals to an ethical militancy of immortal value that operates beyond negative rights and mortal privileges of the Truth. It is by means of being captured by a truth, he holds, that mortals become caught up in the immortality that a truth and its ethic makes possible. Such a truth is revealed by an *event*, a radical break in and from the realm of ordinary, commonsense knowledge. Events form a rupture in the dominance of the supposedly seamless hegemony of the status quo.

For Badiou, events are situated at the edge of a void of incomprehensibility, around which is organized the prevailing hegemony. Badiou understands events, then, as the conditions of possibility for access to the realm of truths. As a sudden, wholly subjective incorporeal transformation, an event is marked by a radical and profound shift that takes place in and on the body and the psyche of a subject. In the radical disorientation of knowledge and desire brought on by an event, a consummating and consuming truth incorporeally transforms a body into its subject and its bearer. That truth subsequently reveals itself with a profound clarity and without any rational bases. Different truths may become apparent to different bodies with respect to different domains of subjectivity, that is, love, art, politics, and science.

A truth thus revealed is, for Badiou, neither good nor evil morally, in and of itself. Instead, an ethic of truths becomes relevant for consideration and judgment in terms of *how* subjects of truth hold that truth. Does one affirm its fidelity or betray it? Does one discern a truth from its "simulacra," or is one deceived? And does one live immortally in a truth of universal singularity, or does one mistake it for the Truth and impose it on others as though it were a universal generality? Fidelity to a truth entails, then, the tireless, passionate work of not betraying or otherwise abandoning it. Discernment thus distinguishes delusion from the immortality of a truth. Attending to differences of banal reality, recognizing details so that their significance can be assessed critically and aesthetically, and noticing approximations of truth are all matters of discernment. A singular truth can have an indefinite number of zones of singular application, but each application of a truth requires subtlety, reflexivity, and discipline to make appropriately nuanced distinctions.

Restraint is the third challenge to an ethic of truths. The thrall of a truth revealed in an event can easily invert itself. Instead of being consumed by it and consummated with its immortality, agency becomes flipped. In this process, the subject to a truth becomes the agent of Truth, consuming Other with Truth by consummating Other as Same. Instead of achieving the universal singularity of a truth, militaristic imposition produces terror—which is to say that it produces Evil in the process of doing Good to/for Other. Recall here that Badiou's provocative claim is that Evil comes from Good, not the other way around. Tragedy is thus produced by assuming that a partisan and singular truth that is universal in its singular address is uniform in its universal application. A truth of immortal and universal address is thus mistaken for the received Truth that ought to be (i.e., that morally deserves to be) uniformly applied. To impose a truth on Other as the Truth is to betray a truth, mistaking it for the transcendent delusions of authoritarianism, imperialism, colonialism, totalitarianism, fascism, and terrorism.

We may see, then, how betrayal, delusion, and terror produce Evil on individual, familial, communal, organizational, institutional, regional, national, and international planes of life. Indeed, we find a multitude of such tragic expressions of goodness in our interdependent "globalized" world. Rather than tasking ethics with the job of valorizing difference by attempting to practice tolerance of the Other, Badiou begins with the assumption that difference is the condition of the world. As such, difference is—in and of itself—not particularly interesting. Of much greater interest for Badiou is the ethically challenging task of recognizing *the coming of the Same* (i.e., that which is not yet, is indifferent to difference, and is becoming). Difference matters, of course, but it is not for Badiou the primary focus, once the coming of the Same (i.e., a truth born of event and which pervades difference) becomes apparent. Instead, it is the coming of the Same that renders difference as indifference by traversing it, cutting across it, and pervading it by means of flowing through it, not by transcending it.

What then is the status of Other, of difference, amid the coming of the Same? For Badiou, any experience whatsoever is the expression of infinite differences. A body's reflexive experience of subjectivity is not evidence of unity, but rather of a labyrinthine system of differentiations. There are as many differences between any two bodies on the planet as there are elements of a singular body; as many, but neither more nor fewer. The difficulty for ethics here lies not on the side of difference but on the side of Same. It is not as if differences do not exist; quite obviously they do—to infinity. And that is Badiou's point. But they are for him of little interest insofar as differences constitute the banal multiplicities of immanence. The principle to be affirmed is that since difference is quite simply what is, and since every truth is a coming to be of what is not yet (i.e., the coming of the Same), differences are precisely what truth procedures depose and render insignificant. A truth is that to which the advent of the Same comes to be. It is in this sense that a truth is indifferent to differences (pp. 25–27). The Same is what must be produced and may come to be through the disciplined adherence to a truth. That truth is not founded on some privileged part of the situation, but is instead born of event. Again, for Badiou, asserting a substantial and/or a communal conformity that aggressively liquidates difference always produces Evil.

Such an ontology assumes that there is no One, no Whole, no Totality, only multiples without One. The law of being, then, is an unbounded multiple of multiples, and its only stopping point is the void, which is the vortex of any organized form of life. Around this void, languages, cultures, and worldviews are organized. Badiou relies here on Pascal for the insight that the infinite is the banal reality, rather than the predicate of transcendence of every situation (p. 25). Every situation, then, is composed of infinite elements, and each element is itself a multiple. Whereas the ethical ideology of difference and of Other holds that one transcends the banal particulars to reach infinity (i.e., the One), an ethic of truths assumes that the banal particulars of difference are infinite. As a result, the coming of the Same is recognized by means of passionately applying a disciplined truth procedure to the infinite elements of a concrete situation.

For an event to have transformational consequences, some body must recognize and name the break *as an event*. This recognizing and naming of an event is what Badiou refers to as an intervention, which is the first moment of a process of fundamental change. An intervention inaugurates a truth procedure, which amounts to a series of inquiries that ask into and map out the implications of the shattering consequences of an event. Those inquiries are what open up and unfold prior singularities as new multiples "stripped bare of any predicates, any identity" (Badiou, 2005, p. 21). Those who recognize and name an event are militants, that is, those who act in fidelity to a truth of an event by inquiring about its situation and entailments. "The object of these enquiries is to work out how to transform the situation in line with what is revealed by the event's belonging to the situation" (Badiou, 2005, p. 21).

To our knowledge, there is currently no published work addressing the implications of Badiou's work for postmodern communication ethics. As an illustration of the possibilities for that application and extension, we briefly explore here contemporary debates surrounding the controversy over universal human rights. We begin by noting that Badiou sees the confusion over the ethics of human rights as stemming largely from four mistaken presumptions: first, that Evil is what predominates in the world; second, that we must recognize Evil; third, that human rights are conceptualized negatively to address and prevent Evil; and finally, as a result, that universal human rights have to do with everyone's being protected from Evil. For Badiou, remember, "evental" sites are situated vulnerably at the edge of a void, break from the categories of approved ordinary knowledge, and thereby evade categorization and classification. As a result, they possess no "ethics in general," no generally universal principles of human rights. What is universally singular is immanence; what is universally general is transcendence. And transcendence to universal generalities accounts for the irony of Evil being produced by attempts to do Good to it.

Let us consider further the specific ideology of the ethics of *human rights*. According to Badiou, this ideology rests on four presuppositions: (1) there is a general human subject that is a passive, pathetic, and reflexive (i.e., a subject who suffers), yet that subject is also an active determining subject of judgment; (2) politics is subordinated to ethics: it is the sympathetic and indignant judgment of the spectator that counts; (3) Evil is that from which Good is derived, not the other way about; and (4) human rights are rights to non-Evil, rights to not be offended or mistreated with respect to one's life, one's body, or one's cultural identity (Badiou, 2005, p. 9). In short, this is a conception of ethics that constitutes humans largely as victims. Ironically, Badiou notes, invoking the prevailing conventional ethical principles in human rights disputes does little other than reinforce the ideology of the status quo. Consequently, an ethics framed as negative human rights is incapable of sustaining carefully situated and decisive interventions insofar as they lack a coherent and sufficiently nuanced conception of Evil. In response, Badiou argues for a superhuman integrity in place of a respect for merely human rights, a partisan universality in place of negotiating merely particular interests, and an "immortal" value in place of our merely mortal privileges.

Against this negative and "victimary" conceptualization of humans, Badiou advances three theses in opposition. Thesis 1: "Man (sic) is to be identified by his affirmative thought, by the singular truths of which he is capable, by the Immortal which makes of him the most resilient and paradoxical of animals" (2005, p. 16). Thesis 2: "It is from our positive capability for Good, and thus from our boundary-breaking treatment of possibilities and our refusal of conservatism, including the conservation of being, that we are to identify Evil—not vice versa" (2005, p. 16). And Thesis 3: "All humanity has its root in the identification of thought [*en pensée*] of singular situations. There is thus no ethics in general. There are only—eventually—ethics of processes by which we treat the possibilities of a situation" (2005, p. 16).

Future communication scholarship could develop this illustration by considering how an increasingly important question in these debates involves the pragmatic consequences of invoking human rights discourse in the midst of conflict. By contrast, invoking it during *post*-conflict peace-building and adjudicatory processes may have quite different consequences. If the objective is to stop or at least curtail abuse and violence, does the reactionary deployment of human rights discourse accomplish that objective? We do not question here whether humans ought to have certain rights recognized and acknowledged. Rather, it is a question of whether making those morally grounded arguments (founded as they are on human rights values, rhetorically deployed as they are by means of human rights discourse) reduces or exacerbates conflict and the violations of human rights overall. There is evidence, for example, that claiming human rights during a conflict actually hardens positions; draws critical fire; widens gaps that separate conflicting factions; raises the stakes at issue; moralizes what had previously been framed in pragmatic, political and economic terms; and abstracts what are singularities and practicalities. As a result, communication scholars might utilize Badiou to problematize naturalized and moralized assumptions about the form and content of "human rights" discourse employed in international conflict. As a result, they may develop a postmodern communication ethic of truths in the immanence of the certain material realities of incommensurable differences. This ethic opens onto very different topologies of scholarship and intervention.

CONCLUSION

Postmodernists have mixed feelings about conclusions, noting that the persistent residues of phenomena often exceed, evade—and return to embarrass—overconfident declarations of "mission accomplished." As a result, we eschew certainty that this—or any other—account will somehow get postmodern ethics "right," once and for all. Instead, this chapter is—à la Geertz (1973)—an enthusiastic imperfection intended to stimulate further, and increasingly useful, disagreement and investigation. We began by arguing that, as the concerns of postmodernism and globalization increasingly merge, the field of communication ethics is challenged to reconsider its modern-ist positions concerning the ethical subject and the practice of discourse in ethical situations. It is a cliché to note that "everything is connected": Nonetheless, this phrase usefully reminds us that, amid the ongoing volatility of global politics, economics, society, and the environment, the study of communication ethics remains *central* for describing, interpreting, critiquing, and intervening in the ways that social actors symbolize phenomena for the purposes of understand-ing and influencing them. If ethics is at least partly implicated by the effects of our actions, then communication undergirds our existence within increasingly complex, sensitive, and powerful networks of responsibility. In this way, our choices may be more important than we know, and if we wish to know more, we can examine how our communication both positions us in a network of relations with Others, and provides us with resources for evaluating that actuality in relation to other possibilities. In considering these alternatives, postmodernism invites us to rely not only on the familiar voices of common sense, but also radical narratives promoted by the wise, angry, incoherent, grief-stricken, consoling, and sublimely indifferent Others who surround us in time and space. Engaging these voices can be Ego-destroying—a profound experience that can be alternately exhilarating, liberating, and terrifying. But, should we muster the courage to risk that experience, we may avoid pointless and destructive repetition, and *account* for our positions in a spirit that is usefully ironic (see Rorty, 1989). That is, postmodern ethical communicators might choose to declare the following: *We commit to exploring the sources and consequences of our actions, and to justifying those actions through an ongoing conversation with those affected. That conversation will proceed under the assumption that any values and truths invoked are not universal, objective, or inevitable, but are resources for practically accomplishing adequate un-derstanding, agreement, and cooperation in the here and now.* Whether we prefer to call it love, democracy, or war, in other words, we can resign ourselves to continuous and humane struggle (Peterson, 2007). Whatever name it is conducted under, that struggle should involve mindful rela-tions with the range of voices that come calling when we seek to do what is called for.

To develop this argument, we reviewed the work of two philosophers with very different re-lationships to postmodern ethics, and considered the implications of their work for scholarship in specifically communicative ethics. Alasdair MacIntyre's work, we saw, imagines how we might respond to—if not escape—the ethical cacophony and amoral rationality of persistent modernity. That response involves rigorous reflection and ongoing accountability to traditional narratives of excellence and virtue that potentially create at-one-ment between the elements of one's autobiog-raphy, and between that autobiography and one's professional and cultural heritage.

Alternately, Alain Badiou's work sustains and revises typical characterizations of "postmod-ern ethics" in several important ways. First, he claims that there are four domains of truth—love, art, science, and politics—in the abyss of a void that an event opens up. This opening thereby makes it possible to reimagine not only a postmodern politics, but postmodern love, art, and science as well. To the extent that postmodernism is confused all too frequently with relative ethics, it has been difficult if not impossible to imagine a postmodern politics. Where was the foundation of such a politics? What were its handholds? We have learned that an event produces a break from ordinary knowledge, and that a named event inaugurates the emergence of a truth that can be betrayed, mistaken, or terrorized—that can be sustained by a truth procedure. As a result, the rhetorical moment of naming of an event is of crucial importance. Badiou refers to this moment as an intervention, that is, the first moment of a process of fundamental change. Such a fundamental change can emerge from the domain of love, art, science, or politics, but an event must be named for a truth procedure to be inaugurated. And a postmodern communication ethics is necessary for any truth procedure to be sustained. As the proposed research program on "human rights" discourse demonstrates, that ethics would concern itself with communicative and rhetorical practices which sustain that truth procedure. Such practices would affirm fidelity, discernment, and restraint of a truth of love, art, science, and politics. A postmodern communication ethics, in this light, would insist on positive rights and on recognizing the coming of the Same. It would not continue along the ideological lines of negating difference and valorizing the Other by insisting on negative rights.

In this way, the work of MacIntyre and Badiou suggests how postmodern ethical theory opens onto several new territories for innovative scholarship and practice in communication ethics. The journey into these territories is not for the faint of heart, or for those seeking (only) the comforts of familiarity, affirmation, and continuity. However, it is increasingly clear that the options for a safe and predictable existence organized around monologue and homogeneity are shrinking, and may only be maintained at great cost to Self and Others. For better and worse, whether we like it or not, we continue to be called upon by difference. This chapter has explored the form and content of a distinctively—although not univocally—*postmodern* response.

NOTES

1. Developed further in the volumes *Whose Justice? Which Rationality?* and *Three Rival Versions of Moral Enquiry: Encyclopaedia, Genealogy, and Tradition.*
2. Here, the issue seems to pivot on ambiguity in Aristotle's work involving (a) his formal distinction between intellectual and moral virtues, (b) his predominant classification of phronesis in the former category, and (c) his linkage of both categories in characterizing the actual practices surrounding phronesis (Tsoukas & Cummings, 1997, p. 666).

REFERENCES

Arneson, P. (Ed.). (2007). *Exploring communication ethics: Interviews with influential scholars in the field.* New York: Lang.

Arnett, R. C. (2001). Dialogic civility as pragmatic ethical praxis: An interpersonal metaphor for the public domain. *Communication Theory, 11,* 315–338.

Arnett, R. (2007). A conversation about communication ethics with Ronald C. Arnett. In P. Arneson (Ed.), *Exploring communication ethics: Interviews with influential scholars in the field* (pp. 53–68). New York: Lang.

Arnett, R. C., Arneson, P., & Bell, L. M. (2006). Communication ethics: The dialogic turn. *Review of Communication, 6,* 62–92.

Aucoin, J. (1992). The Arizona Project as a MacIntyrean moment. *Journal of Mass Media Ethics, 7,* 169–183.

Badiou, A. (2001). *Ethics: An essay on the understanding of evil* (P. Hallward, Trans.). London: Verso. (Original work published 1998)

Badiou, A. (2005*). Badiou: Infinite thought* (O. Feltham & J. Clemens, Trans. & Ed.). London: Continuum.

Baudrillard, J. (1990*). Fatal strategies.* Cambridge, MA: MIT Press.

Bauman, Z. (1993). *Postmodern ethics.* Oxford, UK: Basil Blackwell.

Bauman, Z. (1995). *Life in fragments: Essays in postmodern morality.* Cambridge, UK: Polity.

Bauman, Z., & Tester, K. (2001). *Conversations with Zygmunt Bauman.* Cambridge, UK: Polity.

Benhabib, S. (1992). *Situating the self: Gender, community and postmodernism in contemporary ethics.* Cambridge, UK: Polity Press.

Bernstein, R. J. (1992). *The new constellation: The ethical-political horizons of modernity/postmodernity.* Cambridge, MA: MIT Press.

Best, S., & Kellner, D. (2001). *The postmodern adventure: Science, technology, and culture at the third millennium.* New York: Guilford Press.

Bevir, M. (2007). "A kind of radicality": The avant-garde legacy in postmodern ethics. In M. Bevir, J. Hargis, & S. Rushing (Eds.), *Histories of postmodernism* (pp. 131–148). New York: Routledge.

Bracci, S. L. (2007). A conversation about communication ethics with Sharon L. Bracci. In P. Arneson (Ed.), *Exploring communication ethics: Interviews with influential scholars in the field* (pp. 21–36). New York: Lang.

Butler, C. (1996). Postmodernism and moral philosophy. In G. Hoffmann & A. Hornung (Eds.), *Ethics and aesthetics: The moral turn of postmodernism* (pp. 69–86). Heidelberg: Universitätsverlag C. Winter.

Caputo, J. D. (1993). *Against ethics: Contributions to a poetics of obligation with constant reference to deconstruction.* Bloomington: Indiana University Press.

Carroll, N. (1996). Moral realism in the age of postmodernism. In G. Hoffmann & A. Hornung (Eds.), *Ethics and aesthetics: The moral turn of postmodernism* (pp. 87–96). Heidelberg: Universitätsverlag C. Winter.

Collier, J. (1998). Theorising the ethical organization. *Business Ethics Quarterly, 8,* 621–654.

Cooper, M. (1996). Decentering judgment: Toward a postmodern communication ethic. In J. M. Sloop & J. P. McDaniel (Eds.), *Judgment calls: Rhetoric, politics, and indeterminacy* (pp. 63–83). Boulder, CO: Westview Press.

Deleuze, G. (1984). *Nietzsche and philosophy.* London: Athlone.

Derrida, J. (1978). *Writing and difference* (A. Bass, Trans.). Chicago, IL: University of Chicago Press. (Original work published 1967)

Farrell, T. B. (1984, February). [Review of the book *After virtue: A study in moral theory*, by A. MacIntyre]. *Quarterly Journal of Speech, 70,* 96–98.

Farrell, T. B. (1991). Practicing the art of rhetoric: Tradition and invention. *Philosophy and Rhetoric, 24,* 183–212.

Feldman, S. P. (1998). Playing with the pieces: Deconstruction and the loss of moral culture. *Journal of Management Studies, 35,* 59–79.

Fisher, W. R. (1984). Narration as a human communication paradigm: The case of public moral argument. *Communication Monographs, 51,* 1–22.

Fisher, W. R. (1990, Summer). [Review of the book *Whose justice? Whose rationality?* by A. MacIntyre]. *Philosophy and Rhetoric, 23,* 242–247.

Foucault, M. (1979). *Discipline and punish: The birth of the prison* (A. Sheridan, Trans.). New York: Vintage. (Original work published 1975)

Foucault, M. (1980). *The history of sexuality: Vol. I. An introduction* (R. Hurley, Trans.). New York: Vintage. (Original work published 1976)

Frentz, T. S. (1985). Rhetorical conversation, time, and moral action. *Quarterly Journal of Speech, 71,* 1–18.

Gabriel, B., & Ilcan, S. (Eds.). (2004). *Postmodernism and the ethical subject.* Montreal, Canada: McGill-Queen's University Press.

Geertz, C. (1973). *The interpretation of cultures: Selected essays.* New York: Basic Books.

Hallstein, D. L. O. B. (1999). A postmodern caring: Feminist standpoint theories, revisioned caring, and communication ethics. *Western Journal of Communication, 63,* 32–56.

Hancock, P. (2008). Embodied generosity and an ethics of organization. *Organization Studies, 29,* 1357–1373.

Hawes, L. (1998). Becoming other-wise: Conversational performance and the politics of experience. *Text and Performance Quarterly, 18,* 273–299.

Herrick, J. A. (1992). Rhetoric, ethics, and virtue. *Communication Studies, 43,* 133–149.

Hutcheon, L. (2002). *The politics of postmodernism* (2nd ed.). London: Routledge.

Ilcan, S. (2004a). From modernity to postmodernity. In B. Gabriel & S. Ilcan (Eds.), *Postmodernism and the ethical subject* (pp. 25–37). Montreal, Canada: McGill-Queen's University Press.

Ilcan, S. (2004b). The marginal other: Modern figures and ethical dialogues. In B. Gabriel & S. Ilcan (Eds.), *Postmodernism and the ethical subject* (pp. 227–253). Montreal, Canada: McGill-Queen's University Press.

Johannesen, R. L. (2001). Communication ethics: Centrality, trends, and controversies. In W. B. Gudykunst (Ed.), *Communication Yearbook*. 25, 201–235.

Johnstone, C. L. (2007). A conversation about communication ethics with Christopher Lyle Johnstone. In P. Arneson (Ed.), *Exploring communication ethics: Interviews with influential scholars in the field* (pp. 1–20). New York: Lang.

Jovanovic, S., & Wood, R. V. (2004). Speaking from the bedrock of ethics. *Philosophy and Rhetoric, 37,* 317–334.

Kearney, R. (1999). The crisis of the image: Levinas's ethical response. In G. B. Madison & M. Fairbairn (Eds.), *The ethics of postmodernity: Current trends in continental thought* (pp. 12–23). Evanston, IL: Northwestern University Press.

Lambeth, E. B. (1990). Waiting for a new St. Benedict: Alasdair MacIntyre and the theory and practice of journalism. *Journal of Mass Media Ethics, 5,* 75–87.

Leeper, R. V., & Leeper, K. A. (2001). Public relations as "practice": Applying the theory of Alasdair MacIntyre. *Public Relations Review, 27,* 461–473.

Levinas, E. (1982/1985). *Ethics and infinity: Conversations with Philippe Nemo* (R. A. Cohen, Trans). Pittsburgh, PA: Duquesne University Press.

Lyotard, J. F. (1984). *The postmodern condition: A report on knowledge* (G. Bennington & B. Massumi, Trans.). Minneapolis: University of Minnesota Press. (Original work published 1979)

Lyotard, J. F., & Thébaud, J. L. (1985). *Just gaming.* Minneapolis: University of Minnesota Press.

Macintyre, A. (1981/2007). *After virtue: A study in moral theory* (3rd ed.). Notre Dame, IN: University of Notre Dame Press.

Madison, G. B., & Fairbairn, M. (1999). Introduction. In G. B. Madison & M. Fairbairn (Eds.), *The ethics of postmodernity: Current trends in continental thought* (pp. 1–11). Evanston, IL: Northwestern University Press.

Makau, J. M., & Arnett, R. C. (Eds.). (1997). *Communication ethics in an age of diversity.* Chicago, IL: University of Illinois Press.

McCance, D. (1996). *Posts: Re addressing the ethical.* Albany: SUNY Press.

McMylor, P. (2001). Classical thinking for a postmodern world: Alasdair MacIntyre and the moral critique of the present. In K. Flanagan & P. C. Jupp (Eds.), *Virtue ethics and sociology: Issues of modernity and religion* (pp. 21–34). New York: Palgrave.

McNamee, S., & Gergen, K. J. (1999). *Relational responsibility: Resources for sustainable dialogue.* Thousand Oaks, CA: Sage.

Pearce, W. B., & Freeman, S. (1984). On being sufficiently radical in gender research: Some lessons from critical theory, Kang, Milan, and MacIntyre. *Women's Studies in Communication, 7,* 65–68.

Peters, J. D., Lyne, J. R., & Hariman, R. (1991, February). [Review of the book *Whose justice? Whose rationality?* by A. MacIntyre]. *Quarterly Journal of Speech, 77,* 82–84.

Peterson, T. R. (2007). Response: Nuclear legacies and opportunities for politically and ethically engaged communication scholarship. In B. C. Taylor, W. J. Kinsella, S. P. Depoe, & M. S. Metzler (Eds.), *Nuclear legacies: Communication, controversy, and the U.S. nuclear weapons complex* (pp. 237–254). Lanham, MD: Lexington.

Rorty, R. (1989). *Contingency, irony, and solidarity.* Cambridge, UK: Cambridge University Press.

Rorty, R. (1997). *Truth, politics and "postmodernism".* Assen, the Netherlands: Uitgeverij Van Gorcum.

Rutland, B. (2004). The transject: The ethical subject of postmodernity. In B. Gabriel & S. Ilcan (Eds.), *Postmodernism and the ethical subject* (pp. 75–87). Montreal, Canada: McGill-Queen's University Press.

Shotter, J. (1997). On a different ground: From contests between monologues to dialogical contest. *Argumentation, 11,* 95–112.

Smith, A. R. (1997). The limits of communication: Lyotard and Levinas on otherness. In M. Huspek & G. P. Radford (Eds.), *Transgressing discourses: Communication and the voice of other* (pp. 329–351). Albany: SUNY Press.

Solomon, R. C. (2004). Aristotle, ethics and business organizations. *Organization Studies, 25,* 1021–1043.

Sullivan, D. L., & Martin, M. S. (2001). Habit formation and story telling: A theory for guiding ethical action. *Technical Communication Quarterly, 10,* 251–272.

Tsoukas, H., & Cumming, S. (1997). Marginalization and recovery: The emergence of Aristotelian themes in organization studies. *Organization Studies, 18,* 655–683.

Watson, P. (2001). *The modern mind: An intellectual history of the 20th century.* New York: Harper-Collins.

Wilmott, H. (1998). Toward a new ethics? The contributions of poststructuralism and posthumanism. In M. Parker (Ed.), *Ethics and organizations* (pp. 76–121). London: Sage.

Wyschogrod, E. (1996). Towards a postmodern ethics: Corporeality and alterity. In G. Hoffmann & A. Hornung (Eds.), *Ethics and aesthetics: The moral turn of postmodernism* (pp. 53–68). Heidelberg, Germany: Universitätsverlag C. Winter.

8

Decolonizing Communication Ethics
A Framework for Communicating Otherwise

Debashish Munshi, Kirsten J. Broadfoot,
and Linda Tuhiwai Smith

Communication ethics are always already historically, materially, politically, socially situated and yet the universalizing framework through which they are often constructed is still overwhelmingly Western (Rao & Wasserman, 2007). This largely Western framework is, in some ways, a legacy of communication theory itself which is 'limited by Eurocentric cultural assumptions' (Craig, 2007, p. 256). Our aim in this chapter is to decolonize communication ethics by arguing that Western Enlightenment notions of rationality, justice, and humanity are not necessarily transferable to other contexts and times in their totality without an engagement with issues of social injustice that arise from the ideological, intellectual, and imperial domination of Western thought and theory. Drawing insight from scholars from Asian (e.g. Miike, 2007) and American Indian (Covarrubias, 2007) backgrounds who have sought to 'provincialize communication theory as a Eurocentric field' (Miike, 2007, p. 277), we argue that communication ethics too is largely guided by Western contexts.

Like Rao and Wasserman (2007), we take a postcolonial approach to understanding the nature of ethics. Such an approach explores how individuals and institutions perform active interventions in their worlds focused on the goals of global compassion, justice, and hope (Prasad & Prasad, 2003). As Rao and Wasserman (2007) point out, 'the strength of postcolonial theory is that it provides us with a critical framework that validates the local epistemologies necessary for the formulation of global ethics, and acknowledges the unequal power relationships in which various cultures and nations are historically positioned' (p. 34).

We realize that neither the 'West' nor Enlightenment-influenced notions of liberalism are monolithic. While, on the one hand, subaltern historiographers have established links between liberalism and colonialism (see e.g., Prakash, 1990), other scholars have demonstrated how human rights are indeed an essential part of Western liberal thought (see e.g., Charvet & Kaczynska-Nay, 2008). We also realize that although postcolonial approaches are critical of the 'West', they are not necessarily totally at odds with universalism. As Amselle (2006) points out, the work of the postcolonial scholar Dipesh Chakrabarty, for example, 'tends towards universalism' (p. 191) despite the strong case he makes for 'provincialising' Europe. Further, Ivison (2002) argues that 'the debate between liberals and postcolonial theorists (and other critics of liberalism) is not actually between "universalists" and "particularists," but, it seems, between different conceptions of the universal' (p. 45).

Fundamental to our thesis in this chapter, however, is the argument that Western Enlightenment conceptions of universal have historically been framed as the Universal in discussions of ethical principles. 'In Enlightenment discourse,' Hall (1996) says, 'the West was the model, the prototype, and the measure of social progress' (p. 221). This Western model continues to dictate not only social progress but also moral and ethical progress.

The postcolonial project, in conjunction with Foucauldian ethical analysis, demands that individuals and institutions ask provocative questions and create 'spaces' to reflect on how different forms of communicative practice take on particular moral dimensions. Such a project also examines which moral obligations are recognized, how individuals and institutions can combine intellectual and practical concerns of specific contexts to ethically inform their work and, finally, what kinds of communicative practices they aspire to construct when acting in a moral way.

What we propose in this chapter is to construct a framework for creating ethical spaces and forms of practice that recognize and include unique, subjective experiences and practices that shape individuals and institutions in a diverse, globalizing, world. In order to pursue global social justice, individuals and institutions operating globally need to excavate and elevate the unheard or muted voices within communities that lie subsumed under mainstream discourses of communication ethics. It is this framework that will allow the conceptualization of what we call Communicating *Other*wise to inform and transform communication ethics from a multivocal, postcolonial set of standpoints. More specifically, we use insights from indigenous Kaupapa Maori theory and practice in the country of our birth/residence, Aotearoa-New Zealand, to explore/imagine the communicative practices and ethics necessary to create what Bhabha (1994) calls a 'space in between' for authentic dialogue in a multicultural environment. But before we make this space, let us problematize the ethical ground.

PROBLEMATIZING THE ETHICAL GROUND: ETHICAL ANALYSIS AND THE ETHICAL INDIVIDUAL

While communication ethics expansively incorporates diverse cultural values and transcends particular differences on the ground (see e.g., Christians & Traber, 1997), they remain embedded in a 'capitalist system and globalization theory which speak of ethics' but 'hide the fact that their ethics are those of the marketplace and not the universal ethics of the human person' (Freire, 1998, p. 114).

One example of this manifestation of ethics is the notion of Corporate Social Responsibility (CSR) which, its lofty ideals notwithstanding, is oriented toward maximizing profits for the largely Western shareholders of corporations that continue to disrupt the lives and livelihoods of indigenous and poorer peoples of the Third World (Adeola, 2001; Munshi & Kurian, 2005). The market-driven ethics of CSR, which often leads to cynical 'greenwashing' (Athanasiou, 1996; Beder, 2000), privileges the interests of Western publics and markets over the ones in the Third World (see Munshi & Kurian, 2005, 2007 for an expanded discussion). Similarly, extensive programs under the banner of multiculturalism showcase diversity but as the Australian aboriginal activist, Helena Gulash, points out 'there has been very little practical help forthcoming or offered' from those who organize all-embracing cultural festivals 'to actually help us get our land back' (Cuthbert & Grossman, 1997, p. 57). At the level of scholarly research too, extensive bodies of socially and ethically conscious 'health-related research has been conducted about indigenous populations around the world, but appears to have had little impact on their overall wellbeing' because, in line with a 'Native saying, "researchers are like mosquitoes; they suck your blood and leave"' (Cochran et al., 2008, p. 22). At best, the communicative strategies of expansiveness in the mechanisms of ethics have a self-satisfying effect on dominant groups but do not necessarily encompass the aspirations of social justice for those at the margins.

In essence, therefore, the universal values of communication ethics are weakened by the fact that they are neither political nor contextual. As a result they are tied to the very liberal tradition that is associated with the justification of colonialism (Alfred, 2005). As the Native American scholar Taiaiake Alfred (2005) says, unlike Western ethics, which focuses on acts simplistically labeled 'good' and 'evil', 'non-Western cultures 'put acts in context of a situation' (p. 54). The 'crucial process', he says, is 'contextualizing the whole experience and trying to figure out why the act was done and what made the person do it, so as to determine whether the act was evil or not' (Alfred, 2005, p. 54; Dalai Lama, 1999). It is this lack of adequate contextualizing and reflexivity that allows Western codes of ethics to be habitually breached by dominant groups.

Such ethnocentric positions on 'good' and 'evil' have led to several onslaughts on *Other* peoples in the name of 'Just' wars ranging from colonial invasions (e.g., in Africa, Asia, and the Americas and the present-day conflicts in Iraq) to the 'civilizing missions' in Australasia. However, to unshackle communicative practices and conceptualizations of ethics from what Gonzalez (2003) describes as '"rules" set forth by the imperial force' (p. 83) requires a critical ontology of the self or a '...critique of what we are at one and the same time the historical analysis of the limits imposed on us and an experiment with the possibility of going beyond them' (Foucault, 1984, p. 50). In so doing, ethics becomes an aesthetic phenomenon residing in how individuals should concern themselves with themselves, making themselves subjects of their own attention (Rose, 1996). Such ethical reflection and analysis is rarely undertaken in the construction of argument.

In an insightful examination of predatory vs. dialogic ethics, however, Cannella and Lincoln (2007) actively engage an ethical analysis of Foucault to examine the regulatory and personal ethics which underpin most qualitative research and argue that the embodied moral self is a relational activity. Foucault saw ethical analysis as having four components—ethical substance, mode of subjectivation, ethical work, and *telos* (Rabinow, 1997). The first component, *ethical substance,* is also known as the 'will to truth' or the ways in which individuals constitute themselves as the material of their conduct. The 'will to truth' or 'that which enables one to get free from oneself' is embodied in our curiosity about how forms of thinking take on particular moral dimensions, such as commitments to social justice (Foucault, 1985, p. 9).

The second component, *mode of subjectivation*, relates to the ways in which we as individuals are invited to recognize our moral obligations. Cannella and Lincoln (2007) suggest that these 'accepted rules' vary, and can range from divine law to natural law and rational reason. Here, Foucault encourages scholars and individuals to examine how we construct ourselves as belonging to such sedimented orders of thought, and then transform such relationships to 'invent a different attitude towards the world and the self, one more respectful and difficult to achieve' (Rabinow, 1997, p. xxxii). This new form of thought can be formed in contact with specific social and political contexts and realities (Rabinow, 1997).

The third component of Foucault's ethical analysis is his notion of *ethical work* or the ways by which we can change ourselves to become ethical subjects. For Foucault, this was the relationship between thought and experience. Ethical work has both intellectual and practical dimensions, and 'involves a disentangling of the power relationships within which and from which the self is shaped and takes shape' (Rabinow, 1997, p. xxxvi). This act is a form of self-criticism that knows 'the possibility of no longer being, doing or thinking what we are, do or think" (Foucault, 1986, p. 27).

The last component of ethical analysis for Foucault was that of *telos,* or 'an elaboration of the self by the self, a studious transformation…through a constant care for the truth' (Rabinow, 1997, p. xxxix). This final piece of ethical analysis asks individuals and institutions what kind of beings they aspire to be when acting morally (Rabinow, 1997). As Cannella and Lincoln (2007) suggest, telos establishes a condition that questions and functions to think differently and to form an ethical practice that is flexible and emergent.

In Foucault's eyes, different forms of ethical practice emerge as the telos of ethical analysis changes in society. In order to engage in a 'critical ontology of our selves', Foucault (1984) encourages individuals and institutions to reflect on the arbitrariness, contingency, and precariousness of present practices that come to affect the ways subjectivity is recognized and the possibility of identifying the 'something else' that lies beyond the current way of being (Chan & Garrick, 2002). Since the 1980s and in response to a turbulent cultural milieu, both feminist and postcolonial scholars have engaged in a form of Foucauldian ethical analysis to examine forms of moral reasoning which undergird current conceptualizations and practices involved with communication ethics.

AN 'OTHER' LOOK AT ETHICS: FROM FEMINIST APPROACHES TO POSTCOLONIAL UNDERSTANDINGS

Carol Gilligan (1982) challenged mainstream thought on moral authority by asserting that feminist forms of moral reasoning based in relationships and empathy (the ethic of care) were just as valuable and sophisticated as masculinist forms of moral reasoning based on so-called impartial universalist principles (the ethic of justice). Such an 'ethic of care' challenged individuals to not only feel another's pain but to also assume some responsibility for it; be sensitive to the specific context in which ethical dilemmas emerge; and recognize as well as appreciate, the ethical weight of the perspectives of those involved (Hutchings, 2001). Instead of constructing a list of universal values, this care-based form of moral reasoning is grounded in 'a recognition of responsibility for others…shifting attention from individual and collective rights and interests to questions of relations of recognition and responsibility' (Hutchings, 2001, p. 115). Within the ethic of care, Gilligan invokes the embodied moral self as a relational activity as discussed by both Foucault and Cannella and Lincoln.

Robinson (1999) extended the idea of care as an everyday practice and moral obligation to engage the broader economic, political, and social contexts of the global sphere and the ways in which 'particular patterns of advantage and disadvantage, power and oppression, sameness and difference are institutionalized within it' (Hutchings, 2001, p. 118). As Robinson (1999) states:

> An ethic of care is not about the application of a universal principle ('We all must care about all others') nor is it about a sentimental ideal ('A more caring world will be a better world'). Rather it is a starting point for transforming the values and practices of international society; thus it requires an examination of the contexts in which caring does and does not take place, and a commitment to the creation of more humanly responsive institutions which can be shaped to embody expressive and communicative possibilities between actors on a global scale. (pp. 47–48)

According to this extended version of the ethic of care, the credibility and authority of any ethical claim depends on the meanings it possesses within particular contexts (Urban Walker, 1998). Ethical substance is now considered complex and constructed, with patterns of dependence and responsibility implied therein (Hutchings, 2001). The question now becomes one of 'geographies of responsibility' or as Urban Walker (1998) describes—'how certain values or practices come to be seen as ethically necessary' (as cited in Hutchings, 2001, p. 121). Grounded in a relational ontology (I am because we are), this feminist contribution to global ethics asks scholars to contest assumptions of ethical necessity and consider the ways in which other kinds of worlds could be built. Individual and institutional rights must now be critiqued and judged in relation to the ways in which they intersect with broader context-specific values and structures which infuse actions with meaning.

Moreover, as Anthony Cortese (1990) states in his book *Ethnic Ethics: The Restructuring of Moral Theory*, scholars need to seriously consider 'the possibility that ethnic groups have different moral structures, each adequate to the reproduction of the social life-world found in each ethnic group' (pp. 91–94). Such a perspective is echoed in the Dalai Lama's (1999) book *Ethics for a New Millennium* where he outlines a transcultural ethics, grounded in the basic assumption that all humans desire to be happy and to avoid suffering. In evaluating whether an action is ethical or not, the Dalai Lama (1999), in a similar fashion to Alfred (2005), urges the consideration of whether the act promotes happiness or suffering, the context of the act, the motivation and intention of the act, and the person's degree of freedom in choosing the act. Laying out three ethics of restraint, virtue, and compassion, the Dalai Lama (1999) focuses on the process of discernment in decisions to act and a consideration of an individual's or institution's ultimate concern and their capacity or commitment to universal responsibility.

Ultimate concerns, or long term purposes that override short term goals, are typically related to values central to our identities (Damon & Bronk, 2007). A focus on ultimate concerns begins to reveal the larger cultural and moral logics which govern individual and institutional identity and actions. Responsibility becomes an ultimate concern, for example, when it is motivated by a highly articulated moral identity, the moral purpose at the center of that identity, and supported by a group of respected peers or mentors (Damon & Bronk, 2007). Universal responsibility takes into account the transcendent dimension of every act and the equal right of all others to seek happiness and avoid suffering and assumes that the interests of any particular community cannot be considered to lie solely within its boundaries (Dalai Lama, 1999). Thus, there can be no right or wrong, good or bad, as all acts and phenomena exist within a relationship of dependent origination, where no thing or event comes into existence by itself (Dalai Lama, 1999).

In summary, these formulations of transcultural and feminist ethics bring to light the relationality of the moral self as well as some of the 'truths' willed to and by individuals and institutions. As these scholars begin to engage a global reality, however, it is also easy to see a need to rethink and create new possibilities of being, doing, and thinking to form a flexible, emergent, and contextual form of ethical practice. Such a contextual form of ethical practice is a central part of the postcolonial project. Like the feminist and transcultural project, the postcolonial project contextualizes ethics by focusing on 'the desire for a more just and equitable global order not only in political and economic terms but also in terms that are more cultural, psychological, epistemological and so forth' (Prasad & Prasad, 2003, p. 284). The 'post' of postcolonial here does not suggest that colonialism is over. On the contrary, it exposes, as McClintock (1995) does, the several aspects of colonialism that continue to linger on in the contemporary world. Colonial ideologies remain embedded in social discourse, with communicative processes legitimizing contemporary power structures in the ways they represent individuals, institutions, and their interests (Shome, 1996). The goal of the postcolonial project is not to look at the practices of subaltern groups as 'new objects of study' (Walsh, 2007, p. 234); rather, to draw on other ways of thinking, building connections, and communicating based on lived experiences. In doing so, the postcolonial project provides a platform for articulating resistance to dominant, Eurocentric perspectives that are seen as the norm (see e.g., Chakrabarty, 1992; Said, 1978; Shohat, 1992; Spivak, 1990).

In demonstrating how local values can build independent theorizations of ethics, particularly in the context of the media, Rao and Wasserman (2007) offer the theoretical examples of *Ahimsa*, nonviolence, from India and of *Ubuntu*, 'each individual's humanity is ideally expressed in relationship with others' (Broodryk cited in Rao & Wasserman, 2007, p. 40), from South Africa. Similarly, in an article on Asian communication ethics, Satoshi Ishii (2009) proposes a new paradigm inspired by Buddhist ethics of not only harmony oriented human–human communication but also nonanthropocentric and deep ecological human–nature relationships. Arguing that 'modern and contemporary Euro-US-centric communication ethics have depended largely upon the Ancient Greek and post-Enlightenment philosophy of reason-centrism and the Cartesian dichotomous view of ethics which have conventionally separated ethics from religion' (p. 51), Ishii (2009) states that the Buddhist epistemology of 'oneness' will become increasingly important in the contemporary global context. He concludes that the time has come for a 'non-self-centric, non-anthropocentric and holistic worldview and ethical thought' (p. 58).

So how can we address and analyse communicative practices and ethics in context using a postcolonial perspective? As seen in the examples above of diverse 'wills to truth', indigenous communicative processes and ethics can help in the shaping of a different thought 'constructed and positioned from 'other' histories and subjectivities' (Walsh, 2007, p. 226). Postcolonial theory asks scholars to consider 'the politics of identity and the ethics inherent in encounters of difference…to…emphasize inequality, disjuncture and the impossibility of understanding and accommodation' (Westwood & Jack, 2007, p. 255). This form of engaging 'otherwise' moves understandings of communication ethics toward a form of 'radical co-presence, where practices and agents on both sides are contemporary in equal terms' (de Sousa Santos, 2007, p. 11). As Battiste (2008) says, 'ethical research systems and practices should enable indigenous nations, peoples, and communities to exercise control over information relating to their knowledge and heritage to themselves' (p. 503). Thus, Battiste (2008) argues, a 'postcolonial framework cannot be constructed without indigenous people renewing and reconstructing the principles underlying their own worldview, environment, languages, communication forms, and how these construct their humanity' (p. 508).

When we look at communication ethics through a postcolonial lens we can see gaps between core communication principles and the construction of 'diverse systems of meaning in discursive practices' (Broadfoot & Munshi, 2007, p. 260). For Qing Cao (2007), 'opening up spaces for new voices or different truths to be in dialogue with existing, often dominant ones, represents a productive and empowering engagement in resisting essentialist representation of the Other' (p. 117). In such practices, to be postcolonial is to hover between critique and synthesis and to acknowledge that while all fences/borders/boundaries, be they national, institutional or disciplinary, serve to define what is inside, it is the 'use of space inside and in-between that activates it' (Spivak, cited in Shome & Hegde, 2002, p. 276).

Spivak's discussion of being postcolonial here is different from the radically, politicized, hypercritical one we usually index. This form of postcolonial being while still sensitive to the historical forces and conditions of the emerging global order, is cognizant also of its flows and ephemeral nature. Instead of essentializing or attempting to locate a stable, singular Other, nationally or individually, this form of postcolonialism recognizes Othering practices at work and the ways in which our Others, just as our postmodern selves, are fragmented, dispersed, multiple, and partial. Such a focus on othering practices and how they work enables scholars to 'craft another space for the production of knowledge—an other way of thinking, *un paradigmo otro,* the very possibility of talking about "worlds and knowledges otherwise"' (Escobar, 2007, p. 179). Such 'spaces in-between' (Bhabha, 1994, 1996) are places of translation and negotiation, enabling a blurring of boundaries and a foregrounding of the multiplicity and multidimensionality of cultural meanings and representations in any communicative context. As a result, such spaces enable a 'spatial politics of inclusion rather than exclusion that initiates new signs of identity and innovative sites of collaboration and contestation…and a (re)negotiation of intersubjective and collective experiences of nationness, community interest or cultural values' (Bhabha, 1994, pp. 1–5).

This dynamic engagement with the patterns of relationship is possible by focusing on issues of ethnic relationality and community answerability, according to Shohat and Stam (1994), who propose that multiculturalism, racism, and colonialism need to be discussed together so that the ways in which they interact in any given sphere of communication is illuminated. Such a perspective emphasizes fields of power and struggle as well as issues of differentiation, relationality, and linkages. It is reciprocal and dialogical, considering every act of cultural exchange as an act of cultural interlocution which leaves all who participate, changed. Such an approach, argue Shohat and Stam (1994) focuses on how issues of race and national representations exist '…within a complex and multivalent relationality' (p. 220). It highlights the interethnic and international contradictions and hybridities that exist on what has, until now, been discussed as the margins, or periphery.

Central to understanding global flows and events relationally is a struggle for presence. We all have a role to play in our shared conflictual histories as whole cultures are 'implicated in one another, not only economically but also culturally' (Shohat & Stam, 1994, p. 245). These two concepts from postcolonial thought—'ethnicity in relation/ethnic relationality' and 'spaces in between' with their central commitments to a relational form of moral self, coupled with the allied ethic of care from feminist thought provide a starting point from which communication scholars can begin to construct ethical practices which go past a 'one size fits all' approach as is usually found in traditional ethical discussions. As Frenkel and Shenhav (2003) discuss, attempts to impose 'the one best way' in communication ethics in other parts of the world without any cultural reflexivity not only constitutes a form of personal control over the Other but also exerts cultural control by forcing an adoption and internalization of nonindigenous assumptions. It is important for individuals and institutions communicating in diverse contexts to learn from and support the multiple forms of cultural knowledge around communication ethics native to these contexts instead of immediately adopting 'foreign' forms. In the following section, we envision an alternative form of communication ethics that exists in the Aotearoa-New Zealand context, based on indigenous values and beliefs, and outline examples of individual and institutional communicative practices grounded in Kaupapa Maori.

TOWARDS PRAXIS: INSIGHTS FROM TE KAUPAPA MAORI AND A REVISIONING OF COMMUNICATION ETHICS

Ethics 'is always about the world we inhabit and the world we want to construct' (Hutchings, 2001, p. 130). And yet we need to acknowledge that the '"we" does not emerge outside of the highly complex structures, institutions and practices which make a "we"' (Hutchings, 2001, p. 130). In other words, ethics is grounded in the local context. For most of its history, Aotearoa-New Zealand was narrated by the dominant Pakeha community as White, European, and specifically British—an 'enclave of Europe in the South Pacific' (Laffey, 1999). White and European narratives were rendered plausible by the dispossession of the Maori and the ongoing marginalization of same. However, the velocity and intensity of economic and concomitant social changes rushing through the latter part of the 20th century destabilized the cultural signification of national culture and identity in which Aotearoa-New Zealand, and more specifically, dominant Pakeha institutions, were engaged. As a result, Aotearoa-New Zealand emerged as a dialectical entity of various temporalities—modern, colonial, postcolonial, and native (Bhabha, 1990).

Most histories of Aotearoa-New Zealand begin with the communicative event of the signing of the Treaty of Waitangi in 1840 between the British crown and several Maori chiefs. The intent of the Treaty was to guarantee mutual accommodation and autonomy of Maori people and Pakeha settlers. Two versions of the Treaty were prepared—one in English and the other in Maori. Missionaries translated the Treaty to Maori chiefs throughout the nation to gain their agreement and it has been the translation of the Treaty that has formed the foundation of its contestation by contemporary Maori. As both a symbol of national unity and contestation, the Treaty of Waitangi, has always been a central sign in Maori-Pakeha relationships, as well as a distinct example of a particular ethical logic that accomplished the colonization of a nation. Under its interpretation of unity, the Treaty as cultured/cultural text has facilitated a reimagining of Aotearoa-New Zealand from one nation, one people, one culture to one nation, two people, and biculturalism, in what some argue is a hegemonic attempt to cement a 'partnership' against a sociopolitical background of gross inequality and severe racial tensions (True, 1996). Under the philosophy of first 'biculturalism' and then 'multiculturalism' in the late 20th century, Aotearoa-New Zealand embarked on a series of diverse cultured communicative practices aimed at recentering its multifaceted cultural self into communal and consultative relations between its main population groups. Admittedly, this process has become more complex in recent years and the demographic landscape of the nation has shifted with growth of Pasifika communities and Asian communities.

While colonisation had torn Maori culture asunder, there have been efforts of late to reconstruct it. This process of reconstruction, called *Matauranga Maori*, 'is like a tool for thinking, organising information, considering the ethics of knowledge, the appropriateness of it all and informing us about our world and our place in it' (Mead, 2003, p. 306). As a part of this process, it is now commonplace to see communicative practices drawn from the Maori way of life such as a *powhiri* (a welcome ceremony) or a *hui* (a consultation meeting).

Alongside this process of cultural reconstruction, Kaupapa Maori scholarship has emerged as a resistance to colonialist assumptions of sense-making processes 'which have continued to privilege Western ways of knowing, while denying the validity for Maori of Maori knowledge, language, and culture' (L. T. Smith, 1999, p. 183). This resistance, as several Maori researchers have pointed out, is not reactionary—it 'is one of survival' (Walker, 1996, p. 123). The focus is on developing researchers and scholars to concentrate on the specific needs and priorities of Maori rather than those deemed universal by a colonial mindset. According to Pihama (2001), 'the word *kaupapa* is defined as philosophies or ways of thinking about issues' (p. 78) and it is this awareness of Maori philosophies, principles, and values that allows Kaupapa Maori to actively intervene in the hegemonies of power.

Maori scholar Graham Hingangaroa Smith (2003) highlights six key intervention elements that are integral to Kaupapa Maori: *tino rangatiratanga*, the principle of self-determination; *taonga tuku iho*, the principle of cultural aspirations; *ako Maori*, Maori appropriate pedagogies; *kia piki ake I nga raruraru o te kainga*, socioeconomic mediation; *whanau*, the extended family; and *kaupapa*, the collective philosophy. These principles and commitments are central to Maori ways of being, knowing, and communicating. At individual and institutional levels, these commitments ask how collective responsibility is performed, how relationships are constructed, how individual and collective needs are met, how individuals and institutions can be accountable for generations to come, and where reciprocity lies in communicating collective well-being.

Such an ethical frame aligns itself well with interaction ideals from postcolonial ethnography such as 'accountability', 'context', 'truthfulness', and 'community' (Gonzalez, 2003, pp.

83–85). Within such a frame, individuals and institutions communicate and provide an *account* of how they come to know what they know, the decisions and actions they make, the challenges they face, and things they close themselves from. They also practise a mindfulness of the political, social, environmental, physical, and emotional *context* in which communicative action exists. *Truthfulness* requires individuals and institutions to not only see what is in the context as well as what they have done or said, but also to 'speak nakedly' about issues that are not visible on the surface—the issues that cause them to be afraid, ashamed, or dishonest when confronted by powerful others. Finally, *community* asks individuals and institutions to build 'ecological intimacy' with all those in which they engage, sharing their experiences and lessons learned in order to create, support, and demonstrate just individuals, relationships, and organizations which reflect and respect difference.

These ideals of postcolonial praxis are evident in the growing body of Kaupapa Maori research practices. Such practices involve a reclaiming of indigenous Maori worldviews and concepts that frame Maori values and enable Maori understandings to interrogate Western theories and methodologies that have explained *away* indigenous experiences and positioned them *in the margins*. In line with the postcolonial ethic of *accountability* as 'the ability to account' or 'to tell a story' (Gonzalez, 2003, p. 83) for example, the principle of *ako Maori* asks how we can honor the duality of organizing participants as both learners and teachers by crafting practices that nurture each other. The focus in research settings is, therefore, on relationships between various participants as opposed to traditional Western approaches where 'the position of the researchers is hidden "under a veil of neutrality or objectivity"' (Te Puni Kokiri, 2002, p. 27). The ethic of *context* comes through in the heavy dependence on the physical, social, and spiritual background of narratives in communication practices. The ethic of *truthfulness* is an extension of the ethic of context. For Maori researchers, for example, truthfulness also relates to seeing and framing alternative realities that are more relevant to their cultural survival and safety. As Castellano (2004) points out: 'Just as colonial policies have denied Aboriginal Peoples access to their traditional lands, so also colonial definitions of truth and value have denied Aboriginal Peoples the tools to assert and implement their knowledge' (p. 102). The centrality of the notion of *whanau* or the extended family is connected to the ethic of *community*. The idea of community has multiple layers. It remains 'a persistent way of living and organizing the social world'; it is a 'way of incorporating ethical procedures which report back to the community, a way of 'giving voice' to different sections of Maori communities'; and a 'way of debating ideas and issues' (L. T. Smith, 1999, p. 187).

Indeed, Kaupapa Maori approaches to communication ethics begin by centring Maori or indigenous worldviews and experiences. The act of centring is important because it invites into the centre the complexities of the histories, politics, identities, materialities, aspirations, and capabilities of the Maori people and uses that complex marinade to inform the ways to proceed together in an ethical manner. It is not therefore a romanticised formulation of a cultural worldview but a genuinely decolonised recognition of where we have all come from and where we are at the moment. In this sense it presents that postcolonial possibility of a new space for ethical dialogue that is sharpened by the struggles of survival and polished in the hope of a more ethical and just world.

As Bishop (2003) points out, in 'Kaupapa Maori contexts, the interrelationships and interaction patterns that develop draw on Maori cultural aspirations and sense-making processes (ways of knowing) rather than on those imposed by another culture' (p. 223). Kaupapa Maori is infused with a Maori code of conduct and is dedicated to '...the creation of spaces for Maori realities within wider society' (Pipi et al., 2004). As such it draws on the values and practices of '*aroha ke te tangata*' (a respect for people), '*he kanohi kitea*' (meeting people face to face), '*titiro, whakarongo, korero'* (looking, listening, and finding an appropriate place from which to speak), *'manaaki ki te tangata'* (sharing and collaborating), *'kia tupato'* (being cautious, culturally safe and reflexive), *'kaua e takahia te mana o te tangata'* (not trampling on the *mana* of the people), and *'kia ngakau mahaki'* (being humble) (see e.g., L.T. Smith, 1999, p. 120). This is achieved through the deployment of different discursive rituals, ceremonies, and protocols that constitute speaking subjects in new and expansive ways. The *hui* or the formal gathering of people on a *Marae* (a meeting place) is one such ritual. As Salmond (1983) says, the *hui* is 'a "ritual of encounter" because it is repeated for every group that attends the *hui* and is structured as a balanced exchange between the local people (*tangata whenua*) and the visitors (*manuhiri*)"' (p. 1).

Maori make a point of welcoming and extending hospitality to guests or *manuhiri* through a range of formal and semiformal rituals which often call for the guests, mostly male at this point of the ceremony, to speak drawing on their own language, identifying where they come from, and to sing from their own culture supported by others who accompany them. This engagement by guests is especially welcome if their chosen language is not English and the act of speaking itself draws out surprising reactions from those guests who do speak because it makes them reach inwards and explain in a formal ceremony 'who they are'. There is a diverse range of ways in which men and women, elders and young people are expected to communicate, to speak, to listen, to respond, to tell stories, to sing, to tell jokes, to debate, and while they are performing those tasks there is also an expectation that they will create, enhance, and sustain relationships.

In another sense Maori culture is highly sensitised to the transitions between different human activities; for example, between ceremony and food, between formal interactions and social interactions, and these transitions are often marked by a *karakia*, a prayer or incantation, that acknowledges that people's feelings or state of being has also changed. The marking of the change of context, time, or space, enables people to also change their mode of communication, it lifts the burdens of status and responsibility conducted in one context, and widens the scope for engagement in another context. Acknowledgment of such transitions is a marking of the in-between space.

CONCLUSION

In drawing on insights from indigenous Kaupapa Maori theory and practice in Aotearoa-New Zealand, we have attempted to imagine the communicative practices and ethics necessary to create what Bhabha (1994) calls a 'space in between' for authentic dialogue in a multicultural environment. Constructing such a space enables a form of Communicating *Other*wise that acknowledges the unique and subjective experiences and practices of different cultural groups. This space provides a totally new kind of platform to look at communication ethics—a platform built on a set of postcolonial standpoints.

This space for an ethical dialogue is not a 'Third Space' but a space that Bhabha attempted to describe as '*in-between* the claims of the past and the needs of the present' (Bhabha, 1994. p. 219). It is not an innocent space nor a politically disinterested space, but a space which enables, facilitates, references, activates, frames, and gives voice to the values and practices of all peoples so that they can engage in the world. Further, it is a space in which there is an active intent to disrupt the historic relations of power as they are embodied in particular forms of ethics, to change the rules of engagement and of communication so that new voices emerge. The point is not that the new voices are more or less authentic and will add more or less authenticity to the communication but that the new voices become included and legitimated.

In the Aotearoa-New Zealand context, Kaupapa Maori names the ways of living and being that Maori take for granted. It identifies those practices in particular that draw from a cultural worldview and a set of beliefs and values that have facilitated cultural survival and resiliency and help shape the imagination and sense of possibility that has driven Maori development. When we apply that imagination to ethics it suggests that the in-between space is the very space in which communication ethics resides, caught in translation and negotiation processes between peoples, logics, and values. This is a simultaneously messy and profound space, a protean place where new forms constantly emerge, defying and yet supporting traditional rules and institutions simultaneously. It is a respect-able place also though, a communal space, a collectively conscious space, where as we have seen by the specific communicative practices described here, future, present, and past all combine and transform. Finally, as communication scholarship expands and organizing forms transcend national boundaries, constructing such mutually inclusive spaces with their own logics is important if we are to conduct ourselves ethically in the world.

REFERENCES

Adeola, F. O. (2001). Environmental injustice and human rights abuse: The states, MNCs, and repression of minority groups in the world system. *Human Ecology Review, 8*(1), 39–59.

Alfred, T. (2005). *Wasase: Indigenous pathways of action and freedom.* Peterborough, Ontario, Canada: Broadview Press.

Amselle, J-L. (2006). The world inside out: What is at stake in deconstructing the west? *Social Anthropology, 14*(2), 183–193.

Athanasiou, T. (1996). *Divided planet: The ecology of rich and poor.* Boston, MA: Little, Brown.

Battiste, M. (2008). Research ethics for protecting indigenous knowledge and heritage. In N. K. Denzin, Y. S. Lincoln, & L. T. Smith (Eds.), *Handbook of critical and indigenous methodologies* (pp. 497–509). Los Angeles, CA: Sage.

Beder, S. (2000). *Global spin: The corporate assault on environmentalism.* Foxhole, Dartington, UK: Green Books.

Bhabha, H. (1990). DissemiNation: Time, narrative and the margins of the modern nation. In H. Bhabha (Ed.), *Nation and narration* (pp. 291–321). London: Routledge.

Bhabha, H. (1994). *The location of culture.* London: Routledge.

Bhabha, H. (1996). Culture's in-between. In S. Hall & P. du Gay (Eds.), *Questions of cultural identity* (pp. 53–60). London: Sage.

Bishop, R. (2003). Changing power relations in education: *Kaupapa Maori* messages for 'mainstream'' education in Aotearoa/New Zealand. *Comparative Education 39*(2), 221–238.

Broadfoot, K. J., & Munshi, D. (2007). Diverse voices and alternative rationalities: Imagining forms of post-colonial organizational communication. *Management Communication Quarterly, 21*(2), 249–267.

Cannella, G. S., & Lincoln, Y. S. (2007). Predatory vs. dialogic ethics. *Qualitative Inquiry, 13*(3), 315–335.

Cao, Q. (2007). Western representations of the Other. In Shi-xu (Ed.), *Discourse as cultural struggle* (pp. 105–122). Hong Kong: Hong Kong University Press.

Castellano, M. B. (2004). Ethics of aboriginal research. *Journal of Aboriginal Health 1*(1), 98–114.

Chakrabarty, D. (1992). Postcoloniality and the artifice of history: Who speaks for 'India' pasts? *Representations, 37,* 1–26.

Chan, A., & Garrick, J. (2002). Organization theory in turbulent times: The traces of Foucault's ethics. *Organization, 9*(4), 683–701.

Charvet, J., & Kaczynska-Nay, E. (2008). *The liberal project and human rights: The theory and practice of a new world order.* Cambridge, UK: Cambridge University Press.

Christians, C., & Traber, M. (Eds.). (1997). *Communication ethics and universal values.* Thousand Oaks, CA: Sage.

Cochran, P., Marshall, C., Garcia-Downing, C., Kendall, E., Cook, D., McCubbin, L., et al. (2008). Indigenous ways of knowing: Implications for participatory research and community. *Health Policy and Ethics, 98*(1), 22–27.

Cortese, A. (1990). *Ethnic ethics: The restructuring of moral theory.* Albany: SUNY Press.

Covarrubias, P. (2007). (Un)biased in Western theory: Generative silence in American Indian communication. *Communication Monographs, 74*(2), 265–271.

Craig, R. T. (2007). Issue forum introduction: Cultural bias in communication theory. *Communication Monographs, 74*(2), 256–258.

Cutherbert, D., & Grossman, M. (1997). Crossing cultures: An interview with Helena Gulash. *Hecate: An Interdisciplinary Journal of Women's Liberation, 23*(2), 48–66.

Dalai Lama (1999). *Ethics for a new millennium.* New York: Riverhead Books.

Damon, W., & Bronk, K. C. (2007).Taking ultimate responsibility. In H. Gardner (Ed.), *Responsibility at work: How leading professionals act (or don't act) responsibly* (pp. 21–42). San Francisco, CA: Jossey-Bass.

De Sousa Santos, B. (2007). Beyond abyssal thinking: From global lines to ecologies of knowledge. *Review.* Retrieved from http://www.ces.uc.pt/bss/documentos/AbyssalThinking.pdf

Escobar, A. (2007). Worlds and knowledges otherwise: The Latin American modernity/coloniality research program. *Cultural Studies, 21*(2–3), 179–210.

Foucault, M. (1984). What is Enlightenment? In P. Rabinow (Ed.), *The Foucault reader* (pp. 32–50). New York: Pantheon.

Foucault, M. (1985). *History of sexuality: Vol. 2. The use of pleasure* (R. Hurley, Trans.). New York: Pantheon Books.

Foucault, M. (1986). *History of sexuality: Vol. 3. The care of the self* (R. Hurley, Trans.). New York: Pantheon Books.

Freire, P. (1998). *Pedagogy of freedom: Ethics, democracy, and civic courage.* Lanham, MD: Rowman & Littlefield.

Frenkel, M., & Shenhav, Y. (2003). *Decolonizing organization theory: Between Orientalism and Occidentalism.* Paper presented at the third Critical Management Studies conference at Lancaster University, United Kingdom.

Gilligan, C. (1982). *In a different voice: Psychological theory and women's development.* Cambridge, MA: Harvard University Press.

Gonzalez, M. C. (2003). An ethics for postcolonial ethnography. In R. P. Clair (Ed.), *Expressions of ethnography: Novel approaches to qualitative methods* (pp. 77–86). Albany, NY: SUNY Press.

Hall, S. (1996). The West and the rest: Discourse and power. In S. Hall, D. Held, D. Hubert, & K. Thompson (Eds.), *Modernity: An introduction to modern societies* (pp. 184–228). Malden, MA: Open University Press.

Hutchings, K. (2001). Towards a feminist international ethics. In K. Booth, T. Dunne, & M. Cox (Eds.), *How might we live? Global ethics in a new century* (pp. 111–130). Cambridge, UK: Cambridge University Press.

Ishii, S. (2009). Conceptualising Asian communication ethics: A Buddhist perspective. *Journal of Multicultural Discourses, 4*(1), 49–60.

Ivison, D. (2002). *Postcolonial liberalism.* Cambridge, UK: Cambridge University Press.

Laffey, M. (1999). Adding an Asian strand: Neoliberalism and the politics of culture in New Zealand, 1984–97. In J. Weldes, M. Laffey, H. Austerson, & R. Duvall (Eds.), *Cultures of insecurity: States, communities and the production of danger* (pp. 233–260). Minnesota: University of Minnesota Press.

McClintock, A. (1995). *Imperial leather: Race, gender and sexuality in the colonial context.* London: Routledge.

Mead, H. M. (2003). *Tikanga Maori: Living by Maori values.* Wellington, NZ: Huia.

Miike, Y. (2007). An Asiacentric reflection on Eurocentric bias in communication theory. *Communication Monographs, 74*(2), 272–278.

Munshi, D., & Kurian, P. (2005). Imperializing spin cycles: A postcolonial look at public relations, greenwashing, and the separation of publics. *Public Relations Review, 31*(4), 513–520.

Munshi, D., & Kurian, P. (2007). The case of the subaltern public: A postcolonial investigation of CSR's (o)missions. In S. May, G. Cheney, & J. Roper (Eds.), *The debate over corporate social responsibility* (pp. 438–447). New York: Oxford University Press.

Pihama, L. (2001). *Tihei Mauri Ora: Honouring our voices, Mana wahine as a Kaupapa Maori theoretical framework.* (Doctoral dissertation). The University of Auckland, Auckland, New Zealand. Retrieved from http://www.kaupapamaori.com/assets//PihamaL/tihei_mauri_ora_chpt4.pdf

Pipi, K., Cram, F., Hawke, R., Hawke, S., Huriwai, T., Mataki, T., et al. (2004). A research ethics for studying Maori and Iwi provider success. *Social Policy Journal of New Zealand, 23*(3). Retrieved from http://www.msd.govt.nz/about-msd-and-our-work/publications-resources/journals-and-magazines/social-policy-journal/spj23/23-a-research-ethic-for-studying-mori-and-iwi-provider-success-p141-153.html

Prakash, G. (1990). Writing post-Orientalist histories of the Third World: Perspectives from Indian historiography. *Comparative Studies in Society and History, 32*(2), 383–408.

Prasad, A., & Prasad, P. (2003). The postcolonial imagination. In A. Prasad (Ed.), *Postcolonial theory and organizational analysis* (pp. 283–295). New York: Palgrave-Macmillan.

Rabinow, P. (Ed.) (1997). *Michel Foucault: Ethics, subjectivity and truth.* New York: New Press.

Rao, S., & Wasserman, H. (2007). Global media ethics revisited: A postcolonial critique. *Global Media and Communication, 3*(1), 29–50.

Robinson, F. (1999). *Globalizing care: Ethics, feminist theory and international relations.* Boulder, CO: Westview Press.

Rose, N. (1996). *Inventing our selves: Psychology, power and personhood.* Cambridge, UK: Cambridge University Press.

Said, E. (1978). *Orientalism.* New York: Vintage.

Salmond, A. (1983). *Hui: A study of Maori ceremonial gatherings* (2nd ed.). Wellington, NZ: A. H. & A. W. Reed.

Shohat, E. (1992). Notes on the 'post-colonial." *Social Text, 31–32,* 99–113.

Shohat, E., & Stam, R. (1994). *Unthinking Eurocentrism: Multiculturalism and the media.* London: Routledge.

Shome, R. (1996). Postcolonial interventions in the rhetorical canon: An 'Other" view. *Communication Theory, 6*(1), 40–59.

Shome, R., & Hegde, R. S. (2002). Postcolonial approaches to communication: Charting the terrain, engaging the intersection. *Communication Theory, 12*(3), 249–270.

Smith, G. (2003, December). Kaupapa Maori theory: *Theorizing indigenous transformation of education and schooling.* Paper presented at the Kaupapa Maori symposium, Auckland. Retrieved from http://docs.google.com/viewer?a=v&q=cache:Sw7cb1v_7qcJ:www.aare.edu.au/03pap/pih03342.pdf+Kaupapa+Maori+theory:+theorizing+indigenous+transformation&hl=en&gl=nz&sig=AHIEtbQR8y5l2HvsMs8ssXNJQ56NSaRL6A

Smith, L. T. (1999). *Decolonizing methodologies: Research and indigenous peoples.* London: Zed Books.

Spivak, G. (1990). Poststructuralism, marginality, postcoloniality and value. In P. Collier & H. Geyer-Ryan (Eds.), *Literary theory today* (pp. 219–244). Ithaca, NY: Cornell University Press.

Te Puni Kokiri (2002). Iwi and Maori provider success: A research report of interviews with successful Iwi and Maori providers and government agencies prepared by the International Research Institute for Maori and Indigenous Education, The University of Auckland, in collaboration with Te Ropu Rangahau Hauora A Eeru Pomare, Wellington School of Medicine, the University of Otago. Retrieved from http://www.tpk.govt.nz/publications/research_reports/default.asp

True, J. (1996). 'Fit citizens for the British Empire?": Class-ifying racial and gendered subjects in 'Godzone" (New Zealand). In B. F. Williams (Ed.), *Women out of place: The gender of agency and the race of nationality* (pp. 103–129). New York: Routledge.

Urban Walker, M. (1998). *Moral understandings: A feminist study in ethics.* London: Routledge.

Walker, S. (1996). *Kia tau te rangimarie. Kaupapa Maori theory a resistance against the construction of Maori as the other* (Unpublished master's thesis). The University of Auckland, Auckland, New Zealand. Retrieved from http://www.kaupapamaori.com/assets//WalkerS/kia_tau_te_rangimarie_chpt6.pdf

Walsh, C. (2007). Shifting the geopolitics of critical knowledge: Decolonial thought and cultural studies 'others' in the Andes. *Cultural Studies, 21*(2–3), 224–239.

Westwood, R. I., & Jack, G. (2007). Manifesto for a post-colonial international business and management studies: A provocation. *Critical Perspectives on International Business, 3*(3), 246–265.

Unit 2

CONTEXTS OF APPLICATION AND THEORY DEVELOPMENT

9

Interpersonal Communication Ethics

Sally Planalp and Julie Fitness

What if the mightiest word is love, love beyond marital, filial, national. Love that casts a widening pool of light. (Elizabeth Alexander, "Praise Song for the Day," U.S. Presidential inaugural poem, January 20, 2009)

The need to treat others ethically is all too obvious in interpersonal relationships. The benefits are felt immediately in shared well-being and enjoyment, trust, mutual assistance, and dependably coordinated action. Breaches are also felt directly by experiencing the other's disapproval, disappointment, hurt, righteous indignation, or alienation, but also by feeling one's own regret, guilt, shame, or loneliness. The forces that shaped our emotional lives did not leave us inherently selfish, unjust, or otherwise oblivious to the concerns of others, especially when we interact with them face-to-face. Neither did they guarantee that what is good for the other and the relationship would triumph over what is good only for the self, hence the need for this discussion of ethics in interpersonal communication.

Throughout this chapter, we draw on a variety of established theoretical frameworks for understanding ethics, following from the diverse approaches represented in the research literature. As general ethical guidelines, we can draw on the "golden rule," Kant's categorical imperative (1898/1992), or Rawls's (1971) theory of justice, all of which challenge us to consider whether what is good for ourselves would be good for everyone. Gilligan's (1982) "ethics of caring" are more obviously applicable to interpersonal than to impersonal contexts, though Singer (2002) might challenge us to expand the circle of caring to encompass Mother Earth and all her life forms. A rules approach to ethics (e.g., Kohlberg, 1981) is broadly applicable and has been especially useful to interpersonal communication scholars studying, for example, rules for friendships, rule violations as relational transgressions, rules for fairness, and related topics.

The fundamental premise of these approaches when applied to interpersonal ethics is that negotiating our social lives requires us to consider and balance the interests of all parties (e.g., ourselves, our loved ones, strangers, etc.) and that we frequently draw on socially shared and widely accepted rules (e.g., reciprocity; justice) to guide us. Judgments about interpersonal behaviors that are perceived to be unethical may range from "inconsiderate," to "unforgivable" and responses may range from forgiveness to banishment. Such implicit rules lie at the heart of complex interpersonal issues from "Should I tell the truth about that ugly shirt?" to "What does it mean to be a 'true friend'?"

Our aim in this chapter is to explore the kinds of ethical issues that have been revealed in research in interpersonal communication, defined as dyadic interactions, usually in the context of close relationships. Along with highlighting gaps in our current understanding of such issues, we will argue for the need to recognize the fundamental role of ethics in all aspects of relational communication and to promote a culture of caring that enables human beings to flourish, both individually and in relationship with one another.

BASIC RULES OF COMMUNICATION

Communication functions on the basis of assumed cooperation, but it also holds the potential for advancing one's own interests over those of one's conversational partner. We count on others to share information that is accurate to the best of their knowledge, well founded, and communicated in good faith. It is hard to imagine a workable relationship built on lying, misleading, saying more than you know (aka bullshit), and withholding information, all of which are violations of the conversational maxims posited in the classic work by Grice (1975).

Although cooperation may be the underlying substrate of interactions with others and honesty is believed to be essential in close relationships, deception is also commonplace, whether deliberate or unintentional and whether selfish or unselfish (Knapp, 2006). If indeed, most deception in everyday interaction is made up of "white lies," it seems that the basic ethical imperative to tell the truth may be trumped by the competing ethic of sparing others' feeling or perhaps by the less ethically justifiable motive of sparing oneself the trouble (Bok, 1978). As DePaulo, Morris, and Sternglanz put it: "Sometimes what truth-telling bumps up against is not greed but graciousness" (2009, p. 167).

In fact, people typically report that lying to friends is motivated by wanting to be kindhearted or other-protective whereas lies to strangers or acquaintances are more typically motivated by self-centeredness or the desire to protect oneself (DePaulo & Kashy, 1998; Ennis, Vrij, & Chance, 2008). Even within intimate relationships (close friends, dating partners, and engaged and married couples), greater commitment is positively associated with more partner-focused reasons for deception (Metts, 1989). That said, research shows that greater accuracy in communication is not always associated with relationship satisfaction and stability, and that there are times when empathic inaccuracy (e.g., erroneously believing that one's partner would "never even look at another man") is better for a relationship than knowing the truth (i.e., she does, in fact, look) (Sillars & Scott, 1983; Simpson, Ickes, & Orina, 2001). So honesty may not be the best policy for the health of the relationship (Englehardt, 2001). If deceiving, misleading, or being evasive enhances the other's well-being and makes for a better relationship (e.g., being supportive, protecting privacy), they may not be unethical but instead guided by ethical criteria other than honesty.

As we find time and again, following ethical rules or guidelines is rarely straightforward because rules and guidelines are many and may contradict one another. But even navigating multiple ethical guidelines can be considered from a meta-ethical point of view by asking oneself about rule priorities for oneself, but also for one's partner. Such a consideration may reveal the (perhaps uncomfortable) realization that "meaning well" (i.e., having the other's best interests at heart) is not a legitimate excuse for lying. In a study of marital betrayal, for example, unfaithful respondents reported that they had lied to their partners about infidelity to "spare them pain"; betrayed partners, on the other hand, reported that being lied to was in some respects a greater betrayal than the infidelity, particularly when they realized they were "the last to know" (Fitness, 2001; see also Barbee, Cunningham, Druen, & Yankeelov, 1996).

Given the prevalence and moral ambiguity of lying to protect the other, LaFollette and Graham (1986) make a case for metahonesty, or honest communication about guidelines and reasons for sharing or withholding information, and for developing habits of honesty rather than dishonesty in the interests of greater intimacy. This is consistent with Bok's conclusions that one should seek truthful alternatives whenever possible and lie as a last resort (1978, p. 31). Nevertheless, it is hard to imagine explicitly discussing rules for all dilemmas that might arise, and sometimes metacommunication is impossible without giving away the truth in the moment (e.g., "Would you want me to tell you if you had a terminal disease?" after just meeting with the doctor).

BASIC RULES OF RELATIONSHIPS AND ETHICAL IMPLICATIONS

Although the basic rules of communication transcend contexts, specific kinds of ethical concerns arise most directly and commonly in close relationships. *Connection and inclusion* in personal relationships and society, for example, may be considered a basic human right. Volumes of research on attachment theory (Shaver & Mikulincer, 2006) have documented infants' needs for secure attachments and the emotional damage that is done when attachment is disrupted. Baumeister and Leary (1995) take the argument a step further to posit a fundamental need for humans to be a part of social relations with regular interaction and mutual caring. Extrapolating from their theory, the complete severing of social connections of solitary confinement, ostracism, and abandonment could be considered violations of human rights. Everyday ostracism, rejection, and social exclusion (DeWall, Baumeister, & Masicamp, 2009; Williams, Forgas, & von Hippel, 2005), broken contact (Planalp, Rutherford, & Honeycutt, 1988), and disconfirmation (Dailey, 2006) are milder versions that also cause considerable distress. On the positive side, secure attachment, dependability, and commitment are considered hallmarks of healthy close relationships (Rusbult, Coolsen, Kirchner, & Clarke, 2006).

Akin to the need to belong, there may be a universal human desire for and basic right to *respect and dignity*. Again, its necessity is revealed most strikingly in its violations: humiliation (Miller, 1993), contempt, disrespect (dissing), treating someone as invisible. In his aptly named book *Somebodies and Nobodies*, Fuller (2004, p. 5) calls nobody "another n- word," but it may actually be the mother of all n-words. We see somebodies abusing nobodies in: "a boss harassing an employee, a customer demeaning a waiter, a coach bullying a player, a doctor disparaging a nurse, a teacher humiliating a student, a parent belittling a child" (pp. 173–174). The pernicious effects (including suicide) of such humiliating and disrespectful interactions in organizational and interpersonal contexts have been well documented (e.g., Fitness, 2005, 2008; Tepper, 2000). A growing number of scholars and commentators are likewise concerned about the ways in which modern communication technologies are used to exclude and disrespect others, from severe cases of cyberbullying to more minor but also hurtful instances of text messaging in the middle of a face-to-face conversation (and so sending a message that "you are boring me") (Freeman, 2009; Keith & Martin, 2005). By contrast, in respectful interactions, people listen to one another and respond in a way that lets the other know they have been heard. Everybody is treated like somebody (Bergum & Dossetor, 2005), with the simultaneous humble recognition that everybody is a nobody sometime and somewhere.

Moving beyond basic inclusion and respect, *interdependence* (Kelley et al., 1983) or mutuality (Hinde, 1979) is another basic attribute of human relationships that gives rise to ethical concerns. One-sided caring is the stuff of unrequited love (Baumeister & Wotman, 1992) or arguably infant–caregiver relationships, not mature adult bonds. At a minimum, partners in close relationships are expected to look out for each other's welfare by protecting each other from harm, striving to meet each other's needs, and encouraging each other to flourish. The "ethics of care" is a well-recognized philosophical tradition (Gilligan, 1982) that is founded in interpersonal bonds rather than abstract ethical principles, although there is no reason the two cannot work in concert. Again, the ethical principles at play are most apparent in their violations: intimate violence, neglect, manipulation, one-sided control, monologue rather than dialogue, unilateral decision making, sociopathy, and the like.

When people are interdependent, issues of *fairness* and justice almost inevitably arise, with important implications for ethics, but also for individuals' feelings and relational satisfaction (Kluwer, Tumewu, & Van den Bos, 2009). What constitutes a fair distribution of resources, duties, support, pleasure and pain, and even floor time? There is much indeterminacy both theoretically and practically in ways of assessing value and how to define what is fair in different contexts. According to social psychologists, most people perceive justice as equity—the distribution of rewards in proportion to each partner's contributions. But equity is not the only possible definition of fairness and justice. For example, when resources are distributed in noncapitalist cultures, people frequently favor a norm of equality, giving everybody an equal share, regardless of input. Other cultures or groups, such as charitable institutions, may define justice with respect to need—from each according to his or her abilities, to each according to his or her need. Other groups again may define justice as power—"might is right"—winner takes all (Lerner & Mikula, 1994). There are also various means of attaining fairness, however defined, some of which may be more ethical than others (e.g., turn-taking, reciprocity, equal distribution, drawing on social roles or reworking them).

When fairness almost inevitably falls short sooner or later, the better angels of the overbenefited may lead to repayment in the form of gratitude for what cannot be repaid by other means (Hochschild, 1989). For example, in a recent study of naturally occurring gratitude in college sororities during a week of gift giving from older members to new members, a strong, positive relationship was found between beneficiaries' reported gratitude and the extent to which gift-givers were perceived to have spent more money on, and made more effort on behalf of, the beneficiaries (Algoe, Haidt, & Gable, 2008). The worse angels of the underbenefited, however, may exact revenge based on a subjective and disputable calculus of fairness that may produce vicious cycles of retribution and counterretribution (Baumeister & Catanese, 2001). Further, Frijda (1994) argues that the desire for revenge, while burning enough in its own right, is further enflamed by perceived humiliation.

Finally, connection and interdependence have their limits when they impact too greatly on individuals, hence *autonomy and privacy* arise as ethical concerns in dialectical tension with connection and interdependence (Baxter & Montgomery, 1996; Petronio, 2002). Issues related to openness and closedness have long been addressed under the rubric of self-disclosure (Greene, Derlega, & Mathews, 2006), but Petronio (1991) offers more explicit theoretical statements bearing on ethics in privacy management theory. Privacy rules are developed from cultural, gendered, motivational, contextual, and risk–benefit criteria (Petronio & Durham, 2008, p. 312), which imply no fixed context-free ethical standards for privacy regulation. Along those same lines, the theory is strongly interaction-based, with an emphasis on the coordination and negotiation of privacy boundaries rather than fealty to strict and widely recognized social rules. Although grounded strongly in face-to-face interaction, the theory has also been used to analyze television talk shows (Orrego et al., 2000) and public issues such as sex offender notification policies (Schultz, 2000). New communication venues such as social networking Internet sites blur boundaries between private and public in ways that have interesting ethical implications ("Is it okay to break up over Facebook?") that will continue to challenge privacy theories to evolve (Thompson, 2008).

As stated earlier, however, the rubber meets the road when ethical principles contradict one another. For example, the well-documented demand-withdraw pattern in marital dyads ("Do this!" vs. "Leave me alone!") (Caughlin, 2002) might be viewed as a tension of concern for one partner's needs pulling in one direction and respect for the other partner's privacy or autonomy pulling in the other. Another example that recently attracted a lively debate in an Australian newspaper concerned the dilemma frequently faced by individuals who become aware that their best friend is being betrayed by their romantic partner. Should they tell their friend, in line with the rule that friends should look out for one another, or should they turn a blind eye, in line with the rule that a friend's relationship is her or his own private business? (Not to mention the possibility that the friend will shoot the messenger.) No consensus was reached on the rights and wrongs of this dilemma, at least apparent in public accounts.

TYPES OF RELATIONSHIPS AND FAIRNESS

Fiske and Haslam (2005) have argued for four types of relationships, each with its own set of rules and expectations. *Communal* sharing relationships involve expectations of mutuality, intimacy, and caring, while *authority ranking* relationships involve expectations around issues of power and subordination, leading and following. In *equality matching* relationships, partners follow quid pro quo, or social exchange rules, expecting benefits to be promptly reciprocated, while in *market pricing* relationships partners treat one another as resources to be used as a means for achieving personal goals; for example, cultivating a relationship at work with a disliked colleague who may help get you promoted.

Fiske and his colleagues have found considerable support for their model. For example, they have found that when people get names mixed up, they mix them within categories; for example, if one calls one's current lover the wrong name, it is likely to be the name of an ex-lover rather than the boss's name (Fiske & Haslam, 2005). Further, violating relationship expectations or breaking relationship rules across categories can trigger strong emotional upset and distress. For example, many older wives who have been "traded in" by their husbands for younger women realize that what they thought was a communal sharing relationship was actually a market pricing one in which they were a low-valued commodity. Even so, it is quite rare to find a personal relationship that only ever draws on one model—they're often mixed. For example, parents may love and support their children in a quintessentially communal way, but they also exert authority over their children and expect a degree of obedience and respect, in line with an authority ranking relationship.

There is still much we do not know about the dynamics of these different kinds of relationships, and the ethical implications of different kinds of relationship-specific rules and expectations. However, this model does alert us to the importance of people's beliefs and expectations around such issues as relationship intimacy, power, fairness, and respect—all of which are implied within the various relationship models.

ETHICS IN SPECIFIC TYPES OF CLOSE RELATIONSHIPS

Specific types of relationships such as marriages and friendships not only draw on the general rules for relationships but they also have their own more specific rules that reflect the functions of those particular relationships and carry implications for what constitutes ethical behavior. For example, friendships are guided by rules that revolve around *mutual enjoyment, sharing, and support*. Friends are expected to share news and activities, listen to one another, volunteer help and assistance, offer support, trust and confide in one another, enjoy each other and strive to make each other happy, stand up for each other, and respect each other's privacy (Argyle & Henderson,1984; Davis & Todd, 1985; Fehr, 2004). Violations, especially the most egregious, may significantly harm the relationship. For example, Argyle and Henderson found the rule violation that most strongly contributed to friendship breakdown was that one should *not* be jealous or critical of the partner's other relationships (p. 228).

By contrast, rules for committed romantic relationships, including marriage, focus more on *maintaining the bond and coordinating lives.* One of the most important expectations involves fidelity (Hampel & Vangelisti, 2008, p. 87), and sexual history and extradyadic affairs have been found to be the most common types of secrets kept from partners (Caughlin, Afifi, Carpenter-Theune, & Miller, 2005). In addition, the social roles of spouses and committed romantic partners go well beyond mutual enjoyment and support to the practical concerns of long-term coordination such as eating, maintaining a home, raising children, and so on. Couples can turn to traditional sex-role expectations for guidelines about being a good partner or spouse, but those roles do not necessarily suit everyone, and partners' expectations are not always congruent.

The relational rules that guide specific types of personal relationships, including friendships and marriages undoubtedly involve ethical considerations by varying degrees. Some transgressions may simply make someone "less of a friend" or an "inadequate spouse" while others may be considered truly unethical (for a range of transgressions, see Metts, 1994). Some of the "ethically loaded" rules clearly tie into general ethical concerns such as respect for privacy, trustworthiness, and honesty, others may be specific to intimate relationships (e.g., supportiveness), and still others are clearly relationship specific (e.g., fidelity). Further, there are ethical dilemmas that arise so infrequently that people have no clear ideas about how to deal with them or what the rules are. Such situations may be among the most morally and emotionally difficult that humans have to face; for example, when a dying spouse suffering unremitting pain begs her partner for assistance to die.

NEGOTIATED AND IDIOSYNCRATIC RULES AND ETHICS

Social roles may entail salient and socially accepted ethical guidelines for relating, but partners may find that they don't like the rules and want to ignore them or make up their own. However, it is usually not so simple. Even iconoclasts may find themselves orienting to the general rules by reinforcing, rejecting, or revising them to fit their specific circumstances. Couples may reject exclusiveness (open marriages), friends may add inclusion rules (you must invite me to all your parties), or make finer gradations (you may tell your mother about my drug conviction but don't tell your father).

Particularly interesting are "unscripted" relationships, such as lesbian mothers who embrace, reject, and adjust the rules and role of motherhood to fit in their specific circumstances (Hequembourg, 2004). For example, it would probably not be perceived as ethical to abandon the children of such a union, even though the nonbirth mother may have no legal rights or responsibilities for them. Clearly, the issue of whether and how to apply standard cultural models and their attendant ethical guidelines is a constantly evolving issue in both public and private domains. Consider, as examples, gay marriage, parental roles, or treating employees "like family." Is it ethical to permit same-sex partners to make medical decisions for each other, to give exclusive custody to either mothers or fathers, or to ask employees to keep in touch during their vacations?

Relationship partners may have differing perspectives on such issues, based on their own understandings of "the rules"—which in turn, may differ depending on, for example, who holds more power in the relationship. Further, it is frequently the case that higher-power individuals get to make the rules in the first place, leading to very different perceptions between themselves and their lower-power partners of what is fair, "right," and ethical behavior (see Fitness, 2001, for a discussion of perceived fairness and power in the workplace).

TRANSGRESSIONS, REVENGE, AND REPAIR

Despite our best intentions, ethical violations will inevitably occur and hurt the ones we love, and they will in turn, hurt us. Sometimes we overlook such hurts or explain them away as unintentional and unimportant in the overall context of our relationship. At other times we may feel that the bottom has dropped out of our world—how could someone who loves me have treated me like this? Further, some hurtful behaviors may be judged unforgivable and lead to relationship meltdown; others may be judged forgivable, if not immediately, then over the longer term.

How do suffering partners go about making themselves feel better? One strategy people use to relieve their own distress is to punish, or inflict pain, on the person who most "deserves" it —the partner who caused the distress in the first place. The terms *punishment* and *revenge* tend to be used synonymously, but the constructs can be theoretically distinguished. According to the *Macquarie Dictionary* (1992), to punish means "to subject to a penalty or to pain, loss, confinement, death etc., for some offence, transgression, or fault" with punishment being "that which is inflicted as a penalty" (p. 1428). Revenge, on the other hand, is defined as "retaliation for injuries or wrongs; vindictiveness; to exact expiation on behalf of a person for a wrong, especially in a resentful or vindictive spirit" (p. 1502). Punishment, then, implies a cool, rational and legitimate, if not moral, right to inflict harm on another. Revenge implies spite and the uncontrolled expression of emotions such as resentment and hate. Of course, the boundaries are fuzzy and may depend on the perspectives of the people involved. In particular, punishment may seem morally justified to the punisher, but feel like unwarranted vindictiveness to the target (Kim & Smith, 1993).

In some Islamic, Aboriginal, and Maori cultures, *revenge* in the form of blood retribution and payback are accepted parts of life; in cultures of honor, failures to avenge self/kin are a disgrace and invite further exploitation. Frijda (1994) argues that one of important tasks of civilized society is to serve as a moral arbiter of vengeance, rather than letting the injuring and injured parties (with their separate biases; Baumeister, 1997) negotiate fair payback. To the injured party, revenge can be sweet. It tells the world you are worthy of respect, redresses the power imbalance, asserts dominance, and redeems you from victimhood and humiliation (Baumeister, 1997; Yoshimura, 2007).

Punishment, by contrast, is a much more cooperative and communicative enterprise. Interviews with couples about the role of punishment in their relationship revealed several functions of punishment: to send a signal that something is wrong and a relationship rule has been broken; to "educate" an offending partner about the hurt partner's needs; to rebalance the relationship and restore the wounded partner's power, and to provide opportunities for caring partners to respond with an acknowledgment of the pain they have caused and a willingness to compensate by suffering some pain themselves (see Fitness & Peterson, 2008). Many of the functions of punishment resemble those of revenge (e.g., sharing pain, redistributing power) but with greater emphasis on restraint and relationship.

One of the most serious problems with punishment and revenge concerns the different forms of accounting used by victims and offenders when calculating appropriate punishments (Kim & Smith, 1993). In particular, offenders tend to minimize the harm they have caused, whereas victims tend to maximize their own suffering; thus, victims perceive a great deal more pain and suffering is "owing" than the offender believes is fair and reasonable, and this perceptual mismatch can lead to escalating cycles of revenge and counterrevenge.

Under what circumstances, then, do people forego the pleasures of revenge and choose *forgiveness* or reconciliation instead of or in addition to revenge? One may choose to forgive ethical violations for a number of important reasons, such as commitment to a cherished relationship, or for the sake of children and other family members (Finkel, Rusbult, Kumashiro, & Hannon, 2002; Fitness, 2001). One respondent in a study on marital forgiveness explained, however, that "your heart is not always so ready to forgive," especially when a reminder of the offense triggers fresh pain, anger, and hurt (even years later). Respondents' conclusions about forgiveness in marriage are that it takes time and perseverance, and that one must strive to "let go" of anger and hurt, or at least, allow the intensity of these emotions to diminish, before true forgiveness is possible (Fitness, 2001). Zechmeister, Garcia, Romero, and Vas (2004) also note that the ideal of unconditional forgiveness without some form of punishment or revenge may be just that—an impossible ideal. Participants in their studies required offenders to make amends, particularly following a verbal apology (which ironically, admits accountability). Indeed, they noted that apologies on their own can make a delicate situation worse—offenders need to make amends and "pay" for their crimes if they are to win forgiveness.

Nonetheless, *apologies* may play a critical role in forgiveness and reconciliation and serve some of the same functions as punishment and revenge, albeit with words alone. Lazare (2004) makes the case that successful apologies: (1) restore dignity and respect to the injured party; (2) provide reassurance that both parties have shared values; (3) assure injured parties that offenses were not their fault; (4) assure safety in the relationship; (5) let the injured party see the offender suffer; (6) provide reparation for the harm; and (7) involve meaningful dialogue between injured and offended parties (pp. 44–74). Apologies can go badly wrong, however, causing more damage to the relationship, such as when they are insincere, vague, dodge responsibility, or fail to acknowledge the harm done to the injured party. Effective apologizers must understand the violation and its severity, history, and implications (Tavuchis, 1991). Apologies must also come neither too soon nor too late lest they be seen as preemptive or reluctant. Injured parties may or may not accept even well-crafted apologies, even if done by the book, and relationships may or may not be repaired as a result.

Most of our discussion of ethics to this point has been founded in ways to balance and negotiate the interests of individuals that are represented in a research literature that is dominated by Western perspectives. Shweder, Much, Mahapatra, and Park (1997) proposed that in addition to the autonomy and justice-based morality commonly found in the West, two other moralities are common elsewhere in the world. One is the ethic of divinity, in which humans are believed to be holy and are obliged not to degrade that holiness. The ethic of divinity seems less obviously interpersonal, but it guides sex, food choices, and other personal decisions that are made by couples, families, or friends together and seen as sacred activities but also potentially polluting. The other is the ethic of community, which derives from serving one's role in the community social order, as discussed next.

EXPANDING THE CIRCLE OF INTERPERSONAL ETHICS

Singer (2009) poses a relevant and uncomfortable ethical dilemma. You've bought your dream car, finally, and it cost you many thousands of dollars. On the way home, you get stuck on a railway crossing. The car is wedged there, so you get out to push it off the tracks. As you start to push you see there's a train coming. You've got to get your car off the tracks! And then, to your horror, you see a child lying on the railway tracks unconscious. The train is going to hit the child if you don't grab him—but if you grab him, the train will hit your beautiful new car. What do you do? OK—save the child; of course you do. But hang on—if the child's life is so important, why don't you sell your possessions right now and pour your money into saving some of the children in the world who are suffering right now?

It is an interesting dilemma when the child is a stranger, but it is no dilemma at all if it is your own child. Of course you sell your car to save your own child. But what if the child is your sister's child, your next-door neighbor's child, a child in the next town, a child halfway around the globe? The dilemma becomes increasingly difficult as the distance from you increases.

Clearly close interpersonal relationships, especially family relationships, are privileged. Buss (1999) has hypothesized that when people want or need help, they may even use language that implies a kin relationship—"hey brother, can you spare a dime?" There is much to be said for taking the notion of the "human family" seriously on an ethical level, but is it really feasible to buy birthday presents for 6 billion people? De Waal asks the more practical question of how far we extend the circle of morality before it becomes fragile (de Waal, 2006). He argues that "the biggest step in the evolution of morality was the move from interpersonal relations to a focus on the greater good" (p. 54).

Moving beyond family, people regularly form friendships and cooperative alliances with nonkin. Every day people help their friends in many ways, large and small, from giving advice to sacrificing time and money to help them through a crisis. Why? One answer lies in reciprocal altruism. When times are tough, you can rely on the help of others, just as you have helped others in rough times. The problem lies in enforcement. Some enforcement can be found in the guilt that we feel if we don't repay favors or in the gratitude we feel when others are kind. Another enforcer is reputation. Cheaters may get away with it in the short run but not in the long run if their reputations follow them.

Further, according to this theory, you won't necessarily get help from the same person that you helped; it's more of a "what goes round, comes round" principle (generalized exchange; Blau, 1964). Are there strategies for encouraging cooperation and prosocial behavior in our communities? Axelrod (1984) proposed several: making commitments to future interactions, teaching reciprocity, insisting on no more than equity, responding quickly to cheating, and cultivating a personal reputation as a fair player.

Note that even a sharing and caring community presumes some degree of interaction to make ethical arrangements work. The question that Singer further challenges us to address is whether all human beings can acknowledge that we share the same planet and act as a caring global community, including nonhuman life forms (Singer, 2002). It is a tall order, but one that seems to be met commonly, if not consistently. At the time of this writing, humans are sending aid to Haitian earthquake victims and saving beached whales in New Zealand.

One of the inevitable features of living in groups and communities is that sometimes what's good for us personally will also be good for the group but at other times your individual wants and needs and your social group's wants and needs conflict with the group's—a mixed motive situation. The "tragedy of the commons" (Hardin, 1968) illustrates how individual selfishness can lead to ruinous consequences for the group. Pastures in New England were public areas, called commons, where any sheep or cow herder was allowed to graze his animals, free of charge. On private pastures, herders would only graze as many animals as the land could support, aware that overgrazing quickly destroyed the grass and starved the whole herd. However, herders showed no such restraint with the common areas, and the commons were frequently destroyed by overgrazing. The pursuit of self-interest by individual farmers produced collective disaster.

Most large-scale social and environmental problems today share some features with the tragedy of the commons. Consider, for example, the issue of population control. Many ecologists have argued that people can choose to have as many children as they like because it is a personal right. Yet if everyone has very large families, there may be tremendous pressure on the environment and resources, and ultimately, the whole community suffers. One traditional solution to the problem was to forbid couples to marry unless they had shares to common resources such as woodlands with strong sanctions for procreation out of wedlock (Netting, 1981). Today many would view such a solution as ethically problematic, very much like China's one-child policy.

INTERPERSONAL COMMUNICATION AND THE GREAT ETHICAL ISSUES OF OUR TIMES

Most scholarly work that addresses ethical issues related to interpersonal communication treats close relationships as if they were largely disconnected from the larger physical and social worlds, except for slight expansions to social roles and immediate social networks. Obviously, a relationship does not exist in a bubble. Like an individual, it is embedded in, draws on, and contributes to their greater physical, biological, social, economic, and cultural environments. Rather than review prior bodies of research, in this section we offer suggestions for new directions in research that might link interpersonal communication and the great ethical issues of our day.

Research is needed on the most basic issues related to interpersonal communication about ethical issues that transcend the dyad. Much research addresses ethical issues that pertain to couples, friends, or families, especially those related to personal ethics and health and safety (e.g., safe sex, drug use, etc.). Such work could be extended to address how people talk interpersonally about ethical issues for the larger society and planet. Of course, the first question is what ethical issues they talk about: Global warming? Human rights? Eating meat? Second, what provokes the discussion: A news report? Seeing a gorilla in a zoo? Third, how is the topic discussed: Parents lecturing to children? Couples arguing? Friends trying to persuade each other? Recently, therapists have noted that arguments between couples and among family members about environmental concerns are on the rise (Kaufman, 2010).

How deeply the interpersonal and the more broadly social are and should be intertwined is an important ethical question in its own right, implicating issues of privacy, autonomy, and responsibility. Are personal actions sequestered as largely irrelevant or "not my problem?" Are government policies that interface most closely with personal decisions considered infringements on personal freedoms or justified for the greater good (e.g., abortion, HIV disclosures)? Should people hold each other accountable for acting ethically (e.g., cutting back on consumption of fossil fuels, giving aid in disasters), and if so, how?

Finally, we might consider whether the goal of public policy is to promote the greater good by improving overall quality of life (Diener & Seligman, 2004). If so, support for close relationships needs to be taken seriously because research indicates that healthy relationships are one of the key factors associated with happiness and subjective well-being (Argyle, 1987; Myers, 1999). Public priorities ranging from encouraging social interaction through the design of public squares to providing direct support for families such as the U.S. Family Medical Leave Act might be considered more ethical, in a sense, than those that promote further material acquisition for those whose basic needs are met. In this way, we challenge researchers to think about ethics not just in terms of meeting basic needs, fostering fair play, and creating caring communities, but also in terms of helping humans flourish (Paul, Miller, & Paul, 1999), especially in their close relationships.

REFERENCES

Algoe, S., Haidt, J., & Gable, S. (2008). Beyond reciprocity: Gratitude and relationships in everyday life. *Emotion, 8*, 425–429.

Argyle, M. (1987). *The psychology of happiness*. London: Methuen.

Argyle, M., & Henderson, M. (1984). The rules of friendship. *Journal of Social and Personal Relationships, 1*, 211–237.

Axelrod, R. (1984). *The evolution of cooperation*. New York: Basic Books.

Barbee, A., Cunningham, M., Druen, P., & Yankeelov, P. (1996). Loss of passion, intimacy, and commitment: A conceptual framework for relationship researchers. *Journal of Personal and Interpersonal Loss, 1*, 93–108.

Baumeister, R. F. (1997). *Evil: Inside human cruelty and violence.* New York: W. H. Freeman.

Baumeister, R. F., & Catanese, K. (2001). Victims and perpetrators provide discrepant accounts: Motivated cognitive distortions about interpersonal transgressions. In J. P. Forgas, K. D. Williams, & L. Wheeler (Eds.), *The social mind* (pp. 274–293). New York: Cambridge University Press.

Baumeister, R. F., & Leary, M. R. (1995). The need to belong: Desire for interpersonal attachments as a fundamental human motivation. *Psychological Bulletin, 117*, 497–529.

Baumeister, R. F., & Wotman, S. R. (1992). *Breaking hearts: The two sides of unrequited love.* New York: Guilford.

Baxter, L. A., & Montgomery, B. M. (1996). *Relating: Dialogues and dialectics.* New York: Guilford.

Bergun, V., & Dossetor, J. (2005). *Relational ethics: The full meaning of respect.* Hagerstown, MD: University.

Blau, P. M. (1964). *Exchange and power in social life.* New York: Wiley.

Bok, S. (1978). *Lying: Moral choice in public and private life.* New York: Random House.

Buss, D. (1999). *Evolutionary psychology: The new science of the mind.* Boston, MA: Allyn & Bacon.

Caughlin, J. P. (2002). The demand/withdraw pattern of communication as a predictor of marital satisfaction over time. *Human Communication Research, 28*, 49–85.

Caughlin, J. P., Afifi, W. A., Carpenter-Theune, K. E., & Miller, L. E. (2005). Reasons for, and consequences of, revealing personal secrets in close relationships: A longitudinal study. *Personal Relationships, 12*, 43–59.

Dailey, R. (2006). Confirmation in parent-adolescent relationships and adolescent openness: Toward extending confirmation theory. *Communication Monographs, 73*(4), 434–458.

Davis, K. E., & Todd, M. J. (1985). Assessing friendship: Prototypes, paradigm cases and relationship description. In S. Duck & D. Perlman (Eds.), *Understanding personal relationships* (pp. 17–38). London: Sage.

DePaulo, B. M., & Kashy, D. A. (1998). Everyday lies in close and casual relationships. *Journal of Personality and Social Psychology, 74*, 63–79.

DePaulo, B. M., Morris, W. L., & Sternglanz, R. W. (2009). When the truth hurts: Deception in the name of kindness. In A. L. Vangelisti (Ed.), *Feeling hurt in close relationships* (pp. 167–190). New York: Cambridge University Press.

De Waal, F. (2006). *Primates and philosophers.* Princeton, NJ: Princeton University Press.

DeWall, C. N., Baumeister, R. F., & Masicampo, E. J. (2009). Rejection: Resolving the paradox of emotional numbness after exclusion. In A. L. Vangelisti (Ed.), *Feeling hurt in close relationships* (pp. 123–142). New York: Cambridge University Press.

Diener, E., & Seligman, M. E. P. (2004). Beyond money: Toward an economy of well-being. *Psychological Science in the Public Interest, 5*(1), 1–31.

Englehardt, E. E. (2001). *Ethical issues in interpersonal communication.* Orlando, FL: Harcourt.

Ennis, E., Vrij, A., & Chance, C. (2008). Individual differences and lying in everyday life. *Journal of Social and Personal Relationships, 25*(1), 105–118.

Fehr, B. (2004). Intimacy expectations in same-sex friendships. *Journal of Personality and Social Psychology, 86*(2), 265–284.

Finkel, E. J., Rusbult, C. E., Kumashiro, M., & Hannon, P. A. (2002). Dealing with betrayal in close relationships: Does commitment promote forgiveness? *Journal of Personality and Social Psychology, 82*, 956–974.

Fiske, A., & Haslam, N. (2005). The four basic social bonds: Structures for coordinating interaction. In M. W. Baldwin (Ed.), *Interpersonal cognition* (pp. 267–298). New York: Guilford.

Fitness, J. (2001). Betrayal, rejection, revenge and forgiveness: An interpersonal script approach. In M. Leary (Ed.), *Interpersonal rejection* (pp. 73–103). New York: Oxford University Press.

Fitness, J. (2005). Bye bye, black sheep: The causes and consequences of rejection in family relationships. In K. Williams, J. P. Forgas, & W. von Hippel (Eds.), *The social outcast: Ostracism, social exclusion, rejection, and bullying* (pp. 263–276). Hove, UK: Psychology Press.

Fitness, J. (2008). Fear and loathing in the workplace. In N. Ashkanasy & C. Cooper (Eds.), *Research companion to emotions in organizations* (pp. 127–152). London: Edward Elgar.

Fitness, J., & Peterson, J. (2008). Punishment and forgiveness in close relationships: An evolutionary, social-psychological perspective. In J. P. Forgas & J. Fitness (Eds.), *Social relationships: Cognitive, affective, and motivational perspectives* (pp. 255–269). New York: Psychology Press.

Freeman, J. (2009). *Shrinking the world: The 4000-year story of how email came to rule our lives*. Melbourne, Australia: Text/Penguin Australia.

Frijda, N. H. (1994). The lex talionis: On vengeance. In S. H. M. van Goozen, N. E. van de Poll, & J. A. Sergeant (Eds.), *Emotions: Essays on emotion theory* (pp. 263–289). Hillsdale, NJ: Erlbaum.

Fuller, R. W. (2004). *Somebodies and nobodies*. Gabriola Island, BC, Canada: New Society.

Gilligan, C. (1982). *In a different voice*. Cambridge, MA: Harvard University Press.

Greene, K., Derlega, V. J., & Mathews, A. (2006). Self-disclosure in personal relationships. In A. Vangelisti & D. Perlman (Eds.), *Handbook of personal relationships* (pp. 409–427). New York: Cambridge University Press.

Grice, H. P. (1975). Logic and conversation. In P. Cole & J. L. Morgan (Eds.), *Syntax and semantics: Vol. 9. Pragmatics* (pp. 113–128). New York: Academic Press.

Hampel, A. D., & Vangelisti, A. L. (2008). Commitment expectations in romantic relationships. *Personal Relationships, 15*, 81–102.

Hardin, G. (1968). The tragedy of the commons. *Science, 162*, 1243–1248.

Hequembourg, A. (2004). Unscripted motherhood: Lesbian mothers negotiating incompletely institutionalized family relationships. *Journal of Social and Personal Relationships, 21*, 739–762.

Hinde, R. A. (1979). *Towards understanding relationships*. New York: Academic Press.

Hochschild, A. R. (1989). The economy of gratitude. In D. D. Franks & E. D. McCarthy (Eds.), *The sociology of emotions: Original essays and research papers* (pp. 95–113). Greenwich, CT: JAI Press.

Kant, I. (1992). Duty and reason. In T. C. Denise & S. P. Peterfreund (Eds.), *Great traditions in ethics* (7th ed., pp.180–199). New York: Wadsworth. (Original work published in 1898)

Kaufman, L. (2010, January 18). Preserving the planet, straining the relationship. *The New York Times*, p. A11.

Keith, S., & Martin, M. E. (2005). Cyber-bullying: Creating a culture of respect in a cyber world. *Reclaiming Children & Youth, 13*, 224–228.

Kelley, H. H., Berscheid, E., Christensen, A., Harvey, J. H., Huston, T. L., Levinger, G., et al. (Eds.). (1983). *Close relationships*. New York: W. H. Freeman.

Kim, S., & Smith, R. (1993). Revenge and conflict escalation. *Negotiation Journal, 9*, 37–43.

Kluwer, E. S., Tumewu, M., & Van den Bos, K. (2009). Men's and women's reactions to fair and unfair treatment in relationship conflict. *Personal Relationships, 16*, 455–474.

Knapp, M. L. (2006). Lying and deception in close relationships. In A. Vangelisti & D. Perlman (Eds.), *Handbook of personal relationships* (pp. 517–532). New York: Cambridge University Press.

Kohlberg, L. (1981). *The philosophy of moral development*. San Francisco, CA: Harper & Row.

LaFollette, H., & Graham, G. (1986). Honesty and intimacy. *Journal of Social and Personal Relationships, 3*, 3–18.

Lazare, A. (2004). *On apology*. New York: Oxford University Press.

Lerner, M. J., & Mikula, G. (1994). *Entitlement and the affectional bond: Justice in close relationships*. New York: Springer.

Macquarie Dictionary (2nd ed.). (1992). Sydney, Australia: Macquarie Library, Macquarie University.

Metts, S. (1989). An exploratory investigation of deception in close relationships. *Journal of Social and Personal Relationships, 6*, 159–179.

Metts, S. (1994). Relational transgressions. In W. R. Cupach & B. H. Spitzberg (Eds.), *The dark side of interpersonal communication* (pp. 217–239). Hillsdale, NJ: Erlbaum.

Miller, W. I. (1993). *Humiliation*. Ithaca, NY: Cornell University Press.

Myers, D. G. (1999). Close relationships and quality of life. In D. Kahneman, E. Diener, & N. Schwarz (Eds.), *Well-being: The foundations of hedonic psychology* (pp. 374–391). New York: Sage.

Netting, R. M. (1981). *Balancing on an alp*. New York: Cambridge University Press.

Orrego, V. O., Smith, S. W., Mitchell, M. M., Johnson, A. J., Yun, K. A., & Greenberg, B. (2000). Disclosure and privacy issues on television talk shows. In S. Petronio (Ed.), *Balancing the secrets of private disclosures* (pp. 249–259). Mahwah, NJ: Erlbaum.

Paul, E. F., Miller, F. D., Jr., & Paul, J. (Eds.). (1999), *Human flourishing.* Cambridge, UK: Cambridge University Press.

Petronio, S. (1991). Communication boundary management: A theoretical model of managing disclosure of private information between marital couples. *Communication Theory, 1,* 311–335.

Petronio, S. (2002). *Boundaries of privacy.* Albany, NY: SUNY Press.

Petronio, S., & Durham W. T. (2008). Communication privacy management theory. In L. A. Baxter & D. O. Braithwaite (Eds.), *Engaging theories in interpersonal communication* (pp. 309–322). Thousand Oaks, CA: Sage

Planalp, S., Rutherford, D. K., & Honeycutt, J. M. (1988). Events that increase uncertainty in relationships II: Replication and extension. *Human Communication Research, 14,* 516–547.

Rawls, J. (1971). *A theory of justice.* Cambridge, MA: Harvard University Press.

Rusbult, C. E., Coolsen, M. K., Kirchner, J. L., & Clarke, J. A. (2006). Commitment. In A. Vangelisti & D. Perlman (Eds.), *Handbook of personal relationships* (pp. 615–635). New York: Cambridge University Press.

Schultz, P. D. (2000). Sex offender communication notification policies: Balancing privacy and disclosure. In S. Petronio (Ed.) *Balancing the secrets of private disclosures* (pp. 263–274). Mahwah, NJ: Erlbaum.

Shaver, P. R., & Mikulincer, M. (2006). Attachment theory, individual psychodynamics, and relationship functioning. In A. Vangelisti & D. Perlman (Eds.), *Handbook of personal relationships* (pp. 251–271). New York: Cambridge University Press.

Shweder, R. A., Much, N. C., Mahapatra, M., & Park, L. (1997). The "Big Three" of morality (autonomy, community, divinity) and the "Big Three" explanations of suffering. In A. M. Brandt & P. Rozin (Eds.), *Morality and health* (pp. 119–169). New York: Routledge.

Sillars, A., & Scott, M. (1983). Interpersonal perceptions between intimates: An integrative review. *Human Communication Research, 10,* 153–176.

Simpson, J. A., Ickes, W., & Orina, M. (2001). Empathic accuracy and preemptive relationship maintenance. In J. Harvey & A. Wenzel (Eds.), *Close romantic relationships: Maintenance and enhancement* (pp. 27–46). Mahwah, NJ: Erlbaum.

Singer, P. (2002). *One world: The ethics of globalization.* New Haven, CT: Yale University Press.

Singer, P. (2009). *The life you can save: Acting now to end world poverty.* Melbourne, Australia: Text.

Tavuchis, N. (1991). *Mea culpa: A sociology of apology and reconciliation.* Stanford, CA: Stanford University Press.

Tepper, B. (2000). The consequences of abusive supervision. *The Academy of Management Journal, 43,* 178–190.

Thompson, C. (2008, September 7). Brave new world of digital intimacy. *New York Times.* Retrieved from http://www.nytimes.com

Williams, K. D., Forgas, J. P., & von Hippel, W. (2005). *The social outcast.* New York: Taylor & Francis.

Yoshimura, S. (2007). Goals and emotional outcomes of revenge activities in interpersonal relationships. *Journal of Social and Personal Relationships, 24,* 87–98.

Zechmeister, J. S., Garcia, S., Romero, C., & Vas, S. (2004). Don't apologize unless you mean it: A laboratory investigation of forgiveness and retaliation. *Journal of Social and Clinical Psychology, 23,* 532–564.

10

Ethical Challenges in Small Group Communication

John Gastil and Leah Sprain

By the fall of 2002, Lt. Col. Karen Kwiatkowski had served the U.S. Air Force for 20 years as an intelligence analyst in both the Pentagon and the National Security Agency. After the attacks of September 11, however, she had become increasingly concerned about the changing climate in her workplace. As the Bush administration set the course for war in Iraq, Kwiatkowski saw her "neoconservative" colleagues spend staff meetings reassembling evidence to justify preset conclusions and preparing ideological, often irrational attacks against their critics. She recalled one undersecretary branding a loyal general a "traitor." After General Colin Powell raised questions about the war plan, another colleague quipped that "the best service he could offer would be to quit."[1]

As an attendee at staff meetings, Kwiatkowski felt stifled, and she ultimately decided that she could best serve her country by leaving her intelligence group and retiring from the military. She came to play the role of whistleblower and helped to raise public consciousness of the now infamous Bush administration prewar analysis and planning (Fallows, 2006). Looking back, one can see that Kwiatkowski faced a serious ethical challenge during her Pentagon meetings: Was she obliged to speak up against belligerence, or was her role as Lieutenant Colonel to simply serve the agenda of her employers? Should she have stayed loyal to her group, or did leaving express a higher loyalty to her nation and her conscience?

Few of us will find ourselves in groups that could, by themselves, redirect the flow of history, but the ethical choices we make in small groups shape the course of our lives and those around us. One of the most comprehensive and influential theories used by small group researchers stresses this very point: According to the structuration theory developed by British sociologist Anthony Giddens (1984), the core of any social system consists of individuals choosing how to act in diverse social settings. Small groups prove the most important of these social contexts because it is in the group that we experience a "small-scale society," one large enough to simulate larger social patterns but small enough to change its rules and behavioral patterns. It may seem that there is a "natural" way in which our small group should communicate, but this is a sleight-of-hand that Giddens (1984) calls the "discursive 'naturalization' of the historically contingent circumstances and products of human action" (p. 79). Thus, even when posed with ethical dilemmas in groups, we may fail to recognize—let alone exercise—our freedom of action, but we still have it.

In this chapter, we explore the many ways in which small group research sheds light on the ethical challenges we face in groups. At the same time, we present a broader theoretical approach to groups that may reveal ethical dimensions of group life that past research has failed to explore adequately. We begin with these theoretical considerations, then examine three sets of ethical questions: how to form groups, what rules to set, and how to relate to other groups. In our conclusion, we compile an ethical checklist for working and living in groups, explore connections between the present discussion and other chapters in this volume, and highlight directions for future research on ethical choices in groups.

THEORETICAL OVERVIEW

How one should act in a group depends on one's context because the broad concept of a "small group" contains a tremendous variety of group types. Before exploring those variations, the first task is tracing the boundaries of the small group category.[2]

Defining Small Groups

The *minimum size* of a group is three people. Moving beyond two people makes possible majority–minority splits, introduces potential competition for attention, and changes the fundamental nature of the social unit. On the upper limit of a group, a better way to limit the size of a small group is to require that every group member have a sense of every other member's *copresence*. When people exist as members of a small group, they are together in this minimal sense, each aware of every other individual in the group. A related requirement is that a group's members view it as a *coherent* entity. To count as a small group, a social entity also must have *ongoing interaction* among its members. Most commonly, this means verbal communication, either speaking or typing to one another, but some groups' most important interactions are physical or nonverbal, as in the case of a play group, jazz band, or work crew. What counts as "ongoing" is also a question, but the definition used herein includes even ephemeral "zero-history groups"— those that literally have no history of working together as a group. Small groups must also have a *shared purpose*—at least one goal, aim, or task that brings them together. A small group's task could be to make decisions together, or it might tackle a physical challenge, such as moving a piano. More than simply a set of individual goals, however, to count as a small group a social entity also must have a *collective* goal. That is, the members must have in common the pursuit of some aim that gives their group its sense of purpose or mission. Simply meeting together does not make a social entity a group any more than a pitched street brawl constitutes a fight club.

A final requirement for a social entity to count as a small group holds that members must be interdependent to some degree. In a small group, accomplishment of shared goals depends on group members' contributions. A military unit on patrol counts on each member to watch out for the safety of the entire group, and though each soldier may have a high sense of self-confidence, the personal safety of each may ultimately depend on the alertness and skill of their least capable comrade.

Ethics and Group Variations

There are many ways of classifying the different forms of small group that fit this broad definition. Herein, we suggest a particular typology that highlights three key variations in relation to the different ethical situations that groups present: their origins, process, and external relationships. Table 10.1 shows how different combinations of these three elements yield groups that we readily recognize as fundamentally different.

TABLE 10.1

A Three-Dimensional Typology that Distinguishes Eight Group Types by Their Voluntary or Compulsory Origins, Democratic/Egalitarian or Centralized Authority Structure, and Autonomous or Dependent Relationship with Other Groups and Larger Organizations

	Democratic/Egalitarian		Centralized Authority	
	Autonomous	*Dependent*	*Autonomous*	*Dependent*
Voluntary	consciousness raising group	political party cell	support group	religious study group
Compulsory	self-managing work team	jury	family	task force

For example, in one corner of Table 10.1 lies the consciousness raising group, a voluntary, autonomous, egalitarian group made famous in the women's liberation movement (Shreve, 1989). Such a group might start with a discussion of a recent event or experience, and it would involve "going around the room" to hear members' "personal histories" on topics from childhood to dating to job discrimination or politics (Percy & Freeman, 1972). A democratic ethos might govern these discussions to ensure equal speaking opportunities and respectful listening with limited interruptions. In the opposite corner lies a rigidly structured task force. Joining this group is compulsory for the members assigned to it by a centralized authority, on which it remains dependent. The members of such a group receive their collective task from their employer, who may place an executive member on the task force to exercise any decision-making power it has been granted.

To appreciate the different challenges that contrasting group types present, consider again the painful experiences of Lt. Col. Kwiatkowski, described briefly in the introduction. Kwiatkowski principally worked in groups closer to the task force model, a very distant relative of the consciousness raising group. Had Kwiatkowski been in a relatively democratic group, she might have voiced her concerns more freely. Had her group been voluntary, rather than compulsory, she might have steered clear of the worst group meetings. Had her group been relatively autonomous, it might not have felt such intense pressure from the superiors who insisted on their analysts reaching particular conclusions. In sum, different types of groups present different kinds of challenges and create or foreclose different options for action.

The three dimensions along which groups vary in Table 10.1 also serve to structure our discussion of different ethical dilemmas in groups. The next section of this chapter will examine the ethics involved in group formation. In the case of *voluntary* groups, a number of people resolve to define and address a common purpose by working together. A *compulsory* group, by contrast, has its origin in the directives of one or more persons who require individuals to join a group. Thus, the jury summons calls private citizens to the courthouse, and the manager calls the staff to its mandatory weekly meeting. More subtly, the laws and conventions of society require children to belong to specific families. The difference between a voluntary or compulsory origin has implications for group ethics that we will consider shortly.

After reviewing group origins, we will examine the various process hazards groups encounter as they carry out their tasks. Here again, a fundamental contrast can be helpful. At one end of this continuum lies *democratic/egalitarian* group process. Gastil (1993) provides a detailed account of such processes in his study of a cooperatively managed grocery store, which strove to maintain equal power, nurture respectful relationships, and conduct rigorous and egalitarian deliberations. Even groups less self-consciously democratic still strive to operate by these rules, whether they be juries, nonprofit boards, self-managing work teams, or other quasi-egalitarian groups. Their counterpart has a *centralized* authority, which can come with more autocratic process norms that reinforce unbalanced power relations with asymmetric participation norms. Thus, a support group or religious study group might differentiate the therapist/leader from the patients/clients/ students not only in terms of authority but also in terms of behavioral roles of the different group members. What constitutes an ethical process challenge for diverse small groups will depend, in part, on their basic process rules.

Finally, modern group communication research has emphasized the interconnected nature of small groups (Putnam & Stohl, 1996), and we devote our third main section to the ethical issues related to groups' external relationships. Groups differ here in the degree to which they situate themselves as *autonomous* versus *dependent* groups. The ethics of how one acts in these different groups depends, in part, on their independence or obligations in relation to larger, related organizations and social entities.

GROUP FORMATION

In January 2007, environmental writer and activist Bill McKibben announced an attempt to build a social movement on climate change in the United States centered around a national day of climate action called Step It Up (SIU) (Endres, Sprain, & Peterson, 2009). The day of action was modeled after Earth Day: local actions in iconic places held together by a common call to action. With a small group of recent college graduates working with him as the national organizing team, McKibben established a Web site where individuals interested in planning an event in their town or city could post the details. Other people could go to the site and sign up to participate at an action nearby their home.

Soon, a multitude of small groups were generated. The national organizing team was a small group working closely together to organize the movement. In some cities, multiple people signed up to host actions. Often, these potential organizers decided to join together and organize one action together. In Indianapolis, this meant a small group of organizers led by two primary leaders (Pezzullo, 2009); in Seattle, up to 50 activists attended organizing meetings. On the day of action, some of the local events themselves functioned as small groups. For example, 10 marine activists and artists scuba dived off the coast of Fort Lauderdale, Florida, to explore a coral reef and make a plea—through video and photographic images—for its protection.

The members of these climate change groups were united in their desire to work to curb climate change. In this case, group participation itself was an ethical choice motivated by the desire for collective action on global warming. This desire led each of them to join their respective SIU group by signing up online, attending a meeting, or participating in a group-oriented action. This process of group formation is similar to a lot of voluntary groups that we choose to join.

In voluntary groups, the founders typically negotiate or deliberate about what they want to their group to look like—who can participate, what are the rules, what principles are most important. In compulsory groups, designers make these same decisions on behalf of future members. In both types of groups, this period of decision about what the group will look like and how it will operate poses important ethical dilemmas. Group scholars rarely research the process of group formation, instead focusing on the processes of already established groups or new member socialization in existing groups. This gap in the research highlights potential ethical pitfalls of forming new small groups that theory does not account for.

Membership

At their formation one of the key choices that groups must make centers on membership. The group's founders or designer must decide whom to include, the number of people, and the group's composition. Some groups let anyone who wants to join into the group, like the open invitation for anyone—everyone—to join a SIU action, but an open invitation does not serve the purposes of some groups. A monthly book club cannot include everyone in a discussion in an hour's time if 60 people attend a meeting. Time or resource restrictions may lead the group to limit membership. Restrictions on the composition or diversity of a group may be more controversial. For example, a feminist consciousness raising group may want to ensure that the group is a safe space to empower women and thereby decide to make sure that men (even those with feminist values) do not outnumber women. Honor societies invite only a small number of people, based on specific selection criteria, to join a cohort each year in order to maintain the prestige of membership. In each case, there is an ideological reason for membership restriction. Group ideologies themselves can be unethical; for example, racist skinhead groups who exclude based on race and creed.

Although ethical questions of membership should be discussed during the group formation phase, they should also be revisited throughout the life of the group. Groups may need to revisit membership criteria to ensure that they do not perpetuate historical discrimination by, for example, not allowing women to participate in sports groups or leadership councils in religious organizations. Conversely, assuming that demographic difference necessarily brings new knowledge and expertise also poses an ethical hurdle if the group forms specific—perhaps stereotyped—expectations for what new and demographically different members must bring to the group. Adding one "token" minority member can foster resentment in the person expected to represent minority views and other group members who discount real qualifications believing demographic characteristics are the primary reason for being included in the group (Kanter, 2006).

Groups should also assess their commitment to new member socialization. Traditionally within organizational communication scholarship, socialization is seen as the responsibility of newcomers to understand the organizations they join (Anderson, Riddle, & Martin, 1999). Jablin (1985) has suggested that this process is, and needs to be, mutual; new members influence the group just as the group affects new members. Research has shown that in some understaffed community organizations, for example, people are ready to welcome new staff (Cini, Moreland, & Levine, 1993). In other workplaces, newcomers can threaten existing group relationships leading to skepticism of new coworkers (Moreland & Levine, 1989). Groups need to formulate practices for welcoming new members and educating them about group norms without restricting them to playing the passive role of "newbie." A commitment to socialization should consider not only informational processes, such as training, but also reflection on how to welcome and accommodate new perspectives brought by new members. International work teams face the heightened ethical challenges of how to integrate multiple perspectives when members come to a group with different cultural norms of speaking. For example, North Americans and Western Europeans tend to use more direct speaking styles than Asians and East Indians (Haslett & Ruebush, 1999). In mixed groups, ethical concerns may result in selecting leaders from each group to ensure that multiple ways of relating and communicating can be valued and understood by the team.

Group Contracts

Once membership guidelines are determined, a group needs to determine the basic rules and norms for the group. Sometimes a group elects to formulate a formal set of guiding principles and rules resembling a contract. In political theory, the notion of a social contract suggests that citizens are born into a contract whereby we give up some of our rights as individuals and agree to abide by the rules of government in exchange for rights protection (see Hobbes, 1660/2001; Rousseau, 1762/2001). According to this theory, everyone submits to this contract, a process called "original consent." Some scholars have argued against using the social contract as a justification for governmental practices, like taxation, because not all individuals actually consent to the social contract (for example, anarchists) and the government will punish those who do not pay taxes even if they would not voluntarily submit to the social contract (see Spooner, 2004).

Most groups avoid this critique because group members have the potential to be at the actual signing of a contract or agreement rather than relying on the abstract fiction of "original consent." Historically, groups like the Massachusetts Bay colonists have signed a contract—the Massachusetts Bay Colony Charter—that set the rules for governance and leadership of the group (Vowell, 2008). Cabin groups at a summer camp may devise a covenant, a set of promises for living together, and sign it to illustrate their commitment to treat each other with kindness (and go to sleep when the lights are turned off at 11 p.m.). These different types of contracts demonstrate the range of statements that can be included in a group's founding documents, including a mission statement, structures for governance, and rules for decision making.

Group contracts vary in their degree of formality. Formal contracts can help establish group processes, which can ensure that these processes are in line with the values of the group and necessary tasks get accomplished. (In the next section, we discuss how this sort of contract can help avoid problems when groups that long to be democratic adopt more autocratic structures.) Formal contracts can also help new members understand the goals and rules of a group, particularly in compulsory groups where a member is assigned to a group such as a jury and may not know much about it. Finally, formal contracts can solidify member commitment to the shared purpose of the group, such as having participants at a political rally sign a pledge for future action on behalf of the group. On the other side, formal contracts can limit a group's flexibility, establishing set procedures for who is in charge that cannot always be quickly adapted to changing circumstances. Other groups thrive on a lack of formal commitment. The time and energy spent on a contract would be seen as a waste. For example, a group of friends developing a book club may discuss what they want to get out of the group but never put anything into writing.

Whether the group elects to have formal by-laws or more informal rules, its explicit or implicit contract may include elements about procedure, power structures, and means of revising the contract. The group may choose to be more democratic or more autocratic, by adopting particular voting procedures, rules for representation, and standards for who talks when (these group processes are discussed in more detail in the following section). Power structures can include rules for electing a leader or group of leaders, establishing grievance processes, or forgoing any formal power structures in favor of equality. Finally, the group can establish policies for adapting or amending the group's contract, such as a formal amendment process at an annual meeting or a promise to revisit the contract every three months.

INTERNAL PROCESS AND PRACTICES

Though many groups are quasi-democratic in practice but not in name, some groups are *explicitly* democratic (Gastil, 1993). Fair trade farmer cooperatives are certified as being democratic organizations where members participate in governance and decision making. The fair trade symbol guarantees consumers that the coffee was produced by democratically organized small farmers who were paid a set price for their product, whether it was produced in Ethiopia, Nicaragua, or Uganda. This contracted commitment to democratic process raises the stakes for farmer groups: Failing to allow member participation in governance could undermine their fair trade status and, in turn, their livelihood. In this context, democratic processes focus on representation in cooperative governance, venues for participation like semiannual meetings, and voice through practices such as voting. Some cooperatives expand democratic commitments to explicitly include a certain number of women in formal leadership positions as a means of female empowerment and enactment of the cooperative's values of gender equality (Sprain, 2009).

In other groups, such as some workplaces, the prevailing norms stress rigid structure, sharp role differences, and clear lines of authority. Such systems exist, for instance, within even the smallest typical military units that exist at the bottom of an elaborate hierarchy—from division to brigade to regiment, and on down to squad, crew, fire team, and the like. In these groups, the aim is to perform specific tasks and interpret and carry out orders. Morale and unit cohesion remain important, but such social aims exist only as secondary emphases relative to the unit's principle purpose of efficiently completing assigned tasks. When internal decisions must be made, such as when solutions must be improvised to meet unexpected circumstances, those are made by the unit's leader, who has no obligation to consult the unit's membership before making a determination and giving out commands.

This range of examples represents different practices on the democratic/egalitarian to centralized authority continuum. We do not believe that one or another point on this spectrum is more inherently ethical than another. Instead, we simply argue that the ethical challenges a group faces likely differ depending on its cultural situation.

Setting Procedures

In particular, democratic groups face a distinct challenge when it comes to setting procedure. After all, an autocratic group understood by its members to be legitimate cedes procedural authority to the autocrat, whereas in a democratic group, procedure remains fluid, theoretically at least, owing to both the membership's expectations for securing democratic values and the members' right to alter the process through the democratic process itself.

Democratic norms can include adopting formal group procedures like *Robert's Rules of Order*, decision rules of majority vote or consensus, and formalizing a commitment to a democratic ethos (Gastil, 1993). In practice, this can become quite complicated. For example, Table 10.2 illustrates specific democratic procedures put into place in a Citizens' Jury to ensure a democratic deliberative process. Failure to consider how cultural practices and differences impact democratic processes can result in disenfranchising group members in violation of a group's own aims. A Citizens' Jury in British Columbia, Canada, for example, held small groups in both English and French to accommodate native speakers rather than default to a *lingua franca*; similarly, they ensured that First Nations representatives were included on the jury—even if the members were not randomly selected.

Adopting democratic practices is an ethical choice for many groups, as it embodies their ideas for how the world should be, such as affinity groups in new social movements that use group practices and process to make to create the type of society they would like to see (Evans & Boyte, 1992; Polletta, 2002). Traditionally democratic practices are not, however, inherently ethical. In fact, standardized processes provide a resource that can be used by anyone in the group and can be even appropriated for nondemocratic purposes. School principal Ethel Sadowsky (1992, pp. 248–249) recalls one such occasion at a small "town meeting" on education:

> The procedures of the town meeting often seemed to have a life of their own, separate and distinct from the issues the group was discussing. A kind of half-informed understanding of *Robert's Rules of Order* began to guide the proceedings. Soon, meetings were consumed by such strategies as calling the question, doubting the quorum, and demanding recounts. These complicated delaying tactics frustrated many members who genuinely wanted to address issues of meaning. Those…still in attendance were eventually worn down by these procedures.

TABLE 10.2
Group Procedures Designed to Ensure a Democratic Deliberative Process in a Citizens' Jury

ANALYTIC PROCESS	Citizen Jury Objective	Procedures in Place
Create a solid information base	Combine expertise and professional research with personal experiences to better understand the problem's nature and its impact on people's lives.	Citizens get to cross-examine pro and con witnesses.
Prioritize the key values at stake	Integrate the public's articulation of its core values with technical and legal expressions social, economic, and environmental costs-and-benefits.	Values revealed through structured discussion of evaluation criteria.
Identify a broad range of solutions	Identify both conventional and innovative solutions, including governmental and non-governmental means of addressing the problem.	Initial solutions pre-set, but alternatives may emerge in discussion.
Weigh the pros, cons, and tradeoffs among solutions	Systematically apply the public's priorities to the alternative solutions, emphasizing the most significant tradeoffs among alternatives.	Pros and cons emerge as jury hears testimony and weighs alternatives.
Make the best decision possible	Identify the solution that best addresses the problem, potentially drawing on multiple approaches when they are mutually reinforcing.	Jury votes for a final set of recommendations, sometimes with a written dissent.
SOCIAL PROCESS		
Adequately distribute speaking opportunities	Mix unstructured, informal discussion in smaller groups with more structured discussion in larger groups. Create special opportunities for the reticent.	Mixes formal Q&A with extensive small group deliberation.
Ensure mutual comprehension	Ensure that public participants can themselves articulate general technical points and ensure that experts and officials are hearing the public's voice.	Extensive back-and-forth during Q&A, plus deliberation.
Consider other ideas and experiences	Listen with equal care to both officials and the general public. Encourage the public to speak in their authentic, unfiltered voice.	Citizens have ample time to explore different viewpoints.
Respect other participants	Presume that the general public is qualified to be present, by virtue of their citizenship. Presume officials will act in the public's best interest.	Important and distinct responsibilities given to citizens, experts, and officials help participants respect one another's roles.

Note. Table adapted from Gastil (2008), pp. 185, 207.

Some groups set procedures based on more centralized authority structures and norms that privilege other values above democratic procedure. For example, in some Israeli classrooms, the native term *gibush* (translated as "cohesion" or "crystallization") is a key educational goal: Teachers and students want to form a cohesive class marked by togetherness, involvement in social activities, and caring (Katriel & Nesher, 1986). These values sound as though they could be setting up a democratic ideal. The intergroup harmony of *gibush,* however, is measured by little fighting and group pride rather than the imperative for individuals to voice their concerns in democratic decision making. Sometimes in the aim to create a tightly knit group, placing *gibush* as the ultimate value can lead to problems when new students are not allowed into the group because of the firmly guarded group boundaries. Teachers acknowledge that cohesion is sometimes placed above ethical questions of right and wrong, which leaves students—especially new students—vulnerable.

Group Roles

Both autocratic and democratic groups must consider the procedures for assigning roles and group tasks. An outside authority, like a supervisor, sometimes assigns a group leader. When groups are left to select their own leaders, research has shown that high self-monitors—people who examine a situation and tailor their behavior accordingly—prove most likely to emerge as leaders and successfully navigate a series of group tasks (Zaccaro, Foti, & Kenny, 2006). For the most part, small groups select leaders based on what they do, not what traits they carry. Meta-analyses have shown that people generally find democratic leadership more satisfying (Foels, Driskell, Mullen, & Salas, 2000; Gastil, 1994b), but again, democratic leadership remains an ethical imperative only for those groups already committed to a democratic process (Gastil, 1994a).

Group members adopt many important rules besides leader. Some members take on process roles, such as facilitator or scribe. Some of the roles in groups are impacted by what Paul Moxnes (1999) calls "deep roles," such as gender expectations that are the products of relations over centuries. We have already discussed the danger of selecting a minority to serve as the token member. Groups get into danger when they treat anyone as a stereotype rather than a complex person (Hare, 1999).

Some roles come with status in the group, whether it is leaders who have final veto and control over decisions or a task force head who makes a higher salary than the other members for serving on the task force. If groups grant more respect and power to certain types of people, they run the risk of marginalizing other group members. Unfortunately, we know relatively little about how groups work through persistent status incongruities and interpersonal conflicts over individuals' relative status within the group. One encouraging study suggests that specific characteristics, such as real expertise, can prove the key to settling status conflicts. A pair of laboratory studies found that crude "dominance cues" (e.g., a threat of retribution or reference to one's authority) provide a group member little in terms of prestige and influence, whereas "task cues" (e.g., substantive contributions displaying relevant knowledge) improve one's standing on both dimensions (Driskell, Olmstead, & Salas, 1993; Karakowsky, McBey, & Miller, 2004).

Majority-Minority Relations

For minority members in a group, influencing group decisions is a challenge. To investigate the potential for minority influence, Tanford and Penrod (1984) created a computer simulation model of decision making groups. They found that a minority of one has an exceedingly difficult time prevailing—but add one more to make a coalition of two and the probability of success rises dramatically. They found that minorities have a better chance of success in smaller groups, such as a two-person minority against a six-person group (see also, Bond & Smith, 1996).

The small group literature provides some practical advice for people in minority coalitions who hope to shape and influence decisions (Brashers & Meyers, 1999; Meyers, Brashers, & Hanner, 2000). First, the minority members need to maintain a consistent position, which they express to other group members (and continue to believe themselves). Second, when minority members make their points, it can give them a persuasive boost to use a "tag-team" style, in which more than one member brings forward an argument or series of arguments in rapid succession. Third, researchers have found that group minority members have more success when they put forward high-quality arguments and refutations (as judged by independent observers).

Another line of research probes the effect of group diversity on the emergence of cohesion. The findings of recent research suggest that cohesion forms a bit more rapidly in homogenous groups. For instance, a study of self-managed work team members found that cohesion helped to reduce absenteeism, but cohesion did not form as easily in groups with mixes of men and women and full- and part-time employees (Sanders & Nauta, 2004). Even in more informal groups, member differences can undermine cohesion. In a community walking program, for instance, variation in past fitness experience and biological sex both undermined exercise groups' commitment to their joint activity (Burke et al., 2005; Shapcott, Carron, Burke, Bradshaw, & Estabrooks, 2006). Even the presence of just one "bad apple" can reduce a group's commitment to its task and its sense of togetherness (Wellen & Neale, 2006). But in all of these studies the diversity effect on cohesion is relatively small.

Nonetheless, there exists a widespread belief in the importance of homogeneity as a means of security cohesion. U.S. military officials historically have resisted integrating minorities, women, and now nonheterosexual enlistees for fear of losing "unit cohesion." Preferences for group homogeneity in the name of cohesion appear across the globe and in both formal and informal group settings. In the United States, most people's discussion networks and voluntary associations show tremendous homogeneity (McPherson, Smith-Lovin, & Brashears, 2006; Mutz, 2002). Outside the United States the pattern also occurs, such as in the case of *diwaniyyas*, regular evening discussions among friends and associates that occur in private homes in Kuwait. As described by Tétreault (2003), these meetings were traditionally open only to men, who congregate with one another daily or weekly, sometimes moving among two or more *diwaniyyas* in a single evening. Those reluctant to diversify military squadrons, work teams, or social gatherings fear the loss of cohesion, but the studies cited above suggest that the net loss can be considerably smaller than is imagined, particularly when the nature of the diversification has no relation to the topic or task a group addresses.

EXTERNAL RELATIONSHIPS

Groups distinguish themselves not only in terms their origins and process but also by the company they keep—the connections they make with the larger world. In part, groups forge and break social ties to govern the inward flow of information. In some cases, institutions surrounding the group serve to isolate the group, as when legal codes *prohibit* juries from gathering their own outside knowledge. In a very different way, some parents (and cult leaders) isolate their families (or "families") from the larger social world to better control the messages that reach their charges. For these groups, social sequestration is a legal or ethical imperative.

Isolation, however, presents severe hazards for most groups. Groups that aim to solve complex problems and reach sound judgments, in particular, look to nurture their outside connections. In this spirit, the "X-Team" concept has emerged from organizational research and consulting (Ancona, Bresman, & Kaeufer, 2002). X-Teams distinguish themselves by crossing their group boundaries *constantly* and traveling far outside the organization(s) sponsoring them. Rather than focusing on its internal processes and procedures, X-Teams are "externally oriented" toward their "extensive ties" with people outside the group. In fact, X-Teams focus energy on cultivating and harvesting their members' individual external relationships more than on building their own team's internal relationships and sense of group cohesion. As an example of this approach, the Vehicle Design Summit launched in 2006 tried to design, build, and bring to market a "hyper-efficient" passenger vehicle (see vehicledesignsummit.org). In the spirit of an X-Team, the Summit members deliberately reached outside their core group's expertise, and the Summit made considerable progress, though it did not meet its goal of unveiling a completely functional "concept car" by August 2008.

The Specter of Groupthink

Small group researchers have long recognized the perils of a group limiting its external relationships. Janis (1982) cemented the popular understanding of *groupthink* when he found that under the wrong circumstances, groups of well-intentioned and highly capable experts, policy advisors, and executives could devolve into a kind of discussion that would invariably lead to flawed decisions. Prominent among the underlying causes of groupthink are insularity—the separation of the group from outside voices and critics—and high stress from perceived external threats. In other words, the prototypical groupthink situation involves a group detaching itself from reality, such that it comes to exaggerate its internal morality and rationality, and demonizes its perceived enemies. The historical record of small groups shows full-scale groupthink to be more of a cautionary tale than a common occurrence, but when viewed in more general terms, many decision-making bodies fall into the same pitfalls and experience groupthink, at least by degree (Aldag & Fuller, 1993).

   The groupthink research suggests that neglecting external ties often amounts to an ethical lapse—a failure to maximize the depth and quality of the group's information base. We conceptualize this as both *inherently* and *consequentially* unethical. First, the isolating impulse can exclude from consideration diverse points of view, which amounts to a procedural violation for those groups committed to an inclusive, democratic process. This is also inherently unethical to the extent that the group had a charge—given by its own members of the authority who formed the group—to conduct a rigorous analysis. This amounts to the kind of failure Lt. Col. Karen Kwiatkowski witnessed in the example that began this chapter. More often than not, though, exceedingly weak ties to outside input yields an avoidable negative consequence, as in foreign policy failures that Janis (1982) made famous, such as the Kennedy Administration's reckless Bay of Pigs invasion of Cuba in 1961. In time, the Bush Administration's inept prewar planning in Iraq may well become, literally, another textbook example of the moral cost of such extreme insularity (Woodward, 2006).

   The haunting prospect of groupthink, however, should not hamstring those groups that have very sound reasons for separating themselves from outside scrutiny. In particular, people may choose to join voluntarily groups that give them a kind of social shelter, refuge, or retreat. In consciousness raising and religious study groups, people seek to develop a particular understanding of themselves and their world. Doing so may require the privacy of a group consisting only of fellow seekers and trained guides. Other voluntary groups, such as Alcoholics Anonymous and other support groups, have extensive ties within a larger organization but maintain the privacy of individual chapters or groups (Wuthnow, 1994). Even these groups, though, pose the risk of slipping so far from the external world that their members develop coping skills unsuited for the wider world, potentially yielding deadly consequences for not just their members but for the larger world, as in the case of terrorist cells (National Commission on Terrorist Attacks upon the United States, 2004).

Symbolic Convergence and Separation

More subtly, groups relate to their external environments through their self-representations. Bormann (1996) and others have demonstrated that groups, given a modicum of time, will reach a "symbolic convergence," a shared narrative that gives group members a common set of meanings and dramatic symbols (see Bormann, Cragan, & Shields, 2001). Bormann writes that such a group's members have "jointly experienced the same emotions,…developed common heroes and villains, celebrated certain actions as laudable, and interpreted some aspect of their common experience in the same way" (Bormann, 1996, p. 94). Symbolic convergence principles apply to any group, even those focused only on "work" and "decision making." After all, many work teams distinguish themselves either by their passion for productivity or their exceptional commitment to sloth. In both cases, one finds dramatic stories—whether explicitly celebrated as part of the group's history or unconsciously dragged along as unacknowledged group baggage (e.g., the "hot groups" in Lipman-Blumen & Leavitt, 1999).

This line of research relates explicitly to ethics in the tendency of groups to identify themselves with a popular ethical position, such as the democratic group discussion model described earlier (Bormann, 1996, pp. 110–111; also see Keith, 2007). Groups routinely construct a set of ethical guidelines and warnings through the symbols to which they adhere or stand in opposition. Thus, a band of musicians might identify themselves as "a garage band" to emphasize their commitment to relaxed, friendly relationships and in opposition to the tensions and professional pressures that can come with a drive for achievement. In such a band, showing up late without having practiced may be ethical, whereas replacing an adequate band member with a professional would be seen as a lapse in ethical judgment.

The process of symbolic convergence, per se, however, poses an interesting ethical challenge that goes beyond a group's internal process. In the same structurational sense introduced earlier in this chapter (Giddens, 1984), the process of convergence is really one of appropriating (and potentially modifying) social structures of meaning, norms, and power. In that sense, a group always has the opportunity to draw from and give back to the larger society when it moves toward a symbolic homeostasis. A group may unselfconsciously reproduce symbols that carry derogatory meanings or reinforce oppressive power-relations, or it may converge on more emancipatory themes.

One example is the ways groups reproduce "discourses of power," ways of talking about and understanding people's ability to reshape their sociopolitical environment (see Hindess, 1996). Google lists a quarter-million references to the words attributed to anthropologist Margaret Meade, "Never doubt that a small group of thoughtful, committed citizens can change the world. Indeed, it is the only thing that ever has." Contrast that with the more commonplace portrait of group meetings represented in *Dilbert, The Office*, and corporate folklore, wherein groups have no power and prevent change more often than they engender it. Groups can appropriate one or the other of these contrasting self-representations from their social environment and thereby promote one representation of groups against the other. Such symbolic choices amount to more than accurate self-descriptions; rather, they contribute subtly to the ways in which people accurately recognize constraints placed on them and their opportunities for engendering social change.

Ingroups and Outgroups

At any given time, a society contains a finite but fluid set of categories that mark individuals as members of recognizable social, cultural, political, economic, or demographic classes or groupings. We enter into many others voluntarily, such as when we choose to attend a particular college or move to a new city, either of which might become a part of how we represent ourselves to others. Some social identities, such as those whose formal memberships require considerable economic wealth, might call for considerable effort and remain unavailable to the vast majority of a society's members. In all of these ways, we carry multiple social identities with us wherever we go, and we often enter small groups to deploy, develop, defend, downplay, or even discard them (see Scott, Corman, & Cheney, 1998).

The most pertinent and widely studied theory on this subject is *social identity theory* (Abrams, Hogg, Hinkle, & Otten, 2005). In a small group context, this theory highlights how social comparisons between "ingroups" and "outgroups" (and among group members) shape how we behave in small groups. Group members work hard to demonstrate that their own behavior matches their group's prototype and to show how their group's behavior, attitudes, and values contrast with those typical of disliked "outgroups." Specifically, we strive to show our group as distinctive and just, right, or moral.

This group-comparison process goes well beyond harmless bonding rituals. A pair of meta-analytic summaries covering more than 100 studies between them show that ingroups do, indeed, stereotype and develop prejudices against outgroups; those biases, in turn, result in discriminatory behavior (Mullen & Hu, 1989; Schütz & Six, 1996). Just as group members can denigrate and stereotype the outgroup, so do they reevaluate themselves as individuals. Abrams et al. (2005) explain that within a highly salient group, "perceptions of group members and of the self become *depersonalized*," which means "a person takes the ingroup prototype as a norm" and "the ingroup stereotype as a self-description" (p. 110). The interests of the group become one's self-interest, and "a threat to the ingroup" becomes "a threat to the *self*." This process can create a self-reinforcing cycle, whereby those members who exhibit prototypical opinions and behaviors—particularly those that contrast sharply with outgroup norms—gain ever-more ingroup status and influence.

The use of specific speech styles is associated with particular stereotypes. Patronizing speech—speech marked by simplified grammar and vocabulary, higher and variable pitch, louder volume, and use of endearing terms (e.g. "sweetie")—is sometimes used in response to stereotypes about older individuals (Harwood, Ryan, Giles, & Tysoski, 1997). Research shows that the use of patronizing speech is seen as derogatory, nonetheless there is a tendency to evaluate the victim or target of patronizing speech as a less competent communicator, a "blame the victim" evaluation. This is particularly true in cases where the target is elderly and female. In this case, a stereotype leads to speech behavior that ends up influencing the behavior of the victim and reinforcing the stereotype itself.

This research has important ethical implications for both group researchers and interlocutors. As Harwood and Giles (1996) suggest, an important question for researchers is to investigate how groups of elderly patients can indicate displeasure with their treatment while avoiding negative attributions that come from expressing displeasure. More broadly, researchers should study effective strategies for responding to stereotypes, including strategies that seek to correct misconceptions without perpetuating ingroup/outgroup divisions. In turn, individuals should recognize how stereotypes influence their own behavior and negatively influence others.

Though group identification has its benefits—for individuals and society—examples such as these underscore the danger in these deindividuation, prototyping, and stereotyping processes. As an ethical matter, groups must take these potential side-effects of group identity into account. Better still, groups should think about ways they can reinforce *superordinate identities*, an identity that reaches across conventional lines of in-group/out-group contrast, such as when residents from different parts of a city bond over a shared interest in their local sports team. Research suggests that such identities can promote a cooperative norm based on shared group identity that overrides conflicts of self-interest that would have arisen from separate subordinate identities (Kramer & Brewer, 2006).

CONCLUSION

This review has focused more on the substantive research on groups than on ethics, per se, so we begin this conclusion with a straightforward discussion of the ethical considerations that emerged in the preceding sections. For members of any group, we offer the ethical checklist in Table 10.3. Each of these nine admonitions ties back to the preceding research presented in this chapter. There are many other ethical rules that groups could abide by, and this checklist is certainly partial in this respect. Far from a comprehensive statement of ethics, we instead present it to show how readily one can extract ethical insight from small group research.

With that in mind, we suggest a few directions for future research on groups that could be especially helpful in navigating our ongoing ethical challenges. Generally, we endorse the bona fide group perspective (Putnam & Stohl, 1996), which encourages the study of groups in natural settings. Laboratory studies will continue to add value to our knowledge of groups, but the various methods of field investigation—from interviews and surveys to direct observation—will bring researchers closer to the ethical problems real groups face.

The first line of research we encourage would look at how groups form and establish their initial contracts. This topic may have received less attention to date simply because it is hard to witness an event that often occurs spontaneously. Even if one has to rely on retrospective accounts, this important stage in group development merits study, for the founding period of a group often sets in motion practices and expectations that enable or constrain ethical behavior for the group's entire life.

Second, we think group researchers should further refine the procedural ideal of democracy in small groups. There remains relatively little work on how groups understand themselves in democratic terms (Gastil, 1993), but new lines of study could help us see how groups struggle with democratic norms and procedures. Tracy and Ashcraft (2001), for instance, take on school

TABLE 10.3
An Ethical Checklist for Small Groups

Group Formation
1. When setting group boundaries, think explicitly about the reasons for including or excluding different potential members and reflect on the ideal size of your group.
2. If developing a group contract, ensure that all founding members of the group participate meaningfully in its construction and approval.
3. Make a plan for how to welcome new members that includes planning for their input and potentially adjusting group norms and rules in response.

Process and Procedures
4. Always seek to clarify the appropriate lines of authority and decision making in the group and build procedures accordingly.
5. Consider how group rules and norms impact other members of the group, and establish rules that create a group that respect every role or position in the group.
6. Build a group that can be responsive when a minority of its members advance strong arguments against a majority position.

External Relationships
7. To avoid even mild groupthink, groups should keep their borders permeable to ensure information inflow, regardless of whether the group holds values or views contrary to or in line with prevailing opinion.
8. Groups should recognize that they not only draw on social meanings and norms, but their choices also feed back into the larger society and shape the opportunities and understandings of the wider public.
9. Particularly when building their internal identity, groups must remain vigilant against depersonalizing their members and denigrating other groups, particularly those that fall along other sides of deep social and cultural divisions.

boards, a form of group rarely addressed. Their ethnographic study goes even farther by exploring how internal democratic norms complement (or conflict) with community-wide standards for democratic practice. This is yet one more way in which democratic groups face a special ethical burden owing to their inherent concern with procedural legitimacy.

Finally, the bona fide perspective emphasizes groups' inherently fluid and permeable boundaries, yet in practice, groups can struggle to close and rigidify their borders. Sunwolf and Leets (2004) provide an example of research that investigates the costs of such border management in elementary school, wherein many students feel the sting of rejection from peer groups that deny their entry. Just as the social identity perspective (Abrams et al., 2005) has illuminated the social cost of ingroup/outgroup categorization, so might group researchers look more closely at the *interactive* complement of this social psychological process—the means whereby groups manage their boundaries, sometimes in a struggle to maintain internal identity and cohesion.

These and many other lines of research could clarify how groups conceptualize and confront the ethical dilemmas they face. Understanding such behavior will not only better inform the practice of small groups, per se, but it will also show more clearly how these microdecisions feed into the larger social system. In effect, groups provide their members with daily opportunities to model ethical social behavior. The better we comprehend how and why we resolve our microethical dilemmas the way we do, the better we will understand the ethical character of our wider societies.

NOTES

1. Kwiatkowski has published short memoirs in Salon.com, LewRockwell.com, *Military Week*, and various other outlets. These details come from Kwiatkowski (2004). For the larger context, see Woodward (2006).
2. This definition is adapted from Gastil (2009), as are selected passages presented later in this chapter.

REFERENCES

Abrams, D., Hogg, M. A., Hinkle, S., & Otten, S. (2005). The social identity perspective on small groups. In M. S. Poole & A. B. Hollingshead (Eds.), *Theories of small groups: Interdisciplinary perspectives* (pp. 99–138). Newbury Park, CA: Sage.

Aldag, R. J., & Fuller, S. R. (1993). Beyond fiasco: A reappraisal of the groupthink phenomenon and a new model of group decision processes. *Psychological Bulletin, 113*, 533–552.

Ancona, D. G., Bresman, H., & Kaeufer, K. (2002). The comparative advantage of X-Teams. *MIT Sloan Management Review, 43*, 33–40.

Anderson, C. M., Riddle, B. L., & Martin, M. M. (1999). Socialization processes in groups. In L. Frey (Ed.), *The handbook of group communication theory & research* (pp. 139–166). Thousand Oaks, CA: Sage.

Bond, R., & Smith, P. B. (1996). Culture and conformity: A meta-analysis of studies using Asch's (1952b, 1956) line judgment task. *Psychological Bulletin, 119*, 111–137.

Bormann, E. G. (1996). Symbolic convergence theory and communication in group decision making. In R. Y. Hirokawa & M. S. Poole (Eds.), *Communication and group decision making* (2nd ed., pp. 81–113). Beverly Hills, CA: Sage.

Bormann, E. G., Cragan, J. F., & Shields, D. C. (2001). Three decades of developing, grounding, and using symbolic convergence theory (SCT). *Communication Yearbook, 25*, 271–313.

Brashers, D. E., & Meyers, R. A. (1999). Influence processes in group interaction. In L. R. Frey, *The handbook of group communication theory and research* (pp. 288–312). Thousand Oaks, CA: Sage.

Burke, S. M., Carron, A. V., Patterson, M. M., Estabrooks, P. A., Hill, J. L., Loughead, T. M., et al. (2005). Cohesion as shared beliefs in exercise classes. *Small Group Research*, *36*, 267–288.

Cini, M. A., Moreland, R. L., & Levine, J. M. (1993). Group staffing levels and responses to prospective and new group members. *Journal of Personal and Social Psychology*, *65*, 723–734.

Driskell, J. E., Olmstead, B., & Salas, E. (1993). Task cues, dominance cues, and influence in task groups. *Journal of Applied Psychology*, *78*, 51–60.

Endres, D., Sprain, L., & Peterson, T. R. (Eds.). (2009). *Social movement to address climate change: Local steps for global action.* Amherst, NY: Cambria Press.

Evans, S. M., & Boyte, H. C. (1992). *Free spaces: The sources of democratic change in America.* Chicago, IL: University of Chicago Press.

Fallows, J. (2006). *Blind into Baghdad: America's war in Iraq.* New York: Vintage.

Foels, R., Driskell, J. E., Mullen, B., & Salas, E. (2000). The effects of democratic leadership on group member satisfaction. *Small Group Research*, *31*, 676–701.

Gastil, J. (1993). *Democracy in small groups: Participation, decision-making, and communication.* Philadelphia, PA: New Society.

Gastil, J. (1994a). A definition and illustration of democratic leadership. *Human Relations*, *47*, 953–975.

Gastil, J. (1994b). A meta-analytic review of the productivity and satisfaction of democratic and autocratic leadership. *Small Group Research*, *25*, 384–410.

Gastil, J. (2009). *The group in society.* Thousand Oaks, CA: Sage.

Giddens, A. (1984). *The constitution of society.* Berkeley: University of California Press.

Hare, A. P. (1999). Understanding Paul Moxnes (1999). *Group Dynamics: Theory, Research, and Practice*, *3*, 116–117.

Harwood, J., & Giles, H. (1996). Reactions to older people being patronized: The role of response strategies and attributed thoughts. *Journal of Language and Social Psychology*, *15*, 395–421.

Harwood, J., Ryan, E. B., Giles, H., &Tysoski, S. (1997). Evaluations of patronizing speech and three response styles in a non-service-providing context. *Journal of Applied Communication Research*, *25*, 170–195.

Haslett, B. B., & Ruebush, J. (1999). What differences do individual differences in groups make? The effects of individuals, culture, and group composition. In L. Frey (Ed.), *The handbook of group communication theory & research* (pp. 115–138). Thousand Oaks, CA: Sage.

Hindess, B. (1996). *Discourses of power: From Hobbes to Foucault.* Malden, MA: Blackwell.

Hobbes, T. (2001). Leviathan. In M. L. Morgan (Ed.), *Classics of moral and political theory* (pp 491–621). Indianapolis, IN: Hackett. (Original work published 1660)

Jablin, F. M. (1985). Task/work relationships: A life-span perspective. In M. L. Knapp & G. R. Miller (Eds.), *Handbook of interpersonal communication* (pp. 615–654). Beverly Hills, CA: Sage.

Janis, I. L. (1982). *Groupthink: Psychological studies of policy decision and fiascoes* (2nd ed.). Boston, MA: Houghton Mifflin.

Kanter, R. M. (2006). Some effects of proportions on group life: Skewed sex ratios and responses to token women. In J. M. Levine & R. L. Moreland (Eds.), *Small groups: Key readings* (pp. 37–54). New York: Psychology Press.

Katriel, T., & Nesher, P. (1986). Gibush: The rhetoric of cohesion in Israeli school culture. *Comparative Education Review*, *30*, 216–231.

Karakowsky, L., McBey, K., & Miller, D. L. (2004). Gender, perceived competence, and power displays: Examining verbal interruptions in a group context. *Small Group Research*, *35*, 407–439.

Keith, W. (2007). *Democracy as discussion: The American forum movement and civic education.* Lanham, MD: Rowman & Littlefield/Lexington Books.

Kramer, R. M., & Brewer, M. B. (2006). Effects of group identity on resource use in a simulated commons dilemma. In J. M. Levine & R. L. Moreland (Eds.), *Small groups: Key readings* (pp. 119–132). New York: Psychology Press.

Kwiatkowski, K. (2004, January). Open door policy: A strange thing happened on the way to the war. *The American Conservative.* Retrieved from http://www.amconmag.com/article/2004/jan/19/00027

Lipman-Blumen, J., & Leavitt, H. J. (1999). *Hot groups: Seeding them, feeding them, and using them to ignite your organization.* New York: Oxford University Press.

McPherson, M., Smith-Lovin, L., & Brashears, M. (2006). Social isolation in America: Changes in core discussion networks over two decades. *American Sociological Review, 71*, 353–375.

Meyers, R. A., Brashers, D. E., & Hanner, J. (2000). Majority-minority influence: Identifying argumentative patterns and predicting argument-outcome links. *Journal of Communication, 50*, 3–29.

Moreland, R. L., & Levine, J. M. (1989). Newcomers and oldtimers in small groups. In P. B. Paulus (Ed.), *Psychology of group influence* (2nd ed., pp. 143–186). Hillsdale, NJ: Erlbaum.

Moxnes, P. (1999). Deep roles: Twelve primordial roles of mind and organization. *Human Relations, 52,* 1127–1144.

Mullen, B., & Hu, L. (1989). Perceptions of ingroup and outgroup variability: A meta-analytic integration. *Basic and Applied Social Psychology, 10,* 233–252.

Mutz, D. C. (2002). Cross-cutting social networks: Testing democratic theory in practice. *American Political Science Review, 96*, 111–126.

National Commission on Terrorist Attacks upon the United States. (2004). *9/11 Commission report.* Washington, DC: Author.

Percy, M., & Freeman, J. (1972). Getting together. [Pamphlet originally distributed by Cape Cod Women's Liberation]. Retrieved from http://userpages.umbc.edu/~korenman/wmst/crguide2.html.

Pezzullo, P. (2009). Chapter interlude: Interview with Stephanie Kimball. In D. Endres, L. Sprain, & T. R. Peterson (Eds.), *Social movement to address climate change: Local steps for global action* (pp. 243–252). Amherst, NY: Cambria Press.

Polletta, F. (2002). *Freedom is an endless meeting: Democracy in American social movements.* Chicago, IL: University of Chicago Press.

Putnam, L. L., & Stohl, C. (1996). Bona fide groups: An alternative perspective for communication and small group decision making. In R. Y. Hirokawa & M. S. Poole (Eds.), *Communication and group decision making* (2nd ed., pp. 147–178). Beverly Hills, CA: Sage.

Rousseau, J. J. (2001). On the social contract, or principles of political right. In M. L. Morgan (Ed.), *Classics of moral and political theory* (pp. 771–830). Indianapolis, IN: Hackett. (Original work published 1762)

Sadowsky, E. (1992). Taking part: Democracy in the elementary school. In A. Garrod (Ed.), *Learning for life: Moral education theory and practice* (pp. 246–258). Westport, CT: Greenwood.

Sanders, K., & Nauta, A. (2004). Social cohesiveness and absenteeism: The relationship between characteristics of employees and short-term absenteeism within an organization. *Small Group Research, 35,* 724–741.

Schütz, H., & Six, B. (1996). How strong is the relationship between prejudice and discrimination? A meta-analytic answer. *International Journal of Intercultural Relations, 20,* 441–462.

Scott, C. R., Corman, S. R., & Cheney, G. (1998). Development of a structurational model of identification in the organization. *Communication Theory, 8*, 298–336.

Shapcott, K. M., Carron, A. V., Burke, S. M., Bradshaw, M. H., & Estabrooks, P. A. (2006). Member diversity and cohesion and performance in walking groups. *Small Group Research, 37*, 701–720.

Shreve, A. 1989. *Women together, women alone: The legacy of the consciousness raising movement.* New York: Viking Press.

Spooner, L. (2004). *No treason: The constitution of no authority.* Glacier, MT: Kessinger.

Sprain, L. (2009). *Cultivating cooperativismo: An ethnography of communication in Nicaraguan Fair Trade cooperative meetings.* (Unpublished doctoral dissertation). University of Washington, Seattle.

Sunwolf, & Leets, L. (2004). Being left out: Rejecting outsiders and communicating group boundaries in childhood and adolescent peer groups. *Journal of Applied Communication Research, 32*, 195–223.

Tanford, S., & Penrod, S. (1984). Social influence model: A formal integration of research on majority and minority influence processes. *Psychological Bulletin, 95*, 189–225.

Tétreault, M. A. (2003). Advice and dissent in Kuwait. *Middle East Report, 226,* 36–39.

Tracy, K., & Ashcraft, C. (2001). Crafting policies about controversial values: How wording disputes manage a group dilemma. *Journal of Applied Communication Research, 29*, 297–316.

Vowell, S. (2008). *The wordy shipmates*. New York: Riverhead.

Wellen, J. M., & Neale, M. (2006). Deviance, self-typicality, and group cohesion: The corrosive effects of the bad apples on the barrel. *Small Group Research, 37,* 165–187.

Woodward, B. (2006). *State of denial: Bush at war, Part III*. New York: Simon & Schuster.

Wuthnow, R. (1994). *Sharing the journey: Support groups and America's new quest for community*. New York: Free Press.

Zaccaro, S. J., Foti, R. J., & Kenny, D. A. (2006). In J. M. Levine & R. L. Moreland (Eds.), *Small groups: Key readings* (pp. 357–367). New York: Psychology Press.

11

Communication Ethics and Organizational Contexts

Divergent Values and Moral Puzzles

Matthew W. Seeger and Timothy Kuhn

Ethics have become vogue in the design, management, and external representation of organizations. This new emphasis on ethics might simply be a way to counter the criticism from a steady stream of major corporate scandals and a way to capitalize on new consumer interests. Yet ethics, and the values on which they are based, are much more than corporate window dressing. Rather, they are woven into the fundamental structural/cultural fabric, taken-for-granted assumptions, patterns of language and interaction, and day-to-day routines of organizational life (see Cheney, 1999; Knouse & Giacalone, 1992). They are enacted in the dynamic moment-to-moment processes of organizational operation at deep levels and reflected in a collective value system. Communication plays a central role in constituting this collective value system (Conrad, 1993; Deetz, 1995; Simms & Brinkman, 2002). As we argue later, communication in organizations is both part of the process of constituting an ethical climate and a specific domain of ethical praxis (Seeger, 1997, 2004).

Questions of ethics are, of course, not new; they have surrounded organizations since the development of the modern corporate form during the industrial revolution. Yet they have recently become so endemic that they are now critical social problems (Kuhn & Ashcraft, 2003). Abuses of power by the Robber Barons of the early 1900s, contractor kickbacks in the defense industry, and the moral outrages of the Watergate era spurred the development of ethical codes, training, and programs of research, particularly in the field of management. Ethical issues continue to plague a diverse set of organizations, as evidenced by the ongoing deception in the tobacco industry, the Exxon-Valdez oil spill, the sex scandal in the Catholic Church, the Union Carbide/Bhopal India disaster, food contaminated with the industrial chemical melamine, and the recent financial scandal involving Bernard Madoff. One widely publicized case involved the energy trading firm, Enron; its routine business practices and corporate culture were based on systemic fraud and deception (Eichenwald, 2005), though its public image differed dramatically. Following the disclosure of corrupt business practices, the company collapsed, wiping out billions of dollars in shareholder value and employee retirement funds. Investigations revealed a business model based on political influence, market manipulation, deception, and illegal accounting schemes. Among other things, Enron's practices were designed to create the perception of energy shortages so that the cost of electricity could be inflated. The Enron case illustrates the consequences of failed moral leadership and of privileging a very narrow set of values and stakeholder concerns, particularly in domains with few established rules or ethical standards (Seeger & Ulmer, 2003).

As organizations have become more powerful and prominent in society, both scholars and practitioners have made efforts to justify their activities on grounds other than mere profit making. Organizations, particularly for-profit organizations, have been justified on a wide array of social, religious, philosophical, political, and teleological grounds. Free enterprise, for example, is often associated with ethics of individual freedom, choice and property rights (DeGeorge, 1987). Moreover, much of modern life can only be sustained through the economies of scale and efficiencies created by organizations. This includes the treatment of disease, mass production of food, education of the general public, and the widespread distribution of information. The efficiencies of free market economies, according to this argument, are necessary to humankind reaching its potential (Lipset, 1990).

Many fundamental issues of organization values are addressed in classical models of organization, such as Max Weber's theory of bureaucracy. Organizational legitimacy, derived from the work of Weber (1978) and later Talcott Parsons, for example, argues for the congruence between organizational values and the values of the larger social system within which the organization functions. Because organizations consume society's resources, the larger social system can make judgments about the value and worth of organizational activities and outcomes (Pfeffer & Salancik, 1978). In *The Protestant Ethic and the Spirit of Capitalism* (1958), Weber also connected the development of capitalist systems to Calvinist Christianity. John Calvin's reform theology, along with the writings of other protestant philosophers, helped reposition the concept of work from a degrading and demeaning activity to a religious duty of the devoted. Prior to the reformation, work was largely seen as a necessary evil, primarily reserved for the lower classes, in contrast to the more pure exercise of leisure pursuits reserved for the elite. According to Calvin, worldly success, wealth, and material goods were signs of a person's moral status (Seeger, 1997). Those who were lazy, idle, and unwilling to work hard were not among the elect preordained by God for salvation. Calvinism holds that hard work is God's will and was necessary to build the kingdom of God (Braude, 1975). Greed was still seen as sinful and profits were to be used wisely and reinvested through sound stewardship so that progress and development continued. Charity was not a primary duty of the wealthy, however, as wealth and success were ultimately bestowed by God (Lipset, 1990). While organizational legitimacy requires congruence between the outcomes of profit making organizations and larger social values, the moral justification for capitalist notions of work and material wealth is found in Protestant ideology.

Weber is also known as the seminal theorist of bureaucracy, the formalistic and rationalistic vision of organizational structure. Bureaucracy is based on organizational changes brought about by the industrial revolution as well as forms of military organization. Although Weber is rarely seen as linking bureaucracy with ethics beyond claims that the objective character of rules and structure protects members from capriciousness, he also criticized bureaucratic systems for their potential stultifying effects on persons, and argued for sector-specific ethical practices beyond the rational logic of the bureaucracy (Weber, 1978). In other words, he showed how bureaucracies are substantive ethical domains in their own right, informed and influenced by—but not reducible to—the morals of the surrounding society (du Gay, 2000).

Clearly, then, an interest in organizations, work, and ethics has a long history in social thought. Nevertheless, we hold that there is much to be gained from considering organizational communication as a basis for explaining such issues. This chapter, therefore, is based on the position that organizations are collectives of cooperating (and often conflicting) individuals, practices, and texts; they are also social entities with profound capacity to create a range of ethically compelling and ethically reprehensible outcomes. Moral questions are inherent to, and immanent in, both organizational processes and outcomes. We believe that communication and organizing are connected processes and that changes in communication practices will influence the moral standpoint and ethical climate of the organization. This chapter begins with a consideration of how communication provides a distinctive perspective on organizational ethics, then examines how ethics has been portrayed in studies of organizations and professions. From there, it considers arguments about the morality of organizations and organizing practice, explores perspectives on communication processes and ethical concerns, and concludes with a description of future directions in issues of ethics and organizational communication.

THE CENTRALITY OF COMMUNICATION IN ORGANIZATIONAL ETHICS

Questions regarding the role and function of communication in organizations constitute a major area of inquiry over the last several decades (Deetz, 2001; Jablin, Putnam, Roberts, & Porter, 1987; Putnam & Cheney, 1985). Views have ranged widely, from functionalist perspectives that emphasize the instrumental role of communication to interpretive and critical views that privilege the epistemic and constitutive notions of communication (see Putnam, 1982). Here we review three views of how and why communication is key to understanding organizational ethics.

Communication as a Domain for Ethical Praxis

Communication in organizations is both constitutive of the larger ethical climate and a domain of ethical practice (Seeger, 1997, 2004). Specific standards and traditions for what constitutes good, desirable, and appropriate communication have been developed and refined. Standards such as honesty and truthfulness, for example, have long foundations in philosophy and moral reasoning and provide a fundamental moral underpinning to communicative practices (Haiman, 2000; Nielsen, 1974). Ethics regarding diversity of opinion and perspective have been articulated only more recently but have become important standards for communication in many organizations (Makau & Arnett, 1997). These perspectives, and many others, acknowledge that communication *qua* communication can be good/bad, desirable/undesirable, ethical/unethical, and outline specific standards for communication praxis.

By "the ethics of communication praxis" we mean the communicative actions, activities, and processes, both routine and nonroutine, that may be judged as ethical and result in larger consequences (Seeger, 1997). Organizational members continually make choices about their engagement in communication, and those choices both reflect and reify values. Mumby's (2004) notions of communication and power and the critical discourse movement, for example, have provided extensive critiques regarding the consequential nature of communication in organizations. Mumby reminds us that communicative praxis is manifest in the everyday discursive processes that socially constitute the organization. Thus, the underlying and embedded meanings, ethics, and values that inform both individual and organizational narratives, choices, and actions correspond closely to the morality of the larger system.

Communication praxis in this sense aligns with traditions of Nicomachean ethics and the emphasis on virtuous acts. Aristotle described a theory of ethics rooted in the habits of moral conduct (see Smith, 1946). He believed that all things are judged by their ability to fulfill their specific purpose and a person is good if she or he consistently fulfills that purpose effectively. Thus, the ethical person is one who characteristically acts in a virtuous way as they seek to achieve goals. Nicomachean ethics focuses on the character of the communicators and their habitually behaving (acting) virtuously and developing a virtuous pattern of conduct. Seeger and

Ulmer (2001) applied Nicomachean ethics to the communication of leaders following a crisis. The virtuous acts of these leaders during a crisis were characteristic of their entrepreneurial drive and commitment to stakeholders and resulted in good (positive) outcomes.

George Cheney (2008) recently described this ethical dimension of communication praxis in his review of engaged scholarship. Cheney challenges organizational scholars to both make judgments of their own and other's behaviors while engaging their own practice from the standpoint of integrity. The same standard can be applied to all forms of communication practice. Similar arguments have been made about a social justice orientation in applied communication scholarship (see Frey 1998; Seeger, Sellnow, Ulmer, & Novak, 2009). The meaningful engagement by communication scholars in social problems can be informed by an ethic of social justice (see Frey, 1998). Doing so represents a kind of ethical praxis whereby the actions themselves help constitute virtuous character.

Communication and Organizational Decision Making

Several conceptions of organizations view decision making as the most important "site" for the coordination and control of activity (e.g., Cyert & March, 1963). A key contributor to this line of thought has been Stanley Deetz (1992, 1995), whose work shows decision making to be a complex and inherently political process. Drawing on Foucault, Deetz argues that decision making in contemporary organizations is influenced by a myriad of surrounding discursive formations: culturally specific modes of thought that articulate relations between things, the "nature" of persons, and the "proper" goals for activity. Moreover, discursive formations determine the knowledge considered appropriate and authoritative, as well as who is to be considered an expert, in any given setting.

Discursive formations, moreover, provide the values that influence action as they operate through organizational decision making. In his consideration of decisional practices, Deetz invokes Habermas's (1976/1979, 1981/1984) universal pragmatics to suggest that all utterances in interaction can be interrogated with respect to their ability to satisfy four ethical validity claims, concerning truth, normative legitimacy, sincerity, and comprehensibility (see also Forester, 1993). In organizations—particularly corporate forms—interaction frequently is *systematically distorted* in that it fails to satisfy these validity claims because it is associated with strategic, rather than communicative, action. This means that the parties are under the impression that interaction is consensual, free, and open, but their action serves sectional (often managerial) interests at the cost of another party's desires. The problem is that participants can neither penetrate the ideological apparatus supporting the corporate form (i.e., the surrounding discursive formations) nor overcome informational inequalities, and therefore cannot assess the degree to which interests affect decision making. Deetz's response, then, is to advocate for a model of stakeholder communication that can better include participation in decision making. Moving beyond common models of "dialogue," Deetz argues for the need to question sedimented procedures and rights of participation by (a) recognizing forms of *discursive closure* in decisional conversations, including processes of subjectivation of experience, naturalization, neutralization, and pacification (Deetz, 1992; Thackaberry, 2004); (b) reclaiming deep-seated moral conflicts between stakeholder interests (Benhabib, 1985, 1992); (c) avoiding management projecting supposed interests onto stakeholders; and (d) working toward stakeholders' value inclusion and more fully shared responsibility for shared decision making. Using a multiple stakeholder model (Deetz, 1995) for organizational decision making can, he holds, produce more innovative decisions, more committed stakeholders, and can address moral concerns about organizational dominance in interaction.

Communication and Accountability

Closely associated with the role of communication in constituting ethical practices and decision-making structures is the role of communication as an account of conduct. A primary function of communication within the larger domain of organizational ethics is explaining and justifying the organization's moral stance. In its most literal sense, "accountability refers to the ability and obligation to provide an explanation—to furnish a reckoning or an account of one's behavior" (Seeger, 1999, p. 42). Classical ideas of accountability can be traced to close-knit, traditional agrarian societies where transactions were always face-to-face and where direct causal relations could be drawn between individual actions and outcomes (Petress & King, 1990; Ulmer & Sellnow, 2000). Accountability in this context is both direct and personal. Accountability in corporate usage refers to an obligation, moral, legal, or institutional, to provide explanations or accounts for one's actions to those parties to whom one is answerable (Swift, 2001). It requires the exchange of information between parties and denotes some level of access to information, openness, and system transparency (see Gray, Owen, & Mauders, 1987). These accounts may take various forms including the issue management or public relations campaign, executive speech, legal documents, press releases, and even advertisements. While the gap between organizational speech and action regarding ethics is well documented, these formal accounts are not irrelevant: They lay down a record of expectations and, in some cases, public commitments that may later translate into action and to which the organization may be accountable.

Accounts are generally not offered for routine and expected behaviors, but only for those instances where some perceived offense, ethical wrongdoing, or misbehaviors occurred (Benoit, 1995; Hearit, 2006,). Benoit (1995) notes that a central function of communication is to maintain or restore one's image in light of alleged misconduct, and "accounts involve talk designed to recast the pejorative significance of actions or one's responsibility for it and thereby transform other's negative evaluations" (Buttny, 1993, p. 1). In accounting, communicators frame their interpretations of events around general criteria for holding agents (individuals and organizations) responsible for outcomes. This includes the degree to which the accusations are accurate and truthful, the level of personal freedom and control, the number and nature of extenuating circumstances, and others who are involved. As Benoit (1995) argued, "If several persons jointly committed the act, we might not necessarily hold them all fully responsible, but we may apportion the blame among them" (p. 72).

Benoit (1995, 1997), Benoit and Brinson (1994), Coombs (2006), and Hearit (2006), have described various rhetorical strategies used by both individuals and organizations in response to accusations of wrongdoing, including ethical misconduct. Many of the strategies they describe are grounded in varying degrees of involvement and control. For example, in offering strategic excuses, the organization's responsibility is minimized. Benoit notes that scapegoating as an excuse, must be presented as a plausible explanation. In the strategy of denial, an individual may deny that he or she was responsible for an ethically suspect decision. Benoit uses the example of shifting blame for a plant closure to high taxes or market forces. Finally, the strategy of defeasibility allows for evading responsibility where the "accused alleges a lack of information about or control over important elements of the situation" (p. 267). In organizations, individual managers may claim that subordinates were acting on their own or that they had insufficient knowledge about activities. In fact, maintaining plausible deniability is frequently employed as a corporate strategy.

These rhetorical frameworks of accountability are situated within larger discussions of corporate moral agency described below. The ambiguity surrounding questions of personal and corporate moral standing create an equivocal space for the discursive practices of avoiding blame and shifting responsibility. Theories of image restoration can clarify the function of accounts can help create greater corporate accountability.

OVERVIEW OF ETHICS AND ORGANIZATIONAL COMMUNICATION

When we think about organizational ethics in communicative terms, then, our attention turns to the moral claims we make about organizations and the specific ethical dilemmas that arise. The previous section makes clear that concerns for ethics in organizing are fundamentally communicative; the present section addresses how these issues have generated frameworks for analyzing ethics in organizing.

Materiality and Organizing

A first theme of ethics and organizing involves seeing communication as the nexus of the symbolic and material elements of organizational activity. Communication scholars have, of late, refused to think of the symbolic and material as distinct domains, since assuming that they are opposed risks consigning ethics only to the realm of the symbolic—which, in turn, enables a portrayal of ethics as a secondary or epiphenomenal concern, one not immediately relevant to "real" work or the "natural" order (Adler & Borys, 1993). Instead, they see these forces in constant interplay in producing the conditions of possibility for moral claims about organizing.

Perspectives on organizing derived from Marxist (and neo-Marxist) social theory tend to argue that capitalists occupy a privileged position in shaping the relations of production through their control of the means of production. Capitalists draw upon this position to extract surplus value from workers and assert their right to the profits produced through their work. For Marxists, the prevailing material conditions—of both the workplace and the broader society—are the starting point for any analysis of organizing because they form the substrate upon which class struggles and battles for control over work processes are founded. As an example, research by Dana Cloud (1994, 2001, 2005) provides insight on how labor is both intrinsically material and how struggles for control are, ultimately, ethical concerns. Her work is generally concerned with organized labor and its relationships with corporations, arguing that unions play vital roles in moving corporations toward ethical practices of participation and democracy. She finds, however, that managerial discourse about employee voice is frequently a diversion from actual processes of decision making and power in organizing. Conceiving of the materiality of work from such a Marxist perspective additionally implies a consideration of the surrounding sociomaterial environment (Marens, 2009) and attention to consumerist desires for corporately produced commodities that condition (and also provide cultural schemas for interpreting) labor–management discussions (Cheney & Cloud, 2006). In other words, investigating the nexus of the symbolic and the material in organizing with an eye toward ethics requires starting with a consideration of the economic realities of the workplace itself, but that we additionally move well beyond (artificial) organizational boundaries.

To complement the intersection of economic materiality with production, Ashcraft, Kuhn, and Cooren (2009) provide three categories of materiality through which we can examine ethics in organizing. A first material focus, *objects and artifacts*, directs attention to how the textual and technological enter organizing. Recent scholarship moves beyond merely depicting objects and artifacts as used by people in their activity, beginning instead to theorize the "constitutive entanglement" of the material and the social (Orlikowski, 2007). This means that practices are always a product of both (local and global) social norms and features of a given artifact, and understanding their intersections becomes a key concern. One approach to this topic with clear connections to ethics is the interest in *textual agency*, a view that argues for seeing artifacts as not merely created by humans, but as objects that can display authorial power in the "writing" of organization (Cooren, 2004; Latour, 1996; Law & Singleton, 2005). For instance, Jensen, Sandström, and Helin's (2009) study of the mobilization of a corporate code of ethics between a headquarters and a foreign subsidiary portrayed the document as influencing (moral) practice and transforming the meanings of ethics in the subsidiary independent of the will of its creators. The agency of the material artifact—the code of ethics, in this case—had a direct, but unanticipated, effect on the ethics of organizational practice.

The second theme of materiality Ashcraft et al. (2009) discuss is *sites*, a focus that typically points up locale-specific differences in culture and values, as well as the challenges of coordinating activity across distances. In much research, such concerns reduce material differences to symbolic distinctions, as in research on globalization that foregrounds the inculcation of Western standards for business, the impact of NGOs on marketplace rules, and the distribution of "unskilled" jobs, but which simultaneously ignores the formative power of specific geographic spaces (Frenkel & Shenhav, 2006; Parker & Clegg, 2006). Standing in contrast to this erasure of the material in considerations of sites is research on organizations' stewardship of natural resources. This work recognizes that sites supply particular combinations of physical resources and human artifacts that both shape activity and call forth particular responsibilities on the parts of organizations (Keenoy & Oswick, 2003; Pred, 1990). Stewardship, most broadly, refers to appropriate, responsible, or moral use of resources, usually in ways that are consistent with other obligations and value traditions. This ethic has been generalized to corporate contexts and to a variety of corporate ethical frameworks in part because corporations are primary consumers and producers of material resources. Nicholson (1994), for example, described stewardship as one of the four primary ethical domains for organizational inquiry. Stewardship, Nicholson argues, relates to the "consequences of organizational output of products and services and the ethical values attached to their use" (p. 587). Stewardship, thus, speaks to a variety of issues related to corporate consumption, production, and legitimacy described earlier. This includes the broad issues of natural resources and environmental exploitation, employee and human resources, and larger issues of individual, community, and social benefits of corporate activity, among others. The ethics of how such resources are acquired, apportioned, and used are significant because these processes reify particular value systems which compete with other systems.

A final focus of ethics research examining the material–symbolic nexus is *the body*. Workers' bodies have long been at the center of managerial control efforts, though recent concern has turned toward symbolic forms, such as organizational ideologies, in understanding control (Hassard, Holliday, & Willmott, 2000). Yet bodies remain a nodal point for examinations of ethics in organizing. These interests range from analyses of forms of self-presentation (e.g., attire) in terms of how they expose or conceal of the body (Brewis, Hampton, & Linstead, 1997; Nadesan & Trethewey, 2000; Rafaeli, Dutton, Harquail, & Mackie-Lewis, 1997), to narratives that classify and alter bodily functioning in the organizational interest (Martin, 1990), to sexuality and sexual harassment at work (Brewis & Grey, 1994; Williams, Giuffre, & Dellinger, 1999). In work such as this, ethical concerns for human "nature," personal autonomy, managerial control, and voice meet through the vehicle for the body at work. This conjunction is displayed particularly well in research on workplace surveillance, which combines the materiality of technological objects with efforts to control bodies both within and beyond the formal sites of work. More importantly, the ethical questions it raises are fundamentally communicative, since surveillance alters workers' beliefs about privacy and their patterns of interaction, including their participation in decision making (Botan, 1996), while it also reaches beyond objectively observable behavior into workers' self-conceptions, and occasions various forms of resistance to organizational authority (Ball, 2005).

Across this work, communication can be seen as central in questions of materiality and ethics not simply because economic relations, objects/artifacts, sites, and bodies find expression in interaction. Rather, communication is axial because it is the process through which the material and the moral are organizationally brought to life. From this perspective, communication is not only where the material and the symbolic interpenetrate; it is also the point around which ethical questions and interventions revolve.

Applied Ethics and Organizational Communication

A second theme shaping the framework by which organizational ethics issues are explored is the applied ethics movement. Applied ethics approaches the complexities of morality in organizational and professional contexts from interdisciplinary and practical perspectives by taking up specific ethical problems and questions found in work settings, primarily at the level of the individual (Seeger, Sellow, Ulmer, & Novak, 2009). Applied ethics also critiques traditional philosophy and moral reasoning as disconnected from day-to-day ethical choices and conduct (see Böhme, 1997/2001). Peter Singer (1986), one of the founders of applied ethics, noted that this approach concerns morality in "practical issues—like the treatment of ethnic minorities, equality for women, the use of animals for food and research, the preservation of the natural environment, abortion, euthanasia, and the obligation of the wealthy to help the poor" (p. 1). Most contemporary ethical dilemmas, Singer suggests, have organizational issues at their core.

Applied ethics focuses primarily on the practical norms, standards, guidelines, and processes for promoting ethical decision making (Rosenthal & Shehadi, 1988; Singer, 1986; Winkler & Coombs, 1993). The role of professional codes of conduct in promoting discussion, informing decision making, and resolving ethical dilemmas, for example, is central to applied ethics (Schwartz, 2001; Stevens, 1994). These standards not only help to ensure that ethics are addressed, but may also elevate the credibility and reputation of various professions and help define specific communities of practice. Proponents of applied ethics also suggest that to be relevant to the day-to-day ethical questions that individuals face, codes and standards must accommodate an understanding of organizational and professional life, and adopt a pragmatic stance regarding the issues and dilemmas encountered (Kimmel, 1988; Rest & Navaez, 1994).

Codes of ethical conduct are designed to influence both individual and collective behavior in ways that are consistent with an articulated set of corporate values (Stevens, 1994). These codes are often widely communicated, publicized, and referenced in other documents and executive speeches (Stevens, 1994). Similarly, many organizations conduct corporate training in ethics, codes, and ethical decision making. Sometimes, codes are part of the organization's formal decision process. Yet having ethical codes or attending to value statements and training does not insure ethical conduct: Schwartz (2001) concluded that codes may have an impact on behavior, but the relationship is not direct, and there are important countervailing forces to their effectiveness. Moreover, some of the most vivid examples of corporate misconduct have been accompanied by well-developed and widely referenced ethical codes (Kuhn & Ashcraft, 2003; Seeger & Ulmer, 2003).

The applied ethics movement is also reflected in many contemporary approaches to communication (e.g., Arnett, Harden, & Bell, 2009; Seeger, Sellow, et al., 2009). Some applied communication scholars, for example, have argued for an explicit emphasis on social justice (see Frey, 1998; Frey & Sunwolf, 2009). Journalism and other mass media have long traditions of addressing ethical questions through codes and professional training (Christians, Rotzell, & Fackler; 2001). A number of professional associations, including the International Association of

Business Communication, Society of Professional Journalists, and Public Relations Society of America, have developed sophisticated codes of professional ethics. The National Communication Association adopted a Credo for Ethical Communication in 1999 to address values relevant to teaching, research and service. These and other codes suggest a larger recognition of the need for ethical standards and discourse within the communication professions. While the emphasis on applied ethics and codes of conduct are important developments, larger questions exist about the fundamental nature of corporate moral agency.

Across these two themes—materiality and applied ethics—we see that organizing is a thoroughly communicative process that necessarily implicates ethical concerns (Penman, 1992). Discerning responsibility and accountability for (un)ethical action, however, is complex, dynamic and subject to competing interpretations. With that concern in mind, the next section pursues questions of responsibility through the vehicle of moral agency.

MORALITY OF AND IN ORGANIZATIONS

A key challenge for considering ethics in organizational settings is that identifying unscrupulous action is rarely straightforward. A wide array of activities can be justified with reference to one of many competing behavioral guidelines, and action pursued in the name of the organization can become divorced from the obligations that accompany individuals' choices. The key question, then, is where moral agency and responsibility are to be "located." Hierarchical and divisional corporate forms make identification of moral agency difficult, and the result is that responsibility is distributed and accountability diluted because it is often very difficult to determine who is responsible for a specific organizational outcome. Accordingly, any serious investigation of organizational ethics must begin with the following question: What *is* the organization such that we may make moral claims of it? Such a concern about conceptual roots has been molded through a history of legal decisions in Western (particularly U.S.) courts, where corporations have been treated as *legal fictions* with rights akin to natural persons. In a landmark 1886 case, *Santa Clara County v. Southern Pacific Railroad*, the U.S. Constitution's 14th Amendment and its guarantee of "equal protection to all persons" was deployed to assert that corporations are vehicles for shareholders' rights. Thus, protecting the organization's property was portrayed as a proxy for protecting the property of individuals. In the court reporter's notes, however, the argument was extrapolated (perhaps intentionally: Nace, 2003) to suggest that corporations *are* persons within the meaning of the Amendment. The corporation's rights as a *legal person* have since become doctrine in Western law, though this conclusion was never based on legal or organizational theory, nor was it the subject of debate (Hartmann, 2002; Perrow, 2002).

If organizations can be seen as legal persons, the important question becomes whether they can be held to the same moral obligations as *natural* persons. For scholars, this question usually is framed in terms of collective "moral agency," a move which occasions a consideration of whether the organization demonstrates the qualities of an agent and thus can be held morally accountable for actions. There are three positions one might assume when considering this line of reasoning. First, one could simply deny that organizations qualify as moral agents. Second, one could argue that organizations have a "real" existence that carries ethical responsibilities with it. A third potential response encourages one to put aside the philosophical question of collective moral agency and either (a) assess organizational outcomes, products, and decisions, exclusively, for their adherence to particular ethical principles, or (b) interrogate the ethical dilemmas facing situated individual actors in organizational life and consider the discursive practices in which they engage. The former route, (a), is the more common approach in this third option, but its problem—in addition to the plethora of competing conceptions of ethics as bases for evaluation (Johnson, 2007)—is that attending to outcomes alone tends to render the organization a "black box"; such a move prevents examinations and diagnoses of the organizing practices that produce (un)ethical outcomes. Hence, for the third response, we consider scholarship on the latter route, (b), with particular attention to the claims of critical and postmodern theorists.

Disavowing Collective Moral Agency

The dominant argument about the "nature" of the organization is found in Milton Friedman's (1970) well-known disavowal of the corporation's social responsibility. Friedman, along with a long line of scholars in economics and management (see Lantos, 2001, 2002; Velasquez, 1983), asserted that the organization—specifically, the business firm—has *no* moral agency, and *no* responsibility to a broader public, because it is ontologically distinct from the natural persons on whom the notion of moral agency rests. This view is based on a conception of the firm as a nexus of contracting relationships between suppliers and purchasers of goods and services (including labor), where managers are expected to satisfy the financial interests of its owners and are, in turn, prohibited from using its resources to pursue personal interests (Jensen & Meckling, 1976; Salazar & Husted, 2008; Williamson, 2002). These contracts, in turn, dictate that managers' obligations should be to owners alone, while the marketplace determines whether "socially responsible" interactions with publics are diversions from, or contributions to, that goal (Wempe, 2008). Fischel (1982) explains this view well:

> Those who argue that corporations have a social responsibility and, therefore, that managers have the right, and perhaps the duty, to consider the impact of their decisions on the public interest assume that corporations are capable of having social or moral obligations. This is a fundamental error. A corporation…is nothing more than a legal fiction that serves as a nexus for a mass of contracts which various individuals have voluntarily entered into for their mutual benefit. Since it is a legal fiction, a corporation is incapable of having social or moral obligations much in the same way that inanimate objects are incapable of having these obligations. Only people can have moral obligations or social responsibilities, and only people bear the costs of nonwealth-maximizing behavior. (p. 1273)

In other words, although corporations have been accorded the status of "legal person" in the courts, they are better described as tools—entities actors use to bring about particular desired ends, but which have no unique agency apart from those actors. And the ends they serve, in this theoretical view, should be restricted to those benefiting owners' financial interests. Although some note that their arguments against seeing organizations as moral agents are proffered in the interest of enhancing corporate accountability (e.g., Keeley, 1981), nexus-of-contracts thinkers tend to employ this reasoning to claim that corporations should be free of government control in pursuing these aims.

Beyond nexus-of-contract thinking, the denial of collective moral agency is evident from other theorists of organization as well. Most scholars rely on some form of aggregation theorizing, where organizations are portrayed as merely the sum of their human (and, in some cases, nonhuman) components. For instance, those who view organizations primarily as "sites" for production (e.g., Barney, 1991; Cyert & March, 1963; Ladd, 1970) suggest that organizations are akin to information-processing machines or integrated cultures, and the actors populating them seek to maximize rational utility. They view organizations as consisting of elements such as persons, performance programs, standard operating procedures, divisions of labor, and coalitions, but the general thrust is to show that organizations foster particular types of coordinated effort—they are "impersonal arrangements for the efficient attainment of particular goals" (Keeley, 1981, p. 153)—but are *not* entities with moral standing. Consequently, only the individuals aggregated within organizations may be held morally culpable for harmful actions: "only individual officers, employees, or other agents can be morally responsible for 'corporate' misdeeds, and that responsibility should be determined under the normal standards applicable to natural persons" (Phillips, 1992, p. 439). This model, while culturally prevalent and dominant in economists' thinking, is generally unable to interrogate the powerful influence of organizations, particularly corporate forms, on all aspects of contemporary life; it, therefore, led scholars to suggest seeing the organization as a "real entity."

Embracing Moral Agency through a "Real Entity" Perspective

A second view on the question breaks with the assumption that collective responsibilities must be mapped onto the characteristics defining individual moral agency. Falling under the mantle of what Phillips (1992, 1994) calls a "real entity" theory, some argue not that organizations are conscious agents in philosophical terms, but that they have an ontological standing because (a) their internal relations form an entity that persists beyond the relations' enactment, and (b) these relations become patterned into a *system* which "is a more or less integrated, self-contained, and distinguishable unit with a degree of stability over time [and therefore] it also can be regarded as a distinct entity" (Phillips, 1992, p. 451). Although systems models have long occupied organizational theorists' imaginations, those who employ the notion to assert moral agency make specific claims about these systemic entities. French (1979), for instance, held that organizations have "personalities" or "characters" created by a corporate internal decision structure comprised of formal roles, rules, and responsibilities. An organization's intentions and beliefs, accordingly, are encoded into that decision structure, which leads to the realization of collective goals via the subordination of individual desires—and these are goals *of* the organization, not merely members' goals *for* it. Likewise, Werhane (1985) saw organizations as moral agents in a distinction between "primary" and "secondary" actions. Primary actions are those in which individuals engage with the social world to achieve ends, but when a person acts through the vehicle of another agent—and causal power can thus be attributed to that agent—her action is considered secondary. Werhane, in turn, sees organizations as *secondary* moral agents because they are comprised of persons who draw upon them (e.g., their role structures, cultural and symbolic capital, or potential economic moves) in carrying out situated action. Yet these secondary agents cannot engage in primary action and cannot possess intentionality of their own; in turn, they are accorded few moral *rights* but can be held fully morally culpable for their activity (or activity conducted in their name) by breaking with an anthropomorphic conception of moral agency.

The problems plaguing the real entity view are its questionable foundation of assumed formal (and putatively rational) decision making, unitary and monolithic conceptions of intentions and desires (both collective and individual), and its suggestion that interaction only in particular cases is mediated by other agencies—along with the claim that secondary organizational agency can be separated from the myriad of other agencies. Its argument that organizations can be held responsible for the effects they create is attractive to many, but requires a stronger conception of the constitution of the organization than currently seen in this work.

Shifting Moral Agency to the Situated Subject

A third position on organizational morality is silent on the question of whether organizations can be moral agents, choosing instead to interrogate the morality of individuals and the organizationally situated discursive practices in which they engage. Such a view tends to begin with the claim that despite the recent popularity of programs and codes, what passes for ethics in contemporary organizations usually amounts to little more than a façade to enable the unabated continuation of practices that foster corporate domination over the life-world. Such a cynical conception is most pointed in the work of those operating from the frames of critical and postmodern theory, where a "discourse of suspicion" (Ricouer, 1970) shapes analyses of organizing and organizational action. From these perspectives, ethics initiatives are variously portrayed as alibis that organizations construct to preempt lawsuits, legitimation moves designed to make the organization's image more palatable to its publics, or managerial tools that enhance control over members and other stakeholders (Clegg & Rhodes, 2006; Jermier & Forbes, 2003; Jones, 2003). Kuhn and Deetz (2008) capture this suspicion:

> critical [and postmodern] scholars contend that things are not what they seem: that so-called "socially responsible" activities can obscure the deeper contradictions and systems of valuation that enable corporate socioeconomic domination and, in turn, that such activities actually prevent the creation of a democratic society because they mollify citizens who might otherwise demand systemic change. (p. 174)

The skepticism that ethics programs can be related to substantive organizational change encounters is based on a recognition of the domination of fiduciary responsibilities in determining organizing practices. Thus, Jones (2003) points to a persistent "calculus of advantage" lurking behind (or as centerpiece of) ethics initiatives, in which the costs of an activity are weighed against its fiscal payoff, as in the case of strategic philanthropy (Saiia, Carroll, & Buchholtz, 2003; Stole, 2008). Roberts (2001) calls this the "ethics of narcissus," driven by desires for organizational self-promotion and image construction.

Given these criticisms of the ethics literature, what affirmative claims do those populating this position provide? Although there can be no unitary or agreed-upon stance among the loose association of scholars affiliated with critical and postmodern perspectives, several claims animate their views. Key among these are a desire to eschew general ethical guidelines (including codes of ethics) because of their totalizing and homogenizing character, an interest in advocating for underrepresented or powerless groups, an attention to the subjectivity of those engaged in organizational action, a concern for placing ethics in a discursive context well beyond any particular organization, and an acknowledgment that contesting dominant meaning from a position outside the system can provide new possibilities for practice (Clegg & Rhodes, 2006; Gustafson, 2000; Kuhn, 2008; Parker, 1998; ten Bos, 2006; see also Taylor & Hawes, this volume). These themes are elaborated most pointedly by recent scholarship based on the work of two theorists of ethics, Emmanuel Levinas and Zygmunt Bauman.

Levinas, first, is primarily concerned with individuals' moral choices; for him, *collective* moral agency is an impossibility. For Levinas, corporations are necessarily driven by self-interest and lack the capacity to escape this form of reasoning (i.e., they are "egological"), and thus can be neither subjects nor agents. Levinas builds his theory on a vision of a radical personal moral obligation, in which persons are fundamentally responsible to Others. The self–Other relationship is a phenomenological *a priori*, existing before the self's freedom while it is also the source of the self's uniqueness. Levinas, in particular, sees this responsibility as extending beyond the Other who makes claims on an interactant in face-to-face interaction, to include the responsibility to a "third," the distant Other(s) to whom one is no less accountable (Levinas, 1979). Operating from such a perspective, one is forced to acknowledge the infinite humanity of human beings— ourselves, those with whom we interact, and distant Others (Bevan & Corvellec, 2007).

Such a view stands in direct contrast to the typical assumption in management and economics theorizing about persons as opportunistic, rational, and self-serving (Roberts, 2003). And, although organizations themselves cannot be moral agents, this conception of personhood leads to considerations of the conditions that facilitate or inhibit the obligation associated with being for the Other. Levinas argues that to enact our responsibility for the Other, we often must resort to the use of technical and political systems like organizations, but the challenge is that most such systems—as well as our theorizing about them—rule out the pursuit of such responsibilities. Most versions of stakeholder theory, for instance, advocate managerial assessment and control over the capacities of stakeholder groups to influence an organization's trajectory (Phillips, Freeman, & Wicks, 2003), but a Levinasian version of this thinking would require a consideration of the interests of both powerless stakeholders and *non*-stakeholders in the determination of moral action. Thus, those appropriating Levinas for the study of organizational ethics suggest that organizational structures and practices participate in the acceptance or rejection of responsibilities for the Other, with implications for personal morality (Cohen, 1986; Shearer, 2002; Soares, 2008).

Bauman's work, while established on similar foundations, proceeds in a somewhat different direction. For him, "ethics" is a central concern precisely because it has been taken over by the forces of modernity. The ethical guides and codes found in organizations, the professions, and religions tend to shift moral responsibilities away from individuals and toward collectives, enabling domination because these organizations establish the "rules of the game" (Bauman, 1989, 2001). At the same time, ethical guides constrain the self's moral agency, because their application can result in "adiaphorization," whereby actors become inured to moral concerns because those issues appear fully circumscribed by the system and measurable in the system's terms. Ethics regimes like those offered by organizations, as well as by professions and religions, are about reducing undecidability and ambiguity; they *"make the world of business suitable to anybody.* Its message is that even those who appear to have agonizing moral problems with what business organizations are doing will finally be able to settle down in this world and be comfortable with it" (ten Bos, 2002, p. 62). Yet, for Baumann, ethical justifications cannot bring about individual morality. Morality *is* the struggle over situated action; it is never decidable with reference to a simple logic.

The aim of analyses of morality in organization life should not, therefore, be with determining whether actions meet the standards of codes devised by organizations, religions, or philosophers. Rather, analyses should seek to understand the complexity and ambiguity of practice, of the dilemmas actors—with their fragmented and multiple moral selves—face daily. Bauman (1998) argues that these moral agents are never satisfied when they merely meet their contractual/organizational obligations, but always regret "that they were not moral *enough*" (p. 16). Their ambivalence about their own action "is the only soil in which morality can grow and the only territory in which the moral self may act on its responsibility or hear the voice of the unspoken demand" (p. 22).

Although some express concern about the individualism characterizing his thought (Roberts, 2003; Shilling & Mellor, 1998), Bauman's central contribution to organization scholarship is in the shifting of attention from organizational efforts to display their own virtue to the enabling and constraining effects of "ethics" initiatives on selves. Research following Bauman thus responds to a need to attend to the disorder and uncertainty of situated organizational practice (Bartlett, 2003) and, from this vantage point, scholars have begun to examine contexts and interpretations around ethical practice in organizing. In particular, Bauman encourages us to see how actors make sense of organizational situations in which ethical pluralism exists, yet within which those actors must make decisions that are in some manner morally justifiable—and he argues that *all* situations in which morality is at issue fit this description. Such a view helps us see ethics as *practice*, emphasizing how "formal and informal rules are enacted, how they are implemented and made practical. Rules are resources to legitimize and to negotiate organizational realities; ethics as practice focuses on the use of these resources rather than on their static nature" (Clegg,

Kornberger, & Rhodes, 2007, p. 113). This version of organizational ethics scholarship, then, is a primarily descriptive, rather than normative project, in which attention revolves around the locally available discursive resources and forms of subjectivity (Kornberger & Brown, 2007; Kuhn, 2009) implicated in the conduct of organizing.

Conclusion

The three perspectives offered here present very different visions of morality of, and in, organizations. The focal concern is whether the organization can be seen as an entity akin to a person, against the question of whether organizing practices can be redeemed in the interest of enhancing individual morality. From our perspective, what unites these disparate visions is a consideration of how communication constitutes the ongoing process of organization and the choice contexts in which ethical and unethical action occurs. Communication is thus a central concern, and we next examine programs of organizational ethics scholarship that foreground communication.

ORGANIZATIONAL COMMUNICATION ETHICS IN THEORY AND RESEARCH

Thus far our focus in the discussion of ethics in organizational communication has been on general principles. Here we explore four more focused bodies of inquiry and research traditions; these differ from those offered in our second section because the earlier work tends to be concerned more with frameworks for analysis, whereas the work surveyed here addresses particular topics. In some cases, these traditions concern broad ethics questions and principles with manifestations in organizational settings, such as privacy. In other cases, scholars have examined ethical issues that are inherently grounded in organizations, such as whistle-blowing and stakeholder perspectives. While the areas of inquiry concerning ethics and organizational communication are extensive, these four illustrate prominent and persistent themes.

Stakeholder Perspectives

The integration of stakeholder orientations and stakeholder theory into organizational studies has significantly broadened the range of participation in decision making (Deetz & Cheney, 2008; Freeman, 1984, 1995; Freeman & Gilbert, 1987). Stakeholder theory as a descriptive and normative framework positions a wide array of social actors (groups, agencies, communities, and their associated value positions) as having a legitimate stake in organizational decision-making processes (Donaldson & Preston, 1995). Thus, managers have an obligation to understand these positions, to take them into account, and balance the interests and values of many groups in making decisions. While stakeholder perspectives have not addressed all issues of corporate misconduct, they have expanded the value premise of organizations beyond simple profit making. Stakeholder theory in many ways serves a meta-perspective on ethics and broadens the range of voices and values that organizations should accommodate (Clarkson, 1995; Mitchell, Agle, & Wood, 1997).

Privacy and Employee Rights

The rights of employees, clients, and customers often come into conflict with organizational goals and interests. Privacy in general has become a more critical question in a variety of social contexts and a more central area of communication inquiry (Botan, 1996; Petronio, 2002) concomitant with the rapid expansion of electronic communication (DeSanctis & Monge, 2006;

Herschel & Andrews, 1997). As Sandra Petronio has noted in her theory of communication boundary management, privacy is a function of controlling access to one's self and determining who has access to personal information. Burgoon (1982) identified five factors related to threats to privacy: The degree of control an individual exerts over the release and subsequent use of personal information; the amount of personal information in the hands of others; the number of people with access to personal information; the content of the information; and the nature of the relationship with those possessing or having access to the information. Thus privacy concerns fundamental questions about the relationship of the individual to the organization, where to draw communicative boundaries and about who controls the relationship. Privacy also has important implications about the balance of power between the individual and the organization.

Free Speech/Employee Voice

Issues and dilemmas related to the values of free speech and the relative level of employee input into decisions have been foregrounded in several important programs of scholarship. In fact, early studies of communication climate and information distortion suggested that employee voice was often problematic (Roberts & O'Reilly, 1979). Moreover, free speech has a long tradition in communication scholarship and can be described as a core value of communication. Work on organizational democracy, dissent, and participation all position employee voice as critical processes (see Cheney, 1995; Kassing, 2000; McCall, 2001). Voice is, by definition, associated with participation and the ability of workers to express opinions and attitudes and generally share information. Albert Hirschman's (1970) book provided an important and influential association between job satisfaction and employee voice. Hirschman argued that employees have at least three options in response to dissatisfaction; exit, voice, or loyalty. Voice in this case represents an appeal to authorities for change in the situation. Employee voice is also an important stream of research in the area of procedural justice (Folger, 1977). Generally, the "opportunity to present information relevant to a decision enhances judgments of fairness" (Lind, Kanfer, & Earley, 1990, p. 952). Voice, therefore, is a necessary part of the process to effectively addressing many other issues of ethics.

Whistle-Blowing

Closely associated with free speech and voice are questions of whistle-blowing and employee dissent (Seeger, 1997). Whistle-blowing is an organizational member's "disclosure of immoral, illegal, or illegitimate practices that are under the control of the organization" (Miceli & Near, 1992). As Sissela Bok has noted, "Whistleblowers sound an alarm from within the very organizations in which they work, aiming to spotlight neglect or abuses that threaten the public interest" (1980, p. 10). A number of celebrated cases of organizational ethics have involved whistle-blowing including disclosures about the tobacco industry, Watergate, the Challenger space shuttle disaster, and the Enron collapse. Miceli and Near have conducted extensive examinations of the process of whistle-blowing by describing the contributing factors, identifying who is likely to engage in whistle-blowing, and characterizing what constitutes effective whistle-blowing (Miceli & Near, 1992, 2002).

Dissent is generally viewed more broadly as "the expression of disagreement or contradictory opinions in the workplace" (Kassing & Avtgis, 1999, p. 100). Kassing's work in the area of organizational communication and dissent has included the development of a dissent scale (1998) and investigations of the characteristics of dissenters. Kassing (1997) also concluded that employees make choices about dissent strategies based on individual, relational, and organizational influences. The right to dissent is generally seen as a basic human right necessary for the expression of individual morality.

Both whistle-blowing and dissent have important dimensions as domains of ethical conduct and as areas of ethical praxis. Dissent and voice are generally considered fundamental to a variety of other ethical frameworks and have been privileged in many traditions of communication ethics. Moreover, the ability to speak out in response to some perceived ethical wrongdoing, to call attention to moral misconduct, and to protest such activity is an important area of ethical praxis.

EMERGING TRENDS

We began this discussion by noting that ethics have become vogue for organizations and often serve as a façade designed to mask or legitimize questionable organizational conduct. Scholars have also embraced the study of ethics and organizing and by so doing have revealed a variety of insights regarding how ethics function in organizations, the assessment of moral conduct, and the relationship between ethics and other organizational variables. Here we describe three emerging trends in ethics and organizational communication.

The first trend is that ethics is no longer seen as tangential to the larger issues of organizational effectiveness. Indeed, the effectiveness of organizations is increasingly assessed by the larger social impact and moral grounding of the organization in conjunction with its economic viability. The movement toward social responsibility auditing, including audits of environmental impact, treatment of minorities and women, and philanthropy are illustrative of this trend (see Elkington, 1998, Lovell, 1995). Similarly, organizations are increasingly featuring their ethical stance in advertising and promotion. While many of these efforts constitute façade, others represent substantive efforts to both do the right things and to communicate those efforts to stakeholders. By featuring ethics and values more prominently, organizations position these issues more centrally and lay down the basis for more fully enacting ethics in decision and processes (Seeger, 1997). This is not to suggest, however, that ethical talk translates directly into ethical practice. While a number of scholars have suggested that dialogues of morality many have a positive impact, the relationship is not direct (Carroll, 1979; Orlitzki, Schmidt, & Rynes, 2003; Ruf, Muralidhar, Brown, Janney, & Paul, 2001).

A second trend concerns the willingness of scholars to foreground issues of ethics and values in their own work. Driven primarily by the focus on values inherent to the organizational culture, communication scholars have embraced critical approaches to organizations, social action research, and explicit explorations of ethical misconduct as well as virtuous behavior. By so doing, organizational communication scholars have reversed the trend of ignoring ethics described by Charles Redding (1996) in his critique of the field and the management bias that has dominated organizational communication scholarship (O'Hair & Kreps, 1990). Moreover, communication scholars are actively interrogating and challenging the privileged position of corporate interests (Deetz, 1995; Kuhn, 2009). While these efforts are still nascent when compared to more traditional areas of inquiry, they are expanding. For example, there is an increasingly dominant stream of ethics in applied and engaged communication scholarship (see Cheney, 2008; Seeger, Sellnow, et al., 2009). Communication scholars are increasingly willing to position their scholarship from a particular moral standpoint, most often privileging social justice, democracy, and free speech (see Frey 1998.).

A third trend involves increased attention to the moral standing of the organization itself. Given the immense social power of corporate organizations to which we alluded earlier, it is not surprising to see a good deal of popular literature on the potential to make organizations act ethically (e.g., Frederick, 2006; Hart, 2007; Vogel, 2006). And among scholars of organizations, interest in such issues is likewise strong. The theme can be seen most clearly in literature on organizational democracy, which generates a normative argument for the desirability of more shared governance and member equality, over varying time horizons and contexts (Cheney, 1995, 1999; Deetz, 1992; Iannello, 1992; Stohl & Cheney, 2001). Proponents assert that democratic organizing holds the potential to not only constitute more ethical practices, but also to model a form of social life for all stakeholders. We also see it in the "corporate citizenship" literature, where citizenship refers to "actively engaging in acts or programs to promote human welfare or goodwill" (Carroll, 1991, p. 42) beyond what is legally required. This perspective is based loosely on an affirmative view of the aforementioned collective moral agency question, but emphasizes the organization's embeddedness in a community (Lodgson & Wood, 2002; Matten & Crane, 2005; Melé, 2008). The theme also appears in work on ecological sustainability. Whether the concern is with ethical supply chain management (Millington, 2008) or with developing environmentally sensitive practices (Jermier & Forbes, 2003), scholars are increasingly seeing organizations as key to developing long-term solutions to pressing ecological problems—even problems those organizations themselves helped create.

CONCLUSION

While ethics, morality, and values such as social justice, diversity, and environmentalism have become vogue for organizations, much of the activity and talk has yet to manifest in substantial change. Despite this fact, there have been important developments and promising signs. A diverse and rich body of scholarship in organizational studies generally and in organizational communication specifically has created more meaningful investigations of ethics, greater sensitivity to these issues, and, in some cases, more ethically appealing organizations. A number of challenges and tensions confront efforts to understand how ethics function in organizations and in organizational communication, and to constitute more ethically appealing organization. Dialectic tensions remain between individual values and collective morality, between profitability and social justice, between centralized managerial authority and organizational democracy, and between rhetoric and practice. And despite substantial scholarly attention, organizations continue to stun with decisions and actions that are profoundly immoral. While it is unlikely that these tensions will ever be entirely resolved, exploring how they are manifest will help weave morality more fully into the underlying structural fabric of organizational life.

REFERENCES

Adler, P. S., & Borys, B. (1993). Materialism and idealism in organizational research. *Organization Studies, 14,* 657–679.

Arnett, R., Harden, J. M., & Bell, L. M. (2009). *Communication ethics literacy: Dialogue and difference.* Los Angeles, CA: Sage

Ashcraft, K. L., Kuhn, T., & Cooren, F. (2009). Constitutional amendments: "Materializing" organizational communication. In A. Brief & J. Walsh (Eds.), *Annals of the Academy of Management* (Vol. 3, pp. 1–64). New York: Routledge.

Ball, K. S. (2005). Organization, surveillance and the body: Towards a politics of resistance. *Organization, 12,* 89–108.

Barney, J. (1991). Firm resources and sustained competitive advantage. *Journal of Management, 17,* 99–120.

Bartlett, D. (2003). Management and business ethics: A critique and integration of ethical decision-making models. *British Journal of Management, 14*, 223–235.

Bauman, Z. (1989). *Modernity and the holocaust*. Cambridge, UK: Polity.

Bauman, Z. (1998). What prospects of morality in times of uncertainty? *Theory, Culture, and Society, 15*, 11–22.

Bauman, Z. (2001). *The individualized society*. London: Polity Press.

Benhabib, S. (1985). The utopian dimension in communicative ethics. *New German Critique, 35*, 83–96.

Benhabib, S. (1992). *Situating the self: Gender, community, and postmodernism in contemporary ethics*. Cambridge, UK: Polity Press.

Benoit, W. L. (1995). *Accounts, excuses, and apologies: A theory of image restoration strategies*. Albany, NY: SUNY Press.

Benoit, W. L. (1997). Image repair discourse and crisis communication. *Public Relations Review, 23*, 177–186.

Benoit, W. L., & Brinson, S.L. (1994). AT&T: "Apologies are not enough." *Communication Quarterly, 42*, 75–88.

Bevan, D., & Corvellec, H. (2007). The impossiblity of corporate ethics: For a Levinasian approach to managerial ethics. *Business Ethics: A European Review, 16*, 208–219.

Böhme, G. (2001/1997). *Ethics in context: The art of dealing with serious questions* (E. Jephcott, Trans.). Malden, MA: Blackwell.

Bok, S. (1980). Whistleblowing and professional responsibility. *New York University Education Quarterly, 11*, 2–10.

Botan, C. (1996). Communication work and electronic surveillance: A model for predicting panoptic effects. *Communication Monographs, 63*, 293–313.

Braude, L. (1975). *Work and workers*. New York: Praeger.

Brewis, J., & Grey, C. (1994). Re-eroticizing the organization: An exegesis and critique. *Gender, Work and Organization, 1*, 67–82.

Brewis, J., Hampton, M. P., & Linstead, S. (1997). Unpacking Priscilla: Subjectivity and identity in the organization of gendered appearance. *Human Relations, 50*, 1275–1304.

Burgoon, J. K. (1982). Privacy and communication. In M. K. Burgoon (Ed.), *Communication yearbook* (Vol. 6, pp. 206–249). Beverly Hills, CA: Sage.

Buttny, R. (1993). *Social accountability in communication*. Beverley Hills, CA: Sage.

Carroll, A. B. (1979). A three dimensional conceptual model of corporate social performance. *Academy of Management Review, 4*, 497–505.

Carroll, A. B. (1991, July–August). The pyriamid of corporate social responsibility: Towards the moral management of organizational stakeholders. *Business Horizons*, 39–48.

Cheney, G. (1995). Democracy in the workplace: Theory and practice from the perspective of communication. *Journal of Applied Communication Research, 23*, 167–200.

Cheney, G. (1999). *Values at work: Employee participation meets market pressure at Mondragón*. Ithaca, NY: ILR Press.

Cheney, G. (2008). Encountering the ethics of engaged scholarship. *Journal of Applied Communication Research, 36*, 281–288.

Cheney, G., & Cloud, D. L. (2006). Doing democracy, engaging the material: Employee participation and labor activity in an age of market globalization. *Management Communication Quarterly, 19*, 501–540.

Christians, C. G., Rotzoll, K. B., & Fackler, M. (2001). *Media ethics: Cases and moral reasoning* (6th ed.). New York: Longman.

Clarkson, M. (1995). A stakeholder framework for analyzing and evaluating corporate social performance. *Academy of Management Review, 20*, 92–117.

Clegg, S., Kornberger, M., & Rhodes, C. (2007). Business ethics as practice. *British Journal of Management, 18*, 107–122.

Clegg, S. R., & Rhodes, C. (2006). Introduction: Questioning the ethics of management practice. In S. R. Clegg & C. Rhodes (Eds.), *Management ethics: Contemporary contexts* (pp. 1–9). London: Routledge.

Cloud, D. L. (1994). The materiality of discourse as oxymoron: A challenge to critical rhetoric. *Western Journal of Communication, 58*, 141–163.

Cloud, D. L. (2001). Laboring under the sign of the new: Cultural studies, organizational communication, and the fallacy of the new economy. *Management Communication Quarterly, 15*, 268–278.

Cloud, D. L. (2005). Fighting words: Labor and the limits of communication at Staley, 1993 to 1996. *Management Communication Quarterly, 18*, 509–542.

Cohen, R. A. (1986). *Face to face with Levinas*. Albany: SUNY Press.

Conrad, C. (Ed.). (1993). *The ethical nexus*. Norwood, NJ: Ablex.

Coombs, W. T. (2006). Attribution theory as a guide for post-crisis communication research. *Public Relations Review, 33*, 135–139.

Cooren, F. (2004). Textual agency: How texts do things in organizational settings. *Organization, 11*, 373–393.

Cyert, R. M., & March, J. G. (1963). *A behavioral theory of the firm*. Englewood Cliffs, NJ: Prentice-Hall.

Deetz, S. A. (1992). *Democracy in an age of corporate colonization: Developments in communication and the politics of everyday life*. Albany, NY: SUNY Press.

Deetz, S. A. (1995). *Transforming communication, transforming business: Building responsive and responsible workplaces*. Cresskill, NJ: Hampton Press.

Deetz, S. A. (2001). Conceptual foundations. In F. M. Jablin & L. L. Putnam (Eds.), *The new handbook of organizational communication* (pp. 3–46). Thousand Oaks, CA: Sage.

Deetz , S., & Cheney, G. (2008). Organizational ethics. In W. Donsbach (Ed.), *The international encyclopedia of communication*. Retrieved July 26, 2010, from http://www.communicationencyclopedia.com/public/book?id=g9781405131995_9781405131995

DeGeorge, R. T. (1987). The status of business ethics: Past and future, *Journal of Business Ethics, 6*, 201–211.

DeSanctis, G., & Monge, P. (1999). Introduction to special issue: Communication processes for virtual organizations. *Organizational Science, 10*, 693–703.

Donaldson, T., & Preston, L. (1995). The stakeholder theory of the corporation: Concepts, evidence, implications. *Academy of Management Review, 20*, 65–91.

du Gay, P. (2000). *In praise of bureaucracy: Weber, organization, ethics*. Thousand Oaks, CA: Sage.

Eichenwald, K. (2005). *Conspiracy of fools: A true story*. New York: Broadway Books.

Elkington, J. (1998). *Cannibals with forks: The triple bottom line of 21st century business*. Stony Creek, CT: New Society.

Fischel, D. R. (1982). The corporate governance movement. *Vanderbilt Law Review, 35*, 1259–1288.

Folger, R. (1977). Distributive and procedural justice: Combined impact of "voice" and improvement of experienced inequity. *Journal of Personality and Social Psychology, 35*, 108–119.

Forester, J. (1993). *Critical theory, public policy, and planning practice*. Albany, NY: SUNY Press.

Frederick, W. C. (2006). *Corporation, be good! The story of corporate social responsibility*. Indianapolis, IN: Dog Ear Publishing.

Freeman, R. E. (1984). *Strategic management: A stakeholder approach*. Boston, MA: Pitman.

Freeman, R. E. (1995). Stakeholder thinking: The state of the art. In J. Näsi (Ed.), *Understanding stakeholder thinking* (pp. 35–46). Helsinki, Finland: LSR.

Freeman, R. E., & Gilbert, D. R. (1987). Managing stakeholder relationships. In S. P. Sethi & C. M. Falbe (Eds.), *Business and society: Dimensions of conflict and cooperation* (pp. 397–423). Lexington, MA: Lexington.

French, P. A. (1979). The corporation as a moral person. *American Philosophical Quarterly, 16*, 207–215.

Frenkel, M., & Shenhav, Y. (2006). From binarism back to hybridity: A postcolonial reading of management and organization studies. *Organization Studies, 27*, 855–876.

Frey, L. R. (1998). Communication and social justice research: Truth, justice, and the applied communication way. *Journal of Applied Communication Research, 26*, 155–164.

Frey, L. R., & Sunwolf, (2009). Across applied divides: Great debates in applied communication. In L. R. Frey & K. M. Cissna (Eds.), *Routledge handbook of applied communication research* (pp. 26–54). New York: Routledge.

Friedman, M. (1970, September 13). A Friedman doctrine: The social responsibility of business is to increase its profits. *New York Times Magazine,* SM17, SM21.

Gray, R., Owen , D., & Maunders, K . (1987). *Corporate social reporting: Accounting and accountability.* New York: Prentice-Hall.

Gustafson, A. (2000). Making sense of postmodern business ethics. *Business Ethics Quarterly, 10,* 645–658.

Habermas, J. (1979). *Communication and the evolution of society* (T. McCarthy, Trans.). Boston, MA: Beacon. (Original work published1976)

Habermas, J. (1984). *The theory of communicative action: Vol. 1. Reason and the rationalization of society* (T. McCarthy, Trans.). Boston, MA: Beacon. (Original work published 1981)

Haiman, F. S. (2000). *Freedom, democracy, and responsibility: The selected works of Franklyn S. Haiman.* Cresskill, NJ: Hampton Press.

Hart, S. L. (2007). *Capitalism at the crossroads: Aligning business, earth, and humanity.* Upper Saddle River, NJ: Wharton School Publishing.

Hartmann, T. (2002). *Unequal protection: The rise of corporate dominance and the theft of human rights.* New York: Rodale.

Hassard, J., Holliday, R., & Willmott, H. (Eds.). (2000). *Body and organization.* London: Sage.

Hearit, K. M. (2006). *Crisis management by apology.* Mahwah, NJ: Erlbaum.

Herschel, R. T., & Andrews, P. H. (1997). Ethical implications of technological advances on business communications. *Journal of Business Communications, 34,* 160–170.

Hirschman, A. O. (1970). *Exit, voice and loyalty: Responses to declines in firms, organizations and states.* Cambridge, MA: Harvard University Press.

Iannello, K. P. (1992). *Decisions without hierarchy: Feminist interventions in organizational theory and practice.* New York: Routledge.

Jablin, F., Putnam, L., Roberts, K., & Porter, L. (Eds.). (1987). *Handbook of organizational communication: An interdisciplinary perspective.* Newbury Park, CA: Sage.

Jensen, M. C., & Meckling, W. (1976). Theory of the firm: Managerial behavior, agency costs, and ownership structure. *The Journal of Financial Economics, 3,* 305–360.

Jensen, T., Sandström, J., & Helin, S. (2009). Corporate codes of ethics and the bending of moral space. *Organization, 16,* 529–545.

Jermier, J. M., & Forbes, L. C. (2003). Greening organizations: Critical issues. In M. Alvesson & H. Willmott (Eds.), *Studying management critically* (pp. 157–176). London: Sage.

Johnson, C. E. (2007). *Ethics in the workplace: Tools and tactics for organizational transformation.* Thousand Oaks, CA: Sage.

Jones, C. (2003). As if business ethics were possible, "within such limits"… [?] *Organization, 10,* 223–248.

Kassing, J. (1997). Articulating, antagonizing, and displacing: A model of employee dissent. *Communication Studies, 48,* 311–333.

Kassing, J. (1998). Development and validation of the organizational dissent scale. *Management Communication Quarterly, 12*(2), 183–229.

Kassing, J. W. (2000). Investigating the relationship between superior-subordinate relationship quality and employee dissent. *Communication Research Reports, 17,* 58–69.

Kassing, J. W., & Avtgis. T. A. (1999). Examining the relationship between organizational dissent and aggressive communication. *Management Communication Quarterly, 13*(1), 100–115.

Keeley, M. (1981). Organizations as non-persons. *Journal of Value Inquiry, 15,* 149–155.

Keenoy, T., & Oswick, C. (2003). Organizing textscapes. *Organization Studies, 25,* 135–142.

Kimmel, A. (1988). *Ethics and values in applied social research.* Newbury Park, CA: Sage.

Knouse, S. B., & Giacalone, R. A. (1992). Ethical decision-making in business: Behavioral issues and concerns. *Journal of Business Ethics, 11,* 369–377.

Kornberger, M., & Brown, A. D. (2007). "Ethics" as a discursive resource for identity work. *Human Relations, 60,* 497–518.

Kuhn, T. (2008). A communicative theory of the firm: Developing an alternative perspective on intra-organizational power and stakeholder relationships. *Organization Studies, 29,* 1227–1254.

Kuhn, T. (2009). Positioning lawyers: Discursive resources, professional ethics, and identification. *Organization, 16*, 681–704.

Kuhn, T., & Ashcraft, K. L. (2003). Corporate scandal and the theory of the firm: Formulating the contributions of organizational communication studies. *Management Communication Quarterly, 17*, 20–57.

Kuhn, T., & Deetz, S. A. (2008). Critical theory and corporate social responsibility: Can/should we get beyond cynical reasoning? In A. Crane, A. McWilliams, D. Matten, J. Moon, & D. Siegel (Eds.), *The Oxford handbook of corporate social responsibility* (pp. 173–196). Oxford, UK: Oxford University Press.

Ladd, J. (1970). Morality and the idea of rationality in formal organizations. *Monist, 54*, 488–516.

Lantos, G. P. (2001). The boundaries of strategic corporate social responsibility. *Journal of Consumer Marketing, 18*, 595–630.

Lantos, G. P. (2002). The ethicality of altruistic corporate social responsibility. *Journal of Consumer Marketing, 19*, 205–230.

Latour, B. (1996). On interobjectivity. *Mind, Culture, and Activity, 3*, 228–245.

Levinas, E. (1979). *Totality and infinity: An essay on exteriority.* Boston: Martinus Nijhoff.

Law, J., & Singleton, V. (2005). Object lessons. *Organization, 12*, 331–355.

Lind, A. E., Kanfer, R., & Earley, P. C. (1990). Voice control and procedural justice: Instrumental and noninstrumental concerns in fairness judgments. *Journal of Personality and Social Psychology, 59*(5), 952–959.

Lipset, S. M. (1990, Winter). The work ethic—Then and now. *Public Interest*, 61–69.

Lodgson, J. M., & Wood, D. J. (2002). Global corporate citizenship: From domestic to global level of analysis. *Business Ethics Quarterly, 12*, 155–187.

Lovell, A. (1995). Moral reasoning and moral atmosphere in the domain of accounting. *Accounting, Auditing, & Accountability, 8*, 60–80.

Makau, J., & Arnett, R. (Eds.). (1997). *Communication ethics in an age of diversity.* Urbana: University of Illinois Press.

Marens, R. (2009). It's not just for communists anymore: Marxian political economy and organizational theory. In P. S. Adler (Ed.), *The Oxford handbook of sociology and organization studies* (pp. 92–117). Oxford, UK: Oxford University Press.

Martin, J. (1990). Deconstructing organizational taboos: The suppression of gender conflict in organizations. *Organization Science, 1*, 339–359.

Matten, D., & Crane, A. (2005). Corporate citizenship: Toward an extended theoretical conceptualization. *Academy of Management Review, 30*, 166–179.

McCall, J. (2001). Employee voice in corporate governance: A defense of strong participation rights. *Business Ethics Quarterly, 11*, 195–213.

Melé, D. (2008). Corporate social responsibility theories. In A. Crane, A. McWilliams, D. Matten, J. Moon, & D. Siegel (Eds.), *The Oxford handbook of corporate social responsibility* (pp. 47–82). Oxford, UK: Oxford University Press.

Micili, M. P., & Near, J. P. (1992). *Blowing the whistle: The organization and legal implications for companies and employees.* Lanham, MD: Lexington Books.

Miceli, M. P., & Near, J. P. (2002). What makes whistle-blowers effective? Three field studies. *Human Relations, 55*, 455–479.

Millington, A. (2008). Responsibility in the supply chain. In A. Crane, A. McWilliams, D. Matten, J. Moon, & D. Siegel. (Eds.), *The Oxford handbook of social responsibility* (pp. 363–383). New York: Oxford University Press.

Mitchell, R. K., Agle, B. R., & Wood, D. J. (1997). Toward a theory of stakeholder identification and salience: Defining the principle of who and what really counts. *Academy of Management Review, 22*, 853–886.

Mumby, D. K. (2004). Discourse, power and ideology: Unpacking the critical approach. In D. Grant, C. Hardy, C. Oswick, & L. Putnam (Eds.), *The Sage handbook of organizational discourse analysis* (pp. 237–258). London: Sage.

Nace, T. (2003). *Gangs of America: The rise of corporate power and the disabling of democracy.* San Francisco, CA: Berrett-Koehler.

Nadesan, M. H., & Trethewey, A. (2000). Performing the enterprising subject: Gendered strategies for success (?). *Text and Performance Quarterly, 20,* 223–250.

Nicholson, N. (1994). Ethics in organizations: A framework for theory and research. *Journal of Business Ethics, 13,* 581–596.

Nielsen, T. (1974). *Ethics of speech communication.* Indianapolis, IN: Bobbs-Merrill.

O'Hair, D., & Kreps, G. (Eds.). (1990). *Applied communciation theory and research.* Hillsdale, NJ: Erlbaum.

Orlikowski, W. J. (2007). Sociomaterial practices: Exploring technology at work. *Organization Studies, 28,* 1435–1448.

Orlitzky, M., Schmidt, F. L., & Rynes, S. (2003). Corporate social and financial performance: A meta-analysis. *Organization Studies, 24,* 403–441.

Parker, B., & Clegg, S. (2006). Globalization. In S. R. Clegg, C. Hardy, T. Lawrence, & W. Nord (Eds.), *The Sage handbook of organization studies* (2nd ed., pp. 651–674). Thousand Oaks, CA: Sage.

Parker, M. (1998). Business ethics and social theory: Postmodernizing the ethical. *British Journal of Management, 9,* S27–S36.

Penman, R. (1992). Good theory and good practice: An argument in process. *Communication Theory, 2,* 234–250.

Perrow, C. (2002). *Organizing America: Wealth, power, and the origins of corporate capitalism.* Princeton, NJ: Princeton University Press.

Petress, K., & King, A. (1990). Iran Contra and the defeat of accountability. *Communication Reports, 3,* 15–22.

Petronio, S. (2002). *Boundaries of privacy: Dialectics of disclosure.* Albany, NY: SUNY Press.

Pfeffer, J., & Salancik, G. (1978). *The external control of organizations: A resource dependence perspective.* New York: Harper & Row.

Phillips, M. J. (1992). Corporate moral personhood and three conceptions of the corporation. *Business Ethics Quarterly, 2,* 435–459.

Phillips, M. J. (1994). Reappraising the real entity theory of the corporation. *Florida State University Law Review, 21,* 1061–1123.

Phillips, R., Freeman, R. E., & Wicks, A. C. (2003). What stakeholder theory is not. *Business Ethics Quarterly, 13,* 25–41.

Pred, A. (1990). Context and bodies in flux: Some comments on space and time in the writings of Anthony Giddens. In J. Clark, C. Modgil, & S. Modgil (Eds.), *Anthony Giddens: Consensus and controversy* (pp. 117–129). London: Falmer.

Putnam, L. L. (1982). Paradigms for organizational communication research: An overview and synthesis. *The Western Journal of Speech Communication, 46,* 192–206.

Putnam, L. L., & Cheney, G. (1985). Organizational communication: Historical developments and future directions. In T. W. Benson (Ed.), *Speech communication in the twentieth century* (pp. 130–156). Carbondale, IL: SIU Press.

Rafaeli, A., Dutton, J., Harquail, C. V., & Mackie-Lewis, S. (1997). Navigating by attire: The use of dress by female administrative employees. *Academy of Management Journal, 40,* 9–45.

Redding, C. (1996). Ethics and the study of organizational communication: When will we wake up? In J. Jaksa & M. Pritchard (Eds.), *Responsible communication: Ethical issues in business, industry, and the professions* (pp. 17–40). Cresskill, NJ: Hampton Press.

Rest, J., & Narvaez, D. (Eds.). (1994). *Moral development in the professions: Psychology and applied ethics.* Hillsdale, NJ: Erlbaum.

Ricoeur, P. (1970). *Freud and philosophy: An essay on interpretation* (D. Savage, Trans.). New Haven, CT: Yale University Press.

Roberts, J. (2001). Corporate governance and the ethics of Narcissus. *Business Ethics Quarterly, 11,* 109–127.

Roberts, J. (2003). The manufacture of corporate social responsibility: Constructing corporate sensibility. *Organization, 10,* 249–265.

Roberts, K. H., & O'Reilly, C. A., III. (1979). Some correlates of communication roles in organizations. *Academy of Management Journal, 22,* 42–57.

Rosenthal, D. M., & Shehadi, F. (1988). *Applied ethics and ethical theory*. Salt Lake City: University of Utah Press.

Ruf, B. M., Muralidhar, K., Brown, R. M., Janney, J. J., & Paul, K. (2001). An empirical investigation of the relationship between change in corporate social performance and financial performance: A stakeholder theory perspective. *Journal of Business Ethics, 32*, 143–156.

Saiia, D. H., Carroll, A. B., & Buchholtz, A. K. (2003). Philanthropy as strategy: When corporate charity "begins at home." *Business & Society, 42*, 169–201.

Salazar, J., & Husted, B. W. (2008). Principals and agents: Further thoughts on the Friedmanite critque of corporate social responsibility. In A. Crane, A. McWilliams, D. Matten, J. Moon, & D. Siegel (Eds.), *The Oxford handbook of corporate social responsibility* (pp. 137–155). Oxford, UK: Oxford University Press.

Santa Clara County v. Southern Pacific Railroad Company, 118 394 (U.S. Supreme Court 1886).

Schwartz, M. (2001). The nature of the relationship between corporate codes of ethics and behaviour. *Journal of Business Ethics, 32*(3), 247–262

Seeger, M. W. (1997). *Ethics and organizational communication*. Cresskill, NJ: Hampton.

Seeger, M. W. (2004). Organizational communication ethics: Directions for critical inquiry and application. In D. Tourish & O. Hargie (Eds.), *Key issues in organizational communication* (pp. 220–234.) New York: Routledge.

Seeger, M. W., Sellnow, T. L., Ulmer, R. R., & Novak, J. (2009). Applied communication ethics: A summary and critique of the research literature. In L. R. Frey & K. M. Cissna (Eds.), *Routledge handbook of applied communication research* (pp. 280–305). New York: Routledge.

Seeger, M. W., & Ulmer, R. R. (2001).Virtuous responses to organizational crisis: Aaron Feuerstein and Milt Cole. *Journal of Business Ethics, 31*, 369–376.

Seeger, M. W., & Ulmer, R. R. (2003). Explaining Enron: Communication and responsible leadership. *Management Communication Quarterly*, 17(1), 58–84.

Shearer, T. (2002). Ethics and accountability: From the for-itself to the for-the-other. *Accounting, Organizations and Society, 27*, 541–573.

Shilling, C., & Mellor, P. A. (1998). Durkheim, morality, and modernity: Collective effervescence, homo duplex and the sources of moral action. *British Journal of Sociology, 49*, 193–209.

Simms, R. R., & Brinkmann, J. (2002). Leaders as moral role models: The case of John Gutfreund at Salomon Brothers. *Journal of Business Ethics*, 35, 327–339.

Singer, P. (Ed.). (1986). *Applied ethics*. New York: Oxford University Press.

Smith, J. A. (1946). *The Nicomachean ethics of Aristotle*. New York: E. P. Hutton.

Soares, C. (2008). Corporate legal responsibility: A Levinasian perspective. *Journal of Business Ethics, 81*, 545–553.

Stevens, B. (1994). An analysis of corporate ethical code studies: "Where do we go from here?" *Journal of Business Ethics, 13*, 63–69.

Stohl, C., & Cheney, G. (2001). Participatory processes/paradoxical practices: Communication and the dilemmas of organizational democracy. *Management Communication Quarterly, 14*, 349–407.

Stole, I. M. (2008). Philanthropy as public relations: A critical perspective on cause marketing. *International Journal of Communication, 2*, 20–40.

Swift, T. (2001). Trust, reputation and corporate accountability to stakeholders. *Business Ethics: A European Review, 10,* 16–26.

ten Bos, R. (2002). Machiavelli's kitchen. *Organization, 9*, 51–70.

ten Bos, R. (2006). The ethics of business communities. In S. R. Clegg & C. Rhodes (Eds.), *Management ethics: Contemporary contexts* (pp. 13–31). London: Routledge.

Thackaberry, J. A. (2004). "Discursive opening" and closing in organisational self-study: Culture as trap and tool in wildland firefighting safety. *Management Communication Quarterly, 17*, 319–359.

Ulmer, R. R. (2001). Effective crisis management through established stakeholder relationships: Malden Mills as a case study. *Management Communication Quarterly, 14*, 590–615.

Ulmer, R. R., & Sellnow, T. L. (2000). Consistent questions of ambiguity in organizational crisis communication: Jack in the Box as a case study. *Journal of Business Ethics, 25*, 143–155.

Velasquez, M. G. (1983). Why corporations are not morally responsible for anything they do. *Business and Professional Ethics Journal, 2*, 1–18.

Vogel, D. J. (2006). *The market for virtue: The potential and limits for corporate social responsibility* (Rev. ed.). Washington, DC: Brookings Institution Press.

Weber, M. (1958). *The Protestant ethic and the spirit of capitalism* (T. Parsons, Trans.). New York: Scribners.

Weber, M. (1978). *Economy and society: An outline of interpretive sociology* (Vol. 1 & 2). Berkeley: University of California Press.

Wempe, B. (2008). Contractarian business ethics: Credentials and design criteria. *Organization Studies, 29*, 1337–1355.

Werhane, P. H. (1985). *Persons, rights, and corporations.* Englewood Cliffs, NJ: Prentice-Hall.

Williams, C. L., Giuffre, P. A., & Dellinger, K. (1999). Sexuality in the workplace: Organizational control, sexual harassment, and the pursuit of pleasure. *Annual Review of Sociology, 25*, 73–93.

Williamson, O. (2002). The theory of the firm as governance structure: From choice to contract. *Journal of Economic Perspectives, 16*, 171–195.

Winkler, E. R., & Coombs, J. R. (Eds.). (1993). *Applied ethics: A reader.* Cambridge, MA: Blackwell.

12

Journalism Ethics in Theory and Practice

Clifford G. Christians

This is an account of the state-of-the-art in journalism ethics. Despite 125 years of achievements, journalism ethics faces a heavy agenda today. Theoretical models still require intellectual work. A daunting list of explicit issues needs attention, with four of them of major importance in this global and technologically sophisticated age: social justice, truth, nonviolence, and human dignity. And as these efforts in theory and application are underway, relativism is pushing the entire field to a crossroads. While advancement in any one area does not guarantee success for the whole, the task of journalism ethics will not be complete without all three dimensions of the enterprise flourishing.

JOURNALISM ETHICS THEORY AT PRESENT

Classical Approaches

Ethical thinking in the Western tradition is rooted in the individual decision maker. And this emphasis on individuals makes sense. Persons involved in moral decisions must have the freedom to make choices, otherwise they cannot be held accountable for their actions. Out of this overall focus on the decision maker, three prominent ethical systems have emerged each of which is built on a different appeal: to virtue, consequences, and duty.

Virtue ethics was first developed systematically by Confucius (551–479 BCE; trans., 1991), and a century later in the West by Aristotle (384–322 BCE; trans., 1974). It considers moral behavior in terms of the kind of persons who make decisions. Virtue requires that we be conscientious and morally perceptive—in other words, that we persist in moral behavior until it becomes second nature, habitual, common, the definition of our character. It assumes that when we learn and practice empathy, for example, we will not only understand how our actions affect others but we will feel it and be motivated by it. The practice of piety makes people pious because actions of integrity make for honest people. From this perspective, the journalism profession would be morally overhauled if we trained virtuous people to work in all phases—reporting, editing, and management. Motivated by good intentions, they would transform the news enterprise gradually as they reached a critical mass.

The most common type of moral decision making in the journalism of democratic societies is consequentialism. It thinks in terms of the effects of behavior or a policy and not in terms of the rightness or wrongness of acts themselves. Its most popular form is utilitarianism, as articulated by Jeremy Bentham,where morally acceptable decisions promote the greatest amount of happiness and minimized harm. John Stuart Mill embraced and advanced Bentham's central idea, that is, the greatest balance of good for the whole. "Actions are right in proportion as they tend to promote happiness; wrong as they tend to produce the reverse of happiness" (Mill, 1861/1979, p.7). The balance of pleasure over pain, of benefits over costs, requires only an assessment of an action's consequences, not the character traits of the actor.

Utilitarian ethics works hand-in-glove with the democratic process. The best way to maximize human satisfaction is for everybody to exercise their own preferences. In fact, Mill's *On Liberty* (1859/1975), written 2 years before his *Utilitarianism* (1861/1979), is the Bible of democratic politics, arguing for the greatest possible liberty, limited only by harm to others. It is natural that utilitarian reasoning pervades North American life, politics, and the professions. The mainstream press and its policies, codes of ethics, and media textbooks are dominated by various strains of it.

Duty is a third ethical system that is compelling to many in journalism, and often the strongest opponent of consequentialism. In Immanuel Kant's (1785/1964) famous version, humans live according to formal laws that must be obeyed. Kant was trained in mathematics and physics, and the moral law was the analog of the unchanging law of gravity. "The good will shines like a precious jewel," says Kant, and the obligation of the good conscience is to do its duty for the sake of duty (p. 62). Media professionals are pointed beyond selfish considerations and emotional inclinations to the highest good—living dutifully in accordance with moral absolutes. The news media's decisions and policies can be self-serving, and practitioners defensive when criticized. Competition and careerism often cloud the application of professional codes or ethical guidelines. Making duty nonnegotiable encourages responsible practice whether the circumstances are positive or negative.

Despite their major differences, these three mainstream ethical systems make the individual their centerpiece. Individuals are free to make choices and accountable for doing so. Hence Aristotle's ethics is one of self-realization, Mill's utilitarianism is an ethics of the autonomous individual, and the moral agent in Kant's ethics is a rational being. Journalism ethics that depends on these classical approaches is, therefore, based on rules, principles, and doctrines that guide professional practice. In mainstream professional ethics, codes of ethics are the typical format for moral principles. They provide the basic rules of morality that individuals ought to follow and against them all failures in moral duty can be measured.

Dialogic Ethics

The alternatives to classical approaches are fundamentally social rather than individualist, and these approaches insist on starting over intellectually. Our relation to other selves carries moral obligations. Our duties to others are considered more fundamental to human identity than are individual rights. We are dialogical selves seeking through responsive relations a responsible fit within the life of a community. Moral agents need a context within which to assess what is valuable, and values are nurtured in particular settings. In dialogic ethics, the central questions are simultaneously social and moral in nature. Given the inadequacies of the individualist theories that have dominated journalism ethics historically, it is imperative that we start over conceptually with a media ethics that is fundamentally dialogical. There are several contemporary versions of it, three of them the most noteworthy: discourse, feminist, and communitarian ethics.

Discourse Ethics

The translation of Jürgen Habermas' *Moralbewüsstsein und Kommunikatives Handeln* [*Moral Consciousness and Communicative Action*] in 1990 set the stage for the most important debates in media ethics for more than a decade. In contrast to an ethics of individualism, Habermas situated the moral point of view within the communication practices of a community. Instead of the monologic ethics of the classical approaches, he introduced a dialogic form of moral reasoning. All who are affected by normative claims or moral action must be involved in establishing those norms and in practicing them. A community's members must participate, without exclusion, in a discourse that makes everyone aware of each other's concerns and perspectives. In such discourse we seek to persuade others that they should agree with us about moral norms and public policy. We engage in what Habermas calls communicative action—the process of giving reasons for holding or rejecting particular claims. Such argumentation leads to agreed-on community-held norms. "Justification is tied to reasoned agreement among those subject to the norms in question" (Habermas, 1983/1990, p. 65).

Feminist Ethics

Feminist ethics is a second example of the dialogic alternative. The feminist ethics of Carol Gilligan, Nel Noddings, Edith Wyschogrod, Seyla Benhabib, and Martha Nussbaum fundamentally reconstruct ethical theory in relational terms. They represent a social ethics of self and Other in the dialogic tradition (cf. Koehn, 1998). Reciprocity and caring—rooted in human experience and not in abstract rules—are the basis on which moral discourse is possible. Instead of overriding principles such as the greatest balance of good over evil, feminist theory insists that nurturance and empathy should play the central role in moral decision making across cultural, racial, and historical boundaries.

Communitarian Ethics

Communitarianism presumes that human identity is constituted through the social realm. We are born into a sociocultural universe where values, moral commitments, and existential meanings are negotiated dialogically. Communitarian political philosophy revolves around deliberative democracy and critiques the atomistic ideology that underlies utilitarianism where an aggregate of individual rights is confused with the common good. The communal, our commonness, *communitas*, is the context in which the nature of morality is understood correctly. All moral matters arise from and are resolved in community. Ethics is a shared process of discovery and interpretation. Through dialogic encounter, humans have inescapable claims on one another that cannot be renounced without denying their own humanity.

A dialogic ethics in all three variations is a distinctive model for both ethical theory and professional practice. Journalists committed to a dialogic social ethics seek to open up public life in all its dynamic dimensions. This thick notion of analysis replaces the thinness of the technical, exterior, and statistically precise received view. Dialogic models assume that the people themselves are able to articulate their own needs and possible solutions. The goal for ethical reporting is identifying representative voices and communities rather than spectacular ones that are anecdotal and idiosyncratic. Concepts of the good reflect the values of the community rather than the expertise of news professionals or academic ethicists removed from everyday struggle.

Social Responsibility Theory

One version of professional ethics with credibility is social responsibility. In contrast to classical and dialogic approaches based in philosophy, social responsibility ethics is rooted in professional practice. The foundation of ethics is oriented to duty rather than rights. It has stimulated a heavy emphasis on quality work and integrity, codes of ethics, media councils, better training, and media criticism.

The Hutchins Commission in the United States is one source of this model. After 2 years of debate, the Commission on Freedom of the Press in 1947 published its report, *A Free and Responsible Press*. Instead of facilitating the interests of business or government, the Hutchins Commission insisted on the media's duty to serve society. Believing that the press was caught in the mystique of its own individual rights, the Commission stood both terms on their head with the label *social responsibility*. The Commission worried that the postwar media were becoming big business enterprises. In its view, industrial and technological imperatives could impede truthful and comprehensive reporting. The press must remain free from government and business pressures and serve society instead. Socially responsible news is defined by its duties to the community.

For social responsibility theory, it is the journalists' duty to provide "a truthful, comprehensive, and intelligent account of the day's events in a context which gives them meaning" (Commission, p. 21). The press should serve as a "forum for the exchange of comment and criticism," give a "representative picture of the constituent groups in society," help in the "presentation and clarification of the goals and values of the society" and "provide full access to the day's intelligence" (pp. 23–28). The major mission of mass communication, the Commission argued, is to raise social conflict from levels of violence and vulgarity to the plane of discussion.

Social responsibility has resonated well around the world as a workable philosophy of and policies for the journalism profession. Essentially the same theory of the press has won wide global recognition over the last 50 years in democratic societies, with or without direct references to the Commission (Nordenstreng, 1998). And many of the Hutchins recommendations are still relevant, although they need to be redesigned. In the process of invigorating our moral imagination, the socially responsible press worldwide enables readers and viewers to resonate with other human beings who also struggle in their conscience with human values of a similar sort. Social responsibility theory provides moral guidelines for what Stephen Ward (2005) calls global journalism ethics.

Substantive Issues

While working on theory and ensuring the effectiveness of journalism ethics for the long term, a host of moral issues are obvious as global media empires take shape. Some are new moral problems, such as digital manipulation. Other longstanding issues are being transformed. Privacy, surveillance, deception, gender discrimination, and ethnic diversity are more complicated than ever. On this lengthy agenda, four explicit issues stand out as the most demanding and complicated: social justice, truth telling, nonviolence, and human dignity.

Social Justice

Justice is the defining norm for all social institutions, including media organizations and practices as a social institution. However, while the importance of justice has never been higher as media technologies proliferate, implementing it as a principle has never been more arduous. Globally

194   CLIFFORD G. CHRISTIANS

networked digital systems are producing unmanageable floods of data that make recognizing and evaluating relevant information difficult. For the French thinker, Jacques Ellul, the information explosion produces crystallized humans, not the politically informed. He uses the analogy for overwhelmed audiences of pricking a frog's muscles incessantly in the laboratory until its body freezes (1967, pp. 57–58). Information overload buries us in a world of means, of technical knowledge, or what is typically called instrumentalism. Ends become ephemeral, human values are replaced by machine imperatives.

Bernhard Debatin refers to the paradox of media complexity: "Each and every increase in complexity causes a loss of transparency" (2008, p. 259). In the profusion, anonymity, and decontextualization of digital technology, deep structures and sources are easily hidden and difficult to recover. Rather than clarity about justice and its application, the information sphere build ups "second-order knowledge, that is, knowledge about knowledge. This is the birth of indexes, catalogues, retrieval systems, and information selection systems" (p. 259). For media ethics in an age committed to technical excellence, the challenge is to keep alive a moral vocabulary such as justice and its cognates, making moral distinctions meaningful in education and professional practice.

Justice is of particular importance in the new world information order, and the major issue within this principle is accessibility. In terms of the standard of just distribution of products and services, media access ought to be allocated to everyone according to essential needs, regardless of income or geographical location. Comprehensive information ought to be ensured to all parties without discrimination.

In contrast, the standard conception among privately owned media is allocating to each according to ability to pay. The open marketplace of supply and demand determines who obtains the service. The assumption is that decisions about allocating the consumers' money belong to them alone as a logical consequence of their right to exercise their own social values and property rights without coercion from others. From this perspective, commercial companies are not considered charitable organizations and therefore have no obligation to subsidize the information poor.

An ethics of justice in which distribution is based on need defines fundamental human needs as those related to survival or subsistence. They are not frivolous wants or individual whims or desserts. As a matter of fact, there is rather uniform agreement on a list of most human necessities—food, housing, clothing, safety, and medical care. If we cannot provide them for ourselves because of the limitation of our circumstances, they nonetheless remain as essential goods. Everyone is entitled to them without regard for individual success to that which permits them to live humanely.

The electronic superworld cannot be envisioned except as a necessity. Media networks make the global economy run, they give us access to agricultural and health care information, they organize world trade, and they are the channels through which the United Nations and political discussion flow—through them, we monitor both war and peace. Therefore, as a necessity of life in a global order, the information system ought to be distributed impartially, regardless of income, race, geography, or merit.

But there is no reasonable likelihood that need-based distribution will ever be fulfilled by the marketplace itself. Technological societies have high levels of computer penetration, and nonindustrial societies do not. Digital technology is disproportionately concentrated in the developed world, and under the principle of supply and demand, there are no structural reasons for changing those disproportions. Even in wired societies, the existence of Internet technology does not guarantee it will reach its potential as a democratic medium. There is a direct correlation between per capita Gross National Product and Internet distribution. In the United States, for example,

80% of those households with incomes of $75,000 have computers; only 6% do of those with incomes of $15,000 or less.

There are no grounds for supposing that the geography of the digital world will be fundamentally different from that of the offline world. The history of the communications media indicates that they follow existing political and economic patterns; inequities in society lead to inequities in technology. An ethics of justice requires that we intervene through legislation, government policy, journalism practice, and public ownership to implement open access. To implement this principle, our thinking about media institutions should be modeled after schools, which we accept as our common responsibility, rather than determined by engineers or profits alone.

Given the realities of international politics and limited resources, the need-based principle of social justice must be supplemented by the advocacy standard. In the actual distribution of services under suboptimal conditions, this standard calls for decisions at every level that honor the equal access formula. If providing an entire range of expensive media technologies for everyone is impossible at one time, it is unjust to continue with sophisticated systems for the few and take no initiatives consistent with social justice. The advocacy principle modifies the application of the need-conception of justice in order to address the real world of constraints. But distributive justice remains as the goal due to its moral significance. To realize it only in part or step-by-step is better than jettisoning the principle because of difficulties in implementing the whole.

To make advocacy of social justice vibrant and meaningful, the burden rests finally with citizens. Government censorship of the media has always been an issue in democratic societies, but the dangers are even greater in a digital age within societies at the cutting-edge of the electronic revolution. Ultimately it is the public itself that has responsibility for determining what regulation if any is acceptable for the public good.

One way to keep equal access alive is to establish codes of ethics for the blogosphere with a justice inflection. Rebecca Blood (2002) included a "Weblog Code of Ethics" in the first edition of *The Weblog Handbook* and Jonathon Dube (n.d.), founder of Cyberjournalist.net maintains a code for online journalism patterned after the Society of Professional Journalists Code of Ethics. Both of these are focused on the weblogs that have been integrated into mainstream media corporations and center on news. Martin Kuhn (2007) argues for a broader code that is helpful to political blogs but also credible to bloggers more generally. His "Code of Blogging Ethics" represents the judgment of the computer-mediated world, and focuses on abuses that result from anonymity and lack of accountability. While distributive justice is not as paramount in these efforts as it should be, they do speak to its spirit of inclusiveness and distribution of ideas. It creates, in effect, an A-list of bloggers who are committed to good stewardship of the media resources accessible to them.

The Open Source Software (OSS) movement is consistent also with the advocacy phase of social justice. In 1998 the concept emerged from those working on free distribution of software and opposing license restrictions that unduly benefited the corporate world. Open Source approval allows anyone to create modifications of the software, duplicate it, link it to new processor architectures, or market it. Authors/licensors are understood to own the original copyright, so in effect they are allowing others to use their rights while retaining ownership. In this model, software can become a stepping-stone to a higher-end commercial product or service. The General Public License (GPL) is the most widely used open source label, and together with other such decentralizing codes has saved consumers multiple billions since the OSS initiative began. The circle of software creators has hereby expanded beyond the professional, high-technology circuit, and users are treated as codevelopers of content and structure.

Codes of ethics that promote online technologies for the common good and Open Source Software are two niches of progress consistent with social justice. In the digital age—rooted in computers, the Internet, satellites, and the World Wide Web—ideally all types of persons will use all types of media services for all types of audiences. But universal service is the Achilles heel of new technologies driven by invention, engineering, and markets. Without repeated and aggressive intervention into the commercial system on behalf of distributive justice, the world will remain divided into the technologically elite and those without adequate means to participate.

Truth

Another central issue in journalism ethics is truth. Karl Jaspers (1955) speaks with a German accent, but in world terms: "The moment of communication is at one and the same time the presentation of and a search for the truth" (p. 77).Wherever communication is studied across the human race, truth is the fundamental issue. The press's obligation to truth is a standard part of its rhetoric. Virtually every code of ethics in journalism begins with the newsperson's duty to tell the truth under all circumstances. Credible language is pivotal to the media enterprise. Truth telling is the occupational norm of the media professions.

Historically the mainstream press has defined itself in terms of an objectivist worldview. The facts in news have been said to mirror reality. The aim has been true and incontrovertible accounts of a domain separate from human consciousness. News corresponds to context-free algorithms, and journalistic morality is equivalent to the unbiased reporting of neutral data.

But the mainstream view of truth as accurate information is too narrow for today's social and political complexities. From the perspective of dialogic ethics, a more sophisticated concept of truth is disclosure. Forsaking the quest for precision journalism does not mean imprecision but precision in disclosure and authenticity—in seeing beneath the surface, in getting to the heart of the matter.

An illustration of truth as getting to the nub of the issue is the classic case in television news of Wounded Knee. For the first time in history, broadcast news carried the story every weekday night for 10 weeks, not to be duplicated until nearly 2 decades later with the daily news coverage of the 1991 Gulf War and then the O. J. Simpson trial in 1995. On February 27, 1973, some 200 Native Americans seized the hamlet of Wounded Knee on the Pine Ridge Sioux Indian Reservation in southwest South Dakota. Tension had been growing steadily for 3 weeks, ever since a group of Native Americans clashed with police in Custer, protesting the light second-degree manslaughter charge against a White man accused of stabbing Raymond Yellow Thunder to death. The American Indian Movement (AIM) set up their bunkers at Wounded Knee, which was near Custer, hoping to trade on sympathy for the slaughter of Chief Big Foot there by the U.S. Seventh Cavalry in 1890—the last open hostility between American Indians and the U.S. government until now, 83 years later.

Meanwhile, FBI agents, federal marshals, and police from the Bureau of Indian Affairs surrounded Wounded Knee, hoping to seal off supplies and force a peaceful surrender. News crews from the United States and across the world arrived to cover the story. An incredible 93% of the population claimed to follow the story through television news, but Indian attorney Roman Roubideaux was unimpressed: "Only the sensational stuff got on the air. The facts never really emerged that this was an uprising against Washington's Bureau of Indian Affairs and its puppet government at Pine Ridge" (Hickey, 1973, p. 34). Some reporters did break through the fog with substantive accounts of the history and background—the treaties violated by the U.S. government and the breakdown in the judicial system at Custer. But, on balance, journalists followed the technological imperatives of television, showing primarily the battle action drama.

Truth as authentic disclosure means, in this case, probing through the everyday events to what Charles Taylor (1994) calls the "politics of recognition." Democratic societies are committed by definition to equal representation for all. Each counts for one; in principle everyone is given equal access to democratic institutions—the courts, education, and voting. Therefore, the crucial question: "Is democracy letting its citizens down, excluding or discriminating against them in some morally troubling way, when major institutions fail to take account of their particular identities" (Taylor et al., 1994, p. 3)? Is it necessary that our cultural and social distinctiveness—as African American, Asian Americans, Muslims, the physically disabled—be given a voice? For Taylor, recognizing multicultural groups politically is one of the most urgent and vexing on the democratic agenda at present. Reporters following truth-as-disclosure would give the siege at Wounded Knee a thick reading. They would probe beneath the surface to illumine the politics of identity at the heart of this historic event, knowing that the issue of recognition needs to be solved for democracy to remain vital over the long term.

In terms of disclosing the meaning, reporters will seek what might be called interpretive sufficiency. The best journalists will ensure the news story's deeper reading by understanding from the inside the attitudes, culture, language, and definitions of the people and events they are actually reporting. The truth as authentic disclosure unveils the inner character of a series of events. They generate an insightful picture that gets at the essence of the matter. Rather than reducing social issues to the financial and administrative problems defined by politicians, the news media ought to disclose the depth and nuance that enables readers and viewers to identify the fundamental issues themselves.

Nonviolence

Nonviolence is also an important ethical principle at present, and how to implement it a major challenge. Mahatma Gandhi and Martin Luther King, Jr. developed this principle beyond a political strategy into a philosophy of life. Vaclav Havel and Nelson Mandela were totally committed to it. In Emmanuel Levinas's work, interaction between the self and the Other makes peace normative. "The first word from the Other's face is 'Thou shalt not kill.' It is an order. There is a commandment in the appearance of the face, as if a master spoke to me" (Levinas, 1985, p. 89). In the dialogic face-to-face encounter, the infinite is revealed. The Other's presence involves an obligation to which I owe my immediate attention. In communalistic and indigenous cultures, care of the weak and vulnerable (children, sick, and elderly), and sharing material resources, are a matter of course. Along with *dharma, ahimsa* (nonviolence) forms the basis of the Hindu worldview. For St. Augustine, peace is natural to human relationships. The public's general revulsion against physical abuse in intimate settings and its consternation over brutal crimes and savage wars are glimmers of hope reflecting this principle's validity.

Peace journalism is an illustration of how this principle works itself out for the news in violent conflicts worldwide. As a form of reporting, peace journalism is an interpretive process, and the principle of nonviolence gives the foundation and direction by which the interpretation ought to be done.

The Norwegian scholar Johan Galtung has developed and applied the principle systematically through peace studies, concerned not simply with the standards of war reporting, but positive peace—creative, nonviolent resolution of all cultural, social, and political conflicts (e.g. 2000, 2004). As with Galtung, Jake Lynch recognizes that military coverage feeds the very violence it reports, and therefore he has developed an on-the-ground theory and practice of peace initiatives and conflict resolution (e.g., Lynch, 2008; Lynch & McGoldrick, 2005).

Conflict has significant news value; dramatic violence appeals to journalists and their audiences alike. Standard journalistic norms favor conflict, directly or indirectly (cf. Mitchell, 2007). Peace journalism is a self-conscious, working concept which denies that premise. Galtung (1998) has sought to reroute journalism on the "high road to peace," instead of the "low road" often taken by news media, when they fixate "on a win–lose outcome, and simplify the parties to two combatants slugging it out in a sports arena." In his literature review of war and peace journalism, Seow Ting Lee (2009) sees three contrasting features of each.

The three characteristics of mainstream war journalism are (Lee, 2009): (1) Focus on the here and now, on military action, equipment, tangible casualties, and material damage. Embedding journalists during the Iraq invasion illustrates an effective strategy for meeting this objective. (2) An elite orientation: use official sources, follow military strategy, quote political leaders, and be accurate with the military command perspective. (3) A dichotomy of good and bad. Simplifying the parties to two combatants, them versus us, in a zero sum game—binaries such as Arab intransigence and Israeli militarism.

There are three salient features of peace journalism, grounded in the principle of nonviolence (Lee, 2009): (1) Present context, background, historical perspective following the golden rule. Use linguistic accuracy—not Muslim rebels but rebels identified as dissidents of a particular political group. (2) An advocacy stance editorially for peace, and focusing in news on common values rather than on vengeance, retaliation, and differences. The people's perspective is emphasized. Not just organized violence between nations, but patterns of cooperation and integration among people. (3) A multiplicity orientation: All sides, all parties are represented. Create opportunities for society at large to consider and value nonviolent responses to conflict. Include ways in which the conflict can be resolved without violence (e.g., as in Dayton & Kriesberg, 2009). Consensus building efforts are considered newsworthy.

Peace journalism faces a heavy agenda (cf. Dayton & Kriesberg, 2009). In order to advance it, journalism needs to give up its utilitarian neutrality and detachment, and adopt the principle of nonviolence. Humans are moral beings and this ethical principle can inspire journalists to give peace priority even while reporting on a violent world.

Human Dignity

As with social justice, truth, and nonviolence, the principle of human dignity is basic to journalism ethics. In taking it seriously for itself, journalism is paralleling its escalating importance across the globe. Different cultural traditions affirm human dignity in a variety of ways, but together they insist that all human beings have sacred status without exception. Native American discourse is steeped in reverence for life, an interconnectedness among all living forms so that we live in solidarity with others as equal constituents in the web of life. In communalistic societies, *likuta* is loyalty to the community's reputation, to tribal honor. In Latin American societies, insistence on cultural identity is an affirmation of the unique worth of human beings. In Islam, every person has the right to honor and a good reputation. In Confucius, veneration of authority is necessary because authorities are human beings of dignity. Humans are a unique species, requiring within itself regard for its members as a whole.

From this perspective, one understands the ongoing vitality of the Universal Declaration of Human Rights issued by the United Nations General Assembly in 1948. As the Preamble states, "Recognition of the inherent dignity and of the equal and inalienable rights of all members of the human family is the foundation of freedom, justice and peace in the world" (Universal Declaration of Human Rights, 1988, p. 1). Every child, woman, and man has sacred status, with no exceptions for religion, class, gender, age, or ethnicity. The common sacredness of all human beings regardless of merit or achievement is not only considered a fact but is a shared commitment.

Ethnic self-consciousness these days is considered essential to cultural vitality. The world's cultures each have a distinctive beauty. Indigenous languages and ethnicity have come into their own. Culture is more salient at present than countries. With cultural identity the dominant issue in world affairs after the cold war, social institutions, including the media, are challenged to develop a healthy ethnic diversity and pluralism of ideas. The public sphere is conceived as a mosaic of distinguishable communities, a plurality of ethnic identities intersecting to form a social bond, but each seriously held and competitive as well.

Putting the principle of human dignity to work, Robert Entman and Andrew Rojecki (2000) indicate how the race dimension of cultural pluralism ought to move forward in the media. Race in the 21st-century United States remains a preeminent issue, and their research indicates a broad array of White racial sentiments toward African Americans as a group. They emphasize not the minority of outright racists but the perplexed majority. On a continuum from comity (acceptance) to ambivalence and then racism, a complex ambivalence most frequently characterizes the majority (p. 21). Correcting White ignorance and dealing with ambiguities appear to hold "considerable promise for enhancing racial comity" (p. 21). The reality is, however, that ambivalence shades off into animosity most easily and frequently. In Entman and Rojecki's interviews, personal experiences of Black effort and achievement tend to be discounted "in favor of television images, often vague, of welfare cheats and Black violence.... The habits of local news—for example, the rituals in covering urban crime—facilitate the construction of menacing imagery" (p. 34). Rather than actively following human dignity and enhancing racial understanding among those most open to it, the media tend to tip "the balance toward suspicion and even animosity among the ambivalent majority of Americans" (p. 44). When human dignity is a priority in journalism, this important swing group would be enabled to move forward and cultural pluralism would be enhanced.

RELATIVISM

While working diligently on theory and on the substantive issues, at its deepest level journalism ethics is at a crossroads. Our premiere challenge in metaethics is relativism, and unless we resolve it philosophically the future of journalism ethics is limited. Relativism is a longstanding problem for ethics, but in this first decade of the 21st century, it has reached maturity and has taken on a comprehensiveness that threatens our conceptual progress.

Friedrich Nietzsche

Relativism has been a prominent issue since 19th century Friedrich Nietzsche (1844–1900). In a world where God has died and everything lacks meaning, morality is a fool's paradise. We live in an era beyond good and evil (1886/1966). Since there is no transcendent answer to the why of human existence, we face the demise of moral interpretation altogether. For Nietzsche, morality had reached the end of the line. In its contemporary version, defending a suprasensory good is not beneficent, but imperialism over the moral judgments of diverse communities.

For relativists in the Nietzschean tradition, the right and valid are only known in local space and native languages. A context that is intelligible, a proposition that is true, an argument that is legitimate, and judgments of right and wrong are accepted by their adherents' internal criteria. And therefore these concepts and propositions are considered to have no validity elsewhere. Whatever the majority in a given culture approve is a social good. Since all cultures are equal in principle, all value systems are equally valid. Cultural relativity now typically means moral relativism. Contrary to an ethnocentrism of judging other groups against a dominant Western model, other cultures are not considered inferior only different.

All forms of public communication, including journalism, tend to exacerbate the problem of relativism—journalism's emphasis on particulars, for instance. Reporters work at the juncture of globalization and local identities—both of them happening simultaneously. They are caught in the contradictory trends of cultural homogeneity and resistance. Immigration can no longer be understood in melting-pot terms, for example, for immigrants today insist on honoring their language, culture, and religion. The complexities of an integrated world economy tend to bury the struggle of Aborigines for a viable livelihood. Unique to this complicated age is communication technology on a worldwide scale, but tribalism is fierce at the same time and identity politics has become dominant in world affairs. The integration of globalization and multiculturalism is the extraordinary challenge. But the news media's penchant for everyday affairs makes integration difficult. And in their passion for ethnography, for diversity, for the local—media academics and practitioners typically allow cultural relativity to slide into philosophical relativism.

The preoccupation with narrative in communication studies usually leaves relativism unattended. Stories are symbolic frameworks that organize human experience. Moral commitments are embedded in the practices of particular social groups and they are communicated through a community's stories. But narrative ethics is conflicted in its own terms about which value-driven stories ought to be valued. What in narrative itself distinguishes good stories from destructive ones? On what grounds precisely does narrative require fundamental changes in existing cultural and political practices? Because some customs are relative, it doesn't follow that all are relative. While there are disagreements over details, policies, and interpretations, these differences do not themselves mean that no moral judgments can be made about major historical events—the Holocaust, Stalinism, genocide, genital mutilation, Nazism, apartheid in South Africa, and so forth. The challenge for journalism ethics in a global age is honoring cultural diversity, because of the principle of human dignity, while simultaneously rejecting moral relativism.

When cultural relativism is misconstrued in popular terms as moral relativism, the fallacy of confused categories should be made apparent. Moral relativism justified as cultural diversity yields arbitrary definitions of goodness, as if to say, "This is good because most people in a social group identify it as good." But the communities that journalists describe ethnographically are not necessarily good. From David Hume (1751) through G. E. Moore (1903), we have recognized the fallacy of deriving "ought" statements from "is" statements. To assert prescriptive claims from an experiential base is faulty logic.

Moreover, when popular moral relativism is unquestioned, we have usually not faced up to the pernicious politics that insists on the prerogatives of a nation, caste, religion, or tribe. Cultural relativism turned into a moral claim is stultifying. If moral action is thought to depend on a society's norms, then "one must obey the norms of one's society and to diverge from those norms is to act immorally.... Such a view promotes conformity and leaves no room for moral reform or improvement" (Velaszquez et al., 2009). Ordinarily social consensus does not indicate the wrongness of a society's practices and beliefs.

While continuing to critique relativism on its own terms, the first intellectual step in dealing with the relativism crisis is to separate cultural relativism from philosophical relativism and then deal with the latter epistemologically. The primary challenge here is in metaethics, that is, defending the credibility of realism. A valid realism is the antidote to philosophical relativism, and the next section establishes its possibility.

Realism

Our creative ability works within the limits of an established natural order, creativity within a structured cosmos. People shape their own view of reality and we are under obligation to take each other's cultural worlds seriously. But this fact does not presume that reality as a whole is inherently formless until it is shaped by human language. A world that exists as a given totality forms the presupposition of historical existence. Reality is not merely raw material, but is ordered vertically and through an internal ordering among its parts. Vegetables are ordered to people as food, for example. Some kinds are hierarchical, subspecies within species, and species within genus; but relations among humans are horizontal. There is no slave race to serve a master race, and the human species will not mutate into something else. This coherent whole is history's source, an intelligible order than makes history itself intelligible. From a realist perspective, we discover truths about the world that exist within it.

This is ontological realism. It does not appeal to an objective sphere outside our subjectivity. This is realism inscribed in our very humanness. Among human beings are common understandings entailed by their creatureliness as lingual beings. All human languages are intertranslatable. In fact, some human beings in all languages are bilingual. All languages enable abstraction, inference, deduction, and induction. All human languages serve cultural formation, not merely social functions. All humans know the distinction between raw food and the cooked. Of major importance in our philosophical work is a legitimate realism on this side of Einstein, Freud, and Darwin, and realism grounded in human language qualifies.

In terms of ontological realism, norms can be embedded successfully within culture and history, East and West. As an indicator of its distinctiveness, the human species generates symbolic patterns along the boundaries between moral norms and actual behavior, the deepest self and our collective roles, the intentional and the inevitable (Wuthnow, 1987).Thomas Nagel's *View from Nowhere* (1986) documents those epiphanal moments coming with dynamic force from outside us, though not grounded *a priori*. Through the intrinsic self-reflexivity of natural language, *Homo sapiens* arbitrates its values and establishes the differences and similarities of people's worldviews. In an ironic twist on conventional skepticism, normative claims that presume realism are not a medieval remnant but the catalyst for innovation.

CONCLUSION

This overview of journalism ethics establishes an agenda in three areas: relativism, ethical theory, and moral principles. Specific cases will continue to demand our attention, and ongoing research is necessary on journalism practices across the globe. But whether journalism ethics reaches maturity depends on the quality of our struggle within the bigger picture.

Contending against philosophical relativism through ontological realism opens the right pathway. But a relativism of more than a century in the making will not be discredited overnight. In order to make intellectual work on ethical relativism fruitful, journalism ethics needs to nurture the philosophical imagination across the board. All the ethical issues the media face should be rooted in beliefs about the character of human beings and the meaning of life. Debates over issues such as ethical relativism are not a conceptual exercise only, but a venue for learning how to live. Given the ambiguities within relativism itself, and the possibility of a constructive response through realism, journalism ethics can move forward productively.

In working on theory, journalism educators find classical approaches indispensable; in their absence, we reinvent the wheel or promote theories with no sophistication. But rather than the individualist orientation of the classical models, news reporting as a social practice needs social ethics as its anchor instead. The dialogic alternatives currently are noteworthy—discourse, feminist, and communitarian ethics. Concepts of the good in these approaches reflect the values of the public rather than those of professional practice or academic expertise. Developing one of these, or another, into a distinctive and comprehensive theory of journalism ethics is the heart of the academic task ahead.

Journalism professionals and academics together can clarify, deepen, and apply the principles of social justice, truth, nonviolence, and human dignity. Some of their features were first articulated in terms of print journalism, and several during the broadcast era. These moral norms need to be brought into their own in a technologically sophisticated age. The most productive framework at present for developing each of them is social responsibility theory. Social responsibility thinking has general credibility today internationally, and when it is grounded in justice, truth, nonviolence, and human dignity it can serve as an ethical theory for global journalism.

REFERENCES

Aristotle. (1974). Nicomachean ethics. In R. McKeon (Ed.), *Introduction to Aristotle* (2nd ed.). New York: Modern Library.

Blood,R. (2002). *The weblog handbook: Practical advice on creating and maintaining your blog.* Cambridge, MA: Perseus.

Commission on Freedom of the Press. (1947). *A free and responsible press.* Chicago, IL: University of Chicago Press.

Confucius. (1991). *Four books of the Chinese classics: Confucian analects, the great learning, doctrine of the mean, works of Mencius* (J. Legge, Ed., 4 vols.). Corona, CA: Oriental Book Store.

Dayton, B. W., & Kriesberg, L. (2009). *Conflict transformation and peace building: Moving from violence to sustainable* peace. London: Routledge

Debatin, B. (2008). The future of new media ethics. In T. Cooper, C. Christians, & A. Babbili (Eds.), *An ethics trajectory: Visions of media past, present and yet to come* (pp. 257–263). Urbana: Institute of Communications Research-University of Illinois.

Dube, J. Retrieved from http://www.cyberjournalist.net/category/ethics-and-credibility

Ellul, J. (1967). *The political illusion* (K. Kellen, Trans.). New York: Alfred A. Knopf.

Entman, R. M., & Rojecki, A. (2000). *The black image in the white mind: Media and race in America.* Chicago, IL: University of Chicago Press.

Galtung, J. (1998, December). High road, low road: Charting the course for peace journalism. *Track Two,* 7(4). Retrieved from http://ccrweb.ccr.uct.ac.za/archive/two/7_4/p07

Galtung, J. (2000). *Conflict transformation by peaceful means: A participants' and trainers' manual.* Geneva, Switzerland: UNDP.

Galtung, J. (2004). *Transcend and transform: An introduction to conflict work (Peace by peaceful means).* London: Pluto Press.

Habermas, J. (1990). Discourse ethics: Notes on philosophical justification. In *Moral consciousness and communicative action* (pp. 43–115, C. Lenhart & S. W. Nicholson, Trans.). Cambridge, MA: MIT Press. (Original work published 1983)

Hickey, N. (1973, December 8). Only the sensational stuff got on the air. *TV Guide,* p. 34.

Jaspers, K. (1955). *Reason and existenz* (W. Earle, Trans). New York: Routledge & Kegan Paul.

Kant, I. (1964). *Groundwork of the metaphysic of morals* (H. J. Paton, Trans). New York: Harper Torchbooks. (Original work published 1785)

Koehn, D. (1998). *Rethinking feminist ethics: Care, trust and empathy.* New York: Routledge.

Kuhn, M. (2007). Interactivity and prioritizing the human: A code of blogging ethics. *Journal of Mass Media Ethics,* 22(1), 18–36.

Lee, S. T. (2009). Peace journalism. In L. Wilkins & C. Christians (Eds.), *The handbook of mass media ethics* (pp. 258–275). New York: Routledge.

Levinas, E. (1985). *Ethics and infinity: Conversations with Philippe Nemo.* Pittsburgh, PA: Duquesne University Press.

Lynch, J. (2008). *Debates in peace journalism.* Sydney, Australia: University of Sydney Press.

Lynch, J., & McGoldrick, A. (2005). *Peace journalism.* Glasgow, Scotland: Hawthorn Press.

Mill, J. S. (1975). *On liberty* (D. Spitz, Ed.). New York: Norton. (Original work published 1859)

Mill, J. S. (1979). *Utilitarianism.* Indianapolis, IN: Hackett. (Original work published in three parts in *Fraser's Magazine*; reprinted as a volume in 1861)

Mitchell, J.(2007). *Media violence and Christian ethics.* Cambridge, UK: Cambridge University Press.

Moore, G. E. (1903). *Principia ethica.* Cambridge, UK: Cambridge University Press.

Nagel, T. (1986). *View from nowhere.* New York: Oxford University Press.

Nietzsche, F. 1966. *Beyond good and evil* (W. Kaufmann, Trans.). New York: Random House. (Original work published 1886)

Nordenstreng, K. (1998). Hutchins goes global. *Communication Law and Policy, 3,* 419–438.

Taylor, C., Appiah, K. A., Habermas, J., Rockefeller, S., Walzer, M., & Wolf, S. (1994). *Multiculturalism: Examining the politics of recognition.* Princeton, NJ: Princeton University Press.

Universal Declaration of Human Rights. (1988). *Human rights: A compilation of international instruments.* Geneva, Switzerland: Centre for Human Rights.

Velasquez, M., Andre, C., Shanks, T., & Meyer, M. J. (2009). *Ethical relativism.* Markkula Center for Applied Ethics. Retrieved from http://www.scu.edu/ethics/practicing/decision/ethicalrelativism.html

Ward, S. J. A. (2005). Philosophical foundations for global journalism ethics. *Journal of Mass Media Ethics, 20*(1), 3–21.

Wuthnow, R. (1987). *Meaning and moral order.* Berkeley: University of California Press.

13

Ethical Dimensions
of New Technology/Media

Charles Ess

INTRODUCTION

The emergence of new digital technologies—including computers and computer networks as communication media, as well as Internet-enabled mobile phones—has evoked an extensive range of ethical issues and challenges. Many of these are familiar from earlier technologies; for example, privacy, copyright, pornography, and violence in (computer) games. At the same time, two characteristics of new digital media evoke distinctive ethical difficulties. First, digital devices conjoin or *converge* diverse technologies in a single device, thereby issuing in new combinations of technological possibilities and affordances (Jenkins, 2006). For example, with a standard smartphone, someone may record—with or without others' knowing—either still photographs or motion video, and then upload the photos or video to a publicly accessible site such as YouTube or a moderately restricted social networking site such as Facebook. The device thereby confronts us with a collective of what were once distinct ethical issues surrounding distinct media; that is, questions of permission and consent in connection with photography or videorecording; questions of permission, consent, and copyright in connection with print publication; and questions of harm, including libel and defamation of character following such publication (Ess, 2009a, pp. 9–11; for more critical discussion of convergence and new media, see Nyíri, 2007; Storsul & Studedahl, 2007).

Second, Information and Communication Technologies (ICTs) in the form of the Internet and the World Wide Web now connect over 25% of the world's population ("World Internet Stats," n.d.), a number dramatically increased by the explosive diffusion of mobile phones, which now connect over 4 billion or nearly 60% of humanity (International Telecommunications Union, n.d.). ICTs thus introduce classic ethical dimensions of cross-cultural communication on a massive new scale. Once the concern of only a privileged few (i.e., those persons fortunate enough to physically cross diverse cultures), the ethics of cross-cultural communication now confront many more of "the rest of us" in our daily cross-cultural engagements with one another online. At the same time, these issues are further complicated by the distinctive characteristics of online communication as (largely) *disembodied* (Ess, 2009a, p. 114.).

Finally, many of these issues arise in connection with communications and communication venues that cross sometimes radically divergent cultural domains. So our ethical responses to these issues must recognize how diverse cultural values and communicative preferences shape and influence these responses. This may seem a daunting task but we will see at both a theoretical level and as exemplified in emerging global norms regarding *privacy*, for example, that a *pluralistic* global information and communication ethics is possible. Such pluralism conjoins both shared ethical norms (as required for a genuinely *global* ethics) along with the irreducible differences between diverse cultural traditions and communicative preferences. Pluralism thus respects and fosters the irreducible differences that define individual and cultural identities. At the same time, pluralism thereby avoids both ethical *relativism* (and its tendencies towards cultural isolation and fragmentation) and ethical *monism* (and its correlative tendencies towards homogeneity and cultural imperialism (see Ess, 2009a, pp. 184–86, 190–195).

To explore this emerging digital media ethics more fully, I first take up the issue of privacy. Here I introduce two basic ethical frameworks, *utilitarianism* and *deontology*, that are widely used in modern Western cultures to address and frequently resolve important ethical dilemmas. We will also see an ethical pluralism regarding privacy and data privacy protection emerging between both Western and Eastern countries. As we move on to matters of participation and online democracy, copyright, pornography, violence, and finally, cross-cultural communication online, I then introduce *virtue ethics* as a third ethical framework—one that is enjoying increasing prominence in digital media ethics, in part because it already enjoys a global legitimacy that makes it especially suitable as part of a global media ethics.

MAJOR ETHICAL ISSUES EVOKED BY DIGITAL COMMUNICATION MEDIA: POSSIBLE RESOLUTIONS

Though digital media ethics is a very young field, its issues and relevant literatures are growing rapidly. Hence the following should be understood simply as a representative sample of important issues in digital media ethics, not as a comprehensive survey.

Privacy in the Digital Age?

Modern Western societies—meaning specifically, liberal democratic states whose primary function and justification is to protect the basic rights of the free and autonomous *individual*—have gradually developed distinctive and foundational notions of individual privacy. Briefly, such privacy is justified as protecting a *core space* (my term) in which the individual (in Kant's terms, as a rational *autonomy,* a moral agent capable of rational self-rule) can freely and critically reflect upon possible choices. Privacy is thus essential to the human being as most centrally a *freedom* capable of choosing his or her own conception of the good life, including political, religious, career, and other personal commitments (in Kantian language, one's *ends*) and thus the appropriate and necessary *means* for achieving those ends (see Berlin, 1969, p. 131). Privacy thus safeguards the individual freedom foundational to democratic societies: privacy further makes possible our developing and using the capacities for reflection, dialogue, and debate that are essential to one's participation in the public sphere as a citizen of a democratic society (Johnson, 2001).

In the U.S. context, privacy is initially formulated and defended by Samuel Warren and Louis Brandeis (1890) as the right to "being let alone" (Tavani, 2007, p. 130). Such privacy is also closely tied to *locational privacy,* our ability to prevent others from knowing our physical location, for example, via GPS technology. Tavani (2007) further identifies *decisional privacy* as the freedom from others' interfering in "one's personal choices, plans, and decisions" (p. 131). In the U.S. context, this decisional privacy has been essential in defending decisions regarding contraception, abortion, and euthanasia as matters of a right to *privacy* (Tavani, 2007). Finally,

Tavani (2007) characterizes *informational privacy* as our ability to control what we consider to be our *personal* information. Indeed, Luciano Floridi (2006) has argued that such informational privacy is the most important because in a digital age, at least within the developed world, we increasingly *are* our information (see also Meeler, 2008; for further discussion of the philosophical foundations of modern privacy, see DeCew, 1997).

Given, however, that digital information is "greased"—that is, digital information flows quickly and easily to multiple ports of call (Moor, 1997, p. 27)—threats to these sorts of privacy are now massive and ubiquitous. For example, governments justify attenuating privacy rights for the sake of protecting their citizens from terrorism. As well, many of us are willing to trade off privacy protections for conveniences such as "free" e-mail and web browsing. We do so, however, at the cost of having our IP addresses and search patterns stored and made available to both marketers and governments on demand. Further, our GPS-enabled mobile phones make us prey to automatic surveillance—primarily by the phone companies, but also by the occasional social scientist (Borenstein, 2008; González, Hidalgo, & Barabási, 2008). The rapid diffusion of these devices and thus our ever-greater publicity, along with our voluntary surrender of personal information in other ways, contribute to what Anders Albrechtslund (2008) calls "participatory surveillance."

In contrast with the willingness of some in the United States to give up traditional notions of privacy (see e.g., Springer, 1999), by 1995 the European Union had already established rigorous Data Privacy Protection laws (European Union, 1995) These contrasts are not accidental. To be sure, the liberal democracies of the United States and the European Union share a basic set of assumptions regarding the central importance of the autonomous individual and thereby the function of the state to protect that individual's basic rights: at the same time, however, they have two very different views on how to best *protect* privacy. Dan Burk (2007) characterizes U.S. law as primarily *utilitarian* (p. 98). Briefly, a utilitarian approach aims for "the greatest good for the greatest number." For utilitarians, the happiness of the many can justify risks of serious loss, harm, or even death of the few, if those costs and sacrifices indeed contribute to the greater good. Utilitarianism is perhaps most evident in war: we justify risking the pain and death of the few (primarily combatants) as contributing to the greater good (e.g., security) of the many (see Ess, 2009a, pp. 171–176). With regard to privacy, a utilitarian approach would argue that rigorous privacy protections would result in higher taxes, larger bureaucracies, and economic inefficiencies. Hence, for the sake of greater efficiencies, lower taxes, and smaller bureaucracies (representing the greatest good for the greatest number), less rigorous privacy protections—at least if individuals face as a result only minimal or moderate risk—can be justified. In Burk's phrase, the upshot is a "patchwork" of laws across the state and federal level, leaving individuals largely to fend for themselves such as by "opting out" of certain data-gathering schemes (Burk, 2007, p. 98).

The European Union, by contrast, begins with a clearly *deontological* approach, one that insists on protecting individual rights—including privacy rights—as (nearly) absolute; that is, such rights are to be protected, even if at considerable costs. Again, these rights are essential protections for us as *free* human beings. To override these rights—even if for only a few for the sake of maximizing the happiness of the many—is to thereby violate the very rights and freedoms that both define human beings as free beings and justify the very existence of the liberal democratic state. Hence, these rights—for all, not just the majority—are seen to be (near) absolute; that is, they are not to be eliminated or put at risk, even if for only a few, no matter the possible benefits of doing so (Ess, 2009a, pp. 176–181).

With regard to privacy rights, the result is a comparatively clear definition of personal information that must be protected, including name, address, health status, religious and philosophical beliefs, trade union membership, and sexual identity. Moreover, individuals have the right to be informed when such information is collected about them—and to review and, if necessary, correct that information. In contrast with the U.S. "default" of allowing individuals to opt-out — EU laws hark back to the individual's foundational right to *consent*: individuals must first agree to "opt-in" the collection and processing of their personal information (Burk, 2007, p. 98). A recent dispute between U.S.-based Google and the EU Data Privacy commissioners crystallizes these differences. Google argued that IP addresses are *not* personal information; as such, they would not need the sorts of protections guaranteed by the EU Data Privacy Protection codes. The EU's Data Protection commissioners found, to the contrary, that IP addresses—including the "dynamic" IP addresses that thus change vis-à-vis a specific computer—nonetheless *are* personal information: as such, they require the full protection of the EU privacy laws (White, 2008).

While these contrasts are thus significant, we can now see that these differences can be understood in importantly different ways. Briefly, *ethical relativism* argues that differences such as these result from the *absence* of any universal ethical norms and values that would otherwise count as normative (i.e., having moral force) for all human beings in all cultures. By contrast, *ethical pluralism* holds that these differences represent differences in the *interpretation*, *application*, or *understanding* of what shared and potentially universal norms *mean* within a specific cultural context and time. On this view, we begin with putatively shared norms and beliefs; that is, regarding the primary reality of the autonomous individual, the central importance of privacy and related rights, and the role of the state in defending those rights. But as interpreted and applied in the distinctive contexts of the United States, on the one hand, and the European Union, on the other, these shared norms and ideas thus issue in two distinctive sets of laws and approaches that reflect precisely the larger ethical frameworks (utilitarianism and deontology, respectively) characteristic of each context. A chief advantage of ethical pluralism is that it thereby allows us to avoid both ethical relativism and its opposite—an *ethical monism* that would insist on a single set of norms and practices as applied identically across diverse cultures, thereby threatening to erase differences that are essential to the distinctive identities of each culture. As something of a middle ground between ethical relativism and ethical monism, ethical pluralism thus plays a crucial role in the development of a *global* digital media ethics that allows for both shared norms and practices alongside the diverse interpretations and applications of those norms in specific cultures, so as to thereby preserve the irreducible differences defining distinctive cultural traditions (Ess, 2009a, pp. 184–186, 190–195).

Indeed, such a pluralism is at work in the emerging norms and practices surrounding privacy between both Western and Eastern cultures—and this alongside far greater differences in their initial assumptions regarding the nature of the individual, the community, and the role of the state (Ess, 2006, 2007). To begin with, while distinctive in important ways, Confucian and Buddhist traditions contrast with modern Western emphases on the reality of the autonomous individual—first of all, as they articulate a sense of human beings as *relational* beings. That is, while in the West we might say "I *have* a relationship," for example, with one's spouse, one's friends, one's family, one's colleagues, etc., in Confucian and Buddhist thought, one *is* one's relationships. For the Western self, as an autonomous "psychic atom," the loss of a given relationship, no matter how significant, is the loss of something *extrinsic* to the self. In Buddhist and Confucian thought, by contrast, the loss of a relationship is the loss of an *intrinsic* component of the self. Still more radically, Buddhist traditions argue that the "self" is an *illusion,* indeed, an ultimately insidious and destructive one. To paraphrase the Four-Fold Truth defining Buddhism, the illusory ego is the source of desire, and desire is the source of our suffering or discontentment in life: hence, to escape this suffering, we must overcome the ego-illusion—a task to be achieved by following the Eightfold Path (see Hongladarom, 2007).

In various forms, Confucian and Buddhist traditions—including these basic understandings of the self —have deeply shaped the diverse cultures of Thailand, Japan, and China (among others), at least until recently. Hence, it is not surprising to discover that in these cultures, there simply is no understanding of individual "privacy" as a positive good to be protected. Rather, before Western-style notions of individual privacy are imported into these cultures, anything resembling individual privacy was identified as clearly negative. So, for example, the Chinese philosopher Yao-Hui Lü (2005) has pointed out that until the mid-1980s in China, the only word for privacy—*Yinsi*—meant a "shameful secret" or "hidden, bad things" (p. 14).

In this light, we would hardly expect the emergence of *individual* data privacy protections in these countries. But in fact, under the profound economic, political, and cultural influences of Western societies (as we are increasingly woven together precisely by ICTs), China, Japan, Thailand, and other Asian countries have begun to establish some level of data privacy protection for their citizens (Hongladarom, 2007; Lü, 2005; Nakada &Tamura, 2005). To be sure, *economic* considerations are primary here: very simply, without such privacy protections, citizens will not engage in online commerce, which is seen to be key to further economic development. In addition, countries that wish to do business with EU countries are required by EU data privacy protection laws to offer the same protections to personal information as EU countries, resulting in what Dan Burk (2007) characterizes as the "viral spread" of the EU privacy protection codes (pp. 101–102).

Despite these radical contrasts, then, it appears that a rather remarkable pluralism is emerging between Western and Eastern approaches to data privacy. This pluralism preserves the fundamental and defining differences between the basic conceptions of the individual vis-à-vis the community and the state, while at the same time making possible a set of recognizably similar set of data privacy protections and codes. Such pluralism, I have argued, will become increasingly important first of all within the domains of Information and Computer Ethics, as ICTs continue their rapid diffusion throughout the world. In addition, as digital media, including mobile devices, likewise diffuse throughout the world, most especially in the developing world, a pluralistic approach will be central to a digital media ethics that encompasses ever larger portions of the human population across an ever wider span of cultures and traditions across the globe (Ess, 2009a).

Democracy Online?

The specific focus on privacy rights in the digital age is part of a larger enthusiasm for ICTs as potential "engines of democracy." Especially in the early days of the Internet and the Web, enthusiasts argued that as these communication technologies spread around the globe, they would inevitably bring greater autonomy, freedom of expression, and thereby democracy in their wake (e.g., Negroponte, 1995).

To be sure, in the developed world, ICTs have become increasingly essential to the political process; and striking examples of ICT usage supporting democratization around the globe have been documented (Rheingold, 2002). Broadly speaking, however, the early hopes for greater democratization via ICTs have largely waned in light of subsequent practices emerging online, including rapid commercialization.

It might be thought that the emergence of "Web 2.0," as emphasizing greater interactivity and participation (e.g., in the form of blogging and microblogging such as Twitter, social networking sites, etc.) would revive these earlier hopes, insofar as these more recent innovations highlight how "the many" can participate in and contribute to a larger discussion and deliberation. At the same time, however, many observers note how Web 2.0 also works to shift our focus to other pursuits—commercial as well as social ones. In particular, Axel Bruns's (2006) apt term *produsage* denotes our participation in the construction of media entertainment that we simultaneously consume. The greater participation of Web 2.0 seems to primarily manifest itself in ever more people producing the media entertainments, such as videos posted to YouTube, that we also consume. For every video—say, of the currently famous Iranian protestor Neda—there are thousands more having little, if anything to do with the political sphere. At the time of this writing, while a few of Neda-related videos on YouTube have garnered close to 250,000 views, a tribute to recently deceased Michael Jackson has drawn over 470,000 views, and earlier MJ videos have drawn tens of millions of views.

Whether Web 2.0 will resurrect the earlier democratization potentials of CMC and ICTs or whether we will rather, to paraphrase Neil Postman (1985), increasingly choose to amuse ourselves to death, appears to be an open question. Jennifer Stromer-Galley and Alexis Wichowski (2010), for example, argue that serious political dialogue can be found online, though they acknowledge that it remains largely at the margins of online engagements. Similarly, May Thorseth, earlier a strong proponent of realizing especially feminist and Habermasian forms of deliberative democracy online (e.g., 2008), has concluded that these possibilities will remain largely untapped (forthcoming).

Copyright, Copyleft

A further set of issues opened up by digital media are the ethical matters surrounding copying and distributing various forms of Intellectual Property (IP). With digital technologies it is, of course, trivially easy to copy music and video, much less texts of various sorts (including Web resources)—and then copy and distribute these further. It is equally easy to share such materials through various peer-to-peer networks such as Limewire, BitTorrent, and others. Perhaps influenced by notions of a "gift economy," illegal copying and distribution of digital materials appears to be a common practice, especially among young people around the globe. In the U.S. context, this has led to a long and complicated battle between major corporations, represented by the Recording Industry Association of America (RIAA), and those who argue that illegal downloading, copying, and distribution of music and other forms of IP are justified. As but one example, the Digital Millennium Copyright Act (DMCA) is the primary legal expression of anticopying efforts. The DMCA is opposed not only by scientists and librarians, but also by the Electronic Freedom Foundation (EFF; n.d.) who argues that the "DMCA has been a disaster for innovation, free speech, fair use, and competition" (see http://www.eff.org/issues/drm).

But as with privacy, here again our ethical sensibilities are profoundly shaped by our cultural contexts. To begin with, Dan Burk has argued that—in parallel with its approaches to privacy matters—the U.S. copyright tradition is rooted in a utilitarian sensibility. Most briefly, by protecting intellectual property so that its originators will thereby receive monetary and other sorts of rewards, copyright was originally conceived of as a way of encouraging innovation—and thereby generating the greatest good for the greatest number (Burk, 2007, p. 96). By contrast—again, in parallel with approaches to privacy—European traditions take a more deontological approach, one that insists on the "moral rights" of the individual author as primary. An author's or musician's work is seen as an expression and reflection of the author as an individual. Hence, "*Out of respect for the autonomy* and *humanity* [emphasis added] of the author, that artifact deserves legal recognition" (Burk, 2007, p. 96).

A third set of alternatives to either U.S. or EU forms of copyright protection has emerged in Western countries as well, the "copyleft" and FLOSS (Free/*libre*/Open Source Software) movements. FLOSS refers to both Free Software (FS) and Open Source (OS) software movements as efforts to provide alternative understandings of and methods for both sharing and protecting Intellectual Property (IP) and is affiliated especially with the work of Richard Stallman and Eric

Raymond. Stallman's Free Software (FS) movement has famously defined free software as "…a matter of liberty, not price. To understand the concept, you should think of free as in free speech, not as in free beer" (Stallman/GNU Operating System, n.d.). While Stallman and the FS movement push for a range of freedoms independent of economic interests and rewards, Eric Raymond and his Open Source (OS) movement seek to create mixed models of protecting and distributing software and other forms of IP in ways that would make business involvement with OS software economically attractive. GNU, incidentally, is a "recursive acronym for 'GNU's Not Unix!'" and refers to the FS initiative to develop a free, Unix-like operating system (see www.gnu.org).

Especially in the form of Stallman's GNU General Public License and the Creative Commons' licensing schemes (Creative Commons, n.d.). such copyleft schemes shift from an *exclusive* property right as protected under more traditional copyright to an *inclusive* property right. That is, under these licenses, authors retain important "moral rights" to their creation, including recognition as creators and the right to *prevent* others from making commercial use of and profit from their work; at the same time, however, as long as others respect these restrictions, they are free to make further use of the IP. IP thus becomes a shared or inclusive property.

In these ways, FLOSS returns to the understandings of property that prevailed in the European middle ages, as well as in traditional and Asian societies. For example, the popular *Ubuntu* distribution of the Linux operating system (itself originally licensed by its creator, Linus Torvalds, under Stallman's GNU General Public License) makes this linkage between *inclusive* property rights and distinctive *cultural* traditions explicit. The *Ubuntu* project explains that "Ubuntu is an African concept of 'humanity towards others'. It is 'the belief in a universal bond of sharing that connects all humanity'." (Ubuntu Code of Conduct: http://www.ubuntu.com/community/conduct) This culturally rooted tradition of sharing in order to benefit the larger community then justifies the project's appropriation of central freedoms defined by Stallman and the FS movement (see "Our Philosophy," http://www.ubuntu.com/community/ubuntustory/philosophy).

As we saw with regard to privacy, moreover, the emphasis on *community* that drives the *Ubuntu* project is shared by other cultural traditions as well, including the Confucian and Buddhist traditions. In Confucian tradition, for example, an author would produce a work in part to benefit others, not simply himself or herself. Similarly, a student's appropriation of the beneficent master's text and teaching (for example, in the memorization of the *Analects*) is intended as an act of respect and gratitude for such beneficence. To be sure, obvious economic incentives drive IP piracy in countries such as China and Thailand. At the same time, however, there are clear and deep cultural conflicts between Western and Asian understandings of the nature of property (i.e., *exclusive* vs. *inclusive*) and thereby between our respective approaches to matters of copyright. In this light, FLOSS approaches may be seen as something of a middle ground between Western approaches, on the one hand, and Asian and traditional cultural approaches, on the other.

Dan Burk (2007) argues that currently, at least, the U.S. approach to IP and copyright protection is winning out over the EU approach (pp. 99–100). While the future of such matters is notoriously tricky to predict, it is further apparent, however, that FLOSS approaches are growing in scope and influence, most especially in the developing world where legally free software is crucial to the diffusion of ICTs. And as mobile devices continue their exponential spread throughout the world as "platforms of choice" for connecting with the Internet, and as mobile devices themselves may move more and more to OS software (e.g., Google's Android phone)— FLOSS approaches to copyright and IP seem assured of a strong future as well.

Digital Sex and Games

Perhaps the most common ethical concerns affiliated with digital media surround the easy availability of pornography online—and, increasingly, through mobile devices as well—and violence in video games, including MMOGs (massively multiplayer online games) that link very large numbers of players within a shared gameworld via the Internet.

Pornography The irony for ethicists and researchers is that because pornography (still) represents a taboo subject in the academy, there is very little reliable data regarding its prevalence and availability (Paasonen, 2010). Still, it seems clear that pornography—like other forms of digital media as "greased"—is indeed ubiquitous and easily available online. How do we think ethically about this, especially in light of the large reality that what counts as "pornography" varies widely (wildly?) from culture to culture; for example, so as to include beauty pageants in India (Ghosh, 2006, p. 273)?

To state the obvious: our ethical approaches to pornography begin with our broader and more fundamental understandings and sensibilities regarding sexuality. Hence, it is especially relevant for the online context to note a fundamental difference that deeply shapes subsequent attitudes and responses, both with regard to current debates within Western cultures as well as with regard to larger debates between diverse cultures. So both traditional Christianity and modern Western thought have been largely marked by a strong *dualism*—one that sharply distinguishes between either a soul or a mind (Descartes' *tre raisonnable*) and body (Descartes' *être sensible*). Broadly, this dualism leads to otherwise apparently opposite attitudes and sensibilities. First, such dualism underlies a *contemptus mundi* (contempt of the world) in some expressions of Christianity that works to demonize women, body, and sexuality. But second, this dualism fosters a sense of sexuality as radically divorced from the self: sexuality is thus conceived of as a purely *bodily* experience, to be explored and enjoyed separately from ethical constraints having to do with commitments, obligations, and duties between moral agents as unique and individual *selves*. As long as no one is harmed (or, in the case of sado-masochism, as long as one consents to receiving pain as part of a sexual encounter), sexuality can thus be construed as "an exciting sensuous activity that can be enjoyed in a variety of suitable settings with a variety of suitable partners" (Wasserstrom, 1975/2008, p. 422). On this view, "open marriage" and "cookbook sex" (let's exchange our favorite recipes and techniques) make perfect sense. Similarly, much of the 1990s' discourse regarding our interactions with one another in cyberspace presumed a Cartesian dualism emphasizing a radical difference between the offline and (disembodied) online worlds. On this basis, "virtual sex" with strangers online, and, by extension, the consumption of pornography, could be argued to be radically divorced from our real (embodied) selves, and thereby the real-world moral commitments and ethical constraints we might otherwise agree to.

By contrast, multiple philosophical and religious traditions stress a sense of human identity as *embodied* human beings. This focus on embodiment is particularly prominent in contemporary feminist and phenomenological approaches in the West (e.g., Barney, 2004; Becker, 2002; Borgmann, 1999; Kondor, 2008). Theologically, Judaism has long insisted on the basic goodness of the body and sexuality as part of a creation whose intrinsic goodness reflects that of its Creator. Similarly, some Christian traditions emphasize the significance of *incarnation*—the embodiment of the divine in the *body* (*carne*) and person of Jesus—as thereby sanctifying the human body *per se*. In contrast with dualism and the demonization it sometimes evokes, these emphases on embodiment and the intrinsic goodness of the body further highlight how our specific bodies are inextricably interwoven with how we know and navigate within the world, and thereby how the individual body is intractably interwoven with our unique identities as human beings—and as moral agents (e.g. Stuart, 2008). In particular, the philosopher Sara Ruddick (1975) has argued with especial clarity how such embodiment is thereby essential to what she characterizes as "complete sex." In contrast with somehow "using" our bodies in ways disengaged from our distinctive, unique selves, as embodied beings, we *are* our bodies. Hence sexual engagement with one another is at once an interaction between two persons seamlessly at one with their bodies and the desires at work in them. In Ruddick's phrase, approaching sexuality as embodied beings can thereby issue in "complete sex," a sexual engagement inextricably interwoven and suffused with the distinctive identities of the persons involved. Such engagements thereby embody in turn their unique relationship with and correlative moral commitments to one another, including equality in the form of reciprocal care and concern for one another. Such embodied understandings and practices of sexuality thereby bring into play what Ruddick characterizes as "a preeminently moral virtue [excellence]—respect for persons" (1975, p. 98). *Contra* Descartes and Wasserstrom, Ruddick thus articulates and justifies common moral intuitions that our partner has betrayed or been "unfaithful" to *us* as individual (moral) agents or to our unique commitments and relationships with one another by "having sex" (i.e., where sex, Cartesian style, becomes an object/action separate from one's *self*) with someone else. Such intuitions make sense only if we move beyond Cartesian dualism and take up an understanding of the self as embodied in the ways Ruddick describes.

This broader framework further sheds new light on older debates. That is, to begin with, anti-porn feminists condemn most pornography as reinforcing patriarchal stereotypes of women as primarily sex objects (Adams, 1996). Anti-anti-porn feminists, by contrast, argue that various pornographies allow women and men to explore diverse sexualities and sexual identities (Paasonen, 2009). Both of these views, however, share the assumption that pornography online somehow engages us as real persons. Similarly, the religious conservatives concerned with the pornification of society assume that the consumption of pornography online has real-world (if entirely negative) consequences. By contrast, we can defend pornography as artistic expression by holding to a more Cartesian view that thus undermines both feminist and religious critiques. On this view, what happens is all just pixels on a screen, radically divorced from real persons in the real world, and hence nothing to be concerned about. But if our basic assumptions about body and sexuality moved toward the nondualistic views that emphasize embodiment—these views in turn undermine such Cartesian-based defenses of porn.

Virtue Ethics and Computer Games   As we have seen, utilitarianism and deontology have predominated in ethical reflection on matters of privacy and copyright. Sara Ruddick's account of embodiment and sexuality is important as it further brings to the foreground a virtue ethics. Virtue ethics is at once an ancient and contemporary framework: moreover, it promises to work well as a pluralistic and global ethic; that is, one that conjoins both shared norms and values with a diversity of interpretations that reflect and sustain distinctive cultural traditions.

Briefly, virtue ethics focuses on the habits and abilities that an individual needs to acquire and practice in order to become a *good* human being. "Good" is used here in roughly the same sense as when we say a particular knife is a good knife: "good" means primarily to perform defining functions well. A good knife is one that is handy to use, keeps a sharp blade, and so on. Analogously, a good human being realizes his or her potentials to act rationally and compassionately and to fulfill important ethical commitments to others. In these ways, human beings move toward *eudaimonia*, a sense of contentedness or well-being that comes precisely from realizing our best potentials and abilities, and then exercising these in ways that compliment and reinforce one another. Finally, this individual sense of well-being is inextricably tied up with our interactions with another in *community*: both for Aristotle and Confucius, the excellences or virtues of the individual (understood as a relational rather than an atomistic self) are thereby seen to foster both individual contentment and community harmony.

Recent feminist ethics have emphasized an "ethics of care" and distinctive forms of virtue ethics. And both feminist and environmental ethics stress precisely the ancient understanding of the individual as a relational self inextricably interwoven with community. They thereby contribute to the larger renaissance of virtue ethics over the past few decades in the West (e.g., Hursthouse, 1999). At the same time, virtue ethics are found throughout the globe, not only in Confucian thought, but in Buddhist traditions, multiple indigenous traditions, and in the Abrahamic religions of Judaism, Christianity, and Islam. All agree, to begin with, on the injunction to care for one's neighbor as oneself (the Golden Rule): such an injunction implies the necessity of *practicing* such care so as to acquire it as a habit and excellence (virtue) of the good human being.

Moreover, as virtue ethics emphasizes the individual–community interrelationship—it thereby mirrors recent developments within the domain of digital media and digital media ethics. That is, as more and more of our lives (in the developed world, at least) are spent online (e.g., doing banking and shopping, communicating with friends and family, etc.), and hence as the boundary between our offline and online lives thus blurs (Bakardjieva, 2010)—our sense of identity as connected in these diverse ways with ever more people is thus *distributed* across the computer networks that make such connections possible. In contrast with the atomic self presumed in the modern West, such distributed selves, as now more and more interwoven with larger communities, thus seem to require a "distributed morality," one that is currently only in its beginning stages (Ess, 2009b; Floridi, 2008). Ancient but global versions of virtue ethics thus find new resonance for such selves, as distributed through global computer and communication networks with any number of diverse communities in diverse cultural contexts (Ess, 2009a).

As thus consonant with such networked and increasingly global selves, virtue ethics finds extensive application in digital media ethics. For example, Shannon Vallor (2009) has analyzed mobile phones and their affordances in light of the virtues she identifies as necessary to friendship, including careful listening, patience, and perseverance. Vallor demonstrates that the affordances of mobile devices, as facilitating easy, quick, and short forms of communication reinforce rather opposite habits and practice, as when we prefer to text someone because a phone call is uncomfortable or more time-consuming than we might like. *Contra* these prevailing affordances, Vallor argues that new technologies could be designed in ways that foster the sorts of habits and practices we need to sustain friendship. She thus provides a framework for design as informed by ethical considerations from the outset, rather than relying on ethical reflection and response as solely a response to technologies after their design and diffusion in the marketplace (2009).

Virtue ethics has been especially prominent in application to computer games. In addition to utilitarian and deontological analyses, virtue ethics provides distinctive new defenses and critiques of games. So, for example, Miguel Sicart (2009) has articulated the many virtues or excellences built into games generally—including virtues of fairness, a sense of playing skillfully and creatively (both as an individual and as a cooperative team member), accepting both winning and losing with grace, and avoiding cheating. If we expand our focus beyond the usual target of violent videogames, so as to include what are called serious games (i.e., with one or more educational goals: see Egenfeldt-Nielsen, Smith, & Tosca 2008), then it seems perfectly fair to say that our engagement with such games, as with their preelectronic ancestors, constitutes an important way in which we learn to become more virtuous (excellent) persons; that is, more fully and completely human, especially in concert with one another.

At the same time, however, a virtue ethicist can criticize our use of violent video games in at least two ways. To begin with, virtue ethics stresses the importance of cultivating habits and practices that contribute to both our internal harmony and resonance between our various capacities and drives and to the larger harmony of our surrounding community. A key question here is: how should we approach and respond to "the Other" (Levinas, 1963), the person(s) who are clearly different from us, beginning in terms of gender and sexualities, but certainly also including ethnicity, language, the distinctive behaviors of a given cultural group? Again, the Golden

Rule appears to be a cultural universal: it seems that humanity everywhere must be steered in the direction of *learning* compassion and care for our neighbor, the Other. In the terms of virtue ethics, if we are to treat our neighbors with care and compassion (as well as with respect, humility, forgiveness, etc.), we must acquire these as habits and postures through the hard work of *practicing* these attitudes over time—indeed, a lifetime of intentional and intensive practice.

In marked contrast, much of our enjoyment of violent computer games involves learning the skills and knowledge needed to annihilate Others—at least virtually. Such skills and knowledge have their place in a virtue ethics of just war, as just war requires combatants who are *good*, that is, *excellent*, combatants. Beyond this, however, two difficulties emerge. The first we can think of in terms of an "opportunity cost." Given that we are creatures of finite space and time, every choice we make to pursue one set of practices is at the same time a choice *not* to pursue an alternative set of practices. So a first question would be: in our choosing to spend, say, 2 to 3 hours a day practicing the skill of annihilating Others, am I thereby giving up the opportunity to spend those hours developing other skills and habits—other human excellences or virtues—that contribute both to my own development, balance, and contentment, as well as to the harmony of the larger community around me? A second question is more direct. Playing such games appears to depend upon a basic fear of "the Other"—a fear that justifies our use of violence against *it*; that is, "the enemy" is usually reconstructed to be nonhuman, so as to further legitimate our violence. Insofar as a game rewards and reinforces a violent response to the Other as nonhuman—it arguably cultivates in us habits and practices that work contrary to those we must learn, practice, and perfect for the sake of our own contentment and community harmony (Ess, 2009a).

As virtue ethics thus invokes a central human concern to care for and develop the self in relationship with others, it thus provides ethical guidance and potential motivation to *be* "ethical" that can complement utilitarian and deontological approaches. At the same time, virtue ethics thereby sidesteps some of the more overt (and, in my view, largely ineffective) moralistic condemnation that some other approaches may lead to. Perhaps most importantly, as forms of virtue ethics are found in cultural and religious traditions around the globe, it hence stands as a very strong candidate for a global but pluralistic media ethics for the networked or distributed selves facilitated by our computer and communication networks.

Citizenship in the Global Metropolis

In ways that far exceed even the most utopian dreams of previous generations, the Internet and mobile communication devices now connect staggering numbers of people around the globe. Current estimates suggest that the Internet alone, that is, via "classical" desktop and laptop computers, connects 1.73 billion people, 25.6% of the world's population ("World Internet Stats," as of February 2010). But even more staggering, by 2008, subscriptions to mobile phones amounted to over 4 billion people, very close to 60% of the world's population (International Telecommunications Union, n.d.). Again, this explosive diffusion of ICTs has issued in understandings of both "distributed selves" and "distributed morality"; that is, a sense of self as inextricably interwoven with others across a network or web of relationships that directly mirrors both ancient and modern understandings of the self and community, especially as emphasized in virtue ethics. These new forms of global and thereby cross-cultural webs of relationships, moreover, thus further bring to the foreground in new ways the importance of our attending to the ethics of cross-cultural communication online.

To be sure, such cross-cultural communication has been the concern and interest of a privileged few throughout history, including, in the West, the Renaissance man (and occasional woman) who realized the ancient dream of *cosmo-politanism*, a world citizenship, in part as she or he became familiar with multiple languages and cultures, and thereby learned how to communicate and live with "the Other" in ways that fundamentally respected and preserved the distinctive differences defining diverse cultures. In these terms, the ongoing diffusion of ICTs, including mobile devices, means that what was once the prerogative of a privileged few is increasingly the ethical obligation of very large numbers of the world's population. That is, given that our technologies make cross-cultural communication an ever-more central component of our everyday lives, it would seem that we are thereby obliged to learn at least the rudiments of a cross-cultural communication ethics that avoids ethnocentrism (and, worse, cultural imperialism) and instead fosters mutual respect and recognition of the fundamental differences that define our cultural traditions.

A striking example highlighting the importance of such an ethics is the publication, in 2006 of the "Mohammed cartoons" by the small Danish newspaper, *Jyllands-Posten*. The cartoons' creation and publication were intended to evoke debate about central Western cultural values, including freedom of speech and the press—in part, precisely as the cartoons were perceived by Muslims as blasphemy against the holy Prophet of Islam. In pre-Internet days, the publication of these cartoons perhaps would have passed with little to no notice. But the cartoons inspired far more, thanks to their more or less instantaneous distribution throughout the Islamic world. Once made available online, the cartoons evoked diplomatic furor and violent protest worldwide, resulting in multiple deaths and significant property damage (see Debatin, 2007).

The Mohammed cartoon controversy makes clear some of the deep rifts between diverse cultural values—rifts that, in the end, may be insuperable. Happily, however, most of our efforts at cross-cultural communication are more productive and beneficent, especially as we learn to exercise some elementary sensibilities in our communication online with the Other. A first step is obvious, and yet bears repeating: in order to avoid a naïve ethnocentrism that presumes that our ways, beliefs, and practices are universally shared by all people, we must begin with what I call an epistemological humility. This humility recognizes that our ways of knowing and doing are *not* universal, but are rather limited precisely to those of our own *ethnos*, our own people and traditions. If we wish to communicate with the Other *as* Other (i.e., as irreducibly different from ourselves) our next task is then to learn what we can of the Other's language, customs, and practices and appropriate these into our own "vocabulary" of communicative skills and abilities.

As we saw with regard to the affordances of mobile devices, however, not only our prevailing uses but also the very technologies themselves that make such cross-cultural communication possible may incline us away from practicing exactly the virtues needed to help such communication avoid ethnocentrism and imperialism. So, for example, the use of a given *lingua franca* (e.g., English, Chinese, etc.) is clearly essential to quick and efficient communication. At the same time, however, if we are native English speakers, such a *lingua franca* thus reinforces our own sense that our one language is all we need, and thereby excuses us from the difficult and time-consuming labor of learning another language well. But it is only through acquiring fluency in another language that we thereby gain access to many of the central cultural values and elements of everyday life carried out in another culture; only thus do we begin to acquire an understanding of the Other as Other, as a person whose most important, most intimate thoughts and feelings can only be expressed directly and transparently within her or his native tongue.

At a deeper and subtler level, ICTs may further reinforce cultural and communicative ethnocentrism, as they embed and foster the cultural values and communicative preferences of their designers and primary users. As we have seen, in its earliest days, the Internet was heralded as an engine of freedom of expression and democracy. As originally designed, as a communication network to survive extensive damage in a nuclear war, the Internet was thought to interpret "censorship as damage—and route around it" (Elmer-Dewitt, 1993). And through the anonymity it provided, CMC was thought to foster more egalitarian relationships between employees and their superiors. All well and good, but of course, these are cultural values central but distinctive to the West. As has now been extensively documented, diffusing CMC technologies throughout the globe has resulted in a wide range of cultural conflicts, which have often been fatal for important projects aimed at development; for example, as the recipients of these technologies often found that they clashed with their own distinctive cultural values and communicative preferences in fundamental ways (see Ess, 2008, 2009a, for further discussion). A crucial lesson to be drawn from these experiences is the importance of being aware of our own cultural values and communicative preferences, and, at a deeper level, of how these may be fostered by a given communication medium, and, finally, how these may conflict with the preferences and values of the Others with whom we want to communicate.

A further difficulty facing cross-cultural communication online is that, at least currently, much of this communication occurs via text. Such communication is thus largely *disembodied*. By contrast, especially in non-Western cultures, much of our communication with one another takes place nonverbally *through* the body via gesture, body distance, and gaze. Worst case, an SMS or textual email may appear to communicate successfully across cultures, but the nontextual cues conveyed through the body, thus lost in such a communicative exchange, might tell a very different story indeed. Minimally, the absence of bodily cues in our cross-cultural communication online, like the use of a *lingua franca,* makes it easy to believe (again) that our ways are those of the Other. But again, in fact, by believing so, we only thereby impose our ways on the Other, rather than recognizing and then seeking to preserve and foster the irreducible differences defining the Other as Other (Ess, 2009a; Ploug, 2009).

To be sure, developing an awareness of these manifold elements of culture, communication, and ICTs is by no means an easy matter. At the same time, however, I hope by now it is clear that developing such an awareness is essential if we are to avoid inadvertent ethnocentrism and a correlative imperialism that cheerily imposes our own cultural values and communicative preferences on Others, not because we are creatures of ill-will, but because we remain blithely ignorant of these multiple differences and how they define diverse and distinctive cultural identities. Again, developing such an awareness—along with still more difficult chores such as learning the language and cultural practices of the Other—is no longer the luxury of a privileged few. Rather, if we are to value and *practice* a fundamental respect for the Other and the irreducible differences that define his or her culture and communication preferences, then, as the continued expansion of ICTs throughout our lives and across the cultures of the globe thereby make more and more of us *cosmopolitans*, citizens of the world, those who are thereby enabled to communicate cross-culturally are thus obliged to continuously develop such an awareness, along with ever-greater facility in communicating in ways appropriate to the Other within his or her own cultural setting and language, not simply from within the more comfortable but more superficial framework of a *lingua franca* and unexamined assumptions regarding the cultural values and communicative preferences embedded in ICTs.

CONCLUDING REMARKS: UNEXAMINED DIGITAL MEDIA ARE NOT WORTH USING?

Digital media confront us with sometimes familiar, sometimes novel ethical challenges. Especially as these media are characterized by, one, a *convergence* that brings together into single devices what were once separate technological capabilities and, two, a *global* extension and reach that render more and more of us *cosmopolitans,* they thereby evoke ethical challenges that strain against the capacities of traditional ethical frameworks and approaches. On the one hand, as we've seen, some of the new ethical challenges evoked by these technologies may be met through the emergence of both old and new ethical frameworks, including a resurgent virtue ethics and emerging feminist and environmental ethics: both of these, as a reminder, emphasize the interconnection between self and community that is mirrored and amplified by the networks that interweave our digital media. Moreover, these ethical frameworks are especially promising for a *global* digital media ethics, one that enjoys recognition and application across diverse cultures and traditions around the world, in part because they allow for *pluralistic* interpretations and applications that reflect and foster the irreducible differences that define specific cultural traditions and identities.

At the same time, however, a significant *metaethical* discussion centers on whether we can fully and adequately respond to the ethical dimensions of new digital media through these more familiar ethical frameworks, even if modified and revised in light of new technological affordances and their global reach. In addition to these more traditional frameworks perhaps one or more distinctively new frameworks will be necessary. In the closest analogue to digital media ethics—the older and much more fully developed domain of Information and Computing Ethics (ICE)—this debate is decades old, with no clear resolution. To be sure, as the example of an emerging "distributed morality" for distributed selves suggests, there are efforts to sketch out distinctively new ethical frameworks (e.g., Braidotti, 2006; see also, Ess, 2009b). But it is simply far too early to tell whether these will survive both critical scrutiny and, even more importantly, the crucial test of being fully applicable in *praxis* of successfully meeting the specific ethical challenges evoked by digital media.

These ethical uncertainties are for some the occasion of despair, if not moral panic. At the same time, however, it may be helpful to remember that these concerns are as old as modernity and industrialization, if not older. Indeed, the history of technology is arguably a history of people seeking how to respond ethically to new possibilities and affordances, and with more or less reasonable success. To be sure, the 1990s' utopian dreams of an electronic global village, a democratic, egalitarian, and equitably prosperous world community woven together by ICTs, has proven to be a naïve vision (in part, precisely because of the ethnocentrism and resulting cultural imperialism that prevailed among the early enthusiasts and proponents of "liberation in cyberspace"; Ess & Sudweeks, 2002). At the same time, as digital media and ICTs continue to weave more and more of our lives together, one can be cautiously optimistic that we will learn how to use these technologies effectively and in ethically responsible ways, both as members of our own tribes, and, perhaps, as genuine *cosmopolitans*.

REFERENCES

Adams, C. J. (1996). "This is not our fathers' pornography": Sex, lies, and computers. In C. Ess (Ed.), *Philosophical perspectives on computer-mediated communication* (pp. 147–170). Albany, NY: SUNY Press.

Albrechtslund, A. (2008). Online social networking as participatory surveillance. *First Monday 13*(3). Retrieved from http://www.uic.edu/htbin/cgiwrap/bin/ojs/index.php/fm/article/view/2142/1949

Bakardjieva, M. (2010). The Internet in everyday life: Exploring the tenets and contributions of diverse approaches. In M. Consalvo & C. Ess (Eds.), *The Blackwell handbook of internet studies* (pp. 59–82). Oxford, UK: Blackwell-Wiley.

Barney, D. (2004). The vanishing table, or community in a world that is no world. In A. Feenberg & D. Barney (Eds.), *Community in the digital age: Philosophy and practice* (pp. 31–52). Lanham, MD: Rowman & Littlefield.

Becker, B. (2002). Sinn und Sinnlichkeit: Anmerkungen zur Eigendynamik und Fremdheit des eigenen Leibes [Sense and sensibility: Remarks on the distinct dynamic and strangeness of one's own body]. In L. Jäger (Ed.), *Mentalität und Medialität* (pp. 35–46). München: Fink Verlag.

Berlin, I. (1969). Two concepts of liberty. In *Four essays on liberty* (pp. 118–173). London: Oxford University Press.

Borenstein, S. (2008, June 6). Cell phone users outside U.S. secretly tracked: Study tracking 100,000 raises privacy, ethical questions. *Associated Press*. Retrieved from http://www.msnbc.msn.com/id/24969880/

Borgmann, A. (1999). *Holding onto reality: the nature of information at the turn of the millennium*. Chicago, IL: University of Chicago Press.

Braidotti, R. (2006). *Transpositions: On nomadic ethics*. Cambridge, UK: Polity Press.

Bruns, A. (2006). Towards produsage: Futures for user-led content production. In F. Sudweeks, H. Hrachovec, & C. Ess (Eds.), *Proceedings: Cultural attitudes towards communication and technology 2006* (pp. 275–284). Perth: Murdoch University.

Burk, D. (2007). Privacy and property in the global datasphere. In S. Hongladarom & C. Ess (Eds.), *Information technology ethics: Cultural perspectives* (pp. 94–107). Hershey, PA: IGI Global.

Creative Commons. (n.d.). http://creativecommons.org/licenses/by-nc-sa/3.0/us/

Debatin, B. (Ed.). (2007). *Der Karikaturenstreit und die Pressefreiheit. Wert- und Normenkonflikte in der globalen Medienkultur* [The cartoon debate and the freedom of the press: Conflicting norms and values in the global media culture]. Berlin: LIT Verlag.

DeCew, J. (1997). *In pursuit of privacy: Law, ethics, and the rise of technology*. Ithaca, NY: Cornell University Press.

Egenfeldt-Nielsen, S., Smith, J., & Tosca, S. (2008). *Understanding videogames: The essential introduction*. London: Routledge.

Electronic Freedom Foundation. (n.d.). (see http://www.eff.org/issues/drm).

Elmer-Dewitt, P. (1993, December 6). First nation in cyberspace. *Time, 49*. Retrieved from http://www.time.com/time/magazine/article/0,9171,979768-1,00.html

Ess, C. (2006). Ethical pluralism and global information ethics. *Ethics and Information Technology, 8*(4), 215–226.

Ess, C. (2007). Cybernetic pluralism in an emerging global information and computing ethics. *International Review of Information Ethics, 7*. Retrieved from http://www.i-r-i-e.net/inhalt/007/11-ess.pdf

Ess, C. (2008). Culture and global networks: hope for a global ethics? In J. van den Hoven & J. Weckert (Eds.), *Information technology and moral philosophy* (pp. 195–225). Cambridge, UK: Cambridge University Press.

Ess, C. (2009a). *Digital media ethics*. Cambridge, UK: Polity Press.

Ess, C. (2009b). Floridi's philosophy of information and information ethics: Current perspectives, future directions. *The Information Society, 25*, 159–168.

Ess, C., & Sudweeks, F. (Eds.). (2002). Liberation in cyberspace…Or computer-mediated colonization? Introduction to "Global cultures: collisions and communication." *Electronic Journal of Communication, 12*(3 & 4). Retrieved from http://www.cios.org/EJCPUBLIC/012/3/01236.html

European Union. (1995). Directive 95/46/EC of the European Parliament and of the Council of 24 October 1995. Retrieved from http://eur-lex.europa.eu/LexUriServ/LexUriServ.do?uri=CELEX:31995L0046:EN:HTML

Floridi, L. (2006). Four challenges for a theory of informational privacy. *Ethics and Information Technology, 8*(3), 109–119.

Floridi, L. (2008). Information ethics: A reappraisal. *Ethics and Information Technology, 10*(4), 253–262.

Ghosh, S. (2006). The troubled existence of sex and sexuality: Feminists engage with censorship. In B. Bose (Ed.), *Gender and censorship*, (pp. 255–285). New Delhi, India: Women Unlimited.

González, M. C., Hidalgo, C. A., & Barabási, A-L. (2008, June 5). Understanding individual human mobility patterns. *Nature, 453*, 779–782. doi: 10.1038/nature06958.

Hongladarom, S. (2007). Analysis and justification of privacy from a Buddhist perspective. In S. Hongladarom & C. Ess (Eds.), *Information technology ethics: Cultural perspectives* (pp. 108–122). Hershey, PA: IGI Global.

Hursthouse, R. (1999). *On virtue ethics*. Oxford, UK: Oxford University Press.

International Telecommunications Union. (n.d.). Mobile cellular subscriptions. Retrieved from http://www.itu.int/ITU-D/icteye/Reporting/ShowReportFrame.aspx?ReportName=/WTI/CellularSubscribersPublic&RP_intYear=2008&RP_intLanguageID=1

Jenkins, H. (2006). *Convergence culture: Where old and new media collide*. New York: New York University Press.

Johnson, D. (2001). *Computer ethics* (3rd. ed.). Upper Saddle River, NJ: Prentice-Hall.

Kondor, Z. (2008) Converging theories: The age of secondary literacy. In *Embedded thinking: Multimedia and the new rationality* (pp. 157–164). Frankfurt am Main: Lang.

Levinas, E. (1963, September). La Trace de l'autre [The trace of the other] (A. Lingis, Trans.). *Tijdschrift voor Philosophie*, 605–623.

Lü, Y-H. (2005). Privacy and data privacy issues in contemporary China. *Ethics and Information Technology, 7*(1), 7–15.

Meeler, D. (2008). Is information all we need to protect? *The Monist, 91*(1), 151–169.

Moor, J. (1997). Towards a theory of privacy in the information age. *ACM SIGCAS Computers and Society, 27*, 27–32.

Nakada, M., & Tamura, T. (2005). Japanese conceptions of privacy: An intercultural perspective. *Ethics and Information Technology, 7*(1), 27–36.

Negroponte, N. (1995). *Being digital*. New York: Knopf.

Nyíri, K. (Ed.). (2007). *Integration and ubiquity: Towards a philosophy of telecommunications convergence*. Vienna, Austria: Passagen Verlag.

Paasonen, S. (2010). Online pornography: Ubiquitous and effaced. In M. Consalvo & C. Ess (Eds.), *The Blackwell handbook of internet studies* (pp. 424–439). Oxford, UK: Blackwell-Wiley.

Ploug, T. (2009). *Ethics in cyberspace: How cyberspace may influence interpersonal interaction*. New York: Springer.

Postman, N. (1985). *Amusing ourselves to death: Public discourse in the age of show business*. New York: Penguin.

Rheingold, H. (2002). *Smart mobs: The next social revolution*. New York: Basic Books.

Ruddick, S. (1975). Better sex. In R. Baker & F. Elliston (Eds.), *Philosophy and sex* (pp. 280–299). Amherst, NY: Prometheus Books.

Sicart, M. (2009). *The ethics of computer games*. Cambridge, MA: MIT Press.

Springer, P. (1999, January). Sun on privacy: "Get Over It." *Wired*. Retrieved from http://www.wired.com/politics/law/news/1999/01/17538

Stallman, R./GNU Operating System. (n.d.). http://www.gnu.org/philosophy/free-sw.html

Stromer-Galley, J., & Wichowski, A. (2010). Political discussion online. In M. Consalvo & C. Ess (Eds.), *The Blackwell handbook of internet studies* (pp. 168–187). Oxford, UK: Blackwell-Wiley.

Storsul, T., & Stuedahl, D. (Eds.). (2007). *Ambivalence towards convergence: Digitalization and media change*. Gothenburg, Sweden: NORDICOM.

Stuart, S. (2008) From agency to apperception: Through kinaesthesia to cognition and creation, *Ethics and Information Technology, 10*(4), 255–264.

Tavani, H. (2007). *Ethics and technology: Ethical issues in an age of information and communication technology* (2nd ed.). Hoboken, NJ: Wiley.

Thorseth, M. (2008). Reflective judgment and enlarged thinking online. *Ethics and Information Technology, 10*(4), 221–231.

Thorseth, M. (Forthcoming). Deliberative democracy online. In C. Ess & M. Thorseth (Eds.), *Trust and virtual worlds: Contemporary perspectives*. New York: Lang.

Ubuntu Code of Conduct. (n.d.). http://www.ubuntu.com/community/conduct

Vallor, S. (2009). Social networking technology and the virtues. *Ethics and Information Technology*. doi: 10.1007/s10676-009-9202-1.

Warren, S., & Brandeis, L. (1890). The right to privacy. *Harvard Law Review, 14*(5), 193–220.

Wasserstrom, R. (2008). Is adultery immoral? In J. Boss, *Analyzing moral issues* (4th ed., pp. 420–427). Boston, MA: McGraw-Hill. (Reprinted from R. Baker & F. Elliston, Eds., *Philosophy and sex*, pp. 207–221. Buffalo, NY: Prometheus Books, 1975)

White, A. (2008, January 22). IP addresses are personal data, E.U. regulator says. *Washington Post*. Retrieved from http://www.washingtonpost.com/wp-dyn/content/article/2008/01/21/AR2008012101340.html

World Internet Stats. (n.d.). Retrieved from http://www.internetworldstats.com/stats.htm

14

Public Relations and Marketing

Ethical Issues and Professional Practice in Society

Jacquie L'Etang

INTRODUCTION

The purpose of this chapter is to delineate key ethical issues and debates in relation to public relations and marketing and to reflect upon the methodological and technical challenges, which arise in such analysis. Within a *tour d'horizon*, I highlight key problematics, the reasons for their existence, and angles from which these problems may be tackled. Although much of the chapter is conceptually driven and argumentative in style, I have also attempted to suggest areas for academic and functional change and development, which, I hope, are not naïve, and which might advance debate.

Core ethical challenges to public relations and marketing have included manipulation (of consumers, stakeholders, publics, the general public, and the media), lying, sophistry, pandering, bribery, distorting the channels of public communication or dominating the public sphere, serving the powerful and privileging political and corporate classes, and generating inauthenticity within society through the practices of puffery and the assumptions of promotional culture. Public relations is linked to the media (as a source) and shares some ethical concerns and ideals such as truth telling, which may partly account for media antagonism toward public relations practice expressed by many journalists and media academics who see public relations as a duplicitous and nefarious practice. Public relations and marketing are tied to consumption as a cultural practice underpinned by the ideology of capitalism. Marketing has also been accused of promoting conspicuous consumption, greed, competition, built-in obsolescence, and superficial consumerist lifestyles, which degrade the planet. Critiques of marketing and public relations are, to an extent, a critique of 'promotional culture' (Wernick, 1991) grounded in the market economy and the values of freedom, autonomy, and choice-making (Brenkert, 2008, p. xi) and thus ideologically grounded. On the other hand, it is important to acknowledge the ideologies of public relations and marketing, taking care to distinguish between lofty ideals and practice. In some cultural contexts public relations has been associated with government information and democratic education, and considerable emphasis given to truthfulness. In other words, debate about the ethics of these practices needs to take into account competing multiple discourses including the official occupational aims (encompassed in codes of ethics and the formal statements of professional bodies); the normative literature; empirical evidence regarding aims and impacts.

I begin with some basic definitions and contextual discussion, based on published literature. Thereafter I attempt to synthesize these insights before stripping down to my understanding of the central and underlying concerns regarding these occupations and their role in, and between organizations and society. The concept of 'profession' is relevant, since this occupational category clearly bestows societal and organizational legitimacy, in part because of the notion of public service, but also because of their engagement with, and commitment to, codes of practice or ethics. The ideal of public service seems not unconnected to the practice of corporate social responsibility, which both these disciplines, and others, have claimed as their own, and I consider whether, and why, practitioners of public relations and marketing may, or may not be suitable policy-makers and managers in this area. Finally, I turn my attention to the concept of propaganda, of which public relations and advertising (a subfield of marketing) have been accused, in relation to manipulation and false claims. In this part of the discussion I endeavour to lay out some of the definitional and conceptual problems in order to uncover the problem of agency.

THE ROLE AND SCOPE OF PUBLIC RELATIONS AND MARKETING IN SOCIETY: A CRITICAL REFLECTION

Epistemological and definitional issues arise in any discussion of the roles of marketing or public relations in society, in that although the terms did not become associated with particular organizational and business contexts until the late 19th or early 20th century, it is common for the roots of these activities to be traced back to practices such as political or government communication; citizen action or advocacy; rhetorical and debating skills and events; architecture and monuments. Many of these practices are recorded through literary as well as historical or archaeological sources. In our own times processes of consumption and globalization overlay the historical legacy, which belongs more to public relations via its links to public opinion, political communication and reputation, than to marketing.

According to Jones and Shaw (2002, p. 41), marketing originated in the 7th century BC in Asia Minor (modern Turkey) and then diffused through Greece and the Mediterranean where the new phenomenon, 'represented a strange new form of behaviour. Emphasising individual gain and competition, marketing activity appeared detrimental to maintaining the social bonds uniting the members of societies traditionally based on altruism and co-operation' (Jones & Shaw, 2002, p. 41).

A number of marketing historians have reinterpreted classical literature in relation to trade and what they see as rudimentary marketing concepts. Modern marketing emerged from applied economics, linked to market ideology and the concept of utility. Marketing is grounded in free-market economics and has developed from a consumer focus to sell product into a much broader and more research-led business discipline. It encompasses specialist areas such as consumer behaviour (based on social psychology), supply chain management, logistics, retail studies, personal selling, sales promotion, direct mail, sponsorship, and advertising. Marketing has, to some extent, reinvented itself through the concepts of corporate societal marketing, social marketing, relationship marketing, and customer relationship management. A rather contradictory picture emerges; some interpretations favour justifications for the emergence of the middleman and the division of labour which resulted in the separation of producers and consumers; other readings highlight negative criticism of embryonic markets as parasitic, immoral, and low status; and activist interpretations which perceive imbalances of power between buyers and sellers as marketing malpractice (Jones & Shaw, 2002, pp. 40–42). The notion of 'customer-orientation' was identified as ethically grounded by McKitterick (1957, cited in Webster, 2002, p. 71) as early as the 1950s in the Kantian-inspired idea that the customer should not be treated as a means to an end (Webster, 2002, p. 71) but as an end in him- or herself. The subfield of macromarketing has debated the role and impact of marketing on society and vice versa. Much of this literature considers the implications of, and response to antitrust laws, consumer boycotts, activism, and advocacy.

Currently, however, it would be fair to say that there are more general and persistent societal, media, and academic criticisms of public relations and 'spin doctors' than of advertising. It appears that the public relations occupation has inherited advertising's reputational problems (based on false claims for products, offence to others, and use of subliminal messages). Public relations is, however, a more complex target for analysis and critique. For a start, public relations is known by many different terms: *communication management, corporate affairs, corporate communications, public affairs, stakeholder relations, media manager, press officer, information officer*, all are terms in recent or current use which refer to public relations work, although they may reflect slightly different aspects of that work. Positioning public relations as part of the management function raises the organizational and societal status of the occupation, but as British sociologist Stuart Hall points out, the alignment of managerialism may have wider societal effects: '[The diffusion of] a gentle glow of legitimacy…a highly effective public relations exercise for public relations: the elevation of PR into the ranks of the "management sciences"…. It is impression management raised to the level of ideology, managerial science becoming a reified discourse' (Hall, 1969, pp. 948–949).

There seems little doubt that the constant reinvention of names is a rhetorical strategy to escape or diffuse potential criticism, part of the endless cycle of 'the PR of PR'. The ethics of reinvention, and the consequent proliferation of euphemistic terms to define the practice, are challenging because they suggest a lack of authenticity that seems dishonest and threatens credibility. It also suggests that practitioners experience an underlying discomfort or cognitive dissonance with the occupation (Campbell, 2009).

From a marketing perspective, public relations performs the promotional part of marketing communications to support advertising through the acquisition of media coverage, often interpreted as 'free publicity'. Public relations viewed through the lens of marketing is a useful adjunct of advertising, but is essentially a tactic to be integrated into a range of marketing communications, rather than a separate discipline with its own strategic focus. Marketers often do not recognise that public relations emerged in many cultures as an adjunct of political government; for example, public communications such as health campaigns or citizen information. In this form they predated the free-market, which necessitated the development of the marketing discipline. Since it is the political class and associated ideology which determined economic arrangements, it can be seen that public relations has always had a strategic relationship with power that marketing has not. Indeed, public relations has been critiqued for its promotion of free-market capitalism and corporate power that provided the framework within which the marketing discipline could thrive. It is therefore ironic that, in practice, marketers generally see public relations as but a small component of the whole marketing effort. At least one reason for this may be that historically, in some cultural contexts, public relations consultancy (as opposed to government, public sector, or corporate public relations) emerged partly from advertising consultancies, where public relations services were often offered free to add value. Gradually, the skill of media relations, networking, and hospitality (dominant forms of public relations in the UK in the 1950s and 1960s) came to be recognised as a useful addition.

In some contexts, however, marketers have combined forces with public relations practitioners to unify corporate communications and marketing communications to ensure consistency of messages through 'integrated marketing' or 'marketing-public relations'. Thus critics of globalised consumer culture such as Ritzer (2000, 2002) normally do not distinguish between public relations and marketing.

Public relations—'relations with the public(s)'—notably takes place at points of organizational or societal change. Changes in the global landscape, political, social, environmental, technological, or economic changes require complementary organizational responses, and the articulation of policy through public communication. Public relations is therefore strongly issue-led, and responsive to external circumstance. The function of public relations is ostensibly to provide all stakeholders and the media with clear information to engage in dialogue, and to foster beneficial relationships that support the organizational enterprise.

Public relations is a culturally specific function, however, and has evolved (and continues to evolve) along variable paths in different cultural contexts, even though there is a form of globalized practice carried out by multinational communications consultancies and organizations. One feature of culture's influence is the variable connections to political power and market ideology. Public relations in some cultures has been strongly embedded in government communications and public diplomacy. It is this connection to ideology which has led to one of the major criticisms that public relations is unethical; that it is no more than propaganda, which during the 20th century became a pejorative term as a consequence of the rise of totalitarian powers and international conflict. This issue is taken up in more detail later in the chapter.

Public relations potentially contributes to the effectiveness of organizations by improving organizational relationships and facilitating public conversations and debate. Public relations has a remit for corporate social responsibility through its issues management function and responsibility for reputation, which necessarily means that it has to help organizations change to meet new agendas such as sustainability. In understanding public relations as being, in some aspects, as rhetorical advocacy, public relations practitioners act as 'discourse workers' on behalf of their clients. In theory, such sponsored debate has the potential to contribute to a more enlightened and better-informed society. Public relations takes place at points of change and moments of transformation in complex contemporary societies. Typically, public relations activity clusters around (1) public policy formation; (2) organizational change and development; (3) public issues such as the environment; and (4) major global shifts such as conflict, unstable international environments, globalisation, natural disasters, or human disasters such as war or global financial collapse. Furthermore, in helping organizations and publics to understand each other's points of view, and those of the wider society, much public relations work itself is fundamentally educational.

ETHICAL ISSUES IN PUBLIC RELATIONS AND MARKETING: OPERATIONAL CONTEXTS

While public relations and marketing have distinctive characteristics and trajectories, they have come to share come common concerns; for example, corporate social responsibility (CSR) and cause-related marketing (CRM). Ethical analysis of both disciplines can be conducted at a macrosocietal level as well as a microfunctional level. Both these business and organizational disciplines are necessarily linked to wider concerns as they relate to strategic issues that arise between business and society.

One of the challenges of tackling this subject is that relevant discussions appear in many disciplines. Certain core themes, which are central to public relations and marketing (though they may be given a different emphasis), also appear in general business and management ethics literature. For example, topics such as risk, trust, reputation, regulation, crisis, public opinion, citizenship, activism, sustainability, environmentalism, corporate social responsibility, corporate social performance, stakeholder relations, regulation, cross-cultural and intercultural communication are handled from different perspectives that do not necessarily take account of, or acknowledge the particular interests, concerns, and implications of public relations, or marketing. Public relations, in particular, is often an invisible function in the literature, despite its evident conceptual responsibility for organizational reputation. Within management and marketing literature, public relations is often a basic level discipline of lesser importance. This chapter goes some way to correct that and to foreground public relations while still making appropriate reference to, and highlighting, points of comparison with marketing.

There are many dimensions to business and management ethics literature from the profoundly philosophical exploring notions of obligation and contract (Baier, 1984; Harrington, 1978; Lodge, 1986; Wood, 2000), and their practical implications realised in the practice of CSR, to organizational bullying and politics. Some aspects of business and management literature have particular resonance for marketing and public relations, such as the role of the ethical advocate; the role of public opinion in relation to corporate social responsiveness (Vallentin, 2009); CSR reporting (Chapple & Moon, 2005) or performance (Greening & Turban, 2000); or reputation (Logsdon & Wood, 2002; Puncheva, 2008). Schwartz and Carroll (2008) usefully reviewed the development of the business ethics field and, while they criticised the lack of a clear 'business and society paradigm' proposed a framework, which integrated five key concepts: CSR, business ethics, stakeholder management, sustainability, and corporate citizenship. Their analysis demonstrates how these and other related terms have often been used inconsistently, interchangeably, or metonymically. They might also have mentioned that in practice, terms are used euphemistically, either to avoid direct reference to moral terms such as *good* or *bad* or *right* or *wrong*, or to use a linguistic formula that sounds more in tune with managerialism, such as *integrity* or *values*, terms which have been employed in some business contexts, or competitively, to appear 'ahead of trend'. Schwartz and Carroll (2008) noted that there are varied practices with regard to conceptual hierarchy, so, for example, CSR may be said to include business ethics, or vice versa (Schwartz & Carroll, 2008, p. 149). The literature on CSR is interdisciplinary and extensive encompassing moral theory and contract, corporate citizenship, stakeholders, regulation, activism, antiglobalization, environmentalism, and sustainability.

Marketing ethics has been defined as work which helps corporate marketing managers make more ethical decisions (Wilkie & Moore, 2002, p. 33). Research on marketing ethics includes reflections of the ethics of the market and marketing (Crane, 1997, 2000b; Desmond, 1998); consumer ethics, social capital theory (Glenane-Antoniadis, Whitwell, Bell, & Menguc, 2003); the ethics of relationship marketing vis-à-vis conventional marketing (Andreasen, 2003; Peattie & Peattie, 2003); critical theory and social marketing (Hastings & Saren, 2003); multiculturalism (Burton, 2002; Priem & Shaffer, 2001); environmental marketing and sustainability (Kilbourne, 2004); ethics of representation (Beetles & Harris, 2005); the role of corporate gifts in marketing communications (Fan, 2006); ethical issues in visual representation in marketing communications (Bergerson & Schroeder, 2002; Schroeder & Bergerson, 2005); and trust in information sources following a food scare (Smith, Young, & Gibson, 1999). Brenkert (2008) usefully explored in depth the core values that underpin marketing practice, and which are relevant to a consideration of its ethics such as individual choice, desire satisfaction, noncoercive exchanges, and mutual satisfaction. Relational approaches within both marketing and public relations have emphasised trust, commitment, and integrity (Jahansoozi, 2006, p. 67). Critique and defence of advertising has been an historic theme in the literature (Hulbert, 1968) including product responsibility (Webber, 1966).

Within public relations literature, discussion has focused on a number of themes including:

the reputation of public relations (Nelson, 2003); the ethics of persuasion (Fawkes, 2007; Heath, 2001; Martinson, 1996; Messina, 2007; Miller, 1989; Pearson, 1989a, 1989b; Sullivan, 1965; Toth, 1992); the ethics of the individual practitioner (Odedele, 2005) and communicative action (Holmstrom, 2004); the need for ethics to be integrated into the corporate communication planning process (Parsons, 2007); the enactment of the ethics counsellor role by public relations (Bowen, 2006; L'Etang, 2003); professional status and the public good (Tobin, 2005); codes of ethics (Odedele, 2005); regulation and professional bodies (Avenarius, 2007); licence to operate (Curtin & Boynton, 2001; Day, Dong, & Robins, 2001); corporate social responsibility (L'Etang, 1990, 1994, 1996a, 2006); and crisis and apologia (Hearit, 2001). In particular, scholars operating within the rhetorical paradigm have given close attention to discourse ethics and the application of the German sociologist Jurgen Habermas's theory of communicative action (L'Etang, 1996; Pearson, 1989a, 1990).

The location, processes, and procedures of marketing and public relations also require consideration. In particular, the relationship that these operations have in relation to managerial and societal power; their adaptation of military models (especially psychological operations or psyops, see McLaurin, 1982) notable in issues management and planning models and adoption of militaristic discourses as in 'ambush marketing', 'marketing warfare' (Kolar & Toporišič, 2007), 'guerrilla marketing', 'environmental scanning', 'intelligence'; their covert aspects (networking, lobbying, mystery shopping)—all these run counter to the dialogic discourses espoused by their ideologies ('customer focus', 'mutual understanding', 'exchange', 'two-way symmetrical communication') and suggest diametrically opposed Jekyll and Hyde characteristics. Such dualisms point to a key characteristic of debate in relation to ethics in marketing and public relations: the employment of universalist terms interpreted relativistically. This has led to diverse literature encompassing normative ideals, ideological critique, and business prudentialism. The clarification of rhetorical practices in this domain and greater reflexivity in writing could help make transparent underlying assumptions in debating ethical issues. In practice, this means that all parties lay out their assumptions, goals, values, and beliefs at the outset of policy-formation, and being prepared to share those with communities and stakeholders. In short, a co-orientational process is incorporated into ethical programmes, such as CSR programmes where companies typically engage in nonmarket activities to gain reputational benefit. While there is probably little that can be done about the self-serving motivation that on a Kantian account renders to activities morally worthless, greater transparency with recipients and media might make the exchange more honest.

THE ROLE OF PUBLIC RELATIONS AND MARKETING IN SOCIETY

An analysis of occupational ethics should not be restricted to negative aspects, but also explore the positive. Key marketing values include: profit, exchange, economic transaction, exchange of meaning, shared meaning, customer focus, value delivery, business strategy, and organizational focus. Key public relations values include: mutuality, dialogue, understanding, and reputation.

An examination of the ethics of a practice necessitates consideration of its wider impact (utilitarian considerations), as well as of its intentions (deontological considerations). It is necessary to analyse the purpose of public relations and marketing, on whose behalf the functions operate, and with what impact. In short, a fuller understanding of public relations and marketing ethics requires a combination of empirical research and conceptual analysis, which explores the relationship between such practices and the social world in its global diversity. The relationship between these functions and societal class and caste (power) arrangements also matters since public relations and marketing occupations and their discourses may inadvertently promote the interests of the economically privileged on a global scale. If marketing and public relations are supposed to be adaptive functions capable of responding effectively to change, it may be assumed that they do so in order to ensure the best outcome for their clients/organizations. This intrinsic self-interest (moral egoism) needs to be acknowledged and should be foregrounded in any evaluation of occupational ethics. This broader level of analysis is important as more detailed considerations of particular acts such as potential collusion with journalists (bribery) or the dubious practice of spying that is carried out by marketers who practice 'secret shopping'.

Marketers arose as functionaries of the free-market, facilitating its operation. Thus, marketing is an ideological operation, and not purely about buying and selling, or, as marketers would put it 'meeting customer demand'. This in itself has had a major global impact that has played a role in the downfall of some controlled economies, and infiltrated others, not to mention the sociocultural, economic, and political impacts. Within existing free-market economies, marketing has expanded its influence into the public sector, so that many cultures can be said to be 'promotional cultures' where promotional and marketing activity has become a taken-for-granted assumption that underpins all cultural activity (Wernick, 1991). Neither marketing nor public relations 'produce' material goods, but they do produce 'discourses' on behalf of governmental, organizational, and commercial interests, which are amenable to variable interpretations and re-interpretations. While practitioners might claim to wish to 'share meaning' or achieve 'mutual understanding' they are charged with the responsibility to promote their paymaster's agendas. Thus those with whom the organization commences communication may well be 'Othered'. It is difficult to discern public responsibility or service in such self-interested actions, although there may be exceptions such as community and culturally based health campaigns (Dutta, 2009).

For some critics, marketing and publicity contributed to an inauthentic society through the peddling of images and false aspirations. And, although marketers claim they are focused on the consumers' needs and wants, some have pointed out that marketing cannot supply all human desires. For example, as David Miller, pointed out, 'if people were to say "we want a society where people look after one another, where there is social justice"—then marketers cannot supply that. Marketers treat everything as a commodity…but of course there's more to human society than commodities' (L'Etang, 2008 p. 151).

Yet, eminent marketer William Wilkie did raise the question: 'what type of society do we wish to create and inhabit?' (Wilkie, 2001 p. 33), and defined the notion of corporate societal marketing. One outcome of marketing's expansion into the public sector has been its activity into public information and health campaigns, and the evolution of 'social marketing', which applied marketing concepts and techniques to solve social problems such as tobacco, drug, and alcohol abuse. Social marketing as been defined as helping those who manage social change to be more effective in doing so (Dutta, 2008; Wilkie, 2001, p. 33). Social marketing is seen as a solution to social/health problems in developing countries supplemented by conventional marketing to 'ignite the engine of economic development' (Dhoklia & Dhoklia, 2001, p. 488). In some areas this appears to be seen as a way of rescuing marketing's ethics by showing that marketing can 'do good'. For example, eminent social marketer Hastings subtitled his student textbook 'Why Should the Devil Have All the Best Tunes'? (Hastings, 2007). However, social marketing is but one approach used in health campaigns, and has been criticised for being overly dependent on advertising and publicity and insufficiently grounded in problematized and 'othered' communities with insufficient effort being given to the issues and diverse problems and challenges which face those communities, some of which may be the consequence of political, economic, or social policies, or wider historical transformations. In other words, marketing is thought to be guilty of being too narrow in its approach to such problems and insufficiently culturally contextualised.

While some public relations activity will indeed be supporting marketing aims, it also retains responsibility for organizational reputation (which is distinct from the organizational 'brand' because reputation is the consequence of behaviour, including organizational statements and representations). Its focus on stakeholder relations and issues management requires an adaptability, responsiveness, and engagement with others' perspectives. Public relations ideals are ethically grounded in that they suggest that it seeks 'true dialogue' in order to foster 'mutual understanding'. These ideals are suggestive of Kantian 'respect for others' that would avoid using others for organizational ends. Unfortunately, the reality does not match the ideals, not least because the power relations between organizations and stakeholders is not often given attention or acknowledged.

In concluding these initial remarks I note the distinction between societal levels of analysis and those related specifically to the functional operations of marketing and public relations, which require a different level of analysis. My analysis now proceeds to focus on three cruxes central to a consideration of the marketing and public relations occupations in society: their (questioned) status as professions; their efforts to codify values, ideals, and principles (Bivins, 2003, pp. 18–19) as part of their 'professional project'; their (competing) claims to jurisdiction over CSR; and their historic and political associations with 'propaganda'.

PROFESSIONS AND PROFESSIONALS

Public relations and marketing have become institutions in various ways. As already noted, they have diffused throughout culture via consumerism, free market ideology, and, significantly, into the upper echelons of powerful institutions such as governments and governmental organizations, the military-industrial complex, and corporations. They have entered mainstream popular culture—they are part of the reality of 'everyday life' and are represented in cultural products (film, news media, literature). As a consequence, public relations and marketing have become a synedoche for broader discourses of capitalism and free-market ideology—a taken-for-granted 'status quo' set of assumptions.

Marketing and public relations have also sought to institutionalise themselves—to become institutions—through the formation of 'professional' bodies seeking to enhance status and exert control over practice. As part of this effort the occupations have engaged with educational institutions to develop qualifications that provide intellectual capital for practice. The question of professionalism, however, has not been given particularly detailed treatment and is usually limited to either the platitudinous or the hopeful, although there is a 'sociology of professions' literature available as an analytic source (Pieczka & L'Etang, 2001). However, any such discussion is going to be culturally specific, as is the more detailed analysis that follows which draws on examples from the UK.

Although occupational codes express clear ideals with regard to truth-telling and obligation to public service, the British Chartered Institute of Marketing (CIM) Code of Practice highlights the prudential nature of its code and links its purpose to occupational reputation, 'public confidence is crucial. Obviously anything done without integrity, or which is discreditable, affects the public's perception of marketers when dealing with the next marketer they encounter' (CIM Code of Practice 2.1, n.d.).

The UK-based Chartered Institute of Public Relations (CIPR) (n.d.) states:

> Reputation is every organization's most valuable asset. It has a direct and major impact on the corporate well-being of every organization, be it a multinational, a charity, a Government Depart-

ment or an SME. That is why the professionalism of those people who guard and mould reputation—PR professionals—is so important. As the PR profession continues to grow, the CIPR, as
the voice of public relations practitioners, has an important role to play in ensuring that public
trust and confidence is gained and guarded in the boardroom and on the high-street alike.

Thus both occupational bodies emphasize the (self-interested) necessity for social legitimacy. However, the concept of 'profession' and 'professional' is contentious in relation to both
public relations and marketing, because, according to strict sociological criteria, these occupations do not meet the necessary conditions. These can be summarised as:

A specialised skill and service, an intellectual and practical training, a high degree of professional
autonomy, a fiduciary relationship with the client, a sense of collective responsibility for the
profession as a whole, an embargo on some methods of attracting business, and an occupational
organization testing competence, regulating standards and maintaining discipline. (Elliott, 1972,
p. 5, cited in Pieczka & L'Etang, 2001, p. 224)

Societal legitimacy matters to public relations and marketing, since critiques suggest that
these occupations are fundamentally unethical. Professional status confers societal legitimacy
and is thus a goal of aspirant occupations or those of semiprofessions.
   Professional status is a clear goal of some practitioners and occupational bodies, not least
because professional status delivers a socially elite status and connections to the state and political culture (Pieczka & L'Etang, 2001, p. 228). Some public relations occupational bodies have
sought to put in place relevant qualifications to restrict entry to those bodies, if not to the occupation itself, and thus to begin the process of erecting boundaries. A key element of professional
status is that of jurisdiction—'the hold that a profession establishes over a set of tasks' (Pieczka
& L'Etang, 2001, p. 227) in relation to other occupations, and that is a major problem for public
relations and marketing, both in relation to each other and other business disciplines which are
seen as having 'encroached' upon their territories. The role and scope of public relations and
marketing is inevitably shaped and in some cases limited by organizational structures, cultures,
and politics (unless they work in specialised agencies offering services to the market). Thus an
important question for both occupations is: who should take responsibility for organizational
ethics or act as ethical advocate (Steiner, 1976)? Debates about the role of public relations as the
ethical conscience of the organization have arisen partly because the practice is fundamentally
concerned with reputation and partly because of its aspiration to claim the field of corporate social responsibility as its own (see discussion below).
   A key feature of professions is their possession and policing of codes of conduct, practice,
or ethics. The requirements of these differ in emphasis in relation to their technical, prudential,
and ethical requirements,

Codes of ethics can be distinguished by being a fairly short set of ethical principles expressed
in the imperative mode; codes of conduct are much more specific in detailing exceptions and
particular circumstances and are practical in nature, dealing with the customer/client; codes of
practice may contain ethical principles but relate to technical standards and are often addressed to
customer/clients in terms of the standards that the members of the occupation/profession have a
duty to uphold. (L'Etang, 1992, p. 737, paraphrasing Harris, 1989, pp. 5–6)

Public relations professional bodies often possess codes of practice, which mix these requirements. In practice, they are statements of ideals, such as truth-telling, rather than an aspect
of sound self-regulation, which, since many practitioners are not members of professional bodies

is doomed to failure. There is, however, cultural variance. In the UK, public relations is a poorly regarded occupation and most practitioners are not members of the occupational body; however, this situation may not obtain in other countries. According to the CIPR (n.d.), their code,

> emphasizes that honest and proper regard for the public interest; reliable and accurate information; and never misleading clients, employers and other professionals about the nature of representation or what can be competently delivered or achieved, are vital components of robust professional practice.

Specifically, their code lays out a number of morally based prescriptions, for example, maintaining,

> The highest standards of professional endeavour, integrity, confidentiality, financial propriety and personal conduct…deal honestly and fairly in business with employers, employees, fellow professionals and other professions and the public; respect the customs, practices and codes of clients, employers, colleagues, fellow professionals and in all countries where they practise…checking the reliability and accuracy of information before dissemination…never knowingly misleading clients, employers, employees, colleagues and fellow professionals about the nature of representation or what can be competently delivered and achieved.

Similarly to the CIM, CIPR highlights the importance of,

> Safeguarding the confidences of present and former clients and employers…being careful to avoid using confidential and insider information to the disadvantage or prejudice of clients or employers, or to self-advantage of any kind…not disclosing confidential information unless specific permission has been granted or the public interest is at stake or the law requires it. (CIPR Code, n.d.)

Thus a great deal is left to individual discretion without any guidance. The emphasis given to confidentiality seems to run counter to the value of transparency. Curiously, 'transparency and conflicts of interest' appear as a bullet-pointed issue, but there is no guidance about the application of these concepts to practice. Neither is it clear how the public interest is to be judged. Is it really any surprise that 'it has been left to a presumed adversarial media to test public relations' claims' (L'Etang, 2004, p. 184)?

Analysis of the UK CIPR code reveals that,

> There is little guidance to those working in areas such as government (British or foreign), lobbying or controversial areas such as tobacco or biotechnology…. Although ethical principles are expressed…[such as] 'a positive duty at all times to respect the truth and [not to] disseminate false or misleading information' nothing is said about withholding truth. Some clauses are not binding and leave action to the individual's discretion. (L'Etang, 2004, p.184)

Public relations practice appears so far to have failed to convince its critics (at least in the UK), through its codes, that the practice is anything other than about advocacy for its clients. Ethical issues, which arise from public relations, especially those related to transparency and obligations to publics need to be given further attention, as does the way in which codes themselves are formulated, and the degree to which practitioners, stakeholder groups, and the media are involved.

The Chartered Institute of Marketing (CIM) (UK) requires all members, 'to adhere to our Code of Professional Standards, which requires marketers to be honest, legally compliant and up-to-date' (CIM, n.d.). The CIM Charter states that it aims 'to promote, and maintain high standards of professional skill, ability and integrity among persons engaged in marketing products and services' (Chartered Institute of Marketing Royal Charter). The CIM code, 'requires its members to recognize their responsibility to customers, employers, colleagues and fellow marketers, and to the public in general' (Code of Professional Standards appended to the Royal Charter). Yet the standards, integrity, or responsibilities are not spelt out, thus providing a good example of a code being too general as to be useful.

The CIM code interestingly acknowledges the hidden aspects of marketing practice, 'As is well-known, a marketer's field of work cannot be closely overseen by those who engage their services, neither can they easily perceived whether work has been done unnecessarily, wastefully or unprofessionally' (CIM Code of Practice 2.1). This implies an important role for wider public education about both applied public relations and marketing to develop a more informed and challenging general public.

CIPR and CIM share some common values; for example, those concerning the requirement to act honestly and to refrain from 'knowingly or recklessly' (CIM) disseminating false or misleading information. Marketers are required to avoid conflicts of interest and to keep business information confidential.

Both CIPR and CIM possess disciplinary committees, although it remains the case that both occupations may be practised without membership, and serious offences would be regulated by the law of the land.

To return to reflect at the broader level, the 'professionalising' efforts of occupations such as marketing and public relations also have an impact on other occupations and their respective statuses, and on society more widely.

PROPAGANDA AND PERSUASION, RHETORIC AND MANIPULATION

A key criticism of public relations is that it is no more than propaganda. Distinguishing between these concepts is not an easy matter, because the planning processes and methods of public relations, propaganda and psychological operations, and public communication campaigns (including health campaigns) are virtually identical. McLaurin's classic text on military propaganda, for example, applied communications theory to psychological operations (Katz, 1982, pp. 9–19); linked objective setting and planning to research, evaluation, and effectiveness and reviewed the potential role of the media in campaigns (Katz, 1982). The relationship between public relations and propaganda is contentious, not least because propaganda became a denigrated term during the second half of the 20th century.

As previously noted, ethical issues in public relations and marketing have macro- and microlevel aspects. At the macrolevel both functions may be critiqued for the contribution they may make to structural inequalities. Public relations and marketing industries require resources and sponsors, and depend on sources of political and economic power. Government, political parties, companies, multinationals, financial institutions, and media institutions all employ numbers of public relations and marketing staff. Thus it can be argued that public relations and marketing operate unfairly by largely supporting those already in power and assisting them to sustain and reproduce that dominance. Conceptually, this has been a theme from the Left. Habermas's framework of the public sphere provides a conceptual base from which to argue that public relations and associated disciplines clutter the space that could be used for citizen debate with corporate and political communications (Habermas, 1989). Media dependence on powerful sources exacerbates the promotional advantages that the powerful already possess through the provision of 'information subsidies' (Gandy, 1982, 1992). Power in itself distorts the opportunities for communication that public relations and marketing ostensibly seek to facilitate, a problem often analysed through the lens of Habermas's theory of communicative action (Habermas, 1991) and applied to public relations (L'Etang, 1996a, 2006; Pearson, 1992) through discussion of discourse ethics. Another strand in the debate concerning the role, scope, impact, and ethics of persuasive communicators in society focuses on rhetoric (Heath, 1992, 1993, 2001). Public relations is connected to the classical concept historically, to the Sophists, paid speech consultants whose technical skill laid them open to savage critique by Plato in his dialogue the *Gorgias* (L'Etang, 1996b, 2006). Plato's concerns focused on the influence of persuasive communicators who could convince an audience, and produce conviction, even though they were not expert themselves in a subject. In other words, the deployment of clever argument need not be based on expertise, neither need it be inspired by a desire to establish 'the truth' which was at the root of Plato's discontent. A more recent criticism of public relations consultancy is that it is simply an occupation of 'hired flacks' (Jackall, 1995). Critics such as Mayhew have continued to argue that public relations,

> Has the capacity to persuade and influence without revealing truth or reality of what it is that is the subject of the influence, thus implying that a mass public receives inaccurate information with which to frame its opinions...the communications most reviled by Mayhew are public relations counsellors, advertisers, and marketers, all representing client-based communication as consumable product. (Stanton, 2009, p. 213)

Public relations constructed as rhetoric argues for a particular perspective, that is, it is relative, or a particular interpretation. This is why definitional distinctions, which seek to separate public relations from propaganda on the basis of truth and lies fail to convince. Rhetorical scholars in public relations accept relativism and focus instrumentally on discourse strategies to suggest that rhetoric is a process, which can (or ought) to produce consensus if conducted as ideal speech communication (Heath, 1992, 1997; Toth & Heath, 1992). However, when applied to public relations contexts, this ideal does not take sufficient account of contextual power or hegemony that distorts those relationships. Indeed, Roper (2005) argued that 'symmetrical communication' is more likely to be used as a tool to maintain hegemony (Weaver, Motion, & Roper, 2006) and Weaver et al. argued that public relations power lay in discourse,

> Public relations communication can be understood as the strategic attempt to control the agenda of public discussion and the terms in which discussion takes place. In these terms, public relations practitioners are complicit in the attempt to gain, and maintain, social, political, and/or economic power for the organizations that they represent. (Weaver et al., 2006, p.17)

Discussions of propaganda can never be clear of the historical and political context, and also tend to imply passive or duped audiences. Proponents of propaganda saw it as an essential tool of democracy to ensure better democratic practice (Bernays, 1923, 1955; Ellul, 1966; Grierson, 1933–1934; Lasswell, 1927; Lippman, 1925). Wartime use has seen regimes of many persuasions indulging in 'unacceptable manipulation' (Weaver et al., 2006, p.12) even though propaganda is popularly associated with totalitarian or nondemocratic regimes. Analysis of the relationship between public relations and propaganda requires attention to historical events and political context; cultural mores and values; communicative processes and techniques; epistemological concepts and moral concepts (L'Etang, 2006, p. 24; L'Etang, 2008). Propaganda has become a pejorative term, and this is problematic for public relations practitioners and most academics not least in terms of justifying their career activities to themselves and others. Careless use of the term in a relativist postmodern world leads one to believe that 'one person's public relations is another person's propaganda', but I would argue for the following definition, which is not dependent on the 'truth–lies' dichotomy but is grounded in historical and political events that have afflicted humanity,

> Propaganda is monolithic communication on a grand scale that attempts to encompass all aspects of culture…[and] which…affects [processes of] social construction to such a degree that its assumptions are welded to the taken-for-granted norms and values of the host culture and make it difficult for deviant views to be expressed. Ultimately, there is no 'accommodation' process to be made by individuals [themselves] as the norms and values define their identity. (L'Etang, 2006, p. 24)

This essentialist definition is constructed at the societal level and based upon philosophical principles of individual autonomy and choice, freedom of expression, and includes the intention to dominate. Despite its careful formulation, however, it is still possible to liken some public relations activities to the definition of propaganda, for example those internal public relations campaigns to support 'culture change'.

Thus there are enormous tensions between the ideals of public relations and marketing and the fact that these occupations are not public sector organizations but are outgrowths of power.

CORPORATE SOCIAL RESPONSIBILITY

Business ethicist Velasquez defined business ethics as, 'a specialized study of moral right and wrong. It concentrates on how moral standards apply particularly to business policies, institutions, and behaviour' (Velasquez, 2006, p. 12, cited in Schwartz & Carroll, 2008). This positions business ethics as firmly within the scope of strategic public relations, which, according to the normative literature, counsels management on issues concerned with organizational reputation, derived from organizational behaviour and relationships. However, public relations has largely not achieved the status and consequently is not the naturally accepted leader and manager of corporate social responsibility.

One dimension of the societal focus is the role that marketing and public relations play in corporate social responsibility, a practice grounded in ethical notions of social justice and obligation, and community benefits. Ethical frameworks for corporate social responsibility have been discussed (Bowen, 2004; L'Etang, 1992, 1995; Van de Ven, 2004), also in relation to ethical decision-taking processes at times of organizational crisis (Christensen & Kohl, 2003), not least because there is an intrinsic link between crisis management and communication, which necessitate a consideration of discourse ethics. Some marketing perspectives concentrate on the strategic advantages of CSR (Sirsly & Lamertz, 2008). Lantos (2001) usefully analysed the economic, legal, ethical, and altruistic elements of CSR adopting a deontological perspective and suggested that marketers take a lead role. The ethics of cause-related marketing has also received attention from a marketing perspective (Smith & Higgins, 2000), as has activism (Derry & Waikar, 2008; Rehbein, Waddock, & Graves, 2004).

Literature on corporate social responsibility is multi- rather than interdisciplinary, the historically strategic level at which this activity has been conducted (because only those with power can dispense patronage or instigate organizational direction) means that it has been the subject of border disputes, or at a minimum been a focus for various business disciplines including accountancy, management, as well as marketing and public relations. Curiously, however, communications has not played a major role in this discussion and so this has been foregrounded in this chapter. For example, the landmark volume by May, Cheney, and Roper (2007), scarcely mentions communication (a rare exception is Chavarria's contribution to that volume) and the only contribution which looks at CSR in relation to public relations presents an overall description of CSR practice in Singapore and survey results, but does not engage critically with the philosophical or moral issues in relation to either CSR or discourse ethics, although it does link the practice to communitarianism (Sriramesh, Ng, Ting, &Wanyin, 2007).

CSR is a culturally specific practice that is linked to politics and ideology. Concepts of social justice and moral duties run counter to free market ideology, and this conflict fuelled much of the early debate in the field. The principle of freedom, however, permits individuals or organizations to make philanthropic or charitable donations. CSR, however, can be distinguished from philanthropy on the basis that the CSR concept, embedded in its definition and discourse, does intrinsically recognise some (Kantian) moral obligation. The extent of this moral obligation (direct to key stakeholders; retributive in recognition of negative impacts; or wider supererogatory duties to society) has been much debated. However, communications practice surrounding CSR, and particularly the role of public relations and marketing, and the ethics of their respective involvement has not received so much attention outside public relations, and only limited, generally functional treatments within the field.

Within marketing, the term *corporate societal marketing* covers a range of activities including, 'traditional philanthropy, strategic philanthropy, sponsorships, advertising with a social dimension, cause-related marketing, licensing agreements, social alliances, traditional volunteerism, strategic volunteerism and enterprises' (Drumwright & Murphy, 2001, p. 165).

One feature of this literature is the term *pragmatic idealism* (Drumwright & Murphy, 2001, p. 174) which is rather akin to the oxymoronic phrase 'self- interested altruism', often applied to organizations which have made such discourse part of their branding, such as the oft cited Ben & Jerry's and the Body Shop. While such organizations could be regarded as Aristotelian leaders, the public relations benefits of such market positioning meant that the Body Shop, under Anita Roddick's leadership, claimed never to need to purchase advertising.

Within the public relations context, the crux of the issue lies in the motivation behind CSR communication and the way in which public relations evaluation is conducted. If CSR programmes are well motivated and driven by a sense of duty or philanthropy then it seems not unreasonable for the organization to publicise their work more widely. However, if the motivation behind the publicity is self-interested (improved reputation), then it might be argued that self-interest negates the moral value of the CSR programme. Otherwise it might be claimed that the CSR programme effectively used (or exploited) the recipients of the programmes as a tool to improve organizational status. Furthermore, the way in which such programmes are evaluated is also significant. If they are evaluated in terms of media relations content, that suggests that organizational self-interest has primacy and that the beneficiaries of CSR programmes are not only a means to organisational ends but they are 'Othered' in the process. How many CSR programmes permit recipients to devise the evaluation of the programme as opposed to responding to donor agendas? If, however, CSR objectives and evaluation are coconstructed with potential beneficiaries that suggests a much more genuine attempt to share power and resources and to resolve social issues. Thus, there is room for CSR programmes to follow health communications by taking a more ethnographic and culture-centred approach and to incorporate attention to discourse ethics. Only in this way can recipients of CSR be empowered and donors avoid patronising and 'Othering'. In short the discourse ethics of CSR needs further attention.

PR's claims to the CSR territory are usually based on the notion of stakeholder relations, particularly community relations; the connection between CSR and its reputational impact; and the somewhat controversial idea that public relations should act as the ethical conscience of the organization. The ethical obligations of public relations were the focus of a Special Issue of the *Journal of Communication Management* in 2003. Included in this issue were articles on the ethical obligations of public relations in an era of globalisation (Starck & Kruckeberg, 2003) and an examination of 'the myth of the "ethical guardian"' (L'Etang, 2003). The use of the term *guardian* is interesting, since it implies expertise and responsibility for others. It might also connote Plato's ruling class and the aspirations of public relations practitioners to join the 'dominant coalition'. The use of the term *ethics* suggests the ability and authority to make moral judgements on behalf of others. There are some serious questions to be asked about the legitimacy of public relations practitioners to adopt such a role, especially given the poor reputation of the practice. Although organizational behaviour may be subjected to moral scrutiny, it does not automatically mean that public relations practitioners are qualified as 'reputation managers'. There are interesting questions to be asked of the knowledge, skills, and expertise required for such a role. There are serious questions of credibility in relation to public relations practice regarding its competence in this area, not least since there are applied philosophers who have the intellectual basis to become professional business ethicists (L'Etang, 2003, p. 64). As Bowen (2004, p. 69) pointed out, 'what training gives them [public relations managers] the background to hold this vital responsibility'? This is a question for public relations educators, as much as for practitioners seeking organizational credibility.

PUBLIC RELATIONS AND MARKETING ETHICS IN PROMOTIONAL CULTURE: SOME FINAL THOUGHTS

This chapter has explained the scope of ethical challenges that face marketing and public relations and reviewed a selection of debates to frame a more detailed discussion of three major issues that impact their social legitimacy. It is clear that there are problems of analysis, stemming in part from tensions between essentialism and relativism, in part between functionalism and interpretivism, but also between the macro- and the microlevels of society. In this respect, ethical issues in marketing and public relations could usefully be subjected to empirical research and theoretical critique that links agency, societal structures, institutional networks, transitions, and culture. The use of alternate methodological strategies such as grounded theory, phenomenology, and ethnography could also produce new readings and insights in this direction. Likewise, social theory offers a range of concepts and frameworks with which to analyse ethics in public relations and marketing (Hastings & Saren, 2003; Ihlen, van Ruler, & Frederikson, 2009).

A key problematic for public relations and marketing is that of agency. Although ethical issues arise within the specific practice such as supply chain ethics or source–media relations, a significant ethical burden may be attributed to those whom the occupations service. In other words, public relations and marketing may acquire further ethical burdens from their clients in addition to ethical issues specific to their function. The hierarchical relation between public relations and marketing and their paymasters has been significant in linking these occupations to propaganda and unethical persuasion. In short, it might be argued that public relations and marketing have limited agency within organizations in relation to policy-making, and it is certainly clear in the literature that public relations is often reduced to a technical function. Occupations based on competition in the marketplace may be more concerned to keep clients by delivering (predictable) techniques (communication outputs) they expect and request, rather than acting as independent consultants with specific and recognised expertise (that can diagnose problems and recommend solutions). As one post-World War II British practitioner astutely observed, 'I don't give the client what he asked for…I give him what he needs…not what he wants…(I) was not sycophantic' (Interview/Personal Communication, September 13, 1995). The challenge for theo-reticians is to acknowledge and accommodate the competitive realities and power-plays intrinsic to the marketplace, within a context in which ethical claims are made. Identifying policy-makers and influencers, and their relationship to communicators and marketers, and to the wider soci-ety is crucial to an understanding of ethical dynamics, motivations, self-interests, and impacts (ethical evaluations). Sources of power seek public relations and marketing services and those services are attracted to power as moths to the flame. The ethics of public relations and marketing is thus partly an analysis of the ethics of power.

Given that public relations scholarship has argued strongly for the occupation to be elevated to the 'dominant coalition' (Grunig, 1992) where public relations can indeed exercise power, then it is crucial that its practitioners are sufficiently educated to understand the moral implications and obligations of such a position. Currently, however, public relations lacks the social legitimacy which grants independent status and jurisdiction, or 'official recognition of the sphere of respon-sibility to which the profession owes due attention' (Kipnis, 1983, p.17). Perhaps a way forward for these communication disciplines is for greater reflexivity about in their own discourse work and a clearer separation between professional and organizational or representative identities.

REFERENCES

Andreasen, A. R. (2003). The life trajectory of social marketing: Some implications. *Marketing Theory, 3*(3), 293–303.
Avenarius, H. (2007). German experiences with codes and their enforcement. *Journal of Communication Management, 11*(2), 99–116.
Baier, K. (1984). Duties to one's employer. In T. Regan (Ed.), *Just business: New introductory essays in business ethics* (pp. 60–99). New York: Random House.
Beetles, A. C., & Harris, L. C. (2005). Consumer attitudes towards female nudity in advertising: An empiri-cal study. *Marketing Theory, 5*(4), 397–437.
Bernays, E. (1923). *Crystallizing public opinion.* New York: Liveright.
Bernays, E. L. (1955). *The engineering of consent.* Norman: University of Oklahoma
Bivins, T. (2003). *Mixed media: Moral distinctions in advertising, public relations and journalism.* Mah-wah, NJ: Erlbaum.
Borgersen, J. L., & Schroeder, J. E. (2002). Ethical issues of global marketing: Avoiding bad faith in visual representation. *European Journal of Marketing, 36,* 570–594.
Bowen, S. A. (2004).Organizational factors encouraging ethical decision making: An exploration into the case of an exemplar. *Journal of Business Ethics, 52,* 311–324.
Bowen, S. A. (2006). Autonomy in communication: Inclusion in strategic management and ethical decision-making, a comparative case analysis. *Journal of Communication Management, 10*(4), 330–352.
Brenkert, G. G. (2008). *Marketing ethics,* Malden, MA: Blackwell.
Campbell, F. (2009, September). *Backs to the wall: How PR carries discomfort for organizations.* Paper presented at Stirling 21, UK National Conference, Stirling, Scotland.
Chapple, W., & Moon, J. (2005). Corporate social responsibility (CSR) in Asia: A seven country study of CSR website reporting, *Business and Society, 44*(4), 415–441.
Chartered Institute of Marketing (CIM). (n.d.). Web page. Retrieved from http://www.cim.co.uk/about/mk-tgstandards.aspx.
Chartered Institute of Marketing (CIM). (2008). *Marketing standards.* Retrieved from http://www.cim.co.uk/about/mktgstandards.aspx.
Chartered Institute of Public Relations (CIPR). (n.d.). Web page. Retrieved from http://www.cipr.co.uk/Membership/conduct/index.htm.
Chartered Institute of Public Relations. (n.d.) *CIPR Code of Conduct.* Retrieved from http://www.cipr.co.uk/Membership/conduct/index.htm.

Chavarria, M. P. (2007). Corporate social responsibility in Mexico: An approximation from the point of view of communication. In S. May, G. Cheney, & J. Roper (Eds.), *The debate over corporate social responsibility* (pp. 135–154). Oxford, UK: Oxford University Press.

Christensen, S. L., & Kohl, J. (2003). Ethical decision making in times of organizational crisis: A framework for analysis. *Business and Society, 42*(3), 328–358.

Crane, A. (1997). The dynamics of marketing ethical products: A cultural perspective. *Journal of Marketing Management, 13*(6), 561–577.

Crane, A. (2000a). Marketing and the natural environment: What role for morality? *Journal of Macromarketing, 20*(2), 144–154.

Crane, A. (2000b). *Marketing, morality and the natural environment.* London: Routledge.

Curtin, P. A., & Boynton, L. A. (2001). Ethics in public relations: Theory and practice. In R. L. Heath (Ed.), *Handbook of public relations* (pp. 411–422). Thousand Oaks, CA: Sage.

Day, K., Dong, Q., & Robins, C. (2001). Public relations ethics: An overview and discussion of issues for the 21st century. In R. L. Heath (Ed.), *Handbook of public relations* (pp. 403–410). Thousand Oaks, CA: Sage.

Derry, R., & Waikar, S. (2008). Strategic distrust as a legitimation tool in the 50-year battle between public health activists and Big Tobacco. *Business & Society, 47*(1), 102–139.

Desmond, J. (1998). Marketing and moral indifference. In M. Parker (Ed.), *Ethics and organizations* (pp. 173–196). London: Sage.

Dhoklia, R., & Dhoklia, N. (2001). Social marketing and development. In P. Bloom & G. T. Gundlach (Eds.), *Handbook of marketing and society* (pp. 486–505). London: Sage.

Drumwright, M., & Murphy, P. E. (2001). Corporate societal marketing. In P. N. Bloom & G. T. Gundlach (Eds.), *Handbook of marketing and society* (pp. 162–183). Thousand Oaks, CA: Sage.

Dutta, M. (2009). *Communicating health: A culture-centered approach.* Cambridge, UK: Polity.

Elliott, P. (1972). *The sociology of the professions.* London: Macmillan.

Ellul, J. (1966). *Propaganda* (K. Kellen & J. Lerner, Trans.). New York: Knopf. (Original work published in French 1962)

Fan, Y. (2006). Promoting business with corporate gifts: Major issues and empirical evidence. *Corporate Communications: An International Journal, 11*(1), 43–55.

Fawkes, J. (2007). Public relations models and persuasion ethics: A new approach. *Journal of Communication Management, 11,* 313–331.

Gandy, O. (1982). *Beyond agenda setting: Information subsidies and public policy.* Norwood, NJ: Ablex.

Gandy, O. (1992). Public relations and public policy: The structuration of dominance in the information age. In E. Toth & R. L. Heath (Eds.), *Rhetorical and critical approaches to public relations* (pp. 131–163). Hillsdale, NJ: Erlbaum.

Glenane-Antoniadis, A., Whitwell, G., Bell, S. J., & Menguc, B. (2003). Extending the vision of social marketing through social capital theory: Marketing in the context of intricate exchange and market failure. *Marketing Theory, 3*(3), 323–343.

Greening, D. W., & Turban, D. B. (2000). Corporate social performance as a competitive advantage in attracting a quality workforce. *Business and Society, 39,* 254–280.

Grierson, J. (1933–1934). Propaganda: A problem for educational theory and for cinema. *Sight and Sound,* G3A: 5: 1. John Grierson Archive, University of Stirling, Stirling, Scotland.

Grunig, J. E. (1992). Communications, public relations, and effective organizations: An overview of the book. In J. E. Grunig (Ed.), *Excellence in public relations and communications management* (pp. 1–28). Hillsdale, NJ: Erlbaum.

Habermas, J. (1989). *The structural transformation of the public sphere: An inquiry into a category of bourgeois society.* Cambridge, UK: Polity.

Habermas, J. (1991). *The structural transformation of the public sphere: an inquiry into a category of bourgeois society* (Trans. T. Burger with F. Lawrence). Cambridge, MA: MIT Press.

Hall, S. (1969, December). The technics of persuasion. *New Society,* 948–949.

Harrington, M. (1978). Corporate collectivism: A system of social justice. In R. T. De George & J. A. Pilcher (Eds.), *Ethics, free enterprise and public policy: Original essays and moral issues in business* New York: Oxford University Press.

Harris, J. R. (1989, February). Ethical values and decision processes of male and female business students. *Journal of Education for Business, 64*, 234–236.

Hastings, G., & Saren, M. (2003). The critical contribution of social marketing: Theory and application. *Marketing Theory, 3*, 305–322.

Hastings, G. B. (Ed). (2007). *Social marketing: Why should the Devil have all the best tunes?* Oxford, UK: Elsevier.

Hearit, K. M. (2001). Corporate apologia: When an organization speaks in defense of itself. In R. L. Heath (Ed.), *Handbook of public relations* (pp. 501–511). Thousand Oaks, CA: Sage.

Heath, R. L. (1992). The wrangle of the marketplace: A rhetorical perspective on public relations. In E. L. Toth & R. L. Heath (Eds.), *Rhetorical and critical approaches to public relations* (pp. 17–36). Hillsdale, NJ: Erlbaum.

Heath, R. L. (1993). A rhetorical approach to zones of meaning and organizational prerogatives. *Public Relations Review, 19*, 141–155.

Heath, R. L. (1997). *Strategic issues management: Organizations and public policy challenges.* Thousand Oaks, CA: Sage.

Heath, R. L. (2001). Shifting foundations: public relations as relationship building. In R. L. Heath (Ed.), *The handbook of public relations* (pp. 1–10). Thousand Oaks, CA: Sage.

Holmström, S. (2004). The reflective paradigm of public relations. In B. van Ruler & D. Verčič (Eds.), *Public relations and communication management in Europe* (pp. 121–133). Berlin, Germany: Mouton de Gruyter.

Hulbert, J. (1968). Advertising: Criticism and reply. *Business & Society, 9*(1), 33–38.

Ihlen, Ø., van Ruler, B., & Fredrikson, M. (Eds.). (2009). *Public relations and social theory: Key figures and concepts.* New York: Routledge.

Jackall, R. (Ed). (1995). *Propaganda.* Basingstoke, UK: Macmillan.

Jahansoozi, J. (2006). Relationships, transparency and evaluation: The implications for public relations. In J. L'Etang & M. Pieczka (Eds.), *Public relations: Critical debates and contemporary practice* (pp. 61–92). Mahwah, NJ: Erlbaum.

Jones, D. G. B., & Shaw, E. H. (2002). History of marketing thought. In B. A. Weitz & R. Wensley (Eds.), *Handbook of marketing* (pp. 39–65). London: Sage.

Katz P. (1982). Communications theory and research and their application to psychological operations. In R. D. McLaurin (Ed.), *Military propaganda: Psychological warfare and operations* (pp. 19–41). New York: Praeger.

Kilbourne, W. E. (2004). Sustainable communication and the dominant social paradigm: Can they be integrated? *Marketing Theory, 4*(3), 187–208.

Kipnis, K. (1983). Professional responsibility and the responsibility of professions. In W. Robinson, M. Pritchard, & J. Ellin (Eds.), *Profits and professionals: Essays in business and professional ethics* (pp. 9–22). Clifton, NJ: Humana Press.

Kolar, T. & Toporišič, A. (2007). Marketing as warfare, revisited. *Marketing intelligence and planning, 25*(3), 203–216.

Lantos, G. P. (2001). The boundaries of strategic corporate social responsibility. *Journal of Consumer Marketing, 18*(7), 595–632.

Lasswell, H. (1927). *Propaganda techniques in the world war.* New York: Peter Smith.

L'Etang, J. (1990, June). Doing good or looking good. *New Consumer.*

L'Etang, J. (1992). A Kantian approach to codes of ethics. *Journal of Business Ethics, 11*(10), 737–745.

L'Etang, J. (1994). Public relations and corporate social responsibility: Issues arising. *Journal of Business Ethics, 13*(2), 111–123.

L'Etang, J. (1996a). Public relations and rhetoric. In J. L'Etang & M. Pieczka (Eds.), *Critical perspectives in public relations* (pp. 106–123). London: International Thomson Business Press.

L'Etang, J. (1996b). Corporate responsibility and public relations ethics. In J. L'Etang & M. Pieczka (Eds.), *Critical perspectives in public relations* (pp. 82–105). London: International Thomson Business Press.

L'Etang, J. (2003). The myth of the 'ethical guardian': An examination of its origins, potency and illusions. *Journal of Communication Management, 8*(1), 53–67.

L'Etang, J. (2004). *Public relations in Britain: A history of professional practice in the twentieth century.* Mahwah, NJ: Erlbaum.

L'Etang, J. (2006). Corporate responsibility and public relations ethics. In J. L'Etang & M. Pieczka (Eds.), *Public relations: Critical debates and contemporary practice* (pp. 405–423). Mahwah, NJ: Erlbaum.

L'Etang, J. (2008) *Public relations: Concepts, practice and critique.* London: Sage.

Lippmann, W. (1925). *The phantom public.* New York: Harcourt, Brace.

Lodge, G. C. (1986). The large corporation and the new American ideology. In R. B. Dickie & L. S. Rouner (Eds.), *Corporations and the common good* (pp. 61–77). Notre Dame, IN: University of Notre Dame Press.

Logsdon, J. M., & Wood, D. J. (2002). Business citizenship: From domestic to global level of analysis. *Business Ethics Quarterly, 12*(2), 155–187.

Martinson, D. L. (1996). 'Truthfulness' in communication is both a reasonable and achievable goal for public relations practitioners. *Public Relations Quarterly, 41,* 42–45.

May, S. K., Cheney, G., & Roper, J. (Eds.). (2007). *The debate over corporate social responsibility.* New York: Oxford University Press.

McKitterick, J. B. (1957). What is the marketing management concept? In F. Bass (Ed.), *The frontiers of marketing thought and science* (pp. 71–82). Chicago, IL: American Marketing Association.

McLaurin, R. D. (Ed.). (1982). *Military propaganda: Psychological warfare and operations.* New York: Praeger.

Messina, A. (2007). Public relations, the public interest and persuasion: An ethical approach. *Journal of Communication Management, 11*(1), 29–52.

Miller, G. R. (1989). Persuasion and public relations: Two "Ps" in a pod. In C. H. Botan & V. Hazelton (Eds.), *Public relations theory* (pp. 45–66). Hillsdale, NJ: Erlbaum.

Nelson, R. A. (2003). Ethics and social issues in business: An updated communication perspective. *Competitive Review, 13,* 66–74.

Odedele, S. (2005). Facing the mirror. *Journal of Communication Management, 9*(1), 9–13.

Parsons, P. J. (2007). Integrating ethics with strategy: Analyzing disease-branding. *Corporate Communications: An International Journal, 12,* 267–279.

Pearson, R. (1989a). Beyond ethical relativism in public relations: Coorientation, rules, and the idea of communication symmetry. In J. E. Grunig & L. A. Grunig (Eds.), *Public relations research annual* (Vol. 1, pp. 67–86). Hillsdale, NJ: Erlbaum.

Pearson, R. (1989b). Business ethics as communication ethics: Public relations practice and the idea of dialogue. In C. H. Botan & V. Hazelton (Eds.), *Public relations theory* (pp. 111–131). Hillsdale, NJ: Erlbaum.

Pearson, R. (1990). Ethical values or strategic values? Two faces of systems theory in public relations. In L. Grunig & J. Grunig (Eds.), *Public Relations Research Annual, 2,* 219–235.

Pearson, R. (1992). Perspectives on public relations history. In E. L. Toth & R. L. Heath (Eds.), *Rhetorical and critical approaches to public relations* (pp. 111–130). Hillsdale, NJ: Erlbaum.

Peattie S., & Peattie K. (2003). Ready to fly solo? Reducing social marketing's dependence on commercial marketing theory. *Marketing Theory, 3*(3), 365–385.

Pieczka, M., & L'Etang, J. (2001). Public relations and the question of professionalism. In R. L. Heath (Ed.), *Handbook of public relations* (pp. 223–237). Thousand Oaks, CA: Sage.

Puncheva, P. (2008). The role of corporate reputation in the stakeholder decision-making process. Business & Society, 47(3), 272–290.

Rehbein, K., Waddock, S., & Graves, S. (2004). Understanding shareholder activism: Which corporations are targeted? *Business and Society 43(3),* 239–267.

Ritzer, G. (2000). *The McDonaldization of society.* Thousand Oaks, CA: Pine Forge Press.

Ritzer, G. (Ed.). (2002). *McDonaldization: The reader.* Thousand Oaks, CA: Pine Forge Press

Roper, J. (2005). Symmetrical communication: Excellent public relations or a strategy for hegemony? *Journal of Public Relations Research, 17,* 69–86.

Schroeder, J. E., & Borgerson, J. L. (2005). An ethics of representation for international marketing communication. *International Marketing Review, 22*(5), 578–600.

Schwartz, M., & Carroll, A. (2008). Integrating and unifying competing and complementary frameworks: The search for a common core in the business and society field. *Business & Society, 47*(2), 148–186.

Sirsly, C. T., & Lamertz, K. (2008). When does a corporate social responsibility initiative provide a first-mover advantage. *Business & Society, 47*(3), 343–369.

Smith, A. P., Young, J. A., & Gibson, J. (1999). How now, mad cow? Consumer confidence and source credibility during the 1996 BSE scare. *European Journal of Marketing, 33*, 1107–1122.

Smith, W., & Higgins, M. (2000). Cause-related marketing: Ethics and ecstatic. *Business and Society, 39*(3), 304–322.

Sriramesh, K., Ng, C. W., Ting, S. T., & Wanyin, L. (2007). Corporate social responsibility and public relations: Perceptions and practices in Singapore. In S. May, G. Cheney, & J. Roper (Eds.), *The debate over corporate social responsibility* (pp. 119–134). New York: Oxford University Press.

Stanton, R. C. (2009). On Mayhew: the demonization of soft power and the validation of the new citizen. In Ø. Ihlen, B. van Ruler, & M. Fredrikson (Eds.), *Public relations and social theory: Key figures and concepts* (pp. 212–230). London: Routledge.

Starck, K., & Kruckeberg, D. (2003). Ethical obligations of public relations in an era of globalization. *Journal of Communication Management, 8*(1), 29–40.

Steiner, J. (1976). The prospect of ethical advisors for business corporations. *Business and Society, 16*(2), 5–10.

Sullivan, A. J. (1965). Values in public relations. In O. Lerbinger & A. Sullivan (Eds.), *Information, influence, and communication: A reader in public relations* (pp. 412–439). New York: Basic Books.

Tobin, N. (2005). Can the professionalisation of the UK public relations industry make it more trustworthy? *Journal of Communication Management, 9*(1), 56–64.

Toth. E. (1992). The case for pluralistic studies of public relations: Rhetorical, critical, and systems perspectives. In E. Toth & R. Heath (Eds.), *Rhetorical and critical approaches to public relations* (pp. 3–16). Hillsdale, NJ: Erlbaum.

Toth, E. L., & Heath, R., L. (Eds.). (1992). *Rhetorical and critical approaches to public relations.* Hillsdale, NJ: Erlbaum.

Vallentin, S. (2009). Private management and public opinion: Corporate social responsiveness revisited. *Business & Society, 48*(1), 60–87.

Van de Ven, A. H. (2004). The context-specific nature of competence and corporate development. *Asia Pacific Journal of Management, 21*, 123–147.

Velasquez, M. G. (2006) *Business ethics: Concepts and cases.* Upper Saddle River, NJ: Prentice Hall.

Weaver, C. K., Motion, J., & Roper, J. (2006). From propaganda to discourse (and back again): Truth, power and the public interest, and public relations. In J. L'Etang & M. Pieczka (Eds.), *Public relations: Critical debates and contemporary practice* (pp. 7–21). Mahwah, NJ: Erlbaum.

Webber, R. A. (1966). Advertising and product responsibility. *Business & Society, 7*, 22–32.

Webster, F. E. (2002). The role of marketing and the firm. In B. A. Weitz & R. Wensley (Eds.), *Handbook of marketing* (pp. 66–82). London: Sage.

Wernick, A. (1991). *Promotional culture.* London: Sage.

Wilkie, W. (2001). Foreword. In P. Bloom & G. Gundlach (Ed.), *Handbook of marketing and society* (pp. vii–xi). Thousand Oaks, CA: Sage.

Wilkie, W. L., & Moore, E. S. (2002). Marketing's relationship to society. In B. A. Weitz & R. Wensley (Eds.), *Handbook of marketing* (pp. 9–38). London: Sage.

Wood, G. (2000). A cross cultural comparison of the contents of codes of ethics: USA, Canada, and Australia. *Journal of Business Ethics, 25*(4), 287–298.

15

Visual Communication in Traditional and Digital Contexts

Sean Cubitt and Violeta Politoff

TRADITIONAL CONTEXTS—PREPHOTOGRAPHIC

In Exodus 20: 4–5, God is unambiguous:

4 Thou shalt not make unto thee any graven image, or any likeness of any thing that is in heaven above, or that is in the earth beneath, or that is in the water under the earth:

5 Thou shalt not bow down thyself to them, nor serve them: for I the LORD thy God am a jealous God, visiting the iniquity of the fathers upon the children unto the third and fourth generation of them that hate me;

In case the message failed to get through, the passage is repeated, almost verbatim, in Deuteronomy 5: 8–9. Exodus 34:13 extends the commandment, enjoining the Israelites to break the images of the tribes whose lands they have conquered. The commandments at the core of the religions of the Book—Islam, Judaism, and Christianity—forbid images and their worship. Vicious iconoclasms followed: the Byzantine iconoclasm lasted over a century, between Leo III's edict of 726 CE and its revocation under the empress Theodora in 843 CE (Trakakis, 2004–2005). Dutch Calvinists destroyed statues in 1566. Afghani Taliban dynamited the monumental 5th century CE Buddha at Bamiyan in 2001. For these faiths, God's admonishment against images is clearly stated, even if the practice in the United States of swearing allegiance to the flag, alongside the system of meanings ascribed to the code for folding the flag properly, and the criminal offence of desecrating the flag, all point towards an idolatrous aspect of contemporary North American culture. Proposals to have the Ten Commandments on display in all government buildings would then appear to place the U.S. citizen in an invidious position. Even the apparent clarity of virtue ethics derived from the very word of the deity leads towards uncomfortable ambiguities.

The prohibition on images in the religions of the Book is evidence that images have posed critical problems for ethical thought since the earliest phases of human civilization. Around 360 BCE, Plato too took umbrage at the illusions of painting, arguing through Socrates that

painting or drawing, and imitation in general, when doing their own proper work, are far removed from truth, and the companions and friends and associates of a principle within us which is equally removed from reason, and that they have no true or healthy aim. (Plato, trans., 1994, Book 10)

For Plato, the visible world was already a shadow of a purer world of Forms, such that the artisan who made a table was already an imitator of the ideal table. The painter who imitated the imitation was then guilty not only of doubling the illusion, but of passing the artisan's imitation off as an original, whereas in effect his painting was a work without an original, an *eidolon*, or as the Romans would have it, a *simulacrum*. Despite its apparent proximity to the decalogue, however, Plato's proscription of images from the *Republic* is based on a very different ethic, one of truth and reason opposed to the illusory nature of apparent reality. Such rationalism was not mirrored in other parts of the world. Finlay (2002) reports a Bihari legend concerning the origins of painting, in which the Buddha (d.c. 400 bce) invites the first painter to take his portrait from the reflection in a lake, since his own radiance was too bright for the would-be portraitist to look upon. Thus the Buddha actively participated in the origins of image making, even though he was also the propagator of the belief that the physical world is merely the veil of *maya*, delusion. The more clearly rationalist Confucius (Kǒng Fūzǐ, 551–479 bce) is similarly depicted in early works as engaging in painting with brush and ink. Other ancient civilizations, even the Semitic cultures, seem to have had no problem with the propagation of images, or with their veneration.

Nonetheless, acts of iconoclasm continue, and have not been restricted to religious contexts. Desecrators of graves have targeted the images of hated rulers since the time of the Egyptians. Images as well as books have been the objects of immolations in recent history in Germany under the Nazis, notably as part of the *Entartete Kunst* campaign of 1934, and continue in Christian fundamentalist circles in the United States to this day. The mass destruction of statues throughout the Warsaw Pact nations in the wake of the collapse of Soviet communism in the late 1980s, and the toppling of statues of Hussein in Iraq after the U.S. invasion of 2003, are clearly related secular phenomena. The remnants of idolatry appear here in the negative, as expressions of a residual belief in the magical property of images to hold some part of the spirit of those they depict. This atavistic belief, we will suggest, still has a constituency in the most contemporary of image ethics and the hurt felt in the context even of mutilated photographs.

Other prephotographic tendencies in image ethics are visible in the history of vandalization of artworks. Suffragette Mary Richardson attacked Velasquez's *Rokeby Venus* in the National Gallery in London on March 10, 1914, writing: "I have tried to destroy the picture of the most beautiful woman in mythological history as a protest against the government for destroying Mrs Pankhurst, who is the most beautiful character in modern history" (Gamboni, 1977, p. 94). This proto-feminist assault on "humbug and hypocrisy" echoes a longer tradition of protests against the lubricious and the exploitative. A stranger example is Gerard van Bladeren's attacks on two Barnett Newman abstractions in the Stedelijk Museum in Amsterdam, ripping into *Who's Afraid of Red, Yellow and Blue* in 1986, and *Cathedra* in 1997. The strangeness is heightened by the common opinion (see, for example, Anderson-Reece, 1993; Lyotard, 1998) that Newman's art is deeply informed by Judaism and the prohibition on images. Such individual acts (the latter especially credited to mental illness) may be distinguished from social acts of iconoclasm, but seem to spring from the same deep-seated belief in the power of images, and perhaps from an equally atavistic equation of them with the vulnerability of women's bodies to sexual abuse and violence (McKim-Smith, 2002). This crediting of both power and human presence to images is a significant element in more recent concerns with image ethics.

TRADITIONAL CONTEXTS—PHOTOGRAPHY, FILM AND TELEVISION

Photography

Many of the most frequently discussed ethical questions arising in relation to the photographic image emerge from what Roland Barthes (1981) describes as the photograph's "evidential force" (pp. 88–89). This force refers to the indexicality of the photograph, its capacity to confirm the existence of that which it depicts, even if this confirmation eternally speaks only of an instant. For Herta Wolf (2008), "the language of photography is pure evidence," and it is this characteristic that provides photography with its specific power (p. 83). While the realist position is highly contested, many of the ethical concerns—and possibilities—that arise in relation to the photographic image stem from the perceived evidential quality of photography. It is the ability of the photographic image to "prove" the existence of that which it depicts that enables both the possibility of a moral encounter with the other, as well as the negation of their humanity. As Judith Butler (2004) points out, "it may well be in the domain of representation where humanization and dehumanization occur ceaselessly" (p. 140). Images are implicated in all sides of this process, both in their humanizing and dehumanizing forms.

According to John Tagg (1988), the coupling of evidence and photography began in the second half of the 19th century. Following Foucault, Tagg describes this merger as part of the wider societal emergence of new institutions and practices of observation and record keeping in the West. Photography, as a scientific technology, became understood as capable of communicating reality. This understanding meant that photography could become a means of surveillance, an authoritative and administrative tool that could be used institutionally for recording, observing, cataloguing, witnessing, identifying, and was therefore granted legal status. In this sense, photography is a technology of government, one which is articulated within larger processes that work towards the management and arrangement of things for particular goals. In Tagg's (1988) words, "[t]he photograph is not a magical 'emanation' but a material product of a material apparatus set to work in specific contexts, by specific forces, for more or less defined purposes" (p. 3).

Tagg (1988) explores various institutional practices through which photography's "evidential force" can be understood as a "complex historical outcome" (p. 4). Techniques such as those developed by French photographer Alphonse Bertillon and Italian doctor Cesare Lombroso highlight the troubling past from which notions of photographic evidence emerge. Bertillon pioneered the development of a system for the measurement of the human body, or Anthropometry, intended to enable the scientific identification of individuals and the classification of traits (particularly those of criminality). He used a standardized mode of photography as a means of documentation and classification which could serve as a referential index. Similarly, the theories of Bertillon's contemporary, Cesare Lombroso, sought to identify and document traits of criminality and physiognomy that were considered innate to particular ethic groups and "types" (Breitbart, 1997, p. 25). The physiognomic and typological techniques, backed by the evidential status photography was thought to provide, became highly influential among anthropologists (Breitbart, 1997; Green, 1984). Eric Breitbart makes this connection in his analysis of photographs from the 1904 St. Louis World's Fair. Using photographs from this event as examples, he draws an explicit link between police photography and anthropology revealing how, in this context, these photographs "are not only ethnographic records, but evidence of innate criminality" (Breitbart, 1997, p. 27). The photograph, in this instance, becomes part of the "genre of scientific photography…in which the image is intended to function as a kind of evidence, an irrefutable testimony to the existence of facts" (Green, 1984, p. 8).

Here, the notion of photographic evidence serves to subject particular ethnic groups and individuals to rigid biological classifications which scientifically legitimize oppressive beliefs, actions, and regimes. It is from this photographic and evidentiary mode of biocategorization that eugenics was able to gain scientific and sociocultural legitimacy (see Green, 1984). The example of eugenics, with its linking of photographic evidence to utilitarianism, brings into stark focus the ethical concerns that arise from the marriage of photographic technology with notions of evidence, proof, and truth.

The construction of social faith in the truth of photography is, however, simultaneously the construction of the possibility that a photograph might lie. In the case of propaganda, a term of abuse as much as an analytical category, photography is aligned explicitly with lying. However, as Jaques Ellul (1965) asserts, propaganda is not so much communicating in terms of "truths" and "lies," but rather differing constructions of truths. Goebbels himself insisted that accuracy was of utmost importance for effective communication (Ellul, 1965, p. 53). More recently, the demarcations used to characterize propaganda within academic debates have been expanded and the term has begun to take on a meaning (like the Spanish definition deriving from the Catholic Church's Office for the Propagation of the Faith) which does not exclude public relations and advertising from its conception.

Celebrated among the earliest propaganda photographs are the staged, composite, and montaged images of the Paris Commune made by government supporter and photographer Eugène Appert (English, 1984). Przyblyski (1995) makes the case that Appert was the heir of the engraved magazine illustrators of the midcentury, who derived their authenticity from sketching at the site of actual events, and from either life or portraits of their protagonists, in order to assemble a semblance of the *actualités* being reported. Granted the persuasive task of the images, to condemn the *communards*, Appert's practice fit unobtrusively as professional practice with the institutions of magazine illustration. The use of actors in actual locations, and the technical manipulation of the image, would become mainstays of commercial photography, where fiction has been assimilated and accepted. Propaganda might then be defined as the use of commercial techniques in political reporting, a definition which, however, rests on the diminishing distinction between public life and public relations.

Propaganda is by no means restricted to the fictionalization of photography, however. In many instances photographs of "the decisive moment" (in the phrase made famous by prominent photojournalist Henri Cartier-Bresson) have served propaganda purposes. While many such photographs—Robert Capa's image of a Spanish Civil war soldier at the moment of death, Joe Rosenthal's shot of GIs raising the flag at Iwo Jima, Yevgeny Khaldei's image of the Russian flag over the Reichstag in 1945—have been accused of being staged or, in the latter case, doctored, Capa's famously shaky and damaged image of a GI struggling to shore at Omaha Beach on D-Day, 1944 has not been so maligned. Lauded as a deeply humane image, it was an inspiration for the opening sequence of Spielberg's *Saving Private Ryan*, where its propaganda function as a record of the determination of ordinary people to win the fight against fascism achieved iconic status. At this juncture, the gap between propaganda and the ordinary functioning of ideology is vanishingly small, suggesting merely that any successful photograph, that is, any photograph which succeeds in imparting an affective or conceptual message, by the same token betrays the truth on which it was once based. On the other hand, it may also be said that such images also clarify an oddity about the modernist photographic ethic of the decisive moment, in that the "truth" of a photograph is a result of the necessary relation between it and the light it records, a purely empirical relation grounded in the laws of physics. In Kantian terms, such a relation debars photography from any claim to freedom, which for Kant was first of all freedom from the contingency of natural law. Anchored in the laws of physics, the modernist photograph is unfree and therefore both incapable of action and thus exempt from any ethical claim.

Documentary Photography

Such considerations may then be applied to the documentary photograph more generally. Here the constraint of physics joins the constraints of institutional practices, in ways which extend the institutional framing of Appert's montages in the context of magazine illustration in the 1870s. For John Tagg (1988), embedded in the term *documentary*, coined in the 1920s, is the centrality of photographic technology "within its rhetoric of immediacy and truth" (p. 8). Institutions have the characteristic of producing distinctions between selves and others. Photography allied itself swiftly with such "othering" through the technological distinction between photographer and subject, and the tendency towards the objectification, as a consequence of "objective recording," of the latter.

A telling example occurs in the arguments behind the feuding documentary styles of Margaret Bourke-White and Walker Evans. Both photographers worked throughout the Great Depression to highlight the devastation and harsh living conditions of the rural poor in the United States. The debate concerned the twin risks of the aestheticization of suffering and the exploitation of photographed subjects.

In their book, *Let Us Now Praise Famous Men*, James Agee and Walker Evans (1941) adjure their readers: "Above all else: in God's name don't think of it as Art" (p. 14). These words communicate a sensed need to disassociate their practice of photography from the aesthetic. For Evans it was fundamental that an ethical mode of photography be "objective." According to Stomberg (2007), "Agee and Evans established a new ethic of disengagement and aesthetic of artlessness" (p. 49). Why did aesthetics and beautiful images of suffering draw concern? In the *Critique of Judgment,* Kant (1790/2007) ties the judgment of beauty to disinterested pleasure. Such an understanding of the aesthetic separates beauty from cognition. By permitting the spectacle of suffering as a pleasure, and specifically by reducing it to a matter of the judgment of taste, the aestheticization of documentary images removed them from the realm of ethical action, leaving them as objects of pure contemplation.

Photography has a particularly problematic role in this since it is often considered to be an intrinsically aestheticizing technology. Thus Walter Benjamin accuses the *Neue Sachlichkeit* photographer Renger-Patsch of having "succeeded in transforming even abject poverty—by apprehending it in a fashionably perfected manner—into an object of enjoyment" (Benjamin, 1999, p. 775). Benjamin is clear that there is but a small step from the aestheticization to the commodification of suffering: the claim leveled at Margaret Bourke-White due to the great success and professional aesthetic of her book *You Have Seen Their Faces* (Stomberg, 2007; Weissberg 2000).

Similarly, in the contemporary arena, the moral standing of Brazilian photographer Sebastião Salgado's work has been criticized for being overly aesthetic, a style which has also enabled him to subsidize his work through advertising commissions (Soar, 2003). In *On Photography*, Susan Sontag (1977) points out that the "aestheticizing tendency" of photography is also seen to neutralize the distress that photographs of suffering can effect in the viewer (p. 108). Caroline Brothers (1997) similarly describes, in relation to photojournalism, how the aestheticization of death becomes a "means of deflecting its impact and sheltering the public from scenes considered too gruesome" (p. 172). Hence, the aestheticizing features of photography—particularly through their perceived linkage with "disinterested pleasure"—threaten to neutralize representations of suffering, distance the viewer from the photographed subject, undermine notions of shared responsibility, commodify the image of suffering, and subsequently numb the spectator through the abundance of such spectacles.

Evans is often characterized as approximating a more "honest" or "authentic" image by evading conventions of aestheticization (Stomberg, 2007). Margaret Bourke-White on the other hand "wanted her photographs to be catalysts for change and not 'dispassionate' records" (Stomberg, 2007, p. 42). Stomberg argues that for those critical of this mode of documentary, "Caring, as revealed photographically by the use of flash and dramatic angles, had become an indicator of disingenuousness" (Stomberg, 2007, p. 53). The tendency to perceive the moral power of photography, particularly of the documentary tradition, as deriving from the exposure of something "authentic" has meant that the aesthetic becomes that which distances the viewer from this "authentic" encounter. In *Regarding the Pain of Others* (2003), Susan Sontag notes the exaggeration present in polarizing the photograph's ability to document and to create art. It is felt that a "beautiful photograph drains attention from the sobering subject and turns it toward the medium itself, thereby compromising the picture's status as a document" (p. 77). However, photographic communication cannot cease to be a mediated communication. As David Levi Strauss (2003) points out, "To represent is to aestheticize" (p. 9).

Mediation also occurs in institutional and professional contexts, and to that extent inside regimes of power. John Tagg (1988) argues that the documentary mode works on the evocation of a "politically mobilized rhetoric of Truth" (p. 13). The famous Farm Security Administration (FSA) photography department (where Walker Evans was employed) attempted to mobilize the language of the documentary tradition as a means of intervention. While the FSA photographs are often understood as providing political justification for Franklin D. Roosevelt's New Deal programs, the deployment of these same documentary techniques in the service of colonial intervention has received far less attention. Beginning in the mid-1930s the FSA, as well as other associated government agencies tied to Puerto Rican elites and U.S. government interests, utilized documentary photography in order to provide evidence of progress in "the construction, rehabilitation, and 'improvement' of a colony" (Vázquez, 2002, p. 284). While seemingly depicting the everyday lives of Puerto Rican *campesinos*, these photographic documents appropriated, mobilized, and transformed the figure of the *jíbaro* (the rural laborer of Puerto Rico) from that of resistance and independence, to one of primitivity, poverty, and later, progress. By repositioning the *jíbaro*, and his dwelling (the *bohío*) in terms of "backwardness" and poverty, the *jíbaro* became visualized as a subject in need of intervention. Later, when various New Deal programs were introduced (e.g. agricultural work camps, education, land redevelopments, new housing developments), photography was used to provide evidence of the success of such measures. Positioned as the beneficiary of colonial intervention, the *jíbaro* is again transformed, now depicted in terms of betterment and progress. In this case, photography became a rhetorical strategy used by the U.S. government precisely as a means of "incorporation, homogenization, and proprietorship" (Vázquez, 2002, p. 284). Vázquez points out how such a strategy neutralizes the question of intention, and therefore "the focus remains on the constructed beneficiary—the colonized" (p. 284). These photographs function as institutional documents providing particular evidential knowledge of the lives of Puerto Rican *campesinos*, as well as promoting particular interventions in their name. This visually legitimizes a power dynamic in which the colonized are positioned as the disempowered Other in need of intervention, and those interests of the U.S. government and Puerto Rican elites are then validated as being beneficial for the colonized.

The example of the FSA photography of Puerto Rico highlights the degree to which the positioning of subjects, in this case as objects of the colonial gaze, can work to reproduce particular systems of exploitation. Theorizing position and "the gaze" have become important ways of thinking about visual communication and its role in the reification of exploitative power relations. Feminist film scholar Laura Mulvey (1989) for example, argues that film reproduces patriarchy precisely by positioning the viewer as holder of the "male gaze." Such an understanding means that particular modes of representation (through the positioning of subjects) encourage or entice the viewer to adopt certain kinds of subject positions, which subsequently subject those viewed to specific modes of gazing. The reproduction of modes of domination in the visual field through such technical devices as angle and framing undermine the possibility that these images can communicate in such a way as to enable a relation of care and solidarity between the viewer and the represented subject.

From a deontological perspective, this exploitative relation might be avoided in professional practice: an ethical image must be consensual. When the young, wounded, or dead are photo-graphed or filmed, however, consent cannot always be given, nor is it always unanimous (in the case of crowds or families). Consent given in the heat of the moment may be regretted afterwards, and in many instances the circulation of an image may exceed what the subject believed they were consenting to. Such concerns over the exploitation of subjects become heightened when one considers the economy in which such images circulate. Defending Sebastião Salgado, Uru-guayan writer Eduardo Galeano (1990) describes the dilemma thus:

> Poverty is a commodity that fetches a high price on the luxury market. Consumer-society photog-raphers approach but do not enter. In hurried visits to scenes of despair or violence, they climb out of the plane or helicopter, press the shutter release, explode the flash: they shoot and run. They have looked without seeing and their images say nothing. (p. 11)

At the same time, a utilitarian might argue that without this sea of market driven images we would not know the events of the world. It is commonly believed that this knowledge can open hearts, wallets, and governments. The controversial ethnographic filmmaker Robert Gardner analyzes the aggressive and possessive language of Western "picture *taking*," and argues for the possibility of "image giving" (Gardner, 2007). Implicit in this distinction is the establishment of a more than contractual relationship between photographer and subjects. Thus Walker Evans's work can be characterized as ethical in light of his belief that photographers must familiarize themselves with their subjects before the image can be made (Stomberg, 2007, p. 54). Similarly, Chilean pho-tographer and artist Alfredo Jaar also believes in the importance of becoming "close" with those whom he photographs; however, for Jaar, the problem lies with "the contexts in which these im-ages are disseminated and consumed" (Duganne, 2007, p. 70), leading him in some key works of the 1980s to hide his images from viewers, effectively moving towards the iconoclast position.

The modernist belief in an objective causality running from the real world to the photograph is more difficult to credit in the case of cinematography and moving image media more generally, where the editing process is more evidently on display than in the case of the still image, which hides the selection process preceding publication. Unavoidable once films began to extend more than a few minutes in duration, editing was the subject of extensive experimentation through the silent period. Jean-Luc Godard's epigram, that cinema is truth 24 times a second, indicates some-thing of the ambiguities made possible by the multiple perspectives available to cinema and later television and video editing. Early Soviet experiments like Eisenstein's *Strike!* (*Stachka,* 1925) used cuts to animals to caricature protagonists in a tradition spreading back to early political cartoons. Far more offensive are the visual equations of rats with Jews in the Nazi fiction feature *Jud Süß* (1940). More rhetorical are the montages of *Koyaanisqatsi* (1980), aimed at persuading its audience of ecological and spiritual values. The persuasive aspect of visual communication, like the rhetorical tropes discussed in Plato's debates with the Sophists, remains an ethical issue today. The relation between sound and image, especially in the form of voice-over, has received related attention. One early practitioner went so far as to announce: "If we were living in the twelfth century, a period of lofty civilization, the practitioners of dubbing would be burnt in the market-place for heresy. Dubbing is equivalent to a belief in the duality of the soul" (Renoir, 1974, p. 106). Voice-overs in documentary, especially broadcast documentary, are regarded in some quarters as not merely guiding and explaining but restricting and controlling audience responses.

Dramatic fiction is less prone to disputes over truth, although the realist aesthetic had a significant impact on classical film theorists Siegfried Kracauer (1960) and André Bazin (1967, 1971). Deriving his aesthetics from Catholic existentialist traditions, Bazin argued that the liberty of the audience was at stake in closely edited fictions. The use of long takes and deep focus not only allowed more reality into the image, so liberating the viewer to choose where to look, but also provided the basis on which to form moral judgments about the characters and the fictional worlds they inhabit. Bazin was, however, prescient enough to note that any technique can be fetishized and lose its potency: the prevalence of the long take and deep focus in fantasy and action films of the last two decades demonstrates the point (Bazin, 1971). Particular concerns have been raised in press campaigns over docudrama, where historical knowledge becomes the basis for fictionalized speculation. Controversy rarely arises over simple film biographies, but has instead been typically focused on television and to a lesser extent film accounts of historical episodes, especially military ones such as the mutinies in the last years of World War I, the Dresden fire bombings, and the Irish and Indian wars of independence. The blurring of fact and fiction is felt as morally unsettling too in the case of reality television, particularly shows which select performers on the basis of their propensity to emotional outburst or excessive behavior. Such shows also raise questions concerning their encouragement of prurience, and their emulation of surveillant systems, placing viewers implicitly as well as explicitly (for example, through voting) in positions of power over the contestants.

Some commentators argue for censorship of such programs, and have been successful in the case of several docudramas. Arguments over censorship frequently rest on the popular accusation that films, television, video, and increasingly computer games are causes of either sexual activity or physical violence, or both. From both Left and Right, criticisms of the moral impropriety of audiovisual drama can be distinguished from the causal argument to demonstrate a moral disapproval of the depiction of certain classes of act, especially sexual and violent, but including verbal forms. Criminality, drug abuse, and in some jurisdictions alternative religious practices are similarly subject to both legal and moral opprobrium, on grounds both of virtue and of utilitarian worth. Core to such positions are the ease of availability of domestic-format recordings, and the presence of such material in the home, as opposed to specialized venues such as cinemas and clubs, a theme which places children in the role of the "wives and servants" of the *Chatterley* case (see below).

It is difficult to disentangle behaviorist models of causality associated with utilitarian ethics from atavistic notions of the magical power of images, and both form the sociological credo that audiovisual media are the media of choice for the poor, children, the uneducated and thus ideologically vulnerable. It is notable that three of the four most populous nations, China, India, and Indonesia, have strong legal censorship regimes, as well as traditions of restraint in sexual matters and of highly stylized representations of violence. Mass produced media have been the butt of many moral panics (Pearson, 1983), often involving unlikely alliances of Left and Right. Such is the case of 1950s horror comics (Barker, 1984), where defenders of public morality joined forces with Communist Party unionists seeking to stem the tide of comics depicting negatively the communist side in the Korean War. While detractors point to the supposed right to free speech, which has legal strength in a limited number of jurisdictions and is only arguably a human right, supporters note that censorship precludes extreme exploitation of performers and audiences, and forces creators to more subtle and allusive forms of presentation.

A more politicized criticism points to absences in fictional accounts of contemporary society: the lack of migrants in the Paris of *Amélie* (*Le Fabuleux destin d'Amélie Poulain*, 2001), the lack among Hollywood productions of a Vietnamese perspective on the war until the honorable if late exception of Oliver Stone's *Heaven & Earth* (1993). Few moral campaigns have been launched to secure redress for such omissions, although many advocacy groups now campaign for positive representations in broadcast television on such moral grounds, as well as grounds of social justice (Montgomery, 1989). Alasdair MacIntyre's narrative approach to ethics in *After Virtue* (1984) has had some impact in film studies, not least because the depiction of virtue is clearly a major function of all fictions. The universe of classical narrative cinema (loosely defined as popular pre-1960 films) is basically Manichean, with good and evil clearly demarcated. In recent years, however, while evil continues to be clearly depicted, the hero is less frequently an embodiment of virtue, and more commonly either an innocent forced to take on a heroic role (such as Frodo in *The Lord of the Rings*), or a functionary whose less than ethical actions can be justified as protecting the innocent (such as William Munny in *Unforgiven*). This may suggest that popular cinema has abdicated the role of advocating virtue, or alternatively that previously nonvirtuous motivations, notably revenge, are now considered virtuous in popular media such as cinema and computer games. While it is true that some crossover art house hits, like Iñáritu's *21 Grams* and *Babel*, describe narratives with clearly consequentialist ethics, others such as Tykwer's *Lola Rennt* and Boyle's *Slumdog Millionaire* seem to describe worlds where the results of actions and the rewards once reserved for virtuous fictional heroes are entirely random. As early as the 1930s, the Disney company had discovered that the "niceness" of Mickey Mouse made it increasingly difficult to build stories around his character: such technical problems may explain the abdication of ethical foregrounds in popular film. However, it is also the case that *Slumdog Millionaire*, like previous slum-set fiction films *Pixote* (1981) and *Salaam Bombay* (1988), has been accused of sentimentalizing the plight of slum-dwellers for the delectation of affluent Western audiences.

Colonial and Ethnographic Imaging

Deriving its authority from the emergent discipline of visual anthropology in the 1880s, the earliest colonial photography and film shared techniques with the anthropometric studies of Bertillon and Lombroso. French physician Félix-Louis Regnault used chronophotography—a technique deployed soon after in Taylorist time-and-motion studies—in order to record the bodily movements of West African performers at the Paris Ethnographic Exposition of 1895 (Rony, 1996, p. 23). By comparing the recorded movements of indigenous bodies with the recorded movements of White Europeans, Regnault believed he could map racial difference, and ultimately establish an "evolutionary typology of the races" (Rony, 1996, p. 14). Regnault's faith in the moving image as a tool for anthropological taxonomies of "races" continued through the work of such anthropologists as Margaret Mead and Franz Boas, who "believed that films of gesture and behavior would provide unimpeachable records for the classification of cultures" (Rony, 1996, p. 195).

Even with the discursive shift from race to culture, the continuing positivism of visual anthropology implies that all ethnographic film reasserts narratives of evolution (Rony, 1996, p. 25)—familiar from Robert Flaherty's *Nanook of the North* (1922), as well as popularizations of the ethnographic eye like *The Gods Must Be Crazy* (1980) and *Dances With Wolves* (1990). In this narrative, the colonized become the "primitive," the "vanishing," the "backward" and the "always already dead" (Rony, 1996, p. 198). Observational cinema turns recording into document and document into knowledge along a singular historical timeline, and the specific histories, struggles, and contexts of marginalized and subjugated peoples are rendered invisible. The use of John Marshall's *The Hunters* (1956) and Jamie Uys's *The Gods Must Be Crazy* (1980) by the South African and Namibian governments as documents justifying land seizures from Ju/'hoansi people (Rony, 1996, p. 261) reveals the degree to which such visual constructions can be involved in unethical actions.

Fundamental to the observational mode and its use in power relations is distance from the subjects filmed, a distance which several projects have tried to break down. In *Through Navajo Eyes* (1972), Sol Worth and John Adair gave the camera to the subjects of their study. When a Navajo girl named Maryjane Tsosie chose not to film her grandfather in close-up, Worth found himself so frustrated that he took the camera from her. Rony (1996) points out that Tsosie's reticence can be likened to the desire felt by many indigenous filmmakers to limit what can be seen of their culture (p. 212). Often what is considered photographable by indigenous groups is different from, or at odds with, the conventions of the visual anthropologist or filmmaker. Against the anthropological and voyeuristic desire for an all-seeing, all-knowing gaze, "the importance of *not* photographing certain subjects, whether profane or sacred, is a central theme in the works of many indigenous filmmakers" (Rony, 1996, p. 212). Colonial and ethnographic image practices broadly ignored prohibitions on depicting or circulating images based on sacred sites or objects or the souls of ancestors. Understood as tools for the construction of objective or instrumental knowledge, photography constructed the colonial Other as object rather than subject of knowledge, who was deemed to be wholly known through an external visual discourse and whose own codes of visual communication were excluded from the process (Ginsburg, 2007).

While this ethnographic mode of representation is still active in Western contemporary culture—particularly visible in television adventure and travel documentaries—alternative practices, such as indigenous video, aim to create dignified and faithful self-portraits that represent the community "as they wish to be presented, and so that they can control the way in which their wisdom, spirituality and knowledge are made known" (Montefore, 2002, p. 25). The Zapatistas, for example, as well as many other leftist and populist movements in Latin America, have adopted video technology as a way towards indigenous autonomy through self-determination and self-representation (Fernandez, 2007, p. 229). Here, indigenous communities themselves control their depictions and, to some degree, to whom they are addressed. For example, while indigenous groups like the Quechua have prioritized the creation and circulation of visual media within their own communities (Fernandez, 2007, p. 231), new global media technologies have enabled groups like the Zapatistas to expand their reach, facilitating communication with large numbers outside the community.

NEW CONTEXTS

Apparent in earlier phases of the obscenity debate is a class-based morality. One of its most notorious instances was the UK trial for obscenity of D. H. Lawrence's *Lady Chatterley's Lover*. During the summing up, chief prosecutor Mervyn Griffith Jones asked the jury to consider whether this was a book "you would wish your wife or servants to read." The implication that educated men of a certain class might be unaffected by the book echoes with the amorality proper to the nobility proposed by Nietzsche in *The Genealogy of Morals* (1967), for whom "noble" souls need not be restricted by the "slave" morality of Christianity. Such class distinctions seem to recur in contemporary disputes over the circulation of images in digital form. This is the case, for example, with the 2008 furor over an exhibition of photographs by Australian artist Bill Henson. When campaigners attacked his use of pubescent female models, a key ground for complaint was the circulation of the images on the Internet (Perkin, 2008). *Sydney Morning Herald* journalist David Marr (2008) is one of several commentators to note that the obscenity seems to depend on the circulation rather than on the images themselves (although some campaigners assert that no children should ever be photographed naked in a formal expression of virtue ethics which parallels the "shopping list" approach to banning whole categories of image adopted in the UK Video Recordings Act of 1984). As digital delivery and cataloguing become more prevalent, some commentators (e.g., Zittrain, 2008) fear a move from jury-based decisions on prevailing and changing social mores towards a keyword or semantic tagging of content, with far less opportunity for exploration, challenge, and innovation in audiovisual media.

Like the case of the Video Recordings Act, moral debates surrounding Internet obscenity are exacerbated by the threat of unlimited copying and dissemination, with no controls over where and when such images may be seen. Traditionally, censorship has been able to create sliding scales using such instruments as broadcasting watersheds, hours during which adult materials may be shown, or restricted access venues such as cinema clubs. The Internet, like the grey economy in pirate videos, has few reliable systems for identifying users by age that cannot be circumvented by hackers with even low levels of skill. This is also the case for other identifiers: Internet users may be careless with their data, giving away personal information both through cookie technology and social networking sites like Facebook, but they show a marked distaste for any attempt to track online activities which are regarded as private.

Ancient rock art in the Northern territory of Australia, and many of the earliest representations of human figures, are explicit about the generative organs. By the time of Courbet's *L'origine du monde* (1866), a painting of a naked woman's vagina, such works could only be exhibited behind a curtain, the property of roués and, later in the 20th century, of the psychoanalyst Jacques Lacan (Solomon-Godeau, 1997, pp. 293–296). The problem of obscenity is clearly historical, as the flexibility of legal definitions (e.g., the test of community standards in jury trials) demonstrates. Lacan (1986) and subsequent French theorists proposed a definition of obscenity as excessive visibility. This tradition, traced by Martin Jay (1993), culminates in the proposal that contemporary media are definitionally obscene: "Obscenity begins precisely when there is no more spectacle, no more scene, when all becomes transparence and immediate visibility, when everything is exposed to the harsh and inexorable light of information and communication" (Baudrillard, 1983, p. 130). No longer the special condition of erotic or pornographic images, obscenity describes the relentless visualization of everything that once was private or concealed.

The problem of excessive visibility becomes a practical ethical concern in the case of cyberbullying and the posting of violent attack videos on YouTube and similar user-generated image and video websites. While legislation can place the blame for such cases on the shoulders of Internet service providers and website or portal owners, moral blame quite clearly resides with the poster. Previously, humiliation of peers and defamation of authority figures could be contained either locally or through the gatekeeping functions of centralized media distribution outlets such as TV stations and newspapers. The democratization of the Internet, however, removes such gatekeeping functions, handing them back to users, who are rarely trained in civic or professional ethics.

The more widely disseminated such images become, the greater the damage they may inflict. This may also be the case with the dissemination of images made in the first instance for a particular kind of circulation—for example, in galleries—but which achieve notoriety through public debate and Internet distribution. The further an image circulates, the further it is removed from the informed consent of its subject. Moreover, any ethics of redress is hampered by the difficulty of withdrawing files from circulation once they have entered Internet discourse.

The distributive moment is one of only two major changes to image ethics brought about by digitization. The second change, while not entirely new, relates to the ease with which images can be doctored, and has also been made faster, cheaper, and easier. Thus democratized, the power to falsify images produces on the one hand a harmless quasi-surrealist entertainment, but on the other malicious and damaging uses. Images composited from a celebrity's face and a model's body, or those purporting to show aliens and other monstrous creatures, continue the side-show cruelty of old fairgrounds, and are not often taken seriously even by those who consume them most avidly. Indeed, if the French tradition of philosophical critique is correct, all images are untruthful, and those that are manifestly manipulated, whether painterly or photographic, merely illustrate the point.

A frequent characteristic of such images is their "airbrushed" look, the overly perfect surfaces which they share with the products of commercial photography in the advertising industry. Perhaps as a result, it is frequently the less technically perfect images which convey the greatest sense of authenticity, not least those recorded on domestic-grade equipment: closed-circuit television cameras, portable video handicams, and mobile phones with photographic or video capacity. Images derived from the late 2000s craze in some countries for "happy slapping" (minor but painful and unexpected assaults), or the slightly earlier concern about images sneaked in public toilets, may demean those victimized, but surely also demean those who document, circulate, and condone them. Arendt (2003) notes that literary portrayals of evil are always replete with signs of despair: it may well be that this particular mode of "banal" evil, in its own way, demonstrates a particular kind of moral despair, just as youth riots demonstrate a political and economic one. At the same time, Arendt notes that evil embraces its own despair in the full knowledge of what it is and does: such is not in any sense apparent among cyberbullies or YouTube sex offenders.

Arendt's observations are perhaps most chilling when we turn to one of the most egregious of recent image distributions, the mobile phone pictures of torture victims in the U.S. Army run prison at Abu Ghraib. Through this "grotesque infantile reality-show" (Baudrillard, 2006, p. 86) the torture and the photograph become inextricably linked, the photograph proving and disseminating the degradation of the prisoners:

> In many pictures, the faces of the tortured stare out at us in a moment not only of fear and pain but also of shame, as we, by looking, prolong the shaming. Viewing and disseminating these pictures thus complete the rituals of degradation first enacted in the prison. (Reinhardt, 2007, p. 16)

Grusin (2010) argues that what is so shocking about the images (apart from the representation of torture) is what they share with our everyday media practices, a theme also pursued by news commentaries noting the relation between the Abu Ghraib images and reality television shows. Eisenman (2007) asserts the continuity of these images with an ancient tradition of depicting prisoners gratefully accepting their punishment, Baudrillard (2006) their continuity with violent pornography. Through their transformation into weapons, the photographs compound the humiliation, and the images themselves participate in the annihilation of the prisoner's world.

Scarry (1985) adds that the use of regular everyday objects as weapons of torture make the objects themselves participants in "the annihilation of the prisoners, made to demonstrate that everything is a weapon" (p. 41). According to Scarry, the use of domestic objects in torture externalizes the destruction of the person's world through pain. In the case of Abu Ghraib, the banal digital camera becomes a torture instrument. This is a new dimension of media ethics, one in which not only images and words but the very technological devices of ubiquitous media themselves now become domestic and quotidian, may become instruments of torture. Thus the very presence of cameras, embedded in mobile phones or otherwise, may be as much of a concern for media ethics today as the reproduction and dissemination of images, which in the case of Abu Ghraib became a continuation of that torture. Political concerns with the ubiquity of cameras as instruments of surveillance here meet ethical concerns with the limits of privacy. To what extent is suffering a private event, and to what extent is its undoubted affective power a reason to deploy images of it in the interests of a greater good, whether by encouraging donations in the case of famine images, or political action in the case of abused prisoners? Is the convenience and global reach of the digital camera/photo in the Internet age an instrument of care, or a mechanism of further humiliation, of loss of humanity and world? It is of course widely felt that though the images from Abu Ghraib are exceptionally horrific, their publicity is ethical (and necessary) because of the political ramifications of such an exposure. By revealing what was daily practice at Abu Ghraib, support could be mobilized for its cessation and the global superpower responsible held to account. However, from this utilitarian perspective, the suffering of those depicted is understood in the past tense, the private suffering converted into public symbol, and the pain caused by the act of representation is counted of less importance than disseminating knowledge of the events.

CONCLUSION

Adorno's late lectures on moral philosophy (2000) argue that Kantian deontology is overly ready to sacrifice happiness, and in doing so reduces the yearning of human beings for a better life. Adorno sees a symmetrical fault in utilitarianism's readiness to sacrifice the well-being of others for the greater good, seeing both as faces of a single totalitarianism which, fatalistically, denies any kind of happiness other than that of the state. In this perspective, both entertainment and news media supply minor pleasures in place of happiness, and produce narratives in which forces of order struggle with anomic and anarchic others. Explicit in Adorno's account is the challenge of conceiving an ethics with a claim to universality, a challenge only made greater with the increase in migration, tourism, and conflict, which increasingly bring different ethical traditions into contact. This doubt about universality has attached itself to the project for a universal human rights announced in the 1948 United Nations Declaration. Such rights, Žižek (1993) argues, are like Bentham's "fictions," a category which includes such legal fictions as the "person" (which may be a corporation), the social contract (which no-one has signed), and the principle that ignorance is no defense (though no-one knows the entirety of the law). From this analysis, equating Bentham's fictions with Kant's Transcendental Ideas, Žižek is able to argue that good is capable of turning into evil when, for example, we act out of duty to do an immoral act (such as beating a child), or establish a state which, like the Jacobin dictatorship of virtue, is capable of the utmost evil in the name of the greater good. Like Adorno, Žižek's is ultimately a tragic view of the world, though in his case this depends upon the impossibility of both a full subjectivity capable of judging its own actions and the incapacity of our symbolic resources to complete any communication between people. Both thinkers share a deep suspicion that under contemporary circumstances, individual ethical action is no longer possible, or is so difficult as to require extreme conditions and extreme acts of will.

Against this tragic view can be ranged the egoistic ethics proposed by Nietzsche, a mode of voluntarism frequently evoked in computer games and blockbuster movies. MacIntyre (1984), however, criticizes Nietzsche for reproducing the same subjective fallacy as his Enlightenment forebears, in terms reminiscent of Adorno's and Žižek's critique of Kant. MacIntyre proposes instead a teleological renewal of virtue ethics, grounded in the Aristotelean view that life has as its purpose its own completion in the form of the good life, and that the good life comprises discovering what is good. A similarly social and teleological view informs the ethical work of Alain Badiou (2001), who proposes an ethic of truths, a term which he reserves for love, revolution, and major innovations in science and art. The greatest evils, he argues, are the simulation, betrayal, or authoritarian imposition of truths, while the greatest virtue is to "keep going," to maintain the power and efficacy of these historical truths and their capacity to blast open the surrounding status quo. Arendt (2003) argues for a related praxis whose goal is to make possible the transition from will to action. In their distinctive ways, these three thinkers propose a return to the Aristotelean proposition that the fulfillment of ethics, as philosophy of the good life, is only possible in the transition to politics, the good life of the community. In this case, the obligation of visual media is, as it was held to be in the Renaissance, not to depict the world as it is but, in common with the Aristotelean vision of eudaemonism, to picture the world, and humanity, as they should be. The political aspect of such a project must imply that the evolution of societies capable of generating and sustaining workable ideal forms of virtue is dependent on an already ethical will to communicate such a vision. While desirable, such mutual reinforcement seems unlikely in the period of declining U.S. hegemony in the world system, unless adopted by social movements outside the large media corporations.

Between tragic and teleological approaches to communication ethics lies the case of the individual who suffers. In the influential ethical thought of Emmanuel Levinas (1969, 1989), ethics arises as the obligation to the Other, which arises in the face-to-face confrontation with the simultaneous similarity and difference of the one who stands before us. In visual ethics, however, the other and the other's suffering are always mediated. Even our face-to-face activities are conducted in the light of the representations of behaviors in which we are immersed from infancy. Only in exceptional circumstances are our capacities for responsibility called upon in person: instead we ask ourselves to respond to *images* of natural disaster, war, and disease. The increasing ease of production, manipulation, and circulation of images forms the condition for contemporary ethical obligation. In the case of the Abu Ghraib images, few of the many commentators speak of their obligation to the prisoners; only of the obligation to political action. Such a state of affairs might suggest that once again the prohibition against images might be evoked against their obscene omnipresence, their capacity to wound, and their ability to blunt our sense of mutual debt.

REFERENCES

Adorno, T. W. (2000). *Problems of moral philosophy* (E. Jephcott, Trans.). Cambridge, UK: Polity.

Agee, J., & Evans, W. (1965). *Let us now praise famous men: Three tenant families.* London: Peter Owen. (Original work published 1941)

Anderson-Reece, E. (1993). Who's afraid of corporate culture: The Barnett Newman controversy. *The Journal of Aesthetics and Art Criticism, 51*(1), 49–57.

Arendt, H. (2003). *Responsibility and judgment.* New York: Schocken.

Babenco, H. (Director). (1981). *Pixote* [Motion picture]. Brazil: Embrafilme/HB Filmes.

Badiou, A. (2001). *Ethics: An essay on the understanding of evil* (P. Hallward, Trans.). London: Verso.

Barker, M. (1984). *A haunt of fears: The strange history of the British horror comics campaign.* London: Pluto.

Barthes, R. (1981). *Camera lucida: Reflections on photography* (R. Howard, Trans.). New York: Hill & Wang.

Baudrillard, J. (1983). The ecstasy of communication. In H. Foster (Ed.), *Postmodern culture* (pp. 126–134). London: Pluto Press.

Baudrillard, J. (2006). War porn. *Journal of Visual Culture, 5*(1), 86–88.

Bazin, A. (1967). *What is cinema?* (Vol. 1, H. Gray, Trans.). Berkeley: University of California Press.

Bazin, A. (1971). *What is cinema?* (Vol. 2, H. Gray, Trans.). Berkeley: University of California Press.

Benjamin, W. (1999). The author as producer. In M. W. Jennings, H. Eiland, & G. Smith (Eds.), *Walter Benjamin: Selected writings* (Vol. 2, part 2, 1931–1934, pp. 768–782). Cambridge, MA: Harvard University Press.

Boyle, D., Tandar, L. (Directors). (2008). *Slumdog millionaire* [Motion picture]. UK: Celador Films, Film 4.

Breitbart, E. (1997). *A world on display: Photographs from the St. Louis World's Fair, 1904.* Albuquerque, NM: University of New Mexico Press.

Brothers, C. (1997). *War and photography: A cultural history.* London: Routledge.

Butler, J. (2004). *Precarious life: The power of mourning and violence.* London: Verso.

Costner, K. (Director). (1990). *Dances with wolves* [Motion picture]. USA/UK: Tig Productions, Majestic Films International.

Duganne, E. (2007). Photography after the fact. In M. Reinhardt, H. Edwards, & E. Dugganne (Eds.), *Beautiful suffering: Photography and the traffic in pain* (pp. 57–74). Williamstown, MA: Williams College Museum of Art/ University of Chicago Press.

Eisenman, S. F. (2007). *The Abu Ghraib effect*. London: Reaktion.

Eisenstein, S. M. (Director). (1925). *Stachka* (Strike) [Motion picture]. Russia: Goskino/Proletkult.

Ellul, J. (1965). *Propaganda: The formation of men's attitudes* (D. Kellena & J. Lerner, Trans.). New York: Vintage Books.

Eastwood, C. (Director). (1992). *Unforgiven* [Motion picture]. USA: Malpaso Productions, Warner Bros.

English, D. (1984). *The political uses of photography in the Third French Republic, 1871–1914*. Ann Arbor, MI: UMI Research Press.

Fernandez, C. (2007). Movements and militant media: Communications technology and Latin American grassroots politics. In J. MacPhee & E. Reuland (Eds.), *Realizing the impossible: Art against authority* (pp. 228–235). Oakland, CA: AK Press.

Finlay, V. (2002). *Colour*. London: Sceptre.

Flaherty, R. (Director). (1922). *Nanook of the north* [Motion picture]. USA/France: Les Frères Revillon/ Pathé Exchange.

Galeano, E. (1990). Salgado, 17 Times. In E. Galeano & F. Ritchin (Eds.), *An uncertain grace*. New York: Aperture Foundation. Retrieved from http://teaching.quotidiana.org/150/Galeano_Salgado17Times.pdf

Gamboni, D. (1977). *The destruction of art: Iconoclasm and vandalism since the French Revolution*. New Haven, CT: Yale University Press.

Gardner, R. (2007). The moral nature of film. *Media Ethics, 18*(2), 12–13.

Gardner, R., & Marshall, J. (Directors). (1956). *The hunters* [Motion picture]. USA: Film Study Center, Harvard University, Peabody Museum.

Ginsburg, F. (2007, May). Rethinking the digital age. *Media anthropology network* (Working Paper). Retrieved from http://www.media-anthropology.net/ginsburg_digital_age.pdf.

Green, D. (1984). Veins of resemblance: Photography and eugenics. *Oxford Art Journal, 7*(2), 3–16.

Grusin, R (2010). *Premediation: Affect and mediality after 9/11*. New York: Palgrave Macmillan .

Harlan, V. (Director). (1940). *Jud Süß* [Motion picture]. Germany: Terra-Filmkunst, 1940.

Iñárritu, A. G (Director). (2003). *21 grams* [Motion picture]. USA: This Is That Productions.

Iñárritu, A. G. (Director). (2006). *Babel* [Motion picture]. USA: Paramount Pictures.

Jackson, P. (Director). (2002). *The lord of the rings: The fellowship of the ring* [Motion picture]. New Zealand: Wingnut.

Jackson, P. (Director). (2002). *The lord of the rings: The two towers* [Motion picture]. New Zealand: Wingnut.

Jackson, P. (Director). (2003). *The lord of the rings: The return of the king* [Motion picture]. New Zealand: Wingnut.

Jay, M. (1993). *Downcast eyes: The denigration of vision in twentieth-century French thought*. Berkeley: University of California Press.

Jeunet, J-P. (Director). (2001). *Le fabuleux destin d'Amélie Poulain aka Amélie* [Motion picture]. France: Victoires Productions, Tapioca Films,France 3 Cinéma.

Kant, I. (2007). *Critique of judgment* (J. C. Meredith, Trans.). Oxford, UK: Oxford University Press. (Original work published 1790)

Kracauer, S. (1960). *Theory of film: The redemption of physical reality*. New York: Oxford University Press.

Lacan, J. (1986). *Le Séminaire, livre VII, L'éthique de la psychanalyse*. Paris: Seuil.

Levinas, E. (1969). *Totality and infinity: An essay on exteriority* (A. Lingis, Trans.). Pittsburgh, PA: Duquesne University Press.

Levinas, E. (1989). Reality and its shadow (A. Lingis, Trans.). In S. Hand (Ed.), *The Levinas reader* (pp. 129–143). Oxford, UK: Blackwell.

Lyotard, J. (1988). *L'inhumain: Causeries sur le temps.* Paris: Galilée.

MacIntyre, A. (1984). *After virtue: A study in moral theory* (2nd ed.). Notre Dame, IN: University of Notre Dame Press.

Marr, D. (2008). *The Henson case.* Sydney, Australia: Text.

McKim-Smith, G. (2002). The rhetoric of rape: The language of vandalism. *Women's Art Journal, 23*(1), 29–36.

Montefore, G. (2002). El video indígena: Al margen de todo. [The indigenous video: To the margin of everything]. *Oaxaca Poblacíon En El Siglo, 21* (7), 24–26.

Montgomery, K. (1989). *Target: Prime time—Advocacy groups and the struggle over entertainment television.* New York: Oxford University Press.

Mulvey, L. (1989). *Visual and other pleasures.* Bloomington, IN: Indiana University Press.

Nair, M. (Director). (1988). *Salaam Bombay* [Motion picture]. India/UK/France: Cadragee, Channel Four Films, Doordarshan.

Nietzsche, F. (1967). *On the genealogy of morals and ecce homo* (W. Kaufmann & R. J. Hollingdale, Trans.). New York: Vintage.

Pearson, G. (1983). *Hooligan: A history of respectable fears.* Basingstoke, UK: Macmillan.

Perkin, C. (2008, September 9). Naked girl photo may reignite Bill Henson row. *The Australian,*. Retrieved from http://www.theaustralian.com.au/news/arts/catalogue-may-reignite-henson-row/story-e6frg8n6-1111117429722

Plato (1994). *The republic* (B. Jowett, Trans.). Internet Classics Archive. Retrieved from http://classics.mit.edu/Plato/republic.html (Original work published 1896)

Przyblyski, J. M. (1995). Moving pictures: Photography, narrative and the Paris Commune of 1871. In L. Charney & V. R. Schwartz (Eds.), *Cinema and the invention of modern life* (pp. 253–278). Berkeley: University of California Press.

Reggio, G. (Director). (1980). *Koyaanisqatsi* [Motion picture]. USA: IRE Productions, Santa Fe Institute for Regional Education.

Reinhardt, M. (2007). Picturing violence: Aesthetics and the anxiety of critique. In M. Reinhardt, H. Edwards, & E. Duganne (Eds.), *Beautiful suffering: Photography and the traffic in pain* (pp. 13–36). Williamstown, MA: Williams College Museum of Art/University of Chicago Press.

Renoir, J. (1974). *My life and my films* (Trans. N. Denny). London: Collins.

Rony, F. T. (1996). *The third eye: Race, cinema, and ethnographic spectacle.* Durham, NC: Duke University Press.

Scarry, E. (1985). *The body in pain: The making and unmaking of the world.* New York: Oxford University Press.

Soar, M. (2003). The advertising photography of Richard Avedon and Sebastião Salgado. In L. Gross, J. S. Katz, & J. Ruby (Eds.), *Image ethics in the digital age* (pp. 269–293). Minneapolis: University of Minnesota Press.

Solomon-Godeau, A. (1997). *Male trouble: A crisis in representation.* London: Thames & Hudson.

Sontag, S. (1977). *On photography.* London: Penguin Books.

Sontag, S. (2003). *Regarding the pain of others.* New York: Farrar, Straus & Giroux.

Stomberg, J. (2007). A genealogy of orthodox documentary. In M. Reinhardt, H. Edwards, & E. Duganne (Eds.), *Beautiful suffering: Photography and the traffic in pain* (pp. 37–56). Williamstown, MA: Williams College Museum of Art/University of Chicago Press.

Stone, O. (Director). (1993). *Heaven & earth* [Motion picture]. USA: Alcor Films, New regency Pictures, Warner Bros.

Strauss, D. L. (2003). *Between the eyes: Essays on photography and politics.* New York: Aperture.

Tagg, J. (1988). *The burden of representation: Essays on photographies and histories.* Basingstoke, UK: Macmillan.

Trakakis, N. (2004–2005). What was the iconoclast controversy about? *Theandros, 2*(2). Retrieved from http://www.theandros.com/iconoclast.html

Tykwer, T. (Director). (1999). *Lola rennt* (Run Lola run) [Motion picture]. USA/Germany: Sony Pictures, Bavaria Film International.

Uys, J. (Director). (1980). *The gods must be crazy* [Motion picture]. Botswana: Cat Films, Mimosa.

Vázquez, O. E. (2002). "A better place to live": Government agency photography and the transformations of the Puerto Rican Jíbaro. In E. M. Hight & G. D. Sampson (Eds.), *Colonialist photography: Imag(in) ing race and place* (pp. 281–315). London: Routledge.

Weissberg, L. (2000). In plain sight. In B. Zelizer (Ed.), *Visual culture and the holocaust* (pp. 13–27). New Brunswick, NJ: Rutgers University Press.

Wolf, H. (2008). The tears of photography. *Grey Room 29*, 66–89.

Worth, S., & Adair, J. (1972). *Through Navajo eyes: An exploration in film communication and anthropology*. Bloomington, IN: Indiana University Press.

Zittrain, J. (2008). *The future of the internet and how to stop it*. London: Allen Lane.

Žižek, S. (1993). *Tarrying with the negative: Kant, Hegel and the critique of ideology*. Durham, NC: Duke University Press.

16

The Search for Social Justice and the Presumption of Innocence in the Duke University (USA) Lacrosse Case of 2006–2007

Implications for Contemporary Legal and Ethical Communication

Glen Feighery, Marouf Hasian, Jr., and Richard Rieke

INTRODUCTION

Any incident that involves ethical decisions involves uncertainty, but legal cases present particular challenges. In the United States and elsewhere it is generally asserted that the accused are considered innocent until proved guilty, but reality is more complex. The principle of presumption of innocence can be traced at least to the Code of Hammurabi (1792–1750 BCE). The same principle appeared in ancient Roman law and elsewhere in Western European history. In Canada and Britain, Roach (2005) locates the presumption "against the imposition of punishment without proof of fault" in common law "that existed long before the enactment of formal bills of rights" (p. 733). French legal scholar Quintard-Morenas (2010) argues that the presumption carries two implications: it assigns prosecutors the burden of proof and shields the accused from punishment before conviction. He contends that the second element has had a checkered history. In France, the presumption of innocence was largely inoperative until the 1990s despite its inclusion in the 1789 Declaration of Rights. In the United States, he asserts, it has been reduced to an instrument of proof with little practical protection from punishment before conviction.

In this chapter we use the Duke University lacrosse team case of 2006–2007 to illustrate how academic, legal, and journalistic communicators further undermined that protection. Regardless of intentions, activist academicians, an ambitious prosecutor, and competitive journalists invoked social justice in a manner that undermined formal justice. We begin by reviewing the case and considering how ethical decisions in legal contexts can be treacherous. We then examine views from a university campus, the criminal justice system, and the news media before drawing conclusions. Our analysis reveals not only the importance of multiple perspectives on the communication phenomena themselves in such a case but also highlights the ambiguities surrounding the intersection of legal and ethical assessments.

THE CASE

Early on March 14, 2006, Crystal Mangum, an African American mother of two, was taken to Duke University Medical Center in Durham, North Carolina. Mangum and another exotic dancer, Kim Roberts, had been hired by an escort service and sent to a house rented by Duke University lacrosse team members. The dancers were each paid $400 to dance for a party, and the students thought the show would last 2 hours (Cooper, 2007a, pp. 4–6). It ended after a few minutes. When the banter mentioned sex toys, a student held up a broomstick and suggested that the performers use it. Offended, the dancers locked themselves in a bathroom. Eventually they left the house, but not before someone gibed, "Thank your grandpa for my nice cotton shirt" (Taylor & Johnson, 2007, p. 29). Roberts and Mangum drove away, and Mangum appeared to lapse into semiconsciousness. She was taken to the hospital, where a trainee sexual assault nurse examiner reported that Magnum said she had been raped.

Mangum told police she had been taken to a bathroom and assaulted by three men. Team members presented themselves to investigators for interviews, and 46 players submitted DNA samples. Police showed Mangum photo arrays with Duke lacrosse players, but she could not identify any. Later, investigators showed other player photos, and Mangum identified certain individuals (Chalmers, 2007, p. 3). By May 2006, authorities had charged three players—David Evans, Collin Finnerty, and Reade Seligmann—with first-degree rape, first-degree sexual offense, and first-degree kidnapping (Cooper, 2007a, p. 2). During the next several months, scrutiny from defense lawyers, the news media, and others raised questions about the case. Some charges were dropped in December 2006, and North Carolina Attorney General Roy Cooper dismissed all remaining charges in April 2007. Cooper pointed to the actions of the prosecutor as the primary cause of a "tragic…rush to accuse" (Cooper, 2007b, para. 7).

ETHICAL AND COMMUNICATIVE CHALLENGES OF THIS CASE IN LIGHT OF COMPETING PRINCIPLES

Thanks to televised crime scene investigator dramas, people expect scientifically established facts to be available with which to judge the accused (Byers & Johnson, 2009). This fiction is powerful, but gaps in a narrative are often filled with observers' desires and expectations. Various people advanced their own narratives of "what happened," and some evidently took advantage of knowledge gaps. Communication scholars have used different approaches to what Lehman-Wilzig (2003) has called "professional-ethical questions" (see also Feldstein, 2007; Mueller, 2004; Perkins, 2002). White (1984) argues that legal writers should realize that all judicial rhetorics have some "ethical and political dimension" (p. 17), while Hazard and Dondi (2004) note that legal participants in judicial dramas face normative dilemmas as they attempt to legitimate their decision making in complex public arenas. Such decisions were made in the Duke case, and many looked dubious in hindsight.

For example, some Duke University faculty members apparently sought to overcome long-standing discrimination by giving special attention to those who had been ignored or marginalized. The case played into the worldviews of many people, leading them to believe charges before they were verified. The story provided an extraordinary rhetorical exigence on which to develop a teaching moment to overturn established bias. Some took the position that if the story were not true, it should have been, because it provided too powerful a mechanism for doing good (Baydoun & Good, 2007, pp. 172–174). This desire to right a larger wrong might have overwhelmed the details and normal presumptions. Clearly, then, such a case begs attention for the multiple roles of communication present: interaction within the immediate communities, including the larger academic institution; the articulation and application of legal determinations; and reporting and commentary about the case in the mass media.

In the following sections, we show how academicians, legal actors, and journalists altered their judgmental frameworks as events and evidence influenced how they interpreted the presumption of innocence. Thus, our analysis is as much about three professions—including their principles, practices, and institutional constraints—as it is about three different arenas for communication about the case. As Ugland and Henderson (2007) note, various goals, tactics, and values swirl around those who cover mass-mediated events. Following Menkel-Meadow's (2000) suggestion that legal ethics be taught through case studies, we have chosen the Duke lacrosse case not for its peculiar or anomalous characteristics but for what it demonstrates broadly.[1] We examine issues of truth, duty, and fairness to show how communicators attenuated the defendants' presumption of innocence. This, in turn, yields wider lessons for scholars and the public.

THE ACADEMIC SETTING AND ITS INSTITUTIONAL, COMMUNICATIVE, AND ETHICAL IMPLICATIONS

Because this case involved student athletes at an elite university, it is appropriate to discuss what ought to have happened in contrast with what did. We pose two context-based questions that address first, whether Duke should have structures to address such a conflict and second, whether faculty should subordinate political agendas to students' well-being.

Should an Elite University with a Nationally Competitive Athletic Program Have Structures to Address Conflicts with the Local and Academic Communities?

Among elite universities—Harvard, Princeton, Yale, Massachusetts Institute of Technology, Stanford, California Institute of Technology, University of Pennsylvania, Columbia, and Duke—only Stanford and Duke possess nationally competitive athletic programs. When an institution decides to become elite in both athletics and academics, tensions are likely. Duke should have been prepared to deal with criminal charges against athletes, but what occurred can be described as chaotic or even a grievous failure to fulfill expectations. Most institutions have campus police and a dean of students who work together when students get into trouble. They usually feel successful if the students get fair treatment and the university avoids unfavorable publicity. An ethical trap occurs when the interest in avoiding unfavorable publicity trumps concern for students.

After the party, the director of Duke police notified the dean of students that the allegations were not credible and would probably go away. The dean spoke with the coach and some players, who denied the charges, and the dean said she believed them. The dean advised the players that they did not need attorneys and that they should cooperate with the police. A lawsuit by lacrosse players noted that the dean of students was a lawyer, who "in advising the players not to procure legal representation…violated Rule 4.3 of the North Carolina Rules of Professional Conduct" (*Carrington et al.,* 2008, pp. 45–47). Several days passed without players obtaining lawyers or even telling their parents. The tension was heightened by the activities of public protestors.

They were known as "pot bangers." K. C. Johnson, a Brooklyn College history professor who documented the case in his blog, "Durham-in-Wonderland," traces the term to a protest announcement. It read: "Dress warmly, bring your whole family and bring pots and pans and things to bang them with! We are having a 'Cacerolazo,' or a pots & pans protest, because it is a tool women all over the world use to call out sexual assaulters" (Johnson, 2007, para. 2). The protests split the campus between those who shared the protestors' social-justice goals and those who considered them vigilantes. A local magazine described "Duke's Reign of Terror" (Allen, 2007), while a Duke *Chronicle* writer opined:

> Protesters swarmed our campus and the city streets, they screamed vulgar condemnations, they tarred the whole team as complicit.… Worst of all, as they feverishly disregarded due process, they helped create an atmosphere of hysteria. (Miller, 2007, para. 3)

A sign reading "CASTRATE" appeared at one protest. Other signs read, "You can't rape and run," "It's Sunday morning, time to confess," and "Get a conscience, not a lawyer" (Baydoun & Good, 2007, p. 43).

In a civil case against Duke, lacrosse players charged that President Richard Brodhead "sacrificed the rights and interests of the accused Duke students in an effort to avoid embarrassment to Duke and to minimize criticism of [his] administration" (*Carrington et al.,* 2008, p. 5). The lawsuit claimed that Brodhead had exculpatory information and failed to disclose it. When players' attorneys sought to speak with Brodhead, he refused (*Carrington et al.,* 2008, pp. 5–6). Instead, Brodhead stated, "Physical coercion and sexual assault are unacceptable in any setting and will not be tolerated at Duke," implying that such offenses had occurred. He urged "everyone with information pertinent to the events of March 13 to cooperate with authorities," implying that team members had not (*Carrington et al.,* 2008, p. 8). Although Brodhead eventually apologized, we argue that his administration should have reinforced the players' right to due process, not undermined it.

Should University Faculty Subordinate Their Political Agendas to a Primary Concern for Students' Well-Being?

Among the most troubling elements in this incident is the role played by Duke faculty before charges were filed. There is perennial talk on campuses about social justice. Among all evocative ideas, says Perelman (1980), "justice appears to be one of the most eminent and the most hopelessly confused" (p. 1). He continues: "It is always useful and important to be able to qualify as just the social conceptions which one advocates" (p. 1). Working from a distributive perspective on justice, Perelman identifies some of its conceptions: to each the same; to each according to their merits; to each according to their works; to each according to their needs; to each according to their rank; and to each according to their legal entitlement (p. 2). The last conception, Perelman claims, must be distinguished from all others because legal justice seeks only to apply established rules that reflect what society has identified rather than picking and choosing a conception of justice. This is in contrast with ethics, where there is more freedom to choose the formula of justice one intends to apply.

By contrast, Young (1990) argues that a distributive approach to justice is unproductive. She looks instead at injustice: the play of power in domination and oppression, with the central concept being power. Domination and oppression are understood, says Young, first by considering the relation between justice and the core values necessary for living a good life, and second by defining domination and oppression as the absence of one of the two core values: self-development and self-determination. Young says oppression "refers to the vast and deep injustices some groups suffer as a consequence of often unconscious assumptions and reactions of well-meaning people…and structural features of bureaucratic hierarchies" (p. 41).

We argue that the actions of some faculty and administrators constituted injustice toward the accused students. Specifically, faculty used institutional and coercive power to compromise the accused students' chances for self-development and self-determination. From Perelman's perspective, the appropriate venue to determine their fate was "to each according to their legal entitlement," because that reflects society's established rules. Some faculty denounced those rules as reflecting improperly acquired hegemony, but it was not their place to substitute their own form of justice for that of society.

Could the lacrosse players reasonably have expected different treatment? The Duke faculty handbook states:

> The university…respects the right of each member of the academic community to be free from coercion and harassment. It recognizes that academic freedom is no less dependent on ordered liberty than any other freedom, and it understands that the harassment of others is especially reprehensible in a community of scholars. The substitution of noise for speech and force for reason is a rejection and not an application of academic freedom. (Duke University, 2008, V-1)

On March 28, Brodhead expressed what the lacrosse players should have expected: "While we await the results of the investigation, I remind everyone that under our system of law, people are presumed innocent until proven guilty" (Brodhead, 2006, para. 8–9). However, some faculty actions undermined his words. A chronology shows that those actions occurred before legal charges were filed:

- March 13–14, 2006: Party at 610 N. Buchanan Boulevard.
- March 24: Media coverage began. English Professor Faulkner Fox organized a protest for the next lacrosse game. Other faculty asked Brodhead to punish the team (*Carrington et al.,* 2008, pp. 75–77).
- March 25: Brodhead cancelled two lacrosse games and issued his first public statement.
- March 26: The pot banging began.
- March 27: Faculty participated in a protest of 200 people.
- March 28–30: Protests held on campus.
- March 29: English Professor Houston A. Baker, Jr., wrote an open letter titled "Awaiting the Restoration of Confidence: A Letter to the Duke University Administration." He asked, "How is a Duke community citizen to respond to such a national embarrassment from under the 'cloud of silence' that seeks to protect white, male, athletic violence?" (Baker, 2006, para. 1).
- March 31: History Professor William Chafe wrote in the Duke *Chronicle*, "The real issue is how we will respond to this latest example of the poisonous linkage of race and sex as instruments of power and control" (Chafe, 2006, para. 8).
- April 6: The "listening" statement of the Group of 88 faculty members was published in the Duke *Chronicle*.
- April 17: Finnerty and Seligmann were charged.
- May 15: Evans was charged.

Did the faculty statements constitute a rush to judgment in opposition to legal protections for innocence and intellectual commitments to reflection before action? Faculty claimed they were misunderstood. We reject that, and we look more closely at Baker's letter:

> There is no rush to judgment here about the crime…nor the harms to body and soul allegedly perpetrated by white males at 610 Buchanan Boulevard…. The lacrosse team—15 of whom have faced misdemeanor charges for drunken misbehavior in the past three years—may well feel they can claim innocence and sport their disgraced jerseys on campus…. Young, white, violent, drunk-

en men among us—implicitly boasted by our athletic director and administrators—have injured lives. (Baker, 2006)

Although Baker uses the term *allegedly*, he writes of crimes, injuries, and violence. He suggests that because the players have misdemeanor records, they can be assumed guilty of felonies. The day before Baker wrote, a group called "CrimeStoppers" distributed posters stating that "the victim was sodomized, raped, assaulted and robbed" (*Carrington et al.,* 2008, p. 97). A civil complaint later alleged that some Duke administrators were part of CrimeStoppers and participated in preparing the poster. There was no "allegedly" in this statement, and Baker followed in the same vein. We suggest that a fair reading of Baker's words indicates that he rushed to judgment.

Another controversial example of academic communication was the "listening" statement by the Group of 88 faculty. It reads in part:

We are listening to our students. We are also listening to the Durham community, to Duke staff, and to each other. Regardless of the results of the police investigation, what is apparent everyday now is the anger and fear of many students who know themselves to be objects of racism and sexism, who see illuminated in this moment's extraordinary spotlight what they live with everyday…. [N]o one is really talking about how to keep the young woman herself central to this conversation, how to keep her humanity before us…she doesn't seem to be visible in this…. This is a social disaster. The students know that the disaster didn't begin on March 13th and won't end with what the police say or the court decides…. We're turning up the volume in a moment when some of the most vulnerable among us are being asked to quiet down while we wait. To the students speaking individually and to the protestors making collective noise, thank you for not waiting and for making yourselves heard. (Listening statement, 2006)

In our view, "thank you for not waiting" suggests prejudgment. Allusions to the events of March 13, 2006, speculation about the condition of "the young woman," and the rejection of formal verdicts further reinforce an apparent rush to judgment.

Later, the Group of 88 wrote:

The ad has been read as a comment on the alleged rape, the team party, or the specific students accused. Worse, it has been read as rendering a judgment in the case. We understand the ad instead as a call to action on important, longstanding issues on and around our campus, an attempt to channel the attention generated by the incident to addressing these. We reject all attempts to try the case outside the courts and stand firmly by the principle of the presumption of innocence. (Concerned Faculty)

Did this ex post facto dedication to presumption of innocence ameliorate harm to the accused? Not sufficiently. We believe some faculty sacrificed the interests of some students to advance their political–ethical agendas. Regardless of intention, the result was harm. The team suffered a cancelled season. The defendants lived for a year in fear; they incurred enormous legal expenses; and they face lifetime identification as "those lacrosse players."

LEGAL–ETHICAL CONTEXT AND DIMENSIONS: LESSONS FROM A COMMUNICATIVE PERSPECTIVE

It is too easy to equate the legal significance of the Duke lacrosse case with the misconduct of one person, then-Durham County District Attorney Michael Nifong. The point we make here is far larger. In a democratic society, any system of jurisprudence relies on legitimacy in the eyes of those who live within it. In this incident, legitimacy was severely eroded, not only because of what Nifong said and did, but because he leveraged other communicators to magnify his message. This section briefly describes how he did so, then examines communication strategies through which legal legitimacy was repaired.

In the weeks after Mangum made her accusation, Nifong granted dozens of interviews with news organizations. In these statements, he repeatedly asserted that a particularly brutal rape had occurred and that the lacrosse team was stonewalling his investigation (Mosteller, 2008; Williamson, 2007). This was ethically problematic because he had a duty to refrain from public statements that could prejudice a jury. Extreme examples included Nifong's calling the three defendants "hooligans" whose wealthy "daddies" "could buy them expensive lawyers" ("Complaints against Nifong," 2006, para. 3; "Duke rape suspects," 2006, para. 16–17). In addition, Nifong violated the prosecutor's fiduciary duty to disclose potentially exculpatory evidence. This occurred in late 2006, when he should have informed the defense that tests had found DNA from four men—unrelated to Duke or the lacrosse team—on Mangum and her clothing (Williamson, p. 6). Ultimately, Nifong was undone partly through scrutiny by the very mass media he had used as a soapbox. In 2007 he was formally punished by disbarment and one night in jail. But the public—the group needed to legitimate the overall legal system—had gained their knowledge through the media, and initially that knowledge primarily reflected Nifong's views. The media then joined defense attorneys in uncovering facts that eventually exposed Nifong's lies.

With the tables turned and Nifong facing justice, it was possible to heal the attenuated public confidence in the system. When public arguers address such situations, a range of frameworks are at their disposal. For example, explanatory templates could have highlighted the historical origins of stereotypes that separated town and gown in Durham. These tensions might have helped explain why local law-enforcement officials charged students perceived as privileged elites (Turnage, 2009, pp. 143–145). Rush (2009) concluded that "the town-gown relationship between Durham and Duke continues to reflect a tension associated not only with economic disparities, but also with racial divisions and memories of longstanding injustices" (p. 61). Another explanatory template could have used presentist frameworks to blame amorphous "media," "society," or others. Defendant Reade Seligmann used a permutation of this:

> This entire experience has opened my eyes up to a tragic world of injustice I never knew existed…. If police officers and a district attorney can systematically railroad us with absolutely no evidence whatsoever, I can't imagine what they'd do to people who do not have the resources to defend themselves…. The Duke lacrosse case has shown that our society has lost sight of the most fundamental principle of our legal system: the presumption of innocence. (Quoted in Wilson & Barstow, 2007, para. 11–12)

Thus, public legal vindication of the defendants allowed the rich to pontificate on legal protection for the poor, a move that symbolically closed traumatic social wounds.

At the same time, people sought *individuated* culpability. Cooper, the State Attorney General, faced key decisions about placing blame. Mangum stood by her claims, which was viewed as proof that she believed them. She was not charged with making false statements. Nevertheless, Cooper declared that there was "no credible evidence that an attack had occurred" (Wilson & Barstow, 2007, para. 3). Rather than arguing that prosecutors had failed to make a case, he took the unusual step of declaring the accused players innocent. He had no trouble individuating blame on Nifong. The latter's actions were considered so egregious that Nifong was refused state aid when he faced civil and criminal action (Blythe & Dees, 2008). Chairman F. Lane Williamson, in a June 2007 North Carolina Bar disciplinary hearing, did not focus on decisions made by other legal actors who might have supported the initial rush to judgment, but rather on Nifong's activities. Williamson conjectured that Nifong was swayed by the fact that he faced an election and was "politically naïve" (p. 17). Williamson added:

> This matter appears to be an aberration…in the life and career of Michael Nifong. It appears to be an aberration in the way justice is handled in North Carolina.… [P]robably any one of us could be faced with a situation at some point that would test our good character and we would prove wanting. (Williamson, 2007, p. 19)

Given the context of international media coverage and the accompanying perceptual fallout, we can see why Williamson defended the broader legal community. It was part of necessary repair to the overall system. It was critical to reestablishing the presumption of innocence—and public confidence that the presumption would be respected. Williamson singled out Nifong and juxtaposed him with hardworking prosecutors who were characterized as "ethical" defenders of justice (p. 20). The potential victims, including Mangum and the three former defendants, now included the North Carolina Bar Association—and by extension the entire system of jurisprudence. Williamson used a metaphor of a foundering ship that had "righted itself." Once it had done so, "a declaration of innocence" was warranted (Williamson, 2007, pp. 20–21). This type of declarative framing treated the hearing as a cleansing forum that avoided a "media frenzy" (p. 20). By distancing the system from the aberrant behavior of one rogue prosecutor, legal actors restored the perception of an ethical legal process.

THE JOURNALISTIC CONTEXT AND TREATMENT

Sex and crime have always figured prominently in American journalism. Beyond the salacious nature of the allegations, there were other reasons why news organizations around the world deemed it worth reporting. Many journalists joined what could be termed a "rush to social justice"—coverage that appeared driven by a desire to prevent gender, race, class, and privilege from influencing equal protection of the law. As famously phrased by Finley Peter Dunne's fictitious Mr. Dooley, journalism "comforts th' afflicted [and] afflicts th' comfortable" (Dunne, 1902, p. 240).

Although the Duke case seemed ready-made for journalists to facilitate justice, the opposite happened. The news media empowered Nifong by reporting his falsehoods and distortions. Such coverage indeed afflicted the comfortable—and violated their presumption of innocence. How this happened has more to do with journalists' values and routines than it does with bias. To illuminate those values and routines, this section is organized by three of the four main elements of the Society of Professional Journalists' *Code of Ethics* (SPJ, 1996): "Seek Truth and Report It," "Minimize Harm," and "Be Accountable." The SPJ Code lacks enforcement provisions, but its elements are widely accepted normative guides for individuals and organizations (Meyer, 1987, pp. 17–23; Wilkins & Brennen, 2004). In this case, journalists violated the first and second elements. Journalists had mixed success with the third. Before proceeding, we distinguish between journalists—the news media—and "the media." We do not address pundits, "talking heads," or bloggers—all of whom added fuel to the media firestorm.

Seek Truth and Report It

The first element of the SPJ *Code of Ethics* (1996) begins, "Journalists should be honest, fair and courageous in gathering, reporting and interpreting information." It also enjoins, "Test the accuracy of information from all sources" (SPJ, 1996). The Duke case represented a primary failure. Much reporting was superficial and one-sided, but it is useful to examine it in context.

Typically, a public official on the record constitutes the gold standard of journalistic attribution. Crime reporting is overwhelmingly driven by official sources, as Taslitz (2009) points out: "Reporters are thus dependent, at least early in a news cycle, on police and prosecutors for quick information that the reporters highly prize to meet pressing deadlines. The result is relatively one-sided, antidefendant coverage" (p. 184). But why did journalists fail to "test the accuracy of information from all sources"? Part of the answer lies in journalists' sensitivity to alleged victims of sex crimes—which, as shown below, is precisely what the SPJ Code prescribes. Thus, "cops-and-courts" routines influenced how truth was gathered—how much, and through what figurative (and literal) lenses. Another framework was equally limiting. Some news organizations, including *The New York Times*, assigned sports reporters to the story. That appalled some observers (Barnett, 2008; Taylor & Johnson, 2007, p. 122), but it reflects journalistic routines more than bias. An alleged rape is a crime story; an alleged rape by high-profile athletes falls into a gray area between the crime and sports beats. For reporters outside the area, the involvement of elite athletes was the only newsworthy element.

The above pertains to seeking truth. Reporting truth created additional problems. One provision in the SPJ Code reads, "Make certain that headlines, news teases and promotional material…[do] not oversimplify or highlight incidents out of context" (SPJ, 1996). The nature of the case virtually guaranteed that this would happen. For example, the Raleigh *News & Observer* ran a March 2006 profile of the accuser. Headlined "Dancer Gives Details of Ordeal," the article portrayed her surrounded by team members "barking racial slurs" before she was raped, sodomized, and strangled (Khanna & Blythe, 2006, para. 2 & 6). An editorial in the Durham *Herald-Sun* opined that "There's no question the student-athletes were probably guilty of all the usual offenses—underage drinking, loud partying, obnoxious behavior. But the allegations of rape bring the students' arrogant frat-boy culture to a whole new, sickening level" ("Outrage," 2006, p. A8). Such treatment went national with a May 2006 *Newsweek* cover story headlined "Sex, Lies & Duke" (Meadows & Thomas, 2006).

Ideally, accurate reporting can expedite the search for truth, and several news outlets did. Among them was Duke's student newspaper, *The Chronicle*, which questioned its professional counterparts (Mueller, 2004). Television put a human face on the accused when *60 Minutes'* Ed Bradley interviewed the three defendants, and the Raleigh *News & Observer*'s Joseph Neff amassed evidence to eventually debunk Nifong's assertions (Smolkin, 2007). Overall, then, journalists fulfilled the truth imperative imperfectly, reporting rumors as well as facts and reporting facts without context. Context is key, as the Hutchins Commission on Freedom of the Press (1947) argued in its milestone assessment of journalistic freedom and responsibility. It wrote, "It is no longer enough to report the fact truthfully. It is now necessary to report the truth about the fact" (p. 22). By failing to provide contextual truth, the news media misinformed the public and violated the players' presumption of innocence.

Minimize Harm

This SPJ Code provision reflects the informal utilitarianism commonly found within journalists' ethical reasoning (Elliott, 2007; Wilkins & Coleman, 2005). Rather than a Hippocratic "do no harm," the SPJ Code implies that there are times when journalists will cause harm and presumably justify it by showing how it contributes to a greater good. This section stipulates, "Ethical journalists treat sources, subjects and colleagues as human beings deserving of respect." Subpoints include: "Be cautious about identifying…victims of sex crimes"; "Show compassion for those who may be affected adversely by news coverage"; and "Recognize that gathering and reporting information may cause harm or discomfort" (SPJ, 1996).

Pervasive practice among American news media is not to name victims of sexual assault, but some journalists have challenged it, sparking major debates (Overholser, 1989). The reasoning behind not naming alleged victims is that the nature of sexual assault would subject accusers to humiliation if their names were disclosed—and possibly deter them from reporting assaults. In this case, anonymity complicated the search for truth. Because Mangum was not identified, it was hard to subject her claims to scrutiny. Indeed, "no mainstream outlets released her identity before the prosecution dropped rape charges in December 2006" (Dadisman, 2007, p. 22). *Newsweek* was typical, noting that it, "like most news organizations, does not identify alleged rape victims" (Meadows & Thomas, 2006, para. 13). After all charges were dropped, the Raleigh *News & Observer* named Mangum. The editor explained that senior staffers had "consulted a number of people with an interest in these issues, among them advocates for sexual assault victims, defense lawyers, [and] current and former journalists" (Sill, 2007, para. 4, 6). The Associated Press did not name Mangum until October 2008, when she published a book and "came out publicly on her own" (Walker & Beard, 2008, para. 16).

Some details of the SPJ Code appear almost poignant in this case. Instead of minimizing harm, members of the media subjected the accused to extensive coverage. When the 46 subpoenaed players arrived at a lab to provide DNA samples, they were met by a horde of journalists, and it became "the grandest of perp walks" (Yaeger & Pressler, 2007, p. 76). When lacrosse coach Mike Pressler resigned under pressure, he returned home to find that "TV trucks were everywhere.... There was a...TV helicopter hovering over the house. It was a media circus outside my door" (Yaeger & Pressler, 2007, p. 176). In these incidents there was little "compassion for those who may be affected adversely by news coverage" (SPJ, 1996). It is ironic that Finley Peter Dunne's "comfort the afflicted" quip was originally part of a larger complaint against the excessive power of newspapers. Only later did it become a call for social justice. Had journalists focused their watchdog role on Nifong, they might have helped to more quickly debunk the charges. Instead, they enabled him to actively undermine the presumption of innocence.

In this regard, the Duke case resembled recent celebrity trials, including those of former football player O. J. Simpson in 1995 and basketball star Kobe Bryant in 2004. (In the racial context of this case, it is noteworthy that both men are African American.) Simpson was acquitted of murdering his ex-wife and a friend after a nearly yearlong trial surrounded by blanket media coverage—much of which presumed his guilt. Bryant was accused of raping a hotel employee, but charges were dismissed when his accuser refused to testify. Here, too, the case was subject to pervasive pretrial publicity. Other nations have acknowledged the danger inherent in such publicity. In the United Kingdom, legal tradition favors fair-trial rights over free-press rights. In order to preserve jury impartiality, journalists are routinely barred from reporting on a case until proceedings begin (Bicket, 1998).

Be Accountable

In this case, a key contrast stands out: Nifong was held formally accountable, but journalists were not. There were few consequences for members of the news media who had disseminated his statements. The accountability element of the SPJ Code begins, "Journalists are accountable to their readers, listeners, viewers and each other" (1996). Journalists are urged to "clarify and explain news coverage and invite dialogue with the public over journalistic conduct" and to "admit mistakes and correct them promptly" (SPJ, 1996). Journalists were cool to external criticism, but they critiqued themselves. Self-review occurred on vocational, institutional, and individual levels. The first has been problematic, as reflected in the history of the National News Council, which existed from 1971 to 1982 before dying from lack of support. Self-evaluation on the vocational level has mostly depended upon journalism reviews, media critics like *The Washington Post*'s Howard Kurtz, and associations like the Society of Professional Journalists. Of these, most visible are critics like Kurtz, who attacked what he called "aggravated media assault," predicting that "in all the coverage you read and see about the clearing of these young men, very little of it will be devoted to the media's role in ruining their lives" (Kurtz, 2007, para. 3 & 7).

Accountability was more tangible on institutional and individual levels. *The New York Times* and Raleigh *News & Observer* have reader representatives, and both criticized their newspapers. *Times* public editor Byron Calame skewered an August 2006 story bolstering the prosecution, and he concluded that the story was not presented impartially (Calame, 2007). The *News & Observer*'s Ted Vaden declared, "In that 20-20 rear-view mirror...more skepticism would have been in order" (Vaden, 2007, para. 25). On the individual level, *New York Times* columnist David Brooks (2006) was quick to acknowledge guilt, writing that "simple decency requires that we... correct the slurs that were uttered by millions of people, including me" (para. 2). Ruth Sheehan, a columnist for the Raleigh *News & Observer*, apologized for accusing team members of stonewalling. "Members of the men's Duke lacrosse team: I am sorry," she wrote (Sheehan, 2007, para. 1). "Rest assured, I know my errors" (para. 19). These expressions of accountability reflect an ongoing journalistic interest in transparency and civic engagement seen recently in the public journalism movement in the United States (Merritt, 1998) and international efforts to increase trust between journalists and citizens (Myburg, 2009). In this case, however, apologies did not undo the damage.

CONCLUSIONS

This case illustrates the importance of multiple perspectives on communication and the ambiguities that result when legal and ethical assessments intersect. Individuals in three vocations had guiding principles, but their actions reflected personal agendas and institutional constraints that subsumed good intentions. As shown above, some communication content and strategies caused harm, but there is scant evidence that any academician, lawyer, or journalist was motivated by malice. (Nifong's motives, however, will likely remain a mystery.) *The great irony of the Duke case is that ethical actors trying to achieve social justice undermined formal justice.* That is the crux of our argument: No matter how pure the motives, individuals, groups, and even powerful organizations are not free to impose their sense of justice to replace well-defined, properly established systems of public justice. For example, Black (2000) argues that the International Criminal Tribunal for the Former Yugoslavia did just that. Set up, he claims, largely at the behest of the United States to punish former Serb leader Slobodan Milosevic and his sympathizers, the tribunal meant that "private justice has replaced public justice...even the appearance of fundamental justice has been replaced by an open contempt of justice" (p. 29). "The rhetoric used to justify such a body to the general public," continues Black, "was, of course, heavily seasoned with concerns for human rights, the dignity of the individual...and democracy" (p. 29). The tribunal proclaimed its commitment to the presumption of innocence, yet the court itself leveled charges after a prima facie case had been advanced, and upon arrest, detention was automatic (p. 38).

Black's critique illuminates the Duke case by offering a richer understanding of how individual and group motives interact in the pursuit of justice. Whether through an international tribunal or a "listening" statement, groups sought justice through alternative channels. At Duke, the motives were often as noble as academicians trying to inform the public about larger social issues and to right historical wrongs. But this proved perilous. By the time the formal justice system resolved the situation, the accused had already been punished, violating the full meaning of the presumption of innocence asserted by Quintard-Morenas (2010). He reasons: "If accusation does not equate conviction and if only conviction triggers punishment, it follows that suspects must be treated in a manner consistent with their status" (p. 5). That did not happen here.

This is also significant for people intensely involved in communication with various audiences. Although journalists (unlike lawyers) are not bound by professional rules, most American practitioners claim quasi-professional status, as indicated in the name of the Society of Professional Journalists. Nevertheless, the hallmarks of professionalism—credentialing, licensure, formal censure, or expulsion—would conflict with First Amendment protections and another main element of the SPJ Code of Ethics, "Act Independently." The problem was that the mere existence of a code was insufficient to prevent harm. It did not stop the news media from being used by nonjournalists, Nifong in particular, to advance individual agendas. Lacking formal sanctions by their peers or others, many journalists and news organizations allowed competitive and market forces to guide their coverage. As a result, the defendants suffered humiliation, expense, and uncertain futures in an era when damage to one's reputation can persist via erroneous or outdated information online (Peltz, 2008). Some journalists attempted to mitigate the damage through public apologies. We suggest that had more individuals and news organizations done so, that might have replicated for journalists and their subjects the healing process that symbolically took place in the legal system.

This case also offers lessons relevant to theory about communication ethics. Academicians, lawyers, and journalists declared their dedication to truth, but ironically some communication strategies thwarted the discovery and dissemination of truth. Yaeger and Pressler (2007) underscored this in their book title: *It's Not about the Truth*. They argued that some academic actors were less interested in actual facts than in how they would be perceived. In the legal realm, Nifong was found guilty of sharing incomplete truth in violation of discovery laws. As journalists' apologies indicated, some allowed their desires to beat competitors and tell a good story trump their better judgment about what was factual. In each instance, we believe, the end of social justice was used to justify the means. Although we do not suggest that this lessens the value of consequentialist ethical approaches, it hints at their limitations. Ultimately, this was more than merely an unfortunate collision of events and motives. Similar situations have occurred previously and will again. When they do, we hope that ethical agents will pay particular attention to the effect, not just the intent, of their communication.

NOTE

1. We acknowledge the racial element of this case and argue that it connects to other nations. Although our study of the racialized discourses surrounding Mangum's allegations focuses primary attention on U.S. rhetorics, many of the tropes and other figurations are symbolically linked to a host of global and (post)colonial symbolic constructs. Goldfield (1991) argued that U.S. racial tensions have origins in class conflicts tracing back to European feudalism and persisting in "the ominous rise in racist incidents on campuses and in cities" (p. 133). Gilroy (1999) argued that a "syncretic pattern" (p. 3) existed between racial politics and the ways communities in the Caribbean, Great Britain, the United States, and Africa inscribed class conflicts.

REFERENCES

Allen, A. T., (2007, November). Duke's reign of terror. *Raleigh Metro* magazine. Retrieved from http://www.metronc.com/article/index.aspx?id=1448

Baker, H. A., Jr. (2006, March 29). Awaiting the restoration of confidence: A letter to the Duke University administration. Retrieved from http://www.dukenews.duke.edu/mmedia/features/lacrosse_incident/lange_baker.html

Barnett, B. A. (2008, May). *Sports talk: How the news media framed the Duke University lacrosse case.* Paper presented at the annual meeting of the International Communication Association, Montreal, Canada. Retrieved from http://www.allacademic.com/meta/p230225_index.html

Baydoun, N., & Good, R. S. (2007). *A rush to injustice: How power, prejudice, racism, and political correctness overshadowed truth and justice in the Duke lacrosse rape case.* Nashville, TN: Thomas Nelson.

Bicket, D. (1998). Drifting apart together: Diverging conceptions of free expression in the North American judicial tradition. *Communications & the Law, 20*(4), 1–38.

Black, C. (2000). The International Criminal Tribunal for the former Yugoslavia: Impartial? *Mediterranean Quarterly, 11*(2), 29–40.

Blythe, A., & Dees, M. (2008, January 16). Nifong files for bankruptcy; city replies to suit. *Newsobserver.com.* Retrieved from http://www.newsobserver.com/news/crime_safety/story/91745.html?storylink= mirelated

Brodhead, R. H. (2006, March 28). Duke suspends men's lacrosse games pending clearer resolution of legal situation. Duke Office of News and Communications. Retrieved from http://dukenews.duke.edu/2006/03/lacrossestatement.html

Brooks, D. (2006, May 28). The Duke witch hunt. *Nytimes.com.* Retrieved from http://select.nytimes.com/2006/05/28/opinion/28brooks.html

Byers, M., & Johnson, V. (2009). *The CSI effect.* Lanham, MD: Lexington Books,

Calame, B. (2007, April 22). Revisiting the Times's coverage of the Duke rape case. *The New York Times,* p. 12.

Carrington et al. v. Duke University et al. (2008, February 21). In the United States District Court for the Middle District of North Carolina, No. 1:08-cv-119. *Justia.com.* Retrieved from http://docs.justia.com/cases/federal/district-courts/north-carolina/ncmdce/1:2008cv00119/47871/1/0.pdf

Chafe, W. (2006, March 31). Sex and race. *Duke Chronicle.* Retrieved from http://media.www.dukechronicle.com/media/storage/paper884/news/2006/03/31/Columns/Sex-And.Race-1775544.shtml

Chalmers, S. W. (2007). Police department report on Duke lacrosse investigation. City of Durham Police Department. Retrieved from http://www.durhamnc.gov/news/files/dl_police_report.pdf

Complaints against Nifong. (2006, December 3). *News & Observer.* Retrieved from http://www.newsobserver.com/1185/story/517202.html

Concerned Faculty (n.d.). An open letter to the Duke community. Retrieved from http://www.concerneddukefaculty.org

Cooper, R. (2007a). Durham County Superior Court case file Nos. 06 CRS 4332-4336, 5582-5583. Summary of conclusions. *Findlaw.com.* Retrieved from http://fl1.findlaw.com/news.findlaw.com/hdocs/docs/duke/ncdoj42707rpt.pdf

Cooper, R. (2007b). Comments by Attorney General Roy Cooper: State vs. Finnerty, Evans, Seligmann. *NCDOJ.com.* Retrieved from http://www.ncdoj.com/News-and-Alerts/News-Releases-and-Advisories/Press-Releases/AG-Cooper-dismisses-charges-in-Duke-Lacrosse-case.aspx

Dadisman, S. (2007, August/September). Naming names. *American Journalism Review, 29*(4), 22–23.

Duke rape suspects speak out. (2006, October 15). *CBS News, 60 Minutes.* Retrieved from http://www.cbsnews.com/stories/2006/10/11/60minutes/main2082140.shtml

Duke University (2008). Faculty handbook. Office of the Provost. Retrieved from http://www.provost.duke.edu/pdfs/fhb/FHB.pdf

Dunne, F. P. (1902). *Observations by Mr. Dooley.* New York: Harper & Brothers.

Elliott, D. (2007). Getting Mill right. *Journal of Mass Media Ethics, 22*(2–3), 100–112.

Feldstein, M. (2007, Spring). Media coverage and a federal grand jury: Publication of the secret Watergate transcripts. *American Journalism, 24*(2), 7–33.

Gilroy, P. (1999). *The black Atlantic: Modernity and double consciousness.* Cambridge, MA: Harvard University Press.

Goldfield, M. (1991). The color of politics in the United States: White supremacy as the main explanation for the peculiarities of American politics from colonial times to the present. In D. Lacapra, (Ed.), *The bounds of race: Perspectives on hegemony and resistance* (pp. 104–133). Ithaca, NY: Cornell University Press.

Hazard, G. C., & Dondi, A. (2004). *Legal ethics: A comparative study*. Palo Alto, CA: Stanford University Press.

Hutchins Commission on Freedom of the Press. (1947). *A free and responsible press*. Chicago, IL: University of Chicago Press.

Johnson, K. C. (2007, February 14). When the potbangers were riding high. [Durham-in-Wonderland blog]. Retrieved from http://durhamwonderland.blogspot.com/2007/02/when-potbangers-were-riding-high.html

Khanna, S., & Blythe, A. (2006, March 25). Dancer gives details of ordeal. *Newsobserver.com*. Retrieved from http://www.newsobserver.com/news/crime_safety/duke_lacrosse/story/421799.html

Kurtz, H. (2007, April 12). Media miscarriage. *Washingtonpost.com*. Retrieved from http://www.washingtonpost.com/wp-dyn/content/blog/2007/04/12/BL2007041200585.html

Lehman-Wilzig, S. N. (2003, January/February). Political ill-health coverage: Professional-ethical questions regarding news reporting of leaders' ailments. *Journal of Health Communication*, *8*(1), 59–77.

Listening statement. (2006, April 6). *The Chronicle*, p. 5.

Meadows, S., & Thomas, E. (2006, May 1). What happened at Duke? *Newsweek.com*. Retrieved from http://www.newsweek.com/id/52444output/print

Menkel-Meadow, C. (2000). Telling stories in school: Using case studies and stories to teach legal ethics. *Fordham Law Review*, *69*, 787–816.

Merritt, D. (1998). *Public journalism and public life: Why telling the news is not enough*. Mahwah, NJ: Erlbaum.

Meyer, P. (1987). *Ethical journalism*. New York: Longman.

Miller, S. (2007, February 26). Racial hypocrisy. *Duke Chronicle*. Retrieved from http://media.www.duke-chronicle.com/media/storage/paper884/news/2007/02/26/Columns/Racial.Hypocrisy-2742874.shtml

Mosteller, R. P. (2008). Exculpatory evidence, ethics, and the road to the disbarment of Mike Nifong: The critical importance of full open-file discovery. *George Mason Law Review*, *15*, 257–318.

Mueller, A. G. (2004, Winter). Affirming denial through preemptive apologia: The case of the Armenian Genocide Resolution. *Western Journal of Communication*, *68*(1), 24–44.

Myburg, M. (2009). More public and less experts: A normative framework for reconnecting the work of journalists with the work of citizens. *Global Media Journal*, *3*(1), 1–14.

Outrage at lacrosse players. (2006, March 28). *The Herald-Sun*, p. A8.

Overholser, G. (1989, July 11). Why hide rapes? *The New York Times*, p. A19.

Peltz, R. J. (2008). Fifteen minutes of infamy: Privileged reporting and the problem of perpetual reputational harm. *Ohio Northern University Law Review*, *34*(3), 717–754.

Perkins, M. (2002). International law and the search for universal principles in journalism ethics. *Journal of Mass Media Ethics*, *17*, 193–208.

Perelman, C. (1980). *Justice, law, and argument*. Dordrecht, the Netherlands: Reidel.

Roach, K. (2005). Common law bills of rights as dialogue between courts and legislatures. *University of Toronto Law Journal*, *55*(3), 733–766.

Quintard-Morenas, F. (2010). The presumption of innocence in the French and Anglo-American legal traditions. *American Journal of Comparative Law*, *58*(1), 107–149.

Rush, S. (2009). The town-gown relationship. In M. L. Seigel, (Ed.), *Race to injustice: Lessons learned from the Duke lacrosse rape case* (pp. 55–78). Durham, NC: Carolina Academic Press.

Sheehan, R. (2007, April 23). To Duke accused: I'm sorry. *Newsobserver.com*. Retrieved from http://www.newsobserver.com/news/crime_safety/duke_lacrosse/v-print/story/566959.html

Sill, M. (2007, April 12). N&O's decision to identify accuser was made with care. *Newsobserver.com*. Retrieved from http://www.newsobserver.com/news/crime_safety_duke_lacrosse/v-print/story/563049.html

Smolkin, R. (2007, August/September). Justice delayed. *American Journalism Review*, *29*(4), 18–29.

Society of Professional Journalists (SPJ). (1996). Society of Professional Journalists code of ethics. Retrieved May 23, 2009, from http://www.spj.org/ethicscode.asp

Taslitz, A. E. (2009). The Duke lacrosse players and the media: Why the fair trial-free press paradigm doesn't cut it anymore. In M. L. Seigel (Ed.), *Race to injustice: Lessons learned from the Duke lacrosse rape case* (pp. 175–210). Durham, NC: Carolina Academic Press.

Taylor, S., & Johnson, K. C. (2007). *Until proven innocent: Political correctness and the shameful injustices of the Duke lacrosse rape case*. New York: St. Martin's.

Turnage, A. K. (2009). Scene, act, and the tragic frame in the Duke rape case. *Southern Communication Journal, 72*, 141–156.

Ugland, E., & Henderson, J. (2007). Who is a journalist and why does it matter? Disentangling the legal and ethical arguments. *Journal of Mass Media Ethics, 22*, 241–261.

Vaden, T. (2007, April 15). Assessing the N&O's lacrosse coverage. *Newsobserver.com*. Retrieved from http://www.newsobserver.com/opinion/vaden/v-print/story/564152.html

Walker, M. A., & Beard, A. (2008, October 23). Duke lacrosse accuser pens memoir about case. *USAToday. com*. Retrieved from http://www.usatoday.com/news/nation/2008-10-23-duke-lacrosse_N.htm

White, J. B. (1984). *When words lose their meaning*. Chicago: University of Chicago Press.

Wilkins, L., & Brennen, B. (2004). Conflicted interests, contested terrain: Journalism ethics codes then and now. *Journalism Studies, 5*, 297–309.

Wilkins, L., & Coleman, R. (2005). *The moral media: How journalists reason about ethics*. Mahwah, NJ: Erlbaum.

Williamson, F. L. (2007, June 16). Before the Disciplinary Hearing Commission of the North Carolina State Bar, 06 DHC 35. Excerpt transcript, findings of fact and conclusions of law. Retrieved from http://www.ncbar.com/discipline/printorder.asp?id=505

Wilson, D., & Barstow, D. (2007, April 12). All charges dropped in Duke case. *NYTimes.com*. Retrieved from http://ww.nyt.com/2007/04/12/us/12dukehtml

Yaeger, D., & Pressler, M. (2007). *It's not about the truth*. New York: Simon & Schuster.

Young, I. M. (1990). *Justice and the politics of difference*. Princeton, NJ: Princeton University Press.

17

Political Communication Ethics

Postmodern Opportunities and Challenges

Steven R. Goldzwig and Patricia A. Sullivan

In an article for *Daedalus*, Robert N. Bellah identifies a problem with the study of political communication and ethics that we address on a regular basis in our classrooms. He notes that it is commonplace for U.S. citizens to assume there is no relationship between politics and ethics. He says what the average U.S. citizen assumes about politics and ethics is not "nice." For many U.S. citizens, "Politics is a way some people get what they want by using undue influence, questionable tactics, even thinly veiled forms of bribery" (2007, p. 59). Those questionable tactics of course involve communication. Garofalo (2008) addresses cynicism about political ethics from a global perspective and claims that in "resolving such issues as inequality, poverty, and injustice, as well as corruption, the benefits of moral agency and moral competence, seem obvious" (p. 21).

Questions about political ethics were foregrounded for national and international audiences during the 2008 presidential campaign in the United States. As rhetorical critics our focus has been largely directed toward politics in the United States. However, as a result of the recent changes brought about by the election of Barack Obama to the U.S. presidency, we believe it prudent to focus our attention on the meaning of Obama's new presidency and recent developments in the United States in probing their intriguing implications for international relations. More specifically, we would like to rethink and reconfigure a viable political ethic at what seems to be a particularly opportune moment. Obama is now a world leader and has begun to exercise world leadership. We will argue that thus far Obama's rhetorical leadership has opened up new avenues for developing and extending a political ethic with both national and transnational implications.

In the wake of questions about President George W. Bush's ethics as a political communicator following the 9/11 attacks, audiences looked to Obama for a new type of moral leadership. His election attracted global interest. Modern technology permitted people around the world to participate in the inspirational journey of a young man who came from a humble background and overcame many obstacles to become the first Black man elected to serve as president of the United States. As Al-Ghitany (2008), Chief Editor of a Cairo-based weekly Egyptian newspaper *Akhbar al-Adab*, noted in an article for the Carnegie Endowment for International Peace, Obama's election was an enactment of the power of a democratic system: "There is no doubt that it is this environment that nourishes an individual's potential that allowed the United States to attain its leading place among nations." He further observed:

> If I had had a vote, I would have given it to Obama, with an enthusiasm I share with multitudes across Europe and around the world who understand the significance of such a man's arrival to the White House. The election of Obama is an important moment in human history because Obama's ancestors were slaves, most of whom died during the Middle Passage.

Additionally, Al-Ghitany commented that Obama's election was significant for international audiences because it represented a repudiation of "President [George W. Bush's] disastrous decisions."

Not only did Obama's election have international significance, but an article in *Advertising Age* claimed Obama's victory represented "an instant overhaul for tainted Brand America" (Wentz, 2008). After Obama's victory there was a national holiday declared in Kenya and residents of a town in Japan danced in the streets and did the hula. Certainly references to the efficacy of the Obama brand may detract from a focus on the importance of his power as a mediator and decision maker on the international stage. In a media-saturated age the presidential brand functions in the following way according to Nick Ragone, senior VP-director of client development at Omnicom Group's Ketchum in New York, and a presidential historian: "We've put a new face on [the U.S.], and that face happens to be African-American. It takes a lot of hubris and arrogance of the last eight years to put it in the rearview mirror for us" (as cited in Wentz, 2008).

Although there was an outpouring of sentiment nationally and internationally that Obama's victory represented an enactment of his "Change" slogan, a number of contexts in Campaign 2008 and in the early months of the Obama presidency had the potential to prompt audiences to wonder if ethical political communication could be maintained in an age dominated by mediated communication, especially the Internet. The candidates, their surrogates, media sources, and voters engaged in questionable communication when evaluated from a range of ethical perspectives. Some ethical communication lapses might seem obvious, regardless of perspective. For example, a CD of *Barack the Magic Monkey*, set to the tune of *Puff the Magic Dragon*, was played by U.S. talk radio host Rush Limbaugh in 2007. The tune was a staple on YouTube. During President Obama's first 100 days, the *New York Post* ran a cartoon depicting the president as a monkey. Another example, "Rattling the Cage: Played for a Sucker," an article from the *Jerusalem Post*, was reprinted online at WatchingAmerica.com. The article was accompanied by a digitally modified photo of President Obama wearing a court jester's hat. In the United States a poster depicting President Obama as The Joker, Batman's nemesis, appeared at a number of rallies to protest policy changes advocated by the administration. The image spread virally via the Internet. As euphoria over the President's victory dissipated, inflammatory images of the President served as distractions from and additional impediments to the policies he was advocating.

During Campaign 2008 and in the early months of his presidency more subtle questions were raised about Obama's approach to decision making. These types of questions call for a different type of scrutiny. Depending on the ethical perspective used to frame the analysis, the following communication examples might be judged ethical or unethical. As a candidate, did Obama go "far enough" in addressing racial tensions in the United States when he gave a speech on race on March 18, 2008? Some critics questioned whether Obama's speech was primarily reactive in responding to questions about the Rev. Jeremiah Wright's involvement as an informal advisor to the campaign. He referred to Rev. Wright's sermons and gaffes from the other campaigns as distractions, and offered a litany of parallelisms. Obama said that, "This time we want" to address real questions facing the nation (Obama, 2008). But did he go far enough in addressing racial inequality in the United States? Furthermore, did he have the ethical responsibility to address this issue for national and international audiences?

As Obama advocated for healthcare reform in the early months of his presidency, some observers, including former U.S. President Jimmy Carter, suggested that attacks on Obama were racially motivated. For the most part, however, Obama steered away from discussions about race during the campaign and in the early months of his presidency. Some felt Obama still had an ob-ligation to address issues associated with race more directly. An article in the *Belfast Telegraph* did not question Obama's reticence to address race, but raised a larger question about the quality of his leadership. The article posed this question: "Has Obama got the true grit to show his critics who is boss?" (Dee, 2009).

National and international sources thus have questioned whether President Obama has a responsibility to be more direct in addressing issues. A range of ethical perspectives could be brought to bear to make judgments about what might seem to many like a nonconfrontational, passionless, and therefore impotent approach to policy implementation. Judgments about the ethics of the President's communication may vary. During Campaign 2008, however, some com-munication of Obama's opponents, regardless of perspective, was clearly unethical. For example, McCain supporters and his vice-presidential running mate Sarah Palin referred to Obama as a "terrorist." McCain's response to his supporters concerning the labeling of Obama invites closer scrutiny from a range of ethical perspectives. In October McCain received positive media cover-age for speaking out and defending Obama as a Christian, a "decent family man" (Dougherty, 2008). The defense came in response to a supporter who referred to Obama as an Arab and a "secret Muslim." McCain's response begged the question whether Obama could be an Arab and a Muslim *and* a decent family man. Did media sources covering this defense have an ethical responsibility to further interrogate McCain's response?

As Campaign 2008 concluded, a column published in *The Washington Post* referred to 2008 as a "year of the woman." The writer grouped together the campaigns of Hillary Rodham Clinton and Sarah Palin and declared:

As Election Day nears, it's clear that gender was not a disqualifying factor for either Clinton or Palin. Voters who turned against them did so for other reasons, just as they do with male candi-dates. Women from both parties also perceived with satisfaction a heightened emphasis on their issues in this year's race. (Romano, 2008)

The article was accompanied by a cropped photo of a little girl peering at Sarah Palin's peep-toe shoes. Did commentators have an ethical responsibility to interrogate this image as an appropriate interpretation of the "year of the woman"?

In this essay we will cover perspectives that offer possibilities for judging ethics in a range of political communication contexts. Bellah (2007) suggests current democratic politics "are bad and we need to reform them" (p. 59). Gastil (2008) asks us to consider a reformation of demo-cratic politics to promote ethical communication through deliberation. Bellah (2007) questions if it is even possible to have ethical politics: "Can a society that has become a kind of monarchial machine run by private ambition, effectively lacking in virtue and human goodness, be able to face the enormous ethical problems of the world today?" (p. 65). For Arnett, Arneson, and Bell (2006) the answer to this question is the development of an approach to communication ethics for "an era of competing narrative and virtue structures" (p. 64).

In their review of communication ethics scholarship, Arnett, Arneson, and Bell identify three approaches that mark the writing in this area. A prescriptive approach suggests universal stan-dards to judge communication behaviors as ethical or unethical, and "omits the reality of dif-fering standpoints" (p. 63). A descriptive approach, exemplified in Alasdair MacIntyre's *After Virtue*, looks to communication situations and practices to identify "changing character types" (1984, p. 63). Finally, following Arnett, Arneson, and Bell, the problems identified by Bellah seem to call for a dialogic approach, "a turn responsive to a historical moment in which negotiating contending social goods in an era of narrative and virtue contention is normative communication competence" (p. 63).

When we trace approaches to communication ethics in political contexts, it will become clear that most scholars have moved away from prescriptive models in suggesting possibilities for negotiating ethics along a continuum that balances the interests of individuals and community, private and public spheres. First we provide brief overviews of characterological, feminist, and postmodernist approaches to rhetoric. We then propose a framework for judging the ethicality of political messages in a postmodern era. Finally, we pose questions that point to issues implied in our framework and test it by applying it to illustrations from a range of political communication contexts.

CHARACTEROLOGICAL APPROACHES TO COMMUNICATION ETHICS

A characterological approach to ethics is grounded in the assumption that rhetorical choices and practices reflect a communicator's individual moral compass. Contemporary scholars have turned to the Ancients in formulating ethical approaches centered on the character of the rhetor. Aristotle's *Nichomachean Ethics* (trans., 1980) and *Rhetoric* (trans., 1991) provide inspiration for contemporary scholars to frame ethical approaches grounded in the virtuous conduct of the communicator. In the *Ethics* Aristotle identifies what constitutes virtuous conduct by observing the communication of political actors. Ethical communicators make ethical choices and thus manifest virtuous character. An ethical communicator has internalized virtues to guide his or her rhetorical choices.

For Quintilian the habit of making sound choices translated into the "good man speaking well." The Ancients assumed that a male rhetor from an aristocratic social class would have internalized proper virtues and his actions would be guided by *phronesis* or practical wisdom. Gronbeck (2000) provides an overview of ethical criteria for judging the performance of political candidates:

> The good man, to Quintilian, was the product of a careful upbringing and education, a person steeped in the social wisdom of the culture and tutored for public life.... The person had to be "good" ethically and civically, and the message had to be the product of systematic preparation and doxastic thought, that is, well considered and sensitive to the beliefs, attitudes, and values of the population to which it would be delivered. (p. 9)

Although the concept of a "good man speaking well" might seem antithetical to contemporary audiences for whom, as Bellah (2007) notes, politics comes close to being unethical "almost by definition," Gronbeck observes that there is a tendency among voters to focus on the rhetor in an effort to "hold somebody responsible for campaign messages" (p. 9). In Campaign 2008, for example, John McCain and his supporters suggested that Barack Obama's associations with Jeremiah Wright, a controversial pastor, and Bill Ayers, a cofounder of the Weatherman Underground in the 1960s, said something about character. Critics implied Obama could not be a virtuous person if he had such associations.

Scholars who have turned to the Ancients in theorizing about rhetoric and ethics often have relied on MacIntyre's *After Virtue* for inspiration. Condit (1987) questions this reliance on MacIntyre's work because she claims it encourages the "privatization of morality" and, in like manner, challenges the work of Fisher (1984) and Frentz (1985). For Condit, MacIntyre's virtue ethics speaks to a morality that trades in abstractions about the common good and fails to see how virtue is enacted "as a collective craft" (p. 94). She argues for viewing morality as a craft which allows "a perfecting of action through meaning" (p. 94). Moreover, from our perspective, rhetoric, as an art of crafting community helps build and sustain the polity and thus plays an integral part in building and maintaining ethical principles and practices—both past and present.

A number of feminist scholars have challenged characterological approaches to rhetoric as framed according to masculine-associated values. These feminist scholars agree that ethical rhetoric is an art of crafting community. Although feminist scholars do not reject traditional approaches to rhetoric, they offer additional perspectives, grounded in the experiences of women, in their quest to identify what it means to engage in ethical persuasion.

FEMINIST APPROACHES

Feminist approaches to ethics challenge the traditional Aristotelian definition of rhetoric "as an ability, in each [particular] case, to see the available means of persuasion" (I 13355, pp. 36–37). In an early article challenging traditional approaches to rhetoric as reflecting patriarchal value systems, Gearhart (1979) argues that the Aristotelian approach to persuasion is manipulative and centered on converting the audience to a particular viewpoint. In associating this approach to persuasion with patriarchal value system*s,* Gearhart's assumptions parallel scholars such as Spender (1980) who claims that in Western societies privileged men have had the power to name. Spender says: "When one has the power to name, it appears that one can structure almost any reality without undue interference from the evidence" (p. 176).

Communication scholars, inspired by the work of writers such as Gearhart, Spender, and others (Belenky, Clinchy, Goldberger, & Tarule, 1986; Daly, 1978; Gilligan, 1982; Minow, 1990; Noddings, 1984; Tronto, 1993) attempt to define approaches to persuasion and decision making to reflect alternative value systems (e.g., K. A. Foss & S. K. Foss, 1983, 1989, 1994; S. K. Foss & K. A. Foss, 1988; S. K. Foss & Griffin, 1992, 1995; Sullivan & Goldzwig, 1995; Tonn, 1992, 1996; Wood, 1992, 1994).

Foss and Griffin's (1995) theory of an invitational rhetoric represents one attempt to bring an alternative value system, grounded in an "ethic of relations," to the study of rhetoric. The theory generated controversy and was recently revisited by Bone, Griffin, and Scholz (2008). Foss and Griffin identify qualities which invite communicators to engage in dialogue rather than debate. Although they do not reject traditional approaches to rhetoric, they question a privileging of rhetoric defined as persuasion or a commitment to power over others and changing their viewpoints. Their alternative is defined as "an invitation to understanding as a means to create a relationship rooted in equality, immanent value, and self-determination" (p. 5). They also define external conditions—safety, value, freedom—that invite dialogue.

Feminist perspectives emphasize attention to context and dialogue, and in some ways parallel postmodern theorizing on rhetoric, ethics, and politics. Feminist scholars turn to women's experiences to identify qualities associated with dialogic communication. Scholars who theorize about ethics and postmodernity ask what it means to engage in dialogue and communicate ethically in an era of uncertainty, difference, and diversity.

POSTMODERNIST APPROACHES

As Arnett, Fritz, and Bell (2009) suggest, communication in a postmodern era roughly defined as encompassing the middle of the 20th century to today, is marked by an unusual basis for common ground. Common ground in this era is established through a recognition of "the inability to agree with one another" (p. 13). Furrow (1995) speaks to the importance of this perspective for framing a postmodern ethic and argues: "The virtue of such a position is that it allows us to conceptualize ethics and politics only minimally on shared beliefs" (pp. xix–xx). Just as feminist scholars suggest we can learn by entering into dialogue with those with whom we disagree, so do postmodernist scholars.

A postmodern world of narrative disjunctions and "contending views of the good" (Arnett, Fritz, & Bell, 2009) has implications for political rhetoric and ethics. A postmodern approach to ethics and politics must go beyond the campaign context as a frame for the study of political communication. Texts such as *Handbook of Political Communication Research* (Kaid, 2004) and *Readings on Political Communication* (Sheckels, Muir, Robertson, & Gring-Premble, 2007) use campaigns as a reference point and cover topics such as political messages, public opinion, debates, and advertising. The political campaign approach addresses how communication during elections has been transformed by influences such as the Internet. The campaign frame, however, invites critics to focus on the ethical behavior of the individual as a political communicator. What might a broader approach to political communication suggest for the study of ethics? In seeking to answer this question we acknowledge that critics and audiences alike often adopt characterological frames of reference and there is no reason to assume that these interpretive frames will dissipate in the near future. Nevertheless, we believe the cues we have derived from feminist and postmodern perspectives position us to advance a viable national and international political ethic in an environment of globalization, burgeoning computer mediated technologies, and the complex panoply of emerging forms of social media that are inserting themselves into the mix.

POSTMODERNISM, ETHICS, AND ISSUES IN POLITICAL COMMUNICATION

A postmodern approach invites scholars to frame studies of rhetoric, politics, and ethics more capaciously. How do we move along a continuum of political rhetoric from Quintilian's "good man speaking well" to the influence of the Internet and popular culture? Brummett (2004) speculates that in the 21st century we will continue to study traditional forms of political communication (e.g., campaigns, debates, speeches), but political rhetoric will be studied not according to its context, but according to its function.

> When we say political rhetoric, we are speaking of discourse, of symbolic and significant behavior, that creates, maintains, challenges, and overthrows power; of discourse that creates community in all its complexity; of discourse that creates identity; and of discourse that creates shared definitions of reality, even if increasingly fragmented and parochial communities congeal around those definitions. The functions of managing power, community, identity, and reality have always been key to what is called political rhetoric. (Brummett, 2004, pp. 294–295)

A focus on function permits us to identify common ground for ethics across political communication contexts. Function from an ethical postmodern perspective might center on what Arnett, Fritz, and Bell refer to as a "minimalist" set of "shared goods to coordinate human life" (p. 18). Minimalist values "define common sense for a community" (p. 18).

If we accept the postmodern lack of consensus as a frame for making judgments about ethical political communication what would this mean? Although it is tempting to suggest that technological advances and changes in the delivery of political messages through evolving forms of mass and social media have transformed how we must view ethics in political contexts, if we look to a minimalist set of values it is possible to make headway. What would constitute a minimalist set of shared goods for judging the ethics of political rhetoric?

In identifying the minimalist set of values for communication across political contexts in a postmodern era, we draw on the work of a number of scholars who have speculated on what it means to communicate dialogically in an era of uncertainty, difference, and diversity. As Arnett, Fritz, and Bell (2009) observe, "The loss of a metanarrative—one universally acknowledged position—makes discussion of multiple narratives essential" (p. 216). Arnett, Fritz, and Bell suggest narratives must have coherence and fidelity in Fisher's (1987) words and be enacted through practice accordingly. An emphasis on coherence and fidelity of narratives also encompasses ethos or character of the source and a good faith commitment to inviting critical receivers to engage in dialogue. Communicators and critical receivers embrace alterity or "radical otherness" and are open to learning from it (Arnett, Fritz, & Bell, 2009, p. 114).

Ethics for a postmodern era thus asks communicators to commit to the "responsibility to learn and discern" (Arnett, Fritz, & Bell, 2009, p. 221). From this perspective, unethical communication is defined as "assuming that you know everything, and assuming that what the other knows is not worth knowing" (Arnett, Fritz, & Bell, 2009, p. 221). White (1990) refers to the quality of humility that defines an "ethic of translation" as a recognition of "the impossibility of full comprehension or reproduction" (p. 258). To "speak faithfully means to embrace and honor "diversity and difference" (p. 258). In this spirit, Wyschogrod (1990) calls for a "new altruism" that embraces difference and responds to the challenges of communicating in a fragmented postmodern world. Frost (2009) recommends that "international actors" of all types need a skills set he defines as "ethical competence" (p. 91). He further claims: "Many of the problems that presently beset the world community have arisen because of displays of ethical incompetence by important international actors" (p. 91).

Whether scholars call for a an "ethic of translation," a "new altruism," or "ethical competence," there is a recognition that political communication in a postmodern era is complex and marked by diversity, disagreement, and lack of common ground. In our view, these questions therefore reflect minimalist values for inviting communicators and audiences to come together through dialogue and engage in ethical political rhetoric across contexts:

1. Does the political narrative have integrity?
2. Does the political rhetoric suggest openness to learning and discernment?
3. Are all actors in the political narrative enacting humility?

MINIMALIST VALUES AND CONTEXTS FOR POLITICAL COMMUNICATION

In this section we examine a number of political communication illustrations and use the questions posed in the previous section to comment on ethics. Our illustrations range from a traditional context for political rhetoric (e.g., the United States Presidency) to less traditional ones (e.g., the Internet, YouTube).

The United States President as Actor on National and International Stages

Presidential scholars in the United States have debated the president's role in shaping reality through rhetorical choices. Political scientists (e.g., Edwards, 2003; Edwards & Wood, 1999) have questioned the influence of presidential rhetoric and the extent to which it influences policy. Rhetorical scholars, however, offer powerful arguments for the influence of presidential rhetoric.

Zarefsky (2004), for example, responds to these claims by offering an alternative to the "limited effects" media frame of reference that influences the thinking of scholars such as Edwards (2003, p. 608). Zarefsky claims the study of influence from a rhetorical perspective requires a more nuanced approach than Edwards applies in studying the presidency. From Zarefsky's perspective, "Rhetoric is not only an alleged cause of shifts in audience attitudes. It is also a reflection of a president's values and world view. And it is also a work of practical art, often richly layered and multivocal, that calls for interpretation" (p. 610). From this perspective, a president's rhetoric "defines political reality" (p. 611).

A body of scholarship addresses how United States presidents define reality in crisis situations by framing events as melodramatic, hyperbolic, and polarizing (e.g., Bostdorff, 1993; Wander, 1984). The ethics of how President George W. Bush defined political reality following the attacks on September 11, 2001 has received special attention from scholars. His approach to framing political reality following the attacks on 9/11 had national and international consequences. Numerous scholarly accounts suggest the answer would be "no" to the questions posed in the previous section. His narratives lacked integrity, did not manifest or invite learning and discernment, and did not reflect humility. President Bush violated minimalist values for inviting communicators and audiences to come together. Bostdorff (2003) observes, "His messages to a stunned nation spoke frequently about the 'evildoers' who had carried out the terrorist deeds" (p. 294). After 9/11, he appealed to the myth of American exceptionalism and as Bostdorff suggests, the rhetoric of covenant renewal. In his messages, the president portrayed the U.S. citizenry as a special people watched over by a benevolent God; depicted external evil that necessitated a new national mission; optimistically urged the need for a renewal of the national covenant, particularly by the younger generations; described 9/11 as a successful test of character and opportunity for cultural change; and encouraged acts of faith and "good works" (p. 302).

As scholars continue to evaluate the ethics of how President Bush's rhetoric framed the case for going to war in Iraq, there was jubilation around the world after President Obama was elected. An article in *Advertising Age* focused on the U.S. presidency as a damaged brand internationally and hailed Obama's election as "just the start to repairing America's damaged image abroad" (Wentz, 2008). David Brain, CEO of Edelman Europe, Middle East and Africa, declared that "Brand USA. It's just fantastic" (as cited in Wentz, 2008). Kunai Sinha, an Ogilvy & Mather executive director based in Shanghai, said: "The world is happy for Obama because he represents a break from the past, a hope that he will end the bullying that Bush stood for. From an Indian perspective, also a respect for brains, which everyone thought Bush lacked" (as cited in Wentz, 2008).

Although many scholars have argued that President Bush's narratives lacked integrity, failed to invite learning and discernment, and fell short in enacting humility, it is too early to make judgments about ethics and President Obama's rhetoric. We note in passing that Obama "has made ethics a signature issue" for internal U. S. government reform. His "ethics agenda" has been described as "the most ambitious ever set out by a new administration" (Thompson, 2009, p. 1). We shall see how President Obama's leadership style will be judged in the global arena when measured against the minimalist ethical values identified in this chapter. Bai (2009) has proposed that Obama's approach to governing and decision making "suits our multitasking digital age." He refers to Obama's style as "complicated, even eclectic."

> Obama is the nation's first shuffle president. He's telling lots of stories at once, and in no particular order. His agenda is fully downloadable. If what you care about is health care, then you can jump right to that. If global warming gets you going, then click over there. It's not especially realistic to imagine that politics could cling to a linear way of rendering stories while the rest of American culture adapts to a more customized form of consumption.

It is reasonable to ask these questions. How is Obama's nonlinear approach to storytelling viewed around the world? Do such narratives have integrity? Do they invite openness to learning and discernment? Do they enact humility?

National and international commentaries, however, have raised questions about Obama's leadership style and its possible relation to ethics. As Dee (2009) noted in *The Belfast Telegraph*, "To many Obama's consensus-seeking style is a refreshing break from the bitter partisanship that's dominated Washington for decades." Dee wondered if Hillary Rodham Clinton had a point when she ran against Obama in the primaries and questioned whether there was more to him than the ability to give great speeches. Dee questioned whether Obama had "the political depth to run a wily town like Washington." A commentator for the *Jerusalem Post* raised questions about the President's leadership style and said:

> I'm worried about this guy. He has wonderful goals, but he doesn't seem to have a clue as to how to achieve them. When somebody tells him "no," he's stumped. His instinct is to retreat into his Ivy League professor's mode, turn up his nose, say to himself, "I'm not going to sink to that level," walk away and go on thinking his deep thoughts. (Derfner, 2009)

Regardless of some doubts expressed about President Obama's leadership style, a transatlantic survey conducted a few months into the Obama presidency indicated he had succeeded in repairing damage done by President Bush's rhetoric and actions. An article in *Politico* (Marr, 2009) covered highlights from the survey. The survey found that 77% of Europeans supported Obama's approach to foreign policy and this was a marked contrast with the 19% approval rating Bush received. During the Bush Administration, "disagreements over the Iraq War resulted in record-low European public opinion toward America." Zsolt Nyiri, director of the Atlantic Trends survey said, "The Obama bounce is huge" (quoted in Marr, 2009). Marr's article observed that "Obama notably used more conciliatory language than his predecessor." Marr quoted a passage from the President's G-20 press conference in April 2009e to illustrate the contrast with Bush's rhetoric:

> We exercise our leadership best when we are listening; when we recognize that the world is a complicated place and that we are going to have to act in partnership with other countries; when we lead by example; when we show some element of humility and recognize that we may not always have the best answer, but we can always encourage the best answer and support the best answer.

In speeches targeting international audiences, President Obama has contrasted his approach with that of his predecessor. When he speaks, he suggests that his listeners should trust him. As he spoke in Cairo on June 4, 2009, he invited his audience to move beyond differences and cooperate:

> So long as our relationship is defined by our differences, we will empower those who sow hatred rather than peace, and who promote conflict rather than the cooperation that can help all of our people achieve justice and prosperity. This cycle of suspicion and discord must end. (Obama, 2009c)

His narrative suggested he had integrity and that he was open to dialogue with his audiences. Furthermore, he enacted humility as he called for the United States to have "a new beginning between the United States and Muslims around the world." He called for a new beginning "based upon mutual interest and mutual respect; and one based upon truth that America and Islam are not exclusive, and need not be in competition. Instead, they overlap and share common principles—

principles of justice and progress; tolerance and dignity of all human beings." Obama sought a common ground that privileged cooperation over division and humility over the arrogance of traditional power politics.

When he addressed the United Nations on September 24, 2009 (Obama, 2009d), he conveyed a parallel message. He opened by emphasizing that he was "humbled by the responsibility that the American people have placed upon me, mindful of the enormous challenges of our moment in history, and determined to act boldly and collectively on behalf of justice and prosperity at home and abroad." He identified reasons why many people around the world had lost faith in the United States, and indirectly referenced a violation of the minimalist values for ethical communication, such as openness and humility, that we have featured in this chapter. He said:

> I took office at a time when many around the world had come to view America with skepticism and distrust. Part of this was due to misperceptions and misinformation about my country. Part of this was due to opposition to specific policies, and a belief that on certain critical issues, America has acted unilaterally, without regard for the interests of others. And this has fed an almost reflexive anti-Americanism, which too often has served as an excuse for collective inaction.

Although President Obama has reached out to international audiences who distrusted the United States based on the rhetoric and actions of his predecessor, and his rhetoric seems to fulfill the minimalist ethical criteria outlined in this paper, some critics question his approach to leadership. His narratives seem to have integrity, his communication encourages dialogue, and he speaks with a spirit of humility. While we were writing this chapter, the President faced important decisions regarding preparations for increased troop deployments to Afghanistan. The world will be watching to see if he can translate the values of integrity, openness, and humility into policy. As Traub (2009) wrote in the *New York Times*, the Obama Administration runs the risk of making the same mistakes made by the Bush Administration. President Obama is "accused of ignoring the limits of American power, like Mr. Bush or Lyndon Johnson, in his pursuit of victory in an unwinnable war." Diehl (2009) wrote in *The Washington Post* that "Obama is beginning to resemble the man who just vacated the White House."

As national and international commentators, some expert and some not, assess the Obama presidency, their words will go out over the Internet through web sites, blogs, Twitter, and YouTube. What does it mean for political narratives to have integrity over the Internet? Does political rhetoric via the Internet invite dialogue? Is it possible to discern whether political actors via the Internet are enacting humility?

The Internet, Appeals to Fear, Viral Messages, and Ethical Political Communication

Scholars have debated whether the Internet fosters democracy and a more informed public that is prepared to engage in political life or just the opposite. Turkle (1984, 1995) was prescient in identifying the potential for polarized responses to the Internet and urging her readers to reject such simplistic responses. On one end of the polarized spectrum she identified utopian views of the Internet as the great democratizer. The information superhighway would lead to a global village beyond that ever visualized by McLuhan. The other end of the spectrum, however, offered an apocalyptic scenario and an end to culture as we know it.

Discussions of ethical issues centering on the Internet and its potential for promoting public deliberation continue. Koch (2005) represents an apocalyptic view of the Internet and its potential for contributing to public deliberation. He draws on the work of Baudrillard (1983, 1988a, 1988b, 1993, 1994a, 1994b) and argues that the Internet encourages passive responses from the public and creates the illusion that communication online is a substitute for true deliberation in a public forum. Real democratic politics must be practiced in a public forum rather than in virtual space. For Koch and Baudrillard, simulations become a substitute for real politics. "In this context, political life is not just altered, it is destroyed. Political life, which was characterized by drama of subjects struggling against the alienating components of economic and political repression, now disappears in a digitalized universe" (p. 161).

Koch published his article before candidate Barack Obama used the Internet to great success in communicating his positions and in fundraising. He might respond to the following observation by Jamieson by questioning whether voters felt a true connection with Obama. Jamieson, quoted in an article in *The National Journal* by Simendinger (2008), suggests voters, especially young voters, felt a true connection with Obama that was established via the Internet. "The Obama campaign has really refined e-mail and text messaging to get people connected. He's signaling, I know who you are; you know who I am; we can trust each other" (p. 41).

President Obama will continue to rely on the Internet. The White House web site is much more interactive than previous White House web sites and weekly presidential addresses are posted on YouTube. Koch's fear that the Internet could become "another technology of control" (p. 173) might be considered in light of observations from those in advertising, marketing, and journalism about Obama's reliance on the Internet. Creamer (2008) suggested in an article in *Advertising Age* that Obama engaged in "audacious marketing" and that marketers have much to learn from the "boldness" of the campaign in creating the Obama brand. Fraser and Dutta (2008) turned to the Obama campaign as an illustration of "the general future of marketing" and suggested "From now on, success in electoral politics depends on having friends in low places" (p. 10).

The future of marketing was evident in Obama's viral campaigning. Vargas (2008) recounted how he was driving through Iowa and became aware of how the word about Obama was spreading like a virus. He spoke to college students and realized they were drawn to Obama based on coming to "know" him through the Internet. They became aware of his positions and policies, and in turn, "texted" their friends about Obama. For them, this was a form of dialogue, regardless of how Koch and Baudrillard would view this communication. Vargas identified what he viewed as a new political reality, one in which politics isn't "over there" but "right here" with voters:

> Looking back, I realize that it was on that Thursday night that a new political reality was cemented in my head. In the past, we've thought of politics as something *over there*-isolated, separate from our daily lives, as if on a stage upon which journalists, consultants, pollsters and candidates spun and dictated and acted out the process. Now, because of technology in general and the Internet in particular, politics has become something tangible. Politics is *right here.* You touch it; it's in your laptop and on your cell phone. You control it, by forwarding an e-mail about a candidate, donating money or creating a group. Politics is personal, Politics is viral. Politics is individual. (p. B01)

Obviously, for Vargas real rather than simulated political engagement is promoted by the Internet.

Technology also makes it possible for international audiences to engage with President Obama in ways that were not possible in earlier times. When we opened this chapter, we mentioned worldwide celebrations after the President was elected in November 2008. The President had been in office only a few months when the Nobel Committee announced that he was the recipient of the 2009 Nobel Peace Prize. The Committee proclaimed: "He has created a new international climate. Multilateral diplomacy has regained a central position, with emphasis on the role that the United Nations and other international institutions can play" (as cited in Gibbs & Crowell, 2009). Clearly, the Committee credited the President with helping to restore the credibility of the United States in the eyes of the world. The Committee also "attached special importance to Obama's vision of and work for a world without nuclear weapons" (as cited in Gibbs & Crowell, 2009). There was an implied contrast with his predecessor when the committee noted: "Only very rarely has a person to the same extent as Obama captured the world's attention and given its people hope for a better future. His diplomacy is founded in the concept that those who are to lead the world must do so on the basis of values and attitudes that are shared by the majority of the world's population" (as cited in Gibbs & Crowell, 2009). It is difficult to imagine, however, such recognition coming so early in a presidency without the presence of technology, especially the Internet. The Committee seemed to acknowledge that the President's narratives have integrity and invite learning and discernment. The proclamation also implied that the President enacts humility in his leadership style as he reaches out to people around the world.

Observations by Koch, Baudrillard, and Vargas, however, suggest additional ethical issues centering on the Internet and political engagement. For example, viral attacks are inevitable on the Internet. How is it possible to have serious public deliberation in the face of such attacks? The Internet played a role in the debate over ratification of the Lisbon Treaty in Ireland. Ireland had rejected the Treaty in 2008. The Treaty, designed to make decision making in the European Union "more decisive and effective" ("Irish Vote Again on European Union Reform Treaty," 2009), was controversial in Ireland. Although the Treaty passed in October 2009, this was after advocates used the Internet, including blogs, YouTube, Facebook, and Twitter to advocate for their positions. Shortly before the vote "a rumor emerged that Irish people would be conscripted into a European army if the treaty were adopted" (McGee, 2009). "It was a viral story that started from the ground up" (McGee, 2009). In the end, Irish voters concentrated on the economic benefits of the Treaty and were more informed than during the previous vote ("Voters Concentrated on Economic Issues," 2009). It appears that the high unemployment rate in Ireland inoculated many voters against viral fear appeals that suggested the Treaty would mandate abortion rights, higher taxes, a lower minimum wage, and conscription into a European army.

Scholars such as Koch and Baudrillard suggest that public deliberation will disintegrate in the face of such viral attacks on the Internet. We take a different view. Political communication via the Internet is inevitable. Blogs, e-mail, "tweets," and social networking sites such as Facebook will influence political communication. How is it possible to evaluate an Internet source and determine if that source is responsible and humble? How is it possible to judge the integrity of a political narrative on the Internet? We join Arnett, Fritz, and Bell (2009) in advocating a commitment to cultivating media literacy. Just as there has been an effort to foster other types of literacy in the United States and around the world, there must be an effort to develop media literacy. An educated public, a media literate public, will have the skills to learn and discern in an era dominated by Internet communication.

IMPLICATIONS AND CONCLUSIONS

We opened our discussion of ethics and political communication by referring to Bellah's observation that U.S. citizens find it difficult to visualize ethical political communication. When Bellah talks about the possibility for an ethics in political communication, however, the onus for reform seems to fall on political communicators to reform their practices. Our chapter has foregrounded a postmodern ethic that places equal responsibility on rhetors and audiences to engage in dialogue and together frame ethical political communication. Rhetors have the responsibility to communicate with humility, frame narratives of integrity, and invite critical responses from their audiences. Audiences also have the responsibility to be engaged as critical receivers.

In identifying minimalist values for ethical communication in a postmodern world, we join Arnett, Fritz, and Bell (2009) in emphasizing the need to embrace and learn from the other. As they observe, "the pragmatics of dialogue unites *learning, discernment, and difference*" (p. 211, italics original). The pragmatics of this ethic also calls for us to ask "who is being served and who is being left out and why" as we apply the questions we framed to judge ethical political communication (Goldzwig & Sullivan, 2000).

As we conclude, we point to rhetors and contexts that invite inclusion and the type of dialogue we have mapped in this chapter. Since President Obama was sworn in on January 20, 2009, he has been highly visible as a rhetor through speeches, press conferences, traditional town hall meetings, Internet town hall meetings, and in other communication contexts. His audiences may have differing opinions on the fidelity of his narratives, but there is no question he is a thoughtful communicator who invites his audiences to learn and discern with him. Furthermore, in a spirit of humility he calls for his audiences to join him in seeking common ground in addressing crises he inherited when he entered office. Obama's remarks (2009e) following the announcement that he had been awarded the Nobel Peace Prize reflected a spirit of humility and an invitation for listeners to discern why he had received the award.

> I am both surprised and deeply humbled by the decision of the Nobel Committee.
>   Let me be clear, I do not view it as a recognition of my own accomplishments, but rather as an affirmation of American leadership on behalf of aspirations held by people in all nations.
>   To be honest, I do not feel that I deserve to be in the company of so many of the transformative figures who've been honored by this prize, men and women who've inspired me and inspired the entire world through their courageous pursuit of peace.
>   But I also know this prize reflects the kind of world that those men and women and all Americans want to build, a world that gives life to the promise of our founding documents. (Obama, 2009f, October 9)

Many would argue that Obama's response called for humility. As Becker (2009) reported, the announcement that Obama had received the Prize was met "with a bit of amusement and confusion."

Tweets from the "Twitterverse offered up a slate of modern-day whimsy and rounds of sarcastic comments" (as cited in Becker) in response to the Nobel Committee's announcement. Although some observers considered the award premature, Fuller (2009) offered a different interpretation: "Obama got the prize not for doing, but for being. Not for making peace, but for exemplifying something new on the world stage—the politics of dignity."

Fuller implies that Obama received the award for not being President Bush and setting the stage for a new ethics in Washington, DC. In our section on the presidency, we discussed ethical questions surrounding the Bush Administration's polarizing rhetoric. On the *Lehrer News Hour* (May 22, 2009), Richard Norton Smith, Scholar-in-Residence of History and Public Policy at George Mason University, cast Obama as "educator in chief" and said a speech he gave on national security should be viewed as a response to the rhetoric of the previous eight years.

> When I think what this president excels at—and we saw it today par excellence—is framing the debate or reframing the debate not only along the lines that he's comfortable with, but which in effect define the middle. For a long time in this country, we assumed there wasn't such a thing as the middle. You know, we were 50-50 red and blue. And this whole presidency—in some ways, he came to power asserting that that assumption was wrong, that there was a large what used to be called sensible center. And I think the educator-in-chief role is one that he plays very well, and I think that's what today was all about. ("Obama, Cheney Speeches Reframe Debate on Security Policy," 2009, pp. 3–4)

Although Smith was using Obama's May 21, 2009 "Speech on National Security" (2009b) as a reference point, we would argue that Obama's May 17, 2009 "Notre Dame [commencement] Speech" (2009a) offered a parallel vision and reflected a call for common ground in an era that is marked by lack of consensus.

Just as the Nobel Prize Committee recognized the President's commitment to establishing common ground around the world, he has communicated the same message in the United States. At Notre Dame, the President faced protesters who challenged his prochoice position on abortion. He spoke of education as a tool for helping us carve out common ground in an era dominated by lack of agreement and uncertainty. As his speech was interrupted by protesters, he did not ignore them, but seemed determined to present a narrative of integrity and pressed on: "We're fine, everybody. We're following Brennan's [the class valedictorian] adage that we don't do things easily. We're not going to shy away from things that are uncomfortable sometimes" (p. 1). He posed a series of questions:

> How do we work through these conflicts? Is it possible for us to join hands in common effort? As citizens of a vibrant and varied democracy, how do we engage in vigorous debate? How does each of us remain firm in our principle, and fight for what we consider right, without as Father John [Henkins, Notre Dame University President] said, demonizing those with just as strongly held convictions on the other side? (p. 3)

He seemed to be posing questions that parallel those we have framed concerning ethical political communication.

As Obama addressed the need for common ground, he recounted an experience as a candidate when he had learned and discerned from a doctor who had written to him about the statement on his web site concerning his stance on abortion. The doctor, who was opposed to abortion, suggested that Obama implied that those who are prolife are ideologues. The doctor said he did not ask Obama to oppose abortion, but to "speak about this issue in fair-minded words" (p. 3). Obama engaged in dialogue with the doctor and noted:

> After I read the doctor's letter, I wrote back to him and thanked him. And didn't change my underlying position, but I did tell my staff to change the words on my Web site. And I said a prayer that night that I might extend the same presumptions of good faith to others that the doctor had extended to me. Because when we do that when we open up our hearts and minds to those who may not think precisely like we do or believe precisely what we believe that's when we discover at least the possibility of common ground. (p. 3)

In this speech Obama spoke with humility and made it clear he had entered into dialogue and learned from the doctor. Because he offered an example of how he had communicated in a civil manner with someone with whom he disagreed, his narrative had integrity as he provided evidence he had practiced the fair mindedness he was advocating. Of course his response to the protesters at the commencement also served as an enactment of the principles he was espousing. During this same week, Obama gave a speech in which he espoused the same values, but because it was a policy speech, it invited different types of responses from people who approached it as members of a discerning audience. His May 21, 2009 "Speech on National Security" (2009b) received extensive media coverage because it was followed by a rebuttal from former Vice-President Dick Cheney. In his address at the American Enterprise Institute Cheney's rhetoric paralleled the Bush administration rhetoric discussed earlier in this chapter. As Obama outlined his plans to "clean up the mess at Guantanamo," he emphasized that his decision making and policies would be transparent (p. 9). The president called for common ground and a middle ground in this speech and said:

Both sides may be sincere in their views, but neither side is right. The American people are not absolutist, and they don't elect us to impose a rigid ideology on our problems. They know that we need not sacrifice our security for our values, nor sacrifice our values for our security, so long as we approach difficult questions with honesty and a dose of common sense. (p. 10)

This speech reflected qualities recognized by the Nobel Prize Committee and emphasized the contrast between his approach to representing the United States on the world stage and that of his predecessor.

Obama (2009b) gave this speech at the National Archives with the Constitution as a backdrop. Although the themes resonated with the Notre Dame speech, this was a different situation and required a different type of discernment from the audience in making ethical judgments. In this context, it is much more difficult for a critical receiver to make judgments about the integrity of Obama's narrative and whether he was acting with humility and transparency. Audience members in responding to this context might ask, for example, whether a narrative proposing "prolonged detention" for terrorism suspects who cannot be tried has integrity when viewed through the lens of values expressed in the U.S. constitution. As he spoke, Obama emphasized that the issues he was addressing were not suited to "30-second sound bites" (p. 7) and "our media culture [that] feeds the impulse that lead to a good fight and good copy" (p. 10).

Perhaps as a response to eight years of the presidency of George W. Bush, we have uncovered some powerful evidence that Barack Obama is fashioning a new role as "Educator-in-Chief" by attempting to reestablish the ethos of the U.S. presidency and reconfigure the discursive role of the president to conform to a model of "virtuous statesmanship" wherein more reasoned argument in both domestic and international affairs might prevail (see e.g., Lim, 2008, esp. p. 68). While the history of the success or failure of that endeavor remains to be written, it seems largely indisputable that Obama has rekindled grounds for hope and high expectations.

Although we have turned to President Obama's communication to illustrate possibilities for ethical political communication in a postmodern age, our analysis has broader implications for articulating a global political communication ethics. Goodhart (2008) calls for valuing human rights as central to framing an understanding of democracy from a global perspective and claims:

It is democracy's steadfast opposition to domination and oppression and its promise of a better life for all that makes it so appealing to people around the world. Understanding democracy as a system to protect and promote human rights shifts the focus away from institutions, mechanisms, and procedures and back to the core values underlying them. (p. 416)

He points out that Intergovernmental Organizations (IGOs) and World Trade Organizations (WTOs) often operate outside zones of democratic accountability without a clear focus on whether policies advance and support human rights (p. 397). The minimalist values we identified for a political rhetoric marked by integrity, openness, and humility promote dialogues across political contexts and invite the type of attention to human rights advocated by Goodhart (2008).

Our analysis of President Obama's rhetoric has suggested that he has the potential to enact these minimalist values as an international leader. As we close, however, it is important to note the challenges any political leader will face in enacting integrity, openness, and humility across international contexts. When President Obama accepted the Nobel Prize for Peace on December 10, 2009, his rhetoric reflected the challenges of a leader in a postmodern era. He accepted an award that acknowledged his work as a peacemaker a few days after he announced the deployment of additional troops to Afghanistan. As national and international audiences speculated on the address he would give when he accepted the award, it was apparent that he had been praised for leadership qualities that seemed to directly contradict his actions.

When Obama spoke (2009g), it was apparent he was trying to reconcile what he viewed as the demands of material reality with the qualities that had led to his selection as a Nobel Peace Prize winner. Although he acknowledged the legacies of Martin Luther King, Jr. and Gandhi and their commitment to nonviolence, he went on to say:

> But as the head of a state sworn to protect and defend my nation, I cannot be guided by their examples alone. I face the world as it is, and cannot stand idle in the face of threats to the American people. For make no mistake: Evil does exist in the world. A non-violent movement could not have halted Hitler's armies. Negotiations cannot convince al Qaeda's leaders to lay down their arms. To say that force may sometimes be necessary is not a call to cynicism—it is a recognition of history; the imperfections of man and the limits of reason.

Obama's rhetoric seemed to suggest that it may not be possible to enact the minimalist values of integrity, openness, and humility in the face of war and terrorist threats. National and international audiences might have wondered how his argument for "just war" would interface with his efforts to play a leadership role on issues such as global warming. Kagan (2009), writing for the Carnegie Endowment for International Peace, made the following observations about Obama's speech:

> I don't know what to say about the "Obama doctrine," because based on this speech [Nobel Peace Prize acceptance speech] I think we are witnessing a substantial shift, back in the direction of a more muscular moralism, a la, Truman, Reagan. The emphasis on military power, war for just causes, and moral principles recalls Theodore Roosevelt's phrase, "the just man armed." There is something much more quintessentially American and traditional about this speech, compared to most of his rhetorical approach throughout the year.

"Passion Fades for the Perfect Poster Boy," the title of an article published in *The Daily Telegraph*, reflected questions that international audiences had about Obama's Nobel Prize acceptance speech (Homby, 2009). The world is waiting to see what type of ethic will mark Obama as a political leader.

We opened this chapter with comments from scholars on the difficulty of making judgments about political communication in a postmodern age. In closing, we turned to the discourse of President Obama to illustrate possibilities for judging the ethicality of political communication in strikingly different contexts. Obama's rhetoric reflects the challenges of responding to the questions we have posed for judging the ethicality of political communication in a postmodern age of fragmentation and uncertainty. Although it is commonplace to dismiss politics as a dirty business, devoid of possibilities for ethical communication, we disagree. Rhetors and audiences, however, are equally responsible for engaging in dialogue and actualizing possibilities for ethical communication.

REFERENCES

Al-Ghitany, G. (2008, December 8). Social significance of Obama's election. *Carnegie Endowment for International Peace*. Retrieved from http://www.carnegieendowment.org/publications/index.cfm?fa=view&id=22510

Aristotle. (1980). *The Nicomachean ethics* (D. Ross, Trans.). Oxford, UK: Oxford University Press.

Aristotle. (1991). *On rhetoric: A theory of civic discourse* (G. Kennedy, Trans.). New York, NY: Oxford University Press.

Arnett, R. C., Arneson, P., & Bell, L. M. (2006). Communication ethics: The dialogic turn. *The Review of Communication, 6*(1–2), 62–92.

Arnett, R. C., Fritz, J. M., & Bell, L. M. (2009). *Communication ethics literacy: Dialogue and difference.* Thousand Oaks, CA: Sage.

Bai, M. (2009, July 19). The shuffle president. *New York Times Magazine,* pp. 11–12.

Becker, B. (2009, October 9). The early word: Prize surprise. *The Politics and Government Blog of The New York Times.* Retrieved from http://thecaucus.blogs.nytimes.com/2009/10/09/the-early-word-prize-su

Baudrillard, J. (1983). *Simulations.* New York, NY: Semiotext.

Baudrillard, J. (1988a). *The ecstasy of communication.* New York, NY: Semiotext.

Baudrillard, J. (1988b). *Selected writings* (M. Poster, Ed.). Stanford, CA: Stanford University Press.

Baudrillard, J. (1993). *The transparency of evil.* London, UK: Verso.

Baudrillard, J. (1994a). *The illusion of the end.* Stanford, CA: Stanford University Press.

Baudrillard, J. (1994b). *Simulcra and simulation.* Ann Arbor, MI: University of Michigan Press.

Belenky, M. F., Clinchy, B. M., Goldberger, N. R., & Tarule, J. M. (1986). *Women's ways of knowing: The development of self, voice, and mind.* New York, NY: Basic Books.

Bellah, R.N. (2007). Ethical politics: Reality or illusion. *Daedalus, 136*(4), 59–69.

Bone, J. E., Griffin, C. L., & Scholz, L. (2008). Beyond traditional conceptualizations of rhetoric: Invitational rhetoric and a move toward civility. *Western Journal of Communication, 72*(4), 434–462.

Bostdorff, D. (2003). George W. Bush's post-September 11 rhetoric of covenant renewal: Upholding the faith of the greatest generation. *Quarterly Journal of Speech, 89,* 293–319.

Brummett, B. (2004). Communities, identities, and politics: What rhetoric is becoming in the twenty-first century. In P. A. Sullivan & S. R. Goldzwig (Eds.), *New approaches to rhetoric* (pp. 293–307). Thousand Oaks, CA: Sage.

Condit, C. (1987). Crafting virtue: The rhetorical construction of public morality. *Quarterly Journal of Speech, 73,* 79–97.

Creamer, M. (2008). Barack Obama and the audacity of marketing. *Advertising Age, 79*(42), 1–3.

Daly, M. (1978). *Gyn/ecology: The metaethics of radical feminism.* Boston, MA: Beacon Press.

Dee, J. (2009, September 25). Has Obama got the true grit to show his critics who is boss? *Belfast Telegraph.* Retrieved from http://www.belfasttelegraph.co.uk/opinion/has-obama-got-the-true-grit-to-show-his-critics-who-is-boss-14508275.html

Derfner, L. (2009, September 24). Played for a sucker. *Jerusalem Post.* Retrieved from International Newspapers. doi: 1871862111

Diehl, J. (2009, March 8). George W. Obama. *The Washington Post,* p. 17.

Dougherty, R. (2008). McCain defends Obama against his own supporters..AssociatedContent. Retrieved from www.associatedcontent.com/pop_printshtml?content_type=artic

Edwards, G. C. (2003). *The limits of the bully pulpit.* New Haven, CT: Yale University Press.

Edwards, G. C., & Wood, D. (1999). Who influences whom? The president, Congress, and the media. *American Political Science Review, 93,* 327–44.

Fisher, W. (1984). Narration as a human communication paradigm: The case of public moral argument. *Communication Monographs, 51,* 1–22.

Fisher, W. (1987). *Human communication as narration: Toward a philosophy of reason, value, and action.* Columbia, SC: University of South Carolina Press.

Foss, K. A., & Foss, S. K. (1983). The status of research on women and communication. *Communication Quarterly, 31,* 195–204.

Foss, K. A., & Foss, S. K. (1989). Incorporating the feminist perspective in communication scholarship: A research commentary. In K. Carter & C. Spitzack (Eds.), *Doing research on women's communication: Perspectives on theory and method* (pp. 65–91). Norwood, NJ: Ablex.

Foss, K. A., & Foss, S. K. (1994). Personal experience as evidence in feminist scholarship. *Western Journal of Communication, 58,* 39–43.

Foss, S. K., Foss, K. A. (1988). What distinguishes feminist scholarship in communication studies. *Women's Studies in Communication, 11,* 195–203.

Foss, S. K., & Griffin, C. (1992). A feminist perspective on rhetorical theory: Toward a clarification of boundaries. *Western Journal of Communication, 56*, 330–349.

Foss, S. K., & Griffin, C. (1995). Beyond persuasion: A proposal for an invitational rhetoric. *Communication Monographs, 62*, 1–18.

Fraser, M., & Dutta, S. (2008). *MediaWeek, 18*(42), 10.

Frentz, T. S. (1985). Rhetorical conversation, time, and moral action. *Quarterly Journal of Speech, 71*, 1–18.

Frost, M. (2009, Summer). Ethical competence in international relations. *Ethics and International Affairs, 23*, 91–100.

Fuller, R. (2009, October 9). Obama's Nobel honors his dignitarian politics. *The Huffington Post*. Retrieved from http://www.huffingtonpost.com/searchS/?q=Obama%27s+Nobel+honors+his+dignitarian+politics

Furrow, D. (1995). *Against theory: Continental and analytic challenges in moral philosophy*. New York, NY: Routledge.

Garofalo, C. (2008). Ethical challenges in global governance. *Viesoji Politika Ir Administravimas, 23*, 16–22.

Gastil, J. (2008). *Political communication and deliberation*. Thousand Oaks, CA: Sage.

Gearhart, S. (1979). The womanization of rhetoric. *Women's Studies International Quarterly, 2*, 195–201.

Gibbs, W., & Cowell, A. (2009, October 9). Surprise Nobel for Obama stirs praise and doubts. Retrieved from http://www.nytimes.com/2009/10/10/world/10nobel.html?_r=1&hp=&pagewanted=print

Gilligan, C. (1982). *In a different voice*. Cambridge, MA: Harvard University Press.

Goldzwig, S. R., & Sullivan, P. A. (2000). Electronic democracy, virtual politics, and local communities. In R. E. Denton, Jr. (Ed.), *Political communication ethics* (pp. 51–73). Westport, CT: Praeger.

Goodhart, M. (2008, Winter). Human rights and global democracy. *Ethics and International Affairs, 22*, 395–420.

Gronbeck, B. E. (2000). The ethical performances of candidates in American presidential campaign dramas. In R. E. Denton, Jr. (Ed.), *Political communication ethics: An oxymoron* (pp. 9–21). Westport, CT: Praeger.

Irish vote again on European Union reform treaty (2009, October 2). *Associated Press (AP)*. Retrieved from http://www.npr.org/templates/story/story.php?Id=113422381

Homby, G. (2009, December 12). Passion fades for the perfect poster boy. *The Daily Telegraph*. Retrieved from http://proquest.umi.com.libdatabase.newpaltz.edu/pqdweb?index=0&did=1919994471&Srch

Kagan, R. (2009, December 10). Assess Obama's Nobel Prize acceptance speech. *Politico*. Retrieved from http://www.politico.com/arena/perm/Robert_Kagan_765AA3B7-E28D-4F99-B052-412C7518CEFC.html

Kaid, L. L. (Ed.). (2004). *Handbook of political communication research*. New York, NY: Erlbaum.

Koch, A. (2005). Cyber citizen or cyborg citizen: Baudrillard, political agency, and the commons in virtual politics. *Journal of Mass Media Ethics, 20*(2 & 3), 159–175.

Lim, E. T. (2008). *The anti-intellectual presidency: The decline of presidential rhetoric from George Washington to George W. Bush*. New York, NY: Oxford University Press.

Marr, K. (2009, September 9). Poll: U.S.-Europe ties improve. *Politico*. Retrieved from http://www.politico.com/news/stories/0909/26893.html

MacIntyre, A. (1984). *After virtue* (2nd ed.). Notre Dame, IN: University of Notre Dame Press.

McGee, H. (2009, October 1). Evidence on doorstep suggests slight swing to yes. *Irish Times*. Retrieved from http://irishtimes.com/newspaper/ireland/2009/1001/1224255613292.html

Minow, M. (1990). *Making all the difference: Inclusion, exclusion, and American law*. Ithaca, NY: Cornell University Press.

Noddings, N. (1984). *Caring: A feminine approach to ethics and moral education*. Berkeley, CA: University of California Press.

Obama, B. (2008, March 18). Transcript: Barack Obama's speech on race. Retrieved from http://www.nytimes.com/2008/03/18/us/politics/18text-obama.html?scp=1&sq=Barack%20Obama%27s%20Speech%20on%20Race%20March%2018,%202008

Obama, B. (2009a, May 17) Text of Obama's Notre Dame speech. Retrieved from http://www.nytimes.

com/2009/05/17/us/politics/17text-obama.html?scp=1&sq=Text%20of%20Obama%27s%20 Notre%20Dame%20speech&st=cse

Obama, B. (2009b, May 21). Text: Obama's speech on national security. *The New York Times*. Retrieved from http://www.nytimes.com/2009/05/21/us/politics/21obama.text.html?scp=1&sq=Obama%7s%20 Speech%20on%20National%20Security,%20May%2021,%202009%20%20&st=cse

Obama, B. (2009c, June 4). Text: Obama's speech in Cairo. Retrieved from *The New York Times*http://www. nytimes.com/2009/06/04/us/politics/04obama.text.html?scp=1&sq=Obama%27s%20speech%20 in%20Cairo,%20June%204,%202009&st=cse

Obama, B. (2009d, September 24). Text: Obama's speech to the United Nations General Assembly. Retrieved from http://www.nytimes.com/2009/09/24/us/politics/24prexy.text.html?scp=1&sq=Obama%27s%20 speech%20to%20the%20United%20Nations%20General%20Assembly&st=cse

Obama, B. (2009e, September 25). Remarks by President Obama at G20 closing press conference. Retrieved from http://www.whitehouse.gov/the-press-office/remarks-president-g20-closing-press-conference

Obama, B. (2009f, October 9). President Obama's comments on winning Nobel Prize. Retrieved from http://www.whitehouse.gov/the-press-office/remarks-president-winning-nobel-peace-prize

Obama, B. (2009g, December 10). Remarks by the President at the acceptance of the Nobel Prize. Retrieved from http://www.whitehouse.gov/the-press-office/remarks-president-acceptance-nobel-peace-prize

Obama, Cheney speeches reframe debate on security policy (Transcript). (2009). *The Lehrer News Hour*. Retrieved from http://www.pbs.org/newshour/bb/politics/jan-jun09/speechanlys_05-21.html

Romano, R. (2008, October 24). Election '08: Year of the woman. *Washington Post*. Retrieved from http:// www.cbsnews.com/stories/2008/10/24/politics/washingtonpost/main4543024.shtml?tag=mncol;lst;1

Sheckels, T. F., Muir, J. K., Robertson, T., & Gring-Premble, R. (2007). *Readings in political communication*. State College, PA: Strata.

Simendinger, A. (2008, April 19). New media as the message. *National Journal*, pp. 40–44.

Spender, D. (1980). *Man made language*. Boston, MA: Routledge & Kegan Paul.

Sullivan, P. A., & Goldzwig, S. R. (1995). A relational approach to moral decision-making: The majority approach in *Planned Parenthood v. Casey*. *Quarterly Journal of Speech, 81*, 167–180.

Thompson, D. F. (2009). Obama's ethics agenda: The challenge of coordinated change. *The Berkeley Electronic Press, 7*(1), Retrieved from http://www.bepress.com/forum/vol7/iss1/art8

Tonn, M. B. (1992). Effecting labor reform through stories: The narrative rhetorical style of Mary Harris "Mother Jones." In L. A. M. Perry, L. H. Turner, & H. M. Sterk (Eds.), *Constructing and reconstructing gender: Examining the links among communication, Language, and gender* (pp. 283–293). Albany, NY: SUNY Press.

Tonn, M. B. (1996). Militant motherhood: Labor's Mary Harris "Mother" Jones. *Quarterly Journal of Speech, 82*, 1–21.

Traub, J. (2009, October 4).The distance between "we must" and "we can." *The New York Times*. Retrieved from http://www.nytimes.com/2009/10/04/weekinreview/04traub.html?sq=

Tronto, J. C. (1993). *Moral boundaries: A political argument for an ethic of care*. New York, NY: Routledge.

Turkle, S. (1984). *The second self: Computers and the human spirit*. New York, NY: Touchstone.

Turkle, S. (1995). *Life on the screen: Identity in an age of the Internet*. Berkeley: University of California Press.

Vargas, J. A. (2008, December 28). Politics is no longer local. It's viral. *Washington Post*, p. B01.

Voters concentrated on economic issues. (2009, October 4). *Irish Times*. Retrieved from http://www.irishtimes.com/newspaper/breaking/2009/1004/breaking1_html

Wander, P. (1984). The rhetoric of American foreign policy. *The Quarterly Journal of Speech, 70*(4), 339–361.

Wentz, L. (2008, November 10). An instant overhaul for tainted Brand America, *Advertising Age, 79* (42), 1–54. Retrieved from Communication and Media Complete Database. Retrieved from ("Speech on National Security," May 21, 2009)

White, J. B. (1990). *Justice as translation: An essay on cultural and legal criticism*. Chicago, IL: University of Chicago Press.

Wood, J. T. (1992). Gender and moral voice: Moving from women's nature to standpoint epistemology. *Women's Studies in Communication, 15,* 1–24.

Wood, J. T. (1994). *Who cares? Women, care, and culture.* Carbondale, IL: Southern Illinois University Press.

Wyschogrod, E. (1990). *Saints and postmodernism: Revisioning moral philosophy.* Chicago, IL: University of Chicago.

Zarefsky, D. (2004). Presidential rhetoric and the power of definition. *Presidential Studies Quarterly, 34,* 607–619.

18

Ethics in Health Communication

Nurit Guttman and Teresa L. Thompson

The relevance of ethics to health communication is perhaps more apparent and obvious than is the case for many other areas of study in communication. Although ethics are relevant to all human and communicative behavior, health communication brings special concerns related to life and death, mental and physical well-being that are rarely relevant in other communicative contexts. These concerns are present in both scholarly and practical forums. One prominent dilemma concerns patients' end-of-life decisions, which have become more complex with advances in medical technologies that can prolong life. Additionally, power and status issues, which inherently complicate ethics, consistently are important in health communication. Many health communication encounters and contexts involve those with more power trying to influence or help those with less power. Traditionally, medicine (an important health communication context) has been patriarchal, bringing with it associated power and status differences. Power and status inherently complicate ethics. Makau (2007) reminds us that "postmodern studies have unmasked long-standing privileges, structured relations of inequality, and related relations of power" (p. 76). This is echoed by Breggin's (1997) exhortation that "empathy…. Requires a degree of equality, including similar degrees of power, authority, and vulnerability" (p. 49). Contemporary ethical concerns are reflected in official regulations to ask patients for their "informed consent" before engaging them in various medical treatments, which raises dilemmas regarding the adequacy and appropriateness of how this is practiced.

Additionally, the concept of human rights as an ethical concern is particularly relevant to health communication. One can see the salience of respect for human life as it relates to health and health care within the area of health communication. Are patient rights universal, or is this a Westernized concept? As Macklin (1999) argued,

> If the concept of human rights is meaningful, it follows that we need not hold in high regard cultural beliefs and practices that violate those rights. But the concept of human rights has come under attack too as a peculiarly Western notion that developed out of historical traditions of Western Europe and North America. (p. 80)

A key distinction here may be that between the Western conceptualization of right as autonomy, compared to the more universal notions of dignity and the right to care.

The interrelationships between health communication scholars and practitioners also make evident numerous ethical concerns. Health communication practitioners frequently are frustrated with the emphasis scholars place on ethical concerns, while avoiding a focus on real-world, practical problems. However, practitioners also are frustrated by a lack of attention to relevant cultural factors. All of these issues and more make apparent the important links between health communication and ethics.

Despite this particular relevance and the multitude of studies in health communication, much of the health communication literature does not focus on the broad range of ethical issues that emerge in various health-related contexts. In the medical context, relatively few articles focus on such ethical issues as truth-telling and disclosure, and in the public health communication interventions context often the benevolence of the intervention is taken for granted and ethical issues are minimized (Guttman, 2003; Pollay, 1989; Salmon, 1989).

Health communication as an area of study encompasses such issues as health care provider–patient interaction, health campaigns, health information in the media, health organizations, and everyday health communication (Cline, 2003). By the mid-1980s the primary focus on scholarship in the area was provider (primarily doctor)–patient interaction. Within a short period of time, however, research focusing on health campaigns and health information in the media had become important research foci. Within the two primary health communication journals, *Health Communication* and *Journal of Health Communication,* campaign and media issues now account for the largest percentage of published works. In the broader medical, nursing, and allied health literature, however, provider–patient interaction still dominates the research on communication issues. The present chapter will begin with an examination of the issues that are primarily relevant to the interpersonal and, to a lesser degree, organizational aspects of health communication, and will then turn to health campaign concerns and related social marketing issues.

THEORETICAL FRAMEWORKS

Several theoretical approaches to communication ethics are important as these issues are examined. The primary theoretical foci are feminist ethics and the ethics of caring, narrative ethics, a principalist approach to bioethics, casuistry, and virtue ethics. As most of these frameworks have been discussed in earlier chapters, they will be outlined only briefly within the present chapter. The exception will be principalist bioethics, as that is less relevant to the other topics discussed in this volume but is very important in health communication.

Feminist Ethics/Ethics of Caring

As has been made evident elsewhere in this volume, a feminist approach to ethics diverges from a more traditional ethical focus on justice. It is particularly relevant to health communication because of the focus on caring that is evident in both health care delivery and in feminist ethics. Also relevant is the insight that the detachment typically taught to health care providers is replaced in an ethics of care by a sense of attachment. Tong's (1997) discussion of feminist approaches to bioethics is particularly helpful and relevant here.

Narrative Ethics

One of the more dominant qualitative approaches to the study of health communication in recent years has focused on the value of narrative for understanding health and health care. In addition to providing a very productive approach for examining health communication, a narrative approach offers a particularly relevant conceptualization for the study of ethical concerns. This perspective, too, is commonly seen as a contrast to dominant principalist approaches to bioethics.

Charon and Montello (2002) and others writing about narrative ethics argue that the patient's narrative (story) must be understood before appropriate diagnosis and treatment may be provided. Importantly, ethical dimensions guiding interaction and treatment must also be understood within the context of the patient's narrative.

Bioethics/Principalist Approaches

The dominant theoretical approach to the examination of ethical concerns in health care is exemplified by Beauchamp and Childress's (1994) classic volume *Principles of Biomedical Ethics*. The three fundamental principles upon which a bioethical approach is based are respect for autonomy, beneficence, and justice, and these have been articulated into several major moral obligations, according to which practitioners first and foremost need to do the utmost to better people's health, which impresses upon practitioners the need to be proactive. Second is the obligation to avoid doing harm, which, in the context of health communication, can include emotional or social harm. The third is respect for autonomy and privacy, based on the premise that individuals have an intrinsic right to make decisions for themselves on matters that affect them, at least so far as such decisions do not bring harm to others. This obligation is rooted in a liberal Western tradition that places high importance on individual choice, both regarding political life and personal development; it has been the foundation for the development of important medical care codes such as patients' rights, informed consent, and confidentiality. It also serves as the basis of the obligation to be truthful and refrain from manipulative persuasive tactics. Despite the centrality accorded to the obligation to respect autonomy, there are arguments in favor of infringing upon it in circumstances in which it is believed that people are not able to make decisions about what is good for them, or when they have given the authority to others to do so. Related to justice are the obligations to ensure equity and fairness in the provision of healthcare resources and to provide for those who are particularly vulnerable or have special needs. In addition, there are utilitarian approaches that posit obligations to maximize the greatest utility from health promotion efforts, especially when resources are limited in order to maximize the public good (Daniels, 1985).

Casuistry

Also in contrast to principalist approaches to bioethics is a focus that emphasizes practical application of cases in context, commonly referred to as casuistry. Although casuistry as a philosophical focus in ethics has a long history, with principal importance seen during the medieval and early modern periods, it has become more prominent in medical ethics in the last few decades than it has in most other areas of ethics. The assumption underlying casuistry is that judgments cannot be made on general principles or rules divorced from circumstances or context. Medical students and residents commonly participate in case discussions on a weekly basis, with bioethicists actively participating in such interactions. The case discussions focus not only on the medical aspects of each case, but also place strong emphasis on ethical concerns. Casuists differ from principalists in arguing that ethics is more a matter of wisdom and prudence than it is a science.

Virtue Ethics

Discussions of virtue ethics historically go back to Plato and Aristotle, but are based more recently on writing by Alasdair MacIntyre (1984). The relevance of virtue ethics, sometimes also called character ethics because of its emphasis on the character of the individual, to health communication rests on the assumption that health care providers should be virtuous, and that such

virtue should guide their treatment of and interaction with patients. It is one's motivational structure that matters. In this way, virtue ethics bears some similarity to the ethic of care mentioned
above. Discussing health care providers, Nelson and Nelson (1995) argue that "a desire to do the
right thing, even when it involves a certain amount of personal cost, underscores all analyses of
tough cases or difficult issues, and it has to be instilled as a habit" (p. 78).

THE PROVIDER, THE PATIENT, AND THE DYAD: MOVING FROM INDIVIDUAL TO DIALOGIC PERSPECTIVES

An examination of ethical concerns relevant to provider–patient interaction must take into consideration those issues that are particularly relevant to providers, to patients, and to the dyad.
Writing about ethics and health care providers focuses upon issues such as confidentiality, providing explanations, truth-telling, disclosure, breaking bad news, and informed consent. Additionally, concerns such as whistle-blowing, loyalty to colleagues vs. patients, and stress/burnout
are relevant to ethics and care providers.

Ethical notions relating to confidentiality are central to the provider–patient interaction, as
this relationship is one of the key contexts in which individuals have traditionally been assured
that their communication is confidential. However, in order to behave ethically, a care provider
must not only maintain confidentiality, but must balance this with the greater societal good and the
health and wellness of others. Casuistry, in particular, is replete with cases in which maintaining
patient confidentiality can or does result in harm to others. Lack of disclosure of patients' HIV+
status is just one example of many that demonstrate the difficulty of maintaining this balance.

Bok's (1989) discussion of secrecy notes that "conflicts over secrecy…are conflicts over
power: the power that comes through controlling the flow of information" (p. 19). Similarly,
Bok's (1978) earlier work argued that "Honesty from health professionals matters more to patients than almost everything else that they experience when ill" (p. xvi).

While care providers must maintain patient confidentiality, they are simultaneously faced
with the need to tell the truth to patients about their health status and prognosis. In earlier historical eras, the patriarchal care provider was more likely to make decisions about whether patients
should or should not be told the truth about their health. In most Westernized cultures, however,
this trend has changed in the last few decades. Western cultures generally advocate openness of
diagnosis and prognosis to the patient. However, such an orientation is not true across cultures.
For instance, many Asian cultures regard such communication as completely inappropriate. Another example may be seen in the Navajo culture, which perceives "that thought and language
have the power to shape reality and to control events" (Macklin, 1999, p. 118). In this context,
voicing a negative diagnosis or prognosis would be taboo.

A discussion of truth-telling must confront the reality that it is impossible to ever completely
"tell" the truth (Bok, 1978). One never knows the "truth" and one can never completely tell a
story with all relevant details. We do know from research on Westernized cultures, however, that
attempts at truth-telling are more likely to increase trust in relationships between patients and
care providers, and that this is particularly true for those in high power positions, such as physicians.

Also related to the notions of disclosure and truth-telling is a more specific topic: disclosure
of medical error. Recent research by Hannawa (2009) has provided a model of disclosure of
medical errors that has particular relevance for ethical concerns. Grounded in virtue ethics, the
model describes both the process through which care providers go to make disclosure decisions
and the kind of organizational climate that is necessary to allow such disclosure.

Informed consent, another kind of truth-telling, has been a requirement in both medical treatment and research for quite some time. However, Nelson and Nelson (1995) note that "the process of informed consent has to embrace the notion of informed refusal" (p. 84), as well.

The Patient

The work cited above, while focusing on care providers, also makes evident the ethical responsibilities of patients. Patients do have ethical responsibilities in the health care delivery process. Most notably, they have obligations in regard to making their wishes clear to care providers, to tell the truth, to provide complete and clear information for diagnosis, and to comply with treatment regimens unless communicating to the provider that such will not occur. Concerns with wasting the care provider's time or embarrassment at ignorance may lead patients to not discuss issues that should be discussed.

It has become more common among various healthcare provider and insurance organizations, to propose, and some have actually created what they call "patient charters" regarding patient responsibilities. Specified in these charters are such things as the obligation of people to maintain, improve, and restore their health and to contribute to the efficient operation of healthcare services. More specifically, such charters specify the obligation to keep one's appointments, to follow advice and treatment, to ask about things one does not understand, and to use the hospital emergency department only in case of emergency. Some of the charters include responsibility toward others, for example, to use condoms to prevent the spread of infection and to take care of children. Such charters raise ethical issues associated with equity about the ability of people from different socioeconomic backgrounds to meet these responsibilities and reciprocity regarding the obligation of the healthcare system towards each individual, in particular those with special needs. Critics maintain that appealing to people to live (more) healthily can be perceived as an unwelcome form of paternalism, which can infringe upon people's personal liberties or autonomy. Further, can responsibility be considered retrospectively or prospectively when patients seek treatment?

A Dialogic Perspective

When we combine both provider and patient perspectives it brings one to a dyadic or dialogic perspective on health care. Much of this analysis begins with Buber's (1958, 1965) and Bahktin's (1981) writing and is built upon more recently by Michael Hyde's (2001) work on "the call to conscience" and the import of "physicianship," as well as the writing of Arnett, Arneson, and Bell (2006) on the dialogic turn in communication ethics. Similarly, much work has advocated a patient-centered approach on the part of care providers, making relevant a perspective that focuses the attention of the provider on the patient as a person rather than as a body. It brings to the fore patient involvement in decision making as an ethical responsibility of the dyad, if such is desired by the patient. It also makes evident the ethical concerns of talking about difficult topics. Such topics include end-of-life issues.

End-of-Life Issues and Related Concerns.　Topics related to end of life may be broadly conceptualized as encompassing concerns related to the elderly, pain treatment, palliative care, hospice, end-of-life discussion, and euthanasia and assisted suicide. Much has been written about the treatment of the elderly within health care, and many concerns have been raised about such treatment. The elderly are frequently communicated with as if they are children. Their health concerns are too frequently ignored, or merely attributed to "old age" rather than being taken seriously.

Pain treatment is a topic that is receiving increasing attention within health care, as many writers draw attention to the lack of concern shown by care providers for the intense pain experienced by their patients. Such pain can typically be treated much more effectively than is commonly seen. Rather than being concerned about the pain experienced by patients, care providers may see them as "whiners" and "complainers" and be reluctant to provide appropriate pain relief. Scholars in the area are now drawing attention to lack of adequate pain treatment as an ethical concern. The notion of palliative care builds on such concerns, as well. Palliative care is provided for patients who cannot be cured, but who can be made more comfortable. Care providers specializing in this field argue that this, too, is an ethical responsibility of health care. Hospice care is a particularly important area of palliative care. As the patient moves toward death, communicative and ethical concerns become even more relevant.

Communication with the terminally ill has been an important topic of investigation in the last few decades. Thomassen (1992) argues persuasively that "it is not possible to help a dying person without understanding and sympathy, without seriously investing oneself" (p. 144). Denying communication about impending terminality forces the patient to face "death alone, with the additional burden of cooperating in a conspiracy of silence that requires her [sic] to take care of her caregiver's feelings" (Nelson & Nelson, 1995, p. 103).

As the topics noted above are confronted, a focus of analysis may also turn to the notions of (1) spirituality and health communication, and (2) the families of patients within the health care context. Research has only recently begun to examine the role of spirituality in health communication. Any discussion of spirituality becomes intertwined with ethical issues. As health communication research has moved to a focus on the role played by spirituality in the process, these ethical concerns have come to the fore and been given new meaning and emphasis.

Examination of the patient within the context of the family reminds us that "common morality recognizes duties to parents, siblings, and other relatives" (Nelson & Nelson, 1995, p. 69). Family members are not just random "others"—they are not replaceable by similarly or better qualified people (Nelson & Nelson, 1995). "Bioethics has, however, largely been silent about the moral significance of the family in medical decision making" (Nelson & Nelson, 1995, p. 84). Instead, Nelson and Nelson argue that "people in an intimate relationship have special moral claims on each other—claims that cut into one's personal rights" (p. 111).

Intercultural Concerns

Even within a cultural group, subcultural differences and diversity exist (Macklin, 1999). Health communication research and practice must necessarily take cultural differences into account in all ways, including in terms of ethical issues. Whether one agrees with notions of cultural relativism or leans more toward universalism, there is no doubt that different cultures do have different ethical standards. The most effective health care practitioners take these ethical standards into account during health communication. Additionally, the most effective health communicators take intercultural differences and varying ethical standards into account during health campaigns or other persuasive attempts. What impact do cultural differences have on provider–patient interaction? What responsibility does the care provider have when indigenous practices put the health of a vulnerable member of a population at risk? How can cultural sensitivity be balanced with concerns about potential harm or inhumane behavior?

Other Ethical Issues in Provider–Patient Interaction

Several other ethical issues relevant to health communication should be mentioned before we move to our next major section, focusing on health campaigns. Technological advances in both medical technology and information technology have greatly magnified the number of ethical issues facing those delivering health care or promoting health education. The ethical dimensions of telemedicine, for instance, include confidentiality and privacy issues that are much different than those evident in ordinary health care.

Risk communication is also an area of study closely related to health communication, with important implications for it. Communicating about risk involves ethical decisions for care providers and health communicators. Decisions must be made regarding risk estimates and risk framing. This issue will be discussed in more detail below, in our section on health campaigns.

Whistle-blowing—reporting on wrongdoings within one's own organization—is an ethical dilemma not uncommon amongst health care providers (Bok, 1989; Bolsin, Faunce, & Oakley, 2005). Bok notes that individuals working in health care organizations may have to learn to see no evil or hear no evil. Nurses are particularly likely to be confronted by this concern in regard to reporting wrongdoing or questionable behaviors in which they have seen physicians engage. Fidelity to one's colleagues is a serious consideration (Bok, 1978) and may lead to behaviors contrary to those that are best for patients.

Current cost-containment or managerial developments in the healthcare system give rise to new kinds of ethical issues in the doctor–patient relationship. For example, should doctors tell patients about treatments and medications that are not included in their reimbursement plan? Patients increasingly have come to feel that their doctors' recommendations are clouded by organizational or economic interests. Doctors themselves feel that their communication with their patients is influenced by their conflicting obligations—to their patients on the one hand, and to the organization and healthcare system with its limited means on the other; on the one hand to pursue the best treatment for their patients, and on the other to contain healthcare costs and to adhere to organizational guidelines and restrictions in an era of explicit and implicit rationing (Pellegrino, 1997). Some doctors believe it is morally right to deny patients the information that there are treatments that may be beneficial to them but that are not included in their reimbursement plan or are beyond their financial capabilities, whereas others believe it is their duty to inform them (Marcus, 2007). Still others find ways to manipulate reimbursement rules in order to fulfill what they believe is their obligation to their patients (Wynia, Cummins, VanGeest, & Wilson, 2000).

ETHICS IN HEALTH CAMPAIGNS

People's health behavior has increasingly become a public concern, with significant economic implications, and governments and public organizations enlisting communication strategies as the means to influence people to adopt recommended health practices. There is no dispute that ethical issues play a pivotal role in the design and implementation of health communication campaigns to influence people's health. However, because the goals are presumed to be benevolent, often consideration of ethical issues is obscured. The importance of identifying ethical issues embedded in these communication initiatives is underscored by their increased pervasiveness, via the use of new media channels and marketing tactics. Further, for-profit organizations can also benefit from health messages that predispose people to consume related commercial products and services. Health communication campaigns also raise ethical concerns regarding paternalism, truth-telling, and relativism that correspond to those raised in a medical context. But other types of ethical concerns have been noted, which relate to social norms and values. For example, because health communication interventions have such a strong presence in contemporary society, they compete, along with commercial advertising, in the appropriation of the political, social, and moral realms of the public discourse. Health communication interventions may also have unintended adverse effects on the psychological well-being of individuals or their personal relations (Cho & Salmon, 2007; Guttman, 2000).

The identification and analysis of ethical dilemmas embedded in health communication interventions can be informed not by the stipulations from communication ethics (e.g., to be truthful; to acknowledge that there are alternative ways of framing and prioritizing the health issues; to be accurate; to offer complete, reliable, and relevant information; not to exaggerate; not to be offensive) as well as by principles from bioethics literature noted earlier in the chapter. Further, the task of developing ethically derived public health communication in the 21st century needs to include consideration of issues of diversity and pluralism, amidst mounting social and economic disparities within and across nations.

Moralism and Campaigns

The notion of good health as something that needs to be pursued has an essentially moral and ideological character to it. For centuries health has been associated with what people believe is good, and with moral personal behavior. Correspondingly, engaging in behaviors that lead to illness and contagion has been typified as irresponsible or immoral (Bayer, 2008). Throughout human history, and across civilizations, moral stories have linked certain behaviors with illness, and people have been urged to pursue health as a moral duty. One historical example is the consumption of alcohol that was represented in antialcohol campaigns in the United States in the early 19th century as immoral, rather than as harmful to the body. More recently references to the morality of health-related practices can be found in campaigns that implore people to abstain from using illicit drugs or from engaging in sexual relations before being married, and do not provide intended audiences information on condom use (Underhill, Montgomery, & Operario, 2007).

Ethical Issues Regarding Topics and Information

The mere choice of the topic of the communication intervention and the way the problems are defined present a series of ethical challenges. For example, some people may believe that what is described as a health problem is a normal part of aging, others may feel the issues that are at the center of the campaign are less pertinent than others it does not address, and some may believe the issue is too controversial or opposes their cultural or religious beliefs. Growing economic profits related to prevention also raise a host of ethical issues. Health communication campaigns related to prevention often receive wide publicity, with the backing of organizations that have a financial stake in the topic (e.g., companies that produce diagnostic tests or medications). Current studies point out that regardless of the benefits that preventive measures and diagnostic procedures, there remains uncertainty regarding the scientific basis for generalizing their benefits to a wider population, they may pose a risk to some people, and they may produce unnecessary anxieties because of "false-positive" results (incorrectly indicating the existence of a medical problem).

Reliability and Accuracy   Ethical obligations regarding reliability, accuracy, and certainty may conflict with the health promoters' obligation to maximize the effectiveness of their messages. Various recommended health-related practices based on previous scientific knowledge were found to be unreliable, and even put some of those who adopt them at risk (e.g., regarding diet, HIV prevention, or hormone replacement therapy). Scientific backing for health recommendations may be tentative, and the benefits and risks of adopting certain recommended practices may have a degree of uncertainty. Whereas ethical stipulations derived from communication ethics specify that communicators should avoid asserting certainty when tentativeness and degrees of probability would be more accurate (Johannesen, this volume), such tentativeness can jeopardize the persuasiveness of messages and their potential to be adopted by the intended population. It is not uncommon for health promoters to argue that their ethical obligation is to employ claims that are as persuasive as possible, regardless of their accuracy. Often the inaccuracy is represented in slogans or in misleading visual images. It is also argued that it is more effective to disseminate simple and clear messages, and refrain from more detailed information that may refer to complexity of the issue. Critics maintain, however, that according to the precept of respect for people's autonomy, people should be given information in such a way that it enables them to make informed decisions.

Influence and Persuasion Tactics   The attempt to influence or persuade, by definition, raises ethical issues; thus, communication ethicists have developed various frameworks to help ensure that the persuasive communication process adheres to ethical percepts. In the context of health communication interventions a wide range of ethical concerns has been raised regarding persuasive strategies, including what critics characterized as the use of hyperbole, demagoguery, and praying upon fears and prejudices (Goodman & Goodman, 1986). Health communication campaigns increasingly employ persuasion tactics drawing on behavior-change expertise and on a "social marketing" approach that adopts commercial marketing strategies and tactics for the purpose of advancing social goals (Grier & Bryant, 2005). Commercial marketing strategies have been shown to be hugely successful in influencing people to purchase various products and services and to embrace particular life-style trends. The application of commercial marketing strategies highlights a host of ethical concerns, ranging from the use of manipulative tactics to advancing commercialism. Further, there are significant differences between the goals of communication for health promotion and those of commercial marketing. Whereas the goal of commercial marketing is mainly to get people to purchase a particular product, often by focusing on particular benefits and minimizing discussion of issues, the goals of communication to advance health promotion include enhancing people's knowledge about the issue and their decision-making capacities (Smith, 2000). This raises ethical concerns about whether adopting persuasive tactics may serve to undermine this goal. In particular we note the following three prevalent persuasive tactics: exaggeration, fear appeals and appeals to personal responsibility.

Exaggeration and "Breaking Through the Clutter."   The justification for employing exaggerated messages in health communication campaigns typically draws on the need to compete with other topics for the attention of the intended audiences in what has been characterized as a saturated media environment, as well as with persuasive marketing strategies that forcefully counteract health goals. It is common to find appeals in public health communication campaigns that exaggerate—whether by numbers, analogies, graphs, or other visuals—the magnitude of the problem or the potential negative consequences of not adopting the recommended practices. One example is a U.S. government-sponsored breast-feeding promotion television advertisement that presented a mother's choice not to breast-feed her infant as if she were consciously taking grave risks with the welfare of her child (Wolf, 2007). Thus, ethical issues related to respect for people's autonomy are pitted against arguments regarding effectiveness. But these claims for effectiveness may be contested, as in the case of the use of "strong" fear appeals referred to below.

Presentation of Risk and Scare Tactics.   A common, yet contested, influence approach is to elicit strong emotions of fear and anxiety among the intended population. This is typically done by verbal or visual messages of damaged organs, debilitating injury, or images associated with death or immense grief and remorse. Proponents believe that using such tactics is justified on the basis of utility, and claim they are an effective strategy to achieve prosocial goals. In contrast, critics stress the following suppositions: (1) It is morally wrong to attempt to manipulate people emotionally, because this denies them the opportunity to engage in autonomous decision making; (2) It is wrong to engender anxiety and distress because it may cause certain people to view the risk as higher than it is, and make them feel worried to an extent that it affects their wellbeing; (3) Such appeals may cause needless anxiety among people who are not the at-risk population, and (4) The use of fear appeals may contribute to inequity because people in vulnerable populations are more likely to feel they can do little about the risk, and it may generate a sense of ineptness or even of fatalism. Further, critics challenge the effectiveness of using strong "fear appeals," and maintain that "milder" forms of risk messages or a positive approach can be more or just as effective (e.g., Hastings, Stead, & Webb, 2004). Current theory-based frameworks for the use of fear appeals underscore that for both utilitarian and ethical reasons, when using fear appeals one needs to include elements that relate to people's capacities to adopt risk-reducing practices (Witte, 1992).

Responsibility, Culpability, Guilt and Shame   Similar to the popular use of fear appeals in health communication interventions, appeals to personal responsibility are highly prevalent, and their use clearly is inundated with ethical issues (Guttman & Ressler, 2001). The notion of responsibility on the one hand relates to issues of social solidarity and caring, but, on the other, it can be associated with blame, shame, and guilt. Further, it may distract people from thinking about the structural causes of health and focus attention on individuals' responsibility. The importance accorded to personal responsibility in health is reflected in official documents of healthcare provider or insurance organizations in several countries, including Scotland, Germany, and the United States, which explicitly refer to the responsibility of individuals to adopt a healthy lifestyle, and outline specific practices (Schmidt, 2007). Appealing to people's sense of personal responsibility to care for their own health can be viewed as a way to enhance their sense of autonomy as well as caring for others. However, one of the main ethical concerns is that an emphasis on personal responsibility can serve to blame and shame people for not adopting recommended health behaviors, when in fact they may have wanted to do so, but feel there are social, economic, or cultural factors that prevent them from doing so. This has been referred to as "blaming the victim" (McLeroy, Gottlieb, & Burdine, 1987).

Persuasive appeals associated with the notion of personal responsibility often refer to people's obligation toward family members. Some include a warning that people will become a burden to their family if they fail to adopt recommended health practices. Whereas this type of appeal may resonate with the notion of fairness, it can contribute to people's sense of guilt when they become ill or are injured, regardless of whether they could in fact adopt the recommended health-promoting practices. Or people may be told they have responsibility to others: parents are told they have the obligation to talk to their kids about drugs, women are told to ensure their spouses adopt a healthy lifestyle, friends are told to help a smoker quit smoking (Roy, 2008). Whereas these appeals can be justified on the basis of people having a moral commitment to others, some of these messages may unfairly place a burden on people or serve to reinforce inequity in traditional social roles.

Policy issues also emerge when health communication messages link the failure of people to adopt certain practices to detrimental health outcomes. These messages imply accountability, and can serve to reduce the obligation of society or of health insurance companies to pay for people's health care expenses. Public opinion surveys indicate support for propositions that people who engage in what are considered unhealthy practices should pay higher insurance premiums or copayments or should not be eligible for certain medical procedures. Such public sentiments have raised ethicists' concerns regarding public conceptions of individual culpability in healthcare policies rather than on values related to equity and solidarity (Steinbrook, 2006). Health campaigns thus may contribute to framing certain risks as "irresponsible" and implicitly to blaming people who take them, as well as to the adoption of inequitable health policies. Yet, scholars explain that different societies' definition of what constitute a "legitimate" risk and what is considered "irresponsible" depends on each society's selection of what it considers "risky" (Douglas, 1994; Lupton, 1993). In contrast, there are arguments in favor of drawing upon personal responsibility as the moral basis for rationing services or health insurance payment policies (Cappelen & Norheim, 2005). Finally, a related concern is that health messages, while they may not explicitly blame individuals for not being responsible for their health, may frame the notion of responsibility for disease prevention as if it were primarily under the control of individuals. As such, they may serve to deemphasize the need to change structural factors such as work, housing conditions, or pollution, although these significantly contribute to the etiology of health problems.

Ethical Issues Associated with Stigmatizing and Labeling.   Health communication that portrays a particular illness as something that should be avoided and feared may contribute to an unintended adverse effect of stigmatization of the illness itself or the people who suffer from it. Advocates maintain that stigmatization has contributed to further marginalization and actual discrimination of people who live with stigmatized medical conditions (e.g., AIDS/HIV) (Herek, 1999). Stigma imposes unfair burdens on those who were already at a social disadvantage and the process of stigmatization implicates the human right to dignity (Burris, 2008). People with disabilities (Wang, 1998), people diagnosed with lung cancer who do not want to disclose their condition because they smoked cigarettes (Chapple, Ziebland, & McPherson, 2004), and people with eating disorders feel stigmatized by this attitude. Some advocates nonetheless propose that stigmatization could be enlisted as a health communication tactic to "denormalize" unhealthy practices such as smoking, but others oppose this by arguing that it fails to meet the ethical obligation of human dignity, and that its deterrent effects would not be experienced equally across different socioeconomic and racial/ethnic subgroups (Burris, 2008).

A related phenomenon to grouping people according to a medical condition is "labeling," which occurs when people find that they have been defined and targeted as being part of a particular "risk group." A prominent ethical concern is that labeling can lower people's self-esteem, cause them to feel guilty, or place them in a constant state of anxiety, even if they may never suffer from the potential health threat. This concern relates to those raised regarding the emphasis of early detection believed to predispose people to be more influenced by commercial marketing of products, services, and diagnostic tests that can benefit from people's sense of vulnerability (Dyer, 2006).

Issues of Equity and Autonomy: Health Campaigns and Diverse or Underserved Populations

Drawing both on marketing approaches and on the recognition that health communication needs to consider issues of cultural diversity, many health communication interventions identify various population "segments" and aim to create or adapt the content and messages to the language, images and culture of each. A central underlying assumption is that this type of cultural sensitivity would enable program designers to derive more effective and equitable messages and solutions (Campbell & Quintiliani, 2006; Hornik & Ramirez, 2006). However, several ethical issues have been raised regarding the use of segmentation and culturally sensitive approaches. One concerns considerations of equity or which "segment" will benefit when resources are limited (Rothschild, 2001). Critics also maintain that culturally sensitive approaches may primarily serve the establishment's agenda; they are less likely, however, to address the group members' overall marginalized position or to engage them in a critical dialogue regarding the health issue (Dutta, 2007; Slater, Kelly, & Edwards, 2000). Finally, perhaps the most contentious issue associated with communication interventions in diverse populations is the issue of moral relativism, which is also a contentious issue in the provider–patient relationship. A typical dilemma is whether traditional, cultural mores and norms should be upheld and used as an influence approach even if they may contradict wider societal values (e.g., they undermine gender equality).

Inequity and Social Gaps.   Communication scholars note that considerable gaps can be found between groups of people in the acquisition of and their capacity to act upon pertinent information according to their socioeconomic backgrounds. This gap has been referred to as "the knowledge gap," and its occurrence has been found regarding various health issues, including cancer, heart disease, and breast-feeding (Viswanath & Emmons, 2006). Health communication activities, thus, may inadvertently serve to reinforce existing social disparities (Salmon, Wooten, Gentry et al., 1996). Concerns regarding health communication and social inequities can also occur when health recommendations call upon people to relinquish particular practices they enjoy or have an emotional or social importance to them. People with higher economic means are likely to find it less difficult to substitute practices considered unhealthy, whereas members of vulnerable groups may find that these practices are not merely a means of pleasure, but serve as an important coping mechanism that is not easily substituted.

Cultural and Societal Permeation.   Communication interventions for health behavior change play a critical role in public discourse on health. They present claims and arguments regarding what individuals, group, communities, organizations, as well as the state should do or should refrain from doing, what is important and unimportant in terms of health, and who should be praised or admonished for their practices. Ethical issues therefore transcend concerns about health campaigns' impacts on individuals and concern wide permeation of health communication in social life. Seven are outlined below: (1) Turning people into the "worried well" by bombarding them with health risk messages that construct their well-being as constantly being under threat (Dyer, 2006). (2) Escalating expectations from medicine and the healthcare system, in particular among the more affluent, resulting in a growing demand for costly preventive services, which the healthcare system cannot meet or cannot distribute equitably but which receive a constant emphasis in messages encouraging the adoption of preventive measures. (3) Pharmaceutical and medical technology companies turning to the development of products and services demanded by the more affluent populations (Maynard & Bloor, 2003). (4) The pursuit of health can become an issue of social control or an implicit disciplinary power by the establishment. People's bodies become something to be studied and surveyed, and they feel obligated to follow and regulate themselves according to established norms (Roy, 2008). (5) Health becomes a moral value and "good health" increasingly is viewed as a prerequisite for happiness or signifies virtue, thus communication about the pursuit of health can become a crusade with moral overtones. (6) The prominence of health communication in lifestyle issues may cause resistance, in particular among people considered most at risk who may view resistance as a means to define their own world. (7) The prioritization of health can come at the expense of prioritizing other social issues. Further, adapting tactics that distill the issue to a "single-minded" message and that is repeated as much as possible can result in reducing complex social issues into simple slogans, thus framing certain health issues as "simple" and easy to address through particular individual practices. This can prevent people from discussing structural limitations embedded in their everyday lives, such as limited wages, long work hours, unsafe roads, and pollution.

LOOKING AHEAD: ETHICAL ISSUES RELATED TO THE CHANGING HEALTHCARE CONTEXT, NEW INFORMATION, AND BIOMEDICAL TECHNOLOGIES

Looking ahead, we would like to pose a series of challenges that emerge from current advancements in information and biomedical technologies and developments in the economic context of healthcare.

New Biomedical Technologies and Treatments

In an era dominated by the development of new treatments and biomedical innovations, new challenges include how to obtain in an ethical way informed consent for experimental treatments, clinical trials, or organ donation, or how to communicate about reproductive possibilities or genetic testing, all of which raise ethical dilemmas for present and future generations. Similarly, end-of-life decisions are exacerbated by advances in biotechnology.

Advances in Information Technologies

Advancements in information technologies (e.g., Internet, cellular phones, etc.) present opportunities to customize communication according to people's interests and wants including ways to "tailor" and adopt communication messages to individuals according to their needs and preferences, and thus to enhance their effectiveness and efficiency. These advancements, however, also raise concerns regarding the ability of various companies, organizations, and governments to collect personal information about people which they can use to "tailor" more persuasive communication tactics, and thus raise concerns for respect for people's autonomy and privacy. A related challenge is that new information technologies present opportunities as well as concerns in regard to reaching diverse and underserved populations. New information technologies have the potential to enable people from diverse and marginalized groups to be part of the discourse regarding health communication goals and strategies (thus addressing issues of autonomy), and to be part of the decision-making process with equal access to resources, thus addressing issues of equity, but these processes require facing the challenges of what has been labeled the "digital divide" (Kreps, 2005). Another challenge concerns the use of new information technologies for commercial interests: Will new media channels be used to promote products (e.g., cigarettes, alcoholic drinks, illicit drugs, high-caloric food products with low nutritional value) and practices that may put people's health at risk, in particular the health of children and youth?

Healthcare Policy Issues

As a result of the increasing costs of healthcare and a multitude of new treatment options, the public is enlisted to be a partner in discourse on complex topics such as which medical treatments should be covered by public health insurance, or how to regulate the development of new biomedical technologies. The challenge is how to engage laypeople in a discourse that requires a careful consideration of ethical dilemmas (Florin & Dixon, 2004). Related challenges concern issues of equity and access to healthcare. These include how to ensure culturally sensitive communication both in the provider–patient context and in public information campaigns, as well as communication about health rights and advocacy about health insurance coverage.

Economic and Institutional Factors

As healthcare becomes a major factor in the national and global economy, a wide range of ethical challenges emerge. One particularly contentious topic is the role attributed to pharmaceutical companies who are said to be oriented toward developing medicines and treatments that are likely to be profitable (and neglecting others), their influence on regulatory practices and on academic institutions, and the lack of transparency of their research data (Abraham, 2002; Gale, 2001).

To briefly summarize, ethical concerns in health communication are inherent in nearly every interpersonal interaction between patients and providers and have traditionally been acknowledged in the ancient Hippocratic pledge of doctors not to harm their patients. Ethical concerns in health communication are pervasive even in mundane interpersonal communication on lifestyle practices (e.g., what to eat, what not), which are influenced by information campaigns, and in the various tactics employed by such campaigns, which aim to influence people's health-related behaviors.

Ethical concerns both in interpersonal and organizational communication about health, include concerns regarding power relations, privacy, disclosure, and truth-telling, and range from issues regarding what to tell or not tell to patients, presumably for their own benefit, what to keep confidential, and whether to disclose medical mistakes. They are affected by organizational, economic, and biotechnological advances. Similarly, new types of ethical issues arise because of cost-containment demands in the institutional setting of healthcare. Thus healthcare providers face dilemmas such as whether to tell patients about new costly treatments that are not covered by their insurance plan. Finally, there are numerous ethical concerns regarding pharmaceutical and other for-profit organizations that aim to enhance the consumption of their products through sophisticated marketing and advertising strategies, as well as influence the regulatory process and research agenda.

REFERENCES

Abraham, J. (2002). The pharmaceutical industry as a political player. *The Lancet, 360*, 1498–1502.

Arnett, R. C., Arneson, P., & Bell, L. M. (2006). Communication ethics: The dialogic turn. *The Review of Communication, 6*, 62–92.

Bakhtin, M. M. (1981) *The dialogic imagination: Four essays*. M. Holquist (Ed.), C. Emerson & M. Holquist (Trans.). Austin: University of Texas Press. (Original work published 1975)

Bayer, R. (2008). Stigma and the ethics of public health: Not can we but should we. *Social Science & Medicine, 67*, 463–472.

Beauchamp, T. L., & Childress, J. F. (1994). *Principles of biomedical ethics* (4th ed.). New York: Oxford University Press.

Bok, S. (1978). *Lying: Moral choice in public and private life.* New York: Pantheon Books.

Bok. S. (1989). *Secrets: On the ethics of concealment and revelation.* New York: Vintage Books.

Bolsin, S., Faunce, T., & Oakley, J. (2005). Practical virtue ethics: Healthcare whistleblowing and portable digital technology. *Journal of Medical Ethics, 31*, 612–618.

Breggin, P. R. (1997). *The heart of being helpful: Empathy and the creation of a healing presence.* New York: Springer.

Buber, M. (1958). *I and thou* (2nd ed.). R.G. Smith (Trans.). New York: Scribner's. (Original work published 1958).

Buber, M. (1965). *Between man and man.* New York: Macmillan.

Burris, S. (2008). Stigma, ethics and policy: A commentary on Bayer's "Stigma and the ethics of public health: Not can we but should we." *Social Science & Medicine, 67,* 473–475.

Campbell, M. K., & Quintiliani, L. M. (2006). Tailored interventions in public health: Where does tailoring fit in interventions to reduce health disparities? *American Behavioral Scientist, 49,* 775–793.

Cappelen, A. W., & Norheim, O. F. (2005). Responsibility in health care: A liberal egalitarian approach. *Journal of Medical Ethics, 31,* 476–480.

Chapple, A. Ziebland, S., & McPherson, A. (2004). Stigma, shame, and blame experienced by patients with lung cancer: Qualitative study. *British Medical Journal, 328,* 1470–1473.

Charon, R., & Montello, M. (2002). *Stories matter: The role of narrative in medical ethics.* New York: Routledge.

Cho, H., & Salmon, C. T. (2007). Unintended effects of health communication campaigns. *Journal of Communication, 57,* 293–317.

Cline, R. J. W. (2003). Everyday interpersonal communication and health. In T. Thompson, A. Dorsey, K. Miller, & R. Parrott (Eds.), *Handbook of health communication* (pp. 285–315). Mahwah, NJ: Erlbaum.

Daniels, N. (1985). *Just health care.* New York: Cambridge University Press.

Douglas, M. (1994). *Risk and blame: Essays in cultural theory.* London: Routledge.

Dutta, M. J. (2007). Communicating about culture and health: Theorizing culture-centered and cultural sensitivity approaches. *Communication Theory, 17,* 304–328.

Dyer, O. (2006). Disease awareness campaigns turn healthy people into patients. *British Medical Journal, 332,* 871.

Florin, D. & Dixon, J. (2004). Pubic involvement in health care. *British Medical Journal, 328,* 159–161.

Gale, E.A. (2001). Lessons from the glitazones: A story of drug development. *The Lancet, 357,* 1870–1875.

Goodman, L. E., & Goodman, M. J. (1986). Prevention: How misuse of a concept undercuts its worth. *Hastings Center Report, 16*(2), 26–38.

Grier, S. A., & Bryant, C. A. (2005). Social marketing in public health. *Annual Review of Public Health, 26,* 319–339.

Guttman, N. (2000). *Public health communication interventions: Values and ethical dimensions.* Thousand Oaks, CA: Sage.

Guttman, N. (2003). *Ethics in health communication interventions.* In T. Thompson, A. Dorsey, K. I. Miller, & R. Parrott (Eds.), *Handbook of Health Communication* (pp. 651–679). Mahwah, NJ: Erlbaum.

Guttman, N., & Ressler, W. H. (2001). On being responsible: Ethical issues in appeals to personal responsibility in health campaigns. *Journal of Health Communication, 6,* 117–136.

Hannawa, A. F. (2009). Negotiating medical virtues: Toward the development of a physician mistake disclosure (PMD) model. *Health Communication, 24,* 391–399.

Hastings, G., Stead, M., & Webb, J. (2004). Fear appeals in social marketing: Strategic and ethical reasons for concern. *Psychology and Marketing, 21,* 961–986.

Herek, G. M. (1999). AIDS and stigma, *American Behavioral Scientist, 42,* 1106–1116.

Hornik, R. C., & Ramirez, A. S. (2006). Racial/ethnic disparities and segmentation in communication campaigns. *American Behavioral Scientist, 49,* 868–884.

Hyde, M. J. (2001). *The call of conscience: Heidegger and Levinas, rhetoric and the euthanasia debate.* Columbia, SC: University of South Carolina Press.

Kreps, G.L. (2005). Disseminating relevant information to underserved audiences: Implications from the Digital Divide Pilot Projects. *Journal of the Medical Library Association, 93*(4th Suppl.), S68–S73.

Lupton, D (1993). Risk as moral danger: The social and political functions of risk discourse in public health. *International Journal of Health Services, 23,* 425–435.

MacIntyre, A. (1984). *After virtue* (2nd ed.). Notre Dame, IN: University of Notre Dame Press.

Macklin, R. (1999). *Against relativism: Cultural diversity and the search for ethical universals in medicine.* New York: Oxford University Press.

Makau, J. M. (2007). A conversation about communication ethics with Josina M. Makua. In P. Arneson

(Ed.), *Exploring communication ethics: Interviews with influential scholars in the field* (pp. 69–87). New York: Lang.

Marcus, R. (2007). Should you tell patients about beneficial treatments that they cannot have? Yes. *British Medical Journal, 334*, 826.

Maynard, A., & Bloor, K. (2003). Dilemmas in regulation of the market for pharmaceuticals. *Health Affairs, 22*(3), 31–41.

McLeroy, K. R., Gottlieb, N. H., & Burdine, J. N. (1987). The business of health promotion: Ethical issues and professional responsibilities. *Health Education Quarterly, 14*, 91–109.

Nelson, H. L., & Nelson, J. L. (1995). *The patient in the family: An ethics of medicine and families.* New York: Routledge.

Pellegrino, E. D. (1997). Managed care at the bedside: How do we look in the moral mirror? *Kennedy Institute of Ethics Journal, 7*, 321–330.

Pollay, R. W. (1989). Campaigns, change and culture: On the polluting potential of persuasion. In C. T. Salmon (Ed.), *Information campaigns: Balancing social values and social change* (pp. 185–196). Newbury Park, CA: Sage.

Rothschild, M. L. (2001). Ethical considerations in the use of marketing for the management of public health and social issues. In A. R. Andreasen (Ed.), *Ethics in social marketing* (pp. 39–69). Washington, DC: Georgetown University Press.

Roy, S. C. (2008). "Taking charge of your health": Discourses of responsibility in English-Canadian women's magazines. *Sociology of Health & Illness, 30*, 463–477.

Salmon, C .T. (1989). Campaigns for social "improvement": An overview of values, rationales and impacts. In C. T. Salmon (Ed.), *Information campaigns: Balancing social values and social change* (pp. 19–53). Newbury Park, CA: Sage.

Salmon, C. T., Wooten. K., Gentry, E., Cole, G., & Kroger, F. (1996). AIDS knowledge gaps in the first decade of the epidemic. *Journal of Health Communication, 1*, 141–155.

Schmidt, H. (2007). Patients' charters and health responsibilities. *British Medical Journal, 335*, 1187–1189.

Slater, M. D., Kelly, K. J., & Edwards, R. W. (2000). Integrating social marketing, community readiness and media advocacy in community-based prevention efforts. *Social Marketing Quarterly, 6*, 125–137.

Smith, W. A. (2000). Ethics and the social marketer: A framework for practitioners. In A. R. Andreasen (Ed.), *Ethics in social marketing* (pp. 1–16). Washington, DC: Georgetown University Press.

Steinbrook, R. (2006). Imposing personal responsibility for health. *New England Journal of Medicine, 355*, 753–756.

Thomassen, N. (1992). *Communicative ethics in theory and practice.* New York: St. Martin's Press.

Tong, R. (1997). *Feminist approaches to bioethics: Theoretical reflections and practical applications.* Boulder, CO: Westview Press.

Underhill, K., Montgomery, P., & Operario, D. (2007). Sexual abstinence only programmes to prevent HIV infection in high income countries: systematic review. *British Medical Journal, 335*, 248–259.

Viswanath, K., & Emmons, K. M. (2006). Message effects and social determinants of health: Its application to cancer disparities. *Journal of Communication, 56*, S238–S264.

Wang, C. (1998). Portraying stigmatizing conditions: Disabling images in public health. *Journal of Health Communication, 3*, 149–159.

Witte, K. (1992). Putting the fear back into fear appeals: The extended parallel process model. *Communication Monographs, 59*, 329–349.

Wolf, J. B. (2007). Is breast really best? Risk and total motherhood in the National Breastfeeding Awareness Campaign. *Journal of Health Politics, Policy and Law, 32*, 595–636.

Wynia, M. K., Cummins, D. S., VanGeest, J. B., & Wilson, I. B. (2000). Physician manipulation of reimbursement rules for patients: Between a rock and a hard place. *Journal of the American Medical Association, 283*, 1858–1865.

19

Science, Democracy, and the Prospect for Deliberation

Keith R. Benson and John Angus Campbell

Recent years have seen renewed interest in deliberative democracy.[1] Bill Keith's special edition of Rhetoric and Public Affairs (Keith, 2002) with its essays by scholars from communication, political science, history, and sociology exemplifies this interest as does the Bryan Garsten's *Saving Persuasion: A Defense of Rhetoric and Judgment* (2006) and Keith's book, *Democracy and Discussion: Civic Education and the American Forum Movement* (2007). These and other publications manifest the hope that deliberation will play an enhanced role in contemporary political culture and the anxiety that deliberative democracy is threatened by a combination of technical reason and government by opinion poll. One arena in which the role of deliberation is being contested and defined in scholarship, and in everyday decisions—from the products we buy to the medical procedures or drugs we accept or question, to environmental regulations—is science. Steve Fuller has analyzed philosophic, sociological, and rhetorical issues central to science and democracy in several volumes (Fuller, 2000a, 2000b; Fuller & Collier, 2004). Philip Kitcher examines the terms of engagement between science and democracy in *Science, Truth and Democracy* (2001) while R. H. Brown, one of the authors in the *Rhetoric and Public Affairs* (2002) volume, in *Toward a Democratic Science* (1998) casts the eye of a sociologist and rhetorical theorist on the interplay between scientific and cultural narratives. *In Politics of Nature: How to Bring the Sciences into Democracy* (2004) Bruno Latour develops an environmentally informed philosophy, politics, and ethics of science. As though placing themes from Fuller, Kitcher, Brown, and Latour in a pedagogic setting, Michael J. Zerbe's *Composition and the Rhetoric of Science: Engaging the Dominant Discourse* (2007), proposes a freshman writing course focused on actual science texts and semipopular accounts of science. Supporting all of these themes, Sheila Jasanoff in *States of Knowledge: The Co-Production of Science and Culture* (2004) and in, *Designs on Nature: Science and Democracy in Europe and the United States* (2005), examines how the historical character of science and the cultural specificity of science policy challenge Enlightenment notions of the unity and unique authority of science.

Arguably the philosophic *locus classicus* of philosophic thought on science and deliberative democracy in the second half of the 20th century is the work of Jürgen Habermas (McCarthy, 1978, p. 15). Though Habermas has been roundly criticized by postmodern thinkers as a sponsor of the oppressive rationality that they have sought to expose and overcome (Kapoor, 2002 pp. 32–34), Habermas has been foremost among the opponents of uncritical scientism. While an unapologetic champion of Enlightenment reason, Habermas has equally criticized positivism for having narrowed the scope of epistemology to scientific method, thereby divorcing technical science from the human life-world (Habermas, 1968). Positing an interest in emancipation grounded in reason, Habermas has reaffirmed the importance to the Enlightenment project of meaning over the unmediated scientific aim of technical manipulation and control of nature and human society. Meaning, Habermas emphasizes, does not emerge from science but hermeneutically from the dialogue of historically situated actors (Habermas, 1996, pp. 197–211). Paralleling the emphasis on practice and democracy familiar to students of Dewey, yet emerging from a tradition dominated by Kant and Marx, Habermas attempts through his notion of the ideal speech situation (Habermas, 1984, 1987; McCarthy, 1978, pp. 306–310) to recover the emancipatory interest that was displaced when technical reason, following the political science adumbrated by Hobbes, triumphed over the practical/productive reason it was meant to serve.

Our purpose in this essay is not to explicate Habermas, pertinent as we find his perspective, or to rehearse familiar differences between technical and deliberative reason. Issues in the relation of technical science to popular discourse and governance, no longer academic, now thrust themselves into the fabric of daily life and decision making. Does a nonexpert lay public have a place in shaping science policy? Is the emerging ethic expressed uniquely in the United States that would embrace technical science and popular deliberation, a coherent ethic let alone a sustainable one? Are there scientific topics that so significantly affect culture that they ought to be deliberated by laypeople? Are there circumstances in which laypersons might have the ability and ethical responsibility to initiate a scientific project that neither professional science nor government on its own is likely to pursue? Or, as Niklaus Luhmann has maintained in his critique of Habermas, is it not rather the case that the technical control of society by science is so essential to survival that talk of citizen involvement in directing science is "out of step with social reality" (Luhmann cited in Habermas, 1975, p. 130). These are questions we hope to illuminate if not resolve. We begin by examining the historical conditions under which our theme has emerged, both in recent scholarship and in Enlightenment tensions between elite and popular governance; we examine the delayed appearance in the United States of government funding for science and its initial elite-centered, top-down form; we conclude with reflections on a regional citizen initiative to restore ecological integrity to Puget Sound and Hood Canal and its implications for an ethic of popular deliberation.

HISTORICAL CONTEXT

Congruent with Habermas's examination of tensions between technical science and the life world it may be argued that the single most distinctive change during the 20th century among academics who study the history and philosophy of science has been the emergence of studies placing science in its deeper social and cultural context. While examining the social dimension of science may have always served as an implicit goal of scholars, especially among historians of science who literally adopt the creed of *Isis,*[2] the centrality of this quest has become so paramount that the entire field of investigation is currently referred to as "science studies" or, more programmatically, as "science and technology studies" or "science, technology, and society" (both STS). Thus, it has become increasingly rare to read of science's *longue durée,* of the creative genius of the "great man of science," or of the intricate and detailed internal workings of science. Instead attention is being paid to events taking place over a relatively short time period and how these events reflect attitudes of a particular society or culture, or, alternatively, how science has had an impact on society or culture at a specific time. Macrohistory has been replaced by microhistory, with a predominant concern for the reciprocating influences between science and society.

One often reads in the contemporary literature of the relationship between science and the social or cultural institutions under which science has either blossomed or withered. In its focus on the tension between technical science and culture (Habermas's life world) professional study in the history and philosophy of science reflects an ethical and political concern. The title of this essay focuses on one point of tension in this concern—"democracy"—itself admitting of many specific cultural expressions. The mediating term of our title is *deliberation*. Deliberation connects both the internal operations of science, the complex discussion and debate among an elite set apart from democracy by technical language and expertise, and the many whose willingness to accept that conclusions of science are consequential for themselves, science, and culture. Presumably, science should prosper more under democracies since open societies should be more capable than closed ones of reaching the consensus necessary to embrace the social change science fosters. But does this mean that science is inherently democratic and should become more so? Or, conversely, does it mean that in exchange for scientific benefits democracies should accept the tacit leadership of a scientific elite (Fuller, 2000b, pp. 31–34)? If so, might science progress as successfully under alternative political schemes, preserving the name and form of representative government as when under Augustus the Empire retained the symbolism of the Roman Republic (Grant, 1960, p. 42; Lamp, 2009, pp. 1–24)? While we will not exhaustively treat these general questions they cannot help but inform our analysis as we situate the current interest in "science and democracy" by noting the ethical and political questions raised by the interconnection of science with the institutions that support and shape it.

Science for the People? From the 17th Century to the Mid-20th Century

The work of Francis Bacon is a natural demarcation point for considering "science" and "democracy."[3] It is not that Bacon was a democrat, the loyal if self-interested servant of the crown had too much personally and professionally at stake for that. Nor was he a scientist. Though he successfully popularized induction, his specific ideas were known to be unworkable by the founders of the Royal Society and he opposed Copernicus (Shapiro, 1982, p. 24). Bacon was a late Renaissance man and his worldview was inevitably late medieval. What C. S. Lewis has described in *The Discarded Image* (1979) was not entirely discarded by Bacon, though he was prominent among its undertakers. Bacon was a humanist in the Ciceronian mode and thus a statesman, by talent and by vocation, a prophet, architect, and broker of change. If the *Novum Organum* contains the germ of a new science, the *New Atlantis* is the West's first statement of science policy (Kitcher, 2001, p. 137). *New Atlantis* depicts a society that is neither a democracy nor a tyranny but exemplifies a vision of "science for the people." The culture of *New Atlantis* is a mix of Tudor and Stuart in which the novel element is science as a source of human flourishing and hence of cultural power. From his Tudor legacy, Bacon kept the idea of a class society but one permeable to talent not fixed solely by birth or inheritance. From his Stuart legacy, Bacon anticipates a strong central government able and willing to support science on a scale once enjoyed only by the church.[4] Yet within these familiar cultural bottles, themselves the products of frequent violent change with more violence and change on the horizon, there is something undeniably new. The frontispiece of the *Novum Organum* with its picture of a sailing ship heading out past the pillars of Hercules says it all.[5] Both through his iconography that combines intellectual with physical adventure and the constructive iconoclasm of his "idols of the mind," Bacon presented science as an agent of emancipation. Bacon urged natural philosophers to sail past the horizon of Plato and Aristotle toward a new investigation of nature, marked by an active questioning of nature to tease out the hitherto "occult" knowledge hidden from view. Such a reforming enterprise, Bacon insisted, would not just reveal new knowledge to the investigator but would provide fresh insights into how nature might be tamed or, in a more utilitarian phrase, how nature might be put to use. As natural philosophers adopted the novel Baconian approach and turned to nature for knowledge instead of to the ancients, the 17th century, The Age of Science, was marked by significant advancements in the understanding of the natural world and of humanity's place in it. The mechanical philosophies of both Descartes and Newton were developed within the Baconian ethical and political vision of knowledge for use, as was the work of Galileo, Harvey, and Leibniz, to mention only the most prominent contributors to the new science (Hankins, 1985).

The use of nature to advance human ends in turn had social implications not addressed in the *New Atlantis*. Who was to benefit by the new science? Would it be the few whose discoveries might make the many easier to predict and control? Or would the many somehow be made partners in a new society based on inquiry and innovation? The short answer is that the new knowledge could not be confined to one class. As various facets of the Baconian-inspired program of inquiry became commonplace, spread to different cultures, was revisited in Britain at different times, was transplanted to its American colonies, the new science took on both elitist and egalitarian features.[4]

Consider, for example, the Royal Society (1660). On its face the Royal Society (minus the generous state support Bacon had envisioned) seemed a harmless concession to elitism and eccentricity. Through the ingenious experiments of Robert Boyle conducted with high priced equipment manufactured for him—whether his various microscopes or his celebrated air pump—wealthy gentlemen of the Royal Society could harmlessly amaze themselves with the wonders of the body of a flea seen under high magnification, or seek to weigh, measure, and distinguish various kinds of air (Jardine, 1999, pp. 50–65). Along with the restored Church of England and the monarchy, the Royal Society, however novel its pursuits, appeared an eminently conservative institution. After the disorders of religious opinion through which the nation had just passed, what could be more peace and order making than an institution that foreswore metaphysical speculation and sectarian religion, focusing solely on matters of fact determined by experiment and speaking in a plain style (Sprat, 1966, pp. 111–115)? And, while the fellows of the society abstained from using the Bible to prove science or vice versa, what could be more beneficial to all respectable sects than inquiries into the machinery of the heavens or the earth offering evidence of a supreme architect of the universe, even as there was a supreme ruler of the state? It was not for nothing that the members of the Royal Society were called "Christian virtuosi."

Not everyone agreed. Thomas Hobbes recognized immediately the threat to state power and, hence, in his view to civil peace, of the experimental program of Boyle and his associates. On the one hand, these experiments were supposed to be public, to be seen by anyone. In fact they were conducted only by certain persons, at times convenient to themselves, and only approved individuals could see them. Second, the results of the experiments were not self-evident, they could not be deduced from first principles as in geometry, but required argument and interpretation leading to judgment. When Hobbes put these two things together what he saw was first, a small group of men claiming a source of authority independent of the state, an authority that could be certified only by themselves, and second, a body practicing a form of discourse that, despite its decorum, was aligned with the disputatious parliamentary discourse that, along with the claims to truth of preachers, had contributed to the late Civil War (Shapin & Schaffer, 1985, pp. 110–112). What is remarkable about Hobbes is that he was not antiscientific despite (by our standards) his eccentric view of science, nor was he antimodern. His *Leviathan* is Europe's first attempt to make "political science" a true natural science of motion like physics. Captured iconographically, Hobbes's thesis emblazons the title page of his classic. Leviathan stands dressed in what looks like a coat of mail but on second glance his body is composed of figures of individual men. In the composite sovereign's right hand is a sword and in his left a scepter. For Hobbes if humankind is to avoid civil war there must be an authoritative judge to end disputes engendered by the perpetual and opinionated collisions of individuals. For him, "reason" applied to political science means prohibiting all forms of public deliberation that would lead to the independent judgment of citizens or groups of them claiming special access to truth (Garsten, 2006, pp. 36–45; Shapin & Schaffer, 1985, pp. 99–107, 128–129). Even Aristotle's civically restrained "deliberative" rhetoric is too unrestrained for Hobbes. With Leviathan, the modern civic sphere begins in surrender of individual judgment to the state (Garsten, 2006, p. 27). On the cover of their book, *Leviathan and the Air Pump,* Shapin and Schaffer show Leviathan with a sword in his right hand and an air pump in his left—indicating both the centrality of science to his new system of governance and where its authoritative interpretation is to rest. The claim of the Royal Society to deliberate and pass independent judgment about matters of fact is why Hobbes feared it (Shapin & Schaffer, 1985, pp. 103–107). The details of Hobbes's alternative approach to science based on geometrical axioms need not concern us. As Shapin and Schaffer indicate both through the witnessing of experiments by a public, however elite, and through the broader "virtual witnessing" of experiments made possible through Boyle's often prolix printed descriptions of them, laboratory life carried implications for a model of government that was transparent, representative, deliberative, and intelligible. As Hobbes critique of experimental life and Boyle's defense indicate, in the scientific revolution from its 17th century inception to its flowering in the 18th and beyond, the pursuit of fact and the affirmation of value, politics, and new forms of knowledge would flourish or wither together (Shapin & Schaffer, 1985, pp. 342–344).

No clearer example of the political and ethical implications of science to free thought for new uses and understandings can be found than in the internecine battles to define "reason." From Galileo and Descartes onward, and as exemplified by Hobbes, the dominant model of science was mathematics (Hankins, 1985, pp. 46–47). The era of modern science opened with the challenge to reconcile terrestrial and celestial motion; Newton through his development and use of the calculus (if not quite to the satisfaction of Leibniz, and providing one calculates for just two bodies) had solved it. Yet on the other hand Bacon had not privileged mathematics nor was mathematics at the center of Boyle's experiments. Arguably, even Newton was as empirically scrupulous as he was numerically precise (Hankins, 1985, pp. 46–50). In the century to come neither Montesquieu, "whose The Spirit of the Laws had almost the authority of the Principia" (Commager, 1978, p. 120), nor Buffon, let alone Franklin, would center their studies in mathematics. Voltaire, the man who did as much as any to popularize Newton, might be considered a mathematical rationalist like his friend D'Alembert but for the multiple personae of his many-sided talent and his supreme gift of irony. In his *Philosophic Letters* (1734/1961, originally *Lettres Anglaise,* 1734) that introduced Newton to his countrymen, Voltaire's richly textured portrait of English toleration for diversity in religion, government, and culture seems to blur the difference between rationalism and deliberative experimentalism. In the hands of Voltaire and his fellow *philosophes,* "reason," while reflecting the cachet of mathematics, made science a synonym for emancipation and a narrative of independent thought. Indeed Kant coined the motto of what became known as the Enlightenment—*sapere aude*—"dare to think" (Commager, 1978, p. 261).

With mathematics sometimes as its model and sometimes as its metaphor, the Baconian and Newtonian programs of putting nature to use came into its own in the 18th century and proceeded to put nature in order. Linnaeus, through his so-called natural system, used essential characteristics of the biota to link diverse forms of life and thus displayed a rational pattern behind the mindboggling array of fauna and flora that otherwise seemed scattered randomly along the Creator's *scala naurae.* Not to be outdone, and in contrast to the Swedish botanist's emphasis on a precise system, the keeper of the *Jardin du Roi* in Paris, the Baron Georges Buffon, explained the regularity one could observe in the diversity of the natural world as resulting from Newtonian forcelike organizing principles. Thus, horses had the form they exhibited because of an internal mold that operated on the organization of the horse-body with a regularity as precise as the physical laws in nature. Moreover, Buffon organized his magnum opus, *Histoire naturelle*, according to the usefulness of these natural productions to humans (Farber, 2000).

Though originating in the case of France through state subsidized activities of an unelected elite (in the Royal Society the gentlemen supported themselves), the broader mission of science (in case anyone missed it) was made explicit in Diderot's and d'Alembert's magisterial work, the *Encyclopédie* (1751–1772). Not only did the two editors organize the *Encyclopédie* around Bacon's classification of knowledge but in fine egalitarian fashion they placed the latest science cheek-by-jowl with knowledge of various trades (Hankins, 1985, pp. 164–165). Despite the heavy censorship to which the document was subject (Diderot was jailed repeatedly for displeasing the authorities) the *Encyclopédie* had a clear ethical, cultural, and political message. When the authors discussed "salt," their comments were not restricted to accurate scientific insights into the character of salt, but supported removal of the onerous salt tax, an authoritarian edict at odds with the notion of the Enlightenment's spirit of liberty. For Diderot and d'Alembert, once the human mind became fully developed by observing the natural world it would see through the irrational injustices of established cultural, political, and religious systems.

Despite the implications of Enlightenment science for the removal of prejudice, its belief in progress and its gestures toward egalitarianism, the new science carried its own potential for authoritarianism. When Turgot, who had written the essay on "expansibilité" for the *Encyclopédie* became finance minister to the newly crowned Louis XVI in 1774, the only solution for France's financial crisis that he could suggest was a science of society. While he believed that a science founded in the laws of human nature would appeal to persons of good will, no more than Hobbes did he anticipate an alliance of science and representative government. Turgot had in mind a system in which the king would "govern like God by general laws" (Hankins, 1985, p. 159). It was from the circle around Turgot and Condorcet that the term *social science* originated (Hankins, 1985, p. 159). As Commager (1978) notes, "'Everything for the people and nothing by the people' might have been the motto of the Enlightened Despots" (p. 132).

An implicit ethical/political tension, if not an outright contradiction, was thus present from the first in the new science. Could a philosophy that saw the universe governed by natural law in each of its material particulars, the human person no less than the atom, sponsor (other than rhetorically) a philosophy of political freedom? How could the laws of "Nature and of Nature's God" so eloquently memorialized in the Declaration of Independence set anyone free (Hankins, 1985, p. 7)? As the Enlightenment in Europe was brought to an end in the Terror of the French Revolution and in America expired peacefully in the symbolically condign deaths of Adams and Jefferson within hours of one another on July 4, 1826, different cultures answered such questions in different ways.

Though the home of "laissez faire" was France, its true heartland was Britain and America. As suggested by one of the keenest critics of "political arithmetic," Edmund Burke, the true meaning of an abstract principle is found in the circumstances of its application (Burke, 1790/1955, p. 8). Self-governance was no abstraction to the Scots, their American cousins, or to those English industrialists and free-thinkers who were turning the fruits of the scientific revolution into new forms of wealth (Herman, 2001, pp. 161–167, 229–232). It is in the popular culture of deliberation that flourished through the interplay of scientific, legal, historical, religious, and political discourse that we encounter an odd and international paradox of the classical political liberalism that remains one of the most enduring fruits of the Enlightenment marriage (or *ménage à trois*) of science, an ethic of emancipation and politics. Whereas Hobbes, following the lead of Machiavelli, saw the root of order in fear and not in the Republican virtues that animated Cicero and his close student Thomas Jefferson, classical liberalism famously followed Adam Smith (himself informed by the experimental tradition of Bacon and Boyle) and saw the key to order in liberty (Ezrahi, 1990, p. 19). Though each person individually might seek his personal advantage, all persons operating as part of a system would achieve a generally harmonious outcome as though guided by an invisible hand. That government should be limited was one of the first political deliverances of the new science interpreted from this point of view. Beyond maintaining a baseline necessary for common life, government should let go. Nature and its laws would take care of the rest. In the nascent capitalist culture of late-18th century Britain and her independent-minded American colonies, the mechanistic outlook of scientific determinism sponsored an emancipatory political ethic that championed individual freedom and with it the independence of distinct discourse communities—religious, fraternal, political, legal, and scientific.

The center of this egalitarian perspective was no government and not even one class but the fluid culture of what Habermas has called "the bourgeois public sphere" (Habermas, 1989). In salons often presided over by women, in Masonic lodges, in often scurrilous broadsheets, in coffee houses where such papers were read and fueled by the elixirs of coffee, ale, port, and pipes of tobacco, a growing middle class increasingly became accustomed to voicing opinions about matters, political, religious, historical, philosophic, or scientific that traditionally had been none of their business (Habermas, 1989, pp. 36–37, 94; Johnson, 2008, pp. 17–18; Smith, 1934, pp. 315–319). Steven Johnson's account of the initial meeting between Benjamin Franklin and Joseph Priestly, and of their subsequent collaboration, is instructive. When Priestly in 1765 wrangled an invitation to meet the world-famous Benjamin Franklin at "The Club of Honest Whigs" in the London Coffee House near St. Paul's, he was an erudite if obscure dissenting minister and, though fluent in six languages, in science was a mere dabbler. When he emerged from the establishment a few hours later with a pledge from the members to share their notes and hunches about electricity in return for his promise to publicize their work in a volume and contribute experiments of his own, he was virtually a scientist (Johnson, 2008, p. 28). The resulting volume not only won for Priestly a place in the Royal Society but confirmed Hobbes's worst fears about the connection between experimental science and radically republican politics. In his volume, Priestly carefully described the work of his fellows and his own experiments in a manner worthy of, if more readable than, Boyle in the previous century. In Priestly's narrative it seemed credible that with little or no training an ordinary person might contribute to science. Priestly gave the impression that merely by reading, by keeping abreast of a new field such as electricity, an ordinary person might surpass the understanding of a Newton. The idea of progress, encouraged by the burgeoning discoveries of science, seemed to favor a kind of intellectual democracy; that is, differences in genius would be equalized by history (Johnson, 2008, pp. 32–38).

In subsequent years, Priestly won patrons both noble and industrial; most famously among the latter, the members of the Lunar Society in which Erasmus Darwin and the pottery manufacturer Josiah Wedgwood were central figures (Johnson, 2008, pp. 137–139). But Priestly's overt and public championship of radical politics and dissenting religion—he denied the existence of the soul and the divinity of Christ—ultimately triggered the destruction of his laboratory by an angry Birmingham mob and led to his emigration in 1794 to the now independent United States (Johnson, 2008, pp. 162–172). While welcomed to America by Adams, who compared him to Socrates, under his presidency Priestly, not surprisingly, nearly fell afoul of the Alien and Sedition Acts (Johnson, 2008, pp. 188, 191–195, 208). Only under Jefferson, with whom he exchanged a series of moving letters following his inauguration, did Priestly at last find himself in a country where he could feel at home. The American experiment, and particularly its Constitution, was not unlike the theoretically modest, life-world based Rube Goldberg contraptions Priestly himself had devised for his experiments (Johnson, 2008, p. 199). As Priestly shaped Jefferson's understanding of religion (enabling Jefferson to think of himself as a kind of Christian) as well as his understanding of science, Jefferson's invitation to Priestly to help shape one of his most important intellectual legacies—the curriculum for his new University of Virginia—became a fitting tribute to both men and to the political/cultural genius of the bourgeois public sphere (Johnson, 2008, pp. 199–200).

Though the new Republic had achieved in politics what the European Enlightenment had only imagined, its egalitarianism and distrust of all tradition came at a price. To be secure, scientific inquiry had to establish its own tradition and institutional base. No one had understood that more clearly than Boyle who worked tirelessly to establish experimental science in an elite but publicly credible association dedicated to its cultivation. In 1798 Priestly had urged the American government to invest in libraries and laboratories rather than to waste money on a war with France (Johnson, 2008, p. 187). But in America, aside from its almost exclusively denominational colleges, there were few learned institutions. Long before independence, Franklin had understood the important connection between a free society and the unfettered pursuit of knowledge and had created the American Philosophical Society in Philadelphia (1741) to pursue "useful" knowledge.[6] But this was a long way from an organized, let alone nationally subsidized, institution dedicated to the promotion of experimental science. Some museums sprouted in several of the larger cities, there were a handful of medical schools (most were proprietary, owned by their faculty), and colleges and universities offered limited scientific curricula. Overwhelmingly, and from an Enlightenment standpoint paradoxically, most institutions of higher learning aimed to prepare their students for clerical careers or lives as learned gentlemen. For women educational opportunities were extremely limited and for either gender natural history or natural philosophy received only a perfunctory nod (Daniels, 1994).

By the early 19th century, the lack of government-sponsored institutions of science increasingly made the United States anomalous. Many European countries had already invested in science either through universities, through institutes, or through industry. In the United States as a byproduct of having created a working constitution and a democratic republic there was an acute distrust of any institution that produced elite practitioners of specialized knowledge. Nor did the strict constructionist constitutional philosophy of the great American *philosophe* Jefferson improve the situation. Aside from his Lewis and Clark expedition, the federal government did not invest in science projects. Such projects as it did undertake were heavily cloaked within national goals, such as military survey expeditions or explorations for railroad passages. Integral to the egalitarian Jacksonian democracy of the 1820s, '30s, and '40s, and consonant with the agrarian, limited-government legacy of Jefferson, was the belief that "any man could do anything." Following this maxim, the essence of Enlightenment for Americans was democratization that rested on the decentralization of knowledge and equal access to truth. Even medical training was open to the average citizen (Daniels, 1994). The dark side of America's egalitarianism was a kind of self-congratulatory anti-intellectualism.

On a more positive note, the American Association for the Advancement of Science was founded by midcentury, although the so-called scientific Lazzaroni (named after a Neapolitan intellectual dining society) consisted primarily of geologists in service to the nation's various survey missions instead of scientists employed by colleges and universities. In a retrograde move, two of the country's leading institutions of higher education, Harvard and Yale, marginalized their science offerings within two ancillary structures, Harvard's Lawrence School of Science and Yale's Sheffield School of Science. Similarly when a group of Americans, many of whom had received training either directly or indirectly from Europe, attempted to establish a national university in the nation's capital, the plan was soundly defeated by those who claimed it was elitist. Opponents argued that the constitution of the country did not specify an educational imperative to the federal government; as such, any new university had to be part of a state mandate, not a federal one (Bruce, 1987). A further exception to the government staying out of scientific matters was the formation of the Smithsonian Institution (1848); however, it was founded after a financial bequest from a foreigner (James Smithson, an Englishman) and it took Congress many years to reach a decision to accept the gift, since its aim was at variance with the constitutionally mandated tasks of the government (Ewing, 2007).

A harbinger of how the world wars of the 20th century would transform the relation of science to democracy is seen in the first war of the Industrial Revolution—the America Civil War. During the conflict the navy assumed leadership in developing armament, warships, steam, and related technologies. The Civil War also saw the formation of the National Academy of Sciences (1863). The NAS was designed to advise the government on science topics and was an early effort at centralizing U.S. science. Difficult as it is to believe from a 21st century perspective, a significant science policy debate during the Civil War period was over the creation of the Department of Agriculture (1862). Indeed, critics of the agency objected that its establishment would allow tax money to be spent on scientific research (Kleinman, 1995, p. 47).

By the 1870s, America's refusal to recognize the need for advanced research was no longer sustainable. Reforms that would alter the status quo were already on the minds of many progressive thinkers (Bruce, 1987). Josiah Willard Gibbs, the first U.S. theoretic scientist of international distinction since Franklin, received a PhD from Yale in the late 1860s (Kleinman, 1995, p. 27). But the decisive event that changed the landscape of American higher education was the foundation of a new graduate university in 1876, Johns Hopkins. When the new Baltimore school opened its doors, the vast majority of Americans who held an advanced degree in science had received their instruction in Europe. By the beginning of the 20th century, the majority of those who held higher degrees were American-trained. Indeed, J. McKeen Cattell was inspired to list the newly emerging scientific elite in his *American Men of Science*, a work first appearing at the beginning of the 20th century (Cattell, 1906).

The Progressive movement marked another novel development in the relation of science to liberal democracy. While in the time of Adam Smith and continuing through the age of social Darwinism, the chief political lesson from science was the notion of *laissez faire,* advances in medicine, public health, engineering, and countless other fields suggested to progressive thinkers an alternative: conscious planning to support social betterment (Pease, 1962, pp. 7–10). While even in the era of positivism American science was still a long way from Turgot's top-down version of science as an instrument of state control, for American supporters of science liberty was beginning to mean not just freedom from outworn tradition, but freedom to act effectively on reliable knowledge (Ezrahi, 1990, pp. 9–40). In Dewey's pragmatism there is more than a hint of Jeffersonianism and Jacksonianism updated through mass education to operate in an increasingly urban United States (Dewey, 1927/1954, pp. 174–184).

On a par with the Civil War as prophetic of things to come was the Allison Commission (1884–1886). The commission examined whether federal support creates a "politicized" science and whether government science agencies were doing basic or applied research. Contrary to most government science following the Second World War, the agencies examined claimed their work was practical. Several scientists protested that laypersons could not judge technical subjects and that a special science bureau be created to keep science out of the hands of politicians. On this point opinions differed. "Congressman Hilary A. Herbert, an Alabama Democrat on the commission, insisted on the principle of maintaining direct democratic control over the scientific agencies."[7]

If the U.S. government was slow to recognize that during the second Industrial Revolution advantage would go to nations supporting science—democracy be damned—industrial capitalism soon filled the void. Both Andrew Carnegie and John D. Rockefeller established foundations (respectively 1911, 1913) heavily financed to assist with medical education, biological and physical science field stations, new research institutions, and a variety of other scientific ventures (Kohler, 1991). Those serving on the boards of both foundations were also put to work during the nation's First World War, in large measure because they were aware of where the best science was being done. But even following the successful enlistment of science in what became known as the "Chemists' War," the federal government remained impecunious when it came to supporting science after the war. Science may have demonstrated its importance, but only through the hopes of pragmatists, progressivists, and educators was it linked to democratic institutions.

By the third decade of the 20th century, the cultural prestige of science was at an all-time high. As one foundation board member put it, scientific research was "the method of knowledge" (Kleinman, 1995, p. 37). The Deweyan hope that science pursuing a democratically radicalized version of Bacon's vision would prove an endless source of Enlightenment and public good was hardly credible even as a cultural myth. In 1922, Walter Lippmann stated the obvious. In *Public Opinion,* Lippmann (1922) declared that science and technology had produced a culture so far beyond the comprehension of the common person and mass media created a propaganda apparatus so formidable in shaping public opinion, as to consign hope of a robust union between science and democracy to the status of the naïve illusions of a simpler age. According to Lippmann, modern government required a commanding role for technically trained professionals, if not their actual rule (Lippman, 1922, p. 7). Turgot and the enlightened despots seemed to have been right after all. Dewey's reply to Lippmann, *The Public and Its Problems* (1927/1954), reaffirmed his progressivist faith in the power of science through education to produce citizens whose values would inevitably support progressive change. Granting Lippman's thesis that the public did not exist in an absolute sense, Dewey affirmed that particular publics were summoned by issues and that through discussion and debate, the complex readjustment of attitudes and actions encompassed by communication within a democratic public would prove adequate to the challenges before it (Dewey, 1927/1954, pp. 30–34, 208). A major issue on which Dewey's emergent public would wait was the advent of science questions that would invite its engagement.

The Coming of Big Science

It was neither the Enlightenment nor progressivist belief that understanding nature was necessary for democratic flourishing but fear of foreign invasion that finally brought the U.S. government to support science seriously. Vastly unprepared, both from a military and an industrial perspective, the entrance of the United States into the Second World War required an immediate and immense retooling and reconceptualization of its industrial manufacturing structures. And to this task, the nation's scientists, engineers, and technicians were again put into action. This time the end result was not only victory for the Allied forces, but a new relation between science and government. On the advice of prominent scientists, and well before the war began, President Roosevelt in 1940 created the National Defense Research Committee (NDRC) "to issue defense contracts to universities, research centers and corporate laboratories." Replaced in 1941 by the Office of Scientific Research and Development (OSRD) the NDRC became the coordinator of science and military projects while the much larger OSRD managed daily operations (Maddox, 1992, p. 199).

Whatever the United States lacked in scientific originality it soon more than compensated by its ability born of astute engineering to improve on the ideas of others and to organize and mass-produce the results in mind-boggling quantities. Soon it seemed as if the Americans had invented the relationship between science and government. Americans created the impression, during the war and after it, that they had invented the proximity fuse (a radio device to detonate a bomb or shell over its target) radar, sonar, penicillin, sulfa drugs, and even DDT. All these had been invented elsewhere, the latter in Germany (Maddox, 1992, p. 200). Not only did America and its allies win the Second World War, but it was widely believed that the "Physicist's War," a moniker referring to the Manhattan Project, was won by a prodigious organization of science and engineering leading to the production of nuclear weapons (Kevles, 1979). With the arrival of the Cold War in the immediate aftermath of allied victory, the continued fear of foreign invasion reaffirmed the forced marriage between science and American democracy.

Well before the war's end, it was evident to many policy makers and scientists that government funding for science and technology would be needed after the war (Greenhill, 2000, p. 633). What was not clear was what policies would govern the new science–government–military relationship and how it would be organized. The received view until recently has been that the architect of America's postwar science policy was Vannevar Bush (Greenhill, 2000, p. 634). Bush had headed the OSRD and was a politically well-connected Washington insider. His *Science: The Endless Frontier* (1945) was influential and, in retrospect, became the official rationale for continued federal support for science after the war.[8] Though Bush won most of the key battles to create what eventually became the National Science Foundation (NSF), the agency was not the product of one mind but of a political process that encompassed 8 years and required four attempts before Truman (who had vetoed an earlier version of the bill) signed the final legislation into law in 1950 (Greenhill, 2000, pp. 637–640; Kleinman, 1995, p. 137).

Without mentioning him by name Bush warned against the competing ideas of Harley Kilgore, a New Deal senator from West Virginia, who wanted laypeople to have a substantial voice in shaping postwar science. Kilgore envisioned patents from government-financed science to go to the public rather than being retained by the labs or individuals who discovered them. He did not want large businesses to benefit at public expense but small businesses. He wanted research money to be distributed democratically to universities across the country, not just to elite ones. He wanted an emphasis upon applied rather than basic research and he wanted a predominantly lay board to set the agenda for research. By contrast Bush emphasized basic over applied research, from which, he argued economic benefits would follow. Bush also argued that property rights should go to the inventors not to the public and he emphasized control of the research agenda by elite scientists (Greenhill, 2000, pp. 635–636). According to Bush, science of and by the experts could be the only model of a science reliably for the people (Bush, 1945).

In the end neither man got exactly what he wanted.[9] Despite their different ideas for leadership of the organization, both had advocated nationally centralized scientific research. In the end scientific research remained spread over numerous agencies rather than concentrated in one. Bush had pushed for elite civilian scientific oversight of NSF and in a sense he got it. What he got along with it—Kilgore's biggest revenge—was oversight by the President. Bush had pushed for generation of knowledge as the central mission of the agency, Kilgore for its diffusion. The NSF as realized was responsible for both, though in practice its emphasis would be on basic research. Despite Bush's efforts to achieve stronger civilian control of military research following the Korean War, the Air Force emerged as the most powerful engine of U.S. science with the Navy coming in not far behind and the Atomic Energy Commission also heavily influenced by the military (Greenhill, 2000, p. 636).

As Kleinman (1995) notes in the U.S. context, democratization preceded government bureaucracy. The democracy that generously funded science only under threat of national emergency would not accept, at least in peacetime, exclusive concentration or supervision of science in a single agency. In this sense and despite its populism, Kilgore's New Deal model did not have deep historical roots. In contrast Bush's model of professional science seemed, in historical context, a counterweight to the extension of executive branch power and thus appeared less overtly politicized (Kleinman, 1995, p. 141). The key difference between the equally "top-down" (in the sense of centralized) models of Kilgore and Bush was that Kilgore's approach made lay judgment integral to science policy and Bush's did not; therein settled the philosophic/political fault line of science policy stretching back to the Allison Commission and forward through the remainder of the 20th and the beginning of the 21st century.

The growing tension or cultural lag between the education needed for a world dominated by science (whether administered by one agency or several) and one privileging the humanities—Habermas's tension between technical and life-world interests—was addressed in 1959, two years after Sputnik, by C. P. Snow. Often described as decrying the growing divide between the humanities and the sciences, Snow's (1959) *The Two Cultures* had a rather different intent. Snow underscored the critical role that science played in the emergence of political forces at odds with western democracies, a theme powerfully sounded at the end of World War II by Karl Popper in *The Open Society and Its Enemies* (1945). Going beyond Popper, Snow emphasized the failure of the west to support its scientific institutions adequately and urged greater funding for science (Snow, 1959).

It is difficult to tell whether Snow was ahead of history's curve, slightly behind it, or simply reflecting the anxieties of the Cold-War driven shift in the priorities of the western knowledge enterprise. By 1959 the modern research university was already more identified with state-of-the-art research facilities dedicated to advancing medicine, science, and technology than with literature and the humanities. In less than a decade after World War II, the United States had emerged as the leading scientific country in the world. Students from abroad were competing for opportunities to pursue prestigious degrees in the sciences at numerous American institutions. The conditions that would lead to the fulfillment of President Kennedy's 1961 promise to place a man on the moon by the end of the decade were already in place. Well before Snow's provocative book, university science was associated with and complicit in the unparalleled military build-up that placed nuclear missiles at-the-ready aimed at the country's enemies. Unfortunately its enemies also were armed with the same devastating arsenals of mass destruction.

Return of the Public

The reemergence of the question of how to justify the country's scientific infrastructure at the end of World War II and in the years following marks how significantly the relation of science to American democracy had changed since the debate between Lippmann and Dewey. Experts now appealed to Congress and to the public to support projects that spoke to national needs (Dennis, 2004, pp. 225–253). From the postwar years to the present, the deliberative relation between science and American democracy would unfold in three overlapping stages.

In the first and immediate post-World War II phase, big science clearly arrived and the obvious benefactor was the Department of Defense (Hounshell, 1998, p. 237). Top-down as was this arrangement, it also contained a significant democratic element, however far from ideal its expression. In plain terms the situation was this: through their elected representatives the people said to the military and their scientific/technical experts, "You defend us and we will provide monies for your research even though we do not understand it." On its face the arrangement seemed straight out of *Leviathan,* except, of course, for one distinctly American feature. The details of appropriation, how much for bombers and fighters and of what kind and to be manufactured by whom and where (and eventually for missiles) to say nothing of which service would get what, were subject to negotiation. The very familiarity of the usual pork-barrel political questions made the integration of big science into American life almost natural. The arrangement, though surely not what Dewey had in mind (or Hobbes either), was nothing if not pragmatic.

We may date the beginning of the second phase of the relation between science and democracy in the postwar period (the two periods overlap) with the challenge to and critique of Big

Science by Rachel Carson (1962/1987). Though she was a scientist in the Fish and Wildlife Service, Carson functioned as a voice for laypersons when she drew attention to how the chemical products of World War II were not only eradicating crop pests but they were also silencing populations of birds (Carson, 1962). Her voice was not welcomed by many professional scientists, particularly those associated with chemistry, and her research certainly was not funded by NSF (Waddell, 2000, pp. 1–6). Nevertheless, her critique was embraced by a research panel appointed by President Kennedy (Waddell, 2000, p. 8). Carson's case and virtually the entire history of the environmental movement in the second half of the 20th century mark the beginning of the public's willingness to question the cultural legitimacy of Vannevar Bush's expert-directed model of science policy (Lutts, 2000, pp. 17–41).

Allan Brandt recently raised a similar issue in the relationship between cigarette smoking and the tobacco industry (Brandt, 2007). The contrasting scientific claims that smoking was dangerous or benign could not both be true and seemed to illustrate not "reality" but "the way of the world"; that is, the willingness of scientists to work for whomever paid them. When David Baltimore called upon the public not to become involved in an issue of scientific misconduct in his laboratory, he claimed that science was "self-correcting" (Kevles, 2000). Again, was his claim supported or does science, like any other human institution, reliably correct itself only when its operations are transparent and its leadership credible to the public as in the laboratory practices championed by Boyle and feared by Hobbes or in Kilgore's concerns for lay representation? Currently, when pharmaceutical manufacturers and energy companies are appealing to the public with scientific claims to new technologies of health (drugs) or alternatives for energy (usually involving fossil fuels), are they representing scientific claims or appeals to their benefactors for continuing support in return for researchers giving them scientific legitimacy (Angell, 2004; Avron, 2004)? Similar claims can be made for research on women and in AIDS research where, in both areas, activists variously and vigorously intervened to make science responsible to issues important to specific publics (Berridge, 1992, p. 15; Dranginis, 2002, p. A21; Groopman, 2006; Moss, 1996, pp. 21, 58). Indeed, medicine remains one of the most obvious areas in which the expert-only perspective of "the doctor knows best" has been most thoroughly challenged—indeed discredited. Not only do laypersons regularly consult the Internet concerning their illnesses but they argue with their doctors about the proper course of cure, serve on the internal institutional review boards of hospitals, have a say in judging the ethics and merit of experimental drugs or procedures, sit on NIH committees, and currently are demanding family access to emergency rooms (Gearin-Tosh, 2002, pp. 205–209; Groopman, 2006). This last practice, in particular as Jerome Goopman notes, "reveals the extent to which the power to decide how medicine is practiced is no longer an exclusive prerogative of doctors" (Groopman, 2006).

A third phase in the relation of science to democracy may roughly be said to have begun in the early 1990s. The outward markers of this new phase are the collapse of the Soviet Union and the end of the Cold War (1989). Additional factors include the repudiation by the business-oriented Council on Competitiveness of the primacy given by *Science: The Endless Frontier* to pure research in favor of applied science (1991), the endorsement of the Council's report by Clinton/Gore, along with their call for more centralization and coordination of government science/technology planning (Kleinman, 1995, pp. 192–193), and the refusal of Congress to approve funding for the Superconducting Supercollider (1993). A combination of events seem to have come together not so much to reverse the post World War II relation between science and American democracy but to put it on a new footing. The future had already been signaled by the Mansfield Amendment of 1970, "a watershed of science policy" that required defense-related research to show the "direct and apparent" relation between basic research and military aims (Nichols, 1993, p. 202). If the distinguishing mark of the first or Vannevar Bush stage of the relation between science and American democracy was expert-determined pure research over lay-informed research directed by explicit social aims, (a debate reprising the differences between Michael Polyani and J. D. Bernal in the 1930s) and the second, or Rachel Carson stage, was a bottom-up correction emphasizing lay judgment and agenda shaping, the third and appropriately anonymous "postmodern" phase may be regarded as a mix of elements from the previous two models. A distinctively new element that we will consider presently appeared as well, a skepticism about the transformative possibilities of science that has characterized its triumphalist and emancipatory narrative since the Enlightenment (Nichols, 1993, p. 209).

An important element that characterizes this third phase in the relation between science and democracy is a radicalization of the accountability element already operating in phases one and two (Nichols, 1993, p. 211). Though it first made its appearance as one of the gifts of the progressive movement, governmental statistics is the element that neither Lippman nor Dewey figured in their respective critique and defense of the relation of science and democracy and which has proven each to have been partially right and partially wrong. Lippmann was right in emphasizing the role of popularly unfathomable expertise in the governance of modern society, but premature in assuming that this expertise could not be "rationally," that is, reasonably, corrected by public opinion. Dewey was right in believing events would summon public opinion, though premature in assuming that a scientifically informed people would transform national culture from the ground up. Neither anticipated that, thanks to publicly available statistics, the methods of science, while often beyond popular ken, would, initially at least, produce a culture of spectators (as opposed to Deweyan deliberators) whose judgments on the performance of experts would reestablish democracy, though a deliberatively minimalist one, on uniquely late modern grounds (Ezrahi, 1990, pp. 41–42, 197–199). A public of spectators in the sense of mere bystanders was central to the viability of Bush's model of elite-directed science. Yet under a combination of Lippmanesque conditions of 20th-century publicity and Deweyan conditions of public pressure for results and government transparency, the elitism of the Enlightenment came to fruition in expert knowledge but, in an irony Turgot and Condorcet perhaps would have appreciated, the experts would be the hired servants and not the undisputed masters of the many.

If the report of the Council on Competitiveness and defeat of the Superconducting Supercollider mark a turning point in the public's recognition, growing incrementally since publication of *Silent Spring* (1967/1987) that its interests and those of elite-directed science were not necessarily the same, the question of the rationale of science that Bush's *Endless Frontier* had seemed to settle, once again became open. It is at least worthy of note that one prominent physicist, Stephen Weinberg, in part blamed the defeat of the Superconducting Supercollider on an attitude toward science that had sprung up in the social studies of science and in the humanities in the previous several decades (Fuller, 2000b, p. 2). Even were Weinberg correct, his position would merely underscore the need for a new rationale for the pursuit of science in a postmodern world no longer defined by fear or at least by the old fears, and no longer confident that pure research translates into economic benefits, or that experts left alone, will conduct research that will benefit the public. The questions that remain are the ones with which post-World War II science began. Is democracy capable of articulating a rationale for funding science untethered to national defense? Is there a substantive, ethically appropriate, even imperative, deliberative role for laypeople in a partnership with science?

SCIENCE AND DEMOCRACY IN THE POSTMODERN SCENE

The characteristic feature of science and its relation to democracy, particularly since World War II, has been an increasing emphasis on public accountability. Sometimes this accountability has been merely gestural, as in Vannevar Bush's paternalistic assurance that "pure research" would, of course, produce numerous social benefits if Congress but funded science and let experts, not laypeople, decide what projects to support. Increasingly, however, accountability is substantive (Nichols, 1993, pp. 199–202). One has only to open a newspaper or get online to realize that on almost any subject from automobiles, to electronics, to medicines, to the performance of school districts, to the permitting process for logging companies to harvest timber, or the Forest Service to build or decommission roads, there is a plethora of publicly available information. One must also add "some local restrictions may apply." But even if one imagines Jon Stewart delivering this line with mock straight face while counterexamples flash on the screen, the general trend is clear. Science and government were never bigger or more complex, technology never more ubiquitous or information so plentiful or generally so accessible or experts so accountable. A regime of accountability in which laypeople have a serious voice, what Habermas would call a potential for political will formation, increasingly characterizes the contemporary interaction between science and democracy.

A correlate of government accountability and a consequence of political will is local initiative. Local initiative is important for without it (except for collecting taxes) government will not act. It is not merely or necessarily that government is incompetent, bad, or unresponsive as that without articulate constituencies government may perform its general functions while failing to address specific issues in need of urgent and sustained attention. We believe that citizen problem solvers, mindful of the importance of science for addressing their needs and skeptical of the ability or willingness of top-down science to do so, are currently forging a new 21st century approach to science policy. Both of us were born, have spent most of our careers in, and now are each retiring in the Pacific Northwest (heartland of such direct democracy policies as the initiative and referendum) so we close with a local example.

Citizen Science and the Effort to Save Puget Sound Basin Waterways

Each of us lives on a sensitive marine waterway, respectively Puget Sound (Benson) and Hood Canal (Campbell.) Each of these waterways is currently the focus of major efforts to restore its ecological health: 3.8 million people use the Puget Sound Basin. There have been different degrees of marine habitat loss in Puget Sound and Hood Canal caused from such things as human-caused pollution from storm water run-off, septic systems, industry, logging practices, and significant land-use changes. Though cleanup efforts in the 1970s saw the banning of specific chemicals, toxins dumped over long periods remain mixed with bottom sediments in hotspot areas throughout the region. Inevitably, harmful chemicals have found their way into the iconic symbols of the Pacific Northwest such as salmon, seals, and the killer whale (*Orca*).[10] So contaminated are orcas that there is at least one recorded case of an orca body that had to be treated as toxic waste.[11] According to a recent editorial, "forty species of Puget Sound marine life are listed as threatened, endangered or as candidates for listing on federal or state lists. Some seabird populations have dropped by 50 percent since the 1970s; rockfish and bottom fish populations have also dramatically declined in the past 25 years" (*Kitsap Sun*, see note 12) Under the general leadership of the state sponsored Puget Sound Partnership, educational and scientific efforts are underway to restore Puget Sound by the year 2020. The estimated cost of this endeavor is $8 billion. Jay Manning, director of the Washington State Department of Ecology has referred to Hood Canal as "the canary in the coal mine" for the larger problems of Puget Sound.[12] Because of its importance for the region, the distinctly postmodern conditions under which the efforts to restore it are being made and because one of us (Campbell) is a member of the Lower Hood Canal Watershed Coalition, we will focus on Hood Canal.

Hood Canal is a hook-shaped fjord estuary, 110 km (66 miles long and 2–4 km (1.25 to 4 miles wide. It is located on the west side of Puget Sound and on the east side of the Olympic Mountains. From Admiralty Inlet, which serves as the opening to the larger marine waters, the main channel of the canal travels northeast to southwest making a sharp eastward turn at the Great Bend. Approximately 12 miles later the canal ends at the mouth of the Union River near the unincorporated town of Belfair. Hood Canal reaches its deepest point (180 m) in Dabob Bay and then past the hook travels eastward (roughly the former melt-water of the glacier) becoming increasingly shallow (20m or less) (Simonds, Swarzenski, Rosenberry, Reich, & Paulson, 2008). At low tide the Lynch Cove area at the southeastern end of the canal is a mud flat.

Hood Canal was formed 12 to 17,000 years ago by the Vashon Stade of the Fraser glaciation that covered the entire region in a massive ice-sheet estimated to have been 1,600 m thick in the northern end and 450 m in the southern (Burns, 1985, pp. 42–45). The glacial history of Hood Canal is important for understanding its chief contemporary environmental problem—periodic low dissolved oxygen that can occur in the late summer and early fall—caused by what can only be described as its fish habitat birth defect (Simonds et al., 2008, p. 3). The central problem with Hood Canal is that the marine water at the end of the canal does not exchange very well. At its northeastern entrance near Admiralty Inlet, a shallow sill rises to within 65 m of the surface. The sill extends over an area approximately a mile wide and 3 miles long. The sill slows the tidal flushing of the canal and impedes its mingling with the more open source waters of Puget Sound. Another factor is a marked seasonal difference in temperature that separates warmer surface water from the lower, colder, and more densely saline water. For most of the year in lower Hood Canal, algae grow in large blooms. Algal blooms are good in that they provide oxygen to the upper layers as well as food for other trophic levels in the marine water. But algal blooms also die back, and as they sink to the bottom and decay; the decomposition process takes oxygen from an environment already low in oxygen. In late summer and early autumn a confluence of circumstances can result in a water column briefly deplete of oxygen in certain regions, often resulting in the death of thousands of fish. In leading to these events, prolonged southerly winds can displace the more highly oxygenated surface water northward allowing the denser less oxygenated water to well up from the depth. There is nothing modern or human-caused about this fish-killing feature of Hood Canal. Fish kills have presumably been part of the history of Hood Canal since, with the retreat of the Fraser Glacier, it became a marine body of water (Simonds et. al, 2008, p. 3). Butch Boad, a neighbor (Campbell), fisherman, and life-long resident, tells of seeing rock cod (a bottom fish) gasping for breath on the surface off Bald Point in the late 1950s.

It has been suggested that eliminating the sill—a labor that has been estimated to require the removal of four times as much soil as was removed for the original construction of the Panama Canal—might solve the problem (Dunagan, 2008). Scientific measurements since the 1950s suggest that the appropriate seasonal conditions that lead to fish kill events may become more frequent as drainages from urbanized areas near the canal, residential development along its shores, as well as other land use changes have added to the nutrient load from the natural sources of atmosphere and ocean which help drive the process (Simonds et al., 2008, p. 3). In certain years, the low oxygen conditions have been noted more northward from lower Hood Canal to the deeper stretches of the canal. The most plausible remedial action is to control the human contributions that increasingly push the built-in natural low dissolved oxygen conditions to fatal levels for fish. Understanding the mechanisms that create the low dissolved oxygen in lower Hood Canal has been the key question on the agenda of scientists and citizens who seek to improve the situation.

A Problem Summons Its Public.   In 2002 there was a fish kill in Hood Canal. Another occurred in 2003 and another in 2006.13 After the first kill, a neighbor of mine (Campbell) Bob Hager, who is a retired Project Manager for Boeing and who had been Vice President of the Space and Ballistic Missile Division, thought something ought to be done. Hager had already served on an unrelated Clean Water Advisory committee to Mason County in 1994 when the State Health Department had closed a portion of Hood Canal and established a Shellfish Protection Area charged with fixing the problem. The issue at the time for the Clean Water Advisory Committee was not the cause of low dissolved oxygen but the sources of fecal coliform bacteria polluting the shellfish beds particularly in the area of the Great Bend and Lynch Cove. Because of his involvement in the previous issue, which began winding down in 1998, Hager had become familiar with key state environmental scientists such as Jan Newton, at the time with the Department of Ecology, officials in the Department of Fish and Wildlife, Health, and, of course, he knew his neighbor on Hood Canal, U.S. House of Representatives member Norm Dicks.[14]

Hager conferred with Newton and other colleagues from the earlier project and called a meeting of concerned citizens at North Mason High School. Newton and other scientists made short presentations and the scientists and attendees discussed the nature of the problem and what steps might be taken to address it. Following the meeting, Hager worked with Newton and various state and local agency representatives to outline a program. The Puget Sound Action Team—the umbrella organization for overseeing environmental action in the Puget Sound Basin—became an active partner in the development of the plan. Hager then contacted Norm Dicks, who then called a meeting of state agencies at which Hager gave a presentation summarizing what was known of the problem. A three-year investigation and analysis plan to understand the source of the low dissolved oxygen and develop potential corrective actions was proposed. Representative Dicks committed to providing federal funds of over $1 million per year for 3 years that would fund the newly organized Hood Canal Dissolved Oxygen Program, comprised of nonprofit organizations, state, University of Washington and county agencies, native tribes, the Hood Canal Coordinating Committee (HCCDC), and citizen volunteers.

Clearly citizen-based science, no less than elite-directed science, costs money. An immediate concern was to obtain monitoring buoys and develop the analytic models. Representative Dicks put in a request in the 2004 defense bill to go to the Department of the Navy. The Navy has a history of working with the Applied Physics Lab (APL) at the University of Washington. Newton at the time was in the process of changing positions from Ecology to the UW-APL. It became clear that Newton was the appropriate person to head up analysis and monitoring for the project. When one of the very symbols of top-down science, the Applied Physics Lab at the University of Washington (a site of antiwar protests during the late 1960s), becomes the center of operations for a citizen-led science initiative, it is not for nothing that the current phase in the relation between science and society is called "postmodern." Dan Hannafious, a marine biologist affiliated with the Hood Canal Salmon Enhancement Group, one of the many environmental organizations focusing on Hood Canal, was appointed comanager with Newton. With Representative Dicks gaining funding not only for buoys but for an ambitious computer modeling program and with $200,000 from the Puget Sound Action Team, the initiative that Bob Hager and his colleagues had begun was a credible mix of science and decision makers. Early in the process and repeatedly throughout it, Representative Dicks has said of the ultimate outcome that the science, policy, and legal aspects of the challenge must be addressed together. The nub of the entire project is captured in that formula.[15]

The Marriage of Science and Public Policy.   The central issue in this Hood Canal initiative has not been that the science of previous efforts to address the environmental woes of the hydrological, chemical, and biological features of Hood Canal was wrong. The concern is that previous efforts were driven by the mandates of specific agencies (for example, the Department of Health, Department of Ecology, or the U.S. Geological Survey) with tasks and interests peculiar to their funding agencies and covering everything from the purely practical to the purely scientific. It is only when the whole of Hood Canal and all of the scientific agencies concerned with it are coordinated with the aim of addressing a targeted issue that the peculiar difference of a citizen-motivated postmodern "project" model of science comes into view. The aim of the Lower Hood Canal Watershed Coalition is not merely to advance knowledge. The group also intends to bring attention to the water quality and low dissolved oxygen problems of an inland waterway central to a regional economy, cultural identity, and way of life. That lay-centered political and cultural factors drive the project, in the sense of motivating it, goes without saying. But it is these very factors that are also putting civilian pressure on the scientists to produce results that are not just accurate or true but socially meaningful, persuasive, and when translated into policy, effective. If ever there were a clear illustration of the difference between Habermas's technical reason and practical reason, and of how, through dialogue between scientists and laypeople these two forms of reason can meet without confusion in a way that develops a political will capable of advancing science and the common good, it is here. When Dicks says that the science has to be right, he means it in the sense of one who has invested serious political capital (as well as taxpayer money) and wants to be able soon to point to concrete measurable results. What Dicks and all those connected with the project want is specific, science-backed policies that citizens can believe in, local government and state agencies can support, and that commissioners in counties strapped for cash can enact without losing office. Where the project is most political and cultural, it is also most exactingly scientific.

The premise of the LHCWC may be described as a post-Carson, postmodern version of Bacon's thesis that knowledge is power. Scientific knowledge and the policies that follow from it are powerful when the science is accurate and the policies are sanctioned, however variously, by the deliberative consent of those whom they are to govern. The interrelation between the science of the project and the community response to it is represented in Figure 19.1. The essence of the LHCWC's vision of the union of science and representative governance is captured in a 1-page memo currently under discussion. The memo is divided between "Goals" and "Actions." Under "Goals" are: "Storm Water," "On Site Septic Systems," "Water Quality Monitoring," and "Hood Canal Dissolved Oxygen." Beneath "Storm Water" is a list of ordinances that should apply to Hood Canal. As for septic systems, the goal is to have them operate with minimum impact to their associated freshwater or marine waters. The memo notes that the monitoring of surface water would require coordination between the County and the Department of Health. The final goal is the big ticket science item: "Hood Canal Dissolved Oxygen—Sources and magnitudes of contribution defined. Potential corrective actions defined and cost benefit established, including time to reach recovery. Corrective actions defined and implemented."[16]

"Actions," tightly integrated with the goals, specifies steps to be taken by the county and includes: the passage of ordinances that would apply to storm water in the Hood Canal Marine Recovery Area and the Rural Activity Centers of Union and Hoodsport, and the funding for staff to carry out the inspections, and the importance of the ordinances having teeth for their enforcement. And, not least important, the need for "County [to] develop a plan of incentives and partnering with private owners of existing property to bring their storm water runoff & OSS (On Site Septic Systems) up to the current ordinances." One final item underscores that property owners and developers alone have not been responsible for the problem. "WSDOT (Washington State Department of Transportation) roads and DNR (Department of Natural Resources) forest practices are also contributing to the marine water problems and will need correction in the Hood Canal MRA."

Linking as it does the Goals of the LHCWC and the Actions needed from county government, the memo is remarkable for its unity of vision. Only one single line is dedicated exclusively to the technical science now entering its final stage of completion. On the ability of science to

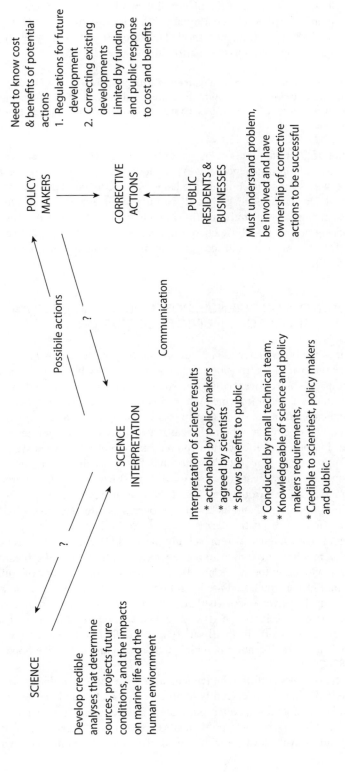

Figure 19.1 Hood Canal Dissolved Oxygen Program, science/action decision model.

deliver on that one "Goal," the success of the plan will depend. Already one can see tensions in the provisions of the plan. The plan will cost money. "Provide funding for adequate, qualified staff for storm water and OSS permitting, monitoring and enforcement. (Utility fee?)"[sic]. There must be ways of making the plan attractive and affordable.

> County develop [sic] a plan of incentives and partnering with private owners of existing property to bring their storm water runoff & OSS up to the current ordinances.... When the nutrient requirement for Hood Canal recovery are established the OSS will probably require plans to assist residents in correction.

As the bare listing of "Action" items suggests, unless all the key constituencies are brought on board early the plan's union of science, lay/expert dialogue, and popular governance could easily unravel. Homeowners might become divided against logging companies or state agencies over who is most to blame. Even if all goes well and the science succeeds in identifying and modeling the sources and amounts of nitrogen (how much from septic systems, how much from the alder trees that spring up from land use changes, and how much nitrogen is fixed in the soil, how much comes in from runoff, etc.) can the coalition maintain the political will to sustain the fruits of its vision over time?

CONCLUSION: MODERN SCIENCE, POSTMODERN SCIENCE AND THE PROSPECT OF CIVIC DELIBERATION

A distinguishing mark of modern science and culture, as Jürgen Habermas (1970) argues, has been the divorce since the rise of positivism in the mid-19th century between the possibilities of technical manipulation and control over nature and society on the one hand, and the ethical need for popular deliberation to create an informed, emancipatory political will on the other. Reason, according to Habermas, cannot achieve its aim unless it distinguishes and reconciles two very different modes of its own operation—the technical reason necessary for mastery of the world of phenomena and in the practical life-world-centered reason necessary to sustain deliberative democratic order. Complicating Habermas's vision has been the abuses of science (its ready subservience to the military and private industry, its elitism, slowness to take environmentalism, women's, gay, and racial issues seriously, etc.) and the rise of postmodernity with its view of Enlightenment reason as oppressive, and its belief in progress as interested and illusory.

The distinguishing feature of postmodern science, as Yaron Ezrahi (1990) contends, is that postmoderns no longer regard science as representing the world but see science as being a product of interpretation as much as any other human endeavor. Politically and ethically pivotal in this new regime of knowledge is the breaking of the correspondence theory of truth that from Bacon and even through Dewey anchored the liberal democratic political heritage in Enlightenment science. Ezrahi wisely leaves open whether this break with realism, rooted in a visually based correspondence between scientific texts and reality, will end in a politics of appearances in which gestures of concern by officials will satisfy a public that no longer believes in truth or in progress, or in a politics of deliberation in which civic action and collective hope are possible (Ezrahi, 1990, pp. 283–284).

Even if realism can be successfully challenged, which we think is dubious, we believe the citizen-based science in the initiatives currently in process in Puget Sound and Hood Canal presage well for deliberative democracy. Though our example is concrete, historically specific, and far from illustrating anything so purely hypothetical as Habermas's "ideal speech situation," we think it supports the normative relevance of his ideal of a scientific philosophy with practical intent explicitly in the service of a deliberative democratic order. Though the centerpiece of the Hood Canal project are computer models based on observations and monitoring aimed at understanding and serving a watershed/marine environment, it seems that both the scientists and the citizens most centrally engaged in their construction are clear about the contingent and circumstanced nature of the models. Most importantly the two parties talk regularly and with candor, sometimes with skepticism, and characteristically with mutual respect. No one we have met believes the models explicitly reproduce the real natural world yet, at the same time, there is a general consensus that however many interpretations and hypothetical assumptions a computer model may entail, at a certain point the model will cross a threshold of scientific and civic confidence that will make it adequate for framing enforceable state and county ordinances.

In the complexity of its interactions between expert and lay knowledge, the deliberation of the LHCWC represents both the elitist and the egalitarian sides of the Enlightenment legacy as well as the legacy of government-sponsored science born of World War II and the Cold War while at the same time embodying and redefining the legacies of Dewey, Kilgore, Carson, and postmodernism. The deliberations of the LHCWC represent the best of the Enlightenment tradition because in a way both Boyle and Priestly would have appreciated they focus in the first instance on matters of fact as these have been determined by numerous, repeated and ongoing observations of a variety of phenomena from fecal coliform bacteria readings to degrees of salinity, wind and tide conditions, and the cycles of algae blooms. That these matters of fact are established by experts, sometimes with lay assistance, through the mediations of technical tests and equipment the deliverances of which are explained to and deliberated by laypersons (and that much or all of this information is available at appropriate web sites) gives a new and expanded meaning to virtual witnessing. While the various tests, charts, and technical reports would have status among credentialed scientific specialists irrespective of their lay acceptance, minus the endorsement of laypeople the entire research and knowledge endeavor they embody would be pointless; it would lack the kind of cultural credibility it needs to bring about specific, and local (to say nothing of regional) environmental change. It is in the practical intent of the LHCWC project where the republicanism that Hobbes feared in the experimental practice of Boyle comes to the fore, along with Carson's science-grounded critique of industrial science. If, as the top-down arrows of the dissolved oxygen discussion chart (Figure 19.1) indicate, members of the LHCWC receive complex data coming from the scientists above them—the pattern of World War II and Cold War science—in another sense as its various levels of audience participation, deliberation, and response indicate, the arrows of technical information reverse their flight. On their return to their expert source these arrows bear cultural and policy data—the fruit and invention of lay deliberation—vital to the direction of additional scientific research and which inform and empower laypeople and scientists alike. Science, no longer an exclusive path to personal or cultural enlightenment, nor merely the preserve of experts, has become an ongoing, never-completed technical and civic process, in which the armamentarium of diverse technical fields summoned by civic will and supported by a cultural ethic funded by tax dollars addresses the people's environmental agenda.

Does this model have a future and what does it tell us of the relation of science and democracy to ethics? The great tension, sometimes amounting to a contradiction, which we have traced from the dawning of the age of science in 17th-century Europe right through our contemporary American example, is between expert judgment based on scientific knowledge and practical lay judgment based on life experience. When framed as stark alternatives, it is hard to avoid sympathizing with Commager's (1978) motto for the enlightened despots "everything for the people and nothing by them." If the ethic of the expert-only model is benignly authoritarian, so be it. If science is too complicated for the public to deliberate about meaningfully, then let public relation techniques reconcile them to a fig-leaf appearance of "democracy" in a world governed by experts.

When, however, we look at a specific case involving scientific knowledge and a challenged natural environment and the kinds of knowledge and actions required to address it, the expert knowledge/lay ignorance model loses much of its force. The expert knowledge/lay ignorance model is simplistic; that is, it vastly underestimates the kinds of knowledge necessary to make cutting edge science succeed (or even to collect its data) and hence underestimates the importance of expert/lay deliberation in securing the integration of science in culture. Considering the care and persuasive skill of his writing, it is difficult to believe that Bacon really believed knowledge was power. Both the artfulness and variety of Bacon's prose and the very real struggles of Boyle to institute what today we regard as experimental science, indicate knowledge becomes power only when it passes through culturally relevant forums of deliberation. When we appreciate the close historical connection between republican politics and the regime of experimental science that Hobbes feared and Franklin, Priestly, and Jefferson, among many others, cheered, and how their themes were championed under different historical conditions by Dewey, Kilgore, Popper, Snow, Carson, Habermas, feminist, AIDs, and environmental activists (just to name a few) then the idea of a serious, stable, and sustainable relation between science and "rhetoric" has deep modern and postmodern scientific precedent, along with deep ethical implications. While the advancement of modern science in the 19th century removed much of science from the lay avocation of the gentleman naturalist—of which Charles Darwin was no doubt both the greatest and the last—the incorporation of science into the fabric of modern culture makes it once again available as an object for public deliberation.

As Stephen Toulmin (2001) has argued, much of our confusion about the nature of science in its relation to the situated judgment of ordinary persons and no small part of its authoritarian appropriation, has stemmed from what he has called "The Physics That Never Was" (Toulmin, 2001, pp. 47–48). Newton could seem to show that our solar system was a stable entity, apparently crafted by a rational mathematical intelligence, so long as he calculated for two, and only two, bodies. But calculating for just two bodies was never good enough for Leibniz who wanted to know not just how to predict the movements of this or that body discretely, but wanted a general equation to show the necessary rationality of the whole system in all of its parts. Repeated and uniformly unsuccessful efforts from Newton's time through the 19th century by the greatest names in mathematics, failed to solve "the three body problem" (Toulmin, 2001, pp. 49–55). The persistence of the three-body problem has led to our own current science of complexity and instability. As our deliberations over global warming illustrate, complexity theory has contributed to our better, if tardy, understanding of the human role in tipping, or righting, the delicate balance between order and chaos.

The ethical implications of our complexity model of science for the relation of science and democracy, expert and lay knowledge, are evident and urgent. Environmental systems are non-Newtonian and the interrelationships they manifest are partly created by the humans who inhabit them. In a dynamic science where many bodies interact, the technical expert/lay ignorance model has, at best, a contextual validity. Seen in broader perspective the expert/lay ignorance model is a relic of Toulmin's "The Physics That Never Was" and risks becoming an obstacle to establishing the "matters of fact" including the "matters of fact/value" that constitute the life worlds of persons whose modes of living and whose relation to valued nonhuman communities are central to addressing our environmental challenge. When human actions shape nature in dangerous and unsustainable ways, nature itself becomes a political scene in which the discourses of reason must encompass many genres—deliberative, judicial, and ceremonial as well as scientific—and in which ethos and pathos may equal logos as modes of proof (Kennedy, 1991, p. 37). In the model of what we may call "The Complexity That Is," the local knowledge of a resident concerned about a mudslide, the erosion of a beach front caused by an unsuitable culvert installed by the county, who notices dead fish, bad smells, algae blooms, a strange color in the water, a stain on the rocks, vibrant green growth on a bulkhead just beneath a drainage pipe, or any number of local particulars of concern, all represent knowledge. This lay knowledge passes through various mediations on its way to becoming cultural power. Heightened lay awareness of local conditions may lead to conversations with neighbors, a fresh interest in the environmental science lessons a child brings home from the North Mason Schools whose science teachers are in partnership with biologists at the nearby newly expanded Northwest Salmon Center. Lay concern once piqued may lead to attendance at a community seminar, an LHCWC meeting, an invitation for an environmental scientist to visit one's property, an interpretation, and the interpretation translated into various readings, points on a graph, absorption into a statistical chart, and the chart into a computer model. When chains of events such as these are common, and when they redefine norms, technical knowledge becomes part of the ethic of a local culture.

The implication of our essay for rhetoric, ethics, and science is guardedly optimistic. Our optimism is guarded because, in the first place, what we describe is an experiment yet in process and is one that may fail and, second, as Pacific Northwesterners we are acutely aware, to take one spectacular counterexample, of democracy's dismal record in the preservation of salmon and their habitat. As David R. Montgomery has shown, monarchy (Edward I in England) and an authoritative central government (the U.S. owns most of Alaska) have far better track records than deliberating, democratic, property-owning citizens in maintaining the conditions necessary for long-term salmon conservation (Montgomery, 2003). In our region where land, water, fish, forest, persistent mist, gray rain, and furtive sun form an ever-present continuum it is just possible that preservationist thinking may become a democratic ethic. If through education, continued stakeholder deliberation, and wise practices and policies this ethic can recreate itself over time, technical science and the life-world of a culture will be united in an ethically, economically, and politically sustainable worldview. This lay-initiated, lay-directed, deliberatively centered, and environmentally conscious worldview would redeem, in a postmodern context, Franklin, Priestly, Dewey, and Carson's belief in the scientific potential of ordinary people and Habermas's hope in the emancipatory power of reason. Expressed in a different political idiom, what Edmund Burke called "just prejudice" would then become deliberative reason's best political gift and environmental science's most stable guarantee (Burke, 1790/1955, p. 99).

ACKNOWLEDGMENTS

The authors would like to thank Mr. Bob Hager co-chair of the Lower Hood Canal Watershed Coalition, Dan Hannafious marine biologist with the Hood Canal Salmon Enhancement Group, and Erin Andrea Falcone of Cascadia Research for their generous assistance.

NOTES

1. Especially important are the works of Eberly (2000), Hauser and Grim (1999), and Hogan (1998).
2. In fact, the official journal of the History of Science Society is named *Isis* and it states its objective to be the study of "science and its social and cultural influences."
3. On Bacon's role in moving science to the public forum, see: Ezrahi (1990). A good general account of Bacon's humanistic foundation and the reception of his method by his immediate successors is Shapiro (1982). As she states, "The Royal Society…quietly abandoned Bacon's philosophy of science while continuing to pursue Baconian projects" (p. 24).
4. The diversification of labor in Salomon's house is clearly not based on birth. The princely trappings of

"one of the fathers" of the house who gives a chosen spokesman of the travelers an audience embodies a society that defers to rank. The rank of the representative presumably is based on merit.

5. The illustration is from http://oregonstate.edu/instruct/phl302/philosophers/bacon
6. For an excellent overview of Franklin and science, see Cohen (1990).
7. From Daniel J. Kevles's web site treatment of the Allison Commission, http://www.answers.com/topic/allison-commission.
8. For a complete version of Bush's influential work, see NSF's web site http://www.nsf.gov/about/history/vbush1945.html
9. or was it entirely original. The Bush/Kilgore debate in turn was prefigured by the prewar differences between Michael Polanyi who stressed pure research and J. D. Bernal who stressed science directed by explicit social aims. Harvey Brooks has written on this and his work is available online as, "Understanding the Bush Report," http://www.cspo.org/ourlibrary/documents/bushconfhighlights.pdf
10. The PCB contamination of Puget Sound orcas was recently documented in Hedrick Smith's PBS Frontline documentary. http://www.pbs.org/wgbh/pages/frontline/poisonedwaters/
11. Personal e-mail communication October 6, 2008 with Erin Andrea Falcone Cascadia Research.
12.. All this material is from the local paper, the *Kitsap Sun*. See its web site, http://www.kitsapsun.com/news/2008/apr/20/editorial-teaming-up-to-resto
13. These kills are archived on the web site, http://www.psparchives.com/our_work/hood_canal.htm
14. All of Hager's insights are from personal (Campbell) communication with Bob Hager September 2008.
15. Personal e-mail from Representative Dicks September 24, 2008.
16. Material concerning an action plan is contained in LHCWC, Goals and Actions September 08.doc

REFERENCES

Angell, M. (2004). *The truth about the drug companies: How they deceive us and what to do about it.* New York: Random House.
Avorn, J. (2004). *Powerful medicines: The benefits, risks, and costs of prescription drugs.* New York: Knopf.
Berridge, V. (1992). Aids, the media and health policy. In P. Aggleton, P. Davies, & G. Hart (Eds.), *Aids, rights, risk and reason* (pp. 13–27). London: Farmer Press.
Brandt, A. (2007).*The cigarette century.* New York: Basic Books.
Brown, R. H. (1998). *Toward a democratic science.* New Haven, CT: Yale University Press.
Bruce, R. V. (1987) *The launching of modern American science.* New York: Knopf.
Burke, E. (1955). *Reflections on the revolution in France* (T. H. D. Mahoney, Ed.). Indianapolis: Bobbs-Merrill. (Original work published 1790)
Burns, R. (1985). *The shape and form of Puget Sound.* Seattle, WA: Puget Sound/Washington Sea Grant.
Bush, V. (1945). *Science the endless frontier: A report to the president by Vannevar Bush, Director of the Office of Research and Development, July 1945.* Washington, DC: U.S. Government Printing Office.
Carson, R. (1987). *Silent spring.* Boston, MA: Houghton Mifflin. (Original work published 1962)
Cattell, J. M. (1906). *American men of science: A biographical dictionary.* Washington, DC: Science Press.
Cohen, I. B. (1990). *Benjamin Franklin's science.* Cambridge, MA: Harvard University Press.
Commager, H. S. (1978). *The empire of reason: How Europe imagined and America realized the Enlightenment.* Garden City, NY: Anchor Books.
Daniels, G. (1994). *American science in the age of Jackson.* Tuscaloosa: University of Alabama Press.
Dennis, M. A. (2004). Reconstructing socio-technical order: Vannevar Bush and U.S. science policy. In S. Jasanoff (Ed.), *States of knowledge: The co-production of science and social order* (pp. 225–253). New York: Routledge.
Dewey, J. (1954). *The public and its problems.* Chicago, IL: Henry Holt. (Original work published 1927)
Dranginis, A. M. (2002, July 15). Why the hormone study finally happened. *New York Times,* p. A21.

Dunagan, C. (2008, July 13). What's the solution to oxygen starvation? *Kitsap Sun,* pp. A1, A3.

Eberly, R. A. (2000). *Citizen critics: Literary public spheres.* Urbana: University of Illinois Press.

Ewing, H. (2007). *The lost world of James Smithson.* London: Bloomsbury Press.

Ezrahi, Y. (1990). *The descent of Icarus: Science and the transformation of contemporary democracy.* Cambridge, MA: Harvard University Press.

Farber, P. L. (2000). *Finding order in nature: The naturalist tradition from Linnaeus to E.O. Wilson.* Baltimore, MD: John Hopkins University Press.

Fuller, S. (2000a). *Thomas Kuhn: A philosophic history of our times.* Chicago, IL: University of Chicago Press.

Fuller, S. (2000b). *The governance of science.* Buckingham, UK: Open University Press.

Fuller, S., & Collier, J. (2004). *Philosophy, rhetoric, and the end of knowledge: A new beginning for science and technology studies* (2nd ed.). Mahwah, NJ: Erlbaum.

Garsten, B. (2006). *Saving persuasion: A defense of rhetoric and judgment.* Cambridge, MA: Harvard University Press.

Gearin-Tosh, M. (2002). *Living proof: A medical mutiny.* New York: Scribner's.

Grant, M. (1960). *The world of Rome.* New York: Mentor Books.

Greenhill, K. M. (2000). Skirmishes on the endless frontier: Re-examining the role of Vannevar Bush as progenitor of U.S. science and technology policy. *Polity, 32,* 633–641.

Groopman, J. (2006, April). Being there; Medical dispatch. *The New Yorker, 82*(7), 34–39.

Habermas, J. (1968). *Knowledge and human interests.* Boston, MA: Beacon Press.

Habermas, J. (1970). *Toward a rational society: Student protest, science and politics* (Trans. J. Shapiro). Boston: Beacon Press.

Habermas, J. (1975). *Legitimation crisis* (T. McCarthy, Trans.). Boston, MA: Beacon Press.

Habermas, J. (1984). *The theory of communicative action: Vol. 1. Reason and the rationalization of society* T. McCarthy, Trans.). Boston, MA: Beacon Press

Habermas, J. (1987). *The theory of communicative action: Vol. 2. Lifeworld and system: A critique of functionalist reason* (T. McCarthy, Trans.). Boston, MA: Beacon Press

Habermas, J. (1989). *The structural transformation of the public sphere: An inquiry into a category of bourgeois society* (T. Burger & F. Lawrence, Trans.). Cambridge, MA: MIT Press..

Habermas, J. (1996). *Between facts and norms: Contributions to a discourse theory of law and democracy* (W. Rehg, Trans.). Cambridge: MIT Press.

Hankins, T. L. (1985). *Science and the enlightenment.* Cambridge, UK: Cambridge University Press.

Hauser, G. A. (1999). *Vernacular voices: A rhetoric of publics and public spheres.* Columbia: University of South Carolina.

Hauser, G. A., & Grim, A. (Eds.). (2004). *Rhetorical democracy: Discursive practices of civic engagement.* Mahwah, NJ: Erlbaum.

Herman, A. (2001). *How the Scots invented the modern world: The true story of how Western Europe's poorest nation created our world and everything in it.* New York: Three Rivers Press.

Hogan, J. M. (1998). *Rhetoric and community: Studies in unity and fragmentation.* Columbia: University of South Carolina Press.

Hounshell, D. (1998). *The Cold War, Rand, and the generation of knowledge, 1946–1962: RAND History Project.* Santa Monica, CA: Rand/RP-729.

Jardine, L. (1999). *Ingenious pursuits: Building the scientific revolution.* New York: Anchor Books.

Jasanoff, S. (2004). *States of knowledge: The co-production of science and social order.* New York: Routledge.

Jasanoff, S. (2005). *Designs on nature: Science and democracy in Europe and the United States.* Princeton, NJ: Princeton University Press.

Johnson, S. (2008). *The invention of air: A story of science, faith, revolution, and the birth of America.* New York: Riverhead Books.

Kapoor, L. (2002). Deliberative democracy or agonistic pluralism? The relevance of the Habermas–Mouffe debate for Third World politics. *Alternatives: Global, Local, Political, 27,* 32–34.

Keith, W. (2002). Introduction: Cultural resources for deliberative democracy. *Rhetoric & Public Affairs, 5,* 219–222.

Keith, W. (2007). *Democracy as discussion: Civic education and the American Forum Movement.* Lanham, MD: Lexington Books.

Kennedy, G. (1991). *Aristotle on rhetoric: A theory of civic discourse.* New York: Oxford University Press.

Kevles, D. J. (1979). *The physicists: The history of a scientific community in modern America.* New York: Basic Books.

Kevles,D. J. (2000). *The Baltimore case: A trial of politics, science, and character.* New York: W.W. Norton.

Kitcher, P. (2001). *Science, truth and democracy.* Oxford, UK: Oxford University Press.

Kleinman, D. L. (1995). *Politics on the endless frontier: Postwar research policy in the United States.* Durham, NC: Duke University Press.

Kohler, R. E. (1991). *Partners in science: Foundations and natural scientists, 1900–1945.* Chicago, IL: University of Chicago Press.

Lamp, K. (2009). The Ara Pacis Augustae: Visual rhetoric in Augustus Principate. *Rhetoric Society Quarterly, 39*(1), 1–24.

Latour, B. (2004). *Politics of nature: How to bring the sciences into democracy.* Cambridge, MA: Harvard University Press.

Lewis, C. S. (1979). *The discarded image: An introduction to Medieval and Renaissance literature.* Cambridge, UK: Cambridge University Press.

Lippmann, W. (1922). *Public opinion.* New York: Free Press.

Lutts, R. H. (2000). Chemical fallout: Silent spring, radioactive fallout, and the environmental movement. In C. Waddell (Ed.), *And no birds sing: Rhetorical analyses of Rachel Carson's* Silent Spring (pp. 17–41). Carbondale: University of Southern Illinois Press.

Maddox, R. J. (1992). *The United States and World War II.* Boulder, CO: Westview Press.

McCarthy, T. (1978). *The critical theory of Jurgen Habermas.* Cambridge, MA: MIT Press.

Montgomery, D. R. (2003). *King of fish: The thousand-year run of salmon.* Boulder, CO: Westview Press.

Moss, K. L. (1996). *Man-made medicine: Women's health, public policy and reform.* Durham NC: Duke University Press.

Nichols, R. (1993). Federal science policies: Consequences of success. *Daedalus, 122,* 197–224.

Pease, O. (1962). *The progressive years: The spirit and achievement of American reform.* New York: Brazillier.

Popper, K. (1945). *The open society and its enemies.* London: Routledge & Kegan Paul.

Shapin, S., & Schaffer, S. (1985). *Leviathan and the air-pump: Hobbes, Boyle, and the experimental life.* Princeton, NJ: Princeton University Press.

Shapiro, B. J. (1982). *Probability and certainty in seventeenth-century England: A study of the relationships between natural science, religion, history, law and literature.* Princeton, NJ: Princeton University Press.

Simonds, F. W., Swarzenski, P. W., Rosenberry, D. O., Reich, C. D., & Paulson, A. J. (2008). *Estimates of nutrient loading by ground-water discharge into the Lynch Cove area of Hood Canal Washington* (Scientific Investigator's Report, 5078). Washington, DC: U.S. Geological Survey

Smith, P. (1934). *The Enlightenment 1687–1776: Vol. 2. A history of modern culture.* New York: Holt, Rinehart & Winston.

Snow, C. P. (1959). *The two cultures and the scientific revolution.* Cambridge, UK: Cambridge University Press.

Sprat, T. (1966). *History of the Royal Society* (J. I. Cope & H. W. Jones, Eds.). Seattle, WA: Washington University Press.

Toulmin, S. (2001). *Return to reason.* Cambridge, MA: Harvard University Press.

Voltaire. (1961). *Philosophical letters.* New York: Bobbs-Merrill. (Original work published 1734)

Waddell, C. (2000). The reception of Silent Spring. In C. Waddell (Ed.), *And no birds sing: Rhetorical analyses of Rachel Carson's Silent Spring.* Carbondale: University of Southern Illinois Press.

Zerbe, M. J. (2007). *Composition and the rhetoric of science: Engaging the dominant discourse.* Carbondale: Southern Illinois University Press.

20

Intercultural Communication Ethics

Multiple Layered Issues

Stella Ting-Toomey

In any ethical dilemma situation, we have to make hard choices in considering the intent, the action, the means, the consequence, the end goal, the situation, and the embedded cultural contexts of the case. In an *intercultural* decision-making context, in particular, we often have to make difficult choices between upholding our own cultural beliefs and values *and* considering the values of the other culture. Much of the complexity of an intercultural ethical decision-making process derives from the tension between whether ethics is a culture-bound concept or whether ethics should be understood apart from the culture.

As cultural beings, we are socialized by the values and norms of our culture to think and behave in certain ways, and to evaluate right from wrong actions. Our family, peer groups, educational institutions, mass media system, political system, and religious institutions are some of the forces that shape and mold our cultural and personal values, and also our everyday decisions. Culture refers to a learned system of traditions, beliefs, values, norms, and shared meanings that fosters a particular sense of group membership identity, communal identity, and communication identity among the majority of its group members within the system. This shared meaning system often frames the outlook, interpretation, and evaluation of an ethical dilemma situation.

Intercultural communication ethics can include topics such as global operational standard and local justice issues, multinational corporate power and responsibility in the local culture scenes, cultural values and communication clashes, and particular ethical issues confronting intercultural communication training and research. This chapter is organized in five sections. First, general contemporary ethical issues that face intercultural communication scholars are explored. Second, specific ethical issues pertaining to intercultural communication training and research are addressed. Third, three intercultural ethical positions, namely, ethical absolutism, ethical relativism, and ethical universalism are discussed. Fourth, the benefits of multilevel theorizing are summarized and the core concepts of a social ecological perspective to the study of intercultural ethics introduced. Fifth, directions for future theorizing in the area of intercultural communication ethics as well as core intercultural communication ethics guidelines are proposed.

INTERCULTURAL COMMUNICATION ETHICS:
SOME CONTEMPORARY ISSUES

What is ethics? *Ethics* is a set of principles of conduct that governs the behavior of individuals and groups. Ethics has been defined as a community's perspective on "what is good and bad in human conduct and it leads to norms (prescriptive and concrete rules) that regulate actions. Ethics regulates what ought to be and helps set standards for human behavior" (Paige & Martin, 1996, p. 36). Thus, ethics is a set of standards that upholds the community's expectations concerning "right" and "wrong" conduct. The concept of ethics becomes more problematic and bewildering when the issue involves the struggle between the interplay of global (or predominantly Western) standards and local justice, corporate responsibility and local practice, and value clash and communication preference issues.

Global Standard Procedure and Local Justice Issues

First, let us check out a summary story excerpted from Oetzel's intercultural text (2009) concerning a real life case that took place in Sudan in November 2007:

> The Teddy Bear Story   Gillian Gibbons is a British woman who was working in a Sudanese school as a teacher of young children. As part of the mandated government curriculum to learn about animals, Gibbons asked one of her students to bring a teddy bear to class. She asked the predominantly Muslim students to identify some names for the bear and then to vote on their favorite names. The voting was a way to introduce the students to democracy. The students, all around 7 years old, identified Abdullah, Hassan, and Muhammad as possible names. Ultimately, the vast majority chose Muhammad. The students took turns taking the teddy bear home and writing a diary, which was labeled "My name is Muhammad."
>   Gibbons was arrested in November 2007 and charged with inciting religious hatred—a crime that is punishable by 40 lashes and 6 months imprisonment. The Prophet Muhammad is the most sacred symbol in Islam and to name an animal Muhammad is insulting to many Muslims. (Oetzel, 2009, p. 2)

Ultimately, Ms. Gibbons was sentenced to 15 days in prison and then deported back to Britain. The case brought forth outcries from both perspectives. From the British perspective, the incident was an innocent cultural misunderstanding and not a major criminal offense. From the Sudanese Muslims' viewpoint, they were offended at such an alarming insult directed at their faith and their sacred spiritual leader, Muhammad. On the day after sentencing, many of the thousands of protestors who marched in the streets demanded Ms. Gibbons be executed by being led to "death by firing squad."

From this news story, you can tell that for each ethical case study, there are multiple perspectives, viewpoints, and layered contexts that frame the interpretation of an ethical dilemma case. For example, Adler and Gundersen (2008) offer another dramatized critical incident to illustrate the clash of global standard procedure and local justice administration:

> The Petty Theft Story   A major North American company operating in Asia discovered one of the local employees stealing company property of minimal value.... Following the company's standard worldwide procedure, the North American managing director reported the case to the local police. Similar to many other North American companies, this company believed that it was best to let officials from the local culture deal with the theft and similar violations in whatever way they found most appropriate, rather than imposing the system of justice from their home culture.

The local police arrived at the company, arrested the employee, took him to the police station, and interrogated him according to local procedures.

The employee confessed. The police then took the employee outside and shot him dead. (p. 215)

Needless to say, the North American managing director was totally devastated and, for the rest of his life felt remorse and guilt about reporting the theft case to the local police that resulted in the loss of a precious life.

As students of intercultural communication ethics, how can we make wise choices that reconcile the differences between global standard procedure and local justice issues? How can we leverage the laws, rules, and norms of the home-based environment with that of the local cultural setting? According to Adler and Gundersen (2008), in approaching the above "theft" case, we can start thinking of a cultural variability framework and applying it systematically to the following five-phase ethical decision-making model: problem recognition, information search, construction of alternatives, choice, and implementation.

In the *problem recognition phase*, we should learn to frame the "petty theft" case from both the North American cultural/legal standpoint and the local cultural/legal (e.g., "serious crime") lens. The cultural variability choice can range from problem solving/change attitude to situational rejection/acceptance. In the *information search phase*, the emphasis is on gathering multiple facts from different sectors of the Western and local cultures, to gathering information concerning diverse ideas, possibilities, and potential consequences. If the North American managing director had searched more closely for additional data, he might have uncovered the harsh punishment of "death" for anyone who violated the local law—whether the meaning of the crime is framed as "petty" or "serious." In the *construction of alternatives phase*, the emphasis is on how the North American company can craft culturally inclusive creative alternatives that reconcile its corporate values (e.g., "individuals can learn and change for the better") and integrity policy with that of the local culture's sense of justice and underlying values (e.g., "once a thief always a thief" notion).

In the *decision making phase*, who assumes primary responsibility for making the process decision and the final outcome decision? Is it an individual or a team? Is the approach used a top-down one or a bottom-up one? Are diverse voices from different sectors of the workplace being heard and responded to in formulating an outcome decision? In applying the cultural variability framework to the "theft" case, for example, a tripartite intercultural decision-making committee (i.e., members from the North American region, Asian region, and a third cultural region group) to review the "petty theft" case might help to bring to light the "death" consequence of the local employee being reported to the local police. Thus, the committee members may want to rotate back to the *construction of alternatives* phase to bounce off some more creative solutions (e.g., devise a first-time warning system, fire the employee but not report the theft, demand personal accountability of full self-disclosure, or deduct money from the employee paycheck as a first-time offense). They may also want to slow down their timing in making a final decision in reporting the theft case in order to understand thoroughly the local legal and cultural punishment ramifications. In the last *implementation phase*, the emphasis is on whether the new global corporate policy (e.g., implementing a first-time warning system for "petty theft") should be implemented from the top-down global headquarters or involve the full participation and feedback cycles from subsidiaries from different cultural regions. Depending on the circumstances of each ethical dilemma case, a layered understanding of the macro- and microfactors (see "a multilayered perspective" in the fourth section) is needed to fine-tune our thinking and interpretation of the complexity of intercultural ethics.

Corporate Responsibility and Local Customary Practice

Another set of contemporary ethical issues concerns the privileged position of a corporate culture in developing countries. Issues such as child labor, women's rights, human rights, working conditions, and corporate responsibility versus local discriminatory policies are waiting to be addressed. For example, during the apartheid period in South Africa, many political groups claimed that international businesses had a "moral duty to boycott the apartheid regime—that is, either not to enter or pull out—while others, and in particular, the staying companies claimed that they were obligated to use their influence to better the life situation for the country's discriminated-against majority" (Brinkmann, 2006, p. 432). Perhaps with global corporate pressure and positive influence via constructive educational programs, social justice and other-awareness issues can be raised. More importantly, it is really through the dedicated commitment and collective action of members inside the local culture scene who fervently want to have a breakthrough change that discriminatory practice in a national culture can be directly confronted.

On a more specific level, on issues of local cultural hiring practices, for example, Donaldson (1989) has developed what he calls an ethical algorithm formula. He identified two conflict types: the country's moral reasoning related to the economic development of the country and the country's moral reasoning not related to economic development. In the first case, for example, a Latin American country has a lower minimum wage than that in the United States because of its lower level of economic development. In the latter case, for example, hiring is done on the basis of clan or family network loyalty rather than based on individual merit. Donaldson's answer to the first case emphasizes that the practice is permissible *if and only if* the members of the home country would, under similar conditions of economic development, regard the practice as permissible. His answer to the "hiring family member" case entails two questions: (1) Is it possible to conduct businesses successfully in the local culture without undertaking this practice? (2) Is the practice a clear violation of a fundamental international human right? The practice is permissible, *if and only if*, the answer to both questions is "no."

Thus, assuming that in Country X, a global company wants to open a manufacturing plant. In Country X, it is strict government policy that women be paid 50% of a man's salary for the same job, thus, applying Donaldson's (1989) situational ethics formula, the answer to the first question is "no." However, the answer to the second question is "yes." Thus, the practice fails the overall situational ethics formula test (Brake, Walker, & Walker, 1995). In addition, Brake et al. (1995) recommend the contemplation of the following questions in making a sound ethical intercultural decision: (1) Are you ethically confident and comfortable in defending your action in both the private and public sectors? Would you want your significant others—your spouse, children, and parents—to know about your problematic behavior? Would you want your colleagues and bosses to know about your shaky practice? Would you be comfortable if your questionable action were on the front page of a major newspaper or become the headline news of CNN? (2) Would you want the same action to be happening to you or directed at a close member of your family? (3) What if everyone acted that way? What are some of the cumulative harms? What are some of the cumulative benefits? Would the resulting consequences be beneficial to the larger community or society on both the tangible and principled ethics levels? Would the benefits sustain themselves without your corporate presence? Would you be comfortable teaching your children to act the same way? If you were designing an ideal global organization, would you want your employees to act that way? Are there better creative alternatives that rest on firmer ethical principles?

Cultural Value Clash and Communication Preference

The third contemporary issue concerns the cultural value clash of universalism and particularism (Parsons, 1951; Triandis, 1995). For example, Trompenaars and Hampden-Turner (1998) offered an intriguing critical incident to 30,000 managers in 30 nations to respond to the following dilemma: You're riding in a car driven by a close friend, and your friend hits a pedestrian. The maximum allowed speed was 20 mph, and your friend was driving at 35 mph. Other than you, there are no witnesses. Your friend's lawyer says that if you testify under oath that your friend was driving at 20 mph, your friend may avoid serious consequences. First, does your friend (a) have a definite right, (b) some right, or (c) no right to expect you to testify to the lower mph figure? Second, what would you do in view of the obligations of a sworn witness and the obligation to your friend: (d) testify that he was driving 20 miles per hour, or (e) not testify that he was driving 20 miles per hour as requested?

According to the authors, if the manager's answer was a (c), or a combination of (b) plus (e), he or she was considered to possess "universalistic" value orientation, that is, a set of consistent rules should apply to all individuals, regardless of relationship types or circumstances. The general principle of what is legal or illegal, right or wrong takes precedence over the particular details of who is involved in the particular situation. If the manager's response was a combination of (a) plus (d), or (b) plus (d), he or she was considered to possess "particularistic" value orientation, that is, the nature of the particular close friendship guided the manager's decision in protecting his or her close friend from legal harm and penalty. More than 90% of the managers in Switzerland, United States, Canada, Ireland, Sweden, Australia, UK, and Netherlands claimed that society's rules were designed for everyone and, therefore, their friend had no right to expect them to testify falsely. On the other hand, less than 55% of managers from Venezuela, Nepal, South Korea, Russia, China, and India made the same claim. While the answers of the Swiss and U.S. managers reflected an "impartial" or "universalistic" value standpoint, the answers of the Venezuelan and Nepalese managers reflected a "particularistic" value pattern. Overall, the North American and Northern European respondents in this particular study tended to be more universalistic-based and individualistic-based in their decision making. Comparatively, the Latin American and Asian managers tended toward subscribing particularistic-based and collectivistic-based value orientations in approaching the car accident scenario. The moral reasoning for the individualistic universalists was: "as the seriousness of the accident increases, the obligation of helping their friend decreases…the law was broken and the serious condition of the pedestrian underlines the importance of upholding the law" (Trompenaars & Hampden-Turner, 1998, p. 34). Comparatively, the moral reasoning of the collectivistic particularists was "my friend needs my help more than ever now that he is in serious trouble with the law." As you can see, a rather straightforward critical incident such as this can generate multiple interpretations, dilemmas, and choices. Thus, a dilemma implies two equally compelling and competing premises and an intercultural communicator has to, at any given moment in time, select one of the two equally appealing or unappealing choices (Gannon, 2008; Williams, 2002). In reality, most intercultural ethical dilemmas have many layers of complexity, gradations, and nuances and are subject to different cultural interpretations from multiple spectrum dimensions.

INTERCULTURAL COMMUNICATION TRAINING AND RESEARCH: PARTICULAR ETHICAL THEMES

Under this broad umbrella, the theorizing of intercultural ethics in the last 20 years or so can be clustered into three themes: The first theme is on the ethics of intercultural communication training. The second theme is on the representative voice of the intercultural communication research field. The third theme is on the various approaches to the study of intercultural ethics. This section covers the first two themes, and the next section reviews the three ethical positions most interculturalists tend to subscribe to in their scholarly writings. While there have been some theorizing efforts concerning ethical issues in the intercultural communication field, there is, unfortunately, a paucity of actual research efforts in investigating the phenomenon of intercultural communication ethics.

Intercultural Communication Training: Specific Ethical Issues

Intercultural communication training is generally defined as an interactive facilitation process in which learners are given the opportunity to acquire culturally relevant knowledge, increase self-awareness and other-awareness, manage emotional challenges, and practice competent intercultural communication skill-sets (Ting-Toomey, 2004, 2007). Through effective intercultural training, trainers can intentionally transform the mindsets, affective habits, and behaviors of the trainees in order for them to communicate competently and adaptively across cultures. For a thorough overview of the history of the intercultural communication training (ICT) field, readers can consult Pusch's (2004) chapter on the historical trends of the ICT field.

The ethical issues involving intercultural communication training are as follows: (1) the competencies of the intercultural trainer; (2) culture contact and training goals; (3) transformative change process; and (4) intercultural training content and pedagogy issues (Hafen, 2005; Paige & Martin, 1996; Ting-Toomey, 2004, 2007). Paige and Martin (1996), for example, offer three concrete guidelines in becoming an ethical intercultural trainer: acquisition of culturally sensitive knowledge, development of relevant and adaptive pedagogical skills, and an active commitment to professional development.

The ethical issues involving culture contact can include issues such as globalization, technological infiltration, dominance of the English language, and religious proselytizing. Thus, ethical intercultural trainers need to understand clearly the ultimate goals of their culture contact or culture adjustment training sessions. They need to develop a set of professional codes to guide their decision to accept the training contract in the first place or to reject the contract outright. They also need to heed the fact that experienced intercultural or diversity trainers

> …do not promote training as the ready solution when the organizational diversity problem or need appears to be institutional, rather than individual…. Institutional cultural changes emerge from changes in organizational policies and practices—the everyday assumptions and interactions that seem "natural" but that can create a climate of exclusion and/or pressured assimilation. (Hafen, 2005, p. 13)

Hafen (2005), thus, makes a strong case for understanding the macrofactors that undergird the immediate context of diversity or intercultural communication training. On the immediate context level, ethical intercultural trainers also need to develop an acute sense of the potential transformational power of an intercultural training workshop (Bennett, 2009). They need to have a clear vision of what changes they want to instill or facilitate in an intercultural training program. They need to learn to facilitate "envisioning skills" in the participants in such a way that they empower organizational members by "involving them in the envisioning process, encourage them to be transcenders, and fostering their capacity for visionist multicultural leadership" (Cortes & Wilkinson, 2009, p. 29). Whether intercultural trainers are designing an intercultural workshop to change behaviors, cognitive frames, or affective habits, they are also "playing" with the mindsets or creating "disjunctions" in the trainees' intrapersonal cognitive and affective system.

Ethical intercultural trainers need to heed the balance between safety and risk factors in the learning process, be mindful of the particular sequencing of the cultural learning modules (e.g., from low risk to high risk learning challenges), and the relevance of the content-activity combination in the context of a culturally diverse audience. They also need to prepare for follow-up support sessions or provide other professional support networks if requested. Ethical intercultural trainers need to know how to sequence the theory–content–activity session in a culturally and professionally intelligent manner so that enough trust and security are in place to counterbalance emotionally charged diversity topics such as stereotyping, prejudice, discrimination, power, privilege, and inclusion–exclusion issues.

Intercultural Communication Research: Specific Ethical Issues

Martin and Butler (2001) theorize about diverse intercultural ethical issues from three research camps: functionalist, interpretive, and critical views. While the functionalist camp emphasizes the role of the researcher as an objective empiricist, researching culture and communication via "quantifiable" dimensions and categories, the interpretive camp emphasizes the role of the researcher as an intersubjective participant, researching the lived cultural experiences of the observed participants in context. While the functionalists emphasize predominantly the strict guidelines of "human subject protection," interpretive ethnographers highlight the importance of practicing "cultural respect" and "cultural humility" in learning from the insiders' views of their stories and metaphors, and their personal experiences of their own cultural worlds and communication codes (Gonzalez, 2000).

From the critical research standpoint which underscores the importance of power struggle in the study of culture, Orbe and Spellers (2005) and Alcoff (1991) further ask the following question: Who can speak for whom in intercultural or interethnic communication research? The question has important intercultural ethical implications for the following question strings: Can a researcher really understand the lived experience of a dissimilar and an unfamiliar cultural group without prolonged immersion in that group? Can a researcher conduct intercultural communication research or fieldwork without first mastering the language or dialect codes of a particular cultural community? Can a researcher legitimately write about another cultural group's lived experience without a deep internalization of that cultural group's histories, traditions, beliefs, and values? Can a researcher write with intercultural empathy and sensitivity when the mere fact of academic writing is a privileged act? Can a researcher truly understand a dissimilar cultural community and its deep-rooted communication patterns when the power differential (or social class issue) between the academic researcher and the disenfranchised groups are vast and deep? These are only some of the beginning ethical questions that an intercultural researcher might want to ponder—whether she or he is interested in conducting quantitative, qualitative, or critical cultural studies.

Martin and Butler (2001) end their analysis of ethical issues in intercultural communication research via the following guidelines: ethical intercultural researchers are self-reflective about their motivations, ethical researchers are self-reflective about their positionality, and ethical researchers attempt at valid, participatory interpretations from members of the cultural community. Moving beyond some of the ethical issues raised concerning the intercultural communication research field, intercultural scholars (Barnlund, 1982; Casmir, 1997; Hall, 1997; Pedersen, 1997; Shuter, 2000) have also explicated three existing positions in the discussion of ethics and culture since the early 1980s.

MULTIPLE ETHICAL POSITIONS: ASSESSING PROS AND CONS

These three ethical positions are: *ethical absolutism, ethical relativism,* and *ethical universalism.* This section defines each position and considers the merits and limitations of each position.

Ethical Absolutism Position

Ethical absolutism emphasizes the principles of right and wrong in accordance with a set of *universally* fixed standards regardless of cultural differences. Under the ethical absolutism position, the importance of cultural context is minimized. Thus, the idea of *universality* means that one set of consistent standards would guide human behavior on a global, universal level (Casmir, 1997).

Ethical absolutists believe that the same fixed standards should be applied to all cultures in evaluating *good* and *bad* behavior. Unfortunately, the dominant or mainstream culture typically defines and dominates the criteria by which ethical behavior is evaluated. Cultural or ethnic differences between membership groups are often minimized (Pedersen, 1997). For example, a dominant culture may view Western medicine as the most "civilized" way of treating a patient and thus impose this view on all groups. If a Hmong woman, for example, gives birth to a new baby and requests the nurse or doctor to give her the placenta, a Western doctor may find this request to be odd, strange, or bizarre and will likely refuse such an "uncivilized" request. However, within the Hmong culture, the act of burying the placenta has extremely important cultural significance and is related directly to the migration of one's soul and also to matters of life after death (Fadiman, 1997).

The positive aspect of ethical absolutism is that one set of fixed standards is applied to evaluate a range of practices, thus preserving cross-situational consistency. The negative aspect is that ethical absolutism is a "culturally imposed" perspective that reflects the criteria set forth by members in the dominant cultures or groups (e.g., First World nations vs. Third World nations). The ethical-absolutism approach often results in marginalizing or muting the voices of nondominant individuals and groups in both domestic and international arenas. It pushes a colonial ethnocentric worldview. Briefly, *colonial ethnocentrism* is defined as the rights and privileges of groups who are in a dominant power position in a society (whether it is at a political, economic, social class, or societal level), and these groups can impose their ethical standards on other nondominant groups or powerless individuals (Munshi, 2005; Ting-Toomey, 1999).

Ethical Relativism Position

A second approach, *ethical relativism* emphasizes the importance of understanding the cultural context in which the problematic conduct is being judged. Under the ethical-relativism position, the critical role of cultural context is maximized. It is important to elicit the interpretations and to understand problematic cases from the cultural insiders' viewpoint. The notion of relativism values understanding and evaluating behavior in accordance with the underlying traditions, beliefs, and values of the particular culture; these factors determine the evaluation of that behavior as appropriate or inappropriate.

Ethical relativists try to understand each cultural group on its own terms. They advocate the importance of respecting the values of another culture and using those value systems as standards for ethical judgments. They emphasize that *ethical* and *unethical* practices should be understood from a cultural insider lens (Barnlund, 1982). The positive implication of this approach is that it takes the role of culture seriously in its ethical decision-making process. It takes into account the importance of ethnorelativism rather than ethnocentrism (Bennett & Bennett, 2004).

However, the danger is that this view encourages too much cultural flexibility and ignores ethical principles that are developed beyond each cultural context. Thus, evaluative standards of ethical behavior are related closely to the conventional customs in each cultural context. These standards can then vary from place to place, group to group, and culture to culture. Furthermore, ethical relativism can continue to perpetuate intolerable cultural practices (e.g., female genital mutilation in Somalia and Sudan). Dominant groups in a society are often the ones that preserve cruel or intolerable cultural practices for their own gratification. They also perpetuate those practices that reinforce the status quo, which maintains its one-upmanship and keeps nondominant groups in subservient, powerless roles.

Ethical Universalism Position

A third approach, a *derived ethical-universalism* position, emphasizes the importance of deriving universal ethical guidelines by placing ethical judgments within the proper cultural context. Evaluations about "good" or "bad" behaviors require knowledge about the underlying similarities across cultures and about the unique features of a culture (Pedersen, 1997). A derived ethical universalism approach highlights an integrative culture-universal and culture-specific interpretive framework. Unfortunately, this is easier said than done.

Although a derived universalistic stance is an ideal goal to strive toward, it demands collaborative dialogue, attitudinal openness, and hard work from members of all gender, ethnic, and cultural groups. It demands that all voices be heard and affirmed. It also demands equal power distributions among all groups that represent a diverse range of cultures (Ting-Toomey & Chung, 2005). Furthermore, under authentic trusting conditions, representatives of diverse groups should also be able to speak up with no fear of sanctions. Most of the current "ethical universalism" approaches, unfortunately, are "imposed ethics" that rely heavily on Eurocentric moral philosophies to the exclusion of many coculture or minority group ethical philosophies or voices (see, for example, Milhouse, Asante, & Nwosu, 2001). Beyond the Western codes of ethics such as virtue ethics, natural laws ethics, and utilitarian ethics, and the occasional inclusion of feminist ethics, ethical codes from other cultural regions such as Confucian ethics, Taoist ethics, Buddhist ethics, Hindu ethics, Jewish ethics, Islamic ethics, Hispanic/Latino ethics, pan-African ethics are seldom seen in the mainstream ethics' readings (Houser, Wilczenski, & Ham, 2006). Ethical universalism is an ideal goal to strive for—especially when multinational and multicultural inclusive efforts have been made to include representative members from all disenfranchised groups to share their visions, dreams, and hopes.

A more analytical perspective for guiding our ethical struggles in contemporary society may be that of the meta-ethics contextualism position (Ting-Toomey, 1999) or, more precisely, the social ecological perspective (Oetzel, Ting-Toomey, & Rinderle, 2006; Rousseau & House, 1994). This approach emphasizes the importance of understanding the problematic practice from a layered, contextual stance. A multilayered contextual approach means that the application of ethics can be understood only through a systematic analysis of the multiple layers of the ethical dilemma—using in-depth case-by-case understanding, layer-by-layer 360-degree analysis, person-by-person consideration, situation-by-situation probes, intention-and-consequence comparative viewpoints, and integrative inclusion of macro-, meso-, and microviewpoints.

INTERCULTURAL COMMUNICATION ETHICS: A MULTILAYERED PERSPECTIVE

Multilevel theorizing approaches such as social ecological frameworks and mesolevel conceptual analysis have been implemented in other fields such as family systems (Brofenbrenner, 1977, 1979; Huston, 2000), organizational behavior (e.g., Klein, Tosi, & Cannella, 1999; Rousseau & House, 1994), and public health (e.g., Williams & Williams-Morris, 2000). More recently, organizational and interpersonal researchers (e.g., Myers & McPhee, 2006; Oetzel, Dhar, &

Kirschbaum, 2007; Oetzel & Duran, 2004; Theiss & Solomon, 2006) also start to pay close attention to the importance of multilevel theorizing in understanding the complexity of human behavior in embedded contexts. Some of the benefits of multilevel theorizing are discussed here.

Benefits of Multilevel Theorizing

There are a number of benefits of multilevel theorizing (see Slater, Snyder, & Hayes, 2006). Any research or practice that focuses on any single level will, by definition, underestimate the effects of other contexts (Klein et al., 1999; Stokols, 1996). The tendency in the intercultural ethics field is to focus on either single case analysis or bemoan the context-free nature of intercultural ethics case analysis. In addition, experts either focus their analysis on microprocesses (e.g., individual behavior) or macroprocesses (e.g., social structures and institutional dominance). In contrast, multilevel theorizing focuses on understanding concepts at multiple levels as well as between different levels. In the context of organizational behavior, for example, Rousseau and House (1994) suggest the importance of "meso organizational" analysis as a third paradigm that challenges the traditional dichotomy of micro- and macroperspectives.

Using the term *meso* to imply the "in-between level" analysis, Rousseau and House (1994) used the concept to refer to an integration of micro- and macrotheory in the study of connective processes specific to organizations which by their very nature are a synthesis of psychological, behavioral, workplace, and the larger socioeconomic systems. More specifically, a mesoconceptual approach considers the following four key issues: (1) the effects of context on individual behaviors; (2) the construction of context by individuals and social dynamics; (3) parallels *and* discontinuities in processes across contexts; and (4) expansion of units of study beyond concrete entities to include more abstract processes (Klein et al., 1999; Rousseau & House, 1994). From this layered contextual lens, multilevel models create a rich tapestry of the phenomenon under study.

Multilevel theorizing fosters synthesis and synergy, creates links and loops where there were none before, and also illuminates reciprocal contextual influences. For example, in the study of intercultural conflict, Ting-Toomey and Oetzel (2001) developed a culture-sensitive situational model to explain the primary socialization factors, situational and relational boundary features, conflict communication process factors, and intercultural conflict competence factors to explain the macro–micro situational nature of studying intercultural conflict. Situational and relational features are viewed as the mediating factors that link primary socialization factors and conflict process factors (Ting-Toomey, 2005). Oetzel, Arcos, Mabizela, Weinman, and Zhang (2006), using a multilevel theorizing process, analyzed the conflict patterns of the Muslim, Chinese, Colombian, and South African cultural worlds. They identified both the macrolevel factors such as historical, spiritual, and political factors, and the microlevel factors such as facework meanings and harmony ideals in shaping major conflict lenses and attitudes in the different cultures.

A multilevel, contextual perspective in analyzing an intercultural ethics case provides the opportunity to understand (and possibly challenge) what are the deeply held assumptions and practiced principles of a particular culture's ethical or unethical practice. A multilevel lens may illustrate that a particular unethical practice has both consistencies and inconsistencies at multiple levels of analysis. Additionally, a multilevel perspective helps to illustrate the multitude of factors that shape system-level, situational-level, and individual-level ethical interpretations within and across distinct levels. For example, if we review "The Teddy Bear" case which involves the character of Ms. Gillian Gibbons in the first section of this chapter and if we dig deeper to study the case from a social ecological lens, we will uncover that multiple perspectives were at work in interpreting this international story. For example, from the Western journalists' lens, they suggested that the case can be understood in the macroideology that the "Sudan President

Omar al-Bashir's Islamic regime has instituted in Sudan: anti-colonialism, a sense that the West in laying harm to Islam, and religious fundamentalism" (Oetzel, 2009, p. 2). From the President's opposition party's (umma) lens, members claimed that the government had deliberately escalated the conflict. From the British viewpoint, the case was interpreted from the lens of a vengeful and challenge position from a former colonized country. In the meantime, from Ms. Gillian Gibbons' viewpoint, she used a forgiving and compassionate position to encourage other individuals to continue visiting the beautiful country of Sudan, and in January 2008, went to China to continue to teaching young children about democracy issues.

Social Ecological Framework: Core Multilevel Concepts

The social ecological framework is an interdisciplinary approach that gained momentum in the mid-1960s and early 1970s to better address the influences of cultural and social contexts on human behavior (Brofenbrenner, 1977, 1979; Stokols, 1996). In family communication, for example, Ihinger-Tallman and Cooney (2005) used the social ecological framework to discuss the family system as an institution and as small groups and how the study of family should be understood within the nested historical, social class, and racial contexts. In a health care communication setting, for example, intimate violence behaviors in Native American communities were analyzed via macro-, meso-, and microconnective factors (Oetzel & Duran, 2004). In the area of intercultural communication research, Kim (2001, 2005) used a macro–micro systems perspective to explain immigrants' adaptation and change processes in a new cultural milieu and emphasized the interdependent effect of multiple-level contextual factors. Ting-Toomey and Takai (2006) identified several theoretical models that hold potential promises to explain macrolevel and microlevel intergroup conflicts in embedded, layering contexts.

At a broad level, Stokols (1996) explains that social ecological perspective consists of five core principles. First, communication outcomes are influenced by the cumulative effect of multiple physical, cultural, social, and temporal factors. Second, communication outcomes are also affected by individual attributes and specific situations. Third, social ecology incorporates concepts from systems theory such as interdependence and homeostasis to understand the relationship between individuals and their broader contexts. Fourth, social ecology recognizes not only the interconnections among multiple settings, but also the interdependence of conditions within particular settings. Fifth, the social ecological perspective is interdisciplinary, involves multilevel domain analysis, and incorporates diverse methodologies.

In examining the reciprocal causation between the individual and the environment (e.g., intergroup conflict in a community setting), two specific types of relationships between and among levels of analysis can be probed: (1) parallels and discontinuities, and (2) cross-level effects (Klein et al., 1999; Rousseau & House, 1994). On the "parallels and discontinuities" relationship type, *parallel models* posit that the relationship between and among variables at one level (e.g., community reaction level—such as the interpretation of the Sudanese Muslim extremists of the actions of Ms. Gillian Gibbons in "The Teddy Bear" story as a religious hate crime) will be the same or similar at another level (e.g., larger institutional/governmental reactions). In contrast, when different types of relationships or reactions are found among concepts at different levels, these are described as *discontinuities* (e.g., Sudan's Foreign Ministry tried to play down the "Teddy Bear" incident as an isolated case and predicted that Gibbons would be released without charges while the local news media played it up).

In the *"cross-level"* relationship type, studying intercultural ethics at any single level underestimates the fact that individuals, organizations, communities, and cultures are interconnected. Multilevel theorizing is influenced by general systems theory principles of interdependence and hierarchy. General systems theory emphasizes that the different analytical levels are nested structures organized hierarchically. Given this assumption, three types of cross-level effects should be considered: (1) top-down effects, (2) bottom-up effects, and (3) interactive effects (Rousseau & House, 1994). *Top-down effects* refer to how larger culture/institutional forces shape the ethical stance or practice—at macro-, exo-, meso-, and microlevels. The "macrolevel" analysis refers to the larger societal and worldview level, the added term *exolevel* refers to the community–level context (Brofenbenner, 1979). In addition, the "mesolevel" analysis refers to the organizational-level system, and the "microlevel" analysis refers to both the intrapersonal and interpersonal levels.

Within this context, individual ethical or unethical practice is shaped by the various layering structures in which people are nested. *Bottom-up effects* focus on how lower levels (e.g., individuals and interpersonal relationships) affect higher levels (e.g., community and culture). These types of effects are not as prevalent in the literature as are top-down, but they are no less important. *Interactive effects* involve simultaneous and mutual effects at more than one level. In some cases, the effects of one level (e.g., culture) moderate the outcomes at another level (e.g., community). Interactive effects differ from top-down (or bottom-up) in that the former assumes simultaneous process effects at multiple levels while the latter assumes some sort of cumulative effect passing down (or up) from one level to the next in a systematic fashion.

Social Ecological Perspective: Applied Questions

Let us check out the following critical incident: "ABC, Inc." (adapted from Moorthy et al., 1998, p. 32) and then use a social ecological perspective to pose some multilevel ethical questions.

ABC, Inc.: Generous Gift-Giving or Bribing?   ABC, Inc. was faced with the issue of needing to pay bribes in a certain country, with full knowledge that they should not do so ethically. The only clear solution seemed to be to forgo business there. But ABC, Inc. used its business savvy. Somehow, ABC, Inc. learned that the bribes were not pocketed by individuals but put into a communal fund for work needed by the local community. Learning of the community's needs, ABC, Inc. offered to help local officials to set up a school and a hospital for the townspeople. Contributions were made openly and were considered part of the company's corporate mission and social responsibility. Subsequently, the company was enthusiastically welcomed and received by the local community. Interestingly enough, there was also no longer a question of being asked to pay bribes in doing business with this particular cultural community. The community was pleased with the generous gift-giving and felt the company had showed "good faith" in developing a potentially, long-term partnership with the community.

At first glance, ABC, Inc. looks like the clear winner in this case, cultivating its image as a benefactor—changing from the possible bribery approach to channeling its funds along alternative routes. When we look at this critical incident from a social ecological framework, the layered contextual reasons have to be placed against the cultural background in which the questionable practice occurs. We should also question the intention-action-consequence dynamics in the case. So we can ask: Is it ethical that ABC, Inc. continues to give money to the cultural community in the name of "charity" now? What is their real motivation and intention? What are their action and consequence? Are they continuing to exploit the local people, or are they actually doing something positive that would benefit the local community in the short and long term?

In applying the *top-down effects* concepts from a comparative social ecological perspective on the *macrolevel* analysis, we can ask the following questions: Is "gift-giving" or "bribery" a common business practice in this particular culture? What are the larger cultural values and norms concerning "gift-giving" in this particular cultural setting? What are the deeper functions and meanings of business "gift-giving" in this culture? What are the cultural values and societal norms concerning "gift-giving" or "bribery" back in the home-based culture? On the *exolevel* community analysis, what are the positive versus negative consequences of "gift-giving" for the local cultural community? What are the positive versus negative consequences for ABC's home-based community? Would the same practice be condoned in the home-based community? Did the local community actually benefit from the "gift" on both short-term and long-term temporal basis? Did the local community have a consensus voice or divergent opinions concerning this "gift-giving" or "charity donation" contribution? Did ABC engage in virtuous, just, and fair practices in taking the interest of the local community into serious consideration? Are there any other sustainable or alternative ways to substitute this monetary "gift-giving" practice and in integrating the ethical standards of both communities?

On the *mesolevel* organizational analysis, what are your company policies and guidelines concerning monetary "gift-giving"? Do members who asked about this "gift-giving" represent the entire company system? Who are your allies if you refuse to engage in this monetary "gift-giving" practice in your company? Who are your opponents? On the *microlevel* analysis, what is your personal meaning for the term *gift-giving* or "bribery"? What do you think is the personal meaning and relevance of the "gift" to the local business people or the local community you are dealing with? How can you communicate in a culturally sensitive manner if you decide to probe deeper into this "gift giving" request by members of this new partnership company?

Similar questions such as these can be applied to *bottom-up effects* concepts, for example: Can we act as change agents from the ground up if we decide not to follow this tradition-honed cultural practice? Of if we realize that "gift-giving" means "building local relationship trust and rapport," are there any other alternatives to reaching this goal without subscribing to this "gift-giving" practice or "bribery"? Or alternatively, should we reexamine our own deeply held assumptions about "bribery," and see things from the other cultural perspective and dig deeper for both the pluses and minuses without cultural prejudgment? In applying the *interactive effects* concepts, ethical intercultural communicators should be mindful that different levels of the social ecological perspective reciprocally influence each other.

In relating the *parallel comparison and discontinuities effects* from the social ecological standpoint, we can also ask: Is "gift-giving" in the business setting similar to "gift-giving" in the everyday interpersonal setting in this particular culture? How are the meanings of "gift-giving," "community contribution," and "bribery" similar in meanings and different in meanings from one's own social construction standpoint? In each problematic ethical case, we have to mindfully place the ethical dilemma against our own personal standards and cultural judgments. We may not personally condone business bribery, but at the minimum we have to understand the societal conditions that contribute to such a practice. We can then reason that "bribery, within this cultural context, is a common practice because of the following reasons…" or "unfair child labor practice originated in this cultural context because…." Once we thoroughly understand the sociohistorical, cultural, political, religious, economic, community, workplace, situational, and realistic reasons for a particular practice, we can then employ creative and imaginative visions in conjunction with the local people in searching for an inclusive, ideal solution. As Cortes and Wilkinson (2009) comment:

> Visionist leaders feel responsibility to the world outside of their organizational boundaries. They guide the organization to act empathetically in that larger world in ways that further justice and equity, embody a respect for human dignity, and reflect an increase understanding of diverse cultural perspectives. (p. 29)

Multilevel theorizing can help provide a more multilayered understanding of how individual meaning, workplace meaning, community meaning, and sociocultural meanings shape our expectations, intentions, viewpoints, and decisions concerning unethical practices and principled stances. Likewise, a comparative social ecological perspective also asks us to extend our imagination to understand the "unethical" practice from multiple levels of analysis and from the other person's cultural frame of reference.

A METAETHICS LENS: RESEARCH DIRECTIONS AND APPLIED GUIDELINES

From this metaethics or layered social ecological perspective, intercultural ethical scholars need to treat each ethical dilemma as a unique case with unique conditions, and each context as a unique ethical context that deserves the full attention, effort, and time commitment of in-depth analysis. *Metaethics* basically refers to the cultivation of an ethical way of thinking in our everyday lives that transcends any particular ideological position. A metaethics lens emphasizes the importance of systematic data collection from a wide range of sources plus the important consideration of taking the total person, the total situation, and the total cultural system into account.

Intercultural Metaethics: Theorizing and Researching Directions

While the theorizing process on intercultural communication has revolved around the different ethical positions, there has been a dearth of research studies on the actual investigation of intercultural communication ethics. For example, on the microlevel analysis, we do not have enough theories and research studies to account for how some individuals develop a principled stance early on in their lives—in the face of making hard choices and tough decisions. How do different cross-cultural family socialization patterns contribute to the nurturing of different ethical standpoints? At the mesolevel, how does workplace diversity or homogeneity impact on the different formulations of ethical policies and decision-making guidelines? At the exolevel, how does a community's socioeconomic outlook in a particular time period influence the ethical integrity or ethical skepticism of an entire generation?

On the macrolevel of change, how does the impact of communication technology create information clarity or information glut in shaping global teams' and individuals' ethical decision-making philosophy? What should be the ethical stance of the intercultural researchers in conceptualizing cultural identity preservation and global identity convergence issues? What are the responsibilities and commitments of global leaders in leveling the technological playing field so that the cyberspace can be a genuine "third cultural space" for dialogue and intercultural collaboration (Casmir, 1997)? How can dialogue conditions be fostered in this "third space" so that no one cultural group monopolizes the airwave or channel because of linguistic or communication fluency advantage? How can diverse modes of communication be honored so that all ethnic and cultural groups have equal access and equal opportunity to discuss ethical–relative and ethical–universal concerns?

Intercultural Metaethics: Applied Guidelines

A metaethics lens encourages the importance of cultivating creative visions and alternative options, and seeking globally inclusive solutions to address diverse ethically wrangling situations. A metaethics standpoint also tries hard to move beyond polarized either-or thinking and advocates the importance of using human imagination and a creative mindset to come to some constructive resolution.

The strength of this approach is that it emphasizes in-depth fact-finding and layer-by-layer interpretations. It also takes into serious consideration the importance of culture, context, persons, intentions, means, consequences, and global humanism. The problem is that the layered contextual perspective is a time-consuming approach that involves lots of human power, hard work, fact-finding, ideas gathering, and collaborative back-and-forth negotiation from diverse cultural groups. The plus side is that, in the long run, the time invested to understand the problematic practice from multiple ecological angles may ultimately help to save time and prevent further human suffering and potential intercultural misattributions.

With clarity of understanding of the embedded social ecological contexts that frame the problematic practice, intercultural visionary leaders can make mindful choices concerning their own degree of commitment in approaching the various ethical situations. Metaethics perspective is really a broader philosophical outlook on how an intercultural ethical dilemma should be envisioned and approached. To engage in a comparative social ecological analysis, here are some final guidelines to help you in framing your intercultural ethical stance:

1.   Who or which group perpetuates this practice within this culture and with what reasons?
2.   Who or which group resists this practice and with what reasons? Who is benefiting? Who is suffering—voluntarily or involuntarily?
3.   Does the practice cause unjustifiable suffering to an individual or a selected group of individuals at the pleasure of another group?
4.   What is my role and what is my "voice" in this ethical dilemma?
5.   Should I condemn/reject this practice publicly and withdraw from the cultural scene?
6.   Should I go along and find a solution that reconciles cultural differences?
7.   Can I visualize alternative solutions or creative outcomes that can serve to honor the cultural traditions and at the same time get rid of the intolerable cultural practice?
8.   At what level can I implement this particular creative solution? Who are my allies? Who are my enemies?
9.   Should I act as a change agent in the local cultural scene via grassroots movement efforts?
10. What systematic changes in the culture are needed for the creative solution to sustain itself and filter through the system?

Many problematic cultural practices perpetuate themselves because of long-standing cultural habits or ignorance of alternative ways of doing things. Education or a desire for change from within the people in a local culture is usually how a questionable practice is ended. From a metaethics social ecological framework, making a sound ethical judgment demands both breadth and depth of culture-sensitive knowledge, context-specific knowledge, and genuine humanistic concern.

A metaethical decision is a discovery process, digging deeper into our own value system to find inconsistencies, resonating points, and creative problem-solving commitments. It also demands us to extend the courtesy and the respect to the other person's cultural frame of reference, and attempting to understand her or his cultural and personal interpretations concerning the problematic practice at multiple levels. After understanding the macro- and microreasons behind an objectionable practice, we can then decide to accept or condemn such problematic "customs," or find reasonable accommodation between both cultural spectrums. A metaethics lens call for the empowerment of the self and others to seek multiple truths, the courage to dialogue side-by-side with culturally unfamiliar others, and the wisdom to make a principled decision once all the social ecological layers from multiple voices are known and respectfully heard.

REFERENCES

Adler, N., with Gundersen, A. (2008). *International dimensions of organizational behavior* (5th edition). Mason, OH: Thomson/Southwest.

Alcoff, L. (1991). The problem of speaking for others. *Cultural Critique, 20,* 5–32.

Barnlund, D. (1982). The cross-cultural arena: An ethical void. In L. Samovar & R. Porter (Eds.), *Intercultural communication: A reader* (3rd ed., pp. 378–383). Belmont, CA: Wadsworth.

Bennett, J. M. (2009). Transformative training: Designing programs for culture learning. In M. A. Moodian (Ed.), *Contemporary leadership and intercultural competence: Exploring the cross-cultural dynamics within organizations* (pp. 95–110). Los Angeles, CA: Sage

Bennett, J. M., & Bennett, M. J. (2004). Developing intercultural sensitivity: An integrative approach to global and domestic diversity. In D. Landis, J. Bennett, & M. Bennett (Eds.), *Handbook of intercultural training* (3rd ed., pp. 147–165). Thousand Oaks, CA: Sage.

Brake, T., Walker, D., & Walker, T. (1995). *Doing business internationally: The guide to cross-cultural success.* Burr Ridge, IL: Irwin Professional.

Brinkmann, J. (2006). Business ethics and intercultural communication: Exploring the overlap between the two academic fields. In L. Samovar, R. Porter, & E. McDaniel (Eds.), *Intercultural communication: A reader* (11th ed., pp. 430–439). Belmont, CA: Thomson/Wadsworth.

Brofenbrenner, U. (1977). Toward an experimental ecology of human development. *American Psychologist, 32,* 513–531.

Brofenbrenner, U. (1979). *The ecology of human development.* Cambridge, MA: Harvard University Press.

Casmir, F. (1997). Ethics, culture, and communication: An application of the third-culture building model to international and intercultural communication. In F. Casmir (Ed.), *Ethics in intercultural and international communication* (pp. 89–118). Mahwah, NJ: Erlbaum.

Cortes, C. E., & Wilkinson, L. (2009). Developing and implementing a multicultural vision. In M. A. Moodian (Ed.), *Contemporary leadership and intercultural competence: Exploring the cross-cultural dynamics within organizations* (pp. 17–31). Los Angeles, CA: Sage.

Donaldson, T. (1989). *Ethics of international business.* New York: Oxford University Press.

Fadiman, A. (1997). *The spirit catches you and you fall down.* New York: Farrar, Straus, & Giroux.

Gannon, M. J. (2008). *Paradoxes of culture and globalization.* Los Angeles, CA: Sage.

Gonzalez, M. C. (2000). The four seasons of ethnography: A creation centered ontology for ethnography. *International Journal of Intercultural Relations, 24,* 623–650.

Hafen, S. (2005). Cultural diversity training: A critical (ironic) cartography of advocacy and oppositional silences. In G. Cheney & G. A. Barnett (Eds.), *International and multicultural organizational communication* (pp. 3–43). Cresskill, NJ: Hampton Press.

Hall, B. J. (1997). Culture, ethics, and communication. In F. Casmir (Ed.), *Ethics in intercultural and international communication* (pp. 11–42). Mahwah, NJ: Erlbaum.

Houser, R., Wilczenski, F., & Ham, M. A. (2006). *Culturally relevant ethical decision-making in counseling.* Thousand Oaks, CA: Sage.

Huston, T. L. (2000). The social ecology of marriage and other intimate unions. *Journal of Marriage and the Family, 62,* 298–320.

Ihinger-Tallman, M., & Cooney, T. (2005). *Families in context: An introduction.* Los Angeles, CA: Roxbury.

Kim Y. Y. (2001). *Becoming intercultural: An integrative theory of communication and cross-cultural adaptation.* Thousand Oaks, CA: Sage.

Kim, Y. Y. (2005). Adapting to a new culture: An integrative communication theory. In W. B. Gudykunst (Ed.), *Theorizing about intercultural communication* (pp. 375–400). Thousand Oaks, CA: Sage.

Klein, K. J., Tosi, H., & Cannella, A. A. (1999). Multilevel theory building: Benefits, barriers, and new developments. *Academy of Management Review, 24,* 243–248.

Martin, J., & Butler, R. (2001). Toward an ethic of intercultural communication research. In V. Milhouse, M. Asante, & P. Nwosu, P. (Eds.), *Transcultural realities: Interdisciplinary perspectives on cross-cultural relations* (pp. 283–298). Thousand Oaks, CA: Sage.

Milhouse, V., Asante, M., & Nwosu, P. (Eds.) (2001). *Transcultural realities: Interdisciplinary perspectives on cross-cultural relations.* Thousand Oaks, CA: Sage.

Moorthy, R., DeGeorge, R., Donaldson, T., Ellos, W., Solomon, R., & Textor, R. (1998). *Uncompromising integrity: Motorola's global challenge.* Schaumberg, IL: Motorola University Press.

Munshi, D. (2005). Through the subject's eye: Situating the other in discourses of diversity. In G. Cheney & G. A. Barnett (Eds.), *International and multicultural organizational communication* (pp. 45–70). Cresskill, NJ: Hampton Press.

Myers, K., & McPhee, R. (2006). Influences on member assimilation in workgroups in high reliability organizations: A multilevel analysis. *Human Communication Research, 32,* 440–468.

Oetzel, J. (2009). *Intercultural communication: A layered approach.* New York: Vango Books.

Oetzel, J., Arcos, B., Mabizela, P., Weinman, A. M., & Zhang, Q. (2006). Historical, political, and spiritual factors of conflict: Understanding conflict perspectives and communication in the Muslim world, China, Colombia, and South Africa. In J. Oetzel & S. Ting-Toomey (Eds.), *The Sage handbook of conflict communication* (pp. 549–574). Thousand Oaks, CA: Sage.

Oetzel, J., Dahr, S., & Kirschbaum, K. (2007). Intercultural conflict from a multilevel perspective: Trends, possibilities, and future directions. *Journal of Intercultural Communication Research, 36,* 183–204.

Oetzel, J. G., & Duran, B. (2004). Intimate partner violence in American Indian and/or Alaska Native communities: A social ecological framework of determinants and interventions. *The American Indian and Alaska Native Mental Health Research: A Journal of the National Center, 11*(3), 49–68.

Oetzel, J., Ting-Toomey, S., & Rinderle, S. (2006). Conflict communication in contexts: A social ecological perspective. In J. Oetzel & S. Ting-Toomey (Eds.), *The Sage handbook of conflict communication* (pp. 727–739). Thousand Oaks, CA: Sage.

Orbe, M., & Spellers, R. (2005). From the margin to the center: Utilizing co-culture theory in diverse contexts. In W. B. Gudykunst (Ed.), *Theorizing about intercultural communication* (pp. 173–191). Thousand Oaks, CA: Sage.

Paige, M., & Martin, J. (1996). Ethics in intercultural training. In D. Landis & R. Bhagat (Eds.), *Handbook of intercultural training* (2nd ed., pp. 35–60). Thousand Oaks, CA: Sage.

Parsons, T. (1951). *The social system.* Glencoe, IL: Free Press.

Pedersen, P. (1997). Do the right thing: A question of ethics. In K. Cushner & R. Brislin (Eds.), *Improving intercultural interactions: Modules for cross-cultural training programs* (Vol. 2, pp. 149–164). Thousand Oaks, CA: Sage.

Pusch, M. (2004). Intercultural training in historical perspective. In D. Landis, J. Bennett, & M. Bennett (Eds.), *Handbook of intercultural training* (3rd ed., pp. 13–36). Thousand Oaks, CA: Sage.

Rousseau, D. M., & House, R. J. (1994). Meso organizational behavior: Avoiding three fundamental biases. In C. L. Cooper & D. M. Rousseau (Eds). *Trends in organizational behavior* (Vol. 1, pp. 13–30). New York: Wiley.

Shuter, R. (2000). Ethics, culture, and communication: An intercultural perspective. In L. Samovar & R. Porter (Eds.), *Intercultural communication: A reader* (9th ed., pp. 443–450). Belmont, CA: Wadsworth.

Slater, M., Snyder, L., & Hayes, A. (2006). Thinking and modeling at multiple levels: The potential contribution of multilevel modeling to communication theory and research. *Human Communication Research, 32,* 375–384.

Stokols, D. (1996). Translating social ecological theory into guidelines for community health promotion. *American Journal of Health Promotion, 10,* 282–298.

Theiss, J., & Solomon, D. (2006). Coupling longitudinal data and multilevel modeling to examine the antecedents and consequences of jealousy experiences in romantic relationships. *Human Communication Research, 32,* 469–503.

Ting-Toomey, S. (1999). *Communicating across cultures.* New York: Guilford.

Ting-Toomey, S. (2004). Translating conflict face-negotiation theory into practice. In D. Landis, J. Bennett, & M. Bennett (Eds.), *Handbook of intercultural training* (3rd ed., pp. 217–248). Thousand Oaks, CA: Sage.

Ting-Toomey, S. (2005). The matrix of face: An updated face-negotiation theory. In W. B. Gudykunst (Ed.), *Theorizing about intercultural communication* (pp. 71–92). Thousand Oaks, CA: Sage.

Ting-Toomey, S. (2007). Intercultural conflict training: Theory-practice approaches and research challenges. *Journal of Intercultural Communication Research, 36,* 255–271.

Ting-Toomey, S., & Chung, L. C. (2005). *Understanding intercultural communication.* Los Angeles, CA: Roxbury /Oxford University Press.

Ting-Toomey, S., & Oetzel, J. (2001). *Managing intercultural conflict effectively.* Thousand Oaks, CA: Sage.

Ting-Toomey, S., & Takai, J. (2006). Explaining intercultural conflict: Promising approaches and directions. In J. Oetzel & S. Ting-Toomey (Eds.), *The Sage handbook of conflict communication* (pp. 691–723). Thousand Oaks, CA: Sage.

Triandis, H. (1995). *Individualism and collectivism.* Boulder, CO: Westview Press.

Trompenaars, F., & Hampden-Turner, C. (1998). *Riding the waves of culture: Understanding cultural diversity in global business* (2nd ed.). New York: McGraw-Hill.

Williams, D., & Williams-Morris, R. (2000). Racism and mental health: The African American experience. *Ethnicity & Health, 5,* 243–268.

Williams, P. (2002). *The paradox of power.* New York: Warner Books.

Unit 3
CONTEMPORARY ISSUES

21

Diversity, Identity, and Multiculturalism in the Media

The Case of Muslims in the British Press

Nasar Meer and Tariq Modood

MULTICULTURALISM, CITIZENSHIP, AND MUSLIMS[1]

Multiculturalism has been described by Bhabha (1998, p. 31) as a "portmanteau term" because it encapsulates a variety of sometimes contested meanings (see Meer & Modood, 2009a for a discussion of some different typologies). In this respect the *idea* of multiculturalism might be said to have a "chameleonlike" quality that facilitates its simultaneous adoption and rejection in the critique or defense of similar social and political projects (e.g., Smith, 2010). At the same time, a widely accepted or central thrust of a great deal of what multiculturalism denotes includes a critique of "the myth of homogeneous and monocultural nation-states," and an advocacy of the right of minority "cultural maintenance and community formation, linking these to social equality and protection from discrimination" (Castles, 2000, p. 5). As such ideas of multiculturalism must necessarily engage with ideas of citizenship when the latter are oriented toward a reciprocal balance of rights and responsibilities, assumptions of virtue, and conceptions of membership or civic status.

While the membership conferred by citizenship should entail equal opportunity, dignity, and confidence, different views remain about the proper ways, in culturally diverse societies, to confer this civic status. Those engaged in the "multicultural turn" maintain that conceptions of citizenship can frequently ignore the sensibilities of minorities marked by social, cultural, and political differences (May, Modood, & Squires, 2004). Hence the *political* multiculturalism of Modood (2006), for example, insists that "when new groups enter a society, there has to be some education and refinement of…sensitivities in the light of changing circumstances and the specific vulnerabilities of new entrants" (p. 61).

In this chapter we use the example of press discourse on Muslims in Britain to explore various intersections between multicultural ethics and communication in the public sphere. Our central argument is that the idea of multiculturalism provides a compelling rationale to seek revisions in the representation of minorities by the mainstream media. This is elaborated through a discussion of dominant characterizations of Muslims in the national press; characterizations that Muslims may seek to challenge through one of two means. The first is to contest negative representations by engaging with the mainstream media. The second is to cultivate a positive difference in alternative public spheres or counterpublics (illustrated by a proliferation of Muslim media). These issues of positive and negative representation herald important implications for wider considerations of citizenship. To elaborate these we first require an explanation of the value of multiculturalism to any theory of communication, as well as some understanding of how this can relate to notions of the public sphere.

In terms of the public philosophy of citizenship in Britain, some have argued that multicultural inclusion would, perhaps uniquely, prove problematic for Muslims. According to Favell (1998), and ever since the *Satanic Verses* affair, "one of the hottest issues thrown up by multiculturalism in Britain has been the growing significance of political and social issues involving Muslims" (p. 38). To be sure, Rushdie's book caused a great deal of anger among British Muslims who felt that "as citizens they [were no less] entitled to equality of treatment and respect for their customs and religion" (Anwar, 1992, p. 9) than either the Christian majority denominations or other religious minorities. As Modood (2005) once asked:

> Is not the reaction to *The Satanic Verses* an indication that the honour of the Prophet or the *imani ghairat* [attachment to and love of the faith] is as central to the Muslim psyche as the Holocaust and racial slavery to others?... Muslims will argue that, historically, vilification of the Prophet and of their faith is central to how the West has expressed hatred for them and has led to violence and expulsion on a large scale. (1993/2005, p. 121)

This experience has helped establish Muslim sensibilities as legitimate and worthy of consideration in mainstream media accounts in Britain. Allied to this recognition has been a cumulative, though by no means unchallenged, acceptance of the empirical reality of Islamophobia (Meer & Modood, 2009b), characterized as an "anti-Muslim prejudice [that] has grown so considerably and so rapidly in recent years that a new item in the vocabulary is needed" (Commission on British Muslims and Islamophobia [CBMI], 1997, p. 4; see also CBMI, 2004).

As such Modood (2007) has argued that what has sometimes been conceived of as a constellation of antiracism and race equality agendas, should be reconciled with more Hegelian inspired dialogic perspectives that speak of minority inclusion through a negotiated and inclusive nation–state citizenship. The many permutations of the former have sought, with mixed success, to prevent and redress involuntary racial identities from becoming a barrier to equality of opportunity, something often conceived as equality of access in the labor market, education, and other public provision (see Meer, 2008). The latter, meanwhile, has championed a "recognition" of minority particularities and sensibilities, in a way that marks a departure from the proscribed universalisms or exclusivity in the unreconstructed accounts of liberalism (Barry, 2001), republicanism (Pettit, 1999), and nationalism (Scruton, 2004).

What an *ethic* of multiculturalism can help establish, therefore, at least in the British context, is the promise of a transformative possibility through which minority negative differences may be turned into positive differences, and show how this is important not only to the well-being of the minorities in question, but also for the quality of membership of that society as a whole (Modood, 2007).

THE PUBLIC SPHERE AND THE ETHICS OF PUBLIC DISCOURSE

These ideational, political, and ethical formulations of multicultural citizenship are important to our discussion because this chapter examines intersections between ethics and communication in the public sphere by examining press discourse on Muslims in Britain. While literature on the idea of the public sphere is lengthy and complex, for the purposes of our discussion it will be conceived as two interdependent possibilities of a communicative and institutional space (e.g., Dahlgren, 1991; Habermas, 1962/1989) where democracy can be *expressed* and civic engagement *practiced*. The notion of the public sphere might well be traced to Kant's (1784/1990) essay on Enlightenment, but it is in Habermas that we find the most widely discussed modern formulation. For Habermas (1962/1989) the public sphere describes an arena that is simultaneously inside and outside civil society. This is because it is not a function of the State, yet it is the canvas upon which a variety of public issues affecting state policy might be drawn.

There is, of course, both a descriptive and normative dimension to Habermas's account and it is the descriptive dimension that we are utilizing here. The normative dimension of Habermas's account sees the public sphere as based upon notions of public good as distinct from private interest and forms of private life (notably families) (see Calhoun, 2000, p. 533). This has been widely criticized by a variety of authors including Fraser (1992, 1995) and Casanova (1994), who either insist that it is undesirable to have public debate confined in this way, or that Habermas ignores how matters of both private and public life, such as religion, have historically played an important role in constituting notions of the public sphere. Indeed, it is striking how during the early 1990s there was a proliferation of critical engagements with the Habermasian characterization of "rational-critical" communication as the ideal standard of modernity. As Anderson (2003) summarizes, Habermas was roundly critiqued "mostly for a narrowness as sexist, classist, Eurocentric" (p. 892). This has often centered on the absence or "audibility" (Bickford, 1996) of a variety of historically marginalized groups that Habermas "leaves out or leaves flattened as objects rather than as constituting subjects" (Anderson, 2003, p. 893). Thus Fraser (1992), amongst others, insisted that any public sphere in a just democracy must necessarily include "subaltern-counter publics" in which a plurality of "identities, interests, and needs" can be cultivated (p. 123). For Benhabib (1992), meanwhile, a permeability and creativity in the public sphere, one that has facilitated access for previously marginalized groups, not least women, who have been able to cultivate novel and critical perspectives, is omitted in Habermas's portrayal. To this we might add the broader argument proposed by Young (1990) who maintained that conceptions of the public sphere that ignore—or view as private matters—certain kinds of expressions from certain kinds of people constitute forms of oppression on a variety of levels, not least since "members of some groups are sometimes in a better position than members of others to understand and anticipate the probable consequences of implementing particular social policies" (p. 158). The interesting point, however, is that

> These critiques pertain more to how Habermas tied this conception of public sphere so tightly and specifically to modernization, and that to rationality, than to the essential identification of the emergence of new public spheres around communications relatively freed from the demands of ritual representation, particularly of mystical authority. (Anderson, 2003, p. 892)

More recently, Habermas has himself led the way in acknowledging that restrictive notions of secularity and public reasoning constitute an epistemological bias against religious citizens by requiring that they present themselves within "secular" terms in the public sphere, thus making "secular" citizens exemplars of rational communication to which others must assimilate (Habermas, 2006). Not all of Habermas's followers or critics are willing to go down this "postsecular" path. Nevertheless one means of attending to Habermas's account, then, is to pluralize it by thinking of multiple public spheres and in this respect Fraser's critique is very much alive in what we detail as the proliferation of Muslim media sources that have emerged *outside* the mainstream public sphere. In either case what is important to note is how the mass media has historically become central to most formulations of the public sphere because of the ways it distributes information to citizens and, at least in theory, facilitates public debate (Curran, 1991), even while this relationship is subject to a variety of well-established critical readings (Nightingale & Ross, 2003). This could be put more strongly in, for example, observing that the permutations of scholarship on the politics of identity, however, have rarely focused on the media, even though they have often specifically been concerned with the issue of representation, and more generally with the claims of new social movements and the politics of recognition as it relates to arenas of education, law, political participation, and so forth. This is despite, as Dreher (2009) argues, "that it is quite clear that media institutions and media representations are central to processes of cultural domination, non-recognition, and disrespect, as well as providing shared resources in struggles of recognition" (pp. 453–454).

It is equally clear that the media devolve access to the consumption and imagination of meta-identities (such as nationhood) to wider circles of people on more occasions and for some time now. Charles Husband (1996) has been arguing for what he terms "the right to be understood" in a "multi-ethnic public sphere" which requires that "all accept the burden of trying to understand" because "without the inclusion of the subordinate claim of the right to be understood the right to communicate becomes too easily unidirectional" (p. 206).

How then will we explore the intersections between ethics and communication in the public sphere? We will do so through focusing upon public discourse, comprising forms of text and talk that contribute to particular modes of understanding our social world (Silverman, 2000). These "modes" might be consensual or critical, established or challenging, with each finding an identity in their public articulation. The national press represents one deep repository or distinct field within which these modes may be observable, and which may self-consciously offer competing perspectives on, and ideals about, identity, citizenship, and belonging, amongst other issues (Meer, Dwyer, & Modood, 2010; Meer & Mouristen, 2009).

This then relates to Allan's (1999) illustration of how the dominant media serve to construct and reconstruct ideas of citizenship and nationhood. In a way this is reminiscent of how Anderson (1983) now famously argued that the rise of the mass press, or "one-day-best-sellers," from the 18th century onward furnished "rational subjects" with the preferred ideologies in which to define themselves as collectivities rather than individuals. This in turn shaped imagined norms and conventions (that had material consequences) which colored the discursive spaces of citizenship one shade instead of another.

An analysis of print media discourses might therefore reveal something valuable about common beliefs and value systems (McQuail, 1994), such that if one was to consider the dynamics of this discourse as being more epiphenomenal with respect to wider societal concerns, analysis would still reveal views held, even if these are not in and of themselves efficacious (and pernicious). This is particularly relevant because the chapter explores some of the commonsense arguments that, as Favell and Modood (2003) have argued, fail to do justice to the complexity of "hard cases," and encourage a conflation between fact and fiction through a reliance "on the unchallenged reproduction of anecdotal facts usually taken from newspapers" (p. 493).

Indeed, and in making a broader point about the currency of press discourse, van Dijk (1999 quoted in Richardson, 2001) supports this view when he states that "speakers routinely refer to… newspapers as their source (and authority) of knowledge or opinions about ethnic minorities" (p. 148). This also lends some support to the view that "social theories are (re)produced in the social worlds by the news media, influencing audience attitudes, values and beliefs" (Richardson, 2001, p. 148). This is a key point because while it is may be difficult to gauge a link between "thought" and "action," or how negative or positive representations of Muslims may translate into their discriminatory or beneficial treatment, what we can point to are the studies of Wilson and Gutierrez (1995, p. 45) which show that "negative, one-sided or stereotypical media portrayals and news coverage do reinforce racist attitudes in those members of the audience who do have them and can channel mass actions against the group that is stereotypically portrayed." To this end this chapter reports on a variety of argumentation strategies evidenced in public and media discourse (for detailed discussion of "argumentation strategies" see Meer, 2006; Poole, 2002; Richardson, 2001). It is in this respect that Elizabeth Poole's (2002) account of "representation" is instructive:

> I use the term representation to mean the social process of combining signs to produce meanings. While it is evident that the media do reproduce the dominant ideologies of the society of which they are a part, I would argue that they also connect their own "meaning" (norms and values) through signifying practices. Representation is not then a transparent process of re-presenting an objective reality. There is always a mediating effect whereby an event is filtered through interpretative frameworks and acquires ideological significance. News, then, provides its audiences with interpretative frameworks, ways of seeing the world and defining reality.... [The task is] to extract the discursive constructions within the texts that are related to wider social processes. (p. 23)

We have indeed endeavored to chart these relationships but also to embed such an approach within our more discrete focus as elaborated below with reference to corresponding material on methods concerning the use of press discourse (e.g., Meer, 2006; Meer & Mouristen, 2009; Richardson, 2001).

CONTEXTUAL POLITICAL DISCOURSE ON MUSLIMS

These theoretical foci are an important means of examining how the public presence of Muslim "difference" in Britain has become increasingly conspicuous, but which also requires some contextualization. For this conspicuousness is not limited to problematizing episodes of violent extremism that have made Muslims more "visible" as a minority. The latter of course inevitably informs part of a broader picture but should not obscure what Modood (1988) once characterized as an "ethnic assertiveness" amongst Muslims themselves. Over the last two decades this assertiveness has translated into forms of mobilization and claims-making which have challenged British citizenship to accommodate Muslim particularities, specifically by contesting the secular and narrowly racial focus of British multiculturalist approaches (Meer & Modood, 2009a).

This was perhaps symbolized by the way in which the Muslim Council of Britain (MCB) developed and emerged as the main interlocutor in State–Muslim engagement, and how it achieved some success in establishing a Muslim voice in the corridors of power (Radcliffe, 2004). The creation of a religion question in the national Census (Aspinall, 2000), achieving state funding for the first Muslim schools (Meer, 2009), and more broadly having socioeconomic policies targeted at severely deprived Muslim groups (Abrams & Houston, 2006; Policy Innovation Unit, 2001) are illustrative of these successes. Simultaneously, and while these modifications of British multiculturalism have been important in projecting a symbolic meaning, they remain comparatively modest when compared with the race-equality components of British multiculturalism (Modood, 2008). It is curious then, given the longevity of its *ethnic* and *racial* focus, that the fate of multiculturalism in Britain should have come to be so intertwined with the political identities of Muslims (Dwyer & Uberoi, 2010).

This linkage corresponds with how the preeminence of the MCB waned in the mid-2000s as it grew critical of the Iraq war and the so-called war on terrorism. Perhaps most importantly for our discussion is how allied to these complaints has been the issue of how "representative" of British Muslims the organization actually is—a question that has plagued it since the early days but which has had a more damaging impact upon its credibility when allied to a handful of other complaints.[2]

One outcome of this political critique has been the extension of the invitation to represent British Muslims in matters of consultation and stakeholders to a plethora of other, though curiously less representative, Muslim organizations (such as the Sufi Muslim Council [SMC] and the Al-Khoie Foundation). At the same time, newer advisory groups (such as the Mosques and Imams National Advisory Body [MINAB]) do not seek the same remit of representation as the MCB, while other older bodies such as the Islamic Sharia Council (ISC) continue to be an affiliate member of the MCB. Muslim assertiveness, therefore, has proven to be patterned by a number of internal differentiations between different Muslim actors, which can be intertwined with external discourses concerning the ascription of names and labels.

Indeed, terms such as *moderate* and *fundamentalism* are amongst many that are highly contested and relational, and therefore demand qualification and contextualization. This point is convincingly made in Denoeux's (2002) insistence that "fundamentalism" can be a highly problematic concept because of the connotations derived from its origins in early 20th century American Protestantism, such that it is not easily applied to Islam and Muslims in Britain (see Modood, 1990 for an early conceptual delineation). Nevertheless, and despite its origins, in the British context it is often the case that fundamentalism is made flesh by drawing upon examples of "Islamic fundamentalism" with the effect that "Islamic fundamentalism has become a metaphor for fundamentalism in general" (Sayyid, 1997, pp. 7–8). Of course the dividing line between categories such as "fundamentalists" and "moderates" is not only context-specific, but also highly porous, constantly shifting and dependent upon subjective value-judgments (Jackson, 2008). Nevertheless, descriptive terms are required and may be appropriated in full knowledge of their contested nature. As, for example, Modood and Ahmad (2007) maintain: "'Moderate Muslim' is obviously a relational term: it only makes sense in terms of a contrast with non-moderates, as is always the case in a moderate–radical couplet (cf. moderate feminist and radical feminist)" (pp. 191–192).

It is our argument that the salience of a "nonmoderate" or "radical" Islam has furnished critics with the means to characterize Muslims as difficult to accommodate (Joppke, 2009; Moore, 2006, 2004; Policy Exchange, 2007). This is particularly the case when Muslims are currently perceived to be—often uniquely—in contravention of liberal discourses of individual rights and secularism that are at risk of being surrendered by concessions implied in multiculturalist approaches (Hansen, 2006; Hutton, 2004; Toynbee, 2004). This is exemplified by the way in which visible Muslim practices such as veiling[3] have in public discourses been reduced to and conflated with alleged Muslim practices such as forced marriages, female genital mutilation, a rejection of positive law in favor of criminal *Shar'ia* law, and so on (Meer, Dwyer, & Modood, 2010). Each suggests a radical "otherness" about Muslims and an illiberality about multiculturalism, and, since the latter is alleged to license these practices, opposition to the practice, it is argued, necessarily invalidates the policy.[4]

A related development derives from global events, and not necessarily from the acts of terrorism undertaken by protagonists proclaiming a Muslim agenda (which are routinely condemned by leading British-Muslim bodies), but from the subsequent conflation of a criminal minority with an assumed tendency inherent to the many. Indeed, in a post 9/11 and 7/7 climate, the explanatory purchase of Muslim cultural dysfunctionality has generated a profitable discursive economy in accounting for what has been described as "Islamic terrorism" (e.g., Cohen, 2007; Gove, 2006; Phillips, 2006).

REPRESENTATION IN THE PRESS

In the following sections we will detail at least three characterizations of Muslims in public discourse. The first includes some of the dominant negative tendencies attributed to Muslims in the national press. The second marks a progressive development in mapping the variety of Muslim voices that can be in invoked in the press. The third, meanwhile, is perhaps the most interesting and reflects the proliferation of Muslim media sources as a means of cultivating a positive representation (in a manner that shares something with Fraser's [1992] description of the emergence of multiple public spheres).

Divided Loyalties

One of the most striking features of the press discourse on Muslims is the extent to which it is marked by a concern over divided loyalties, such that the perception of the threat posed in Muslim disloyalty reduces complex choices to binary options. This is illustrated by the following readers' letters:

Muslim soldiers have expressed their reluctance to fight in Iraq as they may kill fellow Muslims. The old question for these Muslims has become: who is sovereign: Queen (the State) or Mohamed? Unfortunately those who perpetrated the 7/7 bombings clearly gave their answer to that question (Bailey, 2006).

> Muslim fundamentalists feel no loyalty to Britain and the values of democratic and peaceful debate, because they adhere to an ideology which does not see any value in Britishness. ("Muslim Fundamentalists," 2006)

At one level readers' letters by themselves comprise a less significant source of information with which to explore the representation of Muslims. This is because the publication of readers' letters is widely understood to reflect the concerns of a newspaper's core readership. So it is accepted from the outset that, with some variation, a newspaper is much less likely to print readers' letters that criticize an editorial line or leader (the issue of right to reply is a different matter), albeit with exceptions that prove the rule (see Richardson, 2008). It is nevertheless notable that elsewhere in the press, and throughout the discussion of how issues of loyalty may endure, the British Muslim leadership is variously accused of encouraging division.

> If foreign extremists are a major problem so, alas, are a minority of British-born Muslims who place religious fanaticism above any notion of loyalty to their country. In such circumstances one would hope for wise leadership within the Muslim community. Instead, the supposedly "moderate" Sir Iqbal Sacranie pops up to say that the July 7 attacks would not have happened if we had not gone to war in Iraq. What will be the reason given for the next attack; that we are too pro Israeli, or too tough on Iran. This will not do. Those who feel blind loyalty to Islam and none whatever to Britain should go and live in an Islamic country and leave the rest of us in peace. (*Daily Express,* 2006)

This last point licenses a discussion of the ways in which current conceptions of Muslim cultural dysfunction are presented as explanations for what is described as "Islamic terrorism," as elaborated earlier in the discussion. Indeed, some commentators have argued that Muslims are inherently problematical because they are incapable of making certain transcultural changes that other minority communities have undergone:

> When a generation of Lenny Henry and Meera Syals made it possible to invite others to laugh with them about their own communities, those communities entered into the canon of Britishness. …the most dangerous divide now is in culture—and that means Muslim. British Muslims arrested last week as terror suspects had families as British as Meera Syal's—yet culturally they inhabit another universe. (Toynbee, 2004)

While some scholars draw nuanced distinctions between anglicized and religious South-Asian diasporas (Werbner, 2004), in the above extract the center-left columnist Polly Toynbee presents Muslims as particularly problematic because they cannot ridicule themselves. In considering this claim, a multicultural ethic cautions us not to mistake the acceptance of minority cultural expressions by a mainstream orthodoxy as being the sole yardstick of minority integration, particularly since some cultural specificities of one minority identity might not be commodified or consumed by the mainstream in the same way as others.

This suggests that Toynbee is confusing the issue of how certain forms of difference may or may not lend themselves to synthesis, with the separate issue of whether certain forms of difference are exclusionary by their own logic *rather than circumstance* (i.e., in the face of majority contempt). As a form of pathologizing, this represents one of the key techniques within rhetorical argumentation strategies that present a series of general assumptions about Muslim communities in a way that belies internal variation. It is a tendency Toynbee shares with a center-right journalist Charles Moore who, in the following extract, subscribes to an equally revealing fatalism:

> Once there are Islamic financial institutions, how long will it be before Muslims insist that the state and business direct all their monetary dealings with Muslims through these institutions (boycotting businesses with Jewish connections en route)? How long before Muslims, extending the logic of their concentration in places like Bradford and Leicester, seek to establish their own law within these areas, the germ of a state within a state? And how diverse would such a state be? (Moore, 2004)

Moore (2004) emphasises one extreme possibility of many potential outcomes and exaggerates Muslims' actual social, economic, and political power in a manner that is not dissimilar to that of another center-right columnist Richard Littlejohn (2006) who says:

> There must be no more concessions, no special treatment, no more apologies for perceived slights for which we are not responsible. Otherwise where does it end? Will we all have to give up alcohol, will all women have to wear the jilbab, will Britain become a place where everything stops for prayers, simply to satisfy Muslim sensibilities?

A good illustration of how such characterizations can be distilled from broader political debates may be found in the incredibly sensationalist reportage of the Policy Exchange's (2007) notorious report on Muslim social attitudes: *Living Apart Together*. This generated an avalanche of alarming headlines from broadsheets and tabloids across the political spectrum. *The Sun* told its readers that "Islam Kids 'Reject UK'" whilst the normally fair minded *Independent* uncritically adopted Policy Exchange's official line in reporting that "'Young Muslims Are 'More Militant'." The *Daily Mail* went further in characterizing Muslim youth as "A Generation of Outsiders," whilst *The Daily Telegraph* rounded it up by reporting that "'40% Want *Shar'ia* Law in Britain'." One of the astonishing tendencies displayed throughout this reportage was an uncritical acceptance of the findings from a think-tank that has an explicit political agenda. Michael Gove, the Conservative MP and author of the book *Celsius 7/7: How the West's Policy of Appeasement Has Provoked Fundamentalist Terror and What Has to Be Done Now*, is a founding chairperson of the think-tank while Charles Moore, another key figure in the think-tank, and the report's lead author, is a long time critic of Muslim identity politics and race equality.

The report itself confirmed that younger Muslims are more religiously observant than their parents. Thus 37% of their sample of 16- to 24-year-olds would like to see more aspects of *Shar'ia* law in Britain, perhaps also reflected in law, and that this is roughly twice as many as a sample of their parents' age. Yet it is arguable that the vast majority of people who describe themselves as Muslim in Britain already subscribe to a form of *Shar'ia* by fasting during *Ramadan*, eating *Halal* food, donating to charity, observing prayers, celebrating *Eid,* and so forth. Whilst there are undoubtedly problematic aspects of *Shar'ia;* for example, those that concern criminal punishment, these form only a very small part of a vast corpus and are no less internally contested than practices of capital punishment in some non-Muslim democracies. There is nevertheless nothing in the survey that categorically shows that Muslims in Britain want *Shar'ia* incorporated in criminal law as opposed to in relation to aspects of family life.

Such qualifications were omitted in both the report's analysis and the subsequent press coverage, which characterized British Muslims who aspire toward some *Shar'ia* as medieval (indeed the *Daily Star* took its readers back a million years to the Paleolithic era with the headline: "Brit Muslims Want The Stone Age"; Meer & Noorani, 2008, p. 207). This is comparable to denouncing British Christians for believing in the Resurrection and demanding that British Jews abandon the Talmud, and it is arguable that such hyperbole is capable of fuelling moral panics that do more to distort and reify concerns over minority groups than to precipitate solutions. This is particularly so when materially ungrounded claims concerning the disastrous aspirations of minorities are consistently articulated as self-evident truths. Such examples have informed Archer's (2009) insistence that:

> the current media panics are enacting a form of representational violence on Muslims in Britain—calling into question the identities, values and behaviors of *all* Muslims and demanding that they be displayed and opened up for scrutiny. The aim of this audit of Muslim subjectivities is either to provide re-assurances to the non-Muslim majority or to enable intervention and policing of a potential danger. (p. 75)

Indeed, and in a further example of how Muslims and Islam have been characterized as antimodern and antipathetic to democratic and human rights, the center-left commentator Will Hutton (2004), writing in *The Observer* has argued that:

> Islam is predominantly sexist and pre-Enlightenment and that is the core of the problem both within the Islamic world and in its relationship with the West. Thus, the West has to object to Islamic sexism whether arranged marriage, headscarves, limiting career options or the more extreme manifestations, female circumcision and stoning women for adultery.

Hutton assumes and concludes that Islam and "Islamic practices" are predominantly "pre-Enlightenment." The result of this understanding becomes apparent when seeking to explain "Islam's relationship with the West"; the latter he counterposes as a corrective to pre-Enlightenment exemplars of "Islamic sexism" deemed to be the source of Islam's problematic relationship with a nonsexist, egalitarian West. Muslim contributions to British society should thus be scrutinized for they are likely to be antipathetic to "our" beliefs. The centrist Simon Jenkins (2006) of the *Sunday Times*, likewise, concluded that wearing the Muslim veil amounts to "an assertion of cultural separateness" since "to a westerner such conversation is rude. If Muslim women, and it is a tiny number, cannot understand this, it is reasonable to ask why they want to live in Britain." These are precisely the sentiments and characterizations of a common citizenship that our multicultural ethic seeks to challenge and revise.

Including Muslim Voices in Reporting

If we remain with the example of debates surrounding Muslim veiling (see Meer, Dwyer, & Modood, 2010), a series of which were initiated by government minister Jack Straw, who raised concerns over the social impact of veiling, a different (and perhaps emerging) pattern of discourse may be discerned. This was illustrated by the inclusion of a variety of Muslim voices in the newspaper reporting of this story. The first and immediate coverage reported a general Muslim reaction gauged by speaking to Muslim figures who possessed some national standing. This was followed by more specific reporting on the reaction amongst Muslim communities. The effect was that a variety of Muslim positions were being aired in contrast to a sole stereotypical "Muslim view."

More specifically, the immediate news items framed a spectrum of Muslim spokespeople voicing "anger," "ambivalence," and "approval," albeit with different emphases and permutations, in reaction to criticism of the veil. It is worth reflecting on how these might overlap with or deviate from the characterizations of Muslim "fundamentalism" or "moderation" elaborated above. Following Modood and Ahmed's (2007, p. 121) reflexive consideration of these terms, a notion of the former would conceive Islam as a-historical by making no concessions to interpretation and context. It would limit space for critical reasoning and interpretation (*ijtihad*) in the promotion of a dogmatic interpretation. The latter, relationally, would be its opposite. These notions do indeed map onto characterizations of Muslim responses in the news items. So, for example, the *Sun* ("Lift Your Veils…," 2006) structured its reporting with a half-way subheading entitled: "Anger" which included comments from Hamid Quereshi, chairman of the Lancashire Council of Mosques, that: "This has the potential to cause anger. Women believe wearing a veil is God's command." The *Sun* also detailed comments by Massoud Shadjareh of Islamic Human Rights "Foundation" (sic) (the Islamic Human Rights Commission (IHRC) that "it is astonishing Mr Straw chose to selectively discriminate on the basis of religion." So there are two sources of Muslim "anger" here. The first may be characterized as typical "fundamentalist" response, while the latter is suspicious of selective discrimination against Muslims. Indeed, the titles of the immediate news items illustrate this. Interestingly, at least half of the *Sun's* entire news item incorporated comments from different Muslim figures. These included the "ambivalent" admission from Dr. Daud Abdullah, of the Muslim Council of Britain (MCB), that: "The veil does cause some discomfort to non-Muslims. Muslim scholars are divided over whether a woman should cover her face. It is up to the woman to choose." It also included Ghayasuddin Siddiqui, leader of the Muslim Parliament of Great Britain, who—as an exemplar of Muslim "approval"—was described as "welcoming Mr. Straw's comments" before being quoted as stating: "Muslims should recognise that wearing the niqab was a cultural requirement rather than a religious one." The *Sun* interpreted this as evidence that "a small Muslim minority are pressing their views on others [other Muslims]." The crucial point to note is that *more* than Muslim voices of "fundamentalist-anger" are being invoked, and this includes quite a sober disavowal of Straw's criticisms, as well as somebody in between.

During the following day's coverage the *Sun* ("Muslim Fury as…," 2006) opened with the statement: "Jack Straw faced a bitter backlash yesterday as he said ALL British Muslim women should stop wearing veils. Angry Asian groups claimed his remarks were divisive and provocative."[5] It is difficult to discern from the rest of the news item whether the reference to "Asian groups" betrays a conscious attempt to differentiate some Muslim groups from others, or whether it is due more to slippage. Nevertheless, the *Sun* justified its account with some on the ground reporting from Blackburn in a way that most newspapers sought to detail in the days after the initial reaction. These included the following testimonies, attributed to Muslim women in Straw's constituency:

> Shazia Ahmed, 19: Muslim women don't have to wear veils but there are deep religious reasons why they do. What business has Jack Straw to say we should not wear them? I have never met anyone who has considered it a problem. His comments are misjudged and are not helpful in the current climate.

Baksedha Khan, 34: I would refuse to take off my veil if I visited Mr Straw's surgery. We are supposed to live in a free country. I reserve my right to be fully clothed from head to toe. Mr Straw's been MP in this area for a long time so he should know full well why veils are worn. Why is he making a big issue of this now? Does he have an ulterior motive? This is all about his political future and he is looking for publicity.

Fauzia Ali, 23: I choose not to wear a veil or a headscarf. I know some women would refuse to leave the house if they had to remove them. It is trivial to suggest that you need to see someone's face to speak to them freely. People can still communicate with a veil on. (quoted in *The Sun* ("Muslim Fury as …," 2006).

It is worth noting the length of each of these extracts, especially as they were published in a tabloid newspaper and give nuanced voice to Muslim women who hold broadly critical perspectives on Straw's comments. As such this marks a notable contrast with how newspaper editorials broadly cast the veil as an impediment to Muslim women's autonomy (Meer et al., 2010). In the latter case what was observable was a paradoxical tendency to simultaneously cast Muslim women as the main vehicles of integration but also as the first victims of the failure of integration. In this context, freely choosing to wear the veil is, in some ways, a greater offence than being forced to wear it. Or as Khiabany and Williamson (2008) put it: "veiled women are considered to be ungrateful subjects who have failed to assimilate and are deemed to threaten the British way of life" (p. 69). Yet in these news items the reporting of Muslim women's voices lends support to what Malik (2009) conceives as an "iteration of agency" in that Muslim women challenge the assumption of subordination by speaking for themselves.

Further evidence of the tendency within news coverage to frame Muslim voices within a matrix of anger, ambivalence, and support, could be found in the *Mirror's* use of Ghayasuddin Siddiqui's position in full:

What I think we need to recognise is only a very small number of Muslim women put on the veil. It is not an Islamic requirement—it's a cultural thing. A woman who doesn't cover herself is as good a woman as a woman who does. They are equally good Muslims. ("Face to Face…," 2006)

For example, the *Mirror* contrasted this with comments attributed to the MCB: "If anything, this is going to alienate Muslim women and be a catalyst for more to wear the veil. This country is meant to celebrate diversity" (based upon other sources it transpires that these words were specifically spoken by Sheik Ibrahim Dogra). The only exception to the pattern delineated above, and elaborated further below, was the *Daily Star* ("These Veils Stir Up …," 2006) which focused exclusively upon the "angry" variety of Muslim responses. These included Muhammed Umar, chairman of the Ramadhan Foundation, who the paper described as having "hit out" in stating that: "Mr. Straw's stance is disgraceful. For a Muslim woman it is important to wear a veil. Surely statements like this will not help promote racial integration one iota." In support of our analysis of the exceptional stance of the *Daily Star* we can point to how in its reporting this paper gave significant emphasis to Hamid Qureshi, chairman of the Lancashire Council of Mosques, who maintained that:

I don't know what principle he's [Straw] trying to establish. This is not helpful. It is disrespectful and can only cause anger and division. Many Muslim women feel uncomfortable without a veil because they should not expose their face to men who are of an age of marriage (quoted in the *Daily Star,* "These Veils Stir Up…," 2006)

The *Daily Star* ("97% Back...," 2006) then followed this initial coverage with the findings of its poll which it reported as: "Straw's call for Muslim women to remove their veils is backed by a massive 97% of Brits." Notice that this news header ("Get 'Em Off'") reads more like a leader than a news item, and nor is it clear from the item whether the sample of "Brits" referred to included Muslims. Elsewhere, Qureshi and Shadjareh are also included in the *Daily Mail's* ("Take Off Your Veil...," 2006) report subheaded: "Jack Straw Engulfed In Race Row." Despite this emotive header, the paper presented an otherwise sober account that included comments from the Muslim figures elaborated above.

Amongst the broadsheets, during the same period of immediate news reporting, the *Independent* ("Straw: I Feel...," 2006) too referred to Shadjareh and Qureshi but nuanced their positions with other oppositional statements. These included Rajnaara Akhtar, chair of *Protect-Hijab*, who lamented "a deep lack of understanding of the values of this religious choice to many women... the veil is not taken lightly by the vast majority of women who choose to observe it." The *Independent* perhaps also contained the fullest example of an "ambivalent" Muslim response in its reference to Daud Abdullah, introduced as a "spokesman" for the MCB and who "acknowledged" that the veil:

> *can* cause some discomfort to non-Muslims. Even within the Muslim community the scholars have different views on this. There are those who believe it is obligatory for the Muslim woman to cover her face. Others say she is not obliged to cover up. (quoted in the *Independent* ("Straw: I Feel...," 2006; original emphasis)

Elsewhere, the opening sentence of the *Guardian's* ("Take Off the Veil...," 2006) news item read: "Jack Straw provoked anger and indignation among broad sections of the Muslim community." It quoted Shadjareh as asking: "Would he say to the Jewish people living in Stamford Hill that they shouldn't dress like Orthodox Jews?"—before the paper contrasted the views of two Muslim politicians. The first was Khalid Mahmood, Labour MP for Birmingham Perry Barr, who voiced concerns that: "Jack is at risk of providing succor to people who hold anti-Muslim prejudices. Someone of his stature and understanding of the community needs to look at this in a bit more depth." The second figure was the Muslim peer Lady Uddin who the paper described as having "defended Mr. Straw's decision to raise the issue, although she said Muslim women should be able to choose what they wore." The fuller statement attributed to her by the *Guardian* maintained that: "He should have the right to raise this question and people should have a right to disagree. I think the Muslim community needs to address this, not just throw its hands up." The concerns of a third Muslim politician, Shahid Malik, the MP for Dewsbury, were reported in the following edition ("Niquab Controversy...," 2006):

> It's not so much about what he has said as the climate in which he has said it, in which Muslims—and non-Muslims—are getting tired of Muslim stories. The veil isn't the problem; the problem is that people are frightened of it—they've never spoken to someone with a veil. This cannot and must not be about blaming one group, but about saying we have all got to take collective responsibility. (quoted in ("Niqab Controversy...," 2006)

Malik's views were nestled alongside others which included Ghulan Choudhari of Radio Ramadan Blackburn who insisted that while the take up of the face veil had increased, only a small minority of women in Blackburn wore it. The *Guardian* ("Niquab Controversy...," 2006) reported his explanation that: "It's partly down to the increased interest in our religion, especially among young people. But I can see Jack's point about the veil making some people uneasy. To be honest, I get uneasy talking to people who are wearing sunglasses. I don't like not being able to see their eyes." The paper contrasted this with the reactions of other local Muslims, with perhaps the most distinctive attributed to: "one mother wearing a headscarf and shalwar kameez, but not a full veil," who it quoted as maintaining: "when our mums and dads came here it was all work, work, work for them, no time to study and no mosques. Now we have lessons in English, Urdu and Arabic and women are learning what their religion really asks them to do" ("Niqab Controversy…," 2006). The *Daily Telegraph* ("Take Off Your Veils, Says Straw…," 2006) repeated the *Guardian's* characterization that Straw had "provoked anger," though curiously this paper afforded more space than any other national paper in detailing *some* Muslim complaints in full. It did this through concentrating on the reactions of two MCB figures. The first was Sheik Ibrahim Nogra, who stressed the virtues of Britishness as consisting of an acceptance of difference, and elaborated his own conception of multiculturalism contra assimilation:

> On the one hand he says this is a free country. On the other, he is denying that free choice to a woman who chooses to wear the veil. Does Mr Straw mean that people should give up certain cultural and religious customs and practices simply because a vast majority of the country do not share them? That is calling for assimilation. That is saying that one culture or one way of life is superior to another. If we are truly multicultural, we have to accept that there will be women who want to dress in this way. I have a beard and I wear a traditional long shirt. Sometimes I wear a turban and a hat. Am I going to be his next subject of concern? (quoted in "Take Off Your Veils, Says Straw…," 2006)

The second Muslim figure quoted in this news item was Rafeet Drabu, chair of the MCB social and family affairs committee, who repeated Nogra's complaint and emphasized the importance of dialogue. But Drabu also, however, endorsed the view that Muslims who wear the veil are separatist in their intentions:

> If you are trying to build bridges, you need to listen to what Muslims are saying. The problems that alienate women are to do with foreign policy and no one seems to take any notice of that. This country is supposed to celebrate diversity. That is the wonderful thing about this country: that it accepts, that it is tolerant. Women who wear the veil are making the statement that they are separate from society and that is why they wear it. (quoted in "Take Off Your Veils, Says Straw…," 2006)

What is interesting is that this paper routinely and vehemently pushed an antiveil and antimulticultural line through both its leaders and commentators (Meer et al., 2010). Yet it gave much space to detailing the views of Muslim spokespeople who employ a discourse of multiculturalism to defend the wearing of the veil. It is also interesting to note that the *Telegraph*, unlike every other broadsheet, presented the most critical reactions from the MCB when other publications were more likely to cast the MCB as ambivalent on the matter. *The Times* (2006), meanwhile, repeated references to Quereshi, Shadjareh, and Abdullah, but also referred to Salim Mulla, a councillor in Blackburn who represents the Queen's Park ward (home to a high concentration of Muslims) who urged Straw to "respect the decisions women make." This item opened its reporting from Blackburn with the statement that "it might just have seemed this way but every Muslim woman in Blackburn appeared to be wearing a veil yesterday…. In this area a great many abide by the Hanafi philosophy, which advocates the wearing of veils." Its following addition ("Anger and Headscarves," *The Times*, 2006), however, delivered a more embedded, less flippant "ground up approach" in canvassing the views of Blackburn Muslims. Amongst those it included was Rukhsana Aslam, aged 20, who was described as "outraged" and quoted as saying: "He cannot start asking women to remove their veils and scarves, I feel sinful for not wearing my veil all of the time in public" (quoted in "Anger and Headscarves…, 2006).

The Emergence of a British Muslim Press

We must accept, however, that this example begins in response to established news agendas and the perceived concerns of non-Muslim Britons. Paradoxically, however, and as Archer (2009) argues: "the narrow parameters within which this preoccupation takes place are also rendering Muslims profoundly 'invisible'" (p. 75). By this I mean that the terms of reference and debate within which Muslims are "allowed" to speak and appear remain incredibly narrow. Such mainstream press coverage of Islam and British Muslims, specifically a propensity for negative portrayals, that have informed the cultivation of alternative Muslim media sources that are "more aware of and sympathetic to Muslims in the course of reflecting 'the Muslim or Islamic identity of both its producers and readers'" (Ahmed, 2005, p. 111). Publications such as *The Muslim News*, *Q-News*, *Crescent International*, *Impact International,* and *Trends*, media committees at the MCB and FAIR, and radio stations such as *Radio Ummah* and *Radio Ramadan* have increasingly mobilized alternative views to those surveyed above. In truth this agency is not limited to alternative public spheres but is equally discernable amongst a plethora of Muslim organizations seeking to challenge the negative representation of Muslims in the mainstream media. As Inayat Bunglawala formerly of the MCB put it:

> We've often been in a very uneven playing field in the mainstream media, with the Tabloid press often rushing to air the most outlandish voices, the most radical voices at the expense of ordinary Muslims. Because these are often given huge publicity without a necessary context as to how on the fringe the radical groups are or what their numbers amount to compared to the mainstream Muslim view. So in the end the MCB try to counteract that unfair portrayal of the British-Muslim community at the same time as being the focus of it ourselves! (Personal communication, May 21, 2006)

Simultaneously, and as examples of Fraser's (1992) "subaltern-counterpublics," these Muslim media sources "represent an expanding social field characterized by more than contested authority and by more than proliferating voices or blurred boundaries; central to this expanding public sphere of Islam are new media and interest profiles they advance" (Anderson, 2003, p. 888). The content and outlook of each of these media committees and news sources is inevitably informed by the background of the source itself, including the ideological or political stance of its editors and journalists. This is also determined by whether the aim is to provide a current affairs source of information or one more concerned with addressing social and cultural issues. For example, *The Invitation* offers an accessible account of cultural affairs, whilst others, such as *Q-News,* attach much more emphasis to the impact of British and international politics on Muslims in Britain. The latter was created as a fortnightly tabloid publication, before it evolved into its current, monthly magazine format under the present editorship of Fareena Alam. It describes itself as:

> Britain's leading Muslim magazine, providing independent analysis, critique and review of politics, culture and ideas. We are read by second and third generation British Muslims, parliamentarians, policy makers and educators. A third of our readership are not Muslim giving us unique place in the market as a publication which communicates the rich Muslim experience to a diverse audience. The philosophy of *Q-News* is a combination of style, appeal and relevance to the Muslim community living in the west and around the world. Over the years, *Q-News* has repeatedly set the agenda, rather than react to it. Our chief interest lies in the development of a unique and relevant Western Muslim discourse.[6]

Thus, "while the media-savvy militants capture the attention, particularly of analysts, a quieter drama is unfolding" (Anderson, 2003, p. 889). In these terms of encouraging a "Western Muslim discourse," Fareena Alam has herself described the issues that most concerned her before taking editorial control:

> I was struggling with questions of who do I want to be: a Muslim journalist or a journalist who happens to be Muslim? Islam has an incredible capacity to develop distinct cultural forms and expression while maintaining its universal principles… I want British Islam to reflect the best of my—and others'—faith and citizenship.[7]

Whilst such publications are a fairly recent emergence, they convey a clear desire to move beyond solely Muslim audiences, with the editor of *Impact International* describing his belief that "in the course of time, the Muslim media are also going to be part of the mainstream" (quoted in Ahmed, 2005, p. 112). Another publication, the *Muslim News*, epitomizes this conviction in its determination to reach out beyond its constituency of Muslim readers, whilst at the same time taking pride in its role in elevating and accentuating a British Muslim-consciousness. It states that "the Muslim News has been one of the pioneers of recognizing the Muslim community as a diverse faith group with a common British Muslim identity."[8]

Part of this process has been mediated by a remit in which the *Muslim News* "reports on what the non-Muslim media does not report."[9] It insists, for example, that "in its 15 years of publication, it has exposed media establishments' institutionalized Islamophobia on various issues—politics, education, employment and religion."[10] A more recent and perhaps broader development takes the *Muslim News*' concerns and distils them through a movement named ENGAGE.[11] This news collective is oriented toward enhancing the active engagement of British Muslim communities in the fields of politics and the media through such means as running seminars for Muslims on how to engage productively with the media by furnishing Muslim audiences with the means to effectively respond to derogatory and inflammatory news stories. It also organizes forums for journalists to interact with local Muslim communities ensuring greater access to Muslim grass roots.

Perhaps most challengingly, it also highlights the work of journalists and other public figures promoting anti-Muslim sentiment, and was instrumental in uncovering the fabrications surrounding a *Sun* news story claiming that British Muslims had drawn up a "hit-list" of prominent British Jews in retaliation for the Israeli destruction of Gaza. As it transpires, the Press Complaints Commission (PCC) are presently investigating the extent to which the *Sun's* "anti-terror expert" created the initial story by posting anti-Semitic comments on a Muslim web site, using a pseudonym, and proposing that a "hit-list" of Jews should be drawn up.

CONCLUSION

The last example is an illustration of how Muslims are challenging their representation in the mainstream press, specifically on the grounds that as citizens they too are entitled to an unimpaired representation. One means through which they are pursuing this is with the *ethic* of multiculturalism elaborated at the beginning of this chapter. This is a transformative account of how minority negative differences may be turned into positive differences, in the course of achieving a membership that conveys equal opportunity, dignity, and confidence. Media representation can be integral to this process, and in the ways elaborated in this chapter continues to bear profound implications for the study of communication ethics. It was Anderson (1983, p. 36) who now famously argued that the rise of the mass press, or "one-day-best-sellers," from the 18th century onward furnished "rational subjects" with the preferred ideologies with which to define themselves as part of collectivities rather than as individuals. This in turn shaped imagined norms and conventions (that had material consequences) which colored the discursive spaces of citizenship one shade instead of another. It is our argument that if an ethic of multiculturalism were able to permeate the contemporary media it might herald an opportunity to distil a sensitivity that is able to connect with a variety of collectivities in a way that would pluralize the imagination of nationhood and realities of citizenship.

NOTES

1. The research presented in this chapter derives from the EU-funded EMILIE project and from the Bristol-UCL Leverhulme Programme on Migration and Citizenship. We are grateful to the funders and discussions with other project members, particularly Dr. Claire Dwyer of University College London.
2. Though interestingly its regional affiliates such as the Muslim Council of Wales (MCW) have not faced such criticism.
3. Including the headscarf or *hijab*, full face veil or *niqab*, or full body garments such as the *jilbab*.
4. Evidenced not only in public and media but also by academics and intellectuals including Christian Joppke. Writing in the *British Journal of Sociology* he states: "Certain minority practices, on which, so far, no one had dared to comment, have now become subjected to public scrutiny as never before. The notorious example is that of arranged marriage which, to an alarming degree, *seems to be* [emphasis added] forced marriage" (2004, p. 251). Whilst this is an important issue that must never be ignored, on what evidence Joppke bases his assumptions remain undisclosed in the rest of the article. Whilst the conflation between "forced" and "arranged" marriages is unfortunate and misleading, the suggestion that no one has dared to comment on either betrays a surprising unfamiliarity with a British case in which pressure groups and organizations such as Southall Black Sisters and Women Against Fundamentalism (WAF) have led high profile national campaigns. The government, moreover, has established transnational strategies such as the Working Group on Forced Marriage which has seen the creation of the Forced Marriage Unit (FMU), as well as the introduction of the Forced Marriage (Civil Protection) Act 2007.
5. During a BBC Radio Lancashire interview that followed his newspaper article, Straw said: "Communities are bound together partly by informal chance relations between strangers people being able to acknowledge each other in the street or being able to pass the time of day. That's made more difficult if people are wearing a veil. That's just a fact of life. I understand the concerns but I hope there can be a mature debate." When asked if he would rather that veils be discarded, he replied: "Yes. It needs to be made clear I am not talking about being prescriptive but with all caveats, yes, I would rather" (October 6, 2006). Retrieved from http://news.bbc.co.uk/1/hi/uk_politics/5410472.stm).
6. Quoted from the Q-News website: http://www.q-news.com/about.htm
7. Quoted in the NS Interview: "The petrodollar-funded literalists think their version is the real Islam. I'm for an Islam that is at home in Britain" (Rachel Aspden, *New Statesman*, February 27, 2006.
8. See "About Us" at *The Muslim News*, retrieved from http://www.muslimnews.co.uk
9. Ibid.
10. Ibid.
11. See http://iengage.org.uk. Consulted on March 2, 2009.

REFERENCES

Abrams, D., & Houston, D. M. (2006). *Equality, diversity and prejudice in Britain*. London: HM Stationery Office.

Ahmed, T. S. (2005). Reading between the lines: Muslims and the media. In T. Abbas (Ed.), *Muslim Britain: Communities under pressure* (pp. 109–126). London: Zed Books.

Allan, S. (1999). *News culture*. Buckingham, UK: Open University Press.

Anderson, B. (1983). *Imagined communities* London: Verso.

Anderson, J. (2003). New media, new publics: Reconfiguring the public sphere of Islam. *Social Research*, *70*(3), 887–906.

Anger and headscarves on streets of Blackburn. (2006b, October 6). *The Times*. Retrieved from www.timesonline.co.uk

Anwar, M. (1992). Muslims in western Europe. In J. Nielsen (Ed.), *Religion and citizenship in Europe and the Arab world* (pp. 71–94). London: Grey Seal.

Archer, L. (2009). Race, "face", and masculinity. In P. Hopkins & R. Gale (Eds.), *Muslims in Britain: Race, place and identities* (pp. 74–94) Edinburgh, Scotland: Edinburgh University Press.

Aspinall, P. (2000). Should a question on "religion" be asked on the 2001 British Census? A public policy case in favour. *Social Policy & Administration*, *34*(5), 584–600.

Bailey, A. (2006, 10 June). Radical constable [Letter to the editor]. Retrieved from http://www.independent.co.uk

Barry, B. (2001). *Culture and equality: An egalitarian critique of multiculturalism*. London: Polity Press.

Benhabib, S. (1992). *Situating the self: Gender, community and postmodernism in contemporary ethics*. Cambridge, UK: Polity Press.

Bhabha, H. K. (1998). Cultures in between. In D. Bennet (Ed.), *Multicultural states: Rethinking difference and identity* (pp. 29–36). London: Routledge.

Bickford, S. (1996). *The dissonance of democracy: Listening, conflict and citizenship*. London: Cornell University Press.

Calhoun, C. (2000). Social theory and the public sphere. In B. S. Turner (Ed.), *The Blackwell companion to social theory* (pp. 505–544). Oxford, UK: Blackwell.

Casanova, J. (1994). *Public religions in the modern world*. Chicago, IL: University of Chicago Press.

Castles, S. (2000). *Ethnicity and globalization: From migrant worker to transnational citizen*. London: Sage.

Cohen, N. (2007). *What's left? How liberals lost their way*. London: HarperPerennial.

Commission on British Muslims and Islamophobia (CBMI). (1997). *Islamophobia: A challenge for us all*. London: Trentham.

Commission on British Muslims and Islamophobia (CBMI). (2004). *Islamophobia: Issues challenges and action*. London: Trentham.

Curran, J. (1991). Rethinking the media as public sphere. In P. Dahlgren & C. Sparks (Eds.), *Communication and citizenship* (pp. 27–57) London: Routledge.

Dahlgren, P. (1991). Introduction. In P. Dahlgren & C. Sparks (Eds.), *Communication and citizenship* (pp. 1–24). London: Routledge.

Daily Express. (2006, June 3). Untitled leader. Retrieved from http://www.dailyexpress.co.uk/

Denoeux, G. (2002). The forgotten swamp: Navigating political Islam. *Middle East Policy*, *9*(2), 56–81.

Dreher, T. (2009). Listening across difference: Media and multiculturalism beyond the politics of voice. *Journal of Media and Cultural Studies*, *23*(4), 445–458.

Dwyer, C., & Uberoi, V. (forthcoming). British Muslims and community cohesion debates. In R. Phillips (Ed.), *Muslim spaces of hope: Geographies of possibility in Britain and West*. London: Zed Books.

Face to face: Muslim anger as Straw says veils are a barrier. (2006, October 6). *The Mirror*. Retrieved from http://www.mirror.co.uk/

Favell, A., & Modood, T. (2003). The philosophy of multiculturalism: The theory and practice of normative political theory. In A. Finlayson (Ed.), *Contemporary political thought: A reader and guide* (pp. 484–495). Edinburgh, Scotland: Edinburgh University Press.

Fraser, N. (1992). Rethinking the public sphere: a contribution to the critique of actually existing democracies. In C. Calhoun (Ed.), *Habermas and the public sphere* (pp. 289–339). Cambridge MA: MIT Press.

Fraser, N. (Ed). (1995). *Feminist contentions: A philosophical exchange*. New York: Routledge.

Gove, M. (2006). *Celsius* 7/7. London: Weidenfeld & Nicolson.

Habermas, J. (1989). *The structural transformation of the public sphere* (T. Berger, Trans.). Cambridge, UK: Polity. (Original work published 1962)

Habermas, J. (2006). Religion in the public sphere. *European Journal of Philosophy*, *14*(1), 1–25.

Husband, C. (1996). The right to be understood: Conceiving the multi-ethnic public sphere. *Innovation: The European Journal of Social Sciences*, *9*(2), 205–215.

Hutton, W. (2004, January 11). Why the West is wary of Muslims. Retrieved from http://www.guardian.co.uk/

Jackson, R. (2008). Constructing enemies: "Islamic terrorism" in political and academic discourse. *Government and Opposition*, *42*(3), 394–426.

Jenkins, S. (2006, October 8). Under Straw's veil of moderation a fancy piece of political footwork. *The Times*. Retrieved from http://www.timesonline.co.uk/

Joppke, C. (2009). Limits of integration policy: Britain and her Muslims. *Journal of Ethnic and Migration Studies, 35*(3), 453–472.

Kant, I. (1990) *Foundations of the metaphysics of morals* and *what is enlightenment?* (Trans. L. W. Beck). New York: MacMillan. (Original work published 1784)

Khiabany, G., & Williamson, M. (2008). Veiled bodies—Naked racism: Culture, politics and race in the *Sun*. *Race and Class, 2,* 69–88.

Lift your veils. (2006a, October 6). *The Sun*. Retrieved from www.thesun.co.uk

Littlejohn, R. (2006, February 10). What next? Burqas for all? A ban on having a quiet drink? *The Daily Mail*. Retrieved from http://www.dailymailonline.co.uk/

Malik, M. (2009). Feminism and its "other": Female autonomy in an age of "difference." *Cardozzo Law Review*, *30*(6), 2613–2629ardozo L. Rev. 2613 (2008-2009)

May, S., Modood, T., & Squires, J. (Eds.). (2004). *Ethnicity, nationalism, and minority rights*. Cambridge, UK: Cambridge University Press.

McLennan, G. (2004). Travelling with vehicular ideas: The case of the Third Way. *Economy & Society*, *33*(4), 484–499.

McQuail, D. (1994). *Mass communication theory: An introduction*. London: Sage.

Meer, N. (2006). "Get off your knees!" Print media public intellectuals and Muslims in Britain. *Journalism Studies*, *7*(1), 35–59.

Meer, N. (2008). The politics of voluntary and involuntary identities: Are Muslims in Britain an ethnic, racial or religious minority? *Patterns of Prejudice*, *42*(1), 61–81.

Meer, N. (2009). Identity articulations, mobilisation and autonomy in the movement for Muslim schools in Britain. *Race, Ethnicity and Education*, *12*(3), 379–398.

Meer, N., Dwyer, C., & Modood, T. (2010). Embodying nationhood? Conceptions of British national identity, citizenship and gender in the "veil affair." *The Sociological Review, 58(1),* 84–111.

Meer, N., Dwyer, C., & Modood, T. (2010). Beyond "angry Muslims?" Reporting Muslim voices in the press.

Meer, N., & Modood, T. (2009a). Refutations of racism in the "Muslim Question." *Patterns of Prejudice, 43(3–4), 332–351.*

Meer, N., & Modood, T. (2009b). The multicultural state we're in: Muslims, "multiculture," and the civic-rebalancing of British multiculturalism. *Political Studies, 57(1),* 473–479.

Meer, N., & Mouristen, P. (2009). The cartoons in British and Danish press: A comparative political culture perspective. *Ethnicities*, *9*(3), 334–360.

Meer, N., & Noorani, T. (2008). A sociological comparison of anti-Semitism and anti-Muslim sentiment. *The Sociological Review, 56(2),* 195–219.

Modood, T. (1988). "Black", racial equality and Asian identity. *New Community*, *14*(3), 379–404.

Modood, T. (1990). British Asians and the Salman Rushdie affair. In J. Donald & A. Rattansi (Eds.), *"Race", culture and difference* (pp. 260–277) London: Sage.

Modood, T. (2005). *Multicultural politics: Racism, ethnicity and Muslims in Britain*. Edinburgh, Scotland: Edinburgh University Press.

Modood, T. (2006). Obstacles to multicultural integration. *International Migration*, *44*(5), 51–62.

Modood, T. (2007). *Multiculturalism: A civic idea*. London: Polity.

Modood, T.,, & Ahmed, F. (2007). British Muslim perspectives on multiculturalism. *Theory, Culture and Society*, 24(2), 187–213.

Moore, C. (2004, August 21). Islam is not an exotic addition to the English country garden. *The Telegraph*. Retrieved from http://www.telegraph.co.uk/

Moore, C. (2006, June 17). How Cromwell gave us Joan Collins and other luminaries. *The Telegraph*. Retrieved from http://www.telegraph.co.uk/

Muslim fundamentalists. (2006, June 9). [Letters to the editor]. *The Times*. Retrieved from http://www.times.co.uk/

Muslim fury as Straw cranks up row. (2006b, October 7). *The Sun*. Retrieved from www.thesun.co.uk

Nightingale, V., & Ross, K. (2003). *Critical readings: Media and audiences*. Milton Keynes, UK: Open University Press.

97% back Straw's stance on Muslim veils. (2006, October 7). *The Daily Star*. Retrieved from http://www.dailystar.co.uk

Niqab controversy: Dangerous attack or fair point? (2006, October 7). *The Guardian*. Retrieved from http://www.guardian.co.uk/

Pettit, P. (1999). *Republicanism: A theory of freedom and government* (Oxford Political Theory). Oxford, UK: Oxford University Press.

Phillips, M. (2006). *Londonistan: How Britain created a terror state within*. London: Gibson Square Books.

Policy Exchange. (2007). *Living apart together*. London: Author.

Policy Innovation Unit (PIU). (2001). *Improving labour market achievements for ethnic minorities in British society*. London: HM Stationery Office.

Poole, E. (2002). *Reporting Islam: Media representations and British Muslims*. London: I. B. Taurus.

Radcliffe, L. (2004). A Muslim lobby at Whitehall? *Islam and Christian-Muslim Relations*, 15(3), 365–386.

Richardson, J. E. (2001). "Now is the time to put an end to all this": Argumentative discourse theory and "letters to the editor." *Discourse and Society*, 12(2), 143–168.

Sayyid, B. (1997). *A fundamental fear: Eurocentricism and the rise of Islamism*. London: Zed Books.

Scruton, R. (2004). *The need for nations*. London: Civitas.

Silverman, D. (2000). *Doing qualitative research: A practical handbook*. New York: Sage.

Smith, K. (2010). Research, policy and funding: Academic treadmills and the squeeze on intellectual spaces. *The British Journal of Sociology*, 61(1), 176–195.

Straw: I feel uncomfortable with women wearing veils. (2006). *The Independent*. Retrieved from http://www.independent.co.uk/

Straw tells Muslims to lift their veils. (2006, October 6). *The Times*. Retrieved from www.timesonline.co.uk

Take off the veil, says Straw—to immediate anger from Muslims. (2006, October 6). *The Guardian*. Retrieved from http://www.guardian.co.uk

Take off your veil, Straw tells Muslim women. (2006, October 6). *The Daily Mail*. Retrieved from www.dailymail.co.uk.

Take off your veils, says Straw. Minister asks Muslim women to reveal their faces in the interests of race relations but Islamic leaders are outraged. (2006, October 6). *The Daily Telegraph*. Retrieved from http://www.telegraph.co.uk/

These veils stir up race tension. (2006, October 6). *The Daily Star*. Retrieved from http://www.dailystar.co.uk

Toynbee, P. (2004, April 7). Why Trevor is right. *The Guardian*. Retrieved from www.guardian.co.uk

Wilson, C. C. & Gutierrez, F. (1995). *Race, multiculturalism and the media: From mass to class communication* (2nd ed). Thousand Oaks, CA: Sage.

Young, I. M. (1990). *Justice and the politics of difference*. Princeton NJ: Princeton University Press.

22

Hierarchies of Equality

Positive Peace in a Democratic Idiom

Robert L. Ivie

Standing before a convention hall pulsating to the chant of "U.S.A., U.S.A., U.S.A.," John McCain accepted the Republican Party's presidential nomination by declaring to a national television audience, "I hate war" (McCain, 2008). Who in America could be opposed publicly to the ideal of peace? Indeed, Senator McCain insisted, "I know how to secure the peace." Not even the presidential candidate of the political party most closely aligned with the policy of preventative warfare and military victory in Iraq (Keller & Mitchell, 2006) would publicly affirm a love of war that, as Chris Hedges (2003) argues, gives meaning to our lives at the deepest psychological level. As media critic Norman Solomon (2005) points out, U.S. presidents make war easy for us to abide by professing they have done everything possible to avoid it. In the antiwar documentary based on Solomon's book (Alper & Earp, 2007), this point is driven home by a condensed historical sequence of disclaimers from war presidents, assuring Americans that:

> We still seek no wider war—Lyndon Johnson.
> The United States does not start wars—Ronald Reagan.
> America does not seek conflict—George H. W. Bush.
> I don't like to use military force—Bill Clinton.
> Our nation enters this conflict reluctantly—George W. Bush.

Ironically, in the lexicon of American political culture, peace is a national quest that sustains a state of war. As such, it is a paradox that should trouble the nation's collective conscience, which it does, but usually only on the margins of public discourse. The violent quest for peace poses an ethical quandary for all citizens that few wish to acknowledge or address. Thus, my purpose in this chapter is to engage the irony of representing war as a mission of peace. By reviewing the meaning of positive peace in relation to the myth of just war and examining the democratic idiom as a resource for articulating peace-building hierarchies of equality, we can chart a course toward achieving peace by peaceful means.

POSITIVE PEACE

Indeed, relying on violent means poses an ethical quandary that reflects unresolved tensions and instabilities in prevailing conceptions of peace—conceptions which are grounded in the history of Western culture. What is called negative peace today (Barash & Webel, 2009, p. 7; Brunk, 2000, pp. 20–25) resonates with the ancient Greek notion of *eirene* (Bartoli, 2004, p. 154), which designates an absence of war or respite from armed struggle. When it is infused with a sense of imperial power, the idea of negative peace is readily converted into a scheme like that of *pax Romana*, which is a coerced peace or "attempt to avoid war through domination" (Bartoli, 2004, p. 155). Alternatively, the idea of positive peace stipulates a condition of social justice in addition to an absence of military violence. Positive peace is conceived as an absence of all kinds of violence. It is an absence not just of military violence but also the structural violence of human exploitation. It is ideally a peace achieved by the peaceful means of transforming conflict enough to transcend violence (Galtung, 1996, p. 9, pp. 196–197; Galtung, Jacobsen, & Brand-Jacobsen, 2002). As such, it extends the Hebraic notion of *shalom*, understood as "a condition of personal and collective well-being that occurs when justice exists" (Bartoli, 2004, p. 154). Positive peace, more than simply the absence of the killing fields, is the presence of a state of affairs conducive to human fulfillment. Yet, this very aspiration for justice can rationalize a resort to violence in the form of a "just war" or a revolutionary "war of liberation." Fighting for justice under the flag of freedom, for instance, readily inclines a nation toward "ever-increasing levels of violence" (Brunk, 2000, p. 24) rather than greater reliance on nonviolence to achieve a just and stable peace (Boulding, 1978, p. 67).

The doctrine of the just war, which emerged from early Christian pacifism under the strain of citizenship in the Roman Empire, is a case in point. In an effort to control violence while assuming the reality of war, it establishes guidelines for the legitimate use of force, thus designating the conditions under which war may become the ethical instrument of peace or, as Bartoli (2004) puts the matter, indicating when "a violent upheaval" is required "to restore peace to its integrity" (p. 156). In this tradition of Christian ethics, peace may well require violence to conquer evildoers. The religious presumption of nonviolence is thus overturned because the City of Man unlike the City of God is assumed to be founded on war and obliged to struggle against evil (Barash & Webel, 2009, p. 362). In Augustine's words (ca. 410/1958), "A just war...is justified only by the injustice of an aggressor; and that injustice ought to be a source of grief to any good man, because it is human injustice" (p. 447). Thus, the aim of positive peace—justice—is ethically transposed through the lens of this cultural inheritance into a moral impulse to war.

The belief that war is truly virtuous, rather than "morally ambiguous at best," is the just-war myth that Andrew Fiala (2008, pp. 11, vii–viii) subjects to genealogical critique for the purpose of "reduc[ing] our zeal for war," especially since just-war principles are "easily misapplied by both idealists and scoundrels" and readily misconstrued by "a credulous population, who wants to believe the mythic idealism of justice in war," as evidenced by the U.S. invasion of Iraq in the wake of 9/11. Even though the principles of the just-war *theory* should help us to critique a call to arms by revealing how difficult it is to fight a just war, the impetus of the just-war *myth* works to shield war from criticism. In staking out an alternative position of "just-war pacifism," Fiala (2008, pp. x, 162) engages the just-war myth in search of an ethical constraint on war because, he reasons, "there are very few wars (if any) that live up to the standards of the just war ideal." Yet, the force of the myth is not readily overcome within its own circumference of interpretation.

No war—including World War II, which Americans want to remember as the benchmark of a good war—can measure up fully to the standard of a just war. Although just-war theorists, such as Michael Walzer (1977, pp. xiii–xvi, 41, 72; 2004, p. 14), would argue as a matter of practical morality that it must be possible to fight a morally permissible war, Fiala (2008, pp. 29–30) considers this impulse to be more of a mythic compulsion than an ethical reality. Faith in the possibility of a just war is a social formation constituted by a living history of self-justification written by the victors, and thus, as a historical discourse of power, it is a matter for genealogical inquiry and critique (Foucault, 1971/1998).

Such a critical inquiry into the just-war doctrine reveals, among other problems for a liberal democratic society, that this religiously grounded war justification "is linked to [an outmoded] view of sovereignty that holds that political power comes from God" and that "political authorities are ordained and justified by God," thereby giving secular authorities a religious mandate to engage in warfare "sanctified by divine justice" (Fiala, 2008, pp. 30–33). Using the principles of *jus ad bellum* and *jus in bellum* as rhetorical prompts, these same "proper authorities" determine—according to their own perspective, interests, and fallibilities in inherently ambiguous situations—when there is "just cause" and when the ensuing slaughter is guided by "right intention" as a "last resort" to achieve benefits that "proportionally" outweigh the harms of war, while making a good-faith effort to use means in proportion to ends, to avoid the use of inherently wrongful measures such as torture and rape, and to minimize noncombatant casualties, all with a reasonable expectation of "probable success" or victory (see, for example, Ivie, 1979, pp. 312–315). Achieving all of this under the conditions of modern hostilities is impossible to imagine, short of a mythic faith in divine sanction and righteous authority. The sordid reality of warfare simply does not conform to any such ideals of justness. Thus, the theory of just war is a dangerous myth insofar as it rationalizes a state of warfare and displaces an ethic of peace.

Besides perpetuating a religious legitimatization of secular authority which has evolved from medieval origins, the just-war doctrine raises the value of warring states above that of individuals. It disrespects individuality contrary to contemporary standards of liberal democracy, creating a totalizing condition in which individuals are used as functionaries of the state to fight for the state's higher good without due regard for the lives of citizens (Fiala, 2008, pp. 48–49). By extension, "the soldier is a servant of the state, God, and justice" (Fiala, 2008, p. 50). In losing sight of the personal face of war and reducing individuals to dehumanized objects and depersonalized instruments, we lose respect for the dignity of human beings. This is especially problematic in a time when the technology of modern warfare is disproportionate in its extermination of combatants and indiscriminate in its production of widespread collateral damage to noncombatants.

In the United States, this myth of a just war is reinforced by the tradition of American exceptionalism, which raises the nation to the status of a moral force in an immoral world—making it "a moral exemplar with a unique historical mission" (Fiala, 2008, p. 60). This historical narrative underpins the assumption of the state's nobility, bolsters faith in its leaders' wisdom and virtue, and identifies the nation with just-war principles despite recurring lapses such as fire-bombing Dresden, atomic bombing Hiroshima, threatening the Soviet Union with mutual assured destruction, engaging in preventative warfare against Iraq, and disregarding the Geneva Conventions in a global war on terrorism. The mythic force of national exceptionalism and mission conceivably could be aligned with a less confrontational foreign policy (Ivie & Giner, 2009), but typically it serves to sanction and sanctify a resort to arms ostensibly to secure a just peace, make the world safe for democracy, and defend freedom (Hughes, 2003). Likewise, although the just-war theory technically might be deployed to challenge the general legitimacy of war as well as the ethics of particular wars (Fiala, 2008, pp. 166–167), its mythic function is to consecrate a culture of war under the legitimizing sign of reluctant belligerence.

Thinking in terms of the just-war tradition therefore inclines the citizenry and their leaders rhetorically toward an ethic of war rather than an ethic of peace. Whereas the just-war inclination to "conceive, secure, and defend peace by waging a war that must be justified" (Bartoli, 2004, p. 156) habituates the nation to a discourse of fighting for peace, pursuing a positive peace by nonviolent means would shift the emphasis from justifying war to building and sustaining a preventative culture of peace. With positive peace as its telos, peace-building communication works to predispose polities toward better understanding of, more tolerance toward, and increased cooperation with adversaries so that conflict might be managed constructively. It seeks to bridge political divisions enough to prevent armed conflict while advancing the cause of social justice, collective well-being, and human fulfillment.

REDUCING RADICAL OTHERNESS

Accordingly, the United Nations (2010) differentiates peace building from peacekeeping and peacemaking, the latter two terms referring to the prevention of imminent warfare or the resolution of existing hostilities, while peace-building activities in the here and now are undertaken with the longer-term aim of establishing an enduring architecture of peace in countries emerging from conflict and after a peace accord has been secured. Peace building is an ongoing project which entails, beyond its material and institutional dimensions, the challenge of developing an enduring culture of peace—a culture that encompasses a web of constitutive discourses, ranging from everyday interactions between individuals and groups to intergovernmental transactions, all of which address divisive issues of identity that correspond to abiding concerns for social justice and national security.

Relations of war and peace, insofar as they involve different articulations of identities, threats, and injustices, are constituted in discursive practices that produce varying degrees of Otherness through optional "processes of linking and differentiation" (Hansen, 2006, p. 21). These identity constructions mediate perceptions of injury and danger by assigning meaning to material conditions. Accordingly, the production of a culture of peace requires the rearticulation of problematic identities that are deeply embedded in conventional discourses of national insecurity. As Campbell (1998) observes, danger is a product of interpretation that rests historically on "the ability to represent things as alien, subversive, dirty, or sick" (p. 3). Such inscriptions of danger, although naturalized by conventional usage, are necessarily unstable constructions subject to analysis, critique, and reformulation. They can be altered, Campbell (1998) argues, by discourses that advance "claims to shared ethnicity, nationality, political ideals, religious beliefs, or other commonalities" (p. 70), thus creating what Chantal Mouffe (2000, pp. 13, 103) calls a "common symbolic space" or a sufficient measure of "identification" to moderate an Us-versus-Them antagonism. This, in short, is the purpose of bridging (not eliminating) divisions, which Kenneth Burke (1950/1969) assigns to the rhetoric of identification.

Constructing shared symbolic space by articulating points of identification is the work of peaceful persuasion or what Ellen Gorsevski (2004, p. 178) calls nonviolent rhetoric. Consistent with Kenneth Burke's (1937/1984, p. 166) notion of the comic corrective, Gorsevski (2004, pp. 178, 187–188) observes that the goal of a "rehumanizing" rhetoric of nonviolence is to advance "a renewed sense of commonality and humanity" between adversaries. Nonviolent struggle against injustice requires a deep respect for the humanity of others, a recognition that one's own status is debased—not elevated—by debasing others, and a goal of persuading adversaries rather than destroying opponents; that is, of addressing the sources of conflict rather than directing hate and anger toward enemies (Barash & Webel, 2009, pp. 460, 462–463).

Indeed, nonviolent resistance as an approach to positive peace requires a humanizing rhetoric of identification in order to struggle for social justice without triggering the myth of just war—the myth that supposes war is the only practical option for eliminating the threat posed by an enemy who has been reduced to the image of evil savagery. To rely on nonviolent means to secure a just peace between adversaries who are rhetorically constituted as consubstantial rivals averts the cultural proclivity toward destroying a demonized Other who is rhetorically constructed as a sheer enemy (Ivie, 2005, pp. 169–172). As a practice of peace-building dissent from war (Ivie, 2007a), nonviolent rhetoric involves a multiplicity of tactical symbolic actions aimed cumulatively (and thus strategically) at diffusing rituals of redemptive violence (Wink, 1998, pp. 42–62) by transforming dehumanizing discourses.

In promoting the positive conditions of human fulfillment, nonviolent resistance to injustice combined with a humanizing discourse of consubstantial rivalry also provides a solid foundation for enhancing national and international security. In this regard, a potential convergence of interest in peace-building discourse exists between the disciplines of communication and international relations. Specifically, the rhetorical sensibility of the emerging field of critical security studies challenges political realism's reified notion of national security by articulating a broadly defined transnational project of emancipation (Booth, 2005a; Hansen, 2006; Wyn Jones, 1999, 2001). Such a project necessarily entails a concern with bridging or otherwise challenging strict national boundaries that radically divide Us and Them into opposing categories of allies and enemies. These reified binaries are rhetorically constructed and maintained and thus subject to rhetorical revision and reconstruction. Their boundaries are made more or less flexible and permeable by discursive practices that are more or less nuanced and humanizing. In short, the rhetorical entailment of critical security studies is to bring into focus the problem of Othering as it relates to constructions of insecurity—the problem of realism's construction of hostile/enemy Others residing outside strictly drawn national borders—and the corresponding challenge of articulating more constructive agonistic relations into a discourse of security. Focusing critically on the practice of extreme Othering is a pivotal point for moving from a war culture toward a peace-building culture.

Toward this end of building a culture of peace, and given that national identity and foreign policy are intertwined discourses that mediate material conditions (Hansen, 2006, p. 23), critical communication scholarship and critical security studies share a common project of rearticulating terms of *security* into terms of *community* and *emancipation* as a contribution to richer democratic relations (Wyn Jones, 2001, pp. 10, 17). The larger aim is to reconsider global insecurities so that "the global we" might learn to live together more successfully than in the past (Booth, 2005a, p. viii; Booth, 2005b, p. 1). Scholarship of this kind becomes an exercise in rhetorical invention and intervention, which advances cultural critiques aimed at bridging the human divide by challenging articulations of antagonistic identities. We can expect such work to contribute to a liberating understanding of how an Other is alienated from an Us and made to appear threatening by prevailing discourses of insecurity, and how cultural starting points (presumptions, beliefs, values, hierarchies, etc.) can be strategically realigned with humanizing constructions of political relations in the service of justice (Perelman, 1967; Perelman & Olbrechts-Tyteca, 1969).

This critical work, which is itself constitutive, operates within a broad spectrum of official and unofficial political culture. As Hansen (2006) observes:

> Understanding official foreign policy discourse as situated within a wider discursive field opens up a rhetorical and empirical research agenda that examines how foreign policy representations and representations articulated by oppositional political forces, the media, academe, and popular culture reinforce or contest each other. (p. 7)

In this wider context, critical scholarship examines, for example, how facts are formed and coupled with representations of identity in foreign policy discourses and how they are contested by oppositional discourses (Hansen, 2006, p. 32).

As a project in immanent critique of war culture, critical communication scholarship re-thinks security "from the bottom up" and strives to escape the blinders of prevailing structures and orthodoxies in order to construct peace-building alternatives out of the "unfulfilled potential already existing within society" (Booth, 2005b, pp. 11, 14–15). *Security*, in this sense, is un-derstood to be a derivative category with no inherent or neutral meaning (Smith, 2005, p. 28). It is potentially "the object of conflicting theories about what is real, what constitutes reliable knowledge, and what might be done in world politics" and thus is subject to political contestation (Booth, 2005a, p. 21).

The orthodox articulation of security, understood as a discursive formation, produces and naturalizes "a militarized and confrontational mind-set, which defines security questions in an us-versus-them manner," by disregarding the "distinct genealogical trajectories" through which it has acquired its particular meaning within a given security community (Smith, 2005, pp. 34, 50). As Cheeseman (2005, p. 82) observes, the contemporary security environment—where militarized thinking and the use of military force provide little protection against suicide bombers—"requires a much more democratic, empathetic, and cooperative approach to problem-solving" (see also Linklater, 2005; Wyn Jones, 2005), at least as a way of shifting the presumption more toward mini-mizing military violence by maximizing human fulfillment and reducing structural violence.

While the construction of a national self or identity vis-à-vis the articulation of radical Oth-erness is central to conventional expressions of insecurity within a culture of war, this problem-atic pattern of locating danger in the image of a radically threatening Other reflects a strong inclination, or temptation, rather than a necessity (Connolly, 1991, p. 8). Accordingly, the nation-al identity might be constructed otherwise—at least gradually—on lesser degrees of Otherness "that draw upon more ambiguous or complex constructions of difference" (Hansen, 2006, p. 39). Situating the Other in a wider signifying web of identities is a way of diminishing radical de-grees of opposition and alienation. Such a rhetorical turn within established but pliable symbolic dimensions of time and space, for the purpose of articulating more complicated and less threat-ening linkages and differentiations of Self and Other, potentially reconstructs ethical relations of responsibility at the border of national and international realms. Narrowly and definitively drawn, the border between Us and Them locates ethical responsibility within the community of the nation-state, "leaving no space for an international ethics" (Hansen, 2006, p. 50). Defined more ambiguously, the scope of ethical responsibility potentially extends outward to encompass a broader humanitarian concern for preserving human rights, reducing structural violence, and building a positive peace nonviolently.

ARTICULATING HIERARCHIES OF EQUALITY

At a minimum, the rhetorical practices that extend ethical responsibility for human fulfillment beyond national borders, by reducing radical Otherness and moderating antagonistic relations, op-erate purposefully (i.e., strategically and tactically) to deepen and broaden—not eliminate—social and political hierarchies. Hierarchy, as Kenneth Burke (1950/1969) postulates, is endemic to the dramaturgy of symbolic action and "indigenous to all well-rounded human thinking," but "to say that hierarchy is inevitable is not to say that any particular hierarchy is inevitable" (p. 141). There are hierarchies of equality just as there are hierarchies of inequality. Peace-building hierarchies of equality are multifaceted and complementary rather than one-dimensional and unidirectional. They signify mutually enriching intersections among dramatis personae that are otherwise aligned against and alienated from one another. In this way, conceptions of self-interest can be extended by the principle of symbiosis into a conjointly empowering web of interdependencies.

From this perspective, rather than conceptualizing a just peace in strictly leveling terms (i.e., as a condition of sameness devoid of gradations of power, position, and privilege or differences of identity), peace-building communication reduces radical Otherness by articulating hierarchical relations in terms of complementarities and interdependencies within a context of agonistic pluralism. Otherwise, a discourse of equality would prove incompatible with the tenets of liberal democracy, which require a strong regard for individualism no less than, if not more than, community. This is a cultural predisposition that extends beyond personal and partisan relations within the United States to constrain the country's foreign affairs. Short of revolutionizing U.S. political culture, peace building entails a rhetorical sensibility of adaptation to the overall political context in which it operates, even as it contests alienating hierarchies by broadening and deepening them into equalizing hierarchies of human fulfillment.

Discourses of reconciliation that would transform international antagonism—in order to reduce perceptions of insecurity and pursue positive peace nonviolently—are therefore challenged rhetorically to articulate mutually reinforcing conjunctions of differences. Parties in conflict are reconciled not by eliminating their differences or subjugating one party to another but instead by identifying complementarities of differences. Toward this end of transforming antagonisms of radical Otherness, critical attention must be given especially to recognizing and retrieving archetypal projections of the hostile imagination—that is, to acknowledging victimizing projections that perpetuate rites of redemptive violence—so that imperfections and other troubling complexities might be integrated into an otherwise inflated and fragile national identity that ritualistically sacrifices scapegoats to reconfirm its righteous sense of security and well-being.

Retrieving and integrating projections back into the national identity can be facilitated by adopting reflexive perspective-taking practices such as that of the stereoscopic gaze (Ivie, 2007b). This perspective-expanding practice appropriates the language of vision and position to articulate a strategic interdependency between antagonists, thereby circumventing rituals of redemptive violence by confounding the projection of evil. It is, in short, the enactment of a humanizing aesthetic of nonviolent contestation to buffer a demonizing discourse of irreconcilable differences between the forces of good and evil. It is a way of coordinating divergent accounts of disputed events, a method of deescalating struggles over symbolic and material resources, and thus a means of managing schisms by rhetorically constructing empathizing rivals. Adopting this stereoscopic gaze is neither simple nor impossible, as evidenced by the deescalating transactions between John F. Kennedy and Nikita Khrushchev during the Cuban missile crisis and by Jim Wallis's evangelical antiwar discourse after 9/11 (Ivie, 2007b). Indeed, Douglas Fry (2007, p. 216) has mustered anthropological evidence to support the notion that such measures for talking through grievances by promoting "crosscutting ties" between adversaries are bountiful expressions of human ingenuity.

John Paul Lederach (2005) also argues for a grounded approach to peace building that involves the discursive exercise, or creative act, of the moral imagination. He reports stories of people rejecting violence and seeking reconciliation through the "messiness of innovation," stories that provide evidence of the human *"capacity to imagine something rooted in the challenges of the real world yet capable of giving birth to that which does not yet exist"* (Lederach 2005, p. ix; emphasis in the original). Specifically, this is the capacity of a people to embrace complexity enough to imagine themselves in a web of relationships that includes their enemies rather than to revert to the violence of dualistic polarities (Lederach, 2005, pp. 5, 29). Paradoxical curiosity, he suggests, is one such potential resource for aesthetically expanding and constructively complicating perspectives toward others. Yet, the capacity to envision and practice peace building discourse in the public sphere remains decidedly underdeveloped (Lederach, 2005, pp. 60–62). He is convinced, however, that talking in images and listening for metaphors that can clarify crosscutting ties and articulate mutually enriching webs of relationship by synthesizing otherwise befuddling complexities is the aesthetic resource for strategically weaving relational webs in a public sphere where the hostile imagination for protracted violence now dominates (Lederach, 2005, pp. 71– 72, 84). Watching for, invoking, and redeploying such metaphors into peace-building narratives is a creative exercise in immanent critique.

Accordingly, peace-building motifs can be developed by examining the rhetorical ingenuity of adversaries who have succeeded, even if only partially, in reducing radical Otherness. Critical communication scholars can extrapolate from discourse of this kind various strategies of reflexive perspective taking. For example, the image of a stereoscopic gaze can be discerned in the rhetorical efforts of Kennedy to defuse the Cuban missile crisis (Ivie, 2007b, pp. 40–46). Kennedy insisted on understanding Khrushchev's viewpoint, which was a disturbing mystery to the young president. Rather than succumb to simplistic Cold War demonology, he persistently raised the question of motive—asking why his Soviet adversary would place missiles in Cuba—and thus opened a speculative space for discussing the question of perspective expressed in the language of "point of view." Within this discursive space, Kennedy suggested that Western European allies might perceive the United States as demented for assuming a belligerent attitude over missiles in Cuba that did not alter the overall balance of power and that the Soviets could perceive the Western presence in a divided Berlin as bizarre. A purposeful Khrushchev, Kennedy concluded, should be given an opportunity to negotiate a deescalation of the missile crisis. The humanizing aesthetic of Kennedy's crisis-defusing discourse amounted to a double articulation of perspective taking, which involved both speculating on the motives and meaning of adversaries and allies from their presumed vantage point and speaking of oneself critically from the presumed perspective of enemies, allies, and bystanders.

This stereoscopic gaze provided depth of perspective in a crisis situation. It allowed the president to look back at his belligerent stance from the assumed perspective of the other and thus to reflect critically by indirection from that vantage point on his own hostile attitude. It was a metamaneuver which lowered the threshold of constructive self-critique in a context that otherwise promoted the outward projection of evil onto the face of the Soviet enemy.

Four decades later, Jim Wallis relied similarly on this metamaneuver to resist the simplistic projection of evil onto a different enemy (Ivie, 2007b, pp. 46–51). He would humanize the nation's adversaries in a global war on terrorism by gazing at them stereoscopically through the peacemaking lens of a transnational church. As a high-profile peace activist speaking in a prophetic voice to a self-proclaimed Christian people, Wallis invited Americans to acknowledge and heal the darkness that resided within the nation's political soul. Evil, he observed, exists within everyone, and thus it is dangerous to avoid looking inward by projecting darkness outward. He called upon the nation to confront its own sins in a spirit of self-examination and to address the injustices that breed terrorism rather than become the enemy it envisions. His call to choose political healing and reconciliation over closed-minded vengeance and redemptive violence transformed narrow national self-interest by adopting a wider worldview of compassion and humility. It was an exercise in reflective perspective-taking and empathizing self-criticism, which was prompted largely by reminding Christian Americans that they were part of an international faith community made up of multiple perceptions of the U.S. response to terrorism and suggesting that the nation reconnect to its respect for humanity by considering the views of other Christians around the world. By adopting the transnational viewpoint of a worldwide church in order to transform a narrow and self-righteous nationalism, Wallis redirected attention to humanizing values and articulated the interdependency of attending ethically to the common good and enhancing pragmatically global security.

The immediate point here is to illustrate a mode of rhetorical invention, not to assess its impact or chart its uptake in subsequent discourse. The stereoscopic gaze is a basic perspective-taking strategy for articulating crosscutting ties and building hierarchies of equality. It prompts us to look back at our own position from the imagined vantage point of the Other. This exercise in self-critique from an oblique angle may prove in a given setting or particular form of expression to be more or less effective for finessing the demonology of war culture. Moreover, it is not the only conceivable strategy for broadening and deepening a people's perspective, bringing into focus overlooked complementarities and interdependencies within a continuing context of agonistic pluralism, and motivating the nonviolent pursuit of a positive peace. Retrieving and integrating a projected shadow into the national identity requires a full realization of the moral imagination and a continuing exercise of rhetorical ingenuity.

Reconciliation, broadly considered, is a product of rhetorical invention and, as such, a continuous process of imagining, developing, and sustaining an emergent cultural norm through immanent critiques of rhetorical practice. It works to reduce radical Otherness and to build toward a culture of positive peace by constructing and keeping hierarchies of equality in play. As a peace-building discourse, it promotes reflexive perspective taking to broaden and deepen national identities and resists demonizing projections that otherwise inflate perceptions of insecurity. Reconciliation in this sense is an investment in symbolic action, or what Erik Doxtader (2003, pp. 284, 267) calls the tropological and transformational "works of words" that enable us to address, as a "question of *becoming*," the issue of what living in peace might substantively mean. Hence, "there is something inextricably and immanently rhetorical in the midst of reconciliation" (Doxtader, 2003, p. 268). The constitutive work of discourses of reconciliation transforms perspectives and relationships in a context of contestation and difference. It manages the tension between identity and identification as it articulates compensatory points of identification to produce a mutually enriching and empowering unity-in-difference.

As a product of rhetorical invention, the tragicomic discourse of reconciliation is a complex and ongoing process of transforming victim/victimizer relations into mutually enhancing hierarchies of shared humanity and interconnected identities. It does not construct a "fixed and final unity" of identities to manage, at the expense of diversity, the tension between a tragic cry for justice and a comic corrective for peace but instead articulates relations of interdependence and cooperative contention, in a continuing context of diversity, to disrupt "the cycle of violence, aggression, and domination" (Hatch, 2003, pp. 754, 747). The discourse of reconciliation functions as a peace-building sociodrama by refashioning the fabric of extant political culture into a conjointly empowering convergence of material and symbolic interests (Hatch, 2006, pp. 260, 266–267; Wilson, 2004, pp. 368, 371). It is a pragmatic mode of creative symbolic action, which strives nonviolently toward a holistic achievement of positive peace.

As an object of critical communication scholarship, which is itself a productive rhetorical practice (Ivie, 2001), emergent discourses of reconciliation are subject to constructive cultural critique for the purpose of enhancing peace-building possibilities. The work of peace-building scholarship as a rhetorical practice of immanent rather than transcendent cultural critique is to locate emergent articulations of reconciliation and optimize them into hierarchies of equality within their own realms of discourse (a task beyond the scope of this chapter), or at least to facilitate the process as much as possible. Toward this end, productive criticism is a grounded and creative act of extrapolating reflexive perspective-taking strategies, which reduce radical Otherness, from the discourse of adversaries who articulate crosscutting ties. These manifestations of symbolic ingenuity, which realize in varying degrees the capacity of the moral imagination to empathize with a perceived enemy, are the raw material from which to develop the peace-building potential of public discourse. In this way, the scholar-critic coproduces culturally grounded formulations of peace-building strategies and tactics.

PEACE BUILDING IN A DEMOCRATIC IDIOM

A recent example of political campaign discourse in the 2008 U.S. presidential primaries illustrates, albeit imperfectly, a potential for transforming the prevailing war culture. Speaking of national security in what can be characterized as a democratic idiom, Barack Obama invoked the myth of American exceptionalism and turned the national call to mission from a story of moral conquest into a practical vision of working collaboratively on the global scene to promote peace by augmenting social justice (Ivie & Giner, 2009). Rather than defaulting along with other leading candidates in both political parties to a discourse of national insecurity that exaggerates danger by articulating national identity in terms of a demonized enemy—that is, rather than reproducing a fantasy of fear and loathing—candidate Obama distinguished himself from the field by promoting a vision of change and hope over a politics of cynicism and fear. Speaking of the nation's historical mission in familiar democratic overtones, he advanced an alternative attitude toward the problem of terrorism. He would change the basic mindset that got the United States mired in a needless war of choice in Iraq. His vision of sustainable democracy entailed the notion that the United States, mindful of its own imperfections and recognizing the equality and worth of all people, could work more securely in partnership with other nations than by trying to dominate the world. His democratically inflected discourse featured themes of transparency and of uniting a common humanity by bridging differences through sustained efforts to cooperate, discuss, and negotiate—not just with the nation's friends, but also with its enemies. He would promote civil liberties and abandon the use of torture. All of this, he intoned, was the true mission of an exceptional people tasked with promoting freedom and justice in a spirit of mutually reinforcing partnership with a global community. Without global cooperation, the United States would be unable to meet the threats it faced or sustain the prosperity it desires. Only by behaving democratically toward the world at large—all the while working to reduce poverty, protect human rights, and enrich democratic institutions—would the United States see global terrorism reduced and national security improved. Rather than being defined by the terrorists' message of hate, the United States might author its own positive story of mission and security amongst a common humanity—a story of promise and historic mission pursued through the agency of Obama's presidency. The candidate performed his own message by assuming the persona of a calm, collected, and reflective leader and interlocutor who would make diplomacy a top priority.

Candidate Obama's rhetorical achievement in the Democratic Party primaries was to articulate a plausible vision of peace building in a political culture accustomed to the demonizing discourse of war making. His vision was made plausible largely by aligning it with the foundational myth of American exceptionalism and mission as a shift of emphasis rather than as a break with tradition. He would rely more on diplomacy and less on military might, more on convincing and less on bullying, more on the give-and-take of democracy and less on the conceit of ideology, and more on addressing the causes of terrorism than replicating the logic of terrorism. American security and morality, he argued, required global collaboration and partnership consistent with the nation's founding values and aimed at providing for the common good. His message of positive change was mainstream and restorative, not radical or otherwise unrecognizable. It resisted the ritual of redemptive violence by leveraging a foundational myth of exceptionalism to shift expectations for how best to provide for national security rather than accounting for terrorism simplistically by projecting an aura of evil onto the enemy.

Again, the immediate purpose of discussing Obama's admittedly delimited, but nevertheless remarkable, rhetoric is not to determine how effective it was in relation to the complex of factors influencing the outcome of the primaries or even to assess its diminished role in the general campaign, let alone to speculate on how it might play out in his presidency. Rather the purpose is to mark a singular occurrence of peace-building discourse in the midst of a mainstream political campaign. Here we have an artifact of rhetorical invention adapted to contemporary U.S. political culture. This reformulation of the foundational myth of exceptionalism, using a democratic idiom to articulate a practical ethic of multilateral foreign relations and less militarism, reduces polarizing images of radical Otherness and privileges a more reflexive attitude of mutually beneficial cooperation. In this version of a conjointly empowering web of global interdependencies, attending nonviolently to injustices in other parts of the world is represented as a way of investing in world peace and improving national security.

The challenge for critical communication scholars, in addition to locating more cultural artifacts of peace-building discourse in the public sphere, is to refine prototypes of perspective-taking strategies invented by rhetors such as John Kennedy, Jim Wallis, and Barack Obama for elaborating hierarchies of equality into a democratic ethos that can enrich and sustain a democratic practice more conducive to building and maintaining a culture of peace. Working in a democratic idiom of reflexive perspective taking to reduce hostile inclinations by imagining human fulfillment as mutually beneficial to interdependent adversaries is the basic formulation of a discursive construction of positive peace. Finding and refining culturally viable and situation-specific ways of broadening and deepening the national identity—including ways of recognizing, retrieving, and integrating into the collective self-projections of the hostile imagination that perpetuate rituals of redemptive violence—requires a sustained project of productive critique by engaged scholars with a well-developed rhetorical sensibility.

Such peace-building scholarship might ask, for instance, how an Obama presidency could develop the democratic idiom of its campaign rhetoric into a democratic ethos of foreign relations that would resonate with domestic audiences. What specific hierarchies of equality might be crafted between adversaries such the United States and Iran, Israel and the Palestinians, and others that would be mutually beneficial and compatible with public culture? What avenues of reconciliation might the adoption of a stereoscopic gaze toward terrorists and those who support terrorism reveal?

Asking and answering questions such as these involves scholarship deeply grounded in specific contexts and guided by culturally inflected heuristics of observation and innovation. It is a continuous project of rhetorical invention and immanent critique rather than abstract conceptualizing and systematic theory building. Such normative work is guided by the telos of a positive peace constructed nonviolently. It draws on a democratic idiom to articulate a democratic ethos of reflexive perspective-taking. As an exercise of the moral imagination, it reduces tendencies toward demonizing adversaries and promotes empathy in a shared symbolic space to compensate for divisive differences. Peace-building scholars, in this genre of political discourse, are cultural workers who coproduce the strategies they observe.

ETHICAL TRAJECTORY OF DEMOCRATIC PEACE BUILDING

This view of a positive peace derived from the productive analysis of discourses of national identity places critical communication research in a category of ethical intervention, which raises the question of its ethical trajectory and rhetorical commitment to a democratic ethos. What, one might sensibly ask, are the ethical stakes of democratic peace building? The answer lies in the volatility of positive peace as a political objective and the potential of democratic discourse to strengthen the severely stressed linkage between nonviolence and justice.

As an unstable concept, positive peace is readily appropriated to the end of war in the form of a legitimizing rationalization. Fighting wars to obtain a just peace is an all-too-common and seemingly self-sustaining occurrence. Yet, a stable peace cannot be achieved except by peaceful (i.e., nonviolent) means. To the extent that wars are a function of persuasion and symbolic action, managing the tension between a commitment to justice and a goal of nonviolence requires a discourse that reduces inclinations toward radical Othering and thus diminishes overblown perceptions of national insecurity. Operating in a democratic idiom facilitates perspective-taking, which in turn reduces radical Othering by articulating hierarchies of equality.

Given that operating in the democratic idiom is crucial to seeking justice nonviolently, an ethical imperative exists to optimize democratic practice, not as an end in itself but rather as a means to reducing the violence perpetrated by nations against humanity. Thus, integrating a democratic ethos into the national identity—where ethos is taken to mean a customary practice that becomes a distinguishing characteristic and guiding morality of a people—is one very important key to developing a culture of peace conducive to human well-being and fulfillment. This, I submit, is the way to address directly and resolve publicly the ethical paradox of sustaining a state of war in the name of seeking a just peace.

REFERENCES

Alper, L., & Earp, J. (Directors). (2007). *War made easy* [Motion picture]. United States: Media Education Foundation.

Augustine. (1958). *City of God* (G. G. Walsh, Trans.). Garden City, NY: Doubleday. (Original work published 410 CE)

Barash, D. P., & Webel, C.P. (2009). *Peace and conflict studies* (2nd ed). Los Angeles: Sage.

Bartoli, A. (2004). Christianity and peacebuilding. In G. S. Smith & H. Coward (Eds.), *Religion and peacebuilding* (pp. 147–168). Albany, NY: SUNY Press.

Booth, K. (Ed.). (2005a). *Critical security studies and world politics*. Boulder, CO: Lynne Rienner.

Booth, K. (2005b). Critical explorations. In K. Booth (Ed.), *Critical security studies and world politics* (pp. 1–18). Boulder, CO: Lynne Rienner.

Boulding, K. E. (1978). *Stable peace.* Austin: University of Texas Press.

Brunk, C. G. (2000). Shaping a vision: The nature of peace studies. In L. Fisk & J. Schellenberg (Eds.), *Patterns of conflict, paths to peace* (pp. 11–33). Peterborough, Ontario: Broadview Press.

Burke, K. (1984). *Attitudes toward history* (3rd ed.). Berkeley: University of California Press. (Original work published 1937)

Burke, K. (1969). *A rhetoric of motives.* Berkeley: University of California Press. (Original work published 1950)

Campbell, D. (1998). *Writing security: United States foreign policy and the politics of identity* (Rev.ed.). Minneapolis: University of Minnesota Press.

Cheeseman, G. (2005). Military force(s) and in/security. In K. Booth (Ed.), *Critical security studies and world politics* (pp. 63–87). Boulder, CO: Lynne Rienner.

Connolly, W. E. (1991). *Identity/difference: Democratic negotiations of political paradox.* Ithaca, NY: Cornell University Press.

Doxtader, E. (2003). Reconciliation: A rhetorical concept/ion. *Quarterly Journal of Speech. 89*(4), 267–292.

Fiala, A. (2008). *The just war myth: The moral illusions of war.* Lanham, MD: Rowman & Littlefield.

Foucault, M. (1998). Nietzche, genealogy, history. In J. D. Faubion (Ed.), & R. Hurley & others (Trans.). *Michel Foucault: Aesthetics, method, and epistemology* (pp. 369–391). New York: New Press.

Fry, D. (2007). *Beyond war: The human potential for peace.* Oxford, UK: Oxford University Press.

Galtung, J. (1996). *Peace by peaceful means: Peace and conflict, development and civilization.* London: Sage.

Galtung, J., Jacobsen, C. G., & Brand-Jacobsen, K. F. (2002). *Searching for peace: The road to transcend* (2nd ed.). London: Pluto Press.

Gorsevski, E. W. (2004). *Peaceful persuasion: The geopolitics of nonviolent rhetoric.* Albany, NY: SUNY Press.

Hansen, L. (2006). *Security as practice: Discourse analysis and the Bosnian war.* New York: Routledge.

Hatch, J. B. (2003). Reconciliation: Building a bridge from complicity to coherence in the rhetoric of race relations. *Rhetoric & Public Affairs, 6*(4), 737–764.

Hatch, J. B. (2006). The hope of reconciliation: Continuing the conversation. *Rhetoric & Public Affairs, 9*(2), 259–278.

Hedges, C. (2003). *War is the force that gives us meaning.* New York: Anchor Books.

Hughes, R. T. (2003). *Myths America lives by.* Urbana: University of Illinois Press.

Ivie, R. L. (1979). Progressive form and Mexican culpability in Polk's justification for war. *Central States Speech Journal, 30*(4), 311–320.

Ivie, R. L. (2001). Productive criticism then and now. *American Communication Journal, 4*(3). Retrieved from http://www.acjournal.org/

Ivie, R. L. (2005). *Democracy and America's war on terror.* Tuscaloosa: University of Alabama Press.

Ivie, R. L. (2007a). *Dissent from war.* Bloomfield, CT: Kumarian Press.

Ivie, R. L. (2007b). Finessing the demonology of war: Toward a practical aesthetic of humanizing dissent. *Javnost—The Public, 14*(4), 37–54.

Ivie, R. L., & Giner, O. (2009). More good, less evil: Contesting the mythos of national insecurity in the 2008 presidential primaries. *Rhetoric & Public Affairs, 12*(2), 279–301.

Keller, W. W., & Mitchell, G. R. (Eds.) (2006). *Hitting first: Preventive force in U.S. security strategy.* Pittsburgh, PA: University of Pittsburgh Press.

Lederach, J. P. (2005). *The moral imagination: The art and soul of building peace.* Oxford, UK: Oxford University Press.

Linklater, A. (2005). Political community and human security. In K. Booth (Ed.) *Critical security studies and world politics* (pp. 113–131). Boulder, CO: Lynne Rienner.

McCain, J. (2008, September 4). John McCain's acceptance speech. *New York Times.* Retrieved from http://elections.nytimes.com/2008/president/conventions/videos/transcripts/20080904_MCCAIN_SPEECH.html.

Mouffe, C. (2000). *The democratic paradox.* London: Verso.

Perelman, C. (1967). *Justice.* New York: Random House.

Perelman, C., & Olbrechts-Tyteca, L. (1969). *The new rhetoric: A treatise on argumentation* (J. Wilkenson & P. Weaver, Trans). Notre Dame, IN: University of Notre Dame Press.

Smith, S. (2005). The contested concept of security. In K. Booth (Ed.) *Critical security studies and world politics* (pp. 27–62). Boulder, CO: Lynne Rienner.

Solomon, N. (2005). *War made easy: How presidents and pundits keep spinning us to death.* Hoboken, NJ: Wiley.

United Nations. (2010). *Global issues in Africa: Peacekeeping and peacemaking.* Retrieved from http://secint50.un.org/issues/gallery/Africa/chapterpeace.htm

Walzer, M. (1977). *Just and unjust wars: A moral argument with historical illustrations.* New York: Basic Books.

Walzer, M. (2004). *Arguing about war.* New Haven, CT: Yale University Press.

Wilson, K. W. (2004). Is there interest in reconciliation? *Rhetoric & Public Affairs, 7*(3), 367–377.

Wink, W. (1998). *The powers that be: Theology for a new millennium.* New York: Doubleday.

Wyn Jones, R. (1999). *Security, strategy, and critical theory.* Boulder, CO: Lynne Rienner.

Wyn Jones, R. (Ed.). (2001). *Critical theory and world politics.* Boulder, CO: Lynne Rienner.

Wyn Jones, R. (2005). On emancipation: Necessity, capacity, and concrete utopias. In K. Booth (Ed.), *Critical security studies and world politics* (pp. 215–235). Boulder, CO: Lynne Rienner.

23

Democracy, Publicness, and Global Governance

Slavko Splichal

This chapter explores the extent to which the principle of publicity—the defining ethical principle of "the public," "public opinion," and the "public sphere"—is related to personal freedom of expression, the expansion and diversification of (mass) communication, democratic process, and global governance. In the last few decades, technological achievements and globalization have profoundly changed modes of communication in national and transnational contexts. These changes, which created new opportunities for citizens' participation in public discourse beyond national boundaries, may be seen as an opportunity for the construction of a new kind of public sphere(s) that would help materialize the principle of deliberative publicness and the personal right to communicate of which national public spheres largely fall short (Splichal, 2009). The question remains, however, whether the development of new global interactive communication networks and an easier access to communication means can resolve age-old problems of democratic deficit as identified in "old" communication theories.

Based on normative concerns that should help avoid an operational reduction of these issues to the existing social conditions, I begin with a brief discussion of how the ideas of freedom of expression and publication influenced broader social–theoretical conceptualizations of publicness. I then turn to the issue of how the nature of communication in the public sphere has been theorized, and how it has been recently challenged by globalization. The final part is focused on the consequences of global governance for the national and transnational publics and citizen participatory communication, which is constitutive of the public sphere.

FREEDOM OF SPEECH, PUBLICATION, AND CENSORSHIP

It is difficult to say when "communication science" began, but we can clearly point to a number of currents that take us from philosophy into a recognizable body of concepts and ideas specifically related to the phenomena of human communication. The earliest identifiable scholarly interest in communication has been expressed in writings of the great Greek philosophers, such as Plato's *Phaedrus* (trans., 360 BCE/1901) and Aristotle's *Rhetoric*, and from the very beginning, it has been associated with conceptual controversies that have persisted until the 21st century. In a way, Plato may be named the progenitor of communication theory: he was the first to elaborate on communicative persuasion and surveillance. In particular, he addressed the issues of how technology (of writing) affects human communication and interaction, and the value of censorship as a preventive measure against "erroneous representations."

The technical means were long considered secondary and external in relation to the mental dimension of the communication process. In the *Phaedrus*, Plato's Socrates suggests that writing is not a great matter compared with the spoken word. Writing, he says, is inferior to speech because it is silent. Like a painted picture, it can never speak; it cannot answer any questions or come to its own defense, and it has no power of adaptation. Similar kinds of suspicion of technological progress can be found in later periods in many great philosophers, including Hobbes and Hegel. Nevertheless, following Plato's critique of the deficiency of the technology of writing, the question of (the lack of) interactivity remained a major issue in theorizations of public communication.

Plato was also the founder of the aristocratic idea of censorship that has resounded for more than 2,000 years. In *The Republic*, he substantiated the necessity for censorship to prevent narrators and poets from making "an erroneous representation…of the nature of gods and heroes" that young people would not be able to understand. What is needed instead, Plato believed, is

> to establish a censorship of the writers of fiction, and let the censors receive any tale of fiction which is good, and reject the bad; and we will desire mothers and nurses to tell their children the authorized ones only…. [M]ost of those which are now in use must be discarded. (trans., Plato, 360 BCE/1901)

For two millennia, censorship was commonly considered to be socially desirable while official censors were regarded as honorable public *personae*. A consensus existed among early theorists of the press, such as Tobias Peucer (1690) and Caspar Stieler (1695/1969), that rulers and their activities be protected against public exposure. Actions of governments were not to be covered by the press because they were believed to be too complicated and too demanding to be understood by readers. Stieler argued in favor of censorship in order to prevent newspapers from spreading "false, mocking and noxious" news that could "mislead, anger and deceive a simple man" (Stieler, 1695/1969, pp. 164–165).

However, critical intellectuals and rationalists of the 17th century, such as Milton, Spinoza, Locke, and Voltaire, sharply criticized any restraint on free expression and printing, arguing that no administrative regulation is needed for any form of human communication, including the press. Milton claimed in *Areopagitica* (1644) that the press should be freed from authoritarian constraints, such as book and newspaper licensing, which would help attain the "utmost bound of civil liberty." From the postulate that "every man is by indefeasible natural right the master of his own thoughts," which implies his freedom of judgment, Spinoza concluded that "…men thinking in diverse and contradictory fashions" is an unavoidable fact (1670/1883). Consequently, it is a natural condition that "in a free state every man may think what he likes and say what he thinks" (p. 257). Governments should not be allowed to control human minds since this would violate citizens' sovereignty and "natural right" of public speech.

Voltaire and Locke fought for the personal right of free expression and understood criticism as a tool of "moral censorship." This was, essentially, still an aristocratic doctrine allowing authoritative suppression of opinions contrary to "those moral rules which are necessary to the preservation of civil society" (Locke, 1689). In the last instance, their defense of free publication rested on the moral and intellectual superiority of the elite organized in the Court of Honor as conceived by Rousseau in his "The Letter to M. d'Alembert on the Theatre" (1758/1960). Nevertheless, libertarian and rationalist ideas of the 17th century inspired intellectual and political debates on freedom of expression and publicness as an epistemological condition of truth and moral–political condition of justice among generations to come.

In the 18th century, the concept of censorship still did not lose entirely the ancient positive moralistic connotation. Montesquieu (1752), for example, emphasized that "every one knows the wonderful effects of the censorship among the Romans," and Rousseau was no less in favor of it: "As the law is the declaration of the general will, the censorship is the declaration of the public judgment.... Plato banished Homer from his republic and we will tolerate Molière in ours?" (Rousseau, 1758/1960, p. 116). Both Rousseau and Montesquieu saw the value of censorship in fighting against the corruption of morals.

Legal and moral convictions in favor of some form of censorship existed in Europe even after the French Revolution. The European Enlightenment praised Greek and Roman humanism and aristocratic republicanism but closed its eyes to its intolerance of adversarial ideas. Nevertheless, despite the support of "enlightening" forms of censorship, the Enlightenment strongly confronted the royal and ecclesiastic suppression of civil liberties and religious intolerance. The debates on the right to freedom of expression and publication moved ever closer to the idea of freedom of expression and press freedom as fundamental to democratic citizenship.

THE PRINCIPLE OF PUBLICITY AS ETHICAL MAXIM

The 17th century liberal–rationalist ideas on freedom of expression and publication have generated two different intellectual currents of conceptualizing publicness. Immanuel Kant's conceptualization of publicness derives from the transformation of the natural personal right of free expression into the civil right to communicate, as a realization of the generic human ability and need to communicate their spiritual existence and participate in a collective (and particularly political) life. Jeremy Bentham (1791/1994) is the founder of the second conceptualization that rests on functions performed by the public and its immediate instrument, the press, to ensure the surveillance over those in (political) power by the "public opinion tribunal."

Much before "the public" and "the public sphere" became commonly used terms, Kant (1795/1983) defined their core ethical principle—*publicity*—as a "transcendental concept of public justice" based on citizens' fundamental dignity and moral sovereignty. He conceived of publicity as a citizen right to public use of reason and legal norm to legitimize government, as an instrument to achieve both individuals' independent reasoning and legal order in the social realm, arguing that "all actions affecting the rights of other human beings are wrong if their maxim is not compatible with their being made public" (Kant, 1795/1983, p. 135). Kant also argued that individual public use of reason not only must always be free but as a moral action has to be performed out of a sense of duty; thus he declared the motto of enlightenment to be "Have [the] courage to use your own understanding!" (Kant, 1784). Only a free public use of one's reason can stimulate personal enlightenment otherwise hindered by limitations on the private uses of reason. Any regulation of relationships in a (political) community would be contrary to the public interest and citizens' freedom, if citizens are kept alienated from opportunities to discuss matters of common concern in public.

The second stream promoted publicity and a free press as morally justified instruments to establish public surveillance over government because they always produce the greatest balance of pleasure over pain for every citizen. Bentham warned against the permanent danger that the self-interests of governors may be in conflict with the interests of the community for which they are supposed to be responsible. His solution was to ensure that all transactions in the political assembly would be subject to surveillance by the public, which would also secure public confidence (1791/1994, p. 590). Representatives in a political assembly have a *moral obligation* to promote public interests, and the legal system enables citizens to punish those who would fail to do it. Thus it is a *moral duty* of the press to report regularly on government activities and the proceedings of the legislature in a form that is accessible to readers, and to present the public's critical opinions of the legislative process.[1]

Bentham's utilitarian ideas on publicity represent the intellectual foundation of the watchdog concept of the press which served as a powerful means—though not always in the hands of "the public"—of limiting the governmental abuse of power. However, since the mid-1800s, surveillance by the public and the press over political authorities has been increasingly replaced—both in (social-psychological) theory and practice—with press control over individuals. Tocqueville (1856/1955) emphasized the impelling power of public opinion and the press to discipline the people by promoting majority opinions. Tarde (1969) recognized that "the need to agree with the public of which one is a part…becomes all the more strong and irresistible as the public becomes more numerous, the opinion more imposing, and the need itself more often satisfied" (p. 318).

The "disciplinary turn" in public opinion theories followed the historical subordination of press freedom to property rights, and freedom of expression to free enterprise. Whereas in the early stages of the press, the principle of publicity was opposed to the economic sphere and its dominant principle of profitability, in the second half of the 19th century, the press increasingly became "a business pure and simple." This historical transformation led Marx to conclude that, "the primary freedom of the press is in not being a business" (1842/1974, p. 71). Instead, the press should be free, according to Marx, according to its authentic social nature, as a means used by individuals to communicate with each other, since only in community with others—in communication— can the alienated private person achieve emancipation as a citizen.

PUBLIC DISCOURSE: COOPERATION OR ANTAGONISM?

Scholars of the late 18th and 19th century acknowledged that the invention of printing has introduced substantial changes in the way people (inter)act socially, including the emergence of the public (sphere) which has come into existence via its separation from the sphere of public power. With Rousseau and particularly Bentham, the concept of the public as a sort of popular tribunal expressing opinions and representing the general will gained prominence in political–philosophical discourses. The concept of the public was essential for theorizations of public opinion in the 19th and 20th century, in which public opinion was considered a process by which individuals incorporated into the public expressed approval or disapproval of any authoritative actions or abstentions from them.

What forms of communication help to constitute the public, how they inform public opinion, and what is the dominant type of discourse in the public sphere is a matter of enduring scholarly disagreement since Tarde's theory of conversation as imitation. Tarde considered the public a product of "mutual adaptation" between the newspaper and its readers in which the reader selects "his" paper and the paper selects readers it tends to address. Conversation is "the strongest agent of imitation, of the propagation of sentiments, ideas, and modes of action" (p. 308), and so is the press. Both forms of communication are specific instances of the process of imitation, which Tarde defined, along with opposition and innovation, as universal sociological principles central to the human condition.

Tönnies (1922) differentiates between the forms of communication established in the Gemeinschaft and Geselleschaft types of social structure. The difference between community and society has been first and foremost constituted by *writing*. In Gemeinschaft (community), "traditional opinions," such as beliefs and dogmas, are transmitted, primarily from the older to the younger generation and from higher to lower social strata. In Gesellschaft (society), however, tradition and authority "from upside down" give way to verifiable reason and critique in society. The communication of opinions aimed at convincing others is addressed to the very opinion of the addressee or reader. Tönnies notes: "It offers reasons which are supposed to persuade him but which may be checked and discarded, and appeals to his feelings which may change his mind accordingly" (p. 92).

The rationality of discourse among members of the public was further elaborated by Park, who conceptualized the public as a specific social group (opposite to the crowd) in which "discussion among individuals who assume opposing positions…is based upon the presentation of facts" (Park, 1904/1972, p. 57). Essential for the public is the process of reciprocity between different interests; the public expresses criticism and within it, opinions are divided. The process of adaptation through differentiation in the public is similar to that in political life (interaction between opposing political parties) and economy (reciprocal relationship between the buyer and seller). If criticism disappears, the public itself ceases to exist.

Mead perceived the primary aspect of human intelligence to be the capacity of the individual "to put himself to some degree in the experiential places of, or to take the attitudes of, the other individuals belonging to that society" (Mead, 1934, p. 300). By reporting and commenting on significant social situations, public communication serves the function of enabling individuals to "enter into the attitude and experience of other persons" and to take attitudes of "a generalized other"—the community. The social ideal conceived of by Mead would be "the attainment of a universal human society in which all human individuals would possess a perfected social intelligence, …such that the meanings of any one individual's acts or gestures…would be the same for any other individual whatever who responded to them" (p. 310). This, however, does not imply that no conflicts exist in the historical process of social integration based on the growing interdependence of human individuals that social evolution brought about. On the contrary, as Mead argues, social antagonism and social cooperation, conflict and consensus are just two classes of the same "fundamental socio-physiological impulses or behavior tendencies which are common to all human individuals" (p. 303).

Mead's ideas profoundly influenced 20th-century theorizations of public opinion as the main source of coordination, control, and cooperation between individuals, groups, and in society as a whole. Many authors, particularly those defending deliberative democracy, took Mead's ideas as the logical basis of the attainment of consensus in an ideal deliberative situation. The symbolic interactionist tradition and its emphasis on empathy—without its antagonistic dimension—also appear in Habermas's conceptualization of the public. "Citizens behave like a public when they can discuss issues of common interest without pressure, i.e., assured that they can freely gather and assemble, and freely express and publish their opinions" (Habermas, 1962/1989, p. 293), and "everyone is required to take the perspective of everyone else" (1995, p. 117). Habermas defines the public as politically equal citizens participating in free public discussion, freed from any conflict of interest—because they left their private interests in the private sphere—and, therefore, leading to consensus. Despite its counterfactuality, the consensus should be normatively considered attainable for otherwise, "communicative action" oriented toward reaching understanding and consensus would degenerate into "strategic action" aimed at success over a (rational) opponent with competing interests.

Like Habermas, Rawls conceptualizes consensus resulting from rational discourse as a means to provide a justification for political and moral norms in his theory of public reasoning. Public reason is "public," according to Rawls (1997), in three ways:

> as the reason of free and equal citizens, it is the reason of the public; its subject is the public good concerning questions of fundamental political justice, which questions are of two kinds,

constitutional essentials and matters of basic justice; and its nature and content are public, being expressed in public reasoning by a family of reasonable conceptions of political justice reasonably thought to satisfy the criterion of reciprocity. (p. 766)

Rawls applies the idea of public reasoning only to political discussions of fundamental questions in "the public political forum," which consists of three categories of qualified political actors: (1) judges (especially the judges of a supreme court) justifying their decisions; (2) government officials (especially chief executives and legislators); and (3) candidates for public office and their campaign managers (p. 768). A different but supplementary function is attributed by Rawls to "the background culture" or "culture of civil society" of a variety of civic associations, including mass media. "Citizens fulfill their duty of civility and support the idea of public reason by doing what they can to hold government officials to it. This duty, like other political rights and duties, is an intrinsically moral duty" (p. 769).

The main problem with the idea of unforced consensus, either societal consensus at large or among actors of the strong public, is that it cannot accommodate itself for the existing antagonisms in society between individuals and groups with differing interests, which already had been Mead's concern. One way to "solve" this problem is to limit public discourse to identically constructed actors, and thus to *a priori* exclude divergent interests, as Rawls tries with his qualified political actors, but this substantially limits the moral power of the normative idea of consensus. An ideal speech situation as conceived of by Habermas or Rawls—either in interpersonal or mass mediated communication—was already considered by Tönnies, who argued that opinions are determined by interests, to be infeasible in a modern political context .

Another option is to ground a theory of deliberative democracy on a nonconsensual basis that allows for antagonisms, where the (coercive) majority rule rather than (noncoercive) consensus is taken for decision rule. As Mouffe (1999) argues,

the obstacles to the realization of the ideal speech situation are ontological. Indeed, the impediments to the free and unconstrained public deliberation of all on matters of common concern is a conceptual impossibility because, without those so-called impediments, no communication, no deliberation could ever take place. (p. 751)

In that sense, passions and confrontations—as opposed to rationality and cooperation—do not jeopardize democracy but could rather promote it: only when "we accept that every consensus exists as a temporary result of a provisional hegemony, as a stabilization of power and that always entails some form of exclusion, we can begin to envisage the nature of a democratic public sphere in a different way" (Mouffe, 1999, p. 756).

Mouffe's model recurs in Mead's idea of "the ultimate basis of societies" constituted by two fundamental tendencies of human behavior, "those which lead to social cooperation, and those which lead to social antagonism among individuals" (Mead, 1934, p. 304). The solution Mouffe proposes is rather simple: *antagonism* between enemies should be substituted with, or transformed into, *agonism* between adversaries who, "while in conflict, they see themselves as belonging to the same political association, as sharing a common symbolic space within which the conflict takes place" (2005, p. 20). Instead of trying, in vain, institutionally to reconcile all conflicting interests, the democratic project should aim to create a vibrant "agonistic" public sphere of contestation where different hegemonic political projects can be confronted (p. 3). Although at first glance the model of radical agonistic pluralism seems to contradict the model of communicative rationality, we may argue—based on Mead's arguments—that the two models actually represent two complementary perspectives to the democratization of communication. In both instances—to achieve a rational consensus or to keep the democratic contestation alive in the political framework—a *nonexclusive* public sphere is needed.

MEDIATORS BETWEEN CIVIL SOCIETY AND THE STATE: MASS MEDIA AND THE PUBLIC SPHERE

Public phenomena have always been grounded on the most developed modes of (mass) communication. Moreover, since the principle of publicity only makes sense in reference to forms of communication beyond temporary interpersonal interaction, the nature of being public (i.e., publicness) in the strict sense could not have existed before the invention of the first form of mass communication—the press. The invention of printing substantially expanded the social horizon of communication. At the same time, it made it obvious that reading, and particularly, publishing newspapers is not only a matter of individuals' communication abilities but also a matter of ownership (Splichal, 2002, pp. 10–11).

The public could not have been established without the press. Ever since Bentham, first the press and later other media were considered constitutive of the public and public opinion, but only Marx realized that the press is more than just an organ of public opinion. He conceptualized the press in the sense of a *public sphere* mediating between the state and civil society, in which the state and civil society could meet on equal terms, emancipated from their authoritative officiality and private interests:

> The rulers and the ruled alike…are in need of a *third* element, which is *political* without being official, hence not based on bureaucratic premises, an element which is of a *civil* nature without being directly bound up with private interests and their pressing need. This supplementary element…is the *free press*. In the realm of the press, rulers and ruled alike can criticize their principles and demands, yet no longer in a relation of subordination, but on terms of equality as *citizens of the state;* no longer as *individuals*, but as *intellectual forces,* as exponents of reason. The "free press" is the product of public opinion and, at the same time, also produces public opinion; it can transform a particular interest to a common interest. (Marx, 1843a)

The free press, Marx suggests, can mediate between civil society and the state, as it is a medium of rational discourse. The distinctive feature of the press is that it can transform a particular interest to a common interest by confronting the rulers and the ruled, provided that a genuinely public sphere is established in which confrontation between opposing viewpoints is possible. The press is an organ through which the public can express public opinion; it is the condition for public opinion and its creator, the public, to exist—it is a *public sphere*, in which the press "harmoniously combines all the true elements of the popular spirit" (Marx, 1843b).

It took more than a hundred years for Marx's idea of "the third element" to be conceptualized literally as "the public sphere" (Habermas, 1962/1989), which is normatively understood as a specific sphere, domain, or "imagined space" of social life existing between, and constituted by, the state and civil society. It represents an infrastructure for social integration through (mass mediated) public discourse—an opinion market—in contrast to political power in the sphere of politics and market mechanisms in the sphere of economy, both of which represent specific forms of social integration through competition. It is activated in the communicative interdependence and rational–critical discourse among citizens potentially affected by transactions in which they do (or did) not participate, where the legislated laws of the state and the market laws of economy are supposedly suspended.

The public sphere is the arena in which civil society informs itself and exchanges ideas and opinions with other social actors of the two remaining realms, those of the state and the economy. The concept of civil society is closely related and often confused with that of the public sphere since associations that form opinions and serve as a hub for an autonomous public sphere occupy the central part of civil society. As Calhoun (1993) argues:

> the importance of the concept of public sphere is largely to go beyond general appeals to the nature of civil society in attempts to explain the social foundations of democracy and to introduce a discussion of the specific organization within civil society of social and cultural bases for the development of an effective rational-critical discourse aimed at the resolution of political disputes. (p. 269)

Civil society is a form of social organization between, and different from, the state, the economy (the market), and the private domain of family, friendship, and intimacy. It is constituted by uncoerced associations, organizations, and activities that reach beyond economic and political "consumption," through which citizens as economic and political beings contribute to the production of economic (profit) and political power. In contrast, in civil society, opinions are formed and goals defined to influence opinion formation and, consequently, decision making in given institutional and normative frameworks. Civil society is often seen as a locus for limiting the power of the state and capital, but it does not seek to replace either state or commercial actors.

Mass media are constitutive of the public and vitally important for the creation of an institutional (infra)structure of the public sphere. It is their distinctive feature that they can transform a particular interest into a common interest by linking primary publics and confronting (or linking) the rulers and the ruled. Ideally, they channel the flows of discourses from opinion formation in the networks of the public sphere to the political will-formation in the political system and vice versa. It is often claimed, however, that mass media fail to perform their critical role in the public sphere due to the rise of organized particularistic interests in the political decision-making process, media dependence on money and political power, professionalization of public relations in political communication, and commercialization of the media.

Regardless of its immediate consequences, a wide dispersion of communication power among as many actors as possible is a much-desired value in normative theories of democracy because a wide and fair dispersal of power and ubiquitous opportunities to present one's own opinions in public is inherently democratic. Widely dispersed media are also less vulnerable to external political and commercial censorship since they cannot be as easily controlled as heavily concentrated media. On the other hand, global media governance, which is characterized by the absence of effective regulation of transnational media conglomerates, deprives nation-states of two main elements of their media policy: national regulation and control and public service broadcasting.

MEDIA RESPONSIBILITY AND CITIZENS' PARTICIPATION

Prevalent contemporary concerns about mass media appear to conceptualize democratic media and their significance for public engagement and participation by stressing their political independence and the inviolability of the private property right as its prerequisite. The quality of service provided by the media to the public(s) only seldom emerges as essential to democracy. More critical–normative concerns that sustain state "interference" aimed at regulating the media as a public good are strongly opposed by neoliberal forces challenging, in particular, the legitimacy of the public service status of the (broadcast) media and the (proposed) right to communicate. Not surprisingly, however, once hardly imaginable ideas of transforming media into nonprofit, endowed institutions (like universities) are getting more public attention and support in the period of the deep global financial and economic crisis.

The earliest ideas that media freedom can only go together with their social responsibility date from the period of the liberal bourgeois public sphere when the press played a principal part in the rise of liberal economic and democratic political institutions. Despite immense changes in the complexity of the media, the idea of the public as the key player in the public sphere is no less important today, and it is getting even richer in terms of its relevance for democratic political, cultural, and economic processes. The spreading of these processes beyond the nation-states sharpens the tensions between the two main functions which the privately owned "quality media" should fulfill: to provide information, opinion, and education for their audiences, and to secure stable profits for the owners. The tensions are often "solved" in favor of commercial interest: the sensational rather than significant dominates the media; news is decontextualized and thus media do not provide citizens with the information they need to participate in the democratic process. The greater part of all media activities are carried out for profit according to the market rules that should also, as it is often argued, reflect and satisfy consumers' preferences. Research shows, however, that there is increasing skepticism on the part of citizens about the credibility of news media, particularly in the developed part of the world. In a 2008 U.S. poll, just 19.6% of those surveyed could say that they believed all or most news media reporting.[2]

The normative view that mass media have some responsibility to serve the (civil) society in which they operate is considered by its supporters an axiom that hardly needs any additional explanation. For the laissez-faire advocates, however, the idea of social responsibility of the media is an anomaly that has to be challenged in both theory and practice. They argue that production and consumption of media contents should be left to the marketplace in which media enterprises produce programs for viewers and sell their audiences' attention to advertisers.

The first position considers the media an integral part of a modern social system with significant political and cultural functions for individuals and society as a whole. The opposite view

TABLE 23.1
Modes of Media Responsibility (based on Splichal, 2006)

Media responsibility to:	Prevailing type of regulation of obligations	Source of legitimacy of responsibility claims	Normative power of actors to influence the media		
			State/Paternal	*Commercial*	*Public service**
Media owners	Legal	Property right	High	High	Moderate
Corporate economic clients	Contractual (market)	Profit maximization	Low	High/ Moderate	Low
Professions / Content creators / Journalists	Ethical	Professional norms	Low/ None	Moderate	High
Audiences	Cost-effective (market)	Consumers' rights (e.g. right to choose)	Low/ None	High	Moderate
Citizens & civil society	Ethical/political/ legal	Communication rights	None	None	High
State – policy makers and regulatory bodies	Legal/political	Political	High	Moderate	Moderate

* In terms of normative power of actors, 'public service media' to large degree also include 'alternative media.'

holds that a true freedom of expression implies not only the absence of any outside interference (market forces are considered "insiders" in the process), but also no obligation to meet any outside claims, especially any claim "made in the name of the society or state and therefore backed by force as well as authority" (McQuail, 2003, p. 14). This position reflects the rise of a "new First Amendment theology" in the United States (McChesney, 1999, p. 257), which propagates the belief that the First Amendment grants freedom of expression to the media rather than citizens, thus any regulation of the media would be at odds with the First Amendment. If the public speech right, for example, is declared as an abstract goal, it would not conflict with the First Amendment and that would be, in principle, acceptable; yet if it has no concrete meaning and standard to be applied, it cannot contribute to diversity either. On the other hand, if this right is defined in specific terms to encourage a particular kind of expression or contents, or even a specific group of citizens, then it is seen as a content-based violation of the First Amendment.

The outright denial of the laissez-faire campaigners that privately owned media can better serve the public through government regulation, which in itself is a violation of the private property right, is challenged by the social responsibility advocates with the argument that not only public regulation of the media may more resemble shared property rights than governmental regulation, but also that there is no substance in the belief that private property right is inherently superior to the public speech right. The neoliberal laissez-fare criticism of media regulation was perhaps sensible in the 18th and 19th century but it is untenable in modern times, because "with the development of private restraints on free expression, the idea of [a] free marketplace where ideas can compete on their merits has become just as unrealistic in the twentieth century as the economic theory of perfect competition" (Barron, 1967, p. 1653).

The media are irreplaceable in fostering public debate, political pluralism, and awareness of diverse opinions, notably by providing different groups in society—including cultural, linguistic, ethnic, religious, or other minorities—with an opportunity to receive and impart information, to express themselves, and to exchange ideas. At the same time, the idea of the public sphere also includes an aspect of commonality and unity; the media are seen as an important means of social integration, cohesion, and common (national) identity.

The wide-reaching advance of communication technologies makes access to communication means easier and possibilities for media diversity better than any technological revolution in the past. However, while the Internet enables dialogical communication among citizens that cannot be effectively restrained by hierarchical control and external surveillance, it can hardly assure any effect to what citizens publish. Compared with the traditional media, the Internet and web communities can barely perform the role of a watchdog or create moral obligations in a way kthat is similar to the traditional media.

The contrary is even the case: online and offline debates among web users may form a public only when they get together around the issues set on the agenda by the traditional big media. Without the traditional mass media, the public sphere would lack the most effective channel correlating the public(s) with power actors appearing before the public and deriving their legitimacy from it.

> From the perspective of democratic theory, the public sphere must…not only detect and identify problems but also convincingly and *influentially* thematize them, furnish them with possible solutions, and dramatize them in such a way that they are taken up and dealt with by parliamentary complexes. (Habermas, 1996, p. 359)

Despite all technological innovations in computer mediated communication, global media governance rests on rather limited participation by those affected by the consequences of transactions in which they could not participate, to use Dewey's (1927/1991) definition of the public. Instead of providing only passive access to the consumption sphere, a genuine democratization should primarily build up conditions for an active participation of citizens in deliberative communication. A direct and indirect incorporation of citizens into the production and exchange of messages in different forms of communication from interpersonal to mass communication is needed in which the individuals can realize their interests and meet their needs in collaboration with others.

Democratic struggles should not only significantly broaden the social base of mass communication by incorporation of previously excluded social groups, such as the young, women, socially, economically, or politically deprived groups, national, ethnic, linguistic, or religious minorities, but also mobilize citizens around perceived threats that commercial and political party-controlled media pose to the democratic process. Not only is an appropriate institutional environment often missing to democratize the media; even legal restraints may limit citizens' access to the media as the UK Make Poverty History (MPH) case of September 2005 indicates: the UK Office of Communications banned the MPH advertisements that were intended to influence UK national policy on international development, arguing that the MPH aims were "wholly or mainly political" since they aimed to "achieve important changes" and thus violated the Communications Act 2003 which prohibits political advertising.

"Defeudalization" of publicness cannot be created by new modes of communication alone; reminiscent of traditional public factions, web communities which shoot up like mushrooms after the rain on the Internet hardly transcend group particularisms based on racial, gender, age, ideological, religious, professional, and other identities and interests. The democratic merit of CMC is mostly limited to the overturn of suppression and censorship of mass media and public opinion by authoritarian regimes, as for example the "Twitter revolution" of April 2009 in the former Soviet republic of Moldova suggests, where mass protests against the (allegedly forged) parliamentary election results were efficaciously organized by users of social networking web sites Twitter, LiveJournal, and Facebook.

An attempt to (re-)establish publicity in its original "three-dimensional design"—as personal right and moral duty to communicate in public, surveillance of the public over government (governance), and mediation between the state and civil society (Splichal, 2009)—can only be efficacious if firmly rooted in civil society. Social movements are the most important actors in the battle for cultural and political changes in the mainstream media and their economic and political environment, and in establishing alternative media varying from radical to participatory media, and from very loosely structured "activists' media" to firmly institutionalized "civil society media."

Hackett and Carroll (2006, p. 52) identify three possible strategies that media activists can apply to democratize mass communication. (1) One strategy is to reform the media internally by progressive practices of media workers, whether as trade unionists seeking more collective self-determination in the workplace, or as professionals trying to reform the practices and ethos of the media. (2) Creation of new (parallel or alternative) fields to circumvent the established corporate media can significantly influence mainstream media, as the adoption of unconventional (e.g., literary, fanzine-style) techniques of writing, "alternative" design and graphics, and the expansion of "what's on" guides by the "big media" indicate. (3) Another strategy is to change the media environment by policy interventions; for example, to change state or transnational communication policy; to promote critical awareness of media and media literacy in society.

The debates on media democratization also emphasize the need to focus on global processes and work on international policy with a unifying strategic frame, which would allow international coalitions for democratic communication to develop.

GLOBALIZED GOVERNANCE AND TRANSNATIONAL PUBLIC SPHERES

Theories of deliberative democracy claim that democratic legitimation can be achieved through a deliberative process in which a variety of state and nonstate stakeholders participate. However, new forms of global governance often escape traditional mechanisms of public deliberation and accountability, whereas new mechanisms lack in efficiency or even do not (yet) exist. Critics of the global "democratic deficit" argue that globalization actually sacrificed democratic politics to the profitability of global economic transactions: it shook economic security and social equalities, and weakened citizens' participation in decision making and democratic institutions once established within democratic political systems of nation-states.

Powerful transnational actors in globalization undermine national democratic decision-making authorities. A significant part of national political institutions' decision-making power is transferred to those operating at the transnational level, which limits the scope and reach of actions of national governments and, particularly, national legislatures, thus challenging sovereign states' responsibility for the common good.

> The nascent global civil sphere has none of the institutions that, in a fully functioning democracy, allow public opinion to produce civil power and thus regulate the state, such as independent courts, party competition, and elections. Yet this nascent global civil sphere does have access to institutions of a more communicative kind. (Alexander, 2006, p. 523)

The newly developed communicative power of civic actors stimulates the ideas of the development of a transnational public sphere despite the scarcity of global political institutions. Transnational networks may help people to participate in collective actions on transnational or global scale as superior to state sovereignty, referring to human rights, civic equality, and protection against gender, religious, racial, ethnic, or class discrimination.[3]

Since the public can only be effective if its actions have a clearly defined addressee with an effective decision-making power, two aspects of disempowerment of nation-states in global governance are particularly relevant: (1) The loss of state capacities for control requires a kind of transnational equivalent for the nation-state and national public—effective transnational decision-making powers accountable to effective transnational public(s). (2) The growing legitimation deficits in decision-making processes require that decision makers (re-)enter the public sphere to legitimize their decisions and to gain public support (Habermas, 2003, pp. 89–90), as used to be (at least normatively) the case with the nation-state.

In principle, there are two complementary options to reduce the democratic deficit in transnational communities. One is to create democratic institutions analogue to the democratic system of nation-states, but at the moment, it is difficult to imagine how such powerful transnational democratic institutions could be established, despite the decline of nation–state sovereignty. There are no empirical signs of "transplanting" the model of centralized public regulation from the nation-state to the global setting.

A more realistic option is to build a more decentralized and diffuse cosmopolitan system of governance, which ultimately depends upon the creation of a transnational public sphere as an arena for public debates and a medium of social integration fostering solidarity. Global governance should provide opportunities and sites, including mass media, for public deliberation among stakeholders, which would expose the decisions of powerful actors to transnational public scrutiny. By participating in the public discourse, citizens and civic associations can increase transparency, promote accountability, and enhance democratic legitimacy of the rules and institutions of global governance.

Although publicness is a rather weak form of control and influence compared to direct participation in decision making, transnational public spheres could pave the way for the formation of transnational public(s), which could establish a close link between global governance and deliberative democracy. Widespread networks of activists that are most visible in the antiglobalization movement in fact link together many citizens' voices on many different issues related to global governance. By taking an autonomous role of stakeholders in transnational governance, transnational publics would breathe civic engagement into a weak public sphere currently dominated by official state actors, expert elites, and mass media, and strengthen its fourth and most vital component—civil society.

NOTES

1. A recent UK political scandal about outrageous financial claims made by MPs revealed by the *Daily Telegraph* in May 2009 (Moore, 2009) corroborates Bentham's claims that (a) all politicians are potentially corrupted; (b) the transparency of politics is a necessary condition for people to have trust in it; and (**c**) it should be a moral duty of the press to monitor politicians.
2. www.reuters.com/article/pressRelease/idUS160770+08-Jan-2008+PRN20080108.
3. For example, a recent survey of the World Social Forum (WSF) revealed that 76% of the respondents believed that the global reality of the WSF would not have been possible without the Internet, and 47% affirm the positive role of transnational communications and networking in actualizing inclusive and plural spaces (Toor, 2005).

REFERENCES

Aristotle (350 BCE). *Rhetoric* (Trans. W. Rhys Roberts). http://classics.mit.edu//Aristotle/rhetoric.html
Alexander, J. C. (2006). Global civil society. *Theory, Culture and Society, 23*(2–3), 521–524.
Barron, J. A. (1967). Access to the press—A new first amendment right. *Harvard Law Review, 80*, 1641–1678.
Bentham, J. (1994). Of publicity. *Public Culture, 6*(3), 581–595. (Original work published 1791)
Calhoun, C. (1993). Civil society and the public sphere. *Public Culture, 5*(2), 267–280.
Dewey, J. (1991). *The public and its problems*. Athens, OH: Swallow. (Original work published 1927)
Gibson, O. (2005, September 13). Broadcast ban on make poverty history ad campaign. *The Guardian*. Retrieved from http://www.guardian.co.uk/uk/2005/sep/13/g8.advertising
Habermas, J. (1989). *The structural transformation of the public sphere: An inquiry into a category of bourgeois society*. Cambridge, MA: MIT Press. (Original work published 1962)
Habermas, J. (1995). Reconciliation through the public use of reason: Remarks on John Rawls's political liberalism. *The Journal of Philosophy, 92*(3), 109–131.
Habermas, J. (1996). *Between facts and norms*. Cambridge, UK: Polity Press.
Habermas, J. (2003). Toward a cosmopolitan Europe. *Journal of Democracy, 14*(4), 86–100.
Hackett, R. A., & W. K. Carroll (2006). *Remaking media: the struggle to democratize public communication*. New York: Routledge.
Kant, I. (1784). An answer to the question: What is enlightenment? Retrieved from http://www.totalb.com/~mikeg/phil/kant/enlightenment.html#1
Kant, I. (1983). To perpetual peace. In *Perpetual peace and other essays* (pp. 107–144). Indianapolis, IN: Hackett. (Original work published 1795)
Locke, J. (1689). Letter concerning toleration. Retrieved from http://www.constitution.org/jl/tolerati.htm
Marx, K. (1974). Debatten über Pressfreiheit und Publikation der Landständischen Verhandlungen [Debates on press freedom and publication of the discussions of the assembly of the estates]. *Marx-Engels Werke* (Vol. 1, pp. 28–77). Berlin, Germany: Dietz Verlag. (Original work published 1842)

Marx, K. (1843a). The Kölnische Zeitung and the ban on the Leipziger Allgemeine Zeitung. *Rheinische Zeitung* No. 4, January 4, 1843. Retrieved from http://www.marxists.org/archive/marx/works/1842/12/31. htm

Marx, K. (1843b). Justification of the correspondent from the Mosel. *Rheinische Zeitung* No. 19, January 19, 1843. Retrieved from http://marxists.anu.edu.au/archive/marx/works/1843/01/15.htm

McChesney, R. W. (1999). *Rich media, poor democracy: Communication politics in dubious times.* Urbana: University of Illinois Press.

McQuail, D. (2003). Public service broadcasting: both free and accountable. *Javnost—The Public*, *10*(3), 13–23.

Mead, G. H. (1934). *Mind, self, and society* (C. W. Morris, Ed.). Chicago, IL: University of Chicago Press.

Milton, J. (1644). *Areopagitica.* Retrieved from http://www.dartmouth.edu/~milton/reading_room/areopagitica

Montesquieu, C. (1752). *The spirit of laws* (T. Nugent, Trans.). Retrieved from http://www.constitution.org/cm/sol.htm): book viii

Moore, C. (2009). MPs' expenses: We've been paying too much for Labour's morality for too long. Retrieved from http://www.telegraph.co.uk/news/newstopics/mps-expenses/5297557/MPs-expenses-Weve-been-paying-too-much-for-Labours-morality-for-too-long.html

Mouffe, C. (1999). Deliberative democracy or agonistic pluralism? *Social Research*, *66*(3), 745–758.

Mouffe, C. (2005). *On the political.* Abingdon, UK: Routledge.

Park, R. E. (1972). *The crowd and the public* (H. Elsner, Jr., Ed.). Chicago, IL: University of Chicago Press. (Original work published 1904)

Peucer, T. (1690). *Über Zeitungsberichte* [Of news reporting]. Leipzig, Germany: Witttegau.

Plato. (1901). *The republic of Plato* (B. Jowett, Ed. & Trans.). Retrieved from http://classics.mit.edu/Plato/republic.html (Original work published ca.360 BCE)

Rawls, J. (1997). The idea of public reason revisited. *University of Chicago Law Review*, *64*, 765–807.

Rousseau, J. J. (1960). The letter to M. d'Alembert on the theatre (Trans. A. Bloom). In *Politics and the arts* (pp. 3–137). Ithaca, NY: Cornell University Press. (Original work published 1758)

Spinoza, B. (1883). *Theologico-political treatise* (R. H. M. Elwes, Trans.). Retrieved from http://www.spinoza.net/Theworks/index.html (Original work published 1670)

Splichal, S. (2002). *Principles of publicity and press freedom.* Lanham, MD: Rowman & Littlefield.

Splichal, S. (2006). Public media in service of civil society and democracy. In C. Nissen (Ed.), *Making a difference: Public service broadcasting in the European landscape* (pp. 17–34). Eastleigh: John Libbey.

Splichal, S. (2009). "New" media, "old" theories: Does the (national) public melt into the air of global governance? *European Journal of Communication*, *24*(4), 391–405.

Stieler, K. (1969). *Zeitungs Lust und Nutz* [Newspapers' pleasure and use]. Bremen, Germany: Schünemann. (Original work published 1695)

Tarde, G. (1969). *On communication and social influence* (T. N. Clark, Ed.). Chicago, IL: University of Chicago Press.

Tocqueville, A. (1955). *The old regime and the French Revolution* (S. Gilbert, Trans.). New York: Anchor Books. (Original work published 1856)

Tönnies, F. (1922). *Kritik der öffentlichen Meinung* [Critique of public opinion]. Berlin: Julius Springer.

Toor, S. S. (2005). Media for participatory democracy. Retrieved from http://www.mediademocracyproject.org/page01.php?goto=executingInquiry

24

Religion, State, and Secularism

How Should States Deal with Deep Religious Diversity?

Rajeev Bhargava

Since 1980, secular states, virtually everywhere, have come under severe strain. It is hardly surprising then that political secularism, the doctrine that defends them, has also been subjected to severe criticism. Some scholars and public figures have concluded that this critique is ethically and morally so profound and justified that it is time to abandon political secularism. I reject this conclusion. *I argue that the criticism of secularism looks indefensible because critics have focused on mainstream conceptions developed in largely religiously homogenous societies. In this way, the image of and broad-based commitment to secularism have become somewhat detached from the specific versions of it in various national, cultural, and religious contexts.* I claim that it is time we shifted focus away from doctrines underpinning some Western secular states toward the normative practices of a wide variety of states, including the best practices of non-Western states such as India. Once we do this we will begin to see secularism differently from what we have typically conceived and practiced: as a critical ethical and moral perspective not against religion but against religious homogenization and institutionalized (inter- and intrareligious) domination. Of all available alternatives, secularism remains our best bet to help us deal with ever deepening religious diversity and the problems endemic to it. Once these alternative conceptions implicit in the normative practices of states are dredged up, we shall see that we still do not possess a reasonable, morally and ethically sensitive alternative to secularism.

INTRODUCTION

I begin by clarifying some key terms and drawing crucial distinctions. Always and everywhere, human beings relate to each other and the world around them and, however minimal, diffused, and inarticulate, they relate to themselves. In short, their attitudes and actions can be divided into three kinds: those which are self-oriented (intrapersonal), those oriented toward others (interpersonal), and finally those oriented to the nonpersonal world (impersonal). Thus the direction and "target" of the ethical assessment, in terms of consideration of others, is a crucial means of distinguishing different approaches to ethics in practice. Invariably, some relations are seen as possessing greater importance than others. This judgment is made with the help of what may be called a framework of strong evaluation (Taylor, 1989). This framework tells us whether or not something is to be valued; if valued, what its value consists in and why it is valued. Consider for a moment the intrapersonal domain. Here the framework illuminates the kind of life or activity that is worth pursuing, what the ultimate ends of life are, which character and virtues command respect of those around us and are worth nurturing, and therefore, what our dignity consists in. Typically, in the interpersonal domain, we ask what obligations we have toward others, how we should treat others and why, and what should be the appropriate attitude (tolerance? respect?) toward others?

An ethic is flawed if a worthwhile collective life can be properly pursued only by some members of a group and only on condition that other members are excluded, marginalized, or oppressed. But so is an ethic that lacks a proper moral dimension, by allowing the domination of groups with a different vision of worthwhile collective life. An ethic that allows intra- and inter-group domination is seriously deficient. Because all religions purport to be comprehensive ethical visions of collective and individual existence and have a perspective on how to deal with other individuals and groups, they too are flawed if their realization is conditional upon some of their adherents dominating fellow adherents or if they enjoin or permit the domination of other religious groups. Religions that allow interreligious or intrareligious domination must suffer from grave moral or ethical defects. They remain so or become worse if they require or permit force (state power) to be used to initiate or perpetuate either forms of domination.

A need for an alternative ethical and moral vision arises when all existing religions in a society justify or endorse inter- and intrareligious domination. *Appropriately conceived, a critical social secularism purports to provide precisely such an extrareligious alternative vision. This somewhat modest secularism seeks to modify religious ethics, to make them more inclusive by reducing intrareligious domination, or to provide a relatively independent moral standpoint from which to free religions of interreligious domination.* Secularism is against institutionalized religious domination, not necessarily against religion itself. Likewise, political secularism seeks to modify the relationship between states and religions, to prevent states from perpetuating or supporting institutionalized religious domination. It seeks appropriately secular political alternatives to theocracies and states with established religions.

RELIGION-CENTERED STATES

I begin with the assumption that ethical reasoning must be both contextual and comparative. Given this, we must consider the merits and deficits of secular and nonsecular states, exploring what ethical gains or losses might ensue in the movement from a secular state to one that grants more importance to religion or vice versa. What then is wrong if states abandon secularism and become more religion-centered? If we value freedom and equality and are sensitive to religion-related domination, then we must find theocratic states morally and ethically defective; that is, those which have union with a particular religious order and are believed to be governed by divine laws directly administered by a priestly order claiming divine commission (Herberman, 1913), and states with established religions—states not governed by the sacerdotal order but which privilege one or some religions. Such states perpetuate interreligious and intrareligious domination. They have historically recognized a particular version of the religion enunciated by a church as the official religion: compelled individuals to congregate for only one church; punished them for failing to profess a particular set of religious beliefs; levied taxes in support of one particular church; and made instruction of the favored interpretation of the religion in educational institutions mandatory (Levy, 1994). In such cases, not only was there inequality among religions (Christians and

Jews) but also among the churches of the same religion. Societies with such states were either wracked by interreligious or interdenominational wars or persecuted minority religious groups.

States with substantive establishments have not changed with time. In our times, just consider Saudi Arabia (Ruthven, 2002) or consider Pakistan where the virtual establishment of the dominant Sunni sect has proved to be disastrous, even to Muslim minorities. For example, Ahmedis have been deemed as a non-Muslim minority and therefore convicted for calling themselves Muslims or using the word *mosque* to designate their place of worship (Bhargava, 2004, 2010b, p. 30; Malik, 2002, p. 10). I have taken Pakistan as an illustration, but surely the result would be the same if a Hindu state were to be established in India. This would be a threat to religious minorities but also to the plural and tolerant character of Hinduism itself and therefore to a large number of practicing Hindus. The democratic state of Israel suffers from the same problem. Once it was declared a Jewish state it could not but exclude from its full scheme of rights and benefits its own Arab citizens, let alone other Palestinians.

SECULAR STATES

But are secular states really better? To begin with, we should acknowledge that secular states and their underlying ideology, political secularism, appear to be under siege everywhere. They were severely jolted with the establishment of the first modern theocracy in 1979 in Iran. By the late 1980s, Islamic political movements had emerged in Egypt, Sudan, Algeria, Tunisia, Ethiopia, Nigeria, Chad, Senegal, Turkey, Afghanistan, Pakistan, and even in Bangladesh (Ahmed, 1987; Kepel, 1993; Mohsin, 1999; Westerlund, 1996).

Movements challenging secular states were hardly restricted to Muslim societies. Protestant movements decrying secularism emerged in Kenya, Guatemala, and the Philippines. Protestant fundamentalism became a force in American politics. Singhalese Buddhist nationalists in Sri Lanka, Hindu nationalists in India, religious ultra-Orthodoxy in Israel, and Sikh nationalists in the state of Punjab in India, as well as among diasporic communities in Canada and Britain, began to question the separation of state and religion (Juergensmeyer, 1994). In short, Western conceptions of political secularism appear not to have traveled all that well in other societies. What is surprising is that such conceptions and the secular states they underpin are coming under strain even in Europe where they were only some time back believed to be firmly entrenched and secure.

Why so? It is true that substantive secularization of European societies has also brought in its wake extensive secularization of European states. Regardless of their religious affiliation, citizens have a large basket of civil and political rights unheard of in religion-centered states, past or present. But still, two problems remain. First, migration from former colonies and an intensified globalization has thrown together on Western public spaces pre-Christian faiths, Christianity, and Islam (Turner, 2001). The cumulative result is unprecedented religious diversity, the weakening of public monopoly of single religions, and the generation of mutual suspicion, distrust, hostility, and conflict. This is evident in Germany and Britain but was dramatically highlighted by the headscarf issue in France and the murder of filmmaker Theo Van Gogh in the Netherlands shortly after the release of his controversial film about Islamic culture (Barker, 2004; Bowen, 2006; Buruma, 2006; Freedman, 2004; Modood, Trianadafyllidou, & Zapata-Barrero, 2006). Second, despite substantial secularization, the formal establishment of the dominant religion does little to bolster better intercommunity relations or reduce religious discrimination in several European states. As it turns out, the widespread belief of a secular European public sphere is a myth. The religious biases of European states have become increasingly visible with widening and deepening religious diversity. European states have continued to privilege Christianity in one form or another. They have publicly funded religious schools, maintained church real estate and clerical salaries, facilitated the control by churches of cemeteries, and trained the clergy. In short, there has been no impartiality within the domain of religion, and despite formal equality, this continues to have a far reaching impact on the rest of society (Klausen, 2005). In the rest of the paper, I wish to focus on this crisis of secular states in Europe.

To repeat, the crisis of secular states in Europe is in part because the secular humanist ethos endorsed by many citizens is not fully shared, particularly by those who have newly acquired citizenship. Any further secularization along secular humanist lines is not likely to resolve the crisis of European secular states. Second, this is because many of these states have formally or informally established their preferred religion, and establishment of a single religion, even of the weaker variety, is part of the problem, not part of the solution. What, in the face of this imbroglio, are European states to do?

Those reflecting on this crisis have at least four conceptions of secularism staring back at them. To get hold of these conceptions, it is best to examine the conceptual structure of secular states: The state must be separated from religion for the sake of certain ends. The four conceptions flow from the different ways in which the metaphor of separation is unpacked (mutual or one-sided exclusion, opportunistic or principled distance), the levels at which separation is sought (ends, institutions and personnel, law and public policy), and the manner in which ends are conceived (amoral, moral, or ethical). The first of these conceptions of secularism is thoroughly amoral and unethical because it separates religion from the state precisely because of the ethical or moral restrictions that religions place on its ends (wealth, power). Such amoral secular states are inconsistent with the self-organization and self-understanding of most European states, at least to the extent that they appear to have forsaken their imperial pretensions.

MAINSTREAM WESTERN SECULARISMS AS PART OF THE PROBLEM

Indeed, the dominant self-understanding of Western secularism is that it is a *universal* doctrine requiring the strict separation (exclusion) of church/religion and state for the sake of individualistically conceived moral or ethical values. This dominant self-understanding takes two forms, one inspired by an idealized version of the U.S. model of separation and the other of the equally idealized French model. Can European states be reinvigorated by these two forms of Western secularism? Can they then deal better with the new reality of the vibrant presence of multiple religions in public life and accompanying social tensions? In what follows I argue that available mainstream *conceptions* of Western secularism are likely to meet neither the challenge of the vibrant public presence of religion nor of increasing religious diversity.

The Idealized French Model of Secularism

Take first the idealized French conception. For this conception, the state must be separated from religion at the level of (a) ends and (b) institutions and personnel; however, at level (c), the state retains the power to interfere in religion. At the same time, religion is divested of any power to intervene in matters of state. In short, separation means *one-sided exclusion*. The state may interfere in religion to hinder or suppress it or even to help religion, but in all cases only to ensure its control over religion, which becomes an object of law and public policy but only on the state's terms. This conception arose in response to the excessive domination of the Church, encourages an active disrespect for religion, and is concerned solely with preventing the religious order from dominating the secular. It hopes to deal with institutionalized religious domination by taming and marginalizing religion altogether. This may help states to deal with aspects of intrareligious domination: one that exists when some members of a religious community dominate members of their own religion (e.g., anticlericalism in France). However, it has few resources to properly address interreligious domination, when members of one religious community discriminate against, marginalize, or even oppress members of another religious community.

This takes place because issues of radical individual freedom and citizenship equality arose in European societies *after* religious homogenization. The birth of confessional states was accompanied by massive expulsion of subject-communities whose faith differed from the religion of the ruler. Such states found some place for toleration in their moral space but as is well-known, toleration was consistent with deep inequalities and with humiliating, marginalized and virtually invisible existence. The liberal-democratization and the consequent secularization of many European states has helped citizens with non-Christian faiths acquire most formal rights. But such scheme of rights neither embodies a regime of interreligious equality nor effectively prevents religion-based discrimination and exclusion. Indeed, it masks majoritarian, ethnoreligious biases. This is evident in different kinds of difficulties faced by Muslims. For example, in Britain a third of all primary school children are educated by religious communities. Yet applications for state funding by Muslims were frequently turned down. Four years after they were accepted, there were only two Muslim schools compared to 2,000 run by Roman Catholics and 4,700 by the Church of England (Beider, 2007). Similar problems persist in other European countries (Modood, Triandafyllidou, & Barrero, 2006). This is also manifest in the failure of many Western European States to deal with the issue of headscarves (France), demands by the Muslims to build mosques and therefore to properly practice their own faith (Germany, Italy), or to have proper burial grounds of their own (Denmark). In recent times, as Islamophobia grips the imagination of several Western societies (exemplified by the cartoon controversy in Denmark), it is very likely that their Muslim citizens will continue to face disadvantage only on account of membership in a religious community (Barker, 2004; Bowen, 2006; Freedman 2004).

Some segments of European societies, both from the right and the left are tempted to follow the French model largely because they have bought the view that "Islam is a problem" and the only way to straighten the devil is to use the coercive power of the state. But this would be suicidal because it leaves untouched formal and informal establishments of Christianity in these societies. Besides, every attempt to further intervene in religions is likely to meet with resistance not only from Muslims but from non-Muslims too. Any reliance on this model is likely to exacerbate problems.

The Idealized U.S. Model of Secularism

Can these European states turn to the American model? The idealized American self-understanding interprets separation to mean *mutual exclusion*. Neither the state nor religion is meant to interfere in the domain of one another. This mutual exclusion is believed necessary to resolve conflicts between different Christian denominations, to grant some measure of equality between them, but most crucially to provide individuals with the freedom to set up and maintain their own religious associations. Mutual exclusion is believed necessary for religious liberty and for the more general liberties of individuals. This strict, or "perfect separation" as Madison termed it, must take place at each of the three distinct levels: of (a) ends, (b) institutions and personnel, and (c) law and public policy. Levels (a) and (b) make the state nontheocratic and disestablish religion. Level (c) ensures that the state has neither a positive relationship with religion, for example, there should be no policy of granting aid, even nonpreferentially, to religious institutions, nor a negative relationship with it. It is not within the scope of state activity to interfere in religious matters even when some of the values (such as equality) professed by the state are violated within the religious domain. The U.S. Congress simply has no power to legislate on any matter pertaining to religion (Hamburger, 2002; Levy, 1994). This noninterference is justified on the ground that religion is a privileged, private (nonstate) matter, and if something is amiss within this private domain, it can be mended only by those who have a right to do so within that sphere. This, according to proponents of this view, is what religious freedom means. Thus, the freedom that justifies mutual exclusion is negative liberty and is closely enmeshed with the privatization of religion. In my view, this model of secularism encourages the state to have passive respect for religion. Idealized U.S. secularism has some resources to fight interreligious domination (for instance, it necessitates the disestablishment of the dominant religion) but not to wage a struggle against other aspects of the same or against intrareligious dominations. Because the state is unable to facilitate freedoms or equality within religions, it forces people to exit from their religion rather than to press for intrareligious equality.

It is now increasingly clear that both forms of Western secularism have persistent difficulties coping with community-oriented religions such as Roman Catholicism, Islam, some forms of Hinduism, and Sikhism that demand greater public presence and even official recognition for themselves—particularly when they begin to cohabit the same society. Moreover, they were not designed for societies with deep religious diversity. Both these versions developed in the context of a single-religion society and to solve the problems of one religion, namely Christianity. Both understand separation as exclusion and make individualistically conceived values—individual liberty or equality between individuals or both—as the ground for separation. Because of their diveristy-resistant and individualistic character, both these forms of Western secularism have become part of the problem.

The Indian Model of Secularism

Are we caught then between ideologies that legitimate religious domination of the secular and forms of secularisms that are unable to prevent forms of intrareligious or interreligious domination? I believe it is possible to get out of this impasse because although theoretically less developed, there exists another model of secularism, one not generated exclusively in the West, which meets the needs of deeply religiously diverse societies and also complies with principles of freedom and equality: the subcontinental or Indian model found loosely in the best moments of intercommunal practice in India; and in the country's Constitution appropriately interpreted. In India, the existence of deep religious diversity has ensured a conceptual response not only to problems within religions but also between religions. Without taking it as a blueprint, the West must examine the Indian conception and possibly learn from it.

A number of features of the Indian model are striking and relevant to wider discussion, including conceptions of relationships between religious groups and how all of those are governed by a state. First, multiple religions are not extras, added on as an afterthought but present at its starting-point, as part of its foundation. Indian secularism is inextricably tied to deep religious diversity. Second, the Indian model has a commitment to multiple values: liberty and equality, not conceived narrowly as pertaining to individuals but interpreted broadly to cover the relative autonomy of religious communities and equality of status in society, as well as other more basic values such as peace and toleration between communities. It has a place not only for rights of individuals to profess their religious beliefs but for the right of religious communities to establish and maintain educational institutions crucial for the survival and sustenance of their distinctive religious traditions.

The acceptance of community-specific rights brings us to the third feature of Indian secularism. Because it was born in a deeply multireligious society, it is concerned as much with interreligious domination as it is with intrareligious domination. Unlike the two Western conceptions which provided benefits to minorities only incidentally (Jews benefited in some European countries such as France not because their special needs and demands were taken care of but rather because of a change in the general climate of the society), in India, even community-specific political rights (political reservations for religious minorities) were almost granted and were withheld in the last instance only for contextual reasons. In fact, it is arguable that a conceptual space is still available for them within the Indian Constitution.

Fourth, it does not erect an impermeable wall of separation between state and religion. There are boundaries, of course, but they are porous. This allows the state to intervene in religions, to help or hinder them without the impulse to control or destroy them. This involves multiple roles: granting aid to educational institutions of religious communities on a nonpreferential basis; or interfering in socioreligious institutions that deny equal dignity and status to members of their own religion or to those of others (for example, the ban on untouchability and the obligation to allow everyone, irrespective of their caste, to enter Hindu temples, and potentially to correct gender inequalities), on the basis of a more sensible understanding of equal concern and respect for all individuals and groups. In short, it interprets separation to mean not strict exclusion or strict neutrality but rather what I call principled distance, poles apart from one-sided exclusion, mutual exclusion, and strict neutrality or equidistance.

Fifth, it is not entirely averse to the *public* character of practically all religions. Although the state is not identified with a particular religion or with religion more generally (there is no establishment of religion), there is official and therefore public recognition granted to religious communities.

Sixth, this model shows that we do not have to choose between active hostility or passive indifference, or between disrespectful hostility or respectful indifference toward religion. Active respect can be combined with fierce critique: the state may intervene to prevent or respond to malpractices but at the same time offers support for the religious institution (Bhargava, 2009).

Seventh, by not fixing its commitment from the start exclusively to individual or community values or marking rigid boundaries between the public and private, India's constitutional secularism allows decisions on these matters to be taken either within the open dynamics of democratic politics or by contextual reasoning in the courts.

Finally, this commitment to multiple values and principled distance means that the state tries to balance different, ambiguous, but equally important values. This makes its secular ideal more like a contextual, ethically sensitive, politically negotiated arrangement (which it really is), rather than a scientific doctrine conjured by ideologues and merely implemented by political agents.

A somewhat forced, formulaic articulation of Indian secularism goes like this. The state must keep a principled distance from all public or private, individual-oriented or community-oriented religious institutions for the sake of the equally significant (and sometimes conflicting) values of peace, this-worldly goods, dignity, liberty, and equality (in all its complicated individualistic or nonindividualistic versions). Indian secularism then is an ethically sensitive negotiated settlement between diverse groups and divergent values. This model thus embodies what I call contextual secularism. Allow me to elaborate on the two features mentioned above: principled distance and contextual secularism.

PRINCIPLED DISTANCE AS A TEMPLATE FOR RELATIONS AND GOVERNANCE

As seen above, for mainstream western secularism, separation means mutual or one-sided exclusion. The idea of principled distance unpacks the metaphor of separation differently. It accepts a disconnection between state and religion at the level of ends and institutions but does not make a fetish of it at the third level of policy and law (this distinguishes it from all other models of secularism, moral and amoral that disconnect state and religion at this third level). How else can it be in a society where religion frames some of its deepest interests? Recall that political secularism is an ethic whose concerns relating to religion are similar to theories that oppose unjust restrictions on freedom, morally indefensible inequalities, inter-communal domination and exploitation. Yet a secularism based on principled distance is not committed to the mainstream Enlightenment idea of religion. It accepts that humans have an interest in relating to something beyond themselves including God and that this manifests itself as individual belief and feeling as well as social practice in the public domain. It also accepts that religion is a cumulative tradition as well as a source of people's identities (Smith, 1991). But it insists that even if it turned out that God exists and that a particular religion is true and others false, then this does not give the "true" doctrine or religion the right to force it down throats of others who do not believe it. Nor does it give a ground for discrimination in the equal distribution of liberties and other valuable resources.

Similarly, a secularism based on principle distance accepts that religion may not have special public significance antecedently written into and defining the very character of the state or the nation, but it does not follow from this that it has no public significance at all. Sometimes, on some versions of it, the wall of separation thesis assumes precisely that. As long as religion is publicly significant, a democratic state simply has to take it into account. Indeed, institutions of religion may influence individuals as long as they do so through the same process, by access to the same resources as anyone and without undue advantage or unduly exploiting the fears and vulnerabilities that frequently accompany people in their experience of the religious.

But what precisely is principled distance, and what does it mean in terms of communication as well as law and politics? The policy of principled distance entails a flexible approach on the question of inclusion/exclusion of religion and the engagement/disengagement of the state, which at the third level of law and policy depends on the context, nature, or current state of relevant religions (Bhargava, 1998, 2006a, 2006b). This engagement must be governed by principles undergirding a secular state; that is, principles that flow from a commitment to the values mentioned above. This means that religion may intervene in the affairs of the state if such intervention promotes freedom, equality, or any other value integral to secularism. For example, citizens may support a coercive law of the state grounded purely in a religious rationale if this law is compatible with freedom or equality. Equally, the state may engage with religion or disengage from it, engage positively or negatively, but it does so depending entirely on whether or not these values are promoted or undermined. A state that intervenes or refrains from interference on this basis keeps a principled distance from all religions. This is one constitutive idea of principled distance. This idea is different from strict neutrality; that is, the state may help or hinder all religions to an equal degree and in the same manner; if it intervenes in one religion, it must also do so in others. Rather, it rests upon a distinction explicitly drawn by the American philosopher Ronald Dworkin between equal treatment and treating everyone as an equal (Dworkin, 1978). The principle of equal treatment, in the relevant political sense, requires that the state treat all its citizens equally in the relevant respect; for example, in the distribution of a resource of opportunity. On the other hand, the principle of treating people as equals entails that every person or group is treated with equal concern and respect. This second principle may sometimes require equal treatment, say equal distribution of resources but it may also occasionally dictate unequal treatment. Treating people or groups as equals is entirely consistent with differential treatment. This idea is the second ingredient in what I have called principled distance.

I said that principled distance allows in some ways for differential treatment. What kind of treatment do I have in mind, and how might this be framed and argued given an overriding interest in fairness? First, religious groups have sought exemptions from practices in which states intervene by promulgating a law to be applied neutrally to the rest of society. This demand for noninterference is made on the ground either that the law requires them to do things not permitted by their religion or prevents them from doing acts mandated by it. For example, Sikhs demand exemptions from mandatory helmet laws and from police dress codes to accommodate religiously required turbans. Elsewhere, Jews seek exemptions from Air Force regulations to accommodate their yarmulkes. Muslim women and girls demand that the state not interfere in their religiously required chador. Jews and Muslims seek exemption from Sunday closing laws on the ground that this is not required by their religion. Principled distance allows then that a practice that is banned or regulated in one culture may be permitted in the minority culture because of the distinctive status and meaning it has for its members.

For many republican or liberal theories this is a problem because of their simple, somewhat absolutist morality that gives overwhelming importance to one value, in particular to equal treatment or equal liberty. Religious groups may demand that the state refrain from interference in their practices but they may equally demand that the state interfere in such a way as to give them special assistance so that these groups are also able to secure what other groups are able to routinely get by virtue of their social dominance in the political community. It may grant authority to religious officials to perform legally binding marriages, to have their own rules or methods of obtaining a divorce, its rules about relations between ex-husband and ex-wife, its way of defining a will or its laws about postmortem allocation of property, arbitration of civil disputes, and even its method of establishing property rights. Principled distance allows the possibility of such policies on the grounds that it might be unfair to hold people accountable to an unfair law.

However, principled distance is not just a recipe for differential treatment in the form of special exemptions. It may even require state intervention in some religions more than in others, considering the historical and social condition of all relevant religions. For the promotion of a particular value constitutive of secularism, some religions, relative to other religions, may require more interference from the state. For example, suppose that the value to be advanced is social equality. This requires in part undermining caste hierarchies. If this is the aim of the state, then it may be required of the state that it interferes in caste-ridden Hinduism much more than say Islam or Christianity. However, if a diversity-driven religious liberty is the value to be advanced by the state, then it may have to intervene in Christianity and Islam more than in Hinduism. If this is so, the state can neither strictly exclude considerations emanating from religion nor keep strict neutrality with respect to religion. It cannot decide a priori that it will always refrain from interfering in religions or that it will interfere in each equally. Indeed, it may not relate to every religion in society in exactly the same way or intervene in each religion to the same degree or in the same manner. To want to do so would be plainly absurd. All it must ensure is that the relationship between the state and religions is guided by nonsectarian motives consistent with some values and principles. A state interfering in one religion more than in others does not automatically depart from secularism. Indian secularism rejects the assumption that one size fits all.

CONTEXTUAL SECULARISM

Contextual secularism is contextual not only because it captures the idea that the precise form and content of secularism will vary from one to another context and from place to place but also that it embodies a certain model of contextual moral reasoning (Taylor, 1994, pp. 16–43; see also the argument in Parekh, 2000; compare Carens, 2000) out of not only a respect for cultural diversity but also a recognition of differences in communication patterns themselves. This it does because of its character as a multivalue doctrine and by virtue of its commitment to principled distance. To accept that secularism is a multivalue doctrine is to acknowledge that its constitutive values do not always sit easily with one another. On the contrary, they are frequently in conflict. Some degree of internal discord and therefore a fair amount of instability is an integral part of contextual secularism. For this reason, it forever requires fresh interpretations, contextual judgments, and attempts at reconciliation and compromise (Bhargava 2009, 2010). This contextual secularism recognizes that the conflict between individual rights and group rights or between claims of equality and liberty or between claims of liberty and the satisfaction of basic needs cannot always be adjudicated by recourse to some general and abstract principle. Rather they can only be settled case by case and may require a fine balancing of competing claims. The eventual outcome may not be wholly satisfactory to either but still be reasonably satisfactory to both. Multivalue doctrines such as secularism encourage accommodation: not the giving up of one value for the sake of another but rather their reconciliation and possible harmonization; that is, to make each work without changing the basic content of apparently incompatible concepts and values.

This endeavor to make concepts, viewpoints, and values work simultaneously does not amount to a morally objectionable compromise. This is so because nothing of importance is being given up for the sake of a less significant thing, one without value or even with negative value. Rather, what is pursued is a mutually agreed middle way that combines elements from two or more equally valuable entities. The roots of such attempts at reconciliation and accommodation lie in a lack of dogmatism, in a willingness to experiment, to think at different levels and in separate spheres and in a readiness to take decisions on a provisional basis. It captures a way of thinking characterized by the following dictum: "why look at things in terms of this or that, why not try to have both this and that?" (Austin, 1972, p. 318). In this way of thinking, it is recognized that though we may currently be unable to secure the best of both values and therefore be forced to settle for a watered-down version of each, we must continue to have an abiding commitment to search for a transcendence of this second best condition. It is frequently argued against Indian secularism that it is contradictory because it tries to bring together individual and community rights, and that articles in the Indian Constitution that have a bearing on the secular nature of the Indian state are deeply conflictual and at best ambiguous (Tambiah, 1998). This is to misrecognize a virtue as a vice. In my view, this attempt to bring together seemingly incompatible values is a great strength of Indian secularism.

Discerning students of Western secularism may now begin to find something familiar in this ideal. But then, Indian secularism has not dropped fully formed from the sky. It is not entirely *sui generis*. It shares a history with the West, which in part it has learned from and built on. Indian secularism may be seen to be a route to retrieving the rich history of Western secularism: forgotten, underemphasized, or frequently obscured by the formula of strict separation. If so, Western societies can find reflected in Indian secularism not only a compressed version of their own history but also a potential vision of their future (Bhargava, 2006b). Yet it is a mistake to collapse this brand of secularism with mainstream conceptions. Commentators such as Donald Smith (1963), Ashis Nandy (1998), T. N. Madan (1998), and Partha Chatterjee (1998) frequently fail to distinguish Indian secularism from Western conceptions (see also Galanter, 1998).

TWO OBJECTIONS

Two objections might be advanced against my argument. First, it might be said: look at the state of the subcontinent! Look at India! How deeply divided it remains! What about the violence against Muslims in Gujarat and against Christians in Orissa? How can success be claimed for the Indian version of secularism? I do not wish to underestimate the force of this objection. The secular ideal in India is in periodic crisis and is deeply contested. Besides, at the best of times, it generates as many problems as it solves. But it should not be forgotten that a secular state was set up in India *despite* the massacre and displacement of millions of people on ethnoreligious grounds and it has survived in a continuing context in which ethnic nationalism remains dominant throughout the world. Moreover, it was set up to deal with the tensions continuously generated by deep religious diversity, not to offer "a final solution" by expulsion or liquidation of all but the dominant religious group. Yet, regardless of what they did in the past, is it not a fair expectation that European and North American states will not allow any attempt at ethnic cleansing on their soil today? Surely, practitioners of Indian secularism can learn from the institutional mechanism set up by European states to prevent intergroup violence. I agree. Some facets of the institutional basis of Indian secularism can be strengthened by the example of Western states. To consolidate its minimally decent character, India can still learn from the contemporary "West." Yet, as different religious cultures claim their place in societies across the world, it may be India's development of secularism that offers the most peaceful, freedom-sensitive, and democratic way forward. In any case, this account must not be read as an apologia for the Indian state but as a reasonable and sympathetic articulation of a conception which the Indian state frequently fails to realize. My discussion is meant to focus on the comparative value of this conception and its potential for the future and not on how in fact it has fared in India. And why should the fate of ideal conceptions with transcultural potential be decided purely on the basis of what happens to them in their place of origin?

Second, it might be objected that I do not focus here on the best practices of Western states and instead emphasize the more narrow (and vocal) articulations of Western secular conceptions. But that precisely is my point. The dominant conception of Western secularism is derived from an idealized self-understanding of two of its versions rather than from the best practices of Western states, including the practices of the United States and France. It is my view that this doctrinal conception (a) obstructs an understanding of alternative conceptions worked out on the ground by morally sensitive political agents; (b) by influencing politicians and citizens alike, it frequently distorts the practice of many Western and non-Western states; (c) it masks the many ways in which inter- or intrareligious domination persists in many Western societies. Moreover, it is this conception which has traveled to all parts of the world and is a continuing source of misunderstanding of the value of secular states. My objective is to displace these conceptions or at least put them in their place by revealing their moral and practical limits as well as their celebrated advantages.

CONCLUSION

I hope to have demonstrated that there are at least two broad conceptions of secularisms, one mainstream Western (the United States and France) and the other which provides an alternative to it and is embodied in the Indian model. Of these, the Indian conception has better ethical and moral potential to deal with deep religious diversity. I do not wish to suggest that this alternative model is to be found only in India. The Indian case is meant to show that such an alternative exists. It is not meant to resurrect a dichotomy between the "West" and the "East," and I recognize the problematic usage here of these two broad and often unexamined categories. As I have mentioned, I am quite certain that this alternative version of secularism is embedded in the best practices of many states, including those Western states that are deeply enamored by mainstream conceptions of political secularism. My objective in this essay is to draw attention to the frequent inability of ethical and political theorists to see the normative potential in the secular practices of these different states because they are obsessed with the normativity of mainstream conceptions. Thus, we can see how both the images and actual practices of secularism are important here. Western states need to improve the understanding of their own secular practices just as Western secularism needs a better theoretical self-understanding. Rather than become paralyzed by adherence to models they developed at a particular time in their history, they would do well to more carefully examine the normative potential in their own political practices or to learn from the original Indian variant.

REFERENCES

Ahmed, I. (1987). *The concept of an Islamic state: An analysis of the ideological controversy in Pakistan.* London: Frances Pinter.

Austin, G. (1972). *The Indian Constitution: Cornerstone of a nation.* New Delhi, India: Oxford University Press.

Barker, C. R. (2004). Church and state: Lessons from Germany? *The Political Quarterly, 75*(2), 168–176.

Beider, V. (2007). *Secularism or democracy?* Amsterdam, the Netherlands: Amsterdam University Press.

Bhargava, R. (1998). *Secularism and its critics.* New Delhi, India: Oxford University Press.

Bhargava, R. (2006a). Political secularism. In J. Dryzek, B. Honning, & A. Philips (Eds.), *A handbook of political theory* (pp. 636–655). Oxford, UK: Oxford University Press.

Bhargava, R. (2006b). The distinctiveness of Indian secularism. In T. N. Srinivasan (Ed.), *The future of secularism* (pp. 20–58). Delhi, India: Oxford University Press.

Bhargava, R. (2009). Political secularism: Why it is needed and what can be learnt from its Indian version. In G. B. Levey & T. Modood (Eds.), *Secularism, religion and multicultural citizenship* (pp. 82–109). Cambridge, UK: Cambridge University Press.

Bhargava, R. (2010a). *The promise of India's secular democracy.* Delhi, India: Oxford University Press.

Bhargava, R. (2010b). Inclusion and exclusion in South Asia: The role of religion. (Background paper for UNDP Human Development Report). In R. Bhargava, *The promise of India's secular democracy* (pp. 217–248). New Delhi, India: Oxford University Press. (Original work published 2004)

Bowen, J. (2006). *Why the French don't like headscarves: Islam, the state and public space.* Princeton, NJ: Princeton University Press.

Buruma, I. (2006). *Murder in Amsterdam.* London: Penguin Press.

Carens, J. H. (2000). *Culture, citizenship, and community: A contextual exploration of justice as evenhandedness.* Oxford, UK: Oxford University Press.

Chatterjee, P. (1998). Secularism and tolerance. In R. Bhargava (Ed.), *Secularism and its critics* (pp. 345–379). New Delhi, India: Oxford University Press.

Dimova-Cookson, M., & Stork, P., Eds. (2010). *Multiculturalism and moral conflict.* London: Routledge.

Dworkin, R. (1978). Liberalism. In S. Hampshire (Ed.), *Public and private morality* (pp. 113–145). Cambridge, UK: Cambridge University Press.

Freedman, J. (2004). Secularism as a barrier to integration? The French dilemma. *International Migration, 42*(3), 5–27.

Galanter, M. (1998). Secularism, East and West. In R. Bhargava (Ed.), *Secularism and its critics* (pp. 234–267). New Delhi, India: Oxford University Press.

Hamburger, P. (2002). *Separation of church and state.* Cambridge, MA: Harvard University Press.

Herbermann, C. G., Pace, E. A., Pallen, C. B., Shahan, T. J., Wynnn, J. J., et al. (1913). *The Catholic encyclopedia* (Vol. 14). New York: The Encyclopedia Press.

Juergensmeyer, M. (1994). *New cold war? Religious nationalism confronts the secular state.* Berkeley: University of California Press.

Kepel, G. (1993). *The revenge of God: The resurgence of Islam, Christianity, and Judaism in the modern world.* Oxford, UK: Polity Press.

Klausen, J. (2005). *The Islamic challenge: Politics and religion in Western Europe.* Oxford, UK: Oxford University Press

Levy, L. W. (1994). *The establishment clause: Religion and the first amendment.* Chapel Hill: University of North Carolina Press.

Madan, T. N. (1998). Secularism in its place. In R. Bhargava (Ed.), *Secularism and its critics* (pp. 297–320). New Delhi, India: Oxford University Press.

Malik, I. H. (2002). *Religious minorities in Pakistan.* London: Minority Rights Group International.

Modood, T, Trianadafyllidou, A., & Zapata-Barrero, R. (Eds.). (2006). *Multiculturalism, Muslims and citizenship.* Abingdon, UK: Routledge.

Mohsin, A. (1999). National security and the minorities: The Bangladesh case. In D. L. Sheth & G. Mahajan (Ed.), *Minority identities and the nation-state* (pp. 312–332). New Delhi, India: Oxford University Press.

Nandy, A. (1998). The politics of secularism and the recovery of religious toleration. In R. Bhargava (Ed.), *Secularism and its critics* (pp. 321–344). New Delhi, India: Oxford University Press.

Parekh, B. (2000). *Rethinking multiculturalism: Cultural diversity and political theory.* Basingstoke, UK: Macmillan.

Ruthven, M. (2002). *A fury for God: The Islamist attack on America.* London: Granta Books.

Smith, D. (1963). *India as a secular state.* Princeton, NJ: Princeton University Press.

Smith, W. C. (1991). *The meaning and end of religion.* Minneapolis, MN: First Fortress Press

Tambiah, S. (1998). The crisis of secularism in India. In R. Bhargava (Ed.), *Secularism and its critics* (pp. 418–453). Delhi, India: Oxford University Press.

Taylor, C. (1989). *Sources of the self.* Cambridge, UK: Cambridge University Press.

Taylor, C. (1994). Justice after virtue. In J. Horton & S. Mendus (Eds.), *After MacIntyre* (pp.16–43). Notre Dame, IN: University of Notre Dame Press.

Turner, B. S. (2001). Cosmopolitan virtue: On religion in a global age. *European Journal of Social Theory, 4*(2), 131–152.

Westerlund, D. (1996). *Questioning the secular state.* London: Hurst.

25

Truths, Evils, Justice, and the Event of Wild(er)ness

Using Badiou to Think the Ethics of Environmentalism

Kevin Michael DeLuca

Man is the measure of all things.—Plutarch

As the archaeology of our thought easily shows, man is an invention of recent date. And one perhaps nearing its end. —Foucault

In Wildness is the preservation of the World.—Thoreau

On January 15, 2009, on Martin Luther King Jr.'s birthday, on the eve of the opening of the deeper shade of green Sundance Film Festival, leaders of the Congress of Racial Equality (CORE) held a protest march in Salt Lake City to denounce Robert Redford and by extension other wilderness environmentalists as racists. Redford had termed the Bush Administration's last minute gambit to open hundreds of thousands of acres to oil and gas leases, many in the spectacular canyonlands of southern Utah, "morally criminal." CORE national spokesman Niger Innis stated that such opposition "hurts a lot of low-income families at the other end of the natural gas pipeline." Bishop Harry Jackson Jr. of the Hope Christian Church in Beltsville, MD, chairman of the High-Impact Leadership Coalition, upped the ante: "The high energy prices we're going to see this winter are essentially discriminatory." The protest march achieved its media goal in the headline: "Robert Redford Criticized as Racist and 'Enemy of the Poor.'" (Avro, 2009).[1]

These are extraordinary charges. I want to start from this moment not to focus on the charges and responses (Redford spokeswoman Joyce Deep retorted, "They've gotten about $275,000 from Exxon oil in the last five years."), but to try to understand what this moment reveals about the state of environmental politics today. To put it bluntly, the environmental movement is haunted by the chimera of justice—a justice that arises out of the toxic ground of humanism[2] and is framed by the lens of species' solipsism.

At the anti-Redford rally Innis and Harry Jackson Jr. were speaking from the perspective and deploying a key tactic of what is commonly called the environmental justice movement (EJM).[3] In the environmental movement, the concept of justice has become the property of the EJM.

Unfortunately, it is a concept of justice entirely circumscribed by humanism and in the service of identity politics. These are fatal flaws for an environmental movement that is ostensibly about the earth and ecosystems and nonhuman species and the future.

CORE's anti-Redford rant may seem atypical, but it is not. Labeling environmentalists as racists has been at the core of the EJM's political strategy for two decades. In 1982, Benjamin Chavis initially termed EJ "environmental racism." In the famous 1990 letters to the Group of Ten mainstream environmental organizations, the SouthWest Organizing Project (SWOP) indicted wilderness advocacy as racist and colonialist:

> There is a clear lack of accountability by the Group of Ten environmental organizations towards Third World communities in the Southwest, in the U.S. as a whole and internationally. Your organizations continue to support and promote policies which emphasize the clean-up and preservation of the environment on the backs of working people in general and people of color in particular. In the name of eliminating environmental hazards at any cost, across the country industrial and other economic activities which employ us are being shut down, curtailed, or prevented while our survival needs and cultures are ignored.... Racism is a root cause of your inaction around addressing environmental problems in our communities.[4]

This is the clarion call of the EJM? The focus on race by Chavis and in this letter becomes a dominant motif in the EJM. Attempting to curtail sheep grazing, hunting, and fishing to protect endangered species is decried as racist. In EJ activist Dana Alston's renowned 1991 speech, she calls on expanding the definition of endangered species to include people: "It is not just ancient forests; it is not just saving the whales or saving other endangered species.... But our communities and our people are endangered species, too."[5] Campaigns to ban certain poisons or industrial practices have been criticized for costing jobs. Attempts to protect certain landscapes or wilderness areas have brought forth charges of racism.[6]

In what follows, after acknowledging the many important successes of the EJM, I will suggest it is more rightly understood as a social justice movement and that to displace wilderness with social justice cripples the environmental movement. It does this in two major ways—with respect to environmentalism in an international context and, more fundamentally, with respect to the central question of what is an environmental movement. Justice within the frame of humanism and identity politics renders environmentalism incapable of responding to the crucial issues of global warming, ocean pollution/depletion, and other catastrophic global threats. The question becomes: how to think differently? How to think of justice *outside* of justice for humans and how to think politics outside of identity? How to think of ethics outside of humanism, with humanism understood as an orientation that measures all issues by the question of how they affect humans? Or, as the movies constantly put it, "PEOPLE ARE DYING!!!" What I am suggesting is that an ethical environmental orientation by definition cannot pivot on the question of whether people are dying. Indeed, that is an extremely uninteresting and ineffective standard for any sort of ethics since people are always dying.[7] To provide an extrahuman ethical orientation that enables us to see the vital contribution of environmentalism as emerging from the encounter with wild(er)ness, I turn to philosopher Alain Badiou's provocative intervention in ontology and ethics.[8] Badiou makes a radical break with both postmodern philosophy and analytic philosophy. This break is marked by his salvaging and transforming of the concept of truth. *In Logics of Worlds*, Badiou (2009) tosses this ontological brick for a foundation: *"There are only bodies and languages, except that there are truths"* (p. 4). Thus, "Philosophy, in its very essence, elaborates the means of saying 'Yes!' to the previously unknown thoughts that hesitate to become the truths they are" (p. 3). But Badiou's (2007) saving of truth depends on a transformation, "A truth is solely constituted by rupturing with the order which supports it, never as an effect of that order. I have named this type of rupture which opens up truths 'the event'" (p. xii).[9] This engagement with environmentalism will hinge on events, truths, and the subjects that live them.

SOCIAL JUSTICE PARADING AS ENVIRONMENTAL JUSTICE: THE HOSTILE TAKEOVER OF ENVIRONMENTALISM

The EJM in the United States has achieved extraordinary success. Whether one ties its origin to Lois Gibbs, Love Canal, and the antitoxics movement or to Benjamin Chavis, Warren County, and the environmental racism movement, the EJM has made the disproportionate impact of environmental degradation on minorities and lower classes a national issue that has raised public awareness, changed corporate practices, helped pass right-to-know laws, and transformed government policies.[10] Some of the more obvious successes include the stopping of numerous hazardous waste sites, the establishment of the Superfund law, and the signing of Executive Order 12898 Federal Actions to Address Environmental Justice in Minority Populations and Low-Income Populations in 1994. That order mandated that "Each Federal agency shall make achieving environmental justice part of its mission by identifying and addressing, as appropriate, disproportionately high and adverse human health or environmental effects of its programs, policies, and activities on minority populations and low-income populations."[11] The federal government established the National Environmental Justice Advisory Council (NEJAC) and the Interagency Working Group on Environmental Justice (IWG) to help implement EJ goals.

Clearly, the EJM has benefited thousands, even millions, of people. It has changed government policies and laws and it has helped specific communities protect their homeplaces from the depredations of corporate polluters. Lois Gibbs (2006) of Love Canal fame claims that in the past 20 years every new commercial landfill proposal save one has been defeated and that over a thousand landfills have closed. For its many successes, for its dedication, for its effective redress of race and class discrimination, the EJM is to be celebrated.

As it has gained national stature, the EJM has also challenged and transformed the mainstream environmental movement, especially over the issue of their focus on wild(er)ness. This challenge has been both implicit and explicit. EJ activists have redefined "environment" to focus on humans. As Gibbs (1993) wrote, "The Environmental Justice Movement is about people and the places they live, work and play [in]" (p. 2).[12] To a surprising extent, EJ activists have succeeded in shifting the meaning of environmentalism from a wild(er)ness focus to a human and human habitat focus, with one of the unfortunate side effects being the demonizing of environmentalists as racists for focusing on wild(er)ness instead of people and their problems. Academic and EJ advocate Dorceta Taylor's complaint in 1990 is typical: "When forests are threatened, large numbers of people are mobilized to prevent damage. But we have yet to see an environmental group champion human homelessness or joblessness as issues on which they will spend vast resources" (as quoted in Dowie, 1996, p. 126). The irony is that the EJM evinces little if any concern for actual environmental issues. Jose Drummond, professor of sustainable development in Brazil and board member of the fledgling journal *Environmental Justice* rues this fact,

> I have not found a single case designated as being of environmental injustice that is not first and utmost a case of social injustice, political injustice, cultural clash, legal loopholes, or even economic inequality.... From where I stand, adding "environmental" to the designation of thoroughly social issues or to the field as a whole usually amounts to a trivialization of the natural variables possibly involved.... The adjectives "just" or "unjust" simply do not apply to natural variables. (Drummond, 2008, p. 180)

THE EVENT OF WILD(ER)NESS

What are the ethical grounds of an EJM that cares only about people, that takes no heed of other beings, of ecosystems, of anything that is not reduced to serving human interests? Badiou suggest that it is the common ethics of our time, an ethics based on a misunderstanding of the ontological status of difference that results in a veneration of the Other and a commitment to identity politics and multiple rights. In this sense, there is a confluence of a certain type of humanism, a certain orientation toward rights, and a preoccupation with the identities of certain groups. Significantly, the venerated Other must be of a certain type and the rights tend to be negative— rights from certain evils: torture, pollution, discrimination, and so on. Badiou (2001) attempts to rescue philosophy from the incoherence of identity politics and the relativism of postmodernism through an ethics grounded in the assertion that "Man *thinks*, that Man is a tissue of truths" (p.12). Badiou characterizes the current mainstream scene of ethics, philosophy, and politics as one that is consumed with the valorization of differences and human rights. For Badiou, there are several problems with difference and human rights as the ground of practical ethics and related policy. First, ontologically, "Infinite alterity is quite simply what there is…. There are as many differences, say, between a Chinese peasant and a young Norwegian professional as between myself and anybody at all, including myself"(pp. 25–26). On a pragmatic level, respect for differences is limited to "a tourist's fascination for the diversity of morals, customs and beliefs" that make up the world as it is (p. 26). When the differences are serious, the West resorts to its chronic imperialism. Female circumcision in Africa, the Taliban's treatment of women, bride burning in India, honor killings in Pakistan (karo-kari), Chinese totalitarianism, and so on are all condemned as differences that do not deserve respect.[13] Even something as simple as Muslim dress in schools in France is not to be tolerated. As Badiou concludes, the valorization of differences is "the final imperative of a conquering civilization: 'Become like me and I will respect your difference'" (pp. 24–25). Badiou is not making an ethical judgment on practices such as female circumcision, but, rather, is describing the insufficiency of an ethics premised on respect for differences.

Badiou critiques the regime of human rights as a *negative* ethics that reduces humans to only their animal/biological state, occludes the politics of rights in favor of a simple moralism, crushes possibilities by reproducing the status quo, and reduces the Good to merely freedom from Evil. For Badiou (2001), the discourse of human rights posits humans as beings who suffer: "man is the *being who is capable of recognizing himself as a victim*" (p. 10). Human rights are not positive but only derive from evil. They are the rights not be offended, mistreated, oppressed, tortured, and murdered. Badiou considers these as biological rights that attend to humans only as animals, animal-victims. For Badiou, the horror of the negative ethics of human rights is that it reproduces the world as it is:

> Since the barbarity of the situation is considered only in terms of "human rights"—whereas in fact we are always dealing with a political situation, one that calls for a political thought-practice, one that is peopled by its own authentic actors—it is perceived, from the heights of our apparent civil peace, as the uncivilized that demands of the civilized a civilizing intervention. Every intervention in the name of a civilization *requires* an initial contempt of the situation as a whole, including the victims. And this is why the reign of "ethics" coincides, after decades of courageous critiques of colonialism and imperialism, with today's sordid self-satisfaction in the "West", with the insistent argument according to which the misery of the Third World is the result of its own incompetence, its own inanity—in short, of its *subhumanity*. (p. 13)

Many historical examples support Badiou's acidic observation about the West's imposition of human rights around the globe, but the current "War on Terror" suffices, especially its version in Iraq. Among the multiple justifications for the preemptive, nonprovoked, illegal invasion of Iraq was that "we" must depose the dictator Saddam Hussein and teach the Iraqis to respect human rights, freedom, and democracy. The slaughter of the literally uncounted hundreds of thousands of Iraqis in the process was just an incidental cost (The Johns Hopkins University and *Lancet* study estimated between 400,000 to 900,000 casualties by 2006). The obscenity of the lesson was unintentionally illustrated by Thomas Friedman, a neoliberal columnist for *The New York Times* and a chronic cheerleader for the neoliberal imperialist project. On *The Charlie Rose Show* (May 30, 2003), Friedman celebrated the war:

Rose: Now that the war is over, and there's some difficulty with the peace, was it worth do-
           ing?
Friedman: I think it was unquestionably worth doing, Charlie. I think that, looking back, I now
           certainly feel I understand more what the war was about.... What we needed to do was
           go over to that part of the world, I'm afraid, and burst that bubble. We needed to go
           over there basically, and take out a very big stick, right in the heart of that world, and
           burst that bubble.... And what they needed to see was American boys and girls going
           from house to house, from Basra to Baghdad, and basically saying: which part of this
           sentence do you understand? You don't think we care about our open society?... Well,
           Suck. On. This. That, Charlie, was what this war was about. We could have hit Saudi
           Arabia. It was part of that bubble. Could have hit Pakistan. We hit Iraq because we
           could. That's the real truth.

Respect for differences as long as we are all the same suggests the inability to accept the ontological condition of infinite differences. This refusal results in violence on multiple levels. The conversation in environmental communication suggests a much less dramatic yet similar ethics dynamic, wherein scholars explicitly or implicitly posit an ethics of difference and human rights but within a mandatory frame of Western humanism that requires in the end that we all become one through communication practices. Two assumptions are crucial here: the reflexive adoption of Habermas's public sphere and the adherence to a mythic democracy. Both require *a priori* the bracketing of differences (race, class, ethnicity, languages, knowledges, and so on) in the interests of oneness and compromise in an ethics of proceduralism, a hazy ethics enacted through communication processes. As environmental communication scholar Stephen Depoe (2004) rightly notes, "A growing number of scholars are examining the structures and processes of public involvement in the formation of environmental risk policy and the resolution of environmental management disputes" (p. 157). An ethics of proceduralism necessarily obscures questions of why in favor of questions of how.

The "how" focuses on public participation, deliberation, and transparency. Citizens are reduced to stakeholders in a complicated machinery of mechanisms, including public hearings, citizen panels, community advisory boards, citizen task forces, citizen review panels, workshops, collaborative learning, civic discovery, conflict assessment, two-way communication, face-to-face dialogue, and decision spaces. The edited volume of leading environmental communication scholars, *Communication and Public Participation in Environmental Decision Making* (Depoe, Delicath, & Elsenbeer, 2004), exemplifies this focus.[14] The three parts of the book are "Theorizing and Constructing More Effective Public Participation Processes," "Evaluating Mechanisms for Public Participation in Environmental Decision Making," and "Emergent Participation Practices Among Activist Communities." I do not want to suggest that these scholars are engaging in a simple celebration of public participation. Indeed, they often are critical, as these essay titles suggest: "The Roadless Areas Initiative as National Policy: Is Public Participation an Oxymoron"

(Walker, 2004), "Public Participation and (Failed) Legitimation" (Schwarze, 2004), "Public Participation or Stakeholder Frustration" (Toker, 2004). The point is that the focus is on the process itself, with the assumption that a perfected process of public participation would solve environmental crises. New and improved mechanisms of communication and consensus become the goals of ethics.

Somehow the procedural ethics of transparency, deliberation, and participation are deemed able to erase real differences not amenable to compromise. Yet the drive to compromise is dangerously damaging to the very environmental issues that the ethics are purportedly in service of. As NASA scientist James Hansen (2009) notes about climate chaos, "This is analogous to the issue of slavery faced by Abraham Lincoln or the issue of Nazism faced by Winston Churchill. On those kind of issues you cannot compromise. You cannot say let's reduce slavery, let's find a compromise and reduce it 50% or reduce it 40%" (as quoted in Goldenberg, 2009). The examples multiply. The differences are irreconcilable between the animal rights vegetarian and McDonald's, the wilderness activist and Exxon, Captain Paul Watson and the Japanese whaling fleet, an EarthFirst!er occupying an ancient Redwood and the logging corporation wanting to turn it into decks and hot tubs. Forest activist and writer Derrick Jensen (Jensen & Draffan, 2003) describes the process:

> Public participation programs are replacements for genuine democracy. Public relations firms, government agencies, and consensus groups have developed sophisticated techniques for confusing, exhausting, and co-opting the concerned public. The fundamental understanding that guides this participation—and those in power are exquisitely aware of this understanding—is the impossibility of true negotiation between parties of grossly unequal power.... We are "allowed" to "speak truth to power" all we want, but everyone knows that those in power will ignore these truths and go ahead and do whatever the hell they want. (pp. 96–97)

Developing Jensen critique, political science professor Douglas Amy (1987) argues that public participation "is not simply about communication. It's also about power struggles. It is not only about common interests, but also about conflicting interests. And it's not only about horse trading but competition between conflicting values and different moral visions" (p. 228). To impose the ethical conventions of communication in the interests of compromise is to commit violence to truths.

Against the ethics of human rights that posits humans as animal-victims, Badiou insists on the positive conceptualization of each and every human as potentially immortal as a being that thinks. In practical terms, this means that humans transcend their human-animalness and become a human subject when thinking the event that ruptures the situation as it is. It is this thinking from the perspective of the event that produces truths and new worlds. As Badiou (2001) explains, in the situation as it is "every animal gets by as best it can.... Let us say that a subject, which goes beyond the animal (although the animal remains its sole foundation) needs something to have happened, something that cannot be reduced to its ordinary inscription in 'what there is.' Let us call this supplement an event...which compels us to decide a new way of being" (pp. 40–41). Crucially, an event "is committed to chance. It is unpredictable, incalculable. It is beyond what is" (Badiou, 2005, p. 46). Badiou discusses events and their unfolding in four areas—politics, science, love, and art. Examples include the French Revolution, Galileo's work, Einstein's theory of relativity, Cantor's set theory, two people falling in love, Schoenberg's music, Osip Mandelstam's poetry, and Beckett's plays. May '68 was clearly such an event for French intellectuals like Badiou, Baudrillard, Foucault, and Deleuze that forced them to see the world and become who they became through the event of May '68. Arguably, Cubism was such an event that forced the artists of the 20th century to see through the lens of Cubism. Although the consequences of an event unfold over time, an event itself is only a moment, a flash that interrupts the world as it is, a gliff.[15]

For Badiou (2001), truths emerge in the decision to be faithful to the event: "To be faithful to an event is to move within the situation that this event has supplemented, by *thinking* the situation 'according to' the event. And this, of course—since the event was excluded by all the regular laws of the situation—compels the subject to *invent* a new way of being and acting in the situation" (pp. 41–42). It is also through the decision to be faithful to an event that a human-animal becomes a subject.[16] Truths then mark immanent breaks with the situation as it is, for "what enables the truth-process—the event—meant nothing according to the prevailing language and established knowledge of the situation" (p. 43). As I will later elaborate, the invention of new ways of being and acting is intimately connected to performing public acts of communication. Truths are created through the articulation of events.

Environmentalism marks such a break with the established knowledge of the situation, of humanism. *Environmentalism* is the generic term that names the truths of numerous events that subjects have been faithful to. Most pointedly, environmentalism is the truth of the events of encounters of subjects with nonhuman worlds, with wild(er)ness. These events consistently exceeded self-interests and merely human worlds. There are numerous famous examples that illustrate the process that Badiou is conceptualizing. The examples of John Muir, Ansel Adams, Julia Butterfly Hill, and Aldo Leopold will suffice to illustrate this point and suggest the fruitfulness of thinking environmentalism through Badiou's ethical framework.

In 1867, following an industrial accident in Wisconsin, John Muir sets out on a voyage that lands him in San Francisco, from which he walks to the Sierra Nevadas, to Yosemite. His first sight of the Sierra Nevadas is an event, a moment of rapture that disrupts the world as it is and transforms Muir into a subject of the truths of the Sierra Nevadas. His lifelong commitment to the event of meeting the Sierra Nevadas produces a new world, a world with Yosemite National Park and the Sierra Club and a vision (truth) of sublime wilderness that has worth beyond the economic calculations of the industrial juggernaut. Muir (1914/1988) writes of his first encounter with the Sierra Mountains:

> Looking eastward from the summit of the Pacheco Pass one shining morning, a landscape was displayed that after all my wanderings still appears as the most beautiful I have ever beheld. At my feet lay the Grand Central Valley of California, level and flowery, like a lake of pure sunshine, forty or fifty miles wide, five hundred miles long, one rich furred garden of yellow compositae. And from the eastern boundary of this vast golden flowerbed rose the mighty Sierra, miles in height, and so gloriously colored and so radiant, it seemed not clothed with light, but wholly composed of it, like the wall of some celestial city. Along the top and extending a good way down, was a rich pearl-gray belt of snow, below it a belt of blue and dark purple, marking the extension of the forests; and stretching along the base of the range a broad belt of rose-purple; all these colors, from the blue sky to the yellow valley smoothly blending as they do in a rainbow, making a wall of light ineffably fine. Then it seemed to me that the Sierra should be called, not the Nevada or Snowy Range, but the Range of Light. And after ten years of wandering and wondering in the heart of it, rejoicing in its glorious floods of light, the white beams of the morning streaming through the passes, the noonday radiance on the crystal rocks, the flush of the alpenglow, and the irised spray of countless waterfalls, it still seems above all others the Range of Light. (pp. 2–3)

The event of Muir's encounter with the Sierras and his decision to be faithful to that event, to think the world through his encounter with the Sierras, transforms Muir from a machinist to the prophet of Yosemite, the founder of the Sierra Club, the writer of the sublime, and the inventor of environmentalism (then called preservationism).

Famed photographer and environmental activist Ansel Adams experienced a similar event in his encounter with Yosemite. Adams (1985) writes of his first trip to Yosemite National Park in 1916 at the age of 14:

> We finally emerged at Valley View—the splendor of Yosemite upon us and it *was* glorious…. One wonder after another descended upon us; I recall not only the colossal but the little things: the grasses and ferns…. Sentinel Fall and Yosemite Falls were booming in early summer flood, and many small shining cascades threaded the cliffs. There was light everywhere!…How different my life would have been if it were not for these early hikes in the Sierra—if I had not experienced that memorable first trip to Yosemite…. Everything I have done or felt has been in some way influenced by the impact of the Natural Scene…. I knew my destiny when I first experienced Yosemite. (pp, 52–53, 67)

At the time of the event of his encounter with Yosemite, Adams was a sickly, home-schooled, aspiring pianist. When Yosemite punched a hole in the world as it is and inspired Adams to think (and see) from the perspective of the Yosemite mountains, Adams became an immortal subject, a giant of both 20th century photography and environmentalism, the photographer of the sublime. His book, *Sierra Nevadas: The John Muir Trail* (1938) helped establish Kings Canyon National Park. His 1960 book with Nancy Newhall, *This Is the American Earth*, became a national best-seller and a key rhetorical weapon in the passage of the Wilderness Act. In addition, the book's financial and political success as the Sierra Club's first coffee-table book prompted Sierra Club President David Brower to turn the Club into a more overt political direction and led to a series of coffee-table books and the campaign to prevent the damming of the Grand Canyon.

A more contemporary case involves the transformation of Arkansas waitress Julia Hill into eco-activist and speaker for the trees, Julia "Butterfly" Hill. Hill (2000) describes the event that gave birth to Butterfly—her first encounter with redwoods:

> For the first time, I really felt what it was like to be alive, to feel the connection of all life and its inherent truth…. Gripped by the spirit of the forest, I dropped to my knees and began to sob. I sank my fingers into the layer of duff, which smelled so sweet and so rich and so full of life, then lay my face down and breathed it in. Surrounded by these huge, ancient giants, I felt the film covering my senses from the imbalance of our fast-paced, technologically dependent society melt away. I could feel my whole being burst into new life in this majestic cathedral. I sat and cried for a long time. Finally, the tears turned into joy and the joy turned to mirth, and I sat and laughed at the beauty of it all…. I walked out of the forest a different woman. (pp. 8–9)

Butterfly decided to be faithful to the event of her encounter with the Redwoods and joined an EarthFirst! tree-sit. Sitting in a 1,500-year-old redwood called Luna, Butterfly vowed not to leave the tree until it was saved. During her 2-year struggle, Butterfly galvanized support through a worldwide multimedia campaign from her perch 150 feet up in Luna and eventually succeed in getting Maxxam Lumber to capitulate and preserve Luna and her fellow redwoods in a buffer zone.

Perhaps ecologist Aldo Leopold most clearly articulates these events with wild(er)ness and the truths that may emerge through the subject's fidelity to the event in his landmark tome *A Sand County Almanac*. In a section that constitutes the heart of the book, "Thinking Like a Mountain," Leopold (1949/1989) describes coming upon a family of wolves and reflexively shooting at them:

> In those days we had never heard of passing up a chance to kill a wolf…. We reached the old wolf in time to watch a fierce green fire dying in her eyes. I realized then, and have known ever since,

that there was something new to me in those eyes—something known only to her and to the mountain. I was young then, and full of trigger-itch; I thought that because fewer wolves meant more deer, that no wolves would mean hunters' paradise. But after seeing the green fire die, I sensed that neither the wolf nor the mountain agreed with such a view. (Leopold, 1949/1989, p. 130)

Leopold goes on to describe how the widespread slaughter of wolves in the name of farming, sport, and safety have wreaked ruin on mountains and ecosystems across the country. Of course, Leopold is illustrating the concepts of ecological balance (dynamic equilibrium) and trophic cascades. Leopold concludes the section by musing on the dangers of comfort and safety (a world without predators), for "too much safety seems to yield only danger in the long run. Perhaps this is behind Thoreau's dictum: In wildness is the salvation of the world. Perhaps this is the hidden meaning in the howl of the wolf, long known among mountains, but seldom perceived among men" (p. 133).

The event of watching the wolf die rips the fabric of conventional forester Leopold's world as it is, and his response to the event, his effort to think like a mountain, leads to the new Leopold as ecologist and wilderness advocate. Leopold became the architect of the world's first wilderness area in New Mexico's Gila National Forest and cofounder of The Wilderness Society, a key player in the passage of the 1964 Wilderness Act. Finally, in creating the truths of the event, Leopold (1949/1989) invented a new ethic, the land ethic, that has become a cornerstone of much environmental thought: "A thing is right when it tends to preserve the integrity, stability, and beauty of the biotic community. It is wrong when it tends otherwise" (pp. 224–225). Leopold understands himself to be making two key interventions here. First, while ethics has dealt with relations among individuals, relations between the individual and community, and relations among communities, he is expanding ethics to consider relations between humans and the nonhuman. Second, he is expanding the meaning of community "to include soils, waters, plants, and animals, or collectively: the land" (p. 204). When one is able to interrupt the world as it is and to think like a mountain, the hierarchy of being gets toppled: "In short, a land ethic changes the role of *Homo sapiens* from conqueror of the land-community to plain member and citizen of it. It implies respect for his fellow-members, and also respect for the community as such" (p. 204).

These events, these engagements with nonhuman worlds, with wild(er)ness and the truths that emerged through the decisions and acts of these subjects collectively constitute the heart of environmentalism. The articulation of events into truths requires acts, most importantly communication acts. Muir, Adams, Hill, and Leopold use books, articles, photographs, and spoken testimony to bear witness to these events, to articulate the truths of wild(er)ness. The EJM attack on environmentalists for caring for nonhuman worlds, for wild(er)ness, is an attack on the truth of environmentalism, the truth that makes it matter. For Badiou, such attacks are evil.

ETHICS, EVIL, AND THE ENVIRONMENTAL JUSTICE MOVEMENT

Whether or not the EJM is grounded in events and truths is debatable. If we agree that a toxic event is an event in Badiou's sense, the responses of subjects become crucial. If an example of a response is a mother fighting to save her children, that is a rather conventional occurrence and does not disrupt the situation. It is what is to be expected. If, though the toxic event is engaged by the parent as a rupture of the world as it is, as a questioning of the American Dream, as a breaking of the promise of industrialism, then there is an event and the potential process of the unfolding of truths. Lois Gibbs' response in 1978 to her son being sickened by the Love Canal toxic site beneath his school transforms her subjectivity and creates new truths about industrialism and America. Gibbs significantly moves beyond her family and organizes her community but then even moves beyond that. Instead of stopping at NIMBY (Not in My Backyard), Gibbs moves to advocate NIABY (Not In Anyone's Backyard) and founds the Citizens' Clearinghouse for Hazardous Wastes, an act that takes up her encounter with the toxic event as a rupture of the industrial world as it is. Gibbs wins the evacuation and resettlement of her community, prompts President Carter to act, and spurs the passage of Superfund legislation. Love Canal is often seen as the founding moment of the modern EJ movement. But more often it is not.

More often it is the activities at Warren County, NC that are granted founding status as the "symbolic birthplace of the environmental justice movement" (Cox, 2006, p. 294). In her history of the EJM, McGurty (1997) writes, "The events in Warren County are proclaimed by activists and policymakers alike as the birth of the environmental justice movement" (p. 302). In the narrative, African American citizens protest the targeting of their community for toxic wastes. Their actions, though unsuccessful on a local level, spur on a movement concerned with environmental racism—the unequal targeting of minority communities for the siting of toxic industries. As activist Reverend Benjamin Chavis (1993) later defined it,

> Environmental racism is racial discrimination in environmental policymaking. It is racial discrimination in the enforcement of regulations and laws. It is racial discrimination in the deliberate targeting of communities of color for toxic waste disposal and the siting of polluting industries. It is racial discrimination in the official sanctioning of the life-threatening presence of poisons and pollutants in communities of color. And, it is racial discrimination in the history of excluding people of color from the mainstream environmental groups, decisionmaking boards, commissions, and regulatory bodies. (p. 3)

It is revealing that there is no equivalent term *environmental classism*. As already discussed, the EJM ends up having many notable successes. Bullard reframes the movement from environmental racism to environmental justice, but the EJ movement remains focused on race. This can be seen in how racism inflects the more general term of environmental in/justice. Luke Cole and Sheila Foster, in their respected history *From the Ground Up: Environmental Racism and the Rise of the Environmental Justice Movement* (2000), exemplify this dynamic. First, it is obvious in the title. Second, though they do mention class, their focus in case studies and analyses remains on race and is revealed in their use of terms: "We use the terms 'environmental racism' and 'environmental injustice' interchangeably in the book" (p. 15). This privileging of race over class can be seen in origin stories. Consistently, Warren County is posited as the founding act/place of the EJ movement, with Love Canal either ignored or given a secondary status. The Second National People of Color Environmental Leadership Summit's "Environmental Justice Timeline" omits Love Canal altogether. The book title *Transforming Environmentalism: Warren County, PCBs, and the Origins of Environmental Justice* epitomizes this procedure.[17]

There are other histories. Some do give Lois Gibbs and the Love Canal struggle founding status. Others turn to Rachel Carson and the publication of *Silent Spring* in 1962. Still others cite Martin Luther King's support of the Memphis sanitation workers' strike in 1968. In a useful history, Robert Gottlieb (1993) credits Alice Hamilton's work at Hull House in Chicago on the health effects of industrialism starting in the 1890s. All origin stories are always mythic and the choice of origin story reveals less about history and more about the ideological investments and political possibilities of a movement. To start from *Silent Spring* is to suggest a broad concern for all humans and other living beings and ecosystems. The institutional consequences of her book suggest the breadth of purpose. To start with King is to embed the EJM in the civil rights movement. To start with Love Canal is to focus on class in a capitalist society. As Gibbs (2006) herself comments, "Love Canal sparked a new social justice movement nationwide around concerns about environmentally linked health problems and the right of corporations to increase their profits through calculated decisions to sacrifice innocent families" (p. 3). To start with Warren County is to focus on race. It is to see the world through the prism of race. Such a perspective simultaneously reveals and blinds. This race focus is also evident in the "founding document" of the EJ movement, the "Principles of Environmental Justice" issued at the First National People of Color Environmental Leadership Summit in 1991. Obviously, the name of the conference itself suggests the focus on race. These "Principles" are always cited in accounts of the EJM (they are often reprinted in academic books) and are usually described as something akin to the Declaration of Independence. Indeed, the opening words suggest a certain mimicry while notably restricting "We, the people": "We, the people of color, gathered together at the multinational People of Color Environmental Leadership Summit, to begin to build a national and international movement of all peoples of color...." The companion founding document, *Toxic Wastes and Race in the United States* (1987), was directed by Chavis, leader of the United Church of Christ's Commission for Racial Justice, and was designed to prove that race is really the deciding factor in the siting of toxic enterprises. Such proof has been controversial and attempts to confirm or refute such claims have become such a cottage industry among academics that in a recent book one researcher suggests (or hopes) that "academics and activists alike have become concerned that it is time to get beyond the 'race versus class trap' in order to devise practical, yet fair, environmental policies" (Fletcher, 2003, p. 18).

In short, after 3 decades of aggressive promulgation the notion of the EJM as predominantly a race-based movement has carried the day. Putting aside the factual accuracy of such a story, there are significant ethical and political problems in taking a narrow perspective and universalizing it. As it now stands in its raced-base incarnation, the EJM embodies the ethics that Badiou disdains—humans as victims and the valorization of difference-centered ethics. As already discussed, Badiou is not interested in a negative ethics, from which the good is derived from the absence of evil. Instead, he posits a positive good, the creation of truths, from which sometimes evil may emerge. For Badiou, violence in itself is not evil. The violence that the human animal deploys in pursuit of survival and interests is beneath Good and Evil. Instead, "it is only because there are truths, and only to the extent that there are subjects of these truths, that there is evil" (2001, p. 61). Badiou discusses three types of evil, only two of which we will consider here.

Disaster

Under the term *disaster* Badiou describes the attempt to totalize the power of truths. The "language of the situation" is the pragmatic communication that enables the world as it is to go on for human animals. Then there is also the "subject-language" which enables the inscription of truths upon the elements of a situation, the seeing anew of the situation from the perspective of the event. Truths can rename the elements of the situation, such as when the EJM renames the conventional business-as-usual placing of toxic waste sites as social injustices. The subject-language of truths cannot, however, rename the entirety of the world as it is for the event depends on the existence of the situation, the Immortal subject depends on the human animal for its existence, and truths depend on pragmatic opinions, so that "every attempt to impose the total power of a truth ruins the truth's very foundation" (Badiou, 2001, p. 84). As Badiou (2001) concludes, "The world is, will remain, beneath Good and Evil. The Good is Good only to the extent that it does not aspire to render the world good. Its sole being lies in the situated advent of a singular truth" (p. 85). One expansive definition of EJ claims, "Environmental justice is served when people can realize their highest potential, without experiencing the 'isms.' Environmental justice is supported by decent paying and safe jobs; quality schools and recreation; decent housing and adequate health care; democratic decision-making and personal empowerment; and communities free of violence, drugs, and poverty" (Bryant, as quoted in Schlosberg, 2007, pp. 50–51). Clearly, this claim expands the term *environmental justice* to encompass all the ills in society—discrimination, unhappiness, poverty, bad jobs, poor schools, lack of exercise, illness, violence, drug addiction, and so on. Such a move totalizes one truth, thus obscuring the ability to understand the singularity of each situation and slighting other truths. From Badiou's ethics, it is wrong for the race-based EJM to use the social injustice of racism to name all the injustices of the situation of corporate industrialism. As EJ scholars Brulle and Pellow (2005) conclude, "The distribution of environmental harm does involve, and has always involved, both race and class. The social production of environmental inequality cannot be understood through a singularly focused framework that emphasizes one form of inequality to the exclusion of others" (p. 115).

There are additional problems on a pragmatic level. The race-based EJM has wasted time and resources insisting on racism as the primary cause, what Chavis called "the deliberate targeting of communities of color" (1993, p. 3). It has gotten tangled up in failed legal challenges and endless statistical disputes. It has slighted the truths of White working-class and poor people who have also experienced the social injustices of industrialism. For example, mountaintop removal coal mining in Appalachia is invisible from a race-based EJ frame. It has slurred wilderness-based environmentalists as racists. Most importantly, its attempt to totalize the truth of racial social injustices has clouded understanding and responses to the social injustices of industrialism. Quite simply, the environmental racism frame does not have enough explanatory power for understanding social injustices in a transnational corporate industrial world. First, does anyone really think a company like WalMart or GE makes decisions based on racism? Does the GE board get together and say we hate Black people so let's put a toxic waste site in an African American neighborhood? Of course not. For historical reasons is race a factor in an ancillary way in the United States? Yes, but one cannot understand how decisions are made in a capitalist corporate industrial world through the frame of racism.[18] Second, on an international scale the race frame is even more problematic. Around the globe, race is usually not the deciding cause of bias. When Hutus slaughtered Tutsis in the Rwandan genocide, it was not on the basis of race. The Cambodian killing fields are not explained through race. More significantly, not only can the frame of racism not explain most causes of bias and discrimination internationally, it cannot explain global corporate decision making and the resultant injustices. Right now, are multinational corporations shipping e-waste to China because of racial hatred of Asians? Finally, offering racism (or ethnic hatreds) as an universal, transcendent explanation erases the politics and particularity of situations. For example, with respect to the Rwandan genocide, it is crucial to explain it "not as the incomprehensible symptom of ancient and intractable ethnic conflict, but as deliberate state power, a program ruthlessly planned and implemented by Hutu Power" (Hallward, 2003, p. 404).

The example of *climate chaos* (although commonly referred to as global warming or climate change, my term more accurately reflects the science) powerfully illustrates the paucity of a racial EJ frame and the impossibility of identity politics. As just noted, racism does not translate neatly across borders. More significantly, identities shift dramatically when responding to the crisis of climate chaos. Climate chaos is not framed as a Black/White issue but as North/South, developed/developing,[19] rich/poor, or via national identities. In all of these shifting identities, African Americans assume the privileged pole as part of the North or developed world or rich or the United States. The majority of African Americans, and, indeed, the majority of poor Americans, are relatively rich by world standards and have large carbon footprints. According to the World Bank, in 2005 the United States per capita CO_2 emissions was 19.5 metric tons. China was at slightly under 5 metric tons while India was at 2 metric tons. The average in poor countries is *.1* metric tons (New Community Project, n.d.). With respect to the damaging practice of beef production, per capita beef consumption in the United States in 2006 was 43.8 kilograms. In China it was 5.7 kilograms (Livestock and Poultry, 2006). The devastating details of deforestation reveal U.S. citizens as profligate consumers of paper products at 760 pounds per year. The world average is 125 pounds and in the poorest countries the average is less than a pound per year (New Community Project, n.d.). Such vast disparities continue across multiple measures, including energy consumption, water consumption, grain consumption, and waste production. In the calculus of standards of living, the lifestyles of African Americans as well as other Americans is based on the exploitation of the majority of the rest of the world.[20] From the perspective of, say, China, U.S. citizens avoid their responsibilities for climate chaos and refuse to make sacrifices to stop oppressing other people. Even worse, they then blame other countries. Ailun Yang, campaign manager for climate and energy with Greenpeace China, illustrates a common Chinese perspective on global warming and Americans:

> I'll explain the carbon footprint from two perspectives. First, it's true that with China's development, the emission in China is growing very fast. There are studies saying that China maybe has already [over]taken [the] USA to become the world's #1 emitter. However, if we look at the per capita basis, an average American would emit six times more than an average Chinese. What this tells us is that there is still a very big difference in the level and standard of living…. Second, a lot of emissions that are created in China are for the production of products exported to developed countries. Actually, the fact that a lot of developed countries could de-carbonize their own country is because the production, especially those energy-intensive industries, has moved to countries like China. (personal interview, March, 2008)

Betrayal: Abandoning Wild(er)ness

The EJM labeling of mainstream environmentalists as racists has provoked another evil, but this evil is the responsibility of the mainstream environmentalists cowed by such slurs into denying wild(er)ness as the truth of their movement. For Badiou, such betrayal is another form of evil. Ethics requires perseverance to the event and to the truth-process. Badiou (2001) argues that the sole maxim of ethics is: "'Keep going!' Keep going even when you have lost the thread, when you no longer feel 'caught up' in the process, when the event itself has become obscure" (p. 79). A crisis in the face of the regime of opinions can cause a subject to doubt his or her fidelity to the event, leading to giving up and denying the event and one's self as a subject unfolding the truths of the event. The Sierra Club, Muir's legacy, America's preeminent environmental organization both historically and politically, is a prime example of this betrayal.[21] At a Sierra Club centennial celebration, then Executive Director Michael Fischer stated that "The struggle for environmental justice in this country and around the globe must be the primary goal of the Sierra Club during its second century."[22] This marked turn toward social justice was institutionalized by the Board of Directors in 1993: "The Board of Directors of the Sierra Club recognizes that to achieve our mission of environmental protection and a sustainable future for the planet, we must attain social justice and human rights at home and around the globe." This utopian humanitarian mission was elaborated upon with a 2001 declaration of "Environmental Justice Principles."[23]

The Sierra Club is not alone. Three of the world's largest environmental organizations, the World Wildlife Fund, the Nature Conservancy, and Conservation International, have embraced the betrayal of wild(er)ness and the turn to social justice issues. It is a very explicit giving up on wild(er)ness and turn to EJ and an anthropocentric orientation. Conservation International (CI) was founded in 1987 to conserve biodiversity hot spots and has saved over 500 million acres, yet has abandoned this commitment for a new mission: "CI empowers societies to responsibly and sustainably care for nature for the well-being of humanity." As CI cofounder and CEO Peter

Seligmann explains the move away from wild(er)ness, "You look at the issues of climate change, consumption, and the state of the world's oceans and you realize that, although we've succeeded in putting a lot of land and waters into what I like to refer to as 'the conservation pantry,' we haven't changed the hunger of development, nor have we reduced the capacity of development to reach into that pantry whenever they want something and pull it out" (Hightower, 2009). At this moment of crisis, CI has given up its commitment to seeing the world as it is from the perspective of wild(er)ness. The Nature Conservancy (TNC) scientist Peter Kareiva echoes and extends this surrender: "Instead of collecting data to see how the birds and trees are doing, we do household surveys to see, if we set up a marine protected area, whether the people in those communities feel better off…. For me at least the rights of people for self-determination take supremacy over any species" (Hightower, 2009). The extent to which Karieva and the TNC has turned away from wild(er)ness and embraced anthropocentrism is evident in Karieva's response to a classic dilemma:

> You're down to one snow leopard, and that leopard is a pregnant mom. And if she lives and has a litter of four or five, you could maybe recover the whole species. And you're up on a ridge and she's creeping up and about to kill and eat a small two-year-old child. You have a gun, and you have a choice: You can either kill the leopard and save the child's life, or you can sit by and watch the leopard kill it. That's your only choice. I would save the child. (Hightower, 2009)

Kareiva's position is conventionally accepted as the moral one, but if even environmentalists value the life of any single human being over entire species and ecosystems, the mounting ecological devastation is guaranteed to proceed apace. Plus, it is a simplistic moralism that ignores how human lives are actually valued. For example, we value cars over human lives, knowing full well that banning all cars around the world would save millions of lives. Or, we value speed over human lives, for if cars were mechanically limited to not exceed 20 miles per hour, nearly all fatalities would be avoided. The examples multiply. What sort of moralism enables the sanctity of human life to always trump any care for the nonhuman, but such sanctity can be routinely trumped by competing, often trivial, human interests? The West's obsession with iPods, flat-screen TVs, diamonds, Gucci handbags, and other markers of an excessive standard of living guarantees the death of millions around the world, including many small two-year-old children. The West systematically guarantees such misery while prattling on about human rights and respect for differences. The ethics of humanitarianism is a thin veil for the law of profit. As Badiou (2001–2002) archly puts it, "First, liberal capitalism is not at all the Good of humanity. Quite the contrary, it is the vehicle of savage, destructive nihilism…. How long can we accept the fact that what is needed for running water, schools, hospitals, and food enough for all humanity is a sum that corresponds to the amount spent by wealthy Western countries on perfume in a year?" (pp. 4, 8).

The Wildlife Conservation Society (WCS) stubbornly resists the virus of humanism that infects other mainstream environmental organizations, and instead remains faithful to the event of wild(er)ness. In response to TNC's shift to a focus on human needs, WCS Director Kent Redford responds, "We're not doing that, and we're not going to do that. We are a proud and unabashedly a nature-conservation organization focusing on wildlife and wild places" (Hightower, 2009). Redford's rationale is revealing. First, wildlife tend not to live where people are, so a focus on people requires working where wildlife is absent. Second, different organizations have different missions. If the mission is social justice, then focus on people and their issues. If the issue is wild(er)ness, then focus on biodiversity and wild places. This second point requires elaboration. Ecological theorist Andrew Dobson (2003) argues "I have come to the reluctant conclusion that social justice and environmental sustainability are not always compatible objectives…the differences between them are not merely tactical but strategic: their objectives differ in fundamental ways" (p. 83). In fact, Dobson makes the strong claim that there is no evidence of such a relation: "The US environmental justice movement is, therefore, simultaneously a site for extravagant claims regarding the compatability of the justice and environmental agendas and a black hole as far as empirical studies designed to substantiate those claims are concerned" (p. 86). Even staunch advocates of the EJM, Mohai, Pellow, and Roberts (2009), admit that there is no evidence that the EJM does anything for traditional environmental and ecological issues:

> On the basis of environmental justice/social green ideology that environmental problems were at their root based on human oppression of other humans, for years people have acted on the assumption that achieving social justice would move us down the road to environmental sustainability. This is certainly not turning out to be an automatic relationship, and the two can sometimes be quite different endeavors. (p. 19)

In practice, this is quite evident. As McGurty (2007) celebrates, "The Sierra Club, with a legacy of exclusionary membership policies [no evidence provided] and emphasis on wilderness preservation, works to remove lead paint from houses in Detroit, to test air quality in Memphis…" (p. 5). Reverse the question and expectation: when has Chavis or Bullard or any African American EJ group done anything for other species? They do not because they are interested in social justice issues, not wild(er)ness issues. The Second National People of Color Environmental Leadership Summit lists six categories of "Major Findings," with wild(er)ness not included. Even the category "Natural Resources and Ecology" makes no mention of wild(er)ness, focusing instead on human-based issues like the "Asthma Epidemic" from a race-based perspective. Even the subheading of "Energy and Native Americans" is about social justice issues: "Nationwide, Indian lands are grossly underserved by electricity services" (www.ejrc.cau.edu/SummitPolicyExSumm.html). Bullard's Environmental Justice Resource Center (EJRC) focuses on "environmental and economic justice, environmental racism, land use and industrial facility permitting, brownfields redevelopment, community health, transportation equity, suburban sprawl, and smart growth."[24] Wild(er)ness is noticeably invisible. On the EJRC web site they list 316 organizations, only two of which mentions wild(er)ness as part of their mission and one of those is the Sierra Club. Eight groups mention missions that can be understood as involving traditional environmental goals. Four other groups mention biodiversity (www.erjc.cau.edu).[25] The key policy proposals from *Toxic Wastes and Race at Twenty 1987–2007* do not mention biobiversity or any wild(er)ness issues (Mohai et al., 2009). *This is as it should be.* EJM advocates are focused on social justice issues and to demand that they focus on saving grizzlies or protecting the Arctic National Wildlife Refuge would be evil. But the reverse also holds true.

It is important for environmental organizations to keep thinking and acting from the orientation of the event of wild(er)ness, speaking primarily for beings that have no human voice. The Sierra Club Board of Directors is wrong to claim that "to achieve our mission of environmental protection and a sustainable future for the planet, we must attain social justice and human rights at home and around the globe." Democracy is not an *a priori* condition for environmental integrity.[26] Social justice and human rights around the globe are not *a priori* conditions for environmental protection. Indeed, we must recognize the tension that exists in many cases between the advocacy of certain human rights and the protection of a wide array of species. There are human costs involved in preserving biodiversity just as their costs to other species when humans are allowed to develop in sensitive ecological zones. The fact is that environmental protection often increases human sacrifice and suffering. When people are prevented from poaching elephants, human suffering is increased. Some environmental protection requires the shutting down of destructive industries and the loss of jobs. As environmental groups adopt the human-centered perspective of EJ groups, they cannot make the hard decisions that increase human suffering, that require putting other beings and ecosystems, not humans, first. Putting humans first is a crucial cause of the environmental crisis we now face. Environmentalists must be faithful to the truths of wild(er)ness even in the face of the charges of EJ advocates that "in the view of many people of color, environmentalism is associated with the preservation of wildlife and wilderness, which simply is not more important than the survival of people and the communities in which they live; thus the mainstream movement has its priorities skewed" (Austin & Schill, 1991, pp. 69–70). Far from being skewed, such priorities recognize the vital foundations of all life on earth. Life on the planet does not depend on human survival or social justice. The reverse is true. Human survival does depend on nonhuman life, ecosystems, wild(er)ness. Inevitably, wild(er)ness is the ground of possibility for human survival.

The slurs of racism that many EJ groups toss at mainstream environmental groups are particularly pernicious in that this is not an either-or situation. There are already myriad organizations tending to the endless needs of humans. Indeed, the number of organizations caring for humans and the amount of money spent in such causes dwarfs the wild(er)ness focused environmental organizations. If those few groups with their meager resources prioritize social justice issues, no one will be left "speaking for the trees" and the results will be predictably catastrophic. Even with defenders, wild(er)ness is losing badly. If Muir, the Sierra Club, and others had not acted in the 1800s and 1900s wilderness areas would have fallen victim to the despoliations of industrialism. As it is, precious little is left. The decimation of Redwood and Sequoia forests provide a telling example. The fate of the passenger pigeon is a dramatic yet forgotten tale of the dangers of putting human needs ahead of wild(er)ness. Once numbering between 2 to 5 billion and roaming the continent in flocks that stretched for hundreds of miles and blotted out the sun for days, passenger pigeons were slaughtered into extinction in a few short decades in the 1800s in an orgy of blood and money that provided cheap food to working-class immigrants in East Coast cities. The size of the hole in the fabric of life remains impossible to imagine. It brings to mind the opening line of Barbara Kingsolver (1998)'s *The Poisonwood Bible*, "Imagine a ruin so strange it must never have happened" (p. 5). Lest we shake our enlightened heads too comfortably, we need to remember we are doing the same thing right now, this time to the ocean's fish. Cod have collapsed, going from a commercial catch in 1968 of 800,000 tons to a total biomass of 400,000 tons in 1990 to a total biomass of 1,700 tons in 1995. While the cod have collapsed, menhaden, called "the most important fish in the sea" for its dual roles as the keystone of the Atlantic food chain and in filtering waters of algae, has been compared to the passenger pigeon for its prodigious numbers and its equally senseless slaughter, this time as a nonessential but cheap source of fertilizer, livestock feed, pet food, lipstick, and other trivial uses. Best estimates have all the ocean's major fisheries collapsing by 2050.[27] The insatiable appetite of the human maw knows no limits, but the earth does.

CODA

The world is facing multiple unprecedented crises of vast proportions. As documented annually by the World Watch Institute and others, humans are threatening the vital signs of planetary health in a manner and scale unprecedented in human history. Climate chaos, air pollution, water pollution, chemical contamination, topsoil loss, collapse of multiple fisheries, deforestation, desertification, and mass extinctions are the threats that must be confronted in order to achieve environmental protection and a sustainable future for the planet.[28] In *Collapse*, Jared Diamond

(2005) explores how cultures value social survival over biological survival, with catastrophic consequences. Since the Norse colonies on Greenland valued wooden churches, cattle, and not eating fish, they destroyed their habitat and starved to death. Diamond notes of these unfathomable choices, that for the Norse "concerned with their social survival as much as their biological survival, it was out of the question to invest less in churches, to imitate or intermarry with the Inuit, and thereby to face an eternity in Hell just in order to survive another winter on Earth" (p. 247). An adequate response to our ecological crisis is impossible within the calculations of economic profit and human needs. Engaging the world from the orientation of the event of wild(er) ness is absolutely essential in this moment of myriad crises. As Leopold (1949/1989) hopes, "Perhaps such a shift of values can be achieved by reappraising things unnatural, tame, and confined in terms of things natural, wild, and free" (p. ix).

Remember, an event "brings to pass 'something other' than the situation, opinions, instituted knowledges; the event is a hazardous, unpredictable supplement" which both brings into being and needs a subject to faithfully unfold and rethink the situation from the orientation of the event, to produce the truths of the event (Badiou, 2001, pp. 67–68). This unfolding and rethinking occurs publicly through acts of communication. The ethical moment is one of commitment to and articulation of the event. Muir, Adams, Hill, and Leopold remain faithful to their encounter with wild(er)ness by articulating the truths of the event through multiple acts of communication—writing, photographing, speaking. Warren County and the race-based EJM are part of the civil rights movement's unfolding of the unacknowledged event at the heart of the American democratic imaginary—the oppression of black people. This is incredibly important work, but it is not the situation/world of environmental politics. The encounter with wild(er)ness is the event at the heart of environmentalism. Through faithfulness to this event, environmentalists can question the world of industrialism and imagine another world from the imperative and orientation of wild(er) ness.

NOTES

1. The Internet can make for tortured citations. I first read this article under this heading at this site: http://www.consumerenergyreport.com/2009/01/20/robert-redford-criticized-as-racist-and-enemy-of-the-poor/
   All of the quotations are at this site. An almost identical article appeared in the *Salt Lake Tribune* at this site: http://www.sltrib.com/news/ci_11455096.
2. Humanism can be defined in many ways, but the focus is on the centrality of humans: "a philosophy centered on man and human values, exalting human free will and superiority to the rest of nature; man is made the measure of all things" (The *Oxford Desk Encyclopedia*, Presented by *TIME*, 1982, p. 604). Humanism arose in contrast to Christianity, which revolves around God, not humanity. The American Humanist Association's definition is" "Humanism is a progressive philosophy of life that, without supernaturalism, affirms our ability and responsibility to lead ethical lives of personal fulfillment that aspire to the greater good of humanity" (http://www.americanhumanist.org/who_we_are/about_humanism/ Humanist_Manifesto_III). Ambrose Bierce's definition of "man" makes a similar point more archly (*The Devil's Dictionary*, 2003): "An animal so lost in rapturous contemplation of what he thinks he is as to overlook what he indubitably ought to be. His chief occupation is extermination of other animals and his own species, which, however, multiplies with such insistent rapidity as to infest the whole habitable earth and Canada" (p. 79).
3. In my analysis I am not considering Native American EJ groups. Due to historical, cultural, and legal reasons, Native American EJ groups are markedly different from other EJ groups. This difference is perhaps most apparent with respect to attitudes toward nonhuman nature. In addition, the politics are very complicated since Native American reservations are legally independent entities in the United

States, but at best it is a complicated independence and many EJ issues pit different members of the same tribe against each other.

4. The Letter can be found at http://www.swop.net/node/26 and is usually credited to SWOP Co-Director Richard Moore, though it was signed by 105 EJ activists. The hyperbole and hostility of the letter are striking. After claiming that people of color have suffered centuries of racist and genocidal practices and largely attributing these to the U.S. military and mining companies, the letter charges that mainstream environmental groups "play an equal role in the disruption of our communities." The offending environmental activities equivalent to genocidal military practices include opposing sheep grazing in wildlife areas. Besides calling all of the Group of Ten racists, the Letter demands hiring quotas of people of color "to the extent that they make up between 35-40 percent of your entire staff." For an account of the impact of the letter, see "The Letter that Shook a Movement," *Sierra* (May/June 1993), 54.

5. Alston delivered her speech "Moving Beyond the Barriers" at the First National People of Color Environmental Leadership Summit (http://www.ejrc.cau.edu/dana_speech.htm). The SWOP letter makes the same claim: "It is our opinion that people of color in the United States and throughout the world are clearly [an] endangered species" (http://www.swop.net/node/26). Academic and EJ advocate Giovanna Di Chiro (1996) celebrates and sharpens Alston's position, "So the trademark slogans of mainstream environmentalism, such as 'Save the whales' or 'Extinction is forever,' are seen to reflect concerns of white people who are blind to the problems of people of color.... The question of what (and who) counts as an endangered species is therefore another crucial aspect of the environmental justice movement's reconceptualization of the relationships between nonhuman and human nature and the emergence of new ideas of nature and new forms of environmentalism" (pp. 311, 315). This position represents either a stunning stupidity about science or an egregious example of human self-centeredness.

6. Some of the charges defy belief. International Environmental Justice claims that mainstream environmentalism "Trades human health for profit; Promotes unsafe technology; Subsidizes ecological destruction" (Anand, 2004, p. 11).

7. For a fascinating account of how the fetishization of the fear of death has disfigured thinking of human–nature relations, see Kohak's (1987) *The Embers and the Stars*.

8. I am using the awkward neologism of "wild(er)ness" to express both wilderness the place and wildness the quality and how the two are each other's indispensable supplements. The awkwardness forces a moment of reflection on the term each time one trips over it. For my take on the theoretical issues around the concept of wilderness, see DeLuca (2007). Much of the academic critique of wild(er)ness springs from William Cronon's polemical essay, "The Trouble with Wilderness; or, Getting Back to the Wrong Nature" (1996). To move from the deconstruction of wilderness to the dismissal of wilderness in favor of privileging humans and their concerns, however, is to misread Cronon's essay and to misunderstand postmodernism. If postmodernism can be reduced to a central impulse, arguably that impulse would be the questioning of modernism's foundational concepts and truths (Calinescu, 1987; Harvey, 1989; Lyotard, 1984). Far from privileging the human, postmodernism represents an even more sustained questioning of the human than of wilderness. Foucault puts this questioning most succinctly at the end of *The Order of Things* (1973): "Taking a relatively short chronological sample from within a restricted geographical area—European culture since the sixteenth century—one can be certain that man is a recent invention within it.... As the archaeology of our thought easily shows, man is an invention of recent date. And one perhaps nearing its end." Foucault concludes that if the cultural discourses that made possible "man" were to change, "then one can certainly wager that man would be erased, like a face drawn in sand at the edge of the sea" (pp. 386–387). If one accepts the postmodern deconstruction of wilderness, the same logic dictates the deconstruction of the human. Our contact with the world, with the Real, is always already mediated through multiple discourses. This is the meaning of Derrida's famous line, "il n'y a pas de hors-texte [There is nothing outside of the text]" (1976, p. 158). The response, then, is not to dismiss wilderness as a fiction and turn to the human, but, rather, to ask what are the benefits and costs of the fiction of wilderness. To Cronon's credit, this is what he does. It is important to recognize that Cronon is critiquing the idea or concept of wilderness. "By now I hope it is clear that my criticism in this essay is not directed at wild nature per se, or even at efforts to set aside large tracts of wild land, but rather at the specific habits of thinking that flow from

this complex cultural construction called wilderness. It is not the things we label as wilderness that are the problem—for nonhuman nature and large tracts of the natural world do deserve protection." Perhaps the greatest value of wilderness is that it prods us humans out of our infinite self-absorption. "The striking power of the wild is that wonder in the face of it requires no act of will, but forces itself upon us as proof that ours is not the only presence in the universe" (1996, pp. 81, 88).

9. Out of necessity, this essay will not have anything resembling a comprehensive account of Badiou's philosophy. Many of Badiou's shorter books provide exciting exposures to his thought. *Being and Event* (2007) and *Logics of Worlds* (2009) constitute the two foundational tomes.

10. The choice of origins is significant, as I will discuss later. For a definitive history, see Gottlieb (1993).

11. www.epa.gov/fedsite/eo12898.htm

12. Bullard echoes Gibbs: "The environmental justice movement has basically redefined what environmentalism is all about. It basically says that the environment is everything: where we live, work, play, go to school, as well as the physical and natural world" "Environmental Justice: An Interview with Robert Bullard," *Earth First! Journal* July 1999 (www. ejnet.org/ej/bullard.html).

13. The examples are as endless as differences themselves, so I am just mentioning a few prominent examples that are highlighted in the West. So while I mention the Taliban, we could talk about the treatment of women in many other fundamentalist Islamic countries, such as Saudi Arabia. Although I mention China, many other countries would qualify. And so on.

14. I am using this book as a representative example of a trend evident in environmental communication in general. This can be seen in the proceedings of the area's main conference since 1991, the *Biennial Conferences on Communication and Environment* (http://www.esf.edu/ecn/coceconf.htm).

15. The English word *event* implies more of a duration than Badiou is suggesting. For Badiou, the duration is the process of the subject creating the truths of the event. The event itself is ephemeral, a gliff. *A gliff* is a seldom used word that means "a moment; a transient glance; an unexpected view of something that startles one" (www.websters-online-dictionary.org/Gl/Gliff.html). In slang, it means "a nonsense word often used in tests" (www.urbandictionary.com/define.php?term=gliff). I like the word *gliff* because it gets at the unpredictable, contingent, startling, not making sense in the situation as it is, ephemeral qualities of the event. For example, with respect to the mid-20th century Civil Rights movement, for many Americans the initial moment of glimpsing the abject in the monstrous image of Emmett Till's lynched face was an event, a gliff, an unexpected view that startles. While many Americans did not respond to this event and kept living in the White supremacist world as it was, for many others Till's monstrous face ripped the fabric of the world of Jim Crow and called them into becoming subjects creating the truths of equality over the ensuing decades (Harold & DeLuca, 2005).

16. Badiou's philosophy is admittedly difficult and nowhere more so than in his conception of the subject, which is utterly opposed to the dominant "psychological subject." More formally, Badiou writes, "I will call subject the process itself of liaison between the event (thus the intervention) and the procedure of fidelity (thus its operator of connection)" (2007, p. 239). Though too much to unpack here, this sentence is Badiou's most succinct and startling statement on the subject: "We could say that a subject is an operative disposition of the traces of the event and of what they deploy in a world" (2009, p. 33). Badiou evokes the subject on a more poetic register in the concluding chapter of *Logics of Worlds*, "What Is It to Live?" (2009, pp. 507–514).

17. The success of this mythic origin story can be largely attributed to an aggressive propaganda campaign by race-based EJ groups. In addition, two interrelated reasons stand out. Class politics remains the third rail of American politics given its association with communism and socialism. Love Canal was a working class White neighborhood. Identity politics has served to displace class politics, and has often been used by the capitalist class to destroy potential alliances amongst working class folks of different races. Accidentally or out of necessity, the Civil Rights movement made identity politics respectable. It is noteworthy that Martin Luther King Jr. can be canonized for his work on race relations only at the cost of whitewashing his ferocious critiques of class politics in America. In both activism and academia class politics has been eclipsed by identity politics.

18. This is not to downplay the historical and current impact of racism in the United States. Even today, even after the election of President Obama, racism remains a significant cause of social injustices.

19. I vehemently disagree with the conventional labels of "developed" and "developing." It implies a certain hierarchy and level of progress that is simply untrue. For example, I would argue that a non-industrial indigenous culture should be considered developed when it is able to live in balance with its local environment while supporting its members in an egalitarian and sustainable way. Conversely, an industrialized culture should not be considered developed if it is destroying its environment in a nonsustainable manner while generating immense inequalities and miseries among its members.
20. The disparities between the developed and the developing countries in all of the key measures are stunning. These disparities are exacerbated when it is the United States measured against the developing countries. As some of the statistics cited show, this holds true even when the United States is compared to fellow economic superpower China.
21. Other important environmental groups not mentioned here have made the same move, including the National Wildlife Federation, Earth First!, and Greenpeace.
22. "A Place at the Table: A Sierra Roundtable on Race, Justice, and the Environment," *Sierra* (May/June 1993), 51.
23. www.sierraclub.org/policy/conservation/justice.asp
24. Environmental Justice Resource Center, www.ejrc.cau.edu
25. Sixty of the 316 organizations mention "wildlife" under the category of issues. This is suspect, though, since the issues category seems to be a wish list where people checked off items with abandon. So, for example, the Morehouse School of Medicine lists wildlife as an issue even though it is a medical school that claims the mission of training faculty and students in health assessments related to toxics exposure. The Center for Neighborhood Technology claims a focus on Chicago but lists wildlife among 15 other issues. The Cincinnati Women's Health Project also claims wildlife as an issue. And so on.
26. Indeed, in the case of population control, the nondemocratic Chinese government provides a clear counterexample. It is highly doubtful that a democratic China could have curbed its population as effectively as China has through its strict one child policy. Democratic India has been an abject failure at controlling its population. Population control is not a popular idea.
27. The cod collapse is an oft-told tale. For the menhaden story, see H. Bruce Franklin (2007). For the warning of the 2050 fisheries collapse, see Worm et al. (2006) and Pearce (2006).
28. See www.worldwatch.org, especially the new Plan B 2.0: Rescuing a Planet Under Stress and a Civilization in Trouble.

REFERENCES

Adams, A. (1985). *Ansel Adams: An autobiography*. Boston: Little, Brown.

Adams, A. (1938). *Sierra Nevada: The John Muir trail* Berkeley: Archetype Press.

Adams, A., & Newhall, N. (1960). *This is the American earth*. San Francisco, CA: Sierra Club Books.

Amy, D. (1987). *The politics of environmental mediation*. New York City: Columbia University Press.

Anand, R. (2004). *International environmental justice*. Burlington, VT: Ashgate.

Austin, R., & Schill, M. (1991). Black, brown, poor and poisoned: Minority grassroots environmentalism and the quest for eco-justice. *Kansas Journal of Law and Public Policy, 69,* 69–70.

Avro, S. (Jan. 20, 2009). Robert Redford criticized as racist and "Enemy of the poor." http://www.consumerenergyreport.com/2009/01/20/robert-redford-criticized-as-racist-and-enemy-of-the-poor/

Badiou, A. (2001). *Ethics: An essay on the understanding of evil*. New York: Verso.

Badiou, A. (2001–2002). On evil: An interview with Alain Badiou. *Cabinet Magazine*. Retrieved from www.cabinetmagazine.org/issues/5/alainbadiou.php

Badiou, A. (2007). *Being and event*. New York: Continuum.

Badiou, A. (2005). *Infinite thought*. New York: Continuum.

Badiou, A. (2009). *Logics of worlds*. New York: Continuum.

Bierce, A. (2003). *The devil's dictionary*. Bloomsbury, NY: Holtzbrinck.

Brulle, R., & Pellow, D. (2005). Environmental justice: Human health and environmental inequalities. *Annual Review of Public Health, 27,* 103–124.

Bullard, R. D. (n.d.). *Second national people of color environmental leadership summit resource papers: A synthesis (1).* Retrieved from http://www.ejrc.cau.edu/summitPolicyExSumm.html

Calinescu, M. (1987). *Five faces of modernity.* Durham, NC: Duke University Press.

Chavis, Jr., B. (1993). Foreword. In R. Bullard (Ed.), *Confronting environmental racism* (pp. 3–96). Boston, MA: South End Press.

Chavis, Jr., B. F., & Lee, C. (1987).*Toxic wastes and race in the United States.* United Church of Christ Commission for Racial Justice. Author.

Cole, L., & Foster, S. (2001). *From the ground up: Environmental racism and the rise of the environmental justice movement.* New York: New York University Press.

Cox, R. (2006). *Environmental communication and public sphere.* Thousand Oaks, CA: Sage.

Cronon, W. (1996). The trouble with wilderness, or, getting back to the wrong nature. In W. Cronon (Ed.), *Uncommon ground: Rethinking the human place in nature* (pp. 69–90). New York: Norton.

DeLuca, K. (2007). A wilderness environmentalism manifesto. In R. Sandler & P. Pezzullo (Eds.), *Environmental justice and environmentalism* (pp. 27–56). Cambridge, MA: MIT Press.

Depoe, S. P. (2004). Public involvement, civic discovery, and the formation of environmental policy. In S. P. Depoe, J. W. Delicath, & M. A. Elsenbeer (Eds.), *Communication and public participation in environmental decision making* (pp. 157–174). Albany, NY: SUNY Press.

Depoe, S. P., Delicath, J. W., & Elsenbeer, M. A. (Eds.). (2004). *Communication and public participation in environmental decision making.* Albany, NY: SUNY Press.

Derrida, J. (1976). *Of grammatology,* Baltimore, MD: John Hopkins.

Diamond, J. (2005). *Collapse.* New York: Viking.

Di Chiro, G. (1996). Nature as community: The convergence of environment and social justice. In W. Cronon (Ed.), *Uncommon ground* (pp. 298–321). New York: Norton.

Dobson, A. (2003). *Citizenship and the environment.* Oxford, UK: Oxford University Press.

Dowie, M. (1996). *Losing ground: American environmentalism at the close of the twentieth century.* Cambridge, MA: MIT Press.

Drummond, J. (2008). What would I like to see published in *Environmental Justice. Environmental Justice, 1*(4), 179–181.

Fletcher, T. (2003). *From Love Canal to environmental justice.* Ontario, Canada: Broadview Press.

Foucault, M. (1973). *The order of things.* New York: Vintage.

Franklin, H. B. (2007). *The most important fish in the sea: Menhaden and America.* Washington, DC: Island Press.

Freidman, T. (May 30, 2003). *The Charlie Rose Show* [TV series]. New York: WNET.

Gibbs, L. (1993). Celebrating ten years of triumph. *Everyone's Backyard, 11,* 2.

Gibbs, L. (2006). Citizen activism for environmental health. In S. H. Washington, P. Rosier, & H. Goodall, (Eds.), *Echoes from the poisoned well* (pp. 3–16). New York: Lexington Books.

Global Paper Consumption. (2007). Retrieved from http://www.swivel.com/data_sets/spreadsheet/1000519

Goldenberg, S. (2009, December 2). Copenhagen climate change talks must fail, says top scientist. Retrieved from http://www.guardian.co.uk/environment/2009/dec/02/copenhagen-climate-change-james-hansen

Gottlieb, R. (1993). *Forcing the spring.* Washington, DC: Island Press.

Hallward, P. (2003). *Badiou: A subject to truth.* Minneapolis: University of Minnesota Press.

Harold, C., & DeLuca, K. M. (2005). Behold the corpse: Violent images and the case of Emmett Till. *Rhetoric & Public Affairs, 8*(2), 263–286.

Harvey, D. (1989). *The condition of postmodernity.* Cambridge, MA: Basil Blackwell.

Hightower, E. (2009, November). Creating conservation communities. *Outside Magazine.* Retrieved from http://outside.away.com/outside/culture/200911/creating-conservation-communities-1.html

Hill, J. B. (2000). *The legacy of Luna.* San Francisco, CA: Harper.

Jensen, D., & Draffan, G. (2003). *Strangely like war: The global assault on forests.* White River Junction, VT: Chelsea Green.

Kingsolver, B. (1998). *The poisonwood bible.* New York: Faber & Faber.

Kohak, E. (1987). *The embers and the stars.* Chicago, IL: University of Chicago Press.

Leopold, A. (1989). *A Sand County almanac and sketches here and there.* New York: Oxford University Press. (Original work published 1949)

Livestock and poultry: World markets and trade (March, 2006). *Beef: Per Capita consumption summary selected countries.* Retrieved from http://www.fas.usda.gov/dlp/circular/2006/06-03LP/bpppcc.pdf

Lyotard, J. F. (1984). *The postmodern condition.* Minneapolis: University of Minnesota Press.

McGurty, E. M. (2007). *Transforming environmentalism: Warren County, PCBs, and the origins of environmental justice.* New Brunswick, NJ: Rutgers University Press.

McGurty, E. M. (1997). From NIMBY to civil rights: The origins of the environmental justice movement. *Environmental History, 2*(3), 301–323.

Mohai, P., Pellow, D., & Roberts, J. T. (2009). Environmental justice. *The Annual Review of Environment and Resources, 34*(16), 1–26.

Muir, J. (1988/1914). *The Yosemite.* San Francisco, CA: Sierra Club Books.

New Community Project. (n.d.). *Consuming appetites: Global patterns in consumption of the earth's bounty.* Retrieved from http://www.newcommunityproject.org/pdfs/consumingappetites.pdf

Pearce, F. (November, 2006). No more seafood by 2050? *New Scientist.* Retrieved from www.newscientist.com/article/dn10433-no-more-seafood-by-2050.html

Schlosberg, D. (2007). *Defining environmental justice.* New York: Oxford University Press.

Schwarze, S. (2004). Public participation and (failed) legitimation. In S. P. Depoe, J. W. Delicath, & M. A. Elsenbeer (Eds.), *Communication and public participation in environmental decision making* (pp. 137–156). Albany, NY: SUNY Press.

Toker, C. W. (2004). Public participation or stakeholder frustration. In S. P., Depoe, J. W. Delicath, & M. A. Elsenbeer (Eds.), *Communication and public participation in environmental decision making* (pp. 175–200). Albany: State University of New York Press.

Walker, G. B. (2004). The roadless areas initiative as national policy: Is public participation an oxymoron? In S. P. Depoe, J. W. Delicath, & M. A. Elsenbeer (Eds.), *Communication and public participation in environmental decision making* (pp. 113–136). Albany: SUNY Press.

Worm, B., Barbier, E. B., Beaumont, N., Duffy, J. E., Folke, C., Halpern, B. S., et al. (2006). Impacts of biodiversity loss on ocean ecosystem services. *Science, 314,* 787–790.

26

Economic Justice and Communication Ethics

Considering Multiple Points of Intersection

Zachary A. Schaefer, Charles Conrad, George Cheney, Steve May, and Shiv Ganesh

INTRODUCTION: THE RELEVANCE OF COMMUNICATION ETHICS TO ECONOMIC JUSTICE

Markets and Economic Justice

The question of the market's relationship to ethics is long-standing and contested (Kuttner, 1987). The debate shows little sign of resolution today, although some cracks in system-based confidence did appear with the global recession that began in late 2007. In this chapter will we consider the intersection of economy, ethics, and communication while arguing that the triumph of neoliberalism or free-market discourse in the last two decades of the 20th century and the first decade of the 21st represents a case par excellence (a) for the study of persuasion in an economic context; (b) for the obscuring of ethical–moral issues, even as such policies bear directly on human welfare and human rights; and (c) for understanding the interplay of the symbolic and the material dimensions of human experience.

In early formulations of capitalism and indeed in the power struggles in the prior development of mercantilism, a key question arose regarding the concentration of power and the distribution of opportunity. This was clearly evident in the formations of guilds in the late European Middle Ages, where those institutions arose both to assert particular private interests (e.g., for an emerging or established craft) and to generate a countervailing force in what was then a virtually bimodal economic structure. Guilds were in fact the forerunners of both the modern corporation and the modern labor union (e.g., Perelman, 1984).

We argue that the very idea of what constitutes a *just* economy is to a great extent framed by how one thinks of the economy and the market as institutions in themselves. For example, is the market a place where a variety of individual interests and pursuits come in contact and compete with one another? Is the market a site where relationships are built to accomplish avowedly collective as well as personal aims? Is the market the prevailing institution of contemporary society, a crucible of activity and creativity that affords the best chance of confronting global problems? *Each of these views—and there are others—suggests a different locus and role of ethics.*

Although Adam Smith's *The Wealth of Nations* (1776/1976b) often serves as the cultural embodiment of the "invisible hand" of the market and its seeming rational, natural, and essential role as a guiding economic force, his preceding volume, *The Theory of Moral Sentiments* (1759/1976a) offers a countervailing balance with its emphasis on personal bonds and the happiness and good fortune of others.

Part of the difficulty in the study of the ethics of economy derives from the ease with which such classic texts as Adam Smith's (1776/1976b) *The Wealth of Nations* can be taken out of their historical and ideational contexts and appropriated for diverse purposes. In the past 30 years, this text in particular has been employed to support a view of relatively unbridled multinational corporate capitalism under the banners of neoliberal economics, free trade across political and geographic boundaries, and international development. However, even casual research reveals that many of the policy and popular discussions of free-market capitalism have rested on a fundamental misinterpretation of Smith's ideas (see Werhane, 1991). The most important of the dimensions of Smith's economics being overlooked include the central, moderating influence of social bonds in the proper functioning of markets, and the enormous roles accorded to emotional ties such as compassion and empathy. The often misguided ways in which Smith's philosophy of capitalism is invoked, even in some academic circles, points us to the need to include lay discourses as well as academic ones as we consider the interrelations of economy and communication from an ethical standpoint. Smith's ideal political economy would function as a dialectical tension between self-interest and collective interest; the market, as an institution with immediate presence in people's lives, would serve as a tool to negotiate the tensions inherent in a given political and economic system.

A free-market approach that proclaims the ethical triumph of capitalism while overlooking the social inequalities and economic injustices it creates, qualifies in many cases as a form of propaganda (e.g., Altheide & Johnson, 1980). Jowett and O'Donnell (2006) provide a model of propaganda that distinguishes between persuasion, communication, and propaganda, suggesting that the latter does not seek mutual sharing or fulfillment of mutual needs but only to control information, manage public opinion, and manipulate behavior patterns. The problem, ultimately, becomes how to sort out reasonable arguments about the economy and its societal implications from messages aimed at accumulating wealth for private interests and with only passing concern for the broader public good. Moreover, as some scholars have observed, free-market advocacy often resembles theological discourse in the sense that it begins with an assumption that relies on faith rather than necessarily being subject to the test of data (e.g., Cox, 1999; Soros, 1998).

In the United States and in many other industrialized countries, major institutions have combined forces to persuade the broad public that justice somehow "is taken care of" simply through the pursuit of free-market objectives (Beder, 2006, 2007). In fact, the tendency to assume that free markets are the most efficient and effective way to create economic justice represents an underlying premise of contemporary capitalist societies. Further, that assumption makes itself present in a wide range of informal and formal discourses, including vernacular dismissals of government as being "the problem" and business being "the solution." Free-market economic justice has become a taken-for-granted facet of society because of constant messaging from a variety of institutional and informal sources.

The aggressive promotion of free-market values through conservative think tanks is ironic with respect to a state of affairs deemed to be "natural." Economic injustice in today's world is wide-ranging and deeply felt; yet, most citizens have difficulty articulating how ethics applies to institutional arrangements and not only to individual actions typically treated as the spectacle of scandal. Thus, economic justice is an important arena of investigation for communication scholars in part because the very way that ethics enters or does not enter that space is determined by the rhetorical success or failure of particular takes on what economy means for the human experience.

Economic Justice as a Human Rights Issue

Certainly one of the most important movements in recent years in the area of economic justice has been the effort to connect economic rights to human rights. The expansion of economic rights in the past decade especially comes from two main impulses: one deductive, philosophical, and legal; the other grassroots, practical, and extrainstitutional. The first avenue can be seen clearly in discussions of "the third generation" of human rights, where types of positive rights (involving "freedom to") have increased in number and the scope of the relevant constituency has widened to include all of humanity (see, e.g., Stohl, Stohl, & Townsley's, 2007 take on the successive generations of human rights from a communication perspective). The second impulse can be seen in the joining together of a number of social movements with an emphasis on the economy as commonwealth and with a stress on the application of sociopolitical values and systems, such as democracy and solidarity (Tarrow, 2005).

The most prominent example of this connection has been the annual World Social Forum (WSF), launched in 2001 as a counterpoint to the annual World Economic Forum (WEC) in Davos, Switzerland. Vandana Shiva, the noted Indian scientist and activist, explains that the main impulse for the WSF is to keep trade "honest" in the sense of accounting for the human purposes and the actual extent of costs (as cited in Goodman, 2006). This is but one example of how the annual WSF meeting, thus far held in India and Brazil, champions discussions of the social side of economic life in an effort to address ethical gaps in prevailing treatments of corporate globalization. One of the key practical and political questions from this standpoint is about the extent to which principles of economic justice will become widely seen as a priori rights in the global community. Interpretations of the articles of the *Universal Declaration on Human Rights* (1948) vary widely, even where so-called consensus issues such as torture are concerned. Yet, the tendency has been for an expanding circle of rights in political as well as social-movement discourses, and the increasing recognition of global economic inequality helps to support this move.

The Linkage of Economics to Happiness

A very different approach to the study and practice of economic justice has grown out of the interdisciplinary study of happiness. This area has expanded from a few studies in social psychology in the 1970s to a major thrust of work in that discipline and, in fact, to a significant area of attention in fields ranging from philosophy to economics. While initially dismissed as trivial (see Diener & Seligman, 2002), the studies of happiness are now supported by substantial empirical evidence on micro- and macrolevels, showing, for example, only minimal or even no improvements in reported life self-satisfaction for increases in wealth beyond a modest level involving the satisfaction of basic needs and a margin of security.

In a wide ranging book called *The Loss of Happiness in Market Democracies*, political economist Lane (2000) amassed significant research evidence from across disciplines to investigate the profoundly simple question, "If markets exist to maximize happiness, just how are they doing?" The diverse data marshaled by Lane to address this question are mixed, especially insofar as international comparisons reveal anomalies off the regression line that charts the relationship between affluence and reported life satisfaction.

Many neo-Marxists and poststructuralists would concur with Lane (2000), arguing that living in an object-driven society goads people to become more objectlike. Objects have a use value, an exchange value, and a set of symbols associated with status, prestige, and social ranking, which is why consumption is not just material but of course symbolically charged (Veblen, 1899). A great deal of consumption is not, practically speaking, for pleasure anymore because its purpose ironically reduces opportunities for leisure to the extent that access to highly prized goods and services requires more and more hours of work (Schor, 1992, 1997). In the end, reported life satisfaction, or happiness, becomes a fleeting concept as individuals scramble to consume more expensive, more luxurious, and more conspicuous commodities—with an implicit feature of each good "promising" to deliver happiness.

Domains of Symbolic and Material Inquiry

The work on happiness or subjective well-being, and economy, reminds us of the intricate interplay of social and material factors. Folk or lay epistemologies encourage people to dismiss communication and rhetoric as "not the real stuff" (e.g., as heard in "Put your money where your mouth is!"), but we observe that those same epistemologies act ideologically so as to obscure the very influence of the symbolic with respect to the material (Cheney, Christensen, Zorn, & Ganesh, 2010). A good example is the issue of class in the United States where the myth of classlessness persists to some extent even in the face of three decades of a widening gap between the richer and poorer segments of society (e.g., Cheney & Cloud, 2006; Wolff, 2010).

A compilation published by the *New York Times* (2006) presented a series of analyses and studies about whether or not class "matters" in the United States. The report underscored the emphasis that everyday people place on social class and showed that most people associate social class with education, occupation, income, and wealth. It also illustrated that upward social mobility is less likely to happen now than in the late 1970s, when the U.S. income gap ceased to close, and more importantly, people do not just live within objective social class boundaries but rather "perform class" through activities such as child rearing, eating, gift giving rituals, manners, and location of residence. Finally, the *New York Times* compilation captures the essence of Yodanis's (2006) idea that social classes are more than just static structures but rather intricate systems of symbolic interactions and allegiances. Thus, in approaching the ethics of communication in the arena of economic justice, it is crucial that we attend as much to what is unsaid or pushed from view as to what is featured in various discourses.

THE COMPLEX INTERRELATIONS OF ECONOMY, ETHICS, AND COMMUNICATION

Economic Aspects of Discourse, Discursive Aspects of the Economy

The intricate and multiplex relations between economy and society were charted extensively by such theorists as Ricardo (1817/1919), Marx (1867/1930), and Weber (1956/1978). In recent decades, of course, the advancement of materialist analyses of social relations and treatments of the materialistic dimensions of discourse have obviously helped to complicate and refine our understanding of the interplays between the material and the symbolic aspects of human experience. Especially since the 1970s, neo-Marxists have refined our understandings of the ways material conditions constrain rhetorical options and create parameters for the types that emerge (see Cloud, 2001). At the same time, studies of the rhetorical treatments (or lack thereof) of material factors have revealed how the symbolic dimension of human experience directs our attention to some parts of material reality and neglects others. A third type of interplay between the material and the symbolic is relevant here, and that is the rhetorical dimension of what we call the economy, particularly as conceptions of economics are put forth in academic and professional discourses. This type of investigation can be seen as a product of the broader engagement of rhetoric with epistemology, and its offshoots in terms of the analyses of specific disciplines from biology (see Benson & Campbell, this volume) to sociology (Edmondson, 1984).

The Rhetoric of Economy: The Case of Economic Argument

Although communication is one of the few academic disciplines where scholars acknowledge how and to what extent their arguments persuade and affect their audiences, McCloskey (1998) brings this set of insights to a field once considered immune to critical–symbolic investigation. In her treatise on the rhetoric of economics, McCloskey engages in an epistemological expedition to expose how humans can make fallible decisions in the pursuit of science. She argues that the conceptual tools associated with scientific neutrality and validation such as statistical significance and abstract mathematics are, in part, rhetorical enterprises used to persuade specific audiences. The rhetoric of economics, then, becomes a basis for questioning both the presumed epistemology and the implied ontology of economics. Mathematical modeling has supplanted empirical validation in the field of economics, and philosophically inclined economic historians such as Karl Polanyi (1944) have become an archaic part of the discipline. The field of economics, including the "naturalness" and inevitability surrounding market rhetoric, acts as if it is part of the physical world and not the social one.

Working within the framework of the rhetoric of economics, Aune (2001) challenges the notion that markets are the most appropriate way to organize society and demonstrates how a rhetoric of "economic correctness" leads to a society of individualized consumers. Aune maintains that McCloskey (1998) presents an idealized form of economic rhetoric by (a) neglecting how discourses are produced and (b) failing to explore the institutional contexts from which discourse and rhetoric emerge. The rhetoric of economics is also used in the legislative, judicial, and corporate realms to create policy favorable to already powerful interest groups. Aune offers several political lessons for replacing a rhetoric of free markets: (1) Viewing communication as information exchange will limit the possibilities for humans to flourish economically, culturally, and socially. (2) The ideology of "the market" fails to see itself *as* rhetoric and does not acknowledge that "evidence" must be constantly produced to justify this position. (3) Classical economists have crafted a realist style where the economic and social have displaced the political dimension of human action. (4) Modern day heirs of classic economists often equate rhetoric and politics to economic calculation in the name of "liberty" and "efficiency."

Aune's (2001) lessons reveal other virtues that can guide society in addition to prudence. Love, courage, justice, and temperance are also needed for a society to flourish but neoliberal advocates have yet to show how markets can lead to these values (Daly & Cobb, 1989). While the market ironically purports to be directed toward happiness, it often undermines that very pursuit by marginalizing social values which then must be reclaimed through countervailing forces such as simplicity movements or local economies. To truly explore a range of virtues and how humans attain them, we must see past the rhetorical constructions of neoliberal omnipotence. The political, social, and cultural values subsumed under the economic metavalue has neither fulfilled its promise nor encouraged the creativity free-market rhetoric calls its own.

Discourses of the Economy: The Case of the Rhetoric of Neoliberalism

Above we summarized Aune's (2001) critique of the rhetoric of free market economics. In this section we wish to place that analysis in a larger context of contemporary liberalism, focusing on what Ibarra-Colado (2006) has called its "marginal ethical content." Neoliberalism is based on three core means of *presumption*: libertarian economics is legitimized through a particular form of rhetoric; myths of individual freedom are supported by the creation of social structures that privilege large, profit-oriented organizations; and a preference is granted for states whose functions are limited to providing aid for profit-making firms. If left in its "natural" condition, it is argued, capitalist economic systems allow individuals to make economically rational choices, and their free pursuit of individual gain will aggregate to produce economic equilibria that maximize economic growth and individual well-being. Institutional intervention in the process is deemed unnecessary: prices provide economic actors with all of the information they need to make individually rational decisions, and the so-called invisible hand of competition (rhetorically speaking, an almost metaphysical supra-agent; and one invoked only once in each of Smith's major works; see Werhane, 1991) is sufficient to create outcomes that are optimal for the economy as a whole. Every individual should be left free to make choices designed to maximize his or her own utilities, as long as the rules of the economic game are followed. Because the same rules govern every economic actor, fairness is ensured and inequality is naturalized. Justice is defined solely in formal terms. That is, while individuals may differ in individual attributes and as a result may experience disparate outcomes from their efforts, as long as the rules are the same for all competitors, the system is ethical.

Economic neoliberalism includes only a very limited economic role for governments, one oriented toward ensuring that economic exchanges function as they are depicted in the theory. In this way, there is a systemic bias in neoliberalism that a priori elevates one sector over the others. Thus, governments need to ensure that economic markets remain competitive, property rights are protected, and contracts are enforced. In addition to assuming that government action based on any other value or goal inherently impinges on individual liberty, neoliberal ideology assumes that government intervention in the economy will have negative effects. The *futility thesis* states that governments simply cannot effectively direct a society or economy (Hirschman, 1991). The presumed miracle of the free market is that its processes work "invisibly," and thus do not have to be understood or managed (Ostas, 2001); this is analogue to some versions of psychotherapy that eschew insight. The presumed lesson of the demise of the Soviet Union and its client states is that centralized economic planning by a government is doomed to fail. This conclusion is then sloppily applied to all instances of attempts of public management of anything economic.

Neoliberal rhetoric constructs a series of simple, bipolar choices. For instance, in a summarizing statement reminiscent of the-illusion-of-two-alternatives technique of advertising, Milton Friedman (1982) wrote:

> Fundamentally, there are only two ways of co-ordinating the economic activities of millions. One is central direction involving the use of coercion—the technique of the army and the modern totalitarian state. The other is the voluntary cooperation of individuals—the technique of the marketplace. (p. 13)

These choices are indicative of a false dilemma: unfettered freedom *or* outright slavery, growth *or* grinding poverty, with entrepreneurs *or* free-riders, democracy *or* fascism, simple truths *or* convoluted socialist rhetoric (see Collinson, 2005). Although such a simplistic presentation of the "choice" is difficult to sustain in the face of the diversity of human motivations, pursuits, and outcomes, it is compelling because of three rhetorical moves. First, many economists treat their subject matter as if it was part of the physical world, separate from the chaotic, provisional, and imprecise social universe; for example, by sometimes relying almost exclusively on game-theoretic models of human conflict. By extension, free market economics is depicted as a science, and its conclusions as natural and incontrovertibly true. Soros (1998) concludes that, "[fundamentalism] posits an authority that is endowed with perfect knowledge even if that knowledge is not readily accessible to ordinary mortals, one whose persuasive power is that of magic—awe and belief without understanding" (p. 227).

Second, in addition to adopting a rhetorical style that precludes disconfirmation, the sheer amount of persuasive messages produced by free-market think tanks, advocacy programs in universities, and like-minded university faculty saturates public discourse. All of this research is presented in documents that are focused, direct, and simple enough to be easily understood by the general public. When there is a dearth of reliable data on a particular policy question or public debate, or too much information and opinion, this form of rhetoric is especially powerful. Both features applied to the case of health care reform in the United States in 2009–2010.

Third, without a connection between ideology and empirical reality, neoliberalism can become a self-referential system, impervious to critique. For example, Nobel Prize winner Paul Krugman (2009) noted that, "when I first began writing for *The [New York] Times*, I was naïve about many things. But my biggest misconception was this: I actually believed that influential people could be moved by evidence, that they would change their views if events completely refuted their beliefs." He then praises Alan Greenspan, former chairman of the U.S. Federal Reserve Board, for eventually abandoning his faith in the ability of markets to police themselves, but condemns a neoliberalism-dominated U.S. Congress and the presidential administration of Barack Obama for failing to enact substantive regulations in response to the 2010 global recession.

In addition to condemning government intervention into the market, neoliberal rhetoric *ignores* procorporate governmental action. As Michael Perelman (1984, 1989, 2006, 2007) has persuasively argued, free market capitalism has always included a significant role for government as an ally and protector of corporations. This is evident in the economic development of nations as diverse as the United Kingdom, Japan, and Chile. By the late 1800s in the United States the modest governmental function of enforcing economic contracts had been transformed into massive subsidies for trusts on the grounds that industries requiring large capital investments would never be attractive to investors unless adequate profits were guaranteed by government action to limit competition (Prechel, 2000). Over the course of the 20th century, state power was increasingly used to limit the political and economic power of noncorporate interest groups, at the same time that liberal rhetoric increasingly defined organized labor, environmental activists, and other stakeholders as "special interests" that threatened individual liberty and economic growth. Regulations and regulatory agencies were enacted more often to reduce competition and protect existing corporations (Kuttner, 1996; Wilson, 1974) than to protect noncorporate stakeholders, to "shore up the corporate power to the detriment of society" (Perelman, 2007, p. x). As an example, the U.S. Supreme Court ruling in 2010 removing most limits from corporate contributions to political campaigns on the grounds of free speech has further affirmed the status of corporate personhood, while not identifying additional responsibilities that have come with new corporate rights to engage in additional political influence via campaign contributions to political candidates.

Although regulatory bodies—whether they are courts or government agencies—are formally charged with protecting consumers, they function to manage public perceptions and pacify citizens, thus perpetuating the illusion of substantial regulation. Regulation has been rationalized and taken for granted as a legitimate form of control over high-risk industries and institutions. To understand how institutions gain legitimacy and avoid ethical scrutiny, we must explore the processes of rationalization themselves: in other words, the means by which society moves toward greater self-organization along the lines of a particular set of principles that presumably offers the best take on how to link objectives and means to achieve them.

The Broader Colonization of the Lifeworld under Capitalism and Its Attendant Institutions

One of the most significant theoretical explorations of economic discourse comes from the German critical scholar Jürgen Habermas (1983, 1984, 1987, 1989a, 1989b). Habermas, of course, has offered a much broader argument for the inherency of ethics in all communicative activity, of which economic relationships could be seen to be part. Habermas argues that the continuous colonization of the lifeworld within late capitalism alters the way people talk about and experience life and will eventually establish the search for value (i.e., meaningful lives, purpose) solely within a discourse of economic correctness (Aune, 2001). What is paradoxical about the colonization of the lifeworld is that, as the economic system gains more control over how people live and talk about their lives, the system itself appears to detach from society. That is, people follow the technical–rational rules of authoritative institutions while the goals and internal workings of those institutions are of little importance to the flow of everyday life. This illustrates how formal rationality overtakes substantive rationality, or when rules are followed somewhat mindlessly without attention to any ultimate goals (Weber, 1946). To ensure that substantive rationality is achieved in a free society, Habermas (1984, 1987, 1989a, 1989b) argues that well developed and multimodal reasoning must be fostered and practiced.

Deetz (1992, 1995) supports the goals of Habermas's (1983) theory of communicative action but critiques his overreliance on rational consensus-building, arguing that the results of an avowedly pluralist set of relations typically privilege the powerful classes' views. Deetz would rather explore how conflict can be recovered from closure; to accomplish this, he presents a comprehensive analysis of the relationships between communication, democracy, ethics, and corporate value systems. This analysis strives to recapture the radically participatory nature of democracy and cease the private colonization of the public sphere. Deetz's work challenges scholars to understand the meaning-construction processes of everyday people as well as policy makers and offers ways to open up the discursive spaces that the union of technical rationality and corporate dominance has closed.

The rationalization of the economic sphere is represented by organizations and governments seeking out the constant technological innovation that leads to increased profit—all without raising or entertaining questions regarding the ultimate expandability of the market. Schumpeter's (1950) notion of creative destruction similarly addresses how the capitalist system continually advances in spite of its own destructive forces concerning the environment and increased competition. Habermas (1987, 1989a) believes that without a simultaneous rationalization of the lifeworld, its colonization will eventually lead to anomie, or the social instability caused by a loss of morals.

Morality, Amorality, and Immorality in Economic Life: A Case of Master Framing

John Dewey's (1927) *The Public and Its Problems* clearly articulates many of the same problems that today's society is facing: the deficit in political representation, the dichotomy of public vs. private spaces and organizations, and the need to articulate and protect public interests. Dewey says that we must use public institutions to serve societal goals and norms rather than use institutions to limit individual creativity. Interestingly, the theories of neoliberal economics suggest that individuals are far from ignorant and uneducated—by definition consumers (formerly citizens) rationally pursue their self-interests and maximize their utility by relying on perfect information in a marketplace with perfect competition. These free-market rationalizations often entail a tautological paradox that removes the considerations of ethics and morals from organizational and political decision making—even with policies that would affect broad publics. The only logical way to overcome market inefficiencies and maximize consumer utility, or serve the public according to neoliberal theory, would be to marketize and privatize even further. Meanwhile, an entire set of institutions serves to create and not just serve or enhance consumer appetites, and the consumer comes to *see* democracy largely in terms of a widening array of products and services and to use that same lens to apply to other domains of life (Laufer & Paradeise, 1990).

At the level of microinteractions, recent managerial attitudes toward organizational ethics and moral norms illustrate a lack of ethical deliberation and action (Jackall, 1988). Jackall described why many managers and their organizations exhibit an indifference to truth and an allegiance to self-promotion and expediency. He argued that because the sole agenda of for-profit organizations is the pursuit of self-interest, individuals struggle for ways to avoid applying morals to their organizational decisions—they compartmentalize their decision making and ignore higher principles, guidelines, and morals. Managers are indifferent to making moral choices because of the rituals that create the social environment of value-bereft bureaucracies, which Collins (2004) argues are the source of a group's moral standards. Narrowly bureaucratic reward systems are tied to financial results, so there is no need to cultivate moral strength. Within a short-sighted model of capitalism, hypercompetitive and "agile" workplaces can corrode character—the character that binds human beings, brings coherence to lives, and furnishes each person with a sense of sustainable self (Sennett, 1998). Bureaucratic rituals erode the ties that bind and effectively demoralize decisions by keeping morality confined to locales *outside* of corporations. The compartmentalization of ethical talk is an unfortunate but clear distinction between bureaucracy-in-practice and bureaucracy as an ideal type.

Even more unfortunate, bureaucracy-in-practice offers irresponsible organizational actors many discursive opportunities to compartmentalize their unethical decisions. Jackall's (1988) sociobehavioral explanation is reinforced by Mitchell's (2001) structural–legal analysis of the reasons for corporate irresponsibility. The neoliberal economic ideology that guides decision making in the political and organizational spheres privileges one form of logic: immediate capital accumulation and therefore the redirection of other organizational goals along that line. Mitchell focuses on the corporation because it is one of the institutions that determine law-formation, wealth distribution, and public policy creation. Corporations have successfully persuaded individuals that their primary purpose is to fulfill the wealth maximizing goals of *homo economicus*. Mitchell illustrates that the bureaucratic rationality behind the goal of maximizing short-term stock prices for publicly traded companies undermines the moral responsibilities of corporations set up by the corporate legal structure. This arrangement tempts corporate managers and actors to act irresponsibly and takes away from their choices as morally autonomous individuals. *Moral hazards* occur when corporate actors act irresponsibly and shift the costs of their behaviors onto others. Mitchell merely points out that corporations are very efficient externalizing machines; yet, externalization of costs is one of the grand illusions of contemporary corporate capitalism, explains Hawken (1993).

Bureaucratization and Alienation in Economy and Society

Alienation is a polysemic term with resonance in everyday life and academic discussions. For Marx (1844/1988), alienation was the principle at the heart of humankind's problems; that is, insofar as our institutional arrangements serve to separate people from the very products of their labor and, ultimately, from themselves in the sense of their innate yearnings and expressions. The commonality among all individuations of the term is separation and its relationship to human identity—in Burke's (1966) term, humans are defined in part by our being "separated from nature by instruments of our own making." The perspective that is most relevant to an analysis of organizational ethics was articulated by Marx (1867/1930) in response to the work of Hegel (1820/1988) and Feuerbach (1841). Hegel believed that history is the story of the processes through which separate, individual human beings overcome their particular identities to reach a final, universal, shared consciousness—from alienation to identification and freedom. For Hegel, work could make us human, but the institutions we create in the process of working and living can undermine our humanity.

Marx (1867/1930) extended Hegel's (1820/1988) argument by suggesting that work *could* provide us with a way of escaping alienation, but only if it took place in a particular context. First, work cannot be reduced to a means of maintaining one's subsistence. It cannot be solely an instrumental act but must provide us with opportunities to use our creativity—to "transform nature" in Marx's terms—and to celebrate what we have created and the process of creation. Similarly, we must be able to celebrate the ways in which our creative acts help other people satisfy their needs. Second, we must have significant control over our work, both what we create and how we create it. Capitalism, Marx argued, inevitably separates us from our *selves* and from others—it is inherently alienating. Private ownership of property transforms the products of our creative actions into mere commodities, and reduces the "use value" of our efforts to the prices offered by a competitive market. As Burke (1945) stated, "the human personality itself comes to be conceived in the abstract terms of impersonal commodities" (p. 214).

Alienated from our creative potential as human beings, we substitute the pursuit of objects for the pursuit of self and connection with others: consumption of commodities becomes our common neurosis and the engine of contemporary capitalism (Gopnik, 1997). Our neurosis, however, is obscured by capitalist discourse. The dominant ideas of a society, its ideology, are embedded in its language. The most important linguistic process is reification, transforming human creations such as capitalism into "thinglike" entities that *seem* to be objective, unchangeable, and independent of human action (Marx, 1867/1930, Pt. III, ch. 48; also see Lukacs, 1923/1971). By making capitalism seem natural, normal, and moral, discourse perpetuates alienating social and work relationships (Therborn, 1980). One of the many discursive structures that obscure our commodity neurosis is rational-legal discourse in its most typical forms.

The embodiment of rational-legal authority in the modern bureaucracy is supposed to serve as a decision-making structure that leads to avowedly ethical ends (Weber, 1978). Weber's (1930/2002) discussion of the Protestant work ethic was partially an illustration of how the spirit of capitalism—the search for a rational and systematic increase of profit—distorts the range of values and techniques that people use to achieve their goals. Forgetting one's "duty" is the largest infraction possible within the Protestant ethic. To prevent this, organizations began to codify and formalize specific duties to ensure that individuals did not neglect them. The Protestant work ethic has been transformed into bureaucracy throughout the process of global capital expansion. Although the rules, hierarchies, and division of labor are often blamed for societal ills, it is actually the maladministration of the rules that is the cause of many problems (Perrow, 1986).

Within a framework of managerial capitalism, Perrow (1986) argues that the bureaucratic model and its accompanying ethic of rationality create a more thorough check on power imbalances than charismatic or traditional forms of organizing (i.e., nepotism, favoritism, and unjustified routine). Perrow argues that large scale organizing cannot occur without standardization, hierarchies, and rule systems—the hallmarks of a bureaucratic organization. The neo-Weberian approach to rationality and (ethical) decision making argues that *bounded rationality* is a better developed theoretical concept than Weber's bureaucratic model. No one has complete information, stable preferences, or an unlimited knowledge of cause-and-effect relations; thus, decisions are made in dynamic environments. Power thus remains hidden below the surface of bureaucratic procedures. Ethical discussions are not needed when rational-legal rules serve as the guiding logic of organizations because that system is presumed to have handled value commitments a priori, whether the goal is private profit or the provision of public services. Weber's Protestant ethic is complicated through managerial bureaucratization, secular careerism, and rampant consumerism—all ironic from a Weberian perspective because of the presumed grounding of professional and managerial work in a commitment to the common good (Rothschild-Whitt, 1979; Satow, 1975).

Not breaking the formal ethical rules has in many instances replaced systematic moral deliberation in the workplace: as long as the formal rules are not broken, managers and organizations are not acting unethically. The original idea of the calling can then be seen to reside in a distant, idealistic universe. Because bureaucracy is an instrument of unrivaled technical superiority that includes hierarchy, calculability, and rationality (Perrow, 1986; Weber, 1946, 1956/1978), it is difficult to question its self-imposed legitimacy. Friedman's (1970, 1982) narrow view of the role of corporate social responsibility falls in line with the bureaucratic omission of ethical deliberation.

Friedman (e.g., 1982) says that the only responsibility of organizational managers is to maximize shareholder wealth while following the laws of the land, thus minimizing the role of ethical deliberation in the workplace on individual, group, and institutional levels, and increasing managers' incentives to engage in lobbying and other forms of political influence. Free-market fundamentalists (Kuttner, 1996; Soros, 1998) such as Friedman claim that ethics are embedded in the business practices of daily life, and yet it is difficult to find empirical evidence of these claims. Business ethics cannot be equated with laws or codes because judgment entails decision making, action, and some form of accountability. Ethical talk only materializes when immoral actions expose the power structures lurking beneath the surface, and then organizations often use rhetorical strategies to (a) deny wrongdoing, (b) gloss over substantive issues, or (c) create the perception of isolation—that only a few "bad apples" acted unethically. Self-regulating industries create scenarios where organizations aim to avoid unethical (read: illegal) actions rather than strive to act ethically. Organizations that explain their actions by invoking abstract ethical theories sometimes do not meet minimal ethical standards, whereas taking personal responsibility for one's actions as a conscious choice, even when those decisions lead to negative personal consequences for the decision maker, entails substantive ethical action (Bear & Maldonado-Bear, 1994).

Organizational actors are often afraid to *talk* about ethics for fear of questioning the system of authority, damaging social relations, and critiquing the system of formal rationality. There are therefore few incentives to act ethically (compare Gardner, 2008; Jackall, 1988). In addition, bureaucratic ethics replaces the notion of the calling, and its connection to an ascetic view of accomplishing one's duty, with a set of decontextualized rules. There is little need for deliberative democracy within modern bureaucratic organizations because the bureaucratic ethics should always lead to rational outcomes.

ISSUES IN MARKET ETHICS FOR DISCURSIVE-RHETORICAL ANALYSIS

Meanings of the Market in Everyday Life

The market itself is a historically, culturally, and economically embedded concept and term. Its relations with ethics are complex, in large part because of the question of where and how ethical judgments enter the discussion of the market. On this matter, economic theories differ, and part of that difference comes in terms of whether explicit ethics are much highlighted at all. Historically, our cultural understandings of "the market" are varied and complex and are deeply embedded in our assumptions about, and practices of, ethics, rooted in a range of perspectives such as duty, consequence, and virtue, among others.

Although the market is one aspect of human behavior embedded within society, it is often discussed as if it has a life of its own. Capitalism is a socially constructed system of ideas and interactions that include fictitious commodities—land and labor—that were never meant to be bought and sold (Polanyi, 1944). Polanyi argues that the objective of creating a disembedded, self-regulating market economy is a Utopian project because reliance on market capitalism, which includes treating humans like commodities, is in certain ways immoral. Polanyi argues that equilibrium, the theoretical end goal of a capitalist system, is not possible because it is continually being reconstructed by the interactions (and therefore particular interests) of governments, organizations, and individuals. The "obsolete market mentality," or the subordination of people to market needs such as price, supply, and demand—and the international conflicts that accompany this mentality—can be decreased when people realize more economic alternatives exist than simply free markets or Marxism. The laissez-faire movement to expand markets and limit government involvement has always been juxtaposed with a protective countermovement that resists the subordination of people to price. The tensions surrounding this juxtaposition (Polanyi, 1944) need to be more clearly articulated in the lives of everyday individuals, and ethical scholars have a duty to remind individuals that they are more than consumers, they are citizens (e.g., Cheney, 2005).

Yet, currently, the market has been understood as a simultaneously empirical and mysterious vehicle of economic forces that is both impersonal and amoral (McCloskey, 1998). As Cheney, Lair, Ritz, and Kendall (2010) have noted, such cultural understandings of the market, its causes and its consequences, have been influenced by folk claims that support current beliefs that the market is: a means to endless expansion; an idealized mechanism to advocate market solutions as right and true; an overriding frame of interpretation for what constitutes good actions in work settings; and, ultimately, an inevitable and permanent feature of our past, present, and future economic decisions.

"Popular economics," if you will, then appears in media and venues as diverse as reality shows and career web sites (such as for personal branding: see Lair, Sullivan & Cheney, 2005). Importantly, many of these cultural expressions simply reinforce narrow conceptions of ethics when they mention values and morals at all. A classic contemporary example is the wildly successful U.S. TV show *The Apprentice* which proclaims unabashedly, "Nothing personal—it's just business." Such programs offer the potential for ironic, even subversive readings (consider the long-running newspaper-based comic strip *Dilbert*; see Stein, 2008); yet recent studies show that only a small segment of the readership/viewership finds any kind of empowerment from such cultural venues beyond catharsis and cynicism (e.g., Lair, 2007). In general, we find few challenges to the basic tenets which might be derived from a reading of "economic culture," broadly conceived; these are: (1) individuals must "make it" on their own; (2) goods are more important than goodness; and (3) market expansion is inevitable and unending.

The Market, Agency, and Ethical Action

In terms of ethical theory, however, it is important to retain a sense of agency with regard to the market and its impact on economic justice. That is, exploring a range of ethical perspectives can help us better understand, and act upon, the diverse judgments and choices that are available to us in our economic system rather than accepting current decisions as natural and inevitable (May,

2006). The prevailing theoretical perspective that frames our current assumptions regarding the market, consequentialism, produces a narrow set of choices to address the complex ethical dilemmas that arise in any economic system, but particularly capitalist systems that create wide-ranging economic disparities. As a set of ethical theories, consequentialism is distinguished by its focus on ends and, as a result, offers free market proponents the basis for rejecting cultural dialogue regarding the means toward any chosen economic end. The most widely accepted use of this theory has been utilitarianism, as advocated by John Stuart Mill (1863/2002). According to Mill, the purpose of ethical action is to achieve "the greatest overall happiness for the greatest number" and, as such, economic decisions, in the case of economic justice, should be evaluated by the extent to which they contribute to that end. Because happiness, for Mill, is deemed to be "pleasure or the absence of pain," the concept of utility recognizes that different people value happiness in divergent ways. The value of happiness, as a seeming right of an economically privileged, powerful majority, becomes the basis for free market proponents who argue for the universal values of growth and wealth accumulation, with limited regard for the negative externalities produced for marginalized groups in the process.

An alternative to the current, prevailing acceptance of the utility of markets, Kant (1785/1993) advised in his categorical imperative that we should "act only according to that maxim whereby you can at the same time will that it should become a universal law" (p. v). Such an ethical perspective proposes a different understanding of the market, one that focuses not so much on outcomes that may benefit a few powerful elites, but rather on a person's obligation or duty to the collective. An ethical judgment regarding market mechanisms would therefore shift to the motives that compel right economic action, as agents seeking ethical fulfillment not merely for self but also for others. From this perspective, the ethical dimensions of the market are no longer viewed as a means to economic prosperity, per se, but rather as a set of duties that strengthen the intrinsic value of all persons, as a collective.

Choices made related to markets, then, necessarily involve questions related to justice. For Rawls (1971/1999), determinations about actions, in general—or specifically about markets, in this case—require that principles and processes be clearly defined and affirmed in practices of deliberation. His method of reflective equilibrium provides a means for proceeding in particular cases of political economy, for example. Beginning with ideas that are broadly accepted, participants explore the range of judgments about particular cases, acceptable rules, kinds of appropriate reasoning, and reasonable human motivations. An iterative process is used to revise and refine the dimensions, continually seeking coherence among them. From a justice perspective, then, market-related decisions would necessarily have to remain transparent rather than opaque and the processes by which the market functions would be a regular source of deliberation.

An emphasis on economic justice and its relationship to the processes for creating and maintaining human rights, serves as a reminder that the market is but one of many features of our lives. Although we have lately regarded it as an all-powerful, yet external authority beyond our reach, it's dangerous to believe that the market can do everything—or is everything for us. Doing so subverts a broader, fuller understanding of our ethical judgments in life, as a whole, as emphasized in virtue ethics. While market-related decisions seem to have developed as naturalized, sedimented habits, virtue ethics clarifies that a virtue is not a set of habits, but a disposition to act *for reasons* and, thus, a disposition that is exercised through a person's practical reasoning (trans., Aristotle, 2002). This practical reasoning develops over time, in and through decision making and insight. Virtue is accumulated in the ongoing process of action and reflection. Simply put, virtue is the disposition to do the right thing, for the right reason, in the right way, ultimately contributing to *eudaimonia*, or flourishing. In this respect, virtues remind us to consider markets a single component in an overall unity of life, as a whole. The aim is to live a certain kind of life, in which actions are taken for their own sake rather than for instrumental reasons and for which we aspire to be better than we are. In this respect, god-terms common to the market, such as growth, development, and happiness take on new meanings that transcend the typical compartmentalization of ethics as irrelevant to market choices.

Relations of Democracy to Capitalism, and Their Ethical Ramifications

The equation of capitalism and democracy is taken as a given in contemporary industrialized societies (Gray, 1998), yet the ideologically charged linkage obscures not only the diverse forms of democracy and capitalism but also the fact that their impulses are often in tension (Almond, 1991; Cronin, 1987). Often overlooked in passing comments about "capitalist democracy," is relations of power and indeed the concentration of power in systems where actors theoretically have equal agency, or at last equal access to the means by which they can work the system.

In four decades the power theorists and political scientists shifted positions from "everyone has a fair chance" to not only a recognition of the stronghold of corporate interest groups but also to argue that state structures should mediate the consequences of market economies (Lindblom, 2001). For pluralist democracy to succeed, it needs a supporting culture that includes the freedoms found in a bill of rights, a rule of law, and other institutionalized agreements. However, neoliberal economic policies that guide most industrialized governments use these rights as a means to protect corporate interests, which eventually undermines a healthy democracy. Capitalism is a necessary condition for democracy but not a sufficient one, because the cultural variables and institutions that permit and encourage ethical deliberation must be present for the institutionalization of democracy.

One area where democratic ideals are not institutionalized is the modern multinational corporation. Robert Dahl has a large span of work advocating for workplace democracy (Dahl, 1985, 1989, 2002) in these organizations, arguing that the organizational structures that form the backbone of the economy should match the electoral process embodied in the state. Swanson (2007) also says that Dahl's work (1982, 1985, 1989, 1998, 2002; see also Dahl & Lindblom, 1992) points up how neoliberal economic theory conflicts with democracy and fails to accurately describe the U.S. and other laissez-faire economies.

FRAMING AND ASSESSING MARKET GLOBALIZATION

Globalization is Inevitable

Globalization itself is a contested term; moreover, it is far more emotionally charged than is the older term *internationalization* (Fairclough, 2006). Globalization has become, on the one hand, a symbol of the "inevitable" expansion of the market and, on the other, a rallying cry for social movements that unfortunately came to be identified as "antiglobalization" around 1995.

As we look at the period from about 1975 to the present, during which not only the term *globalization* but also the discussion of multinational or transnational corporations has become commonplace, we can see periods in which the dimensions of the discussion were narrowed to a focus on corporate globalization and other aspects such as social exchange, cultural preservation, or the self-determination of peoples were left out of view. This narrowing of the scope of globalization discourses occurred in the early 1980s, especially in the literature of management (see Levitt, 1983), in response to the transformations of Eastern Europe and the breakup of the Soviet Union in between 1988 and 1991, and again in the late 1990s with celebrations of the triumph of free trade and the dot.com "revolution." The period of 1999 to 2001 included several major events that challenged an emerged script or master narrative for globalization: the protests against the WTO meetings in Seattle in November-December 1999; the bursting of the dot.com bubble in March 2000; and the September 11, 2001 terrorist attacks on the United States. In a different way, each of these events called into question U.S.-led corporate globalization, particularly through free-trade regimes and their attendant institutions, as an inevitable march toward further international integration and stabilization.

To fully understand the political, practical, and by extension, ethical dimensions of contemporary globalization, it is important to return to the philosophical underpinnings of neoliberalism. As John Locke would have it, the term *liberal* refers to the rights of individuals against the commands of their rulers. Since Adam Smith (1776/1967b), however, we have also come to associate the term not just with individualism, but with the invisible hand of the market (Hall, 1988). The resurgence of Smith's ideas about the market in the 1970s, especially in American academic circles marks "neoliberalism" which is, in brief, a celebration of the assertion that market forces, left to themselves, will ensure the greatest welfare for all (Williams, 1996).

"Liberalization," a driving force behind worldwide economic change in the last 30 years, is the central policy prescription of the neoliberal model of economic growth supported by such agencies as the World Bank and the International Monetary Fund (IMF). These organizations initially formed as a result of a conference in Bretton Woods in 1944, after World War II, ostensibly to manage the devastation that the war had wreaked in Europe, as well as to manage the impoverishment of former colonies that were emerging as independent countries. That same year, the Global Agreements on Tariffs and Trade (GATT) talks began, ironically enough, in Cuba, which resulted in the formation of the World Trade Organization (WTO) in 1994. The discourse of liberalization that these institutions generated underwrote a shift away from structural or state-sponsored economic development to market-driven capitalism. The move from structure to market has been most evident in the IMF's infamous structural adjustment programs: its advocacy of shifts from import substitution and national self-sufficiency to export orientations and its encouragement of foreign (or international) capital investments, and disinvestment of state and public assets, often at vastly discounted figures, to private capital. Such policies have also been accompanied by an emphasis on maintaining low inflation rates often at the expense of higher rates of unemployment. The predominance of liberalization policies in the third world today as a result of cajoling and coercion on the part of the Bretton Woods institutions as well as GATT and then the WTO highlights the fact that while neoliberalism is understood as a phenomenon evident in the last 3 decades, it has been more than 60 years in the making. It also indicates the pervasiveness of capitalist modernity—that set of historical developments that mark the dominance of the market in all spheres of life.

Market globalization, then, can be understood as the outcome of liberalization policies on the part of states all over the world. *Prima facie* it implies the integration of regional and national economies, and is epitomized by what commentators refer to as the "Washington Consensus": the tacit acceptance of the idea that trade between countries is a significant factor in national economic growth, that legal barriers to trade at the level of the nation-state must be removed, and that nation-states need to develop appropriate organizational and institutional infrastructures to manage free trade. In its purest form, then, market globalization refers to trade that is regulated, not by nation states, but by corporate actors in a global marketplace.

Proponents of market globalization tend to frame it in several ways, but three castings are particularly prominent. First, some frame globalization in purely economic terms, as the inevitable consequence of market expansion and the search for new value, which is itself seen as basic mechanisms of capitalism. A second frame is administrative, and sees globalization as a regulatory regime, which is necessary in order to ensure and protect the free flow of information, goods, and services, thereby helping markets become more "perfect" and democratic. A third frame is couched explicitly in terms of ethics: the globalization of markets has pragmatic consequences for the livelihoods of economically and culturally deprived communities all over the world.

It is evident, however, that market globalization has never just been about the economy. Its origins can be seen as a series of political adjustments effected through Bretton Woods institutions immediately after the Second World War by a group of Western nations—notably the United States, the United Kingdom, and France—as a response to the rising power of the Soviet Union, and a means of preserving dominance in the light of the rising power of emerging countries in the third world. Market globalization is therefore not primarily a result of democratic impulses: rather, it is the result of a series of prevailing articulations of solutions for over 60 years, as discussed earlier (compare Almond, 1991, on the complex interrelations of democracy and capitalism).

Further, proponents of market globalization rest their arguments upon notions of perfect information, which itself is a flawed economic notion that ignores the interpenetration of politics, language, and economy in notions of information. The idea that information has an independent, objective existence from politics, culture, and language has been contested for decades by scholars of communication (Axley, 1984; Klippendorft, 1993) who have instead established that information is also politically inseparable from language and context. Indeed, the breakdown of the Washington Consensus, in the form of increasing protectionism on the part of "advanced" economies in the face of such phenomena as outsourcing and the depletion of the manufacturing base of highly industrialized countries, signals the impossibility of trying to understand contemporary trade without reference to national politics and interests.

Prechel's (2000) structural analysis of the legal relationships between the steel industry and the federal government illustrates the hypocrisy with which advocates of the free market pursue their goals. The conditions under which social classes can unify and state institutions can act autonomously illustrates the historical and legislative transformations of business policy from the 1880s to the 1990s in the steel industry. The U.S.-backed Bretton Woods institutions (i.e., the World Bank, the International Monetary Fund, and the World Trade Organization, as successor to the General Agreements on Tariffs and Trade) originally were charged with alleviating poverty, maintaining a global economic equilibrium, and offering financial aid to developing countries. The agenda that these global financial institutions have pursued, however, is largely one of economic privatization and trade liberalization. Ironically, when the U.S. steel industry was struggling in the 1970s, instead of following the neoliberal logic of deregulation it lobbied for state protection (Prechel, 2000). A global market for steel fostered the development of protectionist rather than liberalized trade policies and revealed the contradiction between institutional rhetoric and action.

Finally, can market globalization be seen as a vehicle to improve livelihoods, benefit marginalized communities, and deal with major contemporary ecological crises? If we follow the logic of the vigorous global protests in the last decade by a wide range of groups, it cannot. The mechanisms that contemporary social movements have used to protest market globalization such as the Internet, have, in a truly dialectical turn of events, been given to them by the very same forces they seek to contest. The scale of contemporary interlocked protests against economic injustices, wars and environmental crises indicates that communities all over the world have not accepted the neoliberal idea that we can treat the economy as something separate and apart from politics, ethics and ecology. The increasing breakdown of the Washington Consensus and the "collapse of globalism" does not mean that the world economy will cease to be global: rather, it is likely that a new, reflexive localism that integrates economics with ecology and politics will become more influential.

We must reveal the strategies used to promote a unilateral understanding of progress and point out the rhetorical nature of such organizational communication and its ethical implications. The Nobel Prize winning economist Joseph Stiglitz (2002) says that regulation and corporate restructuring must accompany privatization in developing nations to ensure a healthy and informed public sphere—even markets in developed countries fail to provide the solution in every situation.

Alternative Economies as Social Movements

Gibson-Graham's (2006) *A Postcapitalist Politics* is an extension of Polanyi's (1944) attempt to reembed the economy within society and show that humans are active agents in economic organizing processes. Several other scholars also contribute to the idea of promoting people over profit by highlighting that the "self-regulating hand of the free market" is connected to a societal body. For instance, Cavanagh and Mander (2004) bring together a wide variety of scholarship and resources to invigorate academic interest and political action around the authoritarian phenomena of corporate globalization. Contrary to the mainstream media, they illustrate an alternative global economic narrative that highlights an increase of world poverty, a decrease of working class bargaining power, and a striking amount of migration and physical relocation. Their findings parallel Gibson-Graham's (2006) analysis, which shows how citizens are forced to enrich their lives by exchanging labor for a predetermined price set by the omnipresent corporate entity. Citizens experience identity paralysis while caught in the process of globalization, and although there does not appear to be an escape to the presence of the community-dividing and identity-subsuming market, Gibson-Graham concludes otherwise.

By using data from their community-based action research programs, Gibson-Graham shows how individuals in local communities around the world currently are implementing alternative visions to the typical capitalist mode. They supplement data from their action research programs with personal reflections, an analysis of the politics of possibility, and an in-depth exploration of the processes for instituting "feminist economies," or modes of organizing that do not operate around a harshly competitive, capital-centric market. They aim to open up directions for new thought and action. Further, they articulate similar conclusions to other scholars about the identity-economy nexus and how this relationship can negatively influence the health of individuals when the economy half is misplaced (see Barber, 2007; Sennett, 1998 for examples of consequences surrounding the economy-identity connection).

While we do not have space to name let alone explain diverse experiments around the world today that are reinvigorating the economic with the social, we wish to simply highlight that these range from gift economies in Peru and South Africa to worker-owned cooperatives in devastated inner cities of the United States; from local currencies in the United Kingdom to alliances of grassroots, indigenous businesses across the South Pacific. Many activities and programs, such as alternative trade organizations (or ATOs) exist outside formal trade regimes and function regionally, for example, in South Asia, without regard for national boundaries. Many such enterprises are not featured in the news, and the mainstream media do not recognize them as constituting a movement as such. Yet we can look to more such grassroots, radical (in the sense of "roots") responses to the dominance of neoliberalism, the prevailing expression of globalization in terms of corporate power, and least-common-denominator approaches to labor and environmental regulations that often characterize specific free-trade policies (see Parker, Cheney, Fournier, & Land, in preparation).

CONCLUSION: ENGAGING THE ETHICS OF ECONOMY IN COMMUNICATIVE TERMS

Moral arguments are often silenced, ignored, or simply relegated to the outcomes of procedural decisions in economics; alternatively, they are assigned to a particular institution (such as a regulatory agency) to decide their merits (Guttman & Thompson, 1996). If we seek organizations and institutions that embody democratic ideals, including notions of democracy as a self-adjusting, self-correcting process, and a progressive realization of our most cherished goals, we must closely examine arguments and images in the economic realm. This means concretely that communication scholars should devote sustained attention to issues such as the framing of economic inequality, the (trans)formation of consumer identities, shifting class-based networks, articulations of globalization and collapse, tensions between local and other levels of economic control, the roles of labor in free-trade agreements, the marginalization of the environment in most industrial and economic policies, and so forth. While we have offered a critique of neoliberal economics from the standpoint of rhetoric and communication, our even larger purpose is to invite empirical and interpretive as well as critical research on at the intersection of economy, ethics, and communication. Above all, we call for the "resocialization" of economic discourse, and suggest it as fertile ground for the further understanding of the interplay of the material and the symbolic.

REFERENCES

Almond, G. A. (1991). Capitalism and democracy. *Political Science and Politics, 24,* 467–474.

Altheide, D. L., & Johnson, J. M. (1980). *Bureaucratic propaganda.* Boston, MA: Allyn & Bacon.

Aristotle. (2002). *Nichomachean ethics* (S. Broadie & C. Rowe, Trans.). Oxford, UK: Oxford University Press.

Aune, J. A. (2001). *Selling the free market: The rhetoric of economic correctness.* New York: Guilford Press.

Axley, S. R. (1984). Managerial and organizational communication in terms of the conduit metaphor. *Academy of Management Review, 9*(3), 428–437.

Barber, B. R. (2007). *Consumed: How markets corrupt children, infantilize adults, and swallow citizens whole.* New York: Norton.

Bear, L. A., & Maldonado-Bear, R. (1994). *Free markets, finance, and law.* Englewood Cliffs, NJ: Prentice-Hall.

Beder, S. (2006). *Suiting themselves: How corporations drive the global agenda.* London: Earthscan.

Beder, S. (2007). *Free market missionaries: The corporate manipulation of community values.* London: Earthscan.

Burke, K. (1945). *A grammar of motives.* Berkeley: University of California Press.

Burke, K. (1966). *Language as symbolic action: Essays on life, literature, and method.* Berkeley: University of California Press.

Cavanagh, J., & Mander, J. (2004). *Alternatives to economic globalization: A better world is possible.* San Francisco, CA: Berrett-Koehler.

Cheney, G. (2005, March). *Is there a citizen in the house?* Annual Humanities Lecture, University of Utah, Salt Lake City.

Cheney, G., Christensen, L. T., Zorn, T. E., Jr., & Ganesh, S. (2010). *Organizational communication in an age of globalization: Issues, reflections and practices.* (2nd ed.). Prospect Heights, IL: Waveland Press.

Cheney, G., & Cloud, D. L. (2006). Doing democracy, engaging the material: Employee participation and labor activity in an age of market globalization. *Management Communication Quarterly, 19,* 501–540.

Cheney, G., Lair, D. J., Ritz, D., & Kendall, B. E. (2010). *Just a job? Communication, ethics, and professional life.* New York: Oxford University Press.

Cloud, D. L. (2001). Laboring under the sign of the new: Cultural studies, organizational communication, and the fallacy of the new economy. *Management Communication Quarterly, 15*(2), 259–278.

Collins, R. (2004). *Interaction ritual chains*. Princeton, NJ: Princeton University Press.

Collinson, D. (2005). Dialectics of leadership. *Human Relations, 58*, 1419–1442.

Cox, H. (1999, March). The market as God: Living in the new dispensation. *The Atlantic*, 18–22.

Cronin, T. (1987). Leadership and democracy. *Liberal Education, 73*, 35–38.

Dahl, R. (1982). *Dilemmas of pluralist democracy*. New Haven, CT: Yale University Press.

Dahl, R. (1985). *A preface to economic democracy*. Berkeley: University of California Press.

Dahl, R. (1989). *Democracy and its critics*. New Haven, CT: Yale University Press.

Dahl, R. (1998). *On democracy*. New Haven, CT: Yale University Press.

Dahl, R. (2002). *How democratic is the American constitution?* New Haven, CT: Yale University Press.

Dahl, R. A., & Lindblom, C. E. (1992). *Politics, economics, and welfare*. New Brunswick, NJ: Transaction.

Daly, H. E., & Cobb, J. (1989). *For the common good: Redirecting the economy towards community, the environment, and a sustainable future*. Boston, MA: Beacon Press.

Deetz, S. A. (1992). *Democracy in an age of corporate colonization: Developments communication and the politics of everyday life*. Albany, NY: SUNY Press.

Deetz, S. A. (1995). *Transforming communication: Transforming business*. Cresskill, NJ: Hampton Press.

Dewey, J. (1927). *The public and its problems*. Athens, OH: Swallow Press.

Diener, E., & Seligman, M. E. (2002). Very happy people. *Psychological Science, 13*(1), 81–84.

Edmondson, R. (1984). *Rhetoric in sociology*. New York: Salem House.

Fairclough, N. (2006). *Language and globalization*. New York: Routledge.

Feuerbach, L. (1841). *The essence of Christianity*. New York: Harper & Row.

Friedman, M. (1970, September 13). The social responsibility of business is to increase profits. *The New York Times Magazine*, 122–126.

Friedman, M. (1982). *Capitalism and freedom*. Chicago, IL: University of Chicago Press.

Gardner, H. (2008, April 10). *What is good work?* Tanner Humanities Lecture, University of Utah, Salt Lake City, United States.

Gibson-Graham, J. K. (2006). *A postcapitalist politics*. Minneapolis: University of Minnesota Press.

Goodman, A. (2006). Democracy now. Retrieved from http://www.democracynow.org/2006/12/13/vandana_shiva_on_farmer_suicides_the

Gopnik, A. (1997, August 4). Trouble at the tower. *The New Yorker*, p. 80.

Gray, J. N. (1998). *False dawn*. New York: New Press.

Guttman, A., & Thompson, D. (1996). *Democracy and disagreement: Why moral conflict cannot be avoided in politics, and what should be done about it*. Cambridge, MA: Belknap Press.

Habermas, J. (1983). *Moral consciousness and communicative action*. Cambridge, MA: MIT Press.

Habermas, J. (1984). *The theory of communicative action: Vol. 1. Reason and the rationalization of society* (T. McCarthy, Trans.). Boston, MA: Beacon Press.

Habermas, J. (1987). *The theory of communicative action: Vol. 2. Lifeworld and system, a critique of functionalist reason* (T. McCarthy, Trans.). Boston, MA: Beacon Press.

Habermas, J. (1989a). Reconstructing historical materialism. In S. Seidman (Ed.), *Jurgen Habermas on society and politics: A reader* (pp. 107–300). Boston, MA: Beacon Press.

Habermas, J. (1989b). *The structural transformation of the public sphere* (T. McCarthy & F. Lawrence, Trans.). Cambridge, MA: MIT Press. (Original work published 1962)

Hall, S. (1988). *The hard road to renewal: Thatcherism and the crisis of the left*. London: Verso.

Hawken, P. (1993). *The ecology of commerce: A declaration of sustainability*. New York: Harper Business.

Hegel, G. (1988). *The philosophy of right* (L. Rauch, Trans.) Indianapolis, IN: Hackett. (Original work published 1820)

Hirschman, A. (1991). *The rhetoric of reaction: Perversity, futility, jeopardy*. Cambridge, MA: Belknap Press.

Ibarra-Colado, E. (2006). The ethics of globalization. In S. Clegg & C. Rhodes (Eds.), *Management ethics* (pp. 32–54). London: Routledge.

Jackall, R. (1988). *Moral mazes: The world of corporate managers.* New York: Oxford University Press.

Jowett, G. S., & O'Donnell, V. (2006). *Propaganda and persuasion* (4th ed.). Thousand Oaks, CA: Sage.

Kant, I. (1993). *Grounding for the metaphysics of morals: On a supposed right to lie because of philanthropic concerns* (3rd ed., J. W. Ellington, Trans.). Indianapolis, IN: Hackett. (Original work published 1785)

Krippendorff, K. (1993). Major metaphors of communication and some constructivist reflections on their use. *Cybernetics and Human Knowing, 2*(1), 3–25.

Krugman, P. (2009). Disaster and denial. Retrieved from www.nytimes.com/2009/12/14/opinion/14krugman.html

Kuttner, R. (1987). *The economic illusion: False choices between prosperity and social justice* (2nd ed.). Philadelphia, PA: University of Pennsylvania Press.

Kuttner, R. (1996). *Everything for sale: The virtues and limits of markets.* Chicago, IL: University of Chicago Press.

Lair, D. J. (2007). *"Survivor for business people": A critical-rhetorical engagement of The Apprentice as popular management discourse* (Unpublished doctoral dissertation). University of Utah, Salt Lake City, Utah.

Lair, D. J., Sullivan, K., & Cheney, G. (2005). Marketization and the recasting of the professional self. *Management Communication Quarterly, 18,* 307–343.

Lane, R. E. (2000). *The loss of happiness in market democracies.* New Haven, CT: Yale University Press.

Laufer, R., & Paradeise, C. (1990). *Marketing democracy.* New Brunswick, NJ: Transaction.

Levitt, T. (1983). The globalization of markets. *Harvard Business Review, 61*(3), 92–102.

Lindblom, C. E. (2001). *The market system: What it is, how it works, and what to make of it.* New Haven, CT: Yale University Press.

Lukacs, G. (1971). *History and class consciousness.* Cambridge, MA: MIT Press. (Original work published 1923)

Marx, K. (1988). *Economic and philosophical essays of 1844: And the communist manifesto* (M. Milligan, Trans.). Amherst, NY: Prometheus Books. (Original work published 1844)

Marx, K. (1930). *Capital* (E. Paul & C. Paul, Trans.). London: J. M. Dent. (Original work published 1867)

May, S. (Ed.). (2006). *Case studies in organizational communication: Ethical perspectives and practices.* Thousand Oaks, CA: Sage.

McCloskey, D. N. (1998). *The rhetoric of economics* (2nd ed.). Madison: University of Wisconsin Press.

Mill, J. S. (2002). Utilitarianism. In *The basic writings of John Stuart Mill* (pp. 233–301). New York: Modern Library. (Original work published 1863)

Mitchell, L. E. (2001). *Corporate irresponsibility: America's newest export.* New Haven, CT: Yale University Press.

New York Times. (2006). *Class matters.* New York, NY: Henry Holt.

Ostas, D. (2001). Deconstructing corporate social responsibility. *American Business Law Journal, 38,* 261–290.

Parker, M., Cheney, G., Fournier, V., & Land, C. (in preparation). *Handbook of alternative organization.*

Perelman, M. (1984). *Classical political economy, primitive accumulation, and the social division of labor.* London: Rowman & Allanheld.

Perelman, M. (1989). Adam Smith and dependent social relations. *History of Political Economy, 21,* 503–520.

Perelman, M. (2006). *Railroading economics: The creation of the free market mythology.* New York: Monthly Labor Review Press.

Perelman, M. (2007). *The confiscation of American prosperity: From right wing extremism and economic ideology to the next great depression.* New York: Palgrave Macmillan.

Perrow, C. (1986). *Complex organizations: A critical essay* (2nd ed.). Detroit: University of Michigan Press.

Polanyi, K. (1944). *The great transformation.* Boston: Rinehart.

Prechel, H. (2000). *Big business and the state: Historical transitions and corporate transformation, 1880s–1990s.* Albany, NY: SUNY Press.

Rawls, J. (1999). *A theory of justice* (Rev. ed.). Cambridge, MA: Harvard University Press. (Original work published 1971)

Ricardo, D. (1919). *Principles of political economy and taxation* (E. C. K. Gonner, Ed.). London: G. Bell. (Original work published 1817)

Rothschild-Whitt, J. (1979). The collectivist organization: An alternative to rational-bureaucratic models. *American Sociological Review, 44*, 509–527.

Satow, V. (1975). Value-rational authority and professional organizations: Weber's missing type. *Administrative Science Quarterly, 20*, 526–531.

Schor, J. B. (1992). *The overworked American: The unexpected decline of leisure.* New York: Harper.

Schor, J. B. (1997). *The overspent American: Why we want what we don't need.* New York: Harper.

Schumpeter, J. A. (1950). *Capitalism, socialism, and democracy.* New York: Harper.

Sennett, R. (1998). *The corrosion of character: The personal consequences of work in the new capitalism.* New York: Norton.

Smith, A. (1976a). *The theory of moral sentiments* (A. L. Macfie & D. D. Raphael, Eds.). Oxford, UK: Oxford University Press. (Original work published 1759)

Smith, A. (1976b). *The wealth of nations* (R. H. Campbell & A. S. Skinner, Eds.). Oxford, UK: Oxford University Press. (Original work published 1776)

Soros, G. (1998). *The crisis in global capitalism.* New York: Public Affairs Press.

Stein, H. (2008). Organizational totalitarianism and the voices of dissent. In S. Banks (Ed.), *Dissent and the failure of leadership* (pp. 73–96). Cheltenham, UK: Edward Elgar.

Stiglitz, J. E. (2002). *Globalization and its discontents.* New York: Norton.

Stohl, M., Stohl, C., & Townsley, N. (2007). A new generation of global corporate social responsibility. In S. May, G. Cheney, & J. Roper (Eds.), *The debate over corporate social responsibility* (pp. 30–44). Oxford, UK: Oxford University Press.

Swanson, J. (2007). The economy and its relation to politics: Robert Dahl, neoclassical economics, and democracy. *Polity, 39*, 208–233.

Tarrow, S. (2005). *The new transnational activism.* Cambridge, UK: Cambridge University Press.

Therborn, G. (1980). *The ideology of power and the power of ideology.* London: Verso.

United Nations. (1948). *The Universal Declaration of Human Rights.* Retrieved from http://www.un.org/Overview/rights.html

Veblen, T. (1899). *Theory of the leisure class: An economic study in the evolution of institutions.* New York: Macmillan.

Weber, M. (1946). *From Max Weber: Essays in sociology* (H. H. Herth & C. Wright Mills, Eds.). New York: Oxford University Press.

Weber, M. (1978). *Economy and society* (Vols. 1 & 2, G. Roth & C. Wittich, Trans.). Berkeley: University of California Press. (Original work published 1956)

Weber, M. (2002). *The Protestant work ethic and the spirit of capitalism.* New York: Routledge. (Original work published 1930)

Werhane, P. C. (1991). *Adam Smith and his legacy for modern capitalism.* New York: Oxford University Press.

Williams, M. (1996). International political economy and global environmental change. In J. Vogler & M. Imber (Eds.), *The environment and international relations* (pp. 44–65). London: Routledge.

Wilson, J. Q. (1974). The politics of regulation. In J. McKie (Ed.), *Social responsibility and the business predicament* (pp. 135–168). Washington, DC: Brookings Institution.

Wolff. R. (2010). Rising income inequality in the U.S.: Divisive, depressing, and dangerous. Retrieved from http://www.rdwolff.com/content/rising-income-inequality-us-divisive-depressing-and-dangerous

Yodanis, C. (2006). A place in town: Doing class in a coffee shop. *Journal of Contemporary Ethnography, 35*, 341–366.

27

The Polyphony of Corporate Social Responsibility

Deconstructing Accountability and Transparency in the Context of Identity and Hypocrisy

Lars Thøger Christensen, Mette Morsing, and Ole Thyssen

Social virtues such as fairness, responsibility, accountability, and community have always informed and shaped human interaction and organization—not least in the area of economic transactions. Over the last few decades, however, significant changes have occurred. Increasingly, the public expects organizations to *explicitly* confirm, demonstrate, and celebrate such virtues as an integral dimension of their business practice. Today, the adherence to social virtues usually takes place under the banner of "corporate social responsibility." Corporate social responsibility refers to activities through which companies contribute to a presumed better society and a cleaner environment by including the public interest into its decision making (see EU's Commission Green Paper, 2001). In the corporate landscape of today, the notion of corporate social responsibility has come to epitomize the growing desire for corporate engagement in social and environmental issues as well as more explicit corporate commitment to questions of ethical concern.

The incorporation of social virtues into the practices of business corporations, however, is less clear-cut than often assumed. As a voluntary and nonstandardized approach to social virtues, corporate social responsibility coexists with other organizational concerns, including economic, legal, and technological considerations. Since these different concerns—or, as we shall call them below, *premises* for decision making—must often be attended to simultaneously, their integration is contextually defined; it cannot be handled in any automatic or technical manner, but must constantly be readdressed and renegotiated. As a consequence, the coexistence of corporate social responsibility with other premises introduces polyphony in organizational decision making. Polyphony, in this context, means that an organization has many premises for its decision making, some imperative and some voluntary.

In spite of these difficulties, the pressure on corporations to demonstrate their responsibility toward society has intensified markedly over the last few years. Under these circumstances, and especially in the wake of the financial crisis, corporate social responsibility is increasingly equated with notions such as *accountability* and *transparency*. The assumption seems to be that true accountability and transparency will reduce or even eliminate the challenges of decisional polyphony and eventually make it possible to assess the right degree of corporate responsibility. We challenge this assumption. Not only because polyphony and ambiguity is inevitable in human communication, but also because the quest for accountability and transparency is bound to fail. In this chapter, we challenge naïve expectations with respect to accountable and transparent organizations in the hope of keeping the debate about business's role in society alive and vibrant.

THE RISE OF CORPORATE SOCIAL RESPONSIBILITY

With the rise of the modern business corporation, social virtues were gradually singled out as explicit areas of managerial as well as political attention and involvement. In the early 19th century, Robert Owen (1813/1972) tried to convince businessmen that fairness and responsibility toward workers were in their own financial interest. Owen managed an experimental spinning mill, New Lanark, where he took care of the workers' whole lives—schools, child labor, homes, infrastructure, leisure activities, and so forth. Paternalistic initiatives such as these were gradually followed by regulatory measures. Toward the end of the 19th century, debates about the effects of business on society as a whole were followed by attempts to regulate corporate practices in areas such as safety, child labor, and concentration of capital (Cheney, Roper, & May, 2007).

According to Marchand (1998), most attempts by business corporations to address ethical issues in the early stages of industrialization were driven by concerns about corporate legitimacy. Realizing that their moral respectability in the eyes of the public was at issue—especially as they grew bigger, accumulated more capital, expanded their social, political, and economic influence, and exhibited their wealth—major business corporations began initiating "welfare programs," addressing dimensions such as employee representation, education, and recreation. In the hope of bolstering their authority and legitimacy in society, major corporations simultaneously began depicting themselves as social institutions with public responsibilities and aspirations beyond their commercial activities. Through extensive PR efforts, corporations sought to demonstrate what Marchand (1998, p. 15) calls a "compassionate concern" for their employees. Although some workers regarded corporate welfare activities as shallow promotion, such activities continued as part of the quest for a more respected corporate personality.

Corporate initiatives inevitably shaped public and political expectations with respect to corporate responsibility and paved the way for more sophisticated initiatives in that arena. Simultaneously, public debate about the social responsibilities of business corporations intensified, especially after World War II. Some scholars—most notably economist and Nobel Prize winner Milton Friedman (2008)—fervently argued against *social* responsibilities of corporations, insisting that business only has one responsibility, to increase its profits. Other scholars claimed that corporations face a broader range of stakeholders (for example, environmental groups, customers, citizens, communities, etc.) whose interests they need to respect and respond to (Freeman, 1984; Post, Preston, & Sachs, 2002).

Although this debate is not yet settled, the notion of corporate social responsibility has gradually caught on as an official descriptor of applied business ethics. During the last decades, a number of prominent scandals, boycotts, and other types of clashes between large corporations and their stakeholders (e.g., the Brent Spar incident involving Royal Dutch Shell and Greenpeace or the Enron and World.com scandals) have reinforced this trend. With the financial crisis of 2008, a broad definition of social responsibility—including concerns about remuneration, labor, and environmental issues—has been accepted and established as an official yardstick for the assessment of ethical corporate behavior in the Western world.

Today, a growing number of social actors—consumers, activists, NGOs, employees, politicians, and journalists—expect corporations to demonstrate their social responsibility on an ongoing basis, both upstream and downstream in the value chain. For example, selection and control of suppliers involve extensive ethical scrutiny. And corporate social responsibilities toward end-users are given unprecedented attention. While there is no guarantee that such activities will fundamentally change the ethical composition of contemporary organizations, the notion of corporate social responsibility has institutionalized the ideal of an ethically alert organization able to balance its financial interests with its concerns for society as a whole.

With the institutionalization of corporate social responsibility, it is increasingly argued that such activities are good not only for society but also for business itself—"the business case" (Epstein & Roy, 2003; Smith, 1993). Most prominently, Harvard professor Michael Porter, a former CSR skeptic, has claimed that "CSR pays off" (Porter & Kramer, 2006). The demand for corporate social responsibility among consumers, Porter points out, represents a potential for growth and product development, which companies need to explore and take advantage of.

Interestingly, the "business-case" perspective of Porter and Kramer does not imply that companies take an ethical position of their own. In *their* rendition, corporate social responsibility is not an independent premise for corporate decision making, but yet another economic criterion, a dependent variable. Corporate social responsibility is a question of market adaptation, not an ethical issue. It is therefore tempting to suggest that Porter and Kramer's position simply is a variety of Friedman's more direct refusal of corporate social responsibility. In fact, Porter and Kramer argue that the most important thing a company can do for society "is to contribute to a prosperous economy" (Porter & Kramer, 2006, p. 91). Yet, such a conclusion—taking Porter and Kramer as proponents of the view that only money counts—misses an important point: even if a corporate social responsibility program is driven by a desire to adapt to new market conditions, it may simultaneously represent a serious attempt to build a visionary corporate identity. As we shall argue in the remainder of this chapter, a continuous development of corporate social responsibility and other types of business ethics is dependent on multiple perspectives, approaches, and voices able to keep the field open and vibrant. Whether corporate social responsibility is taken as an independent premise of decision making or not is an empirical matter. It cannot be decided in the abstract.

ORGANIZATIONS AS SYSTEMS OF COMMUNICATION

In discussing corporate social responsibility, our point of departure is systems theory according to which organizations are *autopoietic systems of communication*. Communication, in this view, is not something an organization does once in a while, in between other important activities, but is constitutive of all organizational life and sense making.

The theory of autopoiesis was originally formulated by Chilean biologists Maturana and Varela (1980). According to them, all living systems are autopoietic. They are not made of pre-existing elements, but create and recreate themselves through operations in self-defined domains. Because the elements of living systems are transitory, new elements must continually be supplied and added. To maintain their identity, living systems must define and nurture a sharp boundary vis-à-vis the environment. All their operations are internal because they cannot mingle with the environment without losing their identity. Internally they must in some way map their external world.

Transferring the theory of autopoiesis to the field of sociology, Luhmann (1990, 1995, 2000) claims that the elements of a social system are communications. Communications, according to Luhmann, are created and linked in self-referential operations that maintain both the distinctiveness and the continuation of the system. Here, we restrict our discussion to the social system called "organization." While an organization, according to Luhmann, is the collective sum of all communications taking place within its contextual framework, it is basically structured around two dimensions: *membership* and *decisions*. On the one hand, an organization must be able to distinguish between itself and the environment, especially between members and nonmembers. On the other hand, it must be able to keep itself in an ongoing movement by organizing its communications around decisions—a movement, which at once includes and excludes alternatives. An organization, in other words, must be able to construct and reconstruct itself using passing communications as its raw material. In its flow of communication, thus, a self-referring chain of decisions is used to organize and move the organization forward.

To claim that an organization is defined and constituted by communication does not imply ignorance of materiality, including such things as resources, geography, architecture, technology, and other material conditions and consequences of organizational life. Rather, conceptualizing organizations as systems of communication means to stress the fact that the social and organizational *significance* of such materiality is produced through communication. "Material conditions," of whatever nature they may be, acquire their meaning only through the labeling, distinctions, and perspectives offered by communication.

If we accept the thesis that communication is the very stuff organizations are made of, we need to reconsider our understanding of corporate ethics and the role communication might play in fostering socially responsible behavior. In particular, we need to be sensitive to the significance of *differences* between types of corporate communication and to the possibility that such differences may generate organizational change. Conventional notions of ethics—especially in the context of organizations—maintain a sharp distinction between communication and action. If an organization, however, is a system of communication, it is not possible to distinguish in a meaningful way between what it says and what it does. According to (Luhmann, 1995), only communications are purely social; actions are not. Moreover, actions are only *organizational* actions when integrated and described in communicative terms.

Communication and action are intimately linked in all processes of organizing, because saying is doing and because actions "speak." As Austin (1962) pointed out, it is possible to "do things with words." The social identity of actions, in other words, is inevitably defined by communication. Moreover, conflicts between communication and action need to be communicated in order to be operative. Thus, *talking* about words and actions, and arguing that they are in conflict, is to communicate about two different modes of communication. This has interesting implications for conventional notions of accountability and transparency and, by extension, for our understanding of corporate social responsibility as a communicative practice with ethical implications.

CSR AS ASPIRATIONAL COMMUNICATION

As organizations enter the scene of social responsibility, they face a growing number of critical voices claiming that their engagements in that arena are merely masquerades designed to deflect criticism and give the false impression that they have nothing to hide. From the political left, represented for example by the antiglobalist movement, as well as from the neoliberal right, corporations are accused of engaging in CSR activities simply to *appear* socially responsible; that is, without changing their behaviors fundamentally.

Ironically, such critiques have made corporations even more concerned about their appearance in the eyes of their stakeholders. As a consequence, corporate social responsibility is increasingly associated with professional communication. While corporations invest huge sums of money in telling about their social deeds on web sites and in corporate CSR reports (see Kolk & Levy, 2001; Morsing & Oswald, 2009; Porter & Kramer, 2006), for example, their engagements in social responsibility programs are increasingly denounced for being *merely communication*. For example, in 2005 *The Economist* stated:

> Under pressure, big multinationals ask their critics to judge them by CSR criteria, and then, as the critics charge, mostly fail to follow through. Their efforts may be enough to convince the public that what they see is pretty, and in many cases this may be all they ever intended to achieve. But by and large CSR is at best a gloss on capitalism, not the deep systematic reform that its champions deem desirable. (Crook, 2005, p. 2)

Such a view of communication is not restricted to the field of corporate social responsibility, but shapes most commonsense notions of business ethics. Ethical organizations, according to such a view, aim for and perhaps succeed in establishing consistency if not identity between words and actions, ideals and practices (Christensen & Langer, 2009). Unethical organizations, on the other hand, maintain loose couplings between the two, thereby fostering pretense and hypocrisy. The philosophy behind this distinction is the principle that "actions speak louder than words." This is a basic assumption behind the accountability research which we will return to later.

Communication, in this view, is usually the culprit. Unethical behavior resides in systematic and deliberate attempts to conceal corporate actions behind misleading messages and self-descriptions. Such ethical charge is doubled: not only are the actions bad, but the organization has explicitly promised to be good. The ideal of corporate social responsibility proceeds from the same split between words and actions: corporate social responsibility, we are told again and again, means *doing* something good to society, not just talking about it (Boatright, 2000). The derogatory notions of "green washing," "blue washing," or "window dressing" bear witness to this fundamental distrust in corporate messages as well as to our propensity to see communication as something external to corporate practices.

Contemporary notions of business ethics, in other words, operate with what Smith (1993) calls a "container metaphor" of organizational communication according to which organizations *produce* communication, not as their general way of being or existence but as something distinct and separate from their organizing practices. Against this container perspective, Taylor and van Every (2000) argue that "it is equally true to say that organizations emerge in communication" (p. 4). *Communication* and *organization*, they claim, are *equivalent* terms. This is not to suggest a simple one-to-one correspondence between what an organization says and what it is. Obviously, an organization that describes itself as a responsible corporate citizen does not emerge as such simply by talking this way. What the perspective implies is that the ways organizations talk about themselves and their communication practices are not neutral undertakings, but constitutive activities that contribute to the continuous enactment of organizational reality (Weick, 1979). Inspired by phenomenology, speech action theory, and conversational analysis, Taylor and van Every show how an organization comes into being through the ways its leaders and members speak about and account for its actions and activities.

If communication is the "essential modality" (Taylor & van Every, 2000) for organizational life, we should not disregard *aspirational talk*, as we often find in programs of corporate social responsibility, as something superficial or detached from organizational practice. Talking about actions is talking about communication, and vice versa. Talk about plans and intentions with respect to corporate social responsibility *is* action just as actions in these areas simultaneously speak. Managerial action needs to be talked about, internally or in public, in order to become part of society. Even when corporate ambitions to do good vis-à-vis society do not reflect managerial action, talk about such ambitions provides articulations of ideals, beliefs, values, and frameworks for decisions—in other words, *raw material for constructing the organization.*

ACCOUNTABILITY, TRANSPARENCY, AND THE MODERNIST MINDSET

In order to earn the patronage of its stakeholders, a responsible organization must *demonstrate* on an ongoing basis that it is "doing the right thing" (Zadek, Pruzan, & Evans, 1997), in other words, that it is *accountable.* While corporate social responsibility activities in principle extend far beyond corporate messaging, in practice they are often equated with procedures through which organizations signal and verify their accountability to society. Power (1997) eloquently refers to the production of such signals as "rituals of verification." Among such rituals, reporting is the most notable, institutionalized, for example, by the UN Global Compact and the Global Reporting Initiative (Henriques, 2007).

Accountability means, as the word suggests, *the ability to account*—for one's actions, ideals, motives, and intentions. In conventional understandings, which we will challenge below, this ability hinges on competences such as seeing, understanding, and explaining. For many years, organizational accountability was practised with only one stakeholder in mind: the shareholder. Regulation and accounting systems have professionalized this activity, and relatively standardized systems have made possible comparisons across years and organizations. Only recently have organizations been encouraged to demonstrate that they are *socially* accountable as well. In 2008 the Danish government made it compulsory by legislation for large companies to annually document their corporate social responsibilities, and The Confederation of British Industry states in a direct fashion how they see corporate social responsibility as a driver for organizations to document their responsibilities toward society:

> CSR requires companies to acknowledge that they should be publicly accountable not only for their financial performance but also for their social and environmental record…CSR encompasses the extent to which companies should promote human rights, democracy, community improvement and sustainable development objectives throughout the world. (*Confederation of British Industry*, 2001, cited in Blowfield & Murray, 2008, p. 13)

In the absence of global standards in the CSR area, much attention is given to the content, production, and completeness of nonfinancial accounts: do they cover the vital issues of the corporate CSR engagement? Are the numbers, figures, and accounts to be trusted? Does the company actually do what it says (Adams & Evans 2004; Livesey & Kearins, 2002; Zadek et al., 1997)? The main concern is that individual organizations are able to decide independently what exactly to report, how to measure social performance, and how to verify and audit the measurements. Still, such voluntary reports play a significant role in corporate self-presentations and claims about accountability. Gradually, however, corporate accountability has become a more structured practice, employing certified tools, standards, and techniques, through which organizations demonstrate their social and environmental engagement (Adams & Evans, 2004). The practice includes codes of conduct, ethical accounting statements, social and environmental reports, and other types of nonfinancial documentation (Adams, 2002). And, to document CSR engagements, the nonfinancial accounting statement has become an institutionalized means embedded in an emerging industry of expert consultants guiding, assessing, and endorsing the processes as well as their results (Crane & Matten, 2007).

Behind the notion of accountability we find the assumption that social actors (persons, organizations, institutions, etc.) are *accessible* to themselves and others; that is, visible, intelligible, and capable of being described accurately in a language that can be meaningfully shared. Accountability, in this rendition, presupposes a high degree of *(self)-transparency* and is, in practice, often operationalized as such (Christensen, Morsing, & Cheney, 2008). Consequently, transparency is one of the most salient issues of contemporary organizations. Although the confidence in big business has been questioned and examined many times during the 20th century (Argenti, 1998; Marchand, 1998), today organizations are exposed even more vehemently to external criticism and assessment. Given the growing attention to corporate business practices, it is not surprising that organizations feel more exposed and transparent than ever before. They are expected to share information with the public on their social and environmental initiatives to improve society, and while this is still largely a voluntary process, there is a growing trend toward legislative involvement and regulation. Given these trends, it may be argued that transparency is becoming one of the most important "account technologies" of our times (Christensen & Cheney, 2009).

Although the notion of transparency epistemologically speaking suggests an ability to see *through* something, in the context of corporate communication it usually implies openness, communication, and accountability and thus easy access to information about all organizational matters (Christensen, 2002). These dimensions are evident in most contemporary understandings. While the European Ombudsman, for example, describes transparency as decision-making processes that are "understandable and open" (Lamming, Caldwell, & Harrison, 2004, p. 299), Williams (2005) defines transparency "as the extent to which the organization provides relevant, timely, and reliable information, in written and verbal form, to investors, regulators, and market intermediaries" (p. 361). In a similar manner Millar, Eldiomaty, Hilton, and Chong (2005) define "institutional transparency" as "the extent to which there is available clear, accurate information, formal and informal, covering practices related to capital markets, including the legal and juridical system, the government's macroeconomic and fiscal policies, accounting norms and practices (including corporate governance and the release of information), ethics, corruption, and regulations, customs and habits compatible with the norms of society" (p. 166). Rawlins (2009) incorporates these dimensions of transparency in the following comprehensive definition:

> Transparency is the deliberate attempt to make available all legally releasable information—whether positive or negative in nature—in a manner that is accurate, timely, balanced and unequivocal, for the purpose of enhancing the reasoning ability of publics and holding organizations accountable for their actions, policies, and practices…to be transparent, organizations should voluntarily share information that is inclusive, auditable (verifiable), complete, relevant, accurate, neutral, comparable, clear, timely, accessible, reliable, honest, and holds the organization accountable. (Rawlins, 2009, pp. 75, 79)

Conventional understandings of accountability, thus, are founded in a modernist epistemology according to which reality is accessible behind its fancy facades and seductive appearances and can be uncovered through a general availability of information. According to this perspective, information reduces opacity and complexity, increases knowledge, and helps diminish the potential for superstition, hypocrisy, corruption, and other types of corporate or institutional evil. Modernity represents what Vattimo (1992) calls the utopian ideal of absolute (self)-transparency—an ideal reflected in positive science and notions of open and unrestricted exchange of information. As Vattimo argues, however, the ideal of (self)-transparency is beyond reach. While the ubiquity of new information technologies suggests that (self)-transparency is possible, in practice the opposite has proved to be the case: increased complexity created by an overload of information. To make the growing amounts of information manageable, complexity needs to be reduced.

And since this can be done in numerous ways, the notion of one single perspective or reality is impossible to sustain (Luhmann 1995; Lyotard, 1984).

Since accountability and transparency have become powerful signifiers of corporate social responsibility, they call for critical reflection able to confront these revered terms with a more sophisticated understanding of communication. As we shall argue in the following section, our understanding of an organization as a system of communication adds further challenges to conventional notions of corporate accountability and transparency.

ORGANIZATIONAL "WHOLENESS" AND THE LIMITS OF OBSERVATION

An important implication of defining an organization as a system of communication is that organizations are *invisible* and only approachable through communicative action (Thyssen, 2005). Although communication has *understanding* as an indispensible element, understanding can only be verified though additional communication.

As an organization cannot be seen, it must be inferred through the use of selective signifiers taken to represent the organization, that is, be *present* on its behalf. Moreover, since we only have partial access to the organization through such signifiers (Christensen & Askegaard, 2001), communicative "tricks" must be used in order to talk about the organization as a whole. Among such tricks we find *the name*, which creates the illusion of access to the organization in its entirety, its past, present, and future. Another trick is the notion of *management*, a part of the organization appointed to reflect and act on behalf of the organization as a whole. The manager represents the organization, that is, is present on its behalf. The notion of "wholeness," however, is merely one local representation among other possible local representations (Andersen, 2003). Epistemologically speaking, top management is only a "part" that aspires to observe, capture, and represent the entire organization. In contrast to other parts, however, top management has the power to claim that it represents the vision of the whole, no matter how limited or provincial its perspective might be.

As a logical consequence, the idea of corporate transparency becomes difficult to uphold. This is true for both theoretical and practical reasons. While Simon (1997) reminded us of our limited capacity to handle information, the systemic perspective of Luhmann presented above implies that we cannot observe the total sum of all communications, no matter how much information we are able to collect, process, and store. In practice, an organization can only be observed partially and selectively by making, on the one hand, a *distinction* between relevant and irrelevant, and on the other hand, by observing from a specific *perspective*. Any observer, in other words, must reduce the complexity of the organization by creating an image of it. Since there is no established consensus about which distinction to use in order to observe an organization—and conflicting views as to what is central and peripheral, important and unimportant—the notion of what the organization "is" remains unclear and uncertain.

Following these comments, we have to ask ourselves how an organization may be transparent if it cannot be observed as one unit and if conflicting views exist as to what is central and peripheral. One answer may be that there is only rhetorical access to the unity of an organization (Luhmann, 2000). The organization as a unified and clear-cut entity is a semantic construct—a trick.

The constructed nature of organizational reality becomes even more evident when we consider the *topic*s that are subject to requests for transparency. Obviously, not everything can be observed and as such become transparent, in terms of being visible, to the organization's environment. Moreover, trivial issues are usually ignored. Requests for transparency, for example, are rarely directed toward issues like the color of the canteen furniture or the number of daily telephone calls. The topics of interest when it comes to organizational transparency are usually issues considered critical in a given cultural and political context, that is, issues that are potentially embarrassing or even scandalous. This, of course, is the very reason why transparency is claimed: "We have nothing hideous to hide." Since we cannot observe everything, the call for transparency is focused on potentially critical dimensions of organizational behavior—and typically on arenas where the organization may have an interest in *hiding* something. To disclose and to conceal, thus, are mirror images of each other.

Observation is selection, and selection implies contingency because something else might have been selected instead. To observe, thus, is not simply to see "what's there." Observing implies selecting a perspective and constructing a unity of attention. However, due to the contingency of construction, the claim of presenting a true picture of an organization is inevitably met with suspicion: what is concealed behind what is made visible? Clearly, processes of selection *may* be nonstrategic. However, in this context of communication ethics it is more interesting and relevant to focus on situations where this is not the case. As we shall see in the following, presenting a picture of an organization is a manner of controlling not just what can be seen, but also what cannot be seen. Claims of transparency, thus, may be strategic attempts to cover embarrassing facts.

Obviously, organizations do not decide themselves exactly how they are seen by others. Communicatively speaking, what an organization "is" depends on how it is described, Descriptions, however, evolve over time and involve many different stakeholders. Self-descriptions normally differ from external descriptions. Looking more specifically at the issue of corporate social responsibility, the evolutionary scheme of variation, selection, and retention implies that many new descriptions are proposed, few are selected, and even fewer are retained and achieve a relative stability (Luhmann, 1995). As long as the content of accountability practices is voluntary, the mechanisms of variation, selection, and retention are not well defined or authorized. Even if an organization chooses to be transparent on critical and hence interesting issues, the organization cannot itself decide where the request for transparency emerges. The selection of criteria of relevance and interest with respect to transparency is negotiated on an ongoing basis between organizations, political institutions, and mass media. In this process, the general public usually plays a passive role—either because it is not interested in the matter altogether or because it is unable to observe and control what organizations claim about themselves. As Henriques (2007) points out, most self-descriptions, no matter how technically accurate they may or may not be, are inaccessible to the average stakeholder. He or she has no direct knowledge of the organizations, but has to rely on mass media, which present simplified descriptions for nonprofessionals. Most audiences, therefore, lack the resources and expert knowledge needed to match corporate initiatives in the area of professional information management (Heald, 2006; O'Neill, 2006). And although journalists and the mass media claim to represent the truth, they can hardly be trusted themselves. Mass media must mediate between the business world and the public, focusing on what is either new-and-interesting or new-and-scandalous. So the problem of estimating whether a "true picture" is really accurate is doubled. To the suspicion against the organization is added the suspicion against the mass media. And behind this lurks the even more complex question: what is "truth" in a world of many interest groups, subcultures, and political factions?

TRANSPARENCY AS CORPORATE IDEALIZATIONS

Organizational self-descriptions are usually administered by corporate managers, acting on behalf of the organization. When a manager communicates about "his" or "her" organization, the task is not simply to inform but also to *motivate* (Thyssen, 2003). Managerial communication is a positive genre in the sense that the task is not to tell the truth, the whole truth, and nothing but the truth, but to present the organization in a favorable light vis-à-vis shareholders, employees, customers, and the general public. A manager, in other words, is not a scientist informing us about the state of the organization, but a motivator telling us what can be *made* true (Weick, 1995).

This observation has several important implications: First, it implies that while the *aspirational reality* of the manager is described as if it is already realized, inconvenient information or information that contradicts this reality is silenced. Second, managers are encouraged to practice hypocrisy not only as a convenient solution but as a duty (Brunsson, 2003a). To tell the whole truth may harm the organization and demotivate stakeholders. These points will be elaborated below.

The managerial task is not to represent "reality." Not only is reality incomprehensible; unconsidered veracity may also be self-destructive. In the current legal environment, for example, the legal consequences of admitting "negative impacts" of one's products or actions are difficult to predict (Fung, Graham, & Weil, 2007). More importantly, a truthful description of reality may prevent a better reality becoming true. An organization normally overestimates its importance and regards its own perspective as self-evident. It takes pleasure, and finds motivation in invoking appealing fictions that compensate for the inaccessibility of reality. Without such fictions, an organization becomes dull and alienated. When an organization describes itself, it not only confirms its identity as it "is," but simultaneously seeks to announce its ideal self-image to the environment. For such an announcement to do more than simply salute the triumphs of the past it needs to hold an element of futuristic aspiration, belief, and hope. A *difference*, in other words, must be created between what the organization is now and what it aspires to be, so that management may be seen as a "process of minimizing differences" (Luhmann 1998, p. 106). Used with caution, such differences can help stimulate and generate change in the interest of both organizations and society (Christensen & Langer, 2009; Thyssen, 2009).

Interestingly, such announcements are often made as if no difference exists: the gap between present and future is made invisible in order to impress and motivate employees and external stakeholders. Self-descriptions, thus, are used by organizations as devices of both autocommunication (Broms & Gahmberg, 1983; Christensen, 1997) and self-seduction (Christensen & Cheney, 2000). In such processes, accuracy and consistency are not the primary drivers. Just like the messages we deliberately convey about ourselves to significant others, corporate messages (advertising, corporate values, mission statements, CSR programmes, etc.) are not perfect mirrors of reality. Rather, they are stories of hopes, dreams, and visions of corporate actors. Often they make use of standardized labels, repetitions, metaphors, and trivialities to eliminate doubt. They create a "true appearance of unambiguity" (Luhmann, 2000, p. 191), which is maintained officially even though insiders treat it with irony or scorn. Rhetoric in this context is not merely communicative tricks, but enables an organization to get access to itself in a simplified form.

In creating such idealizations, the intention of organizations is not necessarily to lie, but to motivate itself to become better. The important distinction, in other words, is not true-false, but real-unreal—with the important addition that what is by now unreal could and *should* be made real in the future. Idealized constructions of corporate reality must be accepted as a particular *genre*, and managers are often encouraged to create illusions. Idealized organizational self-descriptions, thus, are usually tolerated—sometimes even significant deviations from the truth. But this acceptance is not given unconditionally: it must be visible that the motive is not to conceal unpleasant truths, but to reduce the difference between the current and the aspirational reality (Luhmann, 1998; Thyssen, 2003). A manager, thus, is confronted with a double and self-contradictory set of expectations: he or she must at the same time be on earth and in heaven.

The gap between current and aspirational reality therefore is a paradoxical resource: it must simultaneously be reduced and expanded (Thyssen, 2009). The gap motivates by showing that while the organization is not perfect it might come closer to perfection. Without a gap, which includes a vision of a possible future, organizational dynamics are impossible. The idea, thus, is not to reach perfection once and for all, but to keep the difference between real and unreal open as a motive for a permanent effort (Christensen & Langer, 2009).

Livesey and Graham (2007) provide an interesting illustration of this point. In their in-depth study of the Royal Dutch/Shell Group, they show that the talk of large corporations has the potential to transform the perceptions and the practices of social actors, including the organizations themselves. More specifically, their study illustrates how eco-talk emerged in the organization and how this talk gradually became a creative force in shaping the corporation's renewed identity. Instead of seeing eco-talk and corporate initiatives in the area of sustainable development, like many critics would do, as "cheap" public relations maneuvers, the study by Livesey and Graham focuses on the performative, pragmatic dimensions of language and communication:

> Corporate eco-talk participates in (re)creating the firm and (re)constructing its relationship to nature, while opening up novel possibilities of understanding and action at the societal level. (Livesey & Graham, 2007, p. 336)

Based on a thorough examination of selected texts by Shell and its critics, Livesey and Graham illustrated the transformation of Shell's identity toward more sustainable practices. Simultaneously, they show how its new eco-talk at once reflected and shaped the understandings of environmental responsibility in society at large. If this picture of how communication potentially shapes and transforms corporate behavior has any relevance beyond the case of Shell, we need to ask ourselves how much latitude are we willing to grant organizations in experimenting with new ways of talking about their ideas, values, and plans.

Given the *transformative potential* of differences between organizational reality and aspirational self-descriptions, any organization should *nurse* the distinction between real and unreal and avoid dissolving it, *even* if its claims about its CSR engagements are produced without the ambition of being fulfilled. While the maintenance of such differences is usually seen as a sign of insincerity and cynicism, and thus taken to represent unethical behavior, we shall argue below that such behavior is inevitable in complex environments presenting imperative but contradictory demands.

THE INEVITABLE HYPOCRISY

Corporate social responsibility is part of the idealized self-description of many organizations. Together with accountability and transparency it represents values that organizations pledge to fulfil. At the same time organizations have to fulfil other values of an economic, technical, and legal nature. When organizations are faced with conflicting demands, which is often the case in complex environments, they resort to *hypocrisy*, meaning that their words, decisions, and other types of actions are separated (Brunsson, 2003b, p. xii; Luhmann, 2000; March, 1988). In the following section we explore the phenomenon of organizational hypocrisy and argue that the growing demand for corporate social responsibility is likely to force organizations into such behavior.

According to Brunsson, conflicting demands may be divided into two groups. First, the organization must, as we have seen, present an idealized picture of itself in the shape of an image that can motivate internally as well as externally while at the same time accepting less than perfect contingencies and failures of real life. Organizations cannot disclose all the carelessness, contingency, ambiguity, incompetence, indecision, and devious compromises which are part of organizational life. While an organization, of course, must relate to reality, it must simultaneously create a new and intriguing reality that appeals to all its members. It has to "invoke a tempting image of its present state, but also [to] recount of its heroic past and brilliant future" (Thyssen, 2003, p. 166).

Second, organizations must not only measure up to the "soft" and rather vague values of corporate social responsibility and ethics, but also to the "hard" values of economics, technology, and law. A tempting solution to this problem is to address different audiences in different ways, using differentiated messages and rhetoric to give each audience the impression that its most favored values are dealt with by the organization. According to Cicero, the first task of an orator is to know the audience's idea of happiness, so that he can make it "attentive, receptive and well-disposed" (Cicero, 86–83 BC/1989, p. 13). In this manner, for example, organizations may separate the CSR department from the daily operations, so that the "soft" and the "hard" language do not interfere. Also, organizations may engage in corporate social responsibility activities in order to create a public image and an excuse for *not* doing anything serious and substantial on this arena. Often described as "window dressing," "green washing," or "blue washing," such practices are exposed on an almost daily basis by journalists, activists, and other critics, thus reminding corporations that hypocrisy eventually will be revealed.

Yet, even if organizations intentionally are acting hypocritically, they cannot present themselves as such. First, because hypocrisy is not a socially accepted behavior and second, because admitting hypocrisy is self-defeating: to admit hypocrisy is *not* to be hypocritical. Neither can organizations publicly discuss the gap between their image and their daily practices, since that would disclose the image of the organization as an artificial construct and hence weaken its credibility.

Consequently, organizations need to handle truth in a strategic manner. In order to earn a "license to operate," that is, to be perceived as a legitimate societal actor, an organization must demonstrate that it is accountable. But if it is impossible for an organization to be accountable on all expected dimensions, or even to communicate the inevitable compromises that are made, it must *pretend*, that is, operate with differences between its front stage and its backstage. Machiavelli claimed that a prince—that is, a manager—must be able to create illusions and be "a great liar and hypocrite" (Machiavelli, 1985).

At this point, it is important to distinguish between two kinds of hypocrisy. On the one hand, an organization may be involved in direct fraud, for example postulating something which it knows to be untrue. Sometimes lies are trivial and relate to insignificant matters. But as showed earlier, interesting lies usually have to do with behavior known to be unacceptable. We refer to a statement as a lie when the liar is well aware that he or she is concealing something important, which would make a difference to the public. On the other hand, and as we have argued above, an organization can act hypocritically in order to motivate. The two types of hypocrisy have very different effects: whether it takes the form of fraud or window dressing, hypocrisy is bound to create cynicism. In the shape of a visionary picture, hypocrisy may well stimulate motivation. *In practice, however, it is often difficult, even impossible, to distinguish between the two.* The difference is rhetorical, and whether hypocrisy creates motivation or cynicism is an empirical question, depending on so many contingencies that no purely theoretical answer is possible.

In the current demand for corporate social accountability, organizations have become an object for contemporary society's "inflation of demands" (Thyssen, 2009, p. 33), which is characterized by endless demands for "more" in terms of immaterial values such as, for example, health, equality between sexes, environmental issues, and social responsibility. Irrespective of how much corporate social responsibility is delivered, it is not enough or not good enough. Thus, it is difficult to see how organizations may ever satisfy the continuous demand for social responsibility, which *per se* is an area of imperfection. No organization is, and will never be, one hundred percent socially responsible.

However, as the pressure on organizations to demonstrate their engagement with conflicting ideals and demands is intensifying, it seems more likely we will experience a growing gap between organizational realities and idealized corporate self-descriptions. This in turn may lead to more cynicism than motivation.

THE VALUE OF ORGANIZATIONAL TALK

Hypocrisy is only meaningful if talk and decisions have an *intrinsic value,* that is, if there is a strong public interest not only in what, in the vocabulary of Brunsson, organizations do, but also in what they say and decide (Brunsson, 2003b). Stakeholders demand corporate transparency, and organizations view this demand as a demand for communication, assuming that stakeholders are interested in knowing their values and intentions. When it is argued that saying is often more visible than doing, this only means that two kinds of communications are separated. It is significant that even organizational action must be communicated to the public.

So, corporate communication departments are expanding, and like politics in general, much corporate strategy revolves around talking and presenting decisions to convince and impress a variety of audiences. Publicity is often more important than the product (Brunsson, 2003a), and corporate social responsibility seems to follow that trend. While this trend may produce more hypocrisy, it is simultaneously a precondition for organizational identity and change.

In line with this argument, March (1988) recommends a relatively unrestricted articulation of corporate ideals. Like Brunsson, March does not condone hypocrisy as a strategy, but sees it as an inevitable by-product of all organizing—not least in situations where organizations try to improve their practices. A bad person with good intentions, March argues, *may* be a person who is experimenting with the possibilities of becoming a better person. Consequently, it would be more rational to make room for such experiments than to reject them.

These observations speak in favor of more tolerance when observing and evaluating corporate self-descriptions. Such tolerance allows organizations to discover new solutions that benefit not only themselves but also their environment. Such tolerance, however, is difficult to achieve today, in an era shaped by extreme cases of organizational fraud. In the aftermath of the "corporate meltdown" and the financial crisis of 2008, it is not surprising to find a widespread skepticism toward corporate messages and intensified calls for corporate transparency and consistency. In the context of financial deception, as we saw in the Enron scandal, the call for increased transparency and consistency makes perfect sense.

Nevertheless, such calls ignore the fact that organizations change and potentially improve through communication about values. As we have argued, speech is action, just as our acts simultaneously speak. While this is certainly not to suggest a simple one-to-one correspondence between words and action, it is a reminder that the distinction between words and actions is merely a distinction between two communicational domains, which may or may not be separated. It is also a reminder that communication has "organizing properties" (Cooren, 1999) that inevitably shape and generate organizational reality (see also, Fairhurst & Putnam, 2004). Interestingly, however, when it comes to issues of corporate social responsibility, social critics tend to argue that the relationship between words and actions is one of pretense or deceit (e.g., Peterson & Norton, 2007) and that differences between what organizations say and what they do is a problem that needs to be eliminated.

Consequently, organizations and their managers are increasingly expected to "walk their talk"; that is, to practice what they preach. As a general rule, the "walk-the-talk" recipe provides, as Weick (1995) points out, a sensible buffer against the evils of hypocrisy. However, based on his notion that people and organizations act in order to think, Weick argues that the type of consistency prescribed by the walk-the-talk imperative seriously limits the possibility of discovering new solutions or ideas for which the previous words are inadequate (Weick, 1979). To fully benefit from the creative power of language use, organizations should not construe and implement the walk-the-talk imperative too tightly. Talk is action too and organizations learn from the ways they describe themselves and their surroundings—even when those descriptions are not fully accurate. If society only allows people and organizations to articulate and claim ideals, values, and intentions which they already practice, the creative and transformative power of language is seriously curtailed.

THE ETHICS OF CORPORATE SOCIAL RESPONSIBILITY

The arguments presented in this chapter invite us to reconsider conventional notions of ethics in the area of corporate social responsibility. Obviously corporate social responsibility is related to ethics. Both are about values, defined as standards for acceptable behavior (Parsons, 1951). In an organizational context, however, ethical values usually coexist with other values, especially economic and political ones.

It is often assumed that ethics is singular, in other words that it is possible to talk about ethics as if it has one simple meaning that applies to all situations. Moreover, ethics is usually seen as a solution, not as a problem. But this is an unwarranted simplification. Ethics has many meanings, dependent on culture, subculture, profession, and religion. So how is corporate social responsibility related to ethics?

If we take a quick overlook of classical ethical positions, Aristotle argued that ethics consists in the search for virtue in a social setting, but also that the right ethical solution cannot be calculated in a technical manner. It depends on finding the golden mean between extremes. In this search, the example of "good men" should serve as a guideline (Aristotle 1984). This position seems reasonable in the case of corporate social responsibility. Here, too, extremes must be evaded. On the one hand, there is the extreme of corporate social responsibility devoid of ethics, for example when it is reduced to market adaptation; and on the other hand is the extreme of corporate social responsibility without economy, reducing responsibility to good intentions. Also the stress on concrete examples underlines that what is "acceptable behavior" is dependent on context and culture.

Most well-known ethical positions, however, are unfit as guiding principles for complex systems like organizations. Indeed, the Aristotelian position seems more reasonable than the Kantian ethics of duty, as modern corporations face not only one, but many duties. Under such circumstances, Kant's simple question of whether the rule followed can be generalized does not make much sense (Kant, 1785/1967). Likewise, the ethical calculus of John Stuart Mill must be dismissed, because pains and pleasures cannot be defined in the neutral way, he suggests (Mill, 1881/1962). As we saw when discussing transparency, organizational settings are too complex to allow for simple calculations covering economical, political and ethical factors. Also, the Habermasian idea of an ideal speech situation, depending only on good reasons and excluding power, is less than useful in organizations (Habermas, 1990). First, because organizations are, by definition, decision-making systems and thus cannot dismiss power, and second because what counts as "good reasons" varies depending on which group or club one adheres to. There are no second-order good reasons to decide what is a "good reason" writ large, and more discussion and more information may increase conflict instead of reducing it.

But obviously, Aristotle's perspective is not sufficient for our current purpose. Modern society is not an ancient Greek *polis* with an upper class defining what is right and wrong. Democratic societies have rejected the *truth model*, according to which only one set of values is right. While such a model is sometimes applied in subcultures or clubs, it has no legitimacy in the public sphere of modern society. Here prevails the *democratic model*, according to which many positions have to tolerate each other and engage in an ongoing discussion without finite answers (Thyssen, 2009). In this context, unethical behavior means *not* taking the position of other parties and persons seriously; that is, in not listening to them and not considering them worth talking with. According to (Rorty, 1989), cruelty means being inattentive to what is important to others.

So even if it is often assumed that ethics is a simple question of right and wrong, the inherently dynamic and innovative nature of modern societies stimulates transgressions of former borderlines and invites discussion and production of a variety of acceptable ethical solutions. This means that there is no theoretical solution to ethical conflicts. When we talk about creativity, innovation, and pluralism they are different ways of accepting this claim. Therefore we must move from a philosophical to a sociological perspective. In practice, solutions must be found. Here we will point to three types of resources for finding such temporary solutions to ethical dilemmas. The first resource is the commitment and loyalty by strong stakeholders willing to act on and even suffer for their preferred values. Although such preferred values may be philosophically arbitrary, they are practically effective and any solution must take them into consideration. Second, all events can be described in a variety of ways. In the media, some descriptions will dominate and acquire the status of "the normal description." In this way, not only an empirical but an ethical perspective is stabilized. For example, the attack on the Twin Towers in 2001 was defined as a war against Western societies, not as a crime, hence making it an issue for the army and not an issue for the police. Third, in each community or society there are strong emotional feelings defined as a "public opinion" able to arouse strong reactions to ethical transgressions.

These resources are not eternal and may be influenced and changed over time. Still, at any given moment they form a powerful background for solving ethical dilemmas.

CONCLUSION

Corporate social responsibility activities are simultaneously observed and evaluated from many different angles; for example, an ethical perspective of what is acceptable and not, an economic perspective of what is profitable and not, or a political perspective of what may support or harm a political agenda. Adding to these difficulties, the public facing contemporary organizations knows that these different perspectives coexist and that CSR-related behavior as a consequence *may* not be what it claims or appears to be. Corporate social responsibility, thus, is not simply a matter of practicing ethical values, but an arena of complex and strategic decisions and negotiations where outcomes are inevitably ambiguous. There is no way to make it well-defined and clean.

Therefore, any notion of corporate social responsibility will inevitably provoke suspicion. In the interface between an organization and its publics, including its employees and customers, it is always difficult to determine which motives *really* are at play. In the end, however, we may need to ask whether it is important for us to know if corporate initiatives and practices in the area of corporate social responsibility really are expressions of social *responsibility*. Do we, in other words, have to be Protestants, who insist on the purity of the heart, or should we instead be Catholics who argue that motives are less important than acting well?

From a communication perspective, it is obvious that corporate social responsibility is not a formula of perfection. CSR related practices *may* contribute to a better world, but hardly a perfect one. It is always possible to claim that too little is done, that wrong areas are chosen for attention, or that corporate social responsibility is not what it appears to be. Yet, the battery of possible ways of observing—what we have called *the polyphony of corporate social responsibility*— should not be lamented. While we sympathize with concerns that the notion of corporate social responsibility *may* "lose its cutting edge" when applied to many different types of situations and activities (Cheney, Roper, & May, 2007, p. 3), we hope that this chapter has demonstrated the value of differences and polyphony in the process of developing more responsible types of organizing. Such polyphony places corporate social responsibility in a fruitful arena of many different interests, goals, and voices. Within such an arena, corporate social responsibility *may* become a meeting point for vital societal strategies in creating and facilitating a sphere of discussion, without necessarily producing consensus (Hazen, 1993).

The ambiguous nature of corporate social responsibility and the coexistence of many different perspectives on such activities may come across as a limitation. Yet, such polyphony allows social actors to relate to corporate social responsibility in numerous ways and through many types of activities. As such, corporate social responsibility may become an important *resource of social change*, even through the ethical principles behind are constantly disputed and challenged. From this perspective, the problem is not that corporate social responsibility risks being diluted, irrelevant, or used in disingenuous ways. Rather, due to its ambiguous and nonspecialized nature, corporate social responsibility may attract both interest and funding from many different types of sources. It may also attract a shared concern not just for specialized subsystems, but for society as a whole, even if it is hard to be that optimistic. The present discussion on climate changes has not led to unanimity, even if the climate is a shared concern for all human beings.

REFERENCES

Adams, C. A. (2002). Factors influencing corporate social and ethical reporting: Moving on from extant theories. *Accounting, Auditing and Accountability Journal, 15*(2), 223–250

Adams, C. A. , & Evans, R. (2004, Summer). Accountability, completeness, credibility and the audit expectations gap. *Journal of Corporate Citizenship,* 97–115.

Andersen, N. A. (2003). The undecidability of decision. In T. Bakken & T. Hernes (Eds.), *Autopoietic organization theory* (pp. 235–258). Copenhagen: Copenhagen Business School Press/Abstakt, Liber,

Argenti, P. A. (1998). *Corporate communication* (2nd ed.), Boston, MA: Irwin McGraw-Hill

Aristotle (1984). Nicomachean ethics. In *The complete works of Aristotle* (J. Barnes, Ed.). Princeton, NJ: Princeton University Press

Austin, J. L (1962). *How to do things with words.* Oxford, UK: Oxford University Press.

Boatright, J. R. (2000). *Ethics and the conduct of business* (3rd ed.). Upper Saddle River, NJ: Prentice-Hall

Blowfield, M., & Murray, A. (2008). *Corporate responsibility: A critical introduction.* Oxford, UK: Oxford University Press.

Broms, H., & Gahmberg, H. (1983). Communication to self in organizations and cultures. *Administrative Science Quarterly, 28,* 482–495.

Brunsson, N. (2003a). *The organization of hypocrisy: Talk, decisions and actions in organizations* (2nd ed.). Oslo: Liber.

Brunsson, N. (2003b). Organized hypocrisy. In B. Czarnaiwska & G. Sevón (Eds.), *The northern lights— Organization theory in Scandinavia* (pp. 201–222). Copenhagen, Denmark: Copenhagen Business School Press.

Cheney, G., Roper, J., & May, S. (2007). Overview. In S. May, G. Cheney, & J. Roper (Eds.), *The debate over corporate social responsibility* (pp. 3–12). New York: Oxford University Press

Christensen, L. T. (1997). Marketing as auto-communication. *Consumption, Markets & Culture, 1*, 197–227.

Christensen, L. T. (2002). Corporate communication: The challenge of transparency. *Corporate Communications: An International Journal, 7*(3), 162–168.

Christensen, L. T., & Askegaard, S. (2001). Corporate identity and corporate image revisited. A semiotic perspective. *European Journal of Marketing, 35*(4), 292–315.

Christensen, L. T., & Cheney, G. (2000). Self-absorption and self-seduction in the corporate identity game. In M. Schultz, M. Majken, J. Hatch, & M. H. Larsen (Eds.), *The expressive organization* (pp. 246–270). Oxford, UK: Oxford University Press.

Christensen, L. T., & Cheney, G. (2009, July 2–4). *Transparency as societal accountability: A critical analysis of transparency as a corporate account technology.* Paper presented at The 25th EGOS Colloquium, Barcelona.

Christensen, L. T., & Langer, R (2009). Public relations and the strategic use of transparency: Consistency, hypocrisy and corporate change. In E. Toth & R. L. Heath (Eds.), *Critical and rhetorical approaches to public relations* (pp. 129–153). Hillsdale, NJ: Erlbaum.

Christensen, L. T., Morsing, M., & Cheney, G. (2008). *Corporate communications: Convention, complexity and critique.* London: Sage.

Cicero (86–82 bc/1989). *Ad herennium.* (H. Caplan, Trans.). Cambridge, MA: Harvard University Press

Cooren, F. (1999). *The organizing property of communication.* Amsterdam, the Netherlands: Benjamins.

Commission Green Paper. (2001), *Promoting an European framework for corporate social responsibility.* Retrieved from www.emcc.eurofound.eu.int/content/source/eu02002s.html?p1=topic&p2

Crane, A., & Matten, D. (2007). *Business ethics.* Oxford, UK: Oxford University Press.

Crook, C. (2005, January 22). A survey of corporate social responsibility.*The Economist*, 2.

Epstein, M. J., & Roy, M. (2003). Making the business case for sustainability: Linking social and environmental actions to financial performance. *Journal of Corporate Citizenship, 9*, 79–96.

Fairhurst, G., & Putnam, L. (2004). Organizations as discursive constructions. *Communication Theory, 14*(1), 5–26.

Freeman, R. E. (1984). *Strategic management: A stakeholder approach.* Boston. MA: Pittman.

Friedman, M. (2008). The social responsibility of business is to increase its profits. In A. Crane, D. Matten, & L. J. Spence (Eds.), *Corporate social responsibility. Readings and cases in a global context* (pp. 26-32). London: Routledge.

Fung, A., Graham, M., & Weil, D. (2007). *Full disclosure: The perils and promise of transparency.* Cambridge, UK: Cambridge University Press.

Habermas, J. (1990). *Moral consciousness and communicative action.* Cambridge, UK: Polity Press.

Hazen, M. A. (1993). Towards polyphonic organization. *Journal of Organizational Change Management, 6*(5), 15–26.

Heald, D. (2006). Varieties of transparency. In C. Hood & D. Heald (Eds.), *Transparency: The key to better governance?* (pp. 25–43). Oxford, UK: Oxford University Press.

Henriques, A. (2007). *Corporate truth: The limits to transparency.* London: Earthscan.

Kant, I. (1967). Fundamental principles to the metaphysic of morals. In *Kant's critique of practical reason and other works on the theory of* ethics (pp. 1–84; T. K. Abbott, Trans.). London: Longmans. (Original work published in 1785)

Kolk, A., & Levy, D. (2001). Winds of change: Corporate strategy, climate strategy and oil multinationals. *European Management Journal, 19*(5), 501–509.

Lamming, R., Caldwell, N., & Harrison, D. (2004). Developing the concept of transparency for use in supply relationships. *British Journal of Management, 15*(4), 291–302.

Livesey, S. M., & Graham, J. (2007). Greening of corporations? Eco-talk and the emerging social imagery of sustainable development. In S. May, G. Cheney, & J. Roper (Eds.), *The debate over corporate social responsibility* (pp. 336–350). New York: Oxford University Press.

Livesey, S., & Kearins, K. (2002) Transparent and caring corporations? *Organization & Environment, 15*(3), 233–258.

Luhmann, N. (1990). *Essays on self-reference.* New York: Columbia University Press.

Luhmann, N. (1995). *Social systems.* Stanford, CA: Stanford University Press.

Luhmann, N. (1998). *Observations on modernity.* Stanford, CA: Stanford University Press.

Luhmann, N. (2000), *Organisation und entscheidung.* [Organization and Decision]. Opladen, Germany: Westdeutscher Verlag.

Lyotard, J. F. (1984). *The postmodern condition: A report on knowledge.* Minneapolis: University of Minnesota Press.

Machiavelli, N. (1985). *The prince.* Chicago: Chicago University Press.

March, J. G. (1988). *Decisions and organizations.* Oxford, UK: Basil Blackwell.

Marchand, R. (1998). *Creating the corporate soul: The rise of public relations and corporate imagery in American big business.* Berkeley: University of California Press.

Maturana, H. R., & Varela, F. J. (1980). *Autopoiesis and cognition: The realization of the living.* Dordrecht, the Netherlands: D. Reidel.

Mill, J. S. (1861/1962). *Utilitarianism.* London: Fontana.

Millar, C. C. J. M., Eldiomaty, T., Hilton, B. J., & Chong, C. J. (2005). Corporate governance and institutional strategic transparency in emerging markets. *Journal of Business Ethics, 59*(1/2), 163–174.

Morsing, M., & Oswald, D. (2009). Novo Nordisk A/S: Integrating sustainability into business practice. *Journal of Business Ethics Education, 5,* 137–116.

O'Neill, O. (2006). Transparency and the ethics of communication. In C. Hood & D. Heald (Eds.), *Transparency: The key to better governance?* (pp. 75–90). Oxford, UK: Oxford University Press.

Owen, R. (1972). *A new view of society.* London: Everyman's Library.

Parsons, T. (1951). *The social system.* New York: Free Press.

Peterson, T. Rai, & Norton, T. (2007). Discourses of sustainability in today's public sphere. In S. May, G. Cheney, & J. Roper (Eds.), *The debate over corporate social responsibility* (pp. 351–364). Oxford, UK: Oxford University Press.

Porter, M. E., & Kramer, M. R. (2006). Strategy and society: The link between competitive advantage and corporate social responsibility. *Harvard Business Review, 80*(12), 56–68

Post, J. E., Preston, L. E., & Sauter-Sachs, S. (2002). *Redefining the corporation: Stakeholder management and organizational wealth.* Stanford, CA: Stanford Business Books.

Power, M. K. (1997). *The audit society: Rituals of verification.* Oxford, UK: Oxford University Press.

Rawlins, B. (2009). Give the emperor a mirror: Toward developing a stakeholder measurement of organizational transparency. *Journal of Public Relations Research, 21*(1), 71–99.

Rorty, R. (1989), *Irony, contingency and solidarity,* Cambridge, MA: Harvard University Press.

Simon, H. A. (1997). *Administrative behavior* (50th Anniversary ed.). New York: Free Press.

Smith, R. C. (1993). *Images of organizational communication: Root-metaphors of the organization-communication relation.* Paper presented at the annual meeting of the International Communication Association, Washington, DC.

Taylor, J. R., & E. van Every (2000). *The emergent organization: Communication as its site and surface.* Mahwah, NJ: Erlbaum.

Thyssen, O. (2003). Values—The necessary illusions. In M. Morsing & C. Thyssen (Eds.), *Corporate values and responsibility: The case of Denmark* (pp. 163–178). Copenhagen, Denmark: Samfundslitteratur.

Thyssen, O. (2005). The invisibility of the organization. *Ephemera, 5*(3), 519–536.

Thyssen, O. (2009). *Business ethics and organizational values.* Basingstoke, UK: Palgrave Macmillan.

Vattimo, G. (1992). *The transparent society.* Cambridge, UK: Polity Press.

Weick, K. E. (1979). *The social psychology of organizing.* Reading, MA: Addison-Wesley.

Weick, K. E. (1995). *Sensemaking in organizations,* Thousand Oaks, CA: Sage.

Williams, C. C. (2005). Trust diffusion: The effect of interpersonal trust on structure, function, and organizational transparency. *Business and Society, 44*(3), 357–369.

Zadek, S., Evans, R., & Pruzan, P. (2008). How to do it. In A. Crane, D. Matten, & L. Spence (Eds.), *Corporate social responsibility: Readings and cases in a global context* (pp. 400–415). London: Routledge.

28

When Unreason Masquerades as Reason

Can Law Regulate Trade and Networked Communication Ethically?

Radha D'Souza

PROBLEMATIZING REGULATION, TRADE, AND NETWORKED COMMUNICATION

Typically, critical approaches to ethical issues in trade and networked communication view the ethical dilemmas arising from trade and networked communication through the prism of moral philosophy, and seek solutions to ethical problems by using regulatory mechanisms of law, domestic and international. This approach entails a movement from critical engagement with what *is* to what *ought to be,* using Law as the mechanism to realise what *ought to be.* The *is/ought* axis for examining ethical regulation of networked communication and trade invites us to save communication technology, trade, and ethics by harmonising the three. What if the very natures of communication technologies, trade, and regulation make harmonization impossible? What if their very existence is contingent on disharmony between the three? This essay attempts to bring together meta- and microlevel analyses[1] with a view to going beyond familiar conundrums and interrogate a more fundamental tension that underpins the paradigm crisis of our times: the nature of ontological reality and our discourses about the world.

Ethical problems in trade and networked communication are usually examined within disciplinary enclosures of law, trade, and communication technologies, each with its own normative codes. Each one of these fields forms part of a wider field of theoretical inquiry: the field of regulation forms part of a wider field of law and ethics in legal philosophy; the field of trade is part of a wider field of economics and society in social theory; and communication network is part of a wider field of cybernetics and human life in the philosophy of science. Each of these fields makes assumptions about the other fields. The field of cybernetics and human life in science makes assumptions about the economy of which trade is one part. The field of law makes assumptions about the economy including trade and science and technology, of which cybernetics is a part. The field of economics makes assumptions about law/ethics, science/technology/cybernetics, and human purpose. The consequence of disciplines, each with its distinctive normative codes, and the assumptions one discipline makes about others, is that a disjuncture has developed between theoretical and philosophical inquiries in communication ethics on the one hand and applied communication ethics at the user end, on the other.

At the applied end of the spectrum, communication ethics scholarship focuses on law and policy regarding trade, social norms, and state behaviour such as protecting intellectual property, preventing cyber crime, intelligence gathering for state security and such. The focus of applied communication ethics is therefore on the Internet, the technology that allows computers to communicate with each other; the goal is to regulate their behaviour in ways that are consistent with ethical human conduct (e.g. respect for intellectual property, quality of goods and services, and so forth), in other words, make computers behave with each other and with humans the way humans would behave with each other in their social transactions. More fundamentally, the goal of applied ethics in contemporary times is to keep intact the social architecture of capitalism founded on three institutional pillars: Economy-State-Civil Society, an architecture threatened by cyber technology in new ways.

At the theoretical and philosophical end of the spectrum, writings on cyber society tend to give cyber technologies an autonomous status: some dehistoricise and depoliticise technology, others provide post facto phenomenological rationalisations. For example, Manuel Castells (2001, Ch. 1) acknowledges the history of communication technology, which was nurtured within military organisations for military purposes, but does not think that history has any relevance to its subsequent appropriation by monopolistic corporations for economic purposes. Following phenomenological approaches of Heidegger, Rafael Capurro (2006) argues that if all social phenomena can be reconstructed digitally then it invites us to think about a 'digital ontology'. There is a tendency amongst social theorists to take cyber technology as a given condition of social life today, which it is, but to undertheorise and underemphasise the materiality of the technologies and the institutional contexts that make them possible.

The disjuncture between applied and theoretical approaches to regulation of communication technologies and trade points to epistemological problems about the relations between science and society. The solution is often seen to lie in interdisciplinary approaches (Bauer, 1990; Fuller, 1985; Gasper, 2004; Kellog, 2006). Disciplines are an essential feature of modernist knowledge (Giri, 1998). Disciplines in modernist knowledge carve up ontological reality into discrete parts in ways that render their properties and relations opaque. Of these compartmentalised conceptions of Reality,[2] the divide between Science and Society is foundational to modernity. Interdisciplinary approaches proceed on the assumption that Reality can be reconfigured. Interdisciplinary approaches therefore presume epistemology can rectify Reality. In fact, Reality is ontological, with attributes, properties, and relations that cannot be corrected or altered by epistemology. If anything the paradigm crisis we find ourselves in is symptomatic of the failure of such efforts (Schuurman, 1992). It becomes necessary therefore to begin to reverse the process of knowledge creation so that knowledge production is guided by ontological Reality and not the reverse. Stated simply, it is necessary to understanding the nature of the world, what Reality *is,* so that we can better understand *why* our knowledge provides us with a ruptured view of different aspects of lived experiences, and between theory and practice.

The ramifications of disciplinary knowledge, the disciplinary assumptions about the premises of trade/economy, law/ethics, technology/society, are examined in the sections below along three trajectories. First is the trajectory of human relationship with Nature, the subject matter of Science, a trajectory that has presented us with cybernetics, and with the communication technologies used for trade. This relationship is examined in the second section through the life and work of Norbert Wiener the father of cybernetics and campaigner for ethics in Science. Cyber technologies take ethics beyond norms that govern relations between people to norms that govern relations between humans and machines and between machines.

In a social context where scientific and technological innovations are led by militarism is it possible to exclude its social ramification when considering regulation of the economy? The question brings us to the *second* trajectory: "The Economy" as a distinct social sphere with distinctive institutions that make it a hypostatised entity in capitalist societies. The institutional dimensions of monopoly-finance capitalism take ethics beyond relations between human beings and involve regulating relations between human beings and organisations, and between organisations, issues explored in the third section using the case of INTELSAT. The case invites us to reconsider methodological assumptions in social sciences about recurrence of events and precedents as the basis for evaluative judgments about norms.

The *third* trajectory concerns human purpose entailed in ethical judgments. Because of their specific character, the question that cyber technologies pose for ethics is this: can legal persons like incorporated entities make moral judgments and evaluate human purposes in the same way as natural persons? This question is examined in the fourth section. The three trajectories can be pared down to the relationship between Science and Society. The way that relationship is studied in philosophy and theory is addressed in the fifth section drawing insights from Science, Technology, and Society studies in particular by Bruno Latour, and communication theories by Jürgen Habermas. The sixth section reflects on trade, ethics, and networked technology in the light of the arguments made in the preceding sections.

THE SCIENCE AND TECHNOLOGY TRAJECTORY: SCIENTISTS, SOCIETY, AND SOCIAL CONSCIENCE

When we speak of Science 'doing' something, or 'saying' something what exactly do we mean? Who/what exactly is 'acting', and why? Can we separate Science from the agents that produce scientific knowledge: the scientists? This question is examined by contextualising the life and work of Norbert Wiener (1894–1964) because it provides insights into three interrelated questions relevant to scientific innovations and Society: (1) the organisational context and institutional preconditions for cybernetic technologies; (2) the assumptions that the field of science and technology make about 'The Economy'; (3) the assumptions scientists make about ethics in the public sphere.

Wiener is the father of cybernetics. He founded the discipline of cybernetics and gave it the name, a discipline that forms the scientific and technological grid of the world order that emerged at the end of World War II. Wiener believed it was possible to create human beings mechanically as well as biologically, a belief that has since come true as evidenced by new frontiers in the field of robotics and cloning. Wiener discovered that structures must communicate for change/action to occur, whether those structures are machines, biological beings, social structures, or a combination of these. Communication was the key link in systems of command and control that provide movement and bring change, whether such change and movement is brought by machines, by biological activity, or by social institutions.

Wiener was a prodigy, an embodiment of interdisciplinary studies. He was a mathematician, a physicist, a biologist, linguist, social thinker, engineer, and medical researcher. All of these fields he brought to bear in a new field of study: cybernetics, the science of communication between structures, a field that provides the scientific and technological basis for contemporary Network Society, including satellites, the Internet, robotics, and other technologies (Heims 1989). Wiener's innovations helped improve radar systems for the army and navy, to improve fire control systems, and to enhance the effectiveness of antiaircraft fire. His antiaircraft guided missile systems were put into action during World War II. Wiener's statistical theory of communications put communication engineering on a sound mathematical footing and on the road to the Information Age (Heims, 1989).

Like others of his time, Wiener believed that his contributions to Science would help defeat the evil of fascism and that after its defeat Western democracy would ensure that the American war machine together with its scientific and political apparatuses would be dismantled. That far from being dismantled, the scientific, political, and propaganda arms of the war machine grew and expanded after the defeat of fascism troubled Wiener and made him question the social context of cybernetics which he founded. Worried that his efforts to put the genie of fascism back into the bottle may have released yet another, perhaps bigger genie, out of the bottle, Wiener struggled to find ways of reconciling science and technology with social conscience from the end of World War II to the end of his life in 1964.

Wiener began to examine the economic and organisational context for science and technology more critically. Weiner was very conscious that cybernetic technologies centralised power, and that he may have inadvertently contributed to the centralisation of social and economic power by laying the foundations of 'C-Cube' technologies or systems of command-control-communication. Wiener became very suspicious of research funding by private and public sectors at a time when public and private research partnerships burgeoned and scientific research was taken over by large complex research organisations. He riled against what he called 'gadget worshippers' who loved gadgets because they provide 'presumed objectivity' and a cover for actors to avoid moral responsibility (Wiener, 1964, p. 54). More significantly he argued:

> A goal-seeking mechanism…*must foresee all steps* of the process for which it is designed, instead of exercising a tentative foresight which goes up to a certain point and can be continued from that point on *as new difficulties arise* [emphasis added]. The penalties for errors of foresight, great as they are now, will be enormously increased as automatization comes into its full use. (Wiener, 1964, p. 63)

For ethics to inform the agenda of science, scientists must foresee how their work will be appropriated by social institutions in the present and in the future (Wiener, 1964, p. 81). And further, the problem of adapting the machine to the present conditions by the users is not a problem that can be settled once and for all but must be faced again and again. "We cannot be content to assume the all-wisdom of any single epoch" (Wiener, 1964, p. 83). Because it is impossible to predict future social and normative developments with the exactitude demanded by scientific innovations, Weiner's logical and scientific methods required him to confront the paradox of science in the 20th century: it is the business of science to seek knowledge for its own sake yet science must desist from probing certain types of knowledge on ethical grounds.

The more Weiner became aware of the ramifications of his science the more he clung to human will for answers and riled against social institutions. He riled against the "free enterprise and profit-motive economy" (Wiener, 1964, p. 54). Weiner wrote perceptively: 'As engineering technique becomes more and more able to achieve human purposes, *it must become more and more accustomed to formulate human purposes*' [emphasis added] (Wiener, 1964, p. 64).

Like Wiener, many other eminent scientists, including Albert Einstein and Robert Oppenheimer, recognised the social ramifications of their scientific inventions much later when it was too late to put the genie back into the bottle. How should we see the post facto realisation of scientists' social conscience?

The problematic entailed in cyber communication in physical sciences was posed by the specificities of the social, economic, and institutional context of the 20th century. The institutional context was very different from the 18th and 19th century where state and capitalist enterprises were smaller and their boundaries sharply demarcated. Since the 20th century scientific and technological innovations have occurred within what Eisenhower famously called the "military-industrial complex" (Hooks, 2008). These military-industrial complexes are characterised by large research organisations involving multiple research teams, where public institutions like Universities are mobilised for research programmes funded by the state, and where the knowledge produced by scientists is appropriated by organisations public and private, outside the domain of science and scientists (Ritter & McLauchlan, 2008). During the interwar years scientific institutions and universities promoted interdisciplinary approaches, in particular within U.S. institutions, to promote military capabilities, a trend that has grown ever since (Heims, 1989). These interdisciplinary approaches, including sociology, linguistics, and other disciplines, were instrumental in developing fields like cybernetics and robotics and artificial intelligence. Interdisciplinarity begs the question in that it produces the very scientific and technological context that impels social scientists to seek interdisciplinary solutions.

In a prescient comment on social formations marked by private property, in particular the specific typologies of urban-rural relations, Marx says about Greco-Roman societies:

> War is...the great comprehensive task, the great communal labour which is required either to occupy the objective conditions of being there alive, or to protect and perpetuate the occupation. Hence communities in that *social formation are organized in a warlike way...* [emphasis added]. (Marx, 1857–1858/1973/1930, p. 474)

Ex facie, the emergence of military-industrial complexes, research collaborations for developing dual use technologies that enmesh technological advancement and economic growth (Cowan & Foray, 1995; Kulve & Smit, 2003), and the leading role of militarism in technological developments in contemporary times (Udis, 2008) point to an advanced and sophisticated organisation of contemporary society in 'warlike ways'. It is well known that large dams were pioneered by army engineers, not agriculturists (Teclaff, 1967), the science of dietetics developed during World War I (Hodges, 1993), and something as banal as the introduction of the potato to Europe was necessitated by the Napoleonic wars (Reader, 2009). Yet theoretical developments do not provide adequate conceptual resources and analytical frameworks that can integrate accounts of militarism as the engines for innovations in science and technology in their accounts of economy, society, law, and ethics (Lovering, 1987).

Social theory focuses on one field: militarism, technology, trade, whatever, and attempts to study the relationship of that field to the others. These approaches reify the fields as discrete, and atomise aspects of Reality.[2] Epistemological explanations are invoked to reconstruct what appears as fractured Reality. This epistemological unity does not change the ontological Reality, however. The question remains: how come scientists engaged in scientific research, or dual use innovations, do not see the social ramifications of their work? If, hypothetically speaking, social theory had provided a method, a unified, nondualistic account of science and technology, and society and human well-being, would scientists have innovated technologies like atom bombs or C-Cube communication systems?

"If I knew they were going to do this, I would have become a shoemaker," Einstein lamented after Hiroshima and Nagasaki, an outcome made possible by his quantum theory (McCarthy, 2000). We would be right in assuming therefore that the social theories and philosophical orientations that operate in the field of Science are powerful enough to blindfold scientists as to the social consequences of their scientific innovations. The theories and philosophies must be such that segregates science and society in ways that gives ethics an amorphous place. Do social scientists fare better in dealing with society, the object of their studies?

THE TRAJECTORY OF 'THE ECONOMY': MARKET REGULATION AND COMMUNICATION TECHNOLOGIES

Theoretical critique of quantitative methods, empiricism and positivism, development of qualitative methods, efforts to bridge micro- and macrolevels of inquiries, point to problems of extending methods of Science to the study of Society (Bhaskar, 1989; Porter, 1995; Sayer, 1984). Has the critique contributed to the development of frameworks of analyses and conceptual categories that help us address problems of ethical regulation of markets and economies? The extent to which social theories rely on predictability and recurrence of events in Society comparable to those in experimental science can be seen from its reliance on precedents. Legal regulation, in particular, is premised on the expectation that social behaviour can be regulated through deterrence and rewards. Social theory fails to anticipate or address one-off events that transform a social order. The case of INTELSAT, a one-off event, a case without precedent, and one incapable of becoming a precedent, provides insights into the ways in which technology and economic institutions operate to create the context within which we are required to consider ethical regulation of trade in the wake of new communication technologies. The case invites us to question the assumptions we make about the public sphere and ethical interventions.

INTELSAT was a public international treaty organisation, an intergovernmental legal entity created by the United Nations (UN). INTELSAT was privatised by the U.S. Congress and became a U.S. corporate citizen subject to U.S. laws and U.S. Congress through a legal process that began in July 2001 and was completed in January 2005 (Katkin, 2005, p. 4). How are we to understand this extraordinary development? Can an international organisation, a member of the UN system, be privatised by one state? If it has happened, what can we say about regulatory frameworks in the global economy and the assumptions we make about the scope for ethical interventions?

The story of the privatisation of INTELSAT is a long and complex one spanning the entire post-World War era.[3] Briefly, in 1957 the former USSR launched the first space satellite Sputnik1, an event that triggered a competition for the skies, as part of the Cold War, between the United States and the former USSR. Besides sending its own satellites into space, the United States responded with organisational and legal innovation to limit Soviet influence. The United States formed the Communication Satellite Corporation (COMSAT) under the Communication Satellite Act 1962. The scope of COMSAT was global from the outset. In 1961 the UN passed a resolution stating communication satellites must be used in the service of all humanity and in 1967 adopted the Outer Space Treaty.[4] Following an international conference of states, INTELSAT was created to regulate and oversee satellite communication and ensure all states had fair and equitable access to telecommunication infrastructure at reasonable costs. Like other international economic organisations of the post-World War era, such as the World Bank and the International Monetary Fund, INTELSAT too was based on subscriptions to shares by member states with proportionate voting rights. INTELSAT too became another international economic organisation where policy making was dominated by the largest shareholders, the five Western states that used 90% of the telecommunication infrastructure at that time. Thus, INTELSAT was modelled after other institutions in the world order created at the end of World War II. The end of the Cold War restructured that world order.

The end of the politico-military Cold War and the creation of the World Trade Organisation (WTO) form a single moment of regime change in the post-World War order. From its inception, the WTO's mandate was to replace state regulation with market regulation. State regulation as the legal framework in the post-World War world was necessitated by the breakdown of economic institutions during the World Wars. The package of regulatory tools in market regulation is understood as 'neoliberal reforms'. The WTO's mandate was to promote use of market instruments in relations between states, within states, between states and international organisations, and within UN agencies and international organisations.[5] Thus, regulatory and institutional changes between states and economy were at the heart of WTO's purpose.

From its inception telecommunication privatisation was an important part of the WTO agenda and continues to be so.[6] The militaristic moorings of communication technologies meant in most cases only states had the organisational capacity to host telecommunication technologies. Telecommunication providers were invariably state departments or public undertakings. In the United States alone, due to the military-industrial complex with capacities for dual use technologies and legally entrenched state–corporation relations, private corporations were equipped to step into the vacuum created by the withdrawal of the state from regulation of the telecommunications industry. COMSAT was a state owned corporation, an autonomous legal person with private sector participation. In the United States therefore private corporations had the capacity to manufacture and provide satellite communications more than anywhere else.[7] U.S. telecommunication companies were able to insist that INTELSAT was a monopoly and must be privatised.

Market regulation introduced a market logic in the operation of the privatised INTELSAT. In January 2005 INTELSAT was sold to a consortium of private investment companies for a sum of $US5 billion (Katkin, 2005, p.4). Later that year Intelsat, Inc., now a U.S. company, bought out its main U.S. rival, PanAmSat (Belson, 2005). In 2007, BC Partners a British investment equity company bought controlling stakes in Intelsat, Inc. (*Space Mart,* 2007). A large insurance industry has grown around the satellite markets (AON, 2008; Dinerman 2008a, 2008b). The satellite market has increased as have the numbers of satellites in space (*Space Mart,* 2008). Like all commercial ventures the satellite companies must make profits if they are to survive as a market entity in 'The Economy'.

> To make a profit on an investment that has high technological risk and very high up-front demands, a large market is essential.... It can be easily argued that many space services are 'natural monopolies'.... Arguments that the space sector should be 'competitive' and respond fully to market prices sound persuasive, but fail to recognize the reality that *space economic activity is, at best, the province of a handful of companies and is beholden to large purchases from governments—both factors clearly denying space enterprise from fitting any textbook definition of a price-competitive sector* [emphasis added]. (Hertzfeld, 2007)

A satellite industry newsletter informs us that the markets for broadband and Internet communications have reached saturation, nevertheless:

> Increased governmental involvement and spending in military satellite navigation, and positioning systems, and space exploration are expected to prop up demand patterns in the marketplace. (*Space Mart,* 2008; see also Brown 2008; Dinerman 2008c)

Since the invasion of Iraq, there has been a perceptible and increased privatisation of military operations (Brown, 2008; Hartley, 2004; Matthew, 2004; Molas-Gallari, 2001). Boosting demand through government spending in the housing market or the retail market is one thing, boosting demand for the satellite industry through military spending is quite another. Yet, if the satellite industry collapses, the Information Age collapses taking with it the Network Society.

There is a qualitative difference between technology and economy generally, and the character of satellite technology, in particular for communication ethics. As Dinerman (2008a) puts it:

> This is the critical problem for all these companies, US or foreign: none of them could survive without various kinds of government support. The market for private satellite imagery is much too

small to sustain the number of firms in the business today. This is simply due to the fact that these types of spacecraft are essentially military assets. They may have a few civilian applications— GeoEye's list of markets includes state and local governments, forestry, oil and gas, agriculture, real estate, insurance, utilities, and transportation—but they are essentially as military as a bomber or an aircraft carrier. (p. 2)

Satellite technologies have by their very nature dual-use capacities. As Hertzfeld (2007) says: "…because of the dual-use nature of many space activities, there are regulatory and legal limits on the degree of international trade that can occur in this industry" (p. 212). We have come full circle since Wiener's times. Militarism spawned the communication technologies and provided the means for economic recovery in the post-World War world order. Now 'The Economy' must keep the communication satellites in space by spawning new militarisms. The militarist and organisational dimensions of communication technologies is often overshadowed by the excitement of consumerist possibilities opened up by cyber technologies.

If it is true that the need for certain types of technologies is necessitated by specific geo-historical and institutional contexts, it is equally true that technologies impose a social architecture on society and shape and colour its institutions. C-Cube technologies of command-control-communications impose a command-control social architecture sustained by large organisations, state or corporate, public or private. If cybernetics became possible because of scientific research nurtured by military organisations of the state for the explicit purpose of command and control, then, equally, cyber technologies presuppose the existence of large organisations that need communication systems for command and control, whether military or civilian, state or corporate. The precondition for the appropriation and use of cyber technologies by 'The Economy' therefore, is emergence and existence of monopolistic corporate entities (Fortun & Schweber, 1993). The emergence of this form of organisation in the economy ended the era of industrial capitalism and ushered a new stage of capitalism: the monopoly-finance capitalism stage with distinctive features and institutions. Metaphors of 'globalisation', 'network society', 'global commons', 'borderless world', and such, to speak about trade in the contemporary economy deflect attention from the materiality of the technology and economy, their historical and institutional drivers, and render opaque the ramifications for human purpose entailed in ethics.

Liberal philosophy and theory on which legal regulation is founded presupposes citizenship, where citizens are arbiters of ethics, and are able to intervene effectively with the state on the one hand and with civil society organisations on the other to safeguard and promote human purpose. This assumption has become tenuous in the era of monopolistic organisations and states, not least because of another founding principle in law: the myth of the incorporated person.

The law bestows a 'personality' on corporate entities through a legal fiat and equates them with human beings. By putting natural and incorporated persons on a par the law does two things. It marginalises human agents qua citizens as arbiters of ethical questions. This fudges the nexus between ethical deliberations and human purpose. Second, equalising natural and corporate persons fetishizes notions of property. Cyber technologies exacerbate both these problems in law.

Equating corporate property with individual property, Monsanto or Microsoft with the quarter acre plot on which the person from Minnesota or Melbourne builds her home, alters the meaning of 'home' in the economy. Globalisation further aggravates this contradiction by promoting corporatisation of state entities in ways that blur public/private boundaries (cf. Molas-Gallari, 2001; see also *University of Pennsylvania Law Review*, 1982). A public corporate entity functions in pretty much the same ways as a private corporate entity. The fact that COMSAT was a statutory corporation did not exempt it from the economic logic of the satellite markets that led eventually to the privatisation of INTELSAT.

More importantly the conflation of natural and corporate persons insulates "The Economy" and gives to property regimes a privileged place in social relations. Locke argued that property was a 'natural right' on a par with life and liberty, a principle universalised in human rights law. Today, 'The Economy' is life itself. The conception of 'The Economy' as something that operates through the 'invisible hand of the Market' much like god of a previous era, obscures the reality that Markets are nothing more or less than complexes of laws institutionalised through the fiction of the 'legal person', and brought into existence through the legal ritual of incorporation. These insular institutional developments in science and technology and economy present a ruptured view of Science and social life. The rupture is embedded and reified through discourses that refer to 'the state' and 'the economy' as hypostatised entities.

'The Economy' as a hypostatised, omnipresent, omniscient, and institutionally insulated being, *reverses* the moral/ethical questions of our times. 'The Economy's' purpose *becomes* human purpose. Thus, in the INTELSAT case, for states, corporations, and interest groups in society, the perceived economic advantages of satellites were desirable and necessary even when its military potential was known. Those concerned with ethics are therefore required to find answers within the disciplinary remit of the law: how to control the social outcomes without upsetting economic fundamentals. This way of looking at the problem of economy and technology obfuscates a more fundamental ethical paradox and renders it tautological. If to be human is to cast oneself in the image of 'The Economy', can the assumption that human purposes can be effectuated through legal regulation of 'The Economy' remain tenable?

THE TRAJECTORY OF HUMAN PURPOSE: THE DIFFERENCE BETWEEN SOCIETY AND 'CIVIL SOCIETY'

Evaluation of human purposes, at the heart of ethical deliberations, presupposes the existence of Society. Ethics concerns relations of human beings to other human beings, to nature, to social institutions, and the Self. Thus, it invites evaluations of the relationship between Nature (the subject matter of science), Society, its institutional and normative structures (the subject matter of social theory) and Human life, the conditions, including emotional and psychological dimensions, necessary for well-being (the subject matter of ethics); all three, are essential to sustain human life. Ethical evaluations are invariably about sustaining and reproducing conditions conducive to human life, whatever those may be. It is not possible to speak of ethics without having some conception of relations between nature, society, and human life. It is precisely this relation that becomes skewed in the contexts generated by large scale science and large scale social institutions.

Liberal theory substitutes the term *civil society* for *Society*. Civil Society forms the third pillar together with 'the State' and 'the Economy' in the archetype of capitalist society. Civil Society presupposes the existence of a public sphere and citizenship, and is supposed to provide the institutional arrangements through which citizens can bring their human will to bear on regulation of economy and state for human purposes. In the post-World War world order we have seen how human purpose becomes problematic in science and technology and in the economy. The idea of Civil Society to mediate between science and economy is equally problematic.

Following Roy Bhaskar (1989) capitalism reconstitutes communities by uprooting them from preexisting places and histories and grounds them instead in interest-based organisations, incorporated or otherwise. Thus workers have a common interest in the labour market and form trade unions in order to be able to negotiate for better wages; consumers have an interest in cheap high quality goods and services from manufacturers and service providers, and form consumer organisations to articulate their interests in the marketplace; cancer victims and crime victims must form victim support groups to represent their interests where care is provided by states or corporations as opposed to human relationships tied to place, such as extended families, tribes, and similar institutions. The redefinition of communities as groups with common interests vis-à-vis 'the Economy' and markets was facilitated by ideologies of individualism, biological reductionism, and challenges to feudal institutions like family, religion, and ancestral attachments to place. Civil Society becomes a conglomeration of interest based organisations where previous social institutions are replaced with corporate entities within market institutions as the dominant organisational form (D'Souza, 2007).

Community's interests are fragmented into diverse interests, vis-à-vis 'the Economy' and State: as workers, consumers, parents, students, and so on where each interest comes to be cast into distinct organisations: trade unions, consumer organisations, social welfare, student unions, etc. Further, each interest is regulated by a distinct set of laws, such as industrial relations, consumer protection laws, nondiscrimination laws, rules for associations, and so on. In the normative ideal of markets, by affirming their interests, diverse interest groups can ensure that 'the Economy' serves human purposes. An ideal democracy is one where citizens form interest groups and intervene in the public sphere through informed public debate, and the state and economy respect the wishes of 'Civil Society' organisations by reconciling as many contradictory interests as possible. Evaluation of human purpose, at the heart of ethical deliberations, gets conflated to either individual/group purposes, or a deliberation to privilege one or more interests above others. The institutionalisation of human interests into diverse organisations makes it difficult to conceptualise *Society* except as a collection of interest based organisations operating within economic markets regulated by states. In such an institutional context what does human purpose mean in a network society; that is, 'civil societies' reliant on cyber technologies?

Network Societies complement the highly centralised military-industrial complexes that produce communication technologies, the monopolistic corporations that adopt and use them in trade and economy. Network Societies presuppose the reconstitution of society as individuals/interest groups organised around various interest loci, in clusters, groups, or organisations, formal or informal, such that they can be mobilised using communication technologies. Individuals and groups are transformed into 'nodes', 'clusters', and 'fat-tails' of a network that can be mobilised by large social institutions using information technology.

In the post-World Wars world order technology rather than human beings become the conduit for transmission of power and control. In the Fordist era human beings were made to behave like machines through hierarchies of corporate bureaucracies. Bureaucracies constrain human behaviour and subject human will to the logics of economy and state; they do not however *eliminate* human will, human solidarities, or human judgments. Computerisation and automation took roots in the economy by eliminating middle rungs of bureaucracies in command and control systems within large corporations (see also Bagchi, 1995). The purpose was to do away with the unpredictability that human relationships brought to command and control. The elimination of bureaucracies: the tyrannical boss, the egocentric official, does not necessarily result in greater democracy in the sense of an increased capacity to impose human will on corporate entities, scientific or economic or political, as some argue. Instead, communication technologies have polarised economic and political power to the extremes and concentrated it in the hands of a few decision makers, often outside public view, within selective nodes and clusters within and between organisations. The public sphere becomes murky therefore, and dehumanised. This is compounded by the law where the concept of civil society is conflated with humanity (D'Souza, 2007).

Communications technologies do not eliminate uncertainties as they too make mistakes, break down, and result in unpredictable outcomes. They do, however, fudge the domain of ethics: human relationships with other human beings and with nature must now include human relationships with machines and relationships between machines and how all of those relations impinge upon the reproduction of conditions for human life. Ethical deliberations are no longer undertaken by psyche-bearing individuals but by institutions that exist as complexes of laws. While cheering the demise of oppressive hierarchies, the tyrannical boss, the egotistical official, it is necessary to pause and ask what replaces the oppressive system, and whether it is replaced by more or less freedom?

In a controversial TV interview on *60 Minutes* (1996), Lesley Stahl the TV host, when questioning then U.S. Secretary of State Madeleine Albright on U.S. sanctions against Iraq, asked her: "We have heard that a half million children have died. I mean, that's more children than died in Hiroshima. And, you know, is the price worth it'? Her reply was: 'I think this is a very hard choice, but the price—we think the price is worth it'. Was Albright not speaking truthfully about what was needed for the survival of the militaristic state and economy? Yet can we acquiesce to the 'the Economy's' purpose becoming human purpose?

In his book *Love and Sex with Robots: The Evolution of Human Robot Relationship* David Levy predicts that the time is not far off when we will fall in love with robots because they will be designed to be loving and caring in ways that human partners are not (Levy, 2007). In raising a generation of children on virtual pets and tamagotchis are we creating the conditions for human love to be replaced with robot love? Equally, would we not have to purchase the loving robot in the marketplace? And what norms shall we develop for love between robots and humans?

What if we reframe questions about 'individual choice' and ask instead: 'if the price of my beautiful handheld Blueberry, or webcam, or Internet purchases from anywhere in the world, is perpetual war mongering and continuing impoverishment of the majority of human beings, what should I choose'? Posing ethical questions in this manner reveals the extent to which human purpose is lost in the discourses of corporate-economy and militaristic states. Nevertheless, by asking such impossible questions we salvage what there is of a sense of being human.

The problem, as we have seen so far, is not our *desire* to put human purpose at the centre of our deliberations but rather the fault line that runs between Science and Society, between nature and culture. Albright and techno-toys show in different ways how there is a role reversal where economy and technology dictate human purpose instead of the other way around. That fault line invites us to reconsider the epistemologies that have brought about the role reversal.

BETWEEN FATALISM AND FREE WILL: THE STRAITJACKET OF THEORY

At present the fault line between science and society is interrogated by a range of approaches to the science–society divide. At one end of the spectrum of studies are the Science, Technology, and Society studies (STS); at the other end are communication theories, and a range of approaches in between with greater or lesser emphasis on science and technology or human agency. Examining two ends of a spectrum opens up the possibility of probing what is entailed in putting human purpose centre stage in the present context.

At the STS end, Bruno Latour's works offer insights into the science–society divide. Latour puts network society on a theoretical foundation by interrogating the relationship between science and technology and human life; and is one of the leading thinkers on actor-network-theory (ANT). Latour argues that the foundations of modernity rest on the dichotomy between science and society that operate as two distinct conceptual spheres. However, in reality, they exist always as what he calls 'hybrids'; that is, as stabilised relationships between nature and culture, between objects and humans. Social theory, he argues, marginalises the role of objects, artefacts, and technologies in accounts of human life, and obscures the extent to which the artefacts reconstitute human life (Latour, 1993). For Latour the conceptual divide between science and society allows for recombining and reconstituting the nature–culture relationships in innumerable ways.

> ...we can combine associations freely without ever confronting the choice between archaism and modernization, the local and the global, the cultural and the universal, the natural and the social. Freedom...becomes a capacity for sorting and recombining sociotechnological imbroglios. (Latour, 1993, p. 141)

The freedom to sort could also become freedom to manipulate (Schuurman, 1992) the possibility of choices and therefore ethical judgments. For how else can we judge how and what we recombine and re-sort? But for Latour, we must not judge how we reorganise nature–culture relationships and artefacts.

> Protecting human beings from the domination of machines and technocrats is a laudable enterprise, but if the machines are full of human beings who find their salvation there, such a protection is merely absurd.... Every concept, every institution, every practice that interferes with the continuous deployment of collectives and their experimentation with hybrids will be deemed dangerous, harmful, and—we may as well say it—immoral. (Latour, 1993, p.139)

Latour argues for epistemologically equidistance from Science and Society (Latour, 1993, pp. 91–94). Epistemological equidistance between science and society becomes the building block for actors-network-theory wherein we cannot any longer speak about *Society* in the present. As stabilised nature-culture, human-nonhuman relations, a Society can exist only in the past; in the present it is always a process, the future trajectory of which is unpredictable and unknowable. For Latour there are no groups or societies, only transient associations of nonhumans and humans (Latour, 2005; and see Elder-Vass, 2008). There is no room in Latour's network society for a theory of action presupposed in ethics.

> Action is not done under the full control of consciousness; action should rather be felt as a node, a knot, and a conglomerate of many surprising sets of agencies that have to be slowly disentangled.... An 'actor' in the hyphenated expression actor-network is not the source of an action but the moving target of a vast array of entities swarming towards it. (Latour, 2005, pp. 44, 46)

Human agents in Latour's world-view look like the atomised objects they live in association with; the epistemological equidistance makes it impossible to differentiate between humans and nonhumans; in fact, Latour argues, we should not differentiate between them.

> By definition, action is *dislocated.* Action is borrowed, distributed, suggested, influenced, dominated, betrayed, translated.... Like Jesus on the cross, it is of the actor that one should always say: 'Forgive them Father, they know not what they do'....Uncertainty should remain uncertainty because we don't want to rush into saying actors may not know what they are doing, but that we, the social scientists, know that there exists a social force 'making them do' things unwittingly. (Latour, 2005, pp. 46–47)

Latour, correctly identifies the fault line between Science and Society as something foundational, constitutive of modernity, and somehow, a fault line that invests modern societies with extraordinary power, wealth, and capacities. However, from criticising social theorists for sustaining the Science–Society divide he goes on to collapse all distinction between nature and culture; Latour's sociology is left without *Society*: 'there is no society, no social realm, and no social ties, *but there exist translations between mediators that may generate traceable associations'* (Latour, 2005, p. 108).

That human beings are tool-wielding species, that they have always intervened in Nature with tools, and therefore no account of human society is possible without an account of their technological stages, points to ontological attributes of human beings, their relationships to nature, and the contingency of human life on social structures and norms to regulate that relationship. Latour seeks epistemological solutions to ontological problems. Latour's 'hybrids', that is, artefacts that combine human–nonhuman associations, mediate between science and society without consciousness, leaving no room for agency or ethics.

At the other end of the spectrum we have Jürgen Habermas, an influential social philosopher who put communication on philosophical foundations and developed the idea of 'discourse ethics'. Ethics and agency, the critique of capitalism, its institutions, laws, and instrumentalist reasoning, are at the heart of Habermas's work. Habermas recognises a hiatus between 'system', the economic, legal, institutional, and scientific logics of modern society, and 'lifeworld' that encircles 'system' and provides the sociocultural conditions, including language, that make communication possible (Jürgen Habermas, 1984/1986,1987/1989). In modern societies, the economic and administrative 'system' colonizes the 'lifeworld' and stifles communication needed for the 'lifeworld' to flourish. According to Habermas:

> …with the legal institutionalization of the monetary medium, success-oriented action steered by egocentric calculations of utility loses its connection to action oriented mutual understanding.…
> In the instrumental sphere, purposive activity gets free of normative restrictions to the extent that it becomes linked to flows of information from the scientific system. (Habermas, 1987/1989, p. 196)

Habermas acknowledges the fault line between Science and Society from a very different end of the philosophical spectrum. The hallmark of modernity Habermas (1990) argues is sundered reason: Reason has split into three moments: modern science, positive law and posttraditional ethics, and autonomous art and institutionalized art criticism (i.e. aesthetics)' (Habermas, 1990, p. 17). Philosophy, argues Habermas, has very little to do with this compartmentalization of knowledge. It is everyday life that restores a sense of unity at the level of lived experiences and culture. Therefore, the task of philosophy is that of a mediator between sundered reason and unified lived experience. Philosophy can therefore:

> …refurbish its link with the totality by taking on the role of interpreter on behalf of the lifeworld. It might then be able to help set in motion the interplay between the cognitive-instrumental, moral-practical, and aesthetic-expressive dimensions that has come to a standstill today like a tangled mobile. (Habermas, 1990, p. 18)

Ethical communication for Habermas becomes the arbiter between sundered reason and lived experience, between a scientific -economic 'system' and sociocultural 'lifeworld'.

This Habermasean role for philosophy brings us a full circle from Marx's famous dictum that philosophers must not only interpret the world but also engage in social action to change it. By casting themselves in the role of mediators and interpreters between sundered reason and unified life, philosophers open themselves to the charge of manipulating the conceptual threads, the analytical tools, the ideological armoury that connect life experiences with a rational 'system'. A sundered reason is, however, Unreason. Sundered reason is incapable of presenting a comprehensible account of the relations between nature and history, law and ethics, aesthetics and lived experience.

Besides, as Sundar Sarukkai (2002) points out, the language of Science is different from the language of Society. Science speaks in a multisemiotic language of signs, graphs, and experiments through which it claims to translate Nature. Scientific language helps Science make claims about exclusive access to truth. Language in society is unisemiotic and interprets the social world only tentatively. Social science makes claims about approximations to normative ideals. Science and Society speak in different tongues to different ontological entities, one to Nature, the other to Society. Acting as interpreters requires, first of all, the recognition that incommensurable languages sustain the fault line between Science and Society. How do we act as interpreters and mediators without first comprehending what is entailed in the process of translating Nature? The disjuncture between translating Nature and interpreting Society, using very different semiotic strategies, points to the lack of an effective language for communication between Science and Society that manifests as sundered reason.

When Unreason masquerades as Reason it ramifies two effects: first, philosophers reify the disjuncture between reason and everyday life, between science and society, nature and culture; second, human beings become disempowered to transform the realities of lived life through collective action; not because they have failed to recognise the need for collective action, but rather because they continue to seek discursive solutions. Reason is an ontological attribute of being human. When reason, an essential, ontological attribute of being human, appears 'sundered' it signals a rupture between epistemology and ontology. The rupture skews the conceptual lenses through which we see the world.

Nature, society, and people/groups are, as Bhaskar (1989) argues, ontologically distinct with diifferent attributes and properties that are nevertheless relational. Nature exists independently of society or human life. Human life is, however, contingent on Nature *and* Society. Society preexists people/groups, we are always born into a social order of some kind, but at the same time Society is transformed by human beings. It is by coming to grips with the attributes and properties of Nature, Society, and people, and their relationships *inter se*, that we can engage epistemologically with what Science *should* be like, or Society, or what is necessary to create the conditions for human fulfilment. Critique must constantly evaluate the distortions in the ontological relationship between nature/society /people, to create, enhance, and improve the conditions for human flourishing. Modernity undermines, undervalues, and underprivileges ontology and privileges, emphasises epistemology. Consequently either Nature is conflated with society or people/groups conflated with society. We are left either with fatalistic theories that deny agency or voluntaristic theories where actions are unconstrained by context. Consequently we are faced with a paradox at the heart of modern societies: the more we know, the more disempowered we become to transform the conditions of our lives.

CONCLUSION

What can we say about regulating trade and networked communication ethically at the end of meta-micro accounts of the problem? The question itself needs to be considered within the context that gives rise to it: the hiatus between militaristic science and monopolistic economy. Equally, the question arises within knowledge institutions wherein intellectual freedoms exist within institutional constraints of well organised epistemic communities that monitor and discipline, in a myriad ways, how the freedom is exercised: through mechanisms of peer review, academic traditions of locating oneself within existing literatures, research funding, rewards, recognitions, and such (Carter, 2000; Ewick, 2001; May, 2001; Peters, 1992). It is the knowledge economy that gives rise to questions about trade and networked communications in the first place; and in the knowledge economy there is constant need to synchronise and smooth the operations of Science and Society, of technology and economy, networked communication and trade. Individual researchers have no control over the way the knowledge they produce, critical or otherwise, will be mobilised by scientific and economic institutions (D'Souza, 2009b). Assumptions to the contrary are based on conflating individuals with Society, very different types of ontological entities. Wiener's research was used by the military-industrial complex in ways he never foresaw; satellite firms acting in concert transformed the spaces of public spheres and citizenship presenting people with a *fait accompli*. If, however, individuals are ontologically aware, and recognise that their ethical aspirations operate within the constraints of their institutional contexts, then they could insist on altering the rules of engagement. They could insist on consistency between the way they engage with Science, with Society, and with human well-being.

Equating natural and corporate persons, as the law does, is founded on an ontological lie. We know corporations are social institutions; human beings are psyche bearing individuals who feel pain and communities suffer in the present and intergenerationally. Yet, we persist with the lie, find complex epistemological arguments to sustain the ontological lie. To desist from the lie would be to rock the foundations of modern society. We are straightaway terrified of the upheaval and chaos. Yet two thirds of humanity live their lives in daily upheavals and chaos. Half the world's population is displaced due to war, political instability, and poverty (World Bank, 2004, p. 5), and more than half live at levels of poverty where basic biological needs like food and water are unavailable.[8] Policies about science and technology and economy are invariably rationalised in the name of the displaced and the impoverished. As Bauman says, the flip side of modernity is the production of 'wasted humans' (Bauman, 2004).

The Science–Society binary is epistemologically false because nature, society, and human life, despite their distinctive characteristics and attributes exist relationally, interdependently, and inseparably. It follows therefore that the focus of epistemology must turn on the relationships between nature-society and human life. The focus on relationships changes the questions for Science dramatically. No scientific question can be separated from social questions or emotional/ psychological questions (Uberoi, 2002). Science must become nondualistic without becoming deterministic or irrational.

Many will agree with the principle that human well-being should set the agenda for science and technology. That principle, if followed consistently, would alter fundamentally the priorities for Science. The Science that creates ethical dilemmas about networked communications against the backdrop of extensive human misery is premised on what Vandana Shiva (1996) calls 'epistemological violence'; and promotes the 'laboratory state' in development (Visvanathan, 1997) that keeps vast majority of populations in subhuman conditions. Are we prepared to desist from 'epistemological violence'? Are we prepared to leave scientific and technological innovations to the hungry and displaced? Leave farmers to develop water technologies instead of army engineers, electricity conglomerates, and global financial institutions, for example? Leave food production to farmers instead of agribusiness conglomerates and chemical corporations? Eschew knowledge for knowledge's sake and strive for knowledge and well-being of peoples and communities? Spectres of the world plunging into darkness and economic chaos loom large at such suggestions. Indeed modernity itself and Society as we know it will be rocked to its foundations.

If we do not wish to rock the boat as it were, the idea that all human beings are intrinsically valuable and deserve to live fulfilling lives, an idea that informs ethics of modern societies, becomes problematic. If we truly believe in that principle can we continue to privilege the economy, the scientific establishment, the militaristic and corporate institutions, in the way we frame questions for our inquiry? If we accept that human well-being cannot be reduced to economic well-being, can we continue to institutionally segregate and privilege 'the Economy' and in the same breath complain of anomie and alienation and atomised lives? Trade for whom? That question invites us to examine 'us' (the privileged with places in modern institutions) and 'them' (the underprivileged without basic necessities) but tells us very little about how our ill-being is mutually reinforced and contingent.

Instead of asking what regulatory frameworks may we use to regulate trade and communication ethically, may we not turn the question on its head and ask instead: when unreason masquerades as reason, can we regulate trade and communication ethically? May we not point out when Unreason masquerades as Reason fear reigns, nightmares of chaos and upheaval rules? That when Unreason masquerades as Reason we cease to dream of human flourishing?

NOTES

1. On micro and macrolevels in theory see Knorr-Cetina and Cicourel (1981).
2. Here, Reality is capitalised to indicate its use in the ontological sense, referred to in the previous sentence, as is usually the practice when referring to ontological Reality as opposed to the real in everyday life. I have followed this usage throughout the text. Likewise Society and Science are capitalised when used in a metaconcepts sense as opposed to everyday life.
3. For summaries of the proceedings and issues see (Katkin, 2005; Lyall, 2001).
4. Analysis of the character of the United Nations formed by the victors in the World Wars is beyond the scope of this chapter.
5. The role of WTO in the transformation of public international organisations along neoliberal lines and the role of agency in regime changes in relation to the water sector is discussed in D'Souza (2009a).
6. See Uruguay Round ministerial decisions and declarations: Decisions adopted by the Trade Negotiations Committee on December 15,1993 and April 14, 1994: Uruguay round agreement decision on negotiations on basic telecommunications. Retrieved from http://www.wto.org/english/docs_e/legal_e/50-dstel_e.htm
7. The development of U.S. space policy by successive U.S. presidents is provided in Hertzfeld (2007).
8. See *World Development Report* published by World Bank and Human Development Report by UNDP every year.

REFERENCES

Albright, M. (1996, May 12). *60 Minutes* [Television series]. New York: CBS News.

AON. (2008, March 20). Pivotal time for space insurance as insurers look for rates to lift-off [News release]. Retrieved from http://aon.mediaroom.com/index.php?s=43&item=1086

Bagchi, A. K., & Samaddar, R. (Eds.). (1995). *Microelectronics, labour and society*. New Delhi, India: Centre for Studies in Social Sciences/Sage.

Bauer, H. H. (1990). Barriers against interdisciplinarity: Implications for studies of science, technology, and society (STS). *Science, Technology, & Human Values, 15*(1), 105–119.

Bauman, Z. (2004). *Wasted lives: Modernity and its outcasts*. Cambridge, UK: Polity.

Belson, K. (2005). Too many players still shadow satellite industry. *New York Times*. Retrieved from http://www.nytimes.com/2005/08/30/business/30place.html?pagewanted=print

Bhaskar, R. (1989). *Reclaiming reality: A critical introduction to contemporary philosophy*. London: Verso.

Brown, A. (2008, September 15). President Obama's space policy: Learning from Eisenhower. *The Space Review: Essays and Commentary about the Final Frontier*. Retrieved from http://www.thespacereview.com/article/1208/1

Capurro, R. (2006). Towards an ontological foundations of information ethics. *Ethics and Information Technology, 8*, 175–186.

Carter, C. (2000). Keepers of knowledge capital: Legislating for the new millennium. *Management Decision, 38*(3), 179–181.

Castells, M. (2001). *The internet galaxy: Reflections on the internet, business and society.* Oxford, UK: Oxford University Press.

Cowan, R., & Foray, D. (1995). Quandaries in the economics of dual technologies and spillovers from military to civilian research and development. *Research Policy, 24,* 851–868.

Dinerman, T. (2008a, June 16). Basic disappointment? *The Space Review.* Retrieved from http://www.thespacereview.com/article/1217/1

Dinerman, T. 2008b, June 23). Financial risk analysis for the space industry revisited. *The Space Review.* Retrieved from http://www.thespacereview.com/article/1151/1

Dinerman, T. (2008c, September 22). Financial risk analysis for the space industry revisited. *The Space Review: Essays and Commentary about the Final Frontier.* Retrieved from http://www.thespacereview.com/article/1151/1

D'Souza, R. (2007). Looking Into the crystal ball: 'Civil society' and 'humanity' in the 21st century. *Polylog: Journal of Intercultural Philosophy, 18,* 55–62.

D'Souza, R. (2009a). Law and 'development' discourses about water: Understanding agency in regime changes. In U. R. H. Matthew & P. Cullet (Eds.), *Water governance in motion: Towards socially and environmentally sustainable water laws* (pp. 491–522). New Delhi, India: Cambridge University Press.

D'Souza, R. (2009b). The prison houses of knowledge: Activist scholarship and revolution in the era of 'globalisation'. *McGill Journal of Education, 41*(1), 19–38.

Elder-Vass, D. (2008). Searching for realism, structure and agency in Actor Network Theory. *The British Journal of Sociology, 59*(3), 455–473.

Ewick, P. (2001). Mending fences: Beyond the epistemological dilemma. *Law &Soceity Review, 35*(1), 21–24.

Fortun, M., & Schweber, S. S. (1993). Scientists and the legacy of World War II: The case of Operations Research (OR). *Social Studies of Science, 23,* 595–642.

Fuller, S. (1985). Disciplinary boundaries: A critical synthesis. *4S Review, 3*(1), 2–15.

Gasper, D. (2004). Interdisciplinarity: Building bridges and nurturing a complex ecology of ideas. In A. K. Giri (Ed.), *Creative social research: Rethinking theories and methods* (pp. 308–342). New Delhi, India: Sage.

Giri, A. K. (1998). Transcending disciplinary boundaries. *Critique of Anthropology, 18*(4), 379–404.

Habermas, J. (1986). *The theory of communicative action: Reason and the rationalization of society* (T. McCarthy, Trans.). Cambridge, UK: Polity. (Original work published 1984)

Habermas, J. (1989). *The theory of communicative action: The critique of functionalist reason* (T. McCarthy, Trans.). Cambridge: UK: Polity Press. (Original work published 1987)

Habermas, J. (1990). *Moral consciousness and communicative action* (C. Lenhardt & S. W. Nicholsen, Trans.). Cambridge, UK: Polity Press.

Hartley, K. (2004). The economics of military outsourcing. *Defence Studies, 4*(2), 199–206.

Heims, S. J. (Ed.). (1989). *Introduction to the human use of human beings: Cybernetics and society.* London: Free Association Books.

Hertzfeld, H. R. (2007). Globalization, commercial space and spacepower in the USA. *Space Policy, 23,* 210–220.

Hodges, P. (1993). Perspectives on history: Military dietetics in Europe during World War I. *Journal of American Diet Association, 93,* 897–900.

Hooks, G. (2008). Military-industrial complex, organization and history. In L. Kurtz (Ed.), *Encyclopedia of violence, peace and conflict* (pp. 1278–1286). Amsterdam, the Netherlands: Elsevier Science Direct.

Katkin, K. (2005, Autumn). Communication breakdown: The future of global connectivity after the privatization of INTELSAT [Special Issue, Global flow of information]. *International Journal of Communication Law & Policy,* 1–66.

Kellog, D. (2006, Autumn). Toward a post-academic science policy: Scientific communication and the collapse of the Mertonian norms. [Special issue, Access to knowledge]. *International Journal of Communication Law & Policy,* 1–29.

Knorr-Cetina, K., & Cicourel, A. V. (Eds.). (1981). *Advances in social theory and methodology: Towards an integration of micro- and macro-sociologies*. Boston, MA: Routledge & Kegan Paul.

Kulve, H. T., & Smit, W. A. (2003). Civilian-military co-operation strategies in developing new technologies. *Research Policy, 32*, 955–970.

Latour, B. (1993). *We have never been modern* (C. Porter, Trans.). Cambridge, MA: Harvard University Press.

Latour, B. (2005). *Reassembling the social: An introduction to actor-network-theory*. Oxford, UK: Oxford University Press.

Levy, D. (2007). *The evolution of human robot relationships: Love and sex with robots*. New York: HarperCollins.

Lovering, J. (1987). Militarism, capitalism, and the nation-state: Towards a realist synthesis. *Environment and Planning D: Society and Space, 5*, 283–302.

Lyall, F. (2001). On the privatisation of INTELSAT. *Singapore Journal of International and Comparative Law, 5*, 111–132.

Marx, K. (1973[1930]). *Grundrisse: Foundations of the critique of political economy (rough draft)*. Harmondsworth: Penguin. (Original work published 1857–1858)

Matthew, U. R. H. (2004). Private contractors on deployed operations: The United Kingdom experience. *Defence Studies, 4*(2), 145–165.

May, T. (2001). Power, knowledge and organizational transformation: Administration as depoliticization. *Social Epistemology, 15*(3), 171–185.

McCarthy, C. (2000, February 20). Genius of science, genius of peace. Baltimore: Baltimore Sun. Retrieved from http://articles.baltimoresun.com/2000-02-20/topic/0002220301_1_einstein-pacifism-war/3

Molas-Gallari, J. (2001). Government defence research establishments: The uncertain outcome of institutional change. *Defence and Peace Economics, 12*, 417–437.

Public private divide with discussion and debate. (1982). [Special issue]. *University of Pennsylvania Law Review, 130*.

Peters, M. (1992). Performance and accountability in 'post-industrial society': The crisis of the British universities. *Studies in Higher Education, 17*(2), 123–139.

Porter, T. M. (1995). *Trust in numbers: The pursuit of objectivity in science and public life*. Princeton, NJ: Princeton University Press.

Reader, J. (2009). *The untold history of the potato*. London: Vintage.

Ritter, D., & McLauchlan, G. (2008). Military-industrial complex, contemporary significance. In L. Kurtz (Ed.), *Encyclopedia of violence, peace and conflict* (pp. 1266–1278). Amsterdam, the Netherlands: Elsevier Science Direct.

Sarukkai, S. (2002). *Translating the world: Science and language*. Lanham, MD: University Press of America.

Sayer, A. (1984). *Method in social science: A realist approach*. London: Hutchinson

Schuurman, E. (1992). Crisis in agriculture: A philosophical perspective on the relation between agriculture and nature. *Research in Philosophy and Technology, 12* [Special issue: Technology and the Environment], 191–211.

Shiva, V. (1996). Reductionist science as epistemological violence. In A. Nandy (Ed.), *Science, hegemony and violence: A requiem for modernity* (pp. 232–256). Delhi, India: Oxford University Press; Tokyo, Japan: The United Nations University.

Space Mart (2007, June 20). BC partners wins control of satellite group Intelsat. Retrieved from http://www.spacemart.com/reports/BC_Partners_Wins_Control_Of_Satellite_G

Space Mart (2008, November 11). World satellite transponders market to reach 7,262 Units by 2012. Retrieved from http://www.spacemart.com/reports/BC_Partners_Wins_Control_Of_Satellite_G

Teclaff, L. A. (1967). *The river basin in history and law*. The Hague, the Netherlands: Martinus Nijhoff.

Uberoi, J. P. S. (2002). *The European modernity: Science, truth and method*. New Delhi, India: Oxford University Press.

Udis, B. (2008). *Economic conversion. Encyclopedia of violence, peace and conflict*. Amsterdam, the Netherlands: Elsevier Science & Technology.

Visvanathan, S. (1997). *Carnival for science: Essays on science, technology and development*. Delhi, India: Oxford University Press.

Wiener, N. (1964). *God and Golem, Inc.: A comment on certain points where cybernetics impinges on religion*. Cambridge, MA: MIT Press.

Wiener, N. (1989). *The human use of human beings: Cybernetics and society*. London: Free Association Books. (Original work published 1950)

World Bank. (2004). *Involuntary resettlement sourcebook: Planning and implementation in development projects*. Washington DC: Author.

29

Response and Conclusion

A Vision of Applied Ethics for Communication Studies

Josina M. Makau

In the introduction to this volume, the editors highlight key ways in which an applied ethics framework for communication studies may help to bridge historic gaps in the literature and its connections to practice. Pointing to communication as both a discipline and an "interdiscipline" or field offering substantive contributions to ethical inquiry, the editors draw attention to inherent connections between explorations of communication, consciousness, and ethics.

The editors' opening comments feature contributions made possible by drawing on these often overlooked connections. Here they echo insights by philosophers Solomon and Higgins (1997) who observe that:

> Philosophy has always been representative of what is most human about us. Perhaps what we need is not more sophistication, but more openness. We need to be not more clever but, rather, better listeners. What philosophy is, after all, is a thoughtful openness to the world, a passion for wisdom. (p. 128)

The editors underscore the centrality of communicative ethics to this vision of *philosophy in the world*. They note, for example, that an applied ethics of communication is well poised to help move ethical inquiry from the margins to the heart of work probing concrete issues in today's complex world.

The editors suggest in particular than an applied ethics for communication studies promises to integrate theory and practice—recognizing communication *as action*—across contexts. Toward this end, they urge reflective pursuit of connections between work on social justice and related explorations of difference and diversity within communication studies on the one hand, and exploration of ethics and ethical theory on the other. Their comments highlight in particular the significant potential associated with emergent work in multicultural ethics.

Aligned with the editors' visionary call, the chapters throughout the volume deliver lasting insights. Taken together, they contribute valuably to fulfillment of the promise the editors have assigned to applied ethics for communication studies. What follows is intended to build on the volume's contributions in pursuit of this goal.

The volume's reach across widely diverse interpersonal, institutional, civic, mass mediated oral, visual, nonverbal, and written communication contexts highlights the central place of communication in shaping today's globally interdependent world. The authors attend thoughtfully to potential contributions that communication studies may make in helping communication, in all of its forms, support pursuits of justice, peace, truth, and other pathways to human flourishing. Whatever else a vision of applied ethics may offer to this project, helping to enable communication studies' fulfillment of this potential must surely be at the forefront of this work.

A number of the volume's contributors have understandably cautioned against false optimism. As they have reminded us, communication has been and continues to be a tool of choice for tyrants, demagogues, and charlatans. Across continents and contexts, millions of people routinely fall prey to carefully designed propaganda, manipulation, and various forms of communication approaching coercion. Technological as well as financial resources have equipped destructive and misguided leaders to distort issues and mislead people to support potentially devastating courses of action. Much like their counterparts throughout history, skilled practitioners routinely exploit the power and force of communication to serve their purposes or those of their employers. Further, the vastness and complexity of the communication environment today, including media concentration, can undermine even the most dedicated, gifted, and responsible communication practitioners to intervene on behalf of pursuits of truth, justice, or peace.

Technological advancements across sectors have created a compelling force of their own. Robotics, surveillance tools, advanced information networks, sophisticated weaponry, forensics technologies, medical technologies, artificial intelligence, and related leaps within the interdisciplinary fields of neuropsychology and cybernetics are among the many venues of great potential consequence to human destiny. In each of these areas, dangers and opportunities coexist within what some have identified as an *amoral* context, devoid of any meaningful mission or reflective process. As numerous volume contributors have shown, the *machine* advances its cause without consideration of humane values; *techne* serves itself. In her contribution to the volume, D' Souza offers important related insights, providing strong support for her claim that in this historical moment "economy and technology" are dictating "human purpose instead of the other way around." This feature of technological progress—largely invisible in its reach and far outpacing, in many ways, humanity's moral progress—creates a particularly compelling exigency.

At the same time, the globe itself is in peril. In the face of continued population growth, environmental degradation, increasing economic disparity in many parts of the world, and unintended consequences of technological advancement, humankind's seemingly relentless thirst to consume appears to be moving the world as we know it toward an inevitable path to destruction. In light of these realities, efforts to intervene in support of life forces sometimes seem to face seemingly insurmountable obstacles.

Taken together, these circumstances often prove disabling to agents of change seeking to advance humane causes. Further complicating this landscape is the absence of a universal code of conduct aimed at restraint, discipline, or other modifying constraints. Associated, quite rightly, with hegemonic agendas, so-called universal norms no longer serve as sources of moral authority for many around the globe.

Against this backdrop, any effort to provide an applied ethics for communication practice may seem quixotic. Yet, this response to the material realities of the global environment neglects the extraordinary *constructive potential of communication, realized in countless contexts and ways every day around the world.* For, as the editors and many of this volume's contributors have observed, it is through communication that the human heart expresses love, compassion, and care. Communication offers comfort, heals spiritual and emotional wounds, and fosters community building across divides. Each day, communicative acts raise consciousness, shine a light on acts of moral courage, disrupt the forces of corruption, greed, ignorance and tyranny, and create conditions for peaceful, just resolution of conflict. Across the globe, responsible story tellers, parents, community activists, educators, political leaders, artists, scholars and others illuminate, inspire, encourage, and otherwise empower through responsible use of communication's powers.

Against this backdrop of promise and risk, challenge and opportunity, what contribution might an applied ethic for communication studies realistically make to human flourishing in today's world? And what might a vision for such an ethic look like?

APPLIED ETHICS

As the editors have noted, ethics in its most meaningful manifestation provides a guide for responsible and responsive inquiry, deliberation, and action. Among other things, this ancient art provides resources for skillfully discovering (or constructing), interpreting, understanding, and responsibly assessing available options in any given situation. *Applied* ethics, by its nature, provides *viable* means for deliberating and living well—in all the ways potentially entailed by this construct—*across a range of contexts*. A powerful applied ethics framework serves as a beacon for practitioners, as well as for those whose interests are at stake in the outcomes of decision-making processes. As such, development of a proposed vision of applied ethics for communication studies requires, at minimum, responsiveness both to the specifics of the historical moment and to the long-term mission and goals of our shared quest.

Imagining such a framework for communication studies in today's complex world is not for the faint of heart. Obstacles and challenges confront us at every turn. And yet, the promise at the core of the venture beckons. If together we are able to meet the demands of the moment in a meaningful way, taking in and realistically accommodating constraints without acquiescing to the seductive call of nihilism, we may give rise to *legitimate* grounds for hope, one of the most critical qualities of wise, just, and caring practice in any field or endeavor.

Reflecting a wide diversity of orientations, backgrounds, and life experiences, distinct theoretical groundings, standpoints, and perspectives, the contributors to this volume offer a richly diverse—and, in some instances and respects, incompatible—set of pathways for our consideration as we pursue a vision of applied ethics. As such, the volume offers valuable resources for our quest. In important ways, this phenomenon mirrors the essence of the mission itself; engagement of diverse ways of knowing, being, and valuing offers humanity the rich promise of insight required to live well together.

Mining the volume's contents for its potential requires first that we identify common ground, not only within the volume itself but across the terrain covered by its authors. Representing voices from vastly different regions and calling upon the diversity of forebears throughout, the volume offers a glimpse of where the human family might turn for guidance of where and how to shape a shared vision for the future.

To begin, it is important to recognize some of the material realities the authors have highlighted throughout the volume. As noted earlier, a number of authors have drawn attention to stark truths regarding the power and reach of corruption, tyranny, injustice, deception, manipulation, and exploitation in timeless as well as emerging forms.

Contributors have underscored the importance, as well, of recognizing in Buzzanell's words, the apparently "insurmountable barriers to action and lack of accountability erected by institutional hierarchies and community practices."[1] Ivie's instructive exploration of obstacles to positive peace offers another particularly vivid illustration. Through his voice we are able to understand some of the underlying reasons why war, exploitation, and other forms of violence continue to dominate in many parts of the world stage. We are drawn as well to the vivid realization both of communication's historic role in sustaining militarism and its constructive potential in fostering conditions for positive peace.

Related is Schaefer, Conrad, Cheney, May, and Ganesh's incisive look at how communication shapes conditions for the interests of the few to trump the needs of the many in today's global economic landscape. Reflecting on the many ways propaganda is used to "obscure the very influence of the symbolic with respect to the material," for example, they shed light on the gravity of the circumstances. As they reveal, routine discursive practices within dominant institutions and organizations in today's moral order legitimate and foster economic injustice around the globe. At the same time, however, their analysis underscores the *promise* of *communication ethics* as a viable resource for transforming institutional and organizational cultures into more humane and just sites, initially through a critical awareness of rhetoric of economics itself.

Similarly, Splichal writes of the "powerful transnational actors" and related global governance structures inhibiting "those affected by the consequences of transactions" from opportunities to be heard or to participate meaningfully in decision-making processes. And D'Souza writes movingly of Wiener's (1950, 1964) concerted, but unsuccessful, efforts to "find ways of reconciling science and technology with social conscience." Each of these authors underscores the significant place of communication in creating conditions for transformation.

Contributors to this volume offer insights as well regarding a key historical pattern underlying many of these and other obstacles to justice and peace. Troy Duster summarizes the matter succinctly: "As a general phenomenon, elites of every society come to believe that their status, their high position in the social hierarchy, is both natural and just" (Duster, 2009, p. 106). Findings from cross-cultural research reveal illuminating parallels across diverse regions. In Duster's words, "Elites in every society are understandably threatened by insurgent and populist calls for social change, because such changes constitute a possible redistribution of wealth and privilege that have been assumed as established rights and entitlements" (Duster, p. 109)

Duster concludes with a precept shared by nearly all of the volume's contributors. In his words, it is the "task of critical perspectives to reveal the deeper embedded domain assumptions about taken-for-granted privileges that otherwise never ascend to public scrutiny and challenge" (Duster, p. 209). Related are the critical tasks of uncovering and assessing underlying epistemological, ontological, and related ethical assumptions implicit in dominant ways of thinking and accustomed practices. These admonitions, and the material realities outlined above, provide vital starting points for development of a vision of applied ethics for communication studies.

UNCOVERING AND EXAMINING EMBEDDED ASSUMPTIONS

As we begin the process of uncovering and assessing assumptions embedded in approaches to communication study, perhaps one of the most important areas of inquiry is the metaethical (and communicative) question of how ethical issues are *framed*. In response, the volume offers revelations regarding the tenacity with which *individualistic ethical frameworks* continue to retain their hold in dominant Western approaches to communication study and practice. These grounding frameworks—and related master narratives—hold individuals personally responsible for every circumstance shaping their destiny; on these views, neither fate nor chance, societal power relations nor other external constraints can be held to account for the individual's societal standing and experiences. Further, according to individualist frames, the contemporary market provides a "level playing field," in which all who exercise self-responsibility and work hard have equal opportunities to achieve success in their chosen domains.

On the surface, these grounding beliefs may seem invincible in their unflagging calls to accountability for one's personal circumstances. At the same time individualistic accounts of the human condition offer the promise of individual control, with the possibility of good fortune and happiness to all willing to pursue them. When seen from this vantage point, the tenacity of individualism is not difficult to understand.

Individualist ethical frames are attractive to many as well in their presumption that each person has a *natural* right to pursue self-interest even when doing so is at the expense of others. In their most compelling forms, these orientations herald the pursuit of self-interest as the path to personal and collective well-being.

As analyses throughout the volume reveal, however, the foundational assumptions underlying individualism do not hold up under scrutiny. A number of chapters directly challenge, for example, the assumption that the dominant order provides a "level playing field" to all regardless of race, ethnicity, gender, socioeconomic background, or other identities and groupings. As analyses throughout the volume reveal, this assumption grossly distorts the self-perpetuating force of sovereign power and privilege. Explorations of multiple contexts throughout the volume provide strong evidence to support the authors' shared finding that the playing field encountered by countless people around the globe is far from level; access to resources, institutional structures, dominant norms, and the discourses supporting each are skewed sharply in favor of the privileged few at the expense of the many.

Further, as numerous accounts throughout the volume reveal, discourses resting upon and sustaining the illusion of equal or even equitable access to resources and opportunities mask deeply embedded patterns of discrimination and exploitation sustained and reenforced over time and across contexts. Schaefer et al.'s analyses of the dominant "economic culture" reveal, for example, pervasive embedded assumptions in popular culture. The belief that "goods are more important than goodness" is among several tenets propagated with force through media representations across genres. In this and related ways, communicative acts are implicated directly in compromising pathways to human flourishing across the globe.

Schaefer et al. pose further challenges to assumptions at the heart of individualist ethical frameworks. They note, for example, that adherents to individualist frameworks within the economic sphere often cite Adam Smith's philosophy as their guide. Yet, as their analysis reveals, this reading of Smith's philosophy misrepresents and misapplies his work. Among other things, economic practices driven by unfettered pursuit of self-interest fail to account for Smith's strong emphasis on the importance of social bonds, his commitment to the moderating influences of compassion and empathy, and his related focus on fulfillment of humane goals. Smith recognized that economics driven by pursuit of self-interest alone would be devastating to individual and social well-being. Schaefer et al.'s analysis uncovers both the significant harms associated with misappropriation of Smith's philosophy and the potential contributions communication studies may offer in addressing this issue.

Furthermore, and of special import to pursuit of an applied ethic, authors throughout the volume reveal a myriad of harmful consequences associated with relentless pursuit of self-interest without care for and at the expense of others. As chapters throughout the volume reveal, individualistic frameworks applied to communication study demonstrably undermine quests for mutual respect and trust, otherwise jeopardize pathways to human connection, are instrumental in fomenting wars, imperil pursuits of social justice, and otherwise pose significant obstacles to fulfillment of communication's constructive potential. In these and other venues, the human family's short and long-term interests are compromised by communicative acts reflecting limited critical self-awareness, various forms of egoism, and narrow features of individualist frameworks.[2]

Confronting this challenge directly, volume contributors provide valuable insights into an alternative ethical framework. In particular, chapters throughout the volume feature the *inevitability of interdependence* in today's technologically rich global environment, and explore the implications of this finding to communicative ethics.

INTERDEPENDENCE AS A MATERIAL REALITY

In his book, *Ethics for a New Millennium*, cited by volume contributors, the Dalai Lama (1999) offers a particularly concise overview of interdependence as a material phenomenon:

> The universe we inhabit can be understood in terms of a living organism where each cell works in balanced cooperation with every other cell to sustain the whole. If, then, just one of these cells is harmed, as when disease strikes, that balance is harmed and there is danger to the whole. This, in turn, suggests that our individual well-being is intimately connected both with that of all others and with the environment in which we live. It also becomes apparent that our every action, our every deed, word, and thought, no matter how slight or inconsequential it may seem, has an implication not only for ourselves but for all others too. (Dalai Lama, 1999, p. 41)

While the Dalai Lama's commentary is metaphorical in nature, scientific studies using available technologies have provided countless concrete, material examples to illustrate the nature and reach of interdependence in today's world. Journalist Robert Boyd cites work by geologists, for example, revealing that African dust is found in high concentrations in Floridian soil every summer. Similarly, much of Hawaii's soil is native to China and other parts of Asia. In the words of Aerodyne Research Chief Executive Charles Kolb, "The atmosphere connects all regions of the globe…" (Boyd, 2010, p. B2). Similar revelations regarding the inevitability of *connection* appear throughout all of the natural, life, and social sciences.

Placing individualist frameworks under the lens of philosophical scrutiny offers further ground for reconceptualization. For example, epistemological and ontological analyses throughout the volume remind readers that the *individual* exists always in *relation*. Even the most ardent case in support of an ontology resting *exclusively* on consciousness must nevertheless accommodate the *interconnectedness of being*.

Through these and related explorations, the volume offers overwhelming evidence that the atomistic view of life implicit in individualist frameworks cannot be sustained in light of empirical, philosophical, and spiritual interrogation. Further, they reveal the importance of recognizing the inevitability of interconnections between people and their interpretive lenses, individual and communal experiences, ways of knowing, being, and valuing, and the world's material conditions. As we envision an applied ethic for communication studies in today's world, therefore, a critical starting point must be recognition of *interdependence* both as a *material reality* and as an *ethical imperative*.

INTERDEPENDENCE AS AN ETHICAL IMPERATIVE

Although seen by some Western academics as a cutting-edge idea, interdependence as an ethical imperative is a construct with ancient and cross-cultural origins. Several of the volume's contributors remind us, for example, of the central place versions of what is often referred to as the Golden Rule hold in most of the world's philosophic, spiritual, religious, and related faith traditions. The faithful across Christian sects on all of the world's continents, for example, are admonished to "do unto others as you would have them do unto you." This iteration is echoed as well in Western secular humanist writings. Across diverse Native American tribes, for example, communities are bound by the recognition that "what we do to everything, we do to ourselves." In Islam, spiritual leaders across diverse sects teach the sacred lesson that "None of you truly believes until he wishes for his brother what he wishes for himself." These and related concepts of reciprocity, reversibility, and interdependence reflecting shared awareness of humanity's mutual reliance and interconnectedness have retained their place as grounding precepts for tribes, villages, and communities across space and time.

Related are recognitions of needs, interests, and related qualities common to most of humanity. Findings regarding these common bonds shed light on *core values* underlying interdependent approaches to communicative ethics.

CORE VALUES AND ETHICAL REFLECTION

Christians's essay provides a fruitful introduction to this exploration. Invoking the preeminent place of the Golden Rule across cultural boundaries, Christians notes that this principle is "an expression of the common moral wisdom of humanity worldwide." He goes on to remind readers of the "ongoing vitality" of the Universal Declaration for Human Rights issued by the United Nations General Assembly in 1948 and reaffirmed by the international community of nations 50 and 60 years later. This cross-cultural expression of humanity affirms the inherent dignity of all the planet's people, "with no exceptions for religion, class, gender, age, or ethnicity." In Christians's words, "the common sacredness of all human beings regardless of merit or achievement is not only considered a fact but is a shared commitment." Furthermore, "human dignity pushes us to comprehend the demands of cultural diversity, and give up an individualistic morality of rights."

Authors throughout the volume give concrete shape to Christians's vision. Contributors shed light, for example, on qualities and aspirations shared by people across the globe. For example, even people who may cower at the prospect of public visibility of any kind, nevertheless flourish in the face of the gift of acknowledgment; most of humanity yearns to be heard and understood. Further, the human spirit is, in most instances, uplifted in the face of love and imperiled in the face of hatred. Most people, even those complicit in militarism and violent conflict, yearn to live in peace, and wish a peaceful world for their loved ones. Most of humanity wishes to be treated fairly, and most recoil at the prospect of being subjected to injustice at the hands of others. Most people relish the prospect of a safe and secure environment for themselves and those they cherish. For most people, trust is key to meaningful and lasting relationships, and truthfulness is key to trust. People generally crave the experiences of respect and regard. In general, dignity is a vital element of well-being. Most people wish to make wise decisions for themselves and their communities. And most people, when offered the opportunity without compromising the needs and interests of those they love, welcome the prospect of pursuing their passions.

Taken together, these observations regarding the *nature of humanity* provide *grounding for a vision of applied ethics for communication studies*. Among the core values we are able to cull from these revelations are *presumptions* in favor of truthfulness, integrity, courage, humility, care, love, compassion, receptivity, response-ability, and responsibility, justice, and fairness, kindness, and responsiveness.

Importantly, these critical starting points for a vision of applied ethics in communication studies *must not be interpreted or applied either too narrowly or too broadly*. Their application in any specific context must be guided in equal measure both by a recognition of their vital importance on the one hand, and a deep awareness of their limits in the face of diversity on the other. For example, faithfulness to the core values implicit in the Golden Rule conjoins interlocutors to avoid exploitation of another's vulnerabilities in pursuit of self-interest. At the same time, however, application of the Golden Rule in any given context requires consideration of the Other's interests and perspectives *on his or her terms*. In Benhabib's words, ethics in practice calls for connection with the *concrete*, rather than the *generalized* Other (Benhabib, 1992).

Addressing this important caveat requires attentiveness to the role of difference in today's globally interdependent world. In their contribution to the volume, Taylor and Hawes go so far as to suggest that, in their words, "alterity—the conceptualization and practice of Otherness—is the central concern of ethics." Many of the volume's contributors share this sensibility. In response, the volume includes substantive counsel on how to *relate responsibly and responsively to difference* in all of its manifestations.

RELATING WELL TO DIFFERENCE

Recognition of the need to confront difference well reflects responsiveness to the moment. As noted throughout the volume, large-scale climactic, political, and demographic shifts have fundamentally altered the nature of community for people around the globe. Never before have so many been displaced from their ancestral homes; never before have so many lived in proximity with others whose norms and customs are different and, in some cases, at odds with their own. People cast outside familiar ground through a Diaspora or a more localized event often suffer great losses, insecurities, poverty, alienation, identity crises, and other grave hardships. Simultaneously, influxes of newcomers into long-dominant monocultural communities often foster enmity, fear, and xenophobia between newer and older residents. Violence, injustice, exploitation, and in some cases genocide are among the terrible outcomes of these responses.

Among the conditions underlying these phenomena is dominance of the view that difference is inherently dangerous, something to be feared and avoided. Even groups able to overcome primal fears of otherness sometimes succumb to less visceral, but nevertheless potentially debilitating, negative constructions of otherness. For these individuals and groups difference is perceived as inherently problematic, a *deficit* to be overcome rather than an *asset* to be embraced.

Although not difficult to understand, deficit-based orientations to difference significantly compromise fulfillment of communication's potential in today's globally interdependent, technologically interconnected world. Among other things, people encountering difference in these ways find it difficult to build the trust, respect, regard, and mutual understanding required to hear and be heard, to understand and be understood. In these and related ways, relating to difference as something to fear or as an obstacle to overcome compromises abilities to live well together and to collaborate in pursuit of sound decision making.

As chapters throughout the volume reveal, the urgency of the moment demands inclusive and collective efforts to understand and responsibly address the human-made causes of suffering plaguing humanity in this moment. Contributors throughout the volume effectively convey the gravity of this moment. As they reveal, never before has the destiny of the world and the flourishing of its inhabitants depended so strikingly upon humanity's collective will and ability to live well together, and to discern, understand, and responsibly address the issues of the day. Given the centrality of communicative action in each of these processes, never before has humanity's shared state of well being rested so strongly on the clarity, responsibility, and wisdom of the field's response.

Against this backdrop, the authors' collective call to engage difference constructively takes on special meaning. Exploration of the role *partiality* plays in shaping human understanding of issues and circumstances underscores the importance of this insight.

Chapters throughout the volume highlight the significant light shed by rhetorical, phenomenological, postmodernist, postcolonial, and feminist approaches to communication studies regarding the centrality of partiality in informing all human endeavors. Critical analyses of seemingly impartial scholarship within and across the sciences, for example, reveal how researchers' values, interests, and interpretive frames inevitably inform the questions they pose, the methodological tools they employ, and the language used to convey their findings. Similarly, critical analyses of journalistic practice reveal the inevitability of partiality in all facets of the craft, from identifying events worthy of coverage, to preparing narrative accounts, to disseminating the story. The volume offers numerous such windows into the myriad ways discourse both shapes and reveals partiality's inevitable role in framing.

Schaefer et al.'s explorations of the role dominant economic discourses play in shaping widely held perceptions regarding the efficacy of *laissez faire* capitalism vividly illustrate this phenomenon. Their analyses reveal, for example, the instrumental role that discourse from ostensibly impartial and otherwise apparently credible sources plays in *masking* unjust economic policies and practices. As they suggest, critical analysis is required to *unmask* the partiality that informs—and often subsumes—the sanctioned institutional and organizational discourse at the heart of unjust economic relations.

The volume is replete with such examples, reflecting in particular the multiple ways in which partiality is implicated in every facet of scholarly work across the field of communication studies, yet often hidden from view. The myth of neutrality so endemic in many academic circles, for example, often masks the inherently partial nature of all facets of communication study, from the identification and articulation of research questions, the selection and application of research methodologies, the interpretation, analyses, and dissemination, of findings, the content and methods of communication pedagogy, to the framing of guidelines for communicative acts. In each of these vital arenas, communication studies inevitably privilege one set of values, interests, ways of knowing, being, and valuing over others.

Chapters throughout the volume reveal as well the central role of *standpoint* in partiality. Individual standpoint—the intersections of one's race, ethnicity, gender, religious affiliation, tribal identity, socioeconomic standing, hierarchical status within any given social context, age, physical properties, emotional makeup, and related features of one's identity at any given moment—profoundly influences how one takes in cultural artifacts, texts, interactions, news, information, other forms of communication, and direct experiences.

Duster's (2009) observations regarding the tendency of elites to presume that their status is both natural and just point to the role of standpoint in perceptual framing among those at the top of any given hierarchy. However, this phenomenon is not unique to the most powerful and privileged among us. Each and every being's response to any given moment is influenced by all that makes up his or her identity at that time in that context. And as is revealed throughout the volume, *communication is implicated in every facet of identity formation, self-reflection, storytelling, interpretation, being and acting across contexts.*

Importantly, however, *partiality* should not be confused with *partisanship.* As authors throughout the volume have shown, critical self-awareness, moral imagination, shifting of perspective, an ethic of interdependence, dialogic communication skills, compassion, and humility help to mitigate tendencies to collapse one into the other. For example, through *critical self-reflection*, decision makers are able to develop the capacity to recognize the role that standpoint plays in shaping how they take in the world. This process in turn opens the possibility of transformation. Similarly, awareness of how others see us helps to foster conditions for meaningful reciprocal exchanges.

A humble recognition of our partiality and related commitment to fairness paves the way for open hearted, nondefensive, attentive listening. This enactment of *balanced partiality* in turn enables us to reach across differences in pursuit of mutual understanding.

In contrast, partisanship—whether adopted by individuals or groups—inherently compromises abilities to hear and be heard, to understand and be understood. Schaefer et al.'s exploration of differences between propaganda on the one hand and rhetoric on the other within the context of economic discourse provides an illuminating exemplar of this phenomenon. Citing Jowett and O'Donnell's work (2006), they note that propaganda "does not seek mutual sharing or fulfillment of mutual needs but only to control information, manage public opinion, and manipulate behavior patterns." In contrast, responsible and responsive rhetoric takes into account the audience's needs and fosters mutual and open engagement in pursuits of knowledge, truth, and wise deliberations.

An applied ethics for communication studies must therefore carefully *avoid confusing partisanship and propaganda, both obstacles to constructive engagement, with partiality: which, when recognized, offers the promise of constructive engagement.*

Taken together, these insights regarding the inevitability of partiality, the role of standpoint in perceptual framing, and the availability of resources to help avoid collapsing partiality into partisanship provide important starting points for a reframing of difference.

Related is the recognition that, as individuals and a collective, only when we have had the opportunity and ability to take in widely diverse orientations and perspectives do we have reason for confidence that we have done all we can to uncover and responsibly confront the challenges facing humanity in today's globally interdependent context. In important ways, this acknowledgment, and the simple expression of *epistemological humility* it entails, provide the basis for a transformative vision of difference.

Contributors throughout the volume further illuminate the role that communication plays in framing experiences of difference. Ivie's exploration of reconciliation as a peace-building discourse, for example, reveals that this framing "transforms perspectives and relationships in a context of contestation and difference." Through this form of symbolic action, the discourse of reconciliation "manages the tension between identity and identification as it articulates compensatory points of identification to produce a mutually enriching and empowering unity-in-difference." Similarly, Munshi, Broadfoot, and Smith draw on Maori "resiliency, imagination, and sense of possibility" to reveal how communication ethics, "caught in translation and negotiation processes between peoples, logics, and values" may provide an "in-between space" of inestimable value to humanity's quest for a world in which people from diverse backgrounds may live well together.

The volume includes illuminating accounts as well of the role mass media have the potential to play in transforming peoples' experience of difference. Meer and Modood illustrate, for example, how permeating contemporary media with "an ethic of multiculturalism" has the potential to "distil a sensitivity" helping to "pluralize the imagination of nationhood and realities of citizenship" for collectivities around the globe. Entertainment media, literature, journalism, published testimonials, political discourse, advertising, public relations, and other forms of mass communication have the potential to nurture moral imagination, enlarged perspective, creativity, reflection, and other pathways to community building and collaborative decision making, just as they have the power to distort, manipulate, trivialize, demonize, foster war and sustain inequitable power relations.

Discourse's power to shape identities, relationships, markets, communities, and experiences in these ways is not new; oral, written, and visual forms of rhetoric across contexts have been instrumental in framing human experiences and perceptions throughout history. However, the overwhelming control of mass mediated communications networks by a handful of transnational corporate players, the ubiquitous reach of mass media across the globe, and the high stakes involved in decisions regarding how to make use of these resources create unparalleled exigencies for communication studies.

Through these and related reflections, the volume helps to reveal the importance of employing communication resources in service to a transformative vision of difference. *Developing the will and ability to respond skillfully and responsibly to difference* must therefore be a preeminent feature of a vision of applied ethics for communication studies. Toward this end, the exploration below taps insights from the volume regarding development of a transformative framework.

DEVELOPING A CULTURE OF ENGAGEMENT

Many people who are thinking and working in what are generally called Western traditions cling to the view that adversarial communication is ideally designed to help equip the human family with the communicative and deliberative tools needed to confront this historical moment responsibly and well. For example, adversarial communication between opposing counsel in legal contexts continues to be viewed by many in the West as vital for the pursuits of truth and justice. Similarly, within mainstream academic circles, adversarial engagement continues to be perceived by many as essential for successful critical inquiry. The very foundations of reasonable and just exercises of democracy are similarly understood by many to be dependent upon adversarial advocacy.

And yet, several features of the Western adversarial model inevitably constrain fulfillment of this promise. Underlying this model of communication are the assumptions that difference necessarily entails opposition and that opposition necessarily requires adversarial communication. Adversaries within the dominant argument culture are encouraged to associate successful advocacy with being right, with winning an argument or prize, with prevailing on behalf of one's dogma, ideology, or cause, or otherwise satisfying individualistic interests (Makau & Marty, in press).

At its best, this approach to communicating across difference provides training in the skills of research, advocacy, critique, and refutation. Within communication studies programs in North America, Europe, and Australia, this stance is often used to support continued endorsement of adversarial communication models. While theoretically this approach to difference taps important intellectual skills in the service of informed decision making, *in practice* advocates within the argument culture are encouraged to wield their communication skills aggressively. Strategies such as demonizing and vilifying the Other and intimidating one's adversaries are encouraged, especially if doing so supports victory for one's position or cause. Within real-world contexts, this approach inherently fosters hostile communication environments. Participants caught in such circumstances tend to get locked into their positions and avoid reflecting on or reconsidering their values and assumptions. Listening attentively, opening one's heart to the Other, pursuit of mutual understanding, acknowledging the limits of one's perspective, and responding thoughtfully to views potentially at odds with one's own are perceived as weaknesses within such a framework (Makau & Marty, 2010).

As many of this volume's contributors have revealed, mutual trust, respect, meaningful connection, relational integrity, wise deliberations, justice and peace are among the casualties associated with this approach to communication across difference. In light of this recognition and the extraordinary complexity and significance of this historical moment, *fostering a culture of engagement across difference must therefore be a driving force behind development of an applied ethics vision for communication studies.*

In response to this exigency, the volume's contributors offer a diversity of foci, directions, and forms of counsel. Many of the authors write movingly, for example, about the importance of fostering transformative communicative action with particular attention to social justice and care. Rejecting the dominant divide between justice and care as moral orientations, this group of authors underscores the importance of integrating commitments to abstract constructions of justice with careful attention to concrete, material conditions, relational integrity, responsiveness, and care. Planalp and Fitness, for example, provide an integrative analysis featuring recognition of *"connection* and *inclusion* in personal relationships and society" and *respect* and *dignity* as basic human rights. They write further of the roles that interdependence and mutuality play in implicating *fairness* and *justice* as features of relational integrity. Their analysis accounts as well for dialectical tensions between connection and interdependence on the one hand, and appeals to *autonomy* and *privacy* on the other. And their overview of diverse kinds of kinship underscores the importance of taking account of the *particular* while exploring the *transcendent* in fostering *just and caring* relationships.

Elsewhere in the volume, contributors stress the importance of narrative, eschewing particular interpretive frames and counseling against efforts to pursue transcendence. Still other authors feature an emphasis on responsiveness to the needs and interests of the disenfranchised and most vulnerable among us in the face of some centralizing economic and technological tendencies, with special attention to the material consequences of our work. Some of the volume's contributors embrace traditional or adaptive pluralism, some explore cosmopolitan approaches, while still others question the viability of either of these frameworks in the contemporary context. Some of the authors stress the importance of pursuing truth, while others express skepticism and other forms of reservation regarding the promotion of such efforts.

These are among many significant differences of approach and perspective found within the chapters. And yet, the volume as a whole reflects *shared interest in exploring the promise of developing dialogic models of communication.*

TOWARD A DIALOGIC MODEL OF COMMUNICATION

Among the authors emphasizing the importance of such exploration is Arnett. In his vision, "dialogue begins with content, not process or subjective intent." He underscores the importance of taking in "what people consider the good," or in his words, "what they protect and promote." Rather than presume a single orientation or pursue common ground, Arnett proposes a "narrative" approach to dialogic communication featuring multiple pathways to fulfillment of humanity's potential.

Munshi, Broadfoot, and Smith share many precepts with Arnett. However, they guide their exploration of dialogic communication with postcolonial explorations of "how individuals and institutions perform active interventions in their worlds focused on the goals of global compassion, justice, and hope." They emphasize the importance of reflecting on "how different forms of communicative practice take on particular moral dimensions; which moral obligations are recognized and how; how individuals and institutions can begin to combine intellectual and practical concerns of specific contexts to ethically inform their work, and finally, what kinds of communicative practices they aspire to construct when acting in a moral way." The authors are careful to note that their postcolonial project is not designed to "look at the practices of subaltern groups as 'new objects of study,'" but rather "to draw on other ways of thinking, building connections, and communicating based on lived experiences."

Munshi, Broadfoot, and Smith borrow from "indigenous *Kaupapa* Maori theory and practice" and from the work of Bhabha (1990) to "explore/imagine the communicative practices and ethics necessary to create a 'space in between' for authentic dialogue in a multicultural environment." Their work stresses the importance of asking "how collective responsibility is performed, how relationships are constructed, how individual and collective needs are met, how individuals and institutions can be accountable for generations to come, and where reciprocity lies in communicating collective well-being." They offer critical insights into the roles *accountability, context, truthfulness,* and *community* play in framing ethical inquiry and practice. Their research uncovers a "Maori code of conduct" featuring a *respect for people, meeting people face to face, looking and listening to find a place from which to speak, being politically astute, cultural safe and reflexive, not trampling on the mana of people,* and *being humble.*

Mumby's incisive analysis of communication, power, and ethics offers related insights. In his words:

> The study of ethics is centrally concerned with the ways in which one engages with "the other"; to what extent is the other treated as an object to be strategically manipulated or as a human who fully engages and interrogates our own sense of self?

Although different in content and foci, the insights offered by Mumby, Arnett, and Munshi, Broadfoot and Smith reflect shared recognition of the critical role ethical engagement across difference plays in responsible and responsive communicative action. Further, their explorations taken together shed light into the conditions required for meaningful multicultural dialogue.

Taylor and Hawes underscore the importance of such efforts. In their words, "it is increasingly clear that the options for a safe and predictable existence organized around monologue and homogeneity are shrinking, and may only be maintained at great cost to Self and Others." They go on to explore an emerging reconceptualization of "communicative agency following the decentering of the ethical subject." Their analysis probes the importance of developing "a compelling and coherent image of the subject in order to represent the integrity of ethical practice." They note further that in postmodernist accounts, "'responsible' ethical agents are those whose abilities to respond are developed and supervised in ongoing relationships." Citing Bracci (2007), they allude to the virtue of "reflectively nurturing the potential for mutual recognition and transformation that is opened through" dialogic encounters.

These are among the many contributions the volume makes in helping move communication studies toward development and implementation of a multicultural dialogic framework. Yet, even as the scholars represented throughout the volume urge this transformation of vision, they are careful not to overstate the shared ground provided by their collective contributions. Arnett, Bhargava, Mumby, D'Souza, Christians, Stewart, Meer and Modood, Hyde, Ess, Buzzanell, and other contributors are careful to observe, for example, that in our efforts to construct a meaningful ground for multicultural dialogic interaction we cannot assume a shared understanding of the *good,* particularly in light of growing awareness of and sensitivity to human diversity in all of its forms. As these and other authors throughout the volume emphasize, subordinating different ways of being, knowing, and valuing through acculturation, assimilation, or other forms of homogenization will only serve to revitalize cultural hegemony and related forms of social and economic injustice. The volume provides countless concrete illustrations of how such efforts to homogenize inevitably undermine, rather than support, responsible and responsive communicative action. In his contribution, for example, Ess admonishes attentiveness to the diversity of values and preferences at the heart of different responses to new technologies and media. As such, in our pursuit of a vision of applied ethics for communication studies we must *avoid the temptation to imagine a universal conception of the good as its foundation.*

Related are important distinctions between three constructs often confused with one another:

multiculturalism, diversity, and cultural relativism. On the one hand, commitment to multicultural education, scholarship, and engagement entails a diffusion of historic power relations. Placing no single ideology or dogma, value system or perspective at the center of teaching and research, for example, compels inclusiveness of representation and voice. Multicultural approaches to inquiry require attentive listening, open-hearted consideration, shifting of perspective, and balanced partiality in the face of different ways of knowing, being, and valuing.

Diversity as a construct, on the other hand, sits at the confluence of genetic and biological material, ancestral, social, spiritual, and aesthetic propensities, and related interpretive and experiential factors giving shape to narratives and perspectives. The richness and fluidity of each person's identity—finding new shape through each encounter and experience—informs recognition of humanity's extraordinary diversity. As an approach to exploring ways of knowing, being, and valuing, multiculturalism celebrates diversity in all of its forms and embraces the possibilities of new insight made possible through authentic engagements across differences.

However, the *celebration of diversity, commitment to inclusiveness, and related absence of a fixed center associated with multicultural ethics do not entail the absence of criteria or grounds for discerning more or less ethical, sound, or wise decisions.* As the Dalai Lama (1999) observes, the twin hazards of "crude absolutism" and "trivial relativism" inevitably compromise sound deliberative processes. Similarly, in his contribution to the volume, Ess urges pursuit of a pluralistic approach that at once recognizes the irreducibility of differences between cultural traditions and preference without compromising core human values. As these admonitions suggest, the human family's well being rests on implementation of a middle path between the extremes of ethical monism and radical forms of relativism. The exploration below introduces a pathway several volume contributors offer toward pursuit of such a middle ground.

REASONABLENESS AND RESPONSIVENESS

Contributors throughout the volume recount many of the substantive grounds frequently cited for rejecting positivist constructions of rationality as guides for interaction, deliberation, and action. Their analyses provide strong support for abandoning the strangleholds of interpretive frames underlying scientism and positivism within and outside communication studies.

At the same time, however, it is important to distinguish between certain types of rationality within scientism and positivism, on the one hand, and pursuits of reasonableness standards within interdependent ethical frameworks on the other. As critical findings from such pursuits reveal, abandonment of *reasonableness* as a critical guide for interaction, deliberation, and action gravely compromises any hope of grounding for mutually respectful and fulfilling relationships, and for just and wise decision making. Although difficult to define, reasonableness is essential to the quest to develop a viable and credible guide for living well together and for just and wise deliberation in a globally interdependent world.

At a minimum, reasonableness can be understood as an antidote to *arbitrariness*. Whenever someone is subjected to flagrant acts of unfairness, devoid of reasoned and responsive justification, there is great likelihood of suffering. Within an interdependent framework, depriving another of dignity on the basis of the person's creed, ethnicity, or socioeconomic status, for example, inherently jeopardizes the well-being of all. In its starkest forms, arbitrariness inevitably compromises human flourishing within and across cultural boundaries. The volume offers moving testimonials of the profound suffering caused, for example, when those vested with institutional authority wield their power arbitrarily and without accountability. D'Souza's essay provides a particularly incisive look at this phenomenon. In her words: when "Unreason masquerades as reason, fear reigns, nightmares of chaos and upheaval rule," and we otherwise gravely imperil the "dream of human flourishing."

Borrowing insights from Aune (2001), Deetz (1992), Dewey (1927), Habermas (1983), and Weber (1946), Schaefer et al. vividly illustrate the pervasiveness of this phenomenon in today's prevailing economic order. They reveal, for example, how the "union of technical rationality and corporate dominance" has gravely compromised the promotion of public interests. Their analyses reveal further how "narrowly bureaucratic reward systems" ignore "higher principles, guidelines, and morals" and otherwise jeopardize even the most cursory efforts to inculcate moral sensibilities into corporate policies and practices. Simply put, a narrow form of bureaucracy-in-practice, devoid of mitigating reasonableness standards, creates a self-perpetuating paradigm of irresponsibility at all levels of organizational decision making. This graphic case in point underscores the importance of infusing deliberative processes with *legitimate* reasonableness standards responsive to a higher calling.

As many of the volume's contributors have noted, however, standards of reasonableness responsive to humanity's great diversity will not be easy to establish. In their contribution to the volume, for example, Benson and Campbell identify significant threats to deliberative reason in today's mediated political environment. Nor can we expect that those who routinely exercise sovereign power without accountability will acquiesce easily to this call for transformative change. Neither will the strangleholds of technical rationality and bureaucracy-in-practice be easy to overcome.

Seeger and Kuhn, Benson and Campbell, D'Souza, L'Etang, Barghava, Christensen, Morsing, Thyssen, Feighery, Hasian, and Rieke are among the many scholars whose contributions to the volume follow this critical realization. And yet, as is revealed through their analyses and throughout the volume, an ethic of interdependence responsive to this historical moment compels pursuit of just such a transformation. A meaningful vision of applied ethics for communication studies in this historic moment must serve to facilitate development of *viable, responsive standards of reasonableness applicable across cultural boundaries.*

The presumptive status of core values articulated earlier offers a valuable starting point for this work. Importantly, this source of ground integrates logic and emotion, as well as accommodating empirical, aesthetic, materials, and spiritual domains of inquiry, interrogation, and deliberation. Contributors throughout the volume provide thoughtful explorations of related grounding for reasonableness standards. Drawing on insights from studies of casuistry, *phronesis*, dialectic, rhetoric, narrative analysis, cultural studies, linguistics, and philosophy, the authors contribute valuably to the quest to identify *legitimate* tools for assessing the reasonableness of claims, narratives, perspectives, arguments, and decisions in a multicultural society. Whatever else a vision of applied ethics for communication studies offers, *pursuit of viable cross-cultural standards for assessing the reasonableness of arguments and narratives* must surely be a primary goal.

PURSUING TRUTH

Perhaps even more challenging—but no less important—are efforts to pursue truth (or truths). As the volume's contents attest, humanity's inherent fallibility prevents establishing the truth of claims, orientations, interpretations, or narrative accounts with certainty. Within an interdependent multicultural ethical framework, the pursuit of truth is a particularly complex and tenuous undertaking. Given these circumstances, developing viable, responsive criteria for assessing the reliability of empirical claims, the validity of inferences, and related evidentiary standards are daunting tasks. Pursuits of truth(s) in spiritual, aesthetic, and value domains are even more vexing.

And yet, as contributors throughout the volume have shown, the abandonment of these quests promotes arbitrariness, injustice, violent conflicts, and decisions with devastating consequences to the qualities of our relationships, to the destiny of the natural world, and to peace and prosperity across the globe. In his contribution to the volume, Christians underscores the importance of this recognition. Identifying relativism as among the greatest obstacles to human flourishing in the new millennium, Christians admonishes communication scholars, educators, and practitioners to pursue valid realism as an epistemological starting point in pursuits of truth across domains. Simply put, humanity can no longer afford the postmodern inclination to "throw out the" enlightenment baby "with the bathwater."

Christians' insights regarding the role of journalism in pursuits of truth(s) are particularly instructive. He begins by repeating the Hutchins Commission emphasis on the "media's duty to serve society." Within a dialogic ethical framework, this duty requires that journalists enable people "to articulate their own needs and possible solutions." On this view, fulfillment of journalistic goals include "identifying representative voices and communities rather than spectacular ones that are anecdotal and idiosyncratic."

Christians goes on to explore the pivotal role that the search for truth and the corresponding duty to truthfulness play in responsible journalistic practice. As he notes, "virtually every code of ethics in journalism begins with the newsperson's duty to tell the truth under all circumstances." He is careful to observe that "the mainstream view of truth as accurate information is too narrow for today's social and political complexities." In place of this orientation, Christians proposes "disclosure" as the pivotal criterion for journalistic integrity. In his words, "forsaking the quest for precision journalism does not mean imprecision but precision in disclosure and authenticity—in getting to the heart of the matter." Christians offers what he calls "interpretive sufficiency" to frame this feature of the journalist's craft. He adds:

> The best journalists will ensure the news story's deeper reading by understanding from the inside the attitudes, culture, language, and definitions of the people and events they are actually reporting. The truth of authenticity unveils the inner character of a series of events. They generate an insightful picture that gets at the essence of the matter. Rather than reducing social issues to the financial and administrative problems defined by politicians, the news media ought to disclose the depth and nuance that enables readers and viewers to identify the fundamental issues themselves.

Christians concludes his exploration with the observation that "journalism ethics needs to nurture the philosophical imagination across the board." Further, "all the ethical issues the media face should be rooted in beliefs about the character of human beings and the meaning of life."

These insights regarding the nature and role of truth-seeking to responsible and responsive journalistic practice in today's world are applicable to other genres as well. Of particular import are implications to literature, film, and entertainment media. Narratives brought to life through these forms of communication are among the most powerful resources available for ethical inquiry and illumination. Throughout history, storytelling has been instrumental in fulfilling communication's constructive potential. Narratives in literature and film, for example, offer unparalleled potential for cultivating moral imagination and shifting of perspective, nurturing critical self-assessment, and fostering consubstantiation, compassion, care, and loving connection across differences. At the same time, however, narrative's power to illuminate is matched by its power to distort, manipulate, and mislead. An applied ethic for communication studies cannot avoid interrogating intersections between narrative integrity, accountability, responsiveness, and responsibility.

This work offers the corollary promise of promoting exploration of truth and Truth as constructs. Roseanne Cash's response to the depiction of her family in the film *Walk the Line* concisely illustrates this intersection. In an interview with reporter Stephen Dalton (2006), Cash suggests that the portrayal was, to a large extent, *factually correct*. And yet from her perspective, the Hollywood production failed to convey, in her words, *"larger truths."* Conversely, burgeoning genres in historical fiction are often criticized for their failure to remain faithful to empirically verifiable facts. Most docu-dramatists and historical novelists are careful to concede precisely this point in prefaces to their narratives. And yet these genres sometimes offer potentially *illuminating* venues for exploring the nature of the human condition. Barbara Kingsolver's (1998) popular historical fiction, *Poisonwood Bible*, offers a concrete illustration of this complex dynamic.

Related are important intersections between truthfulness and truth, integrity and critical self-awareness, knowledge, understanding, and wisdom. Exploring these, as well as related intersections between accuracy of information, philosophical and spiritual insight, revelation, testimonials, narrative integrity and accountability, and other pathways to illumination will prove critical to human flourishing in the 21st century. Given the centrality of discourse in informing worldview, shaping relationships, creating possibilities between people, and fostering engagement and inquiry, communication studies will be instrumental to these pursuits.

Toward this end, a vision of applied ethics for communication studies must feature cross-disciplinary collaborative efforts to *develop standards for inclusive, meaningful, cross-culturally viable and reliable assessments of narrative fidelity and probability, empirical verifiability, inferential soundness, revelation, and other pathways to truth*. Similarly, *communication scholarship and pedagogy responsive to the moment must find effective ways to collaborate responsibly with other disciplines in fostering development of the knowledge and skills required for information and media literacy.*

These efforts will inevitably confront significant obstacles, particularly in the face of the corporatization of media and the academy. Yet, a meaningful vision for applied ethics in communication studies cannot escape the call today.

Among the obstacles to fulfillment of this vision is the seductive hold instrumental rationality retains among many across the political spectrum. Accepting the precept that the "ends justify the means," many activists representing widely diverse interests and perspectives routinely use communication to deceive, manipulate, or intimidate in pursuit of their goals. Even demonstrably caring, devoted proponents of peace and justice are among those who invoke the nobility of their cause to justify wielding communication's destructive powers. Instrumental rationality—understood specifically here as the notion that one should privilege short-term efficiency over other humane values and interests—cannot withstand critical scrutiny.

This message, conveyed throughout the volume, echoes the voices of great world leaders such as Mahatma Gandhi and Nelson Mandela. As their visionary model of leadership revealed, *the means are the ends in the making*. If we wish to see a world of peace, we must practice peace. If we hope to experience justice, we must practice justice. Every act of exploitation, every demeaning word, every violation of dignity compromises this quest. Whenever we give in to the temptation to deceive, even in the service of a noble cause, we inevitably undermine our own integrity, compromise trust, and shatter the very ground upon which to build connection and community. And whenever we allow partisanship to compromise our abilities to hear and be heard, to understand and be understood, we jeopardize fulfillment of communication's constructive potential. In these and other ways, instrumental rationality inevitably compromises our abilities to hear the twin calls of reason and responsibility, to experience responsiveness, and to embrace the care and compassion compelled by a shared commitment to the core human values explored earlier.

Importantly, renouncing instrumental rationality should not be equated with a call to reject narrowly consequentialist considerations in ethical deliberation. Throughout the volume, contributors feature consequentialist analysis as key to applied ethics. Anticipating, to the best of our abilities, the short and long term consequences of our communicative actions is indeed a central element of any meaningful vision of applied ethics for the field. As the earlier explorations of core humane values reveals, however, consequentialism is a *necessary* but *not sufficient* form of analysis for responsible and responsive communicative action.

Given the nature of the moment, a meaningful vision of applied ethics for communication studies will need to bridge historic gulfs between consequentialist, deontological, virtue, care, and justice ethical paradigms. Tapping each of these domains, without compromising their integrity, will prove challenging. Multicultural dialogic communication—incorporating guidelines for responsible and responsive communication such as those associated with Maori traditions— provides invaluable resources for overcoming this and related obstacles to responsible communicative action.

For example, attentive listening and truthful, open, caring, compassionate, and humble engagement across difference creates conditions required to take in and understand the Other on his or her own terms. Multicultural dialogic engagement encourages critical reflection, fosters moral imagination and shifting of perspective, encourages critical self-reflection, and insists on accountability. Through constructive engagements across differences, participants are enriched by exposure to diverse interpretations and perspectives, and motivated to probe more deeply for hidden truths. Further, this form of reciprocal exchange enables individuals and groups to adapt the Golden Rule and other guides to action to the *particular demands of the moment* without succumbing to a reductionist (absolutist) or (trivial) relativist orientation.

In sum, despite the inherent tenuousness of humanity's efforts to pursue truth and reason in today's complex world, in spite of the apparent incongruities between diverse moral traditions, and although each moment reveals itself *uniquely* to those encountering it, the human family nevertheless has access to *meaningful presumptive starting points for ethical and effective engagement and inquiry.*

In their exploration on communication ethics in organizations, Seeger and Kuhn offer a moving phrase to encapsulate this feature of the vision. Exploring complex issues of moral agency within organizational contexts, they speak of the "infinite humanity of human beings." Citing Roberts (2003), they note that "such a view stands in direct contrast to the typical assumption in management and economics theorizing about persons as opportunistic, rational, and self serving." And while acknowledging "challenges and tensions" in the path to constituting "more ethically appealing organizations" aligned with this vision, they see promise in this pursuit.

As the volume editors suggest in their introductory comments, intimate links between communication, ethics, and dialectic provide means needed to tap these resources effectively. Nowhere are these connections more evident than in the exercise of the ancient art of deliberation.

DELIBERATIVE PARTNERSHIPS

In his contribution to the *21st Century Communication Reference Handbook*, James Klumpp observes that the term *deliberation* is a "Latin verb meaning to weigh, to balance." At the heart of this art is a spirit of critical inquiry directed at sound decision making. Individuals and communities may be said to be deliberative when they tap all available resources in pursuit of the most informed, reasoned, just, and wise decision possible in any given context (Klumpp, 2009, p. 202).

In her exploration of intersections between intercultural training, multicultural theorizing, and deliberative reason, Ting-Toomey in this volume offers valuable related insights. She writes of the important roles that "cultivating creative visions of alternative options and seeking globally inclusive solutions to address diverse ethically wrangling situations" will play in effectively confronting today's complex issues. As noted earlier, dialogic interactions, informed by an interdependent multicultural ethic, and an assets-based orientation toward difference, foster conditions for participants to take in diverse perspectives. Within such a framework, communicators are *motivated* to assess their own and others' views. Under these circumstances, participants are inclined to pursue additional information and insights collaboratively. Through these efforts, they will be equipped to cultivate "creative visions of alternative visions" and to seek "globally inclusive solutions." Similarly, through empathic and compassionate regard and a keen sense of human interdependence, deliberative partners are receptive to openly and honestly examining potential consequences for each proposed alternative (Makau & Marty, 2010).

Importantly, *agreement is not among the purposes* of such interactions; responsiveness and responsibility are not manifested in consensus. Groupthink, acquiescence to authority, coercion, and subordination of insight are among the many harmful outcomes attributable to consensus-driven models of discourse and deliberation. Rather than pursue agreement, responsible and responsive dialogic interactions open the possibilities of constructive engagement across differences, enabling participants to hear and be heard, to understand and be understood. Citing Bok (1995), Arnett in this volume reports that successful dialogue rests on only a *minimalist* expectation of agreement, beginning with "the assumption that we do not have to hold a great deal in common, but we must be willing to learn from the Other as we minimize our impulse to tell, even as we recognize the inevitability of the 'rhetorical' nature of our meeting."

Mumby's essay in this volume offers related insights. In his words, "from a communicative perspective, 'acting ethically' is a dynamic practice that requires an ongoing awareness of the everyday operations of power, and a willingness to engage 'the other' in a manner that is both responsive to his/her/their difference and that opens up the possibility for self-transformation." He goes on to underscore the risks associated with responsible and responsive engagements with others. Unlike the dangers of combative interactions, the risks entailed in such engagements are not that individuals may lose or fail to prevail, but rather that they might *change*.

Initially the fear of change prevents many people from open engagements with one another. Yet, as many of the volume's contributors remind us, nothing is more likely to contribute to fulfillment of communication's constructive potential than the willingness and ability to embrace the possibility of transformation. Responsible and responsive dialogic engagements thus depend on courageous individuals committed to productive change through constructive means. Under these interdependent conditions, deliberative communities flourish and the best decisions for collective well-being are made possible.

In their contribution to the volume, Taylor and Hawes explore the central role rhetoric plays in furthering this effort. As they note, when practiced responsibly and responsively, the art of rhetoric contributes invaluably to the "process of morally deliberating contingent matters of public interest under inevitable conditions of disagreement and uncertainty." Among other things, rhetoric cultivates "practical wisdom and identification in the reasoned interaction between speakers and audiences...." Hyde's transformative vision of "rhetorical competence" offers further insight. Careful to recognize the destructive potential of strategic communication, Hyde identifies appropriateness, truthfulness, and effectiveness as lenses for assessing rhetorical invention and style in service to human flourishing. Passionate, eloquent advocacy—responsive to the moment, truthful, compassionate, engaging, and reflective—contributes invaluably to reasoned, just, and wise deliberations.

When communication fulfills its constructive potential in these ways, people from diverse backgrounds and perspectives, ennobled by a sense of kinship and driven by a shared quest to address the moment responsibly, are empowered to pursue reasoned deliberation *together*. In his contribution to the volume, Hyde writes movingly of deliberative partnerships such as these, describing them as "dwelling places where the well being of humankind is respected and advanced." Hyde highlights the importance of accuracy and integrity as virtues in these contexts, and highlights open-mindedness, conscience-formation, and civility" as related goals. Throughout his contribution, Hyde joins the volume's editors in linking the ancient arts of rhetoric, dialectic, and ethics, observing in particular that "rhetoric is at work whenever language is being employed to open people to ideas, positions, and circumstances that, if rightly understood, stand a better than even chance of getting people to think and act wisely." Hyde concludes his essay by appealing to a recognition that "the otherness of the other is an ontological feature of human existence," ever-present and compelling in its call to conscience, in its call to "create those habitats or openings where collaborative deliberation, moral consciousness, and civility become possible and where a life-giving gift can be shared with others."

REALIZING THE VISION

By shedding light on the nature of the human condition in this historical moment, inculcating an ethic of interdependence, fostering conditions for transformative meetings across difference, developing pathways to meaningful connection, and generating other grounds for responsible and responsive deliberative partnerships, the volume's editors and contributors pave the way for fulfillment of communication's constructive potential.

In their introductory remarks, the volume editors draw attention to important cross-disciplinary studies of happiness, and invite readers to consider intimate connections between the "framing of 'the good life,' the narrative of life's meaning, the articulation of transcendent goals, and the importance of interaction." They go on to offer *human rights* as a representative case study, illustrating through its use the complexity, significance, and power of intersections between communication study, ethics, and pursuits of human flourishing across cultural boundaries. Through these and related explorations, the editors provide moving accounts of the intellectual, material, and spiritual promise afforded by reaching toward a transformative vision of applied ethics for communication study.

As is noted throughout the volume, the path toward fulfillment of this vision is likely to be laden with obstacles. Inequitable power relations reinforced by the tenacity of individualist frames, fear, greed, hostility, technological and instrumental rationality, and related challenges will almost surely pose barriers along the way. Corporate control of government, media, information resources, and educational institutions will no doubt pose particularly significant barriers.

To realize the vision in the face of such foreboding challenges, communication scholars, educators, students, and community partners will be called upon to share insights, gifts, and talents across disciplinary and cultural boundaries. Acknowledgment of the role partiality plays in all facets of communication study and practice will prove critical. Setting constructive limits in the face of structural inequalities, consciousness raising, and pursuit of collective action without falling prey to the seductive calls of partisanship will prove key to success as well.

In her essay, L'Etang draws on Wilkie's (2001, p. 33) work to ask, "What type of society do we wish to create and inhabit?" The volume offers a resounding reply: a world in which people across cultural boundaries come together in pursuit of flourishing for the earth and for all of its inhabitants. Through an integrative, holistic approach to communication study, ethical inquiry, education, dialectic, advocacy, and other forms of communicative action across contexts, this volume offers a critical starting point for realizing this vision, and *legitimate* grounds for hope of its fulfillment. It is difficult to imagine a more valuable contribution.

NOTES

1. Buzzanell cites Johannesen, Valde, and Whedbee (2008) and Redding (1996) in support of this insight.
2. Moral development theory further supports this assessment. For a brief overview of the relationship between moral development theory and communication ethics, see Makau (2009).

REFERENCES

Aristotle. (1954). *Rhetoric (*W. Rhys Roberts, Trans.). New York: Modern Library.

Aune, J. A. (2001). *Selling the free market: The rhetoric of economic correctness.* New York: Guilford Press.

Benhabib, S. (1992). *Situating the self: Gender, communication and postmodernism in contemporary ethics.* New York: Routledge.

Bhabha, H. (1990). DissemiNation: Time, narrative and the margins of the modern nation. In H. Bhabha (Ed.), *Nation and narration* (pp. 291–321). London: Routledge.

Bok, S. (1995). *Common values.* Columbia: University of Missouri Press.

Boyd, R. (2010, Jan. 14,). Tiny particles, big impact. *Monterey Herald*, p. B1.

Bracci, S. (2007). A conversation with Sharon Bracci. In P. Arneson (Ed.), *Exploring communication ethics: Interviews with influential scholars in the field* (pp. 89–105). New York: Lang.

Christians, C. G. (2007). A conversation with Clifford G. Christians. In P. Arneson (Ed.), *Exploring communication ethics: Interviews with influential scholars in the field* (pp. 89–105). New York: Lang.

Dalai Lama (1999). *Ethics for a new millennium.* New York: Riverhead Books.

Dalton, S. (2006, January 13). Walk the line, yes. Toe it, no. *New York Times.* Retrieved from http://www.nytimes.com

Deetz, S. A. (1992). *Democracy in an age of corporate colonization: Developments in communication and politics in everyday life.* Albany, NY: SUNY Press.

Dewey, J. (1927). *The public and its problems.* Athens, OH: Swallow Press.

Duster, T. (2009, Fall). The long path to higher education for African Americans. *Thought and Action, 25,* 99–111.

Habermas, J. (1983). *Moral consciousness and communicative action.* Cambridge, MA: MIT Press.

Johannesen, R. L., Valde, K., & Whedbee, K., (2008). *Ethics in human communication* (6th ed.). Prospects Heights, IL: Waveland.

Jowett, G. S., & O'Donnell, V. (2006). *Propaganda and persuasion* (4th ed.) Thousand Oaks, CA: Sage.

Kingsolver, B. (1998). *Poisonwood bible.* New York: HarperCollins.

Klumpp, J. (2009). Deliberation, debate, and decision making. In W. F. Eadie (Ed.), *21st century communication: A reference handbook* (pp. 202–219). Los Angeles: Sage.

Makau, J. M. (2009). Ethical and unethical communication. In W. F. Eadie (Ed.), *21st century communication: A reference handbook* (pp. 435–443). Los Angeles: Sage.

Makau, J. M., & Arnett, R. C. (Eds.). (1997). *Communication ethics in an age of diversity.* Urbana: University of Illinois Press.

Makau, J. M., & Marty, D. L. (2001). *Cooperative argumentation: A model for deliberative community.* Prospect Heights, IL: Waveland.

Makau, J. M., & Marty, D. L. (2009). *Reuniting communication and reason for a changing world.* Paper presented at the National Communication Association Conference, Chicago, Illinois.

Makau, J. M., & Marty, D. L. (in press). *Dialogue and deliberation.* Prospect Heights, IL: Waveland.

Nussbuam, M. (1997a). *Cultivating humanity: A classical defense of reform in liberal education.* Cambridge, MA: Harvard University Press.

Redding, W. C. (1996). Ethics and the study of organizational communication: When will we wake up? In J. A. Jaksa & M. S. Pritchard (Eds.), *Responsible communication: Ethical issues in business, industry and the professions* (pp. 17–40). Cresskill, NJ: Hampton.

Roberts, J. (2003). The manufacture of corporate social responsibility: Constructing corporate sensibility. *Organization, 10,* 249–265.

Solomon, R. C., & Higgins, K. M. (1997). *A passion for wisdom: A very brief history of philosophy.* New York: Oxford University Press.

Weber, M. (1946). *Max Weber: Essays in sociology* (H. H. Herth & C. Wright Mills, Eds.). New York: Oxford University Press.

Wiener, N. (1964). *God and Golem, Inc.: A Comment on certain points where cybernetics impinges on religion.* Cambridge, MA: MIT Press.

Wiener, N. (1989). *The human use of human beings: Cybernetics and society.* London: Free Association Books. (Original work published 1950)

Wilkie, W. (2001). Foreword. In P. Bloom & G. Gundlach (Ed.), *Handbook of marketing and society* (pp. vii–xi). Thousand Oaks, CA: Sage.

Index

A

Abu Ghraib, 252–253
Academic/philosophical discourses-popular/lay
    discourses, communication ethics, 3–4
Accountability, 170–171
  characterized, 462–463
  corporate social responsibility, 457–458
  Duke University lacrosse case, 267–268
  journalistic ethics, 267–268
  understandings of, 462–463
Accuracy, 300–301
Acknowledgment, 37–41
  recognition, 38
  social death, 38
Adversarial communication, 504–505
Agency, 18
  economic justice, 447–449
  human rights, 9
Alienation, 444–446
Alterity, 100–101
Alternative trade organizations, 452
American Association for the Advancement of
    Science, 316
American exceptionalism, 376
Amorality, 443–444
Answerability, 20–21
Aotearoa-New Zealand, 125–128
Applied ethics, 173–174
  characterized, 496–497
  communication studies, 494–513
    cross-disciplinary collaborative efforts,
      510
    material realities of global environment,
      495–496
    realizing visions, 513
Aristotle, *ethos,* 33
Artworks, vandalization, 242
Authority
  human rights, 9
  small group communication, 150–151
Autonomy, 303–304
  privacy, 205
  relationships, 138
Autopoiesis
  organizations, 459–460
  systems theory, 459–460

B

Badiou, A.
  communication meta-ethics, 110–113
  conceptualization of humans, 419–420
  disaster, 424–426
  environmentalism, 415–416, 419–420, 422,
    424–426
  evil, 424–426
  wild(er)ness event, 417–418
Bias, 45
Bioethics approaches, 295
Biological survival, social survival, compared,
    429–430
Bureaucracy, 167, 444–446
Bush (G.W.) administration
  course for war in Iraq, 148
  political communication, 280

C

Capitalism, 443
  alternative visions, 452
  democracy, relationship, 449
Cartesian *cogito,* effacement, 20
Casuistry, 295
Censorship
  freedom of speech, 387–389
  history, 387–389
  Lady Chatterley's Lover obscenity trial, 250–251
  photography, 248
  publication, 387–389
Change, communication, 477
Characterological approaches
  communication ethics, 276–277
  political communication, 276–277
Choice, 17–22
  communication ethics, individual choices, 22–27
  conceptual invitation from communication
    scholarship to reconsider, 18–21
    invitation refused, 20–21
  culture, 24–25
  effaced, 20
  Enlightenment understanding, 24
  ethics, nexting helix, 22–27
  incomplete analyses, 21–22
  responsiveness, 23–24
  rightness, 26

Cinema, 248–249
Citizenship
    media, 358
    multiculturalism, 355
Citizens' participation, media, 394–397
Civil society, 483–484
    characterized, 394
    state, mediators between, 393–394
Classification, human rights, 9
Climate chaos, 425–426
Codes of ethics, 173–174
    marketing, 229–231
    public relations, 229–231
Colonial imaging, 249–250
Communication, *see also* Specific type
    basic rules, 136–137
    change, 477
    cooperation, 136–137
    dialogic model, 505–507
    ethics, 94–96
        relationship, 1, 46–49
    forms, 390–391
    honesty, 136–137
    lying, 136–137
        moral ambiguity, 136
        prevalence, 136
    power, 94–96
Communication ethics, *see also* Specific type
    academic/philosophical discourses-popular/lay
        discourses, 3–4
    characterological approaches, 276–277
    choice, individual choices, 22–27
    contemporary world, 1–10
    decolonizing, 119–129
    dialogue, interplay, 45–60
    diversity, 49
    economic justice, 436–453
        alienation, 444–446
        alternative economies as social movements,
            452
        amorality, 443–444
        bureaucratization, 444–446
        capitalism, 443
        discursive-rhetorical analysis issues, 446–449
        economic aspects of discourse, 439–442
        economic justice as human rights issue, 438
        framing, 443–444
        immorality, 443–444
        interrelations of economy, ethics, and
            communication, 439–446
        linkage of economics to happiness, 438–439
        market, agency, and ethical action, 447–449
        market globalization, 449–452
        markets, 436–438
        material inquiry domains, 439
        meanings of the market in everyday life,
            446–447
        morality, 443–444

relations of democracy to capitalism, 449
        relevance, 436–439
        rhetoric of economy, 440
        rhetoric of neoliberalism, 440–442
        symbolic inquiry domains, 439
    ethics as content, 49
Eurocentric cultural assumptions, 119
fear appeals, 282–284
feminist approaches, 277
global-local dialectic, 5–7
health communication, 293–306
    accuracy, 300–301
    autonomy, 303–304
    bioethics approaches, 295
    casuistry, 295
    culpability, 302–303
    economic factors, 299, 306
    end-of-life issues, 297–298
    equity, 303–304
    ethics of caring, 294
    exaggeration, 301
    feminist ethics, 294
    guilt, 302–303
    health campaign ethics, 299–305
    healthcare costs, 299, 306
    healthcare policy issues, 305–306
    individual to dialogic perspectives, 296–299
    inequity, 303–304
    influence, 301
    information technology, 305
    institutional factors, 299, 306
    intercultural concerns, 298
    labeling, 303
    moralism, 300
    narrative ethics, 294–295
    new biomedical technologies, 305
    pain treatment, 298
    patient, 296–297
    principalist approaches, 295
    provider–patient interaction, 296–299
    reliability, 300–301
    responsibility, 302–303
    risk communication, 299, 301–302
    shame, 302–303
    social gaps, 303–304
    stigmatizing, 303
    theoretical frameworks, 294–296
    underserved populations, 303–304
    virtue ethics, 295–296
    whistle-blowing, 299
key dialectics, 2–8
multiple, 46–49
multiplicity, 49
organizational contexts, 166–182
    accountability, 170–171
    applied ethics, 173–174
    body, 172–173
    bureaucracy, 167

centrality of communication, 168–171
codes of ethical conduct, 173–174
communication as domain for ethical praxis,
    168–169
decision making, 169
disavowing collective moral agency, 175–176
discursive formations, 169
dissent, 180–181
embracing moral agency through "real entity"
    perspective, 176
emerging trends, 181–182
employee rights, 179–180
employee voice, 180
free speech, 180
materiality, 171–173
morality, 174–179
organizational legitimacy, 167
organization values, 167
organizing, 171–173
privacy, 179–180
research, 179–184
shifting moral agency to situated subject,
    176–179
sites, 172
stakeholder perspectives, 179
textual agency, 172
theory, 179–184
whistle-blowing, 180–181
postcolonial theory, 119–129
    Aotearoa-New Zealand, 125–128
    corporate social responsibility, 120–122
    ethical analysis, 120–122
    ethical ground problematizing, 120–122
    ethical individual, 120–122
    feminist ethics, 122–125
    Foucauldian ethical analysis, 120–122
    'Other' look at ethics, 122–125
    presence, 125
    revisioning of communication ethics, 125–128
    Te Kaupapa Maori, 125–128
    towards praxis, 125–128
    transcultural ethics, 122–125
postmodernism, 277–278
    alterity, 100–101
    Badiou, A., 110–113
    conceptualizing communication, 104–105
    decentering of ethical subject, 104
    deconstruction of moral organization, 102
    discourse, 101–103
    ethics, 278–279
    ethics as central, 100
    issues, 278–279
    MacIntyre, A., 105–110
    Otherness, 100–101
    practice of communication ethics, 104–105
    practice of ethics, 100–103
    reconceptualizing communicative agency, 104
    theory of communication ethics, 104–105

theory of ethics, 100–103
rational-emotional dialectic, 7–8
relational understanding, 21
senses, 1
situating, 119
theoretical-practical dialectic, 2–3
theory, scholarly lineage, 47–48
universalizing framework, 119
universal-particular dialectic, 4–5
values, minimalist values and contexts, 279–284
viral messages, 282–284
vision, 125–128
YouTube, 282–284
Communication meta-ethics
    Badiou, A., 110–113
    MacIntyre, A., 105–110
Communication studies
    applied ethics, 494–513
        cross-disciplinary collaborative efforts, 510
        material realities of global environment,
            495–496
        realizing visions, 513
    embedded assumptions, 497–499
    framing, 497–499
Communicative action, 40–41
Communitarian ethics, journalism ethics, 192
Community
    emancipation, relationship, 378
    security, relationship, 378
Community power debate, 89–92
Compromise
    awareness, 26–27
    procedural ethics, 419
Compulsory groups, 150
Computer games
    new technology, 212–214
    virtue ethics, 212–214
Connection, relationships, 137
Conscience, 34–36
    Heidegger, M., 35
Consciousness raising groups, 150
Consensus, 391–392, 512
    deliberative democracy, 391–392
Constructive engagement, 512
Context, feminist discursive ethics, 71–73
    social construction of context, 71–73
Contextual secularism, 409–410
    objections, 410–411
Cooperation, communication, 136–137
Copyleft, new technology, 209–210
Copyright, new technology, 209–210
Core values, ethical reflection, 500–501
Corporate social responsibility
    accountability, 457–458
    as aspirational communication, 460–462
    ethics of, 470–471
    inevitable hypocrisy, 467–469
    marketing, 224–226, 233–235

Corporate social responsibility (*continued*)
  public relations, 224–226, 233–235
  rise of demand for, 458–459
  social virtues, 457
  transparency, 457–458
    as corporate idealizations, 465–467
  value of organizational talk, 469–470
Culpability, 302–303
Culture
  choice, 24–25
  defined, 335
  influence of, 335
  journalism ethics, 198–199

D
Decentering, 60
Decisional privacy, 205
Decision making, 169
  discursive formations, 169
  intercultural communication ethics, 335, 337
  Obama presidency, 274
  quality decisions, 24
  results, 24
Deconstruction of moral organization, 102
Deference, 25
  nexting helix, 25
Defeudalization
  Internet, 397
  publicity, 397
Deliberation, environmentalism, 418–419
Deliberative democracy, 391
  consensus, 391–392
  globalization, 398
  nonconsensual basis, 392
  science, 309–331
    17th century to mid-20th century, 311–322
    American Association for the Advancement of
      Science, 316
    American Civil War, 317
    big science, 318–320
    cultural prestige of science, 318
    egalitarian perspective, 315
    Habermas, J., 309–310
    history, 309–322
    Hood Canal, 323–328
    industrial capitalism, 317–318
    postmodern scene, 322–331
    post-World War II, 320–322
    Progressive movement, 317
    Puget Sound Basin waterways, 323–328
    reason, 313
    reciprocating influences between science and
      society, 310–311
Deliberative partnerships, 511–513
Democracy, *see also* Deliberative democracy
  capitalism, relationship, 449
Democratic/egalitarian group process, 150
Dependent groups, 150–151

Dialogic confession, 45–60
Dialogic ethics
  dialogic confession
    decentering, 60
    dialogic ethics as content, 56–60
    dialogic ethics as lineage, 54–56
    enlarged mentality, 60
    as ethical rhetorical turn, 53–60
    existential life-world, 57–58
    historicity, 57–58
    minimalist engagement, 57
    multiplicity, 57
  difference, 56
  journalism ethics, 191
  metaphors, 56
  narrative ground, 56
  situating, 45–60
Dialogic theory, 49–53
  dialogue as content, 52–53
  history, 49–51
  scholarly lineage, 51–52
Dialogism, 20–21
Dialogue
  array of approaches, 50–51
  communication ethics, interplay, 45–60
Difference, 501–504
  dialogic ethics, 56
  framing, 503
  media, 503
Dignity
  journalism ethics, 198–199
  relationships, 137
Disaster, Badiou, A., 424–426
Discourse, 101–103
  discursive aspects of the economy,
    439–442
  ethics, 31–42
  feminist discursive ethics, 70–71
  Heidegger, M., 35
  reconciliation, 379–382
  rhetoric, 31–42
    acknowledgment, 37–41
    ancient Greeks, 31
    conscience, 34–36
    intellectual assessments, 31
    language-in-use, 32
    ontological status, 32
    strategic action, 40–41
    truth, 36–37
  strategic action, 40–41
    acknowledgment, 37–41
    ancient Greeks, 31
    conscience, 34–36
    emotion, 36–37
    intellectual assessments, 31
    language-in-use, 32
    ontological status, 32
    truth, 36–37

Discourse ethics, 40–41
  journalism ethics, 192
Discourses of power, small group communication, 159
Discursive formations, decision making, 169
Dissent, 180–181
Documentary photography, 244–249
  mediation, 246
  power, 246
Duke University lacrosse case, 258–269
  academic setting, 260–263
  accountability, 267–268
  communicative challenges, 259–260
  competing principles, 259–260
  ethical challenges, 259–260
  journalistic context, 265–268
  journalistic ethics, 265–268
  journalistic treatment, 265–268
  legal–ethical context and dimensions, 263–265
  political agendas, 261–263
  structures to address local *vs.* academic community conflict, 260–261
  students' well-being, 261–263
  university faculty, 261–263

E
Ecological balance, 422
Economic justice
  communication ethics, 436–453
    alienation, 444–446
    alternative economies as social movements, 452
    amorality, 443–444
    bureaucratization, 444–446
    capitalism, 443
    discursive-rhetorical analysis issues, 446–449
    economic aspects of discourse, 439–442
    economic justice as human rights issue, 438
    framing, 443–444
    immorality, 443–444
    interrelations of economy, ethics, and communication, 439–446
    linkage of economics to happiness, 438–439
    market, agency, and ethical action, 447–449
    market globalization, 449–452
    markets, 436–438
    material inquiry domains, 439
    meanings of the market in everyday life, 446–447
    morality, 443–444
    relations of democracy to capitalism, 449
    relevance, 436–439
    rhetoric of economy, 440
    rhetoric of neoliberalism, 440–442
    symbolic inquiry domains, 439
  markets, 436–438
Emancipation
  community, relationship, 378
    security, relationship, 378
Embedding iterativity, feminist discursive ethics, 76–77
Emotion, truth, 36–37
Employee rights, 179–180
Employee voice, 180
End-of-life issues, 297–298
Enforcement, human rights, 9
Engagement, 512
  developing culture of, 504–505
Entertainment, new technology, 208–209
Environmentalism, 424–429, 495
  Badiou, A., 415–416, 419–420, 422, 424–426
  characterized, 420
  deliberation, 418–419
  hostile takeover, 416
  humanism, compared, 420
  public participation, 418–419
  race, 414–430
  social justice, 415–416
  toxic event, 422
  transparency, 418–419
Environmental justice movement
  environmentalists and, 414, 415
  founding, 423–424
  humanism, 415
  identity politics, 415
  social justice, 415–416
Environmental racism, 423
Equality, hierarchies of, 374, 379–382
Equity, 303–304
Ethical absolutism, 342
Ethical analysis, Foucault, M.
  components, 121–122
  ethical substance, 121–122
  ethical work, 121–122
  mode of subjectivation, 121–122
  telos, 121–122
Ethical challenge, whistleblowers, 148
Ethical integrity, 26
Ethical issues, characterized, 21
Ethical pluralism, 207
Ethical praxis, 15–27
Ethical reflection, core values, 500–501
Ethical relativism, 207, 342–343
Ethical substance, 121–122
Ethical temptation, awareness, 26–27
Ethical theory, 15–27
Ethical universalism, 343
Ethical work, 121–122
Ethics, *see also* Specific type
  choice, nexting helix, 22–27
  communication, 94–96
    relationship, 1, 46–49
  as content, 49
  discourse, 31–42
  ethos, 32–34
  modernity, 85–88

Ethics (*continued*)
  narrow disciplinarity, 15
  organizing, 171–173
  postcolonial approach, 119–129
  power, 85–96
    community power debate, 89–92
    Frankfurt School of Critical Theory, 85–86
    Marxism, 85–86
  rhetoric, 31–42
    acknowledgment, 37–41
    ancient Greeks, 31
    conscience, 34–36
    emotion, 36–37
    intellectual assessments, 31
    language-in-use, 32
    ontological status, 32
    strategic action, 40–41
    truth, 36–37
  strategic action, 40–41
    acknowledgment, 37–41
    ancient Greeks, 31
    conscience, 34–36
    emotion, 36–37
    intellectual assessments, 31
    language-in-use, 32
    ontological status, 32
    truth, 36–37
Ethics of care, 137–138
Ethics of caring, 294
Ethics of environmentalism, wild(er)ness, 414–430
Ethics of public discourse, public sphere, 356–359
Ethnicity, journalism ethics, 198–199
Ethnographic imaging, 249–250
Ethos
  Aristotle, 33
  characterized, 32–34
  ethics, 32–34
  Isocrates, 33
Eurocentric cultural assumptions
  communication ethics, 119
  humanity, 119
  justice, 119
  rationality, 119
Evil, Badiou, A., 424–426
Exaggeration, 301
Existential life-world, 57–58

F
Fairness
  relationships, 138
  types, 139
Fear appeals
  communication ethics, 282–284
  political communication, 282–284
Feminist discursive ethics, 64–78
  context, 71–73
    social construction of context, 71–73
  discourse, 70–71

embedding iterativity, 76–77
gender justice, 64
human values, dialogue, 73–74
intersections of theory–practice dialectics, 64
issues, 64
justice, 66
justice/care tensions, 66
  common images in communication studies, 66–70
process underpinnings, 65–70
public/private tensions, 66
  common images in communication studies, 66–70
reframing, 75–76
transparency
  outcomes, 77
  processes, 77
vision, designing vision, 74–75
Feminist ethics, 122–125, 294
  communication ethics, 277
  journalism ethics, 192
  political communication, 277
FLOSS, new technology, 209–210
Foucault, M.
  ethical analysis, 120–122
    components, 121–122
    ethical substance, 121–122
    ethical work, 121–122
    mode of subjectivation, 121–122
    telos, 121–122
  governmentality, 93
  power, 92–94
    crisis of representation, 92
Framing, 19, 75–76, 443–444
  communication studies, 497–499
  difference, 503
  interdependence, 499
  power, 88
Frankfurt School of Critical Theory, 85–86
Freedom
  media, 395
  power, 93–94
Freedom of speech, 180
  censorship, 387–389
Free Software movement, 209–210

G
Gender, political communication, 275
Gender justice, feminist discursive ethics, 64
Gibush, small group communication, 155–156
Globalization, 16–17
  characterization, 16
  contact with Otherness, 16
  deliberative democracy, 398
  inevitability, 449–452
  postmodernism, 96
Globalized governance, 398–399
Global-local dialectic, communication ethics, 5–7

Global warming, 425–426
Governmentality, Foucault, M., 93
Gratitude, relationships, 138
Great Britain
    media
        including Muslim voices in reporting, 363–367
        Muslim divided loyalties, 361–363
    Muslims, 359–370
        contextual political discourse, 359–360
        emergence of British Muslim press, 368–369
        including Muslim voices in reporting, 363–367
        Muslim divided loyalties, 361–363
        representation in press, 360–369
    newspapers, 359–370
Groupthink
    isolation, 158
    small group communication, 158
Guilt, 302–303

H
Habermas, J.
    moral judgment, 86–87
    power, 86–87
    public sphere, 357
    secularity, 357–358
    social interaction, 86–87
Healthcare costs, 299, 306
Healthcare policy issues, 305–306
Health communication
    communication ethics, 293–306
        accuracy, 300–301
        autonomy, 303–304
        bioethics approaches, 295
        casuistry, 295
        culpability, 302–303
        economic factors, 299, 306
        end-of-life issues, 297–298
        equity, 303–304
        ethics of caring, 294
        exaggeration, 301
        feminist ethics, 294
        guilt, 302–303
        health campaign ethics, 299–305
        healthcare costs, 299, 306
        healthcare policy issues, 305–306
        individual to dialogic perspectives, 296–299
        inequity, 303–304
        influence, 301
        information technology, 305
        institutional factors, 299, 306
        intercultural concerns, 298
        labeling, 303
        moralism, 300
        narrative ethics, 294–295
        new biomedical technologies, 305
        pain treatment, 298

        patient, 296–297
        principalist approaches, 295
        provider–patient interaction, 296–299
        reliability, 300–301
        responsibility, 302–303
        risk communication, 299, 301–302
        shame, 302–303
        social gaps, 303–304
        stigmatizing, 303
        theoretical frameworks, 294–296
        underserved populations, 303–304
        virtue ethics, 295–296
        whistle-blowing, 299
    human rights, 293
Heidegger, M.
    conscience, 35
    discourse, 35
Historical moment
    counter modern, 45–46
    postmodern, 45–46
Historicity, 57–58
Honesty, communication, 136–137
Hood Canal, 323–328
Horizon, 45
Human existence, Otherness, 34
Humanism
    environmentalism, compared, 420
    environmental justice movement, 415
Humanity, Eurocentric cultural assumptions, 119
Human rights
    agency, 9
    authority, 9
    classification, 9
    communication studies standpoint, 8–9
        framing, 8
    economic rights, 438
    enforcement, 9
    health communication, 293
    interpretation, 9
    negotiation, 9
Human values, feminist discursive ethics, dialogue, 73–74

I
Iconoclasm, individual acts, 242
Identity politics, environmental justice movement, 415
Ideology, 33–34
Immorality, 443–444
Inclusion, relationships, 137
Inequity, 303–304
Influence, 301
Informational privacy, 206
Information technology, 305
Ingroups, small group communication, 159–160
Instrumental rationality, 510–511
Integrity, 26

Intellectual property, new technology, 209–210
INTELSAT
    privatisation, 480–482
    regulation, 480–481
Intent, 19
Intentional human actions, 18
Intercultural communication ethics, 335–349
    bribery, 346–347
    communication preference, 338–339
    contemporary issues, 336–339
    corporate culture, 338
    cultural value clash, 338–339
    cultural variability framework, 337
    decision making, 335, 337
    ethical absolutism, 342
    ethical relativism, 342–343
    ethical universalism, 343
    global standard procedure *vs.* local justice,
        336–337
    intercultural meta-ethics
        applied guidelines, 348–349
        theorizing and researching directions, 348
    local cultural hiring practices, 338
    multilayered perspective, 343–348
    multilevel theorizing benefits, 344–345
    multiple ethical positions: assessing pros and
        cons, 341–343
    research: specific ethical issues, 341
    situational ethics formula test, 338
    social ecological framework, core multilevel
        concepts, 345–346
    social ecological perspective, applied questions,
        346–348
    training: specific ethical issues, 340–341
Interdependence
    as ethical imperative, 499–500
    framing, 499
    as material reality, 499
    relationships, 137–138
Internet
    defeudalization, 397
    Obama presidency, 283–284
Interpersonal communication ethics, 135–155, *see
    also* Relationships
    distance and, 142–143
    expanding circle, 142–143
    great ethical issues of our times, 144
    reciprocal altruism, 143
    tragedy of the commons, 143
Interpretation, human rights, 9
Iraq war
    Bush (G.W.) administration, 148
    justifications, 418
    procedural ethics, 418–419
Isocrates, *ethos,* 33
Isolation
    groupthink, 158
    small group communication, 157–158

J
Journalism ethics, 190–202
    accountability, 267–268
    communitarian ethics, 192
    culture, 198–199
    dialogic ethics, 191
    discourse ethics, 192
    Duke University lacrosse case, 265–268
    ethnicity, 198–199
    feminist ethics, 192
    human dignity, 198–199
    nonviolence, 197–198
    race, 198–199
    realism, 200–201
    relativism, 199–200
    social justice, 193–196
    social responsibility theory, 193
    Society of Professional Journalists' *Code of
        Ethics,* 265–266
    substantive issues, 193–199
    theory, 190–193
        classical approaches, 190–191
    truth, 196–197, 265–266, 509
Justice
    Eurocentric cultural assumptions, 119
    feminist discursive ethics, 66
    relationships, 138
Just-war doctrine
    American exceptionalism, 376
    critical inquiry, 376
    disrespects individuality, 376
    religious legitimatization of secular authority,
        376
    standard, 375–376

K
Knowledge, power, 93

L
Labeling, 303
Lady Chatterley's Lover
    censorship, 250–251
    obscenity, 250–251
    obscenity trial, 250–251
Land ethic, 422
Language-in-use, 32
Legal cases, 258–269
Liberty, power, 93–94
Locational privacy, 205
Love Canal, 422–423
Lying, 17–18
    communication, 136–137
        moral ambiguity, 136
        prevalence, 136

M
MacIntyre, A., communication meta-ethics,
    105–110

Majority-minority relations, small group
communication, 156–157
Manipulation
marketing, 231–233
public relations, 231–233
Maori culture, 125–128
Marketing, 221–236
cause-related marketing, 224
codes of ethics, 229–231
core ethical challenges, 221
corporate social responsibility, 224–226, 233–
235
ethical issues, operational contexts, 224–226
ethics in promotional culture, 235–236
ideologies, 221
as profession, 228–231
professionals in, 228–231
propaganda, 231–233
rhetoric, 231–233
role, 222–224, 226–228
scope, 222–224
societal legitimacy, 229–231
values, 226–227
Markets, economic justice, 436–438
Marxism, 85–86
Material inquiry domains, 439
Media, *see also* Journalism ethics
citizenship, 358
citizens' participation, 394–397
difference, 503
freedom, 395
Great Britain
including Muslim voices in reporting, 363–
367
Muslim divided loyalties, 361–363
Muslims, 359–370
contextual political discourse, 359–360
emergence of British Muslim press, 368–369
representation in press, 360–369
nationhood, 358
new technology, 396–397
public sphere, 393–394
representation, 359
responsibility, 394–397
modes, 395
normative view, 395
Mediation, documentary photography, 246
Membership, small group communication, 151–
152
Metaphors, dialogic ethics, 56
Military-industrial complexes, 478–479
Military operations, privatisation, 480–483
Minimalist engagement, 57
Minimalist values, political communication,
279–284
Mode of subjectivation, 121–122
Modernity
ethics, 85–88

power, 85–88
Moralism, 300
Morality, 174–179, 443–444
organizational contexts, 174–179
Moral judgment, Habermas, J., 86–87
Multiculturalism
characterized, 355
citizenship, 355
political, 355
Muslims
Great Britain, 359–370
contextual political discourse, 359–360
emergence of British Muslim press, 368–369
including Muslim voices in reporting, 363–
367
Muslim divided loyalties, 361–363
representation in press, 360–369
media, 359–370
newspapers, 359–370
Mutuality, relationships, 137–138

N
Narrative ethics, 48, 294–295
Narrative ground, dialogic ethics, 56
Nationhood, media, 358
Negotiation, human rights, 9
Neoliberalism, 440–442
Networked communication, regulation, 475–490
difference between society and civil society,
483–485
ethical problems, 475–490
between fatalism and free will, 485–488
market trajectory, 480–483
theory straitjacket, 485–488
trajectory of human purpose, 483–485
New biomedical technologies, 305
Newspapers
Great Britain, 359–370
Muslims, 359–370
New technology, 495
citizenship in global metropolis, 214–216
computer games, 212–214
copyleft, 209–210
copyright, 209–210
as engines of democracy, 208–209
entertainment, 208–209
ethical dimensions, 204–217
FLOSS, 209–210
intellectual property, 209–210
media, 396–397
obscenity, 251
pornography, 210–212
privacy, 205–216
US *vs.* European Union, 206–207
produsage, 208–209
public sphere, 396–397
New Zealand, 125–128
Nexting, characteristics, 22–23

Nexting helix, 22–27
  benefits, 24
  deference, 25
  effectiveness of metaphor, 23
Nietzsche, F., relativism, 199–200
Nonviolence, journalism ethics, 197–198
Nonviolent resistance, 377–378

O

Obama presidency
  decision making, 274
  Internet, 283–284
  peace-building discourse, 383–384
  political communication, 273–274, 280–282,
    284–288
  racially motivated attacks, 274–275
Objective causality, photography, 247
Obscenity
  Lady Chatterley's Lover, 250–251
  new technology, 251
  visual communication, 251
Online communication, 204
Organizational contexts
  communication ethics, 166–182
    accountability, 170–171
    applied ethics, 173–174
    body, 172–173
    bureaucracy, 167
    centrality of communication, 168–171
    codes of ethical conduct, 173–174
    communication as domain for ethical praxis,
      168–169
    decision making, 169
    disavowing collective moral agency,
      175–176
    discursive formations, 169
    dissent, 180–181
    embracing moral agency through "real entity"
      perspective, 176
    emerging trends, 181–182
    employee rights, 179–180
    employee voice, 180
    free speech, 180
    materiality, 171–173
    morality, 174–179
    organizational legitimacy, 167
    organization values, 167
    organizing, 171–173
    privacy, 179–180
    research, 179–184
    shifting moral agency to situated subject,
      176–179
    sites, 172
    stakeholder perspectives, 179
    textual agency, 172
    theory, 179–184
    whistle-blowing, 180–181
  morality, 174–179

Organizations
  autopoiesis, 459–460
  limits of observation, 464–465
  organizational wholeness, 464–465
  systems theory, 459–460
  value of organizational talk, 469–470
Organizing, ethics, 171–173
Other, as term, 51
Otherness, 16, 100–101, 501–504
  human existence, 34
  as moral vocation, 41–42
Outcomes emerging in relationships, 19
Outgroups, small group communication, 159–160

P

Pain treatment, 298
Peace
  articulating hierarchies of equality, 379–382
  democratic peace building, ethical trajectory,
    384–385
  positive peace, 375–377
    in democratic idiom, 383–384
  reducing radical Otherness, 377–379
Philosophy
  centrality of communicative ethics, 494
  narrow disciplinarity, 15
Photography, 242–249, *see also* Documentary
    photography
  censorship, 248
  ethical questions, 242–249
  objective causality, 247
  propaganda, 243–244
Plato
  different types of messages, ethical–moral
    implications, 1
  public moral argument, 31
Political communication, 273–288
  2008 presidential campaign, 273
  Bush (G.W.) administration, 280
  characterological approaches, 276–277
  fear appeals, 282–284
  feminist approaches, 277
  gender, 275
  minimalist values and contexts, 279–284
  Obama administration, 273–274, 280–282,
    284–288
  postmodern approach
    ethics, 278–279
    issues, 278–279
  postmodernist approaches, 277–278
  viral messages, 282–284
  YouTube, 282–284
Political secularism, 401, 403
Pornography, new technology, 210–212
Postcolonial theory, communication ethics, 119–
    129
  Aotearoa-New Zealand, 125–128
  corporate social responsibility, 120–122

ethical analysis, 120–122
ethical ground problematizing, 120–122
ethical individual, 120–122
feminist ethics, 122–125
Foucauldian ethical analysis, 120–122
'Other' look at ethics, 122–125
presence, 125
revisioning of communication ethics, 125–128
Te Kaupapa Maori, 125–128
towards praxis, 125–128
transcultural ethics, 122–125
Postmodernism, 96
communication ethics, 277–278
alterity, 100–101
Badiou, A., 110–113
conceptualizing communication, 104–105
decentering of ethical subject, 104
deconstruction of moral organization, 102
discourse, 101–103
ethics, 278–279
ethics as central, 100
issues, 278–279
MacIntyre, A., 105–110
Otherness, 100–101
practice of communication ethics, 104–105
practice of ethics, 100–103
reconceptualizing communicative agency, 104
theory of communication ethics, 104–105
theory of ethics, 100–103
globalization, 96
political communication, 277–278
ethics, 278–279
issues, 278–279
Power
communication, 94–96
conceptions of, 88–89
disciplinary, positive analytics, 92–93
documentary photography, 246
elitist model, 90
ethics, 85–96
community power debate, 89–92
Frankfurt School of Critical Theory, 85–86
Marxism, 85–86
Foucault, M., 92–94
crisis of representation, 92
framing, 88
freedom, 93–94
Habermas, J., 86–87
knowledge, 93
liberty, 93–94
modernity, 85–88
pluralist view, 89
sovereign models, 92–93
theories of, 88–94
three-dimensional view, 90–91
Presence, 125
Presidential campaign of 2008, political
communication, 273

Presumption of innocence, 258
Principalist approaches, 295
Privacy, 179–180
autonomy, 205
new technology, 205–216
US *vs.* European Union, 206–207
relationships, 138
Privatization
INTELSAT, 480–482
military operations, 480–483
Procedural ethics
compromise, 419
Iraq war, 418–419
public participation programs, 419
Produsage, new technology, 208–209
Propaganda
marketing, 231–233
photography, 243–244
public relations, 231–233
Public, conceptualization, 391
Publication, censorship, 387–389
Public discourse, 390–393
history, 390–391
Publicity
Bentham's utilitarian ideas, 389–390
defeudalization, 397
principle, 387
as ethical maxim, 389–390
Public moral argument
Plato, 31
Socrates, 31
Public opinion, 391
Public participation
environmentalism, 418–419
procedural ethics, 419
Public policy, relationships, 144
Public relations, 221–236
cause-related marketing, 224
codes of ethics, 229–231
core ethical challenges, 221
corporate social responsibility, 224–226, 233–235
ethical issues, operational contexts, 224–226
ethics in promotional culture, 235–236
ideologies, 221
manipulation, 231–233
as profession, 228–231
professionals in, 228–231
propaganda, 231–233
rhetoric, 231–233
role, 222–224, 226–228
scope, 222–224
societal legitimacy, 229–231
values, 226–227
Public sphere
characterized, 394
ethics of public discourse, 356–359
Habermas, J., 357

Public sphere (*continued*)
  media, 393–394
  new technology, 396–397
  transnational, 398–399
Purpose, 19

Q
Quality of life, relationships, 144

R
Race
  environmentalism, 414–430
  journalism ethics, 198–199
  Obama presidency, 274–275
Rational-emotional dialectic, communication
    ethics, 7–8
Rationality, Eurocentric cultural assumptions, 119
Realism, journalism ethics, 200–201
Reason, 18, 313
Reasonableness, 507–508
Reciprocal altruism, interpersonal communication
    ethics, 143
Recognition, acknowledgment, 38
Reconciliation, discourse, 379–382
Reframing, feminist discursive ethics, 75–76
Regulation
  INTELSAT, 480–481
  networked communication, 475–490
    difference between society and civil society,
        483–485
    ethical problems, 475–490
    between fatalism and free will, 485–488
    market trajectory, 480–483
    theory straitjacket, 485–488
    trajectory of human purpose, 483–485
  trade, 475–490
    difference between society and civil society,
        483–485
    ethical problems, 475–490
    between fatalism and free will, 485–488
    market trajectory, 480–483
    theory straitjacket, 485–488
    trajectory of human purpose, 483–485
Relationships
  autonomy, 138
  basic rules, 137–139
    ethical implications, 137–139
  connection, 137
  dignity, 137
  ethics in specific types of close relationships,
      139–140
  fairness, 138
  gratitude, 138
  interdependence, 137–138
  justice, 138
  mutuality, 137–138
  negotiated and idiosyncratic rules and ethics,
      140

  privacy, 138
  public policy, 144
  quality of life, 144
  repair, 141–142
  respect, 137
  revenge, 138, 141–142
  transgressions, 141–142
  types, 139
  unscripted, 140
Relativism
  journalism ethics, 199–200
  Nietzsche, F., 199–200
Reliability, 300–301
Religion
  religious diversity, secular states, 403
  rhetoric of, 35–36
  state and
    principled distance for relations and
        governance, 407–409
    relationship, 401–412
    religion-centered states, 402–403
Representation, media, 359
Respect, relationships, 137
Responsibility, 302–303
  media, 394–397
    modes, 395
    normative view, 395
Responsiveness, 23, 507–508
  choice, 23–24
  vocation, 23–24
Revenge, relationships, 138, 141–142
Rhetoric
  architectural function, 33
  discourse, 31–42
    acknowledgment, 37–41
    ancient Greeks, 31
    conscience, 34–36
    intellectual assessments, 31
    language-in-use, 32
    ontological status, 32
    strategic action, 40–41
    truth, 36–37
  epideictic, 35
  ethics, 31–42
    acknowledgment, 37–41
    ancient Greeks, 31
    conscience, 34–36
    emotion, 36–37
    intellectual assessments, 31
    language-in-use, 32
    ontological status, 32
    strategic action, 40–41
    truth, 36–37
  marketing, 231–233
  public relations, 231–233
  religion, 35–36
  Western rhetorical tradition, 31–32
Rhetoric of economy, 440

Rhetoric of neoliberalism, 440–442
Rightness, choice, 26
Risk communication, 299, 301–302

S
Science
  deliberative democracy, 309–331
    17th century to mid-20th century, 311–322
    American Association for the Advancement of Science, 316
    American Civil War, 317
    big science, 318–320
    cultural prestige of science, 318
    egalitarian perspective, 315
    Habermas, J., 309–310
    history, 309–322
    Hood Canal, 323–328
    industrial capitalism, 317–318
    postmodern scene, 322–331
    post-World War II, 320–322
    Progressive movement, 317
    Puget Sound Basin waterways, 323–328
    reason, 313
    reciprocating influences between science and society, 310–311
  social conscience, 477–479
Secular humanist *ethos,* 403–404
Secularism, 401–412
  conceptions, 404–407
  contextual, 409–410
    objections, 410–411
  Habermas, J., 357–358
  idealized French model, 404–405
  idealized US model, 405–406
  Indian model, 406–411
  mainstream western, 404–407
  principled distance for relations and governance, 407–409
Secular states, 401, 403–404
  movements challenging, 403–404
  religious diversity, 403
  secular humanist *ethos,* 403–404
Security
  articulating hierarchies of equality, 379–382
  community, relationship, 378
  critical communication scholarship, 378–379
  emancipation, relationship, 378
Self-representations, small group communication, 158–159
Separation, small group communication, 158–159
Shame, 302–303
Situational ethics formula test, 338
Small group communication, 148–162
  authority, 150–151
  classifying, 149–151
  defining small groups, 149
  discourses of power, 159
  ethical checklist, 161

  ethics and group variations, 149–151
  external relationships, 157–160, 161
  gibush, 155–156
  group contracts, 152–153
  group formation, 151–152, 161
  group roles, 156
  groupthink, 158
  ingroups, 159–160
  internal process, 153–157
  isolation, 157–158
  majority-minority relations, 156–157
  membership, 151–152
  outgroups, 159–160
  procedures, 161
  process, 161
  requirements, 149
  self-representations, 158–159
  separation, 158–159
  setting procedures, 154–156
  symbolic convergence, 158–159
  theoretical overview, 149–151
  X-Teams, 157–158
Social acts, 242
Social conscience
  science, 477–479
  technology, 477–479
Social death, acknowledgment, 38
Social ecological framework, 345–348
Social gaps, 303–304
Social interaction, Habermas, J., 86–87
Social justice
  environmentalism, 415–416
  environmental justice movement, 415–416
  journalism ethics, 193–196
Social responsibility theory, journalism ethics, 193
Social roles, negotiated and idiosyncratic rules and ethics, 140
Social survival, biological survival, compared, 429–430
Social virtues, corporate social responsibility, 457
Societal legitimacy
  marketing, 229–231
  public relations, 229–231
Society of Professional Journalists' *Code of Ethics,* journalistic ethics, 265–266
Socrates, public moral argument, 31
Stakeholder perspectives, 179
State
  civil society, mediators between, 393–394
  religion and
    principled distance for relations and governance, 407–409
    relationship, 401–412
    religion-centered states, 402–403
Stigmatizing, 303
Strategic action, 40–41
Structuration theory, 148

Symbolic convergence, small group
communication, 158–159
Symbolic inquiry domains, 439
Systems theory
autopoiesis, 459–460
organizations, 459–460

T
Technology, social conscience, 477–479
Telos, 121–122
Text, 45
Theoretical-practical dialectic, communication
ethics, 2–3
Toxic event, environmentalism, 422
Trade, regulation, 475–490
difference between society and civil society,
483–485
ethical problems, 475–490
between fatalism and free will, 485–488
market trajectory, 480–483
theory straitjacket, 485–488
trajectory of human purpose, 483–485
Tragedy of the commons, interpersonal
communication ethics, 143
Transcultural ethics, 122–125
Transparency
characterized, 463–464
corporate social responsibility, 457–458
as corporate idealizations, 465–467
defined, 463
environmentalism, 418–419
feminist discursive ethics
outcomes, 77
processes, 77
limits of observation, 464–465
organizational wholeness, 464–465
(self)-transparency, 463–464
Trophic cascades, 422
Truth, 508–511
emotion, 36–37
journalism ethics, 196–197, 265–266, 509
validity, 37

U
Underserved populations, 303–304
Universal humanitarian, 18
Universal norms, 495
Universal-particular dialectic, communication
ethics, 4–5
Universal truths, 84
crisis of representation, 84

V
Validity, truth, 37

Values
communication ethics, 279–284
minimalist values and contexts, 279–284
political communication, 279–284
Vandalization, artworks, 242
Viral messages
communication ethics, 282–284
political communication, 282–284
Virtue ethics, 295–296
computer games, 212–214
Vision
communication ethics, 125–128
feminist discursive ethics, 74–75
Visual communication, 241–254, *see also* Specific
type
classical theory, 241–242
new contexts, 250–253
obscenity, 251
prephotographic traditional contexts, 241
prohibition on images in religions of the Book,
241
Vocation, responsiveness, 23–24
Voluntary groups, 150

W
War
articulating hierarchies of equality, 379–382
just-war doctrine, 375–377
American exceptionalism, 376
critical inquiry, 376
disrespects individuality, 376
religious legitimatization of secular authority,
376
standard, 375–376
rationales for, 374–382
reducing radical Otherness, 377–379
Web, 204
Western adversarial model, 504–505
Whistleblowing, 180–181, 299
ethical challenge, 148
Wiener, Norbert, 477–478
Wild(er)ness events
abandoning wild(er)ness, 426–429
Badiou, A., 417–418
characterized, 417–418
ethics of environmentalism, 414–430
personal stories, 420–421

X
X-Teams, small group communication, 157–158

Y
YouTube
communication ethics, 282–284
political communication, 282–284